RESOURCES IN ANCIENT PHILOSOPHY:

An Annotated Bibliography of Scholarship in English, 1965-1989

by
Albert A. Bell, Jr.
and
James B. Allis

The Scarecrow Press, Inc.
Metuchen, N.J., & London
1991

British Library Cataloguing-in-Publication data available

Library of Congress Cataloging-in-Publication Data

Bell, Albert A., 1945-
    Resources in ancient philosophy : an annotated bibliography of
scholarship in English, 1965-1989 / Albert A. Bell, Jr., James B.
Allis.
    p.   cm.
    Includes index.
    ISBN 0-8108-2520-1 (alk. paper)
    1. Philosophy, Ancient--Bibliography. 2. Christianity--
Philosophy--History--Bibliography. I. Allis, James B. II. Title.
Z7125.B39   1991
[B171]
016.18--dc20   91-39912

3

For our families,
who have been very philosophical about this whole thing

TABLE OF CONTENTS

	Preface	ix
	List of Abbreviations	xi
1	Introduction and Survey	
	Purpose and Principles of Organization	1
	The Starting Point	4
	General Histories and Reference Works	7
	Collected Essays	11
	Topical Studies	14
2	Doxography; Collected Texts	33
3	The Presocratics: General	40
4	The Milesians	49
	Thales	50
	Anaximander	52
	Anaximenes	55
5	Pythagoras, Xenophanes, and Heraclitus	57
	Pythagoras and the Pythagoreans	57
	Xenophanes	63
	Heraclitus	65
6	The Eleatics	76
	Parmenides	76
	Zeno of Elea	85
	Melissus of Samos	92
7	The Pluralists	94
	Empedocles	94
	Anaxagoras	100
8	The Atomists	105
9	The Sophists	111
	Antiphon	116
	Protagoras	117
	Gorgias	121
	Prodicus	123
10	Socrates	125

11	Minor Socratics	149
	Megarians and Cyrenaics	149
	Cynics	151

12	Plato: Introduction and Topical Studies	156
	Biographical Sketch	156
	Overview of his Thought	156
	Plato: An Assessment	159
	Reference Works and Collected Essays	160
	General	162
	Aesthetics	180
	Epistemology	191
	Ethics	199
	Logic/Dialectic	207
	Metaphysics	213
	Politics	229
	Psychology	237
	Rhetoric	242
	Science (Cosmology and Mathematics)	244
	Theology and Religion	248

13	Plato: Individual Works	252
	Alcibiades I	254
	Apology	255
	Charmides	258
	Clitophon	259
	Cratylus	260
	Critias	264
	Crito	265
	Euthydemus	269
	Euthyphro	270
	Gorgias	274
	Hipparchus	279
	Hippias Major	279
	Hippias Minor	280
	Ion	281
	Laches	282
	Laws	284
	Letters	288
	Lovers	291
	Lysis	292
	Menexenus	293
	Meno	294
	Minos	299
	Parmenides	300
	Phaedo	309
	Phaedrus	318

	Philebus	324
	Protagoras	329
	Republic	334
	Sophist	362
	Statesman	371
	Symposium	374
	Theaetetus	380
	Theages	389
	Timaeus/Critias	389
14	Aristotle	400
	Biographical Sketch	400
	Works	401
	General	403
	The Organization of Knowledge	413
	Aesthetics	416
	Biology	426
	Categories	436
	Epistemology	443
	Ethics	450
	Logic/Dialectic/Language	488
	Mathematics	504
	Metaphysics	506
	Modal Logic	533
	Physics	540
	Politics	550
	Psychology	563
	Rhetoric	573
	Science	581
	Theology	588
	Time	592
15	The Academy and the Peripatetics; Skepticism and Eclecticism	594
	The Academy	594
	Peripatetics	598
	Skepticism	604
	Eclecticism	610
16	Hellenistic Philosophy	612
17	The Stoics	620
	Introduction	620
	General	623
	Zeno of Citium	637
	Cleanthe:.	639
	Chrysippus	640

	Panaetius	641
	Posidonius	642
	Seneca	644
	Epictetus	650
	Marcus Aurelius	652
18	Epicureanism	654
	Epicurus	654
	Lucretius	663
	Philodemus	673
	Diogenes of Oenoanda	674
19	The Late Hellenistic and Roman Era	676
	Neopythagoreanism	676
	Roman Philosophy	679
	Cicero	684
20	Middle Platonism; Neoplatonism	691
	Survey	691
	Middle Platonism	693
	Neoplatonism: General	696
	Plotinus	703
	Porphyry	717
	Iamblichus	720
	Proclus	721
	Philo of Alexandria	724
21	Gnosticism and Christian Philosophy	732
	Gnosticism	732
	Christian Philosophy	735
	Justin Martyr	746
	Athenagoras	748
	Tertullian	749
	Clement of Alexandria	751
	Origen of Alexandria	753
	Marius Victorinus	755
	Augustine	756
	Index	775
	About the Authors	800

PREFACE

Two professors at a small liberal arts college which places a premium on teaching probably should not have undertaken a project of this magnitude. Had we foreseen the scope of it at the outset, we probably would have declined Scarecrow Press's invitation. Like the Savings and Loan bailout, the task grew larger and larger the further we progressed. But, with the help of a number of people, we have endured (like good Stoics) and have reached the goal (the *telos*, as Aristotle would have called it).

We must first thank the reference librarians at Hope College, including Carol Juth-Gavasso, Kelly Gordon-Jacobsma, Margaret Pooler, and Elaine Cline (now director of the library at Augsburg College), who were indefatigable in verifying titles and clearing up obscurities. Their competence and enthusiastic support buoyed us up throughout the ordeal. They also made helpful comments about the format of the book.

Helen Einberger and her staff in the Inter-Library Loan department of Hope's library deserve a paragraph to themselves. We never had to worry about whether we could have access to a book or article. If a copy was available at any library in the U. S., they would get it for us, and cheerfully, no matter how large a stack of ILL cards we dropped on Helen's desk at one time.

We also owe much to Jacob E. Nyenhuis, Provost of Hope College, for his moral and financial support of this project. The college, in general, has provided splendid support facilities for this kind of work, from the library to the computer technology. Kate Maybury, in the office of Computing and Information Technology, designed some special function keys which enabled even computer maladepts such as ourselves to do the very important tasks of numbering the entries and compiling the index in record time. The numbering function worked beautifully; the only problem was that the bold brackets which were a marker for the places where the numbers were to be inserted had not been typed in on a handful of items. We discovered the problem only after we were well into the process of inserting cross-reference numbers. Our only recourse was to add by hand a few numbers with *a*'s on them. We do not think this will cause the users of this tool any problems.

Several student assistants put in long hours compiling entries, typing them into the files, even accompanying us to the libraries at Calvin College or the University of Notre Dame, whose staffs we would also like to thank for their gracious reception and assistance. We would like to express our gratitude to the following student assistants: Brian Paige, Kerstin Byorni, Erika Potts, Yvette van Riper, Pete Johnson, Christine Logan, and Laura Jackson.

Special thanks are due to Bettye Jo Bell for her support during the entire course of the project. In the last stages her editorial and proofreading skills saved us from a number of mistakes and improved the book markedly.

The purposes and scope of this volume are discussed in the first chapter. We hope it proves useful to those who are not experts in ancient philosophy but need to know something about it, as well as to those who are more proficient in the discipline. We have a good deal of ourselves invested in it and would like to know if it is helpful to its intended audience. And we would ask two questions of those who use it: Is there a need for a supplementary volume in a few years? Should we consider converting to an electronic data base? We hope that those who have comments will take the time to contact us or Scarecrow Press, perhaps even to make us aware of items we may have missed.

June, 1991   Albert A. Bell, Jr.
                                                                    James B. Allis

LIST OF ABBREVIATIONS

A&A	Antike und Abendland
ABG	Archiv fuer Begriffsgeschichte
AC	Antiquite Classique
AClass	Acta Classica
ActaPhFenn	Acta Philosophica Fennica
AFC	Anales de Filologia Clasica
AGPh	Archiv fuer Geschichte der Philosophie
AHB	Ancient History Bulletin
AHES	Archive for the History of the Exact Sciences
AIHS	Archives Internationales d'Histoire des Sciences
AJA	American Journal of Archeology
AJAH	American Journal of Ancient History
AJPh	American Journal of Philology
AmJJur	American Journal of Jurisprudence
AmJPhys	American Journal of Physics
AmPhQ	American Philosophical Quarterly
AncPh	Ancient Philosophy
AncSoc	Ancient Society
AncW	The Ancient World
AngThR	Anglican Theological Review
ANRW	Aufstieg und Niedergang der Roemischen Welt
Antich	Antichthon
AntRev	Antioch Review
AnzAlt	Anzeiger fuer die Altertumswissenschaft
Apeir	Apeiron
ArchRechtsSoz	Archiv fuer Rechts und Sozialphilosophie
AS	Anatolian Studies
AUB	Annales Universitatis Budapestinensis
AugStud	Augustinian Studies
AustlJPh	Australasian Journal of Philosophy
BASP	Bulletin of the American Society of Papyrologists
BCPE	Bolletino del Centro internazionale per lo studio dei Papiri Ercolanesi
BHM	Bulletin of the History of Medicine
BICS	Bulletin of the Institute of Classical Studies
Bio&Ph	Biology and Philosophy
BJRL	Bulletin of the John Rylands Library
BLE	Bulletin de Litterature Ecclesiastique
BosUJ	Boston University Journal
BritJAes	British Journal of Aesthetics
BritJHistSci	British Journal for the History of Science
BritJPhSci	British Journal of the Philosophy of Science

BuckRev	Bucknell Review
CanJPh	Canadian Journal of Philosophy
C&M	Classica et Mediaevalia
CB	Classical Bulletin
CF	Classical Folia
ChHist	Church History
ChinStudPhil	Chinese Studies in Philosophy
CJ	Classical Journal
ClAnt	Classical Antiquity (formerly *CSCA*)
ClassOut	Classical Outlook
CompLit	Comparative Literature
CPh	Classical Philology
CQ	Classical Quarterly
CR	Classical Review
CSCA	California Studies in Classical Antiquity
CTM	Concordia Theological Monthly
CultHerm	Cultural Hermeneutics (now Philosophy and Social Criticism)
CW	Classical World
DarshInt	Darshana International
Dial&Hum	Dialectics and Humanism
Dial(Can)	Dialogue: Canadian Philosophical Review
Dial(PST)	Dialogue (Phi Sigma Tau, Marquette University)
Dion	Dionysius
Diot	Diotima
DR	Downside Review
DUJ	Durham University Journal
EducStud	Educational Studies
EducTheor	Educational Theory
EEThess	Epistemonike Epeteris (Thessalonika)
EMC	Echos du Monde Classique
EPh	Etudes Philosophiques
Eranos-Jb	Eranos-Jahrbuch
Euphro	Euphrosyne
ExplorKnowl	Explorations in Knowledge
ExposT	Expository Times
Faith&Ph	Faith and Philosophy
FemStud	Feminist Studies
FoundLang	Foundations of Language
FranStud	Franciscan Studies
FreeInq	Free Inquiry
G&R	Greece and Rome
GB	Grazer Beitraege
GenLing	General Linguistics
GLO	Graecolatina et Orientalia
GM	Giornale di Metafisica
GPhS	Grazer Philosophische Studien

GradFacPhJ	Graduate Faculty Philosophy Journal
GRBS	Greek, Roman and Byzantine Studies
Gregor	Gregorianum
H&PhLog	History and Philosophy of Logic
H&Theo	History and Theory
HastCenRep	Hasting Center Report
HeythJ	Heythrop Journal
HibJ	The Hibbert Journal
HistEurIdeas	History of European Ideas
HPhQ	History of Philosophy Quarterly
HPolTho	History of Political Thought
HR	History of Religions
HSCP	Harvard Studies in Classical Philology
HT	History Today
HThR	Harvard Theological Review
HumStud	Human Studies
ICS	Illinois Classical Studies
IdealStud	Idealistic Studies
ILN	Illustrated London News
IndepJPh	Independent Journal of Philosophy
IndianJofHistofSci	Indian Journal of the History of Science
IndianPhQ	Indian Philosophical Quarterly
InformLog	Informal Logic
Interp	Interpretation
IntJAppliedPh	International Journal of Applied Philosophy
IntJPhRel	International Journal for Philosophy of Religion
IntLogRev	International Logic Review
IntPhQ	International Philosophical Quarterly
IntStudPh	International Studies in Philosophy (also published as SIF)
IntStudPhSci	International Studies in Philosophy of Science
IrishPhJ	Irish Philosophical Journal
JAAC	Journal of Aesthetics and Art Criticism
JAesEduc	Journal of Aesthetic Education
JAULLA	Journal of the Australasian Universities Language and Literature Association
JbAC	Jahrbuch fuer Antike und Christentum
JBL	Journal of Biblical Literature
JBritSocPhen	Journal of the British Society for Phenomenology
JBusEth	Journal of Business Ethics
JChinPh	Journal of Chinese Philosophy
JDharma	Journal of Dharma
JEH	Journal of Ecclesiastical History
JHI	Journal of the History of Ideas
JHistAstr	Journal of the History of Astronomy
JHistBehavSci	Journal of the History of the Behavioral Sciences
JHistBiol	Journal of the History of Biology
JHM	Journal of the History of Medicine and Allied Sciences

JHPh	Journal of the History of Philosophy
JHS	Journal of Hellenic Studies
JIES	Journal of Indo-European Studies
JIndCPhRes	Journal of the Indian Council of Philosophical Research
JLiberStud	Journal of Libertarian Studies
JMedEthics	Journal of Medical Ethics
JNES	Journal of Near Eastern Studies
JPh	Journal of Philosophy
JPhEd	Journal of Philosophy of Education
JPhilLog	Journal of Philosophical Logic
JR	Journal of Religion
JRE	Journal of Religious Ethics
JRelHealth	Journal of Religion and Health
JRS	Journal of Roman Studies
JSpecPh	Journal of Speculative Philosophy
JSymLog	Journal of Symbolic Logic
JTho	Journal of Thought
JThS	Journal of Theological Studies
JValInq	Journal of Value Inquiry
JWI	Journal of the Warburg and Courtauld Institutes
JWVaPhSoc	Journal of the West Virginia Philosophical Society
KyForLangQ	Kentucky Foreign Language Quarterly
LCM	Liverpool Classical Monthly
Log&An	Logique et Analyse
LThPh	Laval Theologique et Philosophique
MainCur	Main Currents
M&W	Man and World
Metaphil	Metaphilosophy
MH	Museum Helveticum
MidwJPh	Midwestern Journal of Philosophy
MidwStudPh	Midwestern Studies in Philosophy
Mnem	Mnemosyne
ModSch	Modern Schoolman
MonStud	Monastic Studies
MPhL	Museum Philologum Londiniense
MusAfr	Museum Africum
Mus&Man	Music and Man
N&C	Nigeria and the Classics
Nat&Sys	Nature and Systems
NDJFormLog	Notre Dame Journal of Formal Logic
NewSchol	New Scholasticism
NovTest	Novum Testamentum
NTS	New Testament Studies
OJRelStud	Ohio Journal of Religious Studies
OSAP	Oxford Studies in Ancient Philosophy

PAA	Praktika tes Akademias Athenon
PACA	Proceedings of the African Classical Association
PacCPh	Pacific Coast Philology
PACPhA	Proceedings of the American Catholic Philosophical Association
PacPhQ	Pacific Philosophical Quarterly (formerly *Pers*)
PaedHist	Paedagogica Historica
PakPhJ	Pakistan Philosophical Journal
P&P	Past and Present
PapBritSchR	Papers of the British School at Rome
PAPhS	Proceedings of the American Philosophical Society
ParPas	La Parola del Passato
PAS	Proceedings of the Aristotle Society
PBA	Proceedings of the British Academy
PBACAPh	Proceedings of the Boston Area Colloquium on Ancient Philosophy
PCPhS	Proceedings of the Cambridge Philological Society
Pers	The Personalist (now *PacPhQ*)
Ph	Philosophy
Ph&Lit	Philosophy and Literature
Ph&PhenRes	Philosophy and Phenomenological Research
Ph&PubAff	Philosophy and Public Affairs
Ph&Rh	Philosophy and Rhetoric
Ph&SocAct	Philosophy and Social Action
PhE&W	Philosophy East and West
PhFor	Philosophical Forum
Phil(Athens)	Philosophia (Athens)
PhilBks	Philosophical Books
PhilFor	Philosophy Forum
PhilInq	Philosophical Inquiry
Phil(Isrl)	Philosophia (Israel)
PhilMath	Philosophia Mathematica
PhilPapers	Philosophical Papers
PhilStud	Philosophical Studies
PhilStud(Ireland)	Philosophical Studies (Ireland)
PhInv	Philosophical Investigations
PhiSci	Philosophy of Science
PhQ	Philosophical Quarterly
PhR	Philosophical Review
PhRef	Philosophia Reformata
PhResArch	Philosophy Research Archives
Phron	Phronesis
Phrontis	Phrontisterion
PhSocSci	Philosophy of the Social Sciences
PhT	Philosophy Today
PolTheo	Political Theory

PRIA	Proceedings of the Royal Irish Academy
ProcPhEd	Philosophy of Education: Proceedings
ProcPhEdSocGB	Proceedings of the Philosophy of Education Society of Great Britain
ProcStud	Process Studies
Prud	Prudentia
QJS	Quarterly Journal of Speech
QS	Quaderni di Storia
QUCC	Quaderni Urbinati di Cultura Classica
RBPh	Revue Belge de Philologie et d'Histoire
RCSF	Rivista Critica di Storia della Filosofia
REA	Revue des Etudes Anciennes
REAug	Revue des Etudes Augustiniennes
RecAug	Recherches Augustiniennes
RecSR	Recherches de Science Religieuse
RecTh	Recherches de Theologie ancienne et medievale
REG	Revue des Etudes Grecques
REJ	Revue des Etudes Juives
RelHum	Religious Humanism
RELO	Revue de l'Organisation Internationale pour l'Etude des Langues Anciennes par Ordinateur
RelStud	Religious Studies
RevW	Revolutionary World
RFIC	Rivista di Filologia e di Istruzione Classica
RFilNeo-Scol	Rivista di Filosofia Neo-Scolastica
RhM	Rheinisches Museum
RIPh	Revue Internationale de Philosophie
RJ	Rechtshistorisches Journal
RMeta	Review of Metaphysics
RMM	Revue de Metaphysique et Morale
RPhA	Revue de Philosophie Ancienne
RPL	Res Publica Litterarum
RSA	Rivista storica dell'Antichita
RSC	Rivista di Studi Classici
SAfrJPh	South African Journal of Philosophy
SCent	Second Century
SCI	Scripta Classica Israelica
SecOrd	Second Order
SicGym	Siculorum Gymnasium
SIF	Studi internazionali di Filosofia (also published as *IntStudPh*)
SIFC	Studi Italiani di Filologia Classica
SJPh	Southern Journal of Philosophy
SM	Speech Monographs
SO	Symbolae Osloenses
SocBiblLitSemPapSer	Society of Biblical Literature Seminar Paper Series

SocPh&Pol	Social Philosophy and Policy
SocRes	Social Research
SouthSpComJ	Southern Speech Communication Journal (formerly *SouthSpJ*)
SouthSpJ	Southern Speech Journal (now *SouthSpComJ*)
SovStudPh	Soviet Studies in Philosophy
SPh	Studies in Philology
StPhilon	Studia Philonica
StudClas	Studii Clasice
StudGen	Studium Generale
StudHist&PhSci	Studies in the History and Philosophy of Science
StudPatr	Studia Patristica
StudPh&HistPh	Studies in Philosophy and the History of Philosophy
StudSovTho	Studies in Soviet Thought
SwJPh	Southwestern Journal of Philosophy
SwPhR	Southwest Philosophy Review
SwPhSt	Southwestern Philosophical Studies
SynPhil	Synthesis Philosophica
TAPhA	Transactions of the American Philological Association
TeachPh	Teaching Philosophy
Thom	The Thomist
ThoughtPrac	Thought and Practice
ThS	Theological Studies
ThZ	Theologische Zeitschrift
TijdFil	Tijdschrift voor Philosophie
TPhS	Transactions of the Philological Society
TPS	Transactions of the Charles S. Peirce Society
Trad	Traditio
TulStudPh	Tulane Studies in Philosophy
UltR&M	Ultimate Reality and Meaning
VigChr	Vigiliae Christianae
WS	Wiener Studien
YCS	Yale Classical Studies
ZAnt	Ziva Antika
ZNTW	Zeitschrift fuer Neutestamentliche Wissenschaft
ZPhilForsh	Zeitschrift fuer Philosophische Forschung
ZWG	Zeitschrift fuer Wissenschaftsgeschichte

Chapter 1

INTRODUCTION AND SURVEY

PURPOSE AND PRINCIPLES OF ORGANIZATION

A bibliography is a tool and, like any tool, it can do some things but is useless for other tasks. Someone needing to drive a nail would not find a screwdriver or a wrench the least bit helpful. Similarly, this tool will be useful for some purposes but not for all. Different users will be able to do different things with it, just as a master carpenter and a weekend thumb-pounder will use the same hammer more or less effectively. We think that non-specialists in the field of ancient philosophy who want a guide to some significant portion of the recent research will find this work helpful, as will the reference librarians to whom they turn for help. We think, however, that it will also prove useful to professionals in the field, simply because the literature in the discipline has grown so vast in recent years that it is now very difficult for anyone to stay current in more than a limited subfield.

A tool of this sort has become a necessity. The last quarter of a century has seen a dramatic rise in interest in ancient western philosophy. English-language scholars have played a significant role in that development. Several English-language journals are now devoted solely to ancient philosophy. A number of important European works have been translated into English, and more European scholars (especially Scandinavian and East European) have begun to publish in English rather than French or German. (It is still true, of course, that no one can *master* this field without a knowledge of the European literature.)

All of these developments mean that just the English-language literature is now so vast that some effort must be made to organize it and make at least some portion of it accessible to a wider academic audience. The need for bibliographic resources of this sort was argued cogently by Radice and Runia in the preface to their work on Philo (cf. #6657), p. xiv:

> We believe that, given the vastly increased productivity of modern scholarship, scholars today will have to pay more attention to the compilation of instruments of research that will enable themselves and their colleagues to surmount the barriers of extreme specialization and to continue to make relevant and effective contributions. The mere listing of works of scholarship will not be enough, for titles can often be insufficiently informative or even positively misleading. Some form of annotation is highly desirable, indeed virtually mandatory.

Our ambitious objective, then, has been to produce a one-volume annotated guide which covers the entire chronological range of ancient western philosophy, from Thales to Augustine. The brief introductions to each figure or school are not meant to present original scholarship, merely to provide a convenient summary of each thinker's major themes and give the user of the guide some idea of the most important questions or problems involved in the study of that philosopher. Their presence should help someone with less experience in the field see how the various pieces of research listed fit into a larger plan and should be more useful than sending users to another reference work, to which they may not have access. We have not tried to summarize the current state of research on any given author because changes in interpretation could outdate our work before it reached publication.

Given the breadth of our objective, we had to impose some limit on ourselves in order to remain within the bounds of even a large single volume. The first was in geographical scope. Though several eastern philosophical schools flourished contemporaneously with the Greco-Roman schools, it would be impossible to cover them adequately and still do justice to the western schools. A number of items in this bibliography deal with points of contact between eastern and western philosophy; they can be located by means of the index. For brevity, the term "ancient philosophy" as used in this volume denotes "ancient Greco-Roman philosophy." Our second limit was chronological. Twenty-five years is a significant period in the history of scholarship in any discipline. In ancient philosophy it encompasses some epoch-making works. But it omits almost as many as it includes. Beginning in 1960 or 1950, however, would still have excluded a number of important English-language studies. Any cut-off date would be somewhat arbitrary.

We have tried to get around the disadvantages of this chronological limit by including older books which have been reprinted since 1965 and articles which have appeared in anthologies. Anyone wanting to consult earlier studies will find references to them in the footnotes or bibliographies of works included here. We have also made a concerted effort to find bibliographies on all the authors covered here, even including some which fall outside our chronological limits.

We began compiling the bibliography by accumulating a list from entries in the *Philosopher's Index* and *Année Philologique*, the annual bibliography of classical studies. We gleaned additional items from footnotes and bibliographies of articles and books as we abstracted them. This sometimes led us to sources overlooked in the two major bibliographical tools. As one small example, our bibliography contains over a dozen items from *Polity* and from the *American Journal of Jurisprudence* which were unearthed in this way. We scanned tables of contents of anthologies and *Festschriften*. We do not, by any means, claim to have compiled an exhaustive bibliography. We are confident, however, that it is thorough.

Several space-saving concessions have been necessary. We have not included texts or translations unless they offer considerable notes or commentary in English. Doctoral dissertations have not been included because they are not easily accessible or intelligible to the non-specialist. We have also excluded surveys which include only a chapter or two on antiquity and works which are strictly textual/philological in orientation. In dealing with Christian thinkers we have listed items that concern their role as continuators of the classical philosophical tradition, not as theologians. We do not include book reviews unless they are article-length discussions. We have set the bibliographical entries in a slightly smaller type than the text of the introductory sections, reasoning that people don't read a bibliography the way they do a section of continuous text.

A few words might be said about the format of the entries. The author's name is given in bold caps, with last name first, then first initial (and middle, if known). Using initials instead of full names is another concession to the size of the volume. If a work has two co-authors, we list both; if more than two, we list the work by the last name of the first author given and designate the others by "et al." We have also abbreviated the names of ancient philosophers in the annotations and the introductions wherever we could do so without causing confusion.

The titles of books are given in italics, followed by full publication information. For books published in the United States the city of publication is given, followed by the state, unless the city is one whose location can be assumed to be known to most people. States are designated by the two-letter Postal Service abbreviations. If the publisher is a university press named after a city (e. g., University of Chicago), the name of the city will be omitted. The words "University" and "Press" will regularly be abbreviated, as will any other terms which can be abbreviated without loss of clarity.

Titles of journal articles are given in quotation marks, followed by the title of the journal, usually in abbreviated form. Some of the abbreviations have been adopted from *Année Philologique* or *Philosopher's Index*, but many have been modified to make them somewhat more self-explanatory. (A full list of abbreviations is included in the front of the book.) Following the title of the journal one will find the volume number, the year (in parentheses), and the inclusive page numbers. One small problem should be noted here. Some journals publish over the calendar year, so they can be listed as: 25(1979). Other journals publish on the academic year, so that their first number appears in the fall. These journals should be listed as: 25(1978-79). It may happen, however, because of the number of entries we have been handling, that the same journal may occasionally appear to have a volume number with two separate years: 25(1978) or 25(1979). This simply means that the article appeared in that portion of the journal published in 1978 or 1979.

Some of the entries are items in anthologies. We list the anthology under the editor's name (if given) in the appropriate section. Each item is then listed under the author's name, with the full title given, followed by the item number of the anthology (e. g., "in #3657") and the page numbers. If an article has appeared in a journal since 1965 and then been anthologized, we give the journal entry first, then the reference to the anthology.

The annotations in the bibliography are written in the most compressed style we could manage and still remain intelligible. They are supposed to represent the author's summation of his/her thesis. The annotations are intended to be informative, not to assess the relative merits of the books or articles being summarized. In some cases we have referred to a work as "somewhat technical" or used some similar phrase to indicate that it is probably not the place a newcomer to the field would want to start. Such a work would, however, be important to consult at some point in one's study of that philosopher. If a book received uniformly bad reviews or had some glaring deficiency noted by several reviewers, we have tried to point out in the annotations what that problem might be. In some cases reviewers have felt that an author's biases so affected his/her perception of the field that we felt it best to give some hint of the bias in the annotation. On the whole we have tried to write the abstracts in a neutral tone. Abstracts of articles are sometimes longer than abstracts of books because an article may sometimes be a more important piece of scholarship than a book. The length of the abstracts is primarily determined by the desire for clarity.

Those wishing to pursue the study of a particular author further should look up that author by name in the *Philosopher's Index* and in *Année Philologique*. Though the latter is published in France, it includes a number of annotations in English in volumes published after 1965. Many (but not all) of the items in those two resources are annotated. Another thorough (but not annotated) listing is the annual *Repertoire Bibliographique de la Philosophie*, which has sections on the various ancient philosophers. Also helpful is the *Bibliographie de la Philosophie*, an annual review of selected books. Books written in English are reviewed in English. *Philosophical Books* also reviews each year's significant publications in the field.

It should be noted that, in this volume, last names beginning with de, des, or du, are alphabetized under the D's; names beginning with van or von are under the V's. Other bibliographies vary in their practice; some are not even internally consistent.

Finally, responsibilities for the work were distributed as follows: Bell covered the pre-Platonic thinkers and post-Aristotelian schools. Allis and Bell worked on Plato and Aristotle with the assistance of several student researchers. Bell compiled the index and produced the camera-ready copy.

THE STARTING POINT

Anyone surveying the discipline of philosophy, looking for some categories and subdivisions — landmarks by which to guide his study — will quickly observe the important role that the Greeks played in its development. One can speak generally of "ancient" philosophy, but the Roman contribution to the field was negligible, consisting largely of the preservation and translation of some of the Greek material, and that not even the best. It was the Arabs, not the Romans, who preserved Plato and Aristotle for the medieval west.

It is to the Greeks, then, that we look as the originators of philosophy. As one scholar put it, by 300 B. C., "the principal problems were raised and were roughly defined. A logical method was evolved to attack them. Systems embracing both macrocosm and microcosm were devised in explanation." Von Weizsacker (#256) agrees that the Greeks "invented what we call philosophy and . . . all the terms we have been using for two thousand years."

The traditional claim is that the early Greek philosophers had no predecessors. They simply invented the discipline outright. But this view has never been a consensus. The ancient Jews, such as Josephus in his *Against Apion*, held that the Greeks had borrowed from the Hebrews. Diogenes Laertius, in the preface to his *Lives of the Philosophers*, concedes the antiquity of Eastern philosophy.

Emile Brehier (#3) contends that the originality of the early Greek philosophers was more a matter of their selection and elaboration of ideas long in circulation among the Mesopotamians and Egyptians. It is undoubtedly significant that the first Greek philosophers known to us came from Ionia, in Asia Minor, the part of the Hellenic world which was in closest contact with Egypt and the East.

Surviving documents do indicate that the Egyptians and Mesopotamians had made observations of natural phenomena and suggested explanations of the origins of the universe. In a limited way they had delved into ethics. The Egyptians, in books such as *The Wisdom of Ptah-Hotep*, had developed maxims or adages designed to guide an observant person through the difficulties of life. But there is a qualitative leap from such things, which most closely resemble the Old Testament books of Genesis and Proverbs, to the efforts of thinkers such as Thales to explain the organization of *physis* (nature), or of Pythagoras to develop a way of daily living based on his understanding of the nature of the universe. No Egyptian or Mesopotamian of whom we have record ever asked the fundamental question: Why do these things exist as they do? Every Egyptian or Mesopotamian explanation of natural phenomena begins with an account of the activity of the gods.

The Greeks, to be sure, had their own myths, formalized by Homer and Hesiod in the late eighth century B. C., and we cannot account for the leap from myth to proto-science which is represented by the Ionian thinkers of the early sixth century B. C. (cf. #392). That is one of the most intriguing aspects of the study of ancient philosophy. Rarely are we privileged to observe the very beginnings of a discipline or a craft. The earliest painters, iron-smelters, and wheelwrights have fallen into oblivion, converted into passive verbs in the textbooks. We know there were poets ere Homer, historians antedating Herodotus, and tragedians who upstaged Aeschylus. But Thales has no traceable ancestor in his intellectual life. Even the ancient sources fail to tantalize us with stories of some semi-legendary founder of philosophy whose work was entirely lost, as they do in other disciplines. All are in agreement: Thales, a citizen of Miletus, was the first philosopher. To him belongs "the prestige inseparable from any supremely original and influential intellectual debut" (#397, p. 93).

Today there is some uncertainty over Thales' claim to the title of first philosopher. But if he was not the first, then the mantle passes to a Milesian of the next generation, Anaximander. Neither man used the term "philosopher" to describe himself, nor did they offer insights on subjects, such as ethics or the purpose of life, which we expect philosophers to deal with today. They attempted to explain what was the basic material from which *physis* was made and what natural, i. e., non-divine, causes governed its operations.

The harder question to answer is, *Why* was an Ionian Greek the first to view the world in these terms? This is the conundrum that the historian of any intellectual discipline inevitably reaches. How does one account for genius, for the insights which one individual achieves which had occurred to no one before him/her? Archeologists digging down through the strata of a site can see how styles of pottery and building changed over the centuries, each generation adding some small new feature or adapting something done by their ancestors. But eventually they reach the level at which it all began. Then they must ask, Why did someone first decide that clay could be used to fashion a container? Did a process of rational deduction lead to that conclusion, or did he/she merely find something that had fallen into a campfire? Was it genius or serendipity? Unfortunately, the world's first potter left no detailed account of his/her work or the motive for undertaking it. The study of ancient Greek pottery makes a nice analogy to the study of Greek philosophy. We can deduce a few things by observing surviving fragments of early pottery, but we're not always entirely sure to whom to attribute them. It is only from the classical period of Greek civilization that we obtain enough samples of pottery to enable us to analyze them with some confidence. The Greeks who came after Alexander, and their Roman conquerers, added little new. In general they debased, if that is not too strong a word, the classical models, exaggerating their less heroic features and creating a realistic and pessimistic style of art.

Now consider the history of western philosophy. All the philosophers before 400 B. C. are grouped together as Presocratics. Their works are fragmentary if they survive at all. The classical period produced Socrates, Plato, and Aristotle, and some studies of Greek philosophy make it appear that all that went before them was a prelude and all that came later, merely an afterthought. (A. N. Whitehead claimed that the history of western philosophy consists of a few footnotes to Plato.) The user of this guide will notice that in sheer bulk the modern studies devoted to these three outweigh all the rest of the authors combined. In the Hellenistic and Roman periods one encounters the copies and exaggerations of the Platonic and Aristotelian systems, as well as the fatalistic Stoic and Epicurean schools.

The analogy to pottery might hold for one more step. Just as clay pots were an essential part of daily life in ancient Greece and Rome, so philosophy was an integral part of their intellectual life, to a degree which we can hardly comprehend today. It had a far wider audience than the discipline has enjoyed at any time since. As Sally Brown once wrote in a school report in a "Peanuts" comic strip, "Ancient Greece was ahead of its time . . . . They had no TV, but they had lots of philosophers. I, personally, would not want to sit around all evening watching a philosopher." The Greeks and Romans would have differed with Sally. They spent a great deal of time listening to philosophers. If Aristophanes' comedies are any indication, even the *hoi polloi* in the theater were familiar enough with philosophers of the day to appreciate jokes at their expense.

The situation changed little over the centuries. The book of Acts mentions Epicureans and Stoics, the dominant schools of that day, and says that the Athenians spent their time in the agora gossiping and listening to such people teach (Acts 17.16-21). Even the pragmatic Romans were eventually attracted to Greek thought. Pliny the Younger, while admitting that "only one philosopher can understand another," was eager to spend "whole days listening" to a contemporary philosopher named Euphrates (*Ep.* 1.10).

Why was philosophy so important to these people? A primary reason may have been the lack of any kind of religious teaching that offered moral guidance. Greco-Roman religious cults were concerned to protect the group by staying on the god's good side. The gods themselves behaved in amoral, sometimes immoral, ways. They were not ultimately powerful. The universe was not their creation, and there was an irresistible Fate which not even they could oppose. Whatever else they may have done, it is clear that those first Milesian philosophers tried to offer a worldview that did not depend on the unpredictable gods and asserted the ability of human rationality to understand the cosmos. Philosophy's role as a kind of secular religion can be emphasized by pointing out that Greeks and Romans could freely worship any number of gods simultaneously but could not be adherents of more than one philosophical school at a time. Many terms which we associate with religion today originated in the ancient philosophical schools. A philosopher taught his *dogma*. A disagreement between two schools was *haeresis* (heresy).

Someone approaching the study of ancient philosophy for the first time is undertaking a difficult but not impossible task. We hope this resource guide will ease the early stages of the journey. To shift from the tool metaphor, we hope this volume will serve as a *pedagogus*, a Greek servant whose task it was to escort the children to school and supervise their studies. For the professional, we hope it will help him/her work more efficiently.

The portion of the bibliography which follows is divided into three sections. The first contains general surveys of ancient philosophy and reference works; the second, volumes of collected essays; and the third, studies of various topics which cover several authors or more than one period. As a general rule, multi-volume works in which the individual volumes do not stand alone are given a single reference number, while those in which the separate volumes can be used independently have a reference number for each volume. We have relaxed the chronological limit in the first section to include some standard surveys.

GENERAL HISTORIES AND REFERENCE WORKS

ARMSTRONG, A. H. *An Introduction to Ancient Philosophy.* Totowa, NJ: Littlefield, Adams, 1981; 3rd ed., rprt. Survey, from Thales to Augustine. Introduction updates and corrects points in each chapter. [1]

BRADY, I. *A History of Ancient Philosophy.* Milwaukee, WI: Bruce, 1959. Standard survey for college students; first of a three-volume set. Looks first at "pre-philosophy" of Israel, Mesopotamia, Egypt, Persia, and the East. Covers major Greek philosophers through Neoplatonists. A Christian philosophy of history underlies entire work. [2]

BREHIER, E. *The History of Philosophy*: Univ. of Chicago Pr.
Vol. I: *The Hellenic Age*, transl. J. Thomas. 1963. Brief but useful treatments of the Presocratics, Socrates, Plato, and Aristotle. [3]

Vol. II: *The Hellenistic and Roman Age*, transl. W. Baskin. 1963. Examines minor Socratics, Stoics, Epicureans, Neoplatonists, Christianity. [4]

BRUMBAUGH, R. S. *The Philosophers of Greece.* New York: Crowell, 1964. Survey which stresses comparison of ancient philosophers (Thales to Aristotle) with modern. Strongest in Aristotle and Atomists. [5]

COPLESTON, F. C. *A History of Philosophy*, vol I: *Greece and Rome.* New York:

Doubleday, 1962; rprt. Traditional survey with somewhat Scholastic bent. Heavy emphasis on Plato and Aristotle.   [6]

CORNFORD, F. M. "The Athenian Philosophical Schools," in #53, pp. 312-365. Survey of the major thinkers, reprinted from *Cambridge Ancient History.*   [7]

————. *Before and After Socrates.* Cambridge Univ. Pr., 1976; rprt. For non-specialists. Chapters on Presocratics, Socrates, Plato, and Aristotle. Socrates' conversion from study of nature to questions of ethics is seen as pivotal.   [8]

DeGEORGE, R. T. *A Guide to Philosophical Bibliography and Research.* New York: Appleton-Century-Crofts, 1971. Lists dictionaries, encyclopedias, bibliographies, and other tools useful to beginning or advanced students.   [9]

DONLAN, W., ed. *The* Classical World *Bibliography of Philosophy, Religion, and Rhetoric.* New York: Garland, 1978. Reprint of bibliographies from various issues of *CW.* Many cover philosophers, such as Presocratics, Epicurus, Seneca.   [10]

Encyclopedia of Philosophy, P. Edwards, editor-in-chief. New York: Macmillan, 1967; 8 vols. Standard reference work. Looks at topics as well as individual thinkers.   [11]

FULLER, B. A. G. *History of Greek Philosophy.* New York: Greenwood, 1969; rprt.:
vol. I: *Thales to Democritus.*
vol. II: *The Sophists, Socrates, Plato.*
vol. III: *Aristotle.* For non-specialists, summary based on Zeller (#39), Gomperz (#14), and Burnet (#312).   [12]

GIRVETZ, H., et al. *Science, Folklore, and Philosophy.* New York: Harper & Row, 1966. Survey which traces development of reasoned approach to knowledge out of cultural folklore. Chapters on Presocratics, Sophists, Plato, and Aristotle.   [13]

GOMPERZ, T. *Greek Thinkers. A History of Ancient Philosophy.* London: Murray, 1964; rprt. Survey typical of solid Germanic scholarship of late nineteenth century. Vol. I covers pre-philosophical Greek thought and Presocratics down to Sophists. Vol. II deals with Socrates, Minor Socratics, early Plato. Vol. III looks at Plato's later work; Vol. IV covers Aristotle and early Lyceum.   [14]

GROOTEN, J., and **STEENBERGEN, G. J.** *New Encyclopedia of Philosophy*, transl. and ed. E. van den Bossche. New York: Philosophical Library, 1972. One volume with survey articles on persons and topics.   [15]

GUTHRIE, W. K. C. *The Greek Philosophers. From Thales to Aristotle.* London: Methuen, 1960; rprt. Survey designed for non-specialists, concentrating on themes: materialism and form among Ionians and Pythagoreans; movement in Heraclitus, Parmenides, and Pluralists; nature of man in Sophists and Socrates.   [16]

————. *A History of Greek Philosophy.* Cambridge Univ. Pr.:
Vol. I: *The Earlier Presocratics and Pythagoreans.* 1962. Relies on Aristotle's doxographies. Stresses originality of Xenophanes. Main section treats Pythagoreans.   [17]

Vol. II: *The Presocratic Tradition from Parmenides to Democritus.* 1965. Parmenides is treated as shaman; reinterprets problem of corporeal or incorporeal being as question of perceptible and intelligible. For Empedocles, problem is to explain evil and to combine necessity and chance. Anaxagoras has Milesian characteristics. To understand him, concept of homoeomerity must be rejected. Democritus' interests were largely ontological. [18]

Vol. III: *The Fifth-Century Enlightenment.* 1969. Discusses Sophists by topics, with biographical data confined to a separate chapter. Compares them to seventeenth-century Enlightenment thinkers. Socrates, though no Sophist, fits better in their intellectual milieu than in Plato's fourth-century world. [19]

Vol. IV: *Plato, the Man and His Dialogues, Earlier Period.* 1975. Chapters 1-3 discuss P's life and philosophical influences on him, his literary style, and chronology of the dialogues. Chapter 4 discusses early Socratic dialogues (*Apology* to *Ion*). Chapter 5 considers dialogues from *Protagoras* to *Menexenus.* Chapter 6 looks at *Phaedo, Symposium, Pheadrus,* while chapter 7 is devoted to *Republic.* P is seen as a religious reformer, with his doctrine of immortal soul. Guthrie shows how Socratic thought "shades into Platonism." [20]

Vol. V: *The Later Plato and the Academy.* 1978. Surveys later dialogues beginning with *Cratylus, Parmenides* and suggests that P may have taught some kind of "esoteric doctrine" based on Pythagorean ideas and passed on orally. The letters attributed to P are treated, particularly 2 and 7. Last chapter is devoted to Speusippus, Xenocrates, and P's other associates in the Academy. [21]

Vol. VI: *Aristotle: An Encounter.* 1981. Surveys Ar's life and early works. Chapter on "The Mind of Aristotle" is especially helpful for non-specialists. Treats Ar's thought by topics: teleology, ethics, logic, etc. Lacks chapters on the *Politics* and *Poetics* because Guthrie suffered a stroke while working on it. [22]

IRWIN, T. *A History of Western Philosophy, I: Classical Thought.* Oxford Univ. Pr., 1989. Chapter on Homer deals with "pre-philosophical" themes; two chapters on Presocratics. Chapter four considers critiques of naturalism in Aeschylus, Democritus, and Protagoras. Chapters five to seven view Socrates, Plato, and Aristotle as a continuous development. Three chapters on Hellenistic philosophy and one on Plotinus. [23]

JASENAS, M. *A History of the Bibliography of Philosophy.* Hildesheim, Ger.: Olm, 1973. Studies origins, biases of bibliographies in field from 1592 to 1960. [24]

JONES, W. T. *A History of Western Philosophy, I: The Classical Mind; II: The Medieval Mind.* New York: Harcourt Brace Jovanovich, 1970; 2nd ed. Standard survey, with generous extracts from ancient sources. Vol. I covers Presocratics to Cicero and Skeptics. Vol. II begins with Gnostics, Plotinus, Augustine. [25]

MARIAS, J. *A Biography of Philosophy,* transl. by H. C. Raley. University, AL: Univ. of AL Pr., 1984. Based on assumption that philosophers' doctrines can be best understood in light of their historical context. Surveys lives and historical background rather than history of ideas. Chapter 1 covers Presocratics, Plato; Chapter 2, historian Herodotus; Chapter 3, Aristotle; Chapter 4, Stoics. Six more chapters deal with medieval and modern philosophy. [26]

OWENS, J. *A History of Ancient Western Philosophy.* New York: Appleton-Century-Crofts, 1959. Differs from standard surveys in emphasis on context of philosophers' teaching and use of excerpts from their works rather than summaries. Four parts: Origins (Thales to Eleatics); Developments (Empedocles to Socrates); Flowering (Plato and Aristotle); Middle and Final Years (Hellenistic schools and Neoplatonism).   **[27]**

PARKER, G. F. *A Short Account of Greek Philosophy.* New York: Barnes & Noble, 1967. Studies Presocratics as investigators of *physis*; Socrates' search for absolutes; three chapters on Plato, four on Aristotle; brief survey of Hellenistic schools.   **[28]**

PETERS, F. E. *Greek Philosophical Terms. A Historical Lexicon.* New York Univ. Pr., 1967. Addressed to non-specialists who do not know Greek. Concentrates on terms used in metaphysics, excluding logic, ethics, and other subfields.   **[29]**

PLOTT, J. C., et al. *Global History of Philosophy, I: The Axial Age; II: The Han-Hellenistic-Bactrian Period.* Delhi, India: Moltilal Banarsidass, 1963 and 1979. Integrated survey of eastern and western philosophies. Vol. I gives slight attention to Presocratics; Vol. II treats Plato, Aristotle, Stoics and Neoplatonists more completely.   **[30]**

RAUCHE, G. A. *A Student's Key to Ancient Greek Thought.*   Fort Hare, S A: Fort Hare Univ. Pr., 1966. Summary descriptions of theories of Presocratics, Sophists, Socrates, Plato and Aristotle, and Hellenistic schools, including Gnostics.   **[31]**

REALE, G. *A History of Ancient Philosophy,* ed. and transl. J. R. Catan. Albany: SUNY Pr.:

Vol. I: *From the Origins To Socrates.* 1986. Noteworthy for introductory chapter on problems of history of philosophy. Eleatics treated at greater length than in most surveys.   **[32]**

Vol. II: *Plato and Aristotle.* 1985. Examines their individual contributions and connections between them.   **[33]**

Vol. III: *Systems of the Hellenistic Age.* 1985. Minor Socratics, Academy, Peripatetics, Epicureans, Stoics, Skeptics, and Eclectics. Hellenistic philosophies arose because political changes brought on by Alexander's conquests made Plato's and Aristotle's doctrines passe even in their own schools.   **[34]**

Vol. IV: *The Schools of the Imperial Age.* 1990. Rebirth of Aristotelianism, Late Epicureanism and Stoicism, Pyrrhonism and Neo-Skepticism; Middle and Neo-Platonism, Neopythagoreanism.   **[35]**

THOMAS, H. *Biographical Encyclopedia of Philosophy.* New York: Doubleday, 1965. Succinct articles on over four hundred philosophers (major and minor) from antiquity to modern times. Emphasis is on each person's biography with a sketch of most important teachings.   **[36]**

TICE, T. N., and **SLAVENS, T. P.** *Research Guide to Philosophy.* Chicago: Amer. Library Assoc., 1983. Discussion of trends in discipline current at time of publication. Several chapters deal with ancient period. Brief, selected bibliographies with each chapter.   **[37]**

WEDBERG, A. *A History of Philosophy, I: Antiquity and the Middle Ages.* Oxford: Clarendon Pr., 1982. Thematic approach: Chapter I discusses physics and natural science; Chapter II, religion and mathematics; III, scientific methodology; IV, concept analysis; V, logic; VI, ethics. [38]

ZELLER, E. *Outlines of the History of Greek Philosophy,* 13th ed., rev. by W. Nestle, transl. L. R. Palmer. Cleveland: World, 1950. Thorough, well-balanced survey. [39]

COLLECTED ESSAYS

ANSCOMBE, G. E. M. *Collected Philosophical Papers,I: From Parmenides to Wittgenstein.* Oxford: Blackwell, 1981. Seven of thirteen essays deal with ancient philosophy (Parmenides, Plato, Diodorus Cronus, and Aristotle). Most are somewhat technical studies of logic. [40]

ANTON, J. P., and KUSTAS, G. L., eds. *Essays in Ancient Greek Philosophy.* Albany: SUNY Pr., 1971. Thirty-five essays, most reprinted from journals, with indices and an introduction. All are abstracted herein. [41]

———., and PREUS, A., eds. *Essays in Ancient Greek Philosophy,* vol. 2. Albany: SUNY Pr., 1983. Twenty-seven papers from Society for Ancient Greek Philosophy's annual meetings; abstracted herein. [42]

ARMSTRONG, A. A., ed. *Classical Mediterranean Spirituality: Egyptian, Greek, Roman.* New York: Crossroad, 1986. Collection of essays emphasizing close link between philosophy and spirituality. Most are abstracted herein. [43]

BAIRD, R. M., et al. eds. *Contemporary Essays on Greek Ideas. The Kilgore Festschrift.* Waco, TX: Baylor Univ. Pr., 1987. Essays on Greek philosophy and its influence. Pertinent ones are abstracted herein. [44]

BOGEN, J., and McGUIRE, J. E., eds. *How Things Are: Studies in Predication and the History of Philosophy and Science.* Dordrecht, Netherlands: Reidel, 1985. Relevant essays in this collection, mostly on Plato and Aristotle, are abstracted herein. [45]

BORZA, E., and CARRUBA, W., eds. *Classics and the Classical Tradition: Festschrift for R. Dengler.* University Park: PA St. Univ. Pr., 1973. Relevant essays abstracted herein. [46]

BOSSIER, F., et al., eds. *Images of Man in Ancient and Medieval Thought. Studia G. Verbeke ab amicis et collegis dicata.* Leuven (Netherlands) Univ. Pr., 1976. Essays in this collection relevant to ancient philosophy are abstracted herein. [47]

BOWERSOCK, G. W., et al., eds. *Arktouros. Hellenic Studies Presented to Bernard M. W. Knox on the Occasion of his 65th Birthday.* Berlin: de Gruyter, 1979. Collection of essays. Those of philosophical interest are abstracted herein. [48]

BRUMBAUGH, R. S. *Platonic Studies of Greek Philosophy: Form, Arts, Gadgets, and Hemlock.* Albany: SUNY Pr., 1989. Collection of Brumbaugh's articles on ancient philosophy. Relevant items abstracted herein. [49]

CAUCHY, V. *Philosophy and Culture. Proceedings of the XVIIth World Congress of Philosophy.* 5 vols. Montreal: Eds. du Beffroi (vol. 1); Eds. de Montmorency (vols 2-5), 1986-1988. Relevant essays in English are abstracted herein.   [50]

CHERNISS, H. F. *Selected Papers*, ed. L. Taran. Leiden: Brill, 1977. Collection of some published articles, most of his longer book reviews, and one previously unpublished lecture. Articles and lecture are abstracted below.   [51]

CORCORAN, J. *Ancient Logic and Its Modern Interpretations. Proceedings of the Buffalo Symposium on Modernist Interpretations of Ancient Logic, 21 and 22 April, 1972.* Dordrecht, Netherlands: Reidel, 1974. Essays on Aristotle, Stoics, mathematics and logic. All are abstracted herein.   [52]

CORNFORD, F. M. *Selected Papers of F. M. Cornford*, ed. A. C. Bowen. New York: Garland, 1987. Reprints of seventeen journal articles and book chapters. Those of philosophic interest are abstracted herein.   [53]

DEPEW, D. J., ed. *The Greeks and the Good Life: Proceedings from the Ninth Annual Philosophy Symposium at Cal State.* Fullerton: CA State Univ. Pr., 1980. Ten papers on Aristotle, Plato, Epicurus, Greek ethics in general. Abstracted herein.   [54]

DE VOGEL, C. J. *Philosophia, I: Studies in Greek Philosophy.* Assen, Netherlands: van Gorcum, 1970. Collected papers, some revisions of earlier publications. Most in English. Subjects include Pythagoras, Socrates, Plato, Aristotle, Plotinus. Two general studies on term *philosophia* and idea of eternal change in Greek and Indian thought.   [55]

DODDS, E. R. *The Ancient Concept of Progress and Other Essays on Greek Literature and Belief.* Oxford: Clarendon Pr., 1973. Relevant essays abstracted herein.   [56]

FREDE, M. *Essays in Ancient Philosophy.* Oxford: Clarendon Pr., 1987. One essay on writing history of philosophy, others on Plato, Aristotle, Stoics, and Sceptics. Emphasis on logic, metaphysics, and epistemology.   [57]

FURLEY, D. *Cosmic Problems: Essays on Greek and Roman Philosophy of Nature.* Cambridge Univ. Pr., 1989. Collection of essays, some previously unpublished. All are abstracted herein.   [58]

GERBER, D. E., ed. *Greek Poetry and Philosophy. Studies in Honor of Leonard Woodbury.* Chico, CA: Scholars' Pr., 1984. Most of essays are literary in nature; two deal with Heraclitus, three with Plato, and are abstracted herein.   [59]

GERSON, L. P., ed. *Graceful Reason. Essays in Ancient and Medieval Philosophy Presented to Joseph Owens on the Occasions of his Seventy-fifth Birthday and the Fiftieth Anniversary of his Ordination.* Toronto: Pontif. Inst. of Medieval Studies, 1983. Twenty essays. Pertinent ones in English abstracted herein.   [60]

HINTIKKA, J., and **KNUUTTILA, S.**, eds. *The Logic of Being.* Dordrecht, Netherlands: Reidel, 1986. Collected essays on ontology; relevant items abstracted herein.   [61]

KAJANTO, I., ed. *Equality and Inequality of Man in Ancient Thought. Papers Read at the Colloquium in Connection with the Assemblee generale of the F. I. E. C. Held in*

Helsinki in August 1982. Helsinki: Finnish Society of Sciences and Letters, 1984. Papers on variety of topics. All are abstracted herein.   [62]

KELLY, M., ed. *For Service to Classical Studies. Essays in Honor of Francis Letters*. Melbourne, Austral.: Cheshire, 1966. Relevant essays are abstracted herein.   [63]

KRETZMANN, N., ed. *Infinity and Continuity in Ancient and Medieval Thought*. Ithaca, NY: Cornell Univ. Pr., 1982. Eleven essays, four on Aristotle, one on influence of ancient math on philosophical discussions of puzzle of infinity. Also discussed: Diodorus Cronus, Zeno of Elea, Alexander of Aphrodisias.   [64]

LEE, E. N., et al., eds. *Exegesis and Argument. Studies in Greek Philosophy Presented to Gregory Vlastos*. *Phronesis* Suppl. 1. Assen, Netherlands: Van Gorcum, 1973. Essays on various writers, abstracted herein. Bibliography of Vlastos' works.   [65]

MACHAMER, P. K., and **TURNBULL, R. G.**, eds. *Studies in Perception: Interrelations in the History of Philosophy and Science*. Columbus: Ohio St. Univ. Pr., 1977. Essays pertinent to ancient philosophers' theories of perception are abstracted herein.   [66]

MANSFELD, J., and **DE RIJK, L. M.**, eds. *Kephalion. Studies in Greek Philosophy and Its Continuation Offered to C. J. de Vogel*. Assen, Netherlands: van Gorcum, 1975. Essays, most abstracted herein, cover Presocratics, Socrates, Plato, Aristotle, Middle Platonism, early Christian philosophy, Neoplatonism, and medieval Platonism.   [67]

MOREWEDGE, P., ed. *Philosophies of Existence. Ancient and Medieval*. New York: Fordham Univ. Pr., 1982. Thirteen essays on ontology. Four deal with ancient period and are abstracted herein.   [68]

OLIVA, P., and **FROLIKOVA, A.** *Concilium Eirene XVI: Proceedings of the 16th International Eirene Conference, Prague 31.8. - 4.9. 1982*. Prague: Kabinet pro studia recka, rimska a latinska CSAV, 1983; 3 vols. Relevant essays in English are abstracted herein.   [69]

OWEN, G. E. L. *Logic, Science, and Dialectic. Collected Papers in Greek Philosophy*, ed. M. C. Nussbaum. Ithaca, NY: Cornell Univ. Pr., 1986. Owen's major philosophical essays. Sections on Presocratics and Plato are chronological. Third section includes studies of Plato and of Aristotle's method and metaphysics.   [70]

PALMER, R. B., and **HAMERTON-KELLY, R.**, ed. *Philomathes: Studies and Essays in the Humanities in Memory of Philip Merlan*. The Hague: Nijhoff, 1971. Relevant essays are abstracted herein.   [71]

PANOU, S., et al. *Philosophy of Law in the History of Human Thought*. Stuttgart, Ger.: Steiner, 1988. Proceedings of a congress in Athens in 1985. Relevant essays in English are abstracted herein.   [72]

PENELHUM, T., and **SHINER, R. A.**, eds. *New Essays in the History of Philosophy*. Guelph, Ont: Canad. Assoc. for Publ. in Philos., 1975; *CanJPh* Supp. 1. Collection of previously unpublished essays; relevant ones abstracted herein.   [73]

ROBINSON, R. *Essays in Greek Philosophy*. Oxford: Clarendon Pr., 1969. Papers, originally published 1936-1956, abstracted herein.[74]

ROSEN, S. *The Quarrel Between Philosophy and Poetry: Studies in Ancient Thought.* London: Routledge, 1988. Reprints of articles, abstracted herein. Attempts to reassert importance of an irrational poetic element.[75]

SCHOFIELD, M., and **NUSSBAUM, M.,** eds. *Language and Logos. Studies in Ancient Greek Philosophy.* Cambridge Univ. Pr., 1982. Fifteen essays: two on Heraclitus, five on Plato, seven on Aristotle, one on Hellenistic philosophy. All focus on function of language in metaphysics and epistemology and are abstracted herein.[76]

SELLARS, W. *Philosophical Perspectives: History of Philosophy.* Reseda, CA: Ridgeview Publ., 1967; rprt. Collection of essays, most previously published, on Plato, Aristotle, and other subjects. Abstracted herein.[77]

SPRUNG, M., ed. *The Question of Being: East-West Perspectives.* University Park: PA St. Univ. Pr., 1978. Essays comparing Western views on being with those of India and China. Relevant ones are abstracted herein.[78]

VESEY, G., ed. *Philosophers Ancient and Modern.* Cambridge Univ. Pr., 1986. Collection of essays aimed at students preparing for exams in the British system. Relevant items, on Plato and Aristotle, are abstracted below.[79]

WALLACH, L., ed. *The Classical Tradition. Literary and Historical Studies in Honor of H. Caplan.* Ithaca, NY: Cornell Univ. Pr., 1966. Collection of essays. Relevant ones are abstracted herein.[80]

WALTON, C., and **ANTON, J. P.,** eds. *Philosophy and the Civilizing Arts: Essays Presented to Herbert W. Schneider.* Athens: Ohio Univ. Pr., 1974. Relevant essays are abstracted herein.[81]

WOOD, O. P., and **PITCHER, G.** *Ryle: A Collection of Critical Essays.* New York: Doubleday, 1970. Collection of essays, most previously published, reacting to work of Gilbert Ryle. Relevant ones abstracted herein.[82]

Zetesis. Album amicorum door vrienden in collega's aangeboden aan Prof. Dr. E. de Strucker. Antwerp: Nederl. Boekhandel, 1973. Festschrift; relevant essays in English are abstracted herein.[83]

TOPICAL STUDIES

ADKINS, A. W. H. "Ethics and the Breakdown of the Cosmogony in Ancient Greece," in *Cosmogony and Ethical Order*, ed. R. W. Lovin (Univ. of Chicago Pr., 1985), pp. 279-309. Divine sanctions against wrongdoing were no longer convincing to articulate fifth-century Greeks. Philosophical concern with ethics attempted to fill this void.[84]

——. "The Greek Concept of Justice from Homer to Plato." *CPh* 75(1980), 256-268. Reply to Havelock (#159).[85]

——. *From the Many to the One. A Study of Personality and Views of Human Nature*

INTRODUCTION: Topical Studies

in the Context of Ancient Greek Society, Values, and Beliefs. Ithaca, NY: Cornell Univ. Pr., 1970. Claims that Greek idea of human personality developed from plurality in Homer to idea of a single *psyche* in Plato and Aristotle. **[86]**

——. "Orality and Philosophy," in #372, pp. 207-227. Greek language itself facilitates philosophical discussion because new words can be coined easily; definite article can be used with adjectives, infinitives, and participles to create abstract terms. Because Greek has certain associations built in (e. g., "see" and "know" come from same root), certain philosophical approaches are favored over others. **[87]**

AFNAN, R. M. *Zoroaster's Influence on Anaxagoras, the Greek Tragedies and Socrates.* New York: Philosophical Library, 1969. Argues that religious fervor aroused by Z's teaching led to Persia's invasion of Greece. Doctrines of universal mind, divine law, and immortality embodied in Zoroastrian hymns appealed to Greek intellectuals but ran contrary to traditional Greek nature worship. Complaints brought against people like A and S included "Medism," which Afnan maintains was Zoroastrianism. **[88]**

AMORY, F. *"Eiron and Eironeia."* *C&M* 33(1981), 49-80. Discussion of necessity of cultural mediators of new ideas among Greeks and Romans. Socrates, other philosophers played this role. **[89]**

ANDERSON, F. M. "Dewey's Experiment with Greek Philosophy." *IntPhQ* 7(1967), 86-100. Dewey saw study of Greek philosophy, especially Plato and Aristotle, as an ongoing reinterpretation which is important for contemporary philosophy. His praise of Plato and Aristotle is balanced, however, by criticism of dualism in Greek thought. **[90]**

ANGELL, J. W., and **HELM, R. M.** *Meaning and Value in Western Thought. A History of Ideas in Western Culture, I: The Ancient Foundations.* Lanham, MD: Univ. Pr. of America, 1981. Survey of development of ancient religious and philosophic concepts and practices. **[91]**

ANTON, J. P. "Aspects of Ancient Ontologies," in #68, pp. 60-77. One must distinguish theories of categories from ontologies, language from reality which it describes. Aristotle, Stoics, Plotinus are examined with this distinction in mind. **[92]**

——. "John Dewey and Ancient Philosophies." *Ph&PhenRes* 25(1965), 477-499. Dewey rejected Greek dualistism but shared some features with Plato and Aristotle. **[93]**

——. "Tragic Vision and Philosophic *Theoria* in Classical Greece." *Diot* 1(1973), 11-31. Tragedians taught principles aimed at self-understanding, avoidance of hybris. Philosophical theories of *mimesis* and *catharsis* supported teaching function of plays. Playwrights instilled an aspiration for perfection. **[94]**

ARIOTTI, P. "The Concept of Time in Western Antiquity," in *The Study of Time,* ed. J. T. Fraser and N. Lawrence (Heidelberg, Ger.: Springer, 1975), II, pp. 69-80. Pre-Aristotelian developments are studied and Aristotle's view of time as celestial reductionism is examined. **[95]**

ARMSTRONG, A. H. "The Divine Enhancement of Earthly Beauties. The Hellenic and Platonic Tradition." *Eranos-Jb* 53(1984), 49-81. Surveys ways in which Greeks perceived nature as embodiment of divine and divinity as beautifying the natural world. **[96]**

––––. "The Hidden and the Open in Hellenic Thought." *Eranos-Jb* 54(1985), 81-117. Belief in reason's ability to comprehend anything is at core of Greek philosophy, but esoteric motifs loom large in Orphism, Pythagoreanism, Platonism, and Plotinus.   [97]

––––. "Philosophy," in *Greek and Latin Literature: A Comparative Study*, ed. J. Higginbotham (London: Methuen, 1969), pp. 1-23. Surveys literary characteristics of Greco-Roman philosophical writing.   [98]

BALDRY, H. C. *The Unity of Mankind in Greek Thought.* Cambridge Univ. Pr., 1965. Broad literary survey shows Greeks maintained various divisions among persons. As one type broke down (e. g., noble/peasant), another arose (Greek/barbarian). Socrates' distinction between wise and foolish became most permanent division. Alexander's "unification" of nations was self-serving, not based on philosophical/religious ideals.   [99]

BALLEW, L. *Straight and Circular. A Study of Imagery in Greek Philosophy.* Assen, Netherlands: Van Gorcum, 1979. Examines straightness/circularity as archetypes of constant battle between forces for order/disorder in universe and human soul.   [100]

BEETS, M. G. J. *The Coherence of Reality. Experiments in Philosophical Interpretation: Heraclitus, Parmenides, Plato.* Delft, Netherlands: Eburon, 1986. Approaches problem of causality and the nature of phenomenal reality on the basis of an "unorthodox" reading of the three authors mentioned in the title. Compares the results with Aristotle's concept of causality in the last chapter.   [101]

BERTI, E. "Ancient Greek Dialectic as Expression of Freedom of Thought and Speech." *JHI* 39(1978), 347-370. Dialectical philosophy, as practiced by Protagoras and Socrates, presupposes variety of opinions and freedom to express them, typical of Athens in fifth/fourth centuries B. C. Plato restricts use of dialectic to philosophers and sets it up against free speech.   [102]

BLUNDELL, S. *The Origins of Civilization in Greek and Roman Thought.* London: Croom Helm, 1986. Studies thought of Presocratics, Plato, Aristotle, Stoics, Epicureans, and others on questions of origins of human race and civilization.   [103]

BOCHNER, S. "The Size of the Universe in Greek Thought." *Scientia* 62(1968), 510-530. Greek concept of an "indefinite" dimension of the universe or a universe "completed" by its dimension fits in with modern theories on the subject.   [104]

BRAGUE, R. "Radical Modernity and the Roots of Ancient Thought." *IndepJPh* 4(1980), 63-74. Heidegger does not return to ancient philosophy for his metaphysical base; shows inadequacy of ancient concepts as foundation for modern thought.   [105]

BROADIE, A., and MACDONALD, J. "The Ancient Near Eastern and Greek Concept of Universal Order." *Prud* 9(1977), 1-14. In ancient Greece concept of order is personified as Logos.   [106]

BRUMBAUGH, R. S. "All the Great Ideas," in #49, pp. 239-249. Surveys importance of Presocratics, Plato, and Aristotle in developing "all the great ideas basic to our modern science and common sense. with not more than four exceptions."   [107]

–––– "Four Definitions of Women in Classical Philosophy," in #49, pp. 209-214. Greek and Roman men seem to have put women in one of four categories: goddess; object of affection; alien, frightening creatures; property, often liabilities. Philosophers discuss the first three categories but not the fourth.   [108]

——. "Philosophy and Literary Style: Two Paradigms of Classical Examples," in #49, pp. 215-225. Literary analysis can be applied to philosophical writing, with sometimes unexpected results. Plato's *Meno* and Aristotle's *Metaphysics* are test cases.   [109]

——. "The World of the Greek Philosophers and the Sense of Form," in #49, pp. 165-176. Examines value of archeological evidence for confirming or correcting what we know about ancient thinkers from their works and what was written about them. [110]

BURNYEAT, M. F. "Conflicting Appearances." *PBA* 65(1979), 69-111. Discusses difficulties arising from contradictory sense impressions for ancient and modern philosophers.   [111]

CALLAHAN, J. F. *Four Views of Time in Ancient Philosophy.* Westport, CT: Greenwood Pr., 1979; 2nd ed. Studies Plato, Aristotle, Plotinus, Augustine. Their views of time differ along with their views of reality as a whole.   [112]

CARRICK, P. *Medical Ethics in Antiquity. Philosophical Perspectives on Abortion and Euthanasia.* Dordrecht, Netherlands: Reidel, 1985. Only for four ancient philosophers or schools can enough evidence be gathered to determine their views on abortion/euthanasia. Pythagoras opposed both. Plato, Aristotle, Seneca sanctioned abortion. Plato and Seneca accepted voluntary euthanasia for terminally ill adults.   [113]

CHERNISS, H. F. "Ancient Forms of Philosophic Discourse," in #51, pp. 14-35. Previously unpublished lecture which surveys use of poetry, dialogue, and letter/treatises by various ancient philosophers and the connection of form with the objectives of the different thinkers or schools.   [114]

CLARK, S. R. L. "The City of the Wise." *Apeir* 20(1987), 63-80. Various philosophers from Presocratics to Roman Stoics described world as city of the wise. This does not mean, however, that all humankind are citizens or that laws of any particular city are viewed as exemplary.   [115]

CLOSE, A. J. "Commonplace Theories of Art and Nature in Classical Antiquity and the Renaissance." *JHI* 30(1969), 467-486. Explores various aspects of relationship of art to nature: art imitates or complements nature; art is based on experience of nature; art has its beginnings in nature; art is inferior to nature; nature is artist.   [116]

——. "Philosophical Theories of Art and Nature in Classical Antiquity." *JHI* 32(1971), 163-184. Plato's assumptions and distinctions dominated ancient theories of art. Influence of Aristotle and Plotinus gradually came to be felt. In Renaissance, propensity toward Plato resurfaced.   [117]

CORRIGAN, K. "Body and Soul in Ancient Religious Experience," in #43, pp. 360-383. From Homer to Neoplatonists concept of soul was expanded but it never completely lost sight of physical aspect of *psyche* or its relationship to body.   [118]

COX, A. "Didactic Poetry," in *Greek and Latin Literature: A Comparative Study*, ed. J.

Higginbotham (London: Methuen, 1969), pp. 124-161. Surveys use of poetry as a teaching tool, with attention to some early Greek philosophers and especially to Lucretius. Brief but useful bibliography appended.   **[119]**

DAUBE, D. "Black Hole." *RJ* 2(1983), 177-193. Expression of wish to die or never to have lived first appears in Greek, Hebrew, Indian thought between 700-500 B. C. Dramatic social changes and cultural contacts explain idea's spread.   **[120]**

DAVIS, S. "Philosophy in Its Originary Pre-Metaphysical Sense," in #535, pp. 155-166. Heidegger views *philia* as "friendship" or "care for" something. "Philosophy" involves a sense of mankind's destiny. Posits end of philosophy as metaphysics.   **[121]**

DENYER, N. "The Origins of Justice," in #6037, pp. 133-152. For Plato and Sophists, justice is matter of people working out a cooperative arrangement. For Hellenistic schools, justice originates when people cluster around a strong ruler.   **[122]**

DE RIJK, L. M. "On Ancient Mediaeval Semantics and Metaphysics (1)." *Vivarium* 16(1978), 81-110. Though ancient sources do not explicitly use distinction between "intension" and "extension," Aristotle and Neoplatonists make use of concept. Ancient semantic theory and its influence on Middle Ages cannot be understood apart from metaphysical theory.   **[123]**

————. "Categorization as a Key Notion in Ancient and Medieval Semantics." *Vivarium* 26(1988), 1-18. Discusses importance of non-statemental predication or categorization in early philosophy.   **[124]**

DE ROMILLY, J. "History and Philosophy." *Diogenes* 88(1974), 50-68. Interest in link between theory and practice led Greeks to create political philosophy.   **[125]**

DICKS, D. R. *Early Greek Astronomy to Aristotle.* London: Thames & Hudson, 1970. Surveys astronomical knowledge from Homer to fourth century B. C. Discounts much written on Presocratic knowledge of heavens, including Thales' prediction of eclipse. Plato and Aristotle established mathematical basis for astronomy, but it quickly advanced beyond what they could master.   **[126]**

DIHLE, A. "The Greek View of Human Action, I and II," in #128, pp. 20-67. Greeks felt moral freedom resulted from free intellectual activity. Social obligations impose duty. Practice leads to moral perfection. Will, or intentionality, is not a factor.   **[127]**

————. *The Theory of Will in Classical Antiquity.* Berkeley: Univ. of CA Pr., 1982. Six lectures, abstracted herein, ranging from classical period to late antiquity.   **[128]**

DODDS, E. R. "The Ancient Concept of Progress," in #56, pp. 1-25. Idea of progress appears to have been popular only during "Golden Age" of Greece in fifth century B. C. Hellenistic philosophers were in varying degrees antipathetic to concept, stressing instead a cycle of events or an earlier idyllic state. Technological progress was usually associated with moral decline.   **[129]**

————. "Euripides the Irrationalist," in #56, pp. 78-91. At very time when Greek philosophers were exalting rationality — *logos* or *nous* — E displays symptoms of an irrationalism that eventually undercut philosophical rationalism. E holds that reason cannot be taught, nor can it hold up against emotion.   **[130]**

DOMBROWSKI, D. A. *The Philosophy of Vegetarianism.* Amherst: Univ. of MA Pr., 1984. Survey of classical debate on vegetarianism, which ran for a millenium, from Hesiod to Porphyry. Various ontologies and ethics supported the position.   **[131]**

DUMITRIU, A. *History of Logic, I: Greece and Rome.* Tunbridge Wells, UK: Abacus Pr., 1977. Logic is difficult to define, but topic can be studied historically. First three chapters consider primitive mentality, Chinese and Indian logic. Rest of book looks at Greco-Roman thinkers, including minor ones, from Presocratics to Augustine.   **[132]**

DUSKA, R. "Philosophy, Literature, and Views of the Good Life." *PACPhA* 15(1980), 181-188. Philosophers differ over whether study of humanities and arts can achieve any sort of genuine knowledge. Plato holds that philosophy leads to truth and poetry distracts us from it, with its tendency to delight. Aristotle believes poetry represents the universal which is the object of knowledge.   **[133]**

DYBIKOWSKI, J. C. "Modern Movements in Ancient Philosophy." *Eidos* 4(1985), 187-199. Looks at important trends and influential scholars in study of ancient philosophy from 1950's to mid-1980's.   **[134]**

EASTWOOD, C. C. *Life and Thought in the Ancient World.* Philadelphia: Westminster Pr., 1967. Wide-ranging survey of Near Eastern, Egyptian, and Greek modes of thought. Brief study of Socrates, Plato, Aristotle, and major Hellenistic schools.   **[135]**

EDELSTEIN, L. *The Idea of Progress in Classical Antiquity.* Baltimore: Johns Hopkins Univ. Pr., 1967. Until nineteenth century most scholars attributed to ancients a concept of continuous progress in human society. Twentieth-century scholarship has largely denied that view. This discussion of various philosophical and literary texts aims to show that "ancient progressivists were not a negligible group."   **[136]**

EHRHARDT, A. *The Beginning. A Study in the Greek Philosophical Approach to the Concept of Creation from Anaximander to St. John.* Manchester (UK) Univ. Pr., 1968. Notion of *arche* is examined in thought of Pythagoreans, Parmenides, Anaxagoras, Atomists, Plato, Aristotle, and Hellenistic schools.   **[137]**

EMERTON, N. E. *The Scientific Reinterpretation of Form.* Ithaca, NY: Cornell Univ. Pr., 1984. Traces development of concept of form through classical and medieval philosophy, and its transformation as it was transferred into a scientific context.   **[138]**

ENGLEBRETSEN, G. F. *Logical Negation.* Atlantic Highlands, NJ.: Humanities Pr., 1981. Compares concepts of negation found in classical and Stoic logic with those of modern mathematics. Aristotle's approach is more useful for philosophical purposes, than the concept of sentential negation which is now favored.   **[139]**

EVANS, E. C. *Physiognomics in the Ancient World.* Philadelphia: Amer. Philosophical Soc., 1969. Analysis of character from physical appearance played major role in oratory, medicine, philosophy, poetry, and theater. Some ancient sources attributed origins of this pseudo-science to Pythagoras.   **[140]**

FERGUSON, J. *"Dinos."* *Phron* 16(1971), 97-115. Many Greek philosophers included concept of a spinning motion (*dinos/dine*) in their cosmogonies. Anaximander compared it to spinning wheel, Empedocles to whirlwind. Atomists equated it with necessity, Plato and Aristotle with fortune.   **[141]**

FINLEY, J. H., Jr. *Four Stages of Greek Thought.* Stanford, CA: Stanford Univ. Pr., 1966. Outlines major features of development of Greek thought: heroic mind (Homer), visionary mind (Aeschylus, Sophocles, Pindar), theoretical mind (Euripides, Thucydides), and rational mind (Plato and Aristotle).   **[142]**

FONTAINE, P. F. M. *The Light and the Dark. A Cultural History of Dualism.* 2 vols. Amsterdam: Gieben, 1986. Vol. I argues that not all dualism is to be traced to Persia. Dualism is natural way of organizing knowledge and perceptions of world. Dualistic systems are characterized by importance of number three, role of fate, concept of restricted knowledge, closed societies or organizations, elitism, downgrading of women, pessimism about life. Pythagoras, Milesians, Eleatics display such tendencies.   **[143]**

FREDE, M. "Philosophy and Medicine in Antiquity," in *Human Nature and Natural Knowledge. Essays Presented to Marjorie Green,* ed. A. Donagan et al. (Dordrecht, Netherlands: Reidel, 1986), pp. 211-230. Surveys, from Presocratics to Galen, the close relationship between philosophy and medicine. Philosophical trends in medicine sometimes evolved independent of traditional philosophers.   **[144]**

FURLEY, D. "The Cosmological Crisis in Classical Antiquity." *PBACAPh* 2(1986), 1-19. Ancients' ways of viewing universe came down to seeing matter in motion, as Atomists taught, or finding a purposive (teleological) explanation, such as Aristotle's.   **[145]**

GADAMER, H.-G. "Natural Science and Hermeneutics. The Concept of Nature in Ancient Philosophy." *PBACAPh* 1(1985), 39-52. Examines use of word *physis* among Presocratics, then explores its development in Aristotle's thought. A turning point was Socrates' complaint in *Phaedo* about answers given by previous natural philosophers to question of cause and generation.   **[146]**

————. "The Relevance of Greek Philosophy for Modern Thought." *SAfrJPh* 6(1987), 39-42. Ancient Greek thought, emphasizing cosmological harmony and virtues such as friendship, could enhance modern scientific thought, with its mathematical basis. **[147]**

GELVEN, M. "The Dionysian Sources in Philosophy." *M&W* 19(1977), 173-193. Dionysian religion underlies comedy, tragedy, philosophy. All three praise something normally rejected. In philosophy, ignorance is valued.   **[148]**

GOSLING, J. C. B., and **TAYLOR, C. C. W.** *The Greeks on Pleasure.* Oxford: Clarendon Pr., 1982. Two chapters study pre-Platonic theories of pleasure, which were didactic or physiological. Democritus first developed system of ethics based on tranquility as goal of life. Two-thirds of book deals with Plato and Aristotle. Plato's view on pleasure was first hedonistic, but pleasures are too varied to serve as criterion for good in life. Aristotle's *NE* 7 and 10 are discussed. Some treatment of Epicurus.   **[149]**

GRAESER, A. "On Language, Thought and Reality in Ancient Greek Philosophy." *Dialectica* 31(1977), 359-388. Greek thought in this area is dominated by perception that words are real things. Parmenides sees them as devoid of sense. Heraclitus sees words and reality as unrelated, opposed. Looks at views of Plato, Aristotle, Stoics.   **[150]**

GRANT, G. P. "Nietzsche and the Ancients: Philosophy and Scholarship." *Dion* 3(1979), 5-16. Discussion of Nietzsche's philosophy and its impact on teaching of ancient philosophy. [151]

GRASSI, E. "Rhetoric and Philosophy." *Ph&Rh* 9(1976), 200-216. Analysis of passages from Plato, Aristotle, and others suggests that rhetoric cannot be studied apart from philosophical problems which it raises. [152]

GRENE, M. *The Knower and the Known.* New York: Basic Books, 1966. Descriptive sketches of epistemologies and ontological underpinnings of several ancient philosophers, especially as they form point of departure for modern reductionistic and mechanistic paradigm of scientific explanation. [153]

GUNNELL, J. G. *Political Philosophy and Time.* Middletown, CT: Wesleyan Univ. Pr., 1968. Analyzes concept and symbols of political organization and time in Egyptian, Mesopotamian, Hebrew societies, and in pre-Platonic Greccc. Two chapters on Plato, one on Aristotle and themes which carry over to later political philosophers. [154]

GYORY, R. A. *The Emergence of Being: Through Indian and Greek Thought.* Washington, DC: Univ. Pr. of Amer., 1978. "Being," the "Absolute," and "God" are taken as synonymous. Indian approach to search for "Being" is considered first, then Greek, beginning with Parmenides and Heraclitus and examining Plato, Aristotle, and Plotinus, whose mysticism is "profound yet often unintelligible or implausible." [155]

HADOT, I. "The Spiritual Guide," in #43, pp. 436-459. Several figures — teacher, musician, poet, king, lawgiver — could serve as spiritual guides, but philosopher comes to dominate in that role. His function is to impart knowledge, awaken self-analysis. [156]

HANKINSON, R. J. "Science and Certainty. The Central Issues." *Apeir* 21(1988), 1-16. Greeks, from Plato to Skeptics, had no firmer notion of what defines science than we do today. [157]

HAVELOCK, E. A. "*Dikaiosune.* An Essay in Greek Intellectual History." *Phoenix* 23(1969), 49-70. Term *dikaiosune* occurs rarely before fourth century B. C. Meaning of morality/righteousness originated in late fifth century. [158]

——. *The Greek Concept of Justice. From Its Shadow in Homer to Its Substance in Plato.* Cambridge Univ. Pr., 1978. Examines differing concepts of justice in Greek society and effect of pre-literate, oral thought on early stages of their development. [159]

HAZO, R. G. *The Idea of Love.* New York: Praeger, 1967. Early chapters define concepts and subcategories. Various thinkers are then surveyed, including Plato, Aristotle, Cicero, Plotinus, Augustine, medieval and modern figures. Discussion of ancient authors appears under headings such as "Love as Acquisitive and Benevolent Desire" and "Judgmental Notions in Relation to Wholly Tendential Conceptions of Love." [160]

HETZLER, F. M. "The Concept of Dynamism in Hellenic Culture. The Samian Paradigm." *Diot* 13(1985), 36-43. Culture of Samos exemplifies Greek blend of quest for knowledge of man, social systems and the absolute with recognition of impossibility of quest. [161]

HINTIKKA, J. "Time, Truth, and Knowledge in Greek Philosophy." *AmPhQ* 4(1967), 1-14; revised version in #4890, pp. 62-92; also in Hintikka *Knowledge and the Known: Historical Perspectives in Epistemology* (Dordrecht, Netherlands: Reidel, 1974), pp. 50-79. For Aristotle and other philosophers, temporally indefinite statements are logically defensible because Greek culture emphasized present time and spoken word.   [162]

HOLLWECK, T. "Truth and Relativity: On the Historical Emergence of Truth," in *The Philosophy of Order: Essays on History, Consciousness and Politics*, ed. P. J. Opitz and G. Sebba (Stuttgart, Ger.: Klett-Cotta, 1981), pp. 125-136. Hesiod is the first to pose the problem of definition of truth and to separate it from divine knowledge. Parmenides gave truth an unchanging quality and identified it with Being. Plato sought to explain why truth was not available to all.   [163]

HUBY, P. M. *Greek Ethics.* New York: St. Martin's Pr., 1967. Short summary of development of ethics from Sophists to Hellenistic schools, emphasizing: law and nature, knowledge and happiness, love and friendship.   [164]

HUGHES, J. D. "Ecology in Ancient Greece." *Inquiry* 18(1975) 115-125. Investigates Greeks' characteristic attitudes towards nature. Most balanced ecological writer was Theophrastus, but his conception of autonomous nature was overshadowed by Aristotle's anthropocentric teleology.   [165]

JOHNSON, D. M. "The Greek Origins of Belief." *AmPhQ* 24(1987), 319-327. What distinguishes Greek thought of sixth century B. C. from that of contemporary peoples is Greek insistence on consistency.   [166]

JOHNSON, J. P. "The Idea of Human Dignity in Classical and Christian Thought." *JTho* 6(1971), 23-37. Greeks saw human worth based on reason, control of material conditions, and contemplation of truth. Christians, especially Augustine, re-interpreted it in terms of free will and soteriology.   [167]

JORDAN, M. D. "Ancient Philosophic Protreptic and the Problem of Persuasive Genres." *Rhetorica* 4(1986), 309-333. Study of protreptic in several Socratic conversations, in Aristotle, Seneca, and Iamblichus.   [168]

JUHASZ, J. B. "Greek Theories of Imagination." *JHistBehavSci* 7(1971), 39-58. Xenophanes and Heraclitus initiate scientific understanding of imagination. For Eleatics it is source of knowledge, a view shared by Empedocles and Anaxagoras. Examines idea as developed by Democritus, Sophists, Plato, Aristotle.   [169]

KAHN, C. H. "The Greek Verb 'To Be' and the Concept of Being." *FoundLang* 2(1966), 245-265. Examines philological basis of Greek ontology and possible ways philosophers were influenced in their formulation of doctrines of Being by pre-philosophical use of verb "to be."   [170]

———. "Linguistic Relativism and the Greek Project of Ontology," in #78, pp. 31-44; also in *Actualitaet der Antike*, ed. R. Bubner et al. (Goettingen, Ger.: Vandenhoeck & Ruprecht, 1979), pp. 20-33. Summarizes results of Kahn's previously published linguistic studies and describes Greek concept of relation between Being and knowledge, especially in Parmenides and Plato. As an Indo-European language, Greek can express concepts of Being in both noun and verb forms more easily than can other languages, but concept of Being as an inquiry after truth transcends language.   [171]

———. "Why Existence Does not Emerge as a Distinct Concept in Greek Philosophy."
AGPh 58(1976), 323-334. In classical Greek thought "existence" as separate concept does
not exist. Notion arises only when ontology becomes tinged with Biblical view of
creation. Closest Greeks come to formulating idea is Aristotle's distinction among types
of questions.   [172]

KANNICHT, R. *The Ancient Quarrel Between Philosophy and Poetry: Aspects of the
Greek Conception of Literature.* Christchurch, New Zealand: Univ. of Canterbury, 1988.
Four lectures tracing *diaphora* between poetry and philosophy from Hesiod through Xen-
ophanes and Gorgias to Plato. At its core is a conflict between knowledge and pleasure.
Aristotle finally proved usefulness of poetry in his *Poetics*.   [173]

KERFERD, G. B. "Reason as a Guide to Conduct in Greek Thought." *BJRL* 64(1981),
141-164. Survey of Platonic, Aristotelian, Stoic views on use of reason in resolving moral
dilemmas. Also looks at Stoics' teaching on suicide.   [174]

KIMPEL, B. *Philosophies of Life of the Ancient Greeks and Israelites.* Lanham, MD:
Univ. Pr. of Amer., 1981. Compares moral philosophies of the two cultures. [175]

KNIGHT, W. F. J. *Elysion. On Ancient Greek and Roman Beliefs Concerning a Life
after Death.* London: Rider, 1970. Wide-ranging survey, from Egypt and Babylon,
through Homer, Hesiod, various Greek philosophers and religious texts, to Cicero,
Lucretius, Neoplatonists, and Christians. Book was put together after Knight's death and
may not represent his best work.   [176]

KOLB, D. A. "Time and the Timeless in Greek Thought." *PhE&W* 24(1974), 137-143.
Neoplatonists combined Platonic view of time as a "moving image of eternity" with
Aristotle's concept of the prime mover's "self-coincident activity" to produce the western
view that timelessness produces patterns of order which can be discerned in temporal
processes.   [177]

LAIN ENTRALGO, P. *The Therapy of the Word in Classical Antiquity,* ed. and transl.
L. J. Rather and J. M. Sharp. New Haven, CT: Yale Univ. Pr., 1970. Considers ability
of the word (*Logos*) to change attitudes and feelings. Plato and Aristotle, as well as Hippocratic writers, consider positive attitudes part of good health. Gorgias and Antiphon,
Sophists, used persuasive techniques to cure the grief-stricken.   [178]

LALUMIA, J. "From Science to Metaphysics and Philosophy." *Diogenes* 88(1974), 1-35.
Philosophy arose from theoretical science. Parmenides and Zeno are first to engage in
logical clarification. Philosophy has been largely misunderstood. Its discoveries are
logical, not scientific. Distinction between philosophy and science can be traced from
Presocratics to present day.   [179]

LeCLERC, I. "The Metaphysics of the Good." *RMeta* 35(1981), 3-26. Considers main
historical theories (Platonic, Aristotelian, Neoplatonic, and Aquinas') which sought to
overcome difficulties of nature of good.   [180]

LLOYD, A. C. "Non-discursive Thought. An Enigma of Greek Philosophy." *PAS*
70(1969-70), 261-274. Non-discursive thought implies intuition/contemplation. Exami-

nation of topic especially in Plato, Aristotle, and Plotinus.   **[181]**

LLOYD, G. E. R. "Aspects of the Interrelations of Medicine, Magic and Philosophy in Ancient Greece." *Apeir* 9 #1(1975), 1-16. Certain Hippocratic treatises are among first efforts to separate medicine from magic and philosophy, but even they rely on vocabulary and assumptions of fields from which they are trying to disengage.   **[182]**

—————. *Early Greek Science: Thales to Aristotle.* New York: Norton, 1970. Thales is first philosopher/scientist due to his distinction between natural and supernatural explanations and use of rational method of criticism. Later Milesians became aware of broader problems. Pythagoreans and Empedocles made important theoretical advances. Socrates changed emphasis of philosophy to human behavior, but Plato advanced development of scientific theory and made astronomy a mathematical science. Aristotle's work in the field was, of course, crucial.   **[183]**

—————. *Magic, Reason and Experience: Studies in the Origin and Development of Greek Science.* Cambridge Univ. Pr., 1979. Studies relationship between what may be called "traditional" and "scientific" patterns of thought.   **[184]**

—————. *Polarity and Analogy: Two Types of Argumentation in Early Greek Thought.* Cambridge Univ. Pr., 1966. Studies development and underlying assumption of these two types of argument. Originated in religious/mythic context. Plato contributed little to analysis of techniques. Aristotle formalized them.   **[185]**

—————. *Science, Folklore and Ideology. Studies in the Life Sciences in Ancient Greece.* Cambridge Univ. Pr., 1983. Examines Greek views on animals, women, and drugs to understand relationship between theory and popular conceptions. Also looks at ideological influences on ancient scientific theory.   **[186]**

LOWRY, S. T. *The Archeology of Economic Ideas. The Classical Greek Tradition.* Durham, NC: Duke Univ. Pr., 1987. Many analytical formulations of modern economic theory originated not in eighteenth century but in ancient Greek philosophy.   **[187]**

MacINTYRE, A. "*Sophrosune*: How a Virtue can Become Socially Disruptive." *MidwStudPh* 13(1988), 1-11. Explores Greco-Roman philosophers' views of *sophrosune* to test thesis that "virtues are qualities which enable one to function well within the forms of common life." In some cases, possession of *sophrosune* can be disruptive to community life.   **[188]**

MANSFELD, J. "Bad World and Demi-urge. A 'Gnostic' Motif from Parmenides and Empedocles to Lucretius and Philo," in #6711, pp. 261-314. Gnostic view of evil physical world is not exactly paralleled by any earlier Greek philosopher. It could have been drawn from cosmologies of several, though.   **[189]**

MASON, J. H. "The Character of Creativity: Two Traditions." *HistEurIdeas* 9(1988), 697-715. Modern positive view of creativity derives from Judeo-Christian thought and Neoplatonism. Classical Greco-Roman world viewed creativity as disruptive.   **[190]**

MASTERS, R. D. "Is Contract an Adequate Basis for Medical Ethics?" *HastCenRep* 5(1975), 24-28. Ancient philosophers, especially Plato and Aristotle, can shed light on problems which arise from the defects of a contractual ethic. The most useful criterion for ethics is the concept of a good or just life.   **[191]**

MAZIARZ, E. A., and **GREENWOOD, T.** *Greek Mathematical Philosophy.* New York: Ungar, 1968. Traces growth of math from mysticism of Thales and Pythagoras to rational approach of Socrates to Aristotle's influence in invention of syllogism.   **[192]**

McEVILLEY, T. "Early Greek Philosophy and Madhyamika." *PhE&W* 31(1981), 141-164. Similarity in dialectic method suggests that Greek thought, especially Eleatic *reductio ad absurdum*, penetrated India, either through Bactria or through commercial contacts in south. After Alexander's conquest process was reversed.   **[193]**

McKEON, R. "The Interpretation of Political Theory and Practice in Ancient Athens." *JHI* 42(1981), 3-11. Examines relation of philosophic speculation to performance and interpretation of practical actions. Discusses alternatives to use of reason — rhetoric and force.   **[194]**

———. "The Methods of Rhetoric and Philosophy: Invention and Judgment," in #80, pp. 365-373. Study of interaction, mutual influence of two fields.   **[195]**

———. "Philosophy and the Development of Scientific Methods." *JHI* 27(1966), 3-22. Wide-ranging survey of methodology which looks at Plato, Aristotle, Epicurus, Cicero, and other, more recent philosophers.   **[196]**

McKINNEY, R. H. "The Origins of Modern Dialectics." *JHI* 44(1983), 179-190. Overview of development of elenchus and dialectic by Socrates and Plato, and Aristotle's efforts at nominal and causal definition. Comments on how Kant and Hegel are indebted to the Greeks.   **[197]**

MEIJER, P. A. "Philosophers, Intellectuals and Religion in Hellas," in *Faith, Hope and Worship. Aspects of Religious Mentality in the Ancient World*, ed. H. S. Versnel (Leiden: Brill, 1981), pp. 216-262. Surveys problems of rationalism and atheism, views of Xenophanes, Heraclitus, Socrates, Plato, Theophrastus, and Plutarch toward prayer and sacrifice.   **[198]**

MENAGE, G. *The History of Women Philosophers*, transl. B. H. Zedler. Lanham, MD: Univ. Pr. of Amer., 1984. Translation of seventeenth-century work.   **[199]**

MERLEAU-PONTY, J. "Ideas of Beginning and Endings in Cosmology," in *The Study of Time*, ed. J. T. Fraser and N. Lawrence (Heidelberg, Ger.: Springer, 1978), III, pp. 333-350. Examines discussions of the beginning of cosmic time in Democritus, Plato, and Aristotle, and its adoption by Augustine and later Christian thinkers. Only Plato among the pre-Christians has anything like a concept of a beginning of the world.   **[200]**

MOORHEAD, J. "The Greeks, Pupils of the Hebrews." *Prud* 15(1983), 3-12. By fifth century Christian thinkers had dropped claim that Greeks borrowed from Jews.   **[201]**

MORRIS, C. *Western Political Thought, I: Plato to Augustine.* New York: Basic Books, 1967. Derivative survey for non-specialists. Traditional organization: Preplatonic, Plato and Aristotle, Hellenistic, Christian. Emphasis on Plato's *Republic*, Aristotle's *Politics*, and Augustine's *City of God*.   **[202]**

MORTLEY, R. *From Word to Silence, I: The Rise and Fall of Logos; II: The Way of Negation, Christian and Greek.* Frankfurt, Ger.: Hanstein, 1986. Early philosophers conceived of discourse (*logos*) as an active process. For Plato and Aristotle it becomes a thing, the essential element sought by Presocratics. Skeptics recognized limitations of *logos* by showing that two *logoi* can be equally convincing. Hellenistic and Christian philosophers lost confidence in language and rational thought, stressing silence and contemplation as equal to Skeptic *epoche* (suspension of judgment).   **[203]**

MULHERN, J. J. "Modern Notations and Ancient Logic," in #52, pp. 71-82. Surveys studies in field from 1945-1970.   **[204]**

MURDOCH, J. "Commentary on Furley's 'The Cosmological Crisis in Classical Antiquity'." *PBACAPh* 2(1986), 20-24. Response to #145. Primacy of opposition between matter-in-motion explanations versus teleological explanations seems to be confirmed by basic reasons which Plato and Aristotle give for rejecting atomism, i. e., that it does not explain purposive behavior characteristic of all animate things.   **[205]**

NEWMAN, H. "Believing Science and Unbelieving Science: Reflections of the Basic Conflict of Ancient and Modern Philosophy of Science." *Zygon* 2(1967), 398-417. Modern ideas of scientific cognition are not as antithetical to biblical faith as concepts of science held by Greek philosophers, particularly Plato and Aristotle.   **[206]**

NORTH, H. F. "Canons and Hierarchies of the Cardinal Virtues in Greek and Latin Literature," in #80, pp. 165-183. Survey of lists of virtues from fifth century B. C. to Christian era. Lists were modified or rearranged as political and philosophical values changed.   **[207]**

———. "The Mare, the Vixen, and the Bee. *Sophrosyne* as the Virtue of Women in Antiquity." *ICS* 2(1977), 35-48. Plato and Stoics thought women capable of same *arete* ("virtue") as men, but majority of ancient writers see women's "wisdom" as limited to domestic crafts.   **[208]**

———. *Sophrosyne. Self-Knowledge and Self-Restraint in Greek Literature.* Ithaca, NY: Cornell Univ. Pr., 1966. Defines *sophrosyne* as "harmonious product of intense passion under perfect control." Greeks valued community and restraint of individualistic impulses. Traces development of idea in Homer, tragedy, Plato, to Hellenistic and Roman eras. *Sophrosyne* not negative concept but energetic creative tension.   **[209]**

NUCHELMANS, G. *Theories of the Proposition, I: Ancient and Medieval Conceptions of the Bearers of Truth and Falsity.* Amsterdam: North Holl. Publ. Co., 1973. To say "x is y" is to formulate a proposition. But is such a formula true in every case of x? That is semantic problem with which philosophers have wrestled since antiquity. Traces development of theories about propositions from Plato and Aristotle through Stoics into early Latin Middle Ages.   **[210]**

NUSSBAUM, M. C. *The Fragility of Goodness. Luck and Ethics in Greek Tragedy and Philosophy.* Cambridge Univ. Pr., 1986. Discusses vulnerability of individual facets of a good life, possibility of irreconcilable conflicts between values, and role of passions and emotions in shaping of rational ideas.   **[211]**

ONIANS, R. B. *The Origins of European Thought About the Body, the Mind, the Soul,* *the World, Time and Fate. New Interpretations of Greek, Roman and Kindred Evidence, also of Some Basic Jewish and Christian Beliefs.* Cambridge Univ. Pr., 1988; 2nd ed. Contains useful information about very early European concepts relating to subjects in title. See index for passages pertaining to particular philosophers.   [212]

ORTEGA Y GASSET, J. *The Origin of Philosophy,* transl. T. Talbot. New York: Norton, 1967. Philosophy originated when mankind felt possibilities exceeded needs. Necessity of choice brought about development of rational method. Heraclitus' use of oracular formulas to express universal wisdom is most apt vehicle for philosophical discourse.   [213]

PATRICIOS, W. N. "The Spatial Concepts of the Ancient Greeks." *AClass* 14(1971), 17-36. Except for Atomists, Greek thinkers saw space in limited terms: sphere, Pythagorean void, Platonic material but invisible substratum.   [214]

PAZDERNIK, V. "Main Aspects of Philosophy of Law from Homer to Aeschylus," in *Antiquitas Graeco-Romana ac Tempora Nostra. Acta Congressus Internationalis habiti Brunae diebus 12-16 mensis Aprilis MCMLXVI,* ed. J. Burian and L. Vidman (Prague: Czechoslov. Akad., 1968), pp. 53-57. Three stages of development: mythological (Homer); beginnings of rationalization of myth (Hesiod, Solon); secularization (Sophists, Aeschylus).   [215]

PEPIN, J. "Cosmic Piety," in #43, pp. 408-435. Some Presocratics talk of a *nous* or world-soul, but Plato is first to speak of world as divine. Aristotle's position is unclear. Stoics saw intellect of world as *the* god who divinizes all other aspects of the world. Also considers theme of world as temple, temple as world.   [216]

PERRY, M. "The Enduring Humanist Legacy of Greece." *FreeInq* 3(1983), 28-32. Greek contribution to Western intellectual development consists mainly of discovery of rational order in nature and society. Greeks did not completely escape religion and myth.   [217]

POHLENZ, M. *Freedom in Greek Life and Thought. The History of an Ideal,* transl. C. Lufmark. Dordrecht, Netherlands: Reidel, 1966. Traces development of concept of freedom — ethical and political — in ancient Greece and Rome. Analyzes passages in poets and tragedians as well as philosophers. Last chapter summarizes and contrasts Greek and Christian concepts of freedom.   [218]

RANKIN, B. "The History of Probability and the Changing Concept of the Individual." *JHI* 37(1966), 482-504. Traces development of concepts of Tyche/Moira.   [219]

RENEHAN, R. "On the Greek Origins of the Concepts Incorporeality and Immateriality." *GRBS* 21(1980), 105-138. Presocratics did not distinguish between body and soul. Plato is first to make ontological division.   [220]

RIST, J. M. *Human Value. A Study in Ancient Philosophical Ethics.* Leiden: Brill, 1982. Modern definitions of human value are alien to those of ancient world. There are, in fact, no Greek words for "values" or "rights." Achievement was basis for value in almost all ancient philosophies. Some chapters of this book focus on individual thinkers (Plato, Aristotle, Plotinus), while others look at topics (Usefulness, Freedom, Social Contracts). Considers Christian as well as Greco-Roman views.   [221]

————. cf. #6523.

ROBB, K. "Greek Oral Memory and the Origins of Philosophy." *Pers* 51(1970), 5-45. Philosophy originated when Greeks were still predominantly oral/aural people, not yet adapted to writing down their ideas. By Aristotle's time mentality of literacy was firmly fixed, making it difficult for later Greeks to understand some early philosophers. [222]

ROCCASALVO, J. F. "Greek and Buddhist Wisdom. An Encounter Between East and West." *IntPhQ* 20(1980), 73-85. Ancient Buddhist dialogue entitled "Milindapanha" demonstrates contact between Greek *sophia* and Buddhist *panna*.   [223]

RODGERS, V. A. "Some Thoughts on *Dike*." *CQ* 21(1971), 289-301. Examination of Hesiod *Works and Days* 202-211 and Plato *Protagoras* 321b*ff*. indicates that Greeks defined *dike* (right) and *aidos* (respect) in terms of consequences of actions, rather than abstract ideals.   [224]

ROSEN, S. "Philosophy and Revolution." *IndepJPh* 3(1979), 71-78. Discusses classical conception of revolutionary nature of philosophy by developing distinction between Presocratic and Socratic conceptions of relation between understanding and political action. Examines three stages in development of Greek teaching about stability and change: 1) men of practical intelligence; 2) rise of Sophists; 3) Plato's publication of his dialogues and the revolution of speech.   [225]

ROTH, N. "The 'Theft of Philosophy' by the Greeks from the Jews." *CF* 32(1978), 53-67. Hellenistic Jewish apologists wanted to prove science and philosophy originated with Abraham and Moses to justify their interest in these topics. Philo wanted to make Torah acceptable to sophisticated audience. Christians took over his claim that Greeks had learned from Jews.   [226]

ROWE, C. "God, Man and Nature. Ancient Greek Views on the Foundation of Moral Values." *Eranos-Jb* 43(1974), 255-291. Studies development of process by which societal norms were justified.   [227]

————. *An Introduction to Greek Ethics.* New York: Barnes & Noble, 1977. Designed for non-specialists. Focuses on Plato, with three brief chapters on Presocratic ethics, Sophists, and post-Aristotelian ethics.   [228]

RUTHERFORD, R. B. "The Philosophy of the *Odyssey*." *JHS* 106(1986), 145-162. Most ancient commentators saw Odysseus as a kind of philosopher, who deals with fate alloted to him and gains greater control over himself.   [229]

SCHOTT, R. M. "Social and Religious Antecedents of Ascetic Greek Philosophy," in *Freedom, Equality, and Social Change*, ed. C. Peden (Lewiston, ME: Mellen Pr., 1989), pp. 385-400. Study of notions of women, embodiment, and impurity. Arising from historic religious practices, they influenced ideas of inferiority of things physical. [230]

SCOTT, C. E. "Psychotherapy: Being One and Being Many." *Review of Existential Psychology and Psychiatry* 16(1978-79), 81-94. Contains comments on Parmenides, Heraclitus, and Plato regarding problem of the one and the many.   [231]

SHIBLES, W. A. *Models of Ancient Greek Philosophy*. London: Vision, 1971. Relates doctrines of early Greek thinkers to modern problems and situations. Deals largely with Presocratics down to Democritus with final chapters on Plato and Aristotle.   [232]

SHIKIBU, H. "The Concept of Man in Greek Philosophy and in Traditional Japanese Thought. A Comparative Study." *Diot* 7(1979), 184-187. Greeks see rational order in universe which man can comprehend. Japanese accept impermanence of things and do not attempt to discover order.   [233]

SINGH, C. S. "The Problems of Change in Greek Philosophy." *DarshInt* 6(1966), 7-10. Non-specialist survey from Ionians and Eleatics to Plotinus.   [234]

SMITH, C. U. M. *The Problem of Life: An Essay in the Origins of Biological Thought.* New York: Wiley, 1975. Historical survey of manner in which scientists and philosophers have viewed life and living processes. Chapters on Ionians, Eleatics, Plato, Aristotle, the Lyceum and Stoa.   [235]

SODIPO, J. O. "The Lighter Side of the Ancient Greek Philosophers." *N&C* 9(1966), 28-37. Humorous anecdotes about philosophers from Thales to Aristotle.   [236]

SOLMSEN, F. "Reincarnation in Ancient and Early Christian Thought," in *Kleine Schriften, III* (Hildesheim, Ger.: Olms, 1982), pp. 465-494. Development of idea in Pythagoras, Plato, and Origen.   [237]

SORABJI, R. "Analyses of Matter, Ancient and Modern." *PAS* 86(1986), 1-22. Discussion of meaning of *hypokeimenon* in Aristotle, who, with Neoplatonists, denies that two bodies can occupy the same space. Stoics argued such a thing was possible. [238]

————. "Closed Space and Closed Time." *OSAP* 4(1986), 215-231. Retraction of author's earlier views on possibility of closed space and time. Various Greek philosophers stand on either side of the issue.   [239]

————. *Time, Creation and the Continuum.* Ithaca, NY: Cornell Univ. Pr., 1983. Surveys Presocratic origins of Aristotle's paradoxes on time, follows development of concept through Plato, Aristotle, later classical writers into Middle Ages. Philosophers saw several problems: Is time real? Does it depend on consciousness? Could it exist in a changeless universe? Greek verb tenses are important in expressing time.   [240]

STEAD, G. C. *Divine Substance.* Oxford: Clarendon Pr., 1977. Offers a sketch of logical patterns involved in history of term *ousia*, deals with ways Plato, Aristotle, and Stoics use term, and deals with doctrine of Trinity in last two chapters.   [241]

STENIUS, E. "Foundations of Mathematics: Ancient Greek and Modern." *Dialectica* 32(1978), 255-290. "Reconstructs" ancient Greek discussion about foundations of geometry and compares it to modern beliefs about mathematics. Refers to Aristotle's discussions involving philosophy of mathematics.   [242]

STROZEWSKI, W. "Man as *Arche.*" *Reports on Philosophy* 8(1984), 73-76. Briefly traces how concept of human beings as object and source of thinking develops from Parmenides to Plato.   [243]

STUNKEL, K. R. *Relations of Indian, Greek, and Christian Thought in Antiquity.*

Washington, DC: Univ. Pr. of Amer., 1979. Sees no important influence of Indian thought on Greek, or vice versa. Parallels can be seen, but no proof of exchange of ideas can be established beyond reasonable doubt.   [244]

SYNODINOU, K. "A Form of Opposition: Small-Big." *Dodone* 16 #2(1987), 9-18. Topos of small cause which has large effects is not Sophistic in origin. Its purpose is to point out contrast between appearance and reality. It can be found in earliest Greek literature and appears particularly often in works of fifth century B. C.   [245]

TALBERT, C. H. "Biographies of Philosophers and Rulers as Instruments of Religious Propaganda in Mediterranean Antiquity." *ANRW* II,16.2,1619-1651. Groups biographies by function instead of form or reliability. Among philosophers' lives five functions are discernible: 1) provide pattern for reader to imitate; 2) dispel false image of the philosopher; 3) discredit a teacher; 4) trace succession to establish authority of a school; 5) provide key to interpreting a philosopher's teaching. All except (4) have parallels among biographies of rulers.   [246]

TANNER, R. G. "Aesthetics in Ancient Philosophy." *Prud* 17(1985), 3-6. Aesthetic views of Plato, Aristotle, Cyrenaics and Megarians, Epicurus, Middle Stoicism and New Academy have one thing in common: a close link to the schools' views on epistemology and ontology, not just to ethics.   [247]

TATARKIEWICZ, W. *History of Aesthetics, I: Ancient Aesthetics; II: Medieval Aesthetics*. The Hague: Mouton, 1970. Surveys authors from Pythagoras to Middle Ages. Texts and translations of passages are given, with analysis, discussion. Presocratics generally paid little attention to aesthetics, then only to poetry. Pythagorean concepts of proportion/measure played major role in later aesthetic theories. Hellenistic period saw no new developments in this field. Neoplatonists saw aesthetics as part of quest for good and beautiful, not an arrangement but a quality. Christian thinkers, to explain ugliness in a world created by God, shifted aesthetic emphasis to divine, transcendent beauty.   [248]

TEJERA, V. *Modes of Greek Thought*. New York: Appleton-Century-Crofts, 1971. Greek philosophy cannot be understood just by looking at work of philosophers. One must also consider thought processes of poets, dramatists, and historians, as well as general aesthetic theory of ancient Greece. Extensive bibliography.   [249]

——. *Nietzsche and Greek Thought*. Dordrecht, Netherlands: Nijhoff, 1987. Analysis of Nietzsche's interest in the past as a model for his own age, which he considered morally bankrupt. Looks at his understanding of Anaximander, Heraclitus, Parmenides, Socrates, Plato, Aristotle.   [250]

TOBEY, J. L. *The History of Ideas. A Bibliographical Introduction, I: Classical Antiquity*. Santa Barbara, CA: Clio Pr., 1975. Studies ideas "used by educated people in each era to comprehend the universe and rationalize their social institutions, arts and religion." Organizes ideas under philosophy, science, aesthetics, and religion. Each topic is given introduction and bibliography. Emphasizes Greece over Rome.   [251]

TRACY, T. "The Soul as Boatman of the Body: Presocratics to Descartes." *Diot* 7(1979), 195-199. Idea of soul inhabiting and steering body is implicit in most Presocratics and enunciated clearly by Plato and Aristotle. It carries over into Neoplatonic and

Christian thought. [252]

URMSON, J. O. "Pleasure and Distress: A Discussion of J. C. B. Gosling and C. C. W. Taylor, *The Greeks on Pleasure*." *OSAP* 2(1984), 209-221. Review essay of #149. [253]

VOEGELIN, E. "Wisdom and the Magic of the Extreme." *Eranos-Jb* 46(1977), 341-409. Imperfection has plagued philosophical search for utopia and total understanding. Will must balance its desire to know reality as an object and its sense that reality is different and unknowable. [254]

VON RINTELEN, F. J. *Values in European Thought, I.* Pamplona, Spain: Ed. Universidad de Navarra, 1972. Begins by defining "value" or "good," admitting that concept is so universal as to be difficult to delimit. Looks at ancient non-European views, covers Socrates, Plato, Aristotle, Hellenistic schools, Middle Ages. [255]

VON WEIZSACKER, C. F. "Greek Philosophy and Modern Physics." *Philosophy in Science* 1(1983), 57-70. Physicists find Greeks, particularly Plato and Aristotle, easy to understand because they were essentially skeptics working on a mathematical foundation. [256]

WAITHE, M. E., ed. *A History of Women Philosophers, I: Ancient Women Philosophers, 600 B. C. - 500 A. D.* Dordrecht, Netherlands: Nijhoff, 1987. Names of many women philosophers, from Pythagoras' wife Theano to Hypatia in Alexandria ca. 400 A. D., are known. Reliable historical data about them is scarce. "Philosopher" is defined more narrowly in this work than it was in ancient world. [257]

WALLIS, R. T. "The Spiritual Importance of Not Knowing," in #43, pp. 460-480. Examines views of Plato, Aristotle, Pyrrho, and Neoplatonists on unknowability of the divine. Four reasons cover most cases: lack of revelation or initiation; the god is unknowable except by inference from his work; his essence cannot be known in positive sense but can be defined in terms of what it is not; the god is unknowable rationally but can be experienced in mystic union. [258]

WENG, S. "A Comparative Study of Natural Philosophy in Pre-Qin China and Ancient Greece." *ChinStudPhil* 21 #2(1989), 3-31. Compares the two traditions in terms of movement from religious view of nature to a natural philosophy. [259]

WESTOBY, A. "Hegel's *History of Philosophy*," in *Philosophy and Its Past*, ed. J. Ree et al. (Atlantic Highlands, NJ: Humanities Pr., 1978), pp. 67-108. Examines importance of Hegel's work on Greek philosophers, especially Thales, Heraclitus, Socrates. [260]

WHITMAN, J. *Allegory. The Dynamics of an Ancient and Medieval Technique.* Cambridge, MA: Harvard Univ. Pr., 1987. Part 1 traces development of allegory in antiquity: Presocratics' reading of Homer; Plato's discussion of bipartite soul; Virgil's view of gods as abstractions; Stoic concept of *mythos*; Seneca's understanding of nature of soul. Christian allegory combined Platonic levels of being with Gnostic typology. [261]

WIDER, K. "Women Philosophers in the Ancient Greek World. Donning the Mantle." *Hypatia* 1(1986), 21-62. Traces lives and work of women philosophers from sixth century B. C. to fourth century A. D. and discusses problem of poor preservation of material by and about them due to gender bias. [262]

WILLIAMS, B. "Philosophy," in *The Legacy of Greece: A New Appraisal*, ed. M. I. Finley (Oxford: Clarendon Pr., 1981), pp. 202-255. Survey of influence of Greek philosophy, especially Platonism, on European thought. **[263]**

WINSTON, D. S. "Freedom and Determinism in Greek Philosophy and Jewish Hellenistic Wisdom." *StPhilon* 2(1973), 40-50. Early Greek philosophers did not treat this problem. Epicurus argued for complete free will. Orthodox Judaism made God responsible for all human actions. Hellenistic Judaism maintained God's sovereignty but also saw man as free, without resolving the conflict. **[264]**

WINTON, R. I., and **GARNSEY, P.** "Political Theory," in *The Legacy of Greece: A New Appraisal*, ed. M. I. Finley (Oxford: Clarendon Pr., 1981), pp. 37-64. Contributions of Sophists, Plato, Aristotle, and others to invention of political science. **[265]**

ZOH, J. "The Oriental Influence on the Origin of Greek Philosophy." *Diot* 8(1980), 164-167. Philosophy originated in Egypt, not Greece. **[266]**

For related items see #5139, #5632.

Chapter 2

DOXOGRAPHY; COLLECTED TEXTS

It has been estimated, on the basis of titles of works compiled from references in ancient and medieval authors, that less than ten percent of the works known to the classical world survive today in even fragmentary form. Philosophical writings have not been immune to loss. We know the names of some 316 philosophers who are believed to have written something in Greek. To that number we can add Cicero, Lucretius, and Seneca in Latin. The works of only two — Plato and Plotinus — are extant today in their entirety. Sixty-one others are represented by one or more reasonably complete works. The other 256 are known to us only through fragments or quotations. (The entire surviving work of Zeno of Elea, for instance, consists of roughly two hundred words; Anaximander's work is voluminous by comparison — two and a half pages of printed text.) The collection and editing of this material occupied scholars before the second World War. The last half of this century has seen less emphasis on this philological side of ancient philosophy, but some significant new editions have appeared in the last two decades.

We have no evidence that any of the Presocratic philosophers before Parmenides wrote anything. Their teachings seem to have been passed along orally (cf. #372, #326). Even after the rediscovery of writing in Greece in the eighth century B. C., oral transmission was still the preferred form of handing on important material. As late as 100 A. D. the Middle Platonist biographer Plutarch maintained that someone writing about the lives of persons from the past should "not only have access to all kinds of books, but through hearsay and personal inquiry . . . uncover facts which often escape the chroniclers and are preserved in *more reliable form* in human memory" (*Demosthenes* 2, italics added). Written texts served primarily as aids in memorization.

It is only in the late classical period that we begin to find written philosophical treatises. But Plato and Aristotle both considered their oral teaching more important than anything written down (cf. #1355). Plato's dialogues — "an amusement," as he styled them — may have been written to defuse suspicion among the common people, the ones who had put Socrates to death because they didn't understand what he taught. He puts into the mouth of Socrates a long discussion of the superiority of memory over reliance on writing (*Phaedrus* 275B) and the importance of being able to question someone about his teaching. Aristotle wrote dialogues for the general public but kept his more important teachings within his school. The treatises which we now have were never intended to circulate. They were probably put together from his lecture notes of those of his students.

Another passage in Plutarch provides insight on this question of secret (oral) versus public (written) teachings:

> It seems clear too that Alexander was instructed by his teacher [Aristotle] not only in the principles of ethics and politics, but also in those secret and more esoteric studies which philosophers do not impart to the general run of students, but only by word of mouth to a select circle of the initiated. Some years later, after Alexander had crossed into Asia, he learned that Aristotle had published some treatises dealing with these esoteric matters, and he wrote to him in blunt language and took him to task for the sake of the prestige of philosophy . . . . [Aristotle] pointed out that these so-called oral doctrines were in a sense both published and not published. For example, it is true that his treatise on metaphysics is written in a style which makes it useless for those who wish to study or teach the subject from the beginning: the book serves simply as a memorandum for those who have already been taught its general principles. (*Alexander* 7)

The ancients were as interested in the origins of philosophy as we are, and as ill-informed. A few writers passed down whatever bits of these early teachings they knew of. Later writers amassed these and tried to extrapolate biographical data from them and postulate the existence of philosophical schools similar to those which flourished in the later antique period. We cannot even date most of the Presocratic philosophers with any confidence. Most of the dates we do have were supplied by Apollodorus, whose *Chronology*, a poem in iambic trimeters to aid memorization, extended to 110 B. C. Based on the third-century work of Eratosthenes of Alexandria, it adopted his method of reckoning an individual's prime of life as age forty. The assumption was that a scholar or writer did his major work at about that time of life. It could be determined that some of the philosophers were active in a particular Olympiad (a system of counting that dated back to 776 B. C.). Thus, if a philosopher mentioned something in his work that was known to have occurred in the sixtieth Olympiad, it could be reckoned that he lived ca. 536 B. C., since 776-(60 x 4)=536.

Information about the early philosophers can be drawn from several types of sources, none of them earlier than Aristotle (ca. 320 B. C.). He usually begins his treatises by summing up the opinions of earlier thinkers before setting forth his own views. The importance of these collected opinions (known as *doxai* or *placita*) for reconstructing the thought of the Presocratic philosophers is discussed in several items in the following section of the bibliography.

Aristotle's pupil Theophrastus followed this precedent in his *Doctrines of the Natural Philosophers*, the first effort at a history of philosophy. One sizeable portion and a few fragments are all that survive of this book. Theophrastus' work provided antiquity's primary source of information about the Presocratics and was excerpted and epitomized by later authors, such as the Stoic compiler of the *Vetusta Placita* in the first century B. C. As late as the second century A. D. this process of compiling the teachings of the Presocratics was still being carried on by writers such as Aetius and the anonymous author of the *Placita Philosophorum* (wrongly attributed to Plutarch).

These late handbooks, edited by H. Diels (cf. #273), are our most important source of information about the teachings of the early philosophers, but the fragments preserved have to be used with caution since the texts have sometimes been contaminated by the interpretations of later philosophical schools. They assume, for example, that if an earlier thinker used the term "cause," he understood that term in the same way that Aristotle or the Stoics did. There is also a problem of selectivity. The texts which survive were often preserved because of the interests of later writers and may not reflect the true emphases of the early philosophers' teaching at all.

This approach to the subject is called doxography, or the writing of opinions. It was not undertaken out of pure academic interest in the lives of the founders of the discipline. Later writers needed to support their own views or refute opposing opinions. Ancient philosophical debate was often bitter, (cf. #5634), and the ability to marshal supporting opinions was an important survival skill.

Other writers had more strictly biographical interests. Aristoxenus of Tarentum, another of Aristotle's pupils, compiled lives of Pythagoras, Socrates, and Plato, among others. He passed along some sensational tidbits about Socrates and charged that Plato had "derived" most of the *Republic* from Protagoras. Alexandrian scholars wrote lives of most of the early philosophers. Most noteworthy among these is probably Hermippus, who lived in the third century B. C. Writers and law-givers as well as philosophers were covered in his huge biographical work. He seems to have enjoyed heightening sensational details and creating poignant death scenes. His work was used by Plutarch and Diogenes Laertius, but only fragments survive today.

Most of the writers who have left biographies of philosophers were from the Peripatetic school, founded by Aristotle. One of the few who viewed things from a different perspective, viz., that of Plato's Academy, was Antigonus of Carystos (ca. 240 B. C.), who was active for a time in Athens and in the kingdom of Pergamum in Asia Minor. His *Lives of Philosophers* consists of character sketches of various thinkers of his own day. To judge from the surviving fragments, his accounts were accurate and well-written.

Polemics was certainly the motivation for early Christian writers to study the Greek philosophers. Hippolytus, bishop of Rome ca. 220 A. D., set out to reply to all the philosophers in his *Refutation of All Heresies*, a work sometimes known by the Greek word *Elenchus*, meaning "refutation"; it is also called the *Philosophoumena*. To see the value of Hippolytus in reconstructing the thought of earlier authors, cf. #291 and #774. In his *Praeparatio Evangelica* the church historian Eusebius (ca. 300 A. D.) used a source similar to Hippolytus'.

The last major strain of information about the early philosophers is heavily biographical. It is made up of writers, beginning with Sotion (ca. 200 B. C.), who presupposed that a "succession" of philosophers in schools, a pattern familiar from Plato's Academy and Aristotle's Lyceum, had existed from the very beginning of the discipline. Sotion divided the early philosophers into two large groups: 1) Ionic, from Thales to the Middle Academy; 2) Italic, from Pythagoras to the Eleatics and Atomists, through the Sophists and Sceptics, on to Epicurus.

On this view, Anaximander was the successor of Thales as head of a Milesian "school." Chapter headings in modern textbooks sometimes give the same impression, but when most scholars use the term "school" in connection with the Presocratics today they mean simply a group of thinkers who came from a certain geographical area. No direct line of teaching is implied. The culmination, at least chronologically, of this interpretation of the history of ancient philosophy is Diogenes Laertius' *Lives of the Philosophers*, a valuable source in spite of the fact that "it has not been digested or composed by any single mind at all, but is little more than a collection of extracts made at haphazard." Another critic made light of Diogenes' "normal abysmal level of incoherence and unreliability," but everyone uses him.

Several doxographic works are known to us only by title or through a quotation or two in later writers. Cleitomachus, an Academician of the second century B. C., and Arius Didymus, who lived in the time of the Roman emperor Augustus, both wrote books on the doctrines of the various philosophical schools. Philodemus of Gadara, in the first century B. C., wrote an *Outline of Philosophy*, and Diocles of Magnesia put together a *Compendium of Philosophy*. Helpful discussions of the doxographers can be found in Burnet (#312), pp. 31-38, and Zeller (#39), pp. 21-24, and the last chapter of Hussey (#338).

The following section of the bibliography pertains to the methodology involved in recovering the texts of the ancient philosophers and to general anthologies of texts in translation from all periods covered by this book. Collections of texts or readings from specific periods are listed in the appropriate chapters.

ALLEN, R. E., ed. *Greek Philosophy: Thales to Aristotle*, 2nd ed. New York: Free Pr., 1985. Selected texts, largely dealing with metaphysics and epistemology. Brief introduction to each author.   [267]

AMUNDSEN, L. "Fragment of a Philosophical Text P. Osl. Inv. 1039." *SO* 41(1966), 5-20. Probably a second-century A. D. text, written by an Epicurean to his students, combatting Stoic ideas on origin of language.   [268]

BARNES, J., ed. *Early Greek Philosophy*. Baltimore: Penguin, 1987. Translation of all surviving Presocratic fragments with extracts from doxographers. Aims not to offer interpretations but to present material on which interpretations must rest.   [269]

BOOTH, N. "Aristotle on Empedokles B 100." *Hermes* 103(1975), 373-375. Ar's citation of a passage helps to clarify E's use of a word.   [270]

CHERNISS, H. F. "The History of Ideas and Greek Philosophy," in #51, pp. 36-61. Ancient doxographers and "historians of philosophy" relied on biographical incidents and had no concept of ideas being passed along in any kind of intellectual history. The limitations of their work "are painfully strict and very dangerous to overstep."   [271]

DE VOGEL, C. J. *Greek Philosophy: A Collection of Texts*. Leiden: Brill, 1969; rprt. Vol. I: *Thales to Plato*; Vol. II: *Aristotle, the Early Peripatetic School and the Early School*; Vol. III: *The Hellenistic-Roman Period*. Title is self-explanatory. Texts intended for students. Commentary and discussion of most important interpretive issues. [272]

DIELS, H. *Doxographi Graeci.* Berlin: De Gruyter, 1965; rprt. Collection of quotations, biographical matter, and other references or allusions to philosophers in later writers. With following item, a standard reference work in the field. [273]

———, and **KRANZ, W.**, eds. *Die Fragmente der Vorsokratiker.* 5th ed., 3 vol. Berlin: Weidmann, 1934. Fragments pertaining to the life and teaching of each philosopher are designated with an A; direct quotations are marked with a B; C indicates imitative or derivative statements. [274]

DILLON, J. "Xenocrates' Metaphysics Fr. 15 (Heinze) Re-examined." *AncPh* 5(1985), 47-52. Text of this frag, preserved by Stobaeus from Aetius, is garbled. [275]

FREEMAN, K. *Ancilla to the Pre-Socratic Philosophers: A Complete Translation of the Fragments in Diels,* Fragmente der Vorsokratiker. Cambridge, MA: Harvard Univ. Pr., 1971; rprt. Translation of all fragments in B section of #274. [276]

———. cf. #328.

HAHM, D. E. "The Diaeretic Method and the Purpose of Arius' Doxography," in #5611, pp. 15-37. Division *(diaeresis)* provides basic structure for presentation of Stoic ethics, moving from things to actions to men, whose value is based on their actions. [277]

HALL, J. J. "Seneca as a Source for Earlier Thought (Especially Meteorology)." *CQ* 27(1977), 409-436. Seneca is as accurate as any doxographer but never precise. He must be used cautiously. [278]

HENRICHS, A. "Two Doxographical Notes. Democritus and Prodicus on Religion." *HSCP* 79(1975), 93-123. Two papyri from Herculaneum refer to D's attempt to prove gods' existence from seasons. Another attests to P's atheism and reliance on Protagoras. [279]

HERSHBELL, J. P. "Plutarch and Democritus." *QUCC* 39(1982), 81-111. P seems to have known several of D's works. He cites D to criticize Stoics and Epicureans. [280]

———. "Plutarch as a Source for Empedocles Re-examined." *AJPh* 92(1971), 156-184. Considers how P uses E and accuracy of his quotations. [281]

KAHN, C. H. "Arius as a Doxographer," in #5611, pp. 3-14. Survey of what can be known of Arius, his methodology, and problems of recovering his text. [282]

KATZ, J., and **WEINGARTNER, R. H.**, eds. *Philosophy in the West: Readings in Ancient and Medieval Philosophy.* New York: Harcourt, Brace and World, 1965. Anthology with chapter introductions. Includes some figures (Origen, Tertullian) and works (Augustine's *De Magistro*) not often anthologized. [283]

KAUFMANN, W., ed. *Philosophic Classics, I: Thales to Ockham.* Englewood Cliffs, NJ: Prentice-Hall, 1968; 2nd ed. Extracts with commentaries. Two-thirds devoted to Plato and Aristotle. [284]

LEBEDEV, A. V. "Did the Doxographer Aetius Ever Exist?" in #50, III, pp. 813-817. Considers difficulties in evaluating the evidence and tenuousness of conclusions. [285]

MAKIN, S. "How Can We Find Out What Ancient Philosophers Said?" *Phron* 33(1988), 121-132. Given limited textual evidence for Presocratics, we must use contemporary techniques of philosophical analysis to reconstruct account of their thought.   **[286]**

MANSFELD, J. "Aristotle, Plato, and the Preplatonic Doxography and Chronography," in *Storiografia e dossografia nella filosofia antica*, ed. G. Cambiano (Turin: Ed. Tirrenia Stampatori, 1986), pp. 1-59. Ar and P gathered doxographical material before Theophrastus. Their material may have been grouped by opposing or similar views rather than concentrating on establishing views of particular philosophers systematically.**[287]**

––––. "Chrysippus and the *Placita*." *Phron* 34(1989), 311-342. C's discussion of the heart as the seat of the soul seems to be based on readings from a doxographic collection from philosophers and doctors.   **[288]**

––––. cf. #537, #539.

MARCOVICH, M. "Hippolytus and Heraclitus." *StudPatr* 8(1966), 255-264. Hippolytus is an excellent source for material from Heraclitus because of accuracy of his quotations and ease with which we can distinguish his paraphrases from direct quotations.   **[289]**

McDERMOTT, J. J. *Cultural Introduction to Philosophy from Antiquity to Descartes*. New York: Texas A&M Univ. Pr., 1985. Selected texts, many complete, with illustrations, maps, and time-line.   **[290]**

OSBORNE, C. *Rethinking Early Greek Philosophy. Hippolytus of Rome and the Presocratics*. Ithaca, NY: Cornell Univ. Pr., 1987. Argues against regarding quotations extracted from later writers as accurate representations of Presocratic thought. Context in which citations occur must be taken into account.   **[291]**

ROBINSON, J. M. *An Introduction to Early Greek Philosophy. The Chief Fragments and Ancient Testimony, with Connecting Commentary*. Boston: Houghton Mifflin, 1968. Aims to introduce non-specialists to early Greek philosophy, using fragments and testimonia joined together with a running commentary. Analyzes individual passages rather than trying to synthesize. Downgrades Thales to an appendix but covers other Presocratics, including Sophists.   **[292]**

RUNIA, D. T. "Xenophanes on the Moon: A *Doxographicum* in Aetius." *Phron* 34(1989), 245-269. X's views on nature of moon are not important in themselves (he thought moon was an ignited cloud that had been condensed). Tracing reports of his views reveals much about how doxographers worked.   **[293]**

SHARPLES, R. W. "Some Aspects of the Secondary Tradition of Theophrastus' *Opuscula*," in #5491, pp. 41-64. Later writers quoted T out of context or gave inaccurate titles of his works, making it difficult to match citations with works whose titles are known.   **[294]**

STEVENSON, J. G. "Aristotle as Historian of Philosophy." *JHS* 94(1974), 138-143. One cannot establish general rules about Ar's use of Presocratic sources. Each passage must be studied individually.   **[295]**

WHEELWRIGHT, P. *The Presocratics*. New York: Odyssey Pr., 1966. Translation of texts, with introduction, notes, glossary of Greek terms, bibliographies. Gives access to English version of doxographical material which tends to get lost in Diels. [296]

WRIGHT, M. R. *The Presocratics. The Main Fragments in Greek.* Bristol, UK: Bristol Class. Pr., 1985. Critical edition with commentary and translation. [297]

YARTZ, F. J. *Ancient Greek Philosophy: Sourcebook and Perspective.* Jefferson, NC: McFarland, 1984. Readings from a wide range of philosophers, emphasizing the theme of Logos. Notes at the end of each section provide research helps for advanced students. [298]

For related items see #612, #670, #828, #851.

Chapter 3

THE PRESOCRATICS: GENERAL

The term "Presocratics" would seem to describe philosophers who lived before Socrates (469-399 B. C.), but included in the category are several thinkers who were contemporary with the old gadfly. Anaxagoras lived in Athens during Socrates' lifetime and Leucippus and Democritus were both born after him.

The term "Presocratic" is thus not purely a chronological designation. The philosophers covered by it were primarily concerned with discovering the principles upon which the world was organized. The term covers a wide range of opinions, from the theory of Heraclitus that the world is in a constant state of flux to the idea of Parmenides and Zeno that change is impossible. These men lived across the Greek world, from Ionia (modern Turkey) to southern Italy and Sicily. The common theme that runs through their work is the effort to answer questions about the nature and matter of the world and the problem of change.

Estimates of the importance of the Presocratics have changed over the past generation of scholarship. Before World War II the emphasis in Presocratic studies was on assembling and analyzing the ancient evidence, with the aim of reconstructing the thought of each individual philosopher. Since the late 1940's the emphasis has shifted to the problem of separating what the Presocratics thought from what Aristotle, Theophrastus, and later doxographers believed that they thought. This is, perhaps, the major difficulty in studying them. Hussey understates the case when he says that "the handling of the evidence is peculiarly difficult" (#338, p. 149).

Scholars of the late nineteenth century, enamored of scientific positivism, saw the Presocratics as their intellectual predecessors. More recently doubt has been cast on just how "scientific" these early thinkers actually were. Mythology and religion seem to play a larger role in their thought and the forms in which it is expressed than the nineteenth century was willing to concede. Hankinson seems to dismiss them altogether as scientists: "Saying that the world is entirely made of water, or air, or fire (or generally of x for some improbable value of x) is no substitute for the type of detailed researches carried out by Aristotle and his colleagues in the Lyceum."(#157, p. 2)

The overarching problems in the study of the Presocratics are the incompleteness of the texts and the extent to which the views of later philosophers have been read back into the fragments which we have. As Tejera points out, "The fraction of their work which has survived is a small one, and we must remember that the way it has been put together actually represents a long series of editorial decisions made by later readers." (#249, p. 2). Though our assessment of them may be in a state of flux, it is certain that the Presocratics "generated some profound and subtle metaphysical arguments and . . . deserve intense philosophical study in their own right." (Moulder #357, p. 88)

ADKINS, A. W. H. "Orality and Philosophy," in #371, pp. 207-227. Reply to Havelock (#331). [299]

ALLEN, R. E., and FURLEY, D. J., eds. *Studies in Presocratic Philosophy.* New York: Humanities Pr.; London: Routledge & Paul:
Vol. I: *The Beginning of Philosophy.* 1970. Collection of essays, reprinted from journals; about half deal with Presocratic thought in general, two with Anaximander, two with the Pythagoreans, and one with Heraclitus. Abstracted herein. [300]

Vol. II: *The Eleatics and Pluralists.* 1975. Collection of journal reprints on Parmenides, Zeno, Empedocles, and Anaxagoras. Abstracted herein. [301]

BARNES, J. "Aphorism and Argument," in #371, pp. 91-109. Though they do not usually figure large in philosophical discourse, pithy, memorable sayings are characteristic of Presocratic philosophers, perhaps because they anticipated an audience of hearers instead of readers. [302]

———. *The Presocratic Philosophers.* London: Routledge & Kegan Paul, 1979; 2nd ed., 1982.
vol. I: *Thales to Zeno.*
vol. II: *Empedocles to Democritus.* Systematic survey of the various philosophers' thought and assessment of their impact on later thinkers. Stresses "the characteristic rationality of Greek thought." Organized by topics rather than individuals or schools. Second edition has extensive bibliography. [303]

———. "The Presocratics in Context." *Phron* 33(1988), 327-344. Review essay of C. Osborne's book (#291). [304]

———. cf. #269.

BENN, A. W. *Early Greek Philosophy.* London: Kennikat Pr., 1969; rprt. Survey of Presocratics for non-specialists. [305]

BICKNELL, P. J. "Early Greek Knowledge of the Planets." *Eranos* 68(1970), 47-54. Reply to Dicks (#321). Ionians did distinguish between stars and planets and knew at least three planets. [306]

———. "*To apeiron, apeiros aer* and *to periechon.*" *AClass* 9(1966), 27-48. Elaboration of ideas of M. C. Stokes (#379) concerning cosmogony and chaos. Relationship of Presocratic concepts to Hesiod's work is discussed. [307]

BLACKER, C., and LOEWE, M., eds. *Ancient Cosmologies.* London: Allen & Unwin, 1975. Surveys creation stories from ancient cultures such as India, China, Egypt. Chapter on Greeks, by G. E. R. Lloyd, focuses on transition from mythical explanations to philosophical. [308]

BREMMER, J. *The Early Greek Concept of the Soul.* Princeton Univ. Pr., 1983. Draws distinction between a soul which endows the body with life and consciousness and a "free" soul, representing the individual personality. Compares concept of soul from other cultures with that of ancient Greece.   [309]

BRENDEL, O. J. *Symbolism of the Sphere: A Contribution to the History of Earlier Greek Philosophy.* Leiden: Brill, 1977; rprt. Focuses on an ancient mosaic, showing Seven Sages of Greece, discussed in connection with written reports of their teaching. Thales, portrayed as an astronomer, is of special interest.   [310]

BROWN, T. S. "The Greek Exiles. Herodotus' Contemporaries." *AncW* 17(1988), 17-28. Discusses process of exile and Herodotus' knowledge of Xenophanes, Anaxagoras, Protagoras, and Empedocles.   [311]

BURNET, J. *Early Greek Philosophy.* 4th ed. New York: Meridian, 1957 (1st ed., 1892). This remains a fundamental study. In format a survey, it stresses Presocratics' separation from religious influences and from Orientalism.   [312]

CHERNISS, H. F. "The Characteristics and Effects of Presocratic Philosophy," in #51, pp. 62-88. Examines problem of how our knowledge of Presocratics is limited by fact that later philosophers quoted them only to suit their own purposes.   [313]

CLAUS, D. B. *Toward the Soul: An Inquiry into the Meaning of Psyche before Plato.* New Haven, CT: Yale Univ. Pr., 1981. Examines words for "soul" used in pre-Platonic Greek writers. Apart from *kardie* and *psyche*, other "soul words" mean thought, life, or personifications of one of those. Most of book traces evolution of *psyche* from "life" or "shade" in Homer to "soul" as opposite of body in Plato.   [314]

CLEVE, F. M. *The Giants of Pre-Sophistic Greek Philosophy. An Attempt to Reconstruct Their Thoughts*; 2 vols. The Hague: Nijhoff, 1965. Using Diels-Kranz texts, attempts purely philosophical (non-philological) reconstruction of Presocratics' ideas, assuming they were genuine philosophers who built coherent systems of thought. Organizes them into religious reformers, philosophers of nature, champions of culture politics.   [315]

COLE, T. "Archaic Truth." *QUCC* 42(1983), 7-28. Word "truth" in Greek (*aletheia*) means "not forgetting," process applicable to persons, not things. Surest means of not forgetting is preservation in writing. Use of this term for "truth," as opposed to other possible words, is measure of progression of Greek thought from oral and mythic to written and rational.   [316]

CORNFORD, F. M. "Innumerable Worlds in Presocratic Philosophy," in #53, pp. 175-190. Defends Zeller's interpretation of Anaximander's innumerable worlds as meaning an endless succession of single worlds. Atomists' view, however, is pluralistic.   [317]

————. "The Invention of Space," in #53, pp. 199-219. Presocratic idea of an unlimited, though finite, spherical universe, is closer to concepts of twentieth-century science than is Euclid's infinite unlimited void.   [318]

————. "Mystery Religions and Pre-Socratic Philosophy," in #53, pp. 36-97. Selections from *Cambridge Ancient History.* Stresses continuity of Ionian and Italian schools of philosophy with earlier mythic patterns of thought. Examines Eleusinian and Orphic mysteries and their connection with philosophers from Thales to Atomists. [319]

DE LUCCA, J. "Three Interpretations of the Pre-Socratic Philosophers." *CJ* 60(1965), 158-163. Discussion of views of H. Bergson, G. Santayana, and B. Russell. [320]

DICKS, D. R. "Solstices, Equinoxes and the Presocratics." *JHS* 86(1966), 26-40. Presocratic astronomy not as scientific as often presented. Pythagoras' theory of spherical earth made astronomy a science. [321]

EMLYN-JONES, C. J. *The Ionians and Hellenism.* London: Routledge & Kegan Paul, 1980. Maintains that Ionians generally, not just gifted individuals, were intellectual adventurers and pioneers, analogous to Homeric heroes. Milesians, Xenophanes, and Heraclitus must be understood against such a background. [322]

FERGUSON, J. "*Dinos* in Aristophanes and Euripides." *CJ* 74(1978-79), 356-359. The source of A's use of term is hard to trace. E may have derived it from Atomists. [323]

——. "Notes on the Early Greek Philosophers." *SO* 3(1974), 38-46. Comments on fragments of Thales, Heraclitus, Empedocles, and Anaxagoras. [324]

——. "The Opposites." *Apeir* 3 #1(1969), 1-17. Awareness of dichotomies is underlying unity among early Greek thinkers, from dialectical ones such as Anaximander and Heraclitus, to dualists like Pythagoras. Opposites considered concrete things. [325]

FERRARI, G. R. F. "Orality and Literacy in the Origin of Philosophy." *AncPh* 4(1984), 194-205. Reply to Robb (#371). Disputes idea, especially as put forth by Havelock (#331), that development of literacy and changing modes of thought can be credited with origins of philosophy. [326]

FRAENKEL, H. *Early Greek Poetry and Philosophy*, transl. by M. Hadas and J. Willis. New York: Harcourt Brace, 1975. Emphasizes intellectual kinship between poets and philosophers from Homer to Pindar. Sections four and five deal most directly with early philosophers, though index will help students locate other references to them. [327]

FREEMAN, K. *The Pre-Socratic Philosophers: A Companion to Diels' Fragmente der Vorsokratiker.* Oxford: Blackwell, 1946. Discusses origins of Presocratic thought, lives of philosophers of sixth and fifth centuries B. C. and Sophists. List at end contains each author's name, place of birth (if known), approximate date, and main works. [328]

FURLEY, D. *The Greek Cosmologists, Vol I: The Formation of the Atomic Theory and its Earliest Critics.* Cambridge Univ. Pr., 1987. Traces cosmological speculation from Milesians to Atomists, showing conflict between those who asserted elements/materials of physics and those who argued for monism. Last two chapters discuss criticisms of Presocratic theories by Plato and Aristotle. [329]

GAGARIN, M. "*Dike* in Archaic Greek Thought." *CPh* 69(1974), 186-197. *Dike* in Parmenides and Heraclitus means universal force of law. For some poets it suggests economic behavior. There is no moral connotation. [330]

HAVELOCK, E. A. "The Linguistic Task of the Presocratics," in #371, pp. 7-82. Epoch-making study of effect of pre-literate modes of thought on Presocratic philosophy.

Education based on written texts cannot be demonstrated earlier than fifth century B. C. Presocratic philosophers had to express their ideas in verse form in competition with — and as corrections of — Homer and Hesiod.   [331]

———. "Pre-Literacy and the Pre-Socratics." *BICS* 13(1966), 44-67. Some aspects of Xenophanes', Heraclitus', and Parmenides' work are shaped by pre-literate modes of thought. Their concerns are not philosophical but linguistic and syntactical.   [332]

HEIDEGGER, M. *Early Greek Thinking: The Dawn of Western Philosophy*, transl. by D. F. Krell and F. A. Capuzzi. San Francisco: Harper & Row, 1975. Studies on Anaximander, Heraclitus, and Parmenides, taken from earlier publications in German. [333]

HEIDEL, W. A. "Qualitative Change in Pre-Socratic Philosophy," in #363, pp. 86-95. Pioneering essay which pointed out that our understanding of elements and change in Presocratics was derived from Aristotle and that his emphases did not necessarily reflect those of early philosophers.   [334]

HERSHBELL, J. P. "The Idea of Strife in Early Greek Thought." *Pers* 55(1974), 205-215. Idea of conflict between elements has Homeric and Hesiodic roots; it becomes important for Plato, Aristotle, and Christian thinkers.   [335]

HETZLER, F. M. "Matter and Spirit: The Ultimate Artistic Realities." *Diot* 10(1982), 26-34. Surveys "first principle" of Presocratics and unity of matter and spirit in Plotinus.   [336]

HOELLER, K. "The Role of the Early Greeks in Heidegger's Turning." *PhT* 28(1984), 44-51. Examines Presocratic influence on development of Heidegger's thought. [337]

HUSSEY, E. *The Presocratics*. London: Duckworth, 1972. Relates Presocratic thought to Near Eastern influences. Surveys major thinkers, pointing out scarcity of reliable information. Concludes with chapters on Sophists and overview of cosmology from Parmenides to Democritus and survey of doxographical problems.   [338]

HYLAND, D. A. *The Origins of Philosophy. Its Rise in Myth and the Pre-Socratics. A Collection of Early Writings Selected, Edited, and with Explanatory Essays.* New York: Putnam, 1973. Philosophical rather than historical approach. Tries to answer question: Can one designate a particular moment as time when philosophy begins? Why does one person begin to think rationally when his society looks at things mythically?   [339]

JAEGER, W. *The Theology of the Early Greek Philosophers*, transl. E. S. Robinson. Oxford: Clarendon Pr., 1967; rprt. Sees Presocratics as neither purely natural scientists nor mystics. Their concept of nature seems to have influenced their understanding of divinity. Chapters are devoted to individual philosophers.   [340]

JEDYNAK, S. "On Humanism before Protagoras (Delphic Circle)." *Studia Filozoficzne* 5(1971), 35-47. Sense of universal morality encouraged by Delphic cult is expressed in tragic poets and in Pythagoreans and Empedocles.   [341]

KAHN, C. H. "On Early Greek Astronomy." *JHS* 90(1970), 99-116. Presocratics should be acknowledged as originators of a genuine astronomical science.   [342]

KERFERD, G. B. "The Image of the Wise Man in Greece in the Period Before Plato," in #47, pp. 17-28. Examines use of terms *sophos, sophistes,* and *sophia* to cover technical ability, as well as political, literary, scientific, and philosophical expertise in Xenophanes, Protagoras, and Aristotle. [343]

———. "Recent Works on Presocratic Philosophy (1953-1962)." *AmPhQ* 2(1965), 130-140. Review essay of a large number of studies. [344]

KIRK, G. S. "Orality and Sequence," in #371, pp. 83-90. Greece's intellectual history underwent important developments during "Dark Age" when Greeks were still illiterate. Several Presocratic philosophers molded and shaped mythic traditions from this era. Oral story-telling emphasizes a sequence of events. Presocratic philosophers had to develop a mind-set that allowed for permanence and lack of change. [345]

———, et al., eds. *The Presocratic Philosophers: A Critical History with a Selection of Texts.* Cambridge Univ. Pr., 1984; 2nd ed. Begins with poetic and religious forerunners of Presocratics and excludes Sophists. Greek text has translation at bottom of page and a commentary and analysis for each thinker. [346]

LEJEWSKI, C. "The Concept of Matter in Presocratic Philosophy," in *The Concept of Matter in Greek and Medieval Philosophy,* ed. E. McMullin (Notre Dame, IN: Univ. of Notre Dame Pr., 1965), pp. 25-36. Presocratic concept of matter was more important philosophically than scientifically because it did not develop understanding of form as opposed to and complementing concept of matter. [347]

LESSER, H. "Nietzsche and the Pre-Socratic Philosophers." *JBritSocPhen* 18(1987), 30-37. Nietzsche's understanding of Presocratic philosophy "as elaborating the paradox that the world is a place of suffering and guilt, but also a place of beauty" influenced his own philosophy. [348]

LLOYD, G. E. R. "Popper versus Kirk. A Controversy in the Interpretation of Greek Science." *BritJourPhSci* 18(1967), 21-38. Disagreement over whether Presocratics were philosophers or scientists centers on role of observation in science. [349]

LONGRIGG, J. "Elements and After. A Study in Pre-Socratic Physics of the Second Half of the Fifth Century." *Apeir* 19(1985), 93-115. Influence of four-element theory on Greek physics and medicine seems to have been immediate, not delayed. [350]

———. "The Sun and the Planets." *Apeir* 1 #1(1966), 19-31. Early philosophers approached study of natural phenomena scientifically, but their assumption of a basic element or unifying hypothesis impeded scientific advance for several centuries. [351]

MARGOLIS, J. "The Emergence of Philosophy," in #371, pp. 228-243. Havelock's theory of connections between literacy and origins of philosophy (#331) is unconvincing. Many elements of Homeric tradition are philosophical in nature. [352]

MATSON, W. I. "From Water to Atoms. The Triumph of Metaphysics," in #371, pp. 255-265. Shows progression from Thales' unscientific but philosophical explanation of nature of universe to Democritus' purely scientific stance. [353]

MILLER, M. H. "The Implicit Logic of Hesiod's Cosmogony. An Examination of

Theogony 116-133." *IndepJPh* 4(1980), 131-142. Though he represents important step between myth and rational accounts of world's origins, Hesiod fails to account for origin of his four primal powers. He seems to have recognized, ontologically, limits of this type of cosmogonic account.   [354]

MINAR, E. L., Jr. "Pre-Socratic Studies, 1953-1966." *CW* 60(1966), 143-163. Annotated bibliography.   [355]

———. "A Survey of Recent Work in Presocratic Philosophy 1945-1952." *CW* 47(1953-54), 161-170, 177-182. Annotated bibliography.   [356]

MOULDER, J. "New Ideas on Early Greek Philosophy." *SAfrJPh* 2(1983), 87-91. Review essay of eleven books.   [357]

———. "The Origins of Early Greek Philosophy." *SAfrJPh* 4(1985), 29-33. Review essay of seven books.   [358]

MOURELATOS, A. P. D. "'Nothing' as 'Not-Being': Some Literary Contexts that Bear on Plato," in #42, pp. 59-69. In Presocratics, especially Parmenides, emphasis is not on "what there *is*" but "*what* it is, on *physis*, not on existence.   [359]

———. "Pre-Socratic Origins of the Principle that There are no Origins from Nothing." *JPh* 78(1981), 649-665. Concept first appears in any developed form in Parmenides but has roots in earlier thinkers.   [360]

———. "The Real, Appearances and Human Error in Early Greek Philosophy." *RMeta* 19(1965-66), 346-365. Presocratic ontologies developed from progressive scepticism about reality of sensible world, which can be broken down to three stages: 1) sensible things are believed to exist in their own right and are usually what they appear to be; 2) only certain kinds of things exist and are what they appear to be; 3) no sensible things exist and never appear as they are. Greek philosophers had moved to second and third stages before they knew why they had abandoned the first.   [361]

———. "Saving the Presocratics." *PhilBooks* 22(1981), 65-77. Comments on #303. Argues book's main weakness is ignoring thinkers' historical context. Discusses treatment of Eleatics at greatest length.   [362]

———., ed. *The Pre-Socratics: A Collection of Critical Essays.* Garden City, NY: Doubleday, 1974. Reprints of journal articles and chapters from books, most of which appear separately in this bibliography.   [363]

O'BRIEN, D. "Derived Light and Eclipses in the Fifth Century." *JHS* 88(1968), 114-127. It is unlikely any philosopher/scientist before Anaxagoras understood eclipses.   [364]

PAQUET, L., et al. *Les Presocratiques: Bibliographie analytique (1879-1980).* Montreal: Bellarmin, 1988. Annotated (in French) survey of work in all languages on Milesians, Pythagoreans, Xenophanes, and Heraclitus.   [365]

POPPER, K. R. "The Pre-Socratics and the Rationalist Tradition." *Etc* 24(1967), 149-172. Thinkers such as Milesians and Heraclitus are philosophers, not scientists. Their rationalist attitude places premium on innovation through criticism. They do not pretend to have achieved certitude. [366]

PRIER, R. A. *Archaic Logic: Symbol and Structure in Heraclitus, Parmenides and Empedocles.* The Hague: Mouton, 1976. Presocratics' thought processes are best understood by emphasizing their concrete, picture-oriented mentality. [367]

——. "*Sema* and the Symbolic Nature of Pre-Socratic Thought." *QUCC* 20(1978), 91-101. Understanding symbolic word use in poets reveals more about meaning of Presocratic usage of words like "air" and "fire" than does study of Aristotle. [368]

——. cf. #952.

REXINE, J. E. "Hesiod as a Thinker." *KyForLangQ* 12(1965), 107-116. H's semi-abstract thought, which lacked suitable language to make it purely philosophical, smoothed way for Presocratics. [369]

RING, M. *Beginning with the Pre-Socratics.* Mountain View, CA: Mayfield, 1987. Survey from Thales to Sophists for non-specialists. Looks at Homer and Hesiod as background for Ionians. [370]

ROBB, K., ed. *Language and Thought in Early Greek Philosophy.* La Salle, IL: Hegeler Inst., 1983. Collection of original essays, abstracted herein, focused on Havelock's theses about orality and modes of thought in archaic Greece. [371]

SANTIROCCO, M. S. "Literacy, Orality, and Thought." *AncPh* 6(1986), 153-160. Havelock (#331) overstresses influence of oral modes of thought on development of Presocratic philosophy. [372]

SELIGMAN, P. "Soul and Cosmos in Presocratic Philosophy." *Dion* 2(1978), 5-17. Anaximenes, Heraclitus, and Empedocles show how soul was regarded as an inner dimension of existence and cosmos an outer dimension. [373]

SINNIGE, T. G. *Matter and Infinity in the Presocratic Schools and Plato.* Assen, Netherlands: van Gorcum, 1968. Studies views of Anaximander, Xenophanes, Pythagoras, Zeno, Empedocles, Anaxagoras, Democritus, and Plato. Considers Anaximander first real philosopher because he developed idea of infinity. Two main theories are traced: matter as "tactile," i. e., a substance, and *apeiron*. The two are combined in Plato's *Timaeus.* Extensive bibliography. [374]

——. "West and East." *Theta Pi* 2(1973), 60-71. Response to #386. [375]

SODIPO, J. O. "Greek Science and Religion." *SecOrd* 1(1972), 66-76. Discussion of Ionians' originality and materialism. [376]

STANNARD, J. "The Presocratic Origin of Explanatory Method." *PhQ* 15(1965), 193-206. Burnet maintains science is a Greek creation. This is true if by "science" is meant development of explanatory method. Presocratic use of classification, hypothesis, and generalization is analyzed. [377]

STARR, C. G. "Ideas of Truth in Early Greece." *ParPas* 23(1968), 348-359. Discussion of poets and Xenophanes, Heraclitus, and Parmenides. [378]

STOKES, M. C. *One and Many in Presocratic Philosophy.* Cambridge, MA: Harvard Univ. Pr., 1971. Presocratics did not appreciate full range of ambiguity of "one" and "many." Plato and Aristotle developed linguistic tools to analyze concepts. Parmenides was not interested in one/many as much as in being/not-being. Material monism developed in reaction to his work. Somewhat technical study of difficult topic. [379]

SWEENEY, L. *Infinity in the Presocratics: A Bibliographical and Philosophical Study.* The Hague: Nijhoff, 1972. Anaximander's *apeiron* is a concept of infinity, built upon by Pythagoreans, Parmenides, Atomists. Anaximander links *apeiron* with perfection and deity; he is not far from idea of God held by Plotinus and Christian thinkers. [380]

TECUSAN, M. "Circle and Line as Patterns in Greek Presocratic Thought." *StudClas* 23(1985), 13-20. Circle/line conflict represents facet of irrational, mythic thought which lingered well into Presocratic period, as intellectual world grew more rationalistic. Geometry held no honored place in mathematics, contrary to common view. [381]

VERDENIUS, W. J. "Hylozoism in Early Greek Thought." *Janus* 64(1977), 25-40. Early Greeks saw matter and life as interrelated, one impossible without the other. This view formed an important link between the mythography of Homer and Hesiod and early "scientific" explanations of nature. [382]

VERNANT, J.-P. *Myth and Thought Among the Greeks.* London: Routledge & Kegan Paul, 1983. Fifteen essays. Most interesting to students of early philosophy are those on positivism in archaic Greece, geometrical space, and Milesian cosmologies. [383]

——. *The Origins of Greek Thought.* Ithaca, NY: Cornell Univ. Pr., 1982. Historical-anthropological approach to question, beginning with collapse of Mycene. Greek rationalism is seen as product of city life. [384]

VON FRITZ, K. "*Nous, Noein,* and Their Derivatives in Pre-Socratic Philosophy (Excluding Anaxagoras)," in #363, pp. 23-85. Surveys vocabulary of cognition in the major Presocratics. [385]

WEST, M. L. *Early Greek Philosophy and the Orient.* Oxford: Clarendon Pr., 1971. Emphasizes period from 550 to 480 B. C. and possible Iranian/Indian influences, especially on Heraclitus and Pherecydes (ca. 550), author of a lost cosmogonic myth. [386]

WILBUR, J. B., and **ALLEN, H. J.** *The Worlds of the Early Greek Philosophers.* Buffalo, NY: Prometheus, 1979. Surveys political and social background of Aegean and southern Italy in sixth and fifth centuries B. C. Relates thought of each philosopher to its context. Generous quotations from primary sources and from modern secondary sources. [387]

WILLARD, D. "Concerning the 'Knowledge' of the Pre-Platonic Greeks," in #371, pp. 244-254. Disputes Havelock's claim (#331) that early Greeks thought in images/narratives and thus could not "know" in a rational sense. [388]

WOODBURY, L. "Two New Works on Early Greek Views of the Soul." *AncPh* 3(1983), 200-210. Discussion of Claus (#314) and Bremmer (#309). [389]

For related items see #291, #296, #297, #593, #1287, #6105, #6142.

Chapter 4

THE MILESIANS

The first group of Presocratic philosophers lived and worked in Miletus, one of a string of cities along the Aegean coast of modern Turkey founded by Greek colonists in the century after 800 B. C. The Milesians are also called Ionians because they spoke that dialect of Greek. Like all Greek cities, they prefered to run their own affairs but had fallen to the Lydian empire around 600. The Lydians proved to be tolerant overlords, and the Greeks of the coast prospered under them, making contact through them with peoples farther to the east. Just how much impact Babylonian or Egyptian learning may have had on Milesian philosophy is still debated. It is noteworthy, though, that Babylonian myths spoke of the world beginning in "the deep," a watery, chaotic mass, and that Thales posited water as the primary element out of which everything else arose.

Were the Milesians prompted by the rebellious, anti-aristocratic spirit spreading over much of the Greek world in the sixth century B. C., making light of the Olympian gods and the nobility who created them? Poets like Archilochus, Semonides, and Sappho, all of whom wrote between 650-600 B. C., rejected the values of the Homeric world and espoused the primacy of the individual. Their poetry was written to express their own feelings, not to entertain noble lords and ladies during dinner. This restless spirit worked itself out in the political sphere as many Greek city-states stripped their kings or aristocratic councils of power and established some sort of proto-democracy, usually led by a *tyrannos*, a Lydian term for a person who assumes power unconstitutionally on the basis of his personal popularity.

What entitles one of these Milesians (either Thales or Anaximander) to be called the first philosopher is his raising of two closely related questions:

1) What is the nature of the universe, i. e., what is the basic element of which it is made? Must we rely on the explanation that it is a cosmic egg or the internal organs of some monster slain by a gigantic god?

2) How can we explain change?

We do not know why it occurred to one of them, first of all people, so far as we know, to ask what was the basic element of which the world was made.

Later historians of philosophy speak of a Milesian "school," but it is highly doubtful that anything so organized existed at the very beginning of the discipline. Nor is it entirely certain that one of these men taught another directly. It is convenient to look at them together and to consider certain common features of their methodology and their teaching.

ALBRIGHT, W. F. "Neglected Factors in the Greek Intellectual Revolution." *PAPhS* 116(1972), 225-242. No satisfactory answer can be found to question, Why was Thales the first philosopher? Some facets of Anaximander's cosmology can be traced to a Phoenician writer named Sanchuniathon, who preserved much older proto-logical and rationalistic explanations of natural phenomena.   [390]

CORNFORD, F. M. "Was the Ionian Philosophy Scientific?" in #53, pp. 191-197. The only genuine scientists in antiquity were physicians. Philosophers began from assumptions which led to conclusions that could easily be refuted by observation.   [391]

DAVIES, J. C. "Mythological Influences on the First Emergence of Greek Scientific and Philosophical Thought." *Folklore* 81(1970), 23-36. While Milesians freed themselves from mythological forms of thought, they did not, and perhaps could not, create new system of thought entirely devoid of such earlier influences.   [392]

FINKELBERG, A. "On the Unity of Orphic and Milesian Thought." *HThR* 79(1986), 321-335. Milesians' question of relationship of individual things to cosmos is analogous to Orphic doctrine about relationship of individual soul to divinity.   [393]

HERSHBELL, J. P. "Plutarch and the Milesian Philosophers." *Hermes* 114(1986), 172-185. Discusses Plutarch's usefulness in reconstructing thought of Thales, Anaximander, and Anaximenes. He knows more about Thales than about the other two.   [394]

LONG, H. S. "The Milesian School of Philosophy." *UltR&M* 3(1980), 256-263. Milesians were primarily interested in cosmogony, best typified by word *physis*. Religion was not excluded but was insignificant to them.   [395]

SODIPO, J. O. "Greek Science and Religion." *SecOrd* 1(1972), 66-76. Ionian thought's impersonal tone, seeing world of natural forces, contrasts to personal, mythic concepts of earlier Greek writers and pragmatism of Babylon and Egypt.   [396]

THALES (640-550 B. C.)

One can say a great deal or very little about T, depending on whether one accepts the claim (made for him by Aristotle) that he was the first philosopher. On a minimalist view he is "among the most overrated figures in the history of philosophy." G. B. Kerferd (#344) concluded that "it is probable that his importance as the founder of Greek philosophical thinking has been exaggerated." The more favorable view was summed up by Friedrich Nietzsche:

Greek philosophy seems to begin with a preposterous fancy, with the proposition that water is the origin and mother-womb of all things. Is it really necessary to stop there and become serious? Yes, and for three reasons: Firstly, because the proposition does enunciate something about the origin of things; secondly, because it does so without figure and fable; thirdly and lastly because in it is contained, although only in the chrysalis state, the idea that everything is one. The first-mentioned reason leaves Thales still in the company of religious and superstitious people; the second, however, takes him out of this company and shows him to us as a natural philosopher; but by virtue of the third, Thales becomes the first Greek philosopher.

Somewhere between those two positions perhaps we can find the real man and assess his work. At worst he seems to have been a clever mathematician (who devised a method of measuring the height of the pyramids), a resourceful businessman (who cornered the market in olive presses just before a record harvest), and an observer of the heavens (who predicted an eclipse). But does any of that make him a philosopher? Some think so: "Thales evidently abandoned mythic formulations: this alone justifies the claim that he was the first philosopher, naive though his thought still was."

Why would he have assumed that there was one element? Not even the ancient sources that record his achievements, not even those who list him among the Seven Sages — the only philosopher so honored — suggest why he concluded that water was the stuff from which all other forms of matter were made.

From traditions handed down about him we know that he concluded that water is the basic element of the universe, but we do not know how much he was aware of earlier Egyptian and Mesopotamian cosmography. It is worth noting that both the Egyptians and Babylonians conceived of water as "the source and also the sustainer of life." Yet neither of those societies produced literature which demonstrates "the discipline, the cogency of reasoning, which we associate with thinking. The thought of the ancient Near East appears wrapped in imagination . . . . tainted with fantasy."

The question of eastern influences on T has been in circulation since antiquity. He lived in Miletus, a racially and culturally diverse city, and most thought his parentage was not purely Greek. By some accounts, T's father was Greek, his mother Lydian. How much, if anything, shall we make of that? (Others argue for a Phoenician background for T.) He is thought to have travelled in Egypt and to have had an interest in various mathematical problems, such as devising navigational aids. The fact that he predicted an eclipse allows us to fix a date for his life, since we know that an eclipse that would have been visible in Asia Minor occurred in 585 B. C.; that date accords well with what scanty biographical information the ancient sources had about him. But we aren't entirely clear how precise T's predictions could have been. If his knowledge of celestial movements was derived from Babylonian or Egyptian sources, he could not have made accurate predictions for other latitudes and longitudes.

What enabled T to view the world differently? Observation of nature may have suggested to him that water exists in solid, liquid, and gaseous states, and nothing lives for long without it. Near Eastern myths, precursors of the Genesis account of creation, all begin with the matter of the universe in a liquid state. In most of these stories "creation" is the process of separating the various elements. T seems to have taken the first step toward science and philosophy by stressing that this process happens without the intervention of a divine power. His observation that a magnetized stone moves pieces of iron led him to the conclusion that there is a *psyche*, a consciousness of some sort, in all things. In his own words, "everything is full of gods," but not arbitrary, Homeric gods. He means by the term an impersonal link between matter and divinity. (The later Stoics took this as an early assertion of their doctrine of the World Soul.)

DAVIES, C. "Thales of Miletus. The Beginnings of Greek Thought." *HT* 20(1970), 86-93. Though Egyptians and Babylonians developed techniques which became basic to Greek science, they did not question ultimate functioning of universe. T presents coherent explanation of nature without recourse to divine action.   [397]

FEINBERG, G. "Physics and the Thales Problem." *JPh* 63(1966), 5-17. A physicist explains how modern science has answered T's question about world origins.   [398]

HAHN, R. "What Did Thales Want to Be When He Grew Up? Or, Re-appraising the Roles of Engineering and Technology on the Origin of Early Greek Philosophy/Science," in #1277, pp. 107-129. Response to #184. T lived at a time when Homeric view of a chaotic universe was giving way to ideas of order and regularity. Large public buildings of the time suggest inspiration for a new worldview. T may have worked on such projects or merely been inspired by them.   [399]

HARTNER, W. "Eclipse Periods and Thales' Prediction of a Solar Eclipse." *Centaurus* 14(1969), 60-71. Given information available to him, T could not have accurately predicted a solar eclipse. At best he might have been able to predict that an eclipse would occur by the end of a certain year.   [400]

MANSFELD, J. "Aristotle and Others on Thales, or the Beginnings of Natural Philosophy, with Some Remarks on Xenophanes." *Mnem* 38(1985), 109-129. Ar attributes to T only an idea of nature which others, such as X, developed.   [401]

MORANO, D. V. "Thales and the Dawn of Western Philosophy." *JTho* 10(1975), 200-205. Dispute over whether T should be called first philosopher is related to one's definition of "religion" and its importance in his thought.   [402]

MOSSHAMER, A. A. "Thales' Eclipse." *TAPhA* 111(1981), 145-155. Present version of story in Herodotus conflates three originally separate incidents.   [403]

ROLLER, D. W. "Some Thoughts on Thales' Eclipse." *LCM* 8(1983), 58-59. There is no evidence that eclipse which T allegedly predicted actually occurred, 585 B. C. [404]

————. "Thales of Miletus. Philosopher or Businessman?" *LCM* 3(1978), 249-253. Doxographic tradition about T usually includes phrases indicating some doubt about his status as first "philosopher." He appears to have been a Milesian politician who gained a reputation as sage or lawgiver.   [405]

ANAXIMANDER (610-545 B. C.)
Some modern scholars would argue that Thales' contributions to rational thought, while significant, do not qualify him as the first philosopher. They consider him an unusually insightful mathematician and natural scientist, but they would award the mantle of first philosopher to a Milesian of the next generation, Anaximander.

A seems to have taught that the *essential* element of the world could not be one of the elements which make up the world, nor could it be something which could not contain its own opposite. Water may be present in most things, but in a rock? So Thales' water would not do as the basal element. In an effort to account for the opposites in the universe, A theorized that the essential element from which everything comes must be something different from any evident "stuff" which we now see and something which can contain opposites, such as hot and cold, wet and dry, heavy and light.

Something that contains all things and all contrary states must be neutral itself and without limits. That is the definition of A's *apeiron*, a material that contains all matter and qualities without having a definite shape or characteristic of its own.

Even though he provided philosophy and physics with their first useful definition of matter, A was not an ivory tower intellectual. Stories were told of Thales falling into a well because he was watching the stars so intently. But A was active in the political life of Miletus and was appointed leader of a new colony, probably on the Black Sea. He drew the first map of the world and made scale models with gears and wheels of various sizes to demonstrate the movement of the planets and stars. He also suggested that animals now on the earth had developed from simpler forms, probably those living in the water.

One of A's most important contributions to the development of later philosophical thought was the notion that laws apply to nature. Thales and the mythographers had accepted an apparently anarchic world, subject to the whims of the gods or some mysterious world-soul. A's thesis was that a law of balance or compensation applied to nature. If the days are long and the nights are short in the summer, the situation is reversed in the winter. Likewise, cold, wet water quenches hot, dry fire.

Although A's notion of the *apeiron* was a step forward in the search for an explanation of the nature of the world, he still faced the question of change. How did matter pass from the chaotic, intermingled state of the *apeiron* to the differentiated condition that we know today? As the motive force in this process A proposed the vortex (*dinos* or *dine*), an eddy or whirlpool, in which the lighter elements (air and fire) were spun off and the heavier elements (earth and water) settled toward the center. The earth, he taught, is a cylinder, supported by nothing. (Thales had thought it floated on water.)

Around the earth circled three wheels of enclosed fire. The material of which the wheels are made conceals the fire and yet gives us the impression that we are looking through it; the best analogy may be to an island hidden in fog. The largest wheel, twenty-seven times the size of the earth (twenty-eight in some ancient citations), is the sun. It has a "breathing hole in it the same size as the earth which allows the fire to show through. The moon is a similar hollow, fire-filled wheel eighteen (or nineteen) times the size of the earth. The two different figures may represent the measurements of the inner and outer diameters of the wheels. Eclipses occur when the breathing holes are covered by clouds. The stars are supposed to be in a wheel nine times the size of the earth. Those numbers, all multiples of three, suggest some mystical implications to A's thought.

A is also credited with the idea that innumerable worlds exist in the *apeiron*.

There is some discussion among scholars as to whether this means a succession of worlds or an infinite number of worlds existing at the same time. His theory of compensation or balance might seem to require that one world come into existence when an older one passed out, but it is also possible that an infinite number of worlds could balance each other in the boundless cosmos; the latter interpretation is current among modern scholars.

ASMIS, E. "What is Anaximander's *Apeiron?*" *JHPh* 19(1981), 279-297. *Apeiron* is not separate reservoir of matter surrounding created things. It is an eternal deity which is one with endless generation of things.   [406]

BICKNELL, P. J. "Seneca and Aetius on Anaximander's and Anaximenes' Account of Thunder and Lightning." *Latomus* 27(1968), 181-184. Seneca's account is more accurate. Both Milesians thought wind striking a cloud produced thunder and that lightning was a kind of fire.   [407]

BODNER, I. M. "Anaximander's Rings." *CQ* 38(1988), 49-51. At very beginning of Greek speculative tradition A can distinguish between an entity itself (celestial rings) and misconception arising from it (holes in the rings).   [408]

BURCH, G. B. "Anaximander and Anaximenes. The Earliest Greek Theories of Change?" *Phron* 22(1977), 89-102. Anaximander's cosmogony focuses on a material substance, leaving no room for theory of change. Positing air as essential element, Anaximenes produces more refined theory which supplied some features of Aristotle's theory of change.   [409]

DAVIES, J. C. "Anaximander of Miletus." *HT* 20(1970), 263-269. Introduction for non-specialists. Also touches on Anaximenes.   [410]

FREUDENTHAL, G. "The Theory of the Opposites and an Ordered Universe: Physics and Metaphysics in Anaximander." *Phron* 31(1986), 197-228. A did not think of a dynamic equilibrium of opposites after they emerge from *apeiron.*   [411]

FURLEY, D. "The Dynamics of the Earth: Anaximander, Plato, and the Centrifocal Theory," in #58, pp. 14-26. A did not hold that earth sits unsupported in center of cosmos, having no sufficient reason to move in any direction.   [412]

GOTTSCHALK, H. B. "Anaximander's Apeiron." *Phron* 10(1965), 37-53. *Apeiron* is material, eternal, indestructible. It is different from all elements known to us. Beings arise from it by a process of separation.   [413]

HALL, J. J. "*Presteros aulos.*" *JHS* 89(1969), 57-59. This phrase, from Aetius 2.20,1, indicates A described sun as a kind of waterspout, i. e., a funnel or column.   [414]

KAHN, C. H. "Anaximander's Fragment: The Universe Governed by Law," in #363, pp. 99-117. Excerpt from Kahn's book *Anaximander and the Origins of Greek Cosmology* (1960). A's concept of ordered universe, with opposites in balance, had direct impact on Plato and Aristotle and on whole train of rationalism in Greek philosophy.   [415]

O'BRIEN, D. "Anaximander's Measurements." *CQ* 17(1967), 423-432. Anaximander began the practice of measuring distances or sizes of heavenly bodies by proportions. Technique was modified by Empedocles and Pythagoras.   [416]

PLASS, P. "A Note on *Presteros aulos*." *JHS* 92(1972), 179-180. Further comments on the funnel-shaped cloud discussed by Hall (#414). Modern eyewitnesses report seeing lightning-like flashes inside tornadoes, much like Anaximander's description.   [417]

ROBINSON, J. "Anaximander and the Problem of the Earth's Immobility," in #41, pp. 111-118. Aristotle understood Anaximander to believe that the earth remained immobile because it has no weight. Anaximander actually thought the earth was flat, so its weight could be supported.   [418]

STOKES, M. C. "Anaximander's Argument," in #1287, pp. 1-22. Attempt to reconstruct A's views on infinite. Best sources are Aristotle and Plato. Aristotle seems to have conflated A with Melissus. Plato had access to more of A's work than did Aristotle. [419]

WHITBY, M. J. "Quasi-elements in Aristotle." *Mnem* 35(1982), 225-247. Aristotle's discussion of elements which are "between" or "alongside" known elements reveals his use of A's work.   [420]

For related item see #6683.

ANAXIMENES (ca. 589-520 B. C.)

The doxographers reckoned Anaximenes as the "successor" of Anaximander in the Milesian school, but the chronology is too neat and the evidence for Anaximenes' dates too imprecise to allow us to accept that assertion unquestioningly. His answers to the two fundamental questions are more akin to Thales' than to Anaximander's. Change results from condensation or rarefaction of *aer*, his name for the one basic element of matter. But he retains the notion that this stretching of the *aer* takes place in the vortex, and he made refined models of it which were parodied in Aristophanes' comedy *Clouds*.

The notion of all things arising from air strikes us as ludicrous. But the Greeks of the sixth century B. C. meant a great deal more than we do when they spoke of this substance. The word *aer* implied a dark mist or fog. Homeric heroes are sometimes hidden by *aer*. Another word, *aither*, described the bright, shining sky, and yet a third word, *pneuma*, was used to talk about the breath or soul. By expanding the meaning of *aer* to take in all these shadings, Anaximenes makes a link between the basic stuff of the universe and life itself. It is as though the whole universe has the breath of life in it.

To the modern mind Anaximenes' cosmology seems a backward step from Anaximander's. The notion of a boundless, indeterminate element offers greater range for explaining the diversity of the universe. But Greek intellectuals emphasized its unity, and Anaximander's *apeiron*, since it contains all the elements, is not a single element in itself. The separation of matter in the vortex can also be seen as a disunifying process, whereas Anaximenes' rarefaction and condensation is a necessary explanation if one starts from the assumption of a single basic element. The observable diversity of the universe must result from the presence of more or less of the primary matter in a particular space.

Anaximenes disagreed with Anaximander in other details as well. He believed that the earth was a table-like disk which floats on the *aer*. In this he resembles Thales, except that the earlier philosopher saw water as the supporting element. The other heavenly bodies, for Anaximenes, were disks of fire floating in the *dine*. Like Anaximander, he did posit other worlds, bodies of "earthy substance" floating among the stars and causing eclipses by blocking our view of the sun and moon. A sample of his cosmology can be found in a passage from Hippolytus' *Refut.* 1.7,5-6:

> And he says that the heavenly bodies do not move under the earth, as others suppose, but around it, as a cap turns around a man's head. The sun is hidden from sight, not because it goes under the earth, but because it is concealed by the higher parts of the earth, and because its distance from us becomes greater. The stars give no heat because of the greatness of their distance.

In some respects the thought of Anaximenes was more influential than that of the other Milesians. Pythagoras and Anaxagoras adopted much of their view of the world from him; Leucippus and Democritus took up his idea of a flat earth. Burnet (p. 79) describes him as "the culminating point of the line of thought which started with Thales." C. Davies, however, says that in comparison to Anaximander, Anaximenes "pales into insignificance" (#410, p. 269).

BICKNELL, P. J. "Anaximenes and the *Gegenschein*." *Apeir* 11 #1(1977), 49-52. Faint elliptical patch of light is sometimes discernible at night in part of the ecliptic opposite sun. A's observation of this phenomenon may have led to his theory of crystal-like firmament. [421]

——. "Anaximenes' Astronomy." *AClass* 12(1969), 53-85. A divided heavenly bodies into two groups: stars, attached to a solid heaven, and sun, moon, and planets, which float on air. [422]

——. "Anaximenes' *pilion* Simile." *Apeir* 1 #1(1966), 17-18. Word *pilion*, found in Hippolytus' account of A's cosmology, refers not to a hat, but to a ribbon. [423]

——. cf. #407.

MORAN, J. "The Priority of Earth in the Cosmogony of Anaximenes." *Apeir* 9 #1(1975), 17-19. Observation that air and water originate from vapors rising from earth led A to conclude earth's priority to other elements. This is inconsistent with other details of his cosmogony. [424]

——. "Ps-Plutarch's Account of the Heavenly Bodies in Anaximenes." *Mnem* 26(1975), 9-14. Anaximenes' views on origins of heavenly bodies were confused with Anaxagoras'. [425]

For related item see #409.

Chapter 5

PYTHAGORAS, XENOPHANES, AND HERACLITUS

PYTHAGORAS AND THE PYTHAGOREANS

Turning to the study of Pythagoras transports us from the eastern edge of the Greek world to the western, and from speculation about the purely material nature of the world to contemplation of its form, expressed in numerical formulae and ratios. We also come upon the first real school, for the Pythagoreans functioned as a semi-secret society with knowledge reserved for their initiates. A probationary period of a year was required, during which candidates for admission were expected to listen to the teachings of the master without speaking or asking questions.

This aristocratic society achieved political power in the Greek city-states of southern Italy before it was overthrown in the democratic revolts which swept over the area soon after 450 B. C. For half a century the society was in eclipse, until a new generation of Pythagoreans dared to identify themselves early in the fourth century. The spread of Pythagorean doctrines, both geographically and chronologically, makes it difficult to differentiate between what Pythagoras himself said and what members of his school later attributed to him.

The key to understanding Pythagoras is his concept that numbers not only describe reality, they have an existence of their own. If we talk of two beans, two shoes, and two dogs, the common factor is the notion of "two-ness." That idea, for Pythagoras, is every bit as real as the physical pairs it is used to describe, and it exists independently of any units of matter. This insight led Pythagoras to suggest numbers as the basic stuff of the universe. In comparison with water, air, or the *apeiron*, numbers have the advantage of being objective. "Two" means the same thing to everyone in every time.

Numbers also express relationship. If a plucked string produces a note and a string twice as long produces the octave of that first note, the relationship between them can be expressed as 2/1. And this ratio holds true for any and all strings. Thus numbers seem to transcend particulars. By using them, one can explain why a general condition is true. This notion led Pythagoras to explore other numerical ratios, such as that between the sides of a right triangle.

Numerical notation itself presented problems to the Pythagoreans. Since the Greeks had no numerals, they used letters of the alphabet to represent numbers. The Pythagoreans found this system cumbersome and preferred to represent numbers by dots. A single dot stood for one, two dots for two, and so on. But the use of such a system requires that one arrange the dots in some fashion. At this point the Pythagoreans developed the idea of numbers that are square or oblong. If twelve is written in the following form,

```
. . . .
. . . .
. . . .
```

it is an oblong number, obtained by starting with two dots (the first two from the left on the bottom row) and adding four dots (the third from the left on the bottom row and the first three on the second row), then six (the top row and the last two on the first and second rows). Nine, written thusly,

```
. . .
. . .
. . .
```

is a square number, built from a similar pattern of one, three, and five dots.

But the most special number of all is ten, written in the form of the "tetractys of the decad":

```
    .
   . .
  . . .
 . . . .
```

Ten is almost a mystical number because it contains within itself $1+2+3+4$, numbers which symbolize a point (1), a line (2), height (3), and depth (4), i. e., reality itself.

While this tetractys becomes a mystic symbol to Pythagoras, it is not a perfect shape. Perfection for the Greeks implies that one cannot detect change in something. The tetractys has sides, and we can determine where one ends and another begins. The only perfect shape is a sphere. On the basis of that assumption and reasoning that the earth, as the center of the universe, should be perfect and equidistant from all points in the universe, Pythagoras concluded that the earth is a sphere. This notion became widespread. Eratosthenes calculated its circumference to within two hundred miles in the third century B. C.

Pythagorean thought, then, contributes the notion of form, as opposed to matter, to the stream of western philosophy. One must be concerned not only with what the universe is made of, but the form in which it is arranged. Pythagoreanism also asserts that the numbers used to describe that form exist in an ideal state open only to contemplation. This is the leap from natural science to philosophy as we understand it today, from physics to metaphysics. At the same time, what makes this school of thought seem unphilosophical is its attachment of religious significance to some of its findings.

Pythagoras was profoundly influenced by the Orphic mystery cult which was enjoying a surge in popularity in the latter half of the sixth century B. C. The primary tenet adopted from the cult was transmigration of the soul. Earlier Greeks had always had a notion of the existence of the *psyche* after death, but never as more than a vague, shadowy "life breath" which passed a dreary existence in Hades. Book XI of Homer's *Odyssey* is the classic description of this unenviable afterlife. Pythagoras elevated the concept of the soul, to a degree, with the notion of transmigration. But in his system it was possible at death for a person's soul to pass into the body of an animal (hence the group's vegetarianism). The idea of the immortality of the soul and its freedom from the body at death had to wait for Socrates.

Pythagoreanism became a religious cult, with initiates living in communities. Some of the dietary regulations seem arbitrary, but modern scholars have discovered possible explanations for some of them. The reverence in which Pythagoras was held by his followers and the quantity of material produced by them in his name makes it difficult to discriminate accurately between what he himself taught and what later generations of Pythagoreans thought. (The Neopythagoreans, for example, have nothing directly to do with Pythagoras. Their school will be covered in its Hellenistic context.) It is clear, however, that Pythagoras contributed the notion of form as independent of physical reality. He makes it possible to talk about the concept of triangularity, for instance, without limiting ourselves to specific triangles. His influence can be seen in Plato's doctrine of the forms as real even if they have no material existence.

BAKER, H. "Pythagoras of Samos." *Sewanee Review* 80(1972), 1-38. Proposes "revisionist" view of P's life, teachings. Non-specialist survey [426]

BARBERA, A. "The Consonant Eleventh and the Expansion of the Musical Tetractys. A Study of Ancient Pythagoreanism." *Journal of Music Theory* 28(1984), 191-223. No one version of *Sectio* served as a model for other two. Document is a Pythagorean composition, put together over several centuries. [427]

———. "Placing *Sectio Canonis* in Historical and Philosophical Contexts." *JHS* 104(1984), 157-161. Pseudo-Euclidean treatise provides introduction to Pythagorean musical theory. Tetractys and two-octave system must be kept in mind when reading it. [428]

———. "*Republic* 530c-531c: Another Look at Plato and the Pythagoreans." *AJPh* 102(1981), 395-410. Some widely held assumptions about relationship between Plato and Pythagoras need to be re-examined. [429]

BOWEN, A. C. "The Foundations of Early Pythagorean Harmonic Science: Archytas, Fragment 1." *AncPh* 2(1982), 79-104. Revised text and translation of fragment from A (early 4th cent. B. C.), which develops a theory of propagation of sound and its quantification by whole-number ratios. [430]

BRUMBAUGH, R. S., and **SCHWARTZ, J.** "Pythagoras and Beans. A Medical Explanation." *CW* 73(1980), 421-423. P's prohibition against eating beans may have been reaction to hereditary enzyme deficiency which leaves some people unable to digest the fava bean. Seizures may result. [431]

BRUNIUS, T. "Pythagoras and the Arts." *M&W* 4(1971), 29-58. Survey of P's life and theories. Particular attention given to aesthetics and question of catharsis in music and medicine. Examines his influence on sculpture, architecture, and music in classical era. [432]

BURKERT, W. "Craft Versus Sect: The Problem of Orphics and Pythagoreans," in #5639, III, pp. 1-22. Orphism seems to have consisted of individualistic practioners of magic and fortune-telling. Within Pythagorean group or "sect" there was a problem defining precisely what a Pythagorean was. Some put emphasis on observing moral teachings of P, others on study of mathematics. [433]

———. *Lore and Science in Ancient Pythagoreanism*. transl. E. L. Minar, Jr. Cambridge, MA: Harvard Univ. Pr., 1972. Analysis of sources on which our knowledge of movement is based. More optimistic about their value than Zeller and others have been. Compares Platonic and Pythagorean number theory, doctrine of metempsychosis and shamanism, astronomy, music. [434]

BURNS, S. A. M. "Virtue and Necessity." *LThPh* 32(1976), 261-275. Examines influence of Pythagoreanism, as developed by Plato, on twentieth-century French writer Simone Weil. [435]

COLE, E. B. "Demonstrating the Pythagorean Intervals." *TeachPh* 11(1988), 128-132. Discusses Greek concept of relation of musical harmony to mathematics. [436]

CORNFORD, F. M. "Mysticism and Science in the Pythagorean Tradition," in #363, pp. 135-160; also in #53, pp. 99-124. Somewhat optimistic view of what can be known of early Pythagoreanism and "number-atomism." Within Pythagoreanism are scientific and religio-mystic strains which cannot be forced into one coherent system. [437]

DEMAND, N. "Plato, Aristophanes and the *Speeches of Pythagoras*." *GRBS* 23(1982), 179-184. The four speeches attributed to Pythagoras may have been written (ca. 400 B. C.) by a conservative Pythagorean to correct Socrates' adaptation of Pythagorean ideas. Aristophanes satirizes Pythagorean ideas and their Socratic development. [438]

———. "Pythagoras, Son of Mnesarchos." *Phron* 18(1973), 91-96. Study of influence of his father's work as an engraver on P's thought. [439]

DE VOGEL, C. J. *Pythagoras and Early Pythagoreanism. An Interpretation of Neglected Evidence on the Philosopher Pythagoras.* Assen: Van Gorcum, 1966. Available sources, often overlooked, include coins, ancient historians/biographers, and Iamblichus. Some conclusions can be reached regarding P's life and teachings, connection with Plato, influence on rhetoric and medicine. [440]

GOODMAN, W. M. "The 'Horseshoe' of Western Science." *JIndCPhRes* 1(1984), 41-60. Metaphorically, history of western science and math is like a horseshoe, moving from monism to dualism and back to monism. P stands at one tip of horseshoe. [441]

GORMAN, P. *Pythagoras: A Life.* London: Routledge & Kegan Paul, 1976. Romanticized interpretation of P as "basically mystical and intuitive, rather than scientific and rationalistic." [442]

———. "Pythagoras Palaestinus." *Philologus* 27(1983), 30-42. Jewish writers claimed P had read Mosaic books, but a separate Hellenistic tradition also connected him with Palestine and attributed to him many Jewish ideas and practices. [443]

———. cf. #6183.

GRANT, R. M. "Dietary Laws Among Pythagoreans, Jews and Christians." *HThR* 73(1980), 299-310. Most restrictions have allegorical and literal meaning. [444]

GUTHRIE, K. S., et al. *The Pythagorean Sourcebook and Library. An Anthology of Ancient Writings which Relate to Pythagoras and Pythagorean Philosophy.* Grand Rapids, MI: Phanes Pr., 1987; rprt. Introduction and selections. [445]

——. cf. #6185.

Homage to Pythagoras: Papers from the 1981 Lindisfarne Corresponding Members Conference, Crestone, Colorado. West Stockbridge, MA: Lindisfarne Pr., 1982. Collection of essays on P and on Pythagorean influences on later thought, emphasizing its mystical aspects. [446]

HUFFMAN, C. "The Role of Number in Philolaus' Philosophy." *Phron* 33(1988), 1-30. Pythagorean axiom that "all things are numbers" seems to derive from Aristotle's interpretation of Pythagoras. For Philolaus things are known *through* numbers. [447]

HUGHES, D. "The Environmental Ethics of the Pythagoreans." *Environmental Ethics* 2(1980), 195-214. Examines two contradictory Pythagorean themes (respect for nature, sense of separation of spirit/body) as they relate to environmental concerns. [448]

JACOBSON, H. "Hermippus, Pythagoras and the Jews." *REJ* 135(1976), 145-149. Certain Jewish elements are discernible in P's thought. Hermippus of Smyrna maintained that several Greek thinkers were similarly influenced. [449]

KAHN, C. H. "Pythagorean Philosophy Before Plato," in #363, pp. 161-185. Surveys evidence relating to Pythagoras and tries to determine which doctrines originated with him and which with his early disciples. [450]

KAKOSY, L. "Egyptian Magic in the Legend of Pythagoras." *Oikumene* 4(1983), 187-189. Discussion of a story in which an eagle obeyed P's voice. [451]

MARCOVICH, M. "Pythagoras as Cock." *AJPh* 97(1976), 331-335. P's appearance as a cock in one of Lucian of Samosota's satires alludes to philosopher/mystic's role as a diviner. [452]

MARTANO, G. "Paron the Pythagorean or the Pythagorean Who Was Present." *Corolla Londiniensis* 2(1982), 123-132. Paron the Pythagorean does not exist. The error is based on a misreading of Greek text of Aristotle's *Physics* IV,222b17. *Paron* is a Greek participle meaning "the one present." [453]

MILLER, J. F. "Time as the Soul of the World. A Meditation on the Pythagorean Conception of Time." *Apeir* 13(1979), 116-123. P claimed that past, present, and future co-exist in divine, eternal present, analogous to stream of light. [454]

MINAR, E. L., Jr. *Early Pythagorean Politics, in Practice and Theory.* New York: Arno Pr., 1979; rprt. Studies organization of "brotherhood," its activities in Samos, Crotona, and Tarentum; dissolution of group; its survival at Tarentum. One chapter discusses Pythagorean political theory and its coherence with group's overall philosophy. Bibliography (through 1939) and various indices. [455]

NABERS, N., and WILTSHIRE, S. F. "The Athena Temple at Paestum and Pythagorean Theory." *GRBS* 21(1980), 207-215. Pythagorean influence is evident in temple's architecture, indicating school's presence in the area.   [456]

NIDDITCH, P. H. "The First Stage of Mathematics: Pythagoreans, Plato, Aristotle." *MidwStudPh* 8(1983), 3-34. Pythagoreans saw numbers as real. Plato took them as immaterial, existing apart from sensibles. Aristotle combined the two ideas.   [457]

PHILIP, J. A. "The 'Pythagorean' Theory of the Derivation of Magnitudes." *Phoenix* 20(1966), 32-50. Theory of derivation of solids, attributed to P by Academy and other Hellenistic philosophers, actually originated after Zeno of Elea's time.   [458]

———. *Pythagoras and Early Pythagoreanism.* Univ. of Toronto Pr., 1966. Discusses how we distinguish Pythagorean doctrine from versions in writers influenced by P. Reconstructs P's thought from extant sources, especially frags of Aristotle's *On the Pythagoreans.* Analyzes cosmology, number theory, astronomy, transmigration of soul.   [459]

RAASTED, J. "A Neglected Version of the Anecdote about Pythagoras' Hammer Experiment." *Cahiers de l'Institut du Moyen Âge grec et latin* 31a(1979), 1-9. Experiment described by Nichomachus of Gerasa is impossible. One of Porphyry's works suggests text should read *sphairai* (spheres), not *sphurai* (hammers).   [460]

RAVEN, J. E. *Pythagoreans and Eleatics: An Account of the Interaction between the Two Opposed Schools during the Fifth and Early Fourth Centuries B. C.* Amsterdam: Hakkert, 1966; rprt. Discusses Cornford's interpretation and studies the development of Pythagoreanism from Parmenides' time to Aristotle's. Assumes that Pythagorean thought can be reconstructed by the study of the Eleatic reaction to it. Aristotle is our primary source.   [461]

SCARBOROUGH, J. "Beans, Pythagoras, Taboos, and Ancient Dietetics." *CW* 75(1982), 355-358. Reviews various theories about why P forbade eating of beans.   [462]

SEIDENBERG, A. "The Origin of Mathematics." *AHES* 18(1977-78), 301-342. Pythagorean and Babylonian mathematics have common source, Vedic Sulvasutra.   [463]

SKOVGAARD JENSEN, S. *Dualism and Demonology: The Function of Demonology in Pythagorean and Platonic Thought with an Introduction on Some Aspects of the General Theory of Metaphysics and Religious Dualism and an Appendix on the Interpretation and Pythagorean Background of Plato's "Rep."* 524d-526c. Copenhagen: Munksgaard, 1966. Plato's dualism is not absolute. Absolute dualism, and the demonology which accompanies it, derives from Pythagorean mathematics.   [464]

SPIERS, J. "Pythagoras: Guru and Absolutist." *Brahmavadin* 12(1977), 236-248. P is best understood as Indian guru, with disciples taught to adore him. He is first Greek to see philosophy as a way of life.   [465]

THESLEFF, H. "The Pythagoreans in the Light and Shadows of Recent Research," in *Mysticism. Based on Papers Read at the Symposium on Mysticism held at Abo on the 7th-9th September, 1968*, ed. by S. S. Hartman and C. M. Edsman (Stockholm: Almqvist & Wiksell, 1969), pp. 77-90. Review of contemporary work.   [466]

VLASTOS, G. "Raven's *Pythagoreans and Eleatics,*" in #301, pp. 166-176. Review essay of #461. **[467]**

WEST, M. L. "Alcman and Pythagoras." *CQ* 17(1967), 1-15. In Alcman's cosmogony opposition of *apeiron* and *peras* suggests connection with Pythagorean number cosmology, in which those two concepts are fundamental. **[468]**

———. "Callimachus on the Pythagoreans." *CR* 21(1971), 330-331. Poet pities rather than criticizes Pythagorean dietary restrictions. **[469]**

ZHMUD', L. J. "'All is Number'?: 'Basic Doctrine' of Pythagoreanism Reconsidered." *Phron* 34(1989), 270-292. Pythagoreans used numbers to express relationships, but were no more mystical or philosophical about them than were other Presocratics. **[470]**

For related items see #652, #6191, #6595, #6598, #6637.

XENOPHANES (540-440 B. C.)

Xenophanes of Colophon is usually described as a younger contemporary of Pythagoras, but there is considerable difficulty about the dates of his life (cf. Thesleff) and about where he lived. To complicate matters even more, some scholars are reluctant to classify him as a philosopher. Even in antiquity Diogenes Laertius put him among the "sporadic" philosophers. Brumbaugh mentions him only in passing in his discussion of Pythagoras (#5, p. 40), and Burnet, while discussing him at some length, admits that the majority of his surviving fragments (about 120 lines) "are not in any way philosophical" (#312, p. 121).

Confusion reigns whether one tries to sort out the details of his long life or the main points of his thought. He seems to have come from Colophon, in Asia Minor, and to have been from a non-aristocratic family, unlike the other Presocratic philosophers. Beyond that we are on uncertain ground. He may have been a rhapsode, a singer of songs who entertained at banquets. He may have lived for a time at Elea, a city in southern Italy that was later home to one of the most influential Presocratic schools of thought. But it cannot be established beyond doubt that he stayed there long or that he was connected with the Eleatic school or had any direct influence on it.

What emerges from the extant fragments of his poetry is a deeply cynical view of the world, critical of social mores, athletic contests, and anthropomorphic beliefs about the gods. Two of his most famous apophthegms deal with this last subject:

> If oxen and horses or lions had hands, and could paint with their hands, and produce works of art as men do, horses would paint the forms of the gods like horses, and oxen like oxen . . . .(frag. 15)

> The Ethiopians make their gods black and snub-nosed; the Thracians say theirs have blue eyes and red hair. (frag. 16)

Diogenes Laertius (9.19) grouped X among the philosophers whose doctrines were difficult to classify as belonging to one of the major schools. He tried to be helpful by summing up X's views that "there are four elements of existent things, and worlds unlimited (*apeiron*) in number but not overlapping in time . . . . The substance of God is spherical, in no way resembling man. He is all eye and all ear, but does not breathe; he is the totality of mind and thought, and is eternal."

Other fragments leave us less certain about whether he saw the world as infinite or finite. This problem of interpretation was exacerbated by the author of a treatise written about the time of Jesus' birth and entitled *On Melissus, Xenophanes, Gorgias*. This anonymous writer read far too much of cosmological theory into some of X's satirical jabs at the early poets and philosophers. Aristotle could find no clear statement by X on this subject (*Metaphysics* A 986b12). All he can deduce from X is the notion that "the Unity is God." Aristotle did not find this idea well-formulated or helpful in his analysis of the nature of the world, so he announced his intention to ignore X.

One philosophical insight which can be drawn from X's work is a three-stage "ascent to the truth," which progresses from seeing to speculating to knowing. Knowledge is based on sense data, he seems to be saying, but it must be interpreted and organized by the mind. In other passages he seems pessimistic about the mind's ability to overcome the obstacle of appearances.

BICKNELL, P. J. "A Note on Xenophanes' Astrophysics." *AClass* 10(1967), 135-136. From its greyish-white appearance in daylight, X concluded moon was a cloud.   **[471]**

———. "Xenophanes' Account of Solar Eclipses." *Eranos* 65(1967), 73-77. New reading of passage preserved in Aetius 2.24,9. X's account of eclipses was rational and consistent with his views on the nature of the sun.   **[472]**

DARCUS, S. M. "The *Phren* of the *Nous* in Xenophanes' God." *SO* 53(1978), 25-39. *Phren* in frag B 25 Diels-Kranz is used instrumentally. It has physical implications and is distinct from *nous*.   **[473]**

DELIGIORGIS, S. "Between Philosophy and Literature: Perspectives on Xenophanes." *Platon* 25(1973), 258-273. X's four-part system has been badly understood by later interpreters.   **[474]**

EISENSTADT, M. "Xenophanes' Proposed Reform of Greek Religion." *Hermes* 102(1974), 142-150. X wanted not to abolish Olympian religion but to expunge stories about gods' immoralities.   **[475]**

FRAENKEL, H. "Xenophanes' Empiricism and his Critique of Knowledge," in #363, pp. 118-131. X's rationalism takes form of critique and rebuttal of mythological ideas. His doctrine of God and his epistemological statements deserve to be called philosophical. His other frags are "expressly unphilosophical."   **[476]**

HERSHBELL, J. P. "The Oral-Poetic Religion of Xenophanes," in #371, pp. 125-133. Havelock's views on orality and literacy help to show that X was not attacking polytheism as much as anthropomorphism in Greek concept of deity. Greek divinities he interpreted as natural phenomena.   **[477]**

JAEGER, W. "Xenophanes and the Beginnings of Natural Theology," in *The Albert Schweizer Jubilee Book*, ed. A. A. Roback (Westport, CT: Greenwood, 1970; rprt.), pp. 397-424. X's inquires not about nature of cosmos but about the divine. [478]

LEBEDEV, A. V. "A New Fragment of Xenophanes," in *Studi filosofia preplatonica*, ed. M. Cappasso et al. (Naples: Bibliopolis, 1985), pp. 13-15. Frag cited anonymously in Philoponus' commentary on Aristotle's *De anima* should be attributed to X. The passage affirms that X equated *theos* with the *holos ouranos*. [479]

LESHER, J. H. "Xenophanes' Scepticism." *Phron* 23(1978), 1-21. X was not a sceptic in the modern sense but revolutionary in his attack on traditional religion, especially divination. [480]

LONG, H. S. "Xenophanes' Concern with Ultimate Meaning and Reality." *UltR&M* 7(1984), 102-116. Summary of X's life and problems attendant on study of his fragmentary work. His most important idea is the significance of the mind and its ability, through speculation, to gain insight on what is useful and of ultimate value. [481]

MANSFELD, J. "Theophrastus and the Xenophanes Doxography." *Mnem* 40(1987), 286-312. The commonly received material about X's ontology and theology comes from a variety of sources, not just Theophrastus. [482]

———. cf. #401.

MARCOVICH, M. "Xenophanes on Drinking Parties and Olympic Games." *ICS* 3(1978), 1-26. Text, translation, and commentary on fragments B1 and B2 Diels-Kranz. B1 describes arrangements for a symposium and moral/religious precepts for participants. Fragment B2 criticizes Olympic games. [483]

MILLER, E. L. "Xenophanes: Fragments 1 and 2." *Pers* 51(1970), 143-147. Overlooked as more poetic than philosophical, two frags shed light on X's concept of God and wisdom. [484]

O'BRIEN, M. J. "Xenophanes, Aeschylus, and the Doctrine of Primeval Brutishness." *CQ* 35(1985), 245-263. Idea can be connected to X only tentatively. Not explicitly stated until late fifth century B. C. [485]

REICHE, H. A. T. "Empirical Aspects of Xenophanes' Theology," in #41, pp. 88-110. X sees human knowledge as unreliable. Divine or absolute knowledge is unattainable, but empirical sense data bring us closest to it. [486]

ROLLER, D. W. "An Imitation of Xenophanes in the *Suppliant Women*." *LCM* 2(1977), 149-150. Compares lines 96-103 of Aeschylus' play with frags 24-26 D-K. [487]

For related item see #293.

HERACLITUS (ca. 544-484 B. C.)

Heraclitus' dates are also insecure. He refers to Pythagoras and Xenophanes in the past tense and is alluded to in the same way by Parmenides, so he must fall somewhere in between them. Sotion thought he was a disciple of Xenophanes, but the latter had left Ionia before H was born. Such a statement arises from the tendency of the doxographers to think in terms of "schools." H does seem to have known Xenophanes' poems and to have been acquainted with the cosmology of the earlier Milesians. Diogenes Laertius states that "he was nobody's pupil, but he declared that he 'inquired of himself,' and learned everything from himself."

He is the first philosopher to write, but we don't know if the phrase "on nature" was the title of his book or just a description of its subject matter; several other titles for it were known to Diogenes, who refers to the book as if it still existed and says that it contained three sections: on the universe, on politics, and on theology. It was couched in a deliberately abstruse style, so that it would not be accessible to the general public. That characteristic earned Heraclitus the sobriquet "the Obscure." One scholar has said, "If his writings were any more obscure, they would be funny." His fragments reveal him as intolerant of what he perceived to be the ignorance of others, even philosophers and poets, and boastful of the originality of his own insights.

He uses the term *logos* to mean his own writings, but that term was interpreted by the Stoics as foreshadowing their doctrine of the Logos as the world soul. That reading of H seems unjustified. Nor does he seem to have influenced the Christian concept of the Logos expressed in the prologue to John's gospel. H uses *logos* and *psyche* in a way no previous philosopher had. He seems to have thought of some rational principle (*logos*) which governed the universe. The human soul (*psyche*) is in some way related to the Logos but is not immortal.

For his basic element H chose fire, fixing on a substance that is constantly in motion and that involves a change. Other things, when consumed by fire, change their form. Many substances liquify, then become gases. This is the "upward path" of H, similar to Anaximenes' rarefaction. His assumption is that the reverse process can also take place, the "downward path."

But should we take H literally when he talks about fire as the basic stuff? Given his penchant for poetry and imagery, perhaps he is using the unceasing activity of fire as a symbol of the state of constant change in which he perceives the world to exist. It would probably be a mistake to think that he is doing merely one or the other. It is helpful to remember that his mind apparently "worked rather by intuition than in concepts."

Since constant motion and change is his perception of the world, it is not surprising that H sees strife and opposition as creative elements in the world. Motion is a kind of strife, and harmony is the resolution of strife. But if everything remains in harmony, stagnation results. Then dissolution sets in; elements are reduced to opposites, and the process of flux continues; e. g., a potion mixed in water settles when the stirring stops, but harmony (the mixture) is restored when the motion (strife) is renewed.

His fragments reveal H as confident that he had discovered something fundamental which even other philosophers had overlooked, though it was staring them in the face. He criticizes them in fragment 16: "The learning of many things does not teach understanding, or else it would have taught Hesiod and Pythagoras, and again Xenophanes and Hecataeus." And in fragment 18: "Of all whose discourses I have heard, there is not one who attains to understanding that wisdom is apart from all."

Philo quotes a passage that sums up H's thought: "For that which is made up of both the opposites is one; and, when the one is divided, the opposites are disclosed. Is not this just what the Greeks say their great and much belauded Heraclitus put in the forefront of his philosophy as summing it all up and boasted of as a new discovery?"

Because of this concept of tension between opposites H is able to maintain that the world is both One and Many. But he is influenced by the Milesians in his choice of a basic element, fire, as the stuff of which the world is made. Like Anaximenes' condensation and rarefaction of *aer*, the fire accounts for change. It consumes materials, changing solids into smoke. Yet the fire itself never seems to change while burning.

Whereas most early philosophers saw change as a problem, H seems to have seen it as the basic state of the universe. One of his most famous fragments (perhaps because it's one of the most lucid) is that we "cannot step twice into the same river." The world is in a constant state of flux. Anaximander had held that the opposites were constantly at war in the *apeiron*. H sees the tension between opposites as constituting the unity of the One.

BEAUFRET, J. "Heraclitus and Parmenides," in #535, pp. 69-86. Supposed conflict between H and P over nature of being arises largely from Plato's reading of H. The "obscure" philosopher actually saw change as resting on layer of permanence. **[488]**

BEREZDIVIN, R. "Fire and Logos," in #571, pp. 68-85. For H fire is without substance. It is only ceaseless change, consuming itself and everything else. For Aristotle fire is an essence. *Logos* is that in us which is like our surroundings and makes contact with them. **[489]**

BRONIAK, C. J. "Heraclitus, Parmenides, and Plato on Living the Good Life." *Dial*(PST) 30(1987), 28-37. For each of these philosophers good life depends on knowing what Good is and, more importantly, knowing how to bring it about. **[490]**

BROWN, C. "Seeing Sleep. Heraclitus Fr. 49 Marcovich (DK 22 B 21)." *AJPh* 107(1986), 243-245. Text of frag needs no emendation. "To see sleep" means simply "to sleep." **[491]**

CAPIZZI, A. "*Opsis akoe*. The Sources of the Problem of Sensations in Heraclitus and Parmenides." *MPhL* 6(1984), 9-35. Neither H nor P perceived an opposition between reason and sensation. Distinction arose in mid-fifth century B. C., probably with Empedocles and Melissus, and was developed by Democritus and Plato **[492]**

CAPUZZI, F. A. "Heraclitus: Fire, Dream, and Oracle," in #571, pp. 135-148. Examination of philosophy as personal experience of philosopher. For H fire symbolizes the thinker and his thought; dream is a "mythos by which the thinker locates himself"; oracle is expression of philosopher's self. **[493]**

CHATTOPADHYAYA, D. "Heraclitus and Hegel." *RevW* 17(1976), 12-31. In H's time philosophy was moving from materialism toward an idealist metaphysic. In Hegel we see movement from metaphysic to dialectic, idealism to materialism.   **[494]**

CLARK, J. "An Inclusive Option within Heraclitean Exclusivity," in #566, pp. 337-345. Study, couched in Heraclitean obscurity, of utility of H's disdain for popular tastes in study of contemporary art and culture.   **[495]**

CLOHESY, W. W. "The Strength of the Invisible. Reflections on Heraclitus." *Auslegung* 13(1987), 175-192. An invisible power holds together the ceaseless activity of the cosmos. Individual things may change or pass away but unity survives. By analogy, an individual person could die, but the community or species is held together by an invisible force.   **[496]**

CONLEY, T. M. "Heraclitus, the Fragments. A Preliminary Study." *CJ* 60(1965), 164-169. Major fragments can be classified in eleven groups. Relationships among groups are discussed.   **[497]**

DARCUS, S. M. "Daimon as a Force Shaping Ethos in Heraclitus." *Phoenix* 28(1974), 390-407. The *daimon* shapes person's character but is not identical with it. Survey of use of term in writers pre-dating H.   **[498]**

————. "Heraclitus the Riddler: B101." *A&A* 24(1978), 40-42. H seems to have taken a deliberately obscure tone, much like Delphic oracle. This frag is in spirit of "know yourself."   **[499]**

————. "Logos of Psyche in Heraclitus." *RSA* 9(1979), 89-93. Man's logos ("order speech") arises from his *daimon*. Divine Logos formed world by speaking. Human speech can approach, though never equal, the divine.   **[500]**

————. "Thumos and Psyche in Heraclitus B 85." *RSC* 25(1977), 353-359. In this frag *thumos* is no longer an independent organ but is becoming a faculty of soul.   **[501]**

————. "What Death Brings in Heraclitus." *Gymnasium* 85(1978), 501-510. H seems to teach that some souls become smoke in afterlife, while some die, and still others become guardians of world from above. Reconciling frags in which these concepts appear is not easy.   **[502]**

DAVENPORT, G. *Herakleitos and Diogenes*. San Francisco: Grey Fox Pr., 1976. Brief introduction to each author. Translation of the 124 frags of H and selected passages attributed to Diogenes the Cynic.   **[503]**

DAVIES, C. "The Beginnings of Greek Thought, III: Heraclitus." *HT* 20(1970), 427-433. General survey for non-specialists. Davies reads into H a bit of mysticism associated with cult of Artemis of Ephesus.   **[504]**

DE MARTINO, F., et al., eds. *Eraclito. Bibliografia 1970-1984 e complementi 1621-1969*. Naples: Ed. Scient. ital., 1986. Thorough but not annotated.   **[505]**

DESAN, W. "Heraclitus and the Space Shuttle: the Anatomy of a Nation." *M&W* 15(1982), 181-188. Reflection on meaning of some Heraclitean terms from longer perspective provided by observation from space.   **[506]**

DUBOSE, S. "Monism, Logos, Fire, and Flux." *TulStudPh* 21(1972), 1-11. Importance for H of nature of logos, status accorded to fire, and concept of flux, which Dubose thinks authentically Heraclitean. Plato's report of H not entirely inaccurate. [507]

EGGERS LAN, C. "Ethical-Religious Meaning of Fr. 30 D.-K.," in #566, pp. 291-299. H is not a cosmologist. Barely ten percent of surviving frags deal with cosmology. His thought is not logical or demonstrative; it is closer to prayer. Frag 30 seems to suggest that world passes through stages. When fire is more active, men are more apt to listen to reason. [508]

EMAD, P. "Heidegger's Originary Reading of Heraclitus Fragment 16," in #535, pp. 103-123. Summary of Heidegger's 1943 lecture course on "The Beginning of Western Thinking: Heraclitus." [509]

———. "Word at the Beginning of Thinking," in #535, pp. 124-134. Heidegger's interpretation of Heraclitus is bound up in the former's view of language. Dialectical thinking is inappropriate for understanding Heraclitus. [510]

EMLYN-JONES, C. J. "Heraclitus and the Identity of Opposites." *Phron* 21(1976), 89-114. H's paradoxical description of opposites as identities and unities is designed to show that people do not understand things most familiar to them. [511]

EVANS, C. "A New Fragment of Heraclitus?" *Pegasus* 9(1968), 28-32. Lucian of Samosota's dialogue between H and slave dealer was perhaps inspired by Stoic interpretation of frag of H. [512]

FAIRWEATHER, J. "The Death of Heraclitus." *GRBS* 14(1973), 233-239. Odd anecdote about his death concocted from illogical deductions from his sayings. [513]

FRAENKEL, H. "A Thought Pattern in Heraclitus," in #363, pp. 214-228. Study of H's use of pattern A/B=B/C. [514]

GUERRIERE, D. "Physis, Sophia, Psyche," in #571, pp. 86-134. Attempts a comprehensive interpretation of H, with emphasis on *physis* (emergence, order) and the need to cohere to it, which is *sophia* (wisdom). On the individual level *psyche* (soul) is the correlate to *physis*. [515]

HEIDEGGER, M., and **FINK, K. E.** *Heraclitus Seminar, 1966/1967,* transl. by C. H. Seibert. Univ. of Alabama Pr., 1979. Papers from seminar analyzing H's text. [516]

HERSHBELL, J. P. "Plutarch and Heraclitus." *Hermes* 105(1977), 179-201. Study of P's possible sources, accuracy and intention of his quotations. List of passages in which P refers to H and discussion of what may have been a biography of him. [517]

HOELSCHER, U. "Paradox, Simile, and Gnomic Utterance in Heraclitus," in #363, pp. 229-238. H's stylistic devices mirror his understanding of world. Similes arise from his idea that phenomena signify underlying meaning; paradoxes illustrate unity of opposites; gnomic or obscure "riddles" force hearer/reader to gain sudden insight. [518]

HUSSEY, E. "Epistemology and Meaning in Heraclitus," in #76, pp. 33-59. Sense perception provides data for understanding the world, but it must be interpreted by recourse to the inner self. Result is an idealist cosmology.   [519]

JONES, H. "Heraclitus, Fragment 31." *Phron* 17(1972), 193-197. Frag should be divided into two parts, both centering on types of transformations of elements.   [520]

——. "-sis Nouns in Heraclitus." *MusAfr* 3(1974), 1-13. H seems to have coined three abstract nouns, *synapsis, gnosis,* and *phronesis,* each of which relates to a theme of his philosophy.   [521]

KAHN, C. H. *The Art and Thought of Heraclitus: An Edition of the Fragments with Translation and Commentary.* Cambridge Univ. Pr., 1979. Introduction to H's background, work; outline of main points of his doctrine. Greek text with facing translation. Sees H as positing analogous structure of "inner personal world of the psyche and the larger natural order of the universe." His art lies in metaphors and puns, which are not obscure but deliberately ambiguous to express multiple meanings of reality.   [522]

——. "Philosophy and the Written Word. Some Thoughts on Heraclitus and the Early Greek Uses of Prose," in #371, pp. 110-124. References in H to "hearing" other men's *logoi* should not be taken too literally. Some conventions of oral composition and presentation remained in force after written works became norm. H's ambiguous language may be partly an effort to preserve some of fluidity of meaning of oral composition.   [523]

——. cf. #1389.

KESSIDIS, T. "The Socio-Political Views of Heraclitus of Ephesus." *Phil*(Athens) 13-14(1983-84), 92-108. H's views, which contain self-contradictions, mark him as moderate aristocrat.   [524]

KIRK, G. S. "Natural Change in Heraclitus," in #363, pp. 189-197. Individual things change in a regulated manner in H's thought, but there is an underlying stability in the single Logos. This explains unity H saw in opposites.   [525]

LAMBEK, J. "The Influence of Heraclitus on Modern Math," in *Scientific Philosophy Today: Essays in Honor of Mario Bunge,* ed. J. Agassi (Dordrecht: Reidel, 1982), pp. 111-122. Technical discussion of H's influence on Marxism, in terms of his dialecitical view. Marxist dialectic has been influential on theory of adjoint functors in modern math.   [526]

LEBEDEV, A. "The Cosmos as a Stadium: Agonistic Metaphors in Heraclitus' Cosmology." *Phron* 30(1985), 131-150. H sees universe as theater where competitions are always taking place (e. g., between day and night). Cosmic god fixes rules for the *agon* and acts as judge.   [527]

LESHER, T. H. "Heraclitus' Epistemological Vocabulary." *Hermes* 111(1983), 155-170. Examination of the terms *xunesis, gnosis,* and *noos* demonstrates H's originality. [528]

MacKENZIE, M. M. "Heraclitus and the Art of Paradox." *OSAP* 6(1988), 1-37. H's paradoxes function on four levels, each demanding a somewhat higher level of understanding of what it means to be an individual. Many of paradoxes were left unresolved to provoke further thought.   [529]

———. "The Moving *posset* Stands Still. Heraclitus Fr. 125." *AJPh* 107(1986), 542-551. Original form of frag can be recovered by comparison with Aristotle as cited in Alexander of Aphrodisias. Passage was first altered by Theophrastus. [530]

MAGNUS, B. "The Connection Between Nietzsche's Doctrine of the Eternal Return, Heraclitus, and the Stoics." *Helios* 3(1976), 3-21. Examination of Nietzsche's claim that H and the Stoics originated idea of the eternal return. [531]

MALY, K. "Man and Disclosure," in #571, pp. 43-60. Study of H's terms *aletheia, lethe, noos, logos* leads to conclusion that *logos* is not rational discourse but a "gathering of the disclosure of things." Humans participate in but do not control it. [532]

———. "The Transformation of 'Logic' in Heraclitus," in #535, pp. 89-102. Somewhat technical summary of Heidegger's 1944 lecture course on meaning of logic/logos. [533]

———., and DAVIS, S. "Reading Heidegger Reading Heraclitus Fragment 112," in #535, pp. 135-154. Joining of concepts such as *logos, aletheia,* and *sophia* in Heidegger's lectures on this frag should be seen as fluid, not static or immobile. [534]

———., and EMAD, P., eds. *Heidegger on Heraclitus. A New Reading.* Lewiston, ME: Mellen Pr., 1986. Collection of essays by various authors, abstracted herein. Includes collection of all frags of Heraclitus which Heidegger quotes. [535]

MANSFELD, J. "*Cratylus* 402A-C: Plato or Hippias?" in #566, pp. 43-55. Plato's source is a work by Sophist Cratylus, a critic of Heraclitus. Cratylus' contemporary Hippias refers to same statement of Heraclitus, but more favorably. [536]

———. "Heraclitus Fr. B 63 D.-K." *Elenchos* 4(1983), 197-205. Frag discusses wakefulness, sleep, death. Christian writer Hippolytus of Rome connected passage with doctrine of resurrection. Suggested emendations of text. [537]

———. "Heraclitus on the Psychology and Physiology of Sleep and on Rivers." *Mnem* 20(1967), 1-29. Group of H's frags seem to link sleep and death. Person sleeping is nearer to death because separated from sun, which warms and dries out soul. But sleeper is also part of timeless river of consciousness and may "see" things even while asleep. [538]

———. "On Two Fragments of Heraclitus in Clement of Alexandria." *Mnem* 37(1984), 447-451. Discussion of frags 22 B 21 and 22 B 20 D-K, pertaining to embodiment of soul as sleep or death. [539]

MARCOVICH, M. *Heraclitus: Greek Text with a Short Commentary.* Merida, Venezuela: Los Andes Univ. Pr., 1967. Frags are grouped under themes: Logos, Fire, and Ethico-political. Marcovich renumbers frags and provides table of concordances with D-K and other editors. Each frag is translated. [540]

———. "Heraclitus. Some Characteristics." *ICS* 7(1982), 171-188. H does not normally use mathematical proportions; relies on paradox, themes from folklore, popular maxims and metrical forms. Uses *logos* on metaphysical level and also to talk about physics, psychology and theology. [541]

———. "On Heraclitus." *Phron* 11(1966), 19-30. Discussion of several frags, some of which are not Heraclitean.   [542]

———. "What Heraclitus Said," in *Proceedings of the Seventh Inter-American Congress of Philosophy* (Quebec: Presses de l'Univ. Laval, 1967), pp. 301-313. Doctrine of Logos is H's most original and valuable contribution to metaphysics. Ideas on fire are less convincing than doctrine of constant measures. He can be viewed as eclectic.   [543]

MARINO, G. D. "An Analysis and Assessment of a Fragment from Jonathan Barnes' Reading of Heraclitus." *Apeir* 18(1984), 77-89. Barnes' formalistic interpretation (cf. #303) obscures H's meaning.   [544]

MICKS LA REGINA, G. "'All Things Give Way, Nothing Remaineth': Walter Pater and the Heraclitean Flux," in #567, pp. 191-208. H's influence on Pater has not been sufficiently recognized. Pater saw H's theme of constant change as a symbol of the state of flux of knowledge in the nineteenth century. References to H appear in Pater's earliest works.   [545]

MILLER, E. L. "The Logos of Heraclitus: Updating the Report." *HThR* 74(1981), 161-176. Resemblances between Logos in H and gospel of John are superficial. No direct connection can be demonstrated.   [546]

MORAVCSIK, J. M. "Heraclitean Concepts and Explanations," in #371, pp. 134-152. Survey of views on H's concepts of understanding, identity, and persistence put forth by Popper, Kirk, and others. H was first to try to formulate principles of identity and persistence, issues still not entirely resolved today.   [547]

MOTTO, A. L., and CLARK, J. B. "Heraclitus and the Ambivalence of Greek Tragic Idealism." *CB* 64(1988), 3-5. H provides an early instance of tendency of Greek thought to strive toward ethics and universal order.   [548]

MOURAVIEV, S. N. "Heraclitus ap. Clem. *Strom.* I, 70.3. A Neglected Fragment?" in #566, pp. 17-36. Passage in Clement is not just allusion or paraphrase but a virtual quotation of H's frag B92.   [549]

———. "Heraclitus B31^b DK (53^b Mch). An Improved Reading?" *Phron* 22(1977), 1-9. Passage must be read in context in which cited, Clement of Alexandria's discussion of Stoic ideas of cyclical transformations. Suggested corrections in text.   [550]

MOURELATOS, A. P. D. "Heraclitus, Fr. 114." *AJPh* 86(1965), 258-266. H's language shows influences of epic. Translations proposed for some key words in frag.   [551]

———. "Heraclitus, Parmenides, and the Naive Metaphysics of Things," in #65, pp. 16-48. Studies link between *pragma* and *logos* in two thinkers. Shows how revolutionary P's metaphysics was by comparison.   [552]

MUTH, R. "Herakleitos, I. Bericht: 1939 bis 1953." *AnzAlt* 7(1954), 65-90. Bibliographic survey.   [553]

NUSSBAUM, M. C. "*Psyche* in Heraclitus, I." *Phron* 17(1972), 1-16. H is first to link *psyche* and *logos* and to conceive of them as animating force of human life.   [554]

————. "*Psyche* in Heraclitus, II." *Phron* 17(1972), 153-169. H does not conceive of life after death. Individual can only aspire to fame or glory. [555]

PRIER, R. A. "Symbol and Structure in Heraclitus." *Apeir* 7 #2(1973), 23-37. H's primary logical symbol is Logos, symbolized by fire. He links opposites by median term, e. g., child is to man as man is to god. [556]

————. cf. #367.

PRITZL, K. "On the Way to Wisdom in Heraclitus." *Phoenix* 39(1985), 303-316. For H wisdom is attained by analysis and correlation of data gathered by hearing and sight. [557]

REEVE, C. D. C. "*Ekpurosis* and the Priority of Fire in Heraclitus." *Phron* 27(1982), 299-305. Modifying Anaximenes' doctrine of transformation of opposites, H posits strife alone as driving force, makes loss or gain of heat the mechanism of change. This, not *ekpurosis*, is why H assigns such importance to fire. [558]

RETHY, R. "Heraclitus Fragment 56. The Deceptiveness of the Apparent." *AncPh* 7(1987), 1-7. H's prefatory comments to riddle of lice-catchers point to riddle's deeper meaning as symbol of elusiveness of Logos itself. [559]

ROBB, K. "Preliterate Ages and the Linguistic Art of Heraclitus," in #371, pp. 153-206. H's literary style is not purely prose or poetry but comes closer to what is called "orational" style, typical of Egyptian and Old Testament wisdom literature. [560]

————. "*Psyche* and *Logos* in the Fragments of Heraclitus. The Origins of the Concept of Soul." *Monist* 69(1986), 315-351. It is tempting, but misleading, to read H's comments on soul as akin to Socrates'. H has many Homeric elements, and is still as close to that end of spectrum of development as he is to Socrates' end. He is first to connect *psyche* with activities involving cognition or rational speech, i. e., *logos*. [561]

ROBINSON, T. M. *Heraclitus: Fragments.* Univ. of Toronto Pr., 1987. Frags with facing-page translation, short essays on various interpretive problems, commentary on frags, and selected bibliography. [562]

————. "Heraclitus on Soul." *Monist* 69(1986), 305-314. Soul is life-principle, informing rationality and morality and is composed of water-vapor. Views on soul's immortality remain unclear. [563]

————. "Heraclitus: Some Soundings," in #59, pp. 229-240. Translation, commentary on several frags. [564]

ROHATYN, D. A. "Heraclitus: Some Remarks on the Political Fragments." *CJ* 68(1972-73), 271-273. List and translation of frags with political overtones. Their general tone is aristocratic, with notion that human law has divine origins. [565]

ROSSETTI, L., ed. *Atti del Symposium Heracliteum, I.* Rome: Ed. dell' Ateneo, 1983. Cf. next item. [566]

————. *Atti del Symposium Heracliteum 1981, II: La 'Fortuna' di Eracliteo nel pensiero moderno*. Rome: Ed. dell' Ateneo, 1984. This and preceding item contain papers read at an international symposium. Those in English are abstracted herein.   [567]

ROUSSOS, E. N. *Heraklit-Bibliographie*. Darmstadt, Ger.: Wissenschaftlichte Buchgesellschaft, 1971. Organized by topics. Some entries have brief annotations (in German). Listings within subjects are chronological.   [568]

SALLIS, J. "Hades: Heraclitus, Fragment B 98," in #571, pp. 61-67. Proposes a Heideggerian translation of the frag, which is usually taken to mean "souls employ the sense of smell in Hades."   [569]

――――. "Heraclitus and Phenomenology," in #567, pp. 267-277. Impact of Heraclitus' thought on Martin Heidegger, who insisted that his reflections on Greek thought lay "at the center" of his work.   [570]

――――., and MALY, K., eds. *Heraclitean Fragments. A Companion Volume to the Heidegger/Fink Seminar on Heraclitus*. University, AL: Univ. of AL Pr., 1980. Collection of essays designed to elaborate on ideas discussed in #516. Relevant ones abstracted herein.   [571]

SCHMIDT, D. J. "On the Obscurity of the Origin." *PhT* 26(1982), 322-331. Examines biases in Hegel's and Heidegger's interpretations of Heraclitus.   [572]

SCOLNICOV, S. "I Searched Myself." *SCI* 7(1983-84), 1-13. H's philosophy is based on observation but validated by insight. Hence his claim to learn from no one.   [573]

SHINER, R. A. "Wittgenstein and Heraclitus: Two River Images." *Ph* 49(1974), 191-197. Both philosophers use image of river to describe mankind's knowledge as constantly in flux. H conceives of river's bed as stone, while W sees it as sand, symbolizing their views of ultimate permanence or its lack in knowledge.   [574]

SHIPTON, R. M. W. "Heraclitus Fragment 10: A Musical Interpretation." *Phron* 30(1985), 111-130. In this frag *synapsis* refers to harmony of two tetrachords, particularly to note common to them. Illustrates H's theory of unity.   [575]

SMITH, C. I. "Heraclitus and Fire." *JHI* 27(1966), 125-127. H's concept of fire was not drawn from the hearth, as some have maintained.   [576]

SNYDER, J. M. "The *Harmonia* of Bow and Lyre in Heraclitus Fr. 51 (DK)." *Phron* 29(1984), 91-95. H's statement that bow and lyre turn back on themselves refers to arc of their frameworks.   [577]

STEIGER, K. "Heraclitus, a Forgotten Fragment (Clement *Paed*. III,1,5)." *AUB* (Phil) 18(1984), 121-129. Discusses reasons for attributing passage to H.   [578]

STEWART, D. "Contradiction and the Ways of Truth and Seeming." *Apeir* 14(1980), 1-14. H was able to accept apparent contradiction that all things are one. Parmenides rejected idea because he could see only contradiction between one and many. Neither man had adequate concept of form as distinct from substance.   [579]

SULLIVAN, S. D. "*To sophon* as an Aspect of the Divine in Heraclitus," in #59, pp.

285-301. On divine level *to sophon* represents knowledge of plan guiding things. It is one. It also exists on level of human psyche and enables persons to understand that all things are one and are guided by a plan, and to live according to the truth. **[580]**

TRIPLETT, T. "Barnes on Heraclitus and the Unity of Opposites." *AncPh* 6(1986), 15-23. Barnes objects to this idea based on narrow reading of doxographies. H teaches contrary qualities exist not at same time but in cyclical process of transformation. **[581]**

VALIULIS, D. J. "Style and Significance. A Note on Heraclitus, Fr. 62," in #566, pp. 163-168. This frag is perhaps H's most obscure. His intention may have been to use literary style — a dense juxtaposition of words having opposite meanings — to reinforce idea that all things are one and that they flow together. **[582]**

VERDENIUS, W. J. "Heraclitus' Conception of Fire," in #67, pp. 1-8. Interpretation of several frags. **[583]**

———. "Some Aspects of Heraclitus' Anthropology," in #47, pp. 29-35. *Psyche* is essential element of a human being. It is connected to world soul, which is fire, and is therefore itself fire. Immortality is not infinite prolongation of human life but passage into absolute life. **[584]**

WHITED, G. L. "The 'Hidden Harmony': A Study of Heraclitus and Parmenides." *SwPhSt* 1(1976), 34-39. Examines element of unity beneath H's doctrine of flux and compares it to P's monadic thought. **[585]**

WIGGINS, D. "Heraclitus' Conceptions of Flux, Fire, and Material Persistence," in #76, pp. 1032. H lacked a vocabulary to speculate but attempted to formulate sufficient reasons for observable phenomena. Result is a realist cosmology. **[586]**

WILLIAMS, H. "Heraclitus' Philosophy and Hegel's Dialectic." *HPolTho* 6(1985), 381-404. H showed Hegel the need for paradox and contradiction. For Hegel, reducing paradox/contradiction to basic elements opens way for knowledge of the Idea. **[587]**

For related items see #1248, #1297, #1859, #5535, #5737.

Chapter 6

THE ELEATICS

If Heraclitus could see change as something positive, other philosophers were perplexed by it. If something changes, they reasoned, then it was not perfect to begin with. And if it changed once, it could change again. Thus how can we be sure of our knowledge if we cannot trust the data on which it is based? A school of philosophy arising at Elea, in southern Italy, approached this problem by denying the possibility of change and using logic to support their position. The Eleatic view held that the world was one (a Monad) and any perceived change or motion was illusory.

BICKNELL, P. J. "Dating the Eleatics," in #63, pp. 1-14. Parmenides' and Zeno's ages, mentioned by Plato in *Parm.* 127A-C, are accurate. Their visit to Athens should be dated to 458 B. C. **[588]**

BOSLEY, R. "Monistic Argumentation," in #1287, pp. 23-44. Analysis of origins of monistic argumentation and of its main points, compared to comments of Plato, Aristotle, and other ancient writers. **[589]**

LACEY, A. R. "The Eleatics and Aristotle on Some Problems of Change." *JHI* 26(1965), 451-468. Parmenides held that Being must be eternal. Aristotle changes emphasis by saying that anything which changes must have some immutable element. Overview of idea of change in several Presocratic philosophers. **[590]**

NUSSBAUM, M. C. "Eleatic Conventionalism and Philolaus on the Conditions of Thought." *HSCP* 83(1979), 63-108. Frags of Philolaus, an obscure Pythagorean, reveal that he countered Eleatic arguments that all *nomoi* are mere human conventions by what is perhaps the first example of a "transcendental argument." **[591]**

SCHWABL, H. "Die Eleaten (Xenophanes, Nachtrag zu Parmenides, Melissos). Forschungsbericht 1939-1956." *AnzAlt* 10(1957), 195-226. Bibliographic survey. **[592]**

THOM, P. "A Lesniewskian Reading of Ancient Ontology. Parmenides to Democritus." *H&PhLog* 7(1986), 155-166. P's ontology was modified by later thinkers. Resulting system can be seen as a type of minimal Lesniewskian ontology. **[593]**

For related items see #461, #599, #618, #653.

PARMENIDES (ca. 500-450 B. C.)
The first exponent of this monadic world view was Parmenides, who chose

to record his views in an epic poem. The first portion of this poem survives under the title "The Way of Truth." Only fragments of the second part, "The Way of Opinion," are extant. In the poem P travels to the palace of the sun, where he receives instruction from a goddess. Her most important revelation to him is that "only Being can exist; not-being cannot be." In less cryptic terms that means that there cannot be a void or an emptiness. Being cannot be divided, the goddess explains. What could separate Being into parts? If Being is the separator, then Being would be separated from Being by Being. But then it would not be separated. If Non-being — pure nothingness — were the separator, then one would be arguing that nothing separates Being, which is another way of saying that Being is not separated.

Being is also eternal and indestructible, P learned from the goddess, for how could Being arise out of non-being? And, if it arose from something else, that something must be Being. It cannot be destroyed, because Being cannot become non-being, and if it becomes anything else, then it is still Being. Change is therefore impossible. Whatever is, has always been, and it has always been everywhere. This doctrine of the oneness of all things is virtually identical to the teaching of the Indian school of Advaita Vedanta.

A corollary from this logical approach is the assertion that, since the world is a material monad, motion is impossible. Being is everywhere. How, then, can something move from one place to another, when all places are occupied by matter?

P's significance is his insistence on the priority of logic, even when it contradicts our most obvious sense perceptions. He also established the principle that only consistent entities can exist and that the validity of statements can be "tested by examining their consistency." What P failed to explain was how the two worlds — that of logical being and that of sense perception — can co-exist.

P is sometimes described as an idealist, i. e., one who asserts the real existence of ideas. He does enunciate a distinction between what can be known by the senses and what is known by the intellect, a fundamental tenet of idealism, especially in Plato. But Parmenides does not distinguish between reason and sense in order to represent the One as self-subsistent Thought, which is Idealism in its developed form. Rather he asserts the distinction to establish a system of Monistic Materialism, in which change and movement are dismissed as illusory. Only reason can apprehend reality, he says, but the reality which reason apprehends is material.

That P regarded Being as material seems to be clearly indicated by his claim that Being, the One, is finite. "Infinite" for him seems to have meant indeterminate and indefinite. Being, as the real, cannot be indeterminate or indefinite; it cannot change, cannot be conceived as expanding into empty space. It must be definite, determinate, and complete. In terms of space, it is finite, but in terms of time, it is infinite, since it has no beginning or end. Furthermore, it is real in all directions, and is thus spherical. As P says, it is "equally poised from the center in every direction: for it cannot be greater or smaller in one place than in another." He is obviously thinking of Being as material.

P's poem is the earliest extant philosophical text which is complete enough to allow us to follow its argument. As C. H. Kahn points, however, we do not get that text free of cost, and "the price we must pay for our good fortune is to face up to a vipers' nest of problems, concerning details of the text and the archaic language but also concerning major questions of philosophic interpretation. These problems are so fundamental that, unless we solve them correctly, we cannot even be clear as to what Parmenides is arguing for, or why. And they are so knotted that we can scarcely unravel a single problem without finding the whole nest in our hands." (#629, p. 700)

ANDRIOPOULOS, D. Z. "Parmenides' Fragment B 16 and His Theory of Perceiving and Knowing," in *Actes de la XIIe Conférence internationale d'Études classiques Eirene, Chij-Napoca, 2-7 octobre 1972*, ed. by I. Fischer. Amsterdam: Hakkert, 1975, pp. 553-561. Reply to Hershbell (#623).   [594]

AUSTIN, S. "Genesis and Motion in Parmenides B8.12-13." *HSCP* 87(1983), 151-168. Frag denies that anything except what-is can come out of what-is.   [595]

———. "Parmenides and Ultimate Reality." *UltR&M* 7(1984), 220-232. Introduction to poem and scholarly debate on it.   [596]

———. *Parmenides: Being, Bounds, and Logic.* New Haven, CT: Yale Univ. Pr., 1986. P saw ontology and logic as one because of his concept of being as bounded. Interpretation of his view and comparison with philosophers who posit an infinite being. One reviewer called book difficult but "essential" for anyone working on P.   [597]

BALLEW, L. "Straight and Circular in Parmenides and the *Timaeus*." *Phron* 19(1974), 189-209. Both P and Plato use the principle "like knows like" in their discussion of human knowledge of the universe. Being is spherical, known by intelligence, whose motion is circular. Objects make straight lines and are perceived by senses, whose movement is also rectilinear.   [598]

BARNES, J. "Parmenides and the Eleatic One." *AGPh* 61(1979), 1-21. Texts usually cited as evidence of P's monism do not actually support assertion.   [599]

BICKNELL, P. J. "A New Arrangement of Some Parmenidean Verses." *SO* 42(1967), 44-50. Rearranging several frags eliminates stylistic problems and clarifies P's opposition to Heraclitus.   [600]

———. "Parmenides, DK 28 B5." *Apeir* 13(1979), 9-11. Placing B 5 before B 2 makes text read more naturally and clarifies meaning of *xunon*.   [601]

———. "Parmenides' Refutation of Motion and an Implication." *Phron* 12(1967), 1-5. Leucippus was not opposed to Melissus' teaching on impossibility of motion. P's refutation, in frag 8 Diels-Kranz v. 33, is quite similar to Melissus', who responded to Atomists in Leucippus' own terminology.   [602]

BLANK, D. L. "Faith and Persuasion in Parmenides." *ClAnt* 1(1982), 167-177. Themes of faith and persuasion loom large in proem because P felt them to be on level with mystery religions and mystical Pythagorean teachings.   [603]

BODNAR, I. "Contrasting Images. Notes on Parmenides B5." *Apeir* 19(1985), 57-63. Translate frag: "Commonly present it is/ wherever I start from, for there I will return again."
[604]

CALVO, T. "Truth and Doxa in Parmenides." *AGPh* 59(1977), 245-260. P is concerned not with an opposition between two forms of knowledge but between two contrasting forms of speech, which he symbolizes in his poem by the opposition between *logos* and *epos*.
[605]

CHAMPLIN, W. W. "Oedipus Tyrannus and the Problem of Knowledge." *CJ* 64(1969), 337-345. Distinction between Oedipus' limited knowledge, which derives from senses, and Teiresias' divinely inspired insight is based on P.
[606]

CLARK, R. J. "Parmenides and Sense-Perception." *REG* 82(1969), 14-32. Survey of interpretations of frag B v. 28-32 (D-K). One can explain P's theory of knowledge without creating contradictions with his cosmology.
[607]

CORNFORD, F. M. "Parmenides' Two Ways," in #53, pp. 129-143. The cosmology which P rejects in the *doxa* part of his poems appears to have been his own construction. He cannot bridge the gap between appearances and Being and can only assert that it cannot be bridged.
[608]

COSGROVE, M. R. "The *Kouros* Motif in Parmenides B 1:24." *HPhQ* 3(1986), 125-136. By calling himself "boy," as opposed to *physikos*, P claims that truth revealed to him is pure, free of preconceived ideas associated with other philosophers.
[609]

COXON, A. H. *The Fragments of Parmenides.* Assen, Netherlands: van Gorcum, 1986. Critical text with translation and commentary.
[610]

DE RIJK, L. M. "Did Parmenides Reject the Sensible World?" in #60, pp. 29-53. P's distinction between route of *aletheia* and routes of *doxa* does not imply distinction between two different domains, one "spiritual," the other "sensible."
[611]

FINKELBERG, A. "The Cosmology of Parmenides." *AJPh* 107(1986), 303-317. Frag 12 and Aetius' account can be reconciled into a consistent cosmology.
[612]

————. "'Like by Like' and Two Reflections of Reality in Parmenides." *Hermes* 114(1986), 405-412. Idea that "like knows like" is not just a doctrine about nature of perception. It is basis of P's teaching. His dualism arises from it and is resolved by it. His theory can be reconstructed based on Theophrastus' account of P's theory of cognition.
[613]

————. "Parmenides: Between Material and Logical Monism." *AGPh* 70(1988), 1-14. P's concept of Being is his effort to overcome difficulty posed by material monism. A true monism should find unity at a higher, logical level.
[614]

FRAENKEL, H. "Studies in Parmenides," in #301, pp. 1-47. Examines several topics: the Ascent, *dike*, human knowledge, world of the senses, relation of P's thought to Anaximander.
[615]

FRINGS, M. S. "Parmenides. Heidegger's 1942-1943 Lecture Held at Freiburg Univ."

JBritSocPhen 19(1988), 15-33. Discusses meanings of *aletheia* and *pseudos* and word "is" in terms of proximity and openness of being.   **[616]**

FURLEY, D. J. "Notes on Parmenides," in #65, pp. 1-15. *Elenchos* originally meant "shame" or "disgrace," but by P's time it had come to mean "refutation." Frag 8 indicates that only one way remains, implying that other ways have been refuted.   **[617]**

FURTH, M. "Elements of Eleatic Ontology." *JHPh* 6(1968), 111-132. Overview of Greek word "being"; interpretation of what is considered P's fundamental concept: "it cannot be said that anything is not." Brief discussion of cosmology and question of whether P really believed his patently absurd doctrines.   **[618]**

GALLOP, D. "'Is' or 'Is Not'?" *Monist* 62(1979), 61-80. Verb *einai* in frag B2.7-8 is existential, not predicative or veridical. It is a conclusion, not a premise.   **[619]**

————. *Parmenides of Elea: Fragments. A Text and Translation with an Introduction.* Univ. of Toronto Pr., 1984. Introduction summarizes basic points of his thought. Text and transl. on facing pages with notes at bottom.   **[620]**

GROARKE, L. "Parmenides' Timeless Universe, Again." *Dial*(Can) 26(1987), 549-552. Reply to #639.   **[621]**

HERSHBELL, J. P. "Parmenides and *Outis* in *Odyssey* 9." *CJ* 68(1972), 178-180. By deceiving Cyclops with name Nobody, Odysseus does not contradict P's dictum that non-being cannot be. Incident actually illustrates P's point.   **[622]**

————. "Parmenides' Way of Truth and B 16." *Apeir* 4 #2(1970), 1-23. This frag, from first part of Way of Truth, affirms affinity between Being and thought.   **[623]**

HINTIKKA, J. "Parmenides' *Cogito* Argument." *AncPh* 1(1980), 5-16. For P thought is goal-directed. One cannot think something untrue or non-existent. His argumentation is genuinely philosophical, using deductions and logic to prove his point.   **[624]**

HUSAIN, M. "The Hybris of Parmenides." *Dial*(Can) 22(1983), 451-460. By claiming to enter divine realm and equating knowledge gained with divine knowledge, P is guilty of excess.   **[625]**

JONES, B. "Parmenides' 'The Way of Truth'." *JHPh* 11(1973), 287-298. P's frags give no evidence of monism or denial of possibility of negative statements.   **[626]**

KAHN, C. H. "Being in Parmenides and Plato." *ParPas* 43(1988), 237-261. Parmenides' use of *esti* is initially veridical, but he develops it into existential concept that nothing real comes to exist or perishes. Plato also moves from an idiomatic usage of *esti* to viewing it metaphysically. Converse idea of not-being is not as well developed in either author.   **[627]**

————. "More on Parmenides." *RMeta* 23(1970), 333-340. Reply to #674, #643.   **[628]**

————. "The Thesis of Parmenides." *RMeta* 22(1969), 700-724. P can be seen as founder of ontology and metaphysics. Key to understanding his thought is the one-word sentence *esti* ("it is"). P is no cosmologist but is wrestling with problem of knowledge. He uses principles of non-contradiction and excluded middle a century before Plato. He connects knowledge of Being with Being itself, a connection elaborated by Aristotle and Neoplatonists. **[629]**

KEMBER, O. "Right and Left in the Sexual Theories of Parmenides." *JHS* 91(1971), 70-79. P seems to have thought that baby's gender is determined by whether it lies on right or left side of womb or by womb's warmth or coldness. **[630]**

LAGAN, W. J. "Parmenides and Mystical Reason. A Metaphysical Dilemma." *ModSch* 60(1982), 30-47. Philosophy confronts a problem of irrationality in mysticism and metaphysics. P was first to outline dilemma. **[631]**

LESHER, J. H. "Parmenides' Critique of Thinking. The *Poluderis Elenchos* of Fragment 7." *OSAP* 2(1984), 1-30. Greek phrase means "the test of many struggles." Like a chariot driver, one must steer a course along a difficult path, not trusting appearances (human *doxa*) but guidance of the goddess (*logos*). This concept of *elenchos* becomes important for Sophists, Socrates, and most later dialecticians. **[632]**

LONG, A. A. "The Principles of Parmenides' Cosmogony," in #301, pp. 82-101. Cosmogony of frag B 8 50-61 is exposition promised by goddess in proem. It serves to offer an exemplar of all false systems, based on appearance and opinion, which can be set against Way of Truth. **[633]**

MacKENZIE, M. M. "Parmenides' Dilemma." *Phron* 27(1982), 1-12. *Aletheia* section of P's poem rejects all physical phenomena, which *Doxa* section describes in detail. P seems to have seen contradiction and exploited it. If Being is one, not even the thinker exists separately; dialectic is impossible. **[634]**

MALY, K. "Parmenides: Circle of Disclosure, Circle of Possibility." *Heidegger Studies* 1(1985), 5-23. Discusses Heidegger's work on P over a period of years, especially his insight that there is more to P's thought than a simplistic contrast between "static being" and "becoming." **[635]**

MANCHESTER, P. B. "Parmenides and the Need for Eternity." *Monist* 62(1979), 81-106. P needed a concept of eternity as a paradigm for numbered time. **[636]**

MASON, R. "Parmenides and Language." *AncPh* 8(1988), 149-166. Human language is meaningless except among humans. Goddess in P's poem speaks meaningfully about constitution of nature, not its descriptive predicates. **[637]**

MATSON, W. I. "Parmenides Unbound." *IntPhQ* 2(1980), 345-360. According to most contemporary interpreters, *Doxa* part of P's poem presents an untrue account of things that have no real existence. But *Doxa* can be seen as having kind or degree of cognitive value. **[638]**

MATTHEN, M. "A Note on Parmenides' Denial of Past and Future." *Dial*(Can) 25(1986), 553-557. P's concept of non-being can be construed too loosely to mean denial of existence of past and future. **[639]**

MILLER, E. L. "Parmenides the Prophet?" *JHPh* 6(1968), 67-69. Taran (cf. #678) stresses logic in P too heavily and overlooks poem's religious tone. **[640]**

MILLER, F. D., Jr. "Parmenides on Mortal Belief." *JHPh* 15(1977), 253-265. P's statement that one cannot know or say what is not is based on his concept of relationship of statements as referring to world and revealing things as they are, though he does not clearly distinguish between reference and insight.   **[641]**

MILLER, M. H., Jr. "Parmenides and the Disclosure of Being." *Apeir* 13(1979), 12-35. In proem P, by his choice of vocabulary and imagery, brings Homer, Hesiod and Ionians to mind, showing how inadequate their understanding of Being was and setting up a progression that culminates in P's disclosure of his own doctrine of Being.   **[642]**

MOURELATOS, A. P. D. "Comments on 'The Thesis of Parmenides'." *RMeta* 22(1968-69), 735-744. Reply to #629.   **[643]**

——. "The Deceptive Words of Parmenides' *Doxa*," in #363, pp. 312-349. Surveys differences in Anglo-American and continental interpretations of second part of P's poem. The *doxa* is an "ironic" explication of a widely-held cosmology, intended to bring out contrasts with P's own views.   **[644]**

——. "Determinancy and Indeterminancy as the Key Contrasts in Parmenides." *Lampas* 8(1975), 334-343. Everything in P's thought is oriented along two "ways," Being and Not-Being, as indicated especially in fragment B2 D-K. Verb *esti* is a bare copula, with no subject.   **[645]**

——. "Determinancy and Indeterminancy, Being and Non-Being in the Fragments of Parmenides," in #1287, pp. 45-60. In "Truth" section of his poem P is not arguing that negative statements fail to refer to real things or states of being but that they are impossibly vague.   **[646]**

——. "Mind's Commitment to the Real: Parmenides B 8.34-41," in #41, pp. 59-80. This frag should be interpreted as asserting that Being not only can be thought about; it is the object of all thought. Mind (*nous*) strives to understand reality. Ordinary speech is too unfocussed to reach the precision necessary to comprehend Being. **[647]**

——. *The Route of Parmenides. A Study of Word, Image and Argument in the Fragments.* New Haven, CT: Yale Univ. Pr., 1970. Places new emphasis on definition of certain key terms: *kinesis, doxa,* and *peithein.* Stresses *hodoi* (ways, routes). Denies that P rejected negative predication. Somewhat slanted toward poetic rather than philosophic side of his thought.   **[648]**

——. "Some Alternatives in Interpreting Parmenides." *Monist* 62(1979), 3-14. P's use of verb *einai* ("to be") is always copulative (joining two ideas), not existential, as some scholars hold. His monism is based on rejection of notion of contraries.   **[649]**

NEHAMAS, A. "On Parmenides' Three Ways of Inquiry." *Deukalion* 33-34(1981), 97-111. In frag B 6 P does not reject any certain method of research. He does, perhaps for the first time in western thought, distinguish between appearance and reality. **[650]**

NORTHRUP, M. D. "Hesiodic Personifications in Parmenides A 37." *TAPhA* 90(1980), 223-232. P's use of deities in his Way of Seeming was inspired by their symbolic use in Hesiod.   **[651]**

OSIER, J. "Parmenides and the Pythagoreans." *CB* 52(1976), 65-66. P was probably a doctor's son and originally Pythagorean.   [652]

OWEN, G. E. L. "Eleatic Questions," in #301, pp. 48-81. P's goddess has no cosmological pretensions. She does not show that world is spherical or eternal. It is useless to try to read P's thought back into earlier cosmological speculation.   [653]

OWENS, J. "Being in Early Western Tradition," in #78, pp. 17-30. P is first western philosopher to try to study things as they really are, to penetrate beneath appearances. He understands Being as whatever is seen as something but is recognized by the enlightened as encompassing everything else. Nothing is outside it except non-Being, which human thought cannot conceive or language express.   [654]

————. "Knowledge and *Katabasis* in Parmenides." *Monist* 62(1979), 15-29. Journey which P describes in his poem should be seen as an ascent, symbolic of upward movement from ignorance to knowledge.   [655]

————. "Naming in Parmenides," in #67, pp. 16-25. Discussion of four passages where idea of naming appears: B 8,38; B 8,53; B9,1; B 18,3 Diels-Kranz.   [656]

————. "The Physical World of Parmenides," in *Essays in Honour of Anton Charles Pegis*, ed. J. R. O'Donnell (Toronto: Pontifical Inst. Mediev. Stud., 1974), pp.378-395. P does not deny existence of physical world. Sense perception, however, cannot give one the truth about its unity.   [657]

PELLIKAAN-ENGEL, M. E. *Hesiod and Parmenides. A New View on Their Cosmologies and on Parmenides' Proem.* Amsterdam: Hakkert, 1978. Attempted rationalization of Hesiod's description of Tartarus and the House of Night and comparison of similarities between H and P. Route of P's journey seems to be linked to H's topography.   [658]

PRIER, R. A. "The Critics on Light and Parmenides." *Platon* 31(1979), 268-274. Surveys scholarly opinion. Light, symbolizing Being/truth, is subordinate to *dike*.   [659]

REINHARDT, K. "The Relation between the Two Parts of Parmenides' Poem," in #363, pp. 293-311. P's problem is to explain how *doxa* arose if there was at first only *aletheia*. He simply says "The [people] came to agree to name two forms." This foreshadows *physis/nomos* dichotomy and epistemological relativism of Sophists.   [660]

RIST, J. M. "Parmenides and Plato's Parmenides." *CQ* 20(1970), 221-229. Views attributed to Parmenides by Plato are related to, but not identical with, those of the historical figure.   [661]

————. cf. #6523.

ROBINSON, T. M. "Parmenides on Ascertainment of the Real." *CanJPh* 4(1975), 623-633. P's argument of a necessary connection — though not an identity — between what is known and what is real is foundation of Plato's and Aristotle's epistemologies. [662]

————. "Parmenides on the Real in its Totality." *Monist* 62(1979), 54-60. The "real" is object of both sections of P's poem. In *Doxa* it is understood only imperfectly. In *Way of Truth* it is seen in its totality, without temporal or spatial limitations.   [663]

ROHATYN, D. A. "A Note on Parmenides B19." *Apeir* 5 #2(1971), 20-22. Frag should be put in first part of P's poem.   [664]

SCHICK, T. "Check and Spur. Parmenides' Concept of (What) Is." *CJ* 60(1965), 170-173. Discussion of P's importance in breaking bonds of materialist thought. He is difficult to understand because he did not distinguish existence and its subjects, as modern philosophy does.   [665]

SCHOFIELD, M. "Coxon's Parmenides." *Phron* 32(1987), 349-359. Discussion of Coxon's edition of frags (#610).   [666]

———. "Did Parmenides Discover Eternity?" *AGPh* 52(1970), 113-135. Claim that P sees Being as outside of time, in a continuous present, is not as well founded as many think. View of Fraenkel (#615) and Taran (#678) that Being is within time but eternal is stronger than they have stated it.   [667]

SCHWABL, H. "Parmenides. Forschungsbericht, 1939-1955." *AnzAlt* 9(1956), 129-156. Bibliographic survey in German.   [668]

———. "Parmenides 1957-1971." *AnzAlt* 25(1972), 15-43. Bibliographic survey in German, updating preceeding item.   [669]

SOLMSEN, F. "Light from Aristotle's *Physics* on the Text of Parmenides B8 D-K." *Phron* 22(1977), 10-12. *Physics* 1,8,191a 23-33 seems to come from P. It denies all becoming, even from Being itself.   [670]

SOLOMON, J. H. M. "Parmenides and the Gurus." *Platon* 30(1978), 157-173. Parallels between P and Hindu thought suggest Indian philosophy may provide more helpful insights into Eleatic thought than western philosophy does.   [671]

SPRAGUE, R. K. "An Anonymous Argument against Mixture." *Mnem* 26(1973), 230-233. Argument in Aristotle's *De gen et corr* 327a35 may be derived from P.   [672]

STEIGER, K. "The Cosmology of Parmenides and Empedocles." *Homonoia* 2(1980), 159-165. Summary of a doctoral dissertation which argues that E's cosmological scheme is identical to P's. Their "closed" cosmology is found in Presocratic thought between Milesians and Anaxagoras.   [673]

STEIN, H. "Comments on 'The Thesis of Parmenides'." *RMeta* 22(1968-69), 725-734. Reply to Kahn (#629).   [674]

STEWART, D. "Contradiction and the Ways of Truth and Seeming." *Apeir* 14(1980), 1-14. Concepts of truth and seeming are best understood in Heraclitean terms of contradictory reality.   [675]

STEWART, R. S. "Say No More. The Relationship Between Parmenides' Ways of Truth and Seeming." *Eidos* 4(1985), 167-186. P used medium of epic poetry (*doxa*) to make his radical thesis (*aletheia*) intelligible to readers of his day.   [676]

STOUGH, C. L. "Parmenides' Way of Truth. B8,12-13." *Phron* 13(1968), 91-107. No need to emend text here. Argument is logically complete as it stands.   [677]

TARAN, L. *Parmenides*. Princeton Univ. Pr., 1965. Text with translation, commentary and critical essays on P's concept of Being; *Aletheia* and *Doxa*; the world of appearance; and P in the ancient philosophical tradition. **[678]**

————. cf. #1473.

TARRANT, H. A. S. "The Conclusion of Parmenides' Poem." *Apeir* 17(1983), 73-84. Coda may have originally stood after B19; B4 and B16 perhaps parts of it. B1.31-32 and B5 may not be authentic. New interpretation of *doxa* based on these readings. **[679]**

————. "Parmenides B1.3. Text, Context, and Interpretation." *Antich* 10(1976), 1-7. No emendation of text necessary. One must put aside preconceptions about divinity's identity. **[680]**

TOWNSLEY, A. L. "Cosmic Eros in Parmenides." *RSC* 23(1975), 337-346. Suggested emendation in frag 1.30. Parmenidean eros is closer to Aristotelian concept than Platonic. **[681]**

————. "Parmenides' Religious Vision and Aesthetics." *Athenaeum* 53(1975), 343-351. P's poem is a religious vision of traditional Greek gods and an aesthetic insight into immutable forms. **[682]**

————. "Some Comments on Parmenidean Eros." *Eos* 64(1976), 153-161. P's cosmic eros is not borrowed from Orphic thought and has no direct link to Platonic Eros. P's association of Eros with wisdom of god brings him closer to Aristotle. **[683]**

VERDENIUS, W. J. "Opening Doors (Parm. B1.17-18)." *Mnem* 30(1977), 287-288. Frag can be understood as meaning that doors referred to are opening by themselves. **[684]**

WHITTAKER, J. *God, Time, Being. Two Studies in the Transcendental Tradition in Greek Philosophy*, with an Appendix: Olympiodorus, *In I Alcib. 141.1ff.* Oslo, Norway: Universitetsforl., 1971. Discusses Parmenides' view of timeless present vs. non-durational eternity. Philo shows some traces of latter concept in some of his works. **[685]**

WOODBURY, L. "Parmenides on Names," in #41, pp. 145-162. Reading *onomastai* in frag B 8.38 allows new interpretation of entire frag on question of link between names and being. **[686]**

————., and **BOWEN, A. C.** (ed). "Parmenides on Naming By Mortal Men: Fr. B8.53-56." *AncPh* 6(1986), 1-13. By naming (and misnaming) things, people create in their own minds the concept of individual entities. P maintains that there is only one true name, which is Being. **[687]**

For related items see #359, #488, #585, #593, #2613, #3233, #3885, #5010, #6340, #6691.

ZENO of ELEA (ca. 490-425 B. C.)

Z is known primarily as the author of several ingenious arguments to prove the impossibility of motion, which we will look at below. He is sometimes dismissed as a clever riddler who delighted in using his wits to puzzle those less clever than himself. But Z had a much more serious purpose in his riddles. He was a disciple of Parmenides, and it is in this light that his work must be understood. His arguments, only about two hundred words of which survive, are not witty toys, but are calculated to prove the position of his master. Parmenides had combated pluralism and had declared change and motion to be illusion. Since plurality and motion seem to be so easily perceived by our sense-experience, these arguments were received with ridicule. Z attempted to prove the existence of the One as taught by Parmenides by showing that such an idea is by no means ridiculous and by demonstrating that the pluralists become involved in insoluble difficulties, and that change and motion are impossible, even on their own pluralistic hypotheses. Z's arguments can be divided into several groups. The first is the arguments against plurality. For reasons of space we will examine only the first.

Pythagoreans hold the world to be made up of units. Z says, let's grant the premise for the sake of argument and see where it leads.

If Being (or Reality) is made up of units, these units either have size or do not have size. If they have size, then a line, for example, made up of units that have size, will be infinitely divisible, since, no matter how far one divides it, the units will still have size and so be divisible. But this will mean that the line will be made up of an infinite number of units, each having size. Thus, the line must be infinitely great. Everything in the world must be infinitely great, then. Indeed, the world itself must be infinitely great. But suppose that the units have no size. In this case the whole universe will be without size, since no matter how many units you add together, if none of them has any size, then the sum will have no magnitude. The Pythagoreans are thus faced with a dilemma: Either everything in the universe is infinitely great or everything is infinitely small. The conclusion Z wants us to draw from this argument is that the dilemma comes from an absurd premise, namely that the world is composed of units.

The second argument against pluralism asks whether one could number all the units which the Pythagoreans claim exist. In the third argument Z asks if a grain of wheat makes a noise when it falls to the ground. Do a bushel of seeds make a noise when they are dumped on the ground? But if the parts make no sound, how can the whole make a sound, when the whole is only composed of its parts? How can $0 + 0^n = 1$?

Z also devised an argument against the Pythagorean doctrine of space. The Pythagoreans held that the world existed in an empty space or void. Parmenides denied the existence of this void and Z tried to uphold this view. Suppose for a moment that there is a space in which things are. If it is nothing, then things cannot be in it. If, however, it is something, then it will itself be in space, and that space will be in space, and so on ad infinitum. Thus, things do not exist in an empty void or in space.

The most celebrated arguments of Z are those concerning motion. Parmenides had denied that motion was possible. Z wanted to prove that it was also impossible on the hypotheses of the Pythagoreans. We will examine only the first, called the race course.

Suppose a runner must cross a race-course. If he were going from point A to point B, he would first have to cross point C, midway between A and B. Going from A to C, he would first have to cross the midpoint D. And so on. If a line is made up of units, as the Pythagoreans claim, the runner must cross an infinite number of points. In order to get anywhere, he must do this in a finite time. This, of course, is impossible. And thus all motion is impossible by the same token.

Another paradox of motion concern a race between Achilles (whom Homer called "the fleet-footed") and a tortoise. Z proves that, if Achilles gives the tortoise a head start, he will never catch him. Yet another paradox designed to refute the possibility of motion purports to show that an arrow cannot move through the air because it must always, at any given instant, be at rest in a particular spot. The most complex of the paradoxes deals with two chariots moving in opposite directions in a stadium. It is discussed by Immerwahr (#711).

Zeno's technique of argumentation laid the foundation for dialectic, the process of reasoning which Socrates and Plato developed to its height. Later generations of thinkers recognized that something had to be wrong with Zeno's conclusions (cf. Lee #716), but they admired the logical rigor with which he defended his position.

ABRAHAM, W. E. "The Nature of Zeno's Argument against Plurality in DK 29 B 1." *Phron* 17(1972), 40-52. Translation of Z's argument as it appears in Simplicius; refutation of arguments against it in Aristotle and Gruenbaum; connection with Atomism. Paradoxes of motion depend on success of this argument.   **[688]**

ADAMS, J. Q. "Gruenbaum's Solution to Zeno's Paradoxes." *Phil*(Isrl) 3(1973), 43-50. Reply to #705.   **[689]**

AHMAD, A. "Change and Time." *PakPhJ* 11(1973), 74-107. Argues change comes instantaneously. "Movement" is a succession of instantaneous periods of rest. Time passes as a static quantity, not continuously. Such an interpretation of change and time solves Z's paradoxes.   **[690]**

ARSENIJEVIC, M. "Solution of the Staccato Version of the Achilles Paradox," in *Contemporary Yugoslav Philosophy*, ed. A. Pavkovic (Dordrecht, Netherlands: Kluwer, 1988), pp. 27-55. Survey of various proposed solutions. Though premises of paradox may be true *per se*, conclusion is not deducible from them.   **[691]**

BOOTH, N. B. "Two Points of Interpretation in Zeno." *JHS* 98(1978), 157-158. Phrase *tou prouchontos* in frag D-K 29 B 1 means "the one leading" or "the next in a sequence." Thus Z did not envision a division resulting in points without magnitude. His error in fourth paradox is result of unfamiliarity with relative motion.   **[692]**

BOSTOCK, D. "Aristotle, Zeno, and the Potential Infinite." *PAS* 73(1972-1973), 37-51. There is no reason why an infinite series cannot be completed unless the curve describing them is mathematically discontinuous.   **[693]**

BURKE, M. B. "The Infinitistic Thesis." *SJPh* 22(1984), 295-306. Aristotle's attempt to describe Z's concept of infinity as potential applies to processes better than to matter.   **[694]**

BUTLER, C. "Motion and Objective Contradictions." *AmPhQ* 18(1981), 131-139.
Defense of Z's refutation of motion in context of "radical event ontology" rather than
Parmenidean monism.   **[695]**

CHAMBERS, C. J. "Zeno of Elea and Bergson's Neglected Thesis." *JHPh* 12(1974), 63-
76. H. Bergson's secondary doctoral thesis, completed in 1889, upholds Z's paradoxes
against a Kantian view.   **[696]**

CHIHARA, C. S. "On the Possibility of Completing an Infinite Process." *PhR* 74(1965),
74-87. One argument advanced in favor of Z's Achilles paradox is that if Achilles could
catch tortoise, completing infinite process, then any being could. Analysis-engendered
concept of space and movement can show that argument's presuppositions about time
and space can be rejected without rejecting conclusion.   **[697]**

CORBETT, S. M. "Zeno's 'Achilles.' A Reply to John McKie." *Ph&PhenRes* 49(1988),
325-331. Reply to #724. "Achilles" paradox is not merely variant of another argument,
the "Dichotomy." In "Achilles" infinite series results from addition, in "Dichotomy" from
division.   **[698]**

DILLON, J. "More Evidence on Zeno of Elea?" *AGPh* 58(1976), 221-222. Passage in
Proclus' commentary on Plato's *Parm* may contain unrecognized frag of Z. **[699]**

———. "New Evidence on Zeno of Elea?" *AGPh* 56(1974), 127-131. A passage in
Proclus' commentary on Plato's *Parm* is actually from Z.   **[700]**

FARIS, J. A. "Zeno's Dichotomy and Achilles Paradoxes." *IrishPhJ* 3(1986), 3-26.
Though apparently different, these two paradoxes make same point about infinite divisibility of line.   **[701]**

FRAENKEL, H. "Zeno of Elea's Attacks on Plurality," in #301, pp. 102-142. It is
difficult to evaluate paradoxes of motion because we have them only as Aristotle preserved them. Z's attacks on plurality survive in his own words. They should be read as
serious arguments, not frivolous puzzles.   **[702]**

GORR, M. "Vlastos and the New Race Course Paradox." *AustlJPh* 54(1976), 244-249.
Vlastos' solution to race course paradox (#748) is shown to be inadequate. **[703]**

GRATTAN-GUINNESS, I. "Achilles is Still Running." *TPS* 10(1974), 8-16. Refutations
of Z's paradox are based on assumptions, such as uniform time, not shared by Z. Models
can be constructed in which Achilles paradox is valid.   **[704]**

GRUENBAUM, A. "Can An Infinitude of Operations Be Performed in a Finite Time?"
BritJPhSci 20(1969), 203-218. Qualified affirmative answer is given. Runner crossing
infinite number of points could rest in an infinity of decreasing pauses. **[705]**

———. *Modern Science and Zeno's Paradoxes.* Middleton, CT: Wesleyan Univ. Pr.,
1967. Three chapters. One deals with general problems of being and coming-into-being
raised by Z. Second shows that his paradoxes of motion can be resolved by emphasizing
sum of infinite sequence, not its discrete parts. Chapter three discusses Z's metrical

paradox of extension.   [706]

———. "Reply to J. Q. Adams' 'Gruenbaum's Solution to Zeno's Paradoxes'." *Phil*(Isrl) 3(1973), 51-57. Reply to Adams' critique (#689).   [707]

HAGER, P. "Russell and Zeno's Arrow Paradox." *Russell* 7(1987), 3-10. Reconstructs B. Russell's account of arrow paradox; argues that Russell was consistent in his various references to it. Reply to Vlastos (#745).   [708]

HAHN, R. "Continuity, Discontinuity, and Some Paradoxes of Motion. Zeno's Arguments in the Light of Quantum Mechanics." *SwPhSt* 7(1982), 115-123. Dichotomy and Achilles-Tortoise paradoxes fail because sum of convergent infinite series $(1/2 + 1/4 + 1/8 \ldots + 1/n)$ has been shown to be finite. Arrow paradox, however, is vindicated by quantum mechanics, which shows that minute particles act irrationally when disturbed by examination.   [709]

HARRISON, A. "Zeno's Paper Chase." *Mind* 76(1967), 568-575. Despite Aristotle's judgment, Achilles paradox is not just a version of Dichotomy. Paradox is designed to make a point not about infinity but about motion, time, and place.   [710]

IMMERWAHR, J. "An Interpretation of Zeno's Stadium Paradox." *Phron* 23(1978), 22-26. The paradox deals not with relative movement or indivisible units but with characteristics of the number zero.   [711]

KAISER, D. N. "Language and the 'Achilles Paradox'." *PhilMath* 5(1968), 11-23. Paradox cannot be solved mathematically, but Z has redefined some commonly used words. Normalizing usage of those terms can open a way to resolve paradox.   [712]

———. "Russell's Paradox and the Residual Achilles." *Apeir* 6 #1(1972), 39-48. B. Russell's discussion, in *Principles of Mathematics*, of Z's first paradox does not resolve difficulty.   [713]

KNORR, W. R. "Zeno's Paradoxes Still in Motion." *AncPh* 3(1983), 55-66. Review essay discussing R. Ferber's *Zenons Paradoxien der Bewegung und die Struktur von Raum und Zeit.*   [714]

LEAR, J. "A Note on Zeno's Arrow." *Phron* 26(1981), 91-104. Discussion of Aristotle's criticism in *Phys* 6.9. A key to Z's argument is to stress idea of present moment in time when the arrow occupies a space.   [715]

LEE, H. N. "Are Zeno's Paradoxes Based on a Mistake?" *Mind* 74(1965), 563-570. Z's mistake was to assume that infinite divisibility can exhaust a continuum. Work of Dedekind and Cantor has shown that irrationals are real numbers, but infinite divisibility as conceived by Z will not yield irrational numbers.   [716]

———. "Comment on 'The Infinitistic Thesis'." *SJPh* 23(1985), 399-400. Reply to M. B. Burke (#694). Z's paradoxes are empty because they ignore fact that every cut in a continuum inevitably produces a gap.   [717]

———. "Zeno Cannot Be Caught on His Own Racetrack." *Mind* 80(1971), 269. Reply to L. van Valen (#743).   [718]

LONGRIGG, J. "Zeno's Cosmology?" *CR* 22(1972), 170-171. Passage in Diogenes Laertius which attributes to Z belief in plurality of worlds may be based on passage in which Z attempted to refute Empedocles.   **[719]**

MABBETT, J. W. "Nagarjuna and Zeno on Motion." *PhE&W* 34(1984), 401-420. Discusses superficial resemblances between the two. Nagarjuna's thought was not mathematically based.   **[720]**

MAKIN, S. "Zeno on Plurality." *Phron* 27(1982), 223-238. Z's arguments against plurality rest on assumption that Being is homogeneous. If any divisibility is possible, it can go on infinitely. Thus, Being is indivisible.   **[721]**

MANSFELD, J. "Digging up a Paradox." *RhM* 125(1982), 1-24. Z's fourth paradox doesn't seem as humorous as the others. Part of problem is that Aristotle's refutation of it (*Phys* Z,9) disturbs text by adding a set of motionless bodies.   **[722]**

MATSON, W. I. "The Zeno of Plato and Tannery Vindicated." *ParPas* 43(1988), 312-336. Z did not think he had proved motion impossible. Paradoxes were merely designed to show that logic of Parmenides' opponents required them to deny motion.   **[723]**

McKIE, J. R. "The Persuasiveness of Zeno's Paradoxes." *Ph&PhenRes* 47(1987), 631-639. Paradoxes are persuasive because of conceptual and linguistic ambiguities inherent in them.   **[724]**

MUELLER, I. "Zeno's Paradox and Continuity." *Mind* 78(1969), 129-131. Reply to H. N. Lee (#716). Paradoxes are problematic only when lines or space are viewed mathematically and motion non-mathematically.   **[725]**

OWEN, G. E. L. "Zeno and the Mathematicians," in #301, pp. 143-165. Aristotle's failure to refute Z's concept of moments as extremely small periods of time led to his failure to deal adequately with acceleration.   **[726]**

PETERSON, S. "Zeno's Second Argument Against Plurality." *JHPh* 16(1978), 261-270. Somewhat technical reconstruction of premises on which Z's argument rested.   **[727]**

POZSGAY, L. J. "Zeno's Achilles Paradox." *ModSch* 43(1966), 375-395. Difficulties in Z's paradoxes of motion arise from our inability to imagine smooth continuous motion based on series of instanteous movements. Mathematics provides better solution than philosophy.   **[728]**

PRIOR, W. J. "Zeno's First Argument Concerning Plurality." *AGPh* 60(1978), 247-256. Reply to Solmsen (#740). Differences between Z and Parmenides demonstrate versatility of Eleatic argumentation.   **[729]**

QUAN, S. "The Solution of Zeno's First Paradox." *Mind* 77(1968), 206-221. Fallacy in paradox is that no effort is made to cross stadium in single movement. The halving which Z posits makes crossing stadium a series of discontinuous movements.   **[730]**

ROSSETTI, L. "The Rhetoric of Zeno's Paradoxes." *Ph&Rh* 21(1988), 145-152. Like Gorgias, Z offered so many paradoxes (perhaps 40) that no one could look too closely at any one; like Socrates he suggested that his argumentation was so simple any one could follow it; like Plato he claimed to be presenting straightforward arguments. [731]

SALMON, W. C. *Zeno's Paradoxes*. Indianapolis: Bobbs-Merrill, 1970. Collection of essays on individual paradoxes and on general problems which they raise. [732]

SEATON, R. "Zeno's Paradoxes. Iteration and Infinity." *Nat&Sys* 6(1984), 229-236. Applying model of computer program which can repeat series of steps *ad infinitum* gives new perspective on basic problem of Z's paradoxes. [733]

SHAMSI, F. A. "Victor Brochard on Zeno's Arguments Against Motion." *IndianPhQ* 15(1988), 1-18. Translation, with brief introduction, of article by Brochard, one of earliest writers to argue for validity of Z's paradoxes. [734]

SHERRY, D. M. "Zeno's Metrical Paradox Revisited." *PhiSci* 55(1988), 58-73. Despite Gruenbaum's claims, modern theory of measure cannot refute Z. [735]

SHIBLES, W. A. "Zeno: How to Become Turtled." *RCSF* 24(1969), 123-134. Z's paradoxes emphasize conceptual errors inherent in human language and abstract theories. What is true of world is not necessarily true of numbers and geometry, which do not designate real things. [736]

SIDERITS, M. "Zeno and Nagarjuna on Motion." *PhE&W* 26(1976), 281-300. The two philosophers conclude that no reasonable account of motion can be given. Z takes that to mean that motion cannot exist. Nagarjuna concludes that no account is possible because a limited description is being stretched too far. [737]

SKYRMS, B. "Zeno's Paradox of Measure," in *Physics, Philosophy and Psychoanalysis. Essays in Honor of Adolf Gruenbaum*, ed. R. S. Cohen and L. Laudan (Dordrecht, Netherlands: Reidel, 1983), pp. 223-254. Z's four paradoxes of motion are merely illustrations of his larger argument against plurality, which rests on paradox of measure. Work of modern mathematicians such as Cantor and Lebesque has provided basis for new approaches to paradox, but it remains unresolved. [738]

SMITH, J. W. "Zeno's Paradoxes." *ExplorKnowl* 2(1985), 1-12. Argues that paradoxes are valid arguments challenging basic ideas of reality. [739]

SOLMSEN, F. "The Tradition about Zeno of Elea Re-Examined." *Phron* 16(1971), 116-141. It is difficult to reconcile accounts of Z's teaching found in Plato's *Parm* and in Simplicius. Z may have been more independent of Parmenides than generally recognized. [740]

STOGRE, M. "Mathematics and the Paradoxes of Zeno." *ModSch* 45(1968), 313-319. Reply to Pozsgay. Solution must be philosophical, rather than mathematical. Z is replying to opponents' arguments, not asserting his own views as truth. [741]

VAN BENDEGEM, J. P. "Zeno's Paradoxes and the Tile Argument." *PhiSci* 54(1987), 295-302. Weyl's rejection of solution of Z's paradoxes does not apply if one stresses the non-zero width of a line. [742]

VAN VALEN, L. "Zeno and Continuity." *Mind* 77(1968), 429. Reply to H. N. Lee (#716). [743]

VLASTOS, G. "A Note on Zeno B 1," in #301, pp. 177-183. Reply to Fraenkel (#702).   [744]

———. "A Note on Zeno's Arrow." *Phron* 11(1966), 3-18. How Z arrived at this paradox can be understood when one distinguishes between individual instances and intervals (or sets of instances).   [745]

———. "Plato's Testimony Concerning Zeno of Elea." *JHS* 95(1975), 136-162. In several passages P presents Z or his teaching as if they are to be taken seriously. His portrayal in *Alcib* 119a as a Sophist teaching for pay is not historically accurate.   [746]

———. "A Zenonian Argument Against Plurality," in #41, pp. 119-144. From conclusions of previous argument Z deduces nullity of size, but involves himself in fallacy which appears to originate with him.   [747]

———. "Zeno's Race Course." *JHPh* 4(1966), 95-108. Race course paradox fails because the impossibility of completing an infinite series of acts in a finite period of time applies only to finite discrete state systems.   [748]

VON FRITZ, K. "Zeno of Elea in Plato's *Parmenides*," in *Serta Turyniana. Studies in Greek Literature and Palaeography in Honor of Alexander Turyn*, ed. J. L. Heller. (Urbana: Univ. of IL Pr.), 1974, pp. 329-341. Plato's picture of relationship between Parmenides and Z is not historically accurate, but ancient traditions connecting the two seem to have factual basis.   [749]

WEDEKING, G. A. "On a Finitist Solution to Some Zenonian Paradoxes." *Mind* 77(1968), 420-426. Effort to distinguish between a mathematical and a common-sense description of linear distances is invalid and cannot be used against Z.   [750]

WHITE, M. J. "Zeno's Arrow, Divisible Infinitesimals, and Chrysippus." *Phron* 27(1982), 239-254. New solution proposed to one of Z's paradoxes and discussion of an explanation of Chrysippus' views on divisibility that may explain puzzling remarks in Plutarch and Sextus Empiricus.   [751]

ZINKERNAGEL, P. "A Note on S. Quan 'The Solution of Zeno's First Paradox'." *Mind* 80(1971), 144. Reply to #730.   [752]

For related items see #2615

MELISSUS OF SAMOS (ca. 440 B. C.)

Melissus of Samos, an admiral who defeated the Athenians in a battle in 441, defended Parmenides' thought against its critics, most notably Empedocles and Leucippus. In a book, the title of which was either *On Nature* or *On Being*, he denied change, since it would mean that something which is passes away and something which was not comes into being. But Being cannot come from or pass into non-Being. Empty space — pure nothingness — is unthinkable and therefore cannot exist. Thus motion is impossible, because there is only undivided Being. M also rejected the evidence of the senses as illusory and deceptive. He went beyond Parmenides in asserting that the universe was physically infinite.

The dialectic of the Eleatic school, their insistence that reason provides the only accurate understanding of the world, even if it is in direct conflict with information received through the senses, paved the way for the relativism of the Sophists. But that same reliance upon logical reasoning, whatever the consequences, was also the forerunner of Platonic-Aristotelian logic.

BICKNELL, P. J. "Melissus' Way of Seeming? A Discussion Note." *Phron* 27(1982), 194-201. Passage in Pseudo-Plutarch *Stromateis* 11 is from M, who may have devoted part of his work to physics.   [753]

FROHN-VILLENEUVE, W. "Space, Time, and Change. Alexander's Interpretation of Melissus," in *Mélanges d'études anciennes offerts à Maurice Lebel*, ed. by J. B. Caron et al. (Quebec: Ed. du Sphinx, 1980), pp. 173-186. Examines importance of Peripatetic commentators as source of knowledge about Presocratics. Alexander of Aphrodisias may have derived his citations from M from a secondary source. M seems to have considered both space and time infinite, and change in Being impossible.   [754]

OBERTELLO, L. "Melissus of Samos and Plato on the Generation of the World." *Dion* 8(1984), 3-18. M held that everything exists eternally; thus the world has not had a generation.   [755]

For related items see #6109.

Chapter 7

THE PLURALISTS

The philosophers who came after the Eleatics, down to Plato and Aristotle, were concerned to show how change was possible. The first two to make the attempt are sometimes lumped together as the Pluralists, for each of them tried to explain change in terms of several ultimate principles. These two, Empedocles and Anaxagoras, will be examined separately below.

DE LEY, H. "Pangenesis versus Panspermia. Democritean Notes on Aristotle's *Generation of Animals.*" *Hermes* 108(1980), 129-153. Term *panspermia* probably originated with Plato. Aristotle read it into his interpretation of Democritus and Anaxagoras. [756]

MOURELATOS, A. P. D. "Quality, Structure, and Emergence in Later Pre-Socratic Philosophy." *PBACAPh* 2(1986), 127-194. Fifth-century Pluralists held that elements making up world are not subject to any kind of genesis when in combination. Explained emergence by preformation or illusion. [757]

WARDY, R. B. B. "Eleatic Pluralism." *AGPh* 70(1988), 125-146. Post-Eleatic philosophers did more than merely react against Eleatic monism, as most histories of philosophy suggest. [758]

EMPEDOCLES (ca. 494-434 B. C.)

The first of the Pluralists was Empedocles of Agrigentum, in Sicily. It is difficult to say when he was born. He lived around the middle of the fifth century B. C., during the time when Pericles was ruling Athens. He seems to have fused scientific and religious thought and left other people with the impression that he had performed miracles. He was a noble and reportedly refused the crown of his native city. He wrote two poems, *On Nature* and *Purifications*. The former is said to have been about two thousand lines long, of which about four hundred lines are extant. According to Diogenes Laertius, the *Purifications* was about three thousand lines long; only about five hundred lines have survived. E seems to have believed in the transmigration of souls. He also spoke of himself as a god. One legend has it that he jumped into the crater of Mt. Aetna in order to convince people that he had returned to his divine home. Timaeus, however, says that he went to the Peloponnesus and never returned. In short, we don't know how he died, though some modern scholars would argue for the volcano.

E did not so much produce a new philosophy as synthesize the thought of his predecessors. Parmenides had held that Being is, and that it is material. E adopted this idea and also the thought of Parmenides that being cannot arise and pass away. But, E goes further. Change, which Parmenides had dismissed as illusory, is too evident a fact to be summarily dismissed. He set out, then, to find a way to reconcile the unity of Being with the fact of change.

This he accomplished by saying that objects as wholes begin to be and pass away, but that they are composed of material particles, which are themselves indestructible. There is only a mingling and interchange of elements. Thales and Anaximenes, we should recall, held water and air to be the primary stuff. These elements changed into the other things in our world. But E says that one element cannot change into another. Therefore, there are four fundamental elements, from heaviest to lightest: earth, water, air, and fire. The four kinds of matter are unchangeable and ultimate particles, which form the concrete objects of the world by their mingling. Objects come to be by the mingling of the elements and pass away by their separation, but the elements are themselves unchangeable.

The Ionian philosophers who had first posited certain elements as the basis of the universe had not tried to explain the processes of Nature. Anaximenes assumed that air transforms itself into other kinds of matter through its own inherent power. But E goes a step further and postulates active forces, which he calls Love (Eros) and Strife (Eris), or Harmony and Discord. In spite of their names, though, the forces are conceived by E as physical and material. Love brings the particles of the four elements together and builds up the world. Strife causes the particles to separate and objects to cease to be.

The world process is cyclical for E. In the beginning the elements are mixed up together in a spherical shape, not separated out to form separate objects. In this primary stage, Love is the governing force. But Strife is around this sphere, and when it penetrates, the process of separation begins. In the end all the water particles, all the fire particles, and so on, are gathered together. Strife reigns, love having been driven out. But Love then begins to penetrate, and the process begins again. The world as we know it is in a halfway stage. Air was the first element to be separated. Then came fire. The earth and water are now being separated.

E made a more concerted effort than his predecessors to explain the process by which we obtain knowledge. Every thing gives off, through its pores, effluvia which may be understood as waves or images. Things made of earth give off earthy effluvia. The earth in us responds to these earthy waves and we perceive the image of the thing creating them.

His concept of the soul, set forth in his *Purifications*, is basically Orphic-Pythagorean. The human *daimon* is a spirit banished from the divine abode because of its faults. It has fallen into a body and become enmeshed in a cycle of rebirths, which will last thirty thousand years. E himself said, "For by now I have been born as a boy, girl, plant, bird, and dumb sea-fish." The *daimon* must be purified by the rules given in his poem before it can return to its divine status.

One of E's most important contributions to philosophy is his emphasis on the senses as assisting reason, not hindering it as Parmenides and Zeno maintained.

But he is no empiricist. The data obtained by the senses must be analyzed by a sound rational method.

ANDRIOPOULOS, D. Z. "Empedocles' Theory of Perception." *Platon* 24(1972), 290-298. Images are composed of same four elements as other objects. One's perception depends on predominance of one element in thing being perceived.   **[759]**

BARNES, H. E. "Unity in the Thought of Empedocles." *CJ* 63(1967), 18-23. *Purifications* and *On Nature* should be seen as complementary. Any structures composed of elements — including *theos* and *daimon* — eventually perish, but elements themselves survive.   **[760]**

BICKNELL, P. J. "The Shape of the Cosmos in Empedocles." *ParPas* 23(1968), 118-119. E derived ideas on shape of cosmos from empirical data, not Orphism.   **[761]**

BOOTH, N. B. "A Mistake to be Avoided in the Interpretation of Empedocles Fr. 100." *JHS* 96(1976), 147-148. Reply to Furley (#769) and O'Brien (#787). In clepsydra simile, water parallels air and air, blood.   **[762]**

————. cf. #270.

BROWN, G. "The Cosmological Theory of Empedocles." *Apeir* 18(1984), 97-101. E thought life should be represented as linear, not a cycle.   **[763]**

CHITWOOD, A. "The Death of Empedocles." *AJPh* 107(1986), 175-191. Traditional story that E leapt into Mt. Aetna is to be preferred.   **[764]**

DARCUS, S. M. "*Daimon* Parallels the Holy *Phren* in Empedocles." *Phron* 22(1977), 175-190. "Holy *phren*" of fragment 134 is not an attribute of God; it *is* God, who initiates Love/Strife cycle. On human level *daimon* is analogous to *phren*.   **[765]**

DAVIES, C. "Empedocles of Acragas." *HT* 21(1971), 708-714. Non-specialist survey of life and teachings.   **[766]**

DE LEY, H. "Empedocles' Sexual Theory. A Note on Fragment B63." *AC* 47(1978), 153-162. His thought is not preformationist, as Aristotle took it; can be characterized as *epigenesis*.   **[767]**

FESHBACH, S. "Empedocles: The Phenomenology of the Four Elements in Literature," in *Analecta Husserliana*, ed. A. T. Tymieniecka (Dordrecht, Netherlands: Kluwer, 1988), pp. 9-63. Four elements are interpreted in terms of Husserl's "natural attitude." Explores motif's use in various European authors, from Homer to modern times. **[768]**

FURLEY, D. J. "Empedocles and the Clepsydra," in #301, pp. 265-274. Clepsydra is used as an analogy, not scientific explanation of phenomenon.   **[769]**

————. cf. Lucretius #6085.

GRAHAM, D. W. "Symmetry in the Empedoclean Cycle." *CQ* 38(1988), 297-312. Reply to Long #778. E's cosmic cycle entails a double creation.   **[770]**

HERSHBELL, J. "Empedoclean Influences on the *Timaeus*." *Phoenix* 28(1974), 145-166. Plato's dialogue contains no direct references or quotations from E, but does reflect his thought on mixture.   **[771]**

————. "Empedocles' Oral Style." *CJ* 63(1968), 351-357. Vocabulary and formulaic character of language suggest that E composed his poems for oral recitation.   **[772]**

————. "Hesiod and Empedocles." *CJ* 65(1970), 145-161. Analysis of H's influence on E in vocabulary and style, major themes, and subsidiary themes. Ideas of roots and Love/Strife have Hesiodic origins.   **[773]**

————. "Hippolytus' *Elenchos* as a Source for Empedocles Re-Examined." *Phron* 18(1973), 97-114; 187-203. H is generally accurate source. Probably drew his Empedoclean quotations from Stoic handbook.   **[774]**

KAHN, C. H. "Religion and Natural Philosophy in Empedocles' Doctrine of the Soul," in #41, pp. 3-38; also in #363, pp. 426-456. Principle unifying E's thought is harmony and life opposed to discord and death. He regarded cosmos as divine. His thought became increasingly spiritual.   **[775]**

LaCROCE, E. "Empedocles' *Sphairos* and Parmenidean Legacy." *Platon* 32-33(1980-81), 114-122. P's Being is replaced in E's system by infinite sphere, not by elements. **[776]**

LAMBRIDIS, H. *Empedocles. A Philosophical Investigation*, with a prefatory essay "Empedocles and T. S. Eliot," by M. McLuhan. University, AL: Univ of AL Pr., 1976. Biography of E, translation of all extant frags, study of his theory of knowledge, biology, cosmology. Reviewers noted inadequate use of recent work on E.   **[777]**

LONG, A. A. "Empedocles' Cycle in the 'Sixties," in #363, pp. 397-425. Review for non-specialists of scholarly opinion during the 1960's on E's cosmology, especially the question of world cycles.   **[778]**

————. "Thinking and Sense-Perception in Empedocles. Mysticism or Materialism?" *CQ* 16(1966), 256-276. Analysis of frags pertaining to these subjects. Discusses relationship of *Purifications* (on religious imagination) to *On Nature*. Sees E's physical and religious doctrines as incompatible.   **[779]**

LONGRIGG, J. "Empedocles's Fertile Fish." *JHS* 94(1974), 173-174. Reply to D. O'Brien (#787). Fertility of fish reveals activity of Eros among them.   **[780]**

————. "Empedocles' Fiery Fish." *JWI* 28(1965), 314-315. Lungs serve to cool inside of body. In fish, gills serve function of lungs. Thus fish must be fiery. Living in water cools their natural heat.   **[781]**

————. "Empedocles, Juno, and *De natura deorum* II.66." *CR* 24(1974), 173. Passage from Cicero's dialogue shows that E identified Aer with Hera.   **[782]**

————. "The 'Roots of All Things'." *Isis* 67(1976), 420-438. Idea of four elements perhaps reflected popular concept of E's day. He does not seem to have thought elements infinitely divisible.   **[783]**

———. cf. #719 and #6108.

MANSFELD, J. "Ambiguity in Empedocles B 17,3-5: A Suggestion." *Phron* 17(1972), 17-39. For E *genesis* is not true birth but combination of elements which are without beginning. Frag. opposes Parmenides' ontology.   **[784]**

———. cf. #6650.

MILLERD, C. E. *On the Interpretation of Empedocles.* New York: Garland, 1980; rprt. Studies his life and character, relations to other thinkers, literary style; analyzes such facets of his thought as elements, mixture, world-cycle.   **[785]**

MINAR, E. L., Jr. "Cosmic Periods in the Philosophy of Empedocles," in #41, pp. 39-58. It is unclear whether E conceives of two or four phases in constant struggle between Love/Strife. Should be possible to have two "golden ages," one just before everything combines into sphere at Love's ascendancy, other just after things begin to break apart but before Strife dominates.   **[786]**

O'BRIEN, D. "The Effect of a Simile. Empedocles' Theories of Seeing and Breathing." *JHS* 90(1970), 140-179. Aristotle's account of E's theories of vision and respiration are his interpretation of similes of lantern and clepsydra. Plato extended meaning of similes in *Tim.*   **[787]**

———. "Empedocles' Cosmic Cycle." *CQ* 17(1967), 29-40. Love's motion is toward and away from center of world. It is confined there when Strife is dominant. Creative/destructive activities of Love/Strife are symmetrical, opposite. Only at point of total unity is world at rest.   **[788]**

———. *Empedocles' Cosmic Cycle. A Reconstruction from the Fragments and Secondary Sources.* Cambridge Univ. Pr., 1969. Defense of traditional view of dual cosmogony or four-stage interpretation of E's thought. Interprets Love as Rest/Unity and Strife as Movement/Plurality and argues this is what E meant by those terms. 60-page bibliography with some annotations.   **[789]**

———. cf. #822.

OSBORNE, C. "Empedocles Recycled." *CQ* 37(1987), 24-50. It is possible that all E's extant frags come from one poem. This would require that cycles of *daimones* and elements be linked and that Love/Strife relationship be re-examined.   **[790]**

OWENS, J. "Aristotle on Empedocles Fr. 8," in #1287, pp. 87-100. Aristotle took *physis* in this frag to mean form or substance. To Empedocles it probably meant "birth," but Aristotle could not have seen it that way.   **[791]**

PANAGIOTOU, S. "Empedocles on his Own Divinity." *Mnem* 36(1983), 276-285. Reply to a point raised by van der Ben (#803). E's reference to himself as *theos* is not ironic or a description of public perception.   **[792]**

PRIER, R. A. "Empedocles 17,1-13. A Suggested Reconstruction and Interpretation."

Platon 28(1976), 214-223. Replacing lines 17.9-10 with 26.7 unifies this passage logically and grammatically, producing triadic description of cosmos. [793]

———. cf. #659.

SIDER, D. "Empedocles B96 (462 Bollack) and the Poetry of Adhesion." *Mnem* 37(1984), 14-24. Suggested emendations for lines in frag, with some discussion of E's theory of pores. [794]

———. "Empedocles' *Persika.*" *AncPh* 2(1982), 76-78. Frag B 34 is from poem on Persian wars, not *Physika.* [795]

SOLMSEN, F. "Empedocles' Hymn to Apollo." *Phron* 25(1980), 219-227. Frags B 131-134 do not fit well into *Peri physeos* or *Katharmoi.* May have come from hymn in which E identified Apollo with divine, non-physical power, akin to Platonic world-soul. [796]

———. "Eternal and Temporary Beings in Empedocles' Physical Poem." *AGPh* 57(1975), 123-145. For E, both eternal and living creatures come into being and pass away. The eternal is not a static quantity but participates in being/change. [797]

———. "Love and Strife in Empedocles' Cosmology." *Phron* 10(1965), 109-148. E's cosmogony is not double. Universe was created by Strife. In response, Love created living things. Appendix discusses order of fragments. [798]

———. "*Zoros* in Empedocles." *CR* 17(1967), 245-246. Comparative form of adjective in frag B 35,15 may mean "more mixed." [799]

SULLIVAN, S. D. "The Nature of *Phren* in Empedocles," in *Studi di filosofia preplatonica,* ed. by M. Capasso et al. (Naples: Bibliopolis, 1985), pp. 119-136. *Phren* appears to be location where perceptions are received and truth discerned. It can be deceived or fail to apprehend. Divine principle is also described as a *phren* moving through the cosmos. [800]

TIGNER, S. S. "Empedocles' Twirled Ladle and the Vortex-Supported Earth." *Isis* 65(1974), 433-447. Aristotle's report (*De caelo* 2.13-14) of E's demonstration of how vortex supports earth is probably inaccurate. [801]

VAN DER BEN, N. "Empedocles' Fragments 8, 9, 10 DK." *Phron* 23(1978), 197-215. Suggestions for emending and interpreting the frags, analyzing how they are quoted, structure of the argument and meaning of some words, particularly *physis*, which seems never to mean "coming-to-be." [802]

———. *The Proem of Empedocles' Peri Physios. Towards a New Edition of All the Fragments.* Amsterdam: Gruener, 1975. Thirty-one frags edited. Introduction and translation. [803]

WEST, M. L. "*Zoros* in Empedocles." *CR* 16(1966), 135-136. Word should be translated "pure," not "mixed" or "unmixed." [804]

WILFORD, F. "Embryological Analogies in Empedocles' Cosmogony." *Phron* 13(1968), 108-118. E buttressed his cosmogony with analogies from human development. Comparison of Hippocratic theory on embryo's breathing with two frags of E.   [805]

WORTHEN, T. D. "Pneumatic Action in the Klepsydra and Empedocles' Account of Breathing." *Isis* 61(1970), 520-530. Ancient water-clocks used syphons to maintain constant water pressure and steady running speed. E compares alternating rhythm of breathing to pneumatic action of clock.   [806]

WRIGHT, M. R., ed. *Empedocles: The Extant Fragments*. New Haven, CT: Yale Univ. Pr., 1981. Reorders frags, provides commentary/discussion of E's life, writings, and various textual matters. Emphasizes Pythagorean influence. History of ideas approach, rather than philosophical analysis.   [807]

For related items see #673, #969, #6061, #6135

ANAXAGORAS (ca. 500-428 B. C.)

A was born at Clazomenae in Asia Minor about 500 B. C. Although a Greek, he was probably a Persian citizen, since his city had been subjugated after the Ionian Revolt. He came to Athens in 480, with the invading Persian army, according to one source. Whatever his origins, he was the first philosopher to settle in Athens and became the teacher of Pericles. That association caused difficulties for him. Unable to attack Pericles directly, his political enemies brought charges of various sorts against friends of his. A was tried for "Medism" and impiety. The former accusation implied that he favored the Persians; it may have arisen from some Oriental influences in his thought.

Though he was a contemporary of Socrates, A is a "presocratic" philosopher in that he was concerned with the origin and nature of the world. He reached some conclusions that were startling for his time, and for any time before the modern era. The Nile River, he said, overflows each spring because of snow melting in the interior of Africa. Ridiculous, said Herodotus (2.22), voicing the standard wisdom of the day: "Since it runs from a very hot to a colder region, how can it flow from snow? Many reasons will readily occur to men of good understanding to show the improbability of its flowing from snow." Not until explorer Richard Burton reached the source of the Nile in the late nineteenth century was A vindicated.

He observed the heavens, too. The moon, he taught, is made of earth and the patterns on its face are caused by mountains and valleys. The sun is a red-hot stone (no one is infallible), and meteorites are not sent by the gods. They are simply chunks of rock that fall from the sky. Such ideas were the basis of the charge of impiety mentioned earlier. His teaching is difficult to assess because so little of it survives and that bit is written in a style "concentrated and compact, without long reasoning." He seems to have written only one book. The extant fragments from it total three and a half pages in a standard printed text. A agrees with Parmenides that Being is unchangeable and neither comes to be nor passes away. But he does not agree with Empedocles that the four elements are the basic stuff. He felt that "hair could not come from that which was not hair, nor flesh from that which was not flesh." He taught that "in everything there is a portion of everything."

In the beginning, A says, particles of all kinds, which he called "seeds" (*spermata*) were mingled together. The objects of sense experience — grass, rocks, etc. — arose when ultimate particles had been brought together so that in the resulting object particles of a certain kind predominated. If, for instance, particles form grass, there are particles of every kind of object in the universe in that grass, but the grass particles predominate. Everything which has parts qualitatively the same as the whole is ultimate and underived. For example, if we cut a piece of gold in two, it is still gold, and is thus underived. But if we cut a dog in half, it is not two equal dogs, and is thus not ultimate.

There is an apparent contradiction between this second principle, which is called homoeomereity (a substance consists only of parts like the whole and like one another) and the idea that "in everything there is a portion of everything." How, or if, A resolved this inconsistency, we cannot tell from our scanty sources.

So far his philosophy is only a variant form of Empedocles'. But when we come to the question of the force responsible for the forming of things out of the first mass, we arrive at A's unique contribution to philosophy. Instead of Love and Hate, A introduces the principle of *Nous* or Mind as the moving force behind the universe. "With A a light, if still a weak one, begins to dawn," Hegel said. A said a great deal about Nous:

Nous has power over all things that have life, both greater and smaller. It had power over the whole revolution, so that it began to revolve at the start . . . and Nous set in order all things that were to be . . . it is infinite and self-ruled, and is mixed with nothing, but is alone, itself by itself.

Nous is present in all things — men, animals, and plants — and is the same in all. Differences between objects are due, then, not to essential differences between their souls, but to differences between their bodies.

Nous is not to be thought of as creating matter. Matter is eternal, and the function of Nous seems to be to set the rotary motion or vortex going in part of the original mixed mass, the action of the vortex itself, as it spreads, accounting for the subsequent motion. Aristotle thus said that Anaxagoras used Nous as a *deus ex machina* to account for the formation of the world, resorting to it only when he could find nothing else. Though he did fail to make full use of the it, A must be credited with the introduction of a principle possessed of the greatest importance for the development of western philosophy.

BICKNELL, P. J. "Did Anaxagoras Observe a Sunspot in 467 B. C.?" *Isis* 59(1968), 87-90. A's observation of a sunspot may be connected to his prediction that a body would fall from sun.   [808]

CLEVE, F. M. *The Philosophy of Anaxagoras.* The Hague: Nijhoff, 1973; rprt. Attempts to go beyond textual concerns to reconstruct A's thought under several headings: elements and nous; primordial condition of the world and creation of cosmos by differentiation and rotation; bodies and souls; infinity of space and time.   [809]

CORNFORD, F. M. "Anaxagoras' Theory of Matter," in #301, pp. 275-322; also in #53, pp. 144-173. The two principles on which A's theory of matter rests (homoeomereity and "a part of everything is in everything") nccd not be contradictory. He intended to deny that anything could come from what was not. Frag 17 seems to mean that there was an original plurality of unalterable things, which were separated by motion, which is not change.   **[810]**

FERGUSON, J. "*Dinos* on the Stage." *CJ* 68(1973), 377-380. Aristophanes and Euripides show the influence of Anaxagoras in their use of this word.   **[811]**

FURLEY, D. J. "Anaxagoras in Response to Parmenides," in #1287, pp. 61-85. A adheres to P's concept of Being more rigidly than other pluralists.   **[812]**

HERSHBELL, J. "Plutarch and Anaxagoras." *ICS* 7(1982), 141-158. Survey of Plutarch's sources for A and effect Plutarch's Platonism had on his recording of information.   **[813]**

KEMBER, O. "Anaxagoras' Theory of Sex Differentiation and Heredity." *Phron* 18(1973), 1-14. Seed is produced by both parents. Gender is determined by whether seed is placed on right or left side of uterus. Proportion of seed given by each parent determines hereditary factors.   **[814]**

KERFERD, G. B. "Anaxagoras and the Concept of Matter Before Aristotle." *BJRL* 52(1969), 129-143. Anaxagoras' views are not logically inconsistent. They share some characteristics of modern phenomenalism.   **[815]**

KONSTAN, D. "Anaxagoras on Bigger and Smaller," in *Studi di filosofia preplatonica*, ed. by M. Capasso et al. (Naples: Bibliopolis, 1985), pp. 137-157. From his theory that things may be indefinitely larger A seems to have reasoned that things could also be indefinitely smaller: "never a least, always a lesser."   **[816]**

MANN, W. E. "Anaxagoras and the Homoiomere." *Phron* 25(1980), 228-249. Discussion of works by Furley (#812) and Schofield (#829).   **[817]**

MANSFELD, J. "Anaxagoras' Other World." *Phron* 25(1980), 1-4. In frag 4 A describes infinity of infinitely small worlds.   **[818]**

———. "The Chronology of Anaxagoras' Athenian Period and the Date of His Trial, I." *Mnem* 22(1979), 36-69. A spent about twenty years in Athens, arriving in 456/5. **[819]**

———. "The Chronology of Anaxagoras' Athenian Period, II: The Plot against Pericles and His Associates." *Mnem* 23(1980), 17-95. A's trial probably took place in 437-436. His book was published around 440.   **[820]**

MASIELLO, R. J. "A Note on Aristotle's Homoemery and the Fragments of Anaxagoras." *ModSch* 46(1969), 135-140. Aristotle is not inaccurate when he calls Anaxagoras' basic particle a homoemery. All he means by the term is "similar part," which is consistent with Anaxagoras' view of the nature of matter.   **[821]**

O'BRIEN, D. "The Relation of Anaxagoras and Empedocles." *JHS* 88(1968), 93-113. Examination of doxographic evidence (Aristotle, Plutarch et al.) and of their theories of vision suggests that A wrote first. E was influenced by him. **[822]**

PAXSON, T. D. "The Holism of Anaxagoras." *Apeir* 17(1983), 85-91. A did not postulate the existence of infinitely many primary substances. His view is actually holistic, with substances within a plenum separated out by *nous*. **[823]**

POTTS, R. "Anaxagoras' Cosmogony." *Apeir* 18(1984), 90-96. A's system is descriptive, not analytic, circular and regressive, yet reasonable and scientific in its denial of a place for the gods. He works backward from the world as it appears to him. **[824]**

REESOR, M. E. "The Problem of Anaxagoras," in #41, pp. 81-88. A had to answer question of whether sensible objects could be equated with being and meet Parmenides' contention that being was not divisible and Protagoras' argument that opposites and qualities were relations. **[825]**

REEVE, C. D. C. "Anaxagorean Panspermism." *AncPh* 1(1981), 89-108. A came closer to accepting Parmenides' denial of non-being than any other Pluralist philosopher. His doctrine of a universal mixture provides better understanding of infinity than other Presocratics achieved. **[826]**

SCHOFIELD, M. "Doxographica Anaxagorea." *Hermes* 103(1975), 1-24. Several writers cite A as deriving his theory of panspermism from observations of nutrition and growth in humans. Their information is derived from Theophrastus and Aristotle. **[827]**

——. *An Essay on Anaxagoras.* Cambridge Univ. Pr., 1980. Points out difficulty of knowing what A thought, due to fragmentary sources and ambiguous nature of much that does survive. Distrusts doxographic matter. **[828]**

SEIDEL, G. J. "Anaxagoras and Hal." *PhT* 29(1985), 319-325. A's model for intelligence, Nous, is closer to modern approaches to the subject than Democritus' mechanistic model. **[829]**

SIDER, D. "Anaxagoras on the Size of the Sun." *CPh* 68(1973), 128-129. A based his view of sun as larger than Peloponnese on his understanding of perspective. **[830]**

——. *The Fragments of Anaxagoras*, ed. with introd. and commentary. Meisenheim am Glan, Ger.: Hain, 1981. Revised text of quotations attributed to A, with translation and commentary. Introduction discusses problems of A's chronology, number of writings, and order of frags. **[831]**

——. "A Note on Anaxagoras Fr. 1." *AGPh* 55(1973), 249-251. Proposed translation of passage. Its meaning depends on how *kateichen* is translated. **[832]**

SILVESTRE, M. L. "*Nous*, the Concept of Ultimate Reality and Meaning in Anaxagoras." *UltR&M* 12(1989), 248-255. A is the first to introduce a meaningful concept of an organizing principle in the cosmos. **[833]**

STEWART, D. J. "*Nous* in Aristophanes." *CJ* 63(1968), 253-255. Several occurences of *nous* in comic poet may be deliberate allusions to Anaxagoras. **[834]**

STOKES, M. C. "Anaxagoras, I: Anaxagoras' Theory of Matter." *AGPh* 47(1965), 1-19.

Analysis of several frags indicates that the traditional view of A's theory is valid. Certain contradictions cannot be resolved.   [835]

———. "On Anaxagoras, II: The Order of Cosmogony." *AGPh* 47(1965), 217-250. Order is: Earth, Sun (and other stars?), Ocean. Testimonies of Hippolytus and Simplicius are evaluated.   [836]

STRANG, C. "The Physical Theory of Anaxagoras," in #301, pp. 361-380. Understanding A's physical theory requires distinction between common substances (visible to the sense) and elemental ones (which cannot be isolated). Term *homoiomere* blurs distinction between the two.   [837]

TEODORSSON, S. T. *Anaxagoras' Theory of Matter.* Goeteborg, Sweden: Acta Univ. Gothoburgensis, 1982. Surveys his life and doctrines. Discusses various critical opinions on him, from late nineteenth century to 1980's. Teodorsson sees A as more closely akin to Eleatics than to Materialists. Appendix gives frags with English translation, brief bibliography.   [838]

THOREN, V. G. "Anaxagoras, Eudoxus, and the Regression of the Lunar Nodes." *JHistAstron* 2(1971), 23-28. A was first to explain moon's phases and to try to explain eclipses. Academic mathematician Eudoxus built on his theories.   [839]

TIGNER, S. S. "Stars, Unseen Bodies and the Extent of the Earth in Anaxagoras' Cosmogony. Three Problems and Their Simultaneous Solution," in #48, pp. 330-335. If one assumes that edge of disk of earth touches the cosmic whirl, stars can be seen as rocks picked up by the whirl and spun ever faster and higher. Until they burst into flame they are "unseen" bodies which cause lunar eclipses.   [840]

VLASTOS, G. "One World or Many in Anaxagoras?" in #301, pp. 354-360. A refers to "another" world in only one text, which need not be taken to refer literally to another *kosmos.*   [841]

———. "The Physical Theory of Anaxagoras," in #301, pp. 323-353. The key term is "seed," which contains the potentiality to become anything.   [842]

WARDEN, J. R. "The Mind of Zeus." *JHI* 32(1971), 3-14. *Nous*, referred to in frag B12 D-K, can be traced back to Homer's *Iliad* 16.688.   [843]

For related items see #1935, #2633, #6058, #6122.

Chapter 8

THE ATOMISTS

We turn now to the last attempt in Presocratic times to answer the question, Of what is the world made? This answer is given by the Atomists. The founder of this school was Leucippus of Miletus. It is not possible to fix his dates; indeed, there is some debate as to whether he ever lived. But it does seem that he did, and probably around 450-430. His work is parodied in Aristophanes' *Clouds*, which was written in 423 B. C., so he must have lived a few years before that. Diogenes Laertius tells us that L was a student of Zeno, who flourished around the middle of the fifth century.

It appears that the *Great Diakosmos*, which was later incorporated in the work of Democritus (460-370 B. C.), was really the work of L. The Democritean body of literature is like the Pythagorean or Hippocritean corpora in that we will never be able to distinguish individual authors of the component parts. The whole corpus is the work of a school. In discussing Atomist philosophy, then, we cannot distinguish between what is due to L and what to D. For that reason, we will not attempt to create separate bibliographies. D does seem to have elaborated the atomist philosophy and extended it to a theory of human conduct. This ethic was hedonistic, i. e., seeing happiness as the goal of human endeavor. But the full development of an "Atomist ethic" had to await Epicurus, and we will discuss it under that heading.

Atomist philosophy is really the logical development of Empedocles' thought. Empedocles had tried to reconcile Parmenides' principle of the impossibility of change with the very obvious fact of change. Empedocles posited the four elements as the basis of Being. He did not, though, really work out his doctrine of particles, nor did he carry the quantitative explanation of qualitative differences to its logical conclusion. Moreover, Empedocles' forces, Love and Strife, were metaphorical devices which would have to be eliminated in a thoroughgoing mechanical philosophy. This is what the Atomists did.

According to L and D there are an infinite number of indivisible units, called atoms (from the Greek word *atomos*, meaning "uncuttable"). Because of their small size, they are imperceptible. The atoms differ in size and shape, and have no quality save that of solidity. They are not particles of any element, as in Empedocles' or Anaxagoras' systems. They are simply atoms. These atoms are infinite in number and move in the void or space. We should note here that Parmenides had denied the reality of space. The Pythagoreans had admitted a void to keep their units apart, but they identified it with atmospheric air. Leucippus, however, affirmed the existence of space and its non-reality, meaning by non-reality non-corporeity. This is what he meant when he said that what is not is just as real as what is. Space, or the void, is not material or corporeal, but it is as real as body. The original Atomists did not assign weight as one of the qualities of atoms. Aristotle says that they accounted for movement of the atoms in the same way that sunbeams move in all directions even when there is no wind.

In whatever way the atoms originally moved in the void, at some point collisions between atoms occurred, and some of them became entangled together. (They have different shapes; some have hooks, others grooves.) In this way the vortex movement began, and the world began to be formed. It is at once noticeable that neither Empedocles' Love and Strife nor the Nous of Anaxagoras appear in Atomist philosophy. L evidently did not consider any moving force to be a necessary hypothesis. The vortex movement brings together atoms of the same size and shape, much like sifting rocks. In this way the four elements are formed. The Atomists did not deny the existence of gods, however. D thought that the dreams or visions which people have are the images emitted by these superhuman beings and received by our souls.

D's work covered much more than physics. The sixty titles known to us range over ethics, mathematics, biology, theories of perception, and a variety of other topics. He wrote an account of the origins of civilization, in which he maintained that people had developed language out of necessity, modeled tools on the movements of animals, and, with the aid of fire, advanced beyond an animalistic level of existence.

D exhibits the most advanced concept of the soul of any philosopher to that time. The soul is composed of small, smooth atoms scattered throughout the body. They are most like air and play a role in perception. Perception is possible because any object gives off images of itself which travel through the air until they meet images given off by our eyes. Each kind of atom in one "recognizes" similar atoms in the other image. Much debate has gone on over the details of this theory.

This, then, represents the climax of pre-Socratic philosophy, at least of that type of philosophy which deals with the nature of reality. The various theories proposed and studied to this point were attempts to answer, without resort to mythology or divine intervention, the questions raised by observation of the world in which these thinkers lived.

AVOTINS, I. "Alexander of Aphrodisias on Vision in the Atomists." *CQ* 30(1980), 429-454. Text, translation and discussion of two passages in which A provides evidence on theory of *eidola* proposed by Democritus, Epicurus, and Lucretius.   **[844]**

BALDES, R. W. "Democritus on Empirical Knowledge. Reflections on DK 68B25 and on Aristotle, *Metaphysics* 4.5." *AncW* 4(1981), 17-34. For D empirical statements are true. Ontological explanations can be based on them.   **[845]**

———. "Democritus on Perception of Size and Distance (Theophrastus *De sensibus* 54)." *CB* 51(1975), 42-44. D apparently thought image of object was originally same size as object but was made smaller by passing through air.   **[846]**

———. "Democritus on the Nature and Perception of Black and White." *Phron* 23(1978),

87-100. Re-evaluation of nature of visual perception and of Theophrastus' remarks on D shows the latter's theory was coherent. [847]

———. "Democritus on Visual Perception: Two Theories or One." *Phron* 20(1975), 93-105. Accounts Theophrastus and Aristotle give of D's theory of rays emitted by objects and by the need are not contradictory. D apparently taught that two rays met immediately in front of pupil of eye. [848]

———. "Divisibility and Division in Democritus." *Apeir* 12 #1(1978), 1-12. While atom is physically and ontologically indivisible, D admits it is conceptually divisible. Against Zeno, he thought an object as it appears can be divided, but that is not the real object. [849]

———. "Subjectivism and Objectively True Observation Statements in Democritus." *AncW* 1(1978), 89-95. D conceded that statements based on observation can be objectively true, within limits. [850]

———. "Theophrastus' Witness to Democritus on Perception by Similars and Contraries." *Apeir* 10 #1(1976), 42-48. In *De sensibus* 49 Theophrastus reports that D did not make clear whether he thought perception occurs through contact with similars or contraries. [851]

BICKNELL, P. J. "Demokritos' Parapsychology Again." *REG* 83(1970), 301-304. Continuation of following item. Examines concept of *nous* in D and its connection with apparent cases of precognition by telepathy. [852]

———. "Demokritos' Theory of Precognition." *REG* 82(1969), 318-326. D admitted prescience of events. People intending to do something give off telepathic messages about their intentions. [853]

———. "Kosmos-sized Atoms in Demokritos." *Apeir* 15(1981), 138-139. Frag DK 68 A 47 can be read to mean that an atom could be as large as a cosmos. It should be taken to mean, however, that a cosmos no larger than a single atom could exist, composed of tiny atoms. [854]

———. "The Seat of the Mind in Demokritos." *Eranos* 66(1968), 10-23. Mind resides in no definite place in body. Spherical atoms making it up are scattered throughout body. [855]

BODEUS, R. "An Iranian Profile of Democritus." *JIES* 2(1974), 63-69. D's lost *Tritogeneia*, which divided ethics into good thinking, speaking, and acting, was probably influenced by Iranian thought on those subjects. [856]

BURKERT, W. "Air-Imprints or *Eidola*. Democritus' Aetiology of Vision." *ICS* 2(1977), 97-109. What may appear to be contradictions in D's theory of vision are developments over time and explanations for physical vision (air-imprints) and parapsychological "vision" (*eidola*). [857]

COLE, T. *Democritus and the Sources of Greek Anthropology.* Cleveland, OH: Case Western Reserve Univ. Pr., 1967. Sees D as originator of Greek speculation about origin and development of human society and technology. Examines later writers who drew from D.   [858]

COSMOPOULOS, A. "Democritian Education. The Way to Happiness through Difficulties." *ZAnt* 27(1977), 337-341. Goal of education is goodness, harmony and justice. Best way to reach goal is to surmount difficulties.   [859]

DE LEY, H. "Democritus and Leucippus. Two Notes on Ancient Atomism." *AC* 27(1968), 620-633. D was approximately same age as Socrates, though he began his activity before Plato's teacher. Historicity of L is probable, though Aristotle does not know his work directly.   [860]

——. cf. #756.

EDMUNDS, L. "Necessity, Chance, and Freedom in the Early Atomists." *Phoenix* 26(1972), 342-357. The "whirl" need not be equated with necessity; it is one possible type of motion. Idea that Atomists believed in chance arises from Aristotle's restatement of their views to suit his purposes in *Phys* 2.4.   [861]

FERGUSON, J. "On the Date of Democritus." *SO* 40(1965), 17-26. Born in 459 B. C. *Mikros Diakosmos* was written in 405. By early fourth century he was concentrating on ethical problems.   [862]

——. cf. 2839.

FERWERDA, R. "Democritus and Plato." *Mnem* 25(1972), 337-378. Opposition between the two is not as strong as sometimes thought. In later dialogues P integrates some aspects of Pluralist and Atomist thought into his own system.   [863]

FOLSE, H. J. "A Reinterpretation of Democritean Atomism." *M&W* 9(1976), 393-417. To reconcile Atomism and Eleaticism, atoms must not be seen as material bodies[864]

FURLEY, D. "The Greek Theory of the Infinite Universe." *JHI* 42(1981), 571-586. Dominant Platonic-Aristotelian theory of a closed universe bounded by the sphere of the stars was contradicted by Atomists, who posited existence of matter outside boundaries of cosmos.   [865]

——. "Weight and Motion in Democritus' Theory. A Discussion of D. O'Brien, *Theories of Weight in the Ancient World, I: Democritus*." *OSAP* 1(1983), 193-209. Review essay of #874. Democritus thought atoms have weight, which explains their tendency to fall down. Since he saw the earth as a flat disk, he did not think atoms fell as a result of the *dine* or vortex movement posited by other Presocratics.   [866]

——. cf. #145, #329, #4956, #5354.

HUSSEY, E. L. "Thucydidean History and Democritean Theory." *HPolTho* 6(1985), 118-138. Influence of D's moral, ethical, psychological concepts on Thucydides. [867]

JOHNSON, H. J. "Three Ancient Meanings of Matter: Democritus, Plato, and Aristotle." *JHI* 28(1967), 3-16. Looks at the three systems in regard to several questions: Are spatial and temporal dimensions separable? Should we conceive of particles conjoined or of fields with local peculiarities? Are laws of other natural sciences reducible to those of physics?   **[868]**

KAHN, C. H. "Democritus and the Origins of Moral Psychology." *AJPh* 106(1985), 1-31. Many Democritean fragments deal with ethics. His ethics appear not to have been teleological but to have emphasized role of reason in life. The more one is able to live a life guided by reason, the happier one will be.   **[869]**

KONSTAN, D. "Ancient Atomism and its Heritage. Minimal Parts." *AncPh* 2(1982), 60-75. Surveys debate over whether atoms are mathematical points or physical particles.   **[870]**

LUCE, J. V. "An Argument of Democritus about Language." *CR* 19(1969), 3-4. In frag preserved by Proclus, D argues that names cannot be attributed to things by nature if things have more than one name.   **[871]**

McGIBBON, D. "The Religious Thought of Democritus." *Hermes* 93(1965), 385-397. Like other Presocratics, D emphasizes soul's divine nature. Also envisions certain intellectual principals which are eternal, unlike gods which embody them temporarily. **[872]**

NOVAK, G. *The Origins of Materialism.* New York: Merit, 1965. Marxist (but not doctrinaire) treatment of Presocratic origins of materialism and religious skepticism. Democritus is high point, Epicurus and Lucretius competent successors.   **[873]**

O'BRIEN, D. "Heavy and Light in Democritus and Aristotle: Two Conceptions of Change and Identity." *JHS* 97(1977), 64-74. D posits correlation between size and weight of atom. A factors in displacement and speed.   **[874]**

————. *Theories of Weight in the Ancient World: Four Essays on Democritus, Plato and Aristotle: A Study in the Development of Ideas.* Leiden: Brill, 1981. Deals with several major points still at issue, especially the question of whether D attributed weight to atoms and whether their motion was always downward. Argues that both qualities are later additions to D's theroy.   **[875]**

Proceedings of the 1st International Congress on Democritus, Xanthi 6-9 October 1983, I. Xanthi, Greece: Internat. Democritean Foundation, 1984. Essays in various languages. Ones in English discuss pleasure, desire, happiness; ethics of D and Aristotle; D's philosophical-historical and sociological views; D on moral psychology; D against scepticism; *physis* and *didache* in D.   **[876]**

REGNELL, H. *Ancient Views on the Nature of Life. Three Studies in the Philosophies of the Atomists, Plato and Aristotle.* Lund, Sweden: Gleerup, 1967. Somewhat limited study of whether life consists of a series of mechanistic connections or whether there is a mental or spiritual dimension fundamental to it. Ancient views on the nature of life are much less metaphysical than is ordinarily believed. They are primitive scientific hypotheses designed to give an integrated explanation of such phenomena as bodily warmth, self-motion, breathing, growth, and decay.   **[877]**

SEDLEY, D. "Two Conceptions of Vacuum." *Phron* 27(1982), 175-193. For D void is not empty space but state of emptiness. Epicurus first thinks of void in geometric terms.   **[878]**

TAYLOR, C. C. W. "Pleasure, Knowledge, and Sensation in Democritus." *Phron* 12(1967), 6-27. Link between D's physics and ethics must be sought in his empirical methodology. [879]

VLASTOS, G. "Ethics and Physics in Democritus," in #301, pp. 381-408. Soul has power to move body but cannot survive without it. Though mortal, soul is divine. Well-being is a healthful balance, and pleasure is awareness of well-being. Soul has some power to change nature but is limited by necessity and subject to chance. Wisdom is insight into natural order. [880]

VOROS, F. K. "The Ethical Fragments of Democritus. The Problem of the Authenticity." *Hellenica* 26(1973), 193-206. Stobaeus seems best source of citations from D's ethical work *Peri euthumias*. [881]

———. "The Ethical Theory of Democritus. On Duty." *Platon* 26(1974), 113-122. Stoics did not originate concept of duty. D is first to give ethical value to certain terms which had previously expressed physical or logical necessity. [882]

———. "The Ethical Theory of Democritus. What is the Criterion?" *Platon* 27(1975), 20-26. D's criterion for determining what is just seems to have been intellectual pleasure derived from an act. This applies to individual as well as political and social acts. [883]

For related items see #279, #825, #929, #950, #5377, #5836, #5988, #5990, #6015.

Chapter 9

THE SOPHISTS

Though concerned with questions of the nature of the universe, Presocratic philosophy never ignored contemporary trends and issues. By the late fifth century B. C. a mood of skepticism prevailed in Greek society, brought on by contact with "barbarians" who had other views of life. An intelligent and reflective people like the Greeks more or less naturally began to ask themselves whether the various national and local ways of life were merely conventions and were subject to change. Were they of a higher moral order?

Another factor in this growing uncertainty about the possibility of gaining sure knowledge may have been the contradictory hypotheses proposed by the early natural philosophers and the vehement arguments over them. Someone who had read Parmenides and Heraclitus could easily come to doubt the validity of sense-perception. If change is illusion, sense-perception is not trustworthy. If everything constantly changes, our sense-perception is worthless and can hardly serve as a basis for epistemology.

The most noteworthy response to this change of attitude was the rise of the movement known as Sophism, from the Greek word meaning a wise man. Sophism differed from the older Presocratic philosophy in regard to the matter with which it dealt, namely mankind and its customs. It treated of the microcosm rather than the macrocosm, as one scholar says. But it also differed in its method. Although the method of the older philosophers by no means excluded empirical observation, it was characteristically deductive. When a philosopher had settled on his primary "stuff," he then proceeded to explain particular phenomena in accordance with the theory. The Sophists, however, sought to amass a wide store of particular observations and facts. They were encyclopaedists. From these accumulated facts they derived conclusions, partly theoretical, partly practical. The method can best be described as empirico-inductive.

The Sophists' practical conclusions were not meant to establish objective norms, founded on necessary truth. This points to a third difference between Sophism and the older philosophy, namely, the difference of end. The early philosophers, the cosmologists, wanted to find the objective truth about the world. The Sophists stressed the difficulty — if not the impossibility — of acquiring such knowledge. They became teachers, travelling from town to town, drawing crowds of students eager to pay for the privilege of listening to them.

Sophistic teaching centered around rhetoric, the art of making of a speech, which played a central role in Greek politics and law. In Greece by the mid-fifth century political life was intensified, particularly in Athens. The free citizen was expected to play a part in the city's public life. The old type of aristocratic education, centered on memorization of Homer and the attainment of *arete* (virtue), proved inadequate to the new situation. What was now required was courses of instruction in grammar, interpretation of the poets, and, above all, rhetoric.

The importance of rhetoric in Athenian society is difficult to explain in a society as indifferent to oratory as ours is. Once every four years we endure a few long speeches at the political nominating conventions, but the candidates then confine themselves to "sound bites" that will fit into thirty-second spots on the evening news. Few of us ever expect to have to make a speech urging someone else to adopt our point of view.

In ancient Greece no one could expect to survive long without the ability to make an effective speech. When summoned to court — as most citizens could expect to be several times during their lives in that litigious society — the requirement was that both plaintiff and defendant present their cases to a jury, usually consisting of several hundred men. Large crowds standing around often expressed their opinions of the merits of the speeches and could sway the jury, who voted in public. Each citizen was also expected to speak in the assembly. By the middle of the fifth century the ability to speak effectively in public was as essential as literacy is today.

This was the skill which the Sophists offered to teach. The important thing, they concluded, was not the intrinsic merit of the case but the skill with which the speaker arranged and presented his arguments. This approach leads inevitably to a kind of relativism. Aristophanes, in the *Clouds*, accuses the Sophists of making the weaker argument appear the stronger. This seems to have been a common perception of them.

The Sophists attracted attention by giving popular lectures in the major cities of Greece, accepting pay from their students, unlike earlier philosophers. Their teaching tended to pull to pieces the traditional ethical code and religious beliefs. It was this skeptical tendency of the Sophists which disturbed more conservative Greeks, especially as the Sophists did not put anything new and stable in place of the old convictions which they had unsettled. The hair-splitting tendencies of some of the later Sophists led to the disparagement of the movement, as reflected in the writings of Aristophanes and Plato. Ambrose Bierce echoed those sentiments in his definition of the Sophists as "a Grecian sect of philosophers who began by teaching wisdom, prudence, science, art and, in brief, whatever men ought to know, but lost themselves in a maze of quibbles and a fog of words." It should be said in their defense, though, that they turned the attention of man to himself, thus setting the stage for Plato and Aristotle.

There is, however, no reason to ascribe to the more notable Sophists the intention of overthrowing religion and morality. They were a great educative force in Hellas, but the rhetoric on which they chiefly based their teaching could be turned to immoral purposes. The evil latent in Sophism lay not in the fact that it asked questions and raised problems, but in that it could not offer satisfactory solutions to the problems it raised.

ALBURY, W. R. "Hunting the Sophist." *Apeir* 5(1971), 1-11. In Plato's *Soph* the Sophists are besieged by definitions, as a sort of military tactic. Sophists based their success on lack of clarity in definition.   [884]

BARRETT, H. *The Sophists: Rhetoric, Democracy, and Plato's Idea of Sophistry.*
Novato, CA: Chandler & Sharp, 1987. Survey for non-specialists, with bibliography and
translations from Gorgias and Prodicus in an appendix.   [885]

BETT, R. "The Sophists and Relativism." *Phron* 34(1989), 139-169. Only Protagoras
can be shown to be relativist in any real sense. Plato's *Theaet* is the only piece of evidence for Sophistic relativism. Plato's antagonism to the Sophists is based on several
points of their teaching.   [886]

BOWIE, E. L. "The Importance of Sophists." *YCS* 27(1982), 29-59. Sophists under
Roman empire were a kind of Greek aristocracy. By Marcus Aurelius' day they were
appointed to some of most important imperial posts.   [887]

BURNS, A. "Athenian Literacy in the Fifth Century B. C." *JHI* 42(1981), 371-387.
Wide-spread literacy among males of fifth-century Athens created interest in, and
demand for, educational skills which Sophists professed to teach.   [888]

CASCARDI, A. J. "The Place of Language in Philosophy; Or, the Uses of Rhetoric."
Ph&Rh 16(1983), 217-227. Socrates' discussion with Sophists sheds light on rhetoric's
ability to overcome linguistic limitations on philosophy.   [889]

CHROUST, A.-H. "The Philosophy of Law of the Early Sophists." *AmJJur* 20(1975), 81-
94. Early Sophists taught that laws were arbitrary decisions of people in power and tried
to establish a concept of "natural" law which respected individual worth and rights.
Despite heavy criticism from Plato and others, their ideas became engrained in the
western tradition.   [890]

CLASSEN, C. J. "Aristotle's Picture of the Sophists," in #905, pp. 7-24. Aristotle
generally uses term *sophistes* for persons contemporary with himself, not for Protagoras,
Gorgias, et al. He defines their fundamental aim as achieving a particular life-purpose,
not striving for truth. He is not objective in his treatment of them but not unduly harsh,
either. He regards their argumentation as inadequate.   [891]

——. "Bibliographie zur Sophistik." *Elenchos* 6(1985), 75-140. Covers over a century
of research on Sophists in general and each separate figure. Not annotated.   [892]

——. "The Study of Language amongst Socrates' Contemporaries," in *Sophistik*
(Darmstadt, Ger.: Wissenschaft. Buchgesell., 1976), pp. 215-247. Increased literacy and
importance of rhetoric in public life led to interest in subtleties of language which
Sophists capitalized on.   [893]

CONLEY, T. M. "Dating the So-Called *Dissoi Logoi.* A Cautionary Note." *AncPh*
5(1985), 59-65. Treatise probably not from late fifth or fourth century B. C.; more likely
Byzantine.   [894]

CRAIK, E. M. "Sophokles and the Sophists." *AC* 49(1980), 247-254. *Philoctetes*
provides allegorical criticism of Sophistic education and its objectives.   [895]

DODDS, E. R. "The Sophistic Movement and the Failure of Greek Liberalism," in #56, pp. 92-105. Sophist stress on living in accord with nature and rejecting conventions of society did produce awareness of importance of individual. But it also exalted individual over community. Stoic humanitarianism and concept of sage who bows to society but does not give up his freedom are offshoots of Sophist teaching. [896]

DUBOSE, S. "Sophistic Measures." *TulStudPh* 17(1968), 13-19. In *Theaet* Plato attempts to show that the concept of a least unit of measure, such as taught by Sophists, is an inadequate basis for knowledge. [897]

GUTHRIE, W. K. C. "The First Humanists." *PCA* 65(1968), 13-25. Sophists' relativistic ethics, religious agnosticism, view of law and justice as established by societal consent, notion of punishment as educative and not retributive, are close to modern attitude known as humanism. [898]

———. *The Sophists.* Cambridge Univ. Pr., 1971. Separate publication of part of vol. III of #19. [899]

HOLMBERG, C. B. "Dialectical Rhetoric and Rhetorical Rhetoric." *Ph&Rh* 10(1977), 232-243. Examines impact which a dialectical or rhetorical world view has on an individual's concept of Being. Sophists, Plato, and Aristotle are studied. [900]

JARRETT, J. L., ed. and transl. *The Educational Theories of the Sophists.* New York: Teachers College Pr., 1969. Sophists, though not profound thinkers, saw importance of professional education. Their emphasis on debate and contrasting arguments broke the hold of oracles and maxims on Greek mind. They were humanists in their rejection of gods and emphasis on what mankind can achieve. Book includes translations of seven significant ancient passges by or about Sophists. [901]

KERFERD, G. B. "The Concept of Equality in the Thought of the Sophistic Movement," in #62, pp. 7-15. Sophists see all Greeks as innately equal but developing at different rates. As teachers they claim to improve pupils' fitness for civic life. [902]

———. "The Future Direction of Sophistic Studies," in #905, pp. 1-6. Tendency in past has been to dismiss Sophists in general as serious philosophers while picking out occasional valid points as exceptions. Sophists are now recognized as forerunners of sociology and as ones who introduced problem of subjectivity in philosophy. More attention should be given to their work on language. [903]

———. *The Sophistic Movement.* Cambridge Univ. Pr., 1981. Reviews earlier assessments of Sophists and reasons for negative evaluations of them. Looks at their efforts in epistemology, dialectic, theory of language, *nomos/physis* debate, views of gods, and question of whether "virtue" can be taught. Stresses importance of rational argumentation and relativism (though not subjectivism). Finds them "a great movement in human thought," which spurred Socrates and Plato to their greatest achievements. [904]

———. *The Sophists and their Legacy. Proceedings of the Fourth International Colloquium on Ancient Philosophy Held in Co-operation with Projectgruppe Altertumswissenschaften der Thyssenstiftung at Bad Homburg, 29th August-1st September, 1979.* Wiesbaden, Ger.: Steiner, 1981. Collection of essays. Those in English are abstracted herein. [905]

———. cf. #343.

MULGAN, R. G. "Lycophron and Greek Theories of Social Contract." *JHI* 40(1979), 121-128. It is questionable whether Lycophron's theory of a social contract, referred to by Aristotle, imposed limits on power of state. **[906]**

POULAKOS, J. "Toward a Sophistic Definition of Rhetoric." *Ph&Rh* 16(1983), 35-48. Discussion of Sophistic views of rhetoric and some important implications of such a definition. **[907]**

RANKIN, H. D. *Sophists, Socratics, and Cynics.* Totowa, NJ: Barnes & Noble, 1983. Examines continuity of thought and method from fifth-century Sophists to Socratic and Cynic schools. All these groups used argument in natural language as their chief investigative technique. **[908]**

RICHARDSON, N. J. "Homeric Professors in the Age of the Sophists." *PCPhS* 21(1975), 65-81. Allegorical, metaphorical, and occasional literal interpretations of Homer made him basis for most pre-Platonic thinkers. **[909]**

ROBINSON, T. M. *Contrasting Arguments. An Edition of the* Dissoi Logoi. New York: Arno Pr., 1979. Introductory section on transmission of text, date, authorship, influences. Text, translation, commentary, bibliography. **[910]**

———. "A Sophist on Omniscience, Polymathy, and Omnicompetence. *D. L.* 8.1-13." *ICS* 2(1977), 125-135. *Dissoi Logoi* 8 depicts ideal sophist-orator-politician. **[911]**

ROSE, P. W. "Sophocles' *Philoctetes* and the Teachings of the Sophists." *HSCP* 80(1976), 49-105. Sophocles seems to have been challenged by Sophistic approach to knowledge and to have been in general agreement with their views on origin of human society and development of human behavior. **[912]**

ROWE, C. J. "Plato on the Sophists as Teachers of Virtue." *HPolTho* 4(1983), 409-427. P and Sophists both defined *arete* as what is necessary for success. They differ over definition of success. **[913]**

SAXONHOUSE, A. W. "Nature and Convention in Thucydides' *History*." *Polity* 10(1978), 461-487. Studies impact of Sophism, especially concept of laws and social mores being conventions instead of natural laws, on Thucydides' account of Peloponnesian War. **[914]**

SHEEKS, W. "Isocrates, Plato, and Xenophon against the Sophists." *Pers* 56(1975), 250-259. Compares P's negative view of Sophists with attitudes of two contemporary writers. **[915]**

SOLMSEN, F. *Intellectual Experiments of the Greek Enlightenment.* Princeton Univ. Pr., 1975. Sees fifth century B. C. as time when Greek intellectuals, exemplified by Sophists, Thucydides, and Euripides, introduced bold innovations in techniques of argumentation and persuasion, experiments in language, utopian schemes, and new psychological insights, all held together by new emphasis on reason. **[916]**

The Sophistic Movement. Athens: Greek Philosophical Association, 1984. Collection of previously unpublished papers; those in English are abstracted herein. **[917]**

SPRAGUE, R. K. "Dissoi Logoi or Dialexeis." *Mind* 77(1968), 155-167. First English translation of this anonymous treatise, Sophistic in origin, written after 400 B. C. **[918]**

——. "Eating, Growth, and Sophists: Some Aristotelian Food for Thought," in #905, pp. 64-80. Aristotle's analysis of growth is unsatisfactory because he did not want to base his arguments on the concepts of mixture and predominance, notions criticized by neo-Eleatic Sophists.   **[919]**

——. *The Older Sophists: A Complete Translation by Several Hands of the Fragments in Die Fragmente der Vorsokratiker ed. Diels-Kranz*, with a new edition of Antiphon and Euthydemus. Columbia: Univ. of SC Pr., 1972. Transl. with brief introduction to each Sophist and some bibliography.   **[920]**

——. "A Platonic Parallel in the *Dissoi Logoi.*" *JHPh* 6(1968), 160-161. Fallacy solution found in 5.15 resembles that found in *Euthyd* 283 B-E.   **[921]**

STANTON, G. R. "Sophists and Philosophers. Problems of Classification." *AJPh* 94(1973), 350-364. In first/second centuries A. D. "Sophist" could be neutral term; it is more often derogatory. Second Sophistic writers preferred to be called philosophers.   **[922]**

TAYLOR, A. E. "The *Dissoi Logoi*," in #1180, pp. 91-128. Surveys contents of this anonymous work and suggests that it was written before Socrates' death by someone with Eleatic sympathies.   **[923]**

UMUKORO, J. A. "The Sophists as Educators." *Phrontis* 4(1966), 23-25. Brief survey of characteristics and contributions.   **[924]**

For related items see #3229, #6202.

ANTIPHON (ca. 450-400 B. C.)

Very little is known about Antiphon the Sophist. He is mentioned by Xenophon and Aristotle as one of Socrates' opponents, but beyond that nothing is certain. Compounding the problem is the existence of another Antiphon, a rhetorician, at the same time. H. C. Avery has suggested that the two Antiphons are in fact one (#925). Works attributed to Antiphon the Sophist include *Truth*, *On the Interpretation of Dreams*, and *Politicus*.

AVERY, H. C. "One Antiphon or Two?" *Hermes* 110(1982), 145-158. Argues for identifying Rhetor and Sophist on basis of similarity of thought and careers.   **[925]**

DILLON, J. "Euripides and Antiphon on Nomos and Physis: Some Remarks," in #917, pp. 127-136. Eteocles in Euripides' *Phoenissae* seems to be a caricature of A's "natural man," who lives according to *physis*, not *nomos*, in the presence of witnesses. A's actual view is not so simplistic.   **[926]**

FURLEY, D. J. "Antiphon's Case against Justice," in #905, pp. 81-91. Antiphon, in frag D-K 87 B 44 argues that to be just is contrary to a person's natural interest. His position is similar to Thrasymachus' in *Rep* 1.   **[927]**

GEORGIADIS, C. "Aristotle's Criticism of Antiphon in *Physics*, Book II, Chapter I," in #917, pp. 108-114. Aristotle pointed out that Antiphon maintained that the nature of something could be defined only as matter, not also as form.   **[928]**

MOULTON, C. "Antiphon the Sophist and Democritus." *MH* 31(1974), 129-139. These two diverge less than has been suggested in their thinking on law and justice.   **[929]**

————. "Antiphon the Sophist, *On Truth*." *TAPhA* 103(1972), 329-366. A's criticism of law on grounds that it is inimical to nature is similar to some trial scenes in Euripides' plays. Both writers are part of general questioning of Athenian legal system in fifth century B. C.   **[930]**

REESOR, M. "The *Truth* of Antiphon the Sophist." *Apeir* 20(1987), 203-218. Work did not describe an ideal society but subjected human actions and concepts of justice to a bitter critique.   **[931]**

SAUNDERS, T. "Antiphon the Sophist on Natural Laws (B44D-K)." *PAS* 78(1977-78), 215-236. New translation of frags of *On Truth*. A tried to show that human laws are inefficient and have unpredictable applications, while natural laws are automatic and work regularly without such unnatural concepts as "justice."   **[932]**

For related items see #950.

PROTAGORAS (ca. 490-420)

One of the earliest to bear the title of Sophist was Protagoras of Abdera, who seems to have come to Athens at about age thirty. Diogenes Laertius says that Protagoras was indicted for blasphemy because of his book on the gods, but that he escaped from Athens before the trial and was drowned while making his way to Sicily. Burnet and Taylor both reject this story. Both also accept the date of ca. 500 for his birth, since Plato represents him as an elderly man in the dialogue named after him, which has a dramatic date of about 435. Plato also says that he died in high repute.

P's best known statement is that "man is the measure of all things, of those that are, that they are, of those that are not, that they are not." There has been considerable controversy as to the interpretation that should be given to this statement. Some hold that "man" means the individual and thus what appears true to you is true for you, while what appears true to me is true for me. Others maintain that "man" means the community or society of man, and thus the group is the judge of truth.

Judging from what Plato says in *Theaet* 152a-b, the individualistic interpretation seems to be the correct one. In this dialogue Socrates observes that when the same wind is blowing, one person may feel chilly and another not, or one may feel slightly cool while the other feels quite cold. He then asks if we should agree with P that the wind *is* cold to the one who feels chilly and not to the other. It is clear in this passage that P is interpreted as referring to the individual. It should also be noted that he does not say that the wind *appears* to be chilly or warm, but that it *is* chilly or warm.

In the *Theaet* P is quoted as saying that ethical judgments are also relative:

"I hold that whatever practices seem right and laudable to any particular State are so for that State, so long as it holds by them." He also urged that the wise man attempts to substitute sound practices for unsound. In other words, there is no question of one ethical view being true and another false. It is a matter of one view being sounder, i. e., more useful or expedient, than another. In another Platonic dialogue, named after him, Protagoras says that Law in general is founded on certain ethical tendencies implanted in all men, but that the individual varieties of Law, as found in particular states, are relative. The law of one state, without being truer than that of another state, may perhaps be sounder. Relativism, then, is the foundation of Protagoras' teaching. He put his views into practice when he was invited to write a constitution for a new Greek colony at Thurii.

Virtually no frags survive from his written works, which included treatises *On Truth*, *On Contradictions*, and *On the Gods*. We do know that he thought ideas about the gods were also conventions, valid only for one group. Users of the bibliography are also referred to the section on Plato's dialogue *Protagoras*.

BEATTIE, P. "Protagoras, the Maligned Philosopher." *ReligHum* 14(1980), 108-115. P's poor reputation stems from Plato's conservative opposition to new thought. Protagorean humanism anticipates all major points of modern humanism.   [933]

BERNSEN, N. O. "Protagoras' Homo-Mensura Thesis." *C&M* 30(1969), 109-144. Plato is primary source for this doctrine, which weakens civil law by its skepticism but provides the critical attitude necessary for intellectual progress.   [934]

COLE, A. T. "The Relativism of Protagoras." *YCS* 22(1972), 19-45. Attempt to resolve seeming contradiction between P the Sophist and relativist as portrayed by doxographers and P the lawgiver and teacher described by Plato.   [935]

———. cf. #3374.

DAVISON, J. A. "Aeschylus and Athenian Politics, 472-456 B. C.," in *Ancient Society and Institutions: Studies Presented to Victor Ehrenberg* (Oxford: Blackwell, 1966), pp. 93-107. In *Prometheus Bound* Pericles is Zeus, the authority figure; Protagoras is Prometheus, who brings civilizing arts to mankind and challenges conventions of society.   [936]

ELDREDGE, L. "Sophocles, Protagoras, and the Nature of Greek Culture: An Introductory Essay." *AntRev* 25(1965), 8-12. Introduction to an issue on cultural relativism. Examines role of human beings in thought of fifth-century Athens and contrasts P's view.   [937]

FRINGS, M. S. "Protagoras Re-discovered. Heidegger's Explication of Protagoras' Fragment." *JVaLInq* 8(1974), 112-123. Heidegger's concern with over-emphasis on subjectivity in metaphysics led him to see P's man-measure statement as applying to Being and not-Being, not to subjective relativism.   [938]

GLIDDEN, D. K. "Protagorean Relativism and Physics." *Phron* 20(1975), 209-227. P's search for truth involves study of nature, not merely of social conventions.   [939]

——. "Protagorean Relativism and the Cyrenaics." *AmPhQ* 9(1975), 113-140. Modern scholars too easily equate P's relativism to Cyrenaic thought. P would maintain that all sense impressions are subjective, while Cyrenaics hold that sense impressions and not physical objects have properties which they seem to us to have. [940]

GOOSSENS, W. K. "Euathlus and Protagoras." *Log&An* 20(1977), 67-75. Analysis of story in which P and a student go to court over payment of a fee. The contract can logically be fulfilled and the debt must be paid. [941]

JORDAN, J. E. "Protagoras and Relativism. Criticisms Bad and Good." *SwJPh* 2(1971), 7-29. Plato's criticism of P is inadequate, as are some modern criticisms. [942]

LENZEN, W. "Protagoras versus Euathlus. Reflections on a So-Called Paradox." *Ratio* 19(1977), 176-180. The paradox is deontological but may be resolved if three court cases can be assumed. P would lose the first and third but win the second. [943]

LEVIN, S. "The Origin of Grammar in Sophistry." *General Linguistics* 22(1982), 41-47. P based some of his clever arguments on gender of nouns and mood of verbs. [944]

LOENEN, D. *Protagoras and the Greek Community.* Ann Arbor, MI: University Microfilms, 1977; rprt. Examines P's ideas on friendship, justice, laws, virtue, and education, and compares them to views of Plato and Aristotle. [945]

MANSFELD, J. "Protagoras on Epistemological Obstacles and Persons," in #905, pp. 38-53. P noted problem of obstacles to knowledge which French philosopher G. Bachelard formulated in detail in 1938. [946]

——. cf. #3401.

MEILAND, J. W. "Is Protagorean Relativism Self-Refuting?" *GPhS* 9(1979), 51-68. Extreme type of relativism first promulgated by P can be defended against charges of self-refutation by distinguishing "X believes y is true" from "y is true for X." [947]

MEJER, J. "The Alleged New Fragment of Protagoras." *Hermes* 100(1972), 175-178. Discusses possible authenticity of new frag and implications for understanding P. [948]

MUIR, J. V. "Protagoras and Education in Thourioi." *G&R* 29(1982), 17-24. City's laws, including grants for education, were created by P. [949]

NILL, M. *Morality and Self-Interest in Protagoras, Antiphon and Democritus.* Leiden: Brill, 1985. Concepts such as "morality" and "altruism" are lacking in ancient Greek thought. P's best justification for an other-regarding act was that it contributed to well-being of community. P failed to define what was moral or to show how acting morally benefitted the agent. A pointed out weaknesses in P's theory and held that acting morally does not always benefit the agent. D defined an inner good which results from moral actions. [950]

PRIER, R. A. "Some Thoughts on the Archaic Use of 'Metron'." *CW* 70(1976), 161-169. For early poets and philosophers *metron* is noetic, dynamic term, not thing or quantity. P's "man-measure" statement should be interpreted against this background. [951]

RITTER, M. R. "In Search of the Real Protagoras." *Dial*(PST) 23(1981), 58-65. Interpretations of P by Plato and Aristotle have left distorted picture of his ethics and epistemology. His positions are more consistent than commonly believed.   **[952]**

ROSEMAN, N. "Protagoras and the Foundations of His Educational Thought." *PaedHist* 11(1971), 75-89. P's educational theory is based on belief in mankind's goodness and possibility of bettering himself. Notes parallels to modern views.   **[953]**

SAUNDERS, T. J. "Protagoras and Plato on Punishment," in #905, pp. 129-141. P seems to be Plato's source for idea that punishment of wrongdoers is cruel and unjustified except for reformatory purposes.   **[954]**

SEGAL, C. "Protagoras' Orthoepeia in Aristophanes' Battle of the Prologues." *RhM* 113(1970), 158-162. *Frogs* 1119-1197 betrays P's influence in more ways than previously recognized. Aristophanes was probably parodying a work of the sophist.   **[955]**

SIMMONS, G. C. "Protagoras on Education and Society." *PaedHist* 12(1972), 518-537. P maintains that the state is necessary to prevent mankind from living in a condition of barbarism. It is thus the primary educational force and the skill involved in running it must be teachable.   **[956]**

TRINKAUS, C. "Protagoras in the Renaissance: An Exploration," in *Philosophy and Humanism: Renaissance Essays in Honor of Paul Oskar Kristeller*, ed. E. P. Mahoney (New York: Columbia Univ. Pr., 1976), pp. 190-213. Renaissance commentators took P to mean what they needed or wanted him to. They did not "misunderstand him any more inadequately" than modern scholars do.   **[957]**

VERSENYI, L. "Protagoras' Man-Measure Fragment," in *Sophistik*, ed. C. J. Classen (Darmstadt, Ger.: Wissenschaft. Buchgesell., 1976), pp. 290-297. The "man" in this statement applies to a real person who makes choices, not to an abstraction.   **[958]**

WHITE, F. C. "Protagoras as a Moral Educator." *PaedHist* 15(1975), 128-141. Defines what is meant by "moral education" and shows how P aims at it by training his students, informing them, and making them rational. Purpose of such education is to build up community.   **[959]**

――. cf. #3431.

WOODRUFF, P. "Didymus on Protagoras and the Protagoreans." *JHPh* 23(1985), 483-497. Though a papyrus attributed to Didymus Caecus is confused, it seems to indicate that P would not have conceded existence of the non-evident.   **[960]**

――. "Protagoras on the Unseen. The Evidence of Didymus," in #917, pp. 80-87. P and Democritus reach opposite conclusions about resolving differences in perceptions because P cannot accept notion of unseen entities.   **[961]**

For related items see #2832, #2850, #2851, #2854, #2869, #2874, #5549.

GORGIAS (ca. 483-375 B. C.)

The other major early Sophist was Gorgias, born in Leontini, in Sicily. He seems to have been a pupil of Empedocles and to have at first been interested in natural science. But the dialectic of Zeno must have won him over to scepticism. While Protagoras taught that everything exists, G taught the opposite. His works include an *Encomium on Helen, Palamedes* and *On That Which is Not, or On Nature* (also translated *On Non-Being*), only frags of which survive. His thought takes this form:

1. Nothing exists, for if there were anything, then it would have either to be eternal or to have come into being. But it cannot have come into being, for neither out of Being nor out of non-Being can anything come to be. Nor can it be eternal, for if it were eternal, then it would have to be infinite. But the infinite is impossible, because it could not be another, nor could it be in itself. Therefore, it would be nowhere, and that which is nowhere is nothing.

2. If anything did exist, then it could not be known. For if there is knowledge of Being, then what is thought must be, and Non-being could not be thought at all. In which case there could be no error, which is absurd.

3. Even if there were knowledge of Being, this knowledge could not be imparted. Every symbol is different from the thing symbolized, e. g., how could we impart knowledge of colors with words, since the ear hears tones, not colors. And how could the representation of Being be in two persons at once, since they are different from one another?

It is uncertain whether G was expressing a serious philosophy of Nihilism, or whether he was simply illustrating the power of rhetoric to make plausible the most absurd hypothesis.

G's most significant philosophical contribution may lie in the area of aesthetics. He is the first to examine the ability of rhetoric and tragedy to persuade their audiences, for good or ill.

ADKINS, A. W. H. "Form and Content in Gorgias' *Helen* and *Palamedes*," in #42, pp. 107-128. Some inconsistencies between G's two works arise from rhetorical emphases, some from presuppositions about human behavior which he shared with other early Greeks. Inconsistencies should make us cautious about trying to reconcile discrepancies between frags of other Presocratics. We may be holding them to a standard of consistency they could not actually reach.   [962]

CALOGERO, G. "Gorgias and the Socratic Principle *Nemo sua sponte peccat*," in #41, pp. 176-186. Examines disagreement between G and Socrates on the question of whether persons can do wrong against their will.   [963]

CASCARDI, A. J. "The Place of Language in Philosophy." *Ph&Rh* 16(1983), 217-227.

Arguing that language has no meaning, G foreshadows modern philosophers such as Derrida.   [964]

DEMAND, N. "Epicharmus and Gorgias." *AJPh* 92(1971), 453-463. Two frags of Epicharmus may be from a play, *Logos and Logina*, about G.   [965]

DE ROMILLY, J. "Gorgias and Magic," in *Magic and Rhetoric in Ancient Greece* (Cambridge, MA: Harvard Univ. Pr., 1975), pp. 1-22. In *Helen* G proposes that rhetoric, with its ability to sway the mind, has magical powers. But such powers can be used for good or ill.   [966]

GRONBECK, B. E. "Gorgias on Rhetoric and Poetic." *SouthSpeechComJ* 38(1972), 27-38. G's agnostic epistemology leads to theories of deceptiveness — understood positively as an aspect of communication — in rhetoric and poetry.   [967]

HUNTER, V. "Thucydides, Gorgias, and Mass Psychology." *Hermes* 114(1986), 412-429. Both the historian and the Sophist see human rational faculties as inadequate, thus vulnerable to fear and persuasion.   [968]

KERFERD, G. B. "Gorgias and Empedocles." *SicGym* 38(1985), 595-605. G probably did know Empedocles personally and was interested in astronomical and physical theories, which he continued to study and teach throughout his life.   [969]

——. "The Interpretation of Gorgias' Treatise *Peri tou me ontos e peri physeos*." *Deukalion* 36(1981), 319-327. Surveys opinion on treatise *On Non-Being*; comments on third part, in which G tries to define parts of communication process.   [970]

——. "Meaning and Reference. Gorgias and the Relation between Language and Reality," in #917, pp. 215-222. G seems to deny referential view of meaning. He sees sense-perceptions as different from thought and thus incommunicable. Though words represent thoughts, they cannot communicate thoughts because thoughts are non-transferable.   [971]

KOHAK, E. "Anti-Gorgias. Being and Nothing as Experience." *HumStud* 4(1981), 209-222. Being and Nothing cannot be converted as lived experiences. Their essential difference creates a non-relative basis for judging true/false, good/evil. Skepticism is thus rejected.   [972]

LONG, A. A. "Methods of Argument in Gorgias, *Palamedes*," in #917, pp. 233-241. This work is not a serious philosophical treatise but purely a rhetorical exercise in making the strongest argument possible.   [973]

MacDOWELL, D. M. *Gorgias:* Encomium of Helen. Bristol (UK):Classical Pr., 1982. Text with transl of *Encomium*; introduction to G's life, works; notes on text.   [974]

MANSFELD, J. "Historical and Philosophical Aspects of Gorgias' 'On What is Not'." *SicGym* 38(1985), 243-271. Outlines treatise's arguments and G's relationship to Protagoras and to Plato's *Parmenides*.   [975]

MOURELATOS, A. P. D. "Gorgias on the Function of Language." *SicGym* 38(1985), 607-638. Examines the apparent contradiction between G's success as an orator and his negative view of the possibility of communicating meaning through language. The positive side of his theory is seen in the *Helen*, the negative, elenctic side in part 3 of his *On Non-Being*. [976]

POULAKOS, J. "Gorgias' *Encomium to Helen* and the Defense of Rhetoric." *Rhetorica* 1 #2(1983), 1-16. G's views on rhetoric can be inferred from the *Encomium*. [977]

ROBINSON, J. M. "On Gorgias," in #65, pp. 49-60. Disputes Guthrie's view (cf. #19) of G as a serious philosopher. He seems to be nothing more than a clever rhetorician. [978]

SAUNDERS, T. J. "Gorgias' Psychology in the History of the Free-Will Problem." *SicGym* 38(1985), 209-228. Comparison of G's views with those of Democritus and Epicurus. [979]

VERDENIUS, W. J. "Gorgias' Doctrine of Deception," in #905, pp. 116-128. G's theory of rhetoric as deception is derived from criticism of the Eleatic theory of knowledge. He cites Homer and Hesiod as support for his concept because the public of his day regarded their work so highly. [980]

For related items see #1049, #1158, #2963.

PRODICUS (late fifth cent. B. C.)

Prodicus seems to have come to Athens from his home city of Ceos as an ambassador, a function he frequently filled. While in Athens he availed himself of the opportunity to teach courses on the proper use of words. He gained a considerable reputation and a fortune to match, for his fees were very high. He professed to teach his students very subtle distinctions among the various possible meanings of words, a sort of preliminary logical exercise. He composed a work *On Nature*, which does not survive. Authorship of a myth entitled "The Choice of Heracles" is attributed to him but we have no complete work of his. In the "Choice" story Heracles comes to a fork in a road. Two women, representing virtue and vice, try to persuade him to follow their respective paths. Heracles chooses the more difficult road of virtue. The story does conflict with P's own reputation for loving luxury. P's idea that gods are personifications of objects and natural forces which people found useful left him open to charges of atheism.

AMBROSE, Z. P. "Socrates and Prodicus in the *Clouds*," in #42, pp. 129-144. P's "Choice of Heracles" may be parodied in *agon* of the *Clouds*. Sophistic doctrine presented in play generally resembles P's. [981]

HENRICHS, A. "The Atheism of Prodicus." *BCPE* 6(1976), 15-21. P denied Olympian pantheon but recognized some gods and allowed for religious practices as social institutions. [982]

———. "Isis," in *Actes du vii͏ᵉ Congrès de la Fédération Internationale des Associations d'Études classiques*, ed. J. Harmatta (Budapest: Akademiai Kiado, 1984), I, pp. 339-353. Five inscriptions pertaining to Isis are inspired by Prodicus' theories on origin of civilization. Slightly revised version appears in *HSCP* 88(1984), 139-158.   [983]

——. cf. #279.

REESOR, M. E. "The Stoic *idion* and Prodicus' Near-Synonyms." *AJPh* 104(1983), 124-133. Alexander of Aphrodisias compares Stoic essential characteristic to P's identifying statement.   [984]

SCHRAM, J. M. "Prodicus' Fifty-Drachma Show-Lecture and the Mytilene Debate of Thucydides. An Account of the Intellectual and Social Antecedents of Formal Logic." *AntRev* 25(1965), 105-130. In light of religious skepticism and doubts about efficacy of law, Greeks turned to logical processes to legitimize social institutions. Early forms of these logical processes are discussed. They culminate in Aristotle's syllogisms.   [985]

WILLINK, C. W. "Prodikos, 'Meteoro-sophists' and the 'Tantalos' Paradigm." *CQ* 33(1983), 25-33. P's ideas and his money-loving reputation form basis of representative Sophist of *Clouds*. Character is called "Socrates" because Athenian comedy sanctioned attacks on citizens, which P was not. In *Protag* 315b-c he is likened to Tantalos because of his wealth and love of luxury.   [986]

Chapter 10

SOCRATES

It was once fashionable to draw parallels between Socrates (hereafter abbreviated S) and Jesus. The poet Shelley called S "the Jesus Christ of Greece," and Thomas Jefferson owned a copy of *Socrates and Jesus Compared*, by J. Priestly (1803). That impulse is not entirely dead today. As recently as 1988 I. F. Stone could begin his book on the trial of S (#1169) by drawing a comparison between these two epochal figures, and P Kreeft could create a fanciful confrontation between the two in *Socrates Meets Jesus* (1987).

Such comparisons occur to people because each of these men made an indelible impact on Western culture, yet both were of humble origins, worked as tradesmen, lived the life of itinerant teachers, and provoked such enmity from the authorities of their day that they were put to death. Both men even had an opportunity to escape the death sentence, but neither took it. Neither man wrote anything, and we are dependent on their disciples for whatever picture we have of them. From those disciples we get portraits which vary greatly. Reading the gospels of Mark and John, one has difficulty recognizing the same man. Reading the accounts of Xenophon and Plato (hereafter P), one can hardly believe they are talking about the same S. Both men suffered the fate of exaltation by later generations. The unorthodox Palestinian rabbi became the divine Logos; the satyr-faced Athenian gadfly became the mouthpiece of Platonic metaphysics.

The early twentieth century saw a "search for the historical Jesus." Some of the same techniques have been applied to the study of S's life, a kind of "demythologizing" process that has sometimes led to radical conclusions. French scholar Eugene Dupreel (1922) was convinced that Aristophanes had created a fictional character called "Socrates" for his play the *Clouds*. P then used that same character in his (fictional) dialogues. Later writers did not know or care whether S had existed. A position at the other extreme was taken by Burnet and Taylor, who held that everything P says about S is historically reliable.

Few serious scholars now would support either of these positions, but the later years of the century have seen a heightening of interest in the historical figure (cf. #1087). Is it possible, scholars wonder, to separate what S himself thought from what P put into his mouth? It may not be entirely possible, but if we confine ourselves to P's earliest dialogues and whatever is most consistently reported by the doxographers (especially Aristotle), we may be able to reconstruct at least an outline of his teaching. It is not difficult to say something about S's method of teaching and the impact he had. What is more elusive is the thought of the man himself. As R. S. Brumbaugh says, "ironically, no figure in the history of thought has appeared in its pages in so many masks."

Biographical data for S are hard to come by. A.-H. Chroust lamented "the paucity of available data which exist on the historical Socrates." They must be gleaned or deduced from passing references in a number of authors. The biography by Diogenes Laertius is no more reliable than his accounts of any of the other philosophers. It seems likely that S was born in 469, the son of a sculptor. He followed his father's profession and served in the Athenian army like any other citizen. He did not exactly cut an impressive figure. He is described as "short, stocky, and stout, blear-eyed and snub-nosed; he had a large mouth and thick lips, and was careless in his dress, clumsy and uncouth." He had a wife (or mistress?) named Xanthippe, a shrew by all accounts. In the prime of his life he was a confidant of the Athenian statesman Pericles. In 399 he was sentenced to death by an Athenian jury after being found guilty of atheism and corrupting the youth of the city. The charges grew out of political conflicts within the city as much as from public irritation with S himself. Even after the conviction he was offered a chance to escape but refused it. He drank a cup of the poison hemlock (which gradually paralyzes the nervous system) and reportedly discoursed on the immortality of the soul as the poison took effect.

The most convenient summary of S's activity is found in P's *Apology*, which purports to be the pupil's record of the speech which his teacher gave in his own defense at his trial. In that speech S says that he had spent his life trying to understand something the god Apollo had said through the oracle at Delphi. A friend of S's had asked the oracle who was the wisest man in Greece, and the priestess had responded, "Socrates." The answer dumbfounded S, who set out to unravel the mystery. It had to be the right answer, he knew, for a god could not lie, but he did not know *why* it was the right answer.

He began his investigation by listening to various teachers who were reputed to be wise (the Sophists, cf. Chapter 9), but when he tried to ask questions about what he saw as weaknesses in their teachings, they became irritated and drove him away, sometimes with brute force. He then talked with craftsmen and artists, thinking that they might have some wisdom derived from their mechanical expertise. But again he was disappointed.

Finally the answer dawned on him. He was wise because he knew that he did not know anything. All the other allegedly wise men in Greece did not really know anything, but they mistook their ignorance for wisdom. He says that after that realization he devoted his life to trying to acquire wisdom. This he did not by propounding a system of thought, but by asking questions and analyzing the answers. He always remained more interested in a sound method of acquiring knowledge than in the knowledge itself.

What S says about his method and purposes in the *Apol* accords well with what we know from other sources. The "Socratic method" of teaching centers on asking questions and leading the student to see weaknesses in his own answers. It also involves a search for definitions that have universal application. If S asks what is justice or courage, he does not want to know what is the just or courageous thing to do in a particular situation. He is trying to find the essence or "virtue" of a thing. There must be some common characteristic underlying all individual acts of justice or courage. If one could understand what that was, he would not have to worry about discovering it again in each particular case.

In questioning others, S assumed an attitude of ignorance. In P's dialogues he usually says that he doesn't know the answer to a particular question and would be grateful if the other party to the conversation could enlighten him. This posture of (mock?) humility is described by the Greek word *eironeia*, meaning the slyness of an animal like a fox. "Socratic irony" is a phrase often encountered in the secondary literature. Once the other party had offered an answer or definition, S began to pick it apart by asking questions about various facets of the reply. In the *Rep* Thrasymachus defines justice as "doing good to your friends and evil to your enemies." S admires the definition, then asks what Thrasymachus means by "doing good" or by "friends" or by other parts of the definition. This technique of refuting (or leading the other person to refute) a statement is called *elenchus*. It is a crucial part of S's method of inquiry. The investigation does not always lead to solid results. At the end of the *Rep*, for example, S and his friends decide that they can't arrive at a satisfactory definition of justice. This situation is called an *aporia*.

Given his primary concerns, it is little wonder that S had no interest in understanding *physis* (nature), the problem which had occupied philosophers before his day. S shifted the entire focus of philosophy to ethics, both individual and corporate. How, he wondered, is one to live the best life (i. e., the life which leads to good for the individual) and how is a community to be organized to allow individuals to do that? This approach is called *eudaimonism*, or a search for the Good. The first step is to know what the Good is, or how will one ever know when it has been found?

S's method of arriving at knowledge is one of his most important contributions to the development of philosophy. He can be credited, as Aristotle noted, with laying the goundwork of an inductive method based on observation of particular instances leading to the formulation of universal principles. As Zeller says, "Behind morals he sought morality, behind prevailing law justice, in the history of existing states fixed principles for the communal life of man and behind the gods divinity."

We can say little of S's thought, interred as it is under the refinements effected by P. He seems to have been fundamentally opposed to the Sophists and their relativism. Knowledge, for S, must have some absolute, unchanging nature, apprehensible by the intellect. Once apprehended, it must have some practical value. He could see no advantage in knowing the elements of the universe or the cause of winds and seasons. But knowing what is piety, the beautiful, the nature of a successful ruler, those things had practical utility. Unlike the Sophists, S did think that such definite knowledge was possible.

On this concept of knowledge S built his ethics. The Sophists maintained that morality was subjective: what pleases any individual is moral for that individual. Other Greeks of the time saw ethics as dictated by convention. S tried to show that a person had to know what virtue was in order to *be* virtuous. No one could live a virtuous life unintentionally or accidentally. On the other hand, no one deliberately seeks evil. People do evil only when they do not know what the good is. These concepts are usually referred to as the Socratic paradoxes: 1) virtue is knowledge; 2) no one does wrong willingly (sometimes seen in its Latin form *nemo sua sponte peccat*).

Fundamental to S's concern with ethics and knowledge is his concept of the soul (*psyche*), which he considered the governing factor of human conduct. The aim of his philosophical inquiry was to improve the souls of his fellow-citizens, like a trainer in a gymnasium. S himself summed up his "mission" in the *Apol*: "I do nothing but go about persuading you all, old and young alike, not to take thought for your persons or properties, but first and chiefly to care about the greatest improvement of the soul. I tell you that virtue is not given by money, but that from virtue comes money and every other good of man, public as well as private." To his contemporaries, however, he appeared something of a meddlesome gnome, an irritant they were unwilling to tolerate any longer.

In compiling this portion of the bibliography we have encountered something of the problem of the historical *vs.* the Platonic S. The items listed here are intended to be more about the former, though there is no absolute dividing line. Socrates will be abbreviated S and Plato P.

ADKINS, A. W. H. "Clouds, Mysteries, Socrates, and Plato." *Antich* 4(1970), 13-24. Portrayal of S in *Clouds* as one who denigrated language of religious initiation was designed to make the audience fear and hate him.   **[987]**

AMORY, F. "Socrates, the Legend." *C&M* 35(1984), 19-56. Because of his irony, original S appears as mediator of intellectual and religious conflicts, a very wise man. Without the irony he becomes an impostor or picture of perfect sage. He can also be seen as passionate and irritable. By early Middle Ages he has become a martyr. **[988]**

ANASTAPLO, G. "Human Being and Citizen: A Beginning to the Study of the *Apology of Socrates*," in G. Anastaplo, *Human Being and Citizen: Essays on Virtue, Freedom and the Common Good* (Chicago: Swallow Pr., 1975), pp. 8-29. *Apol* is intended superficially for the city at large, to make people sympathetic with S. On a deeper level it is aimed at the reader who is attracted to philosophy and self-sacrifice but must be reminded of the demands such a life will place on him.   **[989]**

ANDERSON, A. "Was Socrates Unwise to Take the Hemlock?" *HThR* 65(1972), 437-452. Reasons given in P's dialogues do not justify S's suicide. It can be justified by his own knowledge of his guilt or his desire to advocate an other-worldly morality. **[990]**

ANDERSON, D. E. "Socrates' Concept of Piety." *JHPh* 5(1967), 1-13. In *Euthyphro*, *Apol*, and *Crito*, dialectic process is more important than notion of absolutes. By resigning himself to death, S vindicates his dialectic.   **[991]**

ANSELMENT, R. A. "Socrates and the *Clouds*: Shaftesbury and a Socratic Tradition." *JHI* 39(1978), 171-182. Important issue for Shaftesbury (1621-1683) is not role of Aristophanes' ridicule in damaging S but S's genial response as model for conduct. **[992]**

BARABAS, M. "The Strangeness of Socrates." *PhInv* 9(1986), 89-110. Examines assertion that the philosophical life which S embodies threatens fundamental aspects of human nature, especially physical and sexual.   **[993]**

BARKER, A. "Why Did Socrates Refuse to Escape?" *Phron* 22(1977), 13-28. Escape would have been an unjust act which would have affected S at the core of his being and had negative impact on his friends and children. [994]

BARON, J. R. "On Separating the Socratic from the Platonic in *Phaedo* 118." *CPh* 70(1975), 268-269. Words attributed to S in this passage should be taken as his final words. P merely reports; he does not interpret. [995]

BECK, F. A. "Traditional Elements in the Pedagogy of Socrates." *QUCC* 51(1986), 107-129. S distinguished himself from contemporaneous teachers more by crafty argumentation than by his originality or profundity. [996]

BECKMAN, J. *The Religious Dimension of Socrates' Thought.* Waterloo, Ont.: Wilfrid Laurier Univ. Pr., 1979. Though not pious in the ordinary sense, S is profoundly religious. His philosophy is his religion. Chapters examine historical evidence on S, his *daimonion*, and statements about religion in *Euthyphro* and *Apol.* [997]

BELFIORE, E. "Elenchus, Epode and Magic. Socrates as Silenus." *Phoenix* 34(1980), 128-137. S's words have a magical ability to possess people, like the lute music of a satyr. Once one understands process of elenchus, however, that illusion is dispelled. [998]

BENSON, H. H. "A Note on the Eristic and the Socratic Elenchus." *JHPh* 27(1989), 591-599. Elenchus and eristic both bring an interlocutor to recognize inconsistencies in his statements, but only elenchus penetrates to the level of belief and thus engenders genuine perplexity. [999]

———. "The Problem of the Elenchus Reconsidered." *AncPh* 7(1987), 67-85. If problem with elenchus is that it can establish only inconsistency and not falsehood, this problem cannot be solved because of theoretical constraints S places on elenchus. [1000]

BERLAND, K. J. H. "Bringing Philosophy Down from the Heavens: Socrates and the New Science." *JHI* 47(1986), 299-308. Examines S's ethical emphasis in light of the controversy over moral philosophy and science, especially in 17th- and 18th-century England. [1001]

BERNS, L. "Socratic and Non-Socratic Philosophy: A Note on Xenophon's *Memorabilia* 1.1.13 and 14." *RMeta* 28(1974), 85-88. Socratic moderation is traced to the effort to do justice to cognitive significance of ordinary experience and speech. S tried to find a mean between the common-sense knowledge of experience and the speculations of the cosmologists. [1002]

BERTMAN, M. A. "Socrates' Defense of Civil Disobedience." *StudGen* 24(1971), 576-582. S is right to remain in jail but wrong to see every law as morally binding. [1003]

BETZ, J. "Dewey and Socrates." *TPS* 16(1980), 329-356. Dewey appreciated S as the first true philosopher, who defined the field (as Dewey did) as an examination of traditional values necessitated by scientific progress. But he also criticized S for divorcing thought from action. [1004]

BEVERSLUIS, J. "Socratic Definition." *AmPhQ* 11(1974), 331-336. S rejects every attempt to answer the What-is-X question in terms of examples. But he appeals to particular cases as counter-examples to preferred definition. This ambivalence in S's treatment of definitions is explored.   [1005]

BICKNELL, P. J. "Sokrates' Mistress Xanthippe." *Apeir* 8 #1(1974), 1-5. Xanthippe was probably S's mistress and Myrto his wife. Sources hint at lesbian activity on Xanthippe's part.   [1006]

BLANK, D. L. "Socratics versus Sophists on Payment for Teaching." *ClAnt* 4(1985), 1-49. S refused to teach for money because he wanted to retain freedom to select his associates instead of being compelled to accept anyone who could pay.   [1007]

BLUM, A. F. *Socrates: The Original and its Images.* London: Routledge & Kegan Paul, 1978. Somewhat unorthodox study of S by a sociologist who emphasizes S's ability to integrate theory and life.   [1008]

BONFANTE, L., and RADITSA, L. "Socrates' Defense and His Audience." *BASP* 15(1978), 17-23. *Apol* refers to recent events without clearly taking sides. S could have appeared to be changing positions or to be indifferent to Athens' fate.   [1009]

BRANN, E. "The Offense of Socrates. A Re-reading of Plato's *Apology*." *Interp* 7 #2(1978), 1-21. Work contains P's recognition of civic dangers of philosophy. S's speech offers no plausible defense and is deliberately offensive.   [1010]

BRICKHOUSE, T. C., and SMITH, N. D. "'The Divine Sign Did not Oppose Me.' A Problem in Plato's *Apology*." *CanJPh* 16(1985), 511-526. S relies on silence of his *daimon* as a proof that his death will not be evil. But if *daimon*'s silence can tell S something, how can he remain ignorant of moral truth?   [1011]

―――. "The Formal Charges Against Socrates." *JHPh* 23(1985), 457-481. S's interrogation of Meletus in *Apol* is intended to reveal his accuser's ignorance and to demonstrate that the charges against S are false.   [1012]

―――. "A Matter of Life and Death in Socratic Philosophy." *AncPh* 9(1989), 155-165. In early dialogues S seems to be maintaining that a person who leads a virtuous life will enjoy an even better life after death. In one sense, then, a person could be said to be better off dead than alive.   [1013]

―――. "The Origin of Socrates' Mission." *JHI* 44(1983), 657-666. Even before receiving Delphic evaluation of his sagacity S seems to have believed that piety required service to the god. Oracle convinced him to abandon pretense to wisdom.   [1014]

―――. "The Paradox of Socratic Ignorance in Plato's *Apology*." *HPhQ* 1(1984), 125-132. S professes ignorance but is confident of value of his mission. To resolve paradox one must properly assess S's understanding of divination as giving rise to truth.   [1015]

―――. "Socrates' Evil Associates and the Motivation for his Trial and Condemnation." *PBACAPh* 3(1987), 45-71. Charge that S taught Alcibiades and Critias was not basis of prejudice against him. His refutation of charge of corrupting youth is sufficient to cover his association with these two, without naming them.   [1016]

―――. "Socrates' First Remarks to the Jury in Plato's *Apology* of Socrates." *CJ* 81(1986), 289-298. S's introductory comments are sincere and consistent with his speech as a whole and with what we know of his rhetorical practices.   **[1017]**

―――. "Socrates on Goods, Virtue, and Happiness." *OSAP* 5(1987), 1-27. Coherent account of S's view of relationship between virtue and happiness requires that he conceive of happiness as ensured by virtuous activity. But because virtuous activity can be thwarted by events which virtuous person cannot prevent, S believes that even a good person may, in some circumstances, judge his life as not worth living.   **[1018]**

―――. "Socrates' Proposed Penalty in Plato's *Apology*." *AGPh* 64(1982), 1-22. Fine which S proposes be imposed on him should have been an adequate penalty for his offense. Account of change in jury's vote is probably not historically accurate.   **[1019]**

―――. "Vlastos on the Elenchus." *OSAP* 2(1984), 185-195. Reply to #1204. Vlastos' interpretation of S's sincerity in elenchus requires certain assumptions which not even S is likely to have made.   **[1020]**

―――. cf. #2153.

BRUELL, C. "Xenophon and his Socrates." *Interp* 16(1989), 295-306. Compares X's and P's accounts of S; summarizes contents of X's *Memorabilia*.   **[1021]**

BRUMBAUGH, R. S. "The Trial of Socrates," in #49, pp. 227-238. Surveys the various sources available and the conflicting pictures of S which emerge.   **[1022]**

BURGE, E. L. "The Irony of Socrates." *Antich* 3(1969), 5-17. S's profession of ignorance was sincere. Plato moved from that essentially agnostic position to use elenchus pedagogically.   **[1023]**

BURNYEAT, M. F. "Virtues in Action," in #1199, pp. 209-234. Examines difference between ancient concern with virtues and vices and modern focus on actions through an investigation of S's treatment of virtue.   **[1024]**

CALDER, W. M., III. "Plato's *Apology* of Socrates: A Speech for the Defense." *BosUnivJ* 20(1972), 42-47. Attempts to evaluate the defense as an impartial, analytical member of the jury might have.   **[1025]**

CARAFIDES, J. L. "The Last Words of Socrates." *Platon* 23(1971), 229-232. S's ironic last words should be interpreted in context of Orphic-Pythagorean teachings on purification and immortality.   **[1026]**

CHROUST, A.-H. "A Comment on Aristotle's *On Noble Birth*." *WS* 6(1972), 19-32. Story of S's two wives may derive from a passage in Aristotle. S seems to have lived in a common-law marriage with Xanthippe, then married Myrto, keeping Xanthippe in his house. Myrto died shortly before S's death.   **[1027]**

CIHOLAS, P. "Socrates, Maker of New Gods." *CB* 57(1981), 17-20. S's inner religious experience was interpreted by his enemies as the introduction of new deities which threatened civic life.   **[1028]**

CLAY, D. "Socrates' Mulishness and Heroism." *Phron* 17(1972), 53-60. Shows reasonableness of S's claims about his *daimonion* and his implicit claim to be a hero. **[1029]**

COHEN, M. "Confucius and Socrates." *JChinPh* 3(1976), 159-168. S and Confucius lived in similar situations. Both were pragmatic, not theoretical, and neither outlined a system of thought. Both generated philosophical traditions in which their stress on definition became theoretical.   **[1030]**

COLSON, D. D. "On Appealing to Athenian Law to Justify Socrates' Disobedience." *Apeir* 19(1985), 133-151. Focusing on *Apol* 29C-D and *Crito* 51B-C, author argues that S was at times a civil disobedient out of his own self-interest, not for purely philosophical reasons.   **[1031]**

DANNHAUSER, W. J. *Nietzsche's View of Socrates.* Ithaca, NY: Cornell Univ. Pr., 1974. Aim is to elucidate various central aspects of Nietzsche's writings in light of his understanding of philosophical import of S's existence and reflections.   **[1032]**

DAVIES, C. "Socrates." *HT* 20(1970), 799-805. Non-specialist introduction. One of S's primary objectives was to correct damage done by Sophists. His failure to have wide impact in his own day does not detract from his seminal influence on later philosophical developments.   **[1033]**

DE STRYCKER, E. "The Unity of Knowledge and Love in Socrates' Conception of Virtue." *IntPhQ* 6(1966), 428-444. In identifying virtue and knowledge, S does not mean a knowledge about a special field or about means to an end, but about human life as a whole and about ultimate end of human striving. Virtue is a knowledge about absolute Good and relativity of other values. Virtue is an indissoluble unity of love and knowledge of the Good.   **[1034]**

———. cf. #2157.

DE VOGEL, C. J. "The Present State of the Socratic Problem." *Phron* 1(1955), 26-35. Survey of some then-current work.   **[1035]**

———. "Two Major Problems Concerning Socrates." *ThetaPi* 11(1973), 18-39. Looks at two issues in light of #19: S's ethical utilitarianism; his disdain for the body.   **[1036]**

DILMAN, I. "Socrates and Dostoyevsky on Punishment." *Ph&Lit* 1(1976), 66-78. S saw punishment as a means of reintegrating the miscreant with the good. Its aim is not healing or retribution. Pain necessary for punishment to succeed is derived from moral awakening of individual being punished. Comparison of these ideas to *Crime and Punishment*.   **[1037]**

DIXIT, R. D. "Socrates on Civil Disobedience." *IndianPhQ* 8(1980), 91-98. S's disobedience to law is based on his obedience to his conscience, his willingness to accept calmly whatever penalties may follow, and his refusal to harm others.   **[1038]**

DOVER, K. J. "Socrates in the *Clouds*," in #1199, pp. 50-77. Aristophanes chose S to parody because he was physically unattractive and seemed to conservatives to have an inexplicable appeal to a circle of wealthy young men. He seemed to have no coherent teaching and produced nothing of any literary/artistic value.   **[1039]**

DRENGSON, A. R. "The Virtue of Socratic Ignorance." *AmPhQ* 18(1981), 237-242. Admitting one's ignorance makes it possible to act in a self-enlightening way.   **[1040]**

DUFF, R. A. "Socratic Suicide?" *PAS* 83(1982-83), 35-48. S did intend to die, but character of his intention was different from that of a person who deliberately decides to die. One must define nature of suicide before one can determine if S's death falls in that category.   **[1041]**

DYBIKOWSKI, J. "Socrates, Obedience and the Law: Plato's *Crito*." *Dial*(Can) 13(1974), 519-535. Examines arguments used against escape and shows how each would justify too strong a general view favoring obedience.   **[1042]**

EDMUNDS, L. "Aristophanes' Socrates." *PBACAPh* 1(1985), 209-230. Argues that *Clouds* contains enough historical detail to allow us to reconstruct a picture of S which is similar to that provided by Plato and Xenophon.   **[1043]**

EHRENBERG, V. *From Solon to Socrates.* London: Methuen, 1973; 2nd ed. Discusses Greeks' efforts to understand Delphic oracle's maxim "know thyself" and examines S's efforts to turn Greek investigations to consideration of man rather than the heavens.   **[1044]**

EISNER, R. "Socrates as Hero." *Ph&Lit* 6(1982), 106-118. When S is studied in the context of hero stories, his attributes, character traits, and flaws bear strong resemblance to those of Odysseus.   **[1045]**

ELIOT, A. *Socrates. A Fresh Appraisal of the Most Celebrated Case in History.* New York: Crown, 1967. Introductory, non-specialist essay followed by a dramatic recasting of passages from P's dialogues which pertain to S's death.   **[1046]**

EUBEN, J. P. "Philosophy and Politics in Plato's *Crito*." *PolTheo* 6(1978), 149-172. Examines inconsistency between S's expressed willingness in *Apol* to disobey the jury should they forbid him to practice philosophy and his unwillingness in *Crito* to escape from jail.   **[1047]**

FARNESS, J. "Missing Socrates. Socratic Rhetoric in a Platonic Text." *Ph&Rh* 20(1987), 41-59. Argues that S is unable to deal with transpersonal forces in his defense. His angry reply illustrates various characteristics Athenians had attributed to him. His defense is a personal vindication but a philosophical failure.   **[1048]**

FEAVER, D. D., and **HARE, J. E.** "The *Apology* as an Inverted Parody of Rhetoric." *Arethusa* 14(1981), 205-216. Comparison of *Apol* with Gorgias' *Palamedes* shows S is imitating Gorgias. He is also trying to succeed in terms of telling the truth, not necessarily winning his case.   **[1049]**

FEREJOHN, M. T. "Socratic Virtue as the Parts of Itself." *Ph&PhenRes* 44(1984), 377-388. S never adequately resolved difference between two definitions of "parts": 1) in the sense that ears, nose, mouth, etc., are parts of a face, or 2) in the sense that a piece of gold can be cut into smaller parts.   **[1050]**

————. "The Unity of Virtue and the Objects of Socratic Inquiry." *JHPh* 20(1982), 1-21. Discussion of differing views of Penner (#1138) and Vlastos (#1207). Penner's claim that virtues are identical seems more Socratic.   **[1051]**

FERGUSON, J. *Socrates: A Source Book.* London: Macmillan, 1970. Somewhat

unbalanced collection of sources for study of S, with more than half of authors represented dating from after Aristotle's time. Introduction discusses problem of historical S, but
tends to stress personal facets of his life rather than his thought.   [1052]

FINLEY, M. I. "Socrates and Athens," in *Aspects of Antiquity: Discoveries and Controversies* (Middlesex, UK: Penguin, 1973), pp. 60-73. S's condemnation has been used to
argue against democratic systems, but Athens should be judged on its entire record, not
one incident. Viewed from Athenian standpoint, verdict can be understood.   [1053]

FISCHER, J. L. *The Case of Socrates*, transl. I. Lewitowa. Univ. of Prague, 1969. Tries
to understand S by psychoanalyzing him and reconstructing his youth, family background.
Sees his physical ugliness and social inferiority as producing sense of intellectual superiority. Treats all references to S in ancient sources as historically reliable.   [1054]

FITTON, J. W. "That Was No Lady, that Was . . . ." *CQ* 20(1970), 56-66. Though S
may have had relationships with Xanthippe and Myrto simultaneously, it is also likely that
he married or lived with them in succession. He seems to have had a child by Xanthippe
and several by Myrto.   [1055]

FREY, R. G. "Did Socrates Commit Suicide?" *Ph* 53(1978), 106-108. Analysis of
concept of suicide suggests that S's death should be regarded in that light.   [1056]

GADAMER, H.-G. "Religion and Religiosity in Socrates." *PBACAPh* 1(1985), 53-76.
For S, God is author of all things, not out of necessity or grace, but as perfect craftsman.
This is not proved but is assumed out of piety. S's relationship to Athens' religious
tradition is essential for understanding *Phaedo, Symp.*, and *Phaedrus*.   [1057]

GAVIN, W. "Death: Acceptance or Denial. The Case of Socrates Re-examined."
ReligHum 11(1977), 134-139. S's attitude toward death is not one of acceptance but
irony, which is a form of defiance in an uncertain situation. An idealized portrait, such
as that of S, is in itself a form of denial of death.   [1058]

GILL, C. "The Death of Socrates." *CQ* 23(1973), 25-28. As described in *Phaedo*, S's
death is much calmer than reactions usually produced by hemlock. P has turned the historical event into a philosophical account of the soul's departure from the body.[1059]

GOLD, J. "Socratic Definition: Real or Nominal?" *PhResArch* 10(1985), 573-585.
Argues there is no real/nominal distinction in S's search for definitions.   [1060]

GONTAR, D. P. "The Problem of the Formal Charges in Plato's *Apology*." *TulStudPh*
27(1978), 89-101. Examines S's defense and argues that notion of S as Sophist (as Aristophanes suggested) may not be so far-fetched.   [1061]

GOOCH, P. W. "Socratic Irony and Aristotle's *Eiron*. Some Puzzles." *Phoenix* 41(1987),
95-104. Despite his generally negative view of *eironeia*, Ar applies the term to S in a
positive sense, apparently from his admiration for S.   [1062]

――――. cf. #1367.

GREEN, P. "Strepsiades, Socrates and the Abuses of Intellectualism." *GRBS* 20(1979),
15-25. Strepsiades, in Aristophanes' *Clouds*, is a person not initiated into the New

Learning. S describes such a person in *Theaet.*   [1063]

GUARDINI, R. *The Death of Socrates: An Interpretation of the Platonic Dialogues:* Euthyphro, Apology, Crito *and* Phaedo, transl. B. Wrighton. Cleveland: World, 1969; rprt. Translation of selected passages from these four dialogues interspersed with running commentary to form connected narrative of last phase of S's life.   [1064]

GUILHAMET, L. "Socrates and Post-Socratic Satire." *JHI* 46(1985), 3-12. S is an appropriate target for satire because his life and teachings are profoundly paradoxical: simple, even ludicrous, on the surface, but embodying the most profound search for truth. Survey of later writers' use of S in satiric contexts through Middle Ages, to Erasmus and Rabelais.   [1065]

GULLEY, N. *The Philosophy of Socrates.* London: Macmillan, 1968. Discusses method of elenchus, the aim at definitions, contrasts between dialectic and eristic. Examines paradoxes that virtue is knowledge and that no one does wrong willingly. Also considers S's political and religious views. Pays little attention to biographical matters.   [1066]

GUTHRIE, W. K. C. *Socrates.* Cambridge Univ. Pr., 1971. Portion of vol. III of *History of Greek Philosophy* (#19) reprinted separately.   [1067]

HADEN, J. "On Socrates, with Reference to Gregory Vlastos." *RMeta* 33(1979), 371-389. Reply to #1198. S was not blind to empirical data nor indifferent to human emotion. He masked his tenderness toward others.   [1068]

———. "Socratic Ignorance," in #1083, pp. 17-28. Examines question of what S meant by his professions of ignorance; argues Socratic ignorance is linked with need to establish union between cognitive and emotive dimensions of the human composite.   [1069]

HART, R. E. "Socrates on Trial: Commentary on Brickhouse and Smith," in #1083, pp. 143-150. Reply to #2154; argues that S did not analyze his dilemma at the trial in terms of broadest possible conceptions of truth, justice, and morality.   [1070]

HAVELOCK, E. "The Orality of Socrates and the Literacy of Plato," in #1083, pp. 67-93. Examines parts played by S and P in a process of linguistic and psychological change. Argues that moral philosophy is creation of alphabetic literacy.   [1071]

———. "The Socratic Problem: Some Second Thoughts," in #42, pp. 147-173. Part of difficulty in outlining historic S is problem of understanding the oral mind-set of his age. Aristophanes' *Clouds* can be more useful in this regard than many will allow.   [1072]

———. "The Socratic Self as it is Parodied in Aristophanes' *Clouds*." *YCS* 22(1972), 1-18. Studies similarity, especially in vocabulary, between Aristophanes' S and P's. [1073]

HAWTREY, R. S. W. "Plato, Socrates, and the Mysteries. A Note." *Antich* 10(1976), 22-24. Reply to Adkins (#987). P does not seem to have deliberately avoided use of language associated with mystery cults.   [1074]

———. "Socrates and the Acquisition of Knowledge." *Antich* 6(1972), 1-4. S believed in possiblity of acquiring certain knowledge, but his technique of refutation could lead only to technical, not moral, knowledge.   [1075]

HENRY, M. "Socratic Piety and the Power of Reason," in #1083, pp. 95-106. Seeks to explain Platonic interpretation of Socratic piety (as opposed to Xenophon's) and to show how Athenians were persuaded that S was impious.   **[1076]**

HOGAN, R. "Was Socrates a 'Utilitarian'?" *Auslegung* 5(1978), 118-131. S sought to define what was "useful" on the basis of an objective standard. His definition is unsatisfactory, but it is misleading to call him a utilitarian, as Guthrie (#1067) does.   **[1077]**

IRWIN, T. H. "Socrates and Athenian Democracy." *Ph&PubAff* 18(1989), 184-205. Reply to I. F. Stone (#1170), who fails to grasp some fundamental points of interpretation of P's work.   **[1078]**

JACKSON, D. B. "The Prayers of Socrates." *Phron* 16(1971), 14-37. Examines twenty-one prayers, twelve by S, with regard to their relation to the state cults and to literary usage, their functions in the dialogues, and their place in the portrait of S.   **[1079]**

——. cf. #6759.

KAHN, C. "Socrates and the Rule of Law," in #72, pp. 11-16. Discusses Allen (#2150) and Kraut (#1091). Main points are disobedience as destruction of city, analogy between city and parent, and argument that law depends upon agreement between men and the Law, not a social contract among men.   **[1080]**

KALLICK, D. "The Speakerly Teacher: Socrates and Writing." *Metaphil* 20(1989), 341-346. Criticisms leveled against writing in *Phaedrus* may stem from S himself. Application of his teaching need not mean complete abandonment of writing in education process. He seems to call for a kind of dialogic engagement with a text.   **[1081]**

KARAVITES, P. "Socrates in the *Clouds*." *CB* 50(1973-74), 65-69. The portrait of S in the play differs from others because Aristophanes wanted to parody his physical appearance, not his doctrine.   **[1082]**

KELLY, E., ed. *New Essays on Socrates*. Lanham, MD: University Pr. of America, 1984. Essays are abstracted herein.   **[1083]**

KENDALL, W. "The People versus Socrates Revisited," in *Willmoore Kendall contra Mundum* (New Rochelle, NY: Arlington House, 1971), pp. 149-167. Conservative interpretation maintaining that S was guilty. Liberal bias in modern academic circles has made him champion of free thought.   **[1084]**

KLEVE, K. "Anti-Dover or Socrates in the *Clouds*." *SO* 58(1983), 23-37. Reply to #1039. Evidence suggests Aristophanes' portrait of S is not entirely unreal.   **[1085]**

——. "The Daimon of Socrates." *SIFC* 4(1986), 5-18. Discussion of nature of S's divine voice and modern interpretations, especially Kierkegaard's.   **[1086]**

——. "Did Socrates Exist?" *GB* 14(1987), 123-137. Plato, Xenophon and Aristophanes agree on important points, so that discrepancies in their accounts of S cannot be used as evidence that he did not exist.   **[1087]**

——. cf. #5996.

KLOSKO, G. "Socrates on Goods and Happiness." *HPhQ* 4(1987), 251-264. As depicted by P, S does not hold a consistent position on issue of goods and happiness. Sometimes he seems to say that material things cannot add to happiness. At other times he seems to concede that some material goods can help make a person happy. [1088]

KRAUT, R. "Comments on Gregory Vlastos, 'The Socratic Elenchus'." *OSAP* 1(1983), 59-70. Reply to #1204. Elenchus can establish proof, not merely refute. [1089]

———. *Socrates and the State*. Princeton Univ. Pr., 1984. Maintains that S believed a citizen could disobey a law that was morally wrong if he attempted to persuade the city of the injustice. The city has certain authority, as a parent does, but adult children have the right to make their own decisions. Also discusses S's view that city should be run by moral experts. [1090]

LACEY, A. R. "Our Knowledge of Socrates," in #1199, pp. 22-49. Discusses sources of information about historic S, such as Aristophanes, P, Xenophon, Aristotle, and sophistic *Dissoi Logoi*. [1091]

LESHER, J. H. "Socrates' Disavowal of Knowledge." *JHPh* 25(1987), 275-288. S does not disavow all knowledge, just wisdom (*sophia*) about virtue, i. e., what it is and how it is acquired. Such disavowal does not contradict his view of virtue as an attribute of the soul. [1092]

LUCAS, B. J. "Russell on the Socratic Question." *Russell* (1975), 3-9. Russell's remarks about reliability of Xenophon's portrait of S are not entirely accurate. [1093]

LUKIC, M. "Socrates and Indifference Towards Death." *SJPh* 9(1971), 393-398. S attempted to find a compromise between denial of afterlife and view that earthly life is merely a fragment of a longer process. His effort, however, is inadequate. [1094]

MacKENZIE, M. M. "The Virtues of Socratic Ignorance." *CQ* 38(1988), 331-350. S often does claim to have certain knowledge, but those claims rest on different grounds from his assertion that he knows nothing. [1095]

MAHOOD, G. H. "Socrates and Confucius. Moral Agents or Moral Philosophers?" *PhE&W* 21(1971), 177-188. Moral teaching can be done either by word or deed. S and Confucius are often contrasted on this basis. The contrast is too sharp. S acts out his teaching, just as Confucius gives instruction to supplement his actions. [1096]

MARA, G. M. "Socrates and Liberal Toleration." *PolTheo* 16(1988), 468-495. S's truths are not "dogmatic assertions" but rather aids to learning and improvement. [1097]

MARTIN, H. M. "To Trust (the) God. An Inquiry into Greek and Hebrew Religious Thought." *CJ* 83(1987), 1-10. As examples of their traditions, Abraham and S are similar in their understanding of divine purpose and necessity for obedience to it. They differ in that S believes morality and deity to be separate. [1098]

MARTIN, R. "Socrates on Disobedience to Law." *RMeta* 24(1970), 21-38. In *Crito* S argues that all laws, whether just or not, must be obeyed. Possible weaknesses of this position are explored. [1099]

McLAUGHLIN, R. J. "Socrates on Political Disobedience: A Reply to Gary Young." *Phron* 21(1976), 185-197. Response to #1226. S is not limiting possibility of disobedience to the one order against philosophizing. **[1100]**

McPHERRAN, M. L. "Socrates and the Duty to Philosophize." *SJPh* 24(1986), 541-560. Can everyone be a philosopher, as S seems to maintain in *Apol*? It is possible if philosophy is connected with broader requirements of piety and virtue. **[1101]**

————. "Socratic Piety in the *Euthyphro*." *JHPh* 23(1985), 283-310. S is pious when he criticizes Euthyphro for holding that humans can know divine things. This picture is consistent with our understanding of historic S. **[1102]**

MILLER, J. F. "The Socratic Meaning of Virtue." *SJPh* 9(1971), 141-150. Virtue is not just knowledge that something is true, nor is it knowledge of how to do something. It is knowledge of how to act as a situation requires, founded on knowing what is ultimately right or wrong. **[1103]**

MITSCHERLING, J. "*Phaedo* 118. The Last Words." *Apeir* 19(1985), 161-165. S's instructions to Crito to sacrifice a cock to Asclepius cast doubt on charge of atheism. Practice is consistent with Pythagorean motifs in the work. **[1104]**

MOLINE, J. "Euripides, Socrates and Virtue." *Hermes* 103(1975), 45-67. Euripides does not seem to be engaging in a polemic against S's idea that virtue is knowledge. His characters speak lines appropriate to their dramatic situations. They cannot be assumed to be Euripides' spokespersons. **[1105]**

MOMEYER, R. W. "Socrates on Obedience and Disobedience to the Law." *PhResArch* 8(1982), 21-53. Contradiction between S's pledge to ignore a court order to stop philosophizing and his argument that civic authority compels a citizen to obey cannot be resolved because it is inherent in inconsistencies in S's principles, character. **[1106]**

MONTUORI, M. *Socrates: Physiology of a Myth*, transl. M. Langdale. Amsterdam: Gieben, 1981. Tries to correct what is perceived as an over-emphasis on study of S as a philosopher at the expense of understanding the historical figure. The major obstacle to such a study is that most available accounts about him were written to refute or support charges made at his trial. **[1107]**

MOONEY, C. P. "The Mystical Dimension in Socratic Piety: Response to Henry," in #1083, pp. 161-172. Argues that Henry (#1076) overemphasizes S's rationalism and overlooks mystical or spiritual nature of his vision and method. **[1108]**

MORRIS, T. F. "Kierkegaard's Understanding of Socrates." *IntJPhRel* 19(1986), 105-111. Kierkegaard saw S as upholding a relationship with God because S understood God as giving meaning to all activity. S abstained from desire for physical things precisely because they are less than God. **[1109]**

MORRISON, D. "On Professor Vlastos' Xenophon." *AncPh* 7(1987), 9-22. Challenges claim (#1198) that Xenophon's S has little philosophical or historical interest. **[1110]**

MULGAN, R. G. "Socrates and Authority." *G&R* 19(1972), 208-212. S's assertion that he would refuse to obey an order to stop philosophizing should not be generalized. It applies only to him on this particular issue.   [1111]

MULHERN, J. J. "Aristotle and the Socratic Paradoxes." *JHI* 35(1974), 293-299. Ar exposes first Socratic paradox as too simple to be true by distinguishing cases where virtue can or cannot be equated with knowledge. He dissolves the second — no one does wrong willingly — by noting that disposition is a facet of character but not an inflexible habit and cannot be relied on to lead one to act according to choices. [1112]

———. "A Note on Stating the Socratic Paradox." *JHI* 29(1968), 601-604. Xenophon gives two Socratic paradoxes: "No one does wrong knowingly" and "virtue is knowledge." It is not clear the former is true paradox or that one is derived from the other. [1113]

NADLER, S. "Probability and Truth in the *Apology* (with Reply by Kenneth Seeskin)." *Ph&Lit* 9(1985), 198-202. S tries to persuade Athenians by using "base" rhetoric when addressing alleged reasons for his trial, and a more honest approach when talking about his life, which is the real reason he is being tried.   [1114]

NAGLEY, W. E. "Kierkegaard's Early and Later View of Socratic Irony." *Thought* 55(1980), 271-282. Late in life Kierkegaard admitted that he had undervalued S in his early work. He finally saw S's thought as existential, ethical, deeply religious.   [1115]

NAILS, D. "The Shrewish Wife of Socrates." *EMC* 29(1985), 97-99. P tries to correct negative impression of Xanthippe given by Xenophon.   [1116]

NAKHNIKIAN, G. "Elenctic Definitions," in #1199, pp. 125-157. Seeks to explain nature and availability of elenctic definitions by comparing and contrasting theory and practice of Socratic and Platonic definitions.   [1117]

———. "The First Socratic Paradox." *JHPh* 11(1973), 1-19. S is unsuccessful in defending his paradoxical statement that "no man desires evil, all men desire good." It is related to dictum that virtue is knowledge and vice is ignorance.   [1118]

NAVIA, L. E. "A Reappraisal of Xenophon's *Apology*," in #1083, pp. 47-66. Examines Xenophon's portrait of S and his attempt to clear S from charge of insolent language; argues for a more sympathetic treatment.   [1119]

———. *Socrates: The Man and His Philosophy.* Lanham, MD: University Pr. of America, 1985. Study of major themes of S's life and thought. Stresses his intellectual optimism and moral confidence.   [1120]

NEHAMAS, A. "Socratic Intellectualism." *PBACAPh* 2(1986), 275-316. Argues that S's belief in priority of definition is less radical than is often claimed. Examines issue of S's success or failure as a teacher of virtue. By claiming that virtue is knowledge S seems to make it impossible for anyone to attain to virtue. But P emphasized that S saw knowledge as being within us, so it is ultimately attainable.   [1121]

NEUMANN, H. "Plato's *Defense of Socrates*: An Interpretation of Ancient and Modern Sophistry." *Liberal Education* 56(1970), 458-475. Modern mind associates philosophy with ideology, but Socratic philosophy questions all authority. Maintains that S was not innocent.   [1122]

———. "Socrates and the Tragedy of Athens." *Social Research* 35(1968), 426-444. Many Greek intellectuals favored Sparta with its severe discipline. S, however, finds Athenian candor a philosophic virtue.   [1123]

———. "Socrates in Plato and Aristophanes." *AJPh* 90(1969), 201-214. Compares pictures in *Rep* and *Clouds*. For P, S draws men together around a common good. Aristophanes sees S as sophistic and men as having nothing in common.   [1124]

NICHOLS, M. P. *Socrates and the Political Community: An Ancient Debate.* Albany: SUNY Pr., 1987. Studies Aristophanes, several Platonic dialogues, and Book 2 of Aristotle's *Politics* to see S criticized as one who undermined the state by his search for universals and defended as one who focussed on what really mattered in establishment of a healthy city.   [1125]

NUSSBAUM, M. C. "Commentary on Edmunds' 'Aristophanes' Socrates'." *PBACAPh* 1(1985), 231-240. Disagrees with Edmunds' claim (#1043) that Aristophanes was unable or unwilling to see depth and complexity of Socratic way of life.   [1126]

OBER, W. B. "Did Socrates Die of Hemlock Poisoning?" *AncPh* 2(1982), 115-121. Death narrative in *Phaedo* does not fit with modern understanding of death by hemlock poisoning. P probably enhanced the picture to fit with S's views on death.   [1127]

O'CONNELL, R. J. "God, Gods, and Moral Cosmos in Socrates' *Apology*." *IntPhQ* 25(1985), 31-50. Challenges readings by Grube and Guthrie that *theos* did not have an anthropopsychic (personal) meaning for Plato.   [1128]

OJOADE, J. O. "Socrates: Was He Really a Sophist?" *Phrontis* 5(1967), 48-61. The evidence allows both a positive and a negative answer.   [1129]

ORGAN, T. "The Excellence of Socrates." *DarshInt* 17(1977), 27-34. Examines S's style of questioning and his actions and hints of actions to elucidate how he is a man of excellence.   [1130]

PALMA, A. B. "Socrates: Love, Irony and Philosophy." *Prud* 18(1986), 15-30. Reply to Vlastos (#1198). S should be seen as loving people of Athens, in spite of harshness of his teaching method.   [1131]

PANAGIOTOU, S. "Socrates' Defiance in the *Apology*." *Apeir* 20(1987), 39-61. S does not actually face a situation where he must defy a court order to stop philosophizing. The court offered to be lenient, but this was an offer, not an order.   [1132]

PANGLE, T. L. "The Political Defense of Socratic Philosophy: A Study of Xenophon's *Apology of Socrates to the Jury*." *Polity* 18(1985), 98-114. Xenophon's version of S's last speech concentrates on S's concern with the beauty and importance of his own soul. He seems to transcend political life.   [1133]

PARKER, M. *Socrates: The Wisest and Most Just?* Cambridge Univ. Pr., 1979. Translation of selected passages from Platonic dialogues which present key elements of S's thought. Brief introduction.   [1134]

PATZER, A. *Bibliographia Socratica. Die Wissenschaftliche Literatur ueber Sokrates von*

den Anfaengen bis auf die neueste Zeit in systematisch-chronologischer Anordnung.
Freiburg, Ger.: Alber, 1985. Comprehensive in chronology and scope.   **[1135]**

PENNER, T. "Socrates on the Impossibility of Belief-Relative Sciences." *PBACAPh*
3(1987), 263-325. S rejects rhetoric as a "science" because it relies on assumptions which
the practioner must believe to be true, whether they are or not.   **[1136]**

————. "Socrates on Virtue and Motivation," in #65, pp. 133-151. Examines two of S's
unusual theses: that virtue is an *episteme* or *techne* (a science or art like medicine,
navigation, or carpentry) and that no one errs willingly.   **[1137]**

————. "The Unity of Virtue." *PhR* 82(1973), 35-68. It is difficult to take literally
Socrates' claim that all virtues are one. But the question "what is bravery?" means for
S "what is the psychological condition that produces brave acts?" Identity conditions for
psychological states are wider than those for definitions, so that another word could be
substituted for "bravery" without altering the meaning.   **[1138]**

PESELY, G. E. "Socrates' Attempt to Save Theramenes." *AHB* 2(1988), 31-33. Story
that S tried to save Theramenes from execution by Thirty Tyrants probably comes from
Hermippus, who is noted more for sense of drama than historical accuracy.   **[1139]**

PETERMAN, J. E. "The Socratic Suicide," in #1083, pp. 3-15. In order for his followers
to truly criticize their ideas S must leave their presence, as he is finally the greatest
obstacle to overcoming the natural reluctance to criticize valued ideas.   **[1140]**

POLANSKY, R. M. "Professor Vlastos' Analysis of Socratic Elenchus." *OSAP* 3(1985),
247-259. Points out weaknesses in Vlastos' analysis of elenchus (#1204).   **[1141]**

RANKIN, D. I. "Sokrates, an Oligarch?" *AC* 56(1987), 68-87. S's trial was result of his
close links to oligarchy in Athens. P and Xenophon de-emphasized this part of process,
to protect themselves because their sympathies also lay with oligarchy.   **[1142]**

REILLY, R. "Socrates' Moral Paradox." *SwJPh* 8(1977), 101-107. Paradox that anyone
doing injustice does so unwillingly does not contradict possibility of *akrasia* (weakness of
will). Resolution of paradox lies in recognition of more than one criterion for differentiating better/worse courses of action.   **[1143]**

ROBINSON, R. "Elenchus," in #1199, pp. 78-93. S probably developed elenchus because it was natural to his inquiring mind. It has drawback that it tells a person that he
is wrong but not why. Negative impression it created lingered to end of S's life. In P's
middle and late dialogues elenchus loses its irony and is incorporated into more positive
form of dialectic. By late dialogues it is referred to but not actually used.   **[1144]**

————. "Socratic Definition," in #1199, pp. 110-124. Examines S's use of "What is x?"
question in elenchus as way of searching for essences.   **[1145]**

ROOCHNIK, D. L. "*Apology* 40c4-41e7. Is Death Really a Gain?" *CJ* 80(1985), 212-
220. End of speech is intended to be intelligible to all S's hearers, whether philosophically enlightened or not. It may also demonstrate how he regarded myths.   **[1146]**

RORTY, A. O. "Commentary. The Limits of Socratic Intellectualism: Did Socrates

Teach Arete?" *PBACAPh* 2(1986), 317-330. Response to Nehamas (#1121). Suggests that while S might be an intellectualist about virtue, he may not be an intellectualist about knowledge. Argues that dramatic presentation of S in dialogues undermines his intellectualist views. [1147]

ROSSETTI, L. "The Rhetoric of Socrates." *Ph&Rh* 22(1989), 225-238. Examines S's dialectical practices as rhetorical strategies. [1148]

SANTAS, G. *Socrates: Philosophy in Plato's Early Dialogues.* London: Routledge & Kegan Paul, 1979. Presents a contemporary philosophical analysis of such issues as S as philosopher and citizen, Socratic method and ethics. Emphasizes S's argumentation and how it compares to modern propositional and predicate logic. [1149]

──── . "The Socratic Fallacy." *JHPh* 10(1972), 127-141. Evidence of dialogues leaves it unclear whether S denied examples make adequate definitions. [1150]

SARF, H. "Reflections on Kierkegaard's Socrates." *JHI* 44(1983), 255-276. Kierkegaard found in S an *exemplum* for life devoted to moral improvement. He wanted to make S a living presence in efforts of his age to solve its ethical dilemmas. He saw P as missing essence of S's thought and dogmatizing S's subjective approach to learning. [1151]

SCHARFF, R. C. "Socrates' Successful Inquiries." *M&W* 19(1986), 311-327. S's inquiries can be called successful on his terms, if not ours, because he was aiming at an on-going re-examination of life, not acquisition of a body of knowledge. [1152]

SCHMID, W. T. "The Socratic Conception of Courage." *HPhQ* 2(1985), 113-130. S's concept is examined against historical background of the term, contrasted to Callicles' view, which foreshadows Nietzsche's. P's presentation in early dialogues makes S look ambivalent on subject. [1153]

──── . "Socratic Moderation and Self-Knowledge." *JHPh* 21(1983), 339-348. Old-fashioned notion of *sophrosyne* (moderation) was undergoing significant changes in the late fifth century B. C. But moderation, in sense of humility and self-knowledge, is essential element in Socratic process of learning. [1154]

──── . "Socratic Piety," in #1277, pp. 3-24. Profusely documented study showing that S's piety rests on humble reverence before an unknown God, whose concern for humanity calls people to seek truth and work for welfare of others. [1155]

──── . cf. #2188.

SEESKIN, K. R. "Courage and Knowledge. A Perspective on the Socratic Paradox." *SJPh* 4(1976), 511-521. S's requirement that one know in order to be courageous is where his theory is often criticized. He did not ignore conflict between internal emotions and reason but substituted cowardly behavior for death as ultimate evil. [1156]

──── . *Dialogue and Discovery. A Study in Socratic Method.* Albany: SUNY Pr., 1987. It is no coincidence that S's teaching is presented by P in dialogue form. Socratic *elenchus* requires at least two voices, and aim of S's method is to produce moral reform, i. e., virtue. Aim, methodology, form of presentation are thus integrally linked. Stresses psychological motives of *elenchus*, conflict of personalities as well as ideas. [1157]

———. "Is the *Apology* of Socrates a Parody?" *Ph&Lit* 6(1982), 94-105. *Apol* takes one of Gorgias' speeches as its model and parodies rhetorical commonplaces. Such analysis helps us understand P's attack on rhetoric in his *Gorg*. [1158]

———. cf. #1455.

SEIPLE, G. "The Socratic Method of Inquiry." *Dial*(PST) 28(1985), 16-22. Earlier interpretations of "virtue is knowledge" paradox have failed to explain that elenchus brings realization of ignorance, painful as it may be, and that it is unclear whether "knowledge" means "knowing *that*" or "knowing *how*." [1159]

SENTER, N. W. "Socrates, Rhetoric and Civil Disobedience." *SwPhSt* 1(1976), 50-56. Civil disobedience which S exemplifies in *Apol* is not analogous to modern public protest. It is more closely akin to Thoreau's moral disobedience. [1160]

SESONSKE, A. "To Make the Weaker Argument Defeat the Stronger." *JHPh* 6(1968), 217-231; also in #2081, pp. 71-90. In his defense S says he was accused of this Sophistic trick. He never refutes charge; is actually guilty of it in his speech. [1161]

SILVERBERG, R. *Socrates*. New York: Putnam, 1965. Non-specialist biography of S as philosopher, soldier, Athenian; borders on the novelistic. [1162]

SKEMP, J. B. "The Spirituality of Socrates and Plato," in #43, pp. 102-120. S's *daimonion* suggests that he believed in a divine being which cared for humans. P believed in an eternal existent which exercised benevolent control over sensible world. [1163]

SMITH, M. "Did Socrates Kill Himself Intentionally?" *Ph* 55(1980), 253-254. Fact that S wanted to die and drank poison does not mean he killed himself intentionally.[1164]

SMITH, N. D., and BRICKHOUSE, T. C. "Socrates and Obedience to the Law." *Apeir* 18(1984), 10-18. Understanding S's legal situation is key to resolving apparent contradictions between *Apol* 29c-30c and *Crito* 51b-c. [1165]

SOUPIOS, M. A. "Reason and Feeling in Plato: Response to Haden," in #1083, pp. 137-141. Critically examines Haden's discussion (#1069) of S's profession of ignorance, and challenges Haden's description of reason and feeling. [1166]

STEINKRAUS, W. E. "Socrates, Confucius, and the Rectification of Names." *PhE&W* 30(1980), 261-264. Though there are parallels between thought of S and Confucius, idea that inaccurate naming of things implants evil in men's souls (*Phaedo* 115e) does not seem analogous to Confucius' views on the subject. [1167]

STEPHENS, J. "Socrates on the Rule of Law." *HPhQ* 2(1985), 3-10. Our evidence does not allow us to resolve inconsistency between S's statements on obeying law in *Apol* and *Crito*. [1168]

STONE, I. F. *The Trial of Socrates*. Boston: Little, Brown, 1988. Attempts to understand why the Athenians, who gave the concept of free speech to the western world, could have put S to death for exercising that right. Focuses on primary documents (*Apol*, Xenophon, Aristophanes) rather than secondary literature. [1169]

STRAUSS, L. "On Plato's *Apology of Socrates* and *Crito*," in #2015, pp. 38-66. Survey and comparison of the two dialogues, contrasting public aspects of *Apol* with *Crito's* private character. The *logos* which persuades S to stay in jail is different from that which S uses to persuade Crito. [1170]

———. *Socrates and Aristophanes*. Univ. of Chicago Pr. 1980. Examines confrontation between S and Aristophanes, and shows that this confrontation is one between poetry and philosophy. [1171]

———. *Xenophon's Socrates*. Ithaca, NY: Cornell Univ. Pr., 1972. Endeavors to restore X's reputation as a reliable writer and to recover the historic S. [1172]

———. *Xenophon's Socratic Discourse: An Interpretation of the* Oeconomicus. Ithaca, NY: Cornell Univ. Pr., 1970. Discussion of X's dialogue on farming in which S is depicted as the student. Includes transl. of the document by C. Lord. [1173]

SWAZO, N. K. "Contemporary Politics: Crisis of Infirmity." *M&W* 19(1986), 203-223. S's diagnosis of the Athenian political situation can teach us much about the weaknesses of the contemporary political order. [1174]

SWEENEY, L. "A. E. Taylor on Socrates and Plato." *SwJPh* 8(1977), 79-99. Taylor's view that Theory of Forms is Socratic doctrine cannot be maintained. [1175]

TAYLOR, A. E. "The Impiety of Socrates," in #1180, pp. 1-39. Charges against S were not politically motivated or based on revenge. While S might be considered to have corrupted youth, there is no basis for charge of impiety of word or deed. [1176]

———. "On the Alleged Distinction in Aristotle Between *Sokrates* and *ho Sokrates*," in #1180, pp. 40-90. Virtually every Aristotelian reference to S proves upon inspection to be derived from Plato or some Socratic writer. Aristotle passed on this information, believing it to be historically accurate. [1177]

———. "The *Phrontisterion*," in #1180, pp. 129-177. Careful reading of P's *Phaedo* and Aristophanes' *Clouds* reveals that S is pictured in the same fashion in both documents. This conclusion raises Aristophanes' historical reliability. [1178]

———. *Socrates*. Westport, CT: Greenwood Pr., 1975; rprt. Introduction aimed at non-specialists. Surveys his early life, later life, and his thought. Stresses the importance of his concept of soul. [1179]

———. *Varia Socratica: First Series*. New York: Garland, 1987; rprt. Several essays, abstracted herein, which maintain that P's picture of S is historically accurate. [1180]

———. "The Words *eidos* and *idea* in Pre-Platonic Literature," in #1180, pp. 178-267. These terms appear in writers earlier than P, especially in Pythagoreans. It seems reasonable to conclude that S used the word in sense we associate with P. [1181]

TAYLOR, J. H. "Virtue and Wealth According to Socrates (*Apol*. 30b)." *CB* 49(1973), 49-52. Fortune does not produce virtue. Virtue makes all things good for a person, whether in private or public life. [1182]

TEJERA, V. "Ideology and Literature: Xenophon's *Defense of Socrates* and Plato's *Apology*: Commentary on Navia," in #1083, pp. 151-160. Reply to #1119. Xenophon's *Defense* is viable as ideology. **[1183]**

TELOH, H. *Socratic Education in Plato's Early Dialogues.* Notre Dame, IN: Notre Dame Univ. Pr., 1986. Aims to show what Socrates tries to accomplish educationally by his different verbal maneuvers, and thus focuses less on the logical soundness of the arguments and more on their intended effects on the hearers. **[1184]**

THOMAS, J. E. "On the Duality of Socrates' What-is-X Question." *LThPh* 30(1974), 21-27. The question "what-is-x?" can be taken as a request for some identifying mark of X, or for essence of X. Truly Socratic interpretation maintains this duality. **[1185]**

THOMPSON, H. "Sokrates in the Agora." *PAA* 55(1980), 252-282. One can now follow S's progress around Athenian agora by looking at recently excavated remains. **[1186]**

TOMIN, J. "Aristophanes: A Lasting Source of Reference." *PAS* 88(1987-88), 83-95. Reviews debate over whether Aristophanes is a reliable source of information on historical S. Taylor and Dover have taken positions around which others have rallied. Argues that *Clouds* gives us glimpse of authentic S. **[1187]**

——. "Socratic Gymnasium in the *Clouds.*" *SO* 62(1987), 25-32. Reply to K. Dover's interpretation of S in Aristophanes' play (#1039). Portrayals of S by P and Xenophon should be taken as historically reliable. **[1188]**

——. "Socratic Midwifery." *CQ* 37(1987), 97-102. Reply to Burnyeat (#1316). Midwife analogy comes from Platonic, not historic, S. **[1189]**

TRAINOR, P. "Immortality, Transcendence and the Autobiography of Socrates in the *Phaedo.*" *SJPh* 21(1983), 595-610. Life story of S is presented as an argument for immortality which wins over Cebes and Simmias. **[1190]**

TURLINGTON, B. *Socrates, the Father of Western Philosophy.* New York: Watts, 1969. Non-specialist introduction assuming no knowledge of Greek history or philosophy. Quotes P and other sources extensively (*Apol* in its entirety). Discusses Sophists, question of Platonic elements in Socrates, and his trial. **[1191]**

UMPHREY, S. "Eros and Thumos." *Interp* 10(1982), 353-422. Review essay of #1216 and #2455. Claims S was innocent but points out that he assumes the philosophical way of life is good while admitting that he does not know what the good is. **[1192]**

VANDERPOOL, E. "The Prison of Socrates." *ILN* 264 #6(1976), 87-88. Building called the Poros, outside the agora, fits description of S's prison in P's works. **[1193]**

VLASTOS, G. "Afterthoughts on the Socratic Elenchus." *OSAP* 1(1983), 71-74. Additions to #1204. Elenchus gradually disappears in P's dialogues only to be brought out again in *Meno.* **[1194]**

——. "Happiness and Virtue in Socrates' Moral Theory." *Topoi* 4(1985), 3-22. Happiness or the good is the goal (*telos*) of all human actions, the thing "for whose sake all other dear things are dear." The one thing necessary for happiness is moral virtue.

Other "goods" can make only a minuscule difference in our happiness. **[1195]**

———. "The Historical Socrates and Athenian Democracy." *PolTheo* 11(1983), 495-516. Xenophon's portrait is more accurate because he shows S teaching statecraft. P makes him a master of fiscal responsibility, diplomacy, other manipulative skills. **[1196]**

———. "On 'The Socrates Story'." *PolTheo* 7(1979), 533-536. Reply to #2167. **[1197]**

———. "The Paradox of Socrates," in #1199, pp. 1-21. *Apol* is a reliable portrait of S. It shows him professing a "mission" of care for human soul, but his actions make him appear merely antagonistic. His claim that virtue is knowledge and his admission that he has no knowledge reduce his philosophic approach to a kind of faith. **[1198]**

———. *The Philosophy of Socrates. A Collection of Critical Essays.* Garden City, NY: Anchor Books, 1971. Essays move from historical S to portrait painted by Plato. Some are new, some reprinted. All are abstracted herein. **[1199]**

———. "Socrates' Contribution to the Greek Sense of Justice." *Archaiognosia* 1(1980), 301-324. S's teaching moves far beyond the *lex talonis* (the "eye for an eye" principle), which characterizes the Greek thought of his day. **[1200]**

———. "Socrates' Disavowal of Knowledge." *PhQ* 35(1985), 1-31. S disavows knowledge in the sense of knowing something with certainty, but claims it when it means true belief justified by elenchus. **[1201]**

———. "Socrates on Political Obedience and Disobedience." *Yale Review* (1974), 517-534. Examines conflict between S's statement of duty of political obedience in *Crito* and his statement of right of disobedience in *Apol*. **[1202]**

———. "Socrates on 'The Parts of Virtue'," in #1292, pp. 418-423. Defends claim "Virtue is one thing, and Justice, Temperance, etc. are parts of it" as "standard Socratic doctrine." **[1203]**

———. "The Socratic Elenchus." *OSAP* 1(1983), 27-58. Studies S's use of "What is F?" question; shows elenchus to have double objective: to discover how every person ought to live, and to test person doing the answering to see if he is living as he ought to. S knew that one need only block an opponent's argument and not demonstrate the truth of his own position. He is aware of this fallible point in his method. **[1204]**

———. "The Socratic Elenchus." *JPh* 79(1982), 711-714. Summary of #1204. **[1205]**

———. "Socratic Irony." *CQ* 37(1987), 79-96. In S's hands *eironeia* comes to mean not "deceit" but "saying something contrary to one's intention." Sometimes his irony is unintentionally deceptive. **[1206]**

———. "The Unity of the Virtues," in #1292, pp. 221-269. The virtues form a unity only in the sense that someone who possesses one will possess them all. **[1207]**

———. "What Did Socrates Understand by His 'What is F?' Question?" in #1292, pp. 410-417. Reply to Penner's thesis (#1138) that S, in asking "What is courage?", is seeking a psychological account (explanation) of what it is in men's psyches that makes them brave. Argues that what he wants to know is what "constitutes" courage. **[1208]**

WALLACH, J. R. "Socratic Citizenship." *HPolTho* 9(1988), 393-413. Average Athenian could not comprehend S's view of citizenship. S thought little of participating in government, found public debate lacking in integrity, and denied any skill or virtue in public opinion. His approach exposed weaknesses but could not correct them. **[1209]**

WALSH, J. J. "The Socratic Denial of Akrasia," in #1199, pp. 235-263. Discusses shortcomings of Socratic doctrine that no one does wrong voluntarily. **[1210]**

WALTON, C. "Xenophon and the Socratic Paradoxes." *SJPh* 16(1978), 687-700. Several themes common to Xenophon's and Plato's portraits of S help us to understand the two paradoxes and to see S aiming at becoming a whole man who lives justly. **[1211]**

WALTON, R. E. "Socrates' Alleged Suicide." *JVallnq* 14(1980), 287-300. Xenophon depicts S as using death sentence to achieve a desirable end to his life. Nothing in P's work contradicts that view. Issue cannot be settled from P's early works, which focus on relationship of individual to state, but S does seem to have sanctioned suicide. **[1212]**

WATSON, W. "The Voices of the God: Comments on Kostman," in #1083, pp. 173-180. Challenges Kostman's claim (#2250) that S's refusal to escape from prison constituted an abandonment of his philosophic mission. **[1213]**

WELLMAN, R. R. "Socratic Method in Xenophon." *JHI* 37(1976), 307-318. X's portrayal of S stresses *anamnesis* rather than *elenchus*, and recollection of knowledge is restricted to *physis*. **[1214]**

WEST, T. G. "Defending Socrates and Defending Politics. A Response to Stewart Umphrey." *Interp* 11(1983), 383-397. Reply to review (#1192) of (#1216). **[1215]**

———. *Plato's* Apology of Socrates: *An Interpretation with a New Translation.* Ithaca, NY: Cornell Univ. Pr., 1979. Analyzes dialogue section by section. The speech as given by S was a failure, but P turned it into a manifesto of the philosophic life. **[1216]**

———, and **WEST, G. S.** *Four Texts on Socrates: Plato's* Euthyphro, Apology *and* Crito *and Aristophanes'* Clouds. Ithaca, NY: Cornell Univ. Pr., 1984. Translation, with notes and introduction, of four works which present a reasonable picture of the historic S and the main points of his teaching. Lengthy introduction reviews major themes. Annotated bibliography. **[1217]**

WHELAN, F. G. "Socrates and the 'Meddlesomeness' of the Athenians." *HPolTho* 4(1983), 1-30. S's definitions of justice/injustice implicitly condemn institutions and policies of Athens, but his opposition to democracy is limited. His philosophic life is actually akin to "meddlesomeness" of active life which Athens valued. **[1218]**

WILSON, P. C. *The Living Socrates. The Man Who Dared to Question, as Plato Knew Him.* Owings Mills, MD: Stemmer House, 1975. Attempt to trace a biography of S in context of Athens in late fifth century B. C. Uses excerpts from ancient sources (primarily P) connected by running commentary. **[1219]**

WOOD, E. M., and **WOOD, N.** "Socrates and Democracy. A Reply to Gregory Vlastos."

PolTheo 14(1986), 55-82. Response to #1196. **[1220]**

WOODBURY, L. "Socrates and Archelaus." *Phoenix* 25(1971), 299-309. Fourth-century doxographers created the story of S being Archelaus' student and lover. **[1221]**

——. "Socrates and the Daughter of Aristides." *Phoenix* 27(1973), 7-25. The story of S's marriage to the impoverished Myrto was invented to demonstrate that circumstances have no effect on innate nobility. **[1222]**

WOODRUFF, P. "Socrates on the Parts of Virtue," in #1287, 101-116. If we understand S to mean that the virtues are one in essence, some inconsistencies in P's dialogues can be clarified. **[1223]**

——. "The Socratic Approach to Semantic Incompleteness." *Ph&PhenRes* 38(1978), 453-468. S insists that adjectives, when correctly applied, do not vary in meaning in different contexts. For P this means, metaphysically, that contextually vague sentences are so from the inadequacy of the subjects of the sentences. **[1224]**

——. cf. #2366.

WOOZLEY, A. D. "Socrates on Disobeying the Law," in #1199, pp. 299-318. Attempts to resolve the paradox of S's argument in *Crito* that it would be wrong to break laws by escaping and his statement in *Apol* that he will refuse to obey any ruling that prohibits him from philosophizing. **[1225]**

YOUNG, G. "Socrates and Obedience." *Phron* 19(1974), 1-29. S does not really believe that each citizen should do whatever city commands. His apparent appeal to laws is meant to suffer same difficulties as Crito's appeal to opinions of the many: standard of justice must be found through philosophy, not by appeal to laws. **[1226]**

ZEYL, D. "Socratic Virtue and Happiness." *AGPh* 64(1982), 225-238. In P's early ("Socratic") dialogues virtue seems to be a cause as well as result of happiness. S does not seem to have committed a fallacy but to have allowed for altruism. **[1227]**

ZUCKERT, M. "Rationalism and Political Responsibility: Just Speech and Just Deed in the *Clouds* and the *Apology of Socrates*." *Polity* 17(1984), 271-297. Comparison of the two documents shows that *Apol* was a reply to Aristophanes' charge that rationalism is politically dangerous and epistemologically defective. **[1228]**

For related items see #8, #88, #1783, #2150, #2170, #2251, #2366, #2708, #2862, #3427, #5135, #5607, #5624, #6020, #6246, #6257.

Chapter 11

MINOR SOCRATICS:
MEGARIANS, CYRENAICS, AND CYNICS

Plato was not Socrates' only pupil, but his brilliance and the volume of his work do make his contemporaries seem "minor" by comparison. Some of Socrates' other students founded philosophical schools which stressed certain facets of his thought in ways that did not agree with Plato's interpretation. As Dumitriu (Hist. of Logic I, p. 139) characterized them, "One thing is certain: none of the lesser Socratics understood the ideas of their master." The most prominent of these were the Megarian, Cyrenaic, and Cynic schools. Because so little is known of the first two, they will be considered together. The Cynics will be examined by themselves below. A few studies cover all three.

MERLAN, P. "Minor Socratics." *JHPh* 10(1972), 143-152. Overview of ethical doctrines of Cynics, Cyrenaics, and Megarians. [1229]

ROSSETTI, L. "*Therapeia* in the Minor Socratics. *ThetaPi* 3(1974), 145-157. Consideration of texts, aside from Plato and Xenophon, which give insight on origins of this idea. [1230]

For related item see #5592.

MEGARIANS AND CYRENAICS

Neither of these schools, to judge from the extant fragments, presented a well formulated doctrine. They emphasized instead their opposition to Platonic and Aristotelian thought by devising arguments designed to show up their inconsistencies or absurdities. For this reason the Megarians and Cyrenaics are sometimes called *eristic* schools, from the Greek word *eris* or "strife."

The first representative of the **Megarian** school was Eucleides of Megara (450-380 B. C.), one of Socrates' oldest pupils. He was present at Socrates' death and offered refuge to his panic-stricken students. Eucleides' students developed his philosophy into barren disputations, taking pride in inventing clever but useless fallacies.

Little is known of Megarian doctrine. Eucleides is credited with writing six short dialogues, none of which survive. Diogenes Laertius says only that Eucleides held God, mind, and wisdom to be different names for one thing, the Good. (Plato, by contrast, spent much of his career trying to distinguish among such things and to define the supreme good.) It is known that Eucleides combined

Socrates' insistence on a knowledge of concepts with an Eleatic view that sense perceptions could not be trusted. Only what is real and unchanging can be known, and only the actual is possible. He also rejected the possibility of proof by analogy.

His pupils were not a distinguished lot. Diogenes Laertius mentions several by name but says little more about them than that they engaged in controversy with some particular contemporary (and usually more famous) philosopher.

Megarian argumentation was designed to attack an opponent's conclusions rather than his premises. For example, to show that plurality was impossible they posed this conundrum, called the *sorites*: "One grain of wheat does not make a heap; add another grain, and another, and it still is not a heap. When does it become a heap?" Diodorus Cronus is credited with devising the argument of the horns: "That which you have not lost, you still have. You have not lost horns; therefore you still have horns."

The greatest representative of the school was Stilpo of Megara (389-300 B. C.), who in some ways is not entirely typical of the school's thinking. He combined some features of Cynic thought, especially disdain for worldly goods, with more standard Megarian doctrine. Like other Megarians, his energies were taken up more with contentious opposition to his opponents than with constructive teaching. He resided in Athens for a time until he was banished for his rationalistic views on religion.

The founder of the **Cyrenaic** School, Aristippus of Cyrene (435-356 B. C.), was, according to Guthrie "one who . . . exists only on the margin of philosophy." He saw pleasure as the supreme good of life. Every creature, he argued, instinctively moves toward that which makes it feel good. The wise man will seek whatever pleasure he can find in life, even if he finds it in ways of which society disapproves. But no pleasure, however intense, lasts indefinitely. Thus the sage will always be in pursuit of pleasure and must not let socio-political conventions block him from his objective.

What the philosopher must guard against, Aristippus taught, is letting pleasure take control of his life. His aphorism on the subject was: "I possess, but I am not possessed." The sage must be detached from the very pleasures which are his objective. If he attains them, he is happy. If he does not, he is so indifferent to them that he is content. He can find pleasure anywhere, in a shepherd's hut or a king's palace. Chances of success are obviously greater in the palace, so Cyrenaics did not hesitate to cultivate friendships with the wealthy. Their willingness to do so drew sharp criticism from Diogenes and the Cynics.

Among the followers of the school we know the names of the founder's daughter Arete and her son, also named Aristippus. Theodoros the Atheist (ca. 300 B. C.) spoke of joy and grief instead of pleasure and hardship. Hegesias (ca. 280 B. C.) taught that nothing is pleasant or unpleasant in itself; only circumstances can determine which it will be.

BURNYEAT, M. F. "Gods and Heaps," in #76, pp. 315-338. Study of development of argument of *sorites* from Eubulides of Miletus to Stoics; analysis of its application to gods.   [1231]

CALVERT, B. "Aristotle and the Megarians on the Potentiality-Actuality Distinction." *Apeir* 10 #1(1976), 34-41. Ar's attempt to refute Megarian paradoxes in *Meta* 9.3 is inadequate. It does little more than affirm reality of such processes as movement and becoming. [1232]

DENYER, N. "The Atomism of Diodorus Cronus." *Prud* 13(1981), 33-45. Reconstruction of D's argument against motion and its implications. [1233]

HINTIKKA, J. "Aristotle and the 'Master Argument' of Diodorus," in #4890, pp. 179-213. A reconstruction of D's "Master Argument" is possible from some of Ar's comments on determinism. The Master Argument appears to have been merely another form of one of those arguments. [1234]

MICHAEL, F. S. "What is the Master Argument of Diodorus Cronus?" *AmPhQ* 13(1976), 229-235. Attempt to reconstruct the argument without recourse to assumptions not found in ancient sources. [1235]

MOLINE, J. "Aristotle, Eubulides and the Sorites." *Mind* 78(1969), 393-407. The sorites argument originated with Eubulides as an attack on Ar's theory of the mean. It is possible to reconstruct an Aristotelian solution to the problem raised. [1236]

RESCHER, N. "A Version of the Master Argument of Diodorus." *JPh* 63(1966), 438-455. Reconstruction based on references in Cicero and Epictetus. [1237]

SEDLEY, D. "Diodorus Cronus and Hellenistic Philosophy." *PCPhS* 23(1977), 74-120. Not a Megarian but a Dialectical philosopher. Death between 285-282. Major influence on founders of Hellenistic schools through his paradoxes, theory of minima, modal logic, conditional propositions. Formulated free will/determinism dichotomy as philosophical problem. [1238]

WHEELER, S. C. "Megarian Paradoxes as Eleatic Arguments." *AmPhQ* 20(1983), 287-295. Paradoxes attributed to Megarian philosopher Eubulides are essentially Eleatic and show Megarians as important thinkers. [1239]

WHITE, M. J. "Diodorus' Master Argument. A Semantic Interpretation." *Erkenntnis* 15(1980), 65-72. Somewhat technical discussion of D's three propositions about logical modalities. They can be reconstructed so as not to be inconsistent. [1240]

———. "Facets of Megarian Fatalism: Aristotelian Criticisms and the Stoic Doctrine of Eternal Recurrence." *CanJPh* 10(1980), 189-206. Somewhat technical discussion of influence of Megarian idea that truth of a proposition entails its necessity. [1241]

For related items see #3049, #4867, #5005.

CYNICS

Other thinkers also took certain aspects of Socrates' thought and magnified them into radical systems. Tradition assigns the foundation of the Cynic school to Antisthenes (445-365 B. C.), a native of Athens but the offspring of a Thracian slavewoman and therefore not an Athenian citizen. He studied first with Gorgias the Sophist before being attracted to Socrates' teaching. Plato, elitist that he was, never accepted Antisthenes into his circle.

There is, however, considerable doubt about whether Antisthenes actually founded this school. To judge from surviving accounts of his teaching, his interests seem to have been more speculative than those of the Cynics. Thus it is uncertain whether the distinction of founding the school should go to Antisthenes or to the most famous of the early Cynics, Diogenes (ca. 410-324 B. C.), who is called "Socrates gone mad." The term "Cynic" is derived from the Greek word for a dog. Whether this referred to their lifestyle is unclear. The Cynics themselves adopted the name, interpreting it to mean that they were the watchdogs of philosophy, guarding the true practice of it.

Whoever their founder, the Cynics taught disdain for worldly goods (such as written versions of their teachings), an extension of one of Socrates' themes. Happiness for them consisted of self-sufficiency (*autarkeia*). The true sage is not dependent on other persons or external circumstances for his well-being. Both Plato and Aristotle had taught that the wise man ought to be self-sufficient, but Diogenes supposedly came to this conclusion while watching a mouse go about its business.

Achieving *autarkeia* was not easy in the community-oriented society of ancient Greece. Aristotle had described a human being as "an animal that lives in a city-state," i. e., incomplete unless part of a group. But in the fourth century B. C. the concept of the city-state had fallen on hard times. The disastrous Peloponnesian War (432-404) had left Athens in ruins and Sparta so seriously weakened that it suffered a ruinous defeat at the Battle of Leuctra in 372 at the hands of Thebes, a sister Greek city. Some thinkers, like the orator Isocrates, were advocating a pan-Hellenic union that would supersede the old independent city-states. Diogenes was not so terribly out of step when he called himself not a citizen of a particular city but a "cosmopolitan," a man whose city was the world.

Training was required to reach a state of *autarkeia*. The wise man had to harden himself by living without the luxuries which the Greek world provided in such abundance. Diogenes himself lived in an old wine vat, wore the same clothes year round without regard to the weather, and went without shoes. (Socrates had practiced the latter two forms of asceticism.) But the Cynic must also despise social conventions and be prepared to suffer abuse because he will not conform. In some of these ways the Cynics can be compared to the hippies of the 1960's.

Achieving the goal of the school enabled one to live without fear of reverses of fortune, not enslaved to ambition or greed (and thus not disappointed when he failed to attain his objectives).

This anti-social philosophy had a surprisingly wide and long-lasting effect on ancient society. The doctrine of detachment from worldly concerns became the cornerstone of Stoicism and Epicureanism. The public lectures or diatribes through which the Cynics presented their doctrines became a model for Christian sermons, and their ascetic practices influenced Christian monasticism.

The term Cynic today means one who distrusts other people's motives or doubts their sincerity. That element also appears in the teachings of the ancient school. Diogenes is reported to have walked the streets of Athens in broad daylight carrying a lamp. When asked to explain his odd behavior, he said that he was looking for an honest man.

ATTRIDGE, H. W. *First-Century Cynicism in the Epistles of Heraclitus: Introduction, Greek Text and Translation.* Missoula, MT: Scholars Pr., 1976. In first century A. D. it was common practice to write letters in name of earlier philosophers. Nine such letters attributed to Heraclitus actually were composed by Cynic philosopher(s). Discusses question of authorship and examines Cynic teachings of the letters.   **[1242]**

DOWNING, F. G. "Cynics and Christians." *NTS* 30(1984), 584-593. Cynics' public proclamation of their ethical teachings provided important model for first-century Christian preaching.   **[1243]**

———. cf. #6742.

EMELJANOW, V. "A Note on the Cynic Shortcut to Happiness." *Mnem* 18(1965), 182-184. Cynics saw not two roads, one leading to virtue, the other to vice. Instead, they saw two ways to virtue, one long and winding, the other direct and difficult.   **[1244]**

FINLEY, M. I. "Diogenes the Cynic," in *Aspects of Antiquity: Discoveries and Controversies* (London: Chatto & Windus, 1968), pp. 89-101. Survey for general reader of strengths and weaknesses of D's philosophical position. Most stories about him are probably legendary. Cynics' criticisms of society were too general to be taken seriously by their contemporaries.   **[1245]**

GIANGRANDE, G. "Diogenes' Apophthegm from Herculaneum in the Light of the Ancient *Topoi*." *MPhL* 8(1987), 67-74. This inscription suggests a connection with literary *topos* that woman is worst of evils.   **[1246]**

HOCK, R. F. "Simon the Shoemaker as an Ideal Cynic." *GRBS* 17(1976), 41-53. Accounts of S's relationship to Socrates have been influenced by debate over whether philosophers should associate with people in power.   **[1247]**

KINDSTRAND, J. F. "The Cynics and Heraclitus." *Eranos* 82(1984), 149-178. Cynics claimed H as precursor but were not directly inspired by his teaching, except in their critique of popular religion. There are some resemblances in aggressiveness and contempt for crowd.   **[1248]**

———. "Demetrius the Cynic." *Philologus* 124(1980), 83-98. Discusses Demetrius' motives for participation in a celebrated legal defense in 70 A. D. and considers whether his actions were consistently Cynic.   **[1249]**

MALHERBE, A. J., ed. *The Cynic Epistles.* Missoula, MT: Scholars Pr., 1977. Greek text with facing English translation of letters attributed to Cynics and earlier philosophers. No notes or introduction.   **[1250]**

———. "Pseudo-Heraclitus, Epistle 4. The Divinization of the Wise Man." *JbAC* 21(1978), 42-64. Logical structure of letter is uniform. There are no Jewish, Christian, or Stoic elements in it. Author was a Cynic.   [1251]

———. "Self-Definition Among Epicureans and Cynics," in #5639, III, pp. 46-59; also in #6771, pp. 11-24. Epicureans stressed memorization of founder's teachings and veneration of his image. Cynics, lacking canonical teachings, adapted themselves as conditions changed. More attention given to Cynics than to Epicureans.   [1252]

———. cf. #6765-#6772.

MOLES, J. L. "'Honestius quam ambitiosius'? An Exploration of the Cynic's Attitude to Moral Corruption in his Fellow Men." *JHS* 103(1983), 103-123. Reply to #1249. Demetrius the Cynic could have been inspired in his defense of the Stoic Celer by thoroughly honorable Cynic motives.   [1253]

———. "The Woman and the River. Diogenes' Apophthegm from Herculaneum and Some Popular Misconceptions about Cynicism." *Apeir* 17(1983), 125-130. This saying parodies Cynic teaching and behavior, especially tenet that misfortune is a good.[1254]

RANKIN, H. D. "Absolute Dog. The Life and Thought of Antisthenes." *PCA* 82(1985), 17-18. A may not have been first Cynic nor Diogenes' teacher, but he rejected Homeric notion of shame and did more than anyone except Socrates to provide a practical philosophy.   [1255]

———. "Antisthenes a Near Logician?" *AC* 39(1970), 522-527. All of Aristotle's *Metaphysics* 1043b,23-28 is drawn from Antisthenes.   [1256]

———. "Anthisthenes Fg. 50B (Caizzi), a Possible Section of *Peri tes aletheias*." *AC* 42(1973), 178-180. This frag, not associated earlier with any particular work of A, seems to follow after frag 50A.   [1257]

———. *Antisthenes Sokratikos*. Amsterdam: Hakkert, 1986. Survey of A's life and the main themes of his teaching (Being and not-Being, one god of nature, the virtuous life, etc.). Sees him as follower of Socrates who de-emphasized the city-state but did not go to extreme individualism of Cynics.   [1258]

———. "Irony and Logic. The *antilegein* Paradox and Antisthenes' Purpose." *AC* 43(1974), 316-320. By asserting that contradiction is impossible A was trying to attack logical foundations of Platonic Forms.   [1259]

———. "*Ouk estin antilegein*," in #905, pp. 25-37. Antisthenes seems to have regarded this self-refuting statement as valid. Its origins are obscure, though it resembles early Sophistic paradoxes.   [1260]

———. "That It Is Impossible to Say 'Not' and Related Topics in Anthisthenes." *IntLogRev* 10(1979), 51-98. Denial of predication attributed to A may be seen as continuation of Socratic skepticism, stressing inadequacy of Forms and predication arguments based on them.   [1261]

STEINER, G. "Diogenes' Mouse and the Royal Dog. Conformity in Nonconformity." *CJ* 72(1976), 36-46. Surveys thought of D and Aristippus and suggests reasons for continued interest in Cynics and widespread disinterest in Cyrenaics, who appear hedonists and sycophants. [1262]

STRUGNELL, J., and **ATTRIDGE, H.** "The Epistles of Heraclitus and the Jewish Pseudepigrapha: A Warning." *HThR* 64(1971), 411-413. Epistles 4 and 7 of this collection contain nothing that cannot be explained as Cynic. Nor is there proof of Jewish authorship. [1263]

WINDT, T. O. "The Diatribe: Last Resort for Protest." *QJS* 58(1972), 1-14. Developed by Cynics, diatribe tries to present a counter-culture to protest corruption of speaker's own society. Form knows no limits on slang, obscenity, vituperation. [1264]

XENAKIS, J. "Hippies and Cynics." *Inquiry* 16(1973), 1-15. Hippies of 1960's expressed disdain for society's values in many of same ways Cynics used: long hair, rejection of materialism, performance of private acts in public. [1265]

For related items see #503.

Chapter 12

PLATO: INTRODUCTION
AND TOPICAL STUDIES

BIOGRAPHICAL SKETCH
(Note: S = Socrates; P = Plato; Ar = Aristotle)
 P seems to have been born in 427 B. C., of a noble Athenian family which sided politically with the conservative, anti-democratic faction in the city. One story has it that his name was Aristocles, but that he was given the name Plato (meaning "broad") because of the breadth of his shoulders or his forehead. Educated in the typical Athenian fashion of the time, he studied poetry, painting, and music. He heard S for the first time and became a pupil of his in 407 B. C.
 On the death of S in 399 P (and several other students of S) left Athens for a time. According to stories of dubious value, P traveled in Egypt and Asia. It seems likely that he visited the Pythagoreans in Italy. He did spend some time in Syracuse, on the island of Sicily. His sometimes rocky political connections with that city are discussed in the introduction to his *Letters* (p. 288).
 Returning to Athens, P established a school in a grove dedicated to Academus, a minor divinity. This Academy, which will be discussed in Chapter 15, had a continuous existence until 529 A. D. P left Athens only twice more during his life, both times to visit Syracuse. He died in 347 B. C.
 That synopsis may seem surprisingly brief, but the information available on P's life is scant. A number of his contemporaries, including other students of S's such as Xenophon, left literary remains, but they rarely refer to P. Ar, who spent twenty years in the Academy while P was still living, mentions him only a few times by name and does not seem to know any Platonic doctrine that could not have been derived from P's dialogues. He even raises some confusion by referring to S as the author of the *Republic*.

OVERVIEW OF HIS THOUGHT
 We will try in this introduction to take a respectful, but not reverent, look at some general characteristics of P's thought. It is significant in its effort to resolve several major philosophical problems, and his approach, if not his solutions, still have a currency to them. Specific topics — Ethics, Metaphysics, and the rest — will be discussed at the beginning of the appropriate sections in the bibliography which follows. Each of his dialogues will also be introduced separately in the next chapter.
 To describe P's thought succinctly is not easy. As A. H. Armstrong cautions us:

There was never a less systematic philosopher, and it is often difficult to find out what his final solution of any of the great metaphysical problems which he raises is; and when we find it or think we have found it, it is seldom one which we can accept as finally satisfactory, even if we profess ourselves to be Platonists.

One major obstacle to understanding Platonism is the form in which it is presented to us, the dialogues. P never wrote a treatise which proceeds from certain premises or assumptions, moves logically from one point to the next, and arrives at an inescapable (or at least reasonable) conclusion. Instead he wrote what purport to be records of conversations among S and various individuals, some of them reported by people who claim to have heard them years earlier. Others are reported at second or third hand. The individuals named are historical personages, but whether such conversations actually took place and whether anyone could remember what was said in such detail, we cannot now determine. In some of the dialogues (probably the earlier ones) the discussants engage in genuine interchange of ideas; in others S discourses and the interlocutors merely say "Yes," "No," or "By all means" at the appropriate points.

The dialogues have been compared to dramas. As is true in a Greek tragedy, very little *happens* in a dialogue, though P is quite specific about their settings. One theory holds that the dialogues were read publicly or staged in some fashion. As one scholar says, "In contrast with a playwright, who might philosophize in his plays, Plato is a philosopher who dramatizes his philosophy."

If the dialogues are dramas, what does that make of S? Did P faithfully record his teachings, or was S just a convenient character, as he had been for Aristophanes in his comedy the *Clouds*? Scholars are by no means agreed, but in the earlier dialogues, which attempt to define ethical terms (courage in the *Laches*, piety in the *Euthyphro*, etc.) P seems to represent S's viewpoint and teaching style fairly accurately. In the later dialogues such as the *Sophist* or *Laws* S is a mask through which P speaks or is discarded because P has moved so far beyond Socratic concepts.

Another obstacle to solving the puzzle of P is the question of whether the dialogues represent what he actually thought. As noted in Chapter 2, most ancient philosophers were believed to have presented their real teachings orally to an inner circle of disciples. In *Phaedrus* P denounces the very process of writing; in *Letter* 7, which is widely regarded as genuine, he describes his philosophy in general terms and states that he has never written down the essentials of it:

There does not exist, nor will there ever exist, any treatise of mine dealing therewith. For it does not at all admit of verbal expression like other studies, but, as a result of continued application to the subject itself and communion therewith, it is brought to birth in the soul on a sudden, as light that is kindled by a leaping spark, and thereafter nourishes itself. (341c)

Such a passage makes P sound more like the contemplative mystic whom the

Neoplatonists (cf. Chapter 20) found in his work. Taken uncritically, it could imply that all the dialogues are forgeries or a smoke screen to conceal whatever P was actually teaching.

At the risk of vastly oversimplifying, what emerges from a reading of the dialogues is P's concern with the problem of how one knows, epistemology. A fuller discussion will be given below (p. 191). For now we can say that his answer takes into account both the object known and the knower. The object must be something that *can* be known. For P that requires that the object be unchanging. Since everything in the world perceived by the senses changes, the object of knowledge must be something non-physical. P designates such things as Forms or Ideas. He himself used the words *eide* or *idea*, both of which are derived from a root word meaning "see" or "know." The things we see in the physical world are only copies or shadows of these perfect Forms.

It should be noted at once that *idea* means much more than our word "idea." The Platonic Idea is not a concept in our minds. It is a thing, a substance, that exists in some way entirely independent of our minds. This concept, which has been called "a synthesis between Hellenistic rationalism and Oriental mysticism," is not as far-fetched as it might seem. It is most easily demonstrated in mathematical terms (and P placed great stress on mathematics in the Academy as well as in his utopian schemes). Consider examples such as the circle or equal lines. No circle which we can draw is ever an exact circle. No two equal lines are ever exactly equal, even if the difference is discernible only under a microscope. But there is a notion of Circularity, or of Equality. That, P argues, is how we know a round thing is a circle and has certain properties peculiar to circles. It is how we develop a notion of two things being the same size.

P expands this notion to include ethical concepts. In the dialogues S always reminds his interlocutors not to list examples of some moral quality (courage or justice, for instance) but to tell him what it *is*. P also applies the theory of Forms to classes of phenomena. All dogs, e. g., differ, however slightly. One cannot know what a dog is by trying to develop a definition on the basis of all those individual examples (from chihuahua to Great Dane). But in the realm of the mind there exists the concept of Dog. When we use the word we do not have to qualify or explain it for a reasonably intelligent person to know what we mean. The Forms become the basis for his evaluation of such things as poetry and rhetoric. Since those "arts" focus on imitations, they are inferior and detract the philosopher from the search for the Forms.

We would call such an object of knowledge an abstract concept. But for P the Forms are real. They exist on a level where they cannot be known by physical means, only by a rational method, i. e., dialectic. It was at this point that P's ancient critics found him most vulnerable. Antisthenes the Cynic remarked, "Horses I can see; horse-ness I cannot see." Modern critics have echoed the sentiment. R. E. Allen observes that "no one can scratch Doghood behind the ears."

If the Forms are not physical objects, they cannot be comprehended by the physical mind. They must be comprehended by something similar to them, and the thing most similar to the Forms is the soul. The soul (to be discussed more fully under Psychology, p. 237) can know the Forms because, like them, it — or at least a portion of it — is immortal and has existed in earlier lives. The knowledge which it has gained of the Forms is dormant but can be reawakened by a carefully conducted process of interrogation, as S demonstrates in the *Meno*.

PLATO: AN ASSESSMENT

The praise and attention lavished on P today far exceed extravagance at times. Ralph Waldo Emerson claimed that "Plato is philosophy, and philosophy Plato." Freeman and Appel claim that "there is no problem of philosophy about which the first word was not written by Plato; and there are many who believe that Plato had the last word as well." K. M. Carroll asserts bluntly that "Plato is the world's greatest philosopher."

Those making such claims should recall that P's ideas received vigorous criticism during his lifetime and had little direct impact on ancient philosophy after his death. The Academy dogmatized his teaching and then moved to a skeptical position. Philosophers who are called Middle Platonists or Neoplatonists were actually religious mystics influenced as much by Pythagoras or the mystery cults as by P. They replaced P's logical system with Aristotle's categories. By the early Middle Ages only one of P's dialogues (the *Tim*) had been translated into Latin. That was all western Europe knew of him directly until the thirteenth century. For the medieval Schoolmen the term "the Philosopher" meant Aristotle.

Some modern critics have been less in awe of P. Beattie says that P's "philosophy has been a perpetual source of confusion, in terms of both the subjective and objective world." Bertrand Russell complains:

Plato is always concerned to advocate views that will make people what he thinks is virtuous; he is hardly ever intellectually honest, because he allows himself to judge doctrines by their social consequences. Even about this, he is not honest; he pretends to follow the argument and to be judging by purely theoretical standards, when in fact he is twisting the discussion so as to lead to a virtuous result. He introduced this vice into philosophy, where it has persisted ever since.

In his defense it can be said that he was attempting to provide a solution to political problems which no one in Athens had been able to solve for half a century or more. The old city-state democracy was on the verge of collapse and no one knew how to shore it up. P tried to show that political solutions had to be based on more far-reaching educational reforms. Athens needed a sense of purpose which only an enlightened elite could provide. He was also trying to reconcile two irreconcilable positions on the nature of the world: Heraclitus' doctrine that everything was in a state of flux and Parmenides' monism.

In the late twentieth century P has been the center of controversies over his totalitarian political views and his alleged bias against women. On the other hand, some have realized the value of his holistic view of the cosmos and humankind. Platonic studies have by no means grown stale.

METHODOLOGICAL NOTE
The following bibliography is divided into subsections according to subjects (Aesthetics, Ethics, Metaphysics, etc.) which we hope will allow the non-specialist user to focus on topics of interest as quickly as possible. The abbreviations S, P, and Ar will continue to be used for Socrates, Plato, and Aristotle as long as they do not cause confusion. Titles of the dialogues will be abbreviated. Not included in the Platonic (and Aristotelian) sections of this bibliography are books which survey general topics, e. g., aesthetics or political philosophy, and contain passing comments on P and Ar. Every book on the history of western political philosophy, or any other aspect of philosophy, has a chapter on each of them. We must exclude them to keep this work within the bounds of a single (large) volume.

REFERENCE WORKS AND COLLECTED ESSAYS

ABBOTT, E. *A Subject-Index to the Dialogues of Plato.* New York: Franklin, 1971; rprt. Based on English words.   **[1266]**

ANTON, J. P., and **PREUS, A.,** eds. *Essays in Ancient Greek Philosophy, III: Plato.* Albany: SUNY Pr., 1989. Collection of essays, most not previously published, abstracted herein.   **[1267]**

BAMBROUGH, R., ed. *New Essays on Plato and Aristotle.* London: Routledge & Kegan Paul, 1965. Collection of essays, each abstracted herein.   **[1268]**

BRANDWOOD, L. *A Word Index to Plato.* Leeds, UK: W. S. Maney & Son, 1976. Keyed to Greek words.   **[1269]**

BRISSON, L. "Platon 1958-1975." *Lustrum* 20(1977), 5-304. Annotated bibliography.   **[1270]**

———. "Platon 1975-1980." *Lustrum* 25(1983), 31-320. Cf. #1270.   **[1271]**

CHERNISS, H. F. "Plato (1950-1957)." *Lustrum* 4(1959), 5-308; 5(1960), 323-648. Survey of current work.   **[1272]**

DESCHOUX, M. *Comprendre Platon: Un siècle de bibliographie platonicienne de langue française 1880-1980.* Paris: Les Belles Lettres, 1981. Useful survey of an important body of European studies.   **[1273]**

GADAMER, H.-G. *Dialogue and Dialectic. Eight Hermeneutical Studies on Plato,* transl. P. C. Smith. New Haven, CT: Yale Univ. Pr., 1980. Collection of essays from different stages of Gadamer's career. All are abstracted herein.   **[1274]**

GRISWOLD, C. L., ed. *Platonic Writings, Platonic Readings.* New York: Routledge, 1988. Collection of papers, abstracted herein, focusing on two questions: 1) Why did P write dialogues; 2) How is one to read P's dialogues?   **[1275]**

GROSS, B., ed. *Great Thinkers on Plato.* New York: Putnam's, 1968. Selections from ancient, mediaeval, and modern philosophers evaluating or criticizing P.   **[1276]**

HENDLEY, B. P., ed. *Plato, Time, and Education: Essays in Honor of Robert S. Brumbaugh.* Albany: SUNY Pr., 1987. Collection of original articles and complete bibliography of Brumbaugh's works. Relevant items are abstracted herein. **[1277]**

LINFORTH, I. M., ed. *Studies in Herodotus and Plato.* New York: Garland, 1987; rprt. Collection of Linforth's papers focusing on classical Greece and its religions. Relevant items are abstracted herein. **[1278]**

McKIRAHAN, R. D. *Plato and Socrates: A Comprehensive Bibliography, 1958-1973.* New York: Garland, 1978. Not annotated. **[1279]**

MORAVCSIK, J. M. E., ed. *Patterns in Plato's Thought: Papers Arising out of the 1971 West Coast Greek Philosophy Conference.* Dordrecht, Netherlands: Reidel, 1973. Essays are abstracted herein. **[1280]**

NORTH, H. F., ed. *Interpretations of Plato: A Swarthmore Symposium.* Leiden: Brill, 1977. Four papers, abstracted herein, from symposium held in honor of P's 2,400th birthday. **[1281]**

O'MEARA, D., ed. *Platonic Investigations.* Washington, DC: Catholic Univ. of America, 1985. Collected essays, abstracted herein. **[1282]**

PANAGIOTOU, S., ed. *Justice, Law and Method in Plato and Aristotle.* Edmonton, Alberta: Academic, 1987. Collection of articles, abstracted herein. **[1283]**

PATER, W. *Plato and Platonism: A Series of Lectures.* New York: Chelsea House, 1983. First published in 1901, lectures focus on leading principles of P's doctrine. **[1284]**

PELLETIER, F. J., and **KING-FARLOW, J.**, eds. *New Essays on Plato.* Guelph, Ont.: Canad. Assoc. for Publ. in Philos., 1983; *CanJPh* Suppl. Vol 9. Collection of essays, each abstracted herein. **[1285]**

ROSENMEYER, T. G. "Platonic Scholarship, 1945-1955." *CW* 50(1957), 173-202, 209-211. Bibliographic essay. **[1286]**

SHINER, R. A., and **KING-FARLOW, J.**, eds. *New Essays on Plato and the Pre-Socratics.* Guelph, Ont.: Canad. Assoc. for Publ. in Philos., 1976; *CanJPh* Suppl. Vol. 2. Collection of previously unpublished essays, abstracted herein. **[1287]**

SHOREY, P. *Selected Papers*, Vol. 1 and 2. ed. L. Taran. New York: Garland, 1980. Contains many of Shorey's notes, reviews, and articles on P and Ar. **[1288]**

STOCKHAMMER, M. *Plato Dictionary.* New York: Philosophical Library, 1963. Keyed to Jowett's translation. **[1289]**

VLASTOS, G., ed. *Plato: A Collection of Critical Essays I: Metaphysics and Epistemology.* Notre Dame, IN: Notre Dame Univ. Pr., 1970. Important collection of articles, some previously unpublished; each abstracted herein. Helpful bibliography. **[1290]**

———. *Plato: A Collection of Critical Essays II: Ethics, Politics, and Philosophy of Art and Religion.* Garden City, NY: Anchor Books, 1971. Collection of articles, some

162   PLATO: General

previously unpublished; each abstracted herein. Also includes bibliography.   [1291]

————. *Platonic Studies.* Princeton Univ. Pr., 1981; 2nd ed. Collection of Vlastos' essays, each of which is abstracted herein. Contains good bibliography.   [1292]

WERKMEISTER, W. H., ed. *Facets of Plato's Philosophy.* Assen: Van Gorcum, 1976; *Phron* Suppl. 2. Collection of articles, abstracted herein.   [1293]

GENERAL

ALLEN, R. E. *The Dialogues of Plato.* New Haven, CT: Yale Univ. Pr., 1984. Translations and analyses of *Euthyphro, Apol, Crito, Meno, Gorg, Menex.*   [1294]

AMBROSIO, F. J. "Gadamer, Plato, and the Discipline of Dialogue." *IntPhQ* 27(1987), 17-32. Discusses centrality of Gadamer's interpretations of P in development of Gadamer's ontology of language.   [1295]

ANDERSON, J. M. "On the Platonic Dialogue," in *Essays in Metaphysics*, ed. C. G. Vaught (University Park: PA State Univ. Pr., 1970), pp. 5-17. Overview of the dialogue process and its creative nature. Looks especially at *Rep* and *Tim.*   [1296]

ANDIC, M. "Commentary on 'Plato and Heraclitus'." *PBACAPh* 1(1985), 259-270. Shows that there are many more echoes of Heraclitus in P's dialogues than Kahn (#1389) mentions. Discusses difficulties of interpreting such echoes.   [1297]

ANNAS, J. "Self-Knowledge in Early Plato," in #1282, pp. 111-138. Suggests that apparent isolation and oddity of *Charmides'* discussion of self-knowledge disappears by regaining a wider picture of Platonic corpus. Treats as Platonic two dialogues not generally held to be P's: the *Lovers* and the *First Alcibiades.*   [1298]

ARDLEY, G. "The Role of Play in the Philosophy of Plato." *Ph* 42(1967), 226-244. Discusses P's efforts to heal the dualism between playfulness and seriousness.   [1299]

BAYONAS, A. "The Idea of Legislation in the Earlier Platonic Dialogues." *Platon* 17(1965), 26-116. P viewed law as pedagogic in his early works, with less emphasis on function of punishment than appears in his more mature works, but there is no contradiction between, e. g., *Euthyphro* and *Rep.*   [1300]

————. "The Idea of Legislation in the Earlier Platonic Dialogues, III & IV." *Platon* 18(1966), 103-177. Examines the theme in *Protag* and *Gorg.*   [1301]

BELFIORE, E. "*Elenchus, Epode*, and Magic." *Phoenix* 34(1980), 128-137. Explores P's efforts to oppose philosophy to deceitful magic by comparing definition of deceitful magic in *Rep.* 3 with his statements about "magic" of philosophy.   [1302]

BERGER, H. "Levels of Discourse in Plato's Dialogues," in *Literature and the Question of Philosophy*, ed. A. J. Cascardi. (Baltimore: Johns Hopkins Univ. Pr., 1987), pp. 75-100. P's emphasis is on the creative process, not the philosophical system. Interprets *Theaet* and *Ion* to demonstrate a reading of P which responds to certain feature of the dialogues: they are texts which must perforce be read. [1303]

BERTMAN, M. A. "Plato on Tyranny, Philosophy and Pleasure." *Apeir* 19(1985), 152-160. Participation in Supreme Reality is the ultimate pleasure for men, but pleasure itself is not good unless it is pleasure derived from knowing. [1304]

————. "Wisdom and Philosophy: Plato and Hegel." *IdealStud* 18(1988), 173-179. For P, in our piety and friendship with the divine, "actualized wisdom" guides us and helps save us from personal corruption. For Hegel, achieving wisdom means we operate with and in accordance with divine necessity, and in such a situation the question of personal corruption is an "intellectually retrograde illusion." [1305]

BLUESTONE, N. H. "Why Women Cannot Rule: Sexism in Plato Scholarship." *PhSocSci* 18(1988), 41-60. Discusses P's recommendations for education of women, and treatment of those recommendations in modern scholarship on P. [1306]

BOISVERT, R. D. "Philosophical Themes in Bertolucci's 'Conformist'." *TeachPh* 7(1984), 49-52. Shows how P's Cave Analogy is a central visual image of Bertolucci's film. [1307]

BOSSERT, P. J. "Plato's 'Cave', *Flatland* and Phenomenology," in *Phenomenology in Practice and Theory* by W. S. Hamrick (Dordrecht, Netherlands: Nijhoff, 1985), pp. 53-66. Offers a discussion of P's allegory as an explication of phenomenological philosophy which reflects Husserl's interpretation of phenomenology. [1308]

BOWEN, A. C. "On Interpreting Plato," in #1275, pp. 49-65. Discusses #1482, and argues that authorial intention should not serve as criterion for understanding P[1309]

BOZONIS, G. A. "Platonic Philosophy and Modern Thought." *Diot* 2(1974), 181-201. Examines some themes which modern philosophy and science investigate which, in terms of methodology and selection of problems, are essentially P's problems. [1310]

BROGAN, W. "Plato's *Pharmakon*: Between Two Repetitions," in *Derrida and Deconstruction*, ed. H. J. Silverman (New York: Routledge, 1989), pp. 7-23. Discusses Derrida's deconstructionist approach to P's view of writing. [1311]

BRUMBAUGH, R. S. "The Divided Line and the Direction of Inquiry." *PhFor* 2(1970-1971), 172-199; also in #49, pp. 39-65. Diagram of the divided line can be interpreted in four ways, one for each of its four levels. It functions as a key to reading not only *Rep* but all of P's later dialogues. [1312]

————. "Doctrine and Dramatic Dates of Plato's Dialogues," in #42, pp. 174-185; also in #49, pp. 91-103. Tries to show relationship between dates of composition and development of doctrine of Forms. Explores doctrinal significance of internal cross-references in P's dialogues and his indications of a proper sequence for reader. [1313]

————. "Plato's Ideal Curriculum and Contemporary Philosophy of Education." *EducTheo* 37(1987), 169-177; also in #49, pp. 67-79. Analyzes and defends P's educational theory with respect to twentieth-century philosophies of education, which fall into the same categories P elucidated. [1314]

——. "Time Passes. Platonic Variations." *RMeta* 33(1980), 711-726. Time, an unchanging Form, must mix with non-being in order to change or "pass."   **[1315]**

——. cf. #2437.

BURNYEAT, M. F. "Socratic Midwifery, Platonic Inspiration." *BICS* 24(1977), 7-16. Image of S as midwife must be attributed to P, not to historic S. Image and themes connected with it can be studied in *Theaet, Meno*, and *Symp.*   **[1316]**

BURRELL, D. B. "What the Dialogues Show about Inquiry." *PhFor* 3(1972), 104-125. P is concerned, particularly in early dialogues, to demonstrate his dialectical method than to reach firm conclusions.   **[1317]**

CACOULLOS, A. R. "The Doctrine of Eros in Plato." *Diot* 1(1973), 81-89. P sees *eros*, a tendency toward self-fulfillment and happiness, as driving all persons. *Eros* is need one experiences because of some lack and because it is necessary for growth.   **[1318]**

CALLAHAN, J. F. "Dialectic, Myth and History in the Philosophy of Plato," in #1281, pp. 64-85. Surveys philosophical origins in mythic world view and P's use of non-literal language for philosophic analysis. P uses myths to restate themes he has presented dialectically, present points of doctrine, and provide a setting for his dialectic.   **[1319]**

CAVARNOS, C. *Plato's View of Man.* Belmont, MA: Inst. for Byzantine and Modern Greek Stud., 1975. Focuses on P's primary concern with whole of man's earthly existence considered from cognitive, aesthetic, ethical and religious standpoints.   **[1320]**

CHANG, K. "The Problem of Unity in the Philosophy of Plato." *Philosophical Review* (Taiwan) 6(1983), 61-82. Examines problem of how a unity of determinations can exist in an individual.   **[1321]**

CHERNISS, H. F. "Some War-Time Publications Concerning Plato," in #51, pp. 142-216. Evaluation of several books (European and American) on P published during World War II.   **[1322]**

CHROUST, A-H. "The Organization of the *Corpus Platonicum* in Antiquity." *Hermes* 93(1965), 34-46. Thrasyllus was not first to group dialogues in tetralogies. Practice goes back perhaps to Academy. Others, such as Aristophanes of Byzantium, grouped them in trilogies, using variety of organizational principles.   **[1323]**

——. cf. #3565, #3589.

CLAY, D. "Gaps in the 'Universe' of the Platonic Dialogues." *PBACAPh* 3(1987), 131-157. Argues in favor of taking each dialogue on its own terms rather than trying to construct a Platonic "universe of discourse."   **[1324]**

——. "Platonic Studies and the Study of Plato." *Arion* 2(1975), 116-132. Critical review/discussion of #1292.   **[1325]**

CLEGG, J. S. *The Structure of Plato's Philosophy.* London: Associated Univ. Pr., 1977. Maintains that some central themes can be identified which run consistently through P's philosophy. Ignores questions of chronology and examines P's metaphysics, epistemology, aesthetics, psychology, and politics on the assumption that his views remained essentially the same over his lifetime and that he was defending an urban outlook against the relativism of the Sophists.   [1326]

COOLEY, K. W. "Unity and Diversity of the Virtues in the *Charmides, Laches,* and *Protagoras.*" *Kinesis* 1(1969), 100-106. Shows how physical, or "outer," seems to serve as necessary dialectical stepping stone to mental or "inner" condition of soul.   [1327]

CROMBIE, I. M. *An Examination of Plato's Doctrines, Vol. I: Plato on Man and Society.* London: Routledge & Kegan Paul, 1969; rprt. Discusses P's moral and political philosophy and his philosophy of mind and religion.   [1328]

————. *Ibid., Vol. II: Plato on Knowledge and Reality.* London: Routledge & Kegan Paul, 1979; rprt. Focuses on more technical problems: metaphysics and logic, theory of knowledge, philosophy of nature, methodology of science and philosophy.   [1329]

————. *Plato: The Midwife's Apprentice.* New York: Barnes & Noble, 1965. Stresses importance of Socratic technique of inquiry, and argues that understanding of P has been distorted by Ar's conception of "Platonism" as a set of static dogmas.   [1330]

————. "Ryle's New Portrait of Plato." *PhR* 78(1969), 362-373. Review of Ryle's *Plato's Progress* (#1446); while appreciative of Ryle's novelty and suggestiveness, dissents from his main conclusions.   [1331]

CROPSEY, J. "The Dramatic End of Plato's Socrates." *Interp* 14(1986), 155-175. Examines importance of P's interpretation of S as reconciling Protagorean and Pythagorean thought. Looks at dialogues with dramatic settings between *Theaet* and *Phaedo.* P seems to have kept an open mind in his evaluation of S.   [1332]

CUNNINGHAM, F. J. "Plato: Archaic or Modern Man?" *Thought* 50(1975), 400-417. P's thought is not archaic, i. e., afraid of change and looking to divine sources of meaning. His works suggest he was receptive to creativity and change.   [1333]

DEMOS, R. *The Philosophy of Plato.* New York: Octagon Books, 1966; rprt. Reconstructs P's thought from his own works, without reference to Ar and other ancient interpreters. Surveys dialogues and finds a unity of thought. Chapters cover topics such as Being, Forms and Things, Art and Beauty, etc.   [1333a]

DESJARDINS, R. "Why Dialogues? Plato's Serious Play," in #1275, pp. 110-125. Because discourse is inherently ambiguous we need to appreciate three levels of a Platonic dialogue: 1) S's interpretation of his own tradition; 2) dialogue form of writing which is central to P's interpretation of S; 3) audience's interpretation and dialogue with written texts.   [1334]

DE VOGEL, C. J. "In Search for Unity. Reflections on J. N. Findlay's Plato Book of 1974," in #1338, pp. 57-92. Extended review and discussion of #1355.   [1335]

————. "Notes to W. K. C. Guthrie's Plato," in #1338, pp. 93-118. Expanded version of review of #20 and #21.   [1336]

————. "Plato, The Written and Unwritten Doctrines: Fifty Years of Plato Studies,

1930-1980," in #1338, pp. 3-56. Survey of some seminal works and most important trends in scholarship on this subject.   [1337]

———. *Rethinking Plato and Platonism.* Leiden: Brill, 1986. Collection of lectures, critical notes, and comments on trends in study of P and Platonism. Contains revised versions of some published articles.   [1338]

———. "The *Soma-Sema* Formula: Its Function in Plato and Plotinus Compared to Its Use by Christian Writers," in #6339, pp. 79-95; also in #1338, pp. 233-248. The term *sema* can be variously interpreted as "prison," "temple," or "fence." It is an enclosure of some kind. For P, and for later Platonists, the soul's presence in a body is not necessarily a fall but a challenge, as the soul struggles to gain control over an alien environment. Christian thinkers do not use the image explicitly but seem to have it in mind in several passages.   [1339]

———. "Was Plato a Dualist?" *Theta Pi* 1(1972), 4-60; also in #1338, pp. 159-212. Survey of arguments on each side of question.   [1340]

DE VRIES, G. J. "Colloquialisms in *Republic* and *Phaedrus*," in *Festschrift Hans-Juergen Hundt zum 65. Geburtstag, dargebracht vom Kollegium des Roemisch-Germanischen Zentralmuseums* (Mainz, Ger.: Verl. des Roem.-Germ. Zentralmus., 1977), I, pp. 87-92. Reply to H. Thesleff (#1478).   [1341]

———. "Laughter in Plato's Writings." *Mnem* 38(1985), 378-381. Certain terms for laughter have a negative connotation in dialogues, but others imply only that something is witty or droll.   [1342]

———. "Platonic Dialogues Performed?" *Mnem* 37(1984), 143-145. Reply to H. Thesleff (#1480).   [1343]

DOMBROWSKI, D. A. "Plato and Athletics." *Journal of the Philosophy of Sport* 6(1979), 29-38. P expresses variety of views, none negative, on athletics in education.   [1344]

———. *Plato's Philosophy of History.* Washington, DC: University Pr. of America, 1981. Examines P's view of history through chronological study of dialogues. P is basically a process philosopher and Theory of Forms is compatible with his view of history.[1345]

———. "Rorty and Popper on the Footnotes to Plato." *Dialogos* 22(1987), 135-145. Examines extent to which Rorty and Popper borrow from P.   [1346]

———. "Was Plato a Vegetarian?" *Apeir* 18(1984), 1-9. P was probably not a vegetarian but was favorably impressed by the practice.   [1347]

DYE, J. W. "Plato's Concept of Causal Explanation." *TulStudPh* 27(1978), 37-56. Examination of the way *aitia* is used in Platonic dialogues reveals several meanings, all related to character and intentions of human agents.   [1348]

EISENBERG, P. "*Sophrosune*, Self and State. A Partial Defense of Plato." *Apeir* 9 #2(1975), 31-36. P's reference to concord of superior and inferior about who should rule (*Rep* 432a) means a harmony of interests, not a specific act of consenting. *Sophrosune* can thus apply to an individual or to the *polis*.   [1349]

EPP, R. H. "Katharsis and the Platonic Reconstruction of Mystical Terminology." *Phil*(Athens) 4(1974), 168-179. Discusses P's transformation of religious cult uses of *katharsis* in several of his works. Argues that P borrows heavily, but selectively, from cults. He knows how to retain spiritual significance of these practices, but rejects ritualistic methods associated with their practitioners. [1350]

ESLICK, L. J. "Plato's Dialectic of the Sun," in *History of Philosophy in the Making*, ed. L. J. Thro (Washington, DC: University Pr. of Amer., 1982), pp. 19-34. Examines exact nature of P's earlier dialectic, and in particular, his indebtedness to developments in Greek mathematics. [1351]

FARNESS, J. "Plato's Architexture: Some Problems for Philosophical Interpretation." *Arethusa* 21(1988), 27-46. Examines certain kinds of "linguistic debasing" practiced by P that create difficulties for interpretation. His language is "textually effective" and must be studied in terms of linguistics and rhetoric as well as philosophy. [1352]

FIELD, G. C. *The Philosophy of Plato*. Oxford Univ. Pr., 1969. Discusses main features of P's thought, showing that it is not a fixed and final system but a continually growing and developing body of thought. [1353]

————. *Plato and His Contemporaries: A Study in Fourth-Century Life and Thought*. New York: Barnes & Noble, 1967; rprt. Biography of P and survey of form and chronology of dialogues. Second and third parts look at "moral, political, literary, and philosophical setting of Plato's thought." [1354]

FINDLAY, J. N. *Plato: The Written and Unwritten Doctrines*. London: Routledge & Kegan Paul, 1974. P's dialogues represent not development of his thought but gradual revealing of ideas he held all along. Interpretations of later Platonists, such as Plotinus, are not far-fetched but based on coherent reading of P. [1355]

FISHER, J. "Plato on Writing and Doing Philosophy." *JHI* 27(1966), 163-172. The importance of philosophy justifies the less than desirable fact that it must be put into writing. *Phaedrus* is the best example of this paradox. [1356]

FREELAND, C. "Commentary on Rosen's 'Platonic Hermeneutics: On the Interpretation of a Platonic Dialogue'." *PBACAPh* 1(1985), 289-295. Challenges some of Rosen's points (#1438) on writing and knowledge by measuring them against P's text. [1357]

FRIEDLAENDER, P. *Plato, I: An Introduction*, transl. and rev. H. Meyerhof. Princeton Univ. Pr., 1969. Standard format of discussion of role and influence of S and survey of main points of P's thought. Draws parallels with some modern philosophers, such as Schopenhauer, Bergson, and Heidegger. [1358]

————. *Plato, II: The Dialogues. First Period:* Protagoras, Laches, Republic 1, Charmides, Euthyphro, Lysis, Hippias Major, Hipparchus, Ion, Hippias Minor, Theages, Apology, Crito, Euthydemus, Cratylus, Menexenus, Alcibiades Major, Gorgias, Meno, transl. H. Meyerhof. Princeton Univ. Pr., 1969. Summarizes and discusses the earlier dialogues and reasons for accepting or rejecting some of the dubious works. [1359]

————. *Plato, III: The Dialogues. Second and Third Periods*, transl. H. Meyerhof. Princeton Univ. Pr., 1969. Discusses later dialogues, beginning with *Symposium*. Stresses ethical and political aspects of P's thought, rather than logic or epistemology. Also discusses chronology of dialogues. **[1360]**

FRIES, R., ed. *The Progress of Plato's Progress.* Berkeley: Univ. of CA Dept. of Classics, 1969. Essays reacting to arguments by G. Ryle (#1446). **[1361]**

GADAMER, H.-G. "Plato's Unwritten Dialectic," in #1274, pp. 124-155. Traces importance of number in P's unwritten teaching. What we can know of his oral doctrine does not contradict his written work. **[1362]**

———. "Reply to Nicholas P. White," in #1275, pp. 258-266. Responds to questions raised by White's comments (#1497) on a work of Gadamer. **[1363]**

GAFFNEY, S. K. "Dialectic, the Myths of Plato, Metaphor and the Transcendent in the World." *PACPhA* 45(1971), 77-85. Examines three different levels of dialectic and role of myths in various dialogues. Metaphorical myths solve dichotomy between natural and intelligible worlds. They are means to express vision of the intelligible. **[1364]**

GARSIDE, A. C. "Plato on Women." *FemStud* 2(1975), 131-138. The main passages where P talks about the nature and status of women (in *Tim*, *Rep*, and *Laws*) reveal an inconsistency which proves to be only superficial. **[1365]**

GEDDES, A. "The Philosophical Notion of Women in Antiquity." *Antich* 9(1975), 35-40. Several of P's and Ar's basic assumptions about nature of female were erroneous. These errors created or magnified problems in their philosophical systems. **[1366]**

GOOCH, P. W. "Socrates: Devious or Divine?" *G&R* 32(1985), 32-41. Though S, as P presents him, claims repeatedly not to know, it is clear that P thinks he did have sure knowledge of the things taught in the dialogues. **[1367]**

GOSLING, J. C. B. *Plato.* London: Routledge & Kegan Paul, 1983. Examines P's claims that what all men desire is the good and that all knowledge is knowledge of the good. Explores P's efforts to bring together morality and science. **[1368]**

GOULDNER, A. W. *Enter Plato: Classical Greece and the Origins of Social Theory.* New York: Basic Books, 1965. Sets P's social theory in its sociological and intellectual context. Examines pre-Platonic writers before devoting most attention to P. **[1369]**

GRISWOLD, C. L. "Gadamer and the Interpretation of Plato." *AncPh* 1(1980-81), 171-178. Discusses each of the essays in #1274. Stresses importance of reading each dialogue as a whole and trying to understand why P wrote dialogues. **[1370]**

———. "Plato's Metaphilosophy: Why Plato Wrote Dialogues," in #1275, pp. 143-167. For a good philosophical reason, philosophers cannot defend their own activity non-dialogically; P's decision to write dialogues indicates his awareness of basic difficulty of justifying philosophical reason. **[1371]**

———. "Style and Philosophy: The Case of Plato's Dialogues." *Monist* 63(1980), 530-546. The literary style which a philosopher chooses will reflect the degree of certainty he feels about his ideas. P's choice of an aporetic dialogue form, as exemplified in *Phaedrus*, arises from this connection. **[1372]**

GRUBE, G. M. A. *Plato's Thought.* London: Methuen, 1970; rprt. For non-specialists. Takes a topical approach rather than analyzing dialogues individually. Chapters cover Theory of Ideas, pleasure, eros, the soul, the gods, art, education, statecraft. [1373]

HADEN, T. "On Plato's Inconclusiveness." *CJ* 65(1969), 219-224. The early dialogues are not inconclusive. Just as S's conversations can end on an admission of ignorance, so P's dialogues merely approach the truth but stop short of it. [1374]

HAHN, R. "Being and Non-Being in *Rig Veda X*, in the Writings of the *Lao-Tzu* and *Chuang-Tzu*, and in the 'Later' Plato." *JChinPh* 8(1981), 119-142. Examines *Rig Veda X, Lao Tzu* and *Chuang-Tzu*, and applies perspective on dialectic between Being and Non-Being to creation myth of P's *Tim* and ontological digression of *Philebus*. [1375]

HALL, R. W. *Plato.* London: Allen & Unwin, 1981. Discusses evolution of P's thought through the major dialogues within historical context of actual developments in Athenian democracy. [1376]

HALPERIN, D. M. "Plato and Erotic Reciprocity." *ClAnt* 5(1986), 60-80. P links homosexuality and philosophy because the former creates an atmosphere of reciprocal affection which is conducive to philosophy. [1377]

———. "Platonic *Eros* and What Men Call Love." *AncPh* 5(1985), 161-204. Platonic *eros* is inadequate to task of explicating nature of love, but P never intended to put it to that use. Rather, he attempted and achieved an erotic theory that could account for the metaphysics of desire. [1378]

HARE, R. M. *Plato.* Oxford Univ. Pr., 1982. Non-specialist survey. Examines central problems that led P to become a philosopher: Can human excellence be taught? What would be the qualifications of such a teacher? What sort of knowledge would such a teacher have? What political arrangements are needed to enable such teachers to fulfill their task? [1379]

HARTMAN, M. "The Hesiodic Roots of Plato's Myth of the Metals." *Helios* 15(1988), 103-114. Examines Hesiod's myth of ages of mankind (gold, silver, etc.) to show P's debt to those images. [1380]

HASLAM, M. "Plato, Sophron, and the Dramatic Dialogue." *BICS* 19(1972), 17-38. Publication of a papyrus fragment from Oxyrhynchus which suggests that P derived dramatic element of *dialogikos eidos* from Sophron's mimes. [1381]

HATHAWAY, R. F. "Explaining the Unity of the Platonic Dialogue." *Ph&Lit* 8(1984), 195-208. The unity of a Platonic dialogue arises from P's concept of mimesis, his use of models in philosophic investigation, and the presence of smaller units of discourse ("micro-dialogues") with the larger works. [1382]

HAWTREY, R. S. W. "Dialogue and Education *or* What Plato Did Not Say." *Prud* 10(1978), 57-66. In light of P's disparagement of writing in *Phaedrus* we should ask why he wrote dialogues at all. He seems to have considered them an essential part of educative process, encouraging reader to think through a problem rather than trying to teach "right" answers. [1383]

HYLAND, D. A. "Why Plato Wrote Dialogues." *Ph&Rh* 1(1968), 38-50. Explores P's comments on writing and comic/tragic dialectic in philosophy. Dialogues imitate philosophical situations which may prompt readers to become philosophers. [1384]

IRWIN, T. H. "Reply to David Roochnik," in #1275, pp. 194-199. Response to Roochnik's (#1436) criticisms of Irwin's methodology of reading P. [1385]

JARRETT, J. L. "Dialectic as 'Tao' in Plato and Jung." *Diot* 2(1974), 73-92. Emphasizes one important conception of dialectic — as a logic of progression by means of opposition or contradiction, as a quest for purity and perfection — and compares it to Jung's theory. [1386]

JORDAN, N. *The Wisdom of Plato: An Attempt at an Outline*, 2 vols. Washington, DC: Univ. Pr. of America, 1981. Outlines Platonic thought, and argues that contemporary scholarship is wrong about P in almost everything that matters. [1387]

KAHN, C. H. "Did Plato Write Socratic Dialogues?" *CQ* 31(1981), 305-320. Challenges view that P's motivation in writing Socratic dialogues was primarily historical. Offers new views of chronology of dialogues. [1388]

———. "Plato and Heraclitus." *PBACAPh* 1(1985), 241-258. Seeks to reconstruct from dialogues a true and consistent account of Heraclitus' impact on P and to determine use which P makes of some geniunely Heraclitean ideas. [1389]

KAUFMANN, L. "Scepticism of Essences in Plato." *ModSch* 53(1976), 171-176. Ar's criticism of P shows that P's thought evolved from extreme realism of his youth to position that Forms were only names, a kind of sophisticated skepticism. [1390]

KAYSER, J. R. "Noble Lies and Justice: On Reading Plato." *Polity* 5(1973), 489-515. Difficulties of interpretation arise from dialogue form itself and from P's desire to conceal his thought. [1391]

KOSMAN, A. "Commentary on Teloh's 'The Importance of Interlocutors' Characters in Plato's Early Dialogues.'" *PBACAPh* 2(1986) 39-44. Challenges Teloh's interpretation of the dialogues (#1477) as dramatic representation of philosophical therapy in practice. It is important to recognize S as being also a dramatic character within the Platonic enterprise which takes the form of philosophical poetry. [1392]

KOYRE, A. *Discovering Plato*. New York: Columbia Univ. Pr. 1968. Introductory work that emphasizes the union of politics and philosophy in P. Discusses four dialogues: *Theaet, Meno, Protag,* and *Rep*. [1393]

LAMBERT, G. R. "Plato's Household *Topos*: A Formative Influence on Ancient Educational and Social Theory." *Prud* 16(1984), 17-32. P saw advantages to "having children" in physical and intellectual senses, to immortalize one's name and provide heirs for one's property or teachings. Christian thinkers adopted many of his arguments. [1394]

LANG, B. "Presentation and Representation in Plato's Dialogues." *PhFor* 4(1972-73), 224-240. P sometimes "presents" an idea in an assertive or discursive statement. At other times he uses the technique of representation in an image. [1395]

LAVELY, J. H. "The Turning Point in Plato's Life." *BosUnivJ* 22 #2(1974), 32-36. Illness which prevented P from attending S's last gathering with his disciples may have been severe depression brought on by political chaos in Athens at the time.   **[1396]**

LEDGER, G. R. *Re-counting Plato: A Computer Analysis of Plato's Style.* Oxford: Clarendon Pr., 1989. Thorough discussion of the problems of identifying a writer's style with enough certainty to determine authenticity of any particular work. Somewhat technical explanation of variables considered in such a study. Concludes that several dubious works (*Epinomis* and *Letter 7, Hippias Major, Alcibiades I, Menexenus,* and *Clitophon*) are genuine. Suggests revised chronology for dialogues.   **[1397]**

LEE, E. N. "Reason and Rotation. Circular Movement as the Model of Mind (*Nous*) in the Later Plato," in #1293, pp. 70-102. Examines foundations of P's theory of circular motion and considers why Ar's attacks on the theory are inadequate. Theory represents P's movement to a new phase of considering what philosophic life implies.   **[1398]**

LESSER, H. "Style and Pedagogy in Plato and Aristotle." *Ph* 57(1982), 388-394. P's decision to present his philosophy in dialogue form and Ar's choice of a compressed lecturing style were based more on their pedagogic objectives than on differences in philosophical doctrine.   **[1399]**

MARANHAO, T. *Therapeutic Discourse and Socratic Dialogue.* Madison: Univ. of WI, 1986. Socratic dialogue shares many features with modern psychoanalytic therapy. Like the therapist, the Socratic philosopher cannot persuade or overpower his interlocutor but must help him find his own way to knowledge/understanding. Also compares Sophistic period to age of religious skepticism in which Freud's thought developed.   **[1400]**

MATTEI, J-F. "The Theater of Myth in Plato," in #1275, pp. 66-83. Takes myths to be indispensable elements of dialogues; argues that P's use of myth helps to explain theatrical dimension of dialogues and challenges our understanding of what it means to do philosophy.   **[1401]**

MAULA, E. "The Conquest of Time." *Diot* 11(1983), 130-148. Technical discussion of the relationship between the musical intervals, the "Great Harmonia" (*Tim* 35a-36d), and scientific theories of planetary motion current in P's time.   **[1402]**

MEJER, J. "Plato, Protagoras and the Heracliteans." *C&M* 29(1972), 40-60. Compares P's theory of sensation to certain Presocratics, especially Democritus.   **[1403]**

MELLING, D. J. *Understanding Plato.* Oxford Univ. Pr., 1987. Survey for non-specialists. Biographical sketch, overview of writings. Chapters on teachability of virtue, Sophists, theory of learning/recollection, theory of Forms, and other topics.   **[1404]**

MEYERHOFF, H. "From Socrates to Plato," in *The Critical Spirit: Essays in Honor of Herbert Marcuse*, ed. K. H. Wolff and B. Moore (Boston: Beacon Pr., 1967), pp. 187-201. Development can be traced in P's dialogues and dialectic, from S to P, a movement from uncertainty toward certainty.   **[1405]**

MICHAELIDES-NOUAROS, A. "Causes of War in Plato." *Diot* 2(1974), 61-65. P maintains that when people abandon a simple lifestyle, war results. He disagrees with historian Thucydides, who saw origin of war in socio-economic problems.   **[1406]**

MICHAELSON, S., et al. "The Problem of Plato." *RELO* (1977) #2, 1-28. Divides P's dialogues into two groups, depending on role given to S and views attributed to him. The more "Socratic" dialogues may have been written by another follower of S and wrongly attributed to P.   **[1407]**

MILLER, J. F. "Why Plato Wrote Myths." *SwPhSt* 3(1978), 84-92. Explores how middle dialogues differ from earlier ones by: 1) grounding earlier ethical doctrines on metaphysics; 2) emphasizing both politics and mathematics, and 3) employing myth frequently. Argues P's exposure to Pythagorean teachings accounts for change.   **[1408]**

MILLER, M. "Commentary on Clay's 'Gaps in the "Universe" of Platonic Dialogues'." *PBACAPh* 3(1987), 158-164. Responds to #1324 and discusses difficulties of trying to connect dialogues as steps in a systematic argument.   **[1409]**

MITTELSTRASS, J. "On Socratic Dialogue," in #1275, pp. 126-142. Analyzes how dialogue leads to philosophical knowledge. Brings together notions of dialogue, recollection, elenchus, maieutics, and philosophy as a "way of life" and "disposition of the soul," to show that insight cannot be "proven" discursively.   **[1410]**

MOLINE, J. "Recollection, Dialectic, and Ontology: Kenneth M. Sayre on the Solution to a Platonic Riddle," in #1275, pp. 233-239. Discussion of Sayre's view (#1918) on P's decision to write dialogues and its relation to theory of anamnesis.   **[1411]**

MOORS, K. F. *Platonic Myth: An Introductory Study.* Washington, DC: Univ. Pr. of America, 1982. Advocates contextual study of P's myths. Lists and analyzes passages in which P uses or discusses myth and shows how certain myths relate to broader themes of the dialogues.   **[1412]**

————. "Plato's Use of Dialogue." *CW* 72(1978), 77-93. P felt obliged to write dialogues because it is only through interaction occasioned by discussion that the soul of man is made manifest.   **[1413]**

MORTLEY, R. "Love in Plato and Plotinus." *Antich* 14(1980), 45-52. Idea of love as "lack" is a most important, yet often overlooked, ingredient in accounts of love given by P and Plotinus.   **[1414]**

NEWMAN, J. "Philosophy as a Profession." *Aitia* 7(1980), 18-22. P's effort to draw a clear distinction between S and the Sophists created uncertainty over what it means to be a philosopher which persists until today.   **[1415]**

NOVOTNY, F. *The Posthumous Life of Plato.* The Hague: Nijhoff, 1977. Traces P's influence from Ar to Christianity up to twentieth-century philosophy.   **[1416]**

NUSSBAUM, M. "Aristophanes and Socrates on Learning Practical Wisdom." *YCS* 26(1980), 43-97. Actions and attitudes of ordinary citizens, such as those portrayed in the *Clouds,* make it clear why P considered education of youth and selection of rulers too important to be left to ambition and luck.   **[1417]**

O'NEILL, W. H. "The Love of Wisdom." *Pers* 52(1971), 459-482. Contains a discussion of how P and Ar understand the meaning of "wisdom," and suggests how far contemporary schools in their curricula have departed from that meaning.   **[1418]**

OSWIECIMSKI, S. "The Ancient Testimonies in the Face of the Platonic Apocrypha." *Eos* 67(1979), 233-255. Ancient writers usually cited as authorities for rejecting eight to eleven dialogues attributed to P are late, few in number, of virtually no value. **[1419]**

———. "The Enigmatic Character of Some of Plato's Apocrypha." *Eos* 66(1978), 31-40. Dialogues not listed by Thrasyllus should not be rejected as apocryphal. They may have been school exercises, taken down faithfully by anonymous students of P. **[1420]**

PATTERSON, R. "Plato on Philosophic Character." *JHPh* 25(1987), 325-350. Philosopher needs steadfastness of character because reason's desire for truth may cause it to follow inappropriate leads. **[1421]**

PHILIP, J. A. "The Platonic Corpus." *Phoenix* 24(1970), 296-308. Discusses origins of practice of grouping dialogues by fours, which seems to have originated in a fourth-century B. C. editing of the collection. **[1422]**

PHILIPOUSIS, J. "Heidegger and Plato's Notion of 'Truth'." *Dial*(Can) 15(1976), 502-504. Reexamines Heidegger's interpretation of P's notion of "truth," and argues that P understands *aletheia* not as exactitude but as revelation of *ousia* itself. **[1423]**

PLASS, P. "'Play' and Philosophic Detachment in Plato." *TAPhA* 98(1967), 343-364. Maintenance of delicate poise between purely sensuous and purely rational *eros* depends, in large part, on Socratic irony. While P never defines "irony," he does mention "play" more often. **[1424]**

PLOCHMAN, G. K. "Five Elements in Plato's Conception of Reality." *UltR&M* 4(1981), 24-57. Examines P's treatment of name, sentence, image, knowledge and the real to represent his system. **[1425]**

———. *Plato.* New York: Dell, 1973. Seeks to show that "love of Plato as an artist rests ultimately upon the understanding of him as a thinker." Offers a lengthy discussion of "The Platonic Philosophy" and translations of selected dialogues. **[1426]**

PREUS, A. "The Continuous Analogy. The Uses of Continuous Proportions in Plato and Aristotle." *Agora* 1 #2(1970), 21-42. Examines how P and Ar use arguments by analogy, particularly in *Tim* and *Rep* and in Ar's *Ethics* and biological works. **[1427]**

RANDALL, J. H. "Communication." *JPh* 65(1968), 737-742. Comments on approach taken by Ryle in #1446. **[1428]**

———. *Plato, Dramatist of the Life of Reason.* New York: Columbia Univ. Pr., 1970. Dialogues are dramatic works designed to prompt readers to see important truths. S and other intellectual personalities become vehicles for self-knowledge. **[1429]**

RANKIN, H. D. "Another Look at Kelsen's View of Plato." *Apeir* 2 #1(1967), 18-26. Examines Kelsen's (1944) analysis that P was homosexual and that his inner conflicts externalized themselves in form of: 1) disagreement with society; 2) distaste for sex; 3) theory of *eros* as a pervasive motive force; 4) preoccupation with power and domination. **[1430]**

———. "Laughter, Humour and Related Topics in Plato." *C&M* 28(1967), 186-213. P distinguishes types of laughter, whose significance has been overlooked. [1431]

———. "Plato's Lost Pupil and the Banausic Education." *Apeir* 1(1966), 32. P's unfortunate experience with Dionysius II of Syracuse probably contributed to his disparaging attitude toward manual labor. [1432]

ROBINSON, R., and DENNISTON, J. D. "Plato," in #1290, pp. 7-15. Useful survey of P's life and work. [1433]

ROOCHNIK, D. L. "Plato's Use of *Atechnos*." *Phoenix* 41(1987), 255-263. *Atechnos* may be only an adverb meaning "really," "utterly." But P also seems to use it in its root sense of "without *techne* (skill)." [1434]

———. "Socrates' Use of the Techne-Analogy." *JHPh* 20(1986), 295-310. In early dialogues S is not proposing that moral knowledge is a kind of *techne* (skill, art). Analogy is used to refute those who claim to possess moral knowledge and to encourage those who hesitate to seek it. In an appendix is a statistical analysis of P's use of *techne* and its derivatives. [1435]

———. "Terence Irwin's Reading of Plato," in #1275, pp. 183-193. Critical discussion of #1709. Maintains that the basic weakness of the book is Irwin's interpretive strategy, which sees P's early dialogues as collections of moral axioms. [1436]

ROSEN, S. H. "Heidegger's Interpretation of Plato." *Journal of Existentialism* 7(1967), 477-508; also in *Essays in Metaphysics*, ed. C. G. Vaught (University Park: PA State Univ. Pr., 1970), pp. 51-77; also in #75, pp. 127-147. Offers an outline, not a complete account, looking at concepts of Being and time. Discusses cave image, which is central to Heidegger's understanding of P, to show that Heidegger misinterprets P. [1437]

———. "Platonic Hermeneutics: On the Interpretation of a Platonic Dialogue." *PBACAPh* 1(1985), 271-288. Argues for existence of structural tension in dialogues between rhetoric of mathematics and of poetry. [1438]

———. "Reply by Rosen on Freeland's 'Commentary on Rosen's "Platonic Hermeneutics: On the Interpretation of a Platonic Dialogue"'." *PBACAPh* 1(1985), 296-98. Sharp reply to #1357. [1439]

———. "Return to the Origin. Reflections on Plato and Contemporary Philosophy." *IntPhQ* 16(1976), 151-177. Modern philosophers often speak of finding validity for discipline in a "pre-philosophical situation." P confronted same problem; hence his interest in doxography. [1440]

———. "Self-Consciousness and Self-Knowledge in Plato and Hegel." *Hegel Studien* 9(1974), 109-129. Whereas P accepts phenomenon of self-consciousness, he denies possibility of self-knowledge. For Hegel, self-consciousness is a process of development which culminates in self-knowledge. [1441]

———. "Six Books on Plato by Jacob Klein, Hans-George Gadamer, Ronna Burger, David Bolotin, M. H. Miller, and T. L. Pangle." *Ph&Rh* 18(1981), 112-117. Reviews these six works which show "an admirable interest in P's actual mode of composition." [1442]

ROWE, C. J. *Plato.* New York: St. Martin's Pr., 1984. Non-specialist survey. Places little reliance on efforts to understand historical P or S through dialogues. Summarizes *Euthyphro, Symp,* and *Stsm* as representative works of different stages of P's development. Expresses skepticism about whether there is one Theory of Forms. Other chapters deal with knowledge, pleasure and the good, state and individual, aesthetics, and the soul. **[1443]**

———. cf. #913.

RUDEBUSCH, G. "Plato's Aporetic Style." *SJPh* 27(1989), 539-547. P's earlier dialogues, which often end with the primary problem unsolved, are intended to undermine the readers' confidence in their own wisdom. **[1444]**

RUTTENBERG, H. S. "Plato's Use of the Analogy Between Justice and Health." *JValInq* 20(1986), 147-156. Analogy between justice and health assimilates the physical to the intelligible; consequently P's identification of individual and common good does not produce a tyranny. **[1445]**

RYLE, G. *Plato's Progress.* Cambridge Univ. Pr., 1966. P normally composed his dialogues for oral delivery to audiences. Many of the dialogues were performed at games/festivals. Offers original views on chronology of dialogues. Argues that Ar was never in a strict sense P's disciple. **[1446]**

SADDINGTON, D. B. "The Education of an Ideal Man: The Views of Plato, Cicero, Augustine." *Akroterion* 15(1970), 5-16. Outlines each thinker's views and discusses how their approaches might improve modern education. **[1447]**

SAHAKIAN, W. S., and **SAHAKIAN, M. L.** *Plato.* Boston: Twayne, 1977. Introductory account reviewing the main themes of P's philosophy. Tries to draw parallels between P's thought and that of more modern philosophers and scientists. **[1448]**

SALLIS, J. *Being and Logos: The Way of Platonic Dialogue.* Pittsburgh: Duquesne Univ. Pr., 1975. Radical reinterpretation of *Apol, Meno, Phaedrus, Cratylus, Rep, Soph.* Principal questions are nature of philosophy, of logos, and of being and relation of being to logos. **[1449]**

SANDERS, L. J. "Plato's First Visit to Sicily." *Kokalos* 25(1979), 207-219. Difficulties in relations between P and Dionysius I, tyrant of Syracuse, are tied to vagaries of relations between their two cities. **[1450]**

SAVAN, D. "Socrates' Logic and the Unity of Wisdom and Temperance," in *Analytical Philosophy: Second Series,* ed. R. J. Butler (Oxford: Blackwell, 1965), pp. 20-26. Contrary to much recent scholarship, argues that S's argument at *Rep* 332a-333b demonstrating the unity of wisdom and temperance is clear and sound. **[1451]**

SAYRE, K. M. "Reply to Jon Moline," in #1275, pp. 240-246. Response to #1411. Moline does not give any emphasis himself to the theory of recollection in explaining why P wrote dialogues. **[1452]**

SCHLEIERMACHER, F. E. D. *Introductions to the Dialogues of Plato.* New York: Arno Pr., 1973. Reprint of 1834 edition of essays on the dialogues. Noteworthy as pioneer in the movement to understand dialogues as literature and to re-evaluate their authenticity.   [1453]

SEESKIN, K. R. "Formalization in Platonic Scholarship." *Metaphil* 9(1978), 242-251. Dialogues should not be interpreted with concepts and distinctions which neither P nor anyone living within a thousand years of him could have known about.   [1454]

————. "Socratic Philosophy and the Dialogue Form." *Ph&Lit* 8(1984), 181-194. P's dialogues are literature because they do not preach. They involve the listener, avoiding as much as possible the disadvantages of the written word which S described in *Phaedrus*.   [1455]

————. cf.#2063.

SENTER, N. W. "Plato on Women." *SwPhSt* 2(1977), 4-13. Overview of P's ideas on equal training for men and women. He maintains that the roles people play in social and political life should be determined by skills, not gender.   [1456]

SHOREY, P. *The Unity of Plato's Thought*. New York: Archon, 1968; rprt. Rejects value of stylometric studies and efforts to establish chronology of the dialogues. Maintains that P's ideas were well formed by the time he was thirty or so and that he sets out a coherent body of thought in his dialogues. Examines several topics (Ethics, Ideas, Psychology) and some major dialogues.   [1457]

————. *What Plato Said*. Univ. of Chicago Pr., 1978; rprt. Attempts to distill each of the dialogues, summarizing their main points and including extracts in translation.   [1458]

SIDER, D. "Did Plato Write Dialogues Before the Death of Socrates?" *Apeir* 14(1980), 15-18. Several pieces of evidence suggest that P did compose dialogues in which S appeared while S still lived.   [1459]

SKEMP, J. B. *Plato*. Oxford: Clarendon Pr., 1976. Concise survey of trends in scholarship with discussion of selected books and articles. Looks at topics — e. g. "The Platonic Corpus;" "Plato, Socrates, and the Sophists;" "Plato and Politics;" "Plato's Metaphysical System: The Forms" — instead of individual dialogues.   [1460]

————. cf. #1163, #3520.

SMITH, J. E. "Plato's Myths as 'Likely Accounts' Worthy of Belief." *Apeir* 19(1985), 24-42. Examines certain myths and argues that they are actions which provide a narrative in accord with true opinion. As P's interlocutors advance in dialectical skill they can examine myths and compose new ones.   [1461]

————. "Plato's Use of Myth in the Education of Philosophic Man." *Phoenix* 40(1986), 20-34. In P's dialogues myths introduce hypotheses while avoiding dogmatism, provide playful moments amid serious discussion and reiterate primary themes.   [1462]

SMITH, N. D. "Plato and Aristotle on the Nature of Women." *JHPh* 21(1983), 467-478. Shows how P's and Ar's different prescriptions regarding proper role of women flow from different views of the soul.   [1463]

SOLMSEN, F. "The Academic and the Alexandrian Editions of Plato's Works." *ICS* 6(1981), 102-111. Discusses date of collection of P's works made by Academy and editing done in Alexandria.   [1464]

SOUPIOS, M. A. "Reason and Feeling in Plato: Response to Haden," in #1083, pp. 137-141. Examines Haden's discussion (#1374) of S's profession of ignorance, and challenges Haden's description of reason and feeling.   [1465]

SPELMAN, E. V. "Woman as Body: Ancient and Contemporary Views." *FemStud* 8(1982), 109-132. Examines P's philosophy to suggest why it is important for feminists not only to question what philosophers say about women, but also what philosophers have had to say about the mind/body distinction.   [1466]

SPRAGUE, R. K. "Plato and Children's Games," in #59, pp. 275-284. P regards children's games as beginning of their philosophical education and also uses them analogically in various dialogues.   [1467]

————. "Platonic Unitarianism or What Shorey Said." *CPh* 71(1976), 109-112. Assessment of Shorey's views on P (#1458).   [1468]

SWEENEY, L. "Henry Jackson's Interpretation of Plato." *JHPh* 13(1975), 189-204. Aims at exposing Hegelian and Berkelian idealism which influenced Jackson's approach to Platonic texts in late nineteenth century.   [1469]

————. "Leon Robin's Interpretation of Plato." *IntPhQ* 15(1975), 185-203. Examines Robin's studies to reveal how French idealism has affected exegesis of P.   [1470]

SWIFT RIGINOS, A. *Platonica: The Anecdotes Concerning the Life and Writings of Plato.* Leiden: Brill, 1976. Examines the 148 biographical fragments. Finds nearly all unreliable. Most arose from tendencies to glorify or vilify heads of schools.   [1471]

TAFT, R. "The Role of Compulsion in the Education of the Philosopher-King." *Auslegung* 9(1982), 311-332. Sees no inconsistency between early discussion of education of guardians and later discussion of education of philosopher-king.   [1472]

TARAN, L. "Perpetual Duration and Atemporal Eternity in Parmenides and Plato." *Monist* 62(1979), 43-53. Parmenides seems not to have understood concept of atemporal eternity. P was the first Western philosopher to grasp the notion.   [1473]

TAYLOR, A. E. *Plato: The Man and His Work,* 7th ed. London: Methuen, 1969. Discusses P's thought in context of social, political, economic life of the time. Analyzes dialogues, does not systematize contents under subject headings.   [1474]

TEJERA, V. "Methodology of a Misreading: A Critical Note on Irwin's 'Plato's Moral Theory'." *IntStudPh* 10(1978), 131-136. Challenges Irwin's way of reading Platonic dialogues (#1709).   [1475]

————. *Plato's Dialogues One by One: A Structural Interpretation.* New York: Irvington, 1984. Examines dialogues as dramatized intellectual encounters by considering literary dimension and historical background.   [1476]

TELOH, H. "The Importance of Interlocutors' Characters in Plato's Early Dialogues." *PBACAPh* 2(1986), 25-38. Discusses philosophical importance of fact that "core beliefs" of interlocutors are subjected to scrutiny in a typical Socratic dialogue. No simple logical schema can capture practice of Socratic dialectic which is as complex as the interlocutors' psychic conditions.   **[1477]**

THESLEFF, H. "Colloquial Style and Its Use in Plato's Later Works." *Arctos* 7(1972), 219-227. P juxtaposes colloquial and formal styles to emphasize importance of certain passages. Examines this technique in *Laws*.   **[1478]**

———. "Platonic Chronology." *Phron* 34(1989), 1-26. Expresses reservations about the use of stylistic studies and theories of P's intellectual development as criteria for establishing order of dialogues.   **[1479]**

———. *Studies in Platonic Chronology*. Helsinki: Societas Scientiarum Fennica, 1982. Detailed analysis of order of dialogues; challenges many standard approaches. **[1480]**

———. *Studies in the Styles of Plato*. Helsinki: Suomalassen Kirjallisuuden Kirjapaino, 1967. Studies structure and function of style in P's writings in characterization of speaker. Examines techniques (question and reply, reported dialogue) and classes of style (rhetorical, pathetic, historical).   **[1481]**

TIGERSTEDT, E. N. *Interpreting Plato*. Uppsala, Sweden: Almquist and Wiksell, 1977. General overview of trends in interpretation of P since early nineteenth century, looking especially at question of whether he had a systematic philosophy and, if so, whether it appears in the dialogues.   **[1482]**

TOVAR, A. *An Introduction to Plato*, trans. F. Pino, Jr. Chicago: Argonaut, 1969. Introductory discussion of P's life and works, marred by factual and typographical errors, which argues, "Truth appeared to [Plato] in luminous, integral, and indivisible scenes, but perpetual dissatisfaction moved him to search for another aspect of truth."   **[1483]**

TUTTLE, H. N. "The Negation of History." *SwPhSt* 7(1982), 1-15. Examines philosophy of history of P and several other philosophers.   **[1484]**

VERSVELD, M. "Plato and Confucius." *SAfrJPh* 2(1983), 20-25. Both lived in politically troubled times and tried to link morality and politics. Both believed in basic human goodness and moral order of world. Both also wanted a learned ruler.   **[1485]**

VLASTOS, G. "Elenchus and Mathematics: A Turning-Point in Plato's Philosophical Development." *AJPh* 109(1988), 362-396. Examines why S drops elenchtic method beginning with *Lysis* and *Hipp Maj*, and suggests that P's immersion in mathematical studies leads to this change.   **[1486]**

VOEGELIN, E. *Plato*. Baton Rouge: LA State Univ. Pr., 1966. Contains Voegelin's discussions on S, *Gorg*, *Rep*, *Phaedrus* and *Stsm*, *Tim* and *Critias*, and *Laws*. Argues that order in history depends upon recognition of transcendental source of order. **[1487]**

VON LEYDEN, S. "Time, Number and Eternity in Plato and Aristotle." *PhQ* 14(1968), 35-52. Argues that P's doctrine has less contrast between concepts of eternity and time than is often supposed, and thus the contrast between P and Ar is less.   **[1488]**

WADIA, P. "The Notion of *'Techne'* in Plato." *PhilStud* (Ireland) 31(1986-7), 148-158. Philosopher is a kind of "ideal technician" who seeks by power of thought or dialectic to lift the soul toward the source of all being. [1489]

WALDMAN, T. "A Key to Plato's Early Dialogues," in #81, pp. 60-68. P's early dialogues represent lowest stage of knowledge in several of his allegories, such as divided line and cave. His entire corpus may be structured according to those images. [1490]

WALTER, O. M. "Plato: The Most Maligned Philosopher." *RelHum* 17(1983), 128-133. Some criticism of P arises because he sought to find definitions which would transform his readers' views, especially their values. First step is to reject inadequate definitions. His dialogues often end where search for definition could begin. [1491]

WATSON, G. "Plato and the Story," in #1282, pp. 35-52. Explores why P frequently and deliberately turns to a story in arguments in dialogues. Stories play important role in persuasion. [1492]

————. *Plato's Unwritten Teaching.* Dublin: Talbot Pr., 1973. Examines questions raised by H. J. Kraemer's reassessment of tradition that P, especially in his lecture "On the Good," presented doctrines different from those expounded in his dialogues. P's own arguments against writing in *Phaedrus* and *Letter* 7 must be taken seriously. [1493]

WEINGARTNER, R. H. *The Unity of the Platonic Dialogue: The* Cratylus, *the* Protagoras, *the* Parmenides. Indianapolis: Bobbs-Merrill, 1973. These three dialogues are examined as illustrations of thesis that dialogues must be read holistically. They are not mere dramas or doctrinal expositions. [1494]

WELCH, C. "Plato and Aporia." *GM* 20(1965), 82-90. *Aporiai* result not just from intellect's inability to comprehend reality but from nature of reality itself. [1495]

WENDER, D. "Plato: Misogynist, Paedophile, and Feminist." *Arethusa* 6(1973), 75-90. Favorable attitude toward women expressed in *Rep* conflicts with P's misogyny in other passages. As a homosexual, P disliked women but was not dependent on them and did not fear any (theoretical) improvement in their status. [1496]

WHITE, N. P. "Observations and Questions about Hans-Georg Gadamer's Interpretation of Plato," in #1275, pp. 247-257. Agrees that P embraces a kind of fallibilism, but raises some questions regarding Gadamer's method of interpreting P (#1362). [1497]

WIDULSKI, P. "Platonic Dialogs in the Classroom." *Aitia* 3(1975), 12-15. Brief review of Klein's *A Commentary on Plato's* Meno (#2497), Strauss' *The City and Man* (#3134), and Voegelin's *Order and History* and teaching techniques for P's dialogues. [1498]

WIELAND, G. "Plato or Aristotle? A Real Alternative in Medieval Philosophy," in *Studies in Medieval Philosophy*, ed. J. F. Wippel (Washington, DC: Catholic Univ. of Amer. Pr., 1987), pp. 63-83. Traces impact of P and Ar in medieval thought and implications for a choice to follow one or the other. [1499]

WILBUR, J. B., and **ALLEN, H. J.,** eds. *The Worlds of Plato and Aristotle.* Buffalo: Prometheus Books, 1979. Selected readings from P and Ar on the standard topics: aesthetics, ethics, metaphysics, the soul. Brief introductions. [1500]

WINSPEAR, A. D. *The Genesis of Plato's Thought.* Montreal: Harvest House, 1974; 3rd ed. Survey of P's life, thought and historical background. Analysis of *Rep.* **[1501]**

WISHART, D., and **LEACH, S. V.** "A Multivariate Analysis of Platonic Prose Rhythm." *Computer Studies in the Humanities and Verbal Behavior* 3(1970), 90-99. Certain characteristics of P's prose rhythm can be identified by several different criteria. Such studies suggest that *Phaedrus* is early and that Lysias' speech is genuine.   **[1502]**

WOLZ, H. G. *Plato and Heidegger: In Search of Selfhood.* Lewisburg, PA: Bucknell Univ. Pr., 1981. Tries to emphasize P's dialogues are records of a search, not presentation of a settled dogmatic system. Heidegger's criticisms of Platonism can not be applied to P, if he is understood properly. P and Heidegger are actually fairly close to one another.   **[1503]**

————. "Plato's Doctrine of Truth, *Orthotes* or *Aletheia.*" *Ph&PhenRes* 27(1966), 157-182. Challenges Heidegger's reading of P to the effect that dialogues manifest a change in conception of truth: from "unhiddenness" to "correctness."   **[1504]**

WOODBRIDGE, F. J. E. *"The Son of Apollo": Themes of Plato.* Woodbridge, UK: Ox Bow Pr., 1989; rprt. Interprets P as an artist rather than a metaphysician. Claims that our view of him grows out of biases of later generations.   **[1505]**

WYLLER, E. A. "The Architectonic of Plato's Later Dialogues." *C&M* 27(1966), 101-115; also in *Contemporary Philosophy in Scandinavia*, ed. R. Olson and A. M. Paul (Baltimore: Johns Hopkins Pr., 1972), pp. 381-392. Later dialogues form in themselves a total, if not complete, universe of thought with its center in *Parm.* We can see development from productive stage of the Beautiful, through practical stage of the Good, to theoretical stage of the One.   **[1506]**

ZASLAVSKY, R. *Platonic Myth and Platonic Writing.* Washington, DC: Univ. Pr. of America, 1981. Myths are an important part of P's teaching technique, but he uses the term *mythos* somewhat differently than we do today. For P *mythos* is "an account of the genesis of a phenomenon." By contrast, *logos* is a "descriptive account." Some accounts, such as the "myth" of judgment in *Gorg*, are classed as "paramyths," hypothetical accounts made necessary by the uncertainty of the object of the account or the hearers' inability to comprehend a more exalted account.   **[1507]**

ZUCKERT, C. "Nietzsche's Rereading of Plato." *PolTheo* 13(1985), 213-238. According to Nietzsche, such Platonic doctrines as the "idea of the Good" and the "immortal soul" were teachings which P himself did not believe, designed to conceal his true thought from the public. Later philosophers have erroneously built on this foundation of a "noble lie."   **[1508]**

For related items see #7, #16, #17, #464, #863, #915, #2137, #2435, #2758, #5460, #5607

AESTHETICS

To use the term "aesthetics" in discussing P's view of the arts is not entirely accurate, if "aesthetics" is taken to mean a theory of how art is produced and interpreted. That is not what P discusses in such works as *Ion*, the *Rep*, and the *Laws*. His concern is with the moral and political implications of the arts, especially poetry. The basis of that concern is his doctrine that any form of art is an imitation (*mimesis*), more particularly an imitation of the physical world. Contemplation of such an imitation draws people's attention away from contemplation of the Forms, the only true reality.

The "arts" must be broadly defined, for the Greek term *poetikes* means a "maker" or "producer," without specifying the genre of what is produced. Such artists posed a threat, in P's view, because their work surrounded a Greek throughout his life; their influence was absorbed unconsciously and more readily than ideas which had to be demonstrated by a rational method. Statues, which were painted to appear as lifelike as possible, stood in public buildings and in the marketplace and other open spaces in every Greek town. Poetry was sung at religious and civic celebrations, weddings, and dinner parties. The basic text in the schools was Homer's poetry. Children were forced to memorize large chunks of the *Iliad* and *Odyssey* and were taught to rely on them as a guide in making decisions about politics, morals, and even smaller matters. Greeks quoted snippets from Homer as proof texts much as nineteenth-century American writers quoted or alluded to the Bible. Poetic inspiration was considered a kind of divine madness, worthy of respect.

As an adult, the Greek attended performances of plays and read the texts. A Greek poet, in the stricter sense, wrote music to accompany his lyrics and usually choreographed a dance as well. The themes of the plays were almost exclusively mythical, and the playwrights were considered teachers of the populace at large, as Aristophanes states in no uncertain terms in the *Frogs*:

> A poet whould seek to avoid the depiction of evil — should hide it, not drag into view its ugly and odious features. For children have tutors to guide them aright; young manhood has poets for teachers. And so we must write of the fair and the good.

P's concern with the impact of the arts, especially poetry, on society is roughly analogous to the concerns felt by people today who oppose a literalist interpretation of the Bible. Should one base scientific, political, or economic teaching on ancient texts which were not written with such ends in view, they ask? Should one adopt the ethical standards of a bygone era simply because they are contained in a text which one considers authoritative, perhaps without understanding its origins and the history of its transmission? Would not a rational approach to decision-making be more reliable?

P also recognizes that poetry has persuasive power and can lead people, especially the ill-educated masses, in directions which the philosophically enlightened see as dangerous. The behavior of the gods, reflecting the mores of a rougher age, can be used to justify human behavior which is detrimental to societal progress. For such reasons P concluded that poetry (i. e., the arts in general) should be banished from the ideal state. But something in him must have responded to the beauty of artistic creation. The biographer Olympiodorus claims that he wrote plays as a young man but tore them up upon hearing S for the first time. His own dialogues are masterpieces of literary craftsmanship (some scholars have suggested that they were presented dramatically), and he leaves open in *Rep* 607c the possibility that artists might justify their existence in the state. He would have accepted an art work produced by a philosopher but knew the unlikelihood of such a thing.

In the *Laws*, almost certainly his last work, P assigns art the function of educating young children and providing relaxation for adults. Training in song and dance allows us to control natural impulses which we all have. But the artists must create beautiful works which show what good men do and say, for all people are affected, for good or ill, by what they see and hear. The crucial question here is what type of art will produce the "right" reactions in people, and who is to be the judge. Such decisions cannot be based on the popularity of a type of art or on the will of the masses. The enlightened rulers of a state must see to it that songs and dances and paintings and sculptures are produced which will encourage people to be good citizens.

ADLER, M. J. "Plato," in *Poetry and Politics* (Pittsburgh: Duquesne Univ. Pr., 1965), pp. 1-18. P's attitude toward the arts is ambivalent. He sees poetry as judged primarily by criteria other than its own. His reasons for regulating the arts fall into category of opinion, not knowledge. After decreeing their banishment from the state, he challenges the poets, in *Rep* 607c, to prove their right to exist in a well-ordered city.   **[1509]**

ALEXANDRAKIS, A., and **KNOBLOCK, J.** "The Aesthetic Appeal of Art in Plato and Aristotle." *Diot* 6(1978), 178-185. For P, beauty arises from form, whereas for Ar, an aesthetically appealing art work must have expressive qualities based on representation, action, and life itself, not on merely abstract qualities.   **[1510]**

ANDERSON, W. D. *Ethos and Education in Greek Music: The Evidence of Poetry and Philosophy.* Cambridge, MA: Harvard Univ. Pr., 1966. Examines how music was understood as both expressing and affecting human conduct. Assesses music as part of Greek *paideia* through consideration of works of poets, P, and Ar.   **[1511]**

ANNAS, J. "Plato on the Triviality of Literature," in #1560, pp. 1-28. P maintains that art and literature lose their creative qualities when they become didactic and moralistic. Reform of persons is necessary to achieve moral ends.   **[1512]**

————. cf. #2131.

AVNI, A. "Inspiration in Plato and the Hebrew Prophets." *CompLit* 20(1968) 55-63. Discusses impact of Greek concept of poetic inspiration and inspiration in the prophets on poetic theory and practice. Contrasts Platonic and Hebrew thought.   **[1513]**

BAILIN, S. "Philosophy, Poetry and Plato." *ProcPhEd* 43(1987), 209-212. Response to Swanger (#1598).   **[1514]**

BATTIN, M. P. "Plato on True and False Poetry." *JAAC* 36(1977), 163-174. There is no real contradiction between P's exclusion of Homer's work from his state and his proposal to have state-censored poets create "noble lies" for the populace. Homer is not "true" in a normative sense, i. e., a way which affects how people react. Whether he is historically "true" is irrelevant. [1515]

BELFIORE, E. "Lies Unlike the Truth. Plato on Hesiod, *Theogony* 27." *TAPhA* 115(1985), 47-57. In *Rep* 2(376-383), P criticizes Hesiod because the poet does not tell the truth. Furthermore, his lies do not conform to P's patterns for lies. [1516]

———. "Plato's Greatest Accusation Against Poetry," in #1285, 39-62. P's aesthetic judgments are based on ethical, not ontological, concerns. He objects that poets and artists lead everyone to judge artistic productions on whether they produce pleasure. In *Rep* 605 his "greatest accusation" is that playwrights create situations in which ethical norms appear inapplicable. [1517]

———. "The Role of the Visual Arts in Plato's Ideal State." *Journal of Theory and Criticism of the Visual Arts* 1(1981), 115-127. Analogy between painting and poetry in *Rep* 10 is not as close as is often thought. P does allow for genuine crafts of painting and sculpture in his state, if they emphasize function, not imitation. [1518]

———. cf. #2895.

BRUMBAUGH, R. S. "Plato's Relation to the Arts and Crafts," in #1293, pp. 40-52; also in #49, pp. 195-204. P's negative comments about craft and art are not intended to deny that arts and crafts have utility, interest, and some cognitive value, but to deny that *only* arts and crafts have utility, value, or interest. [1519]

BUFORD, T. "The Parabolic Critique." *Proceedings of the South Atlantic Philosophy of Education Society* 30(1985), 104-112. Examines P's criticisms of poetry and myth; argues that there is a way to evaluate stories and myths by appealing to parables. [1520]

CACOULLAS, A. R. "Truth, Politics and the Artist." *Diot* 6(1978), 135-139. P's real concern in criticizing poetry is with art abused, not art itself. For P, laws of beauty which govern artist's *poesis* are also laws of truth. [1521]

CARTER, R. E. "Plato and Inspiration." *JHPh* 5(1967), 111-121. *Ion* and *Phaedrus*, in particular, show that inspiration and dialectic are complementary, not in opposition. The complete philosopher is also an inspired artist. [1522]

CAVARNOS, C. "Fine Art as Therapy According to Plato." *Phil*(Athens) 7(1977), 266-290. P sees the fine arts as playing an important role in therapy of diseases and more generally in improving condition of soul and body. [1523]

———. "Plato's Critique of the Fine Arts." *Phil*(Athens) 1(1971), 296-314. Presents a systematic overview of P's criticism of fine arts by topics. [1524]

———. *Plato's Theory of Fine Art*. Athens: Astir, 1973. Tries to correct misinterpretations of P's teaching on fine art through systematic examination of what he says about art. P distinguishes true art from pseudo-art and condemns only the latter. [1525]

CUNNINGHAM, F. J. "Mimesis: A Theory of Limited Scope for Plato." *University of Portland Review* 28(1965), 3-15. Attempts to find room within P for a positive approach to creativity by showing that the negative position toward the arts exemplified in the mimesis theory is a limited application.   **[1526]**

DAVIS, W. M. "Plato on Egyptian Art." *Journal of Egyptian Archeology* 65(1979), 121-127. Examines P's few references to Egyptian art to determine what he knew about such art and to add certain details to his aesthetic theory.   **[1527]**

DE LACY, P. "Plato and the Method of the Arts," in #80, pp. 123-132. P described arts by defining and dividing them to their smallest segments and then resynthesizing them. This technique was later applied to medicine and other fields.   **[1528]**

DEMAND, N. "Plato and the Painters." *Phoenix* 29(1975), 1-20. Survey of P's comments on painting suggests that his attitude changed over time, perhaps in reaction to new illusionistic techniques introduced in his day. Study of his attitudes could help in dating dialogues.   **[1529]**

DORTER, K. "Plato and Music: Sensuousness and Spirituality." *Mus&Man* 2(1978), 205-221. P describes philosophy as the highest form of *musike* and makes numerous comparisons between philosophy and what we call music. The key difference is the dominance of the intelligible in philosophy, the sensuous in music.   **[1530]**

————. cf. #2372.

ELIAS, J. A. *Plato's Defence of Poetry.* Albany: SUNY Pr., 1984. Actually a study of P's use of myth, generally criticized by reviewers for defining "myth" so broadly that it loses its meaning.   **[1531]**

ELSE, G. F. *Plato and Aristotle on Poetry*, ed. P. Burian. Chapel Hill: Univ. of NC Pr., 1986. Contains two short works, one on P and one on Ar, left unfinished at Else's death and edited by Burian. Maintains that much of Ar's aesthetic theory was formed in reaction to P's thought, though aesthetics was a relatively unimportant issue for P. P is seen as critical of poetry because it subverts the rational process. Ar defends poetry as a craft with moral implications.   **[1532]**

FARREL, T. B. "Rhetorical Resemblance: Paradoxes of a Practical Art." *QJS* 72(1986), 1-19. P regarded rhetoric as perhaps the most dangerous form of *mimesis* because it involves several of the senses. Ar can approve of all forms of *mimesis* because he believes that people can recognize the difference between imitation and reality in a kind of learning experience.   **[1533]**

FISHER, J. "Did Plato Have a Theory of Art?" *PacPhQ* 63(1982), 93-99. P did not have a coherent theory of art, as is generally believed. This misapprehension has led to misunderstanding of his philosophy.   **[1534]**

FUJITA, K. "God, Man, Musike. An Interpretation of Plato's *Poietike*." *Bigaku* 26(1976), 1-12. Explores ontology, theological facets of P's theory of *poietike*.   **[1535]**

GADAMER, H.-G. "Plato and the Poets," in #1274, pp. 39-72. Discusses P's recognition that traditional education and traditional poetry cannot function in a situation where the common ethos, which gives poetry significance, has been destroyed.   **[1536]**

GILBERT, A. H. "Did Plato Banish the Poets?" *Medieval & Renaissance Studies*

2(1968), 35-55. Statements in P's works which propose banishment of poets cannot definitely be attributed to P, who wrote poetry himself. **[1537]**

GILL, C. "Plato's Atlantis Story and the Birth of Fiction." *Ph&Lit* 3(1979), 64-78. Distinguishes fiction from myth; sees P as pioneer, analyzing nature of truth and falsity in literature and experimenting with genre of fiction in his Atlantis story. **[1538]**

GOLDEN, L. "Plato's Concept of Mimesis." *BritJAes* 15(1975), 118-131. Challenges view that P considered art a trivial activity. Artistic imitation has significant function of aiding us to apprehend ultimate reality. **[1539]**

GOODRICH, R. A. "Plato on Poetry and Painting." *BritJAes* 22(1982), 126-137. *Rep* 10.595a-608b, taken as a separate discussion of aesthetics, raises questions about the relation of the arts to concepts of knowledge, reality, mind, and ethics. Part of the problem arises from difficulties in P's understanding of *mimesis* and the analogy between painting and poetry. **[1540]**

GRISWOLD, C. L. "The Ideas and Criticism of Poetry in Plato's *Republic*, Book 10." *JHPh* 19(1981), 135-150. S's discussion of God and the Forms in *Rep* 10 is ironic, part of his criticism of the imitative arts. **[1541]**

——. "Irony and Aesthetic Language in Plato's Dialogues," in *Philosophy and Literature*, ed. D. Bolling (New York: Haven Press, 1987), pp, 71-99. Platonic dialogue form provides viable and interesting formulation of position that language has an aesthetic dimension. **[1542]**

GULLEY, N. "Plato on Poetry." *G&R* 24(1977), 154-169. Examines assessment of poetry in *Rep* 10 in terms of the aims of poetry, and assessment in Books 2 and 3 in terms of its educational uses. Poetry ranks low as an educational tool but that does not mean it is artistically invalid. **[1543]**

HALL, R. W. "Plato's Theory of Art: A Reassessment." *JAAC* 33(1974), 75-82. P does allow for a normative theory of poetry. Account in *Rep* 2 and 3 is in agreement with Book 10. **[1544]**

HALLIWELL, S. "Plato and Aristotle on the Denial of Tragedy." *PCPhS* 30(1984), 49-71. P sensed a deep contradiction between philosophy and tragedy. Ar tried to make tragedy serviceable to philosophy. **[1545]**

HART, R. L. "The Imagination in Plato." *IntPhQ* 5(1965), 436-461. P never formulated a full-fledged theory of imagination because he appreciated the ontological complexities of such a theory. **[1546]**

IMAMICHI, T. "Mimesis and Expression: A Comparative Study in Aesthetics," in *Facts and Values*, ed. M. Doeser (Dordrecht, Netherlands: Nijhoff, 1986), pp. 139-147. Examines P's and Confucius' treatment of art and enthusiasm. **[1547]**

JAMES, E. F. C. *Plato's Ideas on Art and Education*. Univ. of York Pr., 1975. Brief (21 pp.) sympathetic exploration of thesis that art should be basis of education. **[1548]**

JUDOVITZ, D. "Philosophy and Poetry," in *Literature and the Question of Philosophy*, ed. A. J. Cascardi (Baltimore: Johns Hopkins Pr., 1987), pp. 24-51. P regards poetry and philosophy differently because they represent different types of knowledge. [1549]

KARELIS, C. "Plato on Art and Reality." *JAAC* 34(1976), 315-321. P meant to banish only artistic productions which fail to meet certain criteria, not poetry and art in their entirety. P's claim that the artist's product is two steps removed from the Forms also seems indefensible.   [1550]

KAUFMANN, W. A. *Tragedy and Philosophy*. Garden City, NY: Doubleday, 1968. Examines P's attitude toward tragedy, and in particular the presumption of S and P that their wisdom was superior to that of tragic poets.   [1551]

KEULS, E. *Plato and Greek Painting*. Leiden: Brill, 1978. Argues that *mimesis* means "enactment" rather than "imitation." P probably knew little about developments in painting in his day and was more concerned with assertions of some artists that their work had educational value.   [1552]

————. "Plato on Painting." *AJPh* 95(1974) 100-127. P did not prefer primitive art to that of his day. He objected to role art was assuming in Athenian education.   [1553]

LEAGUE, K. "Plato: No Hope for Painting?" *Auslegung* 15(1989), 165-172. Explains and challenges P's view of painting, and suggests that he may not have really endorsed his strong position on painting in *Rep*.   [1554]

MAGUIRE, J. P. "Beauty and the Fine Arts in Plato: Some Aporiai." *HSCP* 70(1965), 171-193. Discusses eight problems in P's treatment of the fine arts.   [1555]

McCLAIN, E. G. "Plato's Musical Cosmology." *MainCur* 30(1973), 34-41. Study of P's musical metaphors offers new ways to penetrate subtleties of his thought.   [1556]

————. *The Pythagorean Plato: Prelude to the Song Itself*. York Beach, ME: Nicolas-Hays, 1984. Examines the musical examples in the dialogues and their corresponding mathematical equations.   [1557]

MORAVCSIK, J. M. E. "Noetic Inspiration and Artistic Inspiration," in #1560, pp. 29-46. Anything created with inspiration of thought is by nature good. Things created by artistic inspiration are valuable only if they lead people to seek a higher level of knowledge. They are dangerous in that they distract people from moving toward contemplation of Forms.   [1558]

————. "On Correcting the Poets." *OSAP* 4(1986), 35-47. P opposes poets because they arouse people's emotions, blocking their ability to understand intellectually.   [1559]

————. and TEMKO, P., eds. *Plato on Beauty, Wisdom, and the Arts*. Totowa, NJ: Rowman Littlefield, 1982. Six essays, abstracted herein, focused on P's objections to arts as sources of wisdom, and the inconsistency between that position and his use of artistic devices in dialogues.   [1560]

MOSS, L. "Plato and the *Poetics*." *PhQ* 50(1971), 533-542. P's use of "imitation" in his argument against poetry (*Rep* 2, 3, and 10) is inconsistent but anticipates important concepts of Ar's *Poet*.   [1561]

MOUTSOPOULOS, E. "Plato's Ontology of Art." *Diot* 2(1974), 7-17. The very fact that an artistic process — creating something that did not exist and does not actually exist — is possible is an argument for the reality of non-being. Ontological essence of art is thus not entirely positive or negative. **[1562]**

MURDOCH, I. *The Fire and the Sun: Why Plato Banished the Artists.* Oxford: Clarendon Pr., 1977. P's arguments against seductiveness of art are made the basis for probing ability of art to entertain and divert as well as to reveal, highlight and sharpen our awareness, rather than our factual knowledge. Book is aimed at scholars, with no chapters or subdivisions. **[1563]**

MURRAY, M. "The Crisis of Greek Poetics: A Re-interpretation." *JVallnq* 7(1973), 173-187. Examines relations between art and knowledge, the divine and the human, poetry and philosophy. Argues that the real crisis lies much less in P's critique of poetry than in Ar's transvaluation of it. **[1564]**

NEHAMAS, A. "Plato and the Mass Media." *Monist* 71(1988), 214-234. Examines P's rejection of poetry in *Rep* 10 in relation to society's concern over television and mass media in general. **[1565]**

———. "Plato on Imitation and Poetry in *Republic* 10," in #1560, pp. 47-78. P bans poets, but not painters, even though painting is equally *mimesis*. Investigates asymmetry in P's treatment of poetry and painting. **[1566]**

NIARCHOS, C. G. "The Beautiful and the Sublime: From Ancient Greek to Byzantine Art and Thought." *Diot* 10(1982), 81-91. Contains a discussion of P's views of art and the difference from Plotinus' views. **[1567]**

———. "The Philosophy of Art in the Philosophy of Longinus, with Reference to Plato and Aristotle." *Diot* 15(1987), 78-100. Examines "sublimity" as characteristic of a work of art. **[1568]**

NUSSBAUM, M. "Fictions of the Soul." *Ph&Lit* 7(1983), 145-161. Works on connections between view of what a human soul is and how to address that sort of soul in writing. Philosophical protagonist is P, and literary opponent is Proust. **[1569]**

OATES, W. J. *Plato's View of Art.* New York: Scribner, 1972. Challenges view that P was hostile to art, and interprets passages from *Hipp Maj, Ion, Phaedrus* and *Symp* which claim that the creative artist is a philosopher. **[1570]**

OSBORNE, C. "The Repudiation of Representation in Plato's *Republic* and its Repercussions." *PCPhS* 33(1987), 53-73. Criticism of art in *Rep* 10 had impact on Greek understanding of art as late as ninth century A. D. **[1571]**

PAPPAS, N. "Socrates' Charitable Treatment of Poetry." *Ph&Lit* 13(1989), 248-261. S's interpretation of Simonides' poem in *Protag* 338e-348a is not a parody of hermeneutics but use of charity as technique for leading readers away from poetry. **[1572]**

PARTEE, M. H. "Inspiration in the Aesthetics of Plato." *JAAC* 30(1971), 87-95. Examines P's treatment of inspiration, particularly in *Ion*, to explore how he may have thought images of truth and beauty might be communicated. **[1573]**

———. "Plato on the Criterion of Poetry." *PhQ* 52(1973), 629-642. Survey of passages in *Ion, Phaedo,* and *Rep* indicates that P condemns poetry for its power to draw the soul outside itself.   [1574]

———. "Plato on the Rhetoric of Poetry." *JAAC* 33(1974), 203-212; also in #2081, pp. 385-398. P contrasts good and bad rhetorical principles but denies any value whatsoever to any particular embodiment of thought. The dialogues' literary quality testifies that P made no effort to confine himself to the straightforward didactic style endorsed in *Rep* 10.   [1575]

———. "Plato's Banishment of Poetry." *JAAC* 29(1970), 209-222. In *Laws, Rep,* and *Soph* P holds that beautiful language may entice the unenlightened to embrace transient beauty of pleasure instead of contemplating true beauty of virtue. His persistent mistrust reflects his true attitude, in spite of his use of poetry in dialogues.   [1576]

———. *Plato's Poetics: The Authority of Beauty.* Salt Lake City: Univ. of UT Pr., 1981. P distrusts poetry because he ultimately cannot trust language. Discusses function of poetry in educating children and P's concern with moral and political impact of poetry.   [1577]

PATTERSON, R. "The Platonic Art of Comedy and Tragedy." *Ph&Lit* 6(1982), 76-93. Examines what, on Platonic grounds, would be involved in denying or affirming that anyone writes tragedy or comedy by *techne* or *episteme*.   [1578]

PAXSON, T. D., Jr. "Art and Paideia." *JAesEduc* 19(1985), 67-78. Examines P's and Ar's views on function and character of paideia (education) and whether, and how, art can be compatible with it.   [1579]

PICHE, D. R. "Mimesis and Plato's Dialectic." *Proceedings of the New Mexico & West Texas Philosophical Society* (1974), 46-52. Aims to show how *mimesis* or imitation is a functional concept in P's philosophy of the arts.   [1580]

PLOCHMAN, G. K. "Plato, Visual Perception, and Art." *JAAC* 35(1976), 189-200. P's views on visual perception and art can be analyzed on pattern of divided line in *Rep.* Arts lead to lower level of knowledge. Mathematics is final step to knowledge. No artist, no matter how intellectually keen, can impart truth without dialectic.   [1581]

RINGBOM, S. "Plato on Images." *Theoria* 31(1965), 86-109. Examines P's use of concept "picture" in three different contexts: 1) as metaphysical model, 2) as semantic explanation, 3) as argument of value.   [1582]

RIOLA, J. "The Unresolved Paradox in Plato's Aesthetics." *Dial*(PST) 20(1978), 42-49. P sees artists as capable of giving creative expression to the Forms while he paradoxically describes them as mere technicians.   [1583]

ROBINSON, D. "The Ethical Critique of Art in the *Republic*." *Dianoia* (1972), 25-39. Aims to isolate ethical function of art, in answering question, "How can a work of art be considered 'just'?"   [1584]

ROSEN, S. H. "The Quarrel Between Philosophy and Poetry," in #75, pp. 1-26. Starting with S's reference to this quarrel in *Rep* 10, explains the nature of the quarrel.

Notes the paradox that P, creator of the dramatic S, is himself a poet, being the author of philosophical dialogues/dramas. [1585]

RUTHERFORD, R. B. "Plato and Literary Criticism." *Phron* 33(1988), 216-224. Reply to Ferrari (#2747). [1586]

SCHAPER, E. *Prelude to Aesthetics.* London: Allen & Unwin, 1968. Argues that P and Ar provide a key to the interpretation of the aesthetic theories of recent centuries. P defined the field and Ar improved on that definition. Their theories of inspiration and craftsmanship are foundational concepts in the discipline. Separate chapters examine their contributions. [1587]

SCHOEN-NAZZARO, M. B. "Plato and Aristotle on the Ends of Music." *LThPh* 34(1978), 261-273. Examines number and nature of ends of music proposed by P and Ar, and concludes that despite a difference in emphasis, P and Ar have a fundamental similarity regarding how the ends of music ultimately serve to perfect man. [1588]

SEGAL, C. "Logos and Mythos. Language, Reality and Appearance in Greek Tragedy and in Plato," in *Tragique et tragedie dans la tradition occidentale,* ed. P. Gravel and T. J. Reiss (Montreal: Determinations, 1983), pp. 25-41. P and other writers, such as Sophocles and Thucydides, recognized that justice could not be achieved without a vocabulary to express it. Several of P's dialogues attempt to formulate such a language, but he cannot accomplish that objective without resorting to myth. [1589]

———. cf. #3108.

SHERMAN, R. R. "Plato, Aristotle, and the Poets." *EducTheor* 16(1966), 250-261. A key to understanding different interpretations of poets and poetry by P and Ar lies in their interpretation of "imitation." [1590]

SICHEL, B. A. "Comments on Arthur M. Wheeler's 'Creativity in Plato's States'." *EducTheor* 21(1971), 208-218. Provides an alternative analysis of "creativity" in P's philosophic thought (cf. #3156). [1591]

SMALL, I. C. "Plato and the Pater: *Fin-de-Siecle* Aesthetics." *BritJAes* 12(1972), 369-381. Review of Pater's *Plato and Platonism,* his final attempt to define exactly what he meant by terms "moral" and "aesthetic." [1592]

SORBOM, G. *Mimesis and Art: Studies in the Origin and Early Development of an Aesthetic Vocabulary.* Oslo: Universitetsforl., 1966. Explores origin and interpretation of Greek word group to which *mimesis* belongs. Emphasizes particular usage of the word group by Xenophon, P, and Ar in connection with works of art. [1593]

SPARSHOTT, F. E. "The Truth about Gods and Men." *Dial*(Can) 10(1971), 3-11. P's criticisms of poetry need to be studied in light of distinctions he makes between stories about humans and those about gods. [1594]

STEWART, R. S. "Where Have You Been and Where Are You Going: A Question of Consistency in Plato's Aesthetic." *Dial*(PST) 31(1988), 1-10. P's positions on art in *Phaedrus* and *Rep* seem inconsistent, but in *Phaedrus* he is concerned with a type of art which leads to knowledge; in *Rep* he condemns self-absorbed, imitative art. [1595]

STORMER, G. D. "Plato's Theory of Myth." *Pers* 55(1974), 216-223. P's view of poetry is not as negative as usually portrayed. P himself uses poetic myths more innovatively than any previous writer and makes them an integral part of his philosphical enterprise.   **[1596]**

SUNDARA RAJAN, R. "Reversal and Recognition in Plato." *IndianPhQ* 15(1988), 53-73. Uses principles of Reversal and Recognition of Ar's *Poet* for the purpose of understanding the nature of Platonic inquiry and appreciating connections between the discursive, argumentative level and the symbolic expressive level.   **[1597]**

SWANGER, D. "Poetry, Plato and Education: A Reconsideration." *ProcPhEd* 43(1987), 199-207. Analyzes P's rules concerning poetry found in *Rep* and applies them to more modern poetry. Finds his analysis of poetry itself, but not of its place in education, to be accurate.   **[1598]**

THAYER, H. S. "Plato on the Morality of Imagination." *RMeta* 30(1977), 594-618. Arts can contribute to education, even if artists don't use imagination properly.   **[1599]**

————. "Plato's Quarrel with Poetry: Simonides." *JHI* 36(1975), 3-26. Attempts to show why P should think of Simonides as occupying a central place in his thinking about and disagreement with poetry.   **[1600]**

TIGERSTEDT, E. N. *Plato's Idea of Poetical Inspiration*. Helsinki: Centraltryckeriet, 1969. Examines dialogues in which P discusses poetry and its function in the state. P did appreciate poetry but felt that "divine possession" of poets, through which they received inspiration, must be controlled by state, just as oracles such as the Pythia at Delphi were.   **[1601]**

URMSON, J. O. "Plato and the Poets," in #1560, pp. 125-136. P attacks the best of mimetic poets, especially Homer, because they pass off their ignorance as understanding of deep truths. Suggests his argument has contemporary relevance.   **[1601a]**

VERDENIUS, W. J. "Plato's Doctrine of Artistic Imitation," in #1291, pp. 259-273. For P art is inferior because it is a mere shadow of the original, but a successful artist can illuminate the intermediate level of opinion on which he works. The art of P's time was becoming increasingly realistic, and he may have been concerned about artists boasting of their ability to duplicate reality.   **[1602]**

VERSENYI, L. G. "Plato and Poetry: The Academician's Dilemma," in *Ancient and Modern: Essays in Honor of Gerald F. Else*, ed. J. H. D'Arms and J. W. Eadie (Ann Arbor: Univ. of MI, 1977), pp. 119-138. From a Platonic standpoint philosophy and poetry will run into inevitable conflict. Because P's thought is so unified, one cannot reject his attack on poetry without repudiating other facets of his thought.   **[1603]**

————. "The Quarrel Between Philosophy and Poetry." *PhFor* 2(1970-71), 200-212. Various philosophers have assigned different values to poetry and art. Heidegger argued that a work of art's primary function is to reveal truth. Reexamination of P's criticism of such educational claims finds them justified.   **[1604]**

WALSH, D. "Plato's Problem," in *Literature and Knowledge* (Middletown, CT: Wesleyan Univ. Pr., 1969), pp. 16-30. P involves himself in a dilemma when he indicts poetry but then admits that certain kinds of truth can only (or best) be expressed in myths. He never resolves the problem.   [1605]

WOODRUFF, P. "What Could Go Wrong with Inspiration? Why Plato's Poets Fail," in #1560, pp. 137-149. Even though inspiration is a kind of communion with the divine, P judges the inspiration of poets quite harshly because it is not based on love of the beautiful and cannot lead to true knowledge.   [1606]

WRIGHT, R. "How Credible are Plato's Myths?" in #48, pp. 364-371. P generally disparages *mythoi* as harmful but uses them as tools of moral education.   [1607]

For related items see #133, #1681, #2141, #2363, #2783, #2996, #3006, #3093, #3128, #3690.

EPISTEMOLOGY

Every philosopher must answer the question, How do we know, i. e., how do we receive and process the information which leads us to conclusions about particular or larger general issues? Related to that is the question of *what* we can know. Is our knowledge only of things we see and touch or is it of abstract things? The answers to the two questions are closely interrelated.

Though much attention has been given to this problem, the answer boils down to two alternatives: 1) knowledge comes from our senses, and is thus of physical things; 2) knowledge is arrived at through a rational process, and is thus knowledge of general principles or concepts. A possible corollary to the first theory is that, since our senses can be deceived, knowledge may not be reliable, or even possible. The second theory leaves open the possibility that knowledge based on logic may even contradict what our senses tell us.

By P's day several generations of philosophers had wrestled with the problem of how and what we can know and two distinct camps had developed: 1) a Heraclitean view which held that the material world is constantly in a state of flux and that our knowledge of it, derived from the senses, can only be uncertain. The relativism of the Sophists was tied directly to this view; 2) the monism of Parmenides which denied change and asserted that only something unchanging and unchangeable could be a proper object of knowledge. Such things exist, he had shown in his poem, only on a supra-mundane level. The mass of people are content with *doxa* (opinion) about the changing things of this world. The philosopher seeks truth (*aletheia*) about things which always are, and always are the same. Zeno, with his paradoxes, had demonstrated that logic could lead to conclusions that directly contradicted sense perceptions.

P's epistemology is a combination of these two positions. He grants that sense perception affords us knowledge of the changeable physical world. But true knowledge is knowledge of an unchangeable world which exists on a non-physical plane, the world of the Forms. Knowledge of that world is possible only through a rational process. In the early dialogues this process takes the form of *elenchus*, or refutation, the Socratic method of inquiry. A definition is put forward, examined from as many angles as possible, and usually rejected as inadequate. The primary question in these dialogues is whether virtue can be taught. Can a person learn to be courageous, just, good, etc.? In the later dialogues P seems to have moved to his own technique, *diaeresis*, or the collecting of examples and dividing them into cohesive groups (discussed further under Logic/Dialectic).

The *Meno* poses a classic paradox about the acquisition of knowledge: We cannot learn something which we already know, and we cannot learn what we do not know because we cannot recognize it when we see it. S proposes to resolve this paradox with the theory of *anamnesis* or recollection. An individual's soul exists before the person's birth. In its prior states of existence the soul "has seen what is here and in the underworld and everything, and there is nothing which it has not come to know" (*Meno* 81c). Once imprisoned in the body, it loses its awareness of its own knowledge, but that awareness can be re-awakened. In the *Meno* S guides a slave boy through an intricate geometrical demonstration, telling him nothing but asking questions which lead him to solve the problem. This supposedly shows that the boy knows things which he has not consciously learned in this life.

Near the end of the *Meno* S admits that opinion (*doxa*) may be all that one can attain in some matters and that it can be as serviceable as knowledge, though it can be challenged more easily because we are not certain of it. The distinction between *doxa* and true knowledge becomes quite important in the *Theaetetus*, which also discusses the problem of how one can think falsely. The dialogue seems designed to prove that sense perception is not knowledge.

In the *Phaedo* P discusses most fully the relationship between the Forms and knowledge, between intellectual apprehension and sense perception. S asserts that "the purest knowledge will be that of the man who approaches each subject as far as possible with thought alone . . . . For when the body participates, it does not allow the mind to acquire truth and wisdom." The doctrine of anamnesis is linked to the theory of the Forms more closely in this dialogue than in perhaps any other. When we see or experience particular things, we are reminded of the Form of that particular because our soul has known it in a previous life. This is the only way true knowledge is possible.

BALABAN, O. "Relation and Object in Plato's Approach to Knowledge." *Theoria* 53(1987), 141-158. Attempts to settle debate raised by Hintikka (#1628) and Santas (#1657) over whether P saw a difference between the function of knowledge and its object. P's definition of virtue as knowledge results logically from his denial that it is a cognitive relation.　　　　　　　　　　　　　　　　　　　　　　　　　　　　**[1608]**

BALLARD, E. G. *Socratic Ignorance: An Essay on Platonic Self-Knowledge*. The Hague: Nijhoff, 1965. Examines Platonic myths and doctrines which bear upon self-knowledge and self-ignorance.　　　　　　　　　　　　　　　　　　　　　　　　　　　　　　**[1609]**

BEDU-ADDO, J. T. "*Dianoia* and the Images of Forms in Plato's *Republic* VI-VII." *Platon* 31(1979), 89-110. In the line passage P maintains there are four levels of thought and three stages of reality. *Dianoia* is third level of thought, where mind is aware of its quest for knowledge but unable to distinguish Forms from particulars.　　　　　**[1610]**

BENNE, K. D. "Plato's Divided Line: A Dramatic Interpretation." *ProcPhEd* 45(1989), 363-374. A reading of the divided line analogy which shows that the knowledge needed to make one an effective politician or educator is similar to the creative artist's knowledge. It is more than accumulated objective knowledge. Leadership in a community is a creative activity. **[1611]**

BEVERSLUIS, J. "Does Socrates Commit the 'Socratic Fallacy'?" *AmPhQ* 24(1987), 211-223. Socratic fallacy is defined as maintaining that in order to know what it is to be a Thing, one must be able to define criteria for something being a Thing and that one cannot define a Thing by examples. S does not commit this fallacy in P's early dialogues because his concern is with moral knowledge. **[1612]**

BRUMBAUGH, R. S. "Plato: The Fundamentals of Education," in *Philosophers on Education: Six Essays on the Foundations of Western Thought* ed. R. S. Brumbaugh and N. M. Lawrence (Boston: Houghton Mifflin, 1986; rprt), pp. 10-48. Identifies several main themes in P's philosophy (inquiry, form, and value) and shows how his suggested curriculum leads to integrating the three. His view of higher education stresses synthesis, not specialization. **[1613]**

BURNYEAT, M. F. "Examples in Epistemology: Socrates, Theaetetus, and G. E. Moore." *Ph* 52(1977), 381-398. From S to twentieth century, question of relation of examples to definitions remains unsettled. Moore differs with S but seems dissatisfied with his own stand. P changed his view by the end of his life. **[1614]**

———. cf. #3371.

CARBONE, P. F., Jr. "Down Under With Plato." *ProcPhEd* 41(1985), 441-444. Analysis of concept of self-knowledge with respect to P's allegory of the cave. P assumes that people's potential for learning varies and that education will lead only an elite few to knowledge and virtue. **[1615]**

CHAMBLISS, J. J. "Plato: Author of the Philosopher's Tragedy," in *Imagination and Reason in Plato, Aristotle, Vico, Rousseau, and Keats: An Essay on the Philosophy of Experience.* (The Hague: Nijhoff, 1974), pp. 6-19. P sought a kind of "natural" or "pure" knowledge but had to create rational objects of knowledge to express what he had found. His naturalism and rationalism are not mutually exclusive. **[1616]**

CLARK, M. "Plato and the Forms of Geometry," in *Perplexity and Knowledge: An Inquiry into the Structures of Questioning* (The Hague: Nijhoff, 1972), pp. 66-81. P viewed knowledge as personal agency. He seems to have been interested in understanding what it meant to be someone who knows. This makes him largely a spectator giving a report of the process of knowledge, and that viewpoint affects how we understand much of what he says about the duality of universal and particular. **[1617]**

COBB, W. S. "Anamnesis: Platonic Doctrine or Sophistic Absurdity?" *Dial*(Can) 12(1973), 604-628. P does not intend the doctrine of recollection to be a serious epistemological theory but a means of showing the absurdity of some Sophistic arguments. His own theory of knowledge is an analogy with vision. **[1618]**

CROSS, R. C., and **WOOZLEY, A. D.** "Knowledge, Belief and the Forms," in #1290, pp. 70-96. The major weakness of the Theory of Forms as an epistemological tool is that the Forms are expected to explain too much.   **[1619]**

DIGBY, T. "Plato on Instability and Knowledge." *Apeir* 18(1984), 42-45. P rejects radical Heraclitean position that perception is impossible because everything is always changing in every way possible. He seems to accept a position that as things change by degrees some sort of knowledge or true belief about them would be possible.   **[1620]**

DOYLE, K. O. "Theory and Practice of Ability Testing in Ancient Greece." *JHistBehav-Sci* 10(1974), 202-218. Greeks were more familiar with testing for physical than mental abilities. In *Rep* P proposes testing for mental aptitutdes.   **[1621]**

FOTI, V. M. "Presence and Memory: Derrida, Freud, Plato, Descartes." *GradFacPhJ* 11(1986), 67-82. Contains a discussion of P's efforts to safeguard purity of truth and privilege of knowledge by a hierarchical ordering of the kinds and levels of truth, knowledge, and memory.   **[1622]**

FREDE, M. "Observations of Perception in Plato's Later Dialogues," in #57, pp. 3-10. Examines different meanings of *aisthanesthai* in later works, and P's efforts to restrict notion of sense perception so narrowly that we cannot even any longer be said to perceive that something is real.   **[1623]**

GALLOP, D. "Dreaming and Waking in Plato," in #41, pp. 187-201. Reviews evidence for P's conception of dreams; explores his use of analogies from dreaming to express some central ideas in his theory of knowledge and philosophical method.   **[1624]**

GLIDDEN, D. "Mimetic Ignorance, Platonic *Doxa* and *De Re* Belief." *HPhQ* 2(1985), 355-374. Imitation, which does not require understanding, is ignorance. *Doxa* (opinion) must resemble reality at least to some slight degree.   **[1625]**

GOLDEN, L. "Mimesis and Katharsis." *CPh* 64(1969), 145-153. These two concepts are closely linked in P and Ar. The former is a learning process which culminates in the latter, a kind of insight.   **[1626]**

HAHN, R. "A Note on Plato's Divided Line." *JHPh* 21(1983), 235-238. Given different levels of line, and things perceived on those levels, one must consider the object of any individual dialogue. The line is an object on the geometric level.   **[1627]**

HINTIKKA, J. "Knowledge and Its Objects in Plato." *Ajatus* 33(1971), 168-200; also in *Knowledge and the Known: Historical Perspectives in Epistemology.* (Dordrecht, Nether.: Reidel, 1974), pp. 1-30; also in #1280, pp. 1-30. Examines P's treatment of two epistemological problems: 1) possibility of meaningful falsity; 2) distinguishing knowledge from true belief. P saw relation of such *dynameis* as knowledge, belief, saying, etc., to their objects as "aiming at" or "trying to realize themselves in" these objects.   **[1628]**

———. "Plato on Knowing How, Knowing That, and Knowing What," in *Knowledge and the Known* (cf. item #1628), pp. 31-49. Asks: How did P conceive of idea of knowledge? More specifically, what kind of knowledge did S identify with virtue?   **[1629]**

HUNTER, G., and **INWOOD, B.** "Plato, Leibniz, and the Furnished Soul." *JHPh* 22(1984), 423-434. Examines and compares P's and Leibniz's views on whether knowledge is something a person is born with. For P the phenomenon of remembering is an argument for innate knowledge.   [1630]

JOHNSON, P. "Response to Laidlaw-Johnson's 'A Combined Doctrine of Knowledge for Plato'." *Auslegung* 14(1988), 153-157. Challenges "Combined Theory" that argues 1) that we acquire knowledge of Forms through recollection by use of our senses and 2) that only with such knowledge are we able to know cognized external objects. [1631]

KAISER, N. "Plato on Knowledge." *Apeir* 6 #2(1972), 36-43. Theory of knowledge in *Parm* and earlier dialogues seems plagued by unresolved internal problem. P seems to be saying that knowledge is impossible or is based on opinion.   [1632]

KETCHUM, R. J. "Plato on the Unknowability of the Sensible World." *HPhQ* 4(1987), 291-305. Argues for P's thesis that we can have no knowledge of objects of senses because nothing that can be said about them is true in an absolute sense.   [1633]

KOFMAN, S. "Beyond Aporia?" in *Post-structuralist Classics*, ed. A. Benjamin (London: Routledge, 1988), pp. 7-44. P does not intend *aporia* to be a permanent state of lack of knowledge. It is rather a passage from one stage to another.   [1634]

KRELL, D. F. "'Knowledge is Remembrance': Diotima's Instruction at *Symposium* 207c8-208b6," in *Post-structuralist Classics* (cf. item #1634), pp. 160-172. Diotima's epistemology does not accord well with P's *anamnesis*. She wants S to go beyond mere recollection to vision of beauty-in-itself.   [1635]

LAIDLAW-JOHNSON, E. A. "A Combined Doctrine of Knowledge for Plato." *Auslegung* 14(1988), 137-151. Resolves several apparent paradoxes in theory of knowledge which P sets forth in *Theaet*.   [1636]

LESSER, H. "Blake and Plato." *Ph* 56(1981), 223-230. Blake uses the term "imagination" to describe the faculty of intuition, which P calls "reason." For both, this faculty's most important function is to reveal the real world.   [1637]

LESSES, G. "Crafts and Crafts-Knowledge in Plato's Early Dialogues." *SwPhSt* 7(1982), 93-99. Notion of a craft-product is crucial for developing role of *techne* as an epistemic model in early dialogues. Suggests that an expert alone can have genuine knowledge of nature of product in his field, and that knowledge of ends and knowledge of means are not completely unrelated features of expertise.   [1638]

MATTHEWS, G. *Plato's Epistemology and Related Logical Problems.* London: Faber & Faber, 1972. Introduction, selections from various dialogues in translation.   [1639]

MICHELSEN, J. M. "Plato and Santayana: Forms, Flux, and the Ideal of Human Existence." *Diot* 8(1980), 72-80. Traces differences between positions of P and Santayana in philosophy of mind, epistemology, and axiology.   [1640]

MILLER, L. W. "Knowledge, False Belief, and Dialectic in Plato." *TulStudPh* 27(1978), 125-151. S and P view knowledge and ignorance as two sides of the same identity. Claims of knowledge or admissions of ignorance by themselves in the dialogues are ironic. Only through ignorance and dialectic can one achieve knowledge, which is actually recognition of false belief.   [1641]

MOHR, R. D. "The Divided Line and the Doctrine of Recollection." *Apeir* 18(1984), 34-41. Examines usefulness of divided line image from middle dialogues for understanding P's epistemology.   **[1642]**

MOLINE, J. *Plato's Theory of Understanding.* Madison: Univ. of Wisconsin Pr., 1981. Logical positivists, with their concern for verification, misread P and failed to obtain a comprehensive view of his philosophy. Through insight into word *episteme*, one can obtain a more accurate understanding of P's thought.   **[1643]**

MORAVCSIK, J. M. E. "Learning as Recollection," in #1290, pp. 53-69. The theory that learning is recollection is inadequate because it demonstrates only that there is something more than deductive reasoning involved in the learning process.   **[1644]**

———. "Understanding and Knowledge in Plato's Philosophy," in *Aktualitaet der Antike*, ed. R. Bubner et al. (Goettingen, Ger.: vandenHoeck, 1979), pp. 53-69. Maintains that understanding has a non-propositional component, and that P's main concern is with understanding, not with propositional knowledge.   **[1645]**

MORGAN, M. L. "Belief, Knowledge, and Learning in Plato's Middle Dialogues," in #1285, 63-100. Focuses on two questions: (1) Does P's account of *doxa* and knowledge in *Rep* 5-7 make it inconceivable how genuine learning or education can occur?ʳ (2) Can account of *doxa* and knowledge in *Rep* be reconciled with that in *Meno*?   **[1646]**

NAILS, D. "The Erotic Education of the Slave." *SAfrJPh* 4(1985), 1-7. For P, *eros* is fundamental element of human psychology. His epistemology can only be understood in terms of his views about *eros*.   **[1647]**

NEHAMAS, A. "*Episteme* and *Logos* in Plato's Later Thought." *AGPh* 66(1984), 11-36; also in #1267, pp. 267-292. In *Theaet* P reopens S's question of definition. He shows that in order to define something one must master the field to which the object of definition belongs.   **[1648]**

OWEN, D. "Benne's Plato and the Theater of Ideas." *ProcPhEd* 45(1989), 374-377. Reply to #1611. For P knowledge goes beyond words and reason to insight, to a picture.   **[1649]**

POWERS, L. H. "Knowledge by Deduction." *PhR* 87(1978), 337-371. *Meno* illustrates P's claim that one who accepts necessary premises can be brought, by correct sequence of questions, to know anything that can be deduced from those premises.   **[1650]**

PROSCH, H. "Polanyi's Tacit Knowing in the 'Classic' Philosophers." *JBritSocPhen* 4(1973), 201-216. Reviews P's epistemology and compares it to Polanyi's account. Demonstrates how P and Ar make use of tacit elements in their central doctrines. Argues that the inclusion of tacit elements in an epistemological position should not be regarded as shocking or restrictive.   **[1651]**

RIST, J. M. "Knowledge and Value in Plato." *Phoenix* 21(1967), 283-295. Forms exist outside time and space. Descriptions of them are as true as mathematics. "Bad" Forms are only lack of Form of Good. Knowledge of Forms imparts divinity to souls.   **[1652]**

ROSEN, S. "Sophrosyne and Selbstbewusstsein." *RMeta* 26(1973), 617-642. Analyzes

Platonic antecedents of Hegelian doctrine of self-consciousness. Doctrine of Forms makes self-knowledge impossible, but concept of *sophrosyne* does allow for it. P never resolved conflict. **[1653]**

ROUSSEAU, M. F. "Recollection as Realization: Remythologizing Plato." *RMeta* 35(1981), 337-348. Argues for "remythologizing" of doctrine of *anamnesis*. Literal, demythologized interpretations do not solve basic problem of human knowing. **[1654]**

RUDEBUSCH, G. "Plato on Knowing a Tradition." *PhE&W* 38(1988), 324-333. Examination of problem of appropriate object of knowledge, based on *Ion* and *Gorg.* Relativist objects cannot be known without knowledge of a real truth. **[1655]**

——. cf. #3418.

RUNCIMAN, W. G. *Plato's Later Epistemology.* Ann Arbor, MI: Univ. Microfilms, 1978; rprt. In his later epistemology P seems not to have distinguished various uses of the verb "to be" and to have thought of knowledge as gained by acquaintance with something. In *Soph* he moves beyond his earlier atomism with the method of division. He does not seem to have developed a notion of truth value. **[1656]**

SANTAS, G. "Hintikka on Knowledge and its Objects in Plato," in #1280, pp. 31-51. Challenges Hintikka's claim (#1628) to find a confusion in P of function of knowledge with objects of knowledge. **[1657]**

SCHULTZ, J. C. "An Anachronism in Cornford's *Plato's Theory of Knowledge.*" *ModSch* 43(1966), 397-406. Challenges Cornford's interpretation (#3376) that a difficulty about negative facts is the problem P faces when he deals with sophistic difficulties about the possibility of falsehood and error. **[1658]**

SCOLNICOV, S. "Hypothetical Method and Rationality in Plato." *Kantstudien* 66(1975), 157-162. P does not propose an absolute beginning for knowledge. Tension between rationality as given and as merely postulated remains unresolved. **[1659]**

——. "On the Epistemological Significance of Plato's Theory of Ideal Numbers." *MH* 28(1971), 72-97. Ideas are transcendent as well as transcendental and have more than an epistemological function. They are simultaneously relation and substance. **[1660]**

SCOTT, D. "Platonic Anamnesis Revisited." *CQ* 37(1987), 346-366. Theory of recollection may not explain how people are able to develop concepts, but it does account for their ability to move from opinion to knowledge. **[1661]**

SMITH, N. D. "Knowledge by Acquaintance and 'Knowing What' in Plato's *Republic.*" *Dial*(Can) 18(1979), 281-288. In *Rep* 5-7 P compares knowledge to vision, calling both *dynameis* (abilities). This analogy is similar to the concepts of knowledge underlying some modern English expressions which link knowing what a thing is with having some acquaintance with it. **[1662]**

——. "*Republic* 476e-480a: Intensionality in Plato's Epistemology?" *PhilStud* 30(1976), 427-429. Challenges standard interpretation of difference between knowledge and belief as a difference in objects of knowledge and belief. Appropriate distinctions of objects are intensional distinctions. **[1663]**

STEWART, R. S. "The Epistemological Function of Platonic Myth." *Ph&Rh* 22(1989), 260-280. For P myths are first stage in learning to think conceptually, not "physically." They also communicate basic principles of philosophy in symbolic language.   **[1664]**

TANNER, R. G. "*Dianoia* and Plato's Cave." *CQ* 20(1970), 81-91. The sequence of the sun, divided line, and cave has a theological purpose as much as an epistemological one. The Good is the basis of P's ontology as well as a substitute for Zeus.   **[1665]**

THOMAS, J. E. "Anamnesis in New Dress." *NewSchol* 51(1977), 328-349. Overview of some recent interpretations of P's theory.   **[1666]**

TIGNER, S. S. "Plato's Philosophical Uses of the Dream Metaphor." *AJPh* 91(1970), 204-212. Dreams serve in P's dialogues as analogies of process of acquiring knowledge. They are like the sensible world in their unreality and yet can provide a first step toward true knowledge. Process of learning is like awakening from a dream.   **[1667]**

TURNBULL, R. G. "*Episteme* and *Doxa*: Some Reflections on Eleatic and Heraclitean Themes in Plato," in #42, pp. 279-300. Points to some unnoticed features of interrelationships of *episteme* and *doxa* that help explain some difficult texts, and argues that P has means of attaining a "world" that is and a "world" that is and is not.   **[1668]**

———. "The Role of the 'Special Sensibles' in the Perception Theories of Plato and Aristotle," in #66, pp. 3-26. In theories of perception both P and Ar pay more attention to color, sound, odor, etc., than to motion, shape, size because former qualities are what make perception possible and thus need to be explained. Both maintain that senses cannot be mistaken concerning perceptions proper to them.   **[1669]**

VOEGELIN, E. *Anamnesis* , ed. and transl. G. Niemeyer. Notre Dame, IN: Univ. of Notre Dame Pr., 1978. The philosophy of history is developed from the central concept of consciousness, and includes a discussion of the idea of history in P. Also looks at Ar's idea of nature and concept of politics.   **[1670]**

WARE, K. "*Nous* and *Noesis* in Plato, Aristotle and Evagrius of Pontus." *Diot* 13(1985), 158-163. *Nous* does not exclusively signify discursive reason, but rather spiritual understanding, ability to apprehend truth through direct insight and intuition.   **[1671]**

WELLMAN, R. R. "A Note on Platonic *Anamnesis*." *EducTheor* 16(1966), 166-175. Examines doctrine of recollection, avoiding as much as possible questions of metaphysics immanent in P's thought and concentrating on functional aspects of possibility of knowing the Forms.   **[1672]**

WHITE, N. *Plato on Knowledge and Reality*. Indianapolis: Hackett, 1976. Examines P's attempt to show how we can conceive that there is an objective reality, independent of what we may happen to believe, for our efforts at cognition to be right or wrong about. Traces development of this approach through several of his dialogues and shows that P remained, throughout his life, an epistemological realist.   **[1673]**

For related items see #1710, #2934, #3376, #3421, #3974, #3978, #6534, #6548.

ETHICS

The term "ethics" is derived from a Greek word meaning "custom," "habit," or "tradition." It describes one's standards for behavior, how one answers the questions, What do I do in this situation? Why do I do it? What is good or bad? A theory of ethics can stress one of these aspects over the other, but it must ultimately offer some rationale for deciding what is good and some encouragement for people to pursue the good.

The Greeks (and other ancient peoples) based their conduct on maxims — such as the book of Proverbs or the Egyptian *Wisdom of Ptah-hotep* — which represented the accumulated wisdom of earlier generations. In the fifth century B. C., however, the Sophists presented a serious challenge to this traditional concept. Protagoras asserted that societal norms were merely conventions, that each person had to decide for him/herself the principles he/she would live by. Ferguson (#1694, p. 259) says that in P's day ethics were "just in the process of moving from the response to the approbation of others to the response to the approbation of the inward self." S reacted against this absolute relativism with his search for definitions of moral virtues and his overarching concept that there must be some absolute standard of "virtue" (an unfortunate translation of the Greek word *arete*, meaning "goodness," "excellence," or "character"). S thus becomes the first philosopher to pursue ethics methodically.

In P's early dialogues we see this Socratic approach at work in his questions about justice, courage, piety, and other "virtues." He will not accept examples of these behaviors but is always looking for a definition that covers all cases. This fits well with P's concept of Forms, the ideal and ultimate patterns of which all earthly things are imperfect imitations (cf. introduction to Metaphysics, p. 213). In *Rep* 6 P introduces the idea of the Form of the Good, the highest of all the Forms. The other Forms are divided into mathematic and ethical Forms. Mathematics is a type of abstract knowledge, not dependent on particular things. If one examines the properties of a right triangle, e. g., one is not concerned with an individual right triangle but with concepts applicable to all right triangles. Conceptualizing in this way prepares one for the higher level of Forms, the ethical, which deal purely with abstractions such as Piety, Justice, Beauty, etc.

Much of P's ethical thought arises from his efforts to answer certain questions or paradoxes which S raised, but he does not attempt to define rules of conduct. He works his way, by dialectic, toward an insight or realization of the truth. Once that has been achieved, once one knows what courage or justice is, it is easy to determine what to do in any particular case.

J. Ferguson (#1694, p. 261) lamented "how little serious study has been made of Plato's ethics." The following section of the bibliography should lead to more optimism. Scholarly debate on P's ethics has centered around, but has not resolved, questions about whether his ethics can be described as hedonistic (based on what is pleasurable) or utilitarian (the good is what is useful). Passages can be found in the dialogues to support either side on both issues. P does seem to distinguish among various levels of pleasure, from base to noble, and to be opposed to bodily indulgence, which draws one away from contemplation of the Forms. Love and friendship are important topics in P's ethical discussions. The *Symposium* is devoted to the former subject and the *Lysis* to the latter. In each P tries to raise the subject to a higher plane. In the *Symp* love (*eros*) is identified with the Form of Beauty. In the *Lysis* friendship is based on an intellectual bond.

The charge that P's ethics are utilitarian stems from passages such as that in the *Republic* in which he proposes that the philosopher-rulers in his ideal state lie to the populace in order to arrange marriages and other matters to the benefit of the state. Modern readers of P (and any other ancient author) might be less shocked by such proposals when they realize that ethics in ancient Greece and Rome had no religious basis, as they do in the Judeo-Christian tradition. No god gave commands about moral behavior; most of the gods exhibited the same ego-centric, almost animalistic ethics which characterized Greco-Roman society.

In general, P is concerned to show that right action depends on knowledge. People want to do the right thing, he maintains, but cannot if they do not know what the right thing is. He does not attempt to define the right thing in any or every situation but tries to show how people can become the right kind of people.

ADKINS, A. "Plato," in *Ethics in the History of Western Philosophy*, ed. R. J. Cavalier (New York: St. Martins, 1989), pp. 1-31. Studies P's efforts to develop ethical theory out of pre-philosophical concepts bequeathed to him by Homer, tragedians. **[1674]**

ANNAS, J. "Plato and Common Morality." *CQ* 28(1978), 437-451. P tries to redirect ethical emphases from definition of just actions to determining nature of just man. In *Rep* S tries to interpret justice as psychic harmony. **[1675]**

———. cf. #4025.

BECK, R. H. "Responsibility in Homer, Aeschylus and Plato." *ProcPhEd* 43(1987), 401-407. Discusses idea of one's responsibility for his own actions as developed in Homer and Aeschylus, and lack of responsibility of the uninformed in P. **[1676]**

BEIERWALTES, W. "The Love of Beauty and the Love of God," in #43, pp. 293-313. For P and the Platonists Beauty is more an ethical than an aesthetic ideal. It is an expression of the Good. Something is beautiful only if, and as, God is in it. **[1677]**

BRENTLINGER, J. A. "The Nature of Love," in #3304, pp. 113-129; also in *Eros, Agape, and Philia: Readings in the Philosophy of Love*, ed. A. Soble (New York: Paragon House, 1989), pp. 136-148. Discusses such issues as the object of love, what kind of psychological state love is, and the relation of love to desire. Evaluates P's doctrine in comparison to some modern views. **[1678]**

CACOULLOS, A. R. "The Doctrine of Eros in Plato." *Diot* 1(1973), 81-89. P sees "eros," tendency toward self-fulfillment/happiness, as driving all persons. It is a need one experiences because of some lack and because it is necessary for growth. **[1679]**

CAPITAN, W. H. "Can Virtue Be Taught?" *Diot* 1(1973), 101-124. Turns to P for assistance in dealing with certain problems in issue of teachability of morality. **[1680]**

CHERRY, C. "When Is Fantasising Morally Bad?" *PhInv* 11(1988), 112-132. Evaluates several responses to this question, and explores P's account of art and fiction with respect to it.   **[1681]**

COBB, W. S. "Plato on the Possiblity of An Irreligious Morality." *IntJPhRel* 25(1989), 3-12. The distinction between religiousness and justice which is set out in *Euthyphro* involves a logical fallacy which P corrects in *Protag*, leaving no room for conflict between justice and piety.   **[1682]**

COBB-STEVENS, V. "Commentary on Moravcsik's 'Plato's Ethics as Ideal Building'." *PBACAPh* 1(1985), 22-38. Reply to #1724. Challenges impersonality of P's ideal state; argues that the ideal provides inadequate grounds for respecting others as ends. **[1683]**

COOPER, J. M. "Greek Philosophers on Suicide," in *Suicide and Euthanasia: Historical and Contemporary Themes*, ed. B. A. Brody (Dordrecht, Netherlands: Kluwer, 1989), pp. 9-38. P is not dogmatically opposed to suicide. In *Phaedo* he voices opposition through S, but in *Laws* he approves of suicide in certain cases. Ar's opposition to suicide is based on a somewhat confused claim that the person committing suicide injures the state. Stoics did not approve of suicide without qualification.   **[1684]**

CREED, J. L. "Is it Wrong to Call Plato a Utilitarian?" *CQ* 28(1978), 349-365. For P the Good is what one desires, but it is not identical with the pleasurable. He is primarily concerned with good of agent, not of greatest number. Nor does he think that a deed's consequences determine whether it is right or wrong.   **[1685]**

CUMMINS, W. J. "*Eros, Epithumia*, and *Philia* in Plato." *Apeir* 15(1981), 10-18. Meanings of each of these words run across a spectrum. P takes advantage of this feature as he examines topics from various perspectives. He does not rigidly link one theme with one meaning.   **[1686]**

DAVIES, J. C. "Some Thoughts on Plato's View of Pleasure." *Euphro* 4(1970), 173-181. P's idea of love changed from *Gorg*'s idealism to *Laws'* more balanced view.   **[1687]**

DEMOS, R. "Plato on Moral Principles." *Mind* 76(1967), 125-126. P should be judged not only by his professed doctrines but also by his practice. Thus he is not a consequentialist but a deontologist.   **[1688]**

DOVER, K. J. *Greek Popular Morality in the Time of Plato and Aristotle.* Berkeley: Univ. of CA Pr., 1974. Presents the moral assumptions of the average Athenian citizen during the period of the writings of P and Ar.   **[1689]**

DUERLINGER, J. "Ethics and the Divine Life in Plato's Philosophy." *JRE* 13(1985), 312-331. P's ethics are basically religious ethics since the aim of his efforts is to achieve the good and the divine life. Paths of moral training, contemplation, and dialectic to the divine life are explained.   **[1690]**

EPP, R. H. "Plato's Quest for Purification." *Platon* 24(1972), 38-50. S is not an ascetic whose overriding concern is his fate in an afterlife. An ethical sense of *katharsis* sheds light on P's quest for the good life, and there is an interdependence of katharsis with philosophia and dialectic.   **[1691]**

FASTIGGI, R. L. "Law and Morality. The Lessons of Plato and Aristotle." *JDharma* 4(1979), 347-358. Positivist notion that law and morality should remain separate is shown to be contradicted by writings of P and Ar. **[1692]**

FEREJOHN, M. T. "Socratic Thought-Experiments and the Unity of Virtue Paradox." *Phron* 29(1984), 105-122. Reply to #1709. *Euthyd* and *Meno* do not contain redundant versions of one argument for theory of unity of virtues. *Euthyd* distinguishes between goods which are value-indifferent and wisdom, the only true good. *Meno* argues that other virtues are dependent upon wisdom, but do not necessarily make a unity. **[1693]**

FERGUSON, J. "The Ethics of the *Gennaion Pseudos*." *LCM* 6(1981), 259-267. P tolerates inconsistencies in his account of the "noble lie" because of his view that "any action which leads to the most desirable results is the ethically right one." **[1694]**

GADAMER, H.-G. *The Idea of the Good in Platonic-Aristotelian Philosophy*, transl. P. C. Smith. New Haven, CT: Yale Univ. Pr., 1986. Focuses on *Protag, Phaedo, Rep*, and *Philebus*, and on Ar's three moral treatises to show essential continuity of Platonic and Aristotelian reflection on nature of the Good. **[1695]**

GAISER, K. "Plato's Enigmatic Lecture 'On the Good'." *Phron* 25(1980), 5-37. Defends position that P did lecture publicly on his mathematical theory of the Good despite its incomprehensibility to the layman. He would have done so to counter certain theories circulating under his name and to show the public that his school did not hold esoteric doctrines. **[1696]**

GEELS, D. E. "Plato and the Pay-off of Justice." *Pers* 52(1971), 449-458. P fails to refute Glaucon's assertion in *Rep* that an unjust man will be happy because P fails to appreciate the role of reason in making moral decisions. **[1697]**

GERSON, L. P. "Plato on Virtue, Knowledge, and the Unity of Goodness," in #1267, pp. 85-100. P's seemingly paradoxical contentions about the unity of the virtues can be shown to be coherent parts of one ethical doctrine. The concepts of the Form of the Good and tripartite psychology unify P's ethics. **[1698]**

GOULD, J. *The Development of Plato's Ethics*. New York: Russell & Russell, 1972; rprt. P's central concern is how humans can achieve their true moral stature. His answers to this question vary over his career. Traces shift from Socratic ideal of personal decision in early dialogues to institutionalized morality of *Laws*. **[1699]**

GRAHAM, F. B. "A Note on Mr. Demos' Note on Plato on Moral Principles." *Mind* 78(1969), 596-597. Reply to Demos' argument (#1688) that treating P as a consequentialist is misleading. **[1700]**

GULLEY, N. "The Interpretation of 'No one does wrong willingly' in Plato's Dialogues." *Phron* 10(1965), 82-96. As used in *Protag*, phrase is Socratic, meaning that everyone aims for his/her own happiness and does nothing not conducive to it unless compelled. In *Gorg* P's concern with moral responsibility puts new light on phrase. **[1701]**

HARE, R. M. "Platonism in Moral Education: Two Varieties." *Monist* 58(1974), 568-580. P's "What is goodness?" question can be answered descriptively (in terms of its content) and prescriptively (in terms of form). **[1702]**

HARRINGTON, K. W. "John Dewey's Ethics and the Classical Conception of Man." *Diot* 1(1973), 125-148. Contrasts and evaluates two broad types of self-realization theories, one represented by P and Ar, the other by Dewey. [1703]

————. "Santayana and the Humanists on Plato." *Ph&PhenRes* 38(1977), 66-81. Discusses Santayana's "naturalistic" interpretation of P: rejection of view that P's philosophy presupposes a strong ethical or metaphysical dualism, and belief that P's ethics are concerned primarily with achievement of happiness through fulfillment of man's natural powers in context of the political life. [1704]

HUBY, P. M. *Plato and Modern Morality.* London: Macmillan, 1972. Discusses P's views on inequalities of mankind, population control, family and property, education, censorship, and punishment. [1705]

HURSTHOUSE, R. "Plato on Commensurability and Desire, II: Plato on the Emotions." *PAS* Suppl. 58(1984), 81-96. Reply to #1727. Quantitative commensurability cannot be ascribed to P's account of ethical *techne*. [1706]

HUTCHINSON, D. S. "Doctrines of the Mean and the Debate Concerning Skills in Fourth-Century Medicine, Rhetoric and Ethics." *Apeir* 21(1988), 17-52. When P and Ar compare virtue to various skills, especially medical, they are reacting to contemporary discussions in education, rhetoric, and medicine. [1707]

INWOOD, M. J. "Hegel, Plato and Greek 'Sittlichkeit'," in *The State and Civil Society,* ed. Z. A. Pelczynski (Cambridge Univ. Pr., 1984), pp. 40-54. Examines Hegel's distinction between S as self-conscious individualist and P as restorer of harmony to the Greek ethical community. [1708]

IRWIN, T. H. *Plato's Moral Theory: The Early and Middle Dialogues.* Oxford: Clarendon Pr., 1977. Discusses S's theory, P's reactions, and development of P's own position. Shows Theory of Recollection, separation of Forms, account of love and rational desire, and divisions of desires to be P's answers to basic problems in S's theory. [1709]

————. "Recollection and Plato's Moral Theory." *RMeta* 27(1974), 752-772. Examines role of recollection and related doctrine of separated Forms in P's theory of moral knowledge and moral motivation. Attempts to show how P's doctrines are responses to problems arising out of Socratic theories. [1710]

KAHN, C. H. "Plato on the Unity of Virtues," in #1293, pp. 21-39. P conceives of philosophy as an erotic passion for truth and reality that explains doctrine of unity of virtues. It is philosophic wisdom that produces other virtues. [1711]

KLOSKO, G. "The Technical Conception of Virtue." *JHPh* 19(1981), 95-102. Examines Irwin's (#1709) grounds for attributing a "technical conception of virtue" to S in P's early dialogues. Concludes that Irwin's evidence will not bear scrutiny. [1712]

KOSMAN, L. A. "Platonic Love," in #1293, pp. 53-69; also in *Eros, Agape, and Philia: Readings in the Philosophy of Love,* ed. A. Soble (New York: Paragon House, 1989), pp. 149-164. Studies two objections to P's theory of love: 1) love is essentially egotistical and selfish; 2) proper love is not love of an individual, but of Form of love. [1713]

LODGE, R. C. *Plato's Theory of Ethics: The Moral Criterion and the Highest Good.* New York: Archon, 1966; rprt. Examines criteria for distinguishing good from bad, scales of good derived from these criteria, and various highest goods according to discussions in the dialogues. [1714]

LUKES, S. "Moral Weakness." *PhQ* 15(1965), 104-114. S and P approached problem of moral weakness from standpoint of an ideal, viz., that such a condition should not exist in soul of philosopher. Ar was more concerned to describe what did exist. [1715]

MacINTYRE, A. C. "The Virtues at Athens," in *After Virtue: A Study in Moral Theory* (Notre Dame, IN: Univ. of Notre Dame Pr., 1984; 2nd ed.), pp. 131-145. Studies origins of ethical questions and the answers posed by tragedians and by P. [1716]

MacKENZIE, M. M. *Plato on Punishment.* Berkeley: Univ. of CA Pr., 1981. Argues for a dilemma: it is impossible to produce a coherent, consistent theory of punishment that is free from moral outrage; but to practice punishment appears to be irresistible. Then presents this dilemma in operation as theory and tradition. [1717]

————. "Plato's Moral Theory." *JMedEthics* 11(1985), 88-91. Brief discussion of P's moral theory and its relation to medical practice. [1718]

MacKINNON, D. M. "'Thrusting Against the Limits of Language': An Aspect of Plato's *Republic*," in *The Problem of Metaphysics* (Cambridge Univ. Pr., 1974), pp. 17-30. Comparison of just/unjust men in *Rep* 2 is an example of metaphysics in action. [1719]

MADIGAN, A. "Plato, Aristotle and Professor MacIntyre." *AncPh* 3(1983), 171-183. MacIntyre (#1716) is more Platonist than Aristotelian. He fails to deal satisfactorily with the problem of victims of injustice. [1720]

MARGOLIS, J. "Rationality and Weakness of Will." *JChinPh* 8(1981), 9-27. Includes a critical assessment of P's account of weakness of will. [1721]

MILLS, M. J. "*Phthonos* and Its Related *Pathe* in Plato and Aristotle." *Phron* 30(1985), 1-12. Traces development of concept of *phthonos* (malice, jealousy) from *Philebus* to Ar's *Ethics*. Ar seems to have seen how closely *phthonos* and *nemesis* (retribution) are linked, but also managed to distinguish them. [1722]

MOHR, R. D. "A Platonic Happiness." *HPhQ* 4(1987), 131-145. For P, happiness is not psychic harmony but rather self-satisfaction in one's work. [1723]

MORAVCSIK, J. M. E. "Plato's Ethics as Ideal Building." *PBACAPh* 1(1985), 1-21. P's ethics cannot be described as utilitarian or Kantian. They are an effort to define the right or ideal character. P's theory of value is more coherent than those of modern ethical theorists. [1724]

NAKHNIKIAN, G. "Eudaimonism Revisited." *PolTheo* 7(1979), 267-279. Examines Irwin's (#1709) argument that P's moral philosophy is not Socratic. [1725]

————. "Love in Human Reason." *MidwStudPh* 3(1978), 286-317. P maintains that love is an important element in reason. Analyzes what P means by "love." He has no concept of loving a person for his own sake. [1726]

——. cf. #2052.

NUSSBAUM, M. C. "Plato on Commensurability and Desire, I." *PAS* Suppl. 58(1984), 55-80. P tried to base ethical decisions on a system of measurement that denied quantity. Something should be desired because of what it is, without respect to how much of it there is. This is a radical departure from any other ethical foundation.   [1727]

NYGREN, A. "Agape and Eros," in *Eros, Agape, and Philia: Readings in the Philosophy of Love*, ed. A. Soble (New York: Paragon House, 1989), pp. 85-95. Compares and contrasts these two forms of love in P and Paul. Emphasizes egocentric, acquisitive nature of eros in P in contrast to altruism and self-sacrifice of agape.   [1728]

O'BRIEN, M. J. *The Socratic Paradoxes and the Greek Mind*. Chapel Hill: Univ. of NC Pr., 1967. Specialized study of P's ethical theory that examines Socratic paradoxes that virtue is knowledge and that no one does evil voluntarily. Explores their relation to common ethical views held by P's predecessors and contemporaries.   [1729]

O'CONNELL, R. J. "*Eros* and *Philia* in Plato's Moral Cosmos," in #6339, pp. 3-19. Mankind is a mixed creature, attracted to things at first by *eros* but capable of perceiving some things as good, the object of *philia*. To understand the difference one must perceive ultimate unity of Reality, Beauty and the Good.   [1730]

PARRY, A. "A Note on the Origins of Teleology." *JHI* 26(1965), 259-262. Developed concept of an end or objective in ethics cannot be found in Greek thought before S. P and Ar finished this reworking of ethics on a non-Homeric basis.   [1731]

PASSALOGLOU, E. "Definition, Unity of Virtues, and Plato's Development." *Hellenica* 34(1982-83), 331-351. P's concepts of definition and unity of virtues remain virtually unchanged from *Laches* to *Rep*. Later dialogues do not resolve difficulties raised earlier. In this area it seems inaccurate to speak of "development" of P's thought.   [1732]

PELTZ, R. "The True, The Good, and the Humanities." *JAesEduc* 2(1968), 9-20. Examines what P and Ar have to say about the "true," the "good," and the "beautiful," and the impact of their views on general education.   [1733]

PENNER, T. M. I. "Thought and Desire in Plato," in #1291, pp. 96-118. P rejects S's views on *akrasia* (weakness of will) and endorses view that one part of oneself can think one thing while another part thinks something else.   [1734]

PRICE, A. W. *Love and Friendship in Plato and Aristotle*. Oxford: Clarendon Pr., 1989. Both P and Ar maintain that service to another is a form of service to oneself. This concept applies to friends and lovers of either gender, to members of one's family, to fellow-citizens. It breaks down the separation between egoism and altruism.   [1735]

PRICE, K. "Love, Yes, But Maybe Not Sex." *ProcPhEd* 36(1980), 317-321. Challenges P's view of love as the motive for acting rightly.   [1736]

RACHLIN, H. "Maximization Theory and Plato's Concept of the Good." *Behaviorism* 13(1985), 3-20. It is possible to see P's concept of the Good as a forerunner of the modern behavioral theory known as maximization theory, which defines goodness as a quantifiable function of an animal's observable, constrained choices.   [1737]

RIST, J. M. "Knowledge and Value in Plato." *Phoenix* 21(1967), 283-295. The soul is immortal, and it is common sense to care for it. It is improved by contemplation of Forms. Deliberate wrong-doing harms the soul. P does not say that one *must* act morally, but that one is foolish not to.   **[1738]**

RORTY, A. "Plato and Aristotle on Belief, Habit and Akrasia." *AmPhQ* 7(1970), 50-61. P explains why people act contrary to what they know is the better course of action in terms of the effect of belief on action. Ar stresses how desire affects actions.   **[1739]**

ROSEN, F. "Contemplation and Virtue in Plato." *RelStud* 16(1980), 85095. Unless one understands how P views contemplation, several of his ethical and political concepts are difficult to understand.   **[1740]**

ROSENSTEIN, L. "Heidegger and Plato and the Good." *PhT* 22(1978), 332-354. Compares such Platonic virtues as wisdom, courage, temperance to Heidegger's concepts of fundamental thinking, resoluteness, letting-be, and appropriation.   **[1741]**

RUDEBUSCH, G. "Plato, Hedonism, and Ethical Protagoreanism," in #1267, pp. 27-40. Doctrines of pleasure in *Protag* and *Gorg* can be reconciled by examining difference between real and apparent pleasures. P is trying to refute Protagoras' view, not hedonism in general.   **[1742]**

SANTAS, G. "Plato on Goodness and Rationality." *RIPh* 40(1986), 97-114. Before one can decide whether reason is subservient to the passions (as Hume maintains) or dominant over them (as P holds), one must first determine whether practical rationality can be explained in terms of goodness (P), or the reverse (Rawls).   **[1743]**

SCHANKULA, H. A. S. "Plato and Aristotle: *Eudaimonia, Hexis* or *Energeia*?" *CPh* 66(1971), 244-246. Ar based his distinction between potency and act on P's differentiation between *ktesis/chresis* and *hexis*.   **[1744]**

SCHIPPER, E. W. "Motives and Virtues in the Platonic Ethics." *Ratio* 13(1971), 67-75. P assumes that everyone desires the good, though they do not know what it is and often make wrong choices out of ignorance. Personal happiness is not the ultimate motive for virtue. People aspire to knowledge of a wider social good.   **[1745]**

SCRIVEN, T. "Plato's 'Democratic Man' and the Implausibility of Preference Utilitarianism." *Theoretical Decisions* 24(1988), 43-55. If ethics are based on preference, a person must be allowed to change his view constantly or never change his fundamental view at all. The theory is unworkable on either alternative.   **[1746]**

SELLARS, W. "On Knowing the Better and Doing the Worse." *IntPhQ* 10(1970), 5-19; also in (cf. #1748), pp. 27-43. P maintains that one should determine right actions on basis of what benefits the community, but he sets up his own political program on basis of his own pleasure in contemplating the arrangements.   **[1747]**

————. "Reason and the Art of Living in Plato," in *Essays in Philosophy and its History* (Dordrecht, Netherlands: Reidel, 1974), pp. 3-26. Just as every craft has its rules for success, so the art of living a satisfying life has the Form of the Good as its guide. To wish to lead a satisfying life is to will the Good.   **[1748]**

------. "The Soul as Craftsman," in #77, pp. 5-22. In *Rep* the discussion of the state serves as a "large-letter" version of discussion of justice in the soul. Similarly, discussion of Craftsman in *Tim* shows how P's concept of the Good coheres.   [1749]

SHOREY, P. "Plato's Ethics," in #1291, pp. 7-34. Discusses "chief topics" of P's ethics: 1) Socratic paradoxes; 2) definition of virtues and determination of their relation to the good; 3) problem of hedonism; and 4) attempt to demonstrate inseparability of virtue and happiness.   [1750]

SOLOMON, J. H. M. "*Exousia* in Plato." *Platon* 19(1967), 189-197. *Exousia* ("power") is an active quality, limited by capacities of person acting or by laws.   [1751]

SPARSHOTT, F. E. "Five Virtues of Plato and Aristotle." *Monist* 54(1970), 40-65. P mentions four virtues as constituting virtue itself, an idea he may have drawn from a popular catalogue of virtues. Ar has a longer list. Both assume there must be a finite number of virtues or else there can be no study of the subject.   [1752]

TAYLOR, C. C. W. "Plato and Aristotle on the Criterion of Real Pleasures," in *Actes du VIIe Congrès de la Fédération Internationale des Associations d'Études Classiques*, ed. J. Harmata (Budapest: Akademiai Kiado, 1984), II, pp. 345-356. Both P and Ar appeal to the philosopher as judge of what is pleasant and good. Neither is able, however, to establish the validity of the criterion.   [1753]

------. "Plato, Hare and Davidson on Akrasia." *Mind* 89(1980), 499-518. Detailed examination of competing accounts of problem of weakness of will.   [1754]

VLASTOS, G. "The Individual as an Object of Love in Plato," in #1292, pp. 3-42; also in *Eros, Agape, and Philia: Readings in the Philosophy of Love*, ed. A. Soble (New York: Paragon House, 1989), pp. 96-135. Shows that in P's theory of love of persons, what we are to love in other persons is the "image" of the Form in them; hence the individual is never the object of love.   [1755]

------. "Socratic Knowledge and Platonic 'Pessimism'," in #1292, pp. 204-217. Critical discussion of #1699, regarding the development of P's thinking on the relation of virtue and happiness, and the extent to which P maintains his faith in "enlightened absolutism."   [1756]

WALCOTT, P. *Greek Peasants, Ancient and Modern: A Comparison of Social and Moral Values*. Manchester (UK) Univ. Pr., 1970. Comparison of ethical values of modern Greek peasants with those recorded by ancient Greek writers reveals numerous similarities, enabling us to understand world view behind ancient authors' ethical pronouncements.   [1757]

For related items see #191, #490, #1034, $1475, #2031, #2944, #4146, #4937, #5386.

LOGIC/DIALECTIC

P's logic appears almost primitive beside Ar's. In the dialogues S sometimes bullies his interlocutors into conceding points which are not logically consistent at all; or S or the interlocutors will make mistakes in logic which no one seems to notice. P may have been aware of these deficiencies. In *Gorg* 485e Callicles chides S: ". . . you could not conduct an argument in court, nor is it probable that you could make it convincing or give vigorous advice to another."

In the early dialogues S investigates problems by the method of *elenchus* or refutation. This is not a method of logic as much as a technique of dialectic. Someone, often S, will ask a "What is *x*?" question, i. e., a question which calls for a definition, usually of an ethical virtue. S never offers a definition himself — he never admits to knowing anything — but prods someone else into providing one. Then he begins to ask questions about the terms of the definition and their implications, often in the form "Do you mean to say *x*?" The interlocutor agrees or disagrees and S continues leading him in the inquiry until the interlocutor agrees to a proposition which contradicts his original definition. At that point he has been refuted and the definition is seen to be inadequate.

This method has the advantage of involving a person in the examination of something he has said. He does not have an authoritative answer handed to him. If S asks, "Do you agree that . . . ?" the *elenchus* can proceed no further if the person does not agree. S often professes to be just a fellow inquirer, no more certain of where the investigation is going than is the interlocutor (though the sincerity of his professions has been doubted). *Elenchus* is a useful method for dealing with open-ended issues and allows for the possibility that no satisfactory conclusion to the inquiry can be reached, a situation called an *aporia*. P seems not to have wanted to convince his readers or listeners by the power of logic but to lead them to see things for themselves, a kind of enlightenment. Such an approach accords well with his understanding of knowledge (cf. Epistemology).

The primary weakness of this method is its inability to establish definite answers. S usually just points out the weaknesses of his opponent's ideas and does not offer a positively phrased teaching of his own.

Not every *elenchus* works exactly the same way. In some instances S adds up ("syllogizes") the points he has made to conclude the refutation. In others he uses induction (*epagoge*): If something is true in two or three or four cases, wouldn't it also be true in the case we are considering? P uses whatever method worked best, but he has no formal theory of logic, nor does he have the terminology, which Ar developed, of classes of syllogisms with major and minor premises.

As P matured and moved away from S's influence, he seems to have become more optimistic about the possibility of attaining at least some degree of certainty in knowledge. The method he uses in his middle dialogues is still dialectical but with a more constructive tone. His theory of the Forms requires that there be some absolute knowledge which can be found by inquiry. Part of the problem of defining his method is that he uses the term dialectic so loosely. As Robinson says (#1791, p.70), "Plato applied it at every stage of his life to whatever seemed to him at the moment the most hopeful procedure." The closest we come to a statement of his method is the description of a literary composition found in *Phaedrus* 263 ff. A composition must have order, S says, like an animal: a head, body, extremities, all in their proper places. But P does not separate his logical method from his metaphysics, as Ar does. Therefore his method may vary depending on the objective of a particular inquiry.

In the middle dialogues P uses a technique called hypothesis, meaning in this case a proposition assumed or laid down after some consideration as the basis for further investigation, with the realization that it may prove to be false. This method appears in passages which begin "Let us assume (lay down, hypothesize) *x*." This method does not explain as much as it evaluates propositions. Some scholars see it as inconsistent with P's epistemology, which requires sure knowledge of absolutes, and argue that he does not apply the method consistently in those dialogues where it is discussed.

In the *Soph* P introduces a more formal logical method called *diaeresis*, or division, which becomes his primary logical method in the later dialogues. This consists of collecting as many examples of the issue under discussion as possible and dividing them into their natural or logical groups. K. M. Sayre, however, argues that *diaeresis* and hypothesis are simply different names for the same technique (#1796).

ALDERMAN, H. "Dialectic as Philosophical Care." *M&W* 6(1973), 206-219. Examines four dialogues to argue that dialectic is the philosopher's distinctively philosophical mode of caring which insures that we remain open to the dual possibility of knowledge and ignorance and to man's proper role as caretaker of speech.   [1758]

BONDESON, W. B. "Plato and the Foundations of Logic and Language." *SwJPh* 6(1975), 29-41. Compares some arguments in later dialogues with issues in philosophy of logic and language as discussed by contemporary analytic philosophers.   [1759]

BURRELL, D. "Plato: Inquiry as Dialectic," in *Analogy as Philosophical Language* (New Haven, CT: Yale Univ. Pr., 1973), pp. 37-67. P's contribution to philosophical thinking is his recognition that there are various kinds of questions to be asked in the search for truth, but similar principles underlie all of them. Dialectic is not some sort of direct knowing but a reflection on our explanations of what we know.   [1760]

———. cf. #1317.

COHEN, M. "The Logical Background of Plato's Writing." *JHPh* 7(1969), 111-141. Various fifth-century works demonstrate logical and semantic sophistication which suggests that some fallacies in P's early works may be deliberate.   [1761]

COHEN, S. M. "The Logic of the Third Man." *PhR* 80(1971), 448-475. Considers and rejects main lines of interpretation of TMA, and offers a new, set-theoretic reconstruction of the argument.   [1762]

———. "Plato's Method of Division," in #1280, pp. 181-191. Offers alternative models to Moravcsik's account (#1785) of what method of division may be.   [1763]

CORNFORD, F. M. "Mathematics and Dialectic in the *Republic* VI-VII," in #53, pp. 277-310; also in #1809, pp. 61-95. P does not seem to distinguish clearly between *noesis* (intuition) and *dianoia* (deductive reasoning). The apparently redundant descriptions of dialectic in *Rep* 7 actually have two purposes: one relates to education, the other to research.   [1764]

CRAWFORD, T. D. "Plato's Reasoning and the Sapir-Whorf Hypothesis." *Metaphil*

13(1982), 217-227. The very structure of Greek language sometimes leads P into the wrong line of reasoning.   **[1765]**

DAVIES, J. C. "Plato's Dialectic. Some Thoughts on the 'Line'." *Orpheus* 14(1969), 3-11. Universal mathematic/geometric concepts, which have no contact with Forms, are objects of Line's third section (*Rep* 510ff.).   **[1766]**

DESJARDINS, G. "A Gloss on *Republic* 487c." *StudPh&HistPh* 5(1970), 1-12. Examines Adeimantus' complaint that dialectic is just another game, played with words instead of pebbles. P shows that dialectic is a natural kind of division.   **[1767]**

DORTER, K. "The Dialectic of Plato's Method of Hypothesis." *PhFor* 7(1976), 159-187. P's method of hypothesis is neither deductive nor explanatory. It is designed to evaluate explanations and put them to use.   **[1768]**

DuBOIS, P. "On the Invention of Hierarchy." *Arethusa* 15(1982), 203-220. Early Greeks discriminated between things on basis of opposites such as hot/cold, male/female. P and Ar introduced notion of discrimination by ranking, or hierarchy.   **[1769]**

ELIAS, J. A. "'Socratic' vs. 'Platonic' Dialectic." *JHPh* 6(1968), 205-216. In early and middle dialogues P distinguishes between S's essentially negative dialectic and his own positive rationalistic method. Ultimately he despaired of dialectic of either sort.**[1770]**

ENGEL, S. M. "Fallacy, Wit, and Madness." *Ph&Rh* 19(1986), 224-241. P recognizes a connection between logical fallacies and humor which Ar failed to see. Modern studies of the phenomenon need to take the context of a fallacy into account, for that can determine whether it suggests humor or madness.   **[1771]**

ESLICK, L. J. "Plato's Dialectic of the Sun," in *History of Philosophy in the Making*, ed. L. J. Thro (Washington, DC: Univ. Pr. of America, 1982), pp. 19-34. Examines exact nature of P's earlier dialectic, and in particular, his indebtedness to development in Greek mathematics.   **[1772]**

FAJ, A. "Platonic Anticipations of Stoic Logic (Part 1)." *Apeir* 5 #2(1971), 1-19. Traces possible links between Theory of Forms and metaphysics of Stoics, who may have studied *Parm* closely. P also uses propositional logic with Stoic implications.   **[1773]**

————. "Platonic Anticipation of Stoic Logic, II." *Apeir* 6 #1(1972), 1-24. *Parm* is full of pre-formations of Stoic logic.   **[1774]**

GRISWOLD, C. L. "Reflections on 'Dialectic' in Plato and Hegel." *IntPhQ* 22(1981), 115-130. Outlines various senses of "dialectic" in P; examines Hegel's criticisms of them.   **[1775]**

————. cf. #3207.

HAWTREY, R. S. W. "How Do Dialecticians Use Diagrams? Plato, *Euthydemus* 290b-c." *Apeir* 12 #2(1978), 14-18. Investigates P's use of words "diagrams" and "dialecticians." "Dialectics" in this passage has metaphysical implications. P seems to have already held some views which he developed more fully in *Rep*.   **[1776]**

IRWIN, T. H. "Coercion and Objectivity in Plato's Dialectic." *RIPh* 40(1986), 49-74. Explains why and how P forms the aim of transforming conversational argument into compelling argument without lapsing into illegitimately coercive argument. [1777]

KINNEY, A. M. "The Meaning of Dialectic in Plato." *Auslegung* 10(1983), 229-246. Examines P's dialectical method in several later dialogues and seeks to answer questions about his aim, relationship between questioner and respondent, effect of the method on the participants, and the role of metaphor. [1778]

KLOSKO, G. "Criteria of Fallacy and Sophistry for Use in the Analysis of Platonic Dialogues." *CQ* 33(1983), 363-374. Validity of proofs in S's arguments should be determined from interlocutors' viewpoints. Some proofs contain valid and fallacious points side by side, revealing sophistry of S's technique at points. [1779]

———. "Plato and the Morality of Fallacy." *AJPh* 108(1987), 612-626. Argues that P does use fallacious arguments, and discusses the implications of such a view for understanding the dialogues, especially *Hipp Min* and *Euthyd*. [1780]

LEVINSON, R. B. "Language, Plato, and Logic," in #41, pp. 259-284. Though imperfect, human language can represent the Ideal Name. P tries to define objects which words name. He coins words, though he tries not to be careless in use of language. He does not use technical jargon. [1781]

LLOYD, A. C. "Plato's Description of Division," in #1809, pp. 219-230. Language in which dialectic is described in later dialogues presupposes the particular and probably familiar method of illustrating it by way of geometrical illustration. [1782]

MEYER, M. "Dialectic and Questioning. Socrates and Plato." *AmPhQ* 17(1980), 281-290. P wanted to follow S's method of question-answer-question, but his theory of Forms presupposes that there is a definite answer for every question, something by no means assured for S. [1783]

MINARDI, S. "On Some Aspects of Platonic Division." *Mind* 92(1983), 417-423. P's use of *diairesis* (division) seems to change over his life and might provide a useful tool for examining chronology of dialogues and his view of Forms. [1784]

MORAVCSIK, J. M. E. "Plato's Method of Division," in #1280, pp. 158-180. In later dialogues, part of P's dialectic takes form of so-called divisions and collections. Examines products of divisions as well as processes that lead to these. [1785]

———. cf. #1886.

MUELLER, G. E. *Plato, the Founder of Philosophy as Dialectic*. New York: Philosophical Library, 1965. Exposition of underlying unity of P's philosophy, conceived as Hegelian dialectic. [1786]

PHILIP, J. A. "Platonic Diairesis." *TAPhA* 97(1966), 335-358. Examines P's theory and practice of division, and argues that the method of diairesis is an exploratory method that produces insights, not proofs. [1787]

ROBINSON, R. "Elenchus: Direct and Indirect," in #1199, pp. 94-109. Examines degrees of explicitness and tautness in reasoning, and P's answers to the distinction between direct and indirect arguments. Argues that P regards all elenchus as the deduction of a contradiction.   **[1788]**

———. "Hypothesis in the *Republic*," in #1290, pp. 97-131. Examines weakness in P's epistemological method. P thought it possible to establish a hypothesis if no objections to it could be discovered dialectically. What he achieves, however, is only a set of beliefs, not knowledge.   **[1789]**

———. "Plato's Consciousness of Fallacy," in #74, 16-38. Surveys four types of fallacy in P's early dialogues, his conception of fallacy, and the kind of logical apparatus did he had to deal with fallacies.   **[1790]**

———. *Plato's Earlier Dialectic* Oxford: Clarendon Pr., 1984; 2nd ed. Examines logic and methodology of early and middle dialogues, and focuses primarily on elenchus, dialectic, and method of hypothesis.   **[1791]**

ROSEN, S. "Unity and Existence," in *The Limits of Analysis* (New York: Basic Books, 1980), pp. 108-120. Discussion of P's difficulty in defining unity of the whole and how this sum of a thing's parts differs from its essence. The problem has implications for modern philosophers as well.   **[1792]**

ROSENMEYER, T. G. "Plato's Hypothesis and the Upward Path," in #41, pp. 354-366. Seeks to show that Ar's logical terminology, "ontologically conditioned or determined," contrasts with that of P, who, with one or two exceptions, was very careful not to introduce unwarranted ontological perspectives into matters of logic.   **[1793]**

RYLE, G. "Teaching and Training," in #2483, pp. 243-261. Explores question, "How, in logic, can anyone be taught to do untaught things?"   **[1794]**

SAUER, W. "A Note on 'Plato's Reasoning and the Sapir-Whorf Hypothesis.'" *Metaphil* 16(1983), 235-238. Reply to #1765. Criticizes idea that P's dialogues offer support for Sapir-Whorf Hypothesis of linguistic relativity (namely, structures of a person's native language condition how he analyzes raw data of sense experience).   **[1795]**

SAYRE, K. M. *Plato's Analytical Method.* Univ. of Chicago Pr., 1969. In *Theaet* P abandons the method of hypothesis which he had outlined in *Phaedo* 100a-101d and begins to explore the method of division. The technique of collection and division is fully developed in *Soph*, which not only describes the method but exhibits it in its structure. Analysis reveals, however, that the techniques of hypothesis and of collection and division may use different terminology but are merely different manifestations of the same analytical method.   **[1796]**

SPRAGUE, R. K. "Logic and Literary Form in Plato." *Pers* 48(1967), 560-572. P does not merely cast doubt on validity of certain fallacious arguments, but also indicates how fallacies may be cleared up.   **[1797]**

———. "Plato's Sophistry." *PAS* Suppl. 51(1977), 45-61. Reply to Stewart (#2272). P was aware of certain types of fallacious argument.   **[1798]**

STAHL, H. P. "Beginnings of Propositional Logic in Plato," in #2483, pp. 180-197.

Examines logical theory and program of hypothesis, and execution of theory and why it is intertwined with increasingly developing Theory of Ideas. [1799]

STENZEL, J. *Plato's Method of Dialectic*, transl. D. J. Allan. New York: Arno Pr., 1973; rprt. Contains Stenzel's influential essay on literary form and philosophical content of the dialogues, and his studies on P's dialectic. [1800]

SZABO, A. "Hypothesis in Plato's Dialectics and Greek Mathematics." *Epistemologia* 10(1987), 163-170. P's dialectics and foundations of Greek mathematics have same terminology and have a common origin. [1801]

TILGHMAN, B. R. "Parmenides, Plato, and Logical Atomism." *SJPh* 7(1969), 151-160. Like Parmenides, P puzzled over problem of logic of statements and how language means something. His answers resemble those of modern philosophers. [1802]

TREVASKIS, J. R. "Division and Its Relation to Dialectic and Ontology in Plato." *Phron* 12(1967), 118-129. Discusses, using *Phaedrus, Soph,* and *Stsm,* how far the method of division is to be identified with dialectic, what relation, if any, it bears to P's ontology, and what P seeks to gain from it. [1803]

WEDIN, M. V. "Collection and Division in the *Phaedrus* and *Statesman*." *RPhA* 5(1987), 207-233. Extensionalist theory of collection and division set forth in *Stsm* 262a ff. revises views P had expressed in *Phaedrus* 265. [1804]

WOODRUFF, P. "The Skeptical Side of Plato's Method." *RIPh* 40(1986), 22-37. Socratic elenchus of early dialogues was less influential on Stoics than was the *ou mallon* ("no more this than that") strategy used in some of the middle dialogues. [1804a]

For related items see #197, #3186, #3256, #6548

METAPHYSICS

The term "metaphysics" does not appear in P's work (nor in Ar's). It is a much later coinage, as is explained in the introduction to the section on Ar's metaphysics. It is used to describe the study of Being, of what is, of reality. When used in the study of P and other ancient philosophers, metaphysics concerns things that do not change.

The field of metaphysics covers language and logic, for we must talk in a rational fashion about what things are and what their characteristics are. Some terminology which may be unfamiliar to non-specialists is widely used in discussing metaphysics, and a brief explanation may be helpful. The verb "to be" is virtually the foundation of metaphysics. To say that "X is Y" or "X is not Y" is to talk about its being, to predicate something of it. In Greek "to be" is *einai,* while "it is" is *esti* (or *estin*), and the participle "being" is *on,* sometimes used with the article *to,* which means "the" but is often not translated. In the plural the participle becomes *ta onta,* "things which are." From this root the term "ontology" was coined in the seventeenth century. Some scholars use it as a virtual synonym for metaphysics, while others distinguish between the two concepts. The verb "is" can be used in several ways. Used existentially, it asserts that a thing exists: "Socrates is." Used copulatively, it links two things as equal: "Socrates is a man." Used predicatively, it asserts something about a thing: "Socrates is old."

P was not the first metaphysician. The first philosopher worthy of that title was Parmenides (cf. Chapter 6), who asserted that Being is all that exists and that it can be known only through logic. All other sources of knowledge or insight, such as sense impressions or myths, he regarded as merely opinion or illusion. Parmenides made a profound impact on P, who upheld his monism while allowing that the physical world did exist. Knowledge of the world, however, was not true knowledge. What the philosopher must seek is knowledge of true reality.

P's account of reality centers on his theory of Forms (also called Ideas), the unchanging, truly real objects of knowledge. An early version of the theory arguably can be found in S's search for definitions, and the full theory of Forms is developed and made more explicit in the middle dialogues. To what extent P retains or modifies this theory in the later dialogues is a matter of controversy.

In the early dialogues we see S asking questions in the form of "What is x?" where x is usually some ethical concept ("virtue"). In the *Laches* he asks two generals, "What is courage?" In the *Lysis* he asks two friends, "What is friendship?" In the *Hippias Major*, he asks the aesthete Hippias, "What is beauty?" In the *Charmides*, he asks Charmides "What is temperance?" In seeking such definitions S specifies certain conditions which must be met for the definition to be satisfactory. It must be a definition of the essence of a thing, not just an example or several examples.

R. E. Allen (#1808 and #2274) argues that through an investigation of these conditions set forth in the early dialogues we do find a theory of Forms implicit in S's search. This theory involves a metaphysical claim that entities such as courage, friendship, beauty, and holiness actually exist, and that these Forms are universals, standards, and essences. The Forms are universals, S gets Euthyphro to admit in the *Euthyphro*, insofar as the Form of piety is the same in all pious things and that it is something which they all have. The Forms are also standards by which one can tell what things are holy and what are not: "I did not bid you tell me one or two of the many pious actions but that form itself that makes all pious actions pious" (*Euthyphro* 6d-e).

The Forms are, finally, essences. S seeks to discern not just some distinguishing mark of a thing, but its essential nature. The essence of a dog is not its four legs or its tail. To understand the Form of Dogness, one must devise a definition that covers all the individual examples but is not limited by any of them.

While there may be a theory of Forms in the earlier dialogues, with the writing of the *Phaedo* P introduces significant new considerations into his metaphysical thinking which result in what is taken to be *the* Theory of Forms. In the context of arguing that the soul exists prior to birth, S discusses how we come to know Equality:

> We admit, I suppose, that there is such a thing as equality — not the equality of stick to stick and stone to stone, and so on, but something

beyond all that and distinct from it — absolute equality . . . . Was it not from seeing equal sticks or stones or other equal objects that we got the notion of equality, although it is something quite distinct from them. (*Phaedo* 74a-b)

In this passage P is suggesting that there exists a "separation" between Forms and the sensible instances of those Forms. This separation assumes that the sensible instances are in some way deficient or inferior resemblances of the Forms, and these sensible instances are in some way less real than the Forms. These doctrines were not part of the earlier theory, but they constitute the basis of P's "two-worlds" view throughout the middle-period dialogues. There exists the realm of eternal Forms, of which we can have knowledge through reason alone, and there exists the realm of sensible and changing objects, of which we can have only opinion. As P illustrates with the Divided Line Analogy and Cave Analogy in the *Republic*, the intelligible realm of the Forms stands to the visible world of sensibles as originals stand to reflections and shadows, as the fully real to the less real.

The Theory of Forms is the centerpiece of P's metaphysics (as suggested in the introduction to Chapter 12), and thus it is with some surprise that we find in the *Parmenides* what appears to be a searching criticism of the theory. This dialogue begins with the youthful Socrates expressing his commitment to the Theory of Forms, and the elderly Parmenides raising fundamental questions about it. The most famous criticism is what Aristotle termed the Third Man Argument (TMA). It seems to be necessary to assume the existence of a Form to account for the resemblance of different objects in a class. But if this the case, then, Parmenides asks, why not assume the existence of another Form to explain the resemblance between the first Form and the objects, and so on in an infinite regress? The question that arises with respect to the TMA is how does P respond to these criticisms? Is he able to defuse them and maintain the theory? Does he substantially revise the theory? Or does he abandon it altogether?

With this issue the dating of the *Timaeus* becomes important. The *Timaeus* traditionally had been thought to be written late in P's life. The dialogue presents a clear account of the "two-worlds" metaphysics; consequently, it had been believed that P retained his commitment to his metaphysical picture. However, G. E. L. Owen challenged this traditional reading and argued that the *Timaeus* was a middle-period dialogue. This dating has been supported by G. Ryle. If it is correct, then the possibility exists that P rejected the "two-worlds" metaphysics and in the later dialogues began working with a different metaphysics. Nevertheless, H. Cherniss and other scholars have challenged Owen's dating of the dialogue and the suggestion that P gave up his metaphysical theory.

In the *Sophist* we do find an interesting development in P's account of the Forms. In the context of trying to show that negative predications are possible, he introduces the doctrine of the "blending" of the Forms. Heretofore, the Forms had not acted on each other, but now in an effort to address fundamental problems of language and predication, P shows how the Forms can "interact."

ACKRILL, J. L. *"Symploke Eidon,"* in #1809, pp. 199-206; also in #1290, pp. 201-209. This passage, properly understood, indicates that P was moving from the earlier Theory of Forms to a position that discourse depends for its meaning on fixed concepts (*eide*) which can be woven together (*symploke*).   **[1805]**

ALDERMAN, H. "Heidegger on the Nature of Metaphysics." *JBritSocPhen* 2(1971), 12-22. Includes discussion of Heidegger's interpretation of P.   **[1806]**

ALLEN, R. E. "Participation and Predication in Plato's Middle Dialogues," in #1809, pp. 43-60; also in #1290, pp. 167-183. Examines three closely related issues: (1) the nature of Forms, (2) the nature of participation, and (3) the nature of predication. Argues that P is not guilty of confusions surrounding self-predication.   **[1807]**

————. "Plato's Early Theory of Forms," in #1199, pp. 319-334. S works with a Theory of Forms in which Forms are essences, universals, and standards, but these Forms are not same as those in middle dialogues.   **[1808]**

————., ed. *Studies in Plato's Metaphysics.* London: Routledge and Kegan Paul, 1965. Influential collection of articles, each abstracted herein.   **[1809]**

ANNAS, J. "Forms and First Principles." *Phron* 19(1974), 257-283. Translates and discusses twelve neglected arguments from Ar's early polemical work *On the Forms.* Claims arguments show an important shift in P's use of notion of first principle (*arche*) from period of middle dialogues to that of later unwritten doctrines.   **[1810]**

ANSCOMBE, G. E. M. "The New Theory of Forms." *Monist* 50(1966), 403-420. Attempts to delineate the "new" Theory of Forms in two main aspects: participation of one Form in another, and negation and incompatibility.   **[1811]**

BALLARD, E. G. "The Idea of Being. A Platonic Speculation." *TulStudPh* 27(1978), 13-25. Attempts to compose a concept of being from views familiar to readers of P. Good is movement; Rest is the object of intellect. Being is union of these.   **[1812]**

BAMBROUGH, R. "The Disunity of Plato's Thought, or What Plato Did Not Say." *Ph* 47(1972), 295-307. Confusion over whether P held Theory of Forms may arise from his inconsistent use of language of the Theory.   **[1813]**

BESTOR, T. W. "Common Properties and Eponymy in Plato." *PhQ* 28(1978), 189-207. Suggests that for P, Forms are essentially eponyms and particulars are named-after things. He does not seem to have limited eponymous predication to instances where properties are shared. Reply to White (#1952).   **[1814]**

————. "Plato's One/Many Problem and the Question 'What is a Referential Theory of Meaning?'" *PhInv* 4(1981), 1-31. P's worries about One and Many have set pattern for every referential theory of meaning. Priority is usually given to the One, but this pattern should be overturned.   **[1815]**

BIGGER, C. P. *Participation: A Platonic Inquiry.* Baton Rouge: LA State Univ. Pr., 1968. Answer to ontological and epistemological dualism of modernity may be found in pursuit of analogous problem raised by P in his discussion of participation.   **[1816]**

BLUCK, R. S. "Logos and Forms in Plato: A Reply to Professor Cross," in #1809, pp. 33-42. For P, *episteme* of a thing entails ability to give a special kind of logos: not a definition or description that constitutes knowledge, but an explanatory account of the Form in question that indicates its relationship to other Forms. **[1817]**

BOLTON, R. "Plato's Distinction Between Being and Becoming." *RMeta* 29(1975), 66-95. P's conceptions of Being and Becoming change over the dialogues. Final version of distinction between the two remains strong enough to sustain essentials of theory of degrees of reality which the distinction was originally devised to expound. **[1818]**

BONIFAZI, C. *The Soul of the World: An Account of the Inwardness of Things.* Washington, DC: Univ. Pr. of America, 1978. Pursues idea of world-soul from P to Teilhard expressing both a metaphysical dimension in matter and personal character of universe. **[1819]**

BRENTLINGER, J. A. "Particulars in Plato's Middle Dialogues." *AGPh* 54(1972), 116-152. Examines what P means in saying that particulars are less real than forms, his motives for saying this, and how his several motives fit together. **[1820]**

BRINKLEY, R. A. "Plato's Third Man and the Limits of Cognition." *AustlJPh* 60(1982), 152-157. TMA is designed to show that when we think of a Form we transform it into an object, which is all our minds can conceive of. Cognition thus becomes wrapped up in an infinite regress. **[1821]**

CATALDO, P. J. "Plato, Aristotle, and *pros hen* Equivocity." *ModSch* 61(1984), 237-247. Connects Ar's concept of *pros hen* equivocity and P's later metaphysics. **[1822]**

CATAN, J. R. "Plato on Noetic Intermediaries." *Apeir* 3 #2(1969), 14-19. A *physis* is an necessary link between knowledge of Forms and sense awareness. **[1823]**

CAVARNOS, C. *The Classical Theory of Relations: A Study in the Metaphysics of Plato, Aristotle, and Thomism.* Belmont, MA: Inst. for Byzantine & Modern Greek Stud., 1975. Presents views of P, Ar, and Aquinas on relations; argues that the three views have much in common. Challenges claims that P and Ar neglected relations. **[1824]**

CENTORE, F. F. "A Note on T. G. Smith's 'The Theory of Forms, Relations and Infinite Regress'." *Dial*(Can) 8(1970), 678-679. If we assume P's Theory of Forms involves infinite regress, Smith's (#1927a) thesis that there is an infinite regress involved in relations between ideas and their earthly shadows is strengthened. **[1825]**

CHERNISS, H. F. "The Philosophical Economy of the Theory of Ideas," in #1809, pp. 1-12; also in #51, pp. 121-132; also in #1290, pp. 16-27. Reviews motivation for Theory of Forms and how Forms enable P to account for three kinds of phenomena: ethical, epistemological, and ontological. **[1826]**

——. cf. #2031.

CLEGG, J. C. "Self-Predication and Linguistic Reference in Plato's Theory of the Forms." *Phron* 18(1973), 26-43. It is not necessary to attempt to rationalize P's claim that Forms have those properties for which they are Forms (e. g., Justice is just). This is what P means to say. **[1827]**

CODE, A. "Reply to Michael Frede's 'Being and Becoming in Plato'." *OSAP* Suppl. (1988), 53-60. Takes issue with Frede (#1849) on metaphysical conception of realm of becoming when Frede writes, ". . . obviously it is not the case that ordinary objects of experience always are coming into being, but never are." Suggests that P does not agree with this statement.   **[1828]**

CRESSWELL, H. J. "Essence and Existence in Plato and Aristotle." *Theoria* 37(1971), 97-113. P holds that only abstract entities, and not concrete individuals, have essences. Ar maintains that both abstract entities and concrete individuals have essences, but that only the former individuate.   **[1829]**

———. "Is There One or Are There Many One and Many Problems in Plato?" *PhQ* 22(1972), 149-154. Explores difference between the serious form of the problem of the one and the many and trivial form in *Parm, Soph,* and *Philebus.*   **[1830]**

CROSS, R. C. "Logos and Forms in Plato," in #1809, pp. 13-31. Platonic Forms are not universals which exist independently of the sensible world as real entities, but rather Forms are "logical predicates displayed in logoi."   **[1831]**

DE NICOLAS, A. T. "The First Metaphysics: Revisioning Plato," in *New Essays in Metaphysics,* ed. R. C. Neville (Albany: SUNY Pr., 1981), pp. 157-178. Offers an invitation to tackle problem of metaphysics from scratch, and argues that P and his whole project of philosophy has been only partially attended to.   **[1832]**

DENYER, N. "Plato's Theory of Stuffs." *Ph* 58(1983), 315-327. Theory of Forms makes a poor theory of universals, but a good theory of elemental stuffs from which everything is made. Taking Forms as chemical elements instead of universals resolves knottiest problems in the theory.   **[1833]**

DERBOLAV, J. "The Philosophical Origins of Plato's Theory of Ideas." *AGPh* 54(1972), 1-23. P's theory is historical outcome of S's search for absolutes and opposition between Heraclitean and Eleatic views of nature of reality and appearances.   **[1834]**

DEVEREUX, D. T. "Pauline Predications in Plato." *Apeir* 11 #2(1977), 1-4. Challenges Vlastos' claim (#1943) that certain sentences in the dialogues should be read as "Pauline" predications.   **[1835]**

———. cf. #4638.

DE VOGEL, C. J. "Plato's Place in Metaphysics: Italian Reactions to Kraemer's Plato 1982-83," in #1338, pp. 119-127. Review of an important European work. De Vogel finds Kraemer's reading of P too dualistic.   **[1836]**

DOSTAL, R. "Beyond Being: Heidegger's Plato." *JHPh* 23(1985), 71-98. Discusses Heidegger's critique of P and responses to it, primarily by his students. Heidegger seems to have disliked especially P's reliance on myth and his concept of *poiesis* (making or production). Late in his life Heidegger acknowledged some points of contact between his thought and P's.   **[1837]**

EISENBERG, P. D. "More on Non-Being and the One." *Apeir* 10 #1(1976), 6-14. Reply to W. Bondeson (#3187).   **[1838]**

FEIBLEMAN, J. K. "An Updated Version of Plato's Theory of the Ideas." *TulStudPh* 27(1978), 57-67. The empiricist bias of philosophy and science since the seventeenth century has forced P's Theory of Ideas into disfavor. But the results of empirical investigation into the nature of the cosmos suggest the validity, and the need for, P's concept of abstract existents.   [1839]

FINDLAY, J. N. "Essence, Existence and Personality." *IdealStud* 3(1973), 104-116. Attempts to provide a philosophical account of personality within framework of a "more or less" Platonic ontology.   [1840]

——. "The Three Hypostases of Platonism." *RMeta* 28(1974), 660-680. Examines sources in P, especially *Letter* 7, *Tim, Rep, Parm* for Neoplatonic concept of three hypostases: the One, the *Nous*, the *Psyche*. Modern accounts of P have overlooked the ancient Platonic tradition which may have understood him better than we do.   [1841]

FINE, G. "Forms as Causes: Plato and Aristotle," in #4575, pp. 69-112. Ar argues that there are just four sorts of explanatory factors — material, formal, efficient, and final. Platonic Forms are explanatory of sensibles in none of these ways; hence, they contribute nothing to sensibles. Examines how well Ar prosecutes this case.   [1842]

——. "Immanence." *OSAP* 4(1986), 71-97. Certain objections which Ar raises to P's concept of immanence of Forms can be countered by arguments which are implicit in P's writings.   [1843]

——. "The One Over Many." *PhR* 89(1980), 197-240. Reconstructs P's argument that one Form corresponds to every thing for which we have a name and examines Ar's criticism of the argument in the lost *Peri Ideon*.   [1844]

——. "Relational Entities." *AGPh* 65(1983), 225-249. Explores what a relational analysis is, and asks whether P and Ar face certain difficulties with their respective relational accounts.   [1845]

FLOWER, R. J. "The Number of Being." *ModSch* 62(1984), 1-26. Mathematical idea of incommensurable powers sheds light on P's relational concept of "to be."   [1846]

——., and OWEN, G. E. L. "Plato and the Verb 'To Be'." *Apeir* 14(1980), 87-95. P understands "to be" to imply participation, not identity or existence.   [1847]

FORRESTER, J. W. "Some Perils of Paulinity." *Phron* 20(1975), 11-21. Reply to Vlastos (#1943).   [1848]

FREDE, M. "Being and Becoming in Plato." *OSAP* Suppl. (1988), 37-52. P introduces his Forms because he thinks of ordinary objects of experience in a certain way. The many sensible F's display marks of an F without being essentially F.   [1849]

FUJISAWA, N. "*Echein, Metechein*, and Idioms of 'Paradeigmatism' in Plato's Theory of Forms." *Phron* 19(1974), 30-58. Examines "participation" idioms and shows that the Platonic theory is immune to the TMA.   [1850]

GADAMER, H.-G. "Plato and Heidegger," in #78, pp. 45-53. Examines how Heidegger continues certain points of P's doctrines of Being and truth.   [1851]

GOLDSTEIN, L., and MANNICK, P. "The Form of the Third Man Argument." *Apeir* 12 #2(1978), 6-13. In *Parm* S argues for a correlation of Forms and characters. In TMA Parmenides denies that Forms are complete, not that they are unique. He also shows that they cannot have epistemological value which S intends them to. Related aspects of doctrine of Forms are examined in *Soph* and *Philebus*. [1852]

GRISWOLD, C. L. "Plato's Metaphilosophy," in #1282, pp. 1-33. Examines whether P has a "metaphilosophy," what it is, and how he defends it. [1853]

HAMPTON, C. "Plato's Late Ontology: A Riddle Unresolved." *AncPh* 8(1988), 105-116. Reply to K. Sayre (#1918). [1854]

HARE, R. M. "A Question about Plato's Theory of Ideas," in *Essays on Philosophical Method* (London: Macmillan, 1971), pp. 54-79. When P speaks of seeing an Idea he seems to have meant something like "forming a mental image." [1855]

HARPER, A. W. J. "On the Theory of Forms." *Dial*(Can) 10(1971), 558-560. In theorizing about Forms, we do not deal directly with Forms themselves, but with a symbolization of them. [1856]

HEINAMAN, R. "Self-Predication in Plato's Middle Dialogues." *Phron* 34(1989), 56-79. Challenges recent interpretations of various statements "F-ness is F" which argue that P is not asserting that the Form F-ness possesses the property F. [1857]

HINNERS, R. C. *Ideology and Analysis: A Rehabilitation of Metaphysical Ontology.* Paris: Desclée De Brouwe, 1966. In context of attempting to rehabilitate metaphysics, examines P's efforts to develop a formulation of Socratic faith in universal definitions. Focuses on Sun Simile, Divided Line and Cave Analogies. [1858]

IRWIN, T. H. "Plato's Heracleiteanism." *PhQ* 27(1977), 1-13. P's Heracleiteanism, and Ar's account of it, can be understood by reference to arguments for Theory of Forms, quite apart from doctrine of flux in *Theaet.* [1859]

JONES, R. "Plato's Analogy of Beauty." *MidwJPh* 2(1974), 13-21. P uses beauty analogically as a medium through which one can come to see connection between Forms and appearances. [1860]

JORDAN, R.W. *Plato's Arguments for Forms.* Cambridge Philological Soc., 1983. Shows that P's arguments for existence of Forms reveal concern with nature of knowledge and explanation and also interest in analysis of apparent contradictions presented to intellect by sensible world. [1861]

KAHN, C. H. "The Meaning of 'Justice' and the Theory of Forms." *JPh* 69(1972), 567-579. Examines P's theory of meaning, which is essentially a theory of naming,. and applies the concept to discussion of justice in *Rep.* [1862]

————. "Retrospect on the Verb 'To Be' and the Concept of Being," in #61, pp. 1-28. Trying to find in P a distinction between different senses of *esti* (such as the "is" of identity, the "is" of existence, the copulative "is," and the generic "is") is not well suited to way concept of being was actually used by ancients. [1863]

———. "Some Philosophical Uses of 'To Be' in Plato." *Phron* 26(1981), 105-134. Discusses passages where P uses *einai* in connection with notion of truth.   [1864]

KATES, C. A. "Heidegger and the Myth of the Cave." *Pers* 50(1969), 532-548. Critically examines and rejects Heidegger's interpretation of Theory of Ideas and his characterization of P as first metaphysical rationalist.   [1865]

KETCHUM, R. J. "Plato on Real Being." *AmPhQ* 17(1980), 213-220. Defends plausibility of reality doctrine without attributing some special sense to words "real" or "really."   [1866]

KIRWAN, C. "Plato and Relativity." *Phron* 19(1974), 112-129. In its classic form (in *Phaedo* and *Rep*) Theory of Ideas is based on apparently incompatible opposites. But those opposites are seen to be compatible because of their relativity. P's development of this concept was incomplete.   [1867]

LEE, J. S. "D. M. Armstrong and Platonic Realism." *SJPh* 17(1979), 371-385. Attempts to reconstruct an outline of Platonic realism in light of Armstrong's work.   [1868]

LEWIS, F. A. "Did Plato Discover the *Estin* of Identity?" *CSCA* 8(1975), 113-143. Nothing in P's texts nor in his philosophical theories requires a special sense of *estin* ("is") beyond the copulative.   [1869]

———. "Plato on 'Not'." *CSCA* 9(1976), 89-115. P distinguishes between sentences which state non-identity and those with negative predicates. He does not try to analyze such sentences but to explain how negative predicate can have meaning.   [1870]

———. "Plato's Third Man Argument and the 'Platonism' of Aristotle," in #45, pp. 133-174. Ar has no satisfactory argument to show that P must accept a certain principle of predication.   [1871]

LOSONCY, T. A. "The Platonic Ideas: Some Permanent Contributions to Mediaeval Philosophies of Man." *Diot* 7(1979), 105-110. Endeavors to identify Platonic notion of immaterial as such and to show that basic insight remains a key element in medieval philosophies of man.   [1872]

MADIGAN, A. "Syrianus and Asclepius on Forms and Intermediates in Plato and Aristotle." *JHPh* 24(1986), 149-171. Studies commentaries of Syrianus and Asclepius and their respective views on Platonic forms.   [1873]

MALCOLM, J. "On the Place of the *Hippias Major* in the Development of Plato's Thought." *AGPh* 50(1968), 189-195. Dialogue helps us understand transition of P's thought from early to middle periods, especially in terms of theory of Forms.   [1874]

———. "Semantics and Self-Predication in Plato." *Phron* 26(1981), 286-294. Examines connection between predicates and Forms in *Parm* 133d.   [1875]

———. "Vlastos on Pauline Predication." *Phron* 30(1985), 79-91. Reply to #1943 and #2620.   [1876]

MATES, B. "Identity and Predication in Plato." *Phron* 24(1979), 211-229; also in #61,

pp. 29-48. Verb "to be" can be consistently understood as having a single sense throughout P's texts; such an interpretation does less violence to his doctrines than do views
which see "to be" as having two or more senses.   **[1877]**

McPHERRAN, M. L. "Plato's Particulars." *SJPh* 26(1988), 527-553. Argues for a new
theory of P's middle-dialogue particulars. They are "Form-bare" possessors of immanent
characters; "they possess no essential properties for which there exist Forms, and what
few essential properties they do have are not due to participation."   **[1878]**

McTIGHE, T. P. "Scotus, Plato and the Ontology of the Bare X." *Monist* 49(1965), 588-
616. P's One and Quine's referant for singular terms are quite similar.   **[1879]**

MICHAELIDES, C. "The Concept of Not-Being in Plato." *Diot* 3(1975), 19-26.
Examines P's attempts to deal with nihilistic consequences of Parmenides' view that not-
being is inexpressible and unthinkable.   **[1880]**

MICHELSEN, J. M. "Plato and Santayana: Forms, Flux, and the Ideal of Human
Existence." *Diot* 8(1980), 72-80. Traces differences between positions of P and
Santayana in philosophy of mind, epistemology, and axiology.   **[1881]**

MODRAK, F. A. "Forms and Compounds," in #45, pp. 85-100. Examines metaphysical
problem of whether acceptance of "Socrates is a man" involves commitment to a third
type of metaphysical predication, predication of a species or a form of a concrete individual. Considers linguistic problem concerning relationship between linguistic predication
and metaphysical predication.   **[1882]**

MOHR, R. D. "Family Resemblance, Platonism, Universals." *CanJPh* 7(1977), 593-600.
Wittgenstein's theory of family resemblance, though sufficient to refute a theory of universals as common properties, is not sufficient to refute a theory of universals, like P's,
which takes universals as standards.   **[1883]**

──────. "Forms in Plato's *Euthydemus*." *Hermes* 112(1984), 296-300. Proper reading of
300e1-301c2 makes it clear that P sees Forms as real and transcendental.   **[1884]**

──────. "Plato On Time and Eternity." *AncPh* 6(1986), 39-46. Forms of P are eternal in
that they are timeless, not in that they endure infinitely through time.   **[1885]**

MORAVCSIK, J. M. E. "The Anatomy of Plato's Divisions," in #65, pp. 324-348.
Method of Division must be seen as another stage in development of Theory of
Forms.   **[1886]**

──────. "Recollecting the Theory of Forms." in #1293, pp. 1-20. Develops a conceptual
scheme that would account for several functions of Forms and explain why commentators
disagree so widely over role of Forms.   **[1887]**

MOREAU, J. "The Platonic Idea and its Threefold Function: A Synthesis." *IntPhQ*
9(1969), 477-517. The Platonic Idea serves three functions: gnoseological, axiological,
cosmological.   **[1888]**

MORRIS, T. F. "How Can One Form Be in Many Things?" *Apeir* 19(1985), 53-56. It
is possible to say that many things participate in one Form if we say that each thing has

an image of the Form in it.   [1889]

MOURELATOS, A. P. D. "'Nothing' as 'Not-Being': Some Literary Contexts that Bear on Plato," in #48, pp. 319-329; also in #42, pp. 59-69. Earlier writers use terms for "not-being" that can be taken as characterizing rather than predicating, in the way English can say "he's nobody," i. e., unimportant. Such usages prefigure P's concept of degrees of reality.   [1890]

————. cf. #552.

MULHERN, J. J. "Professor Wedberg's Theory of Ideas and Suggestions for Modification." *Apeir* 9(1975), 25-29. Examines Wedberg's (#1948) theory-construction approach to Theory of Ideas and argues that Wedberg's approach fails to reflect that dialogues recognize participation as only one of several relations individuals might have to Ideas.   [1891]

NAILS, D. "*Ousia* in the Platonic Dialogues." *SwJPh* 10(1979), 71-77. P did not consider the concept of *ousia* to be ontologically fundamental. When used without qualifiers, it is not the equivalent of *to on* or *to esti*.   [1892]

NEHAMAS, A. "Confusing Universals and Particulars in Plato's Early Dialogues." *RMeta* 29(1975), 287-306. Contrary to common views, P's early dialogues do not show S's interlocutors as confused between notions of universal and particular.   [1893]

————. "Participation and Predication in Plato's Later Thought." *RMeta* 36(1982), 343-374. In late dialogues, P distinguishes "self-participation" from "self-predication," and thus takes a major step in articulation of notion of predication.   [1894]

————. "Plato on the Imperfection of the Sensible World." *AmPhQ* 12(1975), 105-117. P never held that sensible objects possess their properties only approximately while the Forms possess them exactly. The imperfection consists in that sensible objects possess their properties exactly but accidentally.   [1895]

————. "Self-Predication and Plato's Theory of Forms." *AmPhQ* 16(1979), 93-103. Self-predication is accepted as obvious by both P and his audience. Denies that P had an articulated notion of predication, and his middle Theory of Forms is seen as his attempt to arrive at that notion.   [1896]

O'CONNELL, R. J. *An Introduction to Plato's Metaphysics*. New York: Fordham Univ. Pr., 1985. Chapters discuss *arete*, gods, epistemology, Ideas, soul, and other facets of P's metaphysics. Begins from assumption that P worked his way to metaphysical problems from his concern with ethical and political questions. For non-specialists.   [1897]

OLSHEWSKY, T. M. "The Ideas, the Actual and the Human Condition." *PhInq* 1(1979), 129-140. Compares P's and Ar's views on Form, and explores the different perspectives on the human condition.   [1898]

————. "On the Relations of Soul and Body in Plato and Aristotle." *JHPh* 14(1976), 391-404. Examines P's view that the soul is in the body and Ar's account that the body is in the soul.   [1899]

OSTENFELD, E. N. *Forms, Matter and Mind: Three Strands in Plato's Metaphysics.* The Hague: Nijhoff, 1982. New interpretation of P's conception of man based on an examination of three interrelated strands of Forms, matter, and mind. Argues that P's conception of man is an integrated part of his metaphysics.   [1900]

———. "Plato's Concept of Matter," in *Classica et mediaevalia F. Blatt septuagenario dedicata*, ed. O. S. Due et al (Copenhagen: Gyldendal, 1973), pp. 47-67. P describes matter as a matrix, made up of irregular, undifferentiated bodies, which are transformed into disorganized "powers." Demiurge works on this matter to organize it into solid, regular bodies which are referred to in *Parm* and *Phaedo* as "Forms in *nous*."   [1901]

OWEN, G. E. L. "A Proof in the *Peri Ideon*," in #1809, pp. 293-312. Seeks to show sense and provenance of most complex and puzzling of Ar's surviving arguments against existence of Forms.   [1902]

PANAGIOTOU, S. "Relations and Infinite Regress in Plato." *Dial*(Can) 13(1974), 537-542. By introducing Form of Participation P does not fall into a circular argument, nor does he set up an infinite regress.   [1903]

PATTERSON, R. *Image and Reality in Plato's Metaphysics.* Indianapolis: Hackett, 1985. Examines P's theory of Forms and argues that they should be spoken of as Forms and not as structures or patterns or sets or Fregean concepts.   [1904]

———. "On the Eternality of Platonic Forms." *AGPh* 67(1985), 27-46. Explores in what way Forms are eternal, and how this eternaltiy is related to their "truly real being," their intelligibility, immutability, and separateness from the sensible world.   [1905]

PENNER, T. *The Ascent from Nominalism: Some Existence Arguments in Plato's Middle Dialogues.* Dordrecht, Netherlands: Reidel, 1987. Seeks to discover what Platonic Forms are by asking how P argues for their existence. Examines two middle-period existence arguments and finds them to be anti-nominalist.   [1906]

PINTO, W. "Degrees of Reality in Plato." *JWVaPhSoc* 13(1978), 6-8. Offers explanation of P's degrees of reality theory which need not involve self-predication.   [1907]

PRIOR, W. J. "The Concept of *Paradeigma* in Plato's Theory of Forms." *Apeir* 17(1983), 33-42. Challenges view that P's assertion that Forms are paradigms commits him to view that they are exemplars.   [1908]

———. *Unity and Development in Plato's Metaphysics.* Lasalle, IL: Open Court, 1985. Discusses development of P's metaphysics and focuses òn two central doctrines: the Theory of Forms and doctrine of Being and Becoming. In the *Tim* and *Soph* P augments and clarifies his metaphysics to address objections of *Parm*.   [1909]

RAVEN, J. E. *Plato's Thought in the Making: A Study of the Development of His Metaphysics.* Cambridge Univ. Pr., 1965. Focuses on middle dialogues to discuss development of P's metaphysics. Explores two questions: Where does S end and P begin? What led P beyond his master's positions?   [1910]

RINGBOM, S. "Plato on Images." *Theoria* 31(1965), 86-109. Images serve as metaphysical models; they also provide an explanation of objects they represent and an argument for their value.   **[1911]**

RIST, J. M. "Plato's 'Earlier Theory of Forms'?" *Phoenix* 29(1975), 336-356. Reply to Allen (#2274), No indication of a theory of Forms can be found before *Symp* and *Phaedo*. Early dialogues represent a "period of intellectual puzzlement" as P tried to identify common qualities.   **[1912]**

———. cf. #1652.

ROHR, M. D. "Empty Forms in Plato." *AGPh* 60(1978), 268-283; longer version in *Reforging the Great Chain of Being. Studies in the History of Modal Theories*, ed. S. Knuuttila (Dordrecht, Nether.: Reidel, 1981), pp. 19-56. No Form can be permanently empty, and there can be no Form which never has any particulars as instances. **[1913]**

ROSS, D. *Plato's Theory of Ideas.* Westport, CT: Greenwood Pr., 1976; rprt. Discusses origins and developments of Theory of Forms, and concludes that P "seems never to have brought his 'highest Ideas' into a single system."   **[1914]**

ROSS, R. R. N. "Tillich and Plato." *Sophia* 15(1976), 26-29. Analysis of resemblance between Tillich's concept of "being-itself" and P's theory of Ideas.   **[1915]**

ROSS, S. D. "Plato: The Heresy of Reason," in *Metaphysical Aporia and Philosophical Heresy* (Albany: SUNY Pr., 1989), pp. 31-88. P's philosophical doctrine cannot be separated from the dialogic form in which it is presented. Theory of Forms should be revised to show that the relationship between the eternal and the changeable is aporetic. Reason is a matter of telling stories about the most profound truths. Those truths cannot be restated in words other than P's without imposing doctrine on him. **[1916]**

———. *Transition to an Ordinal Metaphysics.* Albany: SUNY Pr., 1980. Includes discussion of strengths and weaknesses of P's theory of Forms over against other approaches to metaphysics.   **[1917]**

SAYRE, K. M. *Plato's Late Ontology: A Riddle Resolved.* Princeton Univ. Pr., 1983. Maintains that P did not abandon theory of Forms in his late works but did deny their separation from sensibles. Analyzes *Parm* and *Philebus* in particular.   **[1918]**

SCHIPPER, E. W. *Forms in Plato's Later Dialogues.* The Hague: Nijhoff, 1965. Doctrine of Forms is incompletely explained in the dialogues through *Rep*, and is not abandoned in later dialogues, but rather developed and made more precise.   **[1919]**

———. "Is Plato an Idealist?" *StudGen* 24(1971), 583-597. Examination of several dialogues suggests that P is not an idealist but does prefigure idealism.   **[1920]**

———. cf. #3248.

SCOLNICOV, S. *Plato's Metaphysics of Education.* New York: Routledge, 1988. Aims to show how P develops his metaphysics with a view to supporting his deepest educational convictions. Leads from reaction of S against relativism of Sophists to P's mature conception of education as a profound transformation of personality, to his considerations about education as development of reason.   **[1921]**

SEASE, V. W. "The Myth in Plato's Theory of Ideas." *SwJPh* 1(1970), 186-197. Examines P's use of myth and metaphorical, imaginative language, particularly with reference to their implications for interpreting his theory of Ideas. His use of myth provides insufficient evidence for supposing that he considers his Ideas to be in principle extra-logical in character.   **[1922]**

SELIGMAN, P. "Being and Forms in Plato," in #68, pp. 18-32. Platonic Forms, the only things which truly are, are reflected in sensible things which come to be and pass away. Only by having a tenuous link with the Forms can the things of this world be said to exist at all.   **[1923]**

SHARVY, R. "Plato's Causal Logic and the Third Man Argument." *Nous* 20(1986), 507-530. Offers a new analysis of TMA, stressing causal role of Forms and Self-Predication principle as subordinate. TMA does not depend on suppressed premises.   **[1924]**

SHOREY, P. "A Dissertation on Plato's Theory of Forms and on the Concepts of the Human Mind." *AncPh* 2(1982), 1-59. Transl. by R. S. W. Hawtrey of Shorey's 1884 dissertation on Forms which argues that P's initial purpose was to lay foundation of logic and avoid Sophists' objections. This led him to Forms by three main routes: search for definitions, investigation of true causes, and psychological investigation of source and nature of learning and knowledge.   **[1925]**

SMITH, P. C. "H. G. Gadamer's Heideggerian Interpretation of Plato." *JBritSocPhen* 12(1981), 211-230. Examines Heidegger's critique of P as "metaphysical" and Gadamer's expansion and modification of that critique.   **[1926]**

SMITH, R. "Mass Terms, Generic Expressions, and Plato's Theory of Form." *JHPh* 16(1978), 141-153. Attempts to make P's introduction of Forms and his language about them plausibly uncontroversial to common sense.   **[1927]**

SMITH, T. G. "The Theory of Forms, Relations, and Infinite Regress." *Dial*(Can) 8(1969), 116-123. Argues that there is an infinite regress underlying relations between Forms and their images.   **[1927a]**

SPELLMAN, L. "Patterns and Copies: The Second Version of the Third Man." *PacPhQ* 64(1983), 165-175. Likeness is a symmetrical relationship. Parmenides' objection is correct.   **[1928]**

STAHL, D. E. "Nehamas on Platonic Predication." *Apeir* 18(1984), 31-33. Reply to #1893.   **[1929]**

STRANG, C. "Plato and the Third Man," in #1290, pp. 184-200. Discusses why P abandoned Theory of Forms. Its limited epistemological value was the most important reason. The TMA is P's justification for his decision.   **[1930]**

SWEENEY, L. "A. E. Taylor On Socrates and Plato." *SwJPh* 8(1977), 79-99. Examines and challenges Taylor's interpretation of Theory of Forms.   **[1931]**

———. "Participation in Plato's Dialogues: *Phaedo, Parmenides, Sophist, Timaeus.*" *NewSchol* 62(1988), 125-149. Gives an overview of what P intends by "participation" in several dialogues. *Phaedo* shows Forms as present in things; *Parm* adds idea of cause;

Soph stresses reality of Forms and intelligence; in *Tim* Forms are goals. **[1932]**

TELOH, H. *The Development of Plato's Metaphysics.* University Park: Penn. St. Univ. Pr., 1981. P modifies, even changes, his basic metaphysical positions. Focus of early dialogues is *psyche*. Middle dialogues contain two distinct theories of separate Forms. *Soph* and *Philebus* use kinds, not Forms, to solve their respective problems. **[1933]**

———. "The Isolation and Connection of the Forms in Plato's Middle Dialogues." *Apeir* 10 #1(1976), 20-23. In middle dialogues P moves from viewing Forms as separate from physical world and eternal to seeing them as interconnected. **[1934]**

———. "Self-Predication or Anaxogorean Causation in Plato." *Apeir* 9 #2(1975), 15-23. P's self-predicational statements arise from an Anaxagorean account of causation: a cause must have the quality that it produces in something else. **[1935]**

———, and **LOUZECKY, D. J.** "Plato's Third Man Argument." *Phron* 17(1972). 80-84. Examines controversy between Vlastos and Sellars, which began in 1950's. One must take P's phrase *hen hekaston eidos* as one and multiple at same time. **[1936]**

TURNBULL, R. G. "Knowledge and the Forms in the Later Platonic Dialogues." *Proceedings and Addresses of the American Philosophical Association* 51(1978) 735-758. Presents a "big picture" of philosophy of later Platonic dialogues. Argues that P would take seriously possibility that some conventional languages may be quite inadequate as vehicles for exercise of conceptual abilities. **[1937]**

VATER, M. G. "The Human Mind as 'Idea' in the Platonic Tradition and in Spinoza." *Diot* 8(1980), 134-143. Considers teaching, common to P, Plotinus, and Spinoza, that the human mind is not a passive faculty that has ideas, but is itself an idea. **[1938]**

VAUGHT, C. G. "Participation and Imitation in Plato's Metaphysics," in #44, pp. 17-31. Relationship between Forms and things is not satisfactorily explained by P. Metaphors of participation, imitation, resemblance and causality should be taken seriously as explanations. **[1939]**

VLASTOS, G. "Degrees of Reality in Plato," in #1268, pp. 1-19. Examines what is the sense of "real" and "reality" when P says that the Form is "completely" or "purely" or "perfectly" real. Seeks to find why P thinks Forms are "more real" than their sensible instances, and then evaluates doctrine. **[1940]**

———. "A Metaphysical Paradox," in #1292, pp. 43-57. Investigates P's view that Form of the Bed is the "real" bed, while the physical bed is not "perfectly real," and considers different senses of "real." **[1941]**

———. "More on Pauline Predictions in Plato," in #1292, pp. 318-322. Seeks to give a more sympathetic understanding of P's unawareness of ambiguity surrounding different kinds of predication. **[1942]**

———. "A Note on 'Pauline Predications' in Plato." *Phron* 19(1974), 95-101. Argues that we are to read "Justice is pious" as "Justice is such that anyone who has this property is [necessarily] pious." **[1943]**

————. "On a Proposed Redefinition of 'Self-Predication' in Plato." *Phron* 26(1981), 76-79. A logical re-evaluation of self-predication, responding in part to Nehamas (#1894). Challenges Nehamas' proposed account of self-predication ("Justice is just," "Beauty is beautiful").   **[1944]**

————. "Self-Predication and Self-Participation in Plato's Later Period." *PhR* 78(1969), 74-78; also in #1292, pp. 335-341. Challenges thesis that P abandons doctrine of self-predication in *Parm.*   **[1945]**

————. "'Separation' in Plato." *OSAP* 5(1987), 187-195. In Platonic corpus, and also in Ar's testimony about P, same metaphysical claim may be expressed by either "The forms exist 'themselves by themselves'" or "The forms exist 'separately'."   **[1946]**

WATERLOW, S. "The Third Man's Contribution to Plato's Paradigmatism." *Mind* 91(1982), 339-357. TMA provides a transition from metaphysics of *Rep* to P's position in *Tim.* TMA is harmless to *Tim*'s view in which Demiurge is assumed.   **[1947]**

WEDBERG, A. "The Theory of Ideas," in #1290, pp. 28-52. Overview emphasizing importance of math and dialectic in the development of the theory.   **[1948]**

WHITE, D. A. "Truth and Being: A Critique of Heidegger on Plato." *M&W* 7(1974), 118-134. Summarizes Heidegger's interpretation and discusses problems centering on the attitude with which he approached P. His reading of P is flawed by his poor grasp of Theory of Forms.   **[1949]**

WHITE, F. C. "The Compresence of Opposites in *Phaedo* 102." *CQ* 27(1977), 303-311. Reply to #1867. Theory of Forms outlined in *Phaedo* is same as in *Parm.*   **[1950]**

————. "Plato on Naming-After." *PhQ* 29(1979), 255-259. Against T. Bestor (#1814) defends argument that P's theory of eponymous predication could not succeed in freeing him from difficulties of TMA.   **[1951]**

————. "Plato's Middle Dialogues and the Independence of Particulars." *PhQ* 27(1977), 193-213. Reflection doctrine (particulars are reflections which share no properties univocally with their originals) is irrelevant; the theory of eponymous predication means that Forms are only grammatically self-predicating and makes it impossible to see them as causes, transcendent goals, or objects of knowledge.   **[1952]**

————. *Plato's Theory of Particulars.* New York: Arno Pr., 1981. Particulars are as important as Forms in P's metaphysics. Initially P understood particulars as individuals with their own essences. He came to regard them as lacking essences, with nothing but accidents to distinguish them. Finally he dispensed with them altogether.   **[1953]**

————. "Problems of Particulars in Plato's Later Dialogues." *Apeir* 16(1982), 53-62. Examines P's comments about relations of particulars and Forms in *Parm*, *Soph*, and *Philebus* about particulars, which involve two problems, not just one.   **[1954]**

————. "Sensible Particulars in Plato's Ontology." *Antich* 10(1976), 8-21. Examines recent interpretations of P's arguments about particulars and Forms and finds that he distinguishes clearly between them.   **[1955]**

WHITTAKER, J. "The Eternity of the Platonic Forms." *Phron* 13(1968), 131-144. Examines whether Forms are eternal in sense that they endure everlastingly, or whether their eternity is such that it transcends duration; argues that the latter interpretation rests on an insecure basis. [1956]

WOODRUFF, P. "The Socratic Approach to Semantic Incompleteness." *Ph&PhenRes* 38(1978), 453-468. Like S, P tried to apply terms to different objects only when they shared a common characteristic. This approach proved impractical. P did not as a result abandon Theory of Forms but rejected sensible world as imperfect. [1957]

YARTZ, F. J. "Infinite Regress and the Sense World in Plato." *SwJPh* 6(1975), 17-28. P's early attempts to base definitions on division (analysis) leads to an infinite regress which is finally overcome in the intuition of the Ideas. [1958]

ZYCINSKI, J. "A Return to Plato in the Philosophy of Substance?" *NewSchol* 63(1989), 419-434. In the late twentieth century science has moved from viewing nature in Aristotelian terms and has redeveloped an interest in the concept of Forms and mathematical descriptions of reality. [1959]

For related items see #241, #1162, #1762, #2556, #2586, #2935, #3069, #3099, #3499, #3534, #4322, #4413, #4618, #4644

POLITICS

P's reputation as a political philosopher has not fared well in modern times. As one scholar says, it is "not uncommon for a man who is most successful as a moral philosopher to come badly to grief in exploring the principles of politics. Plato is here a classically awful example." He is often depicted as a proto-Nazi, the originator of a rigidly controlled state in which an elite group of Guardians are allowed to lie to the populace at large.

In all fairness to P, one should distinguish between his political theories and his attitude toward politicians. His political thought was profoundly influenced by his reaction against the Athenian democracy which had put S to death and his admiration for the orderly system which had been functioning smoothly in Sparta for several centuries. Sparta limited its citizenship, and its elite group spent their entire lives in military training and running the government. In Athens, as S often points out in the dialogues, the citizen body was much larger and anyone could participate in governing the state, regardless of his background or training. The Athenians expected a shoemaker or stonemason to have some sort of training. There was a skill (*techne*) involved in such occupations, which had to be learned before one was allowed to present oneself as an expert. But everyone was considered an expert in the affairs of the *polis*, i. e., in politics. Most of the offices, except for commanders of the army, were chosen by lot.

This system produced a form of government that appeared chaotic to other Greeks. The Assembly, in which all citizens were free to speak, could vote one way today and be persuaded tomorrow to change its mind. (In one famous instance an execution order was decreed by the assembly. The next day the citizens overturned that decision and had to send out a fast boat in hopes of overtaking the boat sent to carry out the previous day's order.) In the turmoil

of the Peloponnesian War (431-404 B. C.) one faction or another seized control
of the Assembly and prosecuted the war vigorously or sought peace with Sparta.
As a young man P became disgusted with what appeared to him an inefficient,
often inept, form of government and declined to pursue a political career. After
the democracy put S to death, P's hostility to it became absolute. In *Rep* 496c
he sneers at "the madness of the majority, that practically never does one act
sanely in public affairs." The philosophically enlightened man is better off to
remain aloof from the entire process. S expresses a similar sentiment in *Apol*
31d: "no man can remain alive who genuinely opposes you or any other crowd
and prevents you from doing many wrong and unlawful deeds in the state."

But P was faced with a dilemma. People live in communities and, as S had
recognized, improving the community will improve the people who live in it. (Of
course, one could argue the other way around, but the ancient Greeks were
oriented to the community, not given over to individualism, as the modern world
is.) If the community of citizens are not capable of improving themselves and
will not of their own will listen to someone like S, whose divinely inspired mission
in life was to make the citizens of Athens aware of their potential (*Gorgias* 521d),
then it becomes incumbent on those who have been enlightened to direct the
course of the state in the best interests of the unenlightened.

The possibilities for abuse in such an approach are immediately evident to
us, perhaps because we have heard such arguments used as a rationale for
oppressive dictatorships. But P thought it possible to educate an elite class who
could then dedicate themselves to ruling the city, sacrificing their own self-
interest for the benefit of the community. In the *Republic* and the *Laws* he outlines plans for instituting such a state, clearly based on the Spartan model.
Sparta was admired by other ancient Greeks because its form of government resisted revolution for several centuries and its ruling class rejected all notions of
private property.

Did P think that such a state could ever actually exist? That question has
received much attention in modern debates on his political theory. He never attempted to introduce his reforms in Athens itself; the common citizenry would
have had no part of them. He was invited to Syracuse by the tyrant Dionysius
I to instruct his son Dionysius II in statecraft. The younger man, however,
proved a difficult pupil. P made three visits to Syracuse and was treated like a
virtual prisoner on the last. The *Letters* attributed to P discuss his relations with
the Syracusan dynasty and his disappointment in young Dionysius.

Several facets of P's political theory have received close attention from
modern scholars. It is a thorough- going communism. The guardians (the
philosopher-rulers) are to have their necessities provided by the state and to
share everything, including wives. The fact that he allows women a role in
governing his ideal state seems quite extraordinary when one considers that
women were not even citizens in Athens or any other Greek city. (The idea of
women having political power, so utterly ludicrous to the Athenians, formed the
basis of one of Aristophanes' plays, *Women in the Assembly*.) Serious concern
has been expressed over P's advocacy of the "noble lie," the concept that the
guardians may deceive the lower classes for the benefit of the state.

Those interested in P's political views should also see the sections on his dialogues, the *Laws* and the *Republic*.

ADKINS, A. W. H. "*Polupragmosune* and Minding One's Own Business." *CPh* 71(1976), 301-327. By P's time the term *polupragmosune* (interfering in others' business) came to mean the same as *hybris* (excess). He considers *arete* to be a mean between interfering and withdrawing from politics. **[1960]**

BAMBROUGH, R. *Plato, Popper, and Politics: Some Contributions to a Modern Controversy.* New York: Barnes & Noble, 1967. Collected essays, abstracted. **[1961]**

——. "Plato's Modern Friends and Enemies," in #1961, pp. 3-19. Offers general review of main philosophical and political issues which are invloved in the controversy over interpretation of P's "political" doctrines. **[1962]**

——. "Plato's Poltical Analogies," in #1961, pp. 152-170; also #1291, pp. 187-205. P tends to stress definitive answers to deliberative questions. He employs certain analogies repeatedly, especially comparison of state to a ship and political science to medical knowledge. **[1963]**

BARROW, R. "Plato and Politics." *Didaskalos* 5(1977), 410-421. P did not oppose democracy, nor did he favor violent overthrow of a government. The Academy was not a training school for political activists. **[1964]**

BROWNING, G. K. "Plato and Hegel: Reason, Redemption and Political Theory." *HPolTho* 8(1987), 377-393. Compares political theories of P and Hegel, focusing on their common recognition of significance of social life, on their efforts to outline political communities which overcome alienation and disharmony, and their differing conceptions of reason and its role in social life. **[1965]**

CACOULLOS, A. R. "Philosophy and Politics: Some Notes on the Paradox of the Philosopher-King." *Diot* 3(1975), 27-33. For P, philosophy and politics are not logically incompatible, but can be mutually reinforcing. Philosopher is required to govern for good of community. **[1966]**

CAMPBELL, B. "Thought and Political Action in Athenian Tradition: The Emergence of the 'Alienated Intellectual'." *HPolTho* 5(1984), 17-60. P's sense of alienation from contemporary politics resulted not only from a difficult political situation, but also an unrealistic ideal of the politican role of the intellectual. **[1967]**

DERRIDA, J. "Plato's Pharmacy," in *Dissemination*, trans. B. Johnson (Univ. of Chicago Pr., 1981), pp. 61-171. Discusses the "remedy" or "poison" (*pharmakon*) of political lies which P advocates for the rulers of his ideal state. **[1968]**

DOWNEY, G. "The Ethical City, the Secular City, and the City of God." *AngThR* 56(1974), 34-41. Compares concepts of city in P, Ar, and Augustine. **[1969]**

FASTIGGI, R. L. "Law and Morality: The Lessons of Plato and Aristotle." *JDharma* 4(1979), 347-358. P and Ar view law and morality as intimately related. P maintains that the state should pattern its laws on divine *logos*. Ar, more realistically, sees law as providing guidance in formation of ethical habits.   **[1970]**

FEUER, L. S. "Generational Struggle in Plato and Aristotle," in *The Conflict of Generations in Ancient Greece and Rome*, ed. S. Bertman (Amsterdam: Gruener, 1975), pp. 123-127. Both P and Ar see strife between older and younger generations as necessary for political change.   **[1971]**

FIELD, G. C. "On Misunderstanding Plato," in #1961, pp. 71-84. Considers main accusations against P's politics and their validity in light of what P actually says.   **[1972]**

FOSTER, M. *The Political Philosophies of Plato and Hegel.* New York: Garland, 1984; rprt. Contrasts the political philosophies of P and Hegel by distinguishing between Greek conception of *polis* and modern conception of "state."   **[1973]**

FRIEDRICH, C. J. "Plato's Idea of Justice and the Political Elite," in *An Introduction to Political Theory.* New York: Harper & Row, 1967. Discusses P's views in context of a more general theoretical analysis of problems of justice and the elite.   **[1974]**

GILL, C. "Plato and Politics. The *Critias* and the *Politicus*." *Phron* 24(1979), 148-167. Response to G. E. L. Owen (#3505).   **[1975]**

GOLDING, M. P., and **GOLDING, N. H.** "Population policy in Plato and Aristotle. Some Value Issues." *Arethusa* 8(1975), 345-358. P views optimum population as one large enough to defend polis and small enough to live in it. Ar wants a population that is self-sufficient and can be surveyed. Their views on eugenics, abortion, and birth control are too vague to be elaborated.   **[1976]**

GRISWOLD, C. L. "Politike Episteme in Plato's *Statesman*," in #1267, pp. 141-167. P admits that in our mundane world knowledge of "political science" is imperfect. Best government will involve a number of people in an effort to make our knowledge of political science less imperfect. Thus, for P, ideal state would be a democracy. **[1977]**

HAHM, D. E. "Plato's Noble Lie and Political Brotherhood." *C&M* 30(1969), 211-227. Examines literary art P uses to express idea of political brotherhood and not merely idea of general kinship.   **[1978]**

ISRAEL, R. "Plato Versus Popper." *Kinesis* 3(1971), 103-110. Examines P's political philosophy and Popper's attack on this philosophy.   **[1979]**

JACKSON, M. W. "Plato's Political Analogies." *IntStudPh* 20(1988), 27-42. Defends P's use of analogies for describing politics against Bambrough (#1963). The context of the dialogues in which they appear provides a key for their interpretation.   **[1980]**

KALLA, S. "Plato's Political Thought: A Critique of Popper's Interpretation." *JIndCPhRes* 2(1985), 77-88. Challenges Popper's interpretation (#2005) that P was an historicist and a totalitarian.   **[1981]**

KLOSKO, G. *The Development of Plato's Political Theory.* New York: Methuen, 1986. Comprehensive account of P's political theory which explores connections between changes in his political thought and changes in epistemology and moral psychology. His politics must be understood in relation to his concern with moral reform.   **[1982]**

------. "Provisionality in Plato's Ideal State." *HPolTho* 5(1984), 171-193. P posits a rational basis for political authority, making his utopia less authoritarian than it is often depicted.   **[1983]**

------. "Rational Persuasion in Plato's Political Theory." *HPolTho* 7(1986), 15-31. Socratic refutation is effective only when interlocutor takes S seriously. Such a method does not make a secure foundation for political philosophy.   **[1984]**

KRAUT, R. "Egoism, Love, and Political Office in Plato." *PhR* 82(1973), 330-334. For P, self-interest has two facets: what affects one directly ("proper") and what affects one indirectly ("extended"). For a philosopher to be politically active is not in his proper interest, but it is in his extended interest.   **[1985]**

LEE, E. N. "Plato's Theory of Social Justice in *Republic* II-IV," in #1267, pp. 117-140. P's concept of social justice is a contract entered into willingly by all parties. This view may have developed from Sophistic theories of social contracts.   **[1986]**

LEYS, W. A. R. "Was Plato Non-Political?" *Ethics* 75(1965), 272-276; also in #1291, pp. 166-173; 184-186. P's dogmatism makes him anti-political. Second section is a response to Sparshott's criticisms (#2013) of the article.   **[1987]**

LOWENTHAL, D. "Leo Strauss' *Studies in Platonic Political Philosophy*." *Interp* 13(1985), 297-320. Review of #2015.   **[1988]**

MARA, G. "Constitutions, Virtue and Philosophy in Plato's *Statesman* and *Republic*." *Polity* 13(1981), 355-382. Differences between political systems in *Rep* and *Stsm* do not indicate changes in P's political views. They are attributable to classification schemes of their respective spokesmen. P reaffirms his support of position advocated by S. **[1989]**

McKEON, R. "The Interpretation of Political Theory and Practice in Ancient Athens." *JHS* 101(1981), 3-12. Both P and Ar see philosophy as having only limited utility in politics. Without an ethical foundation politics cannot build the kind of good life it promises.   **[1990]**

------. "Person and Community: Metaphysical and Political." *Ethics* 88(1978), 207-217. Discusses two theories of relations of man and society: 1) P analogizes man and society; man's virtues can be discovered writ large in state; associations and communities of men differ in size, not in nature. 2) Ar makes univocal distinctions between virtues and institutions of society.   **[1991]**

MORAVCSIK, J. M. E. "Plato and Pericles on Freedom and Politics," in #1285, pp. 1-18. P's criticisms of democracy are aimed primarily at theory embodied in Pericles' "Funeral Oration" as presented by Thucydides.   **[1992]**

MORPETH, N. A. "Aristotle, Plato, and Self-Sufficiency. Ancient and Modern Controversy in Economic History and Theory." *AncSoc* 12(1982), 34-46. P and Ar began their analyses of functioning of *polis* on a theoretical level. Modern approach emphasizes study of individual cities and their economic and political peculiarities.   **[1993]**

MORROW, G. R. "Plato and the Rule of Law," in #1291, pp. 144-165. Sees *Laws* as a corrective to the picture of P as an apostle of political oppression which is often derived from *Rep*.   [1994]

MULGAN, R. G. "Plato, Aristotle and Political Obligation." *Prud* 6(1974), 59-66. Neither P nor Ar bases his theory of political obligation on idea that law must be obeyed because it is law. Their concepts are inadequate because they cannot distinguish tradition from law.   [1995]

NEUMANN, H. "Goethe's Faust and Plato's Glaucon. The Political Necessity for Philosophy." *StudGen* 19(1966), 627-632. Stresses philosophy's ability to restrain human desire for power.   [1996]

NICHOLS, M. P. "Glaucon's Adaptation of the Story of Gyges and its Implications for Plato's Political Teaching." *Polity* 17(1984), 30-39. Glaucon's adaptation (in *Rep* 2) of story from Herodotus serves to point up danger of an absolutist state.   [1997]

NUSSBAUM, G. B. "Plato and Xenophon. Political Theory and Political Experiment." *LCM* 3(1978), 279-284. X's description of the organization of an army of ten thousand bears close resemblances to P's theoretical organization of the polis.   [1998]

NUSSBAUM, M. C. "Shame, Separateness and Political Unity: Aristotle's Criticism of Plato," in #4312, pp. 395-435. Contrasts P's and Ar's views on individual autonomy, and claims that differences in their views on autonomy lead to their differences about the nature of good political order.   [1999]

OKIN, S. M. "Philosopher Queens and Private Wives: Plato on Women and the Family." *Ph&PubAff* 6(1977), 345-369; also in *The Family in Political Thought* ed. J. B. Elshtain (Amherst: Univ. of MA Pr., 1982), pp. 31-50. Examines how in *Rep*, P abolishes private family while in *Laws*, he reinstates the family and makes it the foundation of his second-best city. His apparent inconsistencies can be clarified.   [2000]

ONYEWUENYI, I. C. "The Education for the Rulers: Plato Revisited." *Ph&SocAct* 4(1978), 11-15. Argues that P's philosophy and its emphasis on education fit the contemporary political culture.   [2001]

OSTWALD, M. "Plato on Law and Nature," in #1281, pp. 41-63. In context of *nomos-physis* debate, P shows rhetoricians/Sophists, by seeing laws as conventions, had perverted Athenian politics. P's efforts to identify objects of moral knowledge, on which valid science of politics could be based, had potential to establish true social justice. [2002]

PANGLE, T. L., ed. *The Roots of Political Philosophy: Ten Forgotten Socratic Dialogues.* Ithaca, NY: Cornell Univ. Pr., 1987. Translations of following dialogues: *Hipparchus, Minos, Lovers, Cleitophon, Theages, Alcibiades I, Laches, Lesser Hippias, Greater Hippias*, and *Ion*, each accompanied by an interpretive essay.   [2003]

PLAMENATZ, J. "The Open Society and its Enemies," in #1961, pp. 136-145. Challenges Popper's (#2005) analysis of P's motives and temperament.   [2004]

POPPER, K. R. *The Open Society and its Enemies, Vol. I: The Spell of Plato.* London: Routledge & Kegan Paul, 1966; 5th ed. Argues that P was anti-democratic and totalitarian regarding structure of society. Attacks his political thinking as a forerunner of modern totalitarianism.   [2005]

———. "Reply to a Critic (1961)," in #1961, pp. 199-219. Response to Levinson's *In Defense of Plato*.
[2006]

REYNOLDS, N. B. "Plato's Defense of Rule of Law," in #72, pp. 16-21. The idea, expounded in *Rep*, that an elite should rule is not P's view. In many of his other writings he advocates rule of law with an objective of happiness for all citizens.
[2007]

ROBINSON, R. "Dr. Popper's Defense of Democracy," in #74, pp. 74-99. Review essay on #2005.
[2008]

SALKEVER, S. G. "Women, Soldiers, Citizens: Plato and Aristotle on the Politics of Virility." *Polity* 19(1986), 232-253. Both P and Ar advocate improvement of status of women not because they believe in inherent equality of sexes, but because they hold that the best human life is that lived by a citizen committed to the community.
[2009]

SAUNDERS, T. J. "'The Rand Corporation of Antiquity'? Plato's Academy and Greek Politics," in *Studies in Honour of T. B. L. Webster*, ed. J. H. Betts et al. (Bristol, UK: Bristol Classical Pr., 1986), I, pp. 200-210. *Laws* and several Platonic *Epistles* provide indirect evidence that members of Academy developed policies and techniques to educate or reform rulers or states who were willing to learn from them.
[2010]

SAXONHOUSE, A. W. "The Philosopher and the Female in the Political Thought of Plato." *PolTheo* 4(1976), 195-212. Questions sincerity of P's attempt to make women equal to men and suggests that P is perverting the female and taking away her peculiar function of childbearing.
[2011]

SIEMSEN, T. I. "Rational Persuasion in Plato's Political Theory: A Reconsideration." *HPolTho* 9(1988), 1-17. Challenges Klosko's (#1984) argument that P's development as a political thinker is marked by rejection of S's reliance on *elenchus* as a way of reforming society.
[2012]

SPARSHOTT, F. "Plato as Anti-Political Thinker." *Ethics* 77(1967), 214-219; also in #1291, pp. 174-183. P makes contribution to study of political problems with his theory that knowledge can eliminate all disputes not based on genuine conflict of interests. But he prefers to solve problems by changing their social context. Reply to #1987. [2013]

SPENGLER, J. J. "Kautilya, Plato, Lord Shang: Comparative Political Economy." *PAPhS* 113(1969), 450-457. Compares governance manuals produced in fourth century B. C. in India, Greece, China. P investigates and generalizes more than other two. Each must be understood in his cultural context, which is still emerging.
[2014]

STRAUSS, L. *Studies in Platonic Political Philosophy*, with an introduction by T. L. Pangle. Univ. of Chicago Pr., 1983. Somewhat inaccurately titled collection of previously published articles. Those pertaining directly to P are abstracted herein.
[2015]

THESLEFF, H. "Plato and Inequality," in #62, pp. 17-29. P never intended for city described in *Rep* to be set up. His purpose in discussing an ideal state was actually to determine what justice is. His interests are speculative, not political.
[2016]

TILES, J. E. "*Techne* and Moral Expertise." *Ph* 59(1984), 49-66. Claims that P confused reasoning about ends with reasoning about means are based on a misunderstanding of P's concept of *techne*.   **[2017]**

UNGER, E. "Contemporary Anti-Platonism," in #1961, pp. 91-108. Examines criticisms
against P that see him as a fascist, or reactionary, or a totalitarian.   **[2018]**

VAN STRAATEN, M. "What Did the Greeks Mean by Liberty? II: Plato and Aristotle." *Theta Pi* 3(1974), 123-144. Greeks saw liberty as restrained by law, which had to be
accepted voluntarily. That latter condition left room for speculation about man's
freedom within himself.   **[2019]**

VEATCH, H. B. "Plato, Popper, and the Open Society: Reflections on Who Might
Have the Last Laugh." *JLiberStud* 3(1979), 159-172. By rejecting any metaphysical
foundation for politics Popper has no basis for an appeal to anything like the nature of
man, or an ideal of what man truly is, to justify political values.   **[2020]**

VLASTOS, G. "Slavery in Plato's Thought," in #1292, pp. 147-163. P's views about slavery, state, man, and world all exhibit same hierarchic pattern based on his idea of *logos*.
Those who do not have logos are to be governed by those who do.   **[2021]**

WARTOFSKY, M. W. "The *Republic* as Myth. The Dilemma of Philosophy and Politics."
PhFor 10(1971), 249-266. In both *Rep* and *Laws* P maintains that deception is a necessary part of ruling. In *Rep* rulers deceive the people. In *Laws* both the rulers and the
ruled are deceived by the myth of the gods. Problem is philosophy's tendency to
challenge orthodoxy and politics' tendency to defend it.   **[2022]**

WEIN, S. "Plato and the Social Contract." *PhResArch* 12(1986-87), 66-77. Argues
superiority of P's contractarian theory of justice over other versions of that theory by
Hobbes, Rousseau, Locke, Rawls, and Gauthier.   **[2023]**

WILD, J. *Plato's Modern Enemies and the Theory of Natural Law.* Univ. of Chicago Pr.,
1971. Investigates those charges that make P out to be an enemy of freedom and an
enemy of democracy. Describes P's views and surveys objections that have been raised
from antiquity to the present day.   **[2024]**

WILLIAMSON, C. "The Social Order and the Natural Order." *PAS* Suppl. 52(1978),
109-126. Attempts to refute arguments put forward by P (and many modern conservatives) which compare social inequality with inequalities of the natural order. **[2025]**

WILSON, J. R. S. "The Basis of Plato's Society." *Ph* 52(1977), 313-320. Passages from
several dialogues show that P conceived of purpose of society as establishing surroundings in which humans can reach their full potential. Acquisition or protection of
property are minor facets, not ultimate purpose of social organization.   **[2026]**

WOOD, E. M., and **WOOD, N.** *Class Ideology and Ancient Political Theory: Socrates,
Plato, and Aristotle in Social Context.* Oxford Univ. Pr., 1978. Marxist reading of class
struggle in Athens; sees S, P, and Ar as spokesmen for reactionary aristocracy. **[2027]**

For related items see #1740, #2395, #2991.

PSYCHOLOGY

The term "psychology" is used in ancient philosophy in its most literal sense of "study of the soul." But "soul" is not the most helpful translation of the term *psyche* because today it carries religious connotations which were lacking in antiquity. In its earliest occurrences in Homer (ca. 750 B. C.) it means little more than a "life breath," a pitiful, ghost-like thing that is expelled from the body at death and lives semi-conscious in Hades until it can sip the blood of a sacrificial offering. With a degree of consciousness restored, it is capable of conversing briefly with a human being. But it is insubstantial, as Odysseus discovers when he attempts to embrace his mother's *psyche* (*Odyssey* 11). Even the life of a slave on earth is preferable to this joyless existence, Achilles tells Odysseus.

With time, and under influences from other cultures, the meaning of *psyche* changed. The Orphic cult, reaching the peak of its popularity before 600 B. C., introduced the idea that at death the soul was released from the body (*soma*) as from a tomb (*sema*). This image became a common way of describing the relation of the soul to the body. The Pythagoreans incorporated Orphic views of the soul into their teaching, which is probably where P originally derived his concept. When S and P use the term *psyche* it seems to have overtones of "intelligence" or "mind." It is still the "life force," the source of all motion. Nothing lives without *psyche*. The notion of its immortality was not widespread before the late fifth century B. C. When S says to Glaucon (*Rep* 608d) "Do you not know that the soul is immortal and is never destroyed?" Glaucon answers "in surprise, 'Heavens no! Can you prove that?'"

It would take too long to trace P's concept of the soul through each dialogue. In many of them P says something which adds some little bit to our understanding of his psychology. In general we can see some development of his view, but no radical contradiction from one work, or one stage of his life, to another. Significant steps in that development are found in the *Phaedo*, which establishes the soul as the means by which the Forms are known; the *Phaedrus*, in which the myth of the charioteer is told to illustrate the tripartite nature of the soul and the need for its reasoning part to control the appetitive; the *Republic*, in which the tripartite nature of the soul is compared to the three parts of a city-state; and the *Timaeus*, in which the immortality of the intellect is asserted.

The most important part of the soul is the intellect, the reasoning faculty. It is the governing part, like the ruling class of the city in the *Republic*. It is the only part able to apprehend universal truth, and the only part which is immortal. It is located in the brain. The second part, situated in the heart, is the "spirited" element of the soul, the part responsible for passions such as courage and ambition. Without the guidance of the intellect it can become absorbed in base desires rather than noble. The lowest part of the soul, located in the liver, is the part which desires the material things of life.

A person's life will reflect the dominance of one part of the soul or another. In the philosopher the three parts work together in harmony, though the intellect is always burdened to some degree by its contact with the other, more physical, elements. At death it is freed and loses its personal identity as it becomes part of the world-soul.

ARANJANIUIL, G. "Transmigration in the Upanishads and the Greek Thought." *JDharma* 4 (1979), 244-254. Attempts to study the Upanishadic and Platonic views of transmigration, and discusses some significant similarities.   [2028]

BEDU-ADDO, J. T. "A Theory of Mental Development, Plato's *Republic* V-VII." *Platon* 28(1976), 288-301. P distinguishes between states of mind as levels of thought and faculties. He puts forward theory of development of mind from infancy.   [2029]

CHEN, L. C. H. "Education in General (*Rep.* 518c4-519b5)." *Hermes* 115(1987), 66-72. The soul, from the beginning, has the power to think (*noein*). Education does not impart this power; it awakens it and channels it in the right direction.   [2030]

CHERNISS, H. F. "The Sources of Evil According to Plato," in #51, pp. 253-260. There must be "negative evil" in a physical world which is an imperfect copy of the ideal. "Positive evil" results from motions of soul which have unintended results.   [2031]

CLEGG, J. S. "Freud and the 'Homeric' Mind." *Inquiry* 17(1974), 445-456. Though he denied influences from earlier thinkers, Freud's theory of the mind draws on Nietzsche's psychology, which ultimately restates P's aesthetic, political and social doctrine. [2032]

COOPER, J. M. "Plato's Theory of Human Motivation." *HPhQ* 1(1984), 3-21. P's understanding of human motivation allows for the desire for esteem derived from competition because of his tripartite psychology.   [2033]

CORNFORD, F. M. "The Division of the Soul," in #52, pp. 242-255. Belief in division of the soul arises from Pythagoras' concept of transmigration, which leads to high valuation of the soul as man's "true self." S further divided the soul by drawing distinction between the moral faculty and desire.   [2034]

———. "Psychology and Social Structure in the *Republic* of Plato," in #52, pp. 256-275. P's psychology of the individual is modeled on his understanding of the political structure of the state.   [2035]

DAWES, R. M. "Plato versus Russell: Hess and the Relevance of Cognitive Psychology." *RelHum* 22(1988), 20-26. Contrary to P and Russell, ethical choice is not a matter of subordinating reason or emotion.   [2036]

DEMOS, R. "Plato's Doctrine of the Psyche as a Self-Moving Motion." *JHPh* 6(1968), 133-145. Examines not P's concept of human soul but of world-soul, which causes all motion, change, and becoming. Demiurge can be taken as a soul.   [2037]

DODDS, E. R. "Plato and the Irrational Soul," in #1291, pp. 206-229. Considers P's reaction to decay of traditional beliefs which set in during fifth century. Focuses on two questions: 1) what importance does P attach to non-rational factors in human behavior? and 2) what concessions is he prepared to make to irrationalism of popular belief for sake of stability?   [2038]

EUCALANO, B. "The Universal Soul." *Dial*(PST) 21(1978), 25-30. Reconciles two opposing views attributed to P regarding immortality of soul: 1) personal immortality of a plurality of souls; 2) existence of a single, universal all-encompassing soul.   [2039]

FERRARI, G. R. F. "The Struggle in the Soul: Plato, *Phaedrus* 253c7-255a1." *AncPh* 5(1985), 1-10. This allegory makes it appear that the charioteer and the bad horse, each striving to realize their own desires, adopt methods which the other ought to use. Examines implications of the passage for P's psychology. [2040]

GAVIN, W. J. "Plato on Death and Dying." *JTho* 9(1974), 237-243. View of death in Socratic death dialogues resembles process of dying outlined by E. Kubler-Ross in *On Death and Dying*: shock, denial, anger, bargaining, acceptance. [2041]

GERSON, L. P. "A Note on Tripartition and Immortality in Plato." *Apeir* 20(1987), 81-96. Consistent account of soul's immortality can be obtained from *Rep, Phaedrus,* and *Tim* by examining whether immortality applies to parts of souls or whole souls. [2042]

———. "Platonic Dualism." *Monist* 69(1986), 352-369. In early dialogues P uses ethical and metaphysical/epistemological arguments for his dualistic view that souls are immaterial and every person is identified with one soul. The tripartite psyche of *Rep* resolves some problems with the earlier doctrine and allows for *akrasia*. Studies development of this idea in later dialogues. [2043]

GRANGE, J. "Lacan's Other and the Factions of Plato's Soul," in *The Question of the Other*, ed. A. B. Dallery (Albany: SUNY Pr., 1989), pp. 157-174. Compares P's notion of tripartite soul with psychoanalytic theory of J. Lacan, stressing the role of culture and the unconscious in human development. [2044]

GUTHRIE, W. K. C. "Plato's Views on the Nature of the Soul," in #1291, pp. 230-243. Examines P's beliefs about whether soul in its own essence is simple or composite, and if it is composite, whether whole soul or just higher part is immortal. P's views are more consistent than commonly supposed. [2045]

KAUFER, D. S. "The Influence of Plato's Developing Psychology on His View of Rhetoric." *QJS* 64(1978), 63-78. P's views on psychology and rhetoric are systematically connected. P knew that words affected the soul for good or evil. [2046]

KENNY, A. J. P. "Mental Health in Plato's *Republic*." *PBA* 55(1969), 229-253; also in *The Anatomy of the Soul: Historical Essays in the Philosophy of Mind* (Oxford: Blackwell, 1973), pp. 1-27. The attempt to assign human activities to different faculties or parts of soul began with P. His metaphor of mental health accomplishes nothing more than Freudian concepts. [2047]

KLOSKO, G. "The 'Rule' of Reason in Plato's Psychology." *HPhQ* 5(1988), 341-356. Examines role of reason in soul and how it rules. Differentiates between rule of reason in philosopher and in typical human. [2048]

MAIDAN, M., and BALABAN, O. "The Problem of the Soul and the Nature of Lies in Plato's Philosophy." *Diot* 14(1986), 182-192. At different periods P's epistemology ranged from extreme anti-subjectivism to moderate subjectivism. Investigates differences between these two conceptions of knowledge as regards two issues: 1) Socratic versus Platonic view of soul; 2) Socratic denial of existence of lies versus P's necessary "noble" lies. [2049]

MOHR, R. D. "The Sources of Evil Problem and the *Arche Kineseos* Doctrine in Plato."

Apeir 14(1980), 41-56; also in #2112. To hold, as some do, that P's doctrine of the soul as cause of motion applies only to orderly motions is to undermine his position on the existence and immortality of the soul.   [2050]

MOLINE, J. "Plato on the Complexity of the Psyche." *AGPh* 60(1978), 1-26. Provides an account of nature and role of parts of psyche in *Rep*, and argues against taking these "parts" as "faculties."   [2051]

NAKHNIKIAN, G. "Reason, Love, and Mental Health." *PhResArch* 5(1979), no. 1349. Discusses connections P makes betwen mental health and love. The flaw in his argument is that the *eros* of the *Symp* cannot be the basis of the mental health which characterizes a rational person.   [2052]

OSTENFELD, E. *Ancient Greek Psychology and the Modern Mind-Body Debate*. Aarhus (Denmark) Univ. Pr., 1986. Attempts to return to a "pre-Cartesian" view of the relationship between body and mind by examining theories of P and Ar. For them the mind informs and directs the informed matter of the body.   [2053]

PATTERSON, R. *Plato on Immortality*. University Park: PA St. Univ. Pr., 1965. Examines passages from *Phaedo* and *Phaedrus* to present P as the first to separate body from soul and to identify death as the moment of separation. Sees P as an ultimate dualist, teaching that both matter and spirit are underived. His picture of the tripartite soul is not to be taken literally, and he believes in the immortality of the individual soul. He connects the immortality of the soul with its relation to the Forms.   [2054]

PAUSON, M. L. "Plato and Madness." *TulStudPh* 27(1978), 153-162. In P's thought madness is a divine gift, an experience of another level of reality. For soul in process of becoming, madness is part of movement toward self-knowledge.   [2055]

PLASS, P. "Anxiety, Repression, and Morality: Plato and Freud." *Psychoanalytic Review* 65(1978), 533-556. Considers P's doctrine of tripartite soul and his broader conception of human development to see whether he has his own version of "civilization and its discontents."   [2056]

RICE, D. H. "Plato on Force: Conflict Between His Psychology and Sociology and His Definition of Temperance in the *Republic*." *HPolTho* 10(1989), 565-576. Without resolving conflict between his psychology of the individual and his understanding of temperate soul, P was unable to integrate knowledge and political coercion.   [2057]

RIDING, S. "Plato's *Kerinon ekmageion* and Memory Models in Current Psychology." *Platon* 37(1985), 101-120. P's comparison of memory to something imprinted in wax endures today among empiricist philosophers and cognitive psychologists.   [2058]

ROBINSON, T. M. *Plato's Psychology*. Univ. of Toronto Pr., 1970. Attempts to give a comprehensive account of what P says in each dialogue on nature of *psyche*, personal and cosmic.   [2059]

———. "Soul and Immortality in *Republic* X." *Phron* 12(1967), 147-151. Argues that 611b-612a can be plausibly interpreted as affirming immortality of entire soul, all three parts, and not just rational part.   [2060]

RUSSELL, G. "Eric Voegelin on the Truth of In-Between Life: A Meditation on Existential Unrest." *Interp* 16(1989), 415-425. Voegelin sees P's thought as occupying an in-between ground, with the immanent/mortal and transcendent/immortal at the poles. *Noesis* is an active search for transcendence. [2061]

SCOLNICOV, S. "Reason and Passion in the Platonic Soul." *Dion* 2(1978), 35-49. Studies impact of contemporary thought on P's concept of relationship between rational and irrational parts of *psyche*. For P reason is not merely deliberation but produces action. [2062]

SEESKIN, K. R. "Platonism, Mysticism, and Madness." *Monist* 59(1976), 574-586. In several dialogues P compares intuitive grasping of Forms to religious ecstasy. This claim is justifiable since acquisition of knowledge has a "religious" effect on the soul and knowledge of Forms is necessary for soul's well-being. [2063]

SHINER, R. A. "Soul in *Republic* X, 611." *Apeir* 6 #2(1972), 23-30. It is difficult to determine what P means when he says that the "true" part of the soul is immortal because he never specifies what he means by the "true" part. [2064]

SOLMSEN, F. "Plato and the Concept of the Soul (Psyche). Some Historical Perspectives." *JHI* 44(1983), 355-367. Examines Burnet's interpretation that supreme value P attached to soul resulted from synthesis of previously distinct religious and secular traditions about psyche. He differs from tragedians and S in role he assigns *nous* in the *psyche*. [2065]

STALLEY, R. F. "Plato's Argument for the Division of the Reasoning and Appetitive Elements within the Soul." *Phron* 20(1975), 110-128. Rejects view that P's argument for division of soul rests on a logical mistake. Because he misunderstands what it means to desire something and to be unwilling to do something, he cannot explain conflicting desires without resorting to divisions of soul. [2066]

STRANG, C. "Tripartite Soul, Ancient and Modern: Plato and Sheldon." *Apeir* 16(1982), 1-11. Maintains that *thumoeides* (spirit) is not a fiction to preserve the tidy correspondence between structure of state and that of soul, but is the one psychic factor that P has accurately observed and described. [2067]

TSIRPANLIS, E. C. "The Immortality of the Soul in *Phaedo* and *Symposium*." *Platon* 17(1965), 224-234. Soul exists infinitely and also closer to the divine. [2068]

WALCOT, P. "Plato's Mother and Other Terrible Women." *G&R* 34(1987), 12-31. Looks at connection between P's account of maternal influence (*Rep* 549c-550b) and stories of powerful mothers in other authors. P shows how the timocratic man is the product of a weak father and domineering mother. [2069]

ZAKOPOULOS, A. N. *Plato on Man: A Summary and Critique of his Psychology with Special Reference to Pre-Platonic, Freudian, Behavioristic, and Humanistic Psychology.* New York: Philosophical Library, 1975. Looks primarily at question of soul's relation to body, its simplicity/complexity, its immortality. Compares P's tripartite psychology with Freud's id, ego, and super-ego. Bibliography and lengthy, thorough notes. [2070]

For related items see #1630, #1899, #1938, #2655, #2975, #3065, #5536.

RHETORIC

It is somewhat surprising that P said much about rhetoric, since he distrusted it profoundly. As with aesthetics, P is more concerned with the moral and political implications of rhetoric than with laying down guidelines for its practice. Two of his dialogues, *Gorg* and *Phaedrus*, discuss the art of public speaking but do not reach consistent conclusions. P's primary concern about rhetoric was its illusionary nature. Like a poem, or a magic trick, it deceives an audience. As S says, "they steal away our souls with their embellished words" (*Menexenus* 234d). Rhetoric has no objective standard of truth but seeks to persuade people by putting together bits and pieces of argument to create an effect, much as the rhapsode stitches together lines and half-lines of poetry or as a seamstress pieces together a quilt. The listener or viewer is supposed to admire the fine craftsmanship and admire the overall effect of the final product. Sophists such as Protagoras, Gorgias, and Hippias made reputations and fortunes for themselves teaching such skills.

Over against the amoral practicioners of this art P depicted S as the unsophisticated seeker after truth, which could only be arrived at through the hard reasoning process known as dialectic. His primary argument against the Sophists was always based on the question "What is it that you claim to teach?" He saw rhetoric and philosophy as unconnected, except that rhetoric had to depend on philosophy for its values, since it had none of its own.

ALEXANDER, J. D. "The Natural Standard of Speech." *CultHerm* 3(1976), 267-294. Examines form of S's speech in dialogues as paradigm for identifying and bringing a standard to bear upon situations of serious speech.   [2071]

ANDERSON, F. D., and ANDERSON, R. L. "Plato's Conception of *Dispositio*." *SouthSpJ* 36(1971), 195-208; also in #2074, pp. 299-311. The comparison of a discourse to a living creature and the harmony of its parts (*Phaedrus* 246c) defines P's view of rhetoric. A speech must be well ordered and internally coherent if it is to lead the hearer to love reason.   [2072]

BATSTONE, W. W. "Commentary on Cooper: Oratory, Philosophy and the Common World." *PBACAPh* 1(1985), 97-114. Reply to #2076. Attempts to appreciate strength of Isocratean position on its own terms, i. e., success of oratory in world of practical affairs.   [2073]

BLACK, E. "Plato's View of Rhetoric," in #2081, pp. 171-191. Obvious inconsistencies between P's view of rhetoric in *Phaedrus* and *Gorg* arise because P is concerned not with describing rhetoric but with defining a "true art" of rhetoric. He does not condemn rhetoric *per se* but worries about ways it can be abused.   [2074]

CONNORS, R. J. "Greek Rhetoric and the Transition from Orality." *Ph&Rh* 19(1986), 38-65. Dialectic as practiced by S and P may have had as one of its objectives to break the sway which rhetoricians still held in a society with a strong oral tradition.   [2075]

COOPER, J. M. "Plato, Isocrates and Cicero on the Independence of Oratory from

Philosophy." *PBACAPh* 1(1985), 77-96. For P oratory is dependent upon philosophy, since oratory has no objective standard of truth. Isocrates offers no counter-argument. Cicero's scepticism leaves him unable to assert independence of oratory.   [2076]

COULTER, J. A. "The Relation of the *Apology of Socrates* to Gorgias' *Defense of Palamedes* and Plato's Critique of Gorgianic Rhetoric," in #2081, pp. 31-69. On one level *Apol* is a refutation of Gorgias' *Palamedes*. The two speeches share vocabulary and structure. P also presents the philosophic way of life as a contrast to the worldly life, devoted to power and wealth, at which rhetoric aims.   [2077]

DE ROMILLY, J. "Plato and Conjurers," in *Magic and Rhetoric in Ancient Greece* (Cambridge, MA: Harvard Univ. Pr., 1975), pp. 23-43; also in #2081, pp. 153-169. Gorgias compared rhetoric to magic in that both aim to create an illusion. P turned that argument against Sophists because of his concern over harm that could be caused by practicing the *techne* of rhetoric.   [2078]

DUFFY, B. K. "The Platonic Functions of Epideictic Rhetoric." *Ph&Rh* 16(1983), 79-83. Contrast between P's purpose of education in rhetoric and Ar's amoral view. P provides examples of two forms, one public (*Menexenus*) and one private (S's second speech in *Phaedrus*).   [2079]

DUNCAN, R. "The Dialectical Destruction of Rhetorical Figures: A Platonic Response to John Kozy, Jr." *Ph&Rh* 4(1971), 175-177. Response to Kozy's general discussion of rhetorical figures. There appears to be a Platonic way of distinguishing philosophy from both poetry and rhetoric while preserving the liberal use of creative metaphor as a part of philosophic method.   [2080]

ERICKSON, K. V. *Plato: True and Sophistic Rhetoric.* Amsterdam: Rodopi, 1980. Collection of previously published essays; abstracted herein.   [2081]

——. "Plato's Theory of Rhetoric: A Research Guide." *Rhetoric Society Quarterly* 7(1977), 78-90. Thorough bibliography, not annotated.   [2082]

FLESHLER, H. "Plato and Aristotle on Rhetoric and Dialectic," in *Communicative Rhetoric: A Workbook*, ed. K. V. Erickson (Berkeley, CA: McCutchan Publ., 1968), pp. 8-12. P grounded rhetoric in dialectic, to give some legitimacy to a technique which he despised. Ar shows rhetoric and dialectic as both amoral, not confined to one subject, and designed to prove arguments. Rhetoric relies on emotional and ethical proofs which dialectic does not need.   [2083]

KELLEY, W. G. "Rhetoric as Seduction." *Ph&Rh* 6(1973), 69-80; also in #2081, pp. 313-323. P sees rhetoric's basic weakness as its lack of genuine affection for truth. Relationship between rhetoric and truth is analogous to that between seduction and love. Rhetoric and seduction both simulate the truer forms.   [2084]

MORROW, G. R. "Plato's Conception of Persuasion," in #2081, pp. 339-354. In P's state persuasion would be a part of the law. Everyone would observe the law because convinced of its rightness. In his rigid system "persuasion" becomes a means of suppressing dissent.   [2085]

MURPHY, J. J. "The Metarhetorics of Plato, Augustine, and McLuhan: A Pointing

Essay." *Ph&Rh* 4(1971), 201-212. "Metarhetoric" attempts to define what one must know to be a rhetorician. One theme is common to three writers studied: images are not reality. Each tried to find a fundamental unity in cosmos. Only Aristotle provides an adequate metarhetoric. [2086]

NORTH, H. F. *"Inutilis sibi periculosus patriae.* A Platonic Argument Against Rhetoric." *ICS* 6(1981), 242-271. Examines arguments against rhetoric current before P's day, in his work, and their survival in Rome. [2087]

QUIMBY, R. W. "The Growth of Plato's Perception of Rhetoric." *Ph&Rh* 7(1974), 71-79; also in #2081, pp. 21-30. *Gorg* and *Phaedrus* give impression that P strongly condemned rhetoric or those who practice it. His statements about it in other dialogues reveal a development of his view on the subject. His attempted resolution of the problem of rhetoric was to divide it into true and false forms, the former being acceptable, the latter not. [2088]

SKOUSGAARD, S. "Genuine Speech vs. Chatter: A Socratic Problematic." *Kinesis* 6(1974), 87-94; also in #2081, pp. 375-383. Social and political implications of speech are paramount for P. S's dialectic is presented as an example of speech which leads to political benefits. Sophists' rhetoric is a paradigm of a corrupt speech form which leads to political chaos. [2089]

VOLPE, M. "Practical Platonic Rhetoric: A Study of the Argumentation of the *Apology*." *SouthSpComJ* 42(1977), 137-150. Though he profoundly opposed Sophistic rhetoric, P used it in defense of philosophy. *Apol* shows value of proof by individual testimony but does not assert that everyone can determine truth for himself. It does show rhetoric as an acceptable form of philosophic investigation. [2090]

WARMAN, M. S. "Plato and Persuasion." *G&R* 30(1983), 48-54. Survey of P's views on rhetoric. He sees it as more effective when practiced on one or a few persons and in form of dialectic rather than oratory. [2091]

For related items see #900, #1048, #1148, #1533, #1575, #2046, #2259, #2335, #2340, #2728, #3347.

SCIENCE (COSMOLOGY AND MATHEMATICS)

P had good reason for neglecting natural science. S, his revered teacher, had turned his back on speculation about the nature of the world, which had occupied the Presocratics (and was still a popular field of research in S's lifetime, as witness the work of S's contemporary, Anaxagoras). In the *Phaedo* a renunciation of scientific research is put into S's mouth, but the dialogue ends with him discussing theories about the earth's shape and structure and the causes of seismic disturbances.

This kind of ambivalence, combined with uncertainty about the dating of the dialogues, makes it difficult to say exactly what P's attitude toward science was. He probably had little background in the sciences, since Athenian education stressed what might be called the liberal arts. Even though he emphasized mathematics and admired Pythagorean number theory, P himself seems to have had only a modest competence in the subject. Two of his students, Eudoxus and

Theaetetus, were the Academy's teachers in that area. Since P believed that the physical, sensible world was of little importance and could not be the object of true knowledge, there was no reason for him to observe and analyze phenomena, as Ar did. In the *Rep* the guardians of his ideal state are to study acoustics and astronomy on a purely theoretical level, without any "hands-on" experience.

In the *Soph*, however, P explicitly says that things which exist and events which occur in time are real. One can attain certainty of knowledge about them. If this dialogue is late, as most scholars maintain, it may signal a new direction in P's intellectual development. The *Tim*, with its creation account, may also represent a movement away from the otherworldly Forms and an admission that natural phenomena are knowable.

ANTON, J. P., ed. *Science and the Sciences in Plato.* Delmar, NY: Caravan Books, 1980. Original essays aimed at restoring P's place in history of scientific thought; abstracted herein. **[2092]**

BRUMBAUGH, R. S. *Plato's Mathematical Imagination: The Mathematical Passages in the Dialogues and their Interpretation.* Millwood, NY: Kraus, 1977; rprt. Reconstructs diagrams and figures which were probably meant to accompany published dialogues. The mathematical passages in the dialogues were meant to be studied seriously. For non-specialists with no knowledge of Greek or philosophy. **[2093]**

BULMER-THOMAS, I. "Plato's Astronomy." *CQ* 34(1984), 107-112. Examines how P based his explanations of motions of stars and planets on mathematics. **[2094]**

———. "Plato's Theory of Number." *CQ* 33(1983), 375-384. Mathematicians in the Academy developed ways of expressing irrational numbers and a theory of number which subsumed commensurables and incommensurables under one definition. **[2095]**

BURNYEAT, M. F. "Platonism and Mathematics: A Prelude to Discussion," in #4575, pp. 213-240. Choice between Aristotelian and Platonic account of objects of mathematics is a choice as to which sciences we should take as most fundamental to our understanding of world and its goodness. **[2096]**

CHERNISS, H. F. "Plato as Mathematician," in #51, pp. 222-252. Though P appreciated the propaedeutic value of mathematics, he carefully distinguished it from, and subordinated it to, dialectic, which he saw as his own field. He was not a productive mathematician. **[2097]**

COLE, R. "Plato and Contemporary Natural Science." *SwJPh* 8(1977), 73-78. Shows how P's image of divided line applies to divisions among contemporary sciences. **[2098]**

FARIS, J. A. *Plato's Theory of Forms and Cantor's Theory of Sets.* Belfast: Queen's Univ., 1968. Inaugural lecture (20 pp.). P's theory of eternal, unchanging Forms provides a better resolution of some metaphysical problems raised by G. Cantor's theory of mathematical sets. **[2099]**

FOLSE, H. J. "Platonic 'Atomism' and Contemporary Physics." *TulStudPh* 27(1978), 69-88. P's atomism in *Tim* 53c-68d is closer to modern physics than is Democritus' atomism.

Its apparent conflict with Theory of Forms is resolved when we realize that it describes a process of becoming and not properties of substantial entities.   [2100]

HARE, R. M. "Plato and the Mathematicians," in #1268, pp. 21-38; also in Hare *Essays on Philosophical Method* (London: Macmillan, 1971), pp. 80-97. Examines P's two criticisms of mathematicians in *Rep* 510b: 1) they use physical diagrams and 2) they are compelled to start their inquiries from hypotheses.   [2101]

HARVEY, F. D. "Two Kinds of Equality." *C&M* 26(1965), 101-146. Looks at problem of geometric and arithmetic proportion and their use as foundations for theories of political equality. Also discusses dating of *Gorg* in relation to P's voyage to Italy and exposure to Pythagorean ideas.   [2102]

JOHNSON, H. J. "Three Ancient Meanings of Matter: Democritus, Plato, and Aristotle." *JHI* 28(1967), 3-16. Concentrates on meanings assigned to concept of matter in cosmologies of these three philosophers and on some peculiarities of method connected with them.   [2103]

KITTS, D. B. "Plato on Kinds of Animals." *Bio&Ph* 2(1987), 315-328. P does not have an explicitly stated doctrine of animal kinds.   [2104]

KUNG, J. "Tetrahedra, Motion, and Virtue." *Nous* 19(1985), 17-27. P's view that some things are transitory and that Forms could be mathematical configurations allows him to integrate his somewhat disparate accounts of soul and to base his curriculum for future rulers on mathematics.   [2105]

LASSERRE, F. *The Birth of Mathematics in the Age of Plato*. Cleveland: World, 1967. Describes the progress of mathematical thought at the time of P.   [2106]

LENNOX, J. G. "Plato's Unnatural Teleology," in #1282, pp. 195-218. Starting with two models of explanation in *Phaedo*, investigates P's explorations of model of an intelligent craftsman in middle and later dialogues to see how they help him develop a more integrated theory of scientific explanation.   [2107]

LLOYD, G. E. R. "Plato as Natural Scientist." *JHS* 88(1968), 78-92. Examines what value P attached to inquiry into nature and how he thought the inquiry should be carried out. His approach to natural science is not eclectic.   [2108]

MARACCHIA, S. "Plato and Russell on the Definition of Mathematics." *Scientia* 65(1971), 216-223. P and Russell share some views on mathematics. For both it is a deductive field, based on unprovable theorems. It is a source of joy and beauty and their underlying truths.   [2109]

MAYR, E. "A Response to David Kitts' 'Plato On Kinds of Animals'." *Bio&Ph* 3(1988), 97-98. P's impact on biology was negative because of his emphasis on cosmos as living organism, his concept of creative Demiurge, and stress on "soul."   [2110]

MOHR, R. D. "The Number Theory in Plato's *Republic* VII and *Philebus*." *Isis* 72(1981), 620-627. In neither dialogue does P maintain that one can abstract mathematical principles from individual phenomena of mathematical operations. The object of mathematical study is Form as number.   [2111]

———. *The Platonic Cosmology.* Leiden: Brill, 1985. Collection of writings on *Tim* 27d-47e, 48a-69a, and other cosmological passages. Some previously published; all abstracted herein.   [2112]

———. "The World-Soul in the Platonic Cosmology." *ICS* 7(1982), 41-48; also in #2112, pp. 171-177. P stresses concept of world-soul, one of more difficult of his ideas to interpret, because it serves in his system to uphold order against physical world's natural tendency to degenerate into chaos.   [2113]

MORTLEY, R. J. "Plato's Choice of the Sphere." *REG* 82(1969), 342-345. P conceived of world as sphere because that shape is most complete and most like itself. Parmenidean influence is discernible.   [2114]

MOURELATOS, A. P. D. "Astronomy and Kinematics in Plato's Project of Rationalist-Explanation." *StudHist&PhSci* 12(1981), 1-32. For P, movements of astral bodies provide most perfect examples of rotary motion. Emphasizes his views in *Rep* 7 and 10. [2115]

———. "Knowledge, Speculation, and Myth in Plato's Account of the Order and the Distances of Celestial Bodies," in #1277, pp. 83-105. Seeks to clarify P's doctrine on order of celestial bodies in cosmos and distances between celestial bodies.   [2116]

———. "Plato's 'Real Astronomy': *Republic* VII 527d-531d," in #2092, pp. 33-73. Argues in favor of an *a priori* astronomy over an astronomy that proceeds by means of problems aiming to "save the phenomena."   [2117]

MUELLER, I. "Ascending to Problems: Astronomy and Harmonics in *Republic* VII," in #2092, pp. 103-121. Examines certain Greek scientific texts to show more clearly the kind of astronomy and harmonics P has in mind. Against this background S's description of astronomy and harmonics is less problematic.   [2118]

NOVAK, J. A. "Plato and the Irrationals." *Apeir* 16(1982), 71-85. Presents overview of development of dialectic in P and discusses problem of irrationals in Greek mathematics as background to understanding their importance in P's dialectic.   [2119]

———. "Plato and the Irrationals — Part 2." *Apeir* 17(1983), 14-27. Highlights importance of mathematics in general and specifically theories about irrationals for P's work. Irrational quantities replace integers as model for interrelationship between the Forms. Presence of Theaetetus and Theodorus in P's dialogues indicates importance he assigns to their mathematical work.   [2120]

POPPER, K. "The Nature of Philosophical Problems and their Roots in Science," in #2483, pp. 128-179. Argues that P's Theory of Forms cannot be understood except in context of critical problem situation which developed as a result of discovery of irrationality of square root of two.   [2121]

ROSE, L. E. "Plato's Unhypothetical Principle." *JHPh* 4(1966), 189-198. Examines P's concept of hypothesis in mathematics and dialectic.   [2122]

SOLMSEN, F. "Plato and Science," in #1281, pp. 86-105. P returned to study of science late in his life, after denigrating it as concerned with mutable things, because his increasing interest in mathematics gave him more confidence in his ability to find unchanging subject matter.   [2123]

TAYLOR, C. C. W. "Plato and the Mathematicians: An Examination of Professor Hare's Views." *PhQ* 17(1967), 193-203. Response to Hare's interpretation (#2101) of P's criticism of mathematicians at *Rep* 510bff, and their use of hypotheses.   [2124]

TURNBULL, R. G. "The Later Platonic Concept of Scientific Explanation," in #2092, pp. 75-101. In the later dialogues, P relies on a certain pattern of explanation which is derived from the method of collection and division (*diaeresis*). He gradually abandons, but does not denigrate, the method of elenchus.   [2125]

VAN DER WAERDEN, B. L. "The Great Year in Greek, Persian, and Hindu Astronomy." *AHES* 18(1978), 359-383. Examination of cosmological theories current in P's day provides useful background to study of his schema.   [2126]

VLASTOS, G. *Plato's Universe*. Seattle: Univ. of WA Pr., 1975. Part I surveys pre-Platonic views of the universe and notes their increasing rationalsim. Part II studies P's explanation of the structure of the universe based on the assumption that clues can be found in God's nature. Part III focuses on P's study of the structure of matter. *Tim* is a primary focus of the book.   [2127]

———. "The Role of Observation in Plato's Conception of Astronomy," in #2092, pp. 1-31. P does not seem to be advocating, in *Rep*. 528e-530c that astronomers abandon observation and rely on speculation. Speculation is true science, but gathering of data by observation must take place first.   [2128]

———. cf. #1486, #3529.

VON WEIZSAECKER, C. F. "Platonic Natural Science in the Course of History." *MainCur* 29(1972), 3-13. In parable of cave, P implies that after the ascent, it will be philosopher's duty to return to the cave and teach, among other things, the limitations of natural science.   [2129]

WHITE, F. C. "Plato on Geometry." *Apeir* 9 #2(1975), 5-14. What P has to say about geometry is often lightly brushed aside, but his theory is still as plausible as many subsequent theories.   [2130]

THEOLOGY AND RELIGION

P's concept of God is, to say the least, difficult to pin down. As Demos says (#1333a, p. 99), "In approaching the topic of the Platonic God, the reader is baffled by the very considerable vagueness of the discussions in the dialogues." This confusion arises in part because of the distinction P makes between the concept of Divinity and the notion of gods such as the Olympians. His lack of precision also creates problems. P uses terminology about "God" and "the gods" and "daimon" so casually that at times he seems to share popular beliefs, at other times to reject them. He condemns myths but creates his own, some of which pertain to divine judgment of humans after death (the myth of Er in *Rep* 10). In *Laws* he speaks, like a dualist, of an evil god and a good god, but in *Stsm* he explicitly denies that evil in the world is the responsibility of a separate evil power.

Confusion also arises because the Forms are the ultimate perfection in P's thought, at least in the middle dialogues, so the role of "God" becomes unclear. The Forms are the real objects of which the world is only an imitation. But in one passage (*Rep* 597b-c) God is described as making the Form of the Bed. Nowhere else in P's dialogues is there any implication that God created the Forms. They are eternal and unchanging. And yet the Forms do not create the material world. In *Rep* 530a P speaks of God as "maker of the heavens." But generally in his works there is no notion of a God who creates the physical world, at least in the Christian sense. Like most ancients, P cannot conceive of a time when absolutely nothing existed, nor can he understand creation of something out of nothing. The matter of which the world is made has always existed. The Greek gods did not create it; they merely ruled over it, and yet themselves were subject to a power of necessity or fate.

By the middle of his life P began to develop a concept of a "world soul" which was designed to answer criticisms that his world of Forms was entirely separated from the sensible world and that there could be no contact between the two and thus no knowledge of one by the other. The human soul and the Divine are similar, in P's view, and that allows for contact between them. The entire world is "ensouled" (*empsychos*). It contains a self-moving principle which directs it toward becoming as much like the Forms as possible.

In the *Tim* P provides his most detailed account of the divine activity, in the myth of the Divine Craftsman, the Demiurge, who is Soul shaping the material of the world (which already exists and is called the Receptacle) according to the pattern of the Forms which he has contemplated. The Demiurge makes as close a copy of the Forms as he can, given the imperfect nature of the Receptacle. This account was not meant to be taken literally. It simply points out that there are three principles — Form, creative activity, and matter — which constitute the world. The Demiurge does try to make the world as good as possible; to that extent he "cares" for it, but he does not govern it or intervene in its functioning in any way familiar from Judeo-Christian theology.

It must be emphasized that P's use of terminology similar to that of Christian theology does not imply that his thought was similar, though later Platonists and Christians did blend the two systems. P is no monotheist. He speaks of gods moving each of the heavenly bodies, and his Demiurge, while a kind of supreme god, is not omnipotent. There is an irrational element present in the matter on which he works, a "disorderly motion," about which he can do nothing. P uses this concept of disorderly motion to account for Necessity, for inexplicable, irrational happenings.

One remaining question, which probably cannot be answered, is whether P conceived of the possibility of a personal relationship with his God. Later Platonists thought they found that concept in his writings; Plotinus and others treated philosophy as a quest for union with God. Some modern commentators have suggested that such an interpretation may be closer to P's meaning than the rather mechanistic viewpoint from which we usually read him. It is very difficult to gauge the effect which Greek mystery cults, Pythagorean mysticism, and Mesopotamian astrology may have had on P's personal view of God.

ANNAS, J. "Plato's Myths of Judgement." *Phron* 27(1982), 119-143. Analyzes judgment myths in *Gorg, Phaedo,* and *Rep.* Shows that philosophical "message" of each myth is different. P's thought in this area developed from simple concept of punishment and reward in *Gorg* to cyclical theory of *Rep.*   [2131]

ARMLEDER, P. J. "Plato on Philosophy versus Theology." *CB* 44(1967), 1-3. Philosophy, for P, is far more able to grasp truths than is theology, particularly those that emphasize relationship between being and becoming. Middle Ages reversed roles of disciplines.   [2132]

BOS, A. P. *Providentia Divina: The Theme of Divine Pronoia in Plato and Aristotle.* Assen, Netherlands: Van Gorcum, 1976. Brief study (36 pp.) which examines doctrine of divine providence presented in *Phaedo, pronoia* in *Tim* and *Laws,* and then explores Ar's alternative to Platonic "physis-theology."   [2133]

———. cf. #5409.

CARMODY, J. "Plato's Religious Horizon." *PhT* 15(1971), 52-68. P balances religious sympathies between inner search for order and effort to gain knowledge of a transcendent deity. This explains importance of religion in his ideal state.   [2134]

CARTER, R. E. "Plato and Mysticism." *IdealStud* 5(1975), 255-268. Reviews criteria of mysticism outlined by several authorities, identifies numerous traits which P shared with great mystics. Challenges Friedlaender's conclusion that P is no mystic.   [2135]

CHROUST, A.-H. "Influence of Zoroastrian Teaching on Plato, Aristotle, and Philosophy." *NewSchol* 54(1980), 342-357. Sees influence of Zoroastrian or Old-Iranian religious teachings in some of P's later dialogues and some of Ar's works. These ideas may have been introduced by Eudoxus of Cnidus, a member of the Academy.   [2136]

DESPLAND, M. *The Education of Desire. Plato and the Philosophy of Religion.* Univ. of Toronto Pr., 1985. Study of P's philosophy of religion is complicated by need to break away from Christian conception of the subject as proving or disproving doctrine and Neoplatonic idea of P as religious philosopher. Object of the study is to show that P was one of first to become conscious of something called "religion," which needed to be studied. Examines several dialogues not usually looked at in this context.   [2137]

EPP, R. H. "Katharsis and the Platonic Reconstruction of Mystical Terminology." *Phil*(Athens) 4(1974), 168-179. P borrows concept of purgation from the mystery cults but bases it on rationalism, not on rituals and sacrifice.   [2138]

ESLICK, L. J. "Plato as a Dipolar Theist." *ProcStud* 12(1982), 213-251. Examines the early Greek connotations for the word *theos,* immortal and soul, and how both meanings "coalesce" in P's philosophy.   [2139]

FINDLAY, J. N. "The Myths of Plato." *Dion* 2(1978), 19-34; also in *Myth, Symbol, and Reality,* ed. A. Olson (Notre Dame, IN: Notre Dame Univ. Pr., 1980), pp. 165-184. P's "myths" are actually serious studies in cosmology, theology, and other areas. Several myths are examined in detail.   [2140]

GREGORY, M. J. "Myth and Transcendence in Plato." *Thought* 43(1968), 273-296. P considers myths more than poetic illustrations. They have a cognitive function which serves the philosopher the same way mystic experience serves initiate of a religious cult. For P, religion and philosophy have same objective, viz., assimilation to God. Knowledge of the transcendent is attainable only through myth.   **[2141]**

HACKFORTH, R. "Plato's Theism," in #1809, pp. 439-447. Same relation is implied in *Laws* between World-Soul and *nous* as in *Philebus* and *Tim*. P says nothing to warrant conception of a hierarchy of souls culminating in a single supreme soul.   **[2142]**

McKOWN, D. B. "Deception and Development of Plato's Theology." *SJPh* 5(1967), 173-179. Investigates P's use of deception in light of his use of religion and vice versa; examines his proofs for existence of God in *Laws*.   **[2143]**

MOHR, R. D. "Plato's Theology Reconsidered. What the Demiurge Does." *HPhQ* 2(1985), 131-144; also in #1267, pp. 293-307. P's craftsman provides knowledge rather than moral guidance. He introduces concepts which are as close a reflection as possible of the Forms.   **[2144]**

———. cf. #2113.

MORROW, G., ed. "Plato's Gods," in *Insight and Vision: Essays in Philosophy in Honor of Radoslav Andrea Tsanoff*, ed. K. Kolenda (San Antonio, TX: Principia Pr. of Trinity Univ., 1966), pp. 121-134. P seems to have seen gods as imitations of divine principle revealed to philosophic intelligence. As imitations they participate in essence of the high God and are worthy of worship.   **[2145]**

QUIGLEY, M. "Which Allegory for Religious Truth: Plato's Cave or Nietzche's Zarathustra?" *Thom* 42(1978), 625-648. Contrasts P's allegory of the cave and Nietzsche's allegory of Zarathustra to investigate whether there is any philosophical sense in which what is "religious" might be opposed to what is Christian.   **[2146]**

SKEMP, J. B. "Plato's Account of Divinity." *DUJ* 29(1967), 26-33. P stressed creator's desire for good as ultimate guarantee for life of creature.   **[2147]**

———. "Plato's Concept of Deity," in #83, pp. 115-121. Discusses P's general concept of divinity as the Form of the Good, especially in *Rep*, and Demiurge of *Tim*.   **[2148]**

———. cf. #1164.

WA SAID, D. *Theosophies of Plato, Aristotle and Plotinus.* New York: Philosophical Library, 1970. Discusses basic principles of early philosophical and natural theology. Focuses on Forms and immortality of the soul, and sees P as father of Christian theology.   **[2149]**

For related items see #1665, #1690, #2399.

Chapter 13

PLATO:
INDIVIDUAL WORKS

Thirty-five dialogues survive under P's name, but no more than twenty-eight are genuine. Many scholars accept only twenty-three or twenty-four. Those mentioned by Aristotle are undisputedly Platonic, but he does not mention all the dialogues by name. Why P chose to write dialogues, we cannot determine. Earlier philosophers had presented their ideas in poetic form or not written anything at all. P puts into the mouth of S some very strong strictures against writing, and the implications of those statements for the interpretation of P's dialogues have been much debated.

The dialogues were almost certainly not written to be read, as we now approach them. In P's day people did not buy books to take home and read or stack on their shelves. "Publication" of a new piece of literature usually took an oral form. Tragedies and comedies were presented annually at festivals in honor of Dionysus. Poets composed pieces for parties, religious festivals, weddings, and other celebrations. Even historians such as Herodotus read their compositions in a public forum of some sort. Against that background it seems likely that P's dialogues may have been read at some kind of gathering, perhaps of his friends and students. Except for the *Republic* and *Laws* they are of such a length that they could have been "performed" in about the same time as a tragedy.

Beyond general agreement that the *Laws* was his last work, there is no consensus about the chronological order of the dialogues. Consequently it is difficult to trace the development of P's thought. As Grube says (#1373, p. xi): "Before we can speak of development in Plato's thought it is obviously necessary to know the order in which the dialogues were written. But that is just what we do not know."

Others place less emphasis on chronological order. H. R. Scodel maintains that "the order in which the dialogues were composed is a red herring insofar as the distillation of Platonic thought from the dialogues is concerned. It is highly inappropriate to redate certain dialogues as is now fashionable, because the traditional dating comports ill with some favored developmental hypothesis." It is possible that P held certain theories in a "mature" form early in his life, while his views on other subjects may have changed. And, as Melling reminds us (#1404, p. 15), "Even if we conclude that Plato is indeed arguing for a particular view, it does not follow he held the same view ever after, any more than the lack of explicit reference to an idea or opinion in a particular dialogue implies Plato did not hold that particular view when writing that dialogue."

It is customary to assign the dialogues to three periods in P's life, but no two scholars agree exactly on which dialogues belong to which period, or which dialogues are spurious. Nor can we assign firm dates to any of these periods nor a firm chronological order to dialogues within a period. The following represents a very general consensus, with certain exceptions noted. The dialogues are listed alphabetically within each period, with no suggestion of chronological order.

EARLY PERIOD: *Apology, Charmides, Crito, Euthydemus, Euthyphro, Gorgias, Hippias Major, Hippias Minor, Ion, Laches, Lysis, Menexenus, Protagoras, Republic 1.*

The unifying characteristic of these dialogues is that S is a major character and engages in examination of definitions put forward by his interlocutors in response to questions of the form "What is x?" or "Is $x y$?" These dialogues may represent the kind of practice sessions that P's students engaged in as they learned the process of *elenchus*, but that is a much debated point. The *Apology* is not a dialogue, but it does seem to come from a time in P's life when S was still his primary inspiration, and this early period seems the most logical time for him to have written it. The *Menexenus* is not accepted as Platonic by many scholars and, like the *Apology*, is not really a dialogue but a speech with a bit of introductory conversation. Book 1 of the *Republic* seems to have been originally composed as a separate piece, probably to be called the *Thrasymachus*. Some scholars also place the *Alcibiades I* and *II* in this period, but the majority opinion holds them to be non-Platonic.

MIDDLE PERIOD: *Cratylus, Parmenides, Phaedo, Phaedrus, Republic 2-10, Symposium, Theaetetus.*

For reasons we do not know, P abandoned the practice of *elenchus* and began to teach the doctrine of the Forms in a more positive manner. The dialogues which reflect this change are designated as the middle dialogues. The *Republic* shows this transition most dramatically. In Book 1 S engages in a lively interchange of ideas with Thrasymachus and the rest, but in Books 2-10 S discourses while the others do little more than nod their heads once in a while. Some scholars would also place the *Timaeus, Critias,* and *Laws* 3-7 in this middle period. The dating of the *Symposium* is particularly problematic. Different scholars consider it Early, Middle, or Late. Some would also argue that the *Parmenides* and *Theaetetus* are late works.

LATE PERIOD: *Critias, Laws, Philebus, Sophist, Statesman (Politicus), Timaeus.*

The dialogues in this group deal largely with methodology and semantics and may have been intended for students in the Academy rather than for a larger general audience. S plays a much smaller role, being reduced to little more than a bystander in the *Sophist*, and P introduces criticisms of his own doctrine of the Forms. Some scholars also place the *Cratylus, Symposium,* and *Theaetetus* in this group.

DUBIOUS: *Alcibiades I* and *II, Clitophon, Epinomis, Hipparchus, Lovers, Minos, Theages.*

Some would also include the *Hippias Major, Ion,* and *Menexenus* in this group.

Also among the writings attributed to P are thirteen letters, the authenticity of which is highly dubious; the seventh is the most likely to be genuine. They are included in the bibliography under "Letters," though they are frequently referred to as "Epistles."

Passages in P's works bear numbers, such as *Euthyphro* 9c or *Parmenides* 331a-c. The numbers refer to the page numbers in the Stephanus edition of the late sixteenth century. Each page was further divided into four sections, lettered a through d. These numbers are used as a form of standard reference, just as chapter and verse numbers are used in the Bible. They were not part of the original work.

In this chapter each dialogue is introduced very briefly and then bibliographic items are listed. If a work discusses two or more dialogues, it will be listed under the first dialogue to appear in the title and cross-referenced under the other dialogue(s). We have also tried to judge whether an item which deals, for example, with the doctrine of the Forms in the *Parmenides* is more about the doctrine or the dialogue. Should it be under the subject "Metaphysics" or under the dialogue? Abundant cross-references have been supplied to help users of the bibliography move between subject and dialogue listings.

We have not attempted to list all the translations and texts with commentaries that are currently available. We have listed a few that have commentaries or notes which can be used by a non-specialist. Each dialogue has been translated afresh at least once in the past twenty-five years. Those who wish to compare such efforts are referred to *Année Philologique*. At the beginning of each year's listing of work on P will be found the texts and translations published in that year, with references to reviews in scholarly journals. The hallmark of translations of P is Benjamin Jowett's, originally published in the late nineteenth century. It holds a place in the history of Platonic translations roughly analogous to the King James Version of the Bible: familiar, majestic, still loved in spite of some antiquated turns of phrase and occasional inaccuracies. Another translation of the complete dialogues can be found in the Loeb Library edition (London: Heinemann; Cambridge, MA: Harvard Univ. Pr.), by Shorey, Lamb, and others. It is a more literal translation, with the Greek on the facing page, and is also showing its age. The Clarendon Plato series provides modern translations with notes, and the major dialogues are also available in Penguin paperback editions.

Alcibiades I

The subtitle of this dialogue is "On the Nature of Man." It was regarded by ancient commentators as a summary of P's philosophy and stood at the head of some collections of his works. It does not have a single theme but moves rapidly from one question or topic to another, sometimes without resolving the issue under discussion. It assumes a close, even intimate, connection between S and Alcibiades, a handsome but erratic young man who led Athens into a disastrous attack on Syracuse during the Peloponnesian War. In the dialogue S attempts to teach Alcibiades what true statesmanship is by teaching him the importance of self-knowledge. At the end of the dialogue Alcibiades has been "converted" to philosophy.

FORDE, S. "On the *Alcibiades I*," in #2003, pp. 222-239. Overview of work. **[2149a]**

Apology

The *Apology* is not a dialogue, in the sense of a conversation (although S does engage in a brief bit of *elenchus* with his accuser). It purports to be the speech which S delivered in his defense when he was being tried in 399 B. C. S certainly made some sort of speech at his trial. Athenian schools taught rhetoric because every citizen of that litigious city expected to be in court several times during his lifetime, on charges great or trivial. That P would have had an accurate copy of his teacher's speech seems unlikely. Nor would anyone have expected him to. In his history of the Peloponnesian war (written just a few years before S's death), Thucydides advised his readers that he had composed speeches befitting the characters and the occasions. To an audience of P's day, then, it would have been perfectly acceptable for him to write something that S *might* or *could* have said at his trial.

Most, though by no means all, scholars concede that the S depicted in this speech is a reasonable facsimile of the historical person, allowing for P's desire to justify his devotion to the old man and to explain his teaching in a calmer atmosphere. He claims to have had no particular wisdom but to have been aware of his ignorance, as other teachers and artisans were not. The speech provides a brief outline of his career, beginning with his exposure to physical ("Presocratic") philosophy, which he found futile. His concern soon turned to what we would call ethical and political matters. Questions such as, What does it mean to be a "good" person? or What is justice? seemed to him more important. He spent the rest of his life in a dogged pursuit of some insight, if not definite answers. And he tried to arouse others from their intellectual and moral lethargy, like a fly that stings a lazy horse. His sense of his mission can be summed up in the question he often addressed to fellow citizens (*Apol* 29d):

> Good sir, you are an Athenian, a citizen of the greatest city with the greatest reputation for both wisdom and power; are you not ashamed of your eagerness to possess as much wealth, reputation and honors as possible, while you do not care for nor give thought to wisdom or truth, or the best possible state of your soul?

Perhaps the most unexpected thing S says is that he has received divine guidance in his quest. The god Apollo, speaking through his oracle at Delphi, first proclaimed S the wisest man in Greece. And S claims to have had his own personal *daimonion*, a kind of guardian angel, who has warned him whenever he has been about to do or say the wrong thing.

The speech failed, however, and S was found guilty of atheism and corrupting the youth of Athens. Under the law he could propose a suitable penalty, such as a fine or a brief period of exile, which the jury could accept or reject. When he suggested that he be supported for the rest of his life at state expense, the jurors reportedly were angered by his gall and voted the death penalty.

ALLEN, R. E. *Socrates and Legal Obligation.* Minneapolis: Univ. of MN Pr., 1980. *Apol* is essentially ironic. S claims no rhetorical skill but his speech is a rhetorical masterpiece. Yet it fails to win him acquittal, because charges against him could not, by their very nature, be refuted. In *Crito* S refuses to escape because that would mean repaying injury with injury and failing to honor certain just agreements. **[2150]**

ARMLEDER, P. J. "Death in Plato's *Apology*." *CB* 42(1966), 46. S's statement that death is sleep or soul's departure to another world is not meant literally. **[2151]**

BRENK, F. E. "Interesting Bedfellows at the End of the *Apology*." *CB* 51(1975), 44-46. S lists various figures with whom he may converse in underworld. Figures mentioned resemble S in being intellectuals and/or unjustly maligned. Sisyphus does not fit these categories, but is clever and in some accounts overcomes death. **[2152]**

BRICKHOUSE, T. C., and **SMITH, N. D.** "Irony, Arrogance, and Truthfulness in Plato's *Apology*." in #1083, pp. 29-46. Challenges view that S defies jury's authority in his defense. **[2153]**

————. *Socrates on Trial.* Oxford Univ. Pr., 1989. Historical, philosophical interpretation of, and commentary on, *Apol.* Argues that S offers a sincere defense. **[2154]**

BUTTREY, T. V. "Plato's *Apology* 23c and the Anger of the Catechized." *LCM* 6(1981), 51-53. Textual note involving the question of the direction of the anger generated by being cross-examined by the young. **[2155]**

DANIEL, J., and **POLANSKY, R.** "The Tale of the Delphic Oracle in Plato's *Apology*." *AncW* 2(1979), 83-85. Delphic oracle section defends philosophy more than S. Everything appearing to pertain especially to the individual man S turns out ironically to concern every man. **[2156]**

DE STRYCKER, E. "The Oracle Given to Chaerephon about Socrates," in #67, pp. 39-49. Examines historicity and meaning of oracle about S's wisdom; looks at its significance both for S's life and for structure of *Apol.* **[2157]**

HATHWAY, R. F. "Law and the Moral Paradox in Plato's *Apology*." *JHPh* 8(1970), 127-142. If accepted as valid, the paradox "no one does wrong willingly" undercuts the law because it removes any justification for punishment. **[2158]**

HOERBER, R. G. "Note on Plato, *Apology* XLII." *CB* 42(1966), 92. Reply to Armleder (#2151). Views on death expressed in passage are not contradictory. **[2159]**

KEANEY, J. J. "Plato's *Apology*, 32c8-d3." *CQ* 30(1980), 296-298. The Meletus who accused S is same as the Meletus who accused Andocides and took part in arrest of Leon of Salamis. **[2160]**

LEADBEATER, L. W. "Platonic Elements in Kafka's 'Investigations of a Dog'." *Ph&Lit* 11(1987), 104-116. Explores influence of P's *Apol* and *Phaedrus* on Kafka's "Investigations of a Dog." The Dog is a S figure. [2161]

MANASSE, E. M. "A Thematic Interpretation of Plato's *Apology* and *Crito*." *Ph&PhenR* 40(1980), 393-400. Discussion of views of L. Noussan-Lettry, who stresses philosophical value of dialogues over historical picture of S. [2162]

McPHERRAN, M. "Commentary on Woodruff's 'Expert Knowledge in the *Apology* and *Laches*." *PBACAPh* 3(1987), 116-130. Reply to #2171. Examines assumption that knowledge and ignorance are mutually exhaustive for S, and attribution to him of a theory of natural ignorance. [2163]

O'CONNELL, R. J. "God, Gods, and Moral Cosmos in Socrates' *Apology*." *IntPhQ* 25(1985), 31-50. Challenges readings by Grube and Guthrie that *theos* did not have an anthropopsychic (personal) meaning for P. [2164]

REEVE, C. D. C. *Socrates in the* Apology: *An Essay on Plato's* Apology of Socrates. Indianapolis: Hackett, 1989. Maintains that S is not being ironic and that his speech is an effective defense against Meletus' accusations. [2165]

SCHMID, W. T. "Socratic Piety," in #1277, pp. 3-24. Explores S's new philosophical account of piety, characterized as "the service of the Unknown God through the care of souls." [2166]

STONE, I. F. "The Socrates Story." *New York Times*, April 8, 1979. Argues that P "turned the trial of Socrates into a trial of Athens and of democracy." [2167]

——. cf. #1169.

TARRANT, H. "Plato's *Apology*. Introduction and Commentary, Part I." *AncSoc* 13(1983), 77-97. Introduction considers historical reliability of *Apol* and P's reasons for writing it. Main problem of interpretation is that we are conditioned to see S quite differently than an ancient Athenian would have seen him. S emerges as tactless and uncompromising. [2168]

——. "Plato's *Apology*: Part II." *AncSoc* 14(1984), 5-11. Continuation of commentary begun in #2168. [2169]

WADE, F. C. "In Defense of Socrates." *RMeta* 25(1971), 311-325. Reply to #2255. Seeks to resolve apparent inconsistency between *Apol* 29 c-d where S says he will refuse to obey the jury if they require him to stop philosophizing and *Crito* 51a-c where he speaks of need to obey law. [2170]

WOODRUFF, P. "Expert Knowledge in the *Apology* and *Laches*: What a General Needs to Know." *PBACAPh* 3(1987), 79-115. For S, having knowledge which qualifies as expert requires being able to define a thing. He discusses a method for obtaining such knowledge (elenchus) in the *Apol* and applies it to the question of courage in the *Laches*. [2171]

For related items see #1025, #1049, #1132, #1158, #1170, #1216, #1217, #2237, #2250, #3250.

Charmides
   This dialogue is an attempt to define *sophrosyne*, which may be variously translated as temperance, moderation, modesty, or even wisdom. For Plato it seems to carry a sense of intellectual virtue, as opposed to the purely moral interpretation which Aristotle later gives it. The handsome youth Charmides offers several definitions, all of which prove unsatisfactory. His mentor, Critias, then offers the definition that *sophrosyne* is self-knowledge, or the knowledge of what one knows and does not know. But Socrates accepts no definition of virtues which lacks scientific overtones. Virtue is knowledge *of* something. It has an object outside itself, just as medicine has health as its object. How, then, can *sophrosyne* be simply knowledge of what one knows? The dialogue ends aporetically.

BENARDETE, S. "On Interpreting Plato's *Charmides*." *GradFacPhJ* 11(1986), 9-36. The dialogue's primary purpose is to study how self-knowledge can be passed on without being transformed into conceptual abstraction. "Know thyself" becomes a "binary construction."   [2172]

BRUELL, C. "Socratic Politics and Self-Knowledge: An Interpretation of Plato's *Charmides*." *Interp* 6(1977), 141-203. P's audience knew that the Charmides whom S tried to lead to moderation became a tyrant. S's futile efforts must be part of his unending quest for self-knowledge.   [2173]

CHEN, C. H. "On Plato's *Charmides* 165c4-175d5." *Apeir* 12 #1(1978), 13-28. Distinctions which P draws between "knowledge of itself" and other special knowledge is unique to Platonic corpus.   [2174]

COOLEY, K. W. "Unity and Diversity of the Virtues in the *Charmides, Laches,* and *Protagoras*." *Kinesis* 1(1969), 100-106. Discusses how physical, or "outer," seems to serve as necessary dialectical stepping stone to soul's mental or "inner" condition.   [2175]

DYSON, M. "Some Problems Concerning Knowledge in Plato's *Charmides*." *Phron* 19(1974), 102-111. Examines four passages to elucidate certain obscure features of P's argument and offer comments on the meaning of "knowledge of knowledge."   [2176]

GRISWOLD, C. L. "Unifying Plato." *JPh* 85(1988), 550-551. Challenges Kahn's use of *Charm* (#2182) to show a thematic unity in the dialogues.   [2177]

HOGAN, R. A. "Soul in the *Charmides*: An Examination of T. M. Robinson's Interpretation." *PhResArch* 2(1976), no. 1095. Reply to #2059. Soul cannot be taken, along with body, as self/person. Soul, body are not related by mutual entailment.   [2178]

———. "The *Techne* Analogy in the *Charmides*." *PhResArch* 3(1977), no. 1225. Reply to #1699. The *techne* analogy itself is not reason for Critias' failure to define temperance. His failure results from not applying analogy rigorously enough.   [2179]

HYLAND, D.A. "Responding to the Tyranny of Scholarship." *AncPh* 5(1985), 157-160. Reply to #2184.   [2180]

——. *The Virtue of Philosophy: An Interpretation of Plato's* Charmides. Athens: Ohio Univ. Pr., 1981. P is arguing for an openness of attitude which does not demand fixed meanings or despair if none can be found. In *Charm* S represents this mean between Chaerophon, who accepts S's teaching without questioning, and Charmides and Critias, who are potential tyrants. **[2181]**

KAHN, C. H. "Plato's *Charmides* and the Proleptic Reading of Socratic Dialogues." *JPh* 85(1988), 541-549. *Charm* is part of a group of dialogues, along with *Laches, Lysis,* and *Euthyd*, which begins to explore ideas set forth more fully in *Rep*. **[2182]**

KOSMAN, L. A. "Charmides' First Definition: Sophrosyne as Quietness," in #42, pp. 203-216. Investigates S's treatment of Charmides' first definition of *sophrosyne* as "a certain quietness" and suggests how S's arguments and alleged fallacies point to an understanding of what *sophrosyne* is. Suggested definitions of *sophrosyne* imply that it is present in Charmides and in his actions. **[2183]**

LEVINE, D. L. "The Tyranny of Scholarship." *AncPh* 4(1984), 65-74. Discusses Hyland's attempt in #2181 to show how Heidegger's work can aid us in interpreting *Charm* and how we can comprehend dialogue's fuller "political" character. **[2184]**

McKIM, R. "Socratic Self-Knowledge and 'Knowledge of Knowledge' in Plato's *Charmides*." *TAPhA* 115(1985), 59-77. S's analysis of why "knowledge of knowledge" fails as a definition of *sophrosyne* functions at the same time as an implicit dramatic analysis by P of the limitations of Socratic self-knowledge as a foundation for philosophic method. **[2185]**

MORRIS, T. F. "Knowledge of Knowledge and of Lack of Knowledge in the *Charmides*." *IntStudPh* 21(1989), 49-61. P draws a clear distinction between being acquainted with something and knowing it. Knowledge of what one knows can be found only through elenchus. **[2186]**

SANTAS, G. "Socrates at Work on Virtue and Knowledge in Plato's *Charmides*," in #65, pp. 105-132. Closely examines S's arguments regarding powers and limits of knowledge in living virtuously. **[2187]**

SCHMID, W. T. "Socrates' Practice of *Elenchus* in the *Charmides*." *AncPh* 1(1980-81), 141-147. To see elenchus as purely destructive is one-sided and ignores S's sensitivity to interlocutor's needs. **[2188]**

——. cf. #1154.

VAN DER BEN, N. *The* Charmides *of Plato: Problems and Interpretations*. Amsterdam: Gruner, 1985. Dialogue is protreptic; it merely touches on topics dealt with more fully in later dialogues, and it is truly aporetic. Investigation into *sophrosyne* is abandoned early in the dialogue. **[2189]**

Clitophon

The authenticity of this shortest of the dialogues attributed to P has been debated in modern times, but ancient critics had no doubt that it was genuine.

Its vocabulary and subject matter cohere well with other dialogues whose authorship is unquestioned. Thrasyllus, the Hellenistic critic who devised the grouping of P's dialogues into tetralogies, linked the *Clitophon* with the *Rep, Tim*, and *Critias*. Like the *Rep*, its theme is justice, and all the named characters in it also appear in the *Rep*. Clitophon is the only character in the *Rep* who does not address S directly.

In this "dialogue" he is the only speaker after a brief statement by S. His speech begins as a reply to S's charge that Clitophon has been defaming him in his conversations with others and speaking highly of Thrasymachus. Clitophon reports what he has said. What begins as an apparent defense of S turns into a reply to several of S's arguments in the *Apol*. Clitophon concludes that S is admirable for his ability to talk *about* justice but cannot define it: "either you don't know or you are unwilling to share the knowledge with me." In either case, Clitophon will continue to consort with Sophists like Thrasymachus, who *can* arrive at answers.

BLITS, J. H. "Socratic Teaching and Justice: Plato's *Clitophon*." *Interp* 13(1985), 321-334. It is just for S not to respond to Clitophon's inept speeches. Clitophon thinks virtue is teachable. S maintains every individual must find it for himself.   **[2190]**

NEUMANN, H. "The Sophistry of Plato's *Protagoras* and *Cleitophon*." *Sophia* 35(1967), 46-55. Similar criticisms of S in *Prot* and *Cleit* argue for authenticity of latter dialogue.   **[2191]**

ORWIN, C. "The Case Against Socrates: Plato's *Cleitophon*." *Canadian Journal of Political Science* 15(1982), 741-753; also in #2003, pp. 117-131. Argues for authenticity of this brief dialogue. It is a mock trial of S, and the "charges" against him are not refuted.   **[2192]**

ROOCHNIK, D. L. "The Riddle of the *Cleitophon*." *AncPh* 4(1984), 132-145. Survey of scholarly opinion on question of why S does not respond to Cleitophon's charges. His very silence may be a kind of response.   **[2193]**

SLINGS, S. R. *A Commentary on the Platonic* Clitophon. Amsterdam: Academische Pers, 1981. Examines attack on S and generally avoids question of authorship. Detailed section-by-section commentary.   **[2194]**

Cratylus

Benjamin Jowett called this dialogue "a source of perplexity to the student of Plato." Much of it is taken up with fanciful etymologies of words which nonetheless contain glimpses of profound insight into the way language works. It is possible that P was not espousing one theory or another but simply presenting the three theories current in his day. One of the speakers, Hermogenes, believes that names of things are purely conventional. Society assigns them without any rational basis. Part of the discussion between S and Hermogenes involves an application of the Heraclitean philosophy of flux to language. Cratylus expounds the view that words are personal and reflective of the character of the things named. Here, too, the ideas of Heraclitus are in the background. Thus there can be only one true name for any given thing. This debate echoes the *nomos/physis* debate among Presocratic philosophers.

At the end of the dialogue S states his belief that the position that all things are in motion and flux is mistaken, for if everything is in motion and flux, there can be no knowledge at all, and the possibility of language and communication becomes quite problematic. Thus S seeks to find out if there is any absolute beauty or good, or any other absolute existence. When Cratylus indicates his support for such fixed entities, S turns the discussion toward a consideration of the true or absolute beauty. But then S closes by saying that whether there are such eternal natures or whether everything is in flux is "a question hard to determine." He urges Cratylus to reflect well with respect to this question.

ANAGNOSTOPOULOS, G. "The Significance of Plato's *Cratylus*." *RMeta* 27(1973), 318-345. The theme of the dialogue is the correctness of names, not the origin of language. P sees that one's understanding of whether a name belongs to a thing naturally or by convention is part of his investigation of the nature of things. He concludes that investigation of names does not lead to knowledge of a thing. **[2195]**

ANNAS, J. "Knowledge and Language: The *Theaetetus* and the *Cratylus*," in #76, pp. 95-114. Suggests that certain passages in *Crat* may give us insight into certain difficulties in "dream" passage in *Theaet*. **[2196]**

BENARDETE, S. "Physics and Tragedy: On Plato's *Cratylus*." *AncPh* 1(1980-81), 127-140. S presents an interpretation of tragedy through his assumption that there is a natural correctness of names. That assumption is interpreted to mean complete coincidence of being and significance. **[2197]**

BERGER, H. "Plato's *Cratylus*: Dialogue as Revision." *PhFor* 2(1970-71), 213-233. Shows how dialogue both considers and dramatizes relation between general problems about language, style, and usage, and problem of style. **[2198]**

BESTOR, T. W. "Plato's Semantics and Plato's *Cratylus*." *Phron* 25(1980), 306-330. The argument over names and the *nomos/physis* debate is reducible to a question of whether names are compressed descriptions or proxies for real things. P seems to have taken them as proxies. **[2199]**

CALVERT, B. "Forms and Flux in Plato's *Cratylus*." *Phron* 15(1970), 26-47. In 389a-390e P introduces a different kind of non-sensible entity ("proper form") similar to the Form but distinguished by its plurality. In 439c-440d, he almost breaks away from Heracliteanism. These are tentative, not final, positions. **[2200]**

CHEN, L. C. H. "Onomatopoeia in the *Cratylus*." *Apeir* 16(1982), 86-101. Making of names discussed in dialogue concerns making of ideal, not actual, names, just as *Rep* deals with an ideal, not an actual, state. **[2201]**

CHURCHILL, S. L. "Nancy Demand on the Nomothetes of the *Cratylus*." *Apeir* 17(1983), 92-93. Reply to #2203. End of *Crat* allows for an interpretation of *nomothetes* on which establishing a custom by nature is not self-contradictory. **[2202]**

DEMAND, N. "The Nomothetes of *Cratylus*." *Phron* 20(1975), 106-109. Examines role of Nomothetes and why P introduces this "embarrassing creature." Nomothetes ("namegiver") is brought in simply because his name itself makes very point which dialogue as a whole makes: that one cannot learn from names. The word itself is a pun. **[2203]**

FERWERDA, R. "The Meaning of the Word *Soma* in Plato's *Cratylus* 400c." *Hermes* 113(1985), 266-279. Examines Pythagorean and Orphic influences on proposed definitions. **[2204]**

FINE, G. "Plato on Naming." *PhQ* 27(1977), 289-301. Explores P's theory of naming. Examines his alleged semantic atomism, his claim in *Crat* that names can be true or false, and his discussions of false belief. P holds that a correct name makes clear the outline of thing named. **[2205]**

GOULD, J. B. "The Ambiguity of Name in Plato's *Cratylus*." *PhilStud* 34(1978), 223-251. Both "name" and "word" are ambiguous. P was aware of ambiguities and used them to develop several important points about language. **[2206]**

———. "Plato: About Language. The *Cratylus* Reconsidered." *Apeir* 3 #1(1969), 19-31. P opposed the idea that names reveal information about the things they name by being likenesses of the things. **[2207]**

KAHN, C. H. "Language and Ontology in the *Cratylus*," in #65, pp. 152-176. P is concerned with two questions: 1) What are some minimum conditions in order for true and false statements to be possible? 2) Of what use is study of names as means for investigating nature of things? **[2208]**

KASULIS, T. P. "Reference and Symbol in Plato's *Cratylus* and Kukai's *Shojijissogi*." *PhE&W* 32(1982), 392-405. Examines pioneering Western and Japanese philosophies of language. Comparisons/contrasts suggest some general observations about nature of comparative philosophy. **[2209]**

KETCHUM, R. J. "Names, Forms, and Conventionalism: *Cratylus* 383-395." *Phron* 24(1979), 133-147. Maintains that the argument that names belong to things by nature and not by convention is neither more nor less valuable nor important than another argument by analogy. **[2210]**

KRETZMANN, N. "Plato on the Correctness of Names." *AmPhQ* 8(1971), 126-138. P's semantic theory is based on his view of the importance of the question "should a name having the force this name has be in use at all?" rather than on the question of whether a name is appropriate for the thing it names. **[2211]**

LORENZ, K., and **MITTELSTRASS, J.** "On Rational Philosophy of Language: The Programme in Plato's *Cratylus* Reconsidered." *Mind* 76(1967), 1-20. Sketches an interpretation of *Crat* as a program for a rational philosophy of language and tries to show how it could be used as framework for further research. **[2212]**

LUCE, J. V. "Plato on Truth and Falsity in Names." *CQ* 19(1969), 223-232. P's view of link between language and reality is based on his understanding of truth and falsity of names. That theme is integral to *Crat*. **[2213]**

——. "The Theory of Ideas in the *Cratylus*." *Phron* 10(1965), 21-36. *Crat* constitutes an important stage in development of P's thought about Ideas (Forms), but a stage distinctly prior to position reached in *Phaedo* inasmuch as Ideas are not as "separated" as those in *Phaedo*.   [2214]

MacKENZIE, M. M. "Putting the *Cratylus* in its Place." *CQ* 36(1986), 124-150. Objections to Forms in *Crat* are serious, suggesting it is a late work.   [2215]

PALMER, M. D. "Bibliography on Plato's *Cratylus*." *PhResArch* 8(1982), suppl. 3. Editions, transl., secondary literature, beginning in late nineteenth century.   [2216]

——. *Names, Reference and Correctness in Plato's* Cratylus. New York: Lang, 1989. P does not presuppose that intensional entities such as concepts or meanings mediate the relation between a name and its nominatum. P thinks reality divides into discrete, natural units and names serve to mark these units. Extensive bibliography.   [2217]

PARTEE, M. H. "Plato's Theory of Language." *FoundLang* 8(1972), 113-132. Discusses P's view that all human representations — "whether poetically of man's actions or verbally of things" — fall short of reality itself, and his awareness of the dangers of the seductive beauty of language.   [2218]

PFEIFFER, W. M. "True and False Speech in Plato's *Cratylus* 385b-c." *CanJPh* 2(1972), 87-104; also in #2081, pp. 355-373. This passage suggests P was first to establish a theory of correspondence between names and objects as linguistic base for truth.   [2219]

REED, N. H. "Plato on Flux, Perception and Language." *PCPhS* 18(1972), 65-77. Seeks to show coherence of thought between *Crat*, *Theaet*, and *Tim* on problems of flux and language, and to suggest that both *Theaet* and *Tim* present versions of P's own theory of perception.   [2220]

RICHARDSON, M. "True and False Names in the *Cratylus*." *Phron* 21(1976), 135-145. Many recent interpreters of the dialogue have erred in trying to make *logos* in 385b-c mean "statement" in modern sense.   [2221]

RIST, J. M. "The Theory and Practice of Plato's *Cratylus*," in #59, pp. 208-218. Language and names do not enable us to know but to express to some degree what we know. Knowing comes from direct contact. Examines how far conclusions of dialogue are relevant to discussion of knowledge in *Rep*.   [2222]

ROBINS, R. H. "The Development of the Word Class System of the European Grammatical Traditions." *FoundLang* 2(1966), 3-19. Discusses how P and Ar made *onomata* and *rhemata* the main constituents of *logos*, the sentence.   [2223]

ROBINSON, R. "A Criticism of Plato's *Cratylus*," in #74, pp. 118-138. P appears not to resolve the question of natural names, but the arguments he presents against it are much stronger than those produced in its favor.   [2224]

——. "The Theory of Names in Plato's *Cratylus*," in #74, pp. 100-117. P does not use *physis* and *nomos* to distinguish between what things are and what people think they are. He seems to hold that there could be more than one correct name of a thing.   [2225]

264 PLATO: *Cratylus*

RUMSEY, W. D. "Plato in the *Cratylus* on Speaking, Language, and Learning." *HPhQ* 4(1987), 385-403. Examines relationship between a dialectician's knowledge of Forms and his knowledge of language in context of arguments of *Crat*. Names cannot be given arbitrarily but must reveal nature of object named. [2226]

SCHOENLY, S. B. "The Etymologies of the Names of the Gods: *Cratylus* 400d-404b." *Dial*(PST) 16(1974), 44-53. Inconsistencies in several of S's etymologies indicate that P uses this technique to illustrate S's philosophical goals. The etymologies are thus not a serious effort at a theory of language. [2227]

SCHOFIELD, M. "The Denouement of the *Cratylus*," in #76, pp. 61-82. Discusses P's treatment of naturalist and conventionalist theories of names, and in particular, focuses on 433-435 to show how P teases reader with argumentation that is ambiguous in direction and equivocal in tone. [2228]

———. "A Displacement in the Text of the *Cratylus*." *CQ* 22(1972), 246-253. Rearranging text in 385 and 387 removes difficulties of interpretation. [2229]

SPRAGUE, R. K. "Reply to Dr. Levinson," in #41, pp. 367-371. Reply to #1781. Concerns with language are subordinate to Theory of Forms in this dialogue. [2230]

THORNTON, M. T. "Knowledge and Flux in Plato's *Cratylus*." *Dial*(Can) 8(1970), 581-591. P should not be taken as saying in *Crat* that the world is in total flux, nor does he maintain that only what is unchanging can be known. [2231]

WARE, J. H. "The *Cratylus* and How Words are Used," in #44, pp. 91-114. Dialogue is structured on orderly progression from naming to names, to ordinary language, and to words. Dilemma of natural vs. conventional meaning of words is not resolved. P's professed intention to charm with his words is often overlooked. [2232]

WEINGARTNER, R. H. "Making Sense of the *Cratylus*." *Phron* 15(1970), 5-25. Sees *Crat* as a unified dialogue in which three theories of language are considered. Hermogenes' "conventionalism" and Cratylus' "representationalism" are criticized as making dialectic impossible. Socrates' position allows for dialectic. [2233]

———. cf. #1494.

WHITE, F. C. "On Essences in the *Cratylus*." *SJPh* 16(1978), 259-274. Early part of dialogue contributes significantly to our understanding of P's thought on status of physical particulars. [2234]

WILLIAMS, B. "Cratylus' Theory of Names and its Refutation," in #76, pp. 83-94. Gives an account of Cratylus' theory of names, and emphasizes distinction between "the name of x" and "the correct name of x" and Cratylus' denial of that distinction. [2235]

For related items see #536, #6635

Critias
   Some scholars question whether this dialogue was even meant to be a

separate work. In many modern discussions it is treated as part of the *Timaeus* (cf. #3471). Users of this bibliography are referred to the section on the *Timaeus* for items which discuss both works.

Crito

The setting of this dialogue is S's cell between the time of his trial and his execution. Around the time of his trial a galley was sent out to the island of Delos as part of a religious festival. While the ship was away, no executions were to take place for fear of ritual pollution. Consequently, S remained in jail for a month after the trial, during which time his friends attempted to persuade him to escape into exile. They have made the necessary arrangements. Now the ship has been sighted and is expected to arrive shortly. S's friend Crito tries to persuade S one more time to escape from jail. Crito is worried about his own reputation. Because Crito is a close friend of S, people will wonder if Crito did enough to keep S alive. But S refuses to cooperate. He asks why Crito pays so much attention to what other people think. The many have no knowledge of matters of justice and virtue, so we should not concern ourselves with their opinion. Whether this indicates a certain anti-democratic spirit in S is the subject of controversy.

S's conversation with Crito turns to the nature of law and the obligation of a citizen to obey the law, regardless of his personal feeling about it. S argues that disobeying the law is unjust, and that injustice is always wrong. No one should commit a minor injustice, even to avoid a greater one. This is a striking example of S's moral integrity. His life is on the line, and yet he insists on looking at the rightness or wrongness of the proposed action solely in terms of rational argument. In 46b-c he sets forth a credo of sorts: "not only now but at all times I am the kind of man who listens only to the argument that on reflection seems best to me. I cannot, now that this fate has come upon me, discard the arguments I used."

In sections 50-54 S imagines the laws of the city themselves addressing him (the "Speech of the Laws") and asking if he did not agree to live by the laws. If he did so, and if he has benefitted from their protection during his long life, he has no right to selectively disobey particular laws. The law has decreed his execution, and the law must be obeyed. If he violates earthly laws, their kin, the laws of the underworld, will receive him harshly.

In S's refusal to disobey the law an apparent tension arises in his position. At *Apol* 29c-d he indicates that if the jury were to acquit him on the condition that he stop philosophizing, he would refuse to obey. "I will obey the God rather than you." In the *Apol* he seems quite willing to go against the legal authorities, but in the *Crito* he is unwilling to do so. There have been numerous scholarly attempts to reconcile these conflicting positions.

ALLEN, R. E. "Law and Justice in Plato's *Crito*." *JPh* 69(1972), 557-567. Examines dialogue's argument to show Socratic revolution in thinking about law, justice. Though condemned unjustly, S accepts the decision because of his view that the wrongfulness of things is judged not by some set of rules but by a standard of justice which is inherent in their nature.   **[2236]**

——. cf. #2150.

CALVERT, B. "Plato's *Crito* and Richard Kraut," in #1283, pp. 17-33. Reply to #1090. Explores whether there is a single, consistent Socratic position on one's legal obligations in *Apol* and *Crito*.   **[2237]**

COLSON, D. D. "*Crito* 51a-c: To What Does Socrates Owe Obedience?" *Phron* 34(1989), 27-55. Starts from apparent tension between *Apol* 29c-d and *Crito* 51a-c to investigate S's understanding of allegiance he owes to his polity. His defiance of the jury is an act of loyalty to the state, properly understood.   **[2238]**

CONGLETON, A. "Two Kinds of Lawlessness: Plato's *Crito*." *PolTheo* 2(1974), 432-446. Only by carefully examining nature of Socratic dialogue and character of Crito can we understand the argument of Speech of the Laws.   **[2239]**

CRAGG, W. "The *Crito* and the Nature of Legal Obligation," in #72, pp. 21-26. S expresses the view that it is sometimes justifiable to oppose unjust laws but not to undermine state's authority to make and enforce law. His position is basically that of non-violent civil disobedience.   **[2240]**

DREISBACH, D. F. "Agreement and Obligation in the *Crito*." *NewSchol* 52(1978), 168-186. P maintains that citizens should obey laws because they depend on them. Disobedience weakens law and is thus harmful to citizen, even if he saves his life by disobedience. Whether it is moral to obey an unjust state is not the issue in *Crito*.   **[2241]**

DYBIKOWSKI, J. "Socrates, Obedience and the Law: Plato's *Crito*." *Dial*(Can) 13(1974), 519-535. Arguments against escape presented in the dialogue lack any fundamental obligation for obedience, showing that S was not actually as democratic as he is often presented.   **[2242]**

DYSON, M. "The Structure of the Laws' Speech in Plato's *Crito*." *CQ* 28(1978), 427-436. Examines three main propositions of the argument attributed to the Laws: 1) disobedience to law harms persons; 2) relationship between citizen and state is analogous to that between child and parent; 3) citizen makes a tacit compact to obey laws. Explores connections between them.   **[2243]**

ERDE, E. L. "Founding Morality: Hume vs. Plato or Hume and Plato." *SwJPh* 9(1978), 19-25. A contractarian theory of society, such as Hume's, can be reconciled with P's view, if one founds the contract on a commitment to the moral validity of promises. Some form of government may be necessary to accomplish this.   **[2244]**

EUBEN, J. P. "Philosophy and Politics in Plato's *Crito*." *PolTheo* 6(1978), 149-172. Examines inconsistency between S's expressed willingness in *Apol* to disobey jury should they forbid him to practice philosophy and his unwillingness in *Crito* to escape from jail.   **[2245]**

FARRELL, D. M. "Illegal Actions, Universal Maxims, and the Duty To Obey the Law: The Case for Civil Authority in the *Crito*." *PolTheo* 6(1978), 173-189. S's arguments against escape, which are more persuasive than is often conceded, rest on his assumption that his reasons for escape would have negative impact for the city if all citizens accepted and acted upon them.   **[2246]**

GAVIN, B. "A Note on Socrates and 'The Law' in the *Crito*." *Aitia* 7(1979), 26-28. S admits laws can be unjust, but no one can justify disobeying spirit of the law.   **[2247]**

GREENBERG, N. A. "Socrates' Choice in the *Crito*." *HSCP* 70(1965), 45-82. *Apol* emphasizes choice between good and evil; *Crito* stresses obedience to law. S resolved conflict to some degree by remaining true to his heroic view of himself.   **[2248]**

KAHN, C. H. "Problems in the Argument of Plato's *Crito*." *Apeir* 22(1989), 29-43. The *Crito* does not support arguments for civil disobedience. Its arguments are specifically for S and his situation and are not to be generalized.   **[2249]**

KOSTMAN, J. "Socrates' Self-Betrayal and the 'Contradiction' Between the *Apology* and the *Crito*," in #1083, pp. 107-130. Sees *Crito* as a philosophical fiction. S submitted to death penalty, not on moral grounds, but for the self-regarding reason that it would be most advantageous for him to die a timely and easy death.   **[2250]**

KRAMER, S. "Socrates' Dream. *Crito* 44a-b." *CJ* 83(1988), 193-197. Whether historical or not, account of S's dream and its interpretation are used dramatically by P to foreshadow the choice S must make between death and flight. Reader is being reminded of Achilles' choice of noble death over life lived in disgrace.   **[2251]**

KRAMM, L. "Plato's *Crito* in Present Perspective." *PhilStud* (Ireland) 31(1986-7), 159-174. *Crito* is a good introduction into philosophical life in a cynical age.   **[2252]**

KRAUT, R. "Reply to Clifford Orwin," in #1275, pp. 177-182. Defends his way of reading *Crito* against Orwin (#2256). Denies that just because a philosophical work is presented as a dialogue, it is not also a treatise.   **[2253]**

LUCAS, B. J. "Plato's *Crito* as Contribution to Philosophy of Law," in #72, pp. 27-31. Reconstructs several claims from S's argument which lead logically to the conclusion that S had a moral duty not to escape and to some broader conclusions about the existence of a necessity to obey the law.   **[2254]**

MARTIN, R. "Socrates on Disobedience to Law." *RMeta* 24(1970), 21-38. In this dialogue S argues that all laws, whether just or not, must be obeyed. Possible weaknesses of this position are explored.   **[2255]**

ORWIN, C. "Liberalizing the *Crito*: Richard Kraut on Socrates and the State," in #1275, pp. 171-176. Challenges Kraut's (#1090) approach to reading *Crito* of not paying sufficient attention to dialogue form and context of particular conversations.   **[2256]**

PANAGIOTOU, S. "Justified Disobedience in the *Crito*," in #1283, pp. 35-50. *Crito* advances the view that a citizen is obligated to obey ultimately any and all laws or orders of the state, but this obligation applies only to citizens of a state which adheres to certain principles and procedures.   **[2257]**

PAYNE, T. "The *Crito* as a Mythological Mime." *Interp* 11(1983), 1-24. Interprets *Crito* as an ironic imitation of *Iliad* 9, in which ambassadors plead with Achilles to accept Agamemnon's authority and return to battle. Some roles are reversed.   **[2258]**

QUANDT, K. "Socratic Consolation: Rhetoric and Philosophy in Plato's *Crito*." *Ph&Rh* 15(1982), 238-256. Speech of Laws fails to satisfy the criteria of valid argumentation which S expounded earlier in dialogue. It maintains that true justice cannot be found in this life.   **[2259]**

RAY, A. C. "The Tacit Agreement in the *Crito*." *IntStudPh* 12(1980), 47-54. S's notion of relationship between citizen and government in *Crito* is more complex than a social contract. Duty of citizen to obey a government which has responsibility to administer laws is part of natural order.   **[2260]**

ROSEN, F. "Obligation and Friendship in Plato's *Crito*." *PolTheo* 1(1973), 307-316. Theme of the dialogue is more subtle than mere principles of political obligation. It is actually about friendship on several levels: person, political, and intellectual.   **[2261]**

ROSIVACH, V. J. "*Hoi Polloi* in the *Crito* 44b5-d10." *CJ* 76(1981), 289-297. Dialogue's purpose is to persuade its audience by rhetoric, not convince them rationally.   **[2262]**

WATSON, W. "The Voices of the God: Comments on Kostman," in #1083, pp. 173-180. Challenges Kostman's claim (#2250) that S's refusal to escape from prison constituted an abandonment of his philosophic mission.   **[2263]**

WEINRIB, E. J. "Obedience to the Law in Plato's *Crito*." *AmJJur* 27(1982), 85-108. Summarizes apparent inconsistencies in speech of Laws, their unexpected brevity, superficiality, and defence of conventional views of legal obligation.   **[2264]**

WEST, E. J. M. "Socrates in the *Crito*: Patriot or Friend?" in #1267, pp. 71-83. Examines relationship between Crito and S in context of larger issue of friendship as basis of Greek politics.   **[2265]**

WOOZLEY, A. D. *Law and Obedience: The Arguments of Plato's* Crito. London: Duckworth, 1979. Detailed discussion of question in *Crito* of whether it would be wrong for S to take advantage of escape from jail which his friends offered him.   **[2266]**

——. cf. #1225.

YAFFE, M. D. "Civil Disobedience and the Opinion of the Many: Plato's *Crito*." *ModSch* 54(1977), 123-136. Approaches the Laws' speech as a kind of introduction to philosophy and that acknowledged circularity of S's argument is deliberately designed for this protreptic purpose.   **[2267]**

For related items see #1101, #1217, #1226, #2162

Epistles (cf. Letters)

Euthydemus

Two young men, one of them the title character, show off the verbal tricks they have learned at the feet of the Sophists. Their primary technique is to present an opponent with alternative positions and to refute whichever he chooses, e. g., do you mean to say x or y? If the opponent chooses x, then another set of alternatives is put forth, supposedly to clarify: do you mean x_1 or x_2? The technique is not totally different from S's, but S has some philosophical insight as his ultimate quest. These young men are simply interested in showing off their ability to do exercises, somewhat like a pianist who can do thunderous chords and runs on the keyboard but cannot interpret the nuances of a piece of music. S shows that their apparent cleverness depends on their opponents' confusion over the meaning of terms. They never produce positive insights but spend their time trying to embarrass others. Their purpose is eristic, i. e., disputatious with no ultimate objective beyond the disputation. Socratic elenchus refutes an opponent's definitions, but with the intention of leading him to refine his own position.

The tone of the *Euthydemus* is that of a satiric play. Leo Strauss called it "the most bantering, not to say frivolous and farcical dialogue." It may have been written shortly before Plato opened the Academy (387 B. C.) and may have been intended as a kind of programmatic announcement for the school.

HAWTREY, R. S. W. *Commentary on Plato's* Euthydemus. Philadelphia: American Philos. Soc., 1981. It is crucial to see dialogue in its historical context and with its intended consequence in "real" world. Gives an exposition of grammatical and lexical points, and in particular use of the particle. **[2268]**

O'SULLIVAN, J. N. "Plato, *Euthydemus* 296c8-10 (Burnet)." *LCM* 4(1979), 61-62. Meaning of the passage can be clarified by changing punctuation. **[2269]**

SCOLNICOV, S. "Plato's *Euthydemus*: A Study on the Relations Between Logic and Education." *SCI* 6(1981-82), 19-29. Purpose of the dialogue is to distinguish between Socratic and Sophistic reasoning. Socratic education is based on irony, which can easily be mistaken for ridicule. **[2270]**

SPRAGUE, R. K. "Plato's Sophistry, II." *PAS* Suppl. 51(1977), 45-61. Reply to Stewart (#2272), citing Aristotle's treatment of arguments in *Euthyd.* **[2271]**

——. cf. #921.

STEWART, M. A. "Plato's Sophistry, I." *PAS* Suppl. 51(1977), 21-44. P largely ignored the nature and importance of ambiguity in the meanings of common words. He was more aware of ambiguities arising from syntax and a speaker's lack of clarity. **[2272]**

STRAUSS, L. "On the *Euthydemus*." *Interp* 1(1970), 1-20; also in #2015, pp. 67-88. Suggests that S and Sophists were not mortal enemies. S acknowledges that every art has good and bad practioners. Philosophy's greatest enemy, in his view, is the unenlightened multitude. **[2273]**

For related items see #1693, #1884.

Euthyphro

This dialogue opens with Euthyphro expressing surprise at finding S at the king-archon's court, where legal disputes are handled. S explains that he has been indicted by Meletus for corrupting the young and for impiety by creating new gods and not believing in the old ones. In response to S's query as to why Euthyphro is at the court, Euthyphro informs him that he is prosecuting his father on a charge of impiety for accidentally killing a laborer who was himself a murderer. Euthyphro's action is denounced by his family and friends, but he takes these objections to be confirmation of their ignorance of the true nature of piety. He is so confident of his own knowledge of piety that he has no doubts about the correctness of his prosecution. Zeus killed his father, who had killed his father. Can it be impious to model oneself on the gods? Euthyphro claims to know the nature of piety better than other men.

S responds to that assertion by asking to become Euthyphro's pupil in order to learn from him the nature of piety and thereby have a better defense at his own trial. (S's irony in this situation has been the subject of much discussion.) S asks Euthyphro, "What is piety?" and the remainder of the dialogue consists in a search for a definition. In the course of responding to Euthyphro's attempted definitions, S spells out certain requirements for a satisfactory definition which have important philosophical implications.

In 6d-e S makes a statement that has far-reaching implications. He says to Euthyphro,

> Bear in mind that I did not bid you tell me one or two of the many pious actions but the form itself that makes all pious actions pious, for you agreed that impious actions are impious and all pious actions pious through one form . . . . Tell me then what this form itself is, so that I may look upon it, and using it as a model, say that any action of yours or another's that is of that kind is pious, and if it is not, that it is not.

S here seems to be committed to some kind of theory of Forms. As R. E. Allen argues, there is an "earlier" theory of Forms in which S takes the Forms to be universals, essences, and standards. The Forms in the *Euthyphro* may not be the separate and transcendent Forms of the *Phaedo*, but Allen maintains that there nonetheless is a genuine theory of Forms in this dialogue.

Another important aspect of the dialogue centers around Euthyphro's third definition of piety as what all the gods love. In response to this definition, S asks whether the gods love what is pious because it is pious or whether what is pious is pious because the gods love it. What S is arguing is that the Form of piety exists independently of the gods, whatever the gods may be. The standards as embodied in the Forms are distinct from the gods themselves, and the gods must conform to these standards.

The dialogue ends with Euthyphro failing to satisfy S's desire to find a satisfactory definition of piety. The self-proclaimed expert is frustrated by his inability to answer the question. What effect the Socratic cross-examination had on Euthyphro's prosecution of his father we do not know.

ALLEN, R. E. *Plato's* Euthyphro *and the Earlier Theory of Forms.* London: Routledge & Kegan Paul, 1970. Translation plus discussion. *Euthyphro* contains a theory of forms which differs from that explicated in *Phaedo, Symp,* and other later dialogues. The earlier version lacks a clear two-world ontology. In *Euthyphro* forms are universals, essences capable of definition. [2274]

ANDERSON, A. "Socratic Reasoning in the *Euthyphro*." *RMeta* 22(1969), 461-481. S's argument at 10a-c is not as weak as many scholars maintain. He teaches Euthyphro as much about formulating a definition as he does about piety. He draws a clear distinction between a thing and its sort and a whole and its part. [2275]

BISHOP, J. "The Reasons of the Gods. A Reply to Robert Nola." *Prud* 15(1983), 13-26. S. M. Cohen's study of the argument in *Euthyphro* (#2281) is stronger than R. Nola's (#2302). [2276]

BLITS, J. "The Holy and Human. An Interpretation of Plato's *Euthyphro*." *Apeir* 14(1980), 19-40. It is necessary to study the dialogue's dramatic situation and S's actions in light of his words. Such an examination can find clues to S's concept of the holy in his refutations. [2277]

BURNS, S. A. M. "Doing Business with the Gods." *CanJPh* 15(1985), 311-326. Though S's attitude toward piety appears negative, *Euthyphro* does offer positive views on the subject. [2278]

CANDISH, S. "*Euthyphro* 6d-9b and its Misinterpretations." *Apeir* 17(1983), 28-32. Claims that argument at 6d-9b has been misinterpreted and mistranslated. The argument is not just an attack on Euthyphro's definition as such; it is directed against Euthyphro himself. [2279]

COBB, W. S. "The Religious and the Just in Plato's *Euthyphro*." *AncPh* 5(1985), 41-46. The view of the relation between justice and piety which S defends in this dialogue is not incompatible with his position in *Protag*. [2280]

COHEN, S. M. "Socrates on the Definition of Piety: *Euthyphro* 10A-11B." *JHPh* 9(1971), 1-13; also in #1199, pp. 158-176. S opposed idea that piety is "what all the gods love." Something must be a loved thing because it is loved, not loved because it is a loved thing. S's argument is valid if "because" is taken equivocally. [2281]

CORNFORD, F. M. "Plato's *Euthyphro* or How to Read a Socratic Dialogue," in #53, pp. 221-238. S's profession of ignorance about divine things would have been taken as a positive claim in ancient Athens. Modern attitudes toward agnosticism prevent us from reading the early Socratic dialogues as P intended them to be understood. [2282]

EGAN, R. B. "Tragic Piety in Plato's *Euthyphro*." *Dion* 7(1983), 17-32. P borrows and adapts a common, familiar theme from tragedy to dramatize dangers and shortcomings of poetry as opposed to philosophical inquiry. [2283]

FINEBURG, S. "Plato's *Euthyphro* and the Myth of Proteus." *TAPhA* 112(1982), 65-70. Examines S's reference to Proteus at 15d; Homeric paradigm points to definition of piety. Like Menelaus struggling with Proteus, S eventually gets from Euthyphro — though grudgingly — a definition of piety linked to *charis* in sense of beauty to which one is devoted because of itself.   [2284]

FRIEDMAN, J. I. "Plato's *Euthyphro* and Leibniz' Law." *Phil*(Isrl) 12(1982), 1-20. Formalizes S's argument, using higher-order Leibniz' Law, and then shows how argument is flawed.   [2285]

FURLEY, W. D. "The Figure of Euthyphro in Plato's Dialogue." *Phron* 30(1985), 201-208. Euthyphro represents traditional religious views, which are shown to be inferior to S's thought on religion.   [2286]

GARRETT, R. "The Structure of Plato's *Euthyphro*." *SJPh* 12(1974), 165-183. There is a subtle geometric structure to the dialogue. The straight-circular structure mirrors a conjunction of opposites in dialogue's subject matter that P later formulated in his distinction between being and becoming. Motion and rest are also important images, as S leads Euthyphro from shifting opinion to stable truth.   [2287]

GEACH, P. T. "Plato's *Euthyphro*: An Analysis and Commentary." *Monist* 50(1966), 369-382; also in *Logic Matters* (Oxford: Blackwell, 1972), pp. 31-44. Emphasizes various elements that tie into contemporary expectations that terms be defined, and alleged distinction between *decidable* factual disputes and *undecidable* moral disputes. [2288]

HADEN, J. "On Plato's Inconclusiveness." *CJ* 64(1969), 219-224. Although argument of *Euthyphro* finally returns to where it started, P wants reader to see that truth can be discerned by following route which Euthyphro refuses to take.   [2289]

HALL, J. C. "Plato, *Euthyphro* 10a1-11a10." *PhQ* 18(1968), 1-11. Examines S's refutation of definition that the pious is "what all the gods love." Examines P's new use of two technical terms and his application of formal logical techniques to a philosophical problem.   [2290]

HENRY, M. "Socratic Piety and the Power of Reason," in #1083, pp. 95-106. Seeks to explain Platonic interpretation of Socratic piety (as opposed to Xenophon's interpretation) and to show how Athenians were persuaded that S was impious.   [2291]

HOLLAND, R. F. "Euthyphro." *PAS* 82(1981-82), 1-15. Euthyphro realizes there is a conflict in his *eusebia* (piety) toward gods and his responsibility to his father, but he is not disturbed by it because he does not understand how deep conflict runs.   [2292]

HOOPES, J. P. "Euthyphro's Case." *CB* 47(1970) 1-6. Euthyphro is dramatic paradigm of *amathia*, while S is revealed as true paradigm of piety: investigating at the god's behest and exhibiting true care of the soul.   [2293]

KLONOSKI, R. "The Portico of the Archon Basileus. On the Significance of the Setting of Plato's *Euthyphro*." *CJ* 81(1986), 130-137. Debate on what is pious is held, ironically, in colonnade of top religious official of Athens.   [2294]

———. "Setting and Characterization in Plato's *Euthyphro*." *Dialogos* 19(1984), 123-140.

Analysis of the settings of the dialogue and the character of Euthyphro himself makes it clear that the dialogue criticizes the decay of religion in P's Athens. **[2295]**

LESHER, J. H. "Theistic Ethics in the *Euthyphro*." *Apeir* 9 #2(1975), 24-30. It does not seem to have been P's intention to suggest that S's arguments against Euthyphro's definition of piety undercut any theistic basis for ethics. **[2296]**

LEWIS, M. "An Interpretation of Plato's *Euthyphro*." *Interp* 12(1984), 225-259. Dialogue reveals that pious devotion to past is in tension with justice and that gods are not concerned for us. Justice is a strictly human affair. **[2297]**

————. "An Interpretation of Plato's *Euthyphro* (Part I, Section 4, to End)." *Interp* 13(1985), 33-64. Running summary and commentary. S's refutation of the view that piety is justice to the gods is based on premises considered valid by most religious persons, in whatever place or time. **[2298]**

MacKINNON, D. M., and MAYNELL, H. "The *Euthyphro* Dilemma." *PAS* Suppl. 46(1972), 211-234. Examines dialogue's central problems in areas of theology and morality. **[2299]**

MOUTAFAKIS, N. J. "Plato's Emergence in the *Euthyphro*." *Apeir* 5(1971), 23-32. This dialogue reflects an early manifestation of P's later thought on moral philosophy and Forms. **[2300]**

NEUMANN, H. "The Problem of Piety in Plato's *Euthyphro*." *ModSch* 43(1966), 265-272. Socratic piety toward an impersonal absolute has no existential value. Euthyphro stresses the personal in his piety. Athenians could not combine the two. **[2301]**

NOLA, R. "Morality and Religion in Plato's *Euthyphro*." *Prud* 14(1982), 83-96. Gods can command us to do what is right, but they cannot provide definition of such terms as piety or a rational explanation for why we should do as they bid. **[2302]**

PANAGIOTOU, S. "Plato's *Euthyphro* and the Attic Code on Homicide." *Hermes* 102(1974) 419-437. Examines legal background of Euthyphro's suit against his father. S criticizes Euthyphro's methodology, not his objective. **[2303]**

PAXSON, T. D. "Plato's *Euthyphro* 10a to 11b." *Phron* 17(1972), 171-190. Shows validity of argument of this passage, which rest on the principle of substitutibility, and explores what it shows about the nature of Platonic ethics. **[2304]**

PRIOR, W. J. "Relations Between Forms and 'Pauline Predication' in *Euthyphro* 11e4-12d4." *AncPh* 1(1980-81), 61-68. Examines question of ambiguity between P's two versions of the statement form "F-ness is g" in *Euthyphro* and *Soph*. P does not seem to have seen any inconsistency in the two accounts. **[2305]**

ROSE, L. E. "A Note on the *Euthyphro*, 10-11." *Phron* 10(1965), 149-150. Euthyphro is involved in three separate inconsistencies. **[2306]**

ROSEN, F. "Piety and Justice: Plato's *Euthyphro*." *Ph* 42(1968), 105-115. For S it is justice, not piety, which links human and divine. **[2307]**

SHARVY, R. "*Euthyphro* 9d-11b: Analysis and Definition in Plato and Others." *Nous* 6(1972), 119-137. S's basic premise in the argument about the definition of piety is not based on substitutivity of definitional equivalents. It is in fact a prototype of a theory of analysis and formal causation. It differs from, and is superior to, some modern theories about defining value terms.   **[2308]**

SPRAGUE, R. K. "Parmenides' Sail and Dionysodorus' Ox." *Phron* 12(1967), 91-98. Similar objections raised in *Euthyphro* and *Parm* to S's arguments are drawn from Eleatics and do not represent P's criticism of his own ideas.   **[2309]**

TAYLOR, C. C. W. "The End of the *Euthyphro*." *Phron* 27(1982), 109-118. Dialogue seems to end aporetically, but the argument suggests piety may be a kind of virtue and may imply doctrine of unity of virtues, prominent in other early dialogues.   **[2310]**

THOMAS, J. E. "On the Duality of Socrates' What-is-X Question." *LThPh* 30(1974), 21-27. Reviews the debate between Allen and Robinson over what S means by the question "what-is-X?" Tries to show that the question can be interpreted in two ways, as asking for an identifying mark of X, or for the essence of X.   **[2311]**

VERSENYI, L. *Holiness and Justice: An Interpretation of Plato's* Euthyphro. Washington, DC: Univ. Pr. of Amer., 1982. A substantive definition of holiness is implicit in the dialogue itself. The conflict between S and Euthyphro is a dichotomy between traditional religious belief and the life of rationalism.   **[2312]**

WEISS, R. "Euthyphro's Failure." *JHPh* 24(1986), 437-452. Euthyphro's failure to justify his case against his father and to define holiness is the result of his belief in morally imperfect gods.   **[2313]**

WELCH, C. "The *Euthyphro* and the Forms." *GM* 22(1967), 228-244. Examines the theme of knowledge/comprehension of Forms.   **[2314]**

WOLZ, H. G. "The Paradox of Piety in Plato's *Euthyphro* in the Light of Heidegger's Conception of Authenticity." *SJPh* 12(1974), 493-511. The problem of the definition of piety is its double meaning of doing the will of the gods and being a kind of virtue. Heidegger's concept of authenticity helps in the resolution of this paradox.   **[2315]**

ZEIGLER, G. "Plato's *Euthyphro* Revisited." *PacPhQ* 61(1980), 291-300. S's two elenchi fail because of an equivocation in his argument and because the argument depends on making substitutions which may not be valid.   **[2316]**

For related items see #1102, #1217, #1332, #1912.

Gorgias

Probably written after the *Protagoras, Meno,* and *Euthydemus,* this dialogue marks P's advancement to a new stage in his development. In it P, apparently despairing of being able to effect any change in Athenian political behavior, signals his intention to withdraw from active participation in the city's life and devote himself to intellectual pursuits. The dialogue aroused considerable interest in his doctrines and seems to have drawn a number of students to the newly opened Academy.

The dialogue's theme is a challenge to the claim of professional rhetoricians (among whom Gorgias was pre-eminent) to teach virtue. S shows that rhetoric is to wisdom as skill in cooking is to an understanding of nutrition. Rhetoric and cooking depend upon clever presentation and require no understanding of the *techne* (art, skill) of education or nutrition. It was probably written as an indictment of the rhetor Isocrates, who opened a school in Athens in 388 B. C., and of the dangers of rhetoric and the power it gives some people over others.

Three sections make up the dialogue. In the first S discusses with the elderly Gorgias the definition and objectives of rhetoric. S argues that, if the rhetorician is to train anyone for public service, he must himself be a good man. Gorgias concedes that not all rhetoricians come up to that standard. In the second section Gorgias' friend Polus relieves the tired Sophist and disputes with S the place of rhetoric among the arts. S brings the discussion around to two of his most fundamental assertions: that no one does evil willingly and that it is better to endure injustice than to commit it. Polus eventually accepts the latter thesis, or at least ceases to offer objections.

Some remarks by Callicles, who has been listening to the debate, provide the transition to the final section, in which S tries to show that the aim of political action should be the improvement of the citizens of a town. Few politicians, however, are genuinely good men, so this objective is rarely, if ever, achieved. Even the most notable leaders, such as Pericles, corrupted the moral character of the citizens rather than improved it. The interlocutors urge S to take an active role in Athenian politics. He declines, but maintains that he is the only true politician in the city, though he has only one supporter, Truth.

Throughout the dialogue, P is intent on developing the contrast between the rhetorician-politician and the philosopher. We see this both in the way in which the different participants conduct the discussion and in the views put forth. P recognizes what is at stake: "Our discussion is about the way we're supposed to live" (500c).

ALGONZIN, K. "Faith and Silence in Plato's *Gorgias*." *Thom* 41(1977),237-246. Suggests that by making a point of Callicles' silence during S's declaration of his ultimate wisdom, P provides, not a signal of Callicles' defeat, but appropriate counter-declaration of tyrannical soul. **[2317]**

ANTON, J. P. "Dialectic and Health in Plato's *Gorgias*: Presuppositions and Implications." *AncPh* 1(1980-81), 49-60. *Gorg* establishes theoretical framework for distinguishing bodily from mental health by combining arts of medicine and dialectic. **[2318]**

ARCHIE, J. P. "Callicles' Redoubtable Critique of the Polus Argument in Plato's *Gorgias*." *Hermes* 112(1984), 167-176. Examines fallacy which Socrates is able to exploit and shows its significance for structure and argument of entire dialogue. **[2319]**

BRICKHOUSE, T. C. "Zeigler on Plato's *Gorgias* and Psychological Egoism." *Pers* 60(1979), 451-454. Response to #2357. **[2320]**

CALVERT, B. "The Politicians of Athens in the *Gorgias* and *Meno*." *HPolTho* 5(1984), 1-16. Concept of true belief is main clue for understanding S's assessments of institutions and politicians of Athens, which are essentially favorable.   **[2321]**

COOPER, J. "The *Gorgias* and Irwin's Socrates." *RMeta* 35(1982), 577-587. Discussion of #2328. S does not see virtue as a means to happiness but as the goal of life.**[2322]**

DILMAN, I. *Morality and the Inner Life: A Study in Plato's* Gorgias. Totowa, NJ: Barnes and Noble, 1979. Examines S's argument for philosophic life, defined as contemplation of other-worldly values. Chapters examine morality in relation to nature, convention, and freedom, and look at S's concept of virtue as knowledge.   **[2323]**

DUNCAN, R. "*Philia* in the *Gorgias*." *Apeir* 8 #1(1974), 23-26. *Philia* serves to limit desire. Callicles is an example of tension an individual feels between desire for friendship and desire to excel over others.   **[2324]**

FRIEDLAENDER, P. "*Gorgias*," in #2081, pp. 91-127. Dialogue's most important themes: struggle between false rhetoric (sophism) and true (philosophy); conflict between pleasure and the good; struggle between S and his fellow citizens.   **[2325]**

GREEN, E. M. "Plato's Use of Three Dramatic Elements in *Gorgias* as Means to Demonstrate his Thought." *SouthSpJ* 33(1968), 307-315. Setting, character, and conflict of ideas enable P to communicate his views in an essentially didactic work.   **[2326]**

HALL, R. W. "*Techne* and Morality in the *Gorgias*," in #41, pp. 202-218. Dialogue displays view of morality that is quite similar to utilitarian ethic grounded on knowledge and values of *techne* characteristic of early dialogues.   **[2327]**

IRWIN, T. H. *Plato:* Gorgias. Oxford: Clarendon Pr., 1979. Transl. for non-specialists, with introduction and notes. Designed for those who do not know P, philosophy, or Greek. Stresses importance for S of the analogy of virtue as a craft.   **[2328]**

JOHNSON, C. N. "Socrates' Encounter with Polus in Plato's *Gorgias*." *Phoenix* 43(1989), 196-216. S's defeat of Polus, though logically flawed, serves to show that philosophy can defeat rhetoric.   **[2329]**

KAHN, C. H. "Drama and Dialectic in Plato's *Gorgias*." *OSAP* 1(1983), 75-121. Refutations of Gorgias, Polus, and Callicles constitute P's fullest portrayal of way in which dialectical encounter with S turns into a critical examination of interlocutor's own life. Thus all three arguments are in deep sense *ad hominem*.   **[2330]**

———. cf. #2846.

KAUFFMANN, C. "Enactment as Argument in the *Gorgias*." *Ph&Rh* 12(1979), 114-129. S's interchanges with various characters in the dialogue mark his failure in dialectic, politics, and rhetoric, at least as measured by the criteria established in the dialogue. P is trying to show that dialectic and rhetoric are dependent on one another and essential to *politike techne*.   **[2331]**

KERFERD, G. B. "Plato's Treatment of Callicles in the *Gorgias*." *PCPhS* 20(1974), 48-52. Callicles, not identifiable with an historical person, is linked with Pericles and accused of playing to galleries instead of effectively leading the people.   [2332]

KIMBALL, B. "The Inclination of Modern Jurists to Associate Lawyers with Doctors: Plato's Response in *Gorgias* 464-465." *Journal of Medical Humanities and Bioethics* 9(1988), 17-31. Explores Gorgias' analogy of association of law and medicine and contrasts it with modern jurists' account.   [2333]

KLOSKO, G. "The Refutation of Callicles in Plato's *Gorgias*." *G&R* 31(1984), 126-139. To refute Callicles' position that a hedonistic life brings more pleasure than a just life would be difficult and time-consuming. P states Callicles' arguments in their most extreme form to make S's task easier.   [2334]

LEWIS, T. J. "Refutative Rhetoric as True Rhetoric in the *Gorgias*." *Interp* 14(1986), 195-210. Examines refutative rhetoric in *Gorg* and constructive rhetoric in *Phaedrus*. S succeeds in making his point in *Phaedrus*, but readers must draw their own conclusions in *Gorg*. S does succeed in attracting those listening to his refutation of Gorgias to the study of philosophy.   [2335]

LINFORTH, I. M. "Soul and Sieve in Plato's *Gorgias*," in #1278, pp. 137-155. P is in fact the unnamed source of this allegedly Pythagorean fable.   [2336]

MacKENZIE, M. M. "A Pyrrhic Victory. *Gorgias* 474b-477a." *CQ* 32(1982), 84-88. P fails to clarify the reference of *kalon* ("good") when shifting from active to passive and thus renders his argument invalid.   [2337]

McKIM, R. "Shame and Truth in Plato's *Gorgias*," in #1275, pp. 34-48. Distinguishes between dialogue carried on "within" P's text and that which P carries on with reader of text. Explores philosophical status of shame and moral insight.   [2338]

McTIGHE, K. "Socrates on Desire for the Good and the Involuntariness of Wrongdoing: *Gorgias* 466a-468e." *Phron* 29(1984), 193-236. Examines logic and dramatic context of argument that neither orators nor tyrants have any great power at all. Challenges a widely accepted interpretation of paradox that no one does wrong voluntarily.   [2339]

MURRAY, J. S. "Plato on Knowledge, Persuasion, and the Art of Rhetoric." *AncPh* 8(1988), 1-10. Analyzes search for definition of rhetoric in *Gorg* 452e9-455a7. Argues that this persuasion is an essential part of true pedagogy. Challenges traditional view that, in P's scheme, rhetoric produces only belief, while true teaching leads to knowledge (*episteme*).   [2340]

PENNER, T. "Socrates on the Impossibility of Belief-Relative Sciences." *PBACAPh* 3(1987), 263-325. Gorgias' rhetoric is a "belief-relative science" in that it aims at persuading people to believe certain things, irrespective of whether these beliefs are true or false. This is what disqualifies it as a true science in the Socratic elenchus, for S denies that there are any such "belief-relative sciences."   [2341]

PLOCHMANN, G. K., and **ROBINSON, F. E.** *A Friendly Companion to Plato's* Gorgias. Carbondale: Southern IL Univ. Pr., 1987. Detailed study arguing that *Gorg* is an "illustration of the peculiar sort of philosophic exploration that Plato advocated" regarding direction successful theorizing about rhetoric ought to take.   [2342]

PRINCIPE, M. A. "Restraint of Desire in the *Gorgias*." *SJPh* 20(1982), 121-132. Challenges Irwin (#2328) by arguing that S presents theses wholly consistent with principle that knowledge is sufficient for virtue. Also argues against Irwin's view that S acknowledges non-rational desires.   **[2343]**

RACE, W. H. "Shame in Plato's *Gorgias*." *CJ* 74(1979), 197-202. Shame, defined by S as ignorance, is central theme of dialogue. Callicles exemplifies this deficiency.   **[2344]**

RENDALL, S. "Dialogue, Philosophy, and Rhetoric. The Example of Plato's *Gorgias*." *Ph&Rh* 10(1977), 165-179. P views philosophy as something that happens in an exchange. Thus rhetoric and dialectic play important roles, as *Gorg* shows, and the dialogue form is the most appropriate mode of expression for his ideas.   **[2345]**

RYAN, E. E. "Plato's *Gorgias* and *Phaedrus* and Aristotle's Theory of Rhetoric: A Speculative Account." *Athenaeum* 57(1979), 452-461. Suggests that some of P's rhetorical theory was developed in reaction to Ar's *Rhet*.   **[2346]**

SAXONHOUSE, A. W. "An Unspoken Theme in Plato's *Gorgias*: 'War'." *Interp* 11(1983), 139-170. Dialogue serves as P's answer to Thucydides' account of Peloponnesian War. Rhetoric and war both express Athens' desire for more. Callicles, the central character, represents Athens.   **[2347]**

SCHMID, W. T. "Philosophy and Moral Commitment." *AncPh* 2(1982), 134-141. Discussion of Dilman *Morality and Inner Life* (#2323).   **[2348]**

SHARIN, D. "Commentary on Penner." *PBACAPh* 3(1987), 326-332. Examines Penner's (#2341) denial of belief-relative sciences, and explores it in relation to interpretation of literary works.   **[2349]**

SHARPLES, R. W. "Condemned Out of His Own Mouth: Two Notes on Callicles in Plato's *Gorgias*." *LCM* 13(1988), 115-116. Notes contradictions between what Callicles says about freedom and the *demos* and the consequences of his positions.   **[2350]**

SPITZER, A. "The Self-Reference of the *Gorgias*." *Ph&Rh* 8(1975), 1-22; also in #2081, pp. 129-151. Sees *Gorg* as self-referential: it not only explicates nature and defects of rhetoric through argument, but also demonstrates them through the characters' words and actions. Three main characters represent rhetoric as art form, self-conscious study, and political tool.   **[2351]**

TARRANT, H. "The Composition of Plato's *Gorgias*." *Prud* 14(1982), 3-22. First part of dialogue (447a-481b) was written before P visited Sicily. Second was composed upon his return, in part in response to Polycrates' charges against S's followers.   **[2352]**

VLASTOS, G. "Was Polus Refuted?" *AJPh* 88(1967), 454-460. It is Polus' inability to keep his "wits about him," not his utterance that suffering wrong would be the "uglier" option, that causes him to lose the argument with S in *Gorg* 474C.   **[2353]**

WEISS, R. "Ignorance, Involuntariness, and Innocence: A Reply to McTighe," *Phron* 30(1985), 314-322. Challenges McTighe's (#2339) claims that "involuntary" wrongdoing means wrongdoing that is exempt from blame and that S regards all wrongdoing as exempt from blame.   **[2354]**

WHITE, N. P. "Rational Prudence in Plato's *Gorgias*," in #1282, pp. 139-162. P does not think he has proved that: one is made better off by acting justly; doing injustice is worse than suffering it; if one does injustice, one is made better off by being punished. He thinks he has shown something about temperance and rational prudence. **[2355]**

WISER, J. L. "The Force of Reason: On Reading Plato's *Gorgias*," in *The Ethical Dimension of Political Life*, ed. F. Canavan (Durham, NC: Duke Univ. Pr., 1983), pp. 49-60. *Gorg* treats the question "Who should rule?" politically and ethically. **[2356]**

ZEIGLER, G. "Plato's *Gorgias* and Psychological Egoism." *Pers* 60(1979) 123-133. Psychological egoism is thesis that people act to their greatest advantage. If that is taken to be soul's good, then S did not believe that people act only to attain it. He did think that people act to attain their greatest benefit if they know what it Is. **[2357]**

———. "Reply to Professor Brickhouse." *Pers* 60(1979), 455-457. Response to #2320, and defense of thesis that P's moral psychology is not egoistic. **[2358]**

ZEYL, D. J., trans. *Gorgias*. Indianapolis: Hackett, 1987. A new translation striving for accuracy and clarity. **[2359]**

For related items see #2102, #2131, #2790, #2920.

Hipparchus

This probably dubious little dialogue is Socratic in form, with S asking a companion to define "profiteering." It fails to resolve the question, largely because no definition of "profit" is ever considered. The career of the sixth-century Athenian tyrant Hipparchus is discussed by S as an example of the ultimate profiteer.

BLOOM, A. "The Political Philosopher in Democratic Society: The Socratic View," in *Mélanges en l'honneur de Raymond Aron*, ed. J.-C. Casanova (Paris: Ed. Calmann-Levy, 1971), pp. 147-166; also in #2003, pp. 32-52. Overview of the dialogue. **[2359a]**

Hippias Major

This is the longer of two dialogues associated with one of the most famous Sophists of the late fifth century. The dramatic date is ca. 420 B. C., when Hippias has supposedly come to Athens on an embassy from his home city, Elis. He vaunts himself on the money he earns as a Sophist and displays his wealth in his clothing and personal ornaments. The dialogue consists of a conversation between Hippias and S. After a lengthy introduction they discuss "the beautiful." Hippias tries to define beauty in terms of appearances and S must show him that some things which seem beautiful on the surface are not really so. The Beautiful is something which must be sought on the level of intellect. In some ways the dialogue provides a corrective to the theme of the *Symposium*, that physical beauty can lead to contemplation of the Form of Beauty.

KAHN, C. H. "The Beautiful and the Genuine." *OSAP* 3(1985), 261-287. Review essay of #2364a.   **[2360]**

MORGAN, M. L. "The Continuity Theory of Reality in Plato's *Hippias Major.*" *JHPh* 21(1983), 133-158. Theory of relations among properties, parts, and whole which is elucidated in this dialogue is predominantly Socrates'. P developed his own views on subject in *Protag, Theaet,* and *Philebus.*   **[2361]**

POLANSKY, R. "Reading Plato: Paul Woodruff and the *Hippias Major,*" in #1275, pp. 200-209. Focuses on three issues regarding #2364: 1) what are interesting questions pertaining to dialogue? 2) how does interpretation of Platonic corpus affect interpretation of a particular dialogue? and 3) are literary elements separable from philosophic content?   **[2362]**

SIDER, D. "Plato's Early Aesthetics: The *Hippias Major.*" *JAAC* 35(1977), 465-470. Assuming the dialogue is an early work of P's, one can summarize several points of his aesthetic theory: an object of beauty remains so; a well made object, no matter how common, is beautiful; a thing with beautiful parts must display artistic arrangement to be thought beautiful. P tries unsuccessfully to draw conclusions about Theory of Forms from these observations.   **[2363]**

SWEET, D. R. "Introduction to the *Greater Hippias,*" in #2003, pp. 340-355. Overview of the dialogue.   **[2363a]**

THESLEFF, H. "The Date of the Pseudo-Platonic *Hippias Major.*" *Arctos* 10(1976), 105-117. Probably written ca. 360 B. C., by one of P's more capable students.   **[2364]**

WOODRUFF, P. *Plato:* Hippias Major. Indianapolis: Hackett, 1982. A translation and commentary with a substantial essay of interpretation.   **[2364a]**

————. "Reply to Ronald Polansky," in #1275, pp. 210-214. Agrees with Polansky's general principles of interpretation, but disagrees on particulars.   **[2365]**

————. "Socrates and Ontology: The Evidence of the *Hippias Major.*" *Phron* 23(1978), 101-117. Forms treated in dialogue are not separate. S shows no interest there in ontological status of Forms.   **[2366]**

————. cf. #2379.

For related item see #1874.

Hippias Minor

In this short dialogue S and the Sophist Hippias debate the virtues of some of Homer's heroes. S confuses Hippias thoroughly by appearing to prove that Odysseus, known for his deceitfulness, is actually the better man and that to do injustice voluntarily is characteristic of a good man. S professes himself disturbed by his own conclusion and disappointed that as wise a man as Hippias has not been able to help him understand the matter any better. What S may actually be trying to demonstrate is the importance of knowledge. One who lies involuntarily, i. e., not knowing that he is lying, lacks knowledge. One who lies deliberately knows the difference between truth and falsehood.

LEAKE, J. "Introduction to the *Lesser Hippias*," in #2003, pp. 300-306. Overview of the main themes of the dialogue and its significance for reading Homer.   [2366a]

MULHERN, J. J. "*Tropos* and *Polytropia* in Plato's *Hippias Minor*." *Phoenix* 22(1968), 283-288. Dialogue's conclusions are based on equivocation in meanings given to each of title terms.   [2367]

WEISS, R. "*Ho Agathos* as *Dunatos* in the *Hippias Minor*." *CQ* 31(1981), 287-304. The "good man" in this dialogue is not just but is capable of acting justly. Charges of equivocation of terms cannot be sustained. Dialogue's arguments are valid.   [2368]

ZEMBATY, S. "Socrates' Perplexity in Plato's *Hippias Minor*," in #1267, pp. 51-69. Builds on Weiss' interpretation (#2368) to show that S's perplexity in the dialogue is not feigned. It is an indication that P was aware of problems arising from S's effort to define virtues "in terms of some characteristic of the agent's psyche."   [2369]

Ion

    In this short dialogue Socrates discusses the interpretation of poetry with the rhapsode Ion. (Rhapsodes were professional singers whose art included the analysis of the text as well as performance of it.) Socrates leads Ion to admit that his poetic art is a kind of inspiration rather than knowledge. To what, then, does this art apply? Ion maintains that he can interpret all parts of Homer better than anyone. But, Socrates counters, would not a chariot driver be better able to explain those passages where Homer talks about driving a chariot? And would not a maker of shields know more about a passage like the description of Achilles' shield? Ion concedes the point. The dialogue ends without achieving a more precise definition of what the poet does. P's primary point seems to be that, since poetry is not an art but a kind of inspiration, the role of the poet needs to be reconsidered. Poetry does not provide us with the knowledge necessary to guide the city. Hence, poetry, and Homer in particular, should not be the source of the standards by which Athenians live.

BLOOM, A. "An Interpretation of Plato's *Ion*." *Interp* 1(1970), 43-62; also in #2003, pp. 371-395. Overview of the dialogue. S tries to show that Ion's lack of understanding is characteristic of the city to which he belongs. Ion is like Proteus, constantly changing his shape as S tries to gain some truth from him.   [2370]

CAMPBELL, P. N. "The *Ion*: Argument and Drama." *RPL* 9(1986), 59-68. P uses certain verbs to describe Ion's rhapsodic efforts either analytically or in terms of performances. Resulting argument against a rhapsodic "art" appears invalid and obscures rhapsodes' importance as earliest text critics.   [2371]

DORTER, K. "The *Ion*. Plato's Characterization of Art." *JAAC* 32(1973), 65-78. *Ion* is P's only dialogue devoted exclusively to art. Art's importance lies in its ability to interpret the divine; its fundamental weakness is that it imitates nature.   **[2372]**

GILBERT, A. H. "Plato's *Ion*, Comic and Serious," in *Studies in Honor of DeW. T. Starnes* (Austin: Univ. of TX, 1967), pp. 259-284. The character of Ion lends comic tone to dialogue, even while P is expounding his view on value of literature.   **[2373]**

MOORE, J. D. "The Dating of Plato's *Ion*." *GRBS* 15(1974), 421-439. An absolute date cannot be established. It is probably not one of the earlier dialogues, nor should it be deemed spurious.   **[2374]**

———. "Limitation and Design in Plato's *Ion*." *PacCPh* 8(1973), 45-51. P bans Homer's poetry from his utopia in *Rep* 10, but in *Ion* he merely questions its educational value and examines specific *technai* mentioned in poems, not the poems themselves.   **[2375]**

PAPPAS, N. "Plato's *Ion*: The Problem of the Author." *Ph* 64(1989), 381-389. *Ion* uses arguments against poetry similar to those of *Rep* 10, viz., that poetry is not merely ignorance; it is seduction away from the search for truth.   **[2376]**

ROOCHNIK, D. L. "Plato's Critique of Post-Modernism." *Ph&Lit* 11(1987), 282-291. P's assertion of Forms against a world of flux forms the basis of a useful criticism of the deconstructionist school of thought.   **[2377]**

WILCOX, J. F. "Cross-Metamorphosis in Plato's *Ion*," in *Literature As Philosophy/Philosophy as Literature*, ed. P. G. Marshall (Iowa City: Univ. of IA Pr., 1987), pp. 155-174. Sees *Ion* as helpful for understanding concerns about poetry in other dialogues, but focuses on P's shaping of S's role and character and how P points toward a union of philosophical and poetic traditions.   **[2378]**

WOODRUFF, P. *Plato, Two Comic Dialogues:* Ion *and* Hippias Major. Indianapolis: Hackett, 1983. Transl. with introduction which maintains authenticity of dialogues and provides background and interpretation. Bibliography also included.   **[2379]**

For related items see #1570, #1573, #1574, #3359.

Laches

The dramatic situation of this dialogue is that two men, Lysimachus and Melesias, ask two distinguished Athenian generals, Nicias and Laches, to an exhibition of men fighting in armor. They extend this invitation to the general in order to consult with them about how best to educate their sons to make them honorable and dutiful men. Laches responds by suggesting that Lysimachus and Melesias consult with S, who agrees to try to offer advice but first wishes to hear from his elders, Nicias and Laches. Nicias supports the idea of instructing young men in the art of fighting in armor, while Laches questions its utility. Lysimachus then asks S to enter the conversation to express his opinion.

S first seeks to expand the topic beyond the issue of teaching the youth how to fight with armor to the issue of the teaching of the virtue of courage. He then suggests that before we can find the best way of teaching the youth to be courageous and before we can find the best teacher for them, we first must try to understand the nature of courage. S professes his ignorance about the nature of this virtue and turns to the two generals in hopes of learning a definition of courage. Since they have demonstrated great courage in battle, they must know what courage is, "and that which we know we must surely be able to tell" (190c). Yet it is not so clear that these two generals *can* define courage.

In response to Laches' first attempt S sets forth certain conditions which a definition must satisfy. Subsequent definitions also fail, but in criticizing them S raises fundamental questions about the relation of courage to other virtues and the relationship of knowledge to virtue. This raises a new problem: can one of the virtues (courage) be the same as virtue in general? None of these questions is answered by the end of the dialogue, but the method of inquiry has been introduced and demonstrated.

BLITZ, M. "An Introduction to the Reading of Plato's *Laches*." *Interp* 5(1975), 185-225. Literary analysis; overview of themes. [2380]

BUFORD, T. O. "Plato on the Educational Consultant: An Interpretation of *Laches*." *IdealStud* 7(1977), 151-171. Main theme is not courage, but the giving of educational advice. [2381]

COOLEY, K. W. "Unity and Diversity of the Virtues in the *Charmides, Laches*, and *Protagoras*." *Kinesis* 1(1969), 100-106. Discusses how the physical, or "outer," seems to serve as a necessary dialectical stepping stone to the mental or "inner" condition of the soul. [2382]

DEVEREUX, D. T. "Courage and Wisdom in Plato's *Laches*." *JHPh* 15(1977), 129-141. P tries to show that courage is a mixture of intellect and temperament and cannot be merely a kind of knowledge. This interpretation suggests that P was doing more than merely expounding S's ideas in the early dialogues. [2383]

GOULD, C. S. "Socratic Intellectualism and the Problem of Courage. An Interpretation of Plato's *Laches*." *HPhQ* 4(1987), 265-279. Though S maintains that courage is knowledge, he appears sympathetic to Laches' argument that courage also requires perseverance. [2384]

GRISWOLD, C. L. "Philosophy, Education, and Courage in Plato's *Laches*." *Interp* 14(1986), 177-193. To understand the unknown requires a certain kind of courage. The philosopher's primary concern is to educate himself, not others. [2385]

HOERBER, R. G. "Plato's *Laches*." *CPh* 63(1968), 95-105. Proper approach to a Socratic dialogue must take into consideration both literary genre and philosophical tenets. In *Laches* meaning of "courage" is revealed partly through literary structure of dialogue. [2386]

KAHN, C. H. "Plato's Methodology in the *Laches*." *RIPh* 40(1986), 7-21. P's decision to write dialogues in which Socrates served as his spokesman allowed him to show his respect for his teacher and to attract a younger generation of readers who had not known S personally. [2387]

KLONOSKI, R. J. "Plato's Discussion of Seers in *Laches* 195e-199a." *AncW* 13(1986), 7-9. P regarded influence of astrologers as highly negative.   **[2388]**

O'BRIEN, M. S. "The Unity of the *Laches*," in #41, pp. 303-315. Shows that in this dialogue, some of P's "laws of composition" can be discovered. Argues that the dialogue is a balanced work of art, in which character and action illuminate the thought, and the thought is in turn a judgment on the characters.   **[2389]**

PASSALOGLOU, E. "On the Argument Structure of Two Debated Passages of Plato's *Peri Andreias*." *EEThess* 21(1983), 379-393. Responds to views of several scholars on interpretaton of *Laches* 192b8-193d10 and 197e.   **[2390]**

SANTAS, G. "Socrates at Work on Virtue and Knowledge in Plato's *Laches*." *RMeta* 22(1969), 433-460; also in #1199, pp. 177-208. Examines doctrine of unity of virtues and relates it to *Protag*, *Rep*, and some of Ar's views. The dialogue constitutes a Platonic investigation of some fundamental difficulties in S's thought.   **[2391]**

SHARPLES, R. W. "Knowledge and Courage in Thucydides and Plato." *LCM* 8(1983), 139-140. Notes similarities between P's dialogue on courage and Pericles' funeral oration as found in Thucydides.   **[2392]**

STOKES, M. C. *Plato's Socratic Conversations: Drama and Dialectic in Three Dialogues.* Baltimore: Johns Hopkins Univ. Pr., 1986. In *Laches*, *Protag*, and *Symp* the interlocutors' views and assumptions (based on their personal background) always shape a Socratic conversation, and some of the confusion which arises is attributable to the interlocutors. S's questions do not put him in the position of commiting himself to any particular answer.   **[2393]**

UMPHREY, S. "Plato's *Laches* on Courage." *Apeir* 10 #2(1976), 14-22. Laches' definition of courage as stamina of soul (190b-194c) is not fully refuted by S.   **[2394]**

―――. "On the Theme of Plato's *Laches*." *Interp* 6(1976), 1-10. The dialogue is actually about Laches' concern for *phylake* (watching, guarding). Discussion of courage arises from that focus.   **[2395]**

Laws

The dialogue opens with three old men discussing the question of whether God or some man is the author of the laws of the city. One of the men is from Crete, one from Sparta, and one an Athenian Stranger. (Whether the Stranger represents S or P is a matter of some controversy.) The three men agree to discuss questions of politics and jurisprudence as they walk from Cnossos up to the cave and chapel of Zeus.

The first three books comprise a kind of introduction to the main project. The Stranger guides the discussion. In so doing, he challenges certain important beliefs held by the Cretan and the Spartan. He leads them to agree that the purpose of laws is not simply to promote courage but the whole of virtue, that education is crucial in the development of virtue, and that drinking has a role in the educational process. Also, the three men examine the time of the founding of Argos, Messene, and Lacedaemon, and why these governments dissolved. They also consider the excesses of the Persian and Athenian regimes and their subsequent destruction. From these historical investigations, they conclude that "the lawgiver must in laying down his laws aim at three things, namely that the city for which he legislates be free, that it be a friend to itself, and that it possess intelligence" (701d).

The three then decide to test their conclusions by finding some way to apply them to an actual city. By fortunate coincidence, the inhabitants of Crete propose to found a new colony in a deserted part of the island. The three decide to use their conclusions to construct a "city in speech," a theoretical constitution for a city, called Magnesia. This they proceed to do in minute detail for the next nine books.

The interpretation of this "second best city" is a matter of significant controversy. Some scholars view the work as a product of P's old age, and thus of vastly inferior quality. Some find in the text substantial and inexplicable deviations from *Rep*, some object to the myriad of legislative details and lack of dramatic vividness, and some find evidence of P's senility. Other scholars argue that the deviations from *Rep* are insignificant and readily explained, that the work shows a dramatic coherence and wholeness as well as a certain stately style, and that it constitutes a virtually complete account of Platonic philosophy and offers solutions to a number of problems posed in earlier dialogues.

BARDIS, P. D. "Overpopulation, the Ideal City, and Plato's Mathematics." *Platon* 23(1971), 120-131. Considers P's claim that the ideal city must consist of 5040 citizens and their respective families. Suggests that P based his choice on his well-known belief in the cosmic properties of seven. **[2396]**

BELFIORE, E. "Wine and Catharsis of the Emotions in Plato's *Laws*." *CQ* 36(1986), 421-437. P's theory of emotions in *Laws* 1 and 3 differs from that in *Rep* in admitting a non-rational element which can lead to an increase in virtue. **[2397]**

BERTMANN, M. A. "Hobbes' Science of Politics and Plato's *Laws*." *IndepJPh* 2(1978), 47-53. Examines crucial differences between Hobbes and P in light of L. Strauss' studies of ancient and modern politics. **[2398]**

CAMPBELL, B. "Deity and Human Agency in Plato's *Laws*." *HPolTho* 2(1981), 417-446. Under the laws proposed for Magnesia, human choice, not divine will, is the highest ethical norm. P may have thought, however, that the population at large were incapable of making rational decisions. **[2399]**

COHEN, D. "The Legal Status and Political Role of Women in Plato's *Laws*." *RIDA* 34(1987), 27-40. P's views on women's legal and political role, which run contrary to those of every Greek city of his time, were based on his philosophical concept that every member of the *polis* should contribute to its life. He is motivated by concern for the state, not by any view of women which is ahead of his time. **[2400]**

————. "Theft in Plato's *Laws* and Athenian Legal Practice." *RIDA* 29(1982), 121-143. Theft is treated in considerable detail in *Laws*, but provisions outlined by P differ dramatically from Athenian laws.   **[2401]**

DAVID, E. "The Spartan Syssitia and Plato's *Laws*." *AJPh* 99(1978) 486-495. Examines P's treatment of *syssitia* (common messes) in *Laws*, and how the common mess is designed to serve as a means of military preparedness and establishment of order in private life. His description is incomplete, perhaps because of complexity of matter. Ar's criticism of P's views are also noted.   **[2402]**

DAVIS, M. "How Many Agronomoi are There in Plato's *Laws*?" *CPh* 60(1965), 28-29. Examines the number of land stewards referred to at 760b ff., and challenges Morrow's claim that there are only 204.   **[2403]**

———. "Monetary Fines and Limitations in Plato's *Magnesia*." *CPh* 65(1969), 98-101. Monetary fines are proportionately heavier for the ruling class, since inappropriate behavior on their part is a more serious problem.   **[2404]**

FORTENBAUGH, W. W. "Plato. Temperament and Eugenic Policy." *Arethusa* 8(1975), 283-305. In *Laws* P recommends marriage between persons of different temperaments, unlike *Rep*. Such unions would produce children of moderate temperaments, benefitting state and avoiding problems often brought on by extraordinary individuals.   **[2405]**

FUKS, A. "Plato and the Social Question: The Problem of Poverty and Riches in the *Laws*." *AncSoc* 10(1979), 33-78. Examines problem of poverty and riches, and P's affirmation of his ideal of Good State in terms of economic-social organization.   **[2406]**

GOLDING, N. H. "Plato as City Planner." *Arethusa* 8(1975), 359-371. Starting from Friedlaender's comments (1958) explores to what extent P continues accepted planning techniques, and to what extent he was an innovator. He never expected that his ideal city could be built.   **[2407]**

McCLAIN, E. G. "Thirty-Seven Musical Guardians in Plato's *Laws*." *Mus&Man* 2(1978), 181-203. Suggests that a number of unsolved mathematical riddles may have a musical rationale and that P may have designed for the interior of Crete his "practicable city of Magnesia" on a musical model.   **[2408]**

MOHR, R. D. "Plato's Final Thoughts on Evil, *Laws* X: 899-905." *Mind* 87(1978), 572-575; also in #2112, pp. 184-188. In this passage P treats evil quite differently from his other major discussion of the problem in *Tim*. His view is somewhere between those who see evil as necessary for the existence of goodness and those who consider evil only an appearance.   **[2409]**

MORROW, G. R. "Plato and the Rule of Law," in #1291, pp. 144-165; also in #1961, pp. 49-70. Follows details of law-enforcing process to determine what rule of law would mean for citizen of P's state. Argues that in *Laws*, P shows strong distrust of absolute power and places sovereignty of law at very basis of political theory.   **[2410]**

———. *Plato's Law of Slavery*. New York, Arno Pr., 1976; rprt. Examines provisions affecting slaves in criminal code of *Laws*.   **[2411]**

PANGLE, T., trans. *The* Laws *of Plato*. New York: Basic Books, 1980. Translation and commentary, with a lengthy interpretive essay.   **[2412]**

PERLMAN, P. "Plato *Laws* 833c-834d and the Bears of Brauron." *GRBS* 24(1983), 115-130. The training of young women described by P may have been modelled on an obscure festival. [2413]

ROBERTS, J. "Plato on the Causes of Wrongdoing in the *Laws*." *AncPh* 8(1987), 23-37. Outlines argument at 860d-864c and argues that P replaces traditional legal distinction between voluntary and involuntary injustice with a distinction between injustice and ignorance. [2414]

SAUNDERS, T. J. "The Alleged Double Version of the Sixth Book of Plato's *Laws*." *CQ* 20(1970), 230-236. *Laws* 751a-755b was not originally two separate plans for organization of state. [2415]

——. "Artisans in the City-Planning of Plato's Magnesia." *BICS* 29(1982), 43-48. Artisans and craftsmen receive better treatment in the *Laws* than is generally recognized, though P never envisions them as citizens of Magnesia. Their techniques provide procedural models for the rulers of the city. [2416]

——. *Bibliography on Plato's* Laws, *1920-1970*. New York: Arno Pr., 1976. Comprehensive listing, with additional items through 1975. [2417]

——. "Notes on Plato as a City Planner." *BICS* 23(1976), 23-26. Geometrical precision of P's ideal state, with twelve sections in circular pattern, would be impossible to achieve. P probably hoped only for an approximation. [2418]

——. *Notes on the* Laws *of Plato*. London Univ. Pr., 1972. Offers detailed interpretation of 130 passages. Notes were compiled during the translation of *Laws* for Penguin Books. Some are brief, others of considerable length, intended as a basis for a philosophical commentary on the dialogue. [2419]

——. "The Penguinification of Plato," in *The Translator's Art: Essays in Honour of Betty Radice*, ed. W. Radice and B. Reynolds (New York: Penguin, 1987), pp. 152-162. Discusses difficulties of translating *Laws*. [2420]

——. "Plato, *Laws* 728bc. A Reply." *LCM* 9(1984), 23-24. Reply to MacKenzie's comments on this passage in her book *Plato on Punishment* (#1717). [2421]

——. "Plato on Killing in Anger: A Reply to Professor Woozley." *PhQ* 23(1973), 350-356. Reply to #2432. P is concerned not with assessing guilt or responsibility for a crime but with reforming or curing the criminal. This passage recognizes four states of mind which could lead to a killing. [2422]

——. "The Socratic Paradoxes in Plato's *Laws*: A Commentary on 859c-864b." *Hermes* 96(1968), 421-434. The paradox "virtue is knowledge" is not abandoned but is modified. Knowledge is necessary for virtue, but because of difficulty of controlling human emotions, knowledge is not sufficient for virtue. [2423]

——. cf. #3518.

SILVERTHORNE, M. J. "Militarism in the *Laws*? *Laws* 942a5-943a3." *SO* 49(1973), 29-38. The passage does not criticize militarism. Its rhetorical style reveals that its purpose is persuasive, not expository. Other passages in dialogue reflect P's views more accurately.   **[2424]**

STALLEY, R. F. *An Introduction to Plato's* Laws. Indianapolis: Hackett, 1983. Several chapters examine the character and context of the work and its relation to P's corpus. Other chapters deal with individual topics, such as nature and aims of law, virtue, pleasure, ideal state, system of government, education and arts, punishment, responsibility, and religion.   **[2425]**

STRAUSS, L. *The Argument and the Action of Plato's* Laws. Univ. of Chicago Pr., 1975. Summarizes the dialogue and offers commentary on a few passages.   **[2426]**

TARAN, L. *Academica: Plato, Philip of Opus, and the Pseudo-Platonic* Epinomis. Philadelphia: Amer. Phil. Soc., 1975. The *Epinomis* was meant by its author to complete the program of P's *Laws*. Examines the question of the authorship and its influence in later schools.   **[2427]**

THOMPSON, W. E. "The Demes in Plato's *Laws*." *Eranos* 63(1965), 134-136. Division of population into tribes and demes influences religious celebrations. Each citizen is obligated to participate in two festivals per month.   **[2428]**

VAN DER WAERDEN, B. L. "On the Motion of the Planets According to Heraclides of Pontus." *AIHS* 28(1978), 167-182. Heraclides' comments help explain *Laws* 821b-822c.   **[2429]**

WHITE, T. I. "Pride and the Public Good: Thomas More's Use of Plato in *Utopia*." *JHPh* 20(1982), 329-354. Explores reasons behind and details of More's use of P, particularly *Laws*. More especially liked P's theme of advancing public good by limiting individual pride.   **[2430]**

WILLETTS, R. F. "A Note on Plato: *Lg* 773b." *JHS* 92(1972), 184-185. Textual note that discusses possible social and political reasons why P used certain terminology in the passage.   **[2431]**

WOOZLEY, A. D. "Plato on Killing in Anger." *PhQ* 22(1972), 303-317. In 866d-867c P discusses killer who does not know what he is doing but who may not be entirely without responsibility.   **[2432]**

For related items see #2143, #3092, #3452, #3461.

Letters

Diogenes Laertius lists among the works of P thirteen letters. The fact that we have thirteen letters attributed to P does not mean that they are the same thirteen which Diogenes knew. Nor does it mean that these letters, or any known to Diogenes, were genuine. Modern scholarly opinion of the letters has fluctuated over time. As Bremer says, "the letters have a curious cycle of falling in and out of favor" (#2908, p. 1).

The problem of determining the genuineness of these letters is complicated by the fact that spurious correspondence was commonly circulated under the names of famous individuals as a way of assuring a readership for an anonymous author's work or to attribute one's idiosyncratic interpretation to an earlier author. The purpose of the anonymous author was not to deceive his audience but to enhance the authority of his work. A fourth-century Christian writer, for example, composed a letter to replace Paul's lost epistle to the church at Laodicea, to which Paul himself refers in Colossians 4.16. Many New Testament scholars think that some of the letters attributed to Paul, especially I and II Timothy and Titus, may have been composed by someone else. Some libraries, such as that at Alexandria, paid well for letters signed by famous people, creating a market for forgeries.

The letters attributed to P have varying degrees of likelihood of actually being written by him. Few scholars today reject *Letter* 7 outright, but opinion on most of the others is divided. Computer technology has been applied to these documents, measuring their vocabulary and literary style against the undoubted works of P. The results have been inconclusive.

The letters are not arranged or numbered in any rational sequence. They could be grouped according to addressees. Numbers 1-3 and 13 are to Dionysius I, tyrant of Syracuse; 4, 7, 8, 10 go to Dion (uncle of Dionysius II) and his friends, making eight of the thirteen addressed to persons in Syracuse, which P visited in 388-387 B. C. and again in 367. He remained in contact with the ruling family, but Dionysius II rebelled against the philosophic lifestyle which P and Dion ordained for him in 367. Dion was exiled and P found it expedient to leave. During a third visit in 361-360 P failed to persuade Dionysius to recall Dion from exile and so antagonized the temperamental young king that he was treated as little more than a prisoner. Dion ultimately attempted to seize control of Syracuse by force. When he failed, a civil war broke out and was still raging when P died in 347 B. C.

Given P's interest in the situation in Syracuse, and his repeated efforts to intervene, it is not unlikely that he wrote letters to other interested parties. Whether the letters we have are those letters cannot be proved.

Letter 7 discusses P's reasons for withdrawing from politics in Athens, describes his visits to Syracuse, dwelling at some length on the third. It also advises Dion's friends to act with restraint. Perhaps the most interesting part of the letter is the digression in 341b-345c. Having said that Dionysius II was a poor student, P goes on to describe his philosophy and to state that he has never written down the essentials of it, in a significant passage which is quoted in the introduction to Chapter 12.

The letter may have been written as a defense to the Athenians and circulated in the city. It refers to a letter from the Syracusans asking for advice. That is likely to be contrived to provide an excuse for P's letter.

AALDERS, G. J. D. "The Authenticity of the Eighth Platonic Epistle Reconsidered." *Mnem* 221969), 233-257. No convincing proof has been offered against genuineness of *Letter* 8. Internal evidence at many points suggests Platonic authorship. [2433]

———. "Political Thought and Political Programs in the Platonic Epistles," in *Pseudepigrapha*, ed. K. von Fritz (Geneva: Fond. Hardt, 1972), I, pp. 145-187. Political thought of

Letter 7 is congruent with that of dialogues, especially *Stsm* and *Laws*. Probable authenticity of other letters, especially 8 and 11, is discussed.   **[2434]**

BEG, A. S. *Plato's Esoteric Logic of Dialogue-Writing: A New Exegesis of His Seventh Epistle 341C-344C.* Aligarh, India: Kitab Ghar, 1984. Reads the passage without reference to dialogues to establish what P himself says about his purpose in writing. P seems to have considered it near madness to put one's thoughts into writing.   **[2435]**

BRANDWOOD, L. "Plato's Seventh Letter." *RELO* (1969) #4, 1-25. Reply to #2447. Letter's style, vocabulary do not differ significantly from P's other works.   **[2436]**

BRUMBAUGH, R. S. "Digression and Dialogue: The Seventh Letter and Plato's Literary Form," in #1275, pp. 84-92. This document uses "digression" and "self-illustration" that are typical of the dialogues, suggesting that literary form is more important than is often supposed.   **[2437]**

CASKEY, E. G. "Again: Plato's Seventh Letter." *CPh* 69(1974), 220-227. If P wrote this letter, it must be contemporaneous with *Laws*, but stylistically the two are quite different.   **[2438]**

DEANE, P. "Stylometrics do not Exclude the *Seventh Letter*." *Mind* 82(1973), 113-117. Comparisons of style and vocabulary of this letter with those of P's known works do not rule out possibility that Seventh Letter was written by P.   **[2439]**

DE BLOIS, L. "Some Notes on Plato's Seventh Epistle." *Mnem* 32(1979), 268-283. Political views expressed in seventh letter are consistent with those in P's known works. *Letter* 7 seems authentic.   **[2440]**

DENNING-BOLLE, S. J. "Wisdom and Dialogue in the Ancient Near East." *Numen* 34(1987), 214-234. Includes analysis of P's concept of wisdom, his understanding of importance of spoken conversation and his rejection of writing. *Letter* 7 in particular is examined.   **[2441]**

EDELSTEIN, L. *Plato's Seventh Letter.* Leiden: Brill, 1966. Examines "autobiography of Plato" and what is told about his intellectual development and his attitude toward philosophy and politics. Explores whether doctrine of dialogues can possibly form a unity with that of the letter. Concludes Letter is not likely to be authentic.   **[2442]**

GADAMER, H.-G. "Dialectic and Sophism in Plato's *Seventh Letter*," in #1274, pp. 93-123. The "digression" in the letter discusses how philosophy originates in and progresses by dialectic, i. e., discussion of opposing opinions undertaken when one is not certain of the truth or essence of something. But Sophism uses the same technique, and philosophy must always be aware that Sophism is its shadow.   **[2443]**

GULLEY, N. "The Authenticity of the Platonic Epistles," in (cf. #2434), pp. 103-143. Internal and external evidence casts doubt on authenticity of *Letters*. Their political ideas do not agree with those set forth in dialogues.   **[2444]**

HACKFORTH, R. *The Authorship of the Platonic Epistles.* Hildesheim, Ger.: Olms, 1976; rprt. Compares the letters to P's known works and concludes that *Letters* 3, 4, 7, 8, 13 are genuine. *Letters* 1, 2, 5, 6, 12 appear to be forgeries; several of them may have been written in Alexandria or Pergamum. *Letters* 9, 10, 11 remain dubious.   **[2445]**

HARWARD, J., trans. *The Platonic Epistles*. New York: Arno Pr., 1976; rprt. Translation, with introductory essay.   **[2446]**

LEVINSON, M., et al. "The Seventh Letter of Plato." *Mind* 77(1968), 309-325. Discusses genuineness of letter and possibility of P's involvement in political affairs. Though inconclusive, evidence points to Speusippus as author.   **[2447]**

MORTON, A. Q., and **WINSPEAR, A. D.** "The Computer and Plato's Seventh Letter." *Computers and the Humanities* 1(1966-67), 72-73. Computer analysis of letter's style raises questions about its authenticity.   **[2448]**

RIST, J. M. "Neopythagoreanism and 'Plato's' Second Letter." *Phron* 10(1965), 78-81. Proposes that Epistle Two, like Epistle Twelve, is of Neopythagorean origin.   **[2449]**

SAYRE, K. "Plato's Dialogues in Light of the Seventh Letter," in #1275, pp. 93-109. The *Letter* does not suggest that oral discourse can articulate truth, whereas written cannot. All discourse suffers from deficiency of its involvement in sense experience, and thus logos is incapable of articulating philosophical vision.   **[2450]**

SCHIFF, J. *A Computerized Word-Index to the Platonic* Epistles. University Park: PA St. Univ. Dept. of Classics, 1973. Useful reference tool.   **[2450a]**

SZLEZAK, T. A. "The Acquiring of Philosophical Knowledge According to Plato's Seventh Letter," in #48, pp. 354-363. Letter contends that philosophical knowledge is acquired by hearing, and that philosophers should not give out their most important doctrines in writing.   **[2451]**

VON FRITZ, K. "The Philosophical Passage in the Seventh Platonic Letter and the Problem of Plato's 'Esoteric' Philosophy," in #41, pp. 408-447. Passage is consistent with other Platonic work and should be considered genuine. Nothing in Platonic corpus suggests that P held back certain teachings for an inner circle.   **[2452]**

For related items see #1478, #6319.

Lovers

This brief dialogue, the authenticity of which is widely doubted, is given this title in all the major manuscripts, with the subtitle "On Philosophy." In Diogenes Laertius' list of P's works, and in a marginal reading in one important manuscript, it is called the *Rivals*. (In Greek "Lovers" is *Erastai*, while "Rivals" is *Anterastai*.) S engages in a discussion with two young men who are the "lovers" of two boys in a school where S stops in to observe the lessons. One man devotes himself to music, the other to athletics. Their conversation becomes the focal point of attention for all those in attendance as they discuss what is more beneficial to the body and the soul — exercise, food, and education in measured doses or in the largest quantity possible. Justice is established as the art by which one learns to "know thoroughly both oneself and others."

BRUELL, C. "On the Original Meaning of Political Philosophy: An Interpretation of Plato's *Lovers*," in #2003, pp. 91-110. Dialogue's authenticity has been doubted largely on basis of concern about content. Its theme is whether philosophy is a noble and good activity suiting philosopher for a role in government. **[2453]**

DAVIS, M. "Philosophy and the Perfect Tense: On the Beginning of Plato's *Lovers*." *GradFacPhJ* 10(1985), 75-97. Examination of this dubious dialogue suggests that nature of a Platonic dialogue reveals something about nature of philosophy. **[2454]**

Lysis

The *Lysis* investigates the question "What is friendship?" It consists of two scenes which have little apparent connection with each other. In the first, S converses with the handsome youth Lysis about the limits which his parents place on his activities because of his limited knowledge of worldly affairs. They are then joined by Lysis' friend Menexenus and S poses the question about the nature of friendship. Since these two young men are friends, surely they can help S define friendship. Who is the friend, the one who loves another, or the one who is loved? Or should both be called friends? What is the basis of the attraction, like to like, or like to unlike? Poets and philosophers are cited in support of each of these positions. S suggests that true friendship is the attraction of the indifferent toward the good. But is that attraction altruistic or self-serving? No adequate answer can be found to the last question, and there the dialogue ends.

BOLOTIN, D. *Plato's Dialogue on Friendship: An Interpretation of the* Lysis, *with a New Translation.* Ithaca, NY: Cornell Univ. Pr., 1979. Sees dialogue as examining relationship between friendship, on the one hand, and wants and needs of imperfect beings, on the other. **[2455]**

GADAMER, H-G. "*Logos* and *Ergon* in Plato's *Lysis*," in #1274, pp. 1-20. Examines S's dialectical *elenchos* and shows reciprocal relationship between the line of his argument and level of insight of his partners in the discussion. **[2456]**

GLIDDEN, D. K. "The Language of Love." *PacPhQ* 61(1980), 276-290. Studies P's grammatical use of *philos* in *Lysis* 212a8-213c9, which is influenced by his interest in incomplete predicates and the logic of relational statements. **[2457]**

——. "The *Lysis* on Loving One's Own." *CQ* 31(1981), 39-59. P is not interested in how lovers of persons and things consciously regard themselves and the objects of their desire. Rather, he is interested in the psychological function achieved by our loving the persons and things we do, regardless of our various motives. **[2458]**

HADEN, J. "Friendship in Plato's *Lysis*." *RMeta* 37(1983), 327-356. Outlines a method of interpreting Socratic dialogues that focuses on concrete details of literary work; applies that method to *Lysis*. **[2459]**

HYLAND, D. A. "*Eros, Epithumia* and *Philia* in Plato." *Phron* 13(1968), 32-46. Examines relation among these three concepts in *Lysis* and *Symp*. They are hierarchical, with *epithumia* the lowest form of love, containing no reason, then *eros* (with an element of reason) and *philia* (the highest because it has more reason).   **[2460]**

LESSES, G. "Plato's *Lysis* and Irwin's Socrates." *IntStudPh* 18(1986), 33-43. Against Irwin (#1709), argues that S in *Lysis* does not hold that moral virtue is an instrumental good by which one obtains happiness.   **[2461]**

LEVIN, D. N. "Some Observations Concerning Plato's *Lysis*," in #41, pp. 236-258. Argues that the search is for definition of friend, not friendship. Dialogue is authentic and earlier than *Symp* and *Phaedrus*.   **[2462]**

MacKENZIE, M. M "Impasse and Explanation: From the *Lysis* to the *Phaedo*." *AGPh* 70(1988), 15-45. *Lysis* does not offer a final definition of friendship, but it does move reader beyond skepticism. It establishes principles of explanation which can be compared to P's methodology in *Phaedo*.   **[2463]**

MORRIS, T. F. "Plato's *Lysis*." *PhResArch* 11(1985), 269-279. Questions raised in dialogue lead to an explanation of ways in which Lysis, Menexenus and S are friends of each other. Motivations for desiring something are also discussed.   **[2464]**

SEDLEY, D. "Is the *Lysis* A Dialogue of Definition?" *Phron* 34(1989), 107-108. P is not seeking a definition of friendship but an answer to the question, "Who or what is a friend to whom or what?"   **[2465]**

TINDALE, C. W. "Plato's *Lysis*: A Reconsideration." *Apeir* 18(1984), 102-109. Challenges traditional view that dialogue fails to come up with concept of friendship. At least one character, Lysis, ultimately realizes what friendship is.   **[2466]**

VERSENYI, L. "Plato's *Lysis*." *Phron* 20(1975), 185-198. The dialogue has more substance, in form and content, than is generally recognized. It can be read coherently by itself but stands philosophically with P's other early dialogues.   **[2467]**

VLASTOS, G. "Is the *Lysis* a Vehicle of Platonic Doctrine?" in #1292, pp. 35-37. Challenges view that Platonic ontology of middle dialogues can be found in this dialogue.   **[2468]**

WENDER, D. "Letting Go. Imagery and Symbolic Naming in Plato's *Lysis*." *Ramus* 7(1978), 38-45. Name "Lysis" has connotations of "driving," "mastering," and "healing," images which play a major role in the dialogue. Lysis cannot do those things but may learn to.   **[2469]**

Menexenus

Though not questioned in antiquity as a work of P, this dialogue has its doubters today. Some facets of its style and theme (a parody of patriotic speeches such as Pericles gives in Thucydides' history) suggest a Platonic origin or a clever forger. The setting of the dialogue is quite simple. S encounters Menexenus, a younger friend of his, and learns that a speaker is to be chosen by the city to deliver a eulogy over the dead. After making some of his customary derogatory comments about rhetoricians, S delivers for Menexenus what he claims is a speech composed by Aspasia, the mistress of Pericles. S identifies her as the author of a number of speeches, including the one attributed to Pericles which commemorated the Athenian dead early in the Peloponnesian War. The speech is an example of what we might call "Fourth of July" rhetoric, with overample references to past military glories and patriotic disregard for any smudges on the escutcheon. As S says, it is easy to praise the Athenians among the Athenians.

BLOEDOW, E. F. "Aspasia and the Mystery of the *Menexenos*." *WS* 9(1975), 32-48. Dialogue attacks rhetoric in general and Sophistic rhetoric in particular. Aspasia represents the Sophistic view.   [2470]

COVENTRY, L. "Philosophy and Rhetoric in the *Menexenus*." *JHS* 109(1989), 1-15. Dialogue uses format of a traditional speech to point up corruption of rhetoric in P's day and assert that S's teaching could lead to renewed vitality of city.   [2471]

HENDERSON, M. M. "Plato's *Menexenus* and the Distortion of History." *AClass* 18(1975), 25-46. Seeks to explain what the work's intention is and to what extent it may be a satire of Athenian political oratory.   [2472]

STERN, H. S. "Plato's Funeral Oration." *NewSchol* 48(1974), 503-508. *Menexenus* is a disguised funeral oration for S. What is often taken as a critique of oratory in the dialogue can be read as clues to P's underlying purpose.   [2473]

VLASTOS, G. "*Isonomia Politike*," in #1292, pp. 164-203. Shows how P parodies idealization of Athens in patriotic oratory.   [2474]

Meno

The *Meno* pursues further the question which the *Protagoras* left unanswered, Can virtue be taught? To answer that question requires first a definition of virtue, then a determination of how we learn anything.

Meno, under the influence of the Sophists, makes several attempts at a definition, none of which satisfies S. Meno finally objects that any definition is futile because it is pointless to look for what one already knows and impossible to inquire after what one doesn't know. How would one know it if one found it? Virtue should be teachable but there are, unfortunately, no teachers of it to be found. S does not claim to know what it is, only to be inquiring.

The answer to the second problem lies in the theory of recollection (*anamnesis*), based on the notion that one could recognize virtue if his soul were immortal and already knew things of which the individual were unaware. S demonstrates *anamnesis* by holding a mathematics lesson with a slave boy. This theory maintains that our soul retains what it learned in previous lives. All a teacher need do is ask questions which will lead the pupil to recall what he already knows. Whether S actually taught such a doctrine is unclear. This dialogue, which some consider early but others date to P's middle period, may mark a transition to the presentation of his own ideas, based on S's thought but advancing beyond it.

ANDERSON, D. E. "The Theory of Recollection in Plato's *Meno*." *SJPh* 9(1971), 225-235. Through theory of recollection P hopes to interact with readers dialectically, leading to conclusion that learning is accomplished through dialectic, not recall. Dialectic can succeed only through knowledge of one's ignorance and a desire to learn.   **[2475]**

ANDIC, M. "Inquiry and Virtue in the *Meno*," in #2483, pp. 262-314. Explores two questions: Does theory of recollection explain how inquiry is possible at all? What other basis besides usefulness is there for believing in truth of theory?   **[2476]**

ANSCOMBE, G. E. M. "Understanding Proofs: *Meno* 85d9-86c2, Continued." *Ph* 54(1979), 149-158. Translation of the passage.   **[2477]**

BEDU-ADDO, J. T. "Recollection and the Argument 'From a Hypothesis' in Plato's *Meno*." *JHS* 104(1984), 1-14. Despite Meno's unwillingness to continue with inquiry into nature of virtue, Socrates artfully introduces the hypothetical method to ensure continuity of Meno's recollection of nature of virtue.   **[2478]**

———. "Sense-Experience and Recollection in Plato's *Meno*." *AJPh* 104(1983), 228-248. Explores S's use of sensible diagrams in course of demonstrating truth of theory of recollection. He does not tell us whether we are to think of sense-experience as an important element in process of recollection. P's epistemology in this dialogue is not different from that of later dialogues.   **[2479]**

BOTER, G. J. "Plato, *Meno* 82c 2-3," *Phron* 33(1988), 208-215. The lines *dia mesou* stand for diagonals, and not transversals.   **[2480]**

BRADIE, M. "Polanyi on the *Meno* Paradox." *PhiSci* 41(1974), 203. Provides counterexample to Polanyi's argument that paradox of inquiry in *Meno* cannot be solved without appeal to notion of tacit knowledge.   **[2481]**

BROWN, M. "Plato Disapproves of the Slave-Boy's Answer." *RMeta* 21(1967), 57-93; also in #2483, pp. 198-242. Slave-boy's lesson is no more successful than is Meno's. Exactly parallel to main discussion, P means to cast suspicion on substantive answer which S and the boy arrive at because inquiry is conducted improperly.   **[2482]**

BROWN, M., ed. *Plato's* Meno. Indianapolis: Bobbs-Merrill, 1971. Contains transl. of dialogue by W. K. C. Guthrie and several critical essays, abstracted herein.   **[2483]**

BRUMBAUGH, R. S. "Plato's *Meno* as Form and Content of Secondary School Courses in Philosophy." *TeachPh* 1-2(1975), 107-115. S teaches virtue by involving people in inquiry, not by lecture. Teaching of values today could use the technique.   **[2484]**

———. "Plato's Philosophy of Education: The *Meno* Experiment and the *Republic* Curriculum." *EducTheor* 20(1970), 207-228. The educational theories set forth in *Meno* and *Rep* are inadequate if taken out of context.   **[2485]**

CAHN, S. M. "A Puzzle Concerning the *Meno* and the *Protagoras*." *JHPh* 11(1973), 535-

537. In *Meno* the answer to S's question whether virtue can be taught is negative. In *Protag* the answer is affirmative, suggesting that *Meno* is earlier of the two.   **[2486]**

CALVERT, B. "Meno's Paradox Reconsidered." *JHPh* 12(1974), 143-152. Meno's paradox, that learning is impossible, is based on a confusion of two claims which can be traced back to Parmenides.   **[2487]**

————. cf. #2321.

CORNFORD, F. M. "Anamnesis," in #2483, pp. 108-127. *Meno* is first work to develop a characteristically Platonic response to problem of knowledge as goodness. Shows how this solution is linked to Theory of Forms and immortal nature of soul.   **[2488]**

DESJARDINS, R. "Knowledge and Virtue: Paradox in Plato's *Meno*." *RMeta* 39(1985), 261-281. *Meno* leaves us with an inconclusive conclusion to question of how we come to lead lives of genuine quality and it is not altogether clear how topics such as definition, recollection, hypothesis, and opinion are related to the main question.   **[2489]**

DEVEREUX, D. "Nature and Teaching in Plato's *Meno*." *Phron* 23(1978), 118-126. S holds virtue is knowledge but says in *Meno* it is not teachable. Two kinds of virtue are meant: one based on right opinion, one on knowledge. Latter is teachable.   **[2490]**

EBERT, T. "Plato's Theory of Recollection Reconsidered: An Interpretation of *Meno* 80a-86c." *M&W* 6(1973), 163-181. In this passage P draws an analogy between moving from error to knowledge and recalling something one has forgotten. Either activity means first becoming aware of a deficiency of knowledge. The geometry lessons serve to make Meno aware of the nature of knowledge.   **[2491]**

ECKSTEIN, J. *The Platonic Method: An Interpretation of the Dramatic-Philosophic Aspects of the* Meno. New York: Greenwood, 1969. Approaches *Meno* on assumption that S's arguments always match competence and attitude of his interlocutors and that his reasoning cannot be properly understood out of context. Argues that P knows recollection is not learning and that S's treatment of the doctrine is designed to show its absurdity. Includes a reprint of Jowett's transl. of dialogue.   **[2492]**

GOFF, R. "The Language of Self-Transformation in Plato and Augustine." *M&W* 4(1971), 413-435. Comparison of *Meno* and *Conf* 10 and 11, looking at the process by which one becomes aware of need for "formal re-presentation of the self." Studies how this passage is carried out in relation of reader and interpreter to these works. **[2493]**

GOOCH, P. W. "Irony and Insight in Plato's *Meno*." *LThPh* 43(1987), 189-204. Examines ironic nature of conclusion that virtue comes through divine dispensation. Meno's mistake is believing that only knowledge (and not virtue) can bc taught.**[2494]**

GOULD, J. B. "Klein on Ethological Mimes; For Example, the *Meno*." *JPh* 66(1968), 253-265. Reply to #2497. The dialogues do not contain enough dramatic setting and distinction among the interlocutors to make them any sort of "morality play" or "ethological mime," which could be acted out.   **[2495]**

HARTMAN, M. "Plato's Philosophy of Education in the *Meno*." *Pers* 57(1976), 126-131. Studies two approaches to education exemplified in *Meno*: the "suitcase" method (collecting opinions but unable to organize or connect them) and Socratic method. But even use of a good method (S's) does not guarantee a student's success.   [2496]

KLEIN, J. *A Commentary on Plato's* Meno. Chapel Hill: Univ. of NC Pr., 1965. A dominant feature of the analysis is the belief that the intent of the dialogue is best seen when the reader becomes a "witness" and is led to continue search for human excellence on his own. Attempts to explain word-play and historical background and introduce characters fully so that reader can participate in the dialogue.   [2497]

MEYERS, J. T. "Plato's Geometric Hypothesis. *Meno* 86e-87b." *Apeir* 21(1988), 173-180. The mathematical problem referred to here presages the procedure S will use to demonstrate teachability of virtue.   [2498]

MIJUSKOVIC, B. "The Synthetic *A Priori* in Plato." *Dial*(PST) 12(1970), 13-22. Relation between color and extension provides key to understanding the necessary and universal connection existing between virtue and knowledge. This connection is essentially an *a priori* synthetic relation.   [2499]

MOLINE, J. "Meno's Paradox." *Phron* 14(1969), 153-161. What some take as a paradox stated by Meno is reasonable response to what Meno thinks is S's irony. S turns Meno's personal question into paradoxical claim with general implications.   [2500]

MOOD, R. A. "The Problem of Inquiry in Plato's *Meno*." *ITA Humanidades* 11(1975), 221-234. Examines difference between "inquiry" (Socratic method of joint investigation) and a rival method of "teaching" (as conceived by Sophists).   [2501]

MORAVCSIK, J. M. E. "Learning as Recollection," in #1290, pp. 53-69. Examines the "Meno Paradox" and investigates explanatory power of the "solution offered."   [2502]

MORGAN, M. L. "How Does Plato Solve the Paradox of Inquiry in the *Meno*?" in #1267, pp. 169-181. Meno's eristic puzzle (80d-86c) is a transitional passage, within dialogue itself and within group of early and middle dialogues, from elenctic inquiry to discussions of more metaphysical import. P is more concerned about the objects of inquiry than the process.   [2503]

NEHAMAS, A. "Meno's Paradox and Socrates as a Teacher." *OSAP* 3(1985), 1-30. P takes Meno Paradox very seriously, for it brings together S's immediate concern with not harming his friends and P's theoretical interest in nature of understanding.   [2504]

PHILLIPS, B. "The Significance of Meno's Paradox," in #2513, pp. 77-83. Challenges view that the paradox is merely a piece of "logic-chopping," and argues that Meno's question is legitimate in context of problem of gaining ethical knowledge.   [2505]

PLOCHMAN, G. K. "Plato's *Meno*: Questions to be Disputed." *JVallnq* 81(1975), 266-282. Tries to clearly frame, not necessarily answer, several questions about *Meno*, organizing them under large headings: drama, dialogue, and dialectic.   [2506]

ROHATYN, D. A. "Reflections on Meno's Paradox." *Apeir* 14(1980), 69-73. P does not introduce *anamnesis* as a serious response to Meno's paradox. The theory is designed merely to make us aware that Meno's argument is self-refuting.   [2507]

ROSE, L. E. "Plato's *Meno* 86-89." *JHPh* 8(1970), 1-8. Surveys interpretations of S's method for determining virtue's teachability; examines use of hypotheses here. **[2508]**

RYLE, G. "Thinking and Self-Teaching." *ProcPhEdSocGB* 5(1971), 216-228. Contains a discussion of slave-boy example and offers a new sequel to dialogue. **[2509]**

────. cf. #1794.

SANTAS, G. "The Socratic Paradoxes," in #2513, pp. 49-64. P does not deny fact of moral weakness. His views regarding relation of knowledge to conduct are more plausible than commonly supposed. **[2510]**

SEESKIN, K. "*Meno* 86c-89a: A Mathematical Image of Philosophic Inquiry," in #1277, pp. 25-41. Method of hypothesis, borrowed from geometers, leads to an *aporia* in regard to teaching of virtue. **[2511]**

SESONSKE, A. "Knowing and Saying: The Structure of Plato's *Meno*," in #2513, pp. 84-96. Discussion of definition, principles of method, and doctrine of recollection represent significant developments in P's thinking. **[2512]**

────., and **FLEMING, N.**, eds. *Plato's* Meno: *Text and Criticism.* Belmont, CA: Wadsworth, 1965. Translation of the dialogue and collection of critical studies, each abstracted herein. **[2513]**

SHANON, B. "*Meno* — A Cognitive Psychological View." *BritJPhSci* 35(1984), 129-147. P's theory of memory is close to the modern materialistic view of mind. **[2514]**

SHARPLES, R. W. "More on Plato, *Meno* 82c2-3." *Phron* 34(1989), 220-226. Reply to Boter (#2480). While attractive, Boter's interpretation of the passage raises problems in understanding the dramatic setting and the irony. **[2515]**

SIMON, H. A. "Bradie on Polanyi on the *Meno* Paradox." *PhiSci* 43(1976), 142-150. Comment on #2481. Meno's paradox does not let us argue that recognizing a problem's solution proves we already know it, what Polanyi calls "tacit knowledge." **[2516]**

STERN, H. S. "Philosophy of Education in Plato's *Meno*." *EducStud* 12(1981), 23-34. P appears to be interested in the nature of virtue but is actually inquiring into how one acquires virtue. This leads to an analysis of the education process, though P throughout conceals his real purpose. **[2517]**

STERNFELD, R. and **ZYSKIND, H.** "Plato's *Meno* 86E-87A: The Geometrical Illustration of the Argument by Hypothesis." *Phron* 22(1977), 206-211. Examines P's application of the geometrical illustration to the question of teachability of virtue. **[2518]**

────. *Plato's* Meno: *A Philosophy of Man as Acquisitive.* Carbondale: S. IL Univ. Pr., 1978. Diversity of methods and dialogue's "descending" dialectic (i. e., movement from definition and recollection downward toward opinion) are in themselves its essential characteristics. Explains construction of dialogue as P's effort to show minimal elements of philosophic content in thought and action. **[2519]**

TEJERA, V. "History and Rhetoric in Plato's *Meno*, or on the Difficulties of Communicating Human Excellence." *Ph&Rh* 11(1978), 19-42. Focuses on historical background of S's interlocutors to illustrate dimension of historical or social allusiveness. [2520]

THOMAS, J. E. "*Anamnesis* in New Dress." *NewSchol* 51(1977), 328-349. Examines attempts of several scholars to "demythologize" P's doctrine of recollection. [2521]

——. "Models for Muddles at *Meno* 75a-77a." *NewSchol* 50(1976), 193-203. After *Meno* fails to provide a workable definition of "virtue," S supplies three model definitions. Examines these attempts and why they fail. [2522]

——. *Musings on the* Meno. The Hague: Nijhoff, 1980. Discussion of background material, translation of the dialogue and commentary by sections. [2523]

——. "Plato's Methodological Device at 84a1." *NewSchol* 45(1971), 478-486. Examines P's shift from arithmetic to geometry at 84a1. [2524]

——. "A Re-Examination of the Slave-Boy Interview." *LThPh* 26(1970), 17-27. S could have made a smoother transition from arithmetic to geometry if he had made use of information already drawn out of the slave-boy. This would avoid difficulties of interpretation suggested by M. Brown (#2483). [2525]

TIGNER, S. S. "On the 'Kinship' of 'All Nature' in Plato's *Meno*." *Phron* 15(1970), 1-4. Reviews scholarly interpretations of what P means by "kinship" of "all nature" at 81d. The assertion serves an argumentative function by showing that all things that can be recalled share an ontological kinship. [2526]

WHITE, N. P. "Inquiry." *RMeta* 28(1974), 289-310. Examines paradox of inquiry in *Meno*, relates it to problems of reference and recognition in work of modern scholars. Studies weaknesses of P's theory of recollection as solution to paradox. [2527]

WILKES, K. "Conclusions in the *Meno*." *AGPh* 61(1979), 143-153. Whatever "knowledge," "teaching," and "learning" may have meant to P, these terms are redefined in light of the theory of recollection and reminding. [2528]

WOODBRIDGE, F. J. E. "Education," in #2514, pp. 38-48. Virtue cannot be taught because it is debatable, but soul may be prepared for virtue through habits of disinterestedness. [2529]

ZYSKIND, H. and STERNFELD, T. R. "Plato's *Meno* 89C: 'Virtue is Knowledge' A Hypothesis?" *Phron* 21(1976), 130-134. Suggests that "virtue is knowledge" is not the primary hypothesis. [2530]

For related items see #1650, #1693.

MINOS

This dialogue, often dismissed as "a fairly able and plausible imitation of P's early work," is atypical in several ways. It begins abruptly, with S asking "What is law, for us?" His interlocutor remains anonymous, and the dialogue is named for a person who is not present or even alive. The interlocutor proposes various definitions of law and notes how widely laws differ among nations. S finds flaws in the definitions which his companion proposes and attempts to answer the question of the nature of law by asking comparable questions, "What is gold? What is stone?" We speak of "gold," but not of "a gold" or "golds." By contrast we do speak of "a stone" and "stones." Is law more like gold or stone? It seems to be some constant element underlying all varieties of law, just as there is some common "distributive skill" behind all types of cooking, gardening, and various other arts. S praises Minos as a lawgiver and the dialogue ends rather ineptly.

BEST, J. "What is Law? The *Minos* Reconsidered." *Interp* 8(1980), 102-113. S concludes that law involves wisdom and consent. Minos section at end of dialogue makes the point that law is a process. Minos' laws are ancient but still in use. Dialogue is coherent and stresses tradition and continuity as vital parts of law. **[2531]**

CHROUST, A.-H. "A Note to the Pseudo-Platonic Dialogue *Minos*." *AmJJur* 15(1970), 171-174. This dialogue "cannot possibly be credited to the authorship of Plato." Perhaps written by someone in the Academy, it takes position that perfect law can only be divinely revealed. **[2532]**

COBB, W. S. "Plato's *Minos*." *AncPh* 8(1988), 187-207. Transl., critical discussion arguing for Platonic authorship. The issue under consideration is relativism. **[2533]**

HATHAWAY, R. F. "*Minos* or *On Law*." *AmJJur* 14(1969), 116-124. Translation of the dialogue. **[2534]**

————., and HOULGATE, L. D. "The Platonic *Minos* and the Classical Theory of Law." *AmJJur* 14(1969), 105-115. Regardless of authorship, *Minos* presents a Platonic theory of law. Laws benefit a community. Intent of law and philosophy is the same. **[2535]**

STRAUSS, L. "On the *Minos*," in *Liberalism Ancient and Modern* (New York: Basic Books, 1968), pp. 65-75; also in #2003, pp. 67-79. Surveys construction and theme of law in the dialogue. Concludes that it "raises more questions than it answers" but that it is Platonic and serves as an introduction to *Laws*. **[2536]**

Parmenides

Many scholars consider this dialogue one of P's later works, written in a group with *Theaet, Cratylus, Soph, Stsm*, and *Philebus*. In form it is a conversation among Parmenides, Zeno, and S, set at a time when Parmenides was reportedly about sixty-five, Zeno forty, and S "a young man." The relative ages of these persons are not altogether improbable, though that is not meant to argue that such a conversation ever actually took place. Also present at this "seminar on Being" was a certain Pythodorus, who often repoeated what he had heard to Antiphon, P's half brother. Cephalus, a friend of P's brothers Glaucon and Adeimantus, is the actual narrator of the dialogue, though it is unclear to whom he is speaking. He has come from his home town of Clazomenae to hear Antiphon relate this conversation. The *Parm* is actually his report of Antiphon's account of what Pythodorus had told him.

In the opening section Zeno reads some of his paradoxes to the assembly. S immediately raises questions and shows that the paradoxes are not paradoxes at all. S and Parmenides then discuss the doctrine of Ideas (Forms), exposing some of its weaknesses. The Eleatic's objections to it are never countered. Parmenides also presents an account of the One and appearances which under-cuts some basic Eleatic positions.

Since the dialogue asserts no Platonic doctrine and, in fact, appears to do nothing but refute some ideas which P held dear, many scholars have wondered about P's purpose in writing it. Much interest in the dialogue has been prompted by Ryle and Vlastos and the study of the regress argument, called the Third Man Argument, which Parmenides poses against the Forms.

ALLEN, R. E. "The Generation of Numbers in Plato's *Parmenides*." *CPh* 65(1970), 30-34. For Parmenides numbers do not seem to have been either pluralities of units or their properties. **[2537]**

——. "Ideas as Thoughts: *Parmenides* 132 b-c." *AncPh* 1(1980-81), 29-38. Examines S's attempt to save unity of Ideas by suggesting that Ideas are thoughts which cannot come to be present anywhere but in minds or souls. **[2538]**

——. *Plato's* Parmenides. *Translation and Analysis*. Minneapolis: Univ. of MN Pr. 1983. Lengthy commentary uses structure of dialogue as a control on interpretation of individual passages. Sees its arguments as aporetic. **[2539]**

——. "Unity and Infinity: *Parmenides* 142b-145a." *RMeta* 27(1974), 697-725. Examines several puzzling features of Parmenides' attempt to prove that Unity is one and many, whole and parts, limited and unlimited in multitude. **[2540]**

AZAR, L. "The Elusive One: Some Historical Explanations." *PhilStud* (Ireland) 16(1967) 104-115. Speculates about P's views on the "One" and its relation to Being and the Good, and contrasts them with the views of other ancient philosophers. **[2541]**

BARFORD, R. "The Context of the Third Man Argument in Plato's *Parmenides*." *JHPh* 16(1978), 1-11. TMA does not reflect P's lack of clarity on the Theory of Forms. He realizes how the Theory could refute TMA but depicts S as lacking the dialectical skill to refute it. **[2542]**

BESTOR, T. W. "Plato's Semantics and Plato's *Parmenides*." *Phron* 25(1980), 38-75. P uses general words in two ways: to name their Form and to designate things which participate in that Form. The objections to Theory of Forms disappear in light of this reading and the dialogue appears to be a pair of workbooks to go along with Aristotle's lectures on fallacious reasoning, now collected in the *Topics*. **[2543]**

BOSTOCK, D. "Plato on Change and Time in the *Parmenides*." *Phron* 23(1978), 224-242. P's discussion of change and temporal relations in the dialogue is largely indepen-dent of any special features of "the One"; the discussion is largely independent of any views one might hold about Forms vis-a-vis their relations to particulars. **[2544]**

BRUMBAUGH, R. S. "History and an Interpretation of the Text of Plato's *Parmenides*." *PhResArch* 8(1982), suppl.; also in #49, pp. 121-126. Contends *Parm* is serious in its intent and logically rigorous. Textual corruptions have clouded interpretation. **[2545]**

———. "The Purposes of Plato's *Parmenides*." *AncPh* 1(1980), 39-48. One purpose is to clarify Theory of Forms. A second is to demonstrate need of something beyond hypothetical-deductive method of *dianoia*. **[2546]**

———. "The Text of Plato's *Parmenides*." *RMeta* 26(1972), 140-148. The interpretive difficulties of the dialogue's hypotheses arise not from textual problems, which are quite minor, but from the philosophical problems under consideration. **[2547]**

CALVERT, B. "A Note on Plato's *Parmenides* 128e5-130a2." *Mnem* 35(1982), 51-59. The phrase *auta ta homoia* does not refer to the Forms. **[2548]**

CHERNISS, H. F. "Parmenides and the *Parmenides* of Plato," in #51, pp. 281-297. Dialogue's are intended to show that Zeno's paradoxes can be used to refute Eleatic view as well as pluralistic. Second part of dialogue parodies Parmenides' poem and Zeno's logic. **[2549]**

CRESSWELL, M. J. "Is There One or Are There Many One and Many Problems in Plato?" *PhQ* 22(1972), 149-154. Explores difference between the serious form of the problem of the one and the many and trivial form in *Parm*, *Soph*, and *Philebus*.**[2550]**

———. "Participation in Plato's *Parmenides*." *SJPh* 13(1975), 163-171. Parmenides is able to pick out flaws in the Theory of Forms because S views them as both immanent and transcendent. This is the same position taken in *Phaedo* 102. **[2551]**

———. cf. #3890.

CURD, P. K. "Parmenidean Clues in the Search for the Sophist." *HPhQ* 5(1988), 307-320. Argues that in neither *Parm* nor *Soph* is P confused about identity and predication. Second part of Parmenides offers insights into Being and non-Being which help to solve the problem of non-Being in *Soph*. **[2552]**

———. "*Parmenides* 131c-132b: Unity and Participation." *HPhQ* 3(1986), 125-136. Two arguments show that S's view of participation implies plurality of Forms. **[2553]**

———. "Some Problems of Unity in the First Hypothesis of the *Parmenides*." *SJPh* 27(1989), 347-359. The dialogue is not a parody. In the first hypothesis P reviews claims about the unity of the Forms which he had made in his middle period. **[2554]**

DIAZ, M. R. "What is the Third Man Argument?" *SJPh* 16(1978), 155-165. Challenges Vlastos' analysis (#2618) of the argument, and offers a new interpretation. **[2555]**

DORTER, K. "The Theory of Forms and *Parmenides I*," in #1267, pp. 183-202. *Parm* examines questions raised about the Forms but does not present full a refutation. It investigates the limits of the theory. This is why P returns to the problem in the later dialogues. **[2556]**

DURRANT, M. "*Parmenides* 127e-130e." *PhilPapers* 4(1975), 105-115. First section of

Parm is intended to produce a serious external objection to Theory of Forms, but it must be read in such a way as to make clear P's respect for Eleatic thought. [2557]

———. "Plato, The Third Man and the Nature of the Forms." *SJPh* 17(1978), 287-304. P did not regard TMA in either version as ultimately valid against his Theory of Forms. Seeks to explain why he offers no formal refutation of the argument. [2558]

FORRESTER, J. W. "Arguments an Able Man Could Refute. *Parmenides* 133b-134e." *Phron* 19(1974), 233-237. Discusses the fallacy of Parmenides' claim that only an intelligent and experienced person could hold the view that Forms are knowable, and therefore any argument against this view must be false. [2559]

———. "Plato's *Parmenides*: The Structure of the First Hypothesis." *JHPh* 10(1972), 1-14. Argues in favor of interpreting the first hypothesis (137c4-142a8) as P's direct expression of what he holds to be truths about "the One." The faulty premise which he knowingly introduces is connected to the structure of the rest of the dialogue. [2560]

GADAMER, H. G. "Plato's *Parmenides* and its Influence." *Dion* 7(1983), 3-16. Examines efforts at distinguishing P from Neoplatonism. [2561]

GEACH, P. T. "The Third Man Again," in #1809, pp. 265-278. Argues that Vlastos (#2620) has not rightly located the inconsistency in the argument and objects to his use of abstract nouns as designations of Forms. Argues that P's tacit assumptions about Forms were not the same as those which come naturally to us when we use abstract nouns. [2562]

GERSON, L. P. "Dialectic and Forms in Part One of Plato's *Parmenides*." *Apeir* 15(1981), 19-28. Arguments in part one of the dialogue fall into two groups, depending on whether or not Forms are present in the sensible world. [2563]

HATHAWAY, R. F. "The Second 'Third Man'," in #1280, pp. 78-100. Analyzes second version of TMA (132c12-133a7), and argues that this argument is the logically appropriate *reductio* against Theory of Forms. [2564]

LEE, E. N. "The Second 'Third Man': An Interpretation," in #1280, pp. 101-122. Examines philosophical strategies behind TMA, and explores metaphysical issues implicit in the argument. [2565]

LEWIS, F. A. "Parmenides on Separation and the Knowability of the Forms: Plato's *Parmenides* 133a ff." *PhilStud* 35(1979), 105-127. Parmenides uses the analogy of mastery and slavery to argue against P's thesis that Forms are separate from sensibles, but the analogy is overdrawn. [2566]

MANN, W. E. "The Third Man. The Man Who Never Was." *AmPhQ* 16(1979), 167-176. The argument at *Parm* 132a-b can be read to show that there are no Forms corresponding to a special class of incomplete predicates, such as "is large," which imply comparison but have no definite upper limit. This argument cannot be applied to other types of predicates. [2567]

McGINLEY, J. *Commentary on* Parmenides. Scranton, PA: McGinley, 1976. Detailed commentary that demonstrates full inter-dependence of the eight hypotheses, and displays their ontological as well as logical significance.   [2568]

McPHERRAN, M. L. "Plato's *Parmenides* Theory of Relations," in #1285, pp. 149-164. A more fully developed version of theory of relations found in *Phaedo* (as interpreted by H.-N. Castaneda) is found in *Parm*. This theory of relations causes epistemological problems of which P is unaware.   [2569]

MILLER, M. H. *Plato's* Parmenides: *The Conversion of the Soul*. Princeton Univ. Pr., 1986. Reads dialogue with "unwavering attention to its dramatic wholeness," for this will reveal definite range of Parmenides' One and function of his hypotheses.   [2570]

MORAVCSIK, J. M. E. "Forms and Dialectic in the Second Half of the *Parmenides*," in #76, pp. 135-154. In second half of dialogue, P is defending and revising his Theory of Forms.   [2571]

MUELLER, I. "*Parmenides* 133a-134e: Some Suggestions." *AncPh* 3(1983), 3-7. Discusses Parmenides' argument against knowability of Forms and finds one reason for its obscurity in its confusion over relational properties.   [2572]

MULHERN, J. J. "Plato, *Parmenides* 130d3-4." *Apeir* 5 #1(1971), 17-22. This passage does not provide grounds for asserting modification of Theory of Ideas. S's speech inclines for representation of even ignoble things in world of ideas.   [2573]

NAILS, D. "Epitaph for the Third Man." *Auslegung* 6(1978), 6-23. TMA holds against any version of Theory of Forms which P has not set down in writing. P knew this, but continued to advocate the theory in its unwritten form, which cannot be refuted by TMA.   [2574]

OWEN, G. E. L. "Notes on Ryle's Plato," in #82, pp. 341-372. Comments on Ryle's discussion of *Parm* (#2596) and argues that the conflicts and paradoxes reveal a plurality of interests, such as confusions between identity-statements and predications, puzzles about non-existence, assumptions about "being" and "becoming."   [2575]

PANAGIOTOU, S. "The Consequences of the Divisibility of Forms in Plato's *Parmenides*." *Phoenix* 36(1982), 45-52. Interpreting *Parm* 131c12-e12 epistemologically instead of ontologically helps to clarify P's purpose.   [2576]

———. "The Day and Sail Analogies in Plato's *Parmenides*." *Phoenix* 41(1987), 10-14. Parmenides' illustration of sail is analogous at relevant points to S's illustration of the day. Both analogies prove to be false.   [2577]

———. "A Note on the Translation and Interpretation of Plato's *Parmenides* 132a 1-4." *CPh* 69(1974), 50-55. Offers a translation which takes all four occurrences of *einai* to be copulative.   [2578]

———. "On the Date of Plato's *Parmenides* ." *C&M* 33(1981-82), 97-117. First part of dialogue, down to 135c, was composed after 365 B. C.   [2579]

———. "The *Parmenides* and the 'Communion of Kinds' in the *Sophist*." *Hermes* 109(1981), 167-171. *Parm* 129d6-e3 does not contradict *Soph* 251c ff. on question of "communion of kinds." *Parm* passage is talking about blending of opposites, not mixture of Forms. [2580]

——. "The *Parmenides* is the *Philosopher*: A Reply." *C&M* 30(1969), 187-210. Challenges interpretation (cf. #2621) that *Parm* is last member of "trilogy" of P's dialogues intended to comprise *Soph*, *Stsm*, and a dialogue dealing with the "philosopher." [2581]

——. "The Relative Order of Plato's *Parmenides* and *Theaetetus*." *CPh* 76(1981), 37-39. Arguments based on attitude toward direct and indirect statement, made for dating first part of *Parm* earlier than *Theaet*, are not valid. [2582]

——. "Vlastos on *Parmenides* 132a1-b2: Some of His Text and Logic." *PhQ* 21(1971), 255-259. Vlastos' evidence (#2618) is not sufficiently strong to justify his interpretation of a crucial passage in the argument. [2583]

PECCORINI, F. "Minding Sciacca's Suggestion on the Platonic 'One' and the *Dialectica Dell Eterno*." *GM* 31(1976), 611-638. Reexamines dialogue in light of Sciacca's book to detect any indication that P is pursuing an anti-conceptualistic understanding of Being even while he is going through the maze of an apparently ultraconceptualistic show of logical games. [2584]

PEMBERTON, H. J. *Plato's* Parmenides: *The Critical Moment for Socrates*. Darby, PA: Norwood, 1984. Dramatic structure reveals dialogue's unity. At end of second hypothesis S sees how he can respond to Parmenides' criticisms. [2585]

PETERSON, S. "The Greatest Difficulty for Plato's Theory of Forms: The Unknowability Argument of *Parmenides* 133c-134c." *AGPh* 63(1981), 11-16. P provides two paths by which we can reach conclusion that Forms are unknowable. One is to maintain that if we can know something, it is not a Form. The other is to assert that if there is such a thing as knowledge of a Form, we cannot have it. P's argument must be taken seriously, though its reconstruction is "complicated." [2586]

——. "A Reasonable Self-Predication Premise for the Third Man Argument." *PhR* 82(1973), 451-470. Proposes a way of understanding self-predication that is not unreasonable in itself, is formally consistent with other premises of TMA, and makes the argument seem to be a threat to Theory of Forms. But does not claim that interpretation gives what P meant. [2587]

PICKERING, F. R. "Plato's 'Third Man' Arguments." *Mind* 90(1981), 263-269. The two versions of TMA in *Parm* 130e-133a, which put up four arguments against Theory of Forms, are not an inconsistent set, as many scholars maintain. [2588]

PINTO, W. "Plato's *Parmenides* and Self-Predication." *JWVaPhSoc* 12(1977), 16-19. Early arguments in dialogue are *reductio ad absurdum* arguments on how not to interpret Forms. P may be questioning that all Forms are self-predicating. [2589]

PRIOR, W. J. "*Parmenides* 132c-133a and the Development of Plato's Thought." *Phron* 24(1979), 230-240. P seems not to accept one premise of arguments against Forms in first part of *Parm* but can still maintain Forms are paradigms. [2590]

RANKIN, K. W. "The Duplicity of Plato's Third Man." *Mind* 78(1969), 178-197. TMA is not designed to prove Theory of Forms false but to show that predication based on Forms is not the same as an explanatory hypothesis.   **[2591]**

———. "Is the Third Man Argument an Inconsistent Triad?" *PhQ* 20(1970), 378-380. Reply to #2620.   **[2592]**

ROCHOL, H. "The Dialogue *Parmenides*: An Insoluble Enigma in Platonism?" *IntPhQ* 11(1971), 496-520. Forms are discussed throughout the dialogue, not just in first portion. P's comments on the One still pose an enigma.   **[2593]**

ROSSVAER, V. *The Laborious Game: A Study of Plato's Parmenides.* Oslo: Univ' Forlaget, 1983. The dialogue is an indirect defense of P's concept of Idea. S and Parmenides reverse positions in the argument and their interchange, the "laborious game," ultimately demonstrates P's point.   **[2594]**

RUNICIMAN, W. G. "Plato's *Parmenides*," in #1809, pp. 149-184. Dialogue contains no fundamental modification of Theory of Forms, but nevertheless represents serious expression of P's own comments on the theory. Second part contains no explicit exposition of doctrinal or metaphysical teaching.   **[2595]**

RYLE, G. "Plato's *Parmenides*," in #1809, pp. 97-147. Dialogue is philosophically serious in sense that P thinks its arguments are valid and its problem is one of philosophical importance. Theory of Forms was intended to answer two questions: 1) How can several things be called by one name or be of one sort of character? 2) How is it that only those systems of propositions express certain knowledge which contain neither names nor descriptions of actual instances of sorts or characters — namely mathematics and philosophy? Shows how dialogue raises problems for the theory.   **[2596]**

SAYRE, K. M. "Plato's *Parmenides*: Why the Eight Hypotheses Are Not Contradictory." *Phron* 23(1978), 133-150. Examines eight hypotheses of second part and challenges view that they comprise series of contradictions. If properly paired, hypotheses are not contradictory.   **[2597]**

SCALTSAS, T. "The Logic of the Dilemma of Participation and of the Third Man Argument." *Apeir* 22(1989), 67-90. Examines P's claims that something cannot participate in part of a Form because the Form is unique. Analyzes logical steps of TMA and shows its assumptions to be absurd.   **[2598]**

SCHOFIELD, M. "The Antinomies of Plato's *Parmenides*." *CQ* 27(1977), 139-158. Views of Ryle and Cornford can be reconciled by understanding complexity of P's treatment of antinomies and development of his argument.   **[2599]**

———. "The Dissection of Unity in Plato's *Parmenides*." *CPh* 67(1972), 102-109. P includes Parmenides' treatment of numbers and division of unity because he wanted to combat a mistaken but widespread notion.   **[2600]**

———. "Eudoxus in the *Parmenides*." *MH* 30(1973), 1-19. *Parm*, especially second part, was "in-house" document for Academy. It discusses topics being debated there. Definition of inequality in 140B6ff. need not be attributed to Eudoxus. The latter's concept of Ideas as immanent in things receives sharp criticism in *Parm*.   **[2601]**

——. "A Neglected Regress Argument in the *Parmenides*." *CQ* 23(1973), 29-44. Parmenides' argument in 142c7-143a3 is undermined by his assumption of identity between "one" and "being" when taken as separate entities and as wholes. [2602]

——. "Plato on Unity and Sameness." *CQ* 24(1974), 33-45. When he wrote *Parm* 139d1-e4 P seems to have thought that sameness was not equivalent to unity. [2603]

SELLARS, W. "Vlastos and 'The Third Man'," in #77, pp. 23-54. Reply to Vlastos (#2620). [2604]

——. "Vlastos and 'The Third Man': A Rejoinder," in #77, pp. 55-72. Continuation of debate in previous item. [2605]

SHINER, R. A. "Self-Predication and the Third Man Argument." *JHPh* 8(1970), 371-386. TMA holds up against any version of Theory of Forms where qualities of Forms are predicated which are not equivocal. [2606]

SINAIKO, H. L. *Love, Knowledge, and Discourse in Plato: Dialogue and Dialectic in* Phaedrus, Republic, Parmenides. Univ. of Chicago Pr., 1965. Attempts to answer the question: If the dialogues are not philosophy, what are they and what is their relation to P's thought? Takes P's reservations about writing (expressed in *Phaedrus*) seriously and looks at each of these three dialogues in its own context, with no concern for overall chronology. [2607]

STERNFELD, R., and ZYSKIND, H. *Meaning, Relation and Existence in Plato's* Parmenides. New York: Lang, 1987. Demonstrates some unifying themes or principles in the dialogue: interrelation between logic and drama; effect of Parmenides' criticisms of Forms; the theory of a "concrete, pluralistic universe" which emerges from the weaving together of the dialogue's metaphysics and logic. [2608]

——. "Plato's *Parmenides* and the Transcendental Conditions for Discourse." *RIPh* 34(1980), 599-609. Dialogue is unified by concept of the One as a unit of significance which can be conveyed by words and makes discourse possible. [2609]

——. "Plato's *Parmenides*: The Drama and the Problem." *RIPh* 40(1986), 140-156. Studies introduction to dialogue to define problems it treats. Suggests the hypotheses lead to a new understanding of language as "logically literal discourse." [2610]

STOUGH, C. "Explanation and the *Parmenides*." *CanJPh* 6(1976), 379-401. Explores P's early claim that Forms are explanatory to the structure and several of the main arguments of *Parm*. Concentrates on what Forms do not explain, and suggests that the burden of much of Parmenides' criticism centers on that issue. [2611]

STRANG, C. "Plato and the Instant, I." *PAS* Suppl. 48(1974), 63-79. Interprets P as holding an atomic conception of time, that the now is not durationless. [2612]

TELOH, H. "Parmenides and Plato's *Parmenides* 131a-132c." *JHPh* 14(1976), 125-130. Parmenides in the dialogue presents strong arguments against modifications P has made of historical Parmenides' theory of Being. *Parm* 131a-132c proves to be a defense of Zeno's arguments supporting historical Parmenides' view of Being. [2613]

———. cf. #1936.

TURNBULL, R. G. "On R. E. Allen's *Plato's* Parmenides." *AncPh* 4(1984), 206-217. Review of Allen's translation of *Parm* (#2539) and challenge to his thesis that dialogue is meant to be aporetic.   **[2614]**

———. "Zeno's Stricture and Predication in Plato, Aristotle, and Plotinus," in #45, pp. 21-58. Examines an argument which P attributes to Zeno, and then investigates responses of P, Ar, and Plotinus.   **[2615]**

———. "The Third Man Argument and the Text of *Parmenides*," in #1267, pp. 203-225. Maintains that G. Vlastos (#2620) has overemphasized importance of the so-called TMA in *Parm* 132A-B2. The discussion provoked by his interpretation is largely irrelevant to understanding the passage and its place in the context of the dialogue.   **[2616]**

VAN STEENBURGH, E. W. "On Spiking the Imitation Regress." *Apeir* 8 #1(1974), 27-30. Outlines the steps necessary to spike the imitation regress argument against the Forms and discusses two important consequences: likeness is not itself a Form and does not lie between sensibles.   **[2617]**

VLASTOS, G. "Plato's 'Third Man' Argument. *PARM* 132A1-B2: Text and Logic." *PhQ* 19(1969), 289-301. Restatement of earlier analysis in light of discussions by Sellars (#2604) and Strang (1963), which resolve inconsistency of argument's premises but do not have much textual support.   **[2618]**

———. "Postscript to the Third Man: A Reply to Mr. Geach," in #1809, pp. 279-292. Response to Geach's technical analysis of TMA (#2562).   **[2619]**

———. "The Third Man Argument in the *Parmenides*," in #1809, pp. 231-264. Analysis of argument which reveals two key assumptions necessary to make TMA valid: Self-Predication Assumption ("Any Form can be predicated of itself") and the Non-Identity Assumption ("If anything has a certain character, it cannot be identical with the Form in virtue of which we apprehend that character"). Shows how those assumed premises are inconsistent. Examines whether, if these assumptions are made explicit, the argument constitutes a valid objection to Theory of Forms.   **[2620]**

———. cf. #746 and #1945.

WYLLER, E. A. "The *Parmenides* is the *Philosopher*." *C&M* 29(1972), 27-39. Argues that the existing dialogue *Parm* is identical with missing third dialogue of the trilogy, *Soph*, *Stsm*, and *Philosopher*.   **[2621]**

YOUNG, J. "*Parmenides* 133A-134B." *Prud* 12(1980), 83-86. This passage's argument succeeds in raising doubts about the possibility of a literal account of our cognitive relations with the Forms.   **[2622]**

For related items see #661, #740, #975, #1494, #1762, #1773, #1774, #1821, #1852, #1874, #1924, #1928, #2791, #3068, #3187, #3885, #5476, #6537, #6540, #6609.

Phaedo

The theme of the *Phaedo* is usually said to be the immortality of the soul, but that point is raised primarily to prove that it is rational for a philosopher to be willing to die. The discussion takes place in S's cell, with a number of his students and friends present, shortly before he swallows the hemlock. The dialogue itself is in the form of Phaedo's report of the conversation to Echecrates, a member of the Pythagorean school.

The dialogue introduces what Cornford calls "the twin pillars of Platonism": the immortality of the soul and the doctrine of the Forms as completely separate from objects. S assures his friends that he is not afraid to die because of his certainty that the soul continues to exist after the death of the body, as it had existed before birth. To prove that point, the dialogue resorts to the Forms. Since, S argues, the soul has not seen the Forms in this life but is nonetheless aware of them, it must have seen them in a prior life (according to P's theory of recollection, discussed at greater length — and in a somewhat different form, according to some scholars — in the *Meno*). But that could just mean that the soul has existed for a long time, not necessarily that it is immortal. To prove this last point, S argues that the Form of which the soul is a particular is Life, and since no particular can contain a Form which is its opposite, the soul cannot contain Death.

Toward the end of the dialogue S describes the abode of the souls in the underworld and the rewards and punishments awaiting the souls, based on their acts in the earthly life.

ACKRILL, J. L. *"Anamnesis* in the *Phaedo*: Remarks on 73c-75c," in #65, pp. 177-195. Analyzes doctrine of reminiscence in *Phaedo*; P is aware that being reminded of something is more complicated than it might appear. **[2623]**

ANTON, J. P. "The Ultimate Theme of the *Phaedo*." *Arethusa* 1(1968), 94-102. Only courage in face of death can qualify to serve as final and ultimate criterion to test man's ability to meet supreme demands of the ethical ideal. **[2624]**

APOLLONI, D. "A Note on *Auta ta Isa* at *Phaedo* 74." *JHPh* 27(1989), 127-134. The puzzling phrase "the equals themselves" is used to show the absurdity of identifying things which are equal with Equality. **[2625]**

BEDU-ADDO, J. T. "On the Alleged Abandonment of the Good in the *Phaedo*." *Apeir* 13(1979) 104-114. There are hints in *Phaedo* that P wants us to understand that S's new method of inquiry is *the* one that can lead the mind to complete recollection of Forms, including the Good. **[2626]**

———. "The Role of the Hypothetical Method in the *Phaedo*." *Phron* 24(1979), 111-132. Examines P's intentions in introducing hypothetical method prior to final proof of immortality of soul in *Phaedo*. Account of method is both a description of the familiarity with death which characterizes philosophy and a description of Socratic quest for cause of man's generation, existence and destruction. **[2627]**

BESTOR, T. W. "Plato's *Phaedo* and Plato's 'Essentialism'." *AustlJPh* 66(1988), 26-51.

Examines issue of why some sensible object (snow) is cold and can never be not-cold. Rejects view that P offers some "Essentialist" doctrine.   **[2628]**

BLANK, D. L. "Socrates' Instructions to Cebes: Plato, *Phaedo* 101d-e." *Hermes* 114(1986), 146-163. Compares use of several terms in *Phaedo* and other dialogues. Some alleged parallels cannot be demonstrated.   **[2629]**

BOLOTIN, D. "The Life of Philosophy and the Immortality of the Soul: An Introduction to Plato's *Phaedo*." *AncPh* 7(1987), 39-56. Presents interpretation that allows for Socratic irony; suggests that S may not have believed in personal immortality.   **[2630]**

BOLTON, R. "On the Argument of *Phaedo* 73c-75c." *PhResArch* 5(1979), no. 1166. Surveys recent discussions of P's contention that all learning is recovery of knowledge which we already possess.   **[2631]**

BOSTOCK, D. *Plato's* Phaedo. Oxford Univ. Pr., 1986. Discussion for non-specialists of all philosophical issues arising in dialogue.   **[2632]**

BRENTLINGER, J. "Incomplete Predicates and the Two-World Theory of the *Phaedo*." *Phron* 17(1972), 61-79. Offers a new interpretation of P's reason for adopting theory of separation of Forms from particulars, according to which flux theory is not a motive for, but a consequence of, the separation doctrine. Reflection on Anaxagoras' philosophy may have led P to accept separation.   **[2633]**

BROWN, M. "The Idea of Equality in the *Phaedo*." *AGPh* 54(1972), 24-36. Explores P's treatment of how one can generalize the standard measure-restricted definition of Equality, and how this applies to P's concern about virtue and standards.   **[2634]**

BURGE, E. L. "The Ideas as *Aitiai* in the *Phaedo*." *Phron* 16(1971), 1-13. *Phaedo* 96ff. should be taken to mean that P considers Ideas causal agents. We can observe similarity between Ideas and particulars, but sense knowledge cannot show causal links.   **[2635]**

BURGER, R. *The* Phaedo: *A Platonic Labyrinth.* New Haven, CT: Yale Univ. Pr., 1984. A Straussian interpretation which challenges traditional view that *Phaedo* contains twin pillars of Platonism: Theory of Forms and immortality of soul. Argues that "Platonism" of first half of dialogue is subject of criticism in second half.   **[2636]**

CAMPBELL, M. "The Meaning of Immortality in the *Phaedo*." *Kinesis* 1(1968), 29-36. Problem of immortality ranges over consideration of Socratic analysis of relations between soul/body, soul/other souls, soul/God.   **[2637]**

CARTER, W. R. "Plato on Essence, *Phaedo* 103-104." *Theoria* 41(1975), 105-111. Regarding P's view of essential properties. Challenges interpretations of Vlastos (#1940), who argues Forms have essential properties although individual particulars do not, and Nehamas (#2692), who argues everyday objects have "natures" consisting of collections of properties upon which identity of thing in question is "grounded."   **[2638]**

CASTANEDA, H. N. "Leibniz and Plato's *Phaedo* Theory of Relations and Predication," in *Leibniz: Critical and Interpretive Essays*, ed. M. Hooker (Minneapolis: Univ. of MN Pr., 1982), pp. 124-159. Examines Leibniz's views about *Phaedo* and the puzzles about relations discussed in *Theaet*.   **[2639]**

──. "The *Phaedo* and the Third-Man Arguments." *ITA Humanidades* 10(1974), 217-236. Seeks to ascertain whether actual Theory of Forms expounded in *Phaedo* is open to kind of attack advanced in TMA. **[2640]**

──. "Plato's *Phaedo* Theory of Relations." *JPhilLog* 1(1972), 467-480; also in *Exact Philosophy: Problems, Tools, and Goals*, ed. M. Bunge (Dordrecht: Reidel, 1973), pp. 201-214. Argues that P did put forward a theory of relations and relational facts, and that this theory is logically sound and ontologically viable. In 102b7-c4 P distinguishes between relations (which are sets of forms) and qualities. **[2641]**

──. "Plato's Relations, Not Essences or Accidents, at *Phaedo* 102b2-d2." *CanJPh* 8(1978), 39-53. Criticizes Gallop's translation (#2673) and Burnet's claim to find contrast between essence and accident in this passage. **[2642]**

COBB, W. S. "Plato's Treatment of Immortality in the *Phaedo*." *SJPh* 15(1977), 173-188. P does not present immortality as philosophically sound doctrine but as "magic charm" designed to calm fear of death which prompts misology. **[2643]**

COBB-STEVENS, V. "*Mythos* and *Logos* in Plato's *Phaedo*," in *The Philosophical Reflection of Man in Literature*, ed. A. T. Tymieniecka (Dordrecht: Reidel, 1982), pp. 391-405. S uses philosophical myths because the soul cannot be separated entirely from the body before death. The *logos* of philosophical insight must determine the structure of a myth, which provides comfort for the fear arising from the body. **[2644]**

COHEN, M. "Dying as Supreme Opportunity: A Comparison of Plato's *Phaedo* and the Tibetan Book of the Dead." *PhE&W* 26(1976), 317-327. Examines two theories of dying in which death is viewed as a culmination of life to be prepared for thoughtfully and rigorously throughout one's adulthood. **[2645]**

CRESSWELL, M. J. "Plato's Theory of Causality: *Phaedo* 95-106." *AustlJPh* 49(1971), 248-249. Reply to #2715. Theory of causality which P presents in *Phaedo*, whether adequate or not, is a sufficient response to Presocratic theories of causation. **[2646]**

──. cf. #2551, #3890.

DALE, A. T. "*Auta ta isa*, *Phaedo* 74c1: A Philological Perspective." *AJPh* 108(1987), 384-399. Discusses meaning of plural phrase for concept of Form of equality. **[2647]**

DALFEN, J. "Kenneth Dorter's Interpretation of the *Phaedo*," in #1275, pp. 215-224. Challenges Dorter's thesis (#2660) that P is not speaking seriously of the personal immortality of the particular soul. **[2648]**

DAVIS, M. "Plato and Nietzsche on Death: An Introduction to Plato's *Phaedo*." *AncPh* 1(1980-81), 69-80. Examines Nietzsche's critique of Platonism, and in particular, P's arguments for immortality of soul. **[2649]**

──. "Socrates' Pre-Socratism: Some Remarks on the Structure of Plato's *Phaedo*." *RMeta* 33(1980), 559-578. Examines S's inquiry into causes of coming-to-be in order to understand need for his turning to consideration of human affairs. **[2650]**

DE VRIES, G. J. "A Note on *Phaedo* 89B." *Mnem* 24(1971), 386-387. Surveys history of interpretation of an important phrase in this passage.   [2651]

DIGBY, T. "The Doctrine of Recollection at *Phaedo* 74a-75d: Coherence is Not Enough." *Phil*(Athens) 10-11(1980-81), 296-303. Doctrine of *anamnesis* fits with rest of *Phaedo* and does not create difficulties for argument that knowledge of Ideas is reserved for philosophers. Self-predication is not at issue in the dialogue.   [2652]

DILMAN, I. "*Phaedo* I: Learning as Recollection," in *Studies in Language and Reason* (Totowa, NJ: Barnes and Noble, 1981), pp. 1-12. P does not believe that people are born virtuous. Love of the Good must be kindled by contact with something from outside. The Forms provide that type of inspiration.   [2653]

———. "*Phaedo* II: Forms and the World of the Senses," in (cf. #2653), pp. 13-33. For P contemplation of the Form is not the same thing as a definition of knowledge. It is the sort of quest visualized in *Symp*.   [2654]

———. "*Phaedo* III: Note on the Immortality of the Soul," in (cf. #2653), pp. 34-38. Survey of the theme in *Phaedo*.   [2655]

DORTER, K. "The Dramatic Aspect of Plato's *Phaedo*." *Dialogue* 8(1970), 564-580. The structure of the dialogue illuminates its arguments, which appear to lull the reader. But the structure encourages him to involve himself in the dialectic.   [2656]

———. "Equality, Recollection, and Purification." *Phron* 17(1972), 198-218. P's theory of recollection, developed as an argument for immortality of soul, does not exclude the argument on purification.   [2657]

———. "The *Phaedo*'s Final Argument," in #1287, pp. 165-180. Examines reasons why S appears to have tricked readers with deliberately fallacious reasoning at the end of the dialogue. The immortality which he argues for is not personal.   [2658]

———. "Plato's Image of Immortality." *PhQ* 26(1976), 295-304. The affinity argument for immortality relies on analogy and is generally considered weak. It needs to be understood in relation to other arguments in the dialogue.   [2659]

———. *Plato's* Phaedo: *An Interpretation*. Univ. of Toronto Pr., 1982. Attempts to synthesize two methods for understanding P's philosophy: analytic approach which isolates individual arguments and evaluates their logical success or failure, and dramatic approach, which views the dialogue as a dramatic unity.   [2660]

———. "The Reciprocity Argument and the Structure of Plato's *Phaedo*." *JHPh* 15(1977), 1-11. Five arguments for immortality of soul are not just a progression but an organic whole. Taken individually, the last is no more successful than the first.   [2661]

———. "Reply to Joachim Dalfen," in #1275, pp. 225-232. Addresses general problem of how to read a Platonic dialogue and responds to Dalfen's "misrepresentations" (#2648). Maintains that Dalfen emphasizes surface meaning of the dialogues, not nuances lying deeper within the text. *Phaedo* serves as a paradigm.   [2662]

———. "Socrates on Life, Death and Suicide." *LThPh* 32(1976), 23-41. The concept of virtue resolves the apparent paradox of death and suicide in 62a-69e.   [2663]

DUNLOP, C. "Anamnesis in the *Phaedo*." *NewSchol* 49(1976), 51-61. Clarifies P's doctrine of recollection and responds to Gulley's assertion (1962) that two incompatible views of sense perception appear in the dialogue. [2664]

ECKSTEIN, J. *The Deathday of Socrates. Living, Dying, and Immortality: The Theater of Ideas in Plato's* Phaedo. Frenchtown, NJ: Columbia, 1981. Includes Jowett's translation of the dialogue and commentary on selected sections. Maintains that P was attempting to refute the idea that S's death was an act of heroism and that the arguments S presents for suicide are to be taken ironically. [2665]

EPP, R. H. "Some Observations on the Platonic Concept of Katharsis in the *Phaedo*." *Kinesis* 1(1969), 82-91. Focuses on scholarly debate over following dilemma: if knowledge is not possible, then S's life was futile; and if knowledge is possible, then S's lifelong quest was unrealized. P concept of *katharsis* serves to resolve the dilemma by offering a new viewing of the dialogue, which integrates concepts of immortality, knowledge, wisdom, and *katharsis*. [2666]

FERGUSON, J. "Plato and Phaedo." *MusAfr* 1(1972), 9-17. *Phaedo* differs from earlier dialogues, especially in views on soul's immortality, because of Pythagorean influences which P absorbed on his trip to southern Italy in 387. Dialogue's dramatic structure is the best developed in P's corpus. [2667]

FREDE, D. "The Final Proof of the Immortality of the Soul in Plato's *Phaedo* 102a-107a." *Phron* 23(1978), 27-41. Final Proof only argues that soul possesses life as its essential attribute. It is not fallacious, as some recent critics have maintained. [2668]

GADAMER, H-G. "The Proofs of Immortality in Plato's *Phaedo*," in #1274, pp. 21-38. Challenges view that S's proofs may be taken as pagan prefiguration of overcoming of death in Christianity. Dialogue raises question of what may be saved of the ancient religious tradition in an age in which scientific explanation and understanding of nature become more dominant. [2669]

GALLOP, D. "Castaneda on *Phaedo* 102b-d." *CanJPh* 8(1978), 55-57. Replies to Castaneda's criticisms (#2642) of the author's earlier paper (#2673). [2670]

———. *Plato:* Phaedo. Oxford: Clarendon Pr., 1975. Translation with notes which include analyses of main arguments and explorations of philosophical issues and problems of interpretation. [2671]

———. "Plato's 'Cyclical' Argument Recycled." *Phron* 27(1982), 207-222. Reexamines P's argument for immortality at *Phaedo* 69e-72c in response to criticisms of his book (#2671). Argument's dialectical function is seen as begging the question. [2672]

———. "Relations in the *Phaedo*," in #1287, pp. 149-163. In 102b-d P is not analyzing relations but outlining difference between essential and accidental predication. [2673]

GOOCH, P. W. "The Relation Between Wisdom and Virtue in *Phaedo* 69a6-c3." *JHPh* 12(1974), 153-159. Discusses two metaphors for wisdom (coin and purgative) and then considers what connection wisdom has with virtue if wisdom is a coin given away. Sees both instrumental and contributory value for wisdom. [2674]

GOSLING, J. "Similarity in *Phaedo* 73b sq." *Phron* 10(1965), 151-161. If S is arguing in this passage that visible equals are never truly equal, nor beautiful things truly beautiful, then either he is inconsistent in his use of notion of similarity, or he makes a highly problematic assumption in his analysis of "being reminded." **[2675]**

HACKFORTH, R. *Plato's* Phaedo. Cambridge Univ. Pr., 1972; rprt. Translation and commentary, with introduction. **[2676]**

HARTMAN, E. "Predication and Immortality in Plato's *Phaedo*." *AGPh* 54(1972), 215-228. Final proof for immortality in *Phaedo* is undermined by P's failure to make a subtle distinction between two sorts of predication. **[2677]**

HOUSE, D. "A Commentary on Plato's *Phaedo*." *Dion* 5(1981), 40-65. Overview of the dialogue which attempts to resolve interpretive problems that arise from looking at its arguments in isolation. **[2678]**

HUFFMAN, C. "Knowledge of Equality Itself at *Phaedo* 74b." *Discorso* 1(1981), 103-108. Analyzes difficulties surrounding concept of equality, in particular tension between 74b where S and Simmias agree that equality itself is known to men, and 76b8-c3, where this agreement seems to be contradicted. **[2679]**

KETCHUM, R. J. "Knowledge and Recollection in the *Phaedo*. An Interpretation of 74a-75b." *JHPh* 17(1979), 243-253. Challenges traditional interpretation that equal things fall short of the Equal itself because equal things are never exactly equal; provides an alternative interpretation that makes argument more plausible. **[2680]**

LINDENMUTH, D. C. "Love and Recollection in Plato's *Phaedo*." *AncPh* 8(1988), 11-18. In S's discussion with Simmias, both of them are "co-creators" of the position eventually developed. Their combined views become a "springboard for mutual philosophical reflection." Doctrine of *anamnesis* constitutes a moderate position between dogmatism and skepticism. **[2681]**

MATTHEN, M. "Forms and Participants in Plato's *Phaedo*." *Nous* 18(1984), 281-298. Reference to "equals" in 74b7-c6 is usually taken to refer to the sticks described earlier in the argument and to lead to the conclusion that Forms and particulars are not identical. But P wants to show that Forms are not knowable by the senses. **[2682]**

———. "Plato's Treatment of Relational Statements in the *Phaedo*." *Phron* 27(1982), 90-100. Any effort to solve the puzzle in *Phaedo* 102b-c is an attempt at a relational statement. It can be solved by denying its presuppositions, as Frege did. P's solution is that in statements such as "x is taller than y" the phrase "than y" modifies the verb. This theory can be connected with theory of Forms. Work of H. N. Castenada (#2641) is examined in this context. **[2683]**

———. "Relationality in Plato's Metaphysics: Reply to McPherran," *Phron* 29(1984), 304-312. Response to #2686. **[2684]**

MATTHEWS, G., and **BLACKSON, T. A.** "Causes in the *Phaedo*." *Synthèse* 79(1989), 581-591. Examines P's turning away from search for definitions as *aitiai* (causes); argues P concludes that search for definitions is not really a search for *aitiai* at all. **[2685]**

McPHERRAN, M. "Matthen on Castaneda and Plato's Treatment of Relational Statements in the *Phaedo*." *Phron* 28(1983), 298-306. Defuses criticisms which Matthen (#2683) makes against Castaneda (#2641) and criticizes Matthen's own understanding of theory of relations. **[2686]**

———. "Participants and Particularizations in the *Phaedo*." *SwPhR* 1(1984), 30-41. Argues for a new view of participation based on P's endorsement of immanent characters. **[2687]**

MENDELSON, A. "Plato's *Phaedo* and the Frailty of Human Nature." *Dion* 5(1981), 29-39. P uses several techniques to support his argument for immortality of the soul. He begins with rational argument, moves to myth, and finally to S's death as a kind of demonstrative action. **[2688]**

MORGAN, M. L. "Sense-Perception and Recollection in the *Phaedo*." *Phron* 29(1984), 237-251. P takes recollection (*anamnesis*) as proof of existence in an earlier life, but it is not same as understanding (*noesis*), which is only produced by dialectic. **[2689]**

MORRIS, M. "Socrates' Last Argument." *Phron* 30(1985), 223-248. Last argument of *Phaedo* is valid, in spite of certain semantic difficulties. **[2690]**

MORRIS, T. F. "The Proof of Pauline and Self-Predication in the *Phaedo*." *PhResArch* 10(1984), 139-152. Focusing on 103e2-5, argues P is discussing Pauline predication and Pauline self-predication but that he poses a series of riddles for the reader. **[2691]**

NEHAMAS, A. "Predication and Forms of Opposites in the *Phaedo*." *RMeta* 26(1973), 461-491. Theory of Forms developed in *Phaedo* is meant to apply only to incomplete predicates. **[2692]**

NOVAK, D. "Suicide and Human Responsiblity in Plato," in *Suicide and Morality: The Theories of Plato, Aquinas and Kant and their Relevance for Suicidology*. New York: Scholars Studies Pr., 1975. Examines P's view that suicide is immoral act in context of three basic human relationships: of person with himself, of person with society, and of person with God. **[2693]**

O'BRIEN, D. "The Last Argument of Plato's *Phaedo*, I." *CQ* 17(1967) 198-231; II, 18 (1968) 95-106. Focuses on how P thought he arrived at his conclusion that the soul is immortal — not on validity of argument. **[2694]**

———. "A Metaphor in Plato: 'Running Away' and 'Staying Behind' in the *Phaedo* and *Timaeus*." *CQ* 27(1977), 297-299. Examination of *Phaedo* 103d10 and *Tim*. 49e4-7 and 57a7-b7. **[2695]**

PREUS, M., and FERGUSON, J. "A Clue to the *Deuteros Plous*." *Arethusa* 2(1969), 104-107. Examines assertions of Simmias and S in *Phaedo* that *logoi* leading to Forms result from divine revelation. **[2696]**

PRUFER, T. "The Dramatic Form of *Phaedo*." *RMeta* 39(1986), 547-551. In its form the dialogue is a mediation of S's message through several individuals. His message is about the mediation of the *auto kath' hauto* to the soul by true *logos*. **[2697]**

RANKIN, H. D. "An Unresolved Doubt: *Phaedo* 76c14-d6." *Apeir* 1 #2(1967), 24-26. Attempts to dispose of objection that knowledge may enter into people at moment of birth and need not have been recollected from ante-natal state.   [2698]

REEVE, M. D. "Socrates' Reply to Cebes in Plato's *Phaedo*." *Phron* 20(1975), 199-208. Examines opinions of various scholars on 103c10-105c9 and concludes that the argument does rely on two fallacies.   [2699]

ROBINSON, T. M. "*Phaedo* 70c: An Error and an Explanation." *Dial*(Can) 8(1969), 124-125. First argument for immortality is invalid. S's claim that "waking up" and "coming back to life" are parallel is based on an erroneous equation of the Greek verbs, which contain a prefix (*ana-*) that can mean "up" or "back."   [2700]

————. cf. #2059, #2774.

ROSE, L. E. "The *Deuteros Plous* in Plato's *Phaedo*." *Monist* 50(1966), 468-473. Challenges "second best way" as hypothetical method; argues P refers rather to explanation of things in terms of formal causes, and means only that this sort of explanation is "second best" to a teleological explanation in terms of final causes.   [2701]

ROSS, D. L. "The *Deuteros Plous*, Simmias' Speech, and Socrates' Answer to Cebes in Plato's *Phaedo*." *Hermes* 110(1982), 19-25. Analysis of several Greek phrases in 99c8-d2 makes clearer what P means by first and second methods.   [2702]

SCHILLER, J. "*Phaedo* 104-105: Is the Soul a Form?" *Phron* 12(1967), 50-58. Examines final argument for immortality of soul, and argues that, contrary to claims of prominent interpretations, P never treats the soul as an immanent form.   [2703]

SHIPTON, K. M. W. "A Good Second-Best: *Phaedo* 99b ff." *Phron* 24(1979), 33-53. "First-best" and "second-best" methods differ not in their goals but in degree of certainty which they attain. Former would attain absolute certainty, but that is impossible. Latter achieves highest degree possible.   [2704]

SMITH, J. E. "The *Hamartia* of *Misologia*," in *Hamartia: The Concept of Error in the Western Tradition. Essays in Honor of John M. Crossett*, ed. D. V. Stump et al. (New York: Mellen, 1983), pp. 73-96. Tragedy of the dialogue is not Socrates' death but the triumph of *misologia* (hatred of reason).   [2705]

SMITH, N. D. "The Various Equals at Plato's *Phaedo* 74b-c." *JHPh* 18(1980), 1-7. Response to #2718. Plural *auta ta isa* is merely an uncommon way of denoting an abstract single entity. P does not use it again in the dialogue.   [2706]

SPITZER, A. "Immortality and Virtue in the *Phaedo*: A Non-ascetic Interpretation." *Pers* 57(1976), 113-125. *Phaedo* shows underlying tendency to equate immortality with "dialectical survival" or power of argument to sustain itself. Knowledge and virtue necessary to sustain the argument involve synthesis of sense and intellect.   [2707]

STEWART, D. J. "Socrates' Last Bath." *JHPh* 10(1972), 253-259. Discusses Orphic doctrines in this dialogue. Bath is part of initiation, purification ritual.   [2708]

STOUGH, C. "Forms and Explanation in the *Phaedo*." *Phron* 21(1976) 1-30. In 95e-

106e P explores how Forms explain some problems related to beliefs and comparisons and arithmetic operations. P solves such problems by emphasizing distinction between Forms and their realization. In his early dialogues P looks at Forms as *archai*, much like Presocratic elements or "causes." [2709]

STRACHEN, J. C. G. "What Did Forbid Suicide at *Phaedo* 62b?" *CQ* 20(1970), 216-220. Orphic prohibition against suicide may have become linked to Pythagoreans, especially Philolaus. [2710]

SWEENEY, L. "'Safe' and 'Cleverer' Answers (*Phaedo*, 100 sqq.) in Plato's Discussion of Participation and Immortality." *SJPh* 15(1977), 239-251. Examines P's "safe" answer to question of how Forms are causes and "cleverer" answer to question about soul's immortality. [2711]

TAIT, W. W. "Plato's Second Best Method." *RMeta* 39(1986), 455-482. Platonic method of reasoning admits that a "mathematical" (Pythagorean) conception of nature is an idealization. Platonic method represents first conceptualization of science as a body of knowledge about which we can reason apart from sense perceptions. [2712]

TARAN, L. "Plato, *Phaedo*, 62A." *AJPh* 87(1966), 326-336. Examines earlier interpretations and shows that S holds suicide to be wrong in any situation. [2713]

TAYLOR, C. C. W. "The Arguments in the *Phaedo* Concerning the Thesis That the Soul is a *Harmonia*," in #42, pp. 217-231. Examines Simmias' argument at 85e-86d that if soul is a *harmonia*, then it cannot be immortal; investigates S's reply. [2714]

——. "Forms as Causes in the *Phaedo*." *Mind* 78(1969), 45-59. Forms are causes either as being essences shared by all their particulars or as being present in some entity which particulars share. Examines how this scheme fits Ar's concept of causation. [2715]

TECUSAN, M. "A Note on *Phaedo*: 81 C FF," in #69, I, pp. 234-240. Reference to ghosts seems not to reflect popular conceptions of ghosts as wrathful spirits. [2716]

VLASTOS, G. "Reasons and Causes in the *Phaedo*." *PhR* 78(1969), 291-325; also in #1290, pp. 132-166; also in #1292, pp. 76-110. P distinguishes causes in a mechanical sense from those of a teleological nature. He also comes close to distinguishing those types of causation from logical causes. He uses the sorts of distinctions which Ar would later formalize. [2717]

WEDIN, M. V. "*Auta ta Isa* and the Argument at *Phaedo* 74b7-c5." *Phron* 22(1977), 191-205. New interpretation of argument for non-identity of Forms with sensible particulars; maintains phrase *auta ta isa* does not refer to equality of form. [2718]

WEISS, R. "The Right Exchange: *Phaedo* 69a6-c3." *AncPh* 7(1987), 57-66. Passage connects wisdom and virtue without equating them. When one properly exchanges pleasures, pains, and fears for their opposites, virtue is achieved. [2719]

——. cf. #2871.

WEST, E. J. M. "Plato and Socrates: The Men and their Methods," in #1083, pp. 131-136. Critically examines Peterman's interpretation of *Phaedo* (#1141) that S "commits suicide" to allow his listeners to think for themselves.   [2720]

WHITE, F. C. "Particulars in *Phaedo* 95c-107a," in #1287, pp. 129-147. Last argument for immortality of the soul which S presents rests on his understanding of the essential properties of particulars, not on the nature and inter-relations Forms.   [2721]

———. "Plato's Essentialism: A Reply." *AustlJPh* 66(1988), 403-413. Argues against Bestor (#2628) that *Phaedo* certainly contains some form of essentialism; it is best interpreted as "particular-essentialism."   [2722]

———. cf. #1950, #1952.

WIGGINS, D. "Teleology and the Good in Plato's *Phaedo*." *OSAP* 4(1986), 1-18. Questions whether at 99c2-d1, S is really prepared to give up search for the "teleological *aitia* itself."   [2723]

WILLIAMS, C. J. F. "On Dying." *Ph* 44(1969), 217-230. Examines P's argument that a thing which begins to be alive at some moment was, before that, dead. These two concepts are not opposites. They are not true predicates, but the meaning of "dead" in this passage is obscure.   [2724]

WOLFE, J. "A Note on Plato's 'Cyclical Argument' in the *Phaedo*." *Dial*(Can) 5(1966), 237-238. Examines the "cyclical argument" for immortality in which the soul is reincarnated after the death of the body.   [2725]

YEAGER, K. L. "Man and Nature in Plato's *Phaedo*." *Interp* 15(1987), 157-178. In this dialogue P breaks down barriers between politics and metaphysics, basing both fields on same set of values.   [2726]

For related items see #995, #1059, #1104, #1141, #1190, #1396, #2041, #2054, #2131, #2463, #3287, #3246, #3303.

Phaedrus

The *Phaedrus* is closely linked to the *Symposium*, but whether it was written before or after the latter dialogue, we do not know. Its ostensible subject is rhetoric and how a scientific study of that art must combine logic with an understanding of human feelings. S shifts the focus of the discussion by asking why someone would study rhetoric except to improve his soul. He tells a myth likening the soul to two winged horses driven by a charioteer. In the souls of the gods both horses are immortal, but in humans one horse is mortal and tends downward, while the other is immortal and strives upward. The charioteer's task is to keep them working together. The successful charioteer, of course, is the philosopher, who knows how to subjugate earthly desires and keep moving toward the heavenly vision.

Also alluded to in this myth of the soul is the idea that the soul existed before its birth into a physical body. In its incorporeal state it contemplates reality, i. e., the Forms. In this life what we call learning is actually the awakening or recollection of things contemplated in that previous existence.

Much of the dialogue consists of a speech allegedly composed by the orator Lysias and read by S's friend Phaedrus. S is dissatisfied with the speech and makes one to rebut it. In the course of this exchange occurs one of the best known passages in the dialogue, the discussion (275ff) of the advantages and disadvantages of writing. S holds that writing does not assist memory but weakens it. Knowledge preserved in writing is not held in the mind, and words in a written text cannot reveal the meaning which the author intended to impart to them. The reader may entirely misinterpret them.

Far more useful, in S's opinion, is dialectic, which "plants and sows in a fitting soil intelligent words." Toward the end of the dialogue he recommends that no one become an orator until he has learned to collect and divide examples by classes, understands the nature of the soul, and can match his rhetoric to the soul of his listener.

BETT, R. "Immortality and the Nature of the Soul in the *Phaedrus*." *Phron* 31(1986), 1-26. Detailed analysis of argument for immortality of soul from formalistic and mythological aspects; comparison of this conception of soul with that in other dialogues leads to conclusion that *Phaedrus* is a late dialogue. [2727]

BROWN, M., and COULTER, J. A. "The Middle Speech of Plato's *Phaedrus*." *JHPh* 9(1971), 405-423; also in #2081, pp. 239-264. Middle speech attacks beliefs central to Athens' rhetorical culture. P's target is Isocrates, or at least his views. [2728]

BROWNSTEIN, O. L. "Plato's *Phaedrus*: Dialectic as the Genuine Art of Speaking." *QJS* 51(1965), 392-398. P is arguing superiority of philosophy and its methodological aspect, dialectic, over rhetoric. [2729]

BURGER, R. *Plato's* Phaedrus. *A Defense of a Philosophical Art of Writing.* University, AL: Univ. of AL Pr., 1980. Argues that the dialogue's various themes — rhetoric, love, the soul — are unified by P's defense of writing. Even though S condemns writing, the overall thrust of the *Phaedrus* is that such a form of communication is valuable, even necessary, as long as it is not taken too seriously. [2730]

————. "Socratic Irony and the Platonic Art of Writing: The Self-Condemnation of the Written Word in Plato's *Phaedrus*." *SwJPh* 9(1978), 113-126. Dialogues are an imitation of Socratic conversation. In *Phaedrus*, story of origin of writing serves as an ironic deprecation of very activity which produces it. [2731]

————. "The Speech of Lysis in Plato's *Phaedrus*." *ClassOut* 55(1978), 81-86. S condemns Lysis' speech, which Phaedrus reads to him from a manuscript. But the speech contains core of P's defense of writing. [2732]

CLAY, D. "Socrates' Prayer to Pan," in #48, pp. 345-353. At beginning of dialogue S seemed a stranger in the countryside. His prayer emphasizes that philosopher is a resident alien in the world, one whose wealth is wisdom. [2733]

COOK, A. "Dialectic, Irony, and Myth in Plato's *Phaedrus*." *AJPh* 106(1985), 427-441. Though it appears disorderly, the dialogue moves from Athens and back to it, from Lysias to Isocrates. S's prayer at the end links together poetry, myth, and love, the three main themes of the work. They have been compared but relationships among them have not been formalized.   [2734]

COULTER, J. A. "*Phaedrus* 279A: The Praise of Isocrates." *GRBS* 8(1967), 225-236. Allusions in passage are designed to hurt Isocrates.   [2735]

CROPSEY, J. "Plato's *Phaedrus* and Plato's Socrates," in *Political Philosophy and the Issues of Politics* (Univ. of Chicago Pr., 1977), pp. 231-251. Aims at reconciling dialogue's two themes: love and verbal utterance, and examines how love is good and speech is good.   [2736]

CURRAN, J. V. "The Rhetorical Technique of Plato's *Phaedrus*." *Ph&Rh* 19(1986), 66-72. P sees dialectic as overcoming problems inherent in written teaching. His views on rhetoric are expounded by using the very techniques he advocates.   [2737]

DE VRIES, J. G. "A General Theory of Literary Composition in the *Phaedrus*," in #67, pp. 50-52. *Phaedrus* 278c suggests that P had a general theory of literary composition embracing oratory, poetry, and other fields.   [2738]

———. "Helping the Writings." *MH* 36(1979), 60-62. Reply to an article (in German) by T. A. Szlezak on P's literary techniques.   [2739]

———. "Isocrates in the *Phaedrus*: A Reply." *Mnem* 24(1971), 387-390. Response to an article (in German) by H. Erbse (1971) on supposed eulogy of Isocrates on which dialogue ends.   [2740]

———. "A Note on Plato, *Phaedrus* 270ac." *Mnem* 35(1982), 331-333. Discusses possible ironic meaning of *meteorologia* and sense in which *physis* is used.   [2741]

———. cf. #1341.

DILLON, J. "Comments on John Moore's Paper," in #1280, pp. 72-77. Response to Moore (#2765) on relationship between *Phaedrus* and *Symp.* Questions arguments based on alleged "logical primitiveness" of *Symp.*   [2742]

DORTER, K. "Imagery and Philosophy in Plato's *Phaedrus*." *JHPh* 9(1971), 279-288. The imagery of the dialogue is too complex and too closely linked to its message for the relationship to be incidental.   [2743]

DU BOIS, P. "Phallocentrism and its Subversion in Plato's *Phaedrus*." *Arethusa* 18(1985), 91-103. P's depiction of S in this dialogue crosses line between homoerotic and heterosexual attraction. S is supposed to draw the reader to him.   [2744]

DUSANIC, S. "The Political Context of Plato's *Phaedrus*." *RSA* 10(1980), 1-26. P tends to communicate his message on contemporary political questions in two implicit ways: (1) by adapting topical matters for major themes of discourse, and (2) by alluding to actual Athenian phenomena and characters.   [2745]

DYSON, M. "Zeus and Philosophy in the Myth of Plato's *Phaedrus*." *CQ* 32(1982), 307-311. Examines a discrepancy between two accounts of origin of philosopher in dialogue's myth. In one, the capacity for philosophy depends upon the identity of the god one follows; in the other, no reference is made to followers of any particular god. **[2746]**

FERRARI, G. R. F. *Listening to the Cicadas: A Study of Plato's* Phaedrus. Cambridge Univ. Pr., 1987. *Phaedrus* must be read with close attention to background, symbolized by cicadas in background of dialogue itself. P intends to say that logical argument can take one only so far toward attainment of philosophical life. One must ultimately, as S does in his speech, rely on myth to communicate one's full meaning. A key element in such a philosophical life is love of another person dedicated to the same goal, though this feeling must be controlled. **[2747]**

———. cf. #2040.

FORTENBAUGH, W. "Plato's *Phaedrus* 235c3." *CPh* 61(1966), 108-109. In response to Phaedrus' demand to identify the old and wise writers who will refute S if he agrees that Lysias' speech is the best, S hesitatingly names Sappho and Anacreon (235c3). Discusses the role the poems of these two have in S's subsequent speeches. **[2748]**

GRISWOLD, C. L. "Plato's *Phaedrus* 230e6-231a3, 262e1-4 and 263e6-264a3." *CB* 55(1979), 68-69. Examines certain inconsistencies in translations of passages. **[2749]**

———. "Self-Knowledge and the *Idea* of the Soul in Plato's *Phaedrus*." *RMM* 86(1981), 477-494. At 246a3 S is taken to indicate that there is an Idea of the Soul, but that interpretation is erroneous. His understanding of the soul is tied in with his concept of self-knowledge. Such a reading helps to underline the unity of the dialogue. **[2750]**

———. *Self-Knowledge in Plato's* Phaedrus. New Haven, CT: Yale Univ. Pr., 1986. Relies on principle that form and content are equally important, and shows how concept of self-knowledge unifies issues set forth in the dialogue. Examines a number of themes: Idea and nature of the soul, P's method of division, the connection between oral and written discourse. Looks at why P wrote dialogues and some larger problems in their interpretation. **[2751]**

———. cf. #1372, #2801.

GUTHRIE, W. K. C. "Rhetoric and Philosophy: The Unity of the *Phaedrus*." *Paideia*, Special Plato Issue (1976), 117-128. *Phaedrus* is not a manual of instruction in rhetoric, but a plea to abandon it for philosophy, which has entirely different aims. **[2752]**

HACKFORTH, R. *Plato's* Phaedrus. Cambridge Univ. Pr. 1979. Translation and commentary. **[2753]**

HAMILTON, W. *Plato*, Phaedrus *and Seventh and Eighth* Letters. Harmondsworth, UK: Penguin, 1973. Transl. with introduction and notes. Discusses problem of P's views on writing in light of *Phaedrus* 275 and *Letter* 7. **[2754]**

HERTER, H. "The Problematic Mention of Hippocrates in P's *Phaedrus*." *ICS* 1(1976), 22-42. Cosmological questions and discussion of *to holon* arise from Platonic concerns and are not derived from Hippocratic school. **[2755]**

HOWLAND, R. L. "The Attack on Isocrates in the *Phaedrus*," in #2081, pp. 265-279. *Phaedrus* contains verbal, thematic allusions to Isocrates, but its attack on rhetoric is an attack on Isocrates himself. P claims Isocrates does not teach rhetoric correctly because he does not base it on *episteme;* his written rhetoric has no serious value.   [2756]

KORITANSKY, J. C. "Socratic Rhetoric and Socratic Wisdom in Plato's *Phaedrus.*" *Interp* 15(1987), 29-53. Seeks to explain why S's rhetoric is oral; analyzes whether deprecation of writing allows for development of genuine art of rhetoric.   [2757]

KRENTZ, A. A. "Dramatic Form and Philosophical Content in Plato's Dialogues." *Ph&Lit* 7(1983), 32-47. P writes dialogues to answer criticisms of written discourse in *Phaedrus.* Form of his works is dialogical; their character is dialectical.   [2758]

LEBECK, A. "The Central Myth of Plato's *Phaedrus.*" *GRBS* 13(1972), 267-290. Studies myth's internal structure and its relation to beginning and end of dialogue. The myth itself is related to P's doctrine of *anamnesis.* By its very beauty it awakens within the reader the insight its author desires to communicate.   [2759]

LEVI, A. W. "Love, Rhetoric, and the Aristocratic Way of Life." *Ph&Rh* 17(1984), 189-208. *Phaedrus* appears to be about love if it is read in connection with *Symp.* If read as a companion piece to *Gorg,* its emphasis appears to be on rhetoric. P's criteria of evaluation, for both love and rhetoric, are determined by his elitist view of life. He defines things not on basis of good/evil, but as noble/base.   [2760]

LINFORTH, I. M. "Telestic Madness in Plato, *Phaedrus* 244D-E," in #1278, pp. 203-212. S tries to justify ritualistic madness by emphasizing divinity of Madness itself.   [2761]

MacKENZIE, M. M. "Paradox in Plato's *Phaedrus.*" *PCPhS* 28(1982), 64-76. Examines antinomy of P writing a book which repudiates writing of books, and how this paradox functions in dialogue as a whole.   [2762]

MANSFELD, J. "Plato and the Method of Hippocrates." *GRBS* 21(1980), 341-362. In *Phaedrus* 269e ff. P describes Hippocrates' work in terms that best fit Hippocratic work, "Airs, Waters, Places."   [2763]

McCUMBER, J. "Discourse and Psyche in Plato's *Phaedrus.*" *Apeir* 16(1982), 27-39. P's claim that rhetoric and *eros* entail one another has its foundation in Theory of Forms and enables P to resolve a "paradox of language."   [2764]

MOORE, J. D. "The Relation Between Plato's *Symposium* and *Phaedrus*," in #1280, pp. 52-71. P wrote *Phaedrus* first; when he came to feel dissatisfied with what he had said there, he wrote *Symp* to complement and to correct earlier impression.   [2765]

MULHERN, J. J. "Socrates on Knowledge and Information (*Phaedrus* 274b6-277a5)." *C&M* 30(1969), 175-186. Examines Thamus myth about invention of writing; point of myth has to do with distinction of knowledge from information. Writing is helpful in amassing information but not in acquiring knowledge.   [2766]

MURRAY, J. S. "Disputation, Deception and Dialectic: Plato On the True Rhetoric (*Phaedrus* 261-266)." *Ph&Rh* 21(1988), 279-289. Recent interpretations of *Soph* show P regards rhetoric as means of leading people to knowledge of Forms.   [2767]

NUSSBAUM, M. C. "'This Story Isn't True': Poetry, Goodness, and Understanding in

Plato's *Phaedrus*," in #1560, pp. 79-124. First speech really expresses P's views and amounts to a kind of recantation of his earlier aesthetic arguments. [2768]

PANAGIOTOU, S. "Lysias and the Date of Plato's *Phaedrus*." *Mnem* 28(1975), 388-398. Dialogue cannot have been written before Lysias' death in 365/364. [2769]

PIEPER, J. *Love and Inspiration: A Study of Plato's* Phaedrus, transl. R. Winston and C. Winston. London: Faber & Faber, 1965. Studies the dialogue "to become aware of certain fundamental aspects of existence which Plato sees, names, and tries to analyze." [2770]

PLASS, P. "The Unity of the *Phaedrus*." *SO* 43(1969), 7-38; also in #2081, pp. 193-221. Examines problem of coherence between discussion of eros and of rhetoric. Inspiration and persuasion are parts of the Divine, aiming to lead soul to philosophy. [2771]

PRICE, C. C., and PRICE, J. T. "The *Phaedrus* and the *Sundiata Epic* on Speech and Writing." *SecOrd* 5(1976), 37-44. Describes similarities between P's *Phaedrus* and *Sundiata: An Epic of Old Mali* on issue of inferiority of writing to speaking. [2772]

ROBINSON, T. M. "The Argument for Immortality in Plato's *Phaedrus*," in #41, pp. 345-353. Examines 245e-246a, and defends original interpretation that argument for soul's immortality stems from an assertion that it was "eternally moving" as opposed to a newer reading that soul was self-moving. [2773]

——. "The Nature and Significance of the Argument for Immortality in the *Phaedrus*." *Apeir* 2 #2(1968), 12-18. Claims the argument has an empirical cast and goes a long way toward solving difficulties presented by psychology of *Phaedo*. [2774]

ROSEN, S. H. "The Argument and Structure of Plato's *Phaedrus*." *PCPhS* 32(1986), 106-125. Examines the role played by the three speeches in the dialogue. [2775]

——. "The Non-Lover in Plato's *Phaedrus*." *M&W* 2(1969), 423-437; also in #75, pp. 78-90; also in #2081, pp. 223-237. Lysias' speech has been overlooked or misunderstood. It teaches us about human baseness and about how philosopher must understand dirt and other low things before he can understand psyche and cosmos. [2776]

——. "Socrates as Concealed Lover," in #75, pp. 91-101. Focuses on second speech to show that philosophical nature must combine natures of lover and nonlover. [2777]

ROWE, C. J., trans. *Plato*: Phaedrus. Wiltshire, UK: Aris and Phillips., 1988. Translation and commentary, for non-specialist. [2778]

SANTAS, G. "Passionate Platonic Love in *Phaedrus*." *AncPh* 2(1982), 105-114. Examines puzzling convergence of *mania* and *nous* in Platonic love. [2779]

SCHAKEL, P. J. "Plato's *Phaedrus* and Rhetoric." *SouthSpJ* 32(1966), 124-132. *Phaedrus* is usually interpreted as maintaining rhetoric, in pure form, is honorable and just. Dialogue actually restates P's opposition to rhetoric, originally set forth in *Gorg*, by constructing an ideal rhetoric which makes real rhetoric appear undesirable. [2780]

SZLEZAK, T. A. "What One Should Know When Reading 'Helping the Writings': A

Reply to J. G. de Vries." *MH* 36(1979), 164-165. Reply to #2739.   [2781]

TEJERA, V. "Irony and Allegory in the *Phaedrus*." *Ph&Rh* 8(1975), 71-87; also in #2081, pp. 281-298. It is unclear whether S is ironic or inspired in the two speeches he composes for Phaedrus. The dialogue may be a jibe at Isocrates or at the young P himself, both of whom relied on writing.   [2782]

THOMPSON, C. A. "Rhetorical Madness. An Ideal in the *Phaedrus*." *QJS* 55(1969), 358-363. Inspired madness is an essential part of true rhetoric as P understands it. Concept is tied in with larger discussion of aesthetics.   [2783]

VERDENIUS, W. J. "Another Note on Plato, *Phaedrus* 270ac." *Mnem* 35(1982), 333-335. Response to de Vries (#2741) on meaning of *physis* and *tou holou*.   [2784]

WEAVER, R. M. "The *Phaedrus* and the Nature of Rhetoric," in *Language Is Sermonic* (Baton Rouge: LA St. Univ. Pr., 1970), pp. 57-83. Offers an "imaginative" interpretation which argues that the dialogue is about one thing: nature of rhetoric, though it appears to touch upon a number of topics.   [2785]

WOLZ, H. G. "Plato's Discourse on Love in the *Phaedrus*." *Pers* 46(1965), 157-170. *Phaedrus*, in dealing with issue of people's relationship to their fellows, has a distinctively modern ring. It addresses itself to those who believe that whatever the conditions into which circumstances beyond their control have thrown them, they are nonetheless responsible for their own mode of being.   [2786]

ZASLAVSKY, R. "A Hitherto Unremarked Pun in the *Phaedrus*." *Apeir* 15(1981), 115-116. Word for plane tree (*platanos*), found several times in *Phaedrus*, is deliberate pun on P's name and suggests the dialogue contains authentic Platonic doctrine.   [2787]

For related items see #1356, #1804, #2076, #2088, #2161 #2335, #2346, #2607, #3279, #3288, #3300, #3303, #3452, #3495, #5125, #6286.

Philebus

S has been discussing with Philebus whether the life of pleasure or the life of reason is the good. As the dialogue begins, Philebus has essentially dropped out of the argument and his friend, Protarchus, has taken over the task of defending Philebus' position that the good for animate creatures consists in enjoyment, pleasure, and delight. S's general aim in the dialogue is to attack the possibility of using pleasure as a standard or criterion for evaluating ways of life.

S attempts to refute the view that pleasure is the good by distinguishing between good and bad pleasures and then arguing that good and bad pleasures are different. But Protarchus will not allow S to make this move, and he maintains that such pleasures are not unlike insofar as they are pleasures. S responds by raising the problem of the one and the many: How can the different forms of pleasure and of knowledge somehow constitute a unity? That is, we can speak of many particular pleasures or many particular instances of knowledge. We can then go on to ask what pleasure is and what knowledge is. But in so doing, we are supposing that there is a one single subject matter to examine. S here seems to be challenging the idea that "pleasure" can denote a single thing, and thus the view that pleasure can be a suitable criterion.

At this point (16c ff.), S puts forward a new method in an apparent attempt to classify the different kinds of pleasures. In developing this method, he introduces the terms *peras* and *apeiron*. P is here commonly interpreted as advancing the division of genera into species and as recommending that the divisions continue into subspecies until no further divisions can be made. Once we have reached this point, then we accept the unlimited number of particular instances. Through such careful classification, we can increase our knowledge.

S then recalls a theory he heard long ago (20b, an apparent reference to *Rep* 505b ff.) that neither pleasure nor knowledge is the good. Rather there is some third thing, different and better than the other two candidates. S indicates that if we could somehow gain a clear account of this third thing, then at the very least, pleasure would have been shown not to be the good. S then, in effect, restates the problem about the different ways of life. There is to be no intelligence in the life of pleasure, and there is to be no pleasure in the life of intelligence. He argues then that neither life in itself contains the good, and that some "mixed" life, involving both intelligence and pleasure, is superior.

S then recalls the terms *peras* and *apeiron*, and pursues the issue of whether intelligence or pleasure is more responsible for the good life in the context of what exists in the universe. Intelligence wins the argument. If the good life is one that is "mixed," then pleasure has a role in that life. But it will be intelligence that determines what kind and how much with respect to that pleasure.

The *Philebus* is a notoriously difficult dialogue, and interpretive controversies are many. Some have viewed the methodological recommendations as supporting the Theory of Forms, and others have argued that these recommendations provide evidence of the abandonment of that theory. The discussion of false pleasures continues to generate much scholarly interest. The overall structure of the dialogue and how different discussions relate to the overall examination of hedonism remains far from clear. As Gosling (#2800, p. 139) writes, the debate about hedonism is "familiar, but is nowhere given such detailed, nor, it must be admitted, such baffling treatment" as in this dialogue.

BARKER, A. "Text and Sense at *Philebus* 56a." *CQ* 37(1987), 103-109. Suggested translation of passage dealing with music.   [2788]

BENITEZ, E. E. *Forms in Plato's* Philebus. Assen, Netherlands: Van Gorcum, 1989. Five interpretive essays on dialogue's epistemology and ontology. Argues that P maintains Theory of Forms despite criticisms raised in *Parm*.   [2789]

BOLOTIN, D. "Socrates' Critique of Hedonism. A Reading of the *Philebus*." *Interp* 13(1985), 1-13. Defense of hedonism by Philebus resembles S's arguments in *Gorg*. Neither statement of case for hedonism is entirely satisfactory.   [2790]

CASPER, D. J. "Is There a Third One and Many Problem in Plato?" *Apeir* 11 #2(1977), 20-26. Problem of one and many can be stated in two questions: 1) how can one changing thing have many characteristics? and 2) how can one Form be in many changing things? *Philebus, Parm* and *Soph*, however, raise a third question: how can one Form have many characteristics? [2791]

COOPER, N. "Pleasure and Goodness in Plato's *Philebus*." *PhQ* 18(1968), 12-15. Shows that words "pleasant" and "good" are not two names for the same thing. A good thing must have some limit. Attempts to show link with *Stsm*. [2792]

CROPSEY, J. "On Pleasure and the Human Good: Plato's *Philebus*." *Interp* 16(1988-89), 167-192. Dialogue goes far beyond definition of human good or pleasure. It tries to bring reader to point of insight into relation between mankind's existence and that of nature as a whole. [2793]

DANCY, R. M. "The One, the Many, and the Forms: *Philebus* 15b1-8." *AncPh* 4(1984), 160-193. The one-many problems in Theory of Forms which occur in this work can be found in other dialogues beginning with *Parm*. [2794]

DAVIS, P. J. "The Fourfold Classification in Plato's *Philebus*." *Apeir* 13(1979), 124-134. *Philebus'* classification system is not related to Theory of Forms. It is devised *ad hoc* to support P's ethical argument. It has no metaphysical implications. [2795]

DYBIKOWSKI, J. C. "False Pleasure and the *Philebus*." *Phron* 15(1970), 147-165. P errs in defending false pleasures; defense can be based on other arguments. [2796]

————. "Mixed and False Pleasures in the *Philebus*: A Reply." *PhQ* 20(1970), 244-247. Reply to #2812. P distinguishes true and false pleasures on one basis and pure and mixed pleasures on another. The fact that he attributes truth to pure pleasures has led some to think the various pleasures are interchangeable. [2797]

FAHRNKOPF, R. "Forms in the *Philebus*." *JHPh* 15(1977), 202-207. Reply to #2821. Discussion of Divine Circle shows P is not advocating Aristotelian immanent realism. Dialogue makes it clear he saw Forms as transcendent throughout his life. [2798]

FREDE, D. "Rumpelstiltskin's Pleasures. True and False Pleasures in Plato's *Philebus*." *Phron* 30(1985), 151-180. Surveys "evolution" of notion of truth and falsity of pleasures and defends P's ethical analysis of pleasures in this way. [2799]

GOSLING, J. C. B. *Plato:* Philebus. Oxford: Clarendon Pr., 1975. Translation with notes and commentary. Examines procedural recommendations that have variously been seen as providing evidence for Theory of Forms and for rejection of that theory, and attempts to make these passages (as nearly as possible) consistent. Discusses problem of true and false pleasures. [2800]

GRISWOLD, C. L. "Soul, Form, and Indeterminacy in Plato's *Philebus* and *Phaedrus*." *PACPhA* 55(1981), 184-194. Examines problem raised by P's use of terms *apeiron* ("unlimited") and *peras* ("limit") in relation to soul. Finds no essential contradiction between P's discussion of soul as a Kind in *Philebus* and an Idea in *Phaedrus*. [2801]

HACKFORTH, R. *Plato's* Philebus. Cambridge Univ. Pr., 1972; rprt 1985. Commentary which suggests that P's motives for writing *Philebus* were not to confute Eudoxus' pronouncement that pleasure is the good, but to restate and modify his own doctrine of pleasure and pain. [2802]

HAHN, R. "On Plato's *Philebus* 15b1-8." *Phron* 23(1978), 158-172. Three complex questions, not two, are posed. Each of them raises epistemological and ontological problems. Examines views of nineteenth- and twentieth-century scholars and includes lengthy bibliography. [2803]

———. "*Synagoge* and the Problem of *to peras* in *Philebus* 25c8-e5." *PhResArch* 5(1979), no 1318. Examines passage which investigates relation between three of four classes of Being introduced at 23c. Focuses on two central problems: significance of the limiting class of Being and the operation of collection, on which P bases his later dialectic. Suggests several textual emendations. [2804]

HAMPTON, C. "Plato's Later Analysis of Pleasure," in #1267, pp. 41-49. P's conception of truth is not based on matters of fact but on the ontological status of things. Pleasures are thus true or false not because a person is mistaken in his beliefs about them but because of their ontological priority. [2805]

———. "Pleasure, Truth and Being in Plato's *Philebus*: A Reply to Professor Frede." *Phron* 32(1987), 253-262. Frede's (#2799) approach to P's calling certain pleasures "false" concedes more to modern ideas of truth and falsity than are found in P. [2806]

KLEIN, J. "About Plato's *Philebus*." *Interp* 2(1972), 157-182. Analyzes dialogue, looking especially at its comic and dramatic features, without presupposing stages in development of P's thought. [2807]

KOLB, D. A. "Pythagoras Bound: Limit and Unlimited in Plato's *Philebus*." *JHPh* 21(1983), 497-512. Offers interpretation of limited and unlimited which gives greater persuasive force to the ethical arguments. [2808]

LEE, J. M. "*Philebus* 35a6-10." *Phron* 11(1966), 31-34. Examines the line of argument from 34e3 to 35d4 which is that desire, since it consists in soul's remembering past replenishment, must be non-bodily. Explores why at 35a6-10, P brings in apparently irrelevant digression about first occasion of depletion, and concludes that "sensation and memory are *prima facie*, the only possible means by which anyone feeling desire can 'have hold of' replenishment." [2809]

LETWIN, O. "Interpreting the *Philebus*." *Phron* 26(1981), 187-206. Response to Gosling's comments about *peras* and *apeiron* in (#2800). P manipulates these terms to make it appear that the good life can be achieved if reason prevails over passion, a point he has explicitly argued against. [2810]

McGINLEY, J. "The Doctrine of the Good in *Philebus*." *Apeir* 11 #2(1977), 27-57. Life of mind rather than of pleasure is closest to the Good, though not identical with it. As subject of all Forms, the One is the Good. [2811]

McLAUGHLIN, A. "A Note on False Pleasure in the *Philebus*." *PhQ* 19(1969), 57-61. Examines some modern comments on P's treatment of false pleasure to show dangers of interpreting him without considering his cultural context. He is more concerned with concept of moral evil than we are. Thus he can classify the pleasure accompanying false belief as wrong and exclude it from the good life simply because it is false. [2812]

MITSIS, P. "Commentary on Sayre's 'The *Philebus* and the Good: The Unity of the

Dialogue in Which the Good is Unity'." *PBACAPh* 2(1986), 72-78. Challenges Sayre's claim (#2818) to find a new ontology in the dialogue, for P is strangely silent about sensible particulars in his account of the four-fold classification.   **[2813]**

MOHR, R. D. "*Philebus* 55c-62a and Revisionism," in #1285, pp. 165-170. Defends unitarian approach to P; discusses knowledge as craft, epistemological dualism, dialectic and its objects, status of flux of phenomena. Reply to #2821.   **[2814]**

MORAVCSIK, J. M. E. "Forms, Nature, and the Good in the *Philebus*." *Phron* 24(1979), 81-104. Harmonizes ontological passages of *Philebus*, relating P's new division technique to Theory of Forms.   **[2815]**

O'CONNELL, S. P. "Plato's *Philebus*." *Auslegung* 10(1983), 247-270. Examines questions about role of pleasure in life of philosophy and the good life.   **[2816]**

PENNER, T. M. I. "False Anticipatory Pleasure: *Philebus* 36a3-41a6." *Phron* 15(1970), 166-178. Offers an interpretation of P's discussion of false pleasures that displays clearly the analogy between pleasure and perception and explains why P gives so much attention to the scribe and painter similes.   **[2817]**

SAYRE, K. M. "The *Philebus* and the Good: The Unity of the Dialogue in Which the Good is Unity." *PBACAPh* 2(1986), 45-71. Examines doctrine of participation and argues that P is reaching a new conception of relationship between Forms and particulars. Not only particular things but also Forms belong to the class of Mixture. The Good is a proportional Unity formed of truth and beauty.   **[2818]**

————. cf. #1918.

SCHOFIELD, M. "Who Were *Hoi Dyschereis* in Plato, *Philebus* 44a ff.?" *MH* 28(1971), 2-20, 181. Philosophical implications of word *dyschereia* ("difficulty") in *Philebus* seem to have been developed by Speusippus.   **[2819]**

SCOLNICOV, S. "*Philebus* 15b1-8." *SCI* 1(1974), 3-13. Passage discusses, though in different order, same problems set forth in *Parm* 128e-130a.   **[2820]**

SHINER, R. A. *Knowledge and Reality in Plato's* Philebus. Assen, Netherlands: Van Gorcum, 1974. Develops interpretation of metaphysical passages of *Philebus* consistent with view that P substantially revised Theory of Forms in later dialogues.   **[2821]**

————. "Knowledge in *Philebus* 55c-62a: A Response to Richard Mohr's '*Philebus* 55c-62a and Revisionism'," in #1285, pp. 171-183. Chief points of debate with #2814 are whether *episteme* and *techne* are interchangeable, whether dialectic in *Philebus* implies two separate worlds, why paradigmatism is not found in *Philebus*.   **[2822]**

————. "Must *Philebus* 59a-c Refer to Transcendent Forms?" *JHPh* 17(1979), 71-77. Reply to Fahrnkopf (#2798). Defends view that in *Philebus*, P need not be read as believing in either immanent or transcendent Forms.   **[2823]**

TALLON, A. "The Criterion of Purity in Plato's *Philebus*." *NewSchol* 46(1972), 439-445. P's primary purpose in *Philebus* is to establish which pleasures are admissible to the good life and which are not. Purity (equated with painlessness) is his main criterion, with knowledge as the prime example of a pure pleasure. But knowledge is usually associated with pain, thus undermining P's argument. [2824]

WATERFIELD, R. A. H. "The Place of the *Philebus* in Plato's Dialogues." *Phron* 25(1980), 270-305. Challenges traditional dating of dialogue. Its immature logic and scientific methodology and its metaphysic point to P's middle period. [2825]

WILLIAMS, C. J. F. "False Pleasures." *PhilStud* 26(1974), 295-297. Argues contrary to P that pleasures can be real, but they cannot be false. [2826]

For related items see #1695, #1954, #2550.

Protagoras

In this dialogue S relates to an unnamed friend how young Hippocrates had come to his door early in the morning with the exciting news that the renowned Sophist Protagoras was in town and with a request that S introduce Hippocrates to Protagoras so the younger man can become a pupil of his. A short discussion leads to Hippocrates' admission that he does not know what Protagoras teaches. S suggests that they find that out before Hippocrates entrusts himself to the visitor.

They visit the house where Protagoras is staying but gain admission only with some difficulty. Inside they find not only Protagoras but also Prodicus and Hippias, two other noted Sophists, and a group of their admirers. S raises the question of what a Sophist is and what he professes to teach. Protagoras replies that people who in the past have been known as poets, religious leaders, by similar designations, were in fact Sophists. Like them, he teaches "civic virtue," i. e., he makes men into good citizens.

S doubts that such a thing can be taught. The Athenian experience suggests that it cannot, for the city's government is based on the assumption that any citizen is capable of giving good advice, without any proof of training. Athenians look for expertise only in the arts and crafts (perhaps a Platonic slap at the democracy which executed S). Furthermore, Athenian statesmen have a sorry record of passing their ability to govern on to their children or proteges. The question thus becomes, Can "civic virtue" be taught? For that matter, can any virtue be taught? And, while they're on the subject, Are all virtues one? These become the thematic questions of the dialogue.

The dialogue becomes a contest between two methods of teaching as well as between two philosophies of what can be taught. Protagoras presents his ideas in speeches, while S attempts to engage him in dialectic. Protagoras' first speech includes a *mythos* relating how human beings progressed from an animalistic condition to the level of civilized society, all made possible because of the ability of one generation to teach what it had learned to the next. In the ensuing *elenchus* S gets Protagoras to admit that the virtues are all parts of one thing, just as the parts of the face are. Protagoras grows weary of the exchange and launches into a speech on the relative meanings of "good" and "beneficial."

After an interlude during which S threatens to leave unless Protagoras will engage in *elenchus* with him, the conversation resumes with an examination of a poem by Simonides, centering on the question of what the poet meant by the expression "it is hard to be good." This section hinges on finding shades of meaning or utterly unlikely meanings in words and is probably meant as a criticism of Prodicus, who based his teaching on such hair-splitting semantics.

In the second section of the dialogue S attempts to refute Protagoras' assertion that all the virtues except courage have something in common. As part of that discussion the two disputants also explore the question of whether pleasure is good and pain evil. By the end of the dialogue the two have exchanged positions. S has defined courage as something like "knowing what is ahead of one and being able to face it." Cowardice is thus lack of knowledge. Courage must be knowledge and must therefore be teachable, the exact opposite of the line he took at the beginning of the dialogue. Protagoras ends by declaring that courage is not knowledge and thus cannot be taught, despite his claim at the beginning of the dialogue to teach such virtues.

ADKINS, A. W. H. "*Arete, Techne*, Democracy and Sophists: *Protagoras* 316b-328d." *JHS* 93(1973), 3-12. Protagoras is vague in defining what he proposes to teach and how, so as to avoid offending Athenians who could vote to expel him. He hopes to gain favor of Athenians by showing that his objectives are appropriate to a democracy.   **[2827]**

ALFORD, C. F. "A Note on the Institutional Context of Plato's *Protagoras*." *CW* 81(1988), 167-176. Protagoras' argument at 318e5-319a6 is not mere sophism. It is the sort of exaggeration considered acceptable in Athenian political debate.   **[2828]**

BALABAN, O. "The Myth of Protagoras and Plato's Theory of Measurement." *HPhQ* 4(1987), 371-384. Myth of Epimetheus, Prometheus and Zeus told by Protagoras reveals that he sees virtue as tripartite. It is not knowledge, but it is teachable.   **[2829]**

BIDGOOD, R. A. "Irwin on Hedonism in Plato's *Protagoras*." *AncPh* 3(1983), 30-32. No passages support claim that for S, every craft must have a determinate product, contrary to Irwin's (#1709) reconstruction of development of Socratic ethics.   **[2830]**

COBB, W. S. "The Argument of the *Protagoras*." *Dial*(Can) 21(1982), 713-731. Argues that S makes no significant logical mistakes in the dialogue.   **[2831]**

——. cf. #2280.

COBY, P. "The Education of a Sophist: Aspects of Plato's *Protagoras*." *Interp* 10(1982), 139-158. In *Protag* P tries to define what a Sophist is, what his intellectual limitations are, and how gulf between sophism and philosophy can be bridged.   **[2832]**

——. *Socrates and the Sophistic Enlightenment. A Commentary on Plato's* Protagoras. London: Associated Univ. Presses, 1987. Discusses how S links his interlocutor's concern for reputation to virtue of courage and how, through an analysis of this virtue, S uncovers the contradictory character of Protagoras.   **[2833]**

CRONQUIST, J. "The Point of the Hedonism in Plato's *Protagoras*." *Prud* 12(1980), 63-81. S does seem serious in asserting hedonism in the dialogue. Its role is to insure that the good is attractive.   **[2834]**

DEVEREUX, D. T. "Protagoras on Courage and Knowledge: *Protagoras* 351a-b." *Apeir* 9 #2(1975), 37-39. Despite appearances, Protagoras has a carefully thought out and consistent view of relationship between courage and knowledge. **[2835]**

DUNCAN, R. "Courage in Plato's *Protagoras.*" *Phron* 23(1978), 216-228. Courage provides a unifying theme in this disjointed dialogue. It is ultimately inconsistent for Protagoras to believe that "Man is the measure of all things" as P interprets maxim in *Theaet*, and believe that there is anything worth dying for. **[2836]**

DYSON, M. "Knowledge and Hedonism in Plato's *Protagoras.*" *JHS* 96(1976), 32-45. Examines P's views on hedonism in 355-358, comparing it with passages in Xenophon and Ar to see what S said about weakness of the will as ignorance. P sees hedonism's main weakness as its claim that right action depends on knowledge and its failure to define objects of knowledge which can help to determine right actions. **[2837]**

EISENSTADT, M. "Protagoras' Teaching in Plato's *Protagoras.*" *SO* 56(1981), 47-61. P seems to suggest that Protagoras personally considered *sophrosyne* compatible with injustice, in spite of his public pronouncements in *Protag* 333c. S attempts to guard against the potential corruption inherent in Protagoras' teaching. **[2838]**

FERGUSON, J. "Plato, Protagoras and Democritus." *BuckRev* 15(1967), 49-58. P's interest in theories which he attributes to Protagoras means that the theories were presented by some fourth-century contemporary thinker, most likely Democritus. **[2839]**

FREDE, D. "The Impossibility of Perfection: Socrates' Criticism of Simonides' Poem in the *Protagoras.*" *RMeta* 39(1986), 729-753. S's comments on poem (334C-348A) are not merely an effort to best Sophists. He notes distinction between being and non-being. Text may be interpolated and suggests connection with *Symp*. **[2840]**

GAGARIN, M. "The Purpose of Plato's *Protagoras.*" *TAPhA* 100(1969), 133-164. Challenges interpretation that views dialogue as contest between S and Protagoras. Rather, P aims at showing basic continuity between Protagorean and Socratic thought, though S advanced beyond Sophists. **[2841]**

GOLDBERG, L. *A Commentary on Plato's* Protagoras. New York: Lang, 1983. Studies dramatic form of the dialogue. Book contains paraphrase of dialogue with comments interspersed and a logical analysis of the dialogue's main arguments. Suggests that it is a kind of response to Aristophanes' *Clouds*, designed to portray S not as a Sophist but as a defender of the city against Sophists. **[2842]**

GULLEY, N. "Socrates' Thesis at *Protagoras* 358b-c." *Phoenix* 25(1971), 118-123. Reply to #2866. When S claims that no one willingly acts contrary to what he knows or believes to be right, the term "believe" involves "believing falsely." Thus a person can voluntarily do what is wrong, but he will believe (falsely) that he is doing right. **[2843]**

HARTMAN, M. "How the Inadequate Models for Virtue in the *Protagoras* Illuminate Socrates' View of the Unity of the Virtues." *Apeir* 18(1984), 110-117. Only a combination of face and gold models can demonstrate S's concept of unity of virtues. **[2844]**

HUBBARD, B. A. F., and **KARNOFSKY, E. S.** *Plato's* Protagoras: *A Socratic Commentary.* Univ. of Chicago Pr., 1982. Non-specialist commentary which asks Socratic-type questions, which readers are expected to answer for themselves, and offers suggestions useful in addressing these questions.   [2845]

KAHN, C. H. "On the Relative Date of the *Gorgias* and the *Protagoras*." *OSAP* 6(1988), 69-102. View that *Protag* is earlier reflects a basic misconception of scope and intent of early Platonic dialogues.   [2846]

———. "Plato and Socrates in the *Protagoras*." *Methexis* 1(1988), 33-51. Defining certain dialogues as "Socratic" involves more than merely looking at the figure of S. Philosophic themes must be examined. *Protag* is studied in those terms.   [2847]

KLOSKO, G. "On the Analysis of *Protagoras* 351b-360e." *Phoenix* 34(1980), 307-322. S argues against the possibility of moral weakness; cites egoism as a basic human motivation.   [2848]

———. "Toward a Consistent Interpretation of the *Protagoras*." *AGPh* 61(1979), 125-142. Discusses use of fallacious arguments in several dialogues, especially *Protag*, which seems to depict some form of organized eristic competition.   [2849]

MAGUIRE, J. P. "Protagoras . . . or Plato?: The *Protagoras*." *Phron* 18(1973), 115-138. Protagoras' two formulae about appearances and man measure are used by Plato as a bridge from Protagoras' subjectivism to Plato's objectivism.   [2850]

——— "Protagoras . . . or Plato? II: The *Protagoras*" *Phron* 22(1977), 103-122. By substituting *aidos* and *dike* for *nomos* in Protagoras' teaching, P is able to shift argument in *Protag* to discussion of unity of those virtues, which is to be thesis of dialogue. Argument has no connection with historical Protagoras.   [2851]

McKIRAHAN, R. D., Jr. "Socrates and Protagoras on Holiness and Justice (*Protagoras* 330c-332a)." *Phoenix* 39(1985), 342-354. S's argument that holiness and justice are identical (*Protag* 330c-332a) is not as weak as commonly supposed. Fallacy which he introduces is used only dialectically. P's picture of Protagoras is more favorable than generally recognized.   [2852]

———. "Socrates and Protagoras on *Sophrosyne* and Justice. *Protagoras* 333-334." *Apeir* 18(1984), 19-25. Puts a conclusion on S's incomplete argument about relationship between these two concepts.   [2853]

McNEAL, R. A. "Protagoras the Historian." *H&Theo* 25(1986), 299-318. Thought patterns of 320c-328d are consistent with intellectual outlook of Athens ca. 450 B. C. as we now understand it.   [2854]

MILLER, C. L. "The Prometheus Story in Plato's *Protagoras*." *Interp* 7 #2(1978), 22-32. The myth which Protagoras tells in his "great speech" (320c-322d) explains the roles which Protagoras and S play in the dialogue. Like Prometheus, both display cleverness, but, like Epimetheus, both are guilty of lack of forethought.   [2855]

———. "Two Midpoints in Plato's *Protagoras*." *ModSch* 55(1977-1978), 71-79. Interlude comprising middle portion of dialogue (334c6-338e5) is crucial for understanding it. Discusses, interprets dramatic interaction of characters at the two midpoints.   [2856]

MOORE, S. "Democracy and Commodity Exchange: Protagoras Versus Plato." *HPhQ* 5(1988), 357-368. Reconstructs Protagoras' social theory from various passages in P's dialogues and opposes it to P's. [2857]

MORTLEY, R. J. "Plato and the Sophistic Heritage of Protagoras." *Eranos* 67(1969), 24-32. Before P, word "sophist" meant either educator or fraud. P pretends to accept first definition when portraying Protagoras but shows that Sophistic "education" is not true education. [2858]

MOSER, S., and KUSTAS, G. L. "A Comment on the 'Relativism' of the *Protagoras*." *Phoenix* 20(1966), 111-115. In this dialogue, P does not present Protagoras as an ethical relativist. [2859]

SALGUERO, C. A. "Plato and the Law. Commentaries on the *Protagoras*." *Athene* 26 #4(1966), 3-7, 15. Looks at Sophistic concepts of law, virtue, and justice. [2860]

SANTAS, G. "Plato's *Protagoras* and Explanations of Weakness." *PhR* 75(1966), 3-33; also in #1199, pp. 264-298; also in *Weakness of Will*, ed. G. Mortimore (London: Macmillan, 1971), pp. 37-62. Examines P's argument that explanations commonly offered for alleged fact that sometimes men act contrary to their knowledge of what is best when they can do otherwise are absurd. [2861]

———. cf. 2391.

SAVAN, D. "Socrates' Logic and the Unity of Wisdom and Temperance," in *Analytical Philosophy: Second Series*, ed. R. B. J. Butler (Oxford: Blackwell, 1965), pp. 20-26. Contrary to much recent scholarship, argues that S's argument at *Protag* 332a-333b demonstrating the unity of wisdom and temperance is valid. It is often faulted, perhaps because S's vocabulary is not technical enough. [2862]

SCODEL, R. "Literary Interpretation in Plato's *Protagoras*." *AncPh* 6(1986), 25-37. S's analysis of Simonides' poem (338e-347e) is intended as a satire of more than just Sophistic methods of textual interpretation. It is a critique of literary exegesis in general, designed to show that knowledge cannot be gained from reading. Only by dialectic can two sides of a question be maintained. [2863]

SPRAGUE, R. K. "An Unfinished Argument in Plato's *Protagoras*." *Apeir* 1 #2(1967), 1-4. Reconstructs argument at 333b-334a to show that justice is temperance. [2864]

TAYLOR, C. C. W. *Plato:* Protagoras. Oxford: Clarendon Pr., 1976. Translation with notes. Examines ethical theories P developed under influence of S, such as nature of human excellence, relation of knowledge to right conduct and place of pleasure in the good life. [2865]

VLASTOS, G. "Socrates on Acrasia." *Phoenix* 23(1969), 71-88. Examination of thesis of *Prot* 352a-358d shows that, though presented hedonistically, i. e., equating good with pleasure and evil with pain, it is valid for a non-hedonist. [2866]

———. "The Unity of the Virtues in the *Protagoras*." *RMeta* 25(1972), 415-458; also in #1292, pp. 221-265. Examines S's argument for unity of virtues in which he employs formulae which seem at odds both with common sense and with procedural assumptions of his own dialectic.   [2867]

WAKEFIELD, J. "Why Justice and Holiness Are Similar: *Protagoras* 330-331." *Phron* 32(1987), 267-276. Reads S's argument regarding relationship of justice and piety in a new way involving states of character and their ability to produce virtuous acts. [2868]

WALSH, J. "The Dramatic Dates of Plato's *Protagoras* and the Lesson of *Arete*." *CQ* 34(1984), 101-106. P probably based dialogue on conversations overheard on more than one occasion when Protagoras visited Athens.   [2869]

WEISS, R. "Courage, Confidence, and Wisdom in the *Protagoras*." *AncPh* 5(1985), 11-24. S's proof that wisdom is courage succeeds and Protagoras' refutation fails. [2870]

———. "The Hedonic Calculus in the *Protagoras* and the *Phaedo*." *JHPh* 27(1989), 511-529. Attempts to reconcile view of pleasure and good in these dialogues must fail. Identification of the two in *Protag* is ironic and is absent from *Phaedo*.   [2871]

———. "Socrates and Protagoras on Justice and Holiness." *Phoenix* 39(1985), 334-341. Argument of 330c ff. serves to examine Protagoras' views, not set out S's. Protagoras finally admits that justice and holiness are related, though not identical.   [2872]

WOLZ, H. G. "Hedonism in the *Protagoras*." *JHPh* 5(1967), 205-217. Theme of hedonism is subordinate to dialogue's main thrust, which is contrast between two concepts of knowledge.   [2873]

ZASLAVSKY, R. "The Platonic Godfather: A Note on the *Protagoras* Myth." *JVallnq* 16(1982), 79-82. Examines S's and Protagoras' positions on the question: Is virtue teachable? It is not for S, since he equates it with knowledge. It is for Protagoras, who regards it as a form of coercion.   [2874]

ZEYL, D. J. "Socrates and Hedonism: *Protagoras* 351b-358d." *Phron* 25(1980), 250-269; also in #1267, pp. 5-25. S argues against *akrasia* in this passage as though he were a hedonist. Such a view need not be attributed to historical S. His arguments are valid regardless of his own view on hedonism.   [2875]

For related items see #955, #1051, #1695, #1742, #1848, #2175, #2191, #2382, #2393, #2486

Republic

The Greek title of this dialogue is *Politeia*, which implies something a bit different from the Latin based word by which we usually denominate it. "Republic" suggests a kind of representative government, chosen by a citizen body. But S and his interlocutors envision no such scheme in either of the ideal states which they discuss. There is some cogency to Bremer's contention (#2908) that the title of the dialogue ought to be something like *Polity* or *Politeia*, to indicate that one of its important themes is what we call politics, but that its approach is quite alien to anything we would recognize by that name.

The dialogue, which probably dates from P's middle period, is structured as a conversation among S, Cephalus, Polemarchus, Thrasymachus, Glaucon, and

Adeimantus, with the last two carrying on most of the interchange. It begins as an effort to define Justice. When that task proves impossible in the abstract, S proposes that they examine the structure of the state because the state is simply a larger version of the soul. If they can determine what causes a state to function justly, they should be able to apply the lesson to the individual soul.

The interlocutors represent various stages in the development of social mores. Cephalus lives without much thought. He is an old man, his time drawing to a close. His son Polemarchus lives by proverbs and maxims, a kind of pre-dialectical mentality, and cannot defend his way of life in a conversation with S. Thrasymachus the Sophist espouses the relativist ideas typical of his school but he does not want to engage in dialogue with S. He wants to make a speech (and be paid for it). He goes into a rage when S draws him into refuting his own definitions and finally refuses to deal any more with S, who then engages Glaucon and Adeimantus in conversation. Of these two brothers Glaucon is the more ambitious, though he has the wit to see the weaknesses of Thrasymachus' claims. He often introduces topics, but Adeimantus is the more serious character, who will not let S get by with superficial replies.

In modern editions the *Republic* is divided into ten books of roughly equal length, but that structure is just as arbitrary as the division of books of the Bible into chapters and sometimes has an equally unfortunate effect on our sense of the work's unity. Different scholars have suggested various ways of subdividing the dialogue. Some see it as having two large sections. Books 1-4 describe an ideal Hellenic *polis* (city-state); Books 5-10 transform that city-state into an ideal state run by philosophers.

Another possibility is to break the dialogue into five sections: 1) Book 1 and the first half of Book 2, consisting of the aporetic discussion of justice; 2) the second half of Book 2 and all of Books 3 and 4, which describe the structure of the first state; 3) Books 5-7, in which the communistic society of the philosopher-kings is constructed; 4) Books 8-9, which consider the perverted forms of government and compare them to the individual's search for pleasure; 5) Book 10, which some scholars consider spurious while others see it as unfinished or badly edited. Its defenders maintain that it draws together various themes discussed in the dialogue and shows, through the myth of Er, how the happiness of the citizens, assured in the ideal earthly city, will be extended after death. Some scholars also maintain that Book 1 was originally composed as a separate Socratic dialogue, to be called the *Thrasymachus*.

How is the dialogue to be interpreted? What was P's purpose in writing it? Such questions have generated a number of answers, which can be grouped under three general categories: 1) P is serious about a blueprint for political reform; 2) his *kallipolis* (good city) is an ideal he takes seriously but doesn't think can be realized; 3) his treatment of justice is ironic.

Of all the important themes that arise from this dialogue perhaps the following should be brought to the non-specialist's attention: P's idea that there is such a thing as the Form of the Good; the problem of the role of the arts in the state; and the Cave analogy, in which P describes people as limited in knowledge to the images or shadows of real things. If a few manage to break free and find knowledge of the real things (the Forms) and become philosophically enlightened, are they obligated to return to the cave and share their knowledge with their fellows? The myth of Er in Book 10, which presents one version of P's view of the afterlife, is also noteworthy.

The *Republic* has spawned imitators (Cicero, Augustine, Thomas More, Huxley) because it focuses on one of the great yearnings of the human heart: a state which overcomes all the problems of the imperfect states which are all we have ever known. It has attracted the attention of commentators because it discusses so many matters that *something* in it is bound to be of interest to every generation. P's treatment of poets raises questions about censorship and about any society's education curriculum. Some have seen Nazi Germany as a terrifying embodiment of his ideal state. His proposals for regulating marriage and family life foreshadow the eugenic plans of several social reformers. Modern feminist scholars have yet to decide whether P actually believed in equality of the sexes or simply advocated it because it served the interests of the state.

Anyone interested in studying this dialogue should also consult the section on "Politics" in the topical portion of the general bibliography on Plato (p. 229). Another important topic is the place of artists in the ideal state; those interested in that topic should consult the "Aesthetics" section in the general bibliography (p. 180).

ACTON, H. B. "The Alleged Fascism of Plato," in #1961, pp. 38-48. Examines fascist philosophy in detail in order to challenge those interpreters who find fascist elements in P's thought.   [2876]

ALEXANDRAKIS, A. "A Differing View: Plato's Books III and X of the *Republic*." *Diot* 8(1980) 196-197. Challenges interpretations of alleged discrepancy between banishment of "all imitative poetry" in Book 3 and allowing of "hymns to the gods and praises of good men" in Book 10.   [2877]

ALLEN, R. E. "The Speech of Glaucon." *JHPh* 25(1987), 3-11; also in #1283, pp. 51-62. Examines Glaucon's version of a "contractarian" account of political association and its Hobbesian conception of human nature, and contrasts it with S's quite different view of human nature and political association. The discussion moves from analysis in terms of desire to analysis in terms of need.   [2878]

ANDERSSON, T. J. *Polis and Psyche: A Motif in Plato's* Republic. Stockholm: Almqvist and Wiksell, 1971. Attempts to show how *polis* (society) illustrates and explains *psyche* (personality) in *Rep*. It remains unclear how valid P's parallelism is and whether P was more concerned with individual or society.   [2879]

ANNAS, J. *An Introduction to Plato's* Republic. Oxford: Clarendon Pr. 1981. Aims to bring out coherence and interest of P's main moral argument, and shows one of his primary concerns to be individual's moral development.   [2880]

———. "Plato on the Triviality of Literature," in #1560, pp. 1-28. Any attempt to harmonize Books 3 and 10 is deeply misconceived. The two arguments in Book 10 show P not to be an advocate of "civic poetry."   [2881]

———. "Plato, *Republic* V-VII," in #79, pp. 3-18. Examines how P's theories of knowledge and reality affect his original claim that it is people with knowledge (philosophers) who should be our rulers.   **[2882]**

———. "Plato's *Republic* and Feminism." *Ph* 51(1976), 307-321. P is not a feminist. His proposals for integrating women into political life are made for the benefit of the state. He never considers women's interests or their rights.   **[2883]**

———. cf. #2131.

ANSBRO, J. J. "Plato's Just Man: A Re-Examination." *NewSchol* 44(1970), 278-285. Response to Hall (#2992), who argues that ordinary citizens in P's utopia have a capacity for justice in their daily lives equal to that of the philosopher-kings.   **[2884]**

———. "Plato's Just Man: A Rejoinder." *NewSchol* 47(1973), 490-500. Response to Hall (#2991). P maintains that all citizens can become just, but that philosopher-king attains the highest degree of justice.   **[2885]**

ARONSON, S. H. "The Happy Philosopher: A Counter-Example to Plato's Proof." *JHPh* 10(1972), 383-398. P's description of the philosopher-king is an effective refutation of his own thesis that justice and the greatest happiness are congruent. For the philosopher the greatest happiness is contemplation, but justice requires him to rule. Thrasymachus is correct: to be just, the philosopher must be unhappy; to be happy, he must be unjust.   **[2886]**

BARKER, A. "*Symphonoi Arithmoi*: A Note on *Republic* 531c1-4." *CPh* 73(1978), 337-342. This phrase seems to describe not numbers that are identical with sounds but those which, like musical notes, belong to a sensible system.   **[2887]**

BARNES, H. "Apotheosis and Deification in Plato, Nietzsche and Huxley." *Ph&Lit* 1(1976), 3-24. Examines P's "Myth of Er," Nietzsche's *Birth of Tragedy*, and Huxley's *Time Must Have a Stop* as philosophic myths. P's concept of the soul falls between Nietzsche's apotheosis and Huxley's deification.   **[2888]**

BARROW, R. *Plato and Education.* London: Routledge & Kegan Paul, 1976. Less technical approach to subject than following item. Examines P's theory of education, then provides introduction to the *Rep*. Comments on distributive justice and state's right to censor are particularly helpful.   **[2889]**

———. *Plato, Utilitarianism and Education.* London: Routledge and Kegan Paul, 1975. Argues that utilitarianism is the only acceptable ethical theory and that P recognized this in *Rep*. Any educational system must aim toward happiness for all, even if this means loss of freedom or self-fulfillment for individuals.   **[2890]**

———. "Who are the Philosopher-Kings?" *ProcPhEdSocGB* 8(1978) 200-221. Argues philosopher-kings are moral experts; specifies six factors of expertise.   **[2891]**

BEATTY, J. "Justice as Dialectic in *Republic* I." *SJPh* 17(1979), 3-17. Definitions of justice refuted by dialectic in *Rep* 1 actually describe dialectic process. **[2892]**

———. "Why Should Plato's Philosopher Be Moral and, Hence, Rule?" *Pers* 57(1976),

132-144. P is an ethical egoist, but he can still maintain that the philosopher should rule, even if that is not in his own best interest. Reason is a key element in justice and happiness and enables a philosopher to experience both. [2893]

BEDU-ADDO, J. T. "Mathematics, Dialectic and the Good in the *Republic* VI-VII." *Platon* 30(1978), 111-127. Each discipline has its own foundations and methods. They are not subordinate to knowledge of the Good, which is culmination of one's dedication to study in various disciplines. [2894]

———. cf. #2029.

BELFIORE, E. "A Theory of Imitation in Plato's *Republic*." *TAPhA* 114(1984), 121-146. The theory of *mimesis* in Books 3 and 10 is more consistent than has generally been recognized. [2895]

———. cf. #1516, #1517, #1518.

BENARDETE, S. *Socrates' Second Sailing: On Plato's* Republic. Univ. of Chicago Pr., 1989. Argues for a distinction between "dialogic city," in which S becomes King, and "city in speech" which S constructs. Discusses double character of Sun Simile, Divided Line, and Cave Analogy, which varies in meaning, depending on whether they are read in terms of the dialogic city or the city in speech. [2896]

BERTMANN, M. A. "Plato on Tyranny, Philosophy, and Pleasure." *Apeir* 19(1985), 152-160. P offers moral and epistemic arguments to link pleasure with thinker's grasp of reality. But this doctrine linking best pleasure to best knowledge seems to offer a fundamentally different S than the S professing ignorance. [2897]

———. "The *Thrasymachus*." *Manuscrito* 11(1988), 7-25. Examines Book 1 of *Rep* as a preparation for the themes and literary techniques of the rest of the dialogue. [2898]

BLOOM, A., trans. *The* Republic *of Plato*. New York: Basic Books, 1968. Translation with lengthy interpretive essay which argues that P is attempting to show impossiblity of realizing perfect justice. [2899]

———. "Response to Hall's 'The *Republic* and the "Limits of Politics"'." *PolTheo* 5(1977), 315-330. Response to #2987a regarding the seriousness with which S puts forward political recommendations. [2900]

BLUESTONE, N. H. *Women and the Ideal Society. Plato's* Republic *and Modern Myths of Gender*. Amherst: Univ. of MA Pr., 1987. Surveys history of scholarship on gender bias in P and Platonic scholarship since 1879. Lengthy bibliography. [2901]

———. cf. #1306.

BOTER, G. J. *The Textual Tradition of Plato's* Republic. Leiden: Brill, 1989. Examines the history of the transmission of the dialogue, an important facet of its interpretation. [2902]

———. "Thrasymachus and *Pleonexia*." *Mnem* 39(1986), 261-281. Review of recent studies of Thrasymachus' vocabulary in *Rep* 1. His view is a combination of ethical

ethical nihilism and psychological egoism. **[2903]**

BOYLE, A. J. "Plato's Divided Line: Appendix." *Apeir* 8 #1(1974), 19-21. Discusses philosophical importance of Line's ontological, epistemological divisions. **[2904]**

——. "Plato's Divided Line, Essay I: The Problem of *Dianoia*." *Apeir* 7 #2(1973), 1-11. Examines ontological and epistemological schema, in particular, nature of cognitive objects of *dianoia*. Considers differences between mathematics and dialectic. **[2905]**

——. "Plato's Divided Line, Essay II: Mathematics and Dialectic." *Apeir* 8 #1(1974), 7-18. Examines two questions: 1) How does dialectician apprehend form of the good by means of unhypothetical first principle? 2) Why does P wish to make the good the "cause" of all forms and identify it with the one? **[2906]**

BRANN, E. "The Music of the *Republic*." *Agon* 1(1967), 1-117. Central books contain dialogue's main pedagogical purpose — conversion to philosophy — not the foundation of a provably unrealizable community. Analyzes structure of dialogue in concentric rings. It begins with descent into Hades, ends with emergence from underworld. **[2907]**

BREMER, J. *On Plato's* Polity. Houston, TX: Inst. of Phil., 1984. *Republic* is a misleading name for this dialogue. *Polity* suggests some of the true themes and connections of the work. This survey examines numbers, patterns and symmetries, the divided dialogue, the universe of Er, and other topics. **[2908]**

BRICKHOUSE, T. C. "More on the Paradox of the Philosopher's Rule." *Pers* 59(1978), 304-306. Response to #2893. If word translated "constrained" is taken to involve a moral constraint, it is not paradoxical for philosopher to rule and be happy. **[2909]**

——. "The Paradox of the Philosopher's Rule." *Apeir* 15(1981), 1-9. Ruling in ideal city does not lessen philosopher-kings' happiness because of their concept of happiness. Ruling under such conditions does not require compulsion of ruler or ruled. **[2910]**

BROWN, G. "The Character of the Individual and the Character of the State in Plato's *Republic*." *Apeir* 17(1983), 43-47. S's comments in *Rep* 9 on the relation between characteristics of a state and of an individual should not be taken as an early version of the Methodological Individualist position. They are simply empirical generalizations, perhaps not clearly formulated. **[2911]**

BROWN, S. "The Social Order and the Natural Order." *PAS* 52 Suppl. (1978), 127-141. Reply to #2025. Argues that P cannot be fairly accused of "ruling class conservatism." **[2912]**

BROWNING, G. K. "Plato and Hegel: Reason, Redemption and Political Theory." *HPolTho* 8(1987), 377-393. Compares political theories of P and Hegel. Focuses on their common recognition of significance of social life, their efforts to outline political communities which overcome alienation and disharmony, and their differing conceptions of reason and its role in social life. **[2913]**

BRUMBAUGH, R. S. "The Divided Line and the Direction of Inquiry." *PhFor* 2(1970-1971), 172-199. The divided line can be interpreted in four ways, one for each of its sections. It may be a picture, a plan of stages of inquiry, a classification of types of knowledge, and a criterion for determining completeness.   **[2914]**

――――. "Interpreting Book V When the *Republic* is Read as Dialectic," in #49, pp. 29-37.
One cannot talk about the philosophical meaning of a Platonic dialogue apart from its
dramatic setting. The characters in the work react dialectically with the ideas P presents.
Rep operates around four organizing principles.   **[2915]**

――――. "The Mathematical Imagery of Plato, *Republic* X." *TeachPh* 7(1984), 223-228.
Cosmic model of *Rep* 10 is part of series of mathematical images with Pythagorean basis.
Commentators, since antiquity, have lost sight of this symbolism.   **[2916]**

――――. "A New Interpretation of Plato's *Republic*." *JPh* 64(1967), 661-670; also in #49,
pp. 17-27. Focuses on three points: 1) P creates interplay of action and argument; 2)
main topics are treated with aesthetic symmetry, each one discussed twice, except the
central point; 3) dialogue as a whole is an example of dialectic and displays the justice
which is its topic.   **[2917]**

――――. "Teaching Plato's *Republic* VIII and IX." *TeachPh* 3(1980), 331-337; revised
version in #49, pp. 81-87. Suggests a diagram which shows transition between Books 7
and 8, and presents another diagram to clarify the mathematical computation offered as
a final proof that the just man lives more happily than unjust man.   **[2918]**

――――. "Time Passes. Platonic Variations." *RMeta* 33(1980), 711-726. Time is understood differently on each level of the divided line. Since language is found on the lowest
level, where the degree of unreality is greatest, it cannot be used to analyze time on the
higher levels of the line.   **[2919]**

――――. cf. #2485.

BURGER, R. "Socratic *Eironeia*." *Interp* 13(1985), 143-146. References to irony in *Rep*
and *Gorg* make charges against S look like indictments against those levelling them. S's
irony is necessitated by ignorance of *demos* and by those whose desire to enslave *demos*
binds them in an essential relation to it.   **[2920]**

BURKHOLDER, P. M. "Plato's Treatment of Invalids in the *Republic* III." *TulStudPh*
27(1978), 27-35. P argues chronic invalids should not be given medical treatment
because they cannot fulfill their function in state and will be useless as well as unhappy.
But his arguments about the soul's good justify treating some invalids.   **[2921]**

BURNS, S. "Women in Bloom." *Dial*(Can) 23(1984), 135-140. Challenges Bloom's
interpretation of *Rep* in his translation and commentary (#2899) that P's recommendations regarding women are intentionally "ridiculous."   **[2922]**

BURNYEAT, M. "Review of L. Strauss' *Studies in Platonic Political Philosophy*." *New
York Review of Books*, May 30, 1985, 30-36. Discusses especially Strauss's view (#3134)
that *Rep* is ironic with its political proposals.   **[2923]**

CADY, D. L. "Individual Fulfillment (Not Social Engineering) in Plato's *Republic*."
IdealStud 13(1983), 240-248. *Rep* is not a vision of an ideal form of government but a
guide for developing individual self-rule, founded on philosophy.   **[2924]**

CALVERT, B. "Plato and the Equality of Women." *Phoenix* 29(1975), 231-243. *Rep* 455d does not apply to all men and women. P maintains equality of genders, despite influences of prejudices of his time, which often impinge on his thought. **[2925]**

———. "Slavery in Plato's *Republic*." *CQ* 37(1987), 367-372. P's utopia has no place or need for slaves. **[2926]**

CAMPBELL, B. "Intellect and the Political Order in Plato's *Republic*." *HPolTho* 1(1980), 361-389. Because he never resolved the tension between his philosophical and political views P is guilty of some inconsistencies in his thinking about the philosopher's duty to participate in politics, the distinction between philosophical and political knowledge, and the concept of justice on the political and personal levels. **[2927]**

CHAUHAN, M. R. "A Comparative Study of Plato's *Republic* and Huxley's *Brave New World*." *PakPhJ* 13(1974), 63-74. Huxley had a better understanding than P of evil effects of welfare tyranny of a utopia. **[2928]**

CHERNISS, H. F. "On Plato's *Republic* X 597 B," in #51, pp. 271-280. In this passage P neither maintains that Ideas arc thoughts of God nor does he identify God as the Ideas. P does contradict what he says in other contexts, due to his overriding concern to attack mimetic arts. **[2929]**

CLAY, D. "Reading the *Republic*," in #1275, pp. 19-33. Argues that deficiencies, paradoxes, tensions, fallacies are set down to invite readers to work through issues for themselves. Also sees the "Kallipolis" as neither a blueprint for a totalitarian state nor some utopia we are to try to realize in practice. **[2930]**

COBY, P. "On Warriors and Artisans: The Case for Moral Virtue in Plato's *Republic*." *Polity* 15(1983), 515-535. The moral virtue which is happiness for the philosopher seems to be a matter of indifference to other classes in P's ideal city. **[2931]**

COOPER, J. M. "Plato's Theory of Human Motivation." *HPhQ* 1(1984), 3-22. P distinguishes three basic kinds of motivation, linked to division of soul. **[2932]**

———. "The Psychology of Justice in Plato." *AmPhQ* 14(1977) 151-157. Examines P's theory of just person's psychology to illuminate his conception of human perfection and to draw out connections between psychology and metaphysics of *Rep*. **[2933]**

COOPER, N. "Between Knowledge and Ignorance." *Phron* 31(1986), 229-242. Studies difference between lovers of knowledge and of appearances in *Rep* 5. **[2934]**

———. "The Importance of *Dianoia* in Plato's Theory of Forms." *CQ* 16(1966), 65-69. Looks especially at *Rep* 6 and 7. **[2935]**

CORNFORD, F. M. *The* Republic *of Plato*. Oxford Univ. Pr. 1972. Translation with notes. **[2936]**

———. cf. #1764 and #2035.

CROMBIE, I. M. "Duff-Forbes on *Republic* 10." *Mind* 80(1971), 286-287. Reply to #2953. We cannot conclude from the passage on the Form of Bed that P saw Forms as both universal characters and also paradigms. It is more accurate to say that he considered them universal characters and, for that reason, not paradigms.   [2937]

CROSS, R. C., and WOOZLEY, A. D. *Plato's* Republic: *A Philosophical Commentary.* New York: St. Martin's Pr., 1979. General discussion on dialogue's major philosophical topics, such as moral and political philosophy, epistemology, metaphysics.   [2938]

CUMMINGS, P. W. "*Republic* 33dB-D." *Apeir* 11 #2(1977), 5-10. Efforts to define the just man in this passage as one who does not harm anyone are undermined by ambiguities of several terms used in the definition.   [2939]

DARLING, J. "Are Women Good Enough? Plato's Feminism Re-examined." *JPhEduc* 20(1986), 123-128. Discusses difficulty of determing whether or not P actually considered women as men's equals; examines Bloom's analysis of this question in #2899.   [2940]

DAVIES, J. C. "A Note on the Philosopher's Descent into the Cave." *Philologus* 112(1968), 121-126. In *Rep* 519c ff. Glaucon objects that philosopher, once enlightened, who is forced to return to cave, suffers injustice. But P holds that philosopher-king benefits city and only achieves his true *telos* as part of a community.   [2941]

————. "The Philosopher and the Cave." *G&R* 24(1977), 23-28. Philosophers do not suffer injustice when they are compelled to return down into the cave because a reclusive life is unnatural and ignores needs of ideal state.   [2942]

DEMOS, R. "A Fallacy in Plato's *Republic*?" in #1291, pp. 52-56. Challenges Sachs' argument (#3097) that P commits "fallacy of irrelevance."   [2943]

DENYER, N. "Ethics in Plato's *Republic*," in #79, pp. 19-33. Studies theory of tripartite soul and how P's moral psychology supports claim that justice is beneficial.   [2944]

DEVEREUX, D. T. "Socrates' First City in the *Republic*." *Apeir* 13(1979), 36-40. Some puzzling aspects of the so-called "pig state" are cleared up when it is seen not merely as the first step in the development of an ideal city but as a response to Glaucon's views of human nature and justice.   [2945]

DICKASON, A. "Anatomy and Destiny: The Role of Biology in Plato's View of Women." *PhFor* 5(1973), 45-53. P has an earlier, more liberal view of women in *Rep*, and a later, more conservative view in *Laws*. This change came about due to a change in his medical theory about reproduction.   [2946]

DIGBY, S. L. "A Comparative Study of Vedic and Platonic Education." *Phil*(Athens) 12(1982), 230-244. In P's ideal state and India's caste system, education serves development of upper classes. Beyond that, the two are more different than alike.   [2947]

DOMBROWSKI, D. A. "MacIntyre, Rawls, and the *Republic*." *PhilStud* (Ireland) 31(1986-1987), 63-68. Criticizes connection between social contract theory of Glaucon and Rawls by appealing to P and MacIntyre.   [2948]

————. "Plato *Republic* 414b-c Again." *LCM* 10(1985), 36-38. Reply to J. Ferguson (#1694).   [2949]

——. "*Republic* 414b-c. Noble *Lies*, *Noble* Lies, or *Noble* 'Lies'?" *CB* 58(1981), 4-6. The stories which P proposes to tell to the masses are not meant to deceive but to educate. They are the only form in which complex ideas can be communicated to the majority of people. [2950]

——. "Two Vegetarian Puns at *Republic* 372." *AncPh* 9(1989), 167-171. S's admiration for a vegetarian diet in this passage can be taken as an expression of P's vegetarianism. The ideal state would be vegetarian. Eating meat destroys man's relationship with nature and fosters greed, and thus war. [2951]

DORTER, K. "Socrates' Refutation of Thrasymachus and Treatment of Virtue." *Ph&Rh* 7(1974), 25-46. Compares and contrasts discussion of justice in *Rep* 1 and 4. S responds to earlier arguments but his definition retains logical coherence. [2952]

DUFF-FORBES, D. R. "The Regress Argument in the *Republic*." *Mind* 77(1968), 406-410. Examines 597c where P advances a regress argument for uniqueness of Forms, which requires him to both assume and argue against self-predication. [2953]

EHRHARDT, E. "The Word of the Muses (Plato, *Rep*. 8.546)." *CQ* 36(1986), 407-420. Argues that there is no hidden number significance in this passage. [2954]

ELLARD, G. "*Eros* and the Ideal State." *JValInq* 8(1975), 283-288. In a Platonic framework, same man can write both comedy and tragedy, despite thesis presented in *Rep* that no one can do so. [2955]

ELSE, G. F. *The Structure and Date of Book 10 of Plato's* Republic. Heidelberg, Ger.: Winter, 1972. Explores question of relation of Book 10 to rest of *Rep*. Suggests that Book 10 consists of four separate sections written at different times and with different purposes and never put into final form by P. [2956]

ESLICK, L. J. "The *Republic* Revisited: The Dilemma of Liberty and Authority." *PhilFor* 10(1971), 171-212. Can virtue be insured for majority if they give up their liberty to an authoritarian elite who supposedly guarantee their rights? *Rep* suggests not. [2957]

EVERS, W. M. "Specialization and the Division of Labor in the Social Thought of Plato and Rousseau." *JLiberStud* 4(1980), 45-68. Striking difference in locus of sovereignty in utopias of two authors can be traced in part to their different attitudes toward specialization. [2958]

FEHL, N. E. *A Guide to the Study of Plato's* Republic. Hong Kong: Chung Chi Publ., 1965. Offers commentary on *Rep*, and considers *Laws* 10, *Euthyphro*, and *Apol* as giving portrait of modest citizen of ideal republic as theologian and philosopher. [2959]

FERGUSON, J., ed. *Plato:* Republic *Book X*. Letchworth, Hertfordshire, UK: Bradda Books, 1978. Examines Book 10 as self-contained; considers P as writer both of dialogue and of myth. Explores his views on aesthetics, metaphysics, human destiny. [2960]

FINE, G. "Knowledge and Belief in *Republic* V." *AGPh* 60(1978), 121-139. In 437c11-480a13 P loosely links knowledge to Forms and belief to sensibles. Before one can know anything, one must know Forms. It is also possible to have belief about Forms. [2961]

FOGELIN, R. J. "Three Platonic Analogies." *PhR* 80(1971), 371-382. Suggests a unified interpretation of analogies of Sun, Divided Line, and Cave. All three deal with proportions.   **[2962]**

FORTENBAUGH, W. W. "On Plato's Feminism in *Republic* V." *Apeir* 9 #2(1975), 1-4. Gorgias connects virtue to an individual's function. P links a person's role to his/her ability and does not distinguish between degrees of ability. Ar concurs but maintains that men and women differ not in degree but in kind.   **[2963]**

FOSTER, M. B. *The Political Philosophies of Plato and Hegel.* New York: Russell & Russell, 1965. Examines P's discussions of justice and freedom in *Rep.*, and investigates Hegel's criticisms of P.   **[2964]**

FRAGOMICHALOS, C. E. "The Question of the Existence of Slaves in Plato's *Republic*." *Platon* 36(1984), 77-96. Close analysis of *Rep* and passages from other dialogues suggests no solid evidence for presence of slaves in P's utopia.   **[2965]**

FUKS, A. "The Conditions of Riches (*Ploutos*) and of Poverty (*Penia*) in Plato's *Republic*." *RSA* 6-7(1976-77), 63-73. Both wealth and poverty are incompatible with *arete*. Wealth hurts not only those who have it but also those who don't. It eventually destroys the state.   **[2966]**

———. "Plato and the Social Question. The Problem of Poverty and Riches in the *Republic*." *AncSoc* 8(1977), 49-83. For P right organization of property ownership is main foundation on which proper civic organization can be built. Examines socio-economic conflict in Greek states, and various political recommendations for resolving tensions arising from economic extremes.   **[2967]**

GADAMER, H.-G. "Plato's Educational State," in #1274, pp. 73-92. Shows how it is philosophy and not poetry that restores soul to focused self-knowledge and thus heals souls of citizens and cures the state.   **[2968]**

GALIS, L. "The State-Soul Analogy in Plato's Argument that Justice Pays." *JHPh* 12(1974), 285-293. Argues (against Sachs #3097, Vlastos #3146) that P's argument connecting two senses of justice, if understood properly, is valid if not strong.   **[2969]**

GALLOP, D. "Image and Reality in Plato's *Republic*." *AGPh* 47(1965), 113-131. Examines numerous allusions to images, especially those of painting and sculpture, in context of exploring apparent paradox presented by *Rep*. Dialogue criticizes imitation and expels dramatists, but P is dramatist himself and past-master of imitation.   **[2970]**

GALSTON, W. A. "Heidegger's Plato: A Critique of Plato's Doctrine of Truth." *PhFor* 13(1982), 371-384. Examines Heidegger's argument that allegory of cave deals with nature of truth, and finds it unconvincing.   **[2971]**

GARLAND, W. J. "Notes on Two Socratic Arguments in *Republic* I." *Apeir* 10 #1(1976), 11-13. Examines fallacies in two of S's arguments at *Rep* 336b-347e. He tries to distinguish between the interests of an art and the interests of those who practice the art, but an art in the abstract has no interests. He argues that craftsmen have two *technai*, one being their craft, the other their status as wage earners. But wage-earning by itself is not a *techne*.   **[2972]**

GEELS, D. E. "Plato and the Pay-off of Justice." *Pers* 52(1971), 449-458. P does not adequately demonstrate that the unjust man whom Glaucon describes is unhappy. He fails because he thinks that reason leads only to knowledge and desire of the Good, when its real function is to evaluate consequences of various actions. **[2973]**

GIBBS, B. R. "Virtue and Reason." *PAS* Suppl. 48(1974), 23-41. Rejects Aristotle's ways of distinguishing virtue from art, and argues that right account of understanding art and virtue is found in *Rep*. **[2974]**

GILL, C. "Plato and the Education of Character." *AGPh* 67(1985), 1-26. P claims to provide in *Rep* an educational program for the whole individual. Books 2-3 concentrate on training emotions; Books 6-7 focus on intellect. It is not clear that P integrated these two aspects. **[2975]**

GLENN, J. "Women in Combat: Plato and the Equal Rights Amendment." *CB* 54(1977), 20-26. Offers comparative synopsis of *Rep* and Equal Rights Amendment on most controversial questions regarding women in military. **[2976]**

GOLD, J. "Bringing Students Out of the Cave." *TeachPh* 11(1988), 25-31. Uses Allegory of Cave to develop teaching strategy aimed at liberation of mind. **[2977]**

GOMBRICH, E. H. "The Open Society: A Comment," in #1961, pp. 146-149. Defends Popper (1948) against critical review of Plamenatz (1952). **[2978]**

GOROSPE, V. R. "Plato's Natural-Law Theory in the *Republic*." *ModSch* 43(1966), 143-178. P argued against Sophists that state's origins and structure are natural and that an absolute norm of morality exists. Knowledge of natural law depends on sure distinction between knowledge and opinion. **[2979]**

GOSLING, J. C. "*Doxa* and *Dunameis* in Plato's *Republic*." *Phron* 13(1968), 119-130. Examines use of *dunamis* to describe *doxa*, and how this has wrongly been taken in support of view that P thought of knowledge as a kind of seeing. Argues that 477ff does not state that knowledge and belief are two quasi-senses with different objects on analogy with sound and color. **[2980]**

———. "Reply to White's 'The "Many" in *Republic* 475a-480A'." *CanJPh* 7(1977), 307-314. Raises six objections to White's view (#3159). **[2981]**

GUTGLUECK, J. "From *Pleonexia* to *Polypragmosune*: A Conflation of Possession and Action in Plato's *Republic*." *AJPh* 109(1988), 20-39. Examines argument at 349b-350c that concludes just man is wise and good and unjust man is ignorant and bad. Focuses on uses of *pleonektein* in analogy between just man and musician or physician. **[2982]**

HADGOPOULOS, D. J. "Thrasymachus and Legalism." *Phron* 18(1973), 204-208. Provides evidence to support interpretation that Thrasymachus is not a legalist. **[2983]**

HAGEN, C. T. "Rationality in Plato's *Republic*." *PhResArch* 11(1985), 611-633. Identifies six elements in Platonic concepts of rationality. **[2984]**

HAHN, R. "A Note on Plato's Divided Line." *JHPh* 21(1983), 235-237. Given different levels of Line and things perceived on those levels, one must consider the object of any individual dialogue. Line itself is an object on the geometric level.   **[2985]**

HALL, D. "Interpreting Plato's Cave as an Allegory of the Human Condition." *Apeir* 14(1980), 74-76. Cave allegory is an image of human condition when philosophy is divorced from politics. Cave's darkness represents belief, but inmates symbolize not just a level of individual belief, but a community deprived of philosophical rule.   **[2986]**

——. "The Philosopher and the Cave." *G&R* 25(1978), 169-173. *Rep* 519c-520d discusses dilemma which philosophers face when they go back into cave to rule. They would prefer to remain outside, contemplating Forms. But their function as rulers in ideal state is to teach.   **[2987]**

——. "The *Republic* and the 'Limits of Politics'." *PolTheo* 5(1977), 293-313. Examines problem of philosophers giving up their contemplation of Forms in order to rule. Ruling is a natural outgrowth of the activity of reason within the soul, so there is no conflict between needs of individual and community.   **[2987a]**

HALL, R. W. "Egalitarianism and Justice in the *Republic*." *Apeir* 6(1972), 7-19. Challenges interpretations which maintain that only philosophers are wise and just; examines political analogy between state and individual.   **[2988]**

——. "The Just and Happy Man of the *Republic*. Fact or Fallacy?" *JHPh* 9(1971), 147-158. Justice in the ideal state is extended to more than philosophers, so P is not guilty of fallacy of irrelevance. Reply to Sachs (#3097) and Schiller (#3104).   **[2989]**

——. "On the Myth of the Metals in the *Republic*." *Apeir* 1(1967), 28-32. Investigates context of myth of metals and argues that it emphasizes fact that men have not only different economic capabilities, but different social abilities which can be roughly classified into the three different orders.   **[2990]**

——. "Plato's Just Man: A Second Look." *NewSchol* 46(1972), 352-367. Responds to #2991; focuses on political analogy between soul and state.   **[2991]**

——. "Plato's Just Man: Thoughts on Strauss' Plato." *NewSchol* 42(1968), 202-225. Relies on Strauss (#3134) to challenge "majority view" that for P, most men are incapable of self-government (individually and politically) and must live under wise rule of philosophers.   **[2992]**

——. "Plato's Political Analogy. Fallacy or Analogy?" *JHPh* 12(1974), 419-435. Though criticized, analogy between soul and state, which is essential to understanding *Rep*'s theory of justice, is valid.   **[2993]**

——. "Plato's Theory of Justice in the *Republic*." *BuckRev* 15(1967), 59-69. Important differences in the political analogy between the city and the individual have been overlooked; justice can be achieved by most individuals, not just philosophers.   **[2994]**

——. cf. #1544.

HAMMOND, L. M. "Classes and Functions in Plato's *Republic*." *SJPh* 4(1966), 242-247. Examines P's claim that justice means minding one's own business; emphasizes certain semantic and ontological distinctions in understanding the claim.   **[2995]**

HANTZ, H. D. "Plato's Ambivalence Toward the Arts." *Diot* 13(1985), 29-35. Examines P's proposed religious and moral restrictions on teaching of arts suggested in *Rep.* Suggests that P, conscious of arts' great power, raised certain significant questions about moral effects of arts, and maintained that in a well-ordered society, arts should foster goodness and beauty. **[2996]**

HARMAN, J. D. "The Unhappy Philosopher: Plato's *Republic* as Tragedy." *Polity* 18(1986), 577-594. In P's state philosophers must be unhappy if they rule, because it is a burden. Unable to avoid the burden, they take on features of a tragic hero. **[2997]**

HARRISON, E. L. "Plato's Manipulation of Thrasymachus." *Phoenix* 21(1967), 27-39. Examines how Thrasymachus is being carefully manipulated by P to meet his own artistic requirements with respect to entire dialogue. **[2998]**

HENDERSON, T. Y. "In Defense of Thrasymachus." *AmPhQ* 7(1970), 218-228. Thrasymachus' argument can be made internally consistent on all important points. S's best arguments are inadequate to refute Thrasymachus. **[2999]**

HENWOOD, K. "Of Philosophers, Kings, and Technocrats." *CanJPh* 9(1979), 299-314. Refutes charge that Platonic account of morals and politics rests on conceptual confusions arising from P's use of analogies with arts and provides an interpretation which displays the utility of those analogies. **[3000]**

HINES, J. N. "Plato's Cave Story. A Dream Interpretation." *Platon* 34-35(1982-83), 145-159. Freudian interpretation of the allegory. **[3001]**

HITCHCOCK, D. L. "The Good in Plato's *Republic*." *Apeir* 19(1985), 65-92. The Good is unity. On a personal level the ultimate *telos* is to become pure reason and contemplate Forms. On level of *polis* the desired form is monolithic. **[3002]**

HOERNLE, R. F. A. "Would Plato Have Approved of the National-Socialist State?" in #1961, pp. 20-37. Examines theory and practice of dictatorship, making P's theory and modern practice mutually throw light on each other. **[3003]**

HOLLANDER, R. "The Golden Ring of Gyges. A Note on the *Republic* II 359." *Eos* 71(1983), 211-213. This story emphasizes man's inability to recognize truth even when confronted directly with it. **[3004]**

HOWLAND, J. "The Cave Image and the Problem of Place: The Sophist, the Poet, and the Philosopher." *Dion* 10(1986), 21-55. Souls of poet, philosopher share orientations; Sophist's soul is disoriented. Philosopher plays most important role in developing framework in which lives can be described as being "in place" or "out of place." **[3005]**

HWANG, P. H. "Poetry in Plato's *Republic*." *Apeir* 15(1981), 29-37. Examines inconsistencies between Books 2 and 3, where P rejects some poetry, and Book 10, where he rejects all. **[3006]**

HYLAND, D. A. "Taking the Longer Road: The Irony of Plato's *Republic*." *RMM* 93(1988), 317-335. Discussion of earlier treatments of irony in P. None sees irony as part of his philosophic intent. Irony in *Rep* is often triadic, not diadic, and is a way of treating the issue of negativity. **[3007]**

INWOOD, B. "Professor Stokes on Adeimantus in the *Republic*," in #1283, pp. 97-103. Reply to #3132. Terms used by Adeimantus about "just" men and "justice" do not necessarily involve admission that justice is a virtue.   **[3008]**

ISRAEL, R. "Plato Versus Popper." *Kinesis* 3(1971), 103-110. Examines P's political philosophy and Popper's attack on it.   **[3009]**

JACKSON, M. W. "Plato's Political Analogies." *IntStudPh* 20(1988), 27-42. Discusses and defends P's use of analogies for describing politics against #1963.   **[3010]**

JACOBS, W. "Plato on Female Emancipation and the Traditional Family." *Apeir* 12 #1(1978), 29-31. *Rep* 5 shows that if men and women have same social roles, traditional family cannot be maintained.   **[3011]**

JEFFREY, A. "Polemarchus and Socrates on Justice and Harm." *Phron* 24(1979), 54-69. Argues against two versions of criticism that S's refutation of Polemarchus hinges on equivocation (*blaptein*). Suggests that refutation is more straightforward than commonly supposed and more straightforwardly fallacious than often supposed. Refutation fails due to unchallenged transitions at several points from examples to definitions.   **[3012]**

JOHNSON, C. "Thrasymachean Justice. The Advantage of the Stronger." *DUJ* 78(1985), 37-49. S and Thrasymachus agree that strength rest on qualities characteristic of a stronger person but they differ over precise nature of those qualities.   **[3013]**

KARASMANIS, V. "Plato's *Republic*: The Line and the Cave." *Apeir* 21(1988), 147-171. Seeks to preserve parallel between two analogies. Argues that *pistis* and *dianoia* deal with applied and pure mathematics, allowing for their equality in the Line.   **[3014]**

KATSOURIS, A. "Some Thoughts About Thrasymachus' Definition of Justice." *Dodone* 12(1983), 75-80. Thrasymachus' definition in *Rep.* 338c-347e is strongly legalistic because it is derived from contemporary Athenian life and reflects ruling class's desire to "neutralize" justice.   **[3015]**

KAYSER, J. R., and **MOORS, K. T.** "*Akribe Logon, Akribologei, Akribestatos* in *Politeia* 340e-3416, 503b*." *Apeir* 8 #1(1974), 31-32. Discusses use of superlative at 503b which may indicate possible difficulties in coincidence of philosophy and political power. Compound *akribologei* seems to be derogatory allusion to S's method.   **[3016]**

KELLY, J. C. "Virtue and Inwardness in Plato's *Republic*." *AncPh* 9(1989), 189-205. Examines S's claim that virtue is something within and compares his understanding of inwardness with that of Descartes and Kant.   **[3017]**

KIRWAN, C. "Glaucon's Challenge." *Phron* 10(1965), 162-173. Examines two interpretations of the challenge, and defends view that throughout *Rep* the brothers require S to show that justice is agreeable, and S attempts to do just what they ask.   **[3018]**

KLOSKO, G. "*Demotike Arete* in the *Republic*." *HPolTho* 3(1982), 363-382. Attempts to describe distinctive characteristics of the third class (producers) in P's state by delineating different functions performed by parts of soul.   **[3019]**

——. "Provisionality in Plato's Ideal State." *HPolTho* 5(1984), 171-194. Refutes charges that P abandons a rational approach to statecraft in *Rep* and assumes an authoritarian stance by examining importance of discursive reason in the dialogue and criticism and modification which its institutions undergo. [3020]

———. "The 'Strassian' Interpretation of Plato's *Republic*." *HPolTho* 7(1986), 275-295. Criticizes arguments of Bloom (#2899) and Strauss (#3134) to effect that *Rep* is a satire designed to show limits of justice. [3021]

———. "Thrasymachos' *Eristikos*: The *Agon Logon* in *Republic* I." *Polity* 17(1984), 5-29. The inconsistency of Thrasymachos' statements is not so surprising if one takes his encounter with S as a dialectical competition. [3022]

KRAUT, R. "Reason and Justice in Plato's *Republic*," in #65, pp. 207-224. Responds to Sachs (#3097), and argues that P does show that it is to one's advantage to be just in a way that addresses Thrasymachus' concerns. [3023]

KUBARA, M. "The Logic of Virtue in the *Republic*," in #73, pp. 11-27. P defines virtue as the ability (*dynamis*) to perform a function (*ergon*) well. Examines how *Rep* works out this definition. P is first concerned with morality of communities, from which morality of individuals is derived. [3024]

LANGE, L. "The Function of Equal Education in Plato's *Republic* and *Laws*," in *The Sexism of Social and Political Theory: Women and Reproduction from Plato to Neitzsche*, ed. L. M. G. Clark and L. Lange (Univ. of Toronto Pr., 1979), pp. 3-15. P's concern with equal education for both genders is to benefit state, not women. Though he grants that some women might share in governing state, it is not clear if he thought this desirable. He appears inconsistent in *Rep* and *Laws* because the two works take different views of public and private life. [3025]

LESSER, H. "Plato's Feminism." *Ph* 54(1979), 113-117. Challenges Annas' claim (#2883) that P's case for sexual equality is inadequate. P is more interested in social good, which ultimately benefits every individual. [3026]

LESSES, G. "Weakness, Reason, and the Divided Soul in Plato's *Republic*." *HPhQ* 4(1987), 147-161. Because P sees parts of soul as having some independent functions he can accept *akrasia* and also S's denial that such behavior is possible. [3027]

LIDOV, J. B. "Justice in Translation." *Interp* 12(1984), 83-106. Examines different translations of *Rep* and different interpretive strategies involved. [3028]

LUBAN, D. "The Form of the Good in the *Republic*." *JVanInq* 12(1978), 161-168. Doctrine of the Good is best understood as an ontological, not a moral, doctrine. The Good in which each of Forms participates adds nothing substantive to any of them: goodness of a Form is nothing more than the Form itself. [3029]

LYCOS, K. *Plato on Justice and Power: Reading Book 1 of Plato's* Republic. Albany: SUNY Pr., 1987. Book 1 does not simply expose inadequacies of popular conceptions of justice, but also shows that "justice is not external to the soul." [3030]

MABBOTT, J. D. "Is Plato's *Republic* Utilitarian?" in #1291, pp. 57-65. In *Rep* 4, P shows justice to be a good in itself. In Book 10 he shows justice to be good for its consequences.   [3031]

MacKENZIE, P. T. "On Praising the Appearance of Justice in Plato's *Republic*." *CanJPh* 15(1985), 617-624. It is fallacious to argue that, in order to show that justice is inherently good, S must prove that the just man who appears to be unjust is happier than the unjust man who appears just.   [3032]

MAGUIRE, J. P. "The Individual and the Class in Plato's *Republic*." *CJ* 60(1965), 145-150. P views society not as a collection of individuals but a blending of groups. The nature of the society is thus determined not by character of individuals but by relationships among groups.   [3033]

———. "Thrasymachus . . . or Plato?" *Phron* 16(1971), 142-163. Examines Thrasymachus' claims about justice in Book 1, and considers to what extent they can be referred to the historical Thrasymachus.   [3034]

MALCOM, J. F. "The Cave Revisited." *CQ* 31(1981), 60-68. Examines P's allegory of cave and focuses on prisoners viewing cave wall and released prisoners looking at puppets which cast shadows. Examines significance of various levels of education or moral awareness portrayed by the analogy. Argues that "converted prisoners" have attained true belief on moral matters.   [3035]

MARTIN, J. "Sex Equality and Education in Plato's Just State," in *Femininity, Masculinity and Androgyny: A Modern Philosophical Discussion*, ed. M. Vetterling-Braggin, (Totowa, NJ: Littlefield Adams, 1982), pp. 279-300. The education P provides for his guardians raises serious questions about extent to which sex equality can be achieved in Just State.   [3036]

MARTIN, R. "The Ideal State in Plato's *Republic*." *HPolTho* 2(1981), 1-30. Surveys P's plan for an ideal state. He regards the philosopher-king as the closest approximation to the ideal one could achieve. Flaws in human nature, however, would lead to corruption of this ideal. Also examines implications of myth of Er for P's theory.   [3037]

McCLAIN, E. G. "Tonal Isomorphism in Plato and the *I Ching*: Brumbaugh as Cultural Anthropologist," in #1277, pp. 131-152. Summarizes a musicological treatment of tyrant's allegory in Book 9 and shows that Chinese *I Ching* is musicalized by same insight which led S to his calculation of measure of tyrant's suffering as exactly 729.   [3038]

MEYERHOFF, H. "Plato Among Friends and Enemies," in #1961, pp. 187-198. Studies criticisms that P is an enemy of democracy and that ideas and values he incorporates in his "ideal" state are totalitarian, reactionary, repressive.   [3039]

MICHAELIDES-NOUAROS, A. "Gifted Youth and Plato." *Diot* 2(1974), 93-115. Analyzes Platonic views related to true nature, education, and future role of the gifted in utopian scheme of *Rep*.   [3040]

———. "A New Evaluation of the Dialogue between Thrasymachus and Socrates." *ArchRechtsSoz* 66(1980), 329-347. Thrasymachus is the pessimist, with his theory that law and justice reflect rulers' viewpoints. S's optimism arises from his philosophical assurance that the state can be structured ethically.   [3041]

MILLER, M. "Platonic Provocations: Reflections on the Soul and the Good in the *Republic*," in #1282, pp. 163-193. Examines P's notion of Good and how proper metaphysical understanding of Forms and Good fulfills search for justice in soul. **[3042]**

MILLS, K. W. "Crombie on *Republic* 597c." *Mind* 82(1973), 602-603. Challenges Crombie's (#2937) reading of argument regarding the Form of the Bed. **[3043]**

————. "Plato's 'Non-Hypothetical Starting Point.'" *DUJ* 31(1970), 152-159. In divided line analogy, P says dialectician ascends beyond hypotheses to a non-hypothetical starting point. Of all Forms, only the Good is non-hypothetical. **[3044]**

MOORS, K. F. "Equality and Cognition in Plato's Divided Line." *QUCC* 45(1984), 147-157. Divided line which S describes in 509d-571e is supposed to have equal subsections in its middle, producing an inequality between first two subsections, which symbolize image and knowledge. Arrangement symbolizes dialogue's basic theme. **[3045]**

————. *Glaucon and Adeimantus on Justice. The Structure of Argument in Book 2 of Plato's Republic*. Washington, DC: Univ. Pr. of Amer., 1981. Analyzes arguments with an examination of connections between them and what occurs in remainder of dialogue. **[3046]**

————. "Justice and Philosophy in Plato's *Republic*: The Nature of a Definition." *Interp* 12(1984), 193-223. Alleged inconsistency between definitions of justice for individual and city is intentional and illustrates difference between knowledge and opinion. **[3047]**

————. "Named Life Selections in Plato's Myth of Er." *C&M* 38(1988), 55-61. Most characters choosing new lives in the myth make their selections on basis of experiences in past lives, as though they have not learned anything. Odysseus, who rejects love of honor and chooses a philosophic life, becomes symbol of Socratic instruction. **[3048]**

————. "Plato's Battle of Megara: *Republic* 368a1." *SJPh* 17(1979), 493-500. Reference to a "battle of Megara" in this passage may apply to P's conflict with Megarian school, not to an historical military encounter. **[3049]**

MORRISON, J. S. "Two Unresolved Difficulties in the Line and the Cave." *Phron* 22(1977), 212-231. Interpretation of these images is difficult because the categories do not seem to correspond. But they are depicted diagrammatically in the Line and pictorially in the Cave. Both illustrate relationship of Forms to universals. **[3050]**

MULGAN, R. "Individual and Collective Virtues in the *Republic*." *Phron* 13(1968), 84-87. Analogy between state and individual should not be taken to mean that all citizens of the ideal state have attained the highest virtue possible. P's theory connects moral excellence with intellect, so that only the guardians can be fully virtuous. **[3051]**

MULHERN, J. J. "Population and Plato's *Republic*." *Arethusa* 8(1971) 265-281. Argues that what S says does contain a population policy, but it has little to do with numbers and food supply. **[3052]**

NACHMAN, L. D. "A Prelude to the *Republic*." *CW* 59(1966), 301-304. Dialogue's main themes are set forth in Book 1. **[3053]**

NAILS, D. "A Little Platonic Heresy for the Eighties." *TeachPh* 8(1985), 33-40. Examines three different approaches to P's account of structure of ideal polis, and suggests that P may not be as totalitarian as is often supposed.   **[3054]**

————. "Teaching Plato in South African Universities." *SAfrJPh* 8(1989), 100-117. Shows how a recasting of Book 1 of *Rep* addresses concerns of relevance.   **[3055]**

NELSON, I. O. "Plato's Cave and the Course of Argument in the *Republic*." *DarshInt* 6(1966), 25-30. Cave analogy not only presents us with P's theory of knowledge and its connection with higher studies of philosopher-kings, but also presents us with his assessment of what has been accomplished so far in *Rep*.   **[3056]**

NEU, J. "Plato's Analogy of State and the Individual: The *Republic* and the Organic Theory of the State." *Ph* 46(1971), 238-254. P does not personify the state or consider it necessarily superior to the individual, except at points where judgments must be made which require the special training of an elite.   **[3057]**

NEUMANN, H. "Plato's Republic: Utopia or Distopia?" *ModSch* 44(1967), 319-330. Interprets roles of Glaucon and Thrasymachus to support view that *Rep* is to be regarded as a tyranny inimical to moral or intellectual growth of most of its citizens.   **[3058]**

NICHOLS, M. P. "The *Republic*'s Two Alternatives: Philosopher-Kings and Socrates." *PolTheo* 12(1984), 252-274. Contrasts mathematical education of philosopher-kings with approach of S.   **[3059]**

————. "Spiritedness and Philosophy in Plato's *Republic*," in *Understanding the Political Spirit*, ed. C. H. Zuckert (New Haven, CT: Yale Univ. Pr., 1988), pp. 48-66. Examines P's treatment of spiritedness (*thymos*) through discussion of guardians.   **[3060]**

————. cf. #1126.

NICHOLSON, P. P. "Unravelling Thrasymachus' Arguments in the *Republic*." *Phron* 19(1974), 210-232. Challenges standard reading of Thrasymachus' definition of justice as "the advantage of the stronger, i. e., ruler." Rather, argues that Thrasymachus means "the advantage of another."   **[3061]**

NORTON, D. "Social Organization and Individual Initiative," in *Organizations and Ethical Individualism*, ed. K. Kolenda, (New York: Praeger, 1988), pp. 107-136. Argues that *Rep* is P's attempt to show what social and political conditions will provide all persons the best opportunity to achieve life akin to that of S.   **[3062]**

O'NEILL, B. "The Struggle for the Soul of Thrasymachus." *AncPh* 8(1988) 167-185. In his method of argument, S seeks to appeal to men who implicitly possess rational structure of human soul, but who do not yet comprehend their true nature. Elenchus then is a kind of "soul-cure."   **[3063]**

O'ROURKE, "*Mythos* and *Logos* in the *Republic*." *Clio* 16(1987), 381-396. Though *Rep* argues for primacy of reason over emotion, P gives vent to his emotions, expressing his love for S and his long-festering anger at those who put him to death.   **[3064]**

OSBORNE, M. L. "On the Image of the Soul as a Stream in Plato's *Republic*." *SJPh*

14(1976), 359-364. Reply to Teloh (#3139), who argues that metaphor of soul as a stream (*Rep* 6) explains its functioning better than the tripartite theory of the soul (*Rep* 4). But one fork of a stream does not control another. Stream image also fails to explain how various classes achieve self-actualization. [3065]

——. "Plato's Unchanging View of Women: A Denial that Anatomy Spells Destiny." *PhFor* 6(1975), 447-452. Challenges Dickason's claim (#2946) that P's view of women changed from *Rep* to *Laws*. [3066]

OSTWALD, M. "The Two States in Plato's *Republic*," in #41, pp. 316-327. Argues that P maintains a clear distinction between Guardians and Philosophers, and that his political doctrine involves not one kind of state but two. [3067]

PARRY, R. D. "The Craft of Justice," in #1285, pp. 19-38. In *Rep* 1-4 P continues to compare virtues and crafts, though he adapts analogy in light of his tripartite psychology. Idea of justice as a craft is basis of P's understanding of virtue. [3068]

——. "The Uniqueness Proof for Forms in *Republic* X." *JHPh* 23(1985), 133-150. Examines third bed argument that shows that the Form of bed is unique, and compares it to first TMA of *Parm*. The argument does not produce an infinite regress. [3069]

PETERS, J. R. "Reason and Passion in Plato's *Republic*." *AncPh* 9(1989), 173-187. As P understands it, reason is a kind of passion which compels the *psyche* to seek order and harmony. The philosopher-king will, therefore, want to rule in order to establish the greatest degree of order. [3070]

PETERS, R. S. "Was Plato Nearly Right about Education," in *Essays on Educators* (Winchester, UK: Allen & Unwin, 1981), pp. 3-14. For P education's central concern is development of reason, but his conception of reason is indefensible. P believed that development of reason culminates in certainty of the sort he found in geometry.[3071]

PFISTER, L. F. "A Study in Comparative Utopias — K'ang Yu-we and Plato." *JChinPh* 16(1989), 59-117. Comparison on seven points of K'ang's (1858-1927 A. D.) *Ta-t'ung shu* and P's *Rep*. [3072]

PIERCE, C. "Equality: *Republic* V." *Monist* 57(1973), 1-11. P does not actually present arguments for inferiority of women. Book 5 is a clever critique of basic assumptions used in such arguments. [3073]

POMEROY, S. B. "Feminism in Book V of Plato's *Republic*." *Apeir* 8 #1(1974), 32-34. Diction P employs in discussing question of women indicates that he is incapable of seeing them as equal to men. [3074]

——. "Optics and the Line in Plato's *Republic*." *CQ* 21(1971), 389-392. Proportions of Divided Line have their origins in optical theory. [3075]

——. "Plato and the Female Physician (*Republic* 454d2)." *AJPh* 99(1978), 496-500. P's statements about women's ability to become doctors are not merely hypothetical, for female physicians existed in Athens during his lifetime. [3076]

QUINCEY, J. H. "Another Purpose for Plato, *Republic* I." *Hermes* 109(1981), 300-315.

Thrasymachus was an historical personage, contemporaneous with S and a teacher in Athens. *Rep* 1 serves not merely to refute Thrasymachus' definition of justice but to oppose his claims about the power of his rhetoric.   [3077]

RANDALL, J. H. "Plato's Treatment of the Theme of the Good Life and His Criticism of the Spartan Ideal." *JHI* 28(1967), 307-324. By examining a Spartan-style system in such detail P is, by irony, defending Athenian system.   [3078]

RANKIN, H. D. "A Modest Proposal about the *Republic*." *Apeir* 2 #2(1968), 20-22. P was a writer of mime and should be read like a satirist. Hence, *Rep* is intended to shock us and make us laugh.   [3079]

———. "*Paradeigma* and Realizability in Plato's *Republic*." *Eranos* 63(1965), 120-133. Discussion of degree to which P thought of his ideal state as a model or potentially realizable plan. Also looks at importance of myth and vision in dialogue.   [3080]

———. "Plato, *Republic* 409a1-b2. An Intersection of Themes." *AClass* 9(1966), 143-147. Examines conflicting motifs in phrase *paradeigmata homoiopathe tois ponerois* "patterns answering to the affections of the bad").   [3081]

———. "Plato's Eugenic *Euphemia* and *Apothesis* in *Republic*, Book V." *Hermes* 93(1965), 407-420. P's reluctance to advocate eugenic approach to population control but his realization of its necessity led him to resort to myth of slavery of souls.   [3082]

RAUBITSCHEK, A. E. "Plato and Minos." *QS* 3(1976), 233-238. Asks if P consciously imitates organization of Minoan Crete in his ideal state and if social, political, and economic life in Minoan Crete was somewhat similar to that of Dorian Cretans and of Spartans, and of ruling class of P's ideal state.   [3083]

REEVE, C. D. C. *Philosopher-Kings: The Argument of Plato's* Republic. Princeton Univ. Pr., 1988. Takes issue with those who see *Rep* as describing a totalitarian state, containing the epitome of P's metaphysics and epistemology, or lacking unity. Tries to show how Book 1 marks P's break with Socratic teaching and raises problems about philosophic method and the definition of justice. Maintains that *Rep* presents theory of Forms which is more plausible than that of earlier dialogues. P's psychology, especially his theory of varieties of desire, is crucial for understanding *Rep* as a unity. His views on education and ethics are also more coherent than generally recognized.   [3084]

———. "Socrates Meets Thrasymachus." *AGPh* 65(1985), 47-64. Book 1 sets forth views opposed to those of S which made P aware of deficiencies in Socratic moral theory. Rest of *Rep* is effort to make up that lack.   [3085]

RICHARDS, I. A., ed. and transl. *Republic*. Cambridge Univ. Pr., 1966. Notes for general reader.   [3086]

ROBINSON, R. "Plato's Separation of Reason from Desire." *Phron* 26(1971), 38-48. Articulates ten propositions by which P establishes reason and desire as different sorts of something in soul, and then considers what these "somethings" are.   [3087]

ROBINSON, T. M. "Professor Allen on Glaucon in the *Republic*," in #1283, pp. 63-66. Reply to #2878. Criticizes Socratic vision of a just society for failing to account for several facets of moral and psychological behavior. **[3088]**

———. cf. #2059, #2060.

ROHATYN, D. A. "Plato and the 'Profession' of Philosophy." *GM* 24(1974), 387-391. Devises an argument on ideal social structure of *Rep* to show that it is possible to justify philosopher's getting paid for his contribution to community. **[3089]**

ROSEN, S. "The Role of Eros in Plato's *Republic*." *RMeta* 18(1965), 452-475.; also #75, pp. 102-118. Contends that for P philosophy includes two basic aspects, poetic and mathematical, and that these philosophical methods represent two fundamentally and mutually complementary inflections of eros. **[3090]**

ROSENSTOCK, B. "Rereading the *Republic*." *Arethusa* 16(1983), 219-246. Examines importance of Book 10 and image of descent into Hades. **[3091]**

ROWE, C. J. "Justice and Temperance in *Republic* IV," in #48, pp. 336-344. In *Laws* P gave up the attempt to separate justice and temperance which he had undertaken in *Rep*. **[3092]**

RUCKER, D. "Plato and the Poets." *JAAC* 25(1966), 167-170. Role of poet in *Rep* is no more restricted than are roles of legislator and philosopher. **[3093]**

RUSSELL, J. R. "The Platonic Myth of Er, Armenian *Ara* and Iranian *Arday Wiraz*." *Revue des Études Arméniennes* 18(1984), 477-485. Examines influence of Zoroastrian thought and Armenian legend on myth in *Rep* 10. **[3094]**

RUTTENBERG, H. S. "Plato's Use of the Analogy Between Justice and Health." *JValInq* 20(1986), 147-156. Analogy between justice and health assimilates physical to intelligible and consequently P's identification of individual and common good does not produce a tyranny. **[3095]**

RYLE, G. "Review of K. R. Popper, *The Open Society and its Enemies*," in #1961, pp. 85-90. Reviews Popper's (1948) very strong attack against *Rep*. **[3096]**

SACHS, D. "A Fallacy in Plato's *Republic*," in #1291, pp. 35-51. P commits a "fallacy of irrelevance" that undercuts *Rep*'s main argument in that his definition of justice departs significantly from ordinary conception of justice. Hence, there is no guarantee that one who is Platonically just will adhere to ordinary canons of justice. **[3097]**

SANKARI, F. A. "Plato and Al-Farabi." *Vivarium* 8(1970), 1-9. Explores some of the parallels between Arab commentator's and P's positions regarding political philosophy, and in particular the ideal state. **[3098]**

SANTAS, G. "The Form of the Good in Plato's *Republic*," in #42, pp. 232-263. Form of the Good is formal cause of ideal attributes of all other Forms. **[3099]**

———. "Justice and Democracy in Plato's *Republic*," in *Antike Rechts- und Sozialphilosophie*, ed. O. Gigon & M. W. Fischer (Frankfurt: Lang, 1988), pp. 37-59. P's analogy between soul and state is applied to democracies in *Rep* 8 to show that being a democratic person is bad for one, because democracy is basically irrational. **[3100]**

―――. "Two Theories of Good in Plato's *Republic*." *AGPh* 67(1985), 223-245. P's initial definition of good is functional but framed in such a way that it will fit with perfectionist theory of Form of Good to which he is leading the reader.　　　　**[3101]**

SARTORIUS, R. "Fallacy and Political Radicalism in Plato's *Republic*." *CanJPh* 3(1974), 349-363. Reply to Sachs (#3097). While Sachs' argument that P commits a fallacy of irrelevance must be rejected, his contention does help make it clear why P's reasons for living justly would seem unconvincing to at least a portion of his audience.　　　　**[3102]**

SATHAYE, S. G. "The *Aitareya Brahmana* and the *Republic*." *PhE&W* 19(1969), 435-441. Gives a critical review of some significant aspects of morals in the *Aitareya Brahmana* and *Rep*.　　　　**[3103]**

SAXONHOUSE, A. W. "The Philosopher and the Female in the Political Thought of Plato." *PolTheo* 4(1976), 195-212. Apparent equality granted women in *Rep* 5 proves to be specious upon closer examination. S denies differences of gender, actually heightening tension between men and women. Gender opposition becomes symbolic of tension between philosophy and politics in later books.　　　　**[3103a]**

SCHILLER, J. "Just Men and Just Acts in Plato's *Republic*." *JHPh* 6(1968), 1-14. Response to earlier arguments that P vacillates between his own and popular concepts of justice.　　　　**[3104]**

SCHIPPER, E. W. "The Relevance of Platonic Justice." *SJPh* 15(1977), 113-116. Reply to #3097. S and his opponents are all interested in the applicability of their definitions of justice to specific acts. S's definition involves the correct ordering of the soul and the application of individual justice to one's work as part of the community.　　　　**[3105]**

SCOLNICOV, S. "Reason and Passion in the Platonic Soul." *Dion* 2(1978), 35-49. P views soul as a complex unity; its "parts" are not heterogeneous. This conception of soul allows him to solve certain Socratic paradoxes.　　　　**[3106]**

SEERY, J. E. "Politics as Ironic Community: On the Themes of Descent and Return in Plato's *Republic*." *PolTheo* 16(1988), 229-256. *Rep* is ironic, but not along Straussian or Derridean lines. Irony is found in descent-return motif (with Orphic overtones), reliance on visual and mathematical imagery, and mocking references/allusions to Homer.　　　　**[3107]**

SEGAL, C. "'The Myth was Saved.' Reflections on Homer and the Mythology of Plato's *Republic*." *Hermes* 106(1978), 315-336. Similarities between Homer and *Rep* point up their common, though not identical, understanding of human condition.　　　　**[3108]**

SHEAR, J. "Mabharishi, Plato and the TM-Sidhi Program on Innate Structures of Consciousness." *Metaphil* 12(1981), 72-84. Conclusion that a certain Transcendental Meditation-Sidhi practice produces experience of an innate structure or archetype finds support in *Rep*.　　　　**[3109]**

SICHEL, B. A. "Self-Knowledge and Education in Plato's Allegory of the Cave." *ProcPhEd* 41(1985), 429-439. Examines how P's ideas bridge a common dichotomy of educational purposes, that between cognitive achievement and self-knowledge.　　　　**[3110]**

SIDER, D. "The Structure of Plato, *Republic* VI." *RSC* 24(1976), 336-348. Discussion of Line's tripartite structure is characteristic of structure of entire book. **[3111]**

SIEMSEN, T. "Thrasymachus' Challenge." *HPolTho* 8(1987), 1-19. The confrontation between S and Thrasymachus is meant to show how philosophy can assert itself over politics, but S's success is only apparent. **[3112]**

SKEMP, J. B. "How Political is the *Republic*?" *HPolTho* 1(1980), 1-7. P's insistence that man is not controlled by material forces and that societal and individual characterstics interact shows that the dialogue is not a political program. **[3113]**

――――. "Individual and Civic Virtue in the *Republic*." *Phron* 18(1969), 107-110. Reply to #3051. In Book 4, P should not be taken to claim that guardians must be morally superior to other citizens, because he separates moral and intellectual qualities. Justice for citizens requires accepting the rule of the guardians. For guardians it means fulfilling their duty to the *polis*. **[3114]**

SMITH, J. F. "Plato, Irony, and Equality." *World Studies International Forum* 6(1983), 597-607. Emphasizes connection between P's analytic probing of nature of sex differences and his radical assertion that society should ideally be arranged to bring out best in each individual, regardless of gender. **[3115]**

SMITH, N. D. "An Argument for the Definition of Justice in Plato's *Republic* (433e6-434a1)." *PhilStud* 35(1979), 373-383. Examines P's argument that justice is "having and doing one's own." Develops an interpretation which preserves validity of P's position and challenges Vlastos' interpretation (#3148). **[3116]**

――――. "The Objects of *Dianoia* in Plato's Divided Line." *Apeir* 15(1981), 129-137. Develops views of Morrison (#3050) and Fogelin (#2962) that objects on second highest portion of the Line (*Rep* 6) are "visible originals taken as images of Forms." **[3117]**

――――. cf. #1663.

――――. and **BRICKHOUSE, T.** "Justice and Dishonesty in Plato's *Republic*." *SJPh* 21(1983), 79-96. What appears to be a paradox between loving the truth and using lies on the part of the Philosopher-Rulers is resolved when one considers the paternalism underlying P's political philosophy. **[3118]**

SOBEL, J. H. "Cephalus: *Republic* 331c-d." *HPhQ* 4(1987), 281-290. In *Crito* S had maintained that disobedience to state is always wrong. In this passage, which probably reflects P's mature thought, he seems to hold that no actions are universally and of necessity unjust. **[3119]**

SPARSHOTT, F. E. "An Argument For Thrasymachus." *Apeir* 21(1988), 55-67. Thrasymachus' argument that justice is the interest of the strong, while confused, need not be seen as self-contradictory. His premises are weak. **[3120]**

――――. "Aristotle's *Ethics* and Plato's *Republic*. A Structural Comparison." *Dial*(Can) 21(1982), 483-499." *Rep* and Ar's *Nicomachean Ethics* can be compared on at least fifteen points, some of which are examined in detail. Three passages in each work have no obvious parallel in the other. **[3121]**

———. "Socrates and Thrasymachus." *Monist* 50(1966), 421-459. S believes that ultimate motivation for "just behavior" is identical with intellect's love of truth. Book 1 could not have been composed separately from rest of dialogue.   [3122]

SPIRO, H. J. *Politics as the Master Science: From Plato to Mao* London: Harper and Row, 1970. Explores analogy between state and *polis*, and argues that P could not conceive of individual apart from *polis*.   [3123]

SPRAGUE, R. K. "A Parallel with *De Anima* III, 5." *Phron* 17(1972), 250-251. Sun analogy in 507a ff. may help explain Ar's comparison of active intellect to light. [3124]

———. *Plato's Philosopher-King: A Study of the Theoretical Background.* Columbia: Univ. of SC, 1976. Philosopher-king is treated as possessor of an art or science, not as head of state. Exhibits the second-order character of statecraft and shows how P distinguishes this art from other second-order arts such as rhetoric and sophistry.   [3125]

STALLEY, R. F. "Mental Health and Individual Responsibility in Plato's *Republic*." *JVallnq* 15(1981), 109-124. P's view of injustice should not be likened to modern concepts of crime as disease. P sees injustice as bad because it upsets the soul's natural condition and hinders worthwhile activity.   [3126]

———. "The Role of the Doctor: Technician or Statesman?" *JMedEthics* 6(1980), 19-22. Considers two possible models for role of doctor in society, one of which is that of philosopher-king, as described in *Rep*.   [3127]

STANFORD, W. B. "Onomatopoetic 'Mimesis' in Plato, *Republic* 396b-397c." *JHS* 93(1973), 185-191. Imitation, which is foundation of poetry, causes persons presenting or hearing a work to identify themselves with persons or animals being represented, which are often base and unworthy of the enlightened soul. Such identification with another is a form of temporary insanity.   [3128]

STEINER, E. E., II. "The Hindu *Republic*." *Dial*(PST) 14(1972), 73-82. Study of *Rep* and *Upanishads* draws attention to points of contact in their social organization, view of human nature, and understanding of how people achieve self-realization.   [3129]

STERLING, K. "Socrates on Rhythm." *AncPh* 1(1980-81), 81-82. Discussion of musical rhythm (*Rep* 400a ff.) foreshadows the three classes who will run the city.   [3130]

STEVENSON, J. "Plato and Political Reaction." *RevW* 33(1979), 22-28. Given a knowledge of social forces in contemporary Greek society, one can read off directly from *Rep* a desire to set up social relations of a previous era.   [3131]

STOKES, M. C. "Adeimantus in the *Republic*." in #1283, pp. 67-96. Examines dialectical role of Adeimantus, and argues that with respect to the question "Is justice a virtue?" P plays off Glaucon and Adeimantus against each other.   [3132]

STRANG, C. "Plato's Analogy of the Cave." *OSAP* 4(1986), 19-34. Examines P's use of analogy, gives *doxa* its proper prominence in the scheme, accounts for some of P's misdirection, interprets Cave story, and places the whole within wider context of P's epistemology.   [3133]

STRAUSS, L. "On Plato's *Republic*," in *The City and Man* (Chicago: Rand McNally, 1968), pp. 50-138; also in *History of Political Thought*, ed. L. Strauss and J. Cropsey. (Univ. of Chicago Pr., 1987) pp. 33-89. In this ironic work P shows impossibility of realizing perfectly just city, showing essential limits of city and of justice. [3134]

STROLL, A. "On a Certain Tension in Plato's *Republic*." *Dial*(Can) 11(1972), 499-508. There are two competing conceptions of human nature in *Rep*. When the ambiguity is exposed, P's defense of anti-democratic society is seen to fail. [3135]

SZE, C. P. "*Eikasia* and *Pistis* in Plato's Cave Allegory." *CQ* 27(1977), 127-138. Interprets shadows in cave as symbolizing myth and poetry. Higher level of originals is Sophistic teaching. [3136]

TAFT, R. "The Role of Compulsion in the Education of the Philosopher-King." *Auslegung* 9(1982), 311-332. No inconsistency exists between early discussion of education of guardians and later discussion of education of philosopher-king. [3137]

TARAN, L. "Platonism and Socratic Ignorance (with Special Reference to *Republic* I)," in #1282, pp. 85-109. *Rep* 1 is test case for certain interpretations of S's profession of ignorance and its relation to *elenchus* throughout Platonic corpus. [3138]

TELOH, H. "Human Nature, Psychic Energy, and Self-Actualization in Plato's *Republic*." *SJPh* 14(1976), 345-358. "Stream of desire" image (*Rep* 485d-e) is psychic energy, a possible meaning of *eros*. The branches of the stream are natural proclivities through which psychic energies are released. Individuals achieve self-actualization (P's goal) by release of energy through their strongest channels. [3139]

———. "A Vulgar and a Philosophical Test for Justice in Plato's *Republic*." *SJPh* 13(1975), 499-510. In response to Sachs' (#3097) charge that P commits fallacy of irrelevance, argues that P is completely disinterested in vulgar justice, and that he does provide a satisfactory criterion for the instantiation of Platonic justice. [3140]

THAYER, H. S. "Models of Moral Concepts and Plato's *Republic*." *JHPh* 7(1969), 247-262. Examines how definitions of justice in *Rep* 1 are constructed. The model P typically uses to test his definitions of justice is *techne*. [3141]

———. "The Myth of Er." *HPhQ* 5(1988), 369-384. Myth is culmination of dialogue's main argument, which is an examination of two fundamental possible choices — a righteous and an unrighteous life. [3142]

TILES, J. E. "The Combat of Passion and Reason." *Ph* 52(1977), 321-330. Discusses passion and reason in relationship to *Rep* 4; argues that P misuses concept of reason. Considers Hume's argument that passion and reason are not opposites. [3143]

VERSENYI, L. G. "Plato and His Liberal Opponents." *Ph* 46(1971), 222-237. Challenges those critics who argue that P's commitment to existence of moral and political knowledge leads to dangerous consequences. One must consider ends when making judgments about the *polis*. [3144]

———. "Virtue as a Self-Directed Art." *Pers* 53(1972), 274-289. Aims at clarifying S's argument against Thrasymachus (338-347) within the context of *Rep*. Attempts to show

that denial of premises of Socratic argument concerning virtue as an art makes a
philosophical determination of human excellence impossible.   **[3145]**

VLASTOS, G. "The Argument in the *Republic* that Justice Pays." *JPh* 65(1968), 665-674.
Examines argument in Book 4 that one has psychic harmony if, and only if, one has
disposition to act justly toward others.   **[3146]**

——. "Does Slavery Exist in Plato's *Republic*?" *CPh* 63(1968), 291-295. Reviews
relevant evidence and answers question affirmatively.   **[3147]**

——. "Justice and Psychic Harmony in the *Republic*." *JPh* 66(1969), 505-521; revised
version in #1291, pp. 66-95. A commonly cited weakness of P's argument that "justice
pays" is his definition of justice as an inner harmony of the psyche, as opposed to a social
relationship. He seems to attempt, not entirely successfully, to link the two senses of
justice in *Rep* 441c-e.   **[3148]**

——. "The Theory of Social Justice in the *Polis* in Plato's *Republic*," in #1281, pp. 1-40.
Argues for existence of theory of social justice in *Rep*, the just relations of persons and
classses *within* the polis and *to* the polis.   **[3149]**

WARREN, E. "The Craft Argument: An Analogy?" in #1267, pp. 101-115. The Craft
argument is not an analogy but a sincere expression of P's view that knowledge is virtue.
There is a craft of governing which only philosopher-kings possess.   **[3150]**

WARTOFSKY, M. W. "The *Republic* as Myth. The Dilemma of Philosophy and Politics."
PhilFor 10(1971), 249-266. In order to rule, one must deceive. *Rep* and *Laws* do not
differ essentially on that point.   **[3151]**

WATERLOW, S. "The Good of Others in Plato's *Republic*." *PAS* 72(1972-3), 19-36. For
P an agent is conceptually prior to action. But reason is prior to both, establishing
connection between justice in agent and in actions. This view, however, eliminates
independence of agent.   **[3152]**

WEINBERGER, D. "Artificial Intelligence and Plato's Cave." *IdealStud* 18(1988), 1-9.
Argues that "the temptation to believe in the possibility of artificial intelligence stems
from a misunderstanding about the nature of ideas" and finds its origins in early
philosophic theories, especially P's Cave metaphor.   **[3153]**

WESTERINK, L. G. "The Title of Plato's *Republic*." *ICS* 6(1981), 112-115. Dialogue
is known by title *Politeia*, a singular noun, until early in sixth century A. D., when title
is pluralized, in accordance with scribal practice of the time.   **[3154]**

WHEELER, A. M. "Creativity: A Rejoinder to Professor Sichel." *EducTheor* 22(1972),
208-211. Reply to #1591. Defends view that censorship powers which P grants to the
state would limit creativity, no matter how "creativity" is defined.   **[3155]**

——. "Creativity in Plato's States." *EducTheor* 19(1969), 249-255. If P's views were put
into practice, creativity would be considerably hampered.   **[3156]**

WHITE, F. C. "J. Gosling on *ta polla kala*." *Phron* 23(1978), 127-132. Challenges
Gosling's (1960) argument that it is difficult to make sense of any interpretation of 479a-

b if we assume that particulars, and not types, are under discussion here. **[3157]**

------. "Justice and the Good of Others in Plato's *Republic*." *HPhQ* 5(1988), 395-410. Justice as P defines it (psychic harmony) and justice as more commonly understood are not incompatible. P shows that a person who is just in his terms will, by reason, be just in terms of regarding the good of others. **[3158]**

------. "The 'Many' in *Republic* 475a-480a." *CanJPh* 7(1977), 291-306. Defends traditional view that this passage concerns the nature of particulars as bearers of opposites. **[3159]**

------. "The *Phaedo* and *Republic* V On Essences." *JHS* 98(1978), 142-156. In *Rep* 5,475-480 P turns away from essentialism because it makes Forms unnecessary. **[3160]**

------. "The Scope of Knowledge in *Republic* V." *AustlJPh* 62(1984), 339-354. Examines what sorts of items (Forms or particulars) are objects of knowledge in *Rep*. 5. **[3161]**

WHITE, N. P. "The Classification of Goods in Plato's *Republic*." *JHPh* 22(1984), 393-422. Explores classification of goods at beginning of Book 2, good "for its own sake" and good "for its consequences," and examines this notion of consequences. **[3162]**

------. *A Companion to Plato's* Republic. Indianapolis: Hackett, 1979. Consists of lengthy introductory essay and commentary with notes. Essay looks in detail at P's overall aim in the dialogue, the Form of the Good, and his ethical theory. The commentary is keyed to Grube's translation, with notes on technical matters. Also contains bibliography. **[3163]**

------. "The Ruler's Choice." *AGPh* 68(1986), 22-46. P holds that being more just is in a person's interest. But, by choosing to rule (which is more just) the philosopher-kings choose what is less good for them. In this case there is another reason besides self-interest for being more just. **[3164]**

WILLIAMS, B. "The Analogy of City and Soul in Plato's *Republic*," in #65, pp. 196-206. The just city must have a majority of appetitive men, but an appetitive man is not a just man. Hence, the city must have a majority of men who are not just. But this contradicts the claim that a city is just if and only if its men are just. **[3165]**

WILSON, J. F. *The Politics of Moderation: An Interpretation of Plato's* Republic. Lanham, MD: Univ. Pr. of America, 1984. *Rep* is a critique of ideas of justice and an endorsement of moderation. Best life is not that of philosopher-king, but of moderate musical human being. Sees the underlying theme as moderation, not justice. The arguments put forward in the first seven books are as provisional as the structure of the ideal state. **[3166]**

WILSON, J. R. S. "The Argument of *Republic* IV." *PhQ* 26(1976), 111-124. Reply to Vlastos (#3146). P distinguishes between the behavior which indicates the presence of a virtue and the structural feature of the soul (or *polis*) in which virtues arise. His argument in Book 4 does not depend on equivocation. **[3167]**

------. "The Contents of the Cave," in #1287, pp. 117-127. New interpretation of various elements of the allegory. Mathematics is not a part of original allegory. **[3168]**

———. "On a Possible Circularity in the *Republic*." *AncPh* 3(1983), 33-54. S argues that a certain condition of the soul is both best for its possessor and source of right action toward others. He also describes an ideal polis, which would produce in its members this condition of the soul. Yet S supports his thesis about soul by means of an analogy with *polis*, which assumes that it is ideal. Explores whether argument is circular.   **[3169]**

———. "Reason's Rule and Vulgar Wrong-doing." *Dial*(Can) 16(1977), 591-604. Someone who is just in P's sense of psychic harmony might commit an injustice to gratify some appetite. P's definition can be amended to resolve this difficulty.   **[3170]**

WOOD, R. E. "Image, Structure and Content: On a Passage in Plato's *Republic*." *RMeta* 40(1987), 495-514. Discusses significance of S's omission of stereometry in his introduction of the quadrivium.   **[3171]**

WU, J. S. "A Note on the Third Section of the Divided Line." *NewSchol* 43(1969), 269-275. Aims to elucidate meaning of "understanding" and "hypotheses" as used in context of the simile.   **[3172]**

YARBROUGH, J. *Plato's* The Republic. New York: Barron's, 1984. Elementary introduction and section-by-section summary of the dialogue.   **[3173]**

YOUNG, C. M. "A Note on '*Republic* 335c9-10' and '335c12'." *PhR* 83(1974), 97-106. Argues for a different translation which does not undercut P's argument that "it is in no way just to damage anybody."   **[3174]**

ZEMBATY, J. S. "Plato's *Republic* and Greek Morality on Lying." *JHPh* 26(1988), 517-545. Discusses claims made about justifiability of lying in *Rep* and what is said regarding lying in Greek tragedies and other Greek writings.   **[3175]**

For related items see #429, #1307, #1308, #1427, #1456, #1541, #1543, #1554, #1565, #1566, #1573-1576, #1598, #1767, #1966, #1986, #2005, #2042, #2047, #2111, #2115-2117, #2146, #2607, #3246, #4014, #4146, #6735.

Sophist

     The dialogue begins with Theodorus, Theaetetus, and S meeting again (after the conversation recorded in the *Theaet*), and being joined by a stranger from Elea who is said to belong to the school of Parmenides and Zeno. The Eleatic Stranger and Theaetetus join together in conversation to "track down" what it means to be a Sophist. One noteworthy aspect of this conversation is the absence of S from the discussion. The significance of his absence is a matter of controversy.

     The Stranger begins with a lengthy illustration of the method of collection and division (first outlined in the *Phaedrus*) that is to be used in defining the Sophist. At least part of the purpose of this discussion is to separate the genuine philosopher from the Sophist. (This brings to mind the *Apol*, where S relates how he has been confused with the Sophists in the minds of many people.) The philosopher engages in cross-examination to expose an interlocutor's ignorance and thus to facilitate learning; the Sophist engages in cross-examination in order to practice "eristic, disputatious, controversial, pugnacious, combative" arguments (226a). At this point, the Sophist turns out to be a maker of appearances. He makes

> it possible to impose upon the young who are still far removed from the reality of things, by means of words that cheat the ear, exhibiting images of all things in a shadow play of discourse, so as to make them believe that they are hearing the truth and that the speaker is in all matters the wisest of men (234c).

But the Stranger then draws a distinction between one who makes likenesses and one who makes semblances (*phantasmata*). The maker of likenesses is one who creates likenesses that conform to the proportions of the original. The maker of semblances creates images that appear to be likenesses, but because they do not conform to the proportions of the original, these images are not likenesses but semblances. The Sophist is one who makes semblances.

Yet the making of semblances involves the making of statements that are false, and this confronts the Stranger and Theaetetus with the problem of whether false statements are even possible. For how can "that which is not" have any being at all. This difficulty has existed since the time of "father Parmenides." To confront this difficulty, the Stranger argues that he and Theaetetus must "establish that what is not, in some respect has being, and conversely that what is, in a way is not" (241e). In developing this position, the Stranger alludes to the battle between those who take being to consist solely of material bodies and those who take reality to consist solely of the immaterial Forms.

In the discussion about the Forms, the Stranger puts forward the important suggestion that it may be possible that the Forms blend or participate in each other. It is this suggestion that enables the Stranger to show how false statements are possible. The *Sophist* thus offers a significant development in P's Theory of Forms.

ACKRILL, J. "In Defence of Platonic Division," in #82, pp. 373-392. Challenges Ryle's attack on the method of division (#2596) as philosophically insignificant, and argues that alleged gap betweeen dividing by kinds and knowing how kinds can and cannot combine is not unbridgeable. [3176]

———. "Plato and the Copula: *Sophist* 251-259," in #1809, pp. 207-218; also in #1290, pp. 210-222. Examines whether P "discovers the copula" or recognizes ambiguity of *estin* as used in statements of identity and in attributive statements. [3177]

ANDIC, M. and BROWN, M. "False Statements in the *Sophist* and Theaetetus' Mathematics." *Phoenix* 27(1973), 26-34. Calls attention to a parallel between P's account of false statement in *Soph* and Theaetetus' study of incommensurables. Studies explicit form of assertions of incommensurability and of falsehood. [3178]

BENARDETE, S., transl. *The Being of the Beautiful: Plato's* Theaetetus, Sophist *and* Statesman. Univ. of Chicago Pr., 1984. A translation of P's *Theaet, Soph,* and *Stsm,* each with a commentary, plus an introduction discussing underlying theme of the three dialogues: relation of the beautiful to problem of being.   [3179]

BERGER, F. R. "Rest and Motion in the *Sophist*." *Phron* 10(1965), 70-77. P maintains that terms of rest and motion are not predicable of each other.   [3180]

BERRY, J. M. "A Deconstruction of Plato's 'Battle of Gods and Giants.'" *SwPhR* 3(1986), 28-39. Reads *Soph* 246-248 in terms of Popper's and Heidegger's work. Concludes that Being is power.   [3181]

_____. "Plato's Forms: A Text that Self-Destructs to Shed Its Light." *SwPhR* 4(1988), 111-119. Reading based on work of Heidegger and Derrida. Taking Being as power leads to the conclusion that to know something is to affect it. Forms cannot be known and remain unchanged.   [3182]

BESTOR, T. W. "Plato on Language and Falsehood." *SwJPh* 9(1978), 23-37. In several dialogues P maintains that false statements are impossible because false names are impossible. In *Soph* he finally concludes that statements are not names but are based on the weaving together of names.   [3183]

BLUCK, R. S. *Plato's* Sophist: *A Commentary*, ed. G. C. Neal. Manchester (UK) Univ. Pr., 1975. Commentary focusing on whether P's Theory of Forms changed or developed after *Rep*. Aims to determine most natural meaning of each argument.   [3184]

BODUNRIN, P. O. "The *Koinonia genon* and Plato's Philosophical Objectives in the *Sophist*." *MusAfr* 4(1975), 47-51. *Soph* 251a-255e attempts to refute extreme logical atomism. Its arguments are not precisely formulated.   [3185]

_____. "Logic and Metaphysics in Plato's *Sophist*." *MusAfr* 7(1981), 23-34. P uses both logical and metaphysical proofs to refute claim that all negatively predicated statements are incoherent.   [3186]

BONDESON, W. B. "Non-Being and the One: Some Connections Between Plato's *Sophist* and *Parmenides*." *Apeir* 7 #2(1973), 13-21. P's concepts of "absolute" non-Being and what is necessary for a thing to be a subject of discourse have implications for the first and sixth hypotheses of *Parm*.   [3187]

_____. "Plato's *Sophist* and the Significance and Truth-Value of Statements." *Apeir* 8 #2(1974), 41-47. Examines 260e ff. to investigate nature of statements, focusing on syntactical issue about functions of kinds of terms in statements.   [3188]

_____. "Plato's *Sophist*. Falsehood and Images." *Apeir* 6 #2(1972), 1-6. Confusion over question of whether non-Being is possible arises in part from analogies to seen images and objects of perception which P attempts to draw.   [3189]

_____. "Some Problems about Being and Predication in Plato's *Sophist* 242-249." *JHPh* 14(1976), 1-10. Definitions of Being at 248c and 249c are compatible but ambiguous. P's problem in *Soph* is failure to resolve question of self-predication.   [3190]

BOSTOCK, D. "Plato on 'Is Not': (*Sophist* 254-9)." *OSAP* 2(1984), 89-119. Elucidates and evaluates P's account of "is not" where the "is" is incomplete (i. e., where the verb requires a complement of some kind). Denies that P means to distinguish the two different senses of is: the "is" of identity and the "is" of predication. [3191]

BROWN, L. "Being in the *Sophist*: A Syntactical Inquiry." *OSAP* 4(1986), 49-70. Examines distinction between "complete" and "incomplete" uses of "to be," which has usually been associated with distinction between the "is" that means "exists" and the "is" of predication. Argues for a new understanding of this distinction. [3192]

BRUMBAUGH, R. S. "Diction and Dialectic: A Note on the *Sophist*," in #371, pp. 266-276; also in #49, pp. 103-111. E. Havelock's observations on language and orality (#331) help us to distinguish between works of P's which are genuine dialogues and those which, though called dialogues, are actually treatises. *Soph* is a conversation. The Eleatic Stranger does not retreat from P's position on the Forms. [3193]

DE RIJK, L. M. "On Ancient and Mediaeval Semantics and Metaphysics (4). Plato's Semantics in his Critical Period." *Vivarium* 19(1981), 1-46. Analyzes *Soph*, examining P's ontology and the ways one can describe an individual thing while still conceiving of it as one thing. [3194]

——. "On Ancient and Mediaeval Semantics (5)." *Vivarium* 19(1981), 81-125. Looks at problem of a thing having several names and its relation to Communion of Kinds. Also examines dialectic and communion of Forms. [3195]

——. "On Ancient and Mediaeval Semantics (6)." *Vivarium* 20(1982), 97-127. Examines communion of different Kinds, being and not-being of Forms. P did not abandon Theory of Forms or attribute change to Forms. [3196]

——. *Plato's* Sophist: *A Philosophical Commentary*. Amsterdam: North Holland Publ., 1986. Studies the dialogue to show that P does not abandon Theory of Forms and that introducing Change and Otherness into the realm of Being does not affect genuine nature of Forms. [3197]

DEVRIES, W. "On *Sophist* 255 B-E." *HPhQ* 5(1988), 385-394. Stranger's "being and identity" and "being and difference" arguments are intrinsically related. [3198]

DUERLINGER, J. "The Ontology of Plato's *Sophist*: The Problems of Falsehood, Non-Being, and Being." *ModSch* 65(1988), 151-184. Examines issue of falsehood independently of modern presuppositions and linguistic frameworks. [3199]

FERG, S. "Plato on False Statement: Relative Being, a Part of Being, and Not-Being in the *Sophist*." *JHPh* 14(1976), 336-342. Dialogue carefully distinguishes false statements from elliptical relational statements which can appear to be false. [3200]

FRANK, D. H. "On What There Is: Plato's Later Thoughts." *Elenchos* 6(1985), 5-18. Fresh examination of *Soph* 246a4-249d4 points up weaknesses of Owen's interpretation (#3231). By end of discussion each of the parties has made an important concession which indicates modifications of P's position on Forms. [3201]

GERSON, L. P. "A Distinction in Plato's *Sophist*." *ModSch* 63(1986), 251-266. Examines P's attempt to respond to criticism of Theory of Forms that Forms must be separate from sensible world and yet also related to it. [3202]

GEVORKIAN, A. T. "Idealism in Plato's *Sophist*." *SovStudPh* 26(1987-88), 43-63. P's true views on question of being do not concur with either of two opposing views presented in this dialogue.   [3203]

GOMEZ-LOBO, A. "Dialectic in the *Sophist*: A Reply to Waletzki." *Phron* 26(1981), 80-83. Formulates three general criteria that a correct interpretation of *Soph* 253d should have to challenge Waletzke's interpretation (in German).   [3204]

——. "Plato's Description of Dialectic in the *Sophist* 253d1-e2." *Phron* 22(1977), 29-47. Opens with a detailed criticism of Stenzel's views (#1800), then argues that passage contains an anticipation of dialectic of greatest kinds which immediately follows in the text. Challenges traditional interpretation that in this passage, P is offering a description of the Method of Division. Rather passage anticipates comparison of Being and Not-Being with other Forms.   [3205]

GOOCH, P. W. "Vice is Ignorance: The Interpretation of *Sophist* 226a-231b." *Phoenix* 25(1971), 124-133. Cross-examination deals with one form of ignorance (stupidity) as though it were a disease in need of correction, not instruction. Wickedness and ignorance cannot therefore be kept completely apart.   [3206]

GRISWOLD, C. L. "Logic and Metaphysics in Plato's *Sophist*." *GM* 32(1977), 555-570. The "greatest genera" of *Soph* are not metaphysical ideas of earlier dialogues. The "participation" of these genera in each other is to be understood from a linguistic or logical, rather than metaphysical, perspective. The Stranger's doctrine of genera means that they cannot be unified, self-predicative, separable, and stable.   [3207]

HEINAMAN, R. E. "Being in the *Sophist*." *AGPh* 65(1983), 1-17. Argues that "being" is used to mean "existence" in the arguments and not "being such and such."   [3208]

——. "Communion of Forms." *PAS* 83(1982-1983), 175-190. This concept is used in 259e5-6 to explain not the meaning of statements but whether or not they are true. It is a reiteration of the idea of participation of the Forms in individual things which P advanced in earlier dialogues.   [3209]

——. "Once More: Being in the *Sophist*." *AGPh* 68(1986), 121-126. Against Malcolm (#3225), defends position that "being" in this dialogue means "existence."   [3209a]

——. "Self-Predication in the *Sophist*." *Phron* 26(1981), 55-66. In spite of criticisms of his theory expressed in *Parm*, P continued to Attempts to show that P continued to accept the notion of self-predication of Forms in *Soph*.   [3210]

JOHNSON, P. A. "Keyt On *heteron* in the *Sophist*." *Phron* 23(1978) 151-157. Response to #3214 over the interpretation of 263 B11-13. If we say that something "is not *x*," do we imply that it is the opposite, or merely different from, *x*?   [3211]

JORDAN, R. W. "Plato's Task in the *Sophist*." *CQ* 34(1984), 113-129. P is trying to prove that whatever is not-being is actually being.   [3212]

KETCHUM, R. T. "Participation and Predication in the *Sophist* 251-260." *Phron* 23(1978), 42-62. Theory of Forms is same in *Soph* as in middle dialogues, though presented in different terms.   [3213]

KEYT, D. "Plato on Falsity: *Sophist* 263b," in #65, pp. 285-305. Examines P's account of falsity and different interpretations that have been offered. [3214]

————. "Plato's Paradox that the Immutable is Unknowable." *PhQ* 19(1969), 1-14. Discussion of recent interpretations of 248a-249b. Argues that P never acknowledged any respect in which a Form can suffer change but that he should have. [3215]

KLEIN, J. *Plato's Trilogy:* Theaetetus, *the* Sophist, *and the* Statesman. Univ. of Chicago Pr., 1977. The three dialogues are unified by question of relationships between sophist, philosopher, and statesman. Concludes that philosopher and statesman are of one kind and that sophist is neither a philosopher nor a statesman. Paraphrases and comments on the three dialogues. Emphasizes number symbolism. [3216]

KOSTMAN, J. P. "The Ambiguity of 'Partaking' in Plato's *Sophist*." *JHPh* 27(1989), 343-363. Examines 255c-e, and argues that the sense of P's partaking-terms switches from a "Pauline" to an "ordinary" usage at a definite point in the text, thus indicating that this switch is deliberate. [3217]

————. "False Logos and Not-Being in Plato's *Sophist*," in #1280, pp. 192-212. While P's reply to sophistic puzzle about false *logos* is philosophically interesting and successful, on deeper level, he is trying to solve a logical difficulty which is illusory. [3218]

LEE, E. N. "Plato on Negation and Non-Being in the *Sophist*." *PhR* 81(1972), 267-304. Analyzes 257c-258c, and tries to address question of what difference there is between the not-Being explicated by means of the Parts of Otherness and the not-Being explicated through Otherness by itself. [3219]

LOGAN, B. "Philosophy and Sophistry: Plato's *Sophist*." *Eidos* 6(1987), 7-19. P, in showing false discourse to be possible, develops a *symploke* or interweaving at the level of the forms and at the level of verbal discourse. [3220]

LOUBET, J. "Plato's *Sophist*: The Theory of Participation." *Dial*(PST) 18(1975), 14-19. Distinguishing between Form as essence and its participatory mode allows P to safeguard its integrity as a Form while also allowing for its presence in another. [3221]

MALCOLM, J. F. "Does Plato Revise his Ontology in *Sophist* 246c-249d?" *AGPh* 65(1983), 115-127. In presenting doctrine of Friends of Forms, P may be presenting ideas which he does not wholeheartedly endorse. He does not appear to be revising his ontology. [3222]

————. "On What is Not in Any Way in the *Sophist*." *CQ* 35(1985), 520-523. Reply to R. W. Jordan (#3212). [3223]

————. "Plato's Analysis of *to on* and *to me on* in the *Sophist*." *Phron* 12(1967), 130-146. Asserts that P does not distinguish existential sense of *einai* from predicative and identifying senses in *Soph*. [3224]

————. "Remarks on an Incomplete Rendering of Being in the *Sophist*." *AGPh* 67(1985), 162-165. Critique of argument that "being" means "existence." Reply to R. Heinaman (#3208) [3225]

McDOWELL, J. "Falsehood and Not-Being in Plato's *Sophist*," in #76, pp. 115-134. Takes dialogue's treatment of not-being as a sustained and organized assault on problem of how falsehood is characterized.   **[3226]**

McPHERRAN, M. L. "Plato's Reply to the 'Worst Difficulty' Argument of the *Parmenides*: *Sophist* 248a-249d." *AGPh* 68(1986), 233-252; also in #1267, pp. 227-246. P does offer a reply to the argument of *Parm* 133a-135a. Shows how that reply saves Theory of Forms.   **[3227]**

MOHR, R. "The Relation of Reason to Soul in the Platonic Cosmology: *Sophist* 248e-249c." *Apeir* 16(1982), 21-25. Passage cannot be cited to prove that P thinks every rational thing is a soul. It commits him only to weaker position that when reason is present in something, what it is in is a soul. Demiurge is not a soul.   **[3228]**

OSCANYAN, F. S. "On Six Definitions of the Sophist: *Sophist* 221c-231e." *PhFor* 4(1972-73), 241-259. The definitions of "Sophist" offered in this passage apply in turn to Gorgias, Protagoras, Hippias, Prodicus, Euthydemus, and Thrasymachus. But the last definition fits Socrates as well as Thrasymachus. This is why P found the method of division inadequate for reaching an acceptable definition of sophistry.   **[3229]**

OWEN, G. E. L. "Plato and Parmenides on the Timeless Present." *Monist* 50(1966), 317-340. Parmenides confuses domains of "statement" and "thing" by translating logical into ontological tenselessness. P, following Parmenides, derives split between timebound and timeless objects from distinction between tensed and non-tensed statements, but in *Soph* seems to recognize his mistake.   **[3230]**

———. "Plato on Not-Being," in #1290, pp. 223-267. Sees *Soph* as primarily an essay in problems of reference and predication and incomplete uses of verb "to be" associated with these. Argument neither contains nor compels any isolation of an existential verb.   **[3231]**

PELLETIER, F. J. "Incompatability in Plato's *Sophist*." *Dial*(Can) 14(1975), 143-146. Interpretation of the dialogue is simplified by translating *heteron* as "non-identical" before 257b as "incompatible" after that point.   **[3232]**

———. "Plato on Not-Being: Some Interpretations of the *Symploke Eidon* (259e) and Their Relation to Parmenides' Problem." *MidwStudPh* 8(1983), 35-66. Focuses on P's response to Parmenides, and in particular P's statement that his opponents cannot overcome his position because he has made allowance for "an interweaving of the forms with one another" and that it is this interweaving of forms that makes all discourse possible.   **[3233]**

PHILIP, J. A. "False Statement in the *Sophistes*." *TAPhA* 99(1968), 315-322. Re-examines P's analysis of false statement, showing steps of argument.   **[3234]**

———. "The *Megista Gene* of the *Sophistes*." *Phoenix* 23(1969), 89-103. The cosmological theory of *Tim*, with its ensouled cosmos, helps us to understand the logic of *Soph*, which is based on the concept of an ensouled *pantelos on*. The *Soph*'s five *megista gene* are equivalent of *Tim*'s three soul components and absolute motion and relative rest of soul. Demiurge is important in both dialogues.   **[3235]**

PIPPIN, R. B. "Negation and Not-Being in Wittgenstein's *Tractatus* and Plato's *Sophist*." *Kantstudien* 70(1979), 179-196. Examines both philosophers' general theory of language to find their solutions to problem of negation and false propositions. They illustrate the difference between "semantic" and "ontological" analyses. [3236]

PRIOR, W. J. "Plato's Analysis of Being and Not-Being in the *Sophist*." *SJPh* 18(1980), 199-211. Most scholars argue that P distinguishes various senses of verb *einai* ("to be"), but he seems to have only one meaning, "to participate in," in *Soph*. The dialogue does not betray changes in his metaphysics. [3237]

——. cf. #1909.

PRZELECKI, M. "On What There is Not." *Dial&Hum* 8(1981), 123-129. Analysis of problems of falsehood and non-being in *Soph* reveals that P is trying to deal with difficulties similar to those which modern logical semantics treats. His proposed solutions are also surprisingly modern. [3238]

RAY, A. C. *For Images: An Interpretation of Plato's* Sophist. Lanham, MD: Univ. Pr. of Amer., 1984. Takes the dialogue as P's defense of his doctrine of Forms. It can be classified as somewhat "conservative," maintaining theory of Forms espoused in middle dialogues but revealing some developments in P's thought, such as increased interest in sensible objects. [3239]

REAGAN, J. T. "Being and Nonbeing in Plato's *Sophist*." *ModSch* 42(1965), 305-314. Suggests that we can attach label "heroic realism" to P's philosophy and that P's rationalism cannot be called "naive." [3240]

REEVE, C. D. C. "Motion, Rest, and Dialectic in the *Sophist*." *AGPh* 67(1985), 47-64. Examines concepts of rest and motion and their relation to dialectic and Theory of Forms. [3241]

ROBERTS, J. "The Problem About Being in the *Sophist*." *HPhQ* 3(1986), 229-243. P does not try to distinguish among various senses of word "is." He attempts to answer Eleatic arguments by showing that Being is something different from anything normally meant by that word. [3242]

ROHATYN, D. A. "Bodunrin on Plato's *Sophist*." *SecOrd* 5(1976), 75-90. Review of Bodunrin's Ph.D. dissertation "Plato and his Contemporaries on the Possibility of False-hood," dealing with P's refutation of Eleaticism. [3243]

ROSEN, S. "Plato's Image of Images," in *The Limits of Analysis* (New York: Basic Books, 1980), pp. 156-175. Based on analysis of the paradigm of the dream of the whole at *Soph* 233c10 ff., originals cannot be seen except through images. Relation between original and image must be expressed mathematically and poetically. [3244]

——. *Plato's* Sophist. *The Drama of the Original and Image*. New Haven, CT: Yale Univ. Pr., 1983. Maintains that dialogue's dramatic structure is designed to emphasize difference between the philosophical and non-philosophical life-styles, but fails to distinguish them clearly because the Eleatic Stranger's Method of Division is inadequate for distinguishing an image from its original. [3245]

SAYRE, K. M. "Falsehood, Forms and Participation in the *Sophist*." *Nous* 4(1970), 81-91. Reviews P's investigation of true and false discourse in *Soph* and compares the conception of Forms which underlies that analysis with theory of Forms in *Phaedo* and *Rep*. [3246]

———. "*Sophist* 263b Revisited." *Mind* 85(1976), 581-586. Analysis of P's use of certain terms of opposition helps resolve apparent paradox in his formulation of truth and falsity of statements in the form "x is a" and "x is not a." [3247]

———. cf. #1796.

SCHIPPER, E. W. "Souls, Forms and False Statements in the *Sophist*." *PhQ* 15(1965), 240-242. Examines passages which raise questions about Turnbull's (1964) position on *Soph*'s account of false statements. Asks whether souls can be "named" or referred to by logos and whether souls "aspire to" the Forms. [3248]

SELIGMAN, P. *Being and Not-Being: An Introduction to Plato's* Sophist. The Hague: Nijhoff, 1974. Gives a critical interpretation of the central sections of *Sophist*. Takes the main point of the dialogue to be to show that being and non-being are interwoven, undercutting Parmenides' arguments. Non-being is actually difference. [3249]

SESONSKE, A. "To Make the Weaker Argument the Stronger." *JHPh* 6(1968), 217-231. This charge is basis of P's complaint against Sophists. Examines how it is developed in *Soph* and *Apol*. [3250]

STARR, D. E. "The Sixth Sophist: Comments on Frederick S. Oscanyan's 'On Six Definitions of the *Sophist*: *Sophist* 221e- 231e.'" *PhFor* 5(1974), 486-492. Reply to #3229. The last Sophist defined is S, not Thrasymachus. [3251]

SWINDLER, J. K. "Parmenides' Paradox." *RMeta* 33(1980), 727-744. Discusses views of several modern scholars on the problem of non-being and shows that P's solution is not linguistic but ontological. [3252]

THORP, J. "Forms, Concepts, and *to me on*." *RPhA* 2 #2(1984), 77-92. Reply to Y. LaFrance's reading (in French) of *Soph* 237b10-239a12. [3253]

TILGHMAN, B. R. "Parmenides, Plato, and Logical Atomism." *SJPh* 7(1969), 151-160. Parmenides' monism arises from his understanding of the meaning of names and sentences. Plato understood this better than modern critics do and rephrases Parmenides' theory in terms to logical atomism of Russell and Wittgenstein. [3254]

TREVASKIS, J. R. "The *Megista Gene* and the Vowel Analogy of Plato, *Sophist* 253." *Phron* 11(1966), 99-116. Investigates *gene* and whether they arc Forms. Examines if some new development in P's thought is taking place in this section. [3255]

VAN FRAASSEN, B. "Logical Structure in Plato's *Sophist*." *RMeta* 22(1969), 482-498. P's discussion of relations among Forms raises at least three problems for logical theory. Theories of modal logic are not adequate to solve them. The "relevant logic" described by Anderson and Belnap provides a better approach to solving at least one of P's problems. [3256]

VLASTOS, G. "An Ambiguity in the *Sophist*," in #1292, pp. 270-308. Investigates development in *Soph* in which P indicates that a Form may participate in another Form, e. g., at 256b where P indicates that Motion participates in Rest. **[3257]**

——. "On the Interpretation of *Sophist* 248d4-e4," in #1292, pp. 309-317. P endorses neither the claim, "when reality is acted upon, it is altered" nor "when reality is known, it is altered." **[3258]**

WEDIN, M. V. "Plato on What *Being* is Not." *Phil*(Athens) 10-11(1980-1981), 265-295. P's purpose here is not to refute views opposed to his but to elucidate his own. The three puzzles posed at *Soph* 243b-245e indicate that P did not take Being as a standard first-order predicate but as a second-order or formal concept. **[3259]**

WIGGINS, D. "Sentence Meaning, Negation, and Plato's Problem of Non-Being," in #1290, pp. 268-303. P's efforts to solve the problem of negation are not fully adequate but do contain the core of modern approaches to the problem. **[3260]**

Statesman

The dialogue is introduced as a continuation of the conversation begun in the *Soph* with the Eleatic Stranger, but this time the main subject is the identification of the statesman (Greek *politikos*, from which the dialogue is sometimes called the *Politicus*) and the Stranger conducts his investigation with the young S.

The Stranger guides young S through the method of collection and division in order to reach a definition of what a statesman is. They reach a preliminary definition of the statesman as the collective herder or shepherd of mankind, but then the Stranger introduces a myth to indicate the shortcomings of this definition. According to the myth, in an earlier era, the universe was governed by the divine ruler. But in the present era, the divine guardianship of men has ceased, and men have to fend for themselves now. Yet the definition of statesman arrived at previously as the shepherd of mankind was based on the idea of the divine ruler in an earlier era (275a).

Consequently, the Stranger suggests that they pursue how a human ruler should govern the polis. They tentatively conclude that the statesman is the tendance or nurture freely accepted by herds of free humans. But this definition is still only an outline sketch.

To illustrate more fully the stateman's art of dealing rightly with the free people he governs, the Stranger focuses on the art of weaving. He devotes much attention to separating the art of weaving from other arts, and weaving turns out to be that art of woolworking that produces a fabric by "the intertwining of warp and woof" (283b). Then as the weaver fashions a piece of clothing out of a number of threads, so, too, the statesman fashions a unified *polis* out of many different individuals and activities.

The Stranger then considers different forms of government, and he argues that the best form of government is one without laws. By virtue of his knowledge of the art of statesmanship, the statesman will govern in such a way that he can give each person his due with accuracy. In a government without laws, the statesman has the flexibility to adapt various measures to different individuals, and thereby develop more effectively the characters of his subjects. The problem with laws is that by their very nature, they are rigid and inflexible, and they fail to acknowledge the differences that arise in different cases. Consequently, a government of laws can perpetuate some very real injustices in the course of upholding the law.

The Stranger does concede that if no true statesman arises, then the next best kind of government is a government of laws. But it is only the government under the leadership of a genuine statesman that can bring together the disparate elements of the *polis* to form a true unity.

Early in the *Soph*, S indicated the difficulty in distinguishing the sophist, the statesman, and the philosopher (216c-217c). This comment has led some commentators to suppose that in addition to the *Soph* and the *Stsm*, there should also be a dialogue entitled the *Philosopher*. Other scholars have suggested that for P, the true statesman and the true philosopher are one and the same (thinking back to the *Rep*), and therefore there is no need for further discussion about who the true philosopher is. This point remains controversial.

BROWN, M. "Plato on Doubling the Cube: *Politicus* 266a-b," in #1277, pp. 43-60. At 266 we have a genuine Platonic text which refers directly to problem of doubling the cube. Later in *Soph* there are indications of P's complaints about one or more of the solutions to it.   [3261]

DAVIS, M. "The *Statesman* as a Political Dialogue." *AJPh* 88(1967), 319-331. Attempts to isolate and discuss those remarks in P's *Stsm* that comprise "a contribution to systematic political science." Discusses: 1) scope of rulership, 2) politics of transition, 3) legal framework, 4) bureaucratic apparatus, and 5) reactions of the public.   [3262]

DORTER, K. "Justice and Method in the *Statesman*," in #1283, pp. 105-122. The method of division is not meant as a replacement for Socratic dialectic, but rather as an introduction to such dialectic. By midway point in dialogue P abandons division in favor of a procedure which resembles more the earlier Socratic ways of inquiry.   [3263]

HITCHCOCK, D. L. "Professor Dorter on Justice and Method in the *Statesman*," in #1283, pp. 123-131. Challenges Dorter's interpretation (#1283) of *Stsm* that two kinds of division exist; sees his explanation for abandonment of division-by-bisection as implausible.   [3264]

KLEIN, S. "Plato's *Statesman* and the Nature of Business Leadership: An Analysis from an Ethical Point of View." *JBusEth* 7(1988), 283-294. P's paradigm for statesmanship, the "weaving" of temperate and courageous properties, provides the contemporary business ethics theorist with an aid for determining certain problems and solutions with regard to business leadership.   [3265]

MILLER, M. H., Jr. *The Philosopher in Plato's* Statesman. The Hague: Nijhoff, 1980. *Stsm* is a dialogue, not a formal treatise, and one must pay attention to dramatic elements. Focuses on P's philosophical aspiration for truth with his pedagogical desire to persuade others to share the aspiration.   [3266]

MOHR, R. D. "Disorderly Motion in the *Statesman*." *Phoenix* 35 (1981), 199-215; also in #2112, pp. 141-157. Analysis of *Stsm* myth indicates that P sees physical objects as moving erratically in and of themselves. They are the source of evil. The World-Soul sustains the order of the cosmos but does not cause motion. The Demiurge is the source of order in both the World-Soul and World-Body. **[3267]**

———. "The Formation of the Cosmos in the *Statesman* Myth." *Phoenix* 32(1978), 250-252. Compares *Stsm*'s creation myth with account in *Tim*, especially on the question of whether *Stsm*'s myth can be read literally because it contains two seemingly contradictory elements. **[3268]**

———. "Plato, *Statesman* 284c-d: An 'Argument from the Sciences.'" *Phron* 22(1977) 232-234. It is likely this passage is source of at least one proof for existence of Ideas which Ar in *Meta* telegraphically calls "the arguments from the sciences." **[3269]**

OSTWALD, M., ed. *Plato's* Statesman, trans. J. B. Skemp. Indianapolis: Bobbs-Merrill, 1979; rprt. A translation with an introduction by Ostwald. **[3270]**

OWEN, G. E. L. "Plato on the Undepictable," in #65, pp. 349-361. Examines P's treatment of Combining and Separating, and what P says about picturing itself and what can be pictured. **[3271]**

ROBINSON, T. M. "Demiurge and World Soul in Plato's *Politicus*." *AJPh* 88(1967), 57-66. *Stsm* incorporates into a single view the cosmology of *Tim* and *Phaedrus'* doctrine of soul to produce a Demiurge who models himself on perfection of Forms and insures that *nous* will ultimately triumph over *anoia*. **[3272]**

ROSEN, S. "Plato's Myth of the Reversed Cosmos." *RMeta* 33(1979), 59-85; also in #75, pp. 56-77. Interprets *Stsm* in terms of a close analysis of myth of reversed cosmos. Political life is separate from nature. Humans thus need some organizational principles to survive. Myths and the arts — philosophy itself — are an effort to supply an ordered framework. Suggests that mixture of precision and confusion in dialogue centers upon problem of relation between theory and productive practice, or alternatively, between physics and politics. **[3273]**

SCODEL, H. R. *Diaeresis and Myth in Plato's* Statesman. Goettingen, Ger.: Vandenhoeck & Ruprecht, 1987. Though it appears digressive, the dialogue uses the technique of division to counter Eleatic reputation for skill in refutation. The Stranger, who does not represent P, confutes himself by his own diaeresis. Though Socrates does not have a part in the dialogue, his elenchtic method is vindicated. **[3274]**

TEJERA, V. "Plato's *Politicus*: An Eleatic Sophist on Politics." *Ph&SocCrit* 5(1978), 83-104. Argues that P is putting a rhetorical sophist's brilliant mix of ideas about government on exhibit before the reader for his reflection. **[3275]**

VIDAL-NAQUET, P. "Plato's Myth of the Statesman: The Ambiguities Of the Golden Age and of History." *JHS* 98(1978), 132-141. Compares P's Golden Age myth to versions in earlier and later writers. P does not see the Golden Age as unmixed blessing. It is an apolitical time. **[3276]**

Symposium

This dialogue consists of a discussion at a banquet about the nature of love. Each of several guests discourses on the topic. S's contribution is to recount a conversation he had with a woman named Diotima, who had taught him that Love is not a god but a *daimon*, an intermediate power who transmits mankind's prayers to the gods and the gods' answers and commands to mankind. Love is desire of the beautiful and the good, S claims to have learned from her. Human beings begin by loving physical beauty in another person, then progress to love of intellect and from that level to see the connection among people. This leads to contemplation of the beauty of institutions such as the law and then the sciences. Ultimately the lover of beauty enjoys a kind of revelation or vision of universal beauty.

This dialogue has been called one of the "few masterpieces of human art which unveil and interpret something of the central mystery of life." Benjamin Jowett said, "If it be true that there are more things in the *Symposium* of Plato than any commentator has dreamed of, it is also true that many things have been imagined, which are not really to be found there."

ALEXANDER, T. M. "Eros and Poiesis in Plato's *Symposium*." *SwPhSt* 7(1982), 100-114. Discusses relation of Eros to *poiesis* (any activity which produces, creates, or makes), and relation of Eros to *mnemosyne*, memory lying in human soul which "links it to truth and which is stirred first and foremost by beauty." [3277]

ALLEN, A. "Plato's Proverbial Perversion." *Hermes* 102(1974), 506-507. P's corruption of proverb at *Symp* 174b is "gently ironic," but "monstrous metrically." [3278]

ALLEN, R. E. "A Note on the Elenchus of Agathon: *Symposium* 199c-201c." *Monist* 50(1966), 460-463. Examines two apparent inconsistencies between the accounts of *eros* in *Symp* and *Phaedrus*, and argues that inconsistencies are merely verbal. [3279]

ANTON, J. P. "The Secret of Plato's *Symposium*." *Diot* 2(1974), 27-47; also in *SJPh* 12(1974), 277-293. Takes a more realistic look at the image of S in the dialogue. His attempt to educate Alcibiades in ethics and politics failed because Alcibiades was an inadequate pupil and because S had not fully internalized what he claimed to have learned about eros from Diotima. [3280]

BEER, S. H. "Two Models of Public Opinion: Bacon's 'New Logic' and Diotima's 'Tale of Love'." *PolTheo* 2(1974), 163-180. Derives a model of public opinion from Diotima's speech in *Symp*. [3281]

BELFIORE, E. "Dialectic with the Reader in Plato's *Symposium*." *Maia* 36(1984), 137-149. The only "dialectic" in this "dialogue" is that which the reader is encouraged to engage in with the text. [3282]

BENJAMIN, W. "Socrates." *PhFor* 15(1983), 52-54. S's discussion of eros in this dialogue displays no sympathy with the human emotion. [3283]

CHEN, L. C. H. "Knowledge of Beauty in Plato's *Symposium*." *CQ* 33(1983), 66-74.

Knowledge can be acquired only when soul is separated from senses. Philosopher can reach such a state before death. **[3284]**

CLAY, D. "The Tragic and Comic Poet of the *Symposium*." *Arion* 2(1975), 238-261. Explores what comedy and tragedy have to do with one another, and how Socratic dialogue combines realms of appearance and reality. Also considers what the last argument of *Symp* has to do with its central argument: the praise of Eros. **[3285]**

COHEN, D. "Law, Society and Homosexuality in Classical Athens." *P&P* 117(1988), 3-21. Athenian attitudes toward homosexuality ranged from P's approval to Aristotle's view of it as a disease. **[3286]**

CORNFORD, F. M. "The Doctrine of Eros in Plato's *Symposium*," in #1291, pp. 119-131. Contrasts ascetic strain in *Phaedo* with theory of Eros developed in *Symp*. Discusses journey of ascent presented by Diotima. **[3287]**

COTTER, J. "*Epapothanein Teteleutekoti* (Plato, *Symp*. 180A)." *Glotta* 62(1984), 161-166. Based on comparison with *Phaedrus* this phrase seems to mean "to die beside and for one who is dead." **[3288]**

———. "The *Symposium*: Plato's Title and Intent," in #46, pp. 33-50. Title was deliberately chosen to arouse comic expectations and it is folly to search for some doctrinal concept at heart of work. **[3289]**

CUMMINGS, P. W. "Eros as Procreation in Beauty." *Apeir* 10 #2(1976), 23-28. Focuses on Diotima's definition of love; shows how love goes beyond egoism. **[3290]**

DE VRIES, G. J. "The Philosophaster's Softness." *Mnem* 22(1969), 230-232. Focusing on introduction, argues that we are to see Apollodorus not as a philosopher, but as a philosophaster. Apollodorus is devoted to Socrates, but he lacks all common sense as well as all philosophical understanding. Reply to #3317. **[3291]**

DORTER, K. "The Significance of the Speeches in Plato's *Symposium*." *Ph&Rh* 2(1969), 215-234. S's speech is a reply to each of the previous speeches, though not in successive order. The speeches progressed up a scale of the criteria of goodness, while S's criterion is the concept of eros. **[3292]**

DOVER, K. J. "Aristophanes' Speech in Plato's *Symposium*." *JHS* 85(1966), 41-50. P believes popular values were committed to the individual, the particular, and the familiar, and that such a morality is irreconciliable with practice of philosophy. **[3293]**

———. "The Date of Plato's *Symposium*." *Phron* 10(1965), 2-20. Internal evidence points to date of ca. 385/4. Yet occasion portrayed in *Symp* is Agathon's first theatrical victory, gained in 416. Compares dialogue's methods of argumentation with those of other dialogues from that period. **[3294]**

DUNCAN, R. "Plato's *Symposium*: The Cloven Eros." *SJPh* 15(1977), 277-290. Suggests that tragedy symbolizes the "Vertical Vector" of eros, while comedy is the "Horizontal Vector", and that the vertical vector is superior. **[3295]**

DYSON, M. "Immortality and Procreation in Plato's *Symposium*." *Antich* 20(1986), 59-

72. Study of 212a shows that philosophers may achieve immortality which is more meaningful than that attained by parents of biological offspring.   [3296]

EISNER, R. "A Case of Poetic Justice. Aristophanes' Speech in the *Symposium*." *CW* 72(1979), 417-418. P indulges in an ironically suitable, but relatively harmless, revenge against Aristophanes in speech he places in poet's mouth.   [3297]

ERDE, E. L. "Comedy and Tragedy and Philosophy in the *Symposium*: An Ethical Vision." *SwJPh* 7(1976), 161-167. *Symp* is a dramatic contest between S and first Agathon, who symbolizes tragedy, then Aristophanes, who symbolizes comedy. By claiming at the end that philosophy is the master of both tragedy and comedy, S shows that love is the subject of all three disciplines, but that only philosophy understands love correctly.   [3298]

EVANGELIOU, C. "Eros and Immortality in the *Symposium* of Plato." *Diot* 13(1985), 200-211. Some have claimed that P's view of immortality in *Symp* is somewhat skeptical. Diotima's arguments for Beauty, however, undergird the theory of Forms, on which P builds his argument for immortality. His position in *Symp* is not inconsistent with that in *Phaedo*.   [3299]

FOTI, V. "Eros, Freedom, and Constraint in Plato's *Symposium* and *Phaedrus*." *Auslegung* 5(1978), 66-100. In *Phaedrus*, duality of *eros* is seen as tension between freedom and constraint, while *Symp* reveals diverse aspects of erotic ambivalence but interprets them in terms of deepened, ontological understanding of freedom and constraint.   [3300]

GAGARIN, M. "Socrates' Hybris and Alcibiades' Failure." *Phoenix* 31(1977), 22-37. Attention is usually given to Alcibiades' praise for S, but his criticisms of his teacher should not be overlooked. He makes us aware of S's hybris, which contributes to his failure as a teacher.   [3301]

GALLAGHER, D. K. "In Praise of Pausanias: Dialectic in the Second Speech of Plato's *Symposium*." *Kinesis* 6(1974), 40-55. Pausanius the degenerate is also Pausanius the philosopher. His speech is as much a genuinely philosophical response to his predecessor, Phaedrus, as it is an apology for pederasty.   [3302]

GELVEN, M. "Eros and Projection: Plato and Heidegger." *SwJPh* 4 (1973), 125-136; also in *Thinking About Being*, ed. R. W. Shahan (Norman: Univ. of OK Pr., 1984), pp. 125-136. Sees Heidegger's theory of existential understanding as formally similar to P's theory of erotic ideality as found in *Phaedrus*, *Phaedo*, and *Symp*.   [3303]

GRODEN, S. Q., and BRENTLINGER, J. A. *The Symposium of Plato.* Amherst: Univ. of MA Pr., 1970. Translation with notes and essays.   [3304]

HALPERIN, D. M. "Platonic *Eros* and What Men Call Love." *AncPh* 5(1985), 161-204. Platonic *eros* is inadequate to task of explicating nature of love, but P never intended to put it to that use. Rather, P attempted and achieved an erotic theory that could account for the metaphysics of desire.   [3305]

HELD, G. F. "Parallels Between the Gilgamesh Epic and Plato's *Symposium*." *JNES* 42(1983), 133-141. Examines similarities in form and theme, especially in teleological views of nature. [3306]

IRIGARAY, L. "Sorcerer Love: A Reading of Plato's *Symposium*, Diotima's Speech." *Hypatia* 3(1989), 32-44. S attributes to Diotima two views of love: it is a mid-point between lovers which teaches immortality; it is a means to the human duty of procreation, and thus is a means to immortality. The two claims are incompatible. [3307]

KAHN, C. H. "Plato's Theory of Desire." *RMeta* 41(1987), 77-103. What P says about eros in *Symp* does not contradict his view in *Rep*. His theory of motivation compares favorably to Freudian exxplanations of desire. [3308]

KONSTAN, D. "Eryximachus' Speech in the *Symposium*." *Apeir* 16(1982), 40-46. Eryximachus' speech is not self-contradictory because he distinguishes between desire and harmony as two senses of *eros*. [3309]

LEVIN, S. "Diotima's Visit and Service to Athens." *GB* 3(1975), 223-240. P provides no definite evidence for or against historic existence of Diotima, but he has made his account of her visit historically and dramatically believable. [3310]

LEVY, D. "The Definition of Love in Plato's *Symposium*." *JHI* 40(1979), 285-291. Definition of love as "seeking for oneself to possess what is beautiful" is inadequate because it is is basically an egocentric conception. Love has, for P, no intrinsic value. But he is wrong to think that one can arrive at knowledge through love and possess the knowledge without love. [3311]

LOWENSTAM, S. "Aristophanes' Hiccups." *GRBS* 27(1986), 43-56. The playwright's hiccups are a linking device between various levels of the speeches in *Symp*. [3312]

——. "Paradoxes in Plato's *Symposium*." *Ramus* 14(1985), 85-104. S changes his answer to the question of who seeks the Good and Beautiful, but neither of his answers is really satisfactory. Problem is examined in the course of the dialogue on several levels: imagistic, mythical, philosophic. One of most important images is that of empty/full. Philosopher is always in a process of gaining and losing knowledge. [3313]

MARKUS, R. A. "The Dialectic of Eros in Plato's *Symposium*," in #1291, pp. 132-143. P's concept of love appealed to later Christian thinkers in part because what he was attempting to identify was the attitude underlying all types of love. [3314]

MILLER, J. F. "The Esoteric Unity of Plato's *Symposium*." *Apeir* 12 #2(1978), 19-25. The dialogue's unity is found in the idea that love is not a god but a Mediating Spirit, through which man finds God. [3315]

MITSCHERLING, J. "Plato's Agathon's Sophocles: Love and Necessity in the *Symposium*." *Phoenix* 39(1985), 375-377. Argues that P's substitution of "love" for "necessity" in a quotation from Sophocles' *Thyestes* attests to P's literary skill and knowledge of his contemporaries. [3316]

MOORE, J. D. "The Philosopher's Frenzy." *Mnem* 22(1969), 225-230. Association which S tries to make between *mantikos* ("prophetic") and *manikos* ("frenzied") in *Phaedrus* 244 may explain link in *Symp* between manic nature of Eros and Diotima's status as a prophetess. [3317]

——. cf. #2765.

MORAVCSIK, J. M. E. "Reason and Eros in the 'Ascent' Passage of the *Symposium*," in #41, pp. 283-302. Reason distinguishes common elements as one moves from one level to another in appreciation of Beauty. Comprehension of Form of Beauty happens suddenly at conclusion of process.   [3318]

MORTLEY, R. "Love in Plato and Plotinus." *Antich* 14(1980), 45-52. Idea of love as "lack" is a most important, yet often overlooked, ingredient in account of love which is given by P and Plotinus.   [3319]

NEHAMAS, A., and **WOODRUFF, P.** *Plato:* Symposium. Indianapolis: Hackett, 1989. New translation with introductory essay and notes.   [3320]

NEUMANN, H. "Diotima's Concept of Love." *AJPh* 86(1965), 33-59. Diotima does not identify Beautiful and Good, and her view of soul's immortality does not accord with S's. It is unclear whether her speech or S's represents P's view.   [3321]

——. "On the Comedy of Plato's Aristophanes." *AJPh* 87(1966), 420-426. Socratic element in Aristophanes' speech must have appeared Socratic to Diotima.   [3322]

——. "On the Madness of Plato's Apollodorus." *TAPhA* 96(1965), 283-289. Apollodorus' madness is his love of philosophy and of S as best practitioner of it.   [3323]

NUSSBAUM, M. C. "The Speech of Alcibiades: A Reading of Plato's *Symposium*." *Ph&Lit* 3(1979), 131-172. Study of entire dialogue shows that P presents a view of the value of love of one unique person for another and also gives us a reason to reject this view in favor of S's view of love.   [3324]

NYE, A. "The Hidden Host: Irigaray and Diotima at Plato's *Symposium*." *Hypatia* 3(1989), 45-61. Understood in historical context, Diotima emerges as hidden host of the banquet who speaks "for a pre-Socratic world view against which classical Greek thought asserted itself."   [3325]

O'BRIEN, M. J. "'Becoming Immortal' in Plato's *Symposium*." *PBACAPh* 2(1986), 185-206. Diotima's statement about immortality at end of *Symp* probably refers to blessedness achieved through a life devoted to philosophy. It does not imply immortality of soul, though it is not inconsistent with it.   [3326]

PENWILL, J. L. "Men in Love. Aspects of Plato's *Symposium*." *Ramus* 7(1978), 143-175. Comparison of the characters' views on love with their actions indicates considerable inconsistency.   [3327]

PLASS, P. C. "Plato's Pregnant Lover." *SO* 53(1978), 47-55. Diotima can describe a male lover as "pregnant" because the more important distinction is mind/body, not male/female. Intellectual reproduction is analogous to biological.   [3328]

PLOCHMAN, G. K. "Interpreting Plato's *Symposium*." *ModSch* 48(1970), 25-43. Discusses strengths and shortcomings of S. Rosen's book on *Symp* (#3333), and expands on several points and criticisms.   [3329]

——. "Supporting Themes in the *Symposium*," in #41, pp. 328-344. P supplies dozens of clues to his double intention to set forth both a doctrine and an embodiment of that doctrine — a "fusion" of philosophy and life. [3330]

PRICE, A. W. "Loving Persons Platonically." *Phron* 26(1981), 25-34. "Platonic" is not egocentric or overly spiritualized. The body participates in the lovers' progress toward mental union. [3331]

ROOCHNIK, D. L. "The Erotics of Philosophical Discourse." *HPhQ* 4(1987), 117-129. S's statement in the *Symp* that he understands "nothing other than things having to do with eros" is made clearer by examining P's concept of philosophical discourse and the close connection which he posits between *eros* and *logos*. [3332]

ROSEN, S. *Plato's* Symposium. New Haven, CT: Yale Univ. Pr., 1968. Detailed discussion of problems, issues, themes, and *dramatis personae*, with special emphasis on fundamental role of dramatic form as an essential part of the argument itself. [3333]

——. "Socrates as Concealed Lover," in #46, pp. 163-177. Contends that concealed lover in first speech is not merely a contingent or totally playful moment on way to more important things in the dialogue. Philosophical nature must combine natures of lover and non-lover. [3334]

SANTAS, G. *Plato and Freud: Two Theories of Love.* Oxford: Blackwell, 1988. Defines questions to be asked to study the topic; examines linguistic background of P's concept of love. Chapters on P look at his theory of eros, friendship, and love within the family. Two chapters discuss Freud and the last chapter compares the two. [3335]

——. "Plato on Love, Beauty, and the Good," in #54, pp. 33-68. P's view can be reconstructed in four stages, forming a ladder of eros. Soul-eros ranks higher. One element of love is the desire for something which one lacks. [3336]

SAXONHOUSE, A. W. "Eros and the Female in Greek Political Thought: An Interpretation of Plato's *Symposium*." *PolTheo* 12(1984), 5-28. *Symp* is used as a paradigm to show how an ancient work can be read differently if the role of women in ancient Greece is properly understood. [3337]

——. "The Net of Hephaestus: Aristophanes' Speech in Plato's *Symposium*." *Interp* 13(1985), 15-32. Discusses net of Hephaestus in Aristophanes' speech where two who need each other are bound together as in politics. [3338]

SCHEIN, S. L. "Alcibiades and the Politics of Misguided Love in Plato's *Symposium*." *Theta Pi* 3(1974), 158-167. Alcibiades represents Athens' imperial democrats, whom P thoroughly despised. [3339]

SIDER, D. "Plato's *Symposium* as Dionysian Festival." *QUCC* 33(1980), 41-56. By setting the scene of the *Symp* during the festival of Dionysus P emphasizes the dialogue's dramatic character. S, like a dramatist, emerges victorious. Several participants in the dialogue are directly connected with various aspects of the Dionysian festival. [3340]

SKEMP, J. B. "The Philosopher's Frenzy." *Mnem* 23(1970), 302-304. Reply to de Vries (#3291). [3341]

SOBLE, A. "Love is not Beautiful: *Symposium* 200c - 201e." *Apeir* 19(1985), 43-52. Examines S's argument that love is not beautiful and not lovable, and suggests that the question of to what extent sexuality can be liberated without undermining social and political cohesion is raised in the dialogue.   **[3342]**

SOLMSEN, F. "Parmenides and the Description of Perfect Beauty in Plato's *Symposium*." *AJPh* 92(1971), 62-70. Compares historic Parmenides' description of Being with account of true Beauty attributed to him in *Symp* 210c2 ff. Eleatic influences are apparent early in Plato's development.   **[3343]**

SPEARRITT, P. "Love Among the Platonists." *DR* 92(1974), 92-101. *Symp* defines love as desire mediating between God and humans. God desires to communicate himself to man, while man fulfills his desire by contemplating truth, beauty, and goodness. Philosopher is person in whom this desire is most fully realized.   **[3344]**

SPRAGUE, R. K. "*Symposium* 211a and Parmenides' Frag. 8." *CPh* 66(1971), 261. Notes similarities in descriptions of Being given by Plato and Parmenides.   **[3345]**

THESLEFF, H. "The Interrelation and Date of the *Symposia* of Plato and Xenophon." *BICS* 25(1978), 157-170. Xenophon probably wrote a short, early version of his work, which influenced P's composition. P's *Symp* in turn influenced Xenophon's final version.   **[3346]**

THOMPSON, W. N. "The *Symposium*: A Neglected Source for Plato's Ideas on Rhetoric." *SouthSpComJ* 37(1972), 219-232; also in #2081, pp. 325-338. Speeches in *Symp* provide verification for what P says about rhetoric in other dialogues. They affirm his insistence on knowing the truth. The Socrates-Diotima speech is best example available of P's ideal speech.   **[3347]**

WARNER, M. "Love, Self, and Plato's *Symposium*." *PhQ* 29(1979), 329-339. Discusses concepts of "love" and "self" as construed by P, Christianity, and Hume. S's speech in *Symp* assumes that someone is loved for his character, not for any sort of metaphysical self.   **[3348]**

WHITE, F. C. "Love and Beauty in Plato's *Symposium*." *JHS* 109(1989), 149-157. Argues that the Form of Beauty is not the ultimate object of love, nor is the Form of Beauty identical with the Form of the Good.   **[3349]**

WOLZ, H. G. "Philosophy as Drama: An Approach to Plato's *Symposium*." *Ph&PhenRes* 30(1970), 323-353. By paying attention to dramatic context, we see that the varieties of Eros discussed in the speeches are transformed by Diotima, who moves from love of a particular beautiful thing to Beauty as an absolute.   **[3350]**

Theaetetus

The dialogue opens with a meeting between Euclides and Terpsion, who are lamenting the grievous wounds suffered in battle and the sickness suffered by Theaetetus. Euclides then recalls the conversation between S, Theodorus (an old man and prominent mathematician), and Theaetetus (a youth at the time and a student of Theodorus). According to Euclides, S mentioned the remarkable promise of Theaetetus. When asked to repeat the conversation, Euclides notes that he has written the conversation down, and he gives his writings to Terpsion (and to us) to read.

Upon meeting Theaetetus, S guides the conversation to the central topic of the dialogue: what is knowledge? In response, Theaetetus provides several examples of knowledge: geometry, arithmetic, astronomy, harmonics, as well as the knowledge exhibited by various craftsmen. S responds by saying that he is not looking for the objects of knowledge, but for the nature of knowledge itself. Theaetetus confesses that while he has often struggled with this question, he has been unable to develop a satisfactory answer.

At this point, S introduces his famous description of himself as a "midwife." He himself is barren of knowledge, but he can assist others in "giving birth" to knowledge. Thus encouraged by S, Theaetetus puts forward his definition that knowledge is perception.

S then begins the exercise of his midwifery by showing that this definition is inadequate. Theaetetus tries two other definitions: knowledge is true opinion and knowledge is true opinion with a rational explanation. These two attempted definitions also fail, and the dialogue ends inconclusively regarding the nature of knowledge. Yet S maintains that the argument serves the two of them well, for at least they do not now think they know what they do not know.

The inconclusive nature of the dialogue has engendered substantial controversy. Some commentators have argued that P intends to show the impossibility of gaining knowledge through perception alone. Knowledge for P can be only of the transcendent, divine Forms, and apprehension of these Forms cannot be gained through sensory perception. Other commentators have argued that this dialogue indicates a rethinking on P's part regarding the nature of knowledge and the role of the Forms in acquiring knowledge.

ACKRILL, J. "Plato on False Belief: *Theaetetus* 187-200." *Monist* 50(1966), 383-402. In earlier sections, P argues that there cannot be false beliefs correctly expressible in sentences like "Beauty is ugly." Examines wax tablet section and P's analysis of ordinary misidentification statements. In aviary section, P tries to explain possibility of purely intellectual error, but fails. [3351]

ANDERSON, R. "The Theory of Perception in Plato's *Theaetetus*," in #1277, pp. 61-81. Investigates whether treatment of perception provides justification of P's critique of perceptual realm in divided line analogy of *Rep.* [3352]

ANGENE, L. E. "False Judgment in *Theaetetus*." *PhilStud* 33(1978), 351-365. P is unable to explain how false judgments can be in the mind, in part because his understanding of what it means to have an object in mind is inadequate. [3353]

ARTHUR, E. P. "Plato, *Theaetetus* 171A." *Mnem* 35(1982), 335-337. S's attempted refutation of Protagoras' relativism is unsuccessful. [3354]

BARKER, A. "The Digression in the *Theaetetus*." *JHPh* 14(1976), 457-462. Digression involving comparison of non-philosopher to philosopher does have relevance to general argument. It introduces subject of universals. [3355]

BARNES, J. "Socrates and the Jury, Part II." *PAS* suppl. 54(1980), 193-206. Response to Burnyeat (#3371) which discusses two paradoxes found at *Theaet* 201b, and argues that neither paradox is particularly puzzling for P or for us.   **[3356]**

BECK, R. H. "Plato's View on Teaching." *EducTheor* 35(1985), 119-134. *Theaet*, not *Meno*, is place to look for P's theory of education.   **[3357]**

BEDU-ADDO, J. T. "Plato on the Object of Knowledge: *Theaetetus* 185eff," in #3809, pp. 301-311. Reviews two different kinds of interpretations of the argument, and suggests that they are not as irreconcilable as they might at first appear. Tries to show proper appreciation of P's conception of nature of philosophical writing.   **[3358]**

BERGER, H. "Plato's Flying Philosopher." *PhFor* 13(1982), 385-407. If P's portrait of S in dialogues illustrates right way to do and live philosophy, then S's portrait of philosopher in *Theaet* and *Rep* must illustrate a wrong way.   **[3359]**

BIERMAN, A. K. "Socratic Humour: Understanding the Most Important Philosophical Argument." *Apeir* 5 #2(1971), 23-42. The laughter provoked in *Theaet* 146c7-147c1 by recognition of Theaetetus' mistake reveals the power of philosophy on the young, which is S's most important argument for the discipline.   **[3360]**

BOGEN, J. "Comments on Lewis," in #1280, pp. 150-157. Examines Lewis' treatment of first paradox (#3399) and argues, contrary to Lewis, that if P had assumed that epistemic contexts are "transparent" (i. e., that substitution of identicals does not alter their truth value), his position would have been inconsistent.   **[3361]**

BOLOTIN, D. "The *Theaetetus* and the Possibility of False Opinion." *Interp* 15(1987), 179-193. Dialogue points up essential similarity between Theaetetus' desire for pure knowledge and Protagoras' relativism.   **[3362]**

BONDESON, W. B. "The Dream of Socrates and the Conclusion of the *Theaetetus*." *Apeir* 3(1969), 1-13. The "dream" passage is interpreted on the basis of the meaning of *logos* and the nature of logical subjects, propositions, and definitions.   **[3363]**

——. "Perception, True Opinion and Knowledge in Plato's *Theaetetus*." *Phron* 14(1969), 111-122. *Theaet* 184b-200d is crucial to understanding the dialogue and argument of *Soph*. P asserts that *episteme* is propositional and distinguishes its objects from those of opinion.   **[3364]**

BOSTOCK, D. *Plato's* Theaetetus. New York: Clarendon Pr., 1988. Full-length study which examines each argument in detail. Discusses relation of dialogue to other dialogues. Designed for those who do not know Greek.   **[3365]**

BROWN, M. "*Theaetetus*: Knowledge as Continued Learning." *JHPh* 7(1969), 359-379. Theaetetus' mathematical method, which takes progress toward a result as equivalent to the result, is similar to S's dialectical method.   **[3366]**

BURNYEAT, M. F. "The Material and Sources of Plato's Dream." *Phron* 15(1970), 101-122. Several reasons are advanced for holding that *Theaet* 201c ff. is original with P. Antisthenes is a particularly unlikely source.   **[3367]**

——. "The Philosophical Sense of *Theaetetus'* Mathematics." *Isis* 69(1978), 489-513. Story told in 147c7-148d8 seems to have historical validity and helps us to understand origins of mathematics. **[3368]**

——. "Plato on the Grammar of Perceiving." *CQ* 26(1976), 29-51. *Theaet* 184c-e argues for a unified sense organ of perception. Greek word for "through" best describes how perception works through this organ. **[3369]**

——. "Protagoras and Self-Refutation in Plato's *Theaetetus*." *PhR* 85(1976), 172-195. *Theaet* 170a-171d makes Protagoras' claim (that a judgment is true for the person whose judgment it is) self-refuting by interpreting it to mean that such judgments are true in a person's world. If one does not accept Protagoras' theory, it does not hold true in his world. **[3370]**

——. "Socrates and the Jury." *PAS* supp. 54 (1980), 173-192. Finds three paradoxes in P's argument at *Theaet* 200d-201c that knowledge is not true belief, and argues that P's epistemology suggests a contrast between knowledge as justified true belief and knowledge as systematic understanding. **[3371]**

CENTORE, F. F. "Atomism and Plato's *Theaetetus*." *PhFor* 5(1974), 475-485. P was indeed referring to the atomists when he discussed how knowledge might be explained by a build-up of elements on the perceptual level. **[3372]**

COBB-STEVENS, V. "Perception, Appearance and *Kinesis*: The Secret Doctrine in Plato's *Theaetetus*," in #1267, pp. 247-265. S actually refutes two doctrines of flux in the early part of the dialogue. He then suggests that Protagoras, whose views have been under consideration, held a doctrine which he propounded only to his intimate disciples, a doctrine with an ontological, not merely epistemological, basis. **[3373]**

COLE, A. T. "The Apology of Protagoras." *YCS* 21(1966), 101-118. In *Theaet* 167a-168c S summarizes Protagoras' position and, while restating it, tacitly assumes that good and bad have an objective character. **[3374]**

COOPER, J. M. "Plato on Sense Perception and Knowledge: *Theaetetus* 184-186." *Phron* 15(1970) 123-146. Challenges interpretations by Cornford (#3376) and others. Offers an interpretation of P's theory of sense perception that emphasizes distinction between the contribution of the senses and that of the mind. **[3375]**

CORNFORD, F. M. *Plato's Theory of Knowledge (The* Theaetetus *and the* Sophist *of Plato)*. Indianapolis: Bobbs-Merrill Pr., 1978; rprt. Translation, commentary. **[3376]**

DeMOSS, D. J. "*Episteme* as *Doxa* in the *Theaetetus*," in #44, pp. 33-54. "Knowledge" in the dialogue seems to be "true opinion." **[3377]**

DESJARDINS, R. "The Horns of Dilemma: Dreaming and Waking Vision in the *Theaetetus*." *AncPh* 1(1981), 109-126. Attempts to make sense of S's Dream and its refutation, and argues that it provides the clue for finally understanding "knowledge" and *logos*. **[3378]**

DOULL, J. A. " A Commentary on Plato's *Theaetetus*." *Dion* 1(1977), 5-47. Overview of dialogue's theme and structure help us see that neither sense perception nor belief is knowledge. This realization prepares us for the next level of inquiry.   [3379]

FINE, G. "False Belief in the *Theaetetus*." *Phron* 24(1979), 70-80. P rejects a view of knowledge in which one has either complete knowledge or complete ignorance of something. This concept of knowledge is the basis of Theaetetus' definition of knowledge as true belief and generates the paradoxes of false belief which appear in the dialogue.   [3380]

――――. "Knowledge and Logos in the *Theaetetus*." *PhR* 88(1979), 366-397. Knowing an object means being able to produce a true account of it, which requires knowing any objects referred to in the account. P manages to avoid the circular argument and the regress which could potentially arise from this argument.   [3381]

――――. "Plato on Perception: A Reply to Professor Turnbull, 'Becoming and Intelligibility'." *OSAP* Suppl. (1988), 15-28. Reply to #3526. Maintains P is not committed to "major features" of theory of perception presented in *Theaet* 150ff.   [3382]

GALLIGAN, E. M. "Logos in the *Theaetetus* and the *Sophist*," in #42, pp. 264-278. Examines theory of S's dream in *Theaet* about knowability of parts and complexes and its reification, and then from vantage point of *Soph*, explores whether and how P changes theory's view of *logos*, and how he deals with dilemma that refutes theory.   [3383]

GLIDDEN, D. K. "Protagorean Obliquity." *HPhQ* 5(1988), 321-340. Protagoras' relativism was probably not put forth as a serious philosophical stance. P's reaction to it holds good for modern philosophies, such as anti-realism, which take a similar approach.   [3384]

HADEN, J. "Did Plato Refute Protagoras?" *HPhQ* 1(1984), 223-240. Study based on James' psychological principles shows that P in *Theaet* did in fact refute Protagoreas' arguments for relativism.   [3385]

HAHN, R. "Knowledge and Death in Plato's *Theaetetus*." *SwPhSt* 6(1981), 82-87. Argues that theory of knowledge must have its roots in study of forgetfulness, or in what "not-knowing" is and how it is possible. This forgetfulness is inextricably tied to problem of "death."   [3386]

HARING, E. S. "The *Theaetetus* Ends Well." *RMeta* 35(1982), 509-528. Most critics hold *Theaet* ends with S's failure to show *episteme* is "true opinion with *logos*." But dialogue has been concerned with eliminating things that are not *episteme*. Theaetetus himself seems to have sure mathematical knowledge, a step in progress toward knowledge.   [3387]

HARRISON, J. C. "Plato's Prologue: *Theaetetus* 142a-143c." *TulStudPh* 27(1978), 103-123. Examines prologue to show how it anticipates dialogue's major themes.   [3388]

HICKEN, W. F. "Knowledge and Forms in Plato's *Theaetetus*," in #1809, pp. 185-198. Attempts to interpret dialogue's last pages in which Socrates presents four versions of a final attempt to define knowledge as true opinion accompanied by logos and rejects them all. Dialogue thus reflects a genuine state of *aporia*.   [3389]

HOLLAND, A. J. "An Argument in Plato's *Theaetetus*, 184-186." *PhQ* 23(1973), 97-116.

P elaborates on arguments from *Rep* against empiricism. His emphasis is different, but he does not abandon position that knowledge through senses is impossible. [3390]

KANAYAMA, Y. "Perceiving, Considering, and Attaining Being (*Theaetetus* 184-186)." *OSAP* 5(1987), 29-81. Examines two questions regarding P's refutation of perception's claim to be knowledge by pointing out its inability to attain being: (1) what is P's idea of perception, and (2) what is meant by "attain being"? [3391]

KLEIN, J. *Greek Mathematical Thought and the Origins of Algebra*, transl. E. Brann. Cambridge, MA: MIT Pr., 1968. Includes discussions of "Logistic and Arithmetic in Plato" and "The Ontological Conception of the Arithmoi in Plato." [3392]

——. cf. #3216.

KRAMER, S. "Education and Digressions in Plato's *Theaetetus*." *EducTheor* 26(1976), 388-394. Presents two contrasting theories of education in dialogue: that of the Socratic midwife and that of the Sophist. [3393]

LANDRY, F. "Fallacy, What Fallacy? *Theaetetus* and the Instances of Knowledge." *Eidos* 4(1985), 135-148. S does not commit fallacy of assuming, as logician P. Geach suggests, either that if one knows that one is correctly predicating a given term 'T,' one must know what it is to be T, or that it is of no use to try to specify meaning of 'T' by giving examples of things that are T. [3394]

LEE, E. N. "'Hoist with His own Petard': Ironic and Comic Elements in Plato's Critique of Protagoras," in #65, pp. 225-261. Examines dramatic structure and ironic dimension of P's arguments against Protagoras. [3395]

LESHER, J. H. "*Gnosis* and *Episteme* in Socrates' Dream in the *Theaetetus*." *JHS* 89(1969), 72-78. P attempts to separate two distinct senses of the comprehensive Greek term for knowledge, *eidenai*, reserving *gnosis* for "knowledge by acquaintance" and employing *episteme* for "intellectual knowledge." [3396]

LEWIS, F. A. "Foul Play in Plato's Aviary: *Theaetetus* 195b ff.," in #65, pp. 262-284. Examines P's efforts to explain false belief in "Aviary theory." [3397]

——. "Knowledge and the Eye-Witness: Plato, *Theaetetus* 201a-c." *CanJPh* 11(1981), 185-197. For P, eyewitnessing has no special role in our knowledge of empirical fact. Also shows that for P, there is an art dedicated to getting beliefs which we suppose can be true even where full knowledge is not available. [3398]

——. "Two Paradoxes in the *Theaetetus*," in #1280, pp. 123-149. Examines first paradox at 188a-c which claims to show quite simply that there can be no false belief. Examines second paradox at 189b that false belief be considered "a sort of allodoxia," a "taking one thing for another." [3399]

MAGUIRE, J. P. "Protagoras ... or Plato?" *Phron* 18(1973), 115-138. Protagoras' two formulae about appearances and man-measure are used by Plato as a bridge from Protagoras' subjectivism to Plato's objectivism. [3400]

MANSFELD, J. "Man the Measure and Sense-Perception." *Theta Pi* 1(1972), 128-139.

Theaet 151e-187a confuses a Protagorean doctrine of sense perception with a theory of how judgments are made.   **[3401]**

——. "Notes on Some Passages in Plato's *Theaetetus* and in the 'Anonymous Commentary'," in #83, pp. 108-114. *Theaet* 146c3-147c6 suggests that P is no longer happy with definition of knowledge as dependent on nature of its objects. He is now interested in propositional aspects of knowledge. Also discusses implications of the "Anonymous Commentary" for understanding the mathematical discussion in 147c7-148b4.   **[3402]**

MARA, G. M. "Socrates and Liberal Toleration." *PolTheo* 16(1988), 468-495. S's truths are not "dogmatic assertions" but rather they help one to learn and improve.   **[3403]**

MATTHEN, M. "Perception, Relativism, and Truth: Reflections on Plato's *Theaetetus* 152-160." *Dial*(Can) 24(1985), 33-58. Examines ontological structure of theory attributed to Protagoras. It is actually relativistic.   **[3404]**

MATTHEWS, G.B. "A Puzzle in Plato: *Theaetetus* 189b-190e," in *Philosophical Analysis*, ed. Austin, D. F. (Norwell Kluwer 1988), pp. 3-15. Explores puzzle of how it is possible to believe falsely of two different things that appear the same, and discusses significance of the puzzle for P.   **[3405]**

McDOWELL, J. "Identity Mistakes: Plato and the Logical Atomists." *PAS* 70(1969-70), 181-196. At 188a-c S sketches an argument which purports to prove that there can be no false judgments.   **[3406]**

——. *Plato's* Theaetetus. Oxford: Clarendon Pr., 1973. Translation with notes for non-specialist.   **[3407]**

MILLS, K. W. "Plato and the Instant." *PAS* Suppl. 48(1974), 81-96. *Theaet* contains no evidence either that P accepted thesis that moving "gets done" at instants, or that this theory was of interest to him, or that he had even heard of it.   **[3408]**

MODRAK, D. K. "Perception and Judgment in the *Theaetetus*." *Phron* 26(1981), 35-54. Aims to elucidate P's conception of perception. Argues that simple judgments about sensible qualities are made through perception.   **[3409]**

MORROW, G. R. "Plato and the Mathematicians: An Interpretation of Socrates' Dream in the *Theaetetus* (201e-206c)." *PhR* 79(1970), 309-333. S's dream puts in generalized form the difficulty P sees in mathematician's procedure of hypothesis, i. e., of positing undemonstrated first principles as starting points of demonstration.   **[3410]**

NEWMAN, J. "The Recoil Argument." *Apeir* 16(1982), 47-52. Analysis and evaluation of P's argument at *Theaet* 170e-171c that Protagoras' epistemological relativism is self-defeating.   **[3411]**

OSKENBERG, R. A. "A Speculative Note on Some Dramatic Elements in the *Theaetetus*." *Phron* 17(1972), 227-238. Investigates why S calls Theaetetus' account (knowledge is true opinion *meta logou*) a dream, and why S calls his own account a dream. What is point of Theaetetus being unable to formulate the theory though he is able to recognize S's dream as the same theory?   **[3412]**

O'TOOLE, E. J. "Forms and Knowledge in the *Theaetetus*." *PhilStud* (Ireland) 19(1970), 102-118. Dialogue is conceived as attack on Heraclitus' metaphysics and on all empiricisms derived therefrom, and thus it cannot give full and adequate details of P's "theory of knowledge." **[3413]**

ROBINSON, R. "Forms and Error in Plato's *Theaetetus*," in #74, pp. 39-73. No certain reference to the Forms or to theory of recollection can be discerned in *Theaet* because Forms do not pertain to the subject of the dialogue, which is the essence of knowledge. P's discussion of error in the dialogue is weakened by his basic assumption that thinking is a matter of sensing without organs. **[3414]**

RORTY, A. O. "A Speculative Note on Some Dramatic Elements in the *Theaetetus*." *Phron* 17(1972), 227-238. Investigates how certain philosophic themes are dramatically presented: 1) can something be simultaneously known and not known? 2) are objects of knowledge the same as those of opinion? 3) does knowing entail knowing that one knows? 4) can things that appear to be different nevertheless be known by the same *logos*. **[3415]**

ROSEN, S. "Socrates' Dream," in *Limits of Analysis* (New York: Basic Books, 1980), pp. 120-129. S's discussion of the alphabet as elements is weakened by the fact that he moves from letters to syllables to sentences, omitting words, which are the crucial point of intersection between elements and statements. **[3416]**

ROWE, C. J., et al. "Knowledge, Perception, and Memory: *Theaetetus* 166b." *CQ* 32(1982), 304-306. In this passage P maintains that memory can be a kind of knowing because of its similarity to visual perception. **[3417]**

RUDEBUSCH, G. "Plato on Sense and Reference." *Mind* 94(1985), 526-537. Frege's strategy for solving a puzzle about false belief is one S considers and rejects. **[3418]**

SCHIPPER, E. W. "Is Plato an Idealist?" *StudGen* 24(1971), 583-597. Interpreting P as an idealist solves problem of how man's thought, expressed in his concepts and theories, can be about the existing world. **[3419]**

SHEA, J. "Judgment and Perception in *Theaetetus* 184-186." *JHPh* 23(1985), 1-14. P does not distinguish two sorts of judgment and truth; perception cannot make any judgment. **[3420]**

STRAMEL, J. S. "A New Verdict on the 'Jury Passage': *Theaetetus* 201a-c." *AncPh* 9(1989), 1-14. S's refutation of the argument that knowledge is true judgment rests on the assumptions that a juror was not an eyewitness and cannot rely on the biased testimony of litigants to gain true knowledge. The argument is valid and is consistent with other statements of the interlocutors and with P's epistemology. **[3421]**

TIGNER, S. S. "The Exquisite Argument at *Theaetetus* 171A." *Mnem* 24(1971), 366-369. There is no need to emend the passage. Protagoras' subjectivism makes it impossible for them to refute his arguments, but it also defeats him as well. **[3422]**

TURNBULL, R. G. "Response to Professor Fine's Critique of 'Becoming and Intelligibility'." *OSAP* Suppl. (1988), 29-36. In response to Fine (#3382), states P's mature account of perception. **[3423]**

WATANABE, K. "The *Theaetetus* on Letters and Knowledge." *Phron* 32(1987), 143-165. Develops a new interpretation of 201d-202c which answers question of how we move from true belief to knowledge.   **[3424]**

WATERLOW, S. "Protagoras and Inconsistency: *Theaetetus* 171a6-c7." *AGPh* 59(1977), 19-36. Inconsistencies in passage arise from Protagoras, not from Plato.   **[3425]**

WAYMACK, M. H. "The *Theaetetus* 172c-177c: A Reading of the Philosopher in Court." *SJPh* 23(1985), 481-489. Digression, in which P argues that philosopher is between brute beasts and gods, is misunderstood.   **[3426]**

WENGERT, R. G. "The Paradox of the Midwife." *HPhQ* 5(1988), 3-10. Examines paradox in which S proclaims himself an intellectual midwife while P inserts messages of his own which denounce S's midwifery.   **[3427]**

WHEELER, S. C. "The Conclusion of the *Theaetetus*." *HPhQ* 1(1984), 355-368. Arguments about knowledge which appear somewhat strange arise from doctrines of P's which can be defended. Because it is one of the foundational principles of the world, knowledge is total knowledge. Because physical things are not stable, real knowledge cannot be about them but must focus on the Forms.   **[3428]**

WHITE, F. C. "'*Hos episteme ousa.*' A Passage of Some Elegance in the *Theaetetus*." *Phron* 17(1972), 219-226. In 151e-152e S appears to claim that perception is infallible because it is knowledge. Refutes this interpretation of S's statement. The phrase *hos episteme ousa* should be deleted from the text.   **[3429]**

———. "The Physical World in the *Theaetetus*." *PhilPapers* 3(1974), 1-16. Many modern philosophers follow P's lead in being critical realists in conceptual terms while holding an ontological position of hypercritical realism.   **[3430]**

———. "Protagoras Unbound," in #73, pp. 1-9. S refers to a thesis attributed to Protagoras — that some perceptual judgments are accurate. While S examines the doctrine closely, he does not refute it.   **[3431]**

———. "The Theory of Flux in the *Theaetetus*." *Apeir* 10 #2(1976), 1-10. P presents this theory with reasonable objectivity. As it is set forth in *Theaet*, one might conclude that perception is knowledge.   **[3432]**

WILLIAMS, C. J. F. "Referential Opacity and False Belief in the *Theaetetus*." *PhQ* 22(1972), 289-302. P's views about false belief are similar to views of modern logician W. V. Quine, but P has not gone as far as Quine.   **[3433]**

YOH, M. "On the Third Attempted Definition of Knowledge: *Theaetetus* 201c-210b." *Dial*(Can) 14(1975), 420-442. Since P sees a fundamental difference between knowledge and true opinion, he cannot define knowledge in terms of true opinion. This does not mean that he would never be able to define knowledge or that he has abandoned the Theory of Forms.   **[3434]**

For related items see #2196, #2582, #2639, #2837, #3179, #3465.

Theages

The authenticity of this minor dialogue was never doubted in antiquity. Modern scholars admit that it does not differ drastically in style from P's other works. Friedrich Schleiermacher seems to have been the first to suggest that the substance of the dialogue did not cohere well with the subject matter of other dialogues which deal with virtues, e. g. *Laches* (courage) and *Euthyphro* (piety). The subject under discussion in *Theages* is wisdom. A man named Demodocus has come to Athens from the country seeking a teacher for his son Theages, who desires to become wise, like his friends who have been listening to Sophists. Demodocus finds rearing a son "vexatious" and turns to S for advice.

The situation is surprisingly similar to the plot of Aristophanes' *Clouds*, where the old rustic Strepsiades brings his troublesome son to S. The dialogue could have been written as a response to Aristophanes' unflattering portrayal, which plagued S the rest of his life. (He even refers to it in the *Apol.*)

PANGLE, T. L. "Socrates on the Problem of Political Science Education." *PolTheo* 13(1985), 112-137; revised version in #2003, pp. 147-174. Argues for authenticity of dialogue and shows how S recognizes dangers of education in political science but serves as a model for such education.   **[3435]**

Timaeus/Critias

According to Paul Shorey (#1458, p. 345), when people move beyond mythological accounts of the workings of the physical world, there remain two competing ways of explaining the origin and development of the universe: 1) one can view the universe as a machine operating according to basic mechanical laws, and when one comprehends those mechanical laws, then one will have an adequate explanation of the universe; 2) one can view the universe as a living organism guided or informed by some higher purpose, and that human ideas of order, right and beauty must stand in some intelligible relation to this purpose.

In the *Phaedo*, S criticizes the philosophy of Anaxagoras for attempting to explain the workings of the physical world mechanistically. On Anaxagoras' view, the cause of S's being in jail is that S's bones and muscles have a certain structure; S's views about what constitutes the best way to live are not part of the explanation of his current situation. S strongly rejects this mechanistic view of causation, and he indicates his support for a more teleological approach. In the *Tim*, we find P providing a detailed application of the teleological view to the universe as a whole. P provides a summary of the imperfect science of his day ("the tale which is probable" [29d]) in the context of his teleological interpretation of the natural world.

The introductory section portrays the *Tim* as the second member of a trilogy of which the *Rep* is apparently the first part. S meets four others who listened to the conversation about the fully good city the previous day. S reviews some of the key features of "the city in words," and then he expresses his desire to find some way of discerning how the citizens of such a city would carry on a struggle against its neighbors, and how "when at war showed by the greatness of her actions and the magnanimity of her words in dealing with other cities a result worthy of her training and education" (19c). Critias then indicates his willingness to recite the tale heard from his grandfather, who had heard it from Solon, about the mighty battle waged by Athens against barbarian forces. This account will provide a historical basis for the city they considered in the previous conversation. But first Timaeus, who "has made the nature of the universe his special study" (27a), will tell the story of the origins of the universe and nature down to the birth of man.

Timaeus then proceeds to show that the universe is the result of intelligent and beneficent design. The Divine Craftsman or Demiurgos uses the eternal Forms as models to give shape and order to a pre-existing chaos. The Demiurgos creates a soul of the universe, and then forms the physical universe within the soul. Within this framework then, Timaeus presents his likely or probable account of the visible world.

One of the most controversial topics regarding the dialogue is its date. The *Tim* contains an account of the distinction between Forms and sensibles, the realm of unchangeable being and the realm of becoming. If, as has been traditionally understood, the dialogue is from P's later period, then the presence of this distinction in this dialogue would indicate that P maintained his commitment to the Forms to the end of his life. But G. E. L. Owen has challenged this view and argued that the *Tim* more suitably belongs to the period shortly after the writing of the *Rep*. If Owen is correct, this dating of the dialogue allows for the possibility that in P's later writing, he seriously modified his Theory of Forms or abandoned it altogether. This question has raised intense controversy in the scholarly literature.

ANDERSON, D. E., and BRENT, J. "The Questioning of the Existence of the Forms in Plato's *Timaeus*." *TulStudPh* 27(1978), 1-12. Examines inconsistency in saying world is in flux, and yet was created according to an immutable model.   [3436]

ANDREWS, P. B. S. "Larger than Africa and Asia?" *G&R* 14(1967), 76-79. P's story of Atlantis may have been colored by his mistaken reading of ms. from which he took story. Instead of being "greater than" Africa and Asia, Atlantis may have been "between" them, i. e., in the Mediterranean.   [3437]

ARCHER-HIND, R. D. *The* Timaeus *of Plato* New York: Arno Pr. 1973; rprt. Transl. with extensive notes and introductory essay.   [3438]

ASHBAUGH, A. F. *Plato's Theory of Explanation: A Study of the Cosmological Account in the* Timaeus. Albany: SUNY Pr., 1988. P tries to restore cognitive balance disturbed by views of Eleatics and Atomists; writes *Tim* in an effort to explain cosmos not objectively but as the soul knows it. Such knowledge is not purely subjective, since the soul is limited by sensible objects in kind of perception it can experience.   [3439]

BENARDETE, S. "On Plato's *Timaeus* and Timaeus' Science Fiction." *Interp* 2(1971), 21-63. Commentary which concludes by claiming that "without political philosophy, cosmology always runs the risk of taking its bearings by the political." Structural divisions of dialogue are analyzed.   [3440]

BODNAR, I. M. "Atomic Shapes and Elementary Triangles in Plato's *Timaeus*." *Doxa Philosophical Studies* 6(1986), 47-57. Surveys scholarly debate on question of P's concept of structure of matter and presents a new interpretation. **[3441]**

BRAGUE, R. "The Body of the Speech: A New Hypothesis on the Compositional Structure of *Timaeus*' Monologue," in #1282, pp. 53-83. At *Phaedrus* 264c2-6 S argues that "any discourse ought to be constructed like a living creature." *Tim* can be seen as embodying this rule most fully. **[3442]**

BRENNAN, J. G. "Whitehead on Plato's Cosmology." *JHPh* 9(1971), 67-78. Transcription, with brief notes, of Whitehead's lectures on P's cosmology, delivered at Harvard in 1934. Most deal with *Tim*. **[3443]**

BROWN, M. "Pappus, Plato, and the Harmonic Mean." *Phron* 20(1975), 173-184. Examines a certain geometrical construction which Pappus preserves, and defends it by showing how it rests on an alternate definition of the third mean. Then relies on this discussion to give a fresh interpretation to the world's body and the world's soul passages in *Tim*. **[3444]**

BRUMBAUGH, R. S. "On the Names of Poseidon's Sons and the Historicity of Atlantis." *AncPh* 1(1980-81), 83-84. Discusses selected passages in *Critias* 114. **[3445]**

———. "Plato's Atlantis: Myth or History?" in #49, pp. 112-119. P's account of Atlantis probably reflects destruction of Thera by volcanic eruption ca. 1450 B. C., but the details which he provides are his own creation, based on his numerology, with some of the less desirable characteristics of Syracuse included. **[3446]**

CHERNISS, H. F. "A Much Misread Passage of the *Timaeus* (*Timaeus* 49c7-50b5)," in #51, pp. 346-363. In this passage P does not contradict what he says in other passages about identifying self-identifying characteristics by reference to their transient phenomenal manifestations. **[3447]**

———. "The Relation of the *Timaeus* to Plato's Later Dialogues," in #1809, pp. 339-378; also in #51, pp. 298-338. Challenges Owen's (#3505) interpretation that *Tim* belongs to middle period of P's thought. Dates it to later period. **[3448]**

———. "*Timaeus* 52c2-5," in #51, pp. 364-375. Examines a clause in which P explains why an image is, properly speaking, in something else. Proposes new translation of the phrase. **[3449]**

———. "*Timaeus* 38a8-b5," in #51, pp. 340-345. This passage need not have been written before *Soph*, as Owen argues (#3505). **[3450]**

CHERRY, R. S. "*Timaeus* 49c7-50b5." *Apeir* 2 #1(1967), 1-11. Examines issue of ontological status of phenomenal world, and in opposition to Cherniss' (1954) extreme flux doctrine, argues for a modified flux doctrine. *Tim* is a late work. **[3451]**

CLEGG, J. S. "Plato's Vision of Chaos." *CQ* 26(1976), 52-61. Though accounts in *Tim*, *Laws*, and *Phaedrus* seem to conflict, P appears to have viewed God's creative activity as bringing order and intelligence into an existing chaotic world, like an animal trainer who guides an organism to realize potential within itself. **[3452]**

DAVID, E. "The Problem of Representing Plato's Ideal State in Action." *RFIC* 112(1984), 33-53. S disqualifies himself and his interlocutors from the task of describing the ideal state because of their lack of political experience. Solon, an experienced ruler but one not associated with events of Athens' recent past, is able to narrate a story, with authoritative Egyptian documents as his source, about an ideal state in a remote time. *Tim-Critias* is utopian literature and was meant to be unfinished. [3453]

DIGBY, T. "*Timaeus* 48e-51b: Plato's Theory of Space." *Phil*(Athens) 13-14(1983-84), 157-162. Studies P's discussion of necessary things, in particular the "third thing" besides the intelligible and always unchangingly real model and the copy of this model. [3454]

DILLON, J. "Tampering with the *Timaeus*: Ideological Emendations in Plato, with Special Reference to the *Timaeus*." *AJPh* 110(1989), 50-72. Examines tendency to alter text to promote one ideological position or another, especially with respect to doctrine of creation of world in time. [3455]

DOMBROWSKI, D. A. "Atlantis and Plato's Philosophy." *Apeir* 15(1981), 117-128. Story of Atlantis is not historical, but P's own literary invention to emphasize what will happen to ideal state. Ideal republic (or its symbol, ancient Athens) is impossible for metaphysical and practical reasons; it must suffer same fate as Atlantis in this story, i. e., destruction at hands of nature. [3456]

DRUMMOND, J. J. "Indivisible Lines and the *Timaeus*." *Apeir* 16(1982), 63-70. Nothing in *Tim* 54d-55c or in Ar's discussion of P's views on points and indivisible lines (*Meta* 992a20-22) demonstrates conclusively that P believed that the void or atomic solids existed. [3457]

DUBOSE, S. "*Poiesis* and *Cosmos*." *TulStudPh* 19(1970), 21-26. Examines beginning of *Tim* and inquiry into making. Points to analogy between construction of cosmos and construction of explanations of it: both are arts which require a full range of techniques. [3458]

DUSANIC, S. "Plato's Atlantis." *AC* 51(1982), 25-52. Atlantis symbolizes both Athens and Syracuse of P's day. One must know history of relations between those two cities in 350's B. C. in order to understand P's story. [3459]

EASTERLING, H. J. "Causation in the *Timaeus* and *Laws* X." *Eranos* 65(1967), 25-38. Literal interpretation of *Tim* does not suggest that it contradicts *Laws* 10. [3460]

FAKHRY, M. "A Tenth-Century Arabic Interpretation of Plato's Cosmology." *JHPh* 6(1968), 15-22. The little-known cosmological writings of al-Razi shed some light on Platonic concept of soul and its relation with God and the Forms. [3461]

GADAMER, H.-G. "Idea and Reality in Plato's *Timaeus*," in #1274, pp. 156-193. The dialogue considers more than just how people can order their lives. The very constitution of the world is examined, especially in light of the role of necessity as limiting possibilities but also providing opportunity for activity. [3462]

GAVIN, W. S. "Science and Myth in the *Timaeus*." *SwJPh* 6(1975), 7-15. Like modern scientists who emphasize the theoretical matrix of their work, P views science as a likely explanation operating within a larger framework of imagination (myth). [3463]

GILL, C. "The Genre of the Atlantis Story." *CPh* 72(1977), 287-304. The Atlantis story appears to be a myth with deliberate political and philosophical overtones. It may provide a cautionary comment on Periclean Athens. **[3464]**

——. cf. #1538.

GILL, M. L. "Matter and Flux in Plato's *Timaeus*." *Phron* 32(1987), 34-53. Removes apparent discrepancy between *Tim* and *Theaet* regarding possibility of making meaningful statements about objects in radical flux. **[3465]**

GREENBERG, N. A. "Sayre and Stylometrics." *AJPh* 106(1985), 227-230. Reply to K. M. Sayre (#1918). Stylistic considerations show *Tim* is later than *Parm*. **[3466]**

GRIFFITS, J. G. "Atlantis and Egypt." *Historia* 34(1985), 3-28. Exploration of numerous possible connections between ancient Egypt and P's Atlantis (numbers, names, political organization, etc.). **[3467]**

HAHN, R. "Being and Non-Being in *Rig Veda X*, in the Writings of the *Lao-Tzu* and *Chuang-Tzu*, and in the 'Later' Plato." *JChinPh* 8(1981), 119-142. Examines *Rig Veda X*, *Lao Tzu* and *Chuang-Tzu*, and applies perspective on dialectic between Being and Non-Being to creation myth of P's *Tim* and ontological digression of *Philebus*. **[3468]**

——. "Material Causality, Non-Being and Plato's *Hypodoche*: A Review of *Timaeus* in Terms of the Divided Line." *Apeir* 14(1980) 57-66. One reading of Divided Line in *Rep* which offers a *theory* of cognition provides an avenue for understanding *Tim*, and in particular the two accounts of principles of creation. **[3469]**

HALL, T. S. "The Biology of the *Timaeus* in Historical Perspective." *Arion* 4(1965), 109-127. *Tim* helps to form a plan for late scientific inquiry. Physiology, when viewed historically, reveals a master tradition, a lasting though flexible strategy of interpretive procedures. P understands these procedures and uses them. **[3470]**

HASLAM, H. W. "A Note on Plato's Unfinished Dialogues." *AJPh* 97(1976) 336-339. There is no internal justification for separation of *Critias* from *Tim* or of *Stsm* from *Soph*. Both pairs of works are unfinished dialogues. **[3471]**

HERSHBELL, J. "Empedoclean Influences on the *Timaeus*." *Phoenix* 28(1974), 145-166. No quotation or verbal allusions to Empedocles can be found in *Tim*, but P's discussion of mixture and his biological concepts reflect E's influence. **[3472]**

KEYT, C. "The Mad Craftsman of the *Timaeus*." *PhR* 80(1971), 230-235. P's failure to distinguish proper and ideal attributes of Forms shows in his fallacies of division. *Tim's* mad craftsman, who copies even useless features of his model, is one example. Logician in *Parm* is another. **[3473]**

KOTRC, R. F. "The Dodecahedron in Plato's *Timaeus*." *RhM* 124(1981), 212-222. Geometrical delineation of dodecahedron and its surfaces offers insight into integrated physical structure of the whole. **[3474]**

KRELL, D. F. "Female Parts in *Timaeus*." *Arion* 2(1975), 400-421. Timaeus' resolution of fundamental ontological problem, generation of visible world from Being through model-forms, requires "female parts." But he degrades the feminine, causing his explanation to fail. [3475]

KUNG, J. "Mathematics and Virtue in Plato's *Timaeus*," in #1267, pp. 309-339. P makes no distinction between soul's function in epistemology and ethics. [3475a]

———. "Why the Receptacle is Not a Mirror." *AGPh* 70(1988), 167-178. P did not compare the Receptacle to a mirror because the analogy does not fit his metaphysics, his epistemology, or the nature of the Receptacle. [3476]

LEE, E. N. "On Plato's *Timaeus* 49d4-e7." *AJPh* 88(1967), 1-28. Careful textual analysis in response to studies of Cherniss (1954) and Gulley (1960) which results in new interpretation regarding P's views about requirements for a *logos* about a phenomenal object. P's point is essentially a logical-semantic contrast "between the combination of subject and attribute and the bare attribute." [3477]

———. "On the 'Gold-Example' in Plato's *Timaeus* (50A5-B5)," in #41, pp. 219-235. Of the two responses given in outline of a dialectical encounter, one is more appropriate, the other acceptable under right conditions. [3478]

———. "On the Metaphysics of the Image in Plato's *Timaeus*." *Monist* 50(1966), 341-368. Analyzes formal structure of *Tim* 48e-52d to show that P expounds meaning of his doctrine that phenomena are images of Forms. His explanation of that doctrine succeeds in avoiding problems posed for his theory in *Parm*. [3479]

———. "Reason and Rotation: Circular Movement as the Model of Mind (Nous) in the Later Plato," in #1293, pp. 70-102. Examines P's decision to represent *nous* itself (mind or intelligence) by model of rotary motion around a fixed center. Considers why Aristotle's attacks on theory are inadequate. Theory represents P's movement to a new phase of considering what philosophic life implies. [3480]

MAULA, E. "The Conquest of Time." *Diot* 11(1983), 130-147. The Grand Harmony which P describes in *Tim* is based on Pythagorean ideas of planetary movements and numerical proportions. [3481]

———. "Eudoxus Encircled." *Ajatus* 33(1971), 201-253. P's cosmological frame of reference in *Tim* must have been Eudoxus' theory of hemocentric spheres. [3482]

———. "Is Time a Child or a Grand-Child of Eternity? (*Timaeus* 37d, 50d)." *Ajatus* 31(1969), 37-61. Forms are said to be "eternal"; their exemplifications are "temporal". Examines interrelation which should explain transition from eternity to time. [3483]

———. "On Plato and Plenitude." *Ajatus* 29(1967), 12-50. Not all Forms are realized in world of sensible particulars. Discusses details of metaphor of Demiurge and the two steps in world of Demiurge. Examines creation myth in *Tim* in light of A. O. Lovejoy's principle of plenitude. [3484]

———. *On the Semantics of Time in Plato's* Timaeus. Abo (Finland) Academy: 1970. Compares *Tim* 38a-b with passages from *Soph* to show P does not hypostatize time but takes it as an attribute. Time may be attributed to sentences or physical things. [3485]

——. "Plato's Agalma of the Eternal Gods." *Ajatus* 31(1969), 7-36. Examines 37c where what craftsman creates is an "agalma," not a likeness or image. Argues that *agalma* is used metaphorically, that it has a special role in P's teachings, and that it is an apt term in discussing interrelations of "eternity" and "temporality." [3486]

——. "Plato's 'Cosmic Computer' (*Timaeus* 35a-39e)." *Ajatus* 32(1970), 185-244. Discusses how P faced some problems created by his basic assumption that knowledge, thought, and belief are *dunameis* ("forces," "faculties," "capacities"). [3487]

——. "Plato's 'Mirror of Soul' in the *Timaeus*." *Ajatus* 32(1970), 160-184. Studies logic of image metaphor, focusing on commoner terms *eikon* and *phantasma*. [3488]

——. *Studies in Plato's Theory of Forms in the* Timaeus. Helsinki: Suomal Tiedeakat, 1970. Brief study examining transition from immutabliity of Forms to changeability of sensibles. [3489]

McCLAIN, E. G. "A New Look at Plato's *Timaeus*." *Mus&Man* 1(1975), 341-360. Aims to reconstruct his "World-Soul" by using insights from musical analysis of related mathematical allegories in *Rep*, *Critias*, and *Laws*. [3490]

MILLS, K. W. "Some Aspects of Plato's Theory of Forms: *Timaeus* 49c ff." *Phron* 13(1968), 145-170. Examines P's doctrine that that which partakes of a Form stands to Form itself as does an image to its original, discusses thesis that P treats predicates as proper names, and argues that this doctrine is immune to TMA regress. [3491]

MOHR, R. D. "Divinity, Cognition, and Ontology: The Unique World Argument," in #2112, pp. 9-52. In *Tim* 30-31 P argues that world is unique because it is only copy of Form of World-as-living-animal. This argument is important in understanding P's concept of objects of knowledge, Forms, and combination of metaphysical speculation and scientific inquiry. [3492]

——. "The Gold Analogy in Plato's *Timaeus* (50a4-b5)." *Phron* 23(1978) 243-252; also in #2112, pp. 99-107. Main point of passage is development of contrast between phenomena taken, on the one hand, as being in flux about which nothing can be said, and phenomena taken, on the other hand, as images. [3493]

——. "Image, Flux, and Space in Plato's *Timaeus*." *Phoenix* 34(1980), 138-152; also in #2112, pp. 85-98. Interprets 49b-50b to show that nothing can be said of phenomena to the extent that they are in flux. But since they are also images, their type can be identified. Delineates ways in which P does not make use of Space. [3494]

——. "The Mechanism of Flux in Plato's *Timaeus*." *Apeir* 14(1980), 96-114; also in #2112, pp. 116-138. Because phenomena move erratically, without any psychic cause, they are a positive source of evil. P's atomistic account of chaos in *Tim* 52d-53a and 58a-c seems to contradict psychic autokinetic doctrine of *Phaedrus* and *Laws* 10. [3495]

——. "Plato on Time and Eternity," in #2112, pp. 53-81. P's views on time and eternity are more coherent than generally recognized. When he says (*Tim* 37c-38c) that the Demiurge makes time, he should be understood to mean that the Demiurge makes a clock. The Forms have a kind of timeless eternity. [3496]

——. "Remarks on the Stereometric Nature and Status of the Primary Bodies in the *Timaeus*," in #2112, pp. 108-115. Argues against Cornford that the primary bodies (earth, water, air, and fire), described in *Tim* 52d-53a, are present in pre-cosmic chaos, though their nature has been largely misunderstood. Examines elemental triangles which make up the primary bodies and their ontological status.   **[3497]**

——. cf. #2050, #2113, #2144, 3268.

MORROW, G. R. "Necessity and Persuasion in Plato's *Timaeus*," in #1809, pp. 421-438. Examines 48a, and asks 1) what has persuasion to do with processes of nature; 2) what kind of necessity is this that can be persuaded?   **[3498]**

——. "Plato's Theory of the Primary Bodies in the *Timaeus* and the Later Doctrine of Forms." *AGPh* 50(1968), 12-28. Concept of primary bodies, which is essentially mathematical, makes Theory of Forms presented in *Tim* rather different from version set out in earlier dialogues.   **[3499]**

MORTLEY, R. "The Bond of the Cosmos: A Significant Metaphor (*Tim.* 31c ff.)." *Hermes* 97(1969), 372-373. P uses term *analogia* as link among the four elements in same way Empedocles used *philia*.   **[3500]**

——. "Primary Particles and Secondary Qualities in Plato's *Timaeus*." *Apeir* 2 #1(1967), 15-17. Considers P's analysis of matter, and asks if primary particles, as well as possessing shapes of cube, octahedron, tetrahedron and icosahedron also possess certain potentialities such as fieriness, wateriness, sweetness, etc.   **[3501]**

MUELLER, I. "Joan Kung's Reading of Plato's *Timaeus*." *Apeir* 22(1989), 1-27. Presentation of writings left by Kung at her untimely death. Among other topics, argues against Owen's claim (#3505) that *Tim* is earlier than generally believed.   **[3502]**

OSTENFELD, E. N. "Disorderly Motion in the *Timaeus*." *C&M* 29(1972), 22-26. In *Phaedrus* and *Laws*, P argues there is no motion without soul. But in *Tim*, he offers an account of world's coming-into-being from mixture and combination of necessity and intelligence which is inconsistent with his doctrine of no motion without soul.   **[3503]**

——. "Plato's Development and the Date of the *Timaeus*." *C&M* 37(1986), 63-87. Comparison with P's later dialogues, especially in mathematic and psychological concepts, indicates that *Tim* is a late dialogue.   **[3504]**

OWEN, G. E. L. "The Place of the *Timaeus* in Plato's Dialogues," in #1809, pp. 313-338. *Tim* belongs to middle period of P's thought. Along with *Critias*, it was constructed as the "crowning work of the *Republic* group" of dialogues and not a reflection of P's maturest thought.   **[3505]**

——. "Plato and Parmenides on the Timeless Present." *Monist* 50(1966), 317-340. In *Tim* P recognizes some kinds of statements as tenseless, based on Parmenides' claim that time distinctions are not tenable. In *Soph* he qualifies this theory.   **[3506]**

PARRY, R. D. "The Unique World of the *Timaeus*." *JHPh* 17(1979), 1-10. In *Tim* 30c1-31b3 P argues that our world is unique because it is copied from a unique model. This argument is not fallacious, as many commentators maintain, because the uniqueness is based on the completeness of the model and the world copied from it. [3507]

PATTERSON, R. "The Unique Worlds of the *Timaeus*." *Phoenix* 35(1981), 105-119. Discusses troublesome issues surrounding arguments supporting P's theory of uniqueness of visible cosmos. [3508]

POHLE, W. "Dimensional Concepts and the Interpretation of Plato's Physics," in #65, pp. 306-323. Examines P's presentation of the physical theory of *Tim* in an uncompromisingly geometric mold. [3509]

––––––. "The Mathematical Foundation of Plato's Atomic Physics." *Isis* 62(1971), 36-46. Response to Cornford's interpretation of P's physics in *Tim*, especially his use of polyhedral particles and triangular elements and his arrangement of them in groups of four and six. [3510]

POPPER, K. R. "Plato, *Timaeus* 54e-55a." *CR* 20(1970), 4-5. New transl. and analysis of sentence describing the oldest stereometric construction. [3511]

PRIOR, W. J. "*Timaeus* 48e-52d and the Third Man Argument," in #1285, pp. 123-148. This passage, introducing Receptacle as part of P's ontology, can support a refutation of TMA. P's vocabulary here shows that Forms are not generally self-predicative. [3512]

REAGAN, J. T. "Plato's Material Principle." *ModSch* 47(1970) 177-193. Delineates status and causal power of material principle, and primarily in work of Necessity in account of world. [3513]

ROBINSON, T. M. "The Argument of *Timaeus* 27d ff." *Phron* 24(1979), 105-109. An apparent inconsistency in this passage can be removed by deleting the adverb "everlastingly" in 28a1. [3514]

––––––. "Understanding the *Timaeus*." *PBACAPh* 2(1986), 103-119. This dialogue should be read "literally." It argues for a real beginning to time and the existence of the Demiurge. Some weaknesses of this approach are considered, especially those pointed out by Taylor (#3525) and Owen (3505). [3515]

ROSS, J. M. "Is There Any Truth in Atlantis?" *DUJ* 38(1977), 189-199. Argues against factuality of Atlantis story, which rightly belongs to realm of myth. [3516]

RYLE, G. "The *Timaeus Locrus*." *Phron* 10(1965), 174-190. This document is a precis-paraphrase of P's *Tim*, probably written during his lifetime. [3517]

SAUNDERS, T. J. "Penology and Eschatology in Plato's *Timaeus* and *Laws*." *CQ* 23(1973), 232-244. In positing an eschatology which omits a personal agent, P parodies Heraclitus' style and his concept that one element can be changed into another.[3518]

SKEMP, J. "The Disorderly Motions Again," in #3809, pp. 289-299. Challenges Vlastos' view (#3528) that the motions are purely material and uncaused. [3519]

––––––. *The Theory of Motion in Plato's Later Dialogues*. Amsterdam: Hakkert, 1967; rev. ed. Book consists of original text, published in 1942, with notes and rethinkings for each chapter in a separate section. Emphasis is on *Tim* and role of *demiourgos*, who is the ultimate cause of movement, though not himself a physical being.   **[3520]**

SOLMSEN, F. "'Beyond the Heavens'." *MH* 33(1976), 24-32. In *Tim* 52b P says that Forms do not exist in a particular place, revising view expressed in *Phaedrus* 247c, where he assigns them to a supracelestial place. Aristotle reflects *Tim* in his *Physics* and *Phaedrus* in his *De Caelo*.   **[3521]**

STEWART, D. J. "Man and Myth in Plato's Universe." *BuckRev* 13 #1(1965), 72-90. P's mastery of craft of myth-making is best seen in *Tim*, less so in *Phaedrus*.   **[3522]**

STRANGE, S. K. "The Double Explanation in the *Timaeus*." *AncPh* 5(1985), 25-39. Analyzes P's notions of *nous* (reason) and *ananke* (necessity). *Nous* is closest to what Ar calls efficient and final causality. *Ananke* is akin to material and formal causality; depends on certain relationships among Forms which govern even Demiurge.   **[3523]**

TARAN, L. "The Creation Myth in Plato's *Timaeus*," in #41, pp. 372-407. Several factors suggest that description of chaos and creation myth are not to be taken literally: reversal of order of creation, lack of reference to soul's self-motion, P's comments about time and creation.   **[3524]**

TAYLOR, A. E. *A Commentary on Plato's* Timaeus. New York: Garland, 1987; rprt. Originally published in 1928.   **[3525]**

TURNBULL, R. G. "Becoming and Intelligibility." *OSAP* Suppl. (1988), 1-14. In *Tim* P has two worlds of becoming: one the deceptive world of sense, the other the mathematized result of demiurge's compromise with necessity.   **[3526]**

VLASTOS, G. "Creation in the *Timaeus*: Is It a Fiction," in #1809, pp. 401-419. Examines P's comments on generation of world, and difficulties with interpretations that take these comments to have only mythical import.   **[3527]**

————. "The Disorderly Motion in the *Timaeus*," in #1809, pp. 379-399. Argues that grounds for interpreting disorderly motion as a mythical symbol are weak and merely avoid obscurities in P's categories of material reality.   **[3528]**

————. "Plato's Supposed Theory of Irregular Atomic Figures." *Isis* 58(1967), 204-209; also in #1292, pp. 366-373. Challenges view that in order to make sense of P's discussion of mechanism of sense of smell, we must interpret him as holding theory of irregular atomic figures.   **[3529]**

WELLIVER, W. *Character, Plot and Thought in Plato's* Timaeus-Critias. Leiden: Brill, 1977. Argues *Tim-Critias* is not an unfinished portion of a projected trilogy but a unified dialogue, illustrating by its characters and its narrative development the underlying philosophical point P wants to make. Atlantis is taken as a symbol of Athens.   **[3530]**

WHITTAKER, J. "Textual Comments on *Timaeus* 27c-d." *Phoenix* 27(1973), 387-391. Provides further evidence that text of *Tim*. 27c-d was deliberately tampered with in later antiquity in order to provide support for non-literal interpretation of account of creation.   **[3531]**

————. "*Timaeus* 27d 5ff." *Phoenix* 23(1969), 181-185. This passage was emended to make it suitable as a proof-text for a non-literal account of creation in *Tim*.   [3532]

WHITTEMORE, R. C. "The Proper Categorization of Plato's Demiurgos." *TulStudPh* 27(1978), 163-166. Challenges Christian attempt to read P as a monotheist in the creationist sense of the term.   [3533]

WILSON, J. C. *On the Interpretation of Plato's* Timaeus *and On the Platonist Doctrine of the* Asymbletoi arthmoi. New York: Garland, 1980. Reprint of two studies from 1889 and 1904. First is a commentary on the dialogue, second a treatment of doctrine that ideal numbers are *symbletoi* and that objects of mathematics are between Ideas and world of sense.   [3534]

WOOD, R. J. "Plato's Atomism." *IntPhQ* 8(1968), 427-441. Geometrical atomism advocated in dialogue mediates distinction between being and becoming.   [3535]

————. "The Demiurge and his Model." *CJ* 63(1968), 255-258. Demiurge, a personification of Form of Good, is mythical. It furnishes its own model for itself.   [3536]

YOUNG, J. "How Chaotic is Plato's Chaos?" *Prud* 10(1978), 77-83. P's Demiurge is not an omnipotent creator. He organizes chaos in the *Tim* because there is order inherent in the universe.   [3537]

ZEMBATY, J. S. "Plato's *Timaeus*: Mass Terms, Sortal Terms and Identity Through Time in the Phenomenal World," in #1285, pp. 101-122. To determine whether P allots a special status to sortal predicates one must distinguish between two sets of identity criteria: those involving mass terms and those linked with sortal terms.   [3538]

ZEYL, D. J. "Commentary on Robinson's 'Understanding the *Timaeus*'." *PBACAPh* 2(1986), 120-126. Generally supportive of #3515, but offers an alternative analysis of 27d and the initial distinction between two general categories of being.   [3539]

————. "Plato and Talk of a World in Flux. *Timaeus* 49a6-50b5." *HSCP* 79(1975), 125-148. P anticipates Ar in distinguishing, by his choice of vocabulary, between attribute of something and thing as an entity in itself.   [3540]

For related items see #374, #598, #1427, #1749, #1947, #2042, #2695, #3235, #3893, #4751.

Chapter 14

ARISTOTLE

BIOGRAPHICAL SKETCH

Aristotle was born in 384 B. C. in Stagira, in Macedonia (northern Greece). His father was a physician, so perhaps Ar's interest in science came about naturally. Both his parents died when he was young; his guardian was a Macedonian court official. (Though Greeks, the Macedonians were ruled by a king, unlike cities in the south of Greece, which tended to be run by councils or have democratic governments.)

At eighteen Ar became a student at Plato's Academy, where he remained until Plato's death in 347 B. C. (For a description of the Academy, cf. Chapter 15. The works which Ar is said to have composed during this early period do not survive. His relationship to P has been a subject of considerable debate. He seems to have been an enthusiastic Platonist at this early stage, though he later came to reject, or at least doubt, some basic Platonic concepts.

Upon P's death his pupil Speusippus was elected his successor as head of the Academy. Ar did not agree with Speusippus' interest in P's number theory and was apparently disappointed at being passed over as head of the school. Furthermore, resentment against Macedonians was growing in Athens at that time, as King Philip II conquered one Greek city after another; by 338 Athens itself would fall. Finding no compelling reason to remain in Athens, Ar accepted the invitation of a former student of the Academy to live in his palace in Asia Minor.

After several years as a guest with different friends (during which time he married and had a daughter), Ar was invited to Macedon to become tutor to the king's son, Alexander. This experiment was not a notable success. Teacher and pupil did not take to one another at all. There is no evidence that either "had any marked effect on the other." Ar wrote a short treatise on monarchy for his pupil; the work is no longer extant and we have no way of gauging its impact on Alexander.

In 335, with Alexander now king, Ar returned to Athens and established his own school in a grove sacred to Apollo Lykeios, a spot which Socrates used to frequent. This Lyceum quickly became a rival to the Platonic Academy, even drawing students away from the older school. In the next decade Ar produced or revised most of the major works attributed to him. His philosophy is called Peripatetic, perhaps from his habit of walking around (*peripateo* in Greek) the grounds of his school while he talked with his disciples. We know very little about him personally except for comments (many of them by his opponents) about his fondness for fine clothes and other luxuries. He was not a citizen of Athens, but his exact legal status there remains uncertain. He could not have owned the grounds of the Lyceum himself, since only Athenian citizens could own property in the city.

Alexander's death in 323 provoked an outbreak of anti-Macedonian sentiment among the Athenians, still desirous of regaining their lost liberty. Persons sympathetic to the Macedonians were objects of suspicion. Charges of "impiety" were levelled against Ar. He fled rather than offer the Athenians the opportunity to execute another philosopher. He spent his last years in the city of Chalcis and died a lonely, withdrawn man in 320 B. C., survived by his daughter, an adoptive son, and a son, Nicomachus, by his mistress.

WORKS

Ancient catalogues of Ar's works list at least two hundred titles. All the works of his earliest period, when he was at the Academy or tutoring Alexander, are lost. His most purely speculative philosophical works belong to this earliest period, when he was still under P's influence. Two of these early works, the *Protrepticus* and *On Philosophy*, were well known in antiquity and even into the early Middle Ages. Attempts have been made to identify fragments and to reconstruct at least their outlines. The works of his middle period were largely research notes. All were thought lost until the *Constitution of Athens* was rediscovered in 1890 in a collection of papyrus documents unearthed in Egypt. This pioneering study in political science was one of 158 studies of the governments of various Greek city states compiled by Ar and his students.

The extant works of Ar seem to have originated as lecture notes for his times with his students. This may account for what may charitably be called their extremely compact style of expression. Even his admirers admit that his treatises are "technical, laborious, and difficult." J. Lear cautions us that "reading Aristotle can be a tricky business. Sometimes a particular passage will look as though Aristotle is clearly asserting something, but when one looks to the larger context in which the passage occurs one can see that he is not asserting anything of the kind" (#3615, p. 239). His students show surprisingly little direct influence of his work in their own writing. Medieval philosopher/theologians such as Thomas Aquinas sound more Aristotelian than the generation of students who studied under the master himself. As one commentator put it, "Once the man was gone, it seemed to be difficult to recapture the original meaning of his words."

All the works of Ar still known to us are from his last period, when he was back in Athens at the Lyceum. They show us his keen interest in what we would call scientific investigation and his fundamental difference from P. Where P sought universal objects of knowledge — the Forms/Ideas — which were separate from the material world and intelligible only to the intellect, Ar held that form — an organizing principle or pattern — could not exist apart from matter. Ar also claimed that P's Forms, if entirely separate from the world, could not explain change and growth. Where P had hoped to arrive at knowledge through an exchange of opinions (dialectic), Ar thought knowledge could be gained by breaking a subject down into its component parts (analytic). W. Jaeger, in his *Aristotle: Fundamentals of the History of his Development* (originally published in German, 1923), was the first modern scholar to trace Ar's movement away from a Platonic world view, based on mathematics and the search for an abstract universal substance, toward his own scientific understanding of the world, focused on biology and specific individual substances. This thesis has not remained unchallenged. Some later scholars have pointed to evidence of sympathetic treatment of P's concepts even in Ar's latest works.

A major stumbling block in the study of Ar's works is the question of how and when they were composed and, in some cases, by whom. Even works which are universally acknowledged as Aristotelian, such as the *Physics* and *Metaphysics*, may contain passages — some think entire chapters — which were not written by Ar, or which were heavily edited by other members of the Lyceum. If ancient stories can be trusted, we do know, in far more detail than we do for any other author, what happened to the mss. of Ar's works. He passed them on to his leading student, Theophrastus, who eventually gave them to a certain Neleus, of the city of Scepsis in northwestern Turkey. Neleus and his descendants hid the mss. in their cellar until about 100 B. C., when they sold them to Apellicon, a book collector. In the 80's the Roman general Sulla brought the mss. to Rome, where an inept edition of them was published. In 70 B. C. Andronicus of Rhodes, head of the Lyceum at that time, attempted to fill in the gaps (*lacunae*) caused by moisture and bugs and published an edition of Ar on which all later mss. seem to depend.

While we cannot establish a definite chronological order for Ar's works, it might be helpful at the outset to see them grouped at least by subjects, an approach he himself probably would have appreciated, given his penchant for classifying things. Some of his works are traditionally known by Latin titles, which will be translated here. The traditional title or an abbreviation will be used in the bibliography. It is customary in Latin to capitalize the first word of a title but no others except names. We will follow that practice.

This also seems an appropriate place for a word of explanation about the system of citing passages from Ar's works. Seeing a reference to "*Metaphysics* Delta 8,1017b23-26" can intimidate the non-specialist. First, Greek letters are often used to distinguish separate books of Ar's longer works. The Greeks had no numerals and used letters in this way themselves. Modern editors sometimes use Roman or Arabic numerals, so Book Delta can also be cited as Book 4 or Book IV. The 8 in this citation refers to a modern division into chapters. These numbers are usually printed in the margin or at the top of the page of an edition or translation. The last part of the citation, 1017b23-26, refers to the page numbers of Bekker's edition of 1831, which is used as an international standard for references to Ar's works. This passage appeared on page 1017 of Bekker's edition, section b, lines 23-26. The Bekker numbers also appear in modern editions or translations.

LOGIC: *Categories, De interpretatione (On Interpretation), Prior Analytics, Posterior Analytics, Topics, De sophisticis elenchis (On Sophistical Refutations).* The logical works as a group are often referred to as the *Organon* ("tool" in Greek).

BIOLOGY (or NATURAL HISTORY): *De partibus animalium (On the Parts of Animals), De motu animalium (On the Movement of Animals), De incessu animalium (On the Progression of Animals), De generatione animalium (On the*

Generation of Animals).

PSYCHOLOGY: *De anima (On the Soul), Parva naturalia,* a collection of short treatises (*On Memory and Recollection, On Dreams, On Prophesying by Dreams,* and similar topics).

PHYSICS: *Physics, De caelo (On the Heavens), De generatione et corruptione (On Coming-to-be and Passing-away), Meteorologica.*

PHILOSOPHY: *Metaphysics, Ethica Nicomachea (Nicomachean Ethics), Ethica Eudemia (Eudemian Ethics), Magna moralia, Politics, Rhetoric, Ars poetica (Art of Poetry).*

It would be natural at this point to begin a survey or summary of the main points of Ar's thought, but the words of David Ross, in the *Oxford Classical Dictionary,* prove a daunting obstacle: "It is impossible in a few pages to offer any useful summary of Aristotle's philosophy; for a philosopher's conclusions are worth little without his reasons for them, and Aristotle's reasons cannot be stated briefly." But, having said that, Ross goes on to outline the main features of Ar's system. We will discuss individual topics briefly in the introductions to each section of the bibliography.

GENERAL

ACKRILL, J. L. *Aristotle the Philosopher.* Oxford Univ. Pr., 1981. Introduction seeking to convey the force and excitement of Ar's philosophical investigations.   [3542]

ADLER, M. J. *Aristotle for Everybody: Difficult Thought Made Easy.* New York: Macmillan, 1978. Non-specialist survey.   [3543]

ALLAN, D. J. "Critical and Explanatory Notes on Some Passages Assigned to Aristotle's *Protrepticus.*" *Phron* 21(1976), 219-240. Suggests emendations to Greek text, offers a new grammatical analysis at some points. A passage which Stobaeus attributes to "Aristotle" probably belongs to Themison of Cyprus.   [3544]

——. *The Philosophy of Aristotle.* Oxford Univ. Pr., 1979. Outlines Ar's principal doctrines with references to the circumstances in which they were formed.   [3545]

ANNAS, J. "An Encounter with Aristotle." *Phron* 27(1982), 82-89. Review essay of Guthrie's book on Ar (#22).   [3546]

ATHERTON, P. "Aristotle," in #43, pp. 121-134. Ar's "first philosophy" is essentially theology, or the science of God. He is confident of close connection between human reason and divine *nous.* Later philosophical schools including his own, abandoned his teleological view of the world.   [3547]

BARNES, J. *Aristotle* Oxford Univ. Pr., 1982. Seeks to show Ar as "philosopher scientist," in whose thought empirical research and theoretical speculation are complementary parts of a unified whole.   **[3548]**

——. *Complete Works of Aristotle. The Revised Oxford Translation.* Princeton Univ. Pr., 1984. 2 vols. Revision of Ross' transl. Probably the standard transl. of the entire corpus.   **[3549]**

BOS A. P. "Aristotle on Myth and Philosophy." *PhRef* 48(1983), 1-18. Examines whether Ar's use of mythical themes harmonizes with his statements on "myth," especially his remark that a "philomythos" is in a sense a philosopher.   **[3550]**

——. "Aristotle's *Eudemus* and *Protrepticus*: Are They Really Two Different Works?" *Dion* 8(1984), 19-51. Frags commonly attributed to *Protrep* and *Eudemus* probably originated in only the latter, a discussion of soul similar to P's *Phaedo*.   **[3551]**

——. "The Relation Between Aristotle's Lost Writings and the Surviving Aristotelian Corpus." *PhRef* 52(1987), 24-40. Ar may have used myths more regularly in dialogues than in treatises. He did not change his approach to philosophy but later generations did and thus lost interest in his early works and did not preserve them.   **[3552]**

BRENTANO, F. *Aristotle and His World View*, ed. and transl. R. George and R. M. Chisholm. Berkeley: Univ. of CA Pr., 1978. Presents essential features of Ar's philosophy and presents them as a unified whole. Begins with his ontology and theory of manifold sense of being, discusses theory of knowledge, examines concepts of substance, matter, and form, and considers his theology and theory of man.   **[3553]**

BRUMBAUGH, R. S. "If Aristotle Had Become Head of the Academy . . . ," in *Energeia: Études aristotéliciennes offertes à Mgr. Antonio Jannone* (Paris: Vrin, 1986), pp. 102-116; also in #49, pp. 129-140. Shows how Ar might have modified P's thought without breaking from him. Some of Ar's "anti-Platonism" may have been prompted by his need to distinguish his teachings from those of older Academy (which was already moving away from P's thought by the time Ar opened his school).   **[3554]**

CHAMBERS, M. M. "Aristotle's Historical Method," in *Panhellenica: Essays in Ancient History and Historiography in Honor of Truesdale S. Brown*, ed. S. M. Burstein and L. A. Okin (Lawrence, KS: Coronado Pr., 1980), pp. 57-68. Ar applies the same scientific methodology to his historical researches that he employs in his biological and other scientific treatises.   **[3555]**

CHROUST, A.-H. "Aetius, *De Placitis* I,7, 7-9: A Fragment of Aristotle's *On Philosophy*." *NewSchol* 49(1975), 211-218. This passage, drawn from an Epicurean attack on P's creationist theory, appears to be an authentic frag of Ar's lost dialogue.   **[3556]**

——. "Aristotle and Athens. Some Comments on Aristotle's Sojourns in Athens." *LThPh* 22(1986), 186-196. Explores various reasons for Ar's different visits to and departures from Athens.   **[3557]**

——. "Aristotle and the 'Philosophies of the East'." *RMeta* 18(1965), 572-580. Discusses passages which suggest that Ar was familiar with Zoroastrian thought, especially the idea of cosmic cycles.   **[3558]**

——. "Aristotle, *De Caelo* 279a 18-35(or 279b3), a 'Fragment' of the Lost Aristotelian

On Philosophy." *Thom* 39(1975), 332-340. Passage seems to be a compressed restatement of what Ar said about eternity of cosmos in Book 3 of *On Philosophy*.   [3559]

——. "Aristotle Enters the Academy." *CF* 19(1965), 21-29. Ar's journey to Athens to enter Academy in 367 may not have been his first visit to the city. He may have previously studied in Isocrates' school.   [3560]

——. "Aristotle Leaves the Academy." *G&R* 14(1967), 39-43. Ar fled from Athens, perhaps in fall of 348, to escape strong anti-Macedonian sentiments.   [3561]

——. *Aristotle: New Light on His Life and on Some of His Lost Works*, Vols. I & II. Notre Dame, IN: Notre Dame Univ. Pr., 1973. Collection of previously published papers. Vol. I is biographical; Vol. II deals with lost works.   [3562]

——. "Aristotle Returns to Athens in the Year 335 B.C." *LThPh* 23(1967), 244-254. Ar's mysterious trip to Athens may have been undertaken to plead the city's case with Alexander upon Athenian surrender to Macedon.   [3563]

——. "Aristotle's Alleged 'Revolt' Against Plato." *JHPh* 11(1973), 91-94. Tradition that Ar "revolted" against P may have arisen from desire of Ar's followers to show that he was not intellectually dependent on P, or from intention of Ar's detractors to show that he did not deserve to succeed P as head of the Academy.   [3564]

——. "Aristotle's Flight from Athens in the Year 323 B. C." *Historia* 15(1966), 185-192. Because of his close links to the Macedonian court Ar found it expedient to leave Athens in face of anti-Macedonian reaction after Alexander's death.   [3565]

——. "Aristotle's *On Philosophy*." *LThPh* 29(1973), 19-22. A passage from Cicero *De nat deor* 2.37,95-96 resembles Ar's *Meta* 982b12 ff. Both suggest men became interested in philosophy only after reaching a certain level of material culture.   [3566]

——. "Aristotle's *On Philosophy* and Plutarch's *De Facie in Orbe Lunae*." *WS* 11(1977), 69-75. Plutarch quotes Ar without naming him. Philo, in *De aet mundi* also cites Ar's lost dialogue.   [3567]

——. "Aristotle's 'Self-Portrayal'." *LThPh* 21(1965), 161-174. Examines Ar's own writings to "reconstruct" his main traits of character.   [3568]

——. "Aristotle's Sojourn in Assos." *Historia* 21(1972), 170-176. The purpose of this trip was diplomacy on behalf of Macedon, not philosophical study.   [3569]

——. "A Brief Account of the Reconstruction of Aristotle's *Protrepticus*." *CPh* 60(1965), 229-239. Modern efforts to reconstruct this lost work from the *Protrepticus* of Iamblichus have paid dividends.   [3570]

——. "Did Aristotle Own a School at Athens?" *RhM* 115(1972), 310-318. It appears that Ar's base was a house near the Lyceum.   [3571]

——. "An Emendation to Fragment 13 of Aristotle's *Protrepticus*." *TijdFil* 28(1966), 366-377. Sections 55,7-56,2 might be from *Pol* rather than *Protrepticus*.   [3572]

———. "The First Thirty Years of Modern Aristotelian Scholarship (1912-1942)." *C&M* 24(1963), 27-57. Surveys trends and important figures.   [3573]

———. "A Fragment of Aristotle's *On Philosophy*? Aristotle, *Metaphysics* 982b11-983a11." *RSF* 27(1972), 287-292. Passage in *Meta* speaks of "astonishment" as beginning of philosophy. Frag from *On Philosophy* treats astonishment as leading to knowledge of God. We do not know which passage is derived from the other.   [3574]

———. "The Genealogy of Aristotle." *CF* 19(1965), 139-146. Reviews what is known of Ar's family history and details of his own life.   [3575]

———. "The Great Deluge in Aristotle's *On Philosophy*." *AC* 42(1973), 113-122. In Book 1 of this lost work Ar seems to have explained cycles of human progress and decline as caused by periodic great floods.   [3576]

———. "The Myth of Aristotle's Suicide." *ModSch* 44(1967), 177-178. Stories about Ar's suicide are not trustworthy because of their late date and the fact that they resemble too closely the story of Socrates' death.   [3577]

———. "A Note on Some of the Minor Lost Works of the Young Aristotle." *TijdFil* 27(1965), 310-319. Argues that frags deserve more attention, though we have little more than titles of works such as *On Prayer*, *On Education*, and others.   [3578]

———. "On Master's 'The Case of Aristotle's Missing Dialogues . . .'." *PolTheo* 7(1979), 537-547. Challenges Master's (#3621) argument that P's *Sophist* and *Statesman* were actually composed by Ar.   [3579]

———. "The Probable Date of Aristotle's Lost Dialogue *On Philosophy*." *JHPh* 4(1966), 283-292. Challenges Jaeger's original dating. Most likely date is between 350/49, or perhaps 348/47, and 347/46.   [3580]

———. "The Probable Dates of Some of Aristotle's Lost Works." *RCSF* 22(1967), 3-23. Suggests dates for *Gryllus*, *On Ideas*, *On the Good*, and others.   [3581]

———. "The Problems of the *Aristotelis librorum fragmenta*." *CJ* 62(1966), 71-74. Studies V. Rose's impact on collection of Ar's frags, state of problem by mid-1960's.   [3582]

———. "Some Additional Fragments of Aristotle's *On Philosophy* in Iamblichus' *Protrepticus* and Iamblichus' *De communi mathematica scientica*." *TijdFil* 37(1975), 89-94. Identifies and discusses several passages.   [3583]

———. "Some Comments on Aristotle's Sojourns in Athens." *LThPh* 22(1966), 186-196. Offers another explanation for Ar's departure from Athens after P's death, and discusses other evidence for his leaving and returning to Athens at various points.   [3584]

———. "Some Comments on Philo of Alexandria, *De Aeternitate Mundi*." *LThPh* 31(1975), 135-145. Sections of the work containing arguments on createdness and indestructibility of the world may be authentic frags of Ar's *On Philosophy*.   [3585]

———. "A Tentative Outline for a Possible Reconstruction of Aristotle's Lost Dialogue *On Philosophy*." *AC* 44(1975), 553-569. Book 1 may have treated origins and history of philosophy; Book 2 probably contained criticisms of P; Book 3 may have been cosmological and theological. **[3586]**

———. "The Term 'Philosopher' and the Panegyric Analogy in Aristotle's *Protrepticus*." *Apeir* 1(1966), 14-17. Description of philosophic way of life by Cicero derives ultimately from Ar's *Protrepticus* and from P. **[3587]**

———. "Was Plato One of the Discussants in Aristotle's Dialogue *On Philosophy*?" *RCSF* 29(1974), 284-287. Ar does appear to have followed P's model and used his teacher as an interlocutor in this dialogue. **[3588]**

———. "Werner Jaeger and the Reconstruction of Aristotle's Lost Works." *SO* 42(1967), 7-43. Discusses importance of Jaeger's work for clarifying Ar's relationship to Platonic thought in his early years. **[3589]**

———. cf. #2136 and #5553.

CLARK, S. R. L. *Aristotle's Man: Speculations Upon Aristotelian Anthropology.* Oxford: Clarendon Pr., 1975. Combines themes from Ar's ethics, biology, and metaphysics to define his position on man and his place in the universe. **[3590]**

CLINE HOROWITZ, M. "Aristotle and Woman." *JHistBiol* 9(1976), 183-213. Surveys Ar's views on nature of women and effect those views have had over centuries. **[3591]**

DAVIES, J. C. "Aristotle's Conception of Function and its Relation to His Empiricism." *Emerita* 37(1969), 55-62. Unlike modern empiricists, Ar subordinates his empiricism to function or teleology, which are more important hallmarks of his system. **[3592]**

DE SMET, R. "The Aristotelian-Thomist Conception of Man." *IndianPhQ* 32(1975), 307-318. Ar's concept of *energeia* and *dynamis* overcomes dualism and enables him to form a "holistic" view of man. **[3593]**

DUERING, I. *Aristotle in the Ancient Biographical Tradition.* New York: Garland, 1987; rprt. Collects and translates biographical references to Ar from wide range of ancient sources, including Arabic and Syriac. Analyzes importance of the material for reconstructing Ar's biography and development of his thought. **[3594]**

———. "Notes on the History of the Transmission of Aristotle's Writings," in *Aristotle and His Influence* (New York: Garland, 1987; rprt), pp. 37-70. Explores which works of Ar were known to Polybius, Posidonius or Cicero because direct and definable quotations from Ar are exceedingly rare. **[3595]**

EDEL, A. *Aristotle.* New York: Dell, 1967. Introductory essays on Ar's life and work followed by representative passages in translation; aimed at non-specialists. **[3596]**

———. *Aristotle and His Philosophy.* Chapel Hill: Univ. of NC Pr., 1982. Survey which assumes no philosophical expertise. Does not cover all aspects of Ar's thought, such as biology. Stresses Ar's thought as a means of unifying fields of knowledge which have been split apart today. Examines different historical interpretations of Ar's philosophy. Useful bibliography. **[3597]**

EVANS, J. D. G. *Aristotle.* Sussex, UK: Harvester Pr., 1987. Presents a comprehensive account of leading theories and arguments in Ar's work. Emphasis is placed on dialectical nature of Ar's philosophy. **[3598]**

——. "Aristotle on Relativism." *PhQ* 24(1974), 193-203. Ar attempts to find a mediating position between Protagorean relativism and Platonic realism. He grants a larger part to human faculties in determining objects of truth, assuming that they are faculties of a good man. **[3599]**

FARRINGTON, B. *Aristotle: Founder of Scientific Philosophy.* London: Weidenfeld 1965. Presents Ar as one who revolutionized thought by uniting the two streams of thought of his predecessors: material science and idealistic philosophy. **[3600]**

FERGUSON, J. *Aristotle.* Boston: Twayne, 1972. Primarily an introduction to help the non-specialist through Ar. Introductory chapter on his life; chapters on his logic, metaphysics, rhetoric, politics, and other standard topics. **[3601]**

GADAMER, H.-G. *"Amicus Plato Amica Veritas,"* in #1274, pp. 194-218. Surveys question of Ar's relation to P, especially in area of P's number theory and Ar's concept of *logos ousias*; finds "an ultimate common ground" between them. **[3602]**

——. "Practical Philosophy As a Model of the Human Sciences." *Research in Phenomenology* 9(1979) 74-86. Discusses how Ar's philosophy lends itself to development of a better understanding of humanities than those found using other methodologies. *Phronesis, techne,* and *episteme* are discussed. **[3603]**

GERSON, L. P. "The Aristotelianism of Joseph Owens." *AncPh* 3(1983), 72-81. Surveys Owens's contribution to Aristotelian scholarship, especially in interpretation of his metaphysics, ethics, and philosophy of nature. **[3604]**

GRAHAM, D. W. *Aristotle's Two Systems.* Oxford: Clarendon Pr., 1987. Scholars, noting inconsistencies in Ar's philosophy, posit stages of development in his thought. But differences between logical works and physical-metaphysical ones are so profound that we can speak of two separate systems of thought. Ar originally held views espoused in his logical works but later moved to his metaphysical positions. **[3605]**

GROTE, G. *Aristotle.* New York: Arno Pr., 1973. Reprint of 1880 edition. **[3606]**

HAHM, D. E. "The Fifth Element in Aristotle's *De philosophia*: A Critical Re-examination." *JHS* 102(1982), 60-74; also in #42, pp. 404-428. Comparison of Ar's concept of fifth element in *De phil* and *De caelo* suggests former work was written first. **[3607]**

HALPER, E. "Ackrill, Aristotle, and Analytic Philosophy." *AncPh* 2(1982), 142-151. Response to #3542. Ar is primarily concerned with essences, not linguistics. **[3608]**

HUXLEY, G. "Aristotle's Interest in Biography." *GRBS* 15(1974), 203-213. Ar's interest in biography, especially of poets and earlier philosophers, is not surprising in light of his stress on significance of individuals. **[3609]**

——. "On Aristotle's Historical Method." *GRBS* 13(1972), 157-170. Ar gathered and analyzed information about the past as carefully as he sought out scientific data. **[3610]**

IRWIN, T. *Aristotle's First Principles.* Oxford Univ. Pr., 1989. Explores Ar's philosophical method, and shows how he defends dialectic against the objection that it cannot justify a metaphysical realist's claims. [3611]

KENNY, A. J. P. "A Stylometric Comparison Between Five Disputed Works and the Remainder of the Aristotelian Corpus," in #3624, pp. 345-366. Examines use of four common particles and twenty less common ones in established Aristotelian works; compares results to several dubious works. Usage in *Meta* K and *De motu animalium* compares well to that of acknowledged works. *Cat* and *Meteor* 4 are "suspicious" and usage of particles in *Meta* A differs noticeably from that in genuine works. [3612]

——. "The Stylometric Study of the Aristotelian Writings." *Cirpho Review* 3(1975-76), 5-32. Presents results of applications of two stylometric tests to Aristotelian corpus performed to determine authorship of works. Evaluates usefulness of this technique for authenticating Ar's works. [3613]

KLUBACK, W. "A Few Thoughts on Eric Weil's Interpretation of Aristotle." *RIPh* 34(1980), 472-481. Reply to #4560 and several other publications by Weil. [3614]

LEAR, J. *Aristotle: The Desire to Understand.* Cambridge Univ. Pr. 1988. Philosophical introduction which focuses on Ar's treatment of following questions: What is it for us to be animated by desire to understand? What is it for a creature to have a nature? What is our human nature? What must the world be like to be intelligible? [3615]

LLOYD, G. E. R. *Aristotle: The Growth and Structure of His Thought.* Cambridge Univ. Pr., 1968. Non-specialist study. First part criticizes Jaeger's theory of Ar's intellectual development. Second part discusses Ar's works on logic, metaphysics, physics, aesthetics, and other topics and provides a survey of his mature system. [3616]

LOHR, C. H. "Some Early Aristotelian Bibliographies." *Nouvelle de la République des Lettres* 1 #1(1981), 87-116. Of interest largely to specialists. [3617]

LONG, H. S. "A Bibliographical Survey of Recent (1945-54) Work on Aristotle." *CW* 51(1957-58), 47-51; 57-60; 69-76; 96-98; 117-119; 160-162; 167-168; 193-194; 204-209. Lists and discusses major American and European studies. [3618]

LORD, C. "On the Early History of the Aristotelian Corpus." *AJPh* 107(1986), 137-161. Considers hypotheses regarding early history of preservation and transmission of Ar's works. Ar may have played a more active role than generally assumed. [3619]

LOWRY, J. M. P. "Aristotle and Modern Historical Criticism." *LThPh* 36(1980), 17-27. Ar's concepts are not historically conditioned but transcend temporal limitations[3620]

MASTERS, R. D. "The Case of Aristotle's Missing Dialogues: Who Wrote the *Sophist*, the *Statesman*, and the *Politics*?" *PolTheo* 5(1977), 31-60. Suggests that some difficulties in Ar's *Pol* can be resolved if Books 4-6 are assumed to be by Theophrastus and that Ar may have written P's *Soph* and *Stsm*. Maintains that Ar was substantially closer to P than is generally assumed. [3621]

——. "On Chroust: A Reply." *PolTheo* 7(1979), 545-547. Reply to #3580. Abandons hypothesis that *Soph* and *Stsm* were written by the young Ar. [3622]

McKEON, R. "The Hellenistic and Roman Foundations of the Tradition of Aristotle in the West." *RMeta* 32(1979), 677-715. Discusses how Ar's philosophy was interpreted and developed during Hellenistic/Roman periods. These translations and interpretations dominated in Middle Ages even after original texts were available again. [3623]

———. *Introduction to Aristotle.* Univ. of Chicago Pr., 1973; 2nd ed. Introductory essay with selections in transl. Includes readings from *Meta*, *Phys*, and *Rhet*, along with *Poetics*, *Topics*, *Nicomachean Ethics*, *De anima* in their entirety. [3623a]

MORAUX, P., and **WIESNER, J.,** eds. *Zweifelhaftes im Corpus Aristotelicum: Studien zu einigen Dubia. Akten des 9. Symposium Aristotelicum (Berlin, 7.-16. September 1981).* Berlin: De Gruyter, 1983. Collection of essays on five of Ar's disputed works. Those in English are abstracted herein. [3624]

MORAVCSIK, J. M. E., ed. *Aristotle: A Collection of Critical Essays.* Notre Dame, IN: Univ. of Notre Dame Pr., 1967. Papers are abstracted herein. [3625]

MORRALL, J. B. *Aristotle.* London: Allen & Unwin, 1976. Sketches background and origins of Greek political tradition. Examines early tradition, and especially S, before considering Ar's views. Examines what can be known of political outlook which characterized early Ar. Traces significance of his career in general. [3626]

MURCHLAND, B. "Aristotle, Metaphor and the Task of Philosophy." *Diot* 3(1975), 95-104. Metaphors play an essential role in philosophy. P's Forms and Ar's Unmoved Mover are metaphors as much as doctrines. Ar's use of such devices accords well with what he says about metaphor in *Poet*. [3627]

NIEBYL, P. H. "Old Age, Fever, and the Lamp Metaphor." *JHM* 26(1971), 351-368. Extinguished lamp, used as metaphor for death by Ar, is picked up by Cicero and by later philosophers and medical writers. [3628]

NOVAK, J. A. "Brentano's *Ueber Aristoteles.*" *Apeir* 21(1988), 69-95. Review and discussion of the German original of #3554. [3629]

O'CONNOR, D. J. "Aristotle," in *A Critical History of Western Philosophy*, ed. D. J. O'Connor (New York: Free Pr., 1968), pp. 36-61. Useful overview, with discussions of formal logic, scientific background, nature of knowledge, substance and cause, mind and body, God, and moral philosophy. [3630]

O'MEARA, D. J., ed. *Studies in Aristotle.* Washington, DC: Catholic Univ. of America Pr., 1981. Collection of essays, which are abstracted herein. [3631]

OWENS, J. "Aristotle: Teacher of Those Who Know," in #3634, pp. 1-13. Brief overview of Ar's approach to philosophical investigations. [3632]

———. "Aristotle's Notion of Wisdom." *Apeir* 20(1987), 1-16. Notion of *sophia* originated as skill in arts and handicrafts. Only later did it come to have the sense in which Ar uses it of the highest practical and theoretical wisdom. [3633]

———. *Aristotle: The Collected Papers of Joseph Owens*, ed. J. R. Catan. Albany: SUNY Pr., 1981. Items are abstracted individually herein. [3634]

PARSONS, H. L. "The Contradictory Humanism of Aristotle's Thought." *RevW* 4/5(1973), 126-162. Ar's individualism, egoism, and elitism are incompatible with humanism that proclaims full development of man. [3635]

PAVLOVSKIS, Z. "Aristotle, Horace and the Ironic Man." *CPh* 63(1968), 22-41. Ar considers an ironic person false, though less objectionable than a braggart, and even somewhat attractive when he controls his use of irony. Horace uses this model in his *Satires*, apparently without consciously borrowing from Ar. [3636]

PELLETIER, F. J., and KING-FARLOW, J., eds. *New Essays on Aristotle*. Guelph, Ont.: Canad. Assoc. for Publ. in Phil., 1984; *CanJPh* Suppl. 10. Collection of essays, each abstracted herein. [3637]

POWELL, C. T. "Why Aristotle Has no Philosophy of History." *HPhQ* 4(1987), 343-357. Discusses Ar's reasons for considering history as having less philosophic significance than poetry. History examines particulars, not universals. Ar does, however, use historical examples to illustrate arguments about universals. [3638]

PRUFER, T. "Aristotelian Themes." *StudPh&HistPh* 5(1970), 73-78. Survey of major topics and problems in Ar's thinking. [3639]

QUANDT, K. *"Hai gar ton enantion apodeixeis aporiai peri ton enantion eisin.* Philosophical Program and Expository Practice in Aristotle." *ClAnt* 2(1983), 279-298. A passage from *De caelo* shows how Ar tried to define a problem by reviewing earlier thought on it. His selection of material, however, is not objective and is done solely for purposes of rebuttal. [3640]

——. "Some Puns in Aristotle." *TAPhA* 111(1981), 179-196. Puns serve several functions in Ar: to ridicule ideas different from his, particularly in his predecessors; to teach; to provide comic relief. [3641]

——. cf. #4524.

RIST, J. M. "The End of Aristotle's *On Prayer.*" *AJPh* 106(1985), 110-113. What some take as a frag of a lost Aristotelian work on prayer is actually a piece of *Peri Eutuchias* ("On Good Fortune"), corrupted by a Platonic transmission. [3642]

RIST, J. M. *The Mind of Aristotle: A Study in Philosophical Growth*. Univ of Toronto Pr., 1989. Seeks to chart Ar's philosophical progress, using both philology and philosophical analysis. [3643]

ROHATYN, D. A. "The Protreptic Argument." *IntLogRev* 8(1977), 192-204. Ar's argument that there is a necessity for philosophizing is shown to be inadequate, whether taken as a deductive statement or a claim about human obligation. It none the less deserves more study than it has received. [3644]

ROSEMANN, P. W. "Averroes and Aristotle's Philosophical Dictionary." *ModSch* 66(1989), 95-115. Examines importance of Averroes' work for determining Ar's text and meaning. [3645]

ROSEN, S. H. "Much Ado about Nothing: Aristotle contra Eleaticism," in #75, pp. 148-

192. Overview of the question of whether nothing can be, which is a question about the possibility of philosophy.   **[3646]**

ROSS, W. D. "The Development of Aristotle's Thought," in #5336, pp. 1-13. Reviews different attempts to discover line of development of Ar's thought, and critically examines Jaeger's (1923) thesis that Ar moved from a Platonic, other-worldly view to one for which problems of physical world mattered a great deal.   **[3647]**

SCHOTT, R. "Aristotle on Women." *Kinesis* 11(1982), 69-84. Ar's view on subordination of women is developed to support status Greek society imposed on them.   **[3648]**

STIGEN, A. *The Structure of Aristotle's Thought: An Introduction to the Study of Aristotle's Writings.* Oslo: Universtetsforl., 1966. An exposition of how and why Ar says what he says, relying largely on paraphrase and quotations.   **[3649]**

THOM, P. "Stiff Cheese for Women." *PhFor* 8(1976), 94-107. Ar's theory of sexual reproduction is an example of his effort to "save the phenomena," i. e., construct a theory that does not contradict appearances. The "appearances" in this case are the sexist views of his culture.   **[3650]**

TURNBULL, R. G. "Aristotle and Philosophy Now: Some Critical Reflections," in *Doing Philosophy Historically,* ed. P. H. Hare (Buffalo, NY: Prometheus Pr., 1988), pp. 117-126. Surveys points of contact between Ar's thought and modern ways of doing philosophy.   **[3651]**

VEATCH, H. B. *Aristotle: A Contemporary Appreciation.* Bloomington: IN Univ. Pr., 1974. Traces philosophy of common sense in *Phys* with notion of change and four causes, in *De Anima* with notion of *psyche* explaining animate objects, in *Ethics* with notion of final cause, in *Meta* with notions of substance, matter, and form, and in *Organon* with unity of categories and concrete reality through the inductive method. Takes Ar as philosopher who speaks directly to common sense of mankind, and argues that he is "a truly live option in philosophy" today.   **[3652]**

VERDENIUS, W. J. "The Nature of Aristotle's Scholarly Writings," in #3657, pp. 12-21. Discusses problems arising from the traditional view that Ar or some of his associates wrote down "lecture notes" which have come down to us. Suggests that Ar thought in terms of written books (as opposed to strong oral elements in P) but that he did not live long enough to bring all of his treatises to a finished state.   **[3653]**

WASSERSTEIN, A. "The Development of Aristotle's Thought." *PACA* 8(1965), 35-37. Reviews earlier publications on Ar's movement away from Platonism.   **[3654]**

WEIL, R. "Aristotle's View of History," in #4036, pp. 202-217; transl. J. and J. Barnes. Discusses relation between history and philosophy in Ar's thought, and argues that his historical researches show scholarly seriousness and philosophical vision of nature of human history.   **[3655]**

WHITEHEAD, D. "Aristotle the Metic." *PCPhS* 21(1975), 94-99. Nothing in Ar's writings supports idea that he held resident alien status in Athens.   **[3656]**

WIESNER, J., ed. *Aristoteles Werk und Wirkung. Paul Moraux Gewidmet, I: Aristoteles* *und seine Schule.* Berlin: De Gruyter, 1985. Collection of previously unpublished papers. Those in English are abstracted herein.   [3657]

WINN, C., and JACKS, M. *Aristotle: His Thought and its Relevance Today.* London: Methuen, 1967. Examines Ar's approach to education in which theory and practice of education must be built upon a solid foundation of a philosophy of life, especially in fields of ethics and politics.   [3658]

WOODBRIDGE, F. J. E. *Aristotle's Vision of Nature,* ed. J. H. Randall et al. New York: Columbia Univ. Pr., 1965. Non-specialist lectures, delivered in 1930, on 1) Ar's logic and language; 2) his psychology (stressing the soul as part of the process of nature); 3) his physics and metaphysics (emphasizing his unitary theory of nature and theory of motion which leads to theology); 4) ethics and aesthetics.   [3659]

ZUBIRI, X. "The Idea of Philosophy in Aristotle," in *Nature, History, and God,* trans. T. B. Fowler (Lanham: Univ. Pr. of America, 1981), pp. 89-96. Examines why Ar called philosophy *zetoumene episteme,* the "sought-after science."   [3660]

For related items see #7, #22, #295, #1177, #1288, #1418, #1463, #1499, #5503, #5512, #5773, #6014,

THE ORGANIZATION OF KNOWLEDGE

While P had sought some principle of unity underlying all knowledge and considered that one could not know something about one subject without knowing all subjects, Ar emphasized grouping and categorizing the various facets of knowledge.

Ar divided knowledge into three general categories: 1) *Theoretical* (Metaphysics, Mathematics, Physics; 2) *Productive* (Aesthetics and Rhetoric); and 3) *Practical* (Ethics and Politics). To illustrate the differences among these types of sciences, we might imagine someone studying the color green. He/she might ask questions such as: How do we perceive that something is green? Is "green" inherent in something or is it a quality we attribute to that thing? Those questions are purely *theoretical.* Answering them does not produce or create anything, nor does it make the investigator's life materially better. If our investigator goes on to consider how he/she might produce the color green in a pigment or dye, or what shade of green to use in a painting, the inquiry becomes *productive,* in the domain of aesthetics. If the investigator goes further to ask what effect the painting or other product might have on those who view it or use it, he/she is moving into the realm of the *practical* (ethics or politics).

This section will discuss Ar's rationale for grouping the "sciences" this way. The bibliography that follows contains sections on each of these topics as well as some subdivisions which modern scholars regularly use, e. g., Biology and Psychology. There is also a section on Logic, which Ar called Analytics and which he considered a study preliminary to philosophy. Some of the sections are given titles which Ar used (e. g., Physics). Others are given titles used by modern scholars (e. g., Metaphysics, a word which never appears in Ar's works).

The sections in the bibliography are arranged alphabetically because the connections which Ar makes among the various subcategories are not always as clear to the modern mind as they were to his (e. g., Ethics and Politics are not usually linked today, nor is Biology considered a subcategory of Physics). Not all scholars agree on exactly how various subcategories should be grouped. Rather than use an arrangement which endorses one view or another, and in order to make things easier for the non-specialist, we have chosen to arrange the topics alphabetically. Let's proceed now to examine Ar's classification of the sciences.

Theoretical Sciences

Under theoretical knowledge Ar includes intellectual activities which do not produce change or motion and which are undertaken purely for themselves, with no ulterior motives. The term "theoretical" is derived from the Greek word meaning to "see" or "contemplate" something. The most important of the theoretical sciences is Metaphysics, called by Ar "first philosophy" or theology, or simply "wisdom" (*sophia*). It is the study of the fundamentals of Being, of what-is, a field which modern philosophers are more likely to describe as ontology, though some use those that term in distinction from "metaphysics." Metaphysics, in Ar's system, is concerned with those things which do not change or move.

The second most important theoretical science is Physics, the study of various kinds of change, especially motion and growth. The etymology of the word can help us once again to understand what Ar intends by this term. The Greek word *physis* means "nature." But Ar approaches the study of nature somewhat differently than we do today. He is not primarily interested in collecting data or doing experiments, though he did do both, to a limited extent. Nor does he want to harness natural forces for the benefit of humanity. This is, we must remember, a *theoretical* science. Ar intends merely to observe and try to understand causes and purposes on the basis of his theories about how nature *should* function.

Mathematics, the third theoretical science, is less important for Ar than it was for Plato and the Pythagoreans. He does not attribute an independent existence to lines and points apart from the sensible objects in which they occur.

Productive Sciences

This branch of knowledge is concerned with *poiesis*, making or creating something. The word has broader connotations than "poetics," and we should not think that Ar's work by that name is devoted solely to writing words in a rhythmic pattern. We have chosen, as many scholars do today, to use the more inclusive term "aesthetics" in order to get beyond this semantic problem.

The two productive sciences, then, are Aesthetics/Poetics and Rhetoric. These two cover all aspects of human creativity, since aesthetics includes painting, sculpture, music, and literature, while Rhetoric pertains to oral communication, particularly in formal, public situations. These two areas were far more important to the Greeks because they formed the basis of their educational and political systems. Education consisted largely of memorizing the works of the great poets/tragedians (with a bit of mathematics and gymnastics thrown in). Our surviving sources show that the poets were quoted or alluded to in writing and conversation as commonly as the Bible was in an earlier age in western European and American literature. Statuary and paintings were on display in temples and other public places, so an educated person was expected to have some informed opinion about their worth.

Rhetoric plays so small a part in our lives (the word even has negative connotations today) that it is difficult for us to appreciate its importance to the ancient Greeks. As an adult, a Greek male could expect to make speeches in his city's political processes, and he could count on being in court often, as juror, defendant, or plaintiff. The Greeks, especially the Athenians, sued one another over even the most trivial issues. Their judicial process made very little use of evidence or testimony of third parties. Normally the plaintiff made a speech, followed by the defendant's *apologia*, or defense. Most trials were held out of doors, with hundreds of people (in addition to the four or five hundred jurors) milling around, ready to voice their reaction when the verdict was reached. Being able to sway those crowds meant the difference between victory and defeat. It is little wonder, then, that Ar devotes an entire work to the techniques of constructing an effective speech and analyzing the psychology behind effective rhetoric.

Practical Sciences
    The last field of knowledge, the practical sciences, concerns the end or objective for which one does something and the use of reason to organize one's knowledge. Practical sciences do not deal with theoretical knowledge or the techniques of production. They focus on how to live the best possible life. Ethics is the study of how the individual lives the good life; politics broadens the question to look at the entire community. We must bear in mind, however, that the only "community" Ar could conceive of was the *polis* or city-state.
    The following few items discuss one aspect or another of Ar's general view of the division of the sciences, as he uses that word.

BENARDETE, S. "On Wisdom and Philosophy." *RMeta* 32(1978), 205-215. At the beginning of *Meta* Ar links wisdom with wonder and claims that wisdom is sought for its own sake. It leaves the philosopher in a sense a stranger.   [3661]

GOMEZ-LOBO, A "Aristotle's First Philosophy and the Principles of Particular Disciplines: An Interpretation of *Metaphysics* E 1, 1025b10-18." *ZPhilForsch* 32(1978), 183-194. Presents a new interpretation of the passage that focuses on two central points in Ar's theory of science: the attitude of different kinds of sciences towards their principles and the meaning of alleged subordination of particular disciplines.   [3662]

GRENE, M. "About the Division of the Sciences," in #3809, pp. 9-13. Discusses *Parts of Animals* 640a1 where Ar appears to distinguish natural science and theoretical sciences. Compares Aristotelian sciences in a number of respects.   [3663]

KUNG, J. "Aristotle's *De Motu Animalium* and the Separability of the Sciences." *JHPh* 20(1982), 65-76. Response to #3845. In this work Ar does not depart significantly from his earlier views on scientific methodology and relation of the sciences.   [3664]

LOUDEN, R. B. "Aristotle's Practical Particularism." *AncPh* 6(1986), 123-138. Ar's claim that practical and theoretical knowledge differ is based on his observation that practical knowledge relates to particulars, not kinds, and that the agent knows the particulars through intiuition, not reasoning.   **[3665]**

OWENS, J. "The Aristotelian Conception of the Sciences," in #3634, pp. 23-34. Reconsiders general conception of scientific knowledge that emerged among the Greeks and was given relatively fixed contours in Ar's philosophical treatises.   **[3666]**

AESTHETICS

Most of what Ar has to say about aesthetic theory is contained in the work known as the *Poetics*, which appears to have been compiled from his lecture notes, perhaps in the mid-340's, and edited or added to later. It is a difficult work, in terms of both establishing the correct text and interpreting crucial points of that text, and yet its impact on western thought has been unparalleled by any other study of the subject.

The most notable difference between Ar's concept of art and P's might be that P was afraid of the power of art while Ar is curious about how works of art are produced. Starting from a moralistic point of view, P wondered about the ultimate purpose of art and its possible negative effect on its audience. As imitation (*mimesis*) it seemed to him to draw people's attention away from the real things which it attempted to imitate.

Ar, as always, takes the more pragmatic view. What kinds of art are there? he wants to know. How are they produced? What is the purpose of artistic creation? Making or production (*poiesis*) seemed to him to involve some kind of skill or craft (*techne*) and yet to be more than the mechanical skill of a workman. Since he believes that everything has a goal or purpose, he wants to find a purpose for art. It appears to him to serve to complete nature. Nature is creative, bringing animate and inanimate objects into existence. But a rock or a tree can be carved into something other than what nature made it. His most oft-quoted example is that of building a house. A house is not natural. It does not grow from a foundation. It is a completion of a process of "growth" imposed by art.

Though *poiesis* could be applied to any type of production, in the *Poetics* Ar confines himself to analyzing what we would call poetry. For the Greeks the term did have a broader meaning than it does for us. Poetry was always sung to a musical accompaniment. In the case of dramatic poetry (tragedy and comedy), which is Ar's specific concern in the *Poetics*, the poet also created dances and may have had a hand in designing the costumes and masks. The portion of the work which survives deals with tragedy; there has been much speculation over what Ar might have said about comedy in Book 2.

Ar discerns two causes that prompt people to create tragedies: the natural impulse toward imitation, and the pleasure of recognition which arises when viewing an imitation. The most problematic points of his definition are the idea that pleasure arises from the "pity and fear" which tragedy evokes and the exact meaning of "catharsis." The definitions offered include "purgation," "purification," and "pruning."

Various explanations of that apparent paradox of pleasure arising from a painful action have been offered. Ar's explanation emphasizes the pleasure derived from a pleasing representation of even an unpleasant subject. In modern terms, a viewer might react positively to a compelling depiction of the crucifixion of Jesus.

ABOUSENNA, M. "Metaphysics of the Absolute in Aristotle's *Poetics*." *Diot* 12(1984), 29-32. Ar sees art as imitation, a type of contemplation (but not change) of reality. Art has universal implications and is organically related to metaphysics. **[3667]**

ADKINS, A. W. H. "Aristotle and the Best Kind of Tragedy." *CQ* 16(1966), 78-102. Ar's ethical values differ enough from those of fifth-century Athenian playwrights to weaken his interpretation in *Poet.* **[3668]**

ADLER, M. J. "Aristotle," in *Poetry and Politics* (Pittsburgh: Duquesne Univ. Pr., 1965), pp. 19-51. Ar sees people as imperfect, except for philosophers. The latter do not need theater or other forms of art. Arts are imitations and exist in a hierarchy. Their function as purgation of emotion is, in a sense, an answer to P. **[3669]**

ALLAN, D. J. "*Eide Tragodias* in Aristotle's *Poetics*." *CQ* 22(1972), 81-88. Though part of text is lost, Ar's definition of types of poetry can still be determined. **[3670]**

ANTON, J. P. "*Mythos, Katharsis*, and the Paradox of Tragedy." *PBACAPh* 1(1985), 299-326. Catharsis is an integral feature of the *structure* of tragedy much more than some emotional purgation in the spectator. Through fulfilment of *mythos*, catharsis becomes part of consciousness of *dramatis personae*, and only secondarily, through compassionate identification with imitated action, is it perceived. **[3671]**

ARMSTRONG, D., and PETERSON, C. W. "Rhetorical Balance in Aristotle's Definition of the Tragic Agent: *Poetics* 13." *CQ* 30(1980), 62-71. *Hamartia* is not the only element accounting for tragic agent's downfall. It should be viewed in relation to other elements Ar introduces to provide a kind of balance typical of rhetorical composition. **[3672]**

ARVANITAKIS, K. "Aristotle's *Poetics*: The Origins of Tragedy and the Tragedy of Origins." *American Imago* 39(1982), 255-268. Overview of psychological implications of Ar's theory of tragedy. **[3673]**

BATTIN, M. P. "Aristotle's Definition of Tragedy in the *Poetics*." *JAAC* 33(1975), 155-170. Somewhat technical discussion of Ar's use of *diaeresis* ("division") and classification to construct the definition which underlies his study of poetry. **[3674]**

———. "*Ibid.*, Part II." *JAAC* 33(1975), 293-302. The concept of *catharsis*, however defined, does not fit logically in Ar's definition of tragedy. The fact that he includes it indicates he was moving away from *diaeresis*, the Platonic method of constructing a definition which he found inadequate. **[3675]**

BELFIORE, E. "Aristotle's Concept of Praxis in the *Poetics*." *CJ* 79(1983), 110-124. Ar considers action the primary element in drama, more important than *ethos*, which concerns choices. Lists occurences of *praxis* and related words in *Poet.* **[3676]**

———. *"Peripeteia* as Discontinuous Action. Aristotle *Poetics* II.1452a22-29." *CPh* 83(1988), 183-194. *Peripeteia* is not "reversal of fortune" but a kind of break in dramatic action by which an agent is prevented from achieving his intended result. **[3677]**

———. "Pleasure, Tragedy and Aristotelian Psychology." *CQ* 35(1985), 349-361. Reading *Poet* in light of such works as *De anima* helps us to see how Ar could argue for the importance of both pleasure and pain in tragedy. **[3678]**

BENNETT, K. C. "The Purging of Catharsis." *BritJAes* 21(1981), 204-213. Explores difficulties in Ar's discussion of catharsis, and offers suggestions for direction of future scholarship. **[3679]**

BERNAYS, J. "Aristotle on the Effect of Tragedy," in #5158, pp. 154-165. Translation of 1889 work. Substitutes for more romantic accounts of *catharsis* the suggestion that *catharsis* is a medical analogy, implying relief. It is spectators who are relieved by having pity and fear aroused in them; and what they are relieved of is their excessive disposition to pity and fear. **[3680]**

BREMER, J. M. *Hamartia: Tragic Error in the* Poetics *of Aristotle and in Greek Tragedy.* Amsterdam: Hakkert, 1969. Concludes that for Ar *hamartia* is not a moral flaw but a flaw due to ignorance. Surveys history of interpretation of this point, beginning in Middle Ages; examines various Greek tragedies to test hypothesis. **[3681]**

BRUNIUS, T. *Inspiration and Katharsis. The Interpretation of Aristotle's* The Poetics *VI 1449b26.* Uppsala: Almqvist & Wiksell, 1966. Somewhat disjointed study which begins by examining Plato's theory of inspiration (especially in *Ion*). Argues that Ar's doctrine of catharsis is based on therapeutic ideas of cult of Asclepius. Physicians (such as Ar's father) used various cathartic techniques, so the term can have different meanings at different times for Ar. **[3682]**

CAREY, C. "'Philanthropy' in Aristotle's *Poetics*." *Eranos* 86(1988), 131-139. This term, as used in chapters 13 and 18, seems to refer to a quality in a play rather than a feeling aroused in a viewer. **[3683]**

CAVARNOS, C. "Art as a Means of Therapy According to Aristotle." *ClassOut* 56(1978-79), 25-32. Ar's theory of man and of the arts generally fits well with his theory of education. Painting serves for enjoyment (hence health); music can produce powerful emotional effects; poetry can impart general truths. **[3684]**

CRAIK, E. M. *"Diplous Mythos."* *CQ* 20(1970), 95-101. Ar expresses highest admiration for tragedies with simple plots. But many Greek tragedies, to judge by those which survive, had a double plot. So long as it is unified, Ar prefers that to an episodic structure. **[3685]**

DAVIES, J. C. "Aspects of Aristotelian Aesthetics." *Euphro* 5(1972), 111-120. Ar's aesthetic views, which cannot be separated from his metaphysics, emphasize pleasure and utility. **[3686]**

DE SAINTE CROIX, G. E. M. "Aristotle on History and Poetry (*Poetics* 9, 1451a36-b11)," in *The Ancient Historian and His Materials: Essays in Honour of C. E. Stevens*, ed. B. Levick (Farnborough, UK: Gregg Internat., 1975), pp. 45-58. For Ar history has less philosophical value than poetry, but he does not denigrate it entirely.   **[3687]**

DES BOUVRIE, S. "Aristotle's *Poetics* and the Subject of Tragic Drama: An Anthropological Approach." *Arethusa* 21(1988), 47-73. Ar defines tragic drama as a symbolic expression of Athenian culture. Its subject is social reality and values.   **[3688]**

DEVEREUX, G. "The Structure of Tragedy and the Structure of the Psyche in Aristotle's *Poetics*," in *Psychoanalysis and Philosophy*, eds. C. Hanly and M. Lazerowitz (New York: International Univ. Pr., 1970), pp. 46-75. Studies problem of replication of structure of psyche in work of art with special reference to Greek tragedy as analyzed by Ar. Argues that Ar's concept of *mimesis* is essentially psychological.   **[3689]**

DEWEY, E. W. "Aristotle's Aesthetics: A Fulfillment of the Platonic Position." *DarshInt* 6(1966), 75-84. We can find a general theory of aesthetics in Ar's works taken as a whole; his position is a development of the Platonic position.   **[3690]**

DOWNING, E. "*Hoion psyche*: An Essay on Aristotle's *muthos*." *ClAnt* 3(1984), 164-177. Examines various uses of *muthos* in Ar and their relationships.   **[3691]**

DYER, R. R. "*Hamartia* in the *Poetics* and Aristotle's Model of Failure." *Arion* 4(1965), 658-664. Term *hamartia* occurs only twice in *Poet*. Ar placed more stress on hero's shift from success to failure than he did on the "flaw" or "error" which caused it.   **[3692]**

EDEN, K. "Poetry and Equity. Aristotle's Defense of Fiction." *Trad* 38(1982), 17-43. Because catharsis involves both pity and fear, the spectator can arrive at a balanced judgment of intentions and moral character of persons represented in a dramatic performance.   **[3693]**

ELSE, G. F. "Persuasion and the Work of Tragedy," in *Tragique et tragédie dans la tradition occidentale*, ed. P. Gravel and T. J. Reiss (Quebec: Déterminations, 1985), pp. 63-68. Examines close connections between *Rhet* and *Poet* and the role of persuasion in both. P feared the seductive power of tragedy, while Ar wanted to show the practical value of art and its usefulness to the common people.   **[3694]**

————. "A Survey of Work on Aristotle's *Poetics*, 1940-1954." *CW* 48(1954-55), 73-82. Annotated.   **[3695]**

————. cf. #1532.

FALUS, R. "Some Remarks on Aristotle's Theory of Catharsis." *Homonoia* 2(1980), 57-88. In *Pol* 8 Ar discusses in instrumental terms the effect of the arts, especially music, on the soul. In *Poet* he fails to define catharsis.   **[3696]**

FERGUSON, F. "On Certain Technical Concepts," in #3736, pp. 142-156. Definitions of plot (form and purpose), action, and mimesis.   **[3697]**

FRIEDRICH, R. "*Epeisodion* in Drama and Epic: A Neglected and Misunderstood Term of Aristotle's *Poetics*." *Hermes* 111(1983), 34-52. Ar uses this term somewhat differently when talking about drama and about epic. With some qualifications, *epeisodion* is roughly equivalent to modern term "episode."   **[3698]**

GELLRICH, N. W. "Aristotle's *Poetics* and the Problem of Tragic Conflict." *Ramus* 13(1985), 155-169. Ar's definition of tragedy does not include a component of conflict or struggle. Considers influence of P's aesthetic views on Ar and asks why conflict is considered so important in modern, but not classical, drama.   **[3699]**

GOLDEN, L. "Aristotle and the Audience for Tragedy." *Mnem* 29(1976), 351-359. Examines current European debate on the subject.   **[3700]**

————. "Aristotle on Comedy." *JAAC* 42(1984), 283-290. Tries to reconstruct Ar's theory of comedy by examining his comments in *Poet* and *Rhet*. He seems to have regarded "indignation" in comedy as the analogue to pity in tragedy.   **[3701]**

————. "The Clarification Theory of Katharsis." *Hermes* 104(1976), 437-452. Katharsis should be taken to mean intellectual clarification, not emotional purgation.   **[3702]**

————. "Comic Pleasure." *Hermes* 115(1987), 165-174. Ar sees pity and fear as appropriate reactions to the tragic hero's nobility. In comedy the protagonist's meanness or ordinariness provokes resentment/indignation.   **[3703]**

————. "Epic, Tragedy, and Catharsis." *CPh* 71(1976), 77-85. Defends interpretation of catharsis as intellectual, as well as physical, cleansing.   **[3704]**

————. "Is *Poetics* 1447b9-23 a Digression?" *RhM* 122(1979), 190-192. The section belongs here and contributes to Ar's argument.   **[3705]**

————. "Is Tragedy the Imitation of a Serious Action?" *GRBS* 6(1965), 283-289. Ar's view of tragedy has been obscured by inaccurate translation of word *spoudaios* in opening lines of *Poet*. The word means "noble," not "serious."   **[3706]**

————. "Katharsis as Clarification. An Objection Answered." *CQ* 23(1973), 45-46. By elevating perception from the individual level to the universal, art enables us to master emotions.   **[3707]**

————. "The Purgation Theory of Catharsis." *JAAC* 31(1973), 473-479. The idea that "catharsis" in Ar means "purgation" can be traced back to Bernays (#3680). But Bernays based his theory on the meaning of the word in *Pol*. In *Poet* it should be taken to mean "intellectual clarification."   **[3708]**

————., and **HARDISON, O. B., Jr.** *Aristotle's Poetics: A Translation and Commentary for Students of Literature*. Englewood Cliffs, NJ: Prentice-Hall, 1968. Translation and section-by-section commentary, looking especially at catharsis.   **[3709]**

GOLDSTEIN, H. D. "Mimesis and Catharsis Re-examined." *JAAC* 24(1966), 567-578. Mimesis is imitation in the sense of purposive creation; catharsis should be derived from a word meaning to prune or shape something.   **[3710]**

GRIFFITH, J. G. "Aristotle's *Megalopsuchos* and Greek Tragedy," in *Festinat senex, or an Old Man in a Hurry, Being an Assortment of Unpublished Essays on Problems in Greek and Latin Literature and Archaeology, Together with Reprints of Three Articles* (Oxford: Oxbow Books, 1988), pp. 36-43. The "great-souled" man of the ethical works is to be compared to the tragic heroes of the *Poet*. This characteristic was more admirable to an ancient audience than it is to us.   [3711]

GULLEY, N. *Aristotle on the Purposes of Literature.* Cardiff: Univ. of Wales Pr., 1971; also in #5158, pp. 166-176. Discusses role of poetry in education and, in particular, in regulating emotions, Also studies Ar's conception of poetry as imitation concerned with moral aspects of human behavior. His opinion of it is relatively low.   [3712]

HAGBERG, G. L. "Mimesis and Abstract Art." *Ph* 59(1984), 365-372. The claim that non-representational art is incompatible with imitation arises out of a misapprehension of what Ar means by *mimesis*.   [3713]

HALLIWELL, S. *Aristotle's* Poetics. Chapel Hill: Univ. of NC Pr., 1986. Overview of Ar's purpose in writing *Poet*; links its doctrines to the whole of his work. Chapters on Ar's aesthetic theory, mimesis, action and character, and other topics. Traces influence of *Poet* on later thinkers.   [3714]

——. cf. #1545.

HANSEN, F. "A Broadway View of Aristotle's Poetics." *JAesEduc* 3(1969) 85-91. Claims that students could gain a better understanding of Ar's method through critical study of Broadway musicals. Technique would also show that Ar's rules of tragedy, derived from one author, do not apply well to others.   [3715]

HASSAN, R. *Practical Criticism and Some Aspects of Aristotle's 'Poetics'.* Lahore, Pakistan: Imperial, 1967. Aims to give readers some introduction to applied criticism and to main issues involved in *Poet*.   [3716]

HELD, G. F. "*Spoudaios* and Teleology in the *Poetics*." *TAPhA* 114(1984), 159-176. Lesky and Kommerell maintain that Ar's theory of tragedy was never meant to be applied beyond stage presentations. But the word *spoudaios* has ethical implications which transcend the usual translation ("serious"). It suggests that, for Ar, tragedy is directed toward the end of producing good actions.   [3717]

HOGAN, J. C. "Aristotle's Criticism of Homer in the *Poetics*." *CPh* 68(1973), 95-108. Ar saw epic and tragedy as closely related and especially certain devices which Homer used that are similar to those of tragedy.   [3718]

HUTTON, J. *Aristotle's* Poetics. New York: W. W. Norton, 1982. Translation with notes and introductory essay.   [3719]

HUXLEY, G. L. "Historical Criticism in Aristotle's Homeric Questions." *PRIA* 79(1979), 73-81. Ar often relies on antiquarian knowledge picked up in his other researches to broaden his interpretation of Homer in *Poet*.   [3720]

JANKO, R. *Aristotle on Comedy: Towards a Reconstruction of* Poetics II. Berkeley: Univ. of CA Pr., 1984. The *Tractatus Coislinianus*, a tenth-century Byzantine ms, preserves a summary of *Poetics* 2 and reveals Ar's views on nature of comedy, humor, and catharsis. On this reading, Ar took Aristophanes as the high point (*entelechy*) of Greek comedy.   [3721]

KARGOPOULOS, P. V. "Mythos and Tragedy in the *Poetics* of Aristotle." *Phil*(Athens)

4(1974), 259-273. Plot is organizing principle of tragedy. It is the beginning because it makes up unity and order of play, and as a complete whole, it is the end. One need not distort them by forcing comparisons to modern terms.   [3722]

KITTO, H. D. F. "Aristotle and Fourth-Century Tragedy," in #63, pp. 113-129. Ar views tragedy as cathartic because drama of his day aimed only at arousing emotions. He failed to grasp that fifth-century tragedy dealt with basic questions of life.   [3723]

LANG, H. S. "An Homeric Echo in Aristotle." *PhQ* 61(1982), 329-339. Ar alludes to a planted bed, like the one in *Odyssey* 23, showing how Homer joined by a simple sign the formal and material elements which Ar considered the components of any work of art.   [3724]

LEVIN, S. R. "Aristotle's Theory of Metaphor." *Ph&Rh* 15(1982), 24-46. Ar's discussion of four types of metaphor in *Poet* 1457b7 has been criticized as unsystematic. It can be better understood if it is seen as a teaching tool, designed to promote awareness of relationships between objects and concepts.   [3725]

LORD, C. "Aristotle's History of Poetry." *TAPhA* 104(1974), 195-229. Ar's theory of tragedy is consistent with what we know of its historical development.   [3726]

———. "Tragedy Without Character: *Poetics* VI. 1450a 24." *JAAC* 28(1969) 55-62. Ar claims that plot, not character, is essential to tragedy. A literal reading of this passage reveals the role that each of the six parts of tragedy play in his system.   [3727]

LOSONCY T. A. "The Being of the Work of Art: Aristotle on His Predecessors." *Diot* 15(1987), 60-65. Examines reason's role with regard to Aristotelian view that art imitates nature. Notes degree to which Ar surpasses earlier positions.   [3728]

MARGON, J. S. "Aristotle and the Irrational and Improbable Elements in *Oedipus Rex*." *CW* 70(1976), 249-255. Ar valued this play precisely because of its emphasis on irrational acts and coincidences.   [3729]

MARSHALL, D. G. "Aristotelian Imitation as Non-Positivist Representation." *Annals of Scholarship* 2(1981), 85-95. Examines how Ar's use of term *mimesis* ranges from a technical sense to fairly loose meanings.   [3730]

McKEON, R. "Rhetoric and Poetics in the Philosophy of Aristotle," in #3736, pp. 201-236. Ar's treatment of arts is set in four "progressively narrowing contexts": 1) particular instances of productive or poetic powers; 2) instances of rational productive powers which are sources of all human actions; 3) instances of rational powers which result in some artificial product apart from the activity itself; and 4) the particular art analyzed in the specific subject matter and objects proper to it.   [3731]

McNALLY, J. R. "Characteristics of Art in the Text of Aristotle." *JAAC* 29(1971), 507-514. Examines Ar's view of art as action, habit, a kind of knowledge, and a human perfection.   [3732]

MISRA, K. S. *Modern Tragedies and Aristotle's Theory*. Atlantic Highlands, NJ: Humanities Pr,, 1981. If Ar is interpreted undogmatically, his theory has great relevance to literature of our time.   [3733]

MOLES, J. "Notes on Aristotle, *Poetics* 13 & 14." *CQ* 29(1979), 77-94. Critical discussion of Stinton's (#3767) analysis of Ar's treatment of *hamartia*. Focuses specifically on interpretation of examples at 13,53a11 and 13,53a20 and problem of contradiction between 13,53a13-15 and 14,54a4-9. [3734]

———. "*Philanthropia* in the *Poetics*." *Phoenix* 38(1984), 325-335. Tragedians try to satisfy our natural urge to love our fellow beings but cannot do this entirely or feelings of pity are lost. Tragedy's primary purpose is aesthetic but it does have moral implications. [3735]

OLSON, E. *Aristotle's* Poetics *and English Literature: A Collection of Critical Essays.* Univ. of Chicago Pr., 1965. Fourteen essays, some dating to eighteenth century. Most use Ar only as point of departure. Relevant ones are abstracted herein. [3736]

———. "The Poetic Method of Aristotle: Its Powers and Limitations," in #3736, pp. 175-191. Tries to define art in Aristotelian philosophic terms to determine what it is able to contribute to human quest for knowledge. [3737]

ØSTERUD, S. "*Hamartia* in Aristotle and Greek Tragedy." *SO* 51(1976), 65-80. Ar's theories are not meant to apply to fifth- or fourth-century plays. He is writing about a kind of perfect tragedy and what is necessary to create it. *Hamartia* need not be a moral failing, as long as the hero is not too good or bad. [3738]

PACKER, M. "The Conditions of Aesthetic Feeling in Aristotle's *Poetics*." *BritJAes* 24(1984), 138-148. Ar fails to specify how viewers of tragedy make connection between cognition and emotion, which is vital if tragedy is to have aesthetic value. A practical syllogism, reasoned by the viewer, seems the only way to establish connection. [3739]

PAPANOUTSOS, E. P. "The Aristotelian Katharsis." *BritJAes* 17(1977), 361-364. It is passions, not dramatic happenings, that are purified by the "form" with which the poet endows them. [3740]

PAUW, D. A. "The Rigorism of Aristotle in His *Poetics*: Fact or Fiction?" *AClass* 21(1978), 71-81. Survey of Ar's interpretive method. [3741]

PELTZ, R. "Classification and Evaluation in Aesthetics: Weitz and Aristotle." *JAAC* 30(1971), 69-78. Unlike modern students of aesthetics, such as Weitz, Ar thinks of classification and evaluation as separate processes. [3742]

POTTS, L. J. *Aristotle on the Art of Fiction.* Cambridge Univ. Pr., 1968. Transl. of *Poetics* with introductory essay and notes. [3743]

QUILLER-COUCH, A. "A Note on the *Poetics*," in #3736, pp. 101-107. Non-specialist overview of Ar's purposes and the outline of the work. [3744]

REES, B. R. "Aristotle's Approach to Poetry." *G&R* 28(1981), 23-39. Ar's approach to poetry is just as analytical as his biological methodology. [3745]

———. "Pathos in the *Poetics* of Aristotle." *G&R* 19(1972), 1-11. Ar gave little attention to pathos because of preference for complex plots. Pathos is action resulting in harm. It is the essence of tragedy. [3746]

————. "Plot, Character and Thought," in *Le monde grec. Pensée, littérature, histoire, documents: Hommages à Claire Preaux*, ed. J. Bingen et al. (Brussells: Ed. de l'Univ., 1975), pp. 188-196. Discusses first three categories in Ar's analysis of tragedy. [3747]

ROSENMEYER, T. G. "Design and Execution in Aristotle, *Poetics* ch. xxv." *CSCA* 6(1973), 231-252. Examines use of terms such as *adunata, techne, hamartia*. [3748]

ROSENSTEIN, L. "On Aristotle and Thought in the Drama." *Critical Inquiry* 3(1977), 543-565. Shows how thought, the third subject or component of the action in drama (first and second being plot and character) is expressed in art form of tragedy. [3749]

RYE, H. J. *A Commentary Illustrating the Poetic of Aristotle*. New York: Garland, 1971. Reprint of 1792 edition which seeks to "render the precepts of Aristotle clear to the English" and to enable those who are conversant only with poets of the 18th century to judge how far Ar's rules "are really consonant with truth and nature." [3750]

SANTORO, L. "Aristotle and Contemporary Aesthetics." *Diot* 10(1982), 112-121. Ar's understanding of art and his concerns about poetry are still reflected in contemporary discussions of aesthetic theory. [3751]

————. "Some Remarks on Aristotle's Concept of Mimesis." *REA* 82(1980), 31-40. For Ar mimesis is a particular activity, a kind of artistic *techne*. [3752]

SCHAPER, E. "Aristotle's Catharsis and Aesthetic Pleasure." *PhQ* 18(1968) 131-143. Catharsis means more than purging. It implies viewer/reader's involvement in understanding the work. [3753]

————. cf. #1587.

SCHRIER, O. J. "A Simple View of *Peripateia*. Aristotle, *Poet*. 1452 A 22-29." *Mnem* 33(1980), 96-118. Text of passage does not need to be emended. Ar's meaning is clear and simple. [3754]

SCHUETRUMPF, E. "The Meaning of *Ethos* in the *Poetics*. A Reply." *Hermes* 115(1987), 175-181. Reply to Held (#3717). [3755]

————. "Traditional Elements in the Concept of *Hamartia* in Aristotle's *Poetics*." *HSCP* 92(1989), 137-156. Legal terminology cannot be overlooked as a source for Ar's concept of *hamartia*. Sophocles' *Oedipus at Colonnus* also helped shape his views. [3756]

SIFAKIS, G. M. "Learning from Art and Pleasure in Learning: An Interpretation of Aristotle *Poetics* 4,1448b8-19," in *Studies in Honour of T. B. L. Webster*, ed. J. H. Betts et al (Bristol, UK: Bristol Classical Pr., 1986), I, pp. 211-222. Art gives pleasure and teaches by extracting the universal meaning from something and allowing the viewer/reader to learn from it without being bothered by trivialities. [3757]

SIMPSON, P. "Aristotle on Poetry and Imitation." *Hermes* 116(1988), 279-291. Ar's definition of poetry as imitation seems to apply best to dramatic and narrative poetry, which sustain emotion and show consequences of action. This didactic function is one element of *catharsis*. [3758]

SMITHSON, I. "The Moral View of Aristotle's *Poetics*." *JHI* 44(1983), 3-18. Offers a detailed analysis of Ar's theory of aesthetics to show that modern commentators have paid too little attention to moral assumptions underlying his thought.   [3759]

SPIEGEL, N. "The Aesthetic, Intellectual and Moral Effects of Tragedy According to Aristotle." *RFIC* 94(1966), 415-423. For Ar several factors influence one's aesthetic reaction to a tragedy. It should also cause one to reflect on the human condition. Catharsis is the most important reaction one might experience. It is therapeutic and has ethical overtones.   [3760]

——. "Aristotle's Theory of the Perception of the Tragedy." *Eos* 55(1965), 44-56. Those who perceive a work of art experience, in varying degrees, emotions and thoughts which are directed to their souls by the work of art itself.   [3761]

——. "The Nature of Katharsis According to Aristotle." *RBPh* 43(1965), 22-39. Based on reading of Ar and other philosophers and poets, catharsis seems to be a process of ridding the soul of disease-like elements.   [3762]

——. "On Aristotle's Definition of Tragedy: A Reconsideration." *RBPh* 49(1971), 14-30. Attempts to clarify definition of various elements of tragedy, such as *mimesis*, which can be translated variously, according to context, and *praxis spoudaia* ("serious plot"). Also examines the spectator's role.   [3763]

SRIVASTAVA, K. G. "How Does Tragedy Achieve *Katharsis* According to Aristotle?" *BritJAes* 15(1975), 132-143. Explores how a tragic play achieves *katharsis* and by what means. Realization of *katharsis* by a tragic play is not itself tragic pleasure; rather it is a guarantee to pleasure proper to tragedy.   [3764]

——. "A New Look at the 'Katharsis' Clause of Aristotle's *Poetics*." *BritJAes* 12(1972), 258-275. Ar held an "organistic" view of tragedy consistently and the catharsis clause should not be given a purification interpretation, but an aesthetic one.   [3765]

STABRYLA, S. "Some Remarks on the Genological Theory in the *Poetics*." *Eos* 65(1977), 25-39. Ar does not have names for various literary genres. He did not intend to create a system but to allow for natural growth of types of literature.   [3766]

STINTON, T. C. W. "*Hamartia* in Aristotle and Greek Tragedy." *CQ* 25(1975), 221-254. Meaning of *hamartia* ranges from "ignorance of fact" to "moral defect." Whether or not agent is responsible for his act, his downfall alienates audience's sympathies.   [3767]

TRIMPI, W. "The Ancient Hypothesis of Fiction: An Essay on the Origins of Literary Theory." *Trad* 27(1971), 1-78. Examines early terms of expectation concerning function of literature. Discusses antagonistic nature of disciplines from which these terms are derived and defines types of "hypothetical activity" characteristic of these disciplines in relation to *Poet*.   [3768]

TSAGARAKIS, O. "Aristotle *Poetics* 1451a24-30." *Phoenix* 22(1968), 159-162. Discusses Ar's views on unity of plot to determine what it consists of. He uses *Iliad* to show that Homer includes only episodes which contribute to unity of his narrative.   [3769]

——. "*Katachresis* of the Aristotelian Term *Epeisodion* as Applied to Homer." *REG*

86(1973), 294-307. Modern critical theory which sees episodes in Homer as virtually independent is entirely contrary to Ar's emphasis on unity of action and the purpose of such episodes. [3770]

TWINING, T. *Aristotle's Treatise on Poetry.* New York: Garland, 1971. Reprint of 1789 translation and notes, a landmark study. [3771]

URBAN, R. T. "All or Nothing at All. Another Look at the Unity of Time in Aristotle." *CJ* 61(1966), 262-264. Reference to unity of time in *Poetics* 1449b12-16 should be understood as applying to time of performance, not time elapsed in play. [3772]

VAN BENNEKOM, R. "The Definitions of *Syndesmos* and *Arthron* in Aristotle, *Poetics* Ch. 20." *Mnem* 28(1975), 399-411. Ar's second definition of *syndesmos*, while still deficient, improves upon his first. Section on *arthron* was written not by Ar but by a Peripatetic well versed in his thought (possibly Theophrastus). [3773]

VAN DER BEN, N. "Aristotle's *Poetics* 1449b27-28," in *Miscellanea Tragica in Honorem J. C. Kamerbeek*, ed. J. M. Bremer et al. (Amsterdam: Hakkert, 1976), pp. 1-15. Discusses interpretation of the passage, especially terms *eleos, phobos, miaros* and *katharos*, in comparison with 1452b28-1454a15. [3774]

VAN DER EIJK, P. J. "Aristotle, *Poetics* 1452b34-36. A Discrepancy Between Wording and Meaning?" *Mnem* 39(1986), 390-394. The apparent contradiction between this passage and others on the same subject arises from the dogmatic fashion in which Ar confuses several terms. [3775]

WELCH, L. M. "Catharsis, Structural Purification, and Else's Aristotle." *BuckRev* 19(1971), 31-50. Discussion of Else's *Aristotle's Poetics* (1958). [3776]

YANAL, R. "Aristotle's Definition of Poetry." *Nous* 16(1982), 499-526. Poetry is not a form as much as a type of literature that makes us aware of moral choices. It is written about types of persons, while history, e. g., is about individuals. [3777]

ZOUMPOS, A. N. "The *Anaisthetos Chronos* in the Art. An Aesthetical Interpretation of Aristotle." *Platon* 18(1966), 277-278. Discusses Ar's concept of beauty as symmetry and proportion. Concept is important in studying other facets of his thought. [3778]

For related items see #133, #1510, #1511, #1561, #1564, #1568, #1579, #1588, #1590, #1597, #3627, #3824, #5158, #5316, #5323.

BIOLOGY

Approximately one-third of Ar's surviving work deals with biological matters. His collection of data, the *Historia animalium*, is his longest single work (though the authenticity of Book 10 has been questioned). It is often noted that there may be some connection between those facts and the fact that his father was a physician. One need not press the issue. It is enough to say that, wherever the impulse came from, observation of plants and animals is a fundamental part of Ar's philosophical theorizing.

The importance of biological observation in Ar's thought could be better appreciated if we knew at what stage of his life he did most of it. Jaeger, Ross, and others who hold to a theory that Ar's thought moved away from Platonism to a more empirical approach, assign the biological works to the last phase of Ar's life, when he had returned to Athens to establish the Lyceum. The significance of this interpretation is its implication that Ar would have approached the study of biology with his theoretical views already formed.

As long ago as 1910, however, D. W. Thompson pointed out that most of the place references in the biological works are to places in Asia Minor and Macedonia, not to Greece. Thompson concluded, and others have concurred, that the biological works were composed in the period between P's death and Ar's return to Athens (347-335 B. C.). D. M. Balme would even date the biological treatises to Ar's days as a member of the Academy. It seems likely, then, that Ar's observations of living creatures shaped his philosophical development, rather than the other way around.

The *Historia animalium* provides a foundation for Ar's biological work. The Greek word *historia* actually means "inquiry" or "research," so the title should not be taken to mean that this is some chronological study of the animal kingdom. It is in fact a collection of data on which Ar planned to base his further study. The results of his interpretation of that data are found in various treatises, primarily *De partibus animalium, De motu animalium, De incessu animalium,* and finally *De generatione animalium.*

In all of these works Ar is concerned to find causes for the phenomena which he has observed. As he says at one point, "to know is to know by means of causes." He groups things into large groups (*megista gene*) and breaks them down into smaller groups (*eide*), similar to our species. But taxonomy is not his primary concern. He does not describe things in absolute terms of size or weight. His descriptions tend to be comparative: this animal is bigger/smaller than that one. Precise measurements are insignificant to him because he is trying to understand the creature's function and its ultimate purpose (*telos*). His biology, like all other facets of his thought, is inescapably teleological, a feature which some see as a shortcoming.

The application of the four causes to biology can be seen in the example of reproduction. The Efeecient (or Motive) cause of a new animal is the male parent; the Material cause is the menstrual flow of the female (which Ar thought played a part in reproduction); the Formal cause is the embryo and the process of development which makes the animal a member of the proper species (Soul is involved in this part of the process); the Final cause, the goal, is the mature, fully developed animal.

It would be easy to pick out points where Ar was totally wrong about the functions of biological parts (he thought the brain served only to cool the body). But he also observed phenomena which were not taken seriously again until the nineteenth century, and his mistakes are generally the result of inadequate data on which to base his judgments.

ATRAN, S. "Pre-Theoretical Aspects of Aristotelian Definition and Classification of Animals: The Case for Common Sense." *StudHist&PhSci* 16(1985), 113-164. All systems of animal classification assume a common nature of animals which appear the same, in spite of surface differences. Ar's doctrine of essences finds the unity of nature in these underlying similarities.   [3779]

BALME, D. M. "Aristotle and the Beginnings of Zoology." *Journal of the Society for the Bibliography of Natural History* 5(1970), 272-285. Examines Ar's biological theory in context of his corpus and compares it to scientific knowledge of his time.   [3780]

―――. "Aristotle *Historia Animalium* Book Ten," in #3657, pp. 191-206. Discusses authenticity and interpretation of this disputed text. It may have originated as a separate treatise on generation, written by Ar before *De gener animal.*   [3781]

―――. "Aristotle's Biology Was Not Essentialist." *AGPh* 62(1980), 1-12; also in #3814, pp. 291-312. Argues that essentialist identification of form and species traditionally attributed to Ar is not to be found in his biological works.   [3782]

―――. "Aristotle's Use of Differentiae in Zoology," in #5158, pp. 183-193. If we view Ar's biological works as aiming at complete classification of animals, they are disappointing. But Ar undertakes other important tasks, such as identifying differences between species and seeking reasons why these differentiating features go together in some combinations and not others.   [3783]

―――. "Aristotle's Use of Division and Differentiae," in #3814, pp. 69-89. Places *Hist. Animal.* in context of theoretical concerns about causal explanation. Traces Ar's reforms of Platonic *diairesis* from *Topics* through *Analytics* and *Meta* Z to critique of dichotomy and presentation of concept of "simultaneous, multi-axis division" in *PostAn.*   [3784]

―――. *Aristotle's Use of the Teleological Explanation.* Univ. of London, 1965. Brief (27 pp.) study of how Ar argues for concept of an end (*telos*) as governing biological development but does not extend principle to metaphysics.   [3785]

―――., trans. *De Partibus Animalium, Book I: De Generatione Animalium, Book I.* Oxford: Clarendon Pr., 1972. Translation and notes.   [3786]

―――. "The Place of Biology in Aristotle's Philosophy," in #3814, pp. 9-20. Reconsiders aims of "biological" treatises. These works are not simply primitive counterparts to contemporary biological investigations, but are philosophical theses in themselves. Work which these treatises embody dates from Ar's time in Academy.   [3787]

―――. "Teleology and Necessity," in #3814, pp. 275-285. Teleological control is not merely in a basic potential borne by movements, but in its characteristic material base: in character of "self-limiting conplex" of movements.   [3788]

―――. cf. #4596.

BOLTON, R. "Definition and Scientific Method in Aristotle's *Posterior Analytics* and *Generation of Animals*," in #3814, pp. 120-166. Challenges view that Ar's primary method of establishing results in study of nature was dialectic. Even in *Phys*, his method is empirical in ways that dialectic cannot be.   [3789]

BOYLAN, M. "Mechanism and Teleology in Aristotle's Biology." *Apeir* 15(1981), 96-102.

Examines Ar's proposed solution to the difficulty of maintaining mechanistic and purposive views of nature.   [3790]

——. *Method and Practice in Arisototle's Biology.* Washington, DC: Univ. Pr. of America, 1983. In the context of his larger philosophical system Ar is seen as a critical empiricist. Chapters discuss his taxonomy, his use of teleological and empirical explanations, and his application of his method in several specific instances. Attempts to counter claims by modern critics that Ar's theory and practice are not coherent. Delineates some crucial aspects of biological methodology which have significance to those interested in the problems of contemporary biology.   [3791]

——. "The Place of Nature in Aristotle's Teleology." *Apeir* 18(1984), 126-140. Summary of several previous publications. Ar uses *physis* (nature) in several ways, including the notion of something that regulates the form of a species.   [3792]

CHARLTON, W. "Aristotle and the *Harmonia* Theory," in #3809, pp. 131-150. Explores whether Ar rejects *harmonia* theory mentioned at *De Anima* I.407b27-30 for its deterministic implications.   [3793]

——. "Aristotle on the Place of Mind in Nature," in #3814, pp. 408-423. Through an examination of three theses about *nous*, shows Ar to have a philosophy of mind that is neither Cartesian nor materialist.   [3794]

CHROUST, A.-H. "Which Came First, the Chicken or the Egg? Censorinus *De die natali* iv,3-4: A Fragment of Aristotle's *On Philosophy*." *C&M* 32(1980), 221-225. This passage seems to be a portion of Ar's lost dialogue which discussed the uninterrupted cycle of generation and the continuation of species.   [3795]

COHEN, S. "Aristotle on Heat, Cold, and Teleological Explanation." *AncPh* 9(1989), 255-270. Examines two of Ar's claims: (1) things that have functions are not made by fire alone and (2) heat and cold can produce some of the characteristics of flesh and bone, but not their logoi.   [3796]

COOPER, J. M. "Aristotle on Natural Teleology," in #76, pp. 197-222. Sketches Ar's theory that living things have two natures, material and formal, and explains how his belief in goal-directedness of nature derives from this theory. Then considers his reasons for doctrine that living things do have these two different natures, with its teleological implications.   [3797]

——. "Hypothetical Necessity and Natural Teleology," in #3814, pp. 243-274. Suggests that Ar has two distinct lines of argument for irreducibility of teleological explanation: one rests on insufficiency of material natures to explain formation of precisely structured outcomes; the other stresses need to explain why outcomes are good for organism which possesses them.   [3798]

DROSSART LULOFS, H. J. "Aristotle, Bar Aebraeus, and Nicolaus Damascenus on Animals," in #3809, pp. 345-357. Textual analysis of *De gen anim* 487b33-488a10 and how man is used in numerous examples.   [3799]

EYBEN, E. "Antiquity's View of Puberty." *Latomus* 31(1972), 677-697. Looks at Ar's explanation in context of an overview of ancient attitudes toward the biological phenomenon. [3800]

FRANKLIN, J. "Aristotle on Species Variation." *Ph* 61(1986), 245-252. Response to Granger (#3821). Things can differ from one another by degree (continuously) or by essence (discretely). Ar maintains that species can vary continuously, foreshadowing Darwin's position. [3801]

———. "Species in Aristotle." *Ph* 64(1989), 107-108. Reply to Granger's (#3818) challenge to view that Ar admits continuous variation between species. [3802]

FREELAND, C. "Aristotle on Bodies, Matter, and Potentiality," in #3814, pp. 392-407. Stresses that matter embodies capacities to be things, which capacities persist in things. Thus develops an argument for blood being both matter for and matter of organic substances. [3803]

FRIEDMAN, R. "Necessitarianism and Teleology in Aristotle's Biology." *Bio&Ph* 1(1986), 355-365. Ar seems to contradict himself in several passages when talking about hypothetical and simple necessity, especially since simple necessity is not compatible with the notion of teleology. The apparent contradiction is resolved by Ar's concept of coincidental sameness. [3804]

———. "Simple Necessity in Aristotle's Biology." *IntStudPh* 19(1987), 1-9. Ar does recognize simple necessity and does not appeal to hypothetical necessity to account for some biological phenomena. [3805]

FURLEY, D. J. "The Mechanics of *Meteorologica* IV. A Prolegomenon to Biology," in #3624, pp. 73-93. The concept of motion expounded in *Meteor* 4 does not contradict what Ar says on the subject elsewhere. The introduction to the work promises that biology will be treated after meteorology. For those reasons Book 4 appears to be Aristotelian and in its proper place. [3806]

FURTH, M. "Aristotle's Biological Universe: An Overview," in #3814, pp. 21-52. Explores thesis that Ar's metaphysics of substance itself was "to a great extent motivated . . . as a deep theoretical foundation . . . for the biological sciences." [3807]

GILSON, E. "Aristotelian Prologue," in *From Aristotle to Darwin and Back Again: A Journey in Final Causality, Species, and Evolution*, transl. J. Lyon (Notre Dame, IN: Notre Dame Univ. Pr., 1984), pp. 3-18. Examines Ar's doctrine of teleology in nature in *Hist animal* as a preface to survey of problem of evolutionary theory. [3808]

GOTTHELF, A., ed. *Aristotle on Nature and Living Things: Philosophical and Historical Studies Presented to David M. Balme on his Seventieth Birthday.* Pittsburgh: Mathesis, 1985. A collection of papers focusing on Ar's biological works; abstracted herein. Contains good bibliography. [3809]

———. "Aristotle's Conception of Final Causality," in #3814, pp. 204-242. An outcome which is not wholly the result of material necessity is the actualization of an "irreducible potential for form," a potential transmitted from parent to offspring via a certain heat and set of "movements." [3810]

———. "First Principles in Aristotle's *Parts of Animals*," in #3814, pp. 167-198. This work exemplifies an axiomatic structure, and thus satisfies central necessary condition for a science organized on principles set forth in *Post An.*   [3811]

————. "Notes towards a Study of Substance and Essence in Aristotle's *Parts of Animals* ii-iv," in #3809, pp. 27-54. Examines each explanation offered in *Parts Animal* 2-4 and to determine which one of three modes of explanation is at work, to specify which feature of the kind of animal in question is being explained, and by reference to which feature this feature is being explained.   [3812]

————. "Teleology and Spontaneous Generation in Aristotle: A Discussion." *Apeir* 22(1989), 181-193. Examines account of spontaneous generation in *De gen anim* 3.1,1, and attempts to resolve tensions between Ar's doctrine that spontaneous generations occur and his denial that they have teleological significance.   [3813]

————. cf. #5501.

————., and **LENNOX, J. G.,** eds. *Philosophical Issues in Aristotle's Biology.* Cambridge Univ. Pr., 1987. Collection of essays, abstracted herein, which gives substantial attention to the whole of Ar's biology, in matters both of detail and of general purpose and direction.   [3814]

GRACIA GUILLEN, D. "The Structure of Medical Knowledge in Aristotle's Philosophy." *ZWG* 62(1978), 1-36. Medicine is included in list of "virtues" in *EN* 6 and list of "sciences" in *Meta* 6 and 11. One need not assume separate authorship of these lists, merely development of Ar's views.   [3815]

GRAHAM, D. W. "Some Myths About Aristotle's Biological Motivation." *JHI* 47(1986), 529-545. Challenges the claim that Ar's biological interests shaped the character of his philosophy. His view of the world as behaving like a biological organism was developed before he began his studies.   [3816]

GRANGER, G. G. "The Differentia and the per se Accident in Aristotle." *AGPh* 63(1981), 118-129. According to Ar the characteristics which distinguish one species from another are not elements of the essence of the genus but rather are "accidental" features of the genus.   [3817]

GRANGER, H. "Aristotle and the Finitude of Natural Kinds." *Ph* 62(1987), 523-526. Challenges Franklin's (#3801) interpretation that Ar holds that natural kinds form a continuous series, one composed of an infinite number of natural kinds. Defends view that natural kinds form a finite series of contiguous and discrete kinds.   [3818]

————. "Aristotle and the Genus-Species Relation." *SJPh* 18(1980), 37-50. By *genos-eidos* Ar does not mean the same thing that we mean by genus-species. His classification system depends on the assumption that the distinguishing characteristics of a genus (its *diaphorai*) must be logically dependent on the *genos*.   [3819]

————. "Deformed Kinds and the Fixity of Species." *CQ* 37(1987), 110-116. Ar's classification scheme has a place for "deformed" kinds. He uses the same terms to describe abnormalities that he uses for certain species like moles. Apparently he understood "natural kinds" in a broader sense than has been realized.   [3820]

――――. "The *Scala Naturae* and the Continuity of Kinds." *Phron* 30(1985), 181-200. The concept of continuity from one kind to another which underlies Ar's biology is not inconsistent with his logical and metaphysical classifications, in which kinds are distinct from one another.   [3821]

――――. cf. #4685.

GRENE, M. "Aristotle and Modern Biology." *JHI* 33(1972), 395-424; also in *Topics In the Philosophy of Biology*, ed. M. Grene and E. Mendelsohn (Dordrecht, Netherlands: Reidel, 1976), pp. 3-36. Ar's most important contribution is in methodology. He shows that not every branch of science deals with same subject or uses same method. [3822]

HULL, D. L. "The Conflict Between Spontaneous Generation and Aristotle's Metaphysics," in *Proceedings of the Seventh Inter-American Congress of Philosophy* (Quebec: Universitie de Laval Pr., nd.), pp. 215-250. Prevalence of equivocal generation in Ar's biology conflicts with his metaphysics.   [3823]

JACOBS, W. "Art and Biology in Aristotle." *Paideia* Special Issue (1978), 16-29. Examines Ar's use of concepts of mimesis and teleology in these areas.   [3824]

――――. "Preus on Aristotle's *Eide*." *Nat&Sys* 3(1981), 115-118. Against Preus (#3858), defends the traditional reading that Ar believes that each biological species is rigidly separate and distinct from every other, with all members of a species exhibiting the same essential nature.   [3825]

KOSMAN, L. A. "Animals and Other Beings in Aristotle," in #3814, pp. 360-391. Asks what distinguishes being of organisms from that of artifacts, such that the former but not the latter are paradigmatic substances. Focuses especially on analysis of potentiality and actuality.   [3826]

KUNG, J. "Some Aspects of Form in Aristotle's Biology." *Nat&Sys* 2(1980) 67-90. Delineates some of Ar's complaints against his predecessors and describes ways that he uses the idea of form as functional organization in the biological discussions.   [3827]

LANG, H. S. "Aristotle and Darwin: The Problem of Species." *IntPhQ* 23(1983), 141-153. Ar's concept of species solves philosophical and biological problems about study of individuals and groups which plagued Darwin and still lack definite solutions.   [3828]

LANGE, L. "Woman is not a Rational Animal: On Aristotle's Biology of Reproduction," in *Discovering Reality: Feminist Perspectives on Epistemology, Metaphysics, Methodology, and Philosophy of Science*, ed. S. Harding and M. B. Hintikka (Dordrecht, Netherlands: Reidel, 1983), pp. 1-16. Examines Ar's theories of generation and sex distinction and considers their implications. Ar regards it as a virtue for a man to dominate a woman. Treating a woman as an equal would be shameful.   [3829]

LEE, H. D. P. "The Fishes of Lesbos Again," in #3809, pp. 3-8. Explores the question of whether Ar's pursuit of empirical investigations can be dated back at least to his time in Lesbos.   [3830]

LENNOX, J. G. "Are Aristotelian Species Eternal?" in #3809, pp. 67-94. For Ar there is an eternal generation of organisms which are one in form; consequently, kinds, including species, are eternal. [3831]

——. "Aristotle on Genera, Species and 'the More and the Less'." *JHistBiol* 13(1980), 321-346. Like modern evolutionsts, Ar emphasizes importance of adaptation in differentiating between species of same genus. [3832]

——. "Divide and Explain: the *Posterior Analytics* in Practice," in #3814, pp. 90-119. Argues that *PostAn* 2.14-18 explores nature of explanation based on distinction between "incidental" and "unqualified" understanding. Unqualified understanding requires locating widest kinds to which differentiae belong universally. Suggests that *Hist Animal* organizes information about animals in accordance with this methodology. [3833]

——. "Kinds, Forms of Kinds, and the More and the Less in Aristotle's Biology," in #3814, pp. 339-359. Revision of 1980 work. Traces development of notion of kinds with forms varying by the more and less and its use to express the way in which *eide* of a *genos* are related to each other, and examines implications of its role in the biology for traditional views of Aristotelian essentialism. [3834]

——. "Recent Philosophical Studies of Aristotle's Biology." *AncPh* 4(1984), 73-82. Surveys several recent publications and discusses implications of Ar's biology for other facets of his philosophical thought. [3835]

——. "Teleology, Chance, and Aristotle's Theory of Spontaneous Generation." *JHPh* 20(1982), 219-238. Offers an interpretation of Ar's teleology which allows A to distinguish between different kinds of organic generation. [3836]

LLOYD, G. E. R. "Empirical Research in Aristotle's Biology," in #3814, pp. 53-63. Excerpt from *Magic, Reason, and Experience* (1979) which explores whether Ar's biological investigations really constitute an empirical science, and if so, what is the relationship to Ar's theoretical interests and preoccupations. [3837]

——. cf. #4212.

LONGRIGG, J. "Roots." *CR* 17(1967), 1-4. Attempts to resolve apparent inconsistencies in A's reading of Empedocles in *De gen et corr*. [3838]

——. "A Seminal 'Debate' in the Fifth Century B.C.?" in #3809, pp. 277-287. A adopts for his own use Diogenes' specific modification of Empedocles' seminal theory in the light of Hippon's critique. [3839]

MATTHEN, M. "The Four Causes in Aristotle's Embryology." *Apeir* 22(1989), 159-179. Ar's explanation of animal powers is undercut by his reliance on teleology at every level of the account. Reproduction is not a striving of the animal for immortality. [3840]

MEPHAM, J. K. "Aristotle's Biological Researches," in *The Sciences: Their Origin and Methods*, ed. R. Harre (Glasgow, UK: Blackie, 1967), pp. 13-43. Reviews Ar's biological works to show his patient empiricism and the analytical power of his method. [3841]

MORSINK, J. *Aristotle on the Generation of Animals: A Philosophical Study.* Washington, DC: Univ. Pr. of America, 1982. Ar used dialectical method to establish general scientific principles and *archai* of biology. He studied opinions of earlier philosophers dialectically to arrive at new scientific insights, though he did not neglect inductive method. He understands the male as providing the form and the female the matter in reproduction. [3842]

——. "Was Aristotle's Biology Sexist?" *JHistBiol* 12(1979), 83-112. Ar's theory on roles which each gender plays in reproduction, though not accurate, was more enlightened than that of earlier scientists. [3843]

NUSSBAUM, M. C. "The 'Common Explanation' of Animal Motion," in #3624, pp. 116-156. Examines Ar's effort to develop account of movement and action in animal kingdom as a whole and explores role of this study in trying to understand the good life for humans and the making of ethical assessments. [3844]

——. *De motu animalium*. Princeton Univ. Pr., 1978. New edition of Greek text with translation, philological and philosophical commentary, and interpretive essays. Argues the work represents a radical but "deliberate and fruitful" rejection of Ar's earlier philosophy of science, for he arrives at a significantly "less departmental and more flexible picture of scientific study." [3845]

OPPENHEIMER, J. M. "Aristotle as a Biologist." *Scientia* 65(1971), 649-658. Discusses Ar's work as biologist and how his willingness to rely on sense organs over reason influenced other scientists. Also explores how Ar's work was influenced by fishermen, hunters, and herdsmen. [3846]

——. "When Sense and Life Begin: Background for a Remark in Aristotle's *Politics* (1335b24)." *Arethusa* 8(1975), 331-343. At some points Ar seems to think human life begins when fetus acquires a soul, probably when it begins to move. At other points he seems to equate life with birth. [3847]

ORGAN, T. "Nature and Non-Nature in Aristotle." *Thom* 39(1975), 575-601. In Ar's view there are only three ways that something can come to exist non-naturally: artificially, by luck, or haphazardly. He does not define coming-into-being naturally beyond saying that it is the negation of the non-natural ways. [3848]

OWENS, J. "The Teleology of Nature in Aristotle." *Monist* 52(1968), 159-173; also in #3634, pp. 136-147. Ar's view of ultimate purpose of nature does not esteem man highly enough, but it does help us discern an organizational principle that emphasizes value and interrelatedness of all nature. [3849]

PELLEGRIN, P. "Aristotle: A Zoology without Species," in #3809, pp. 95-115. Focuses on concept of animal species to show that lack of taxonomy in Ar is not caused by a problem of language. [3850]

——. *Aristotle's Classification of Animals. Biology and the Conceptual Unity of the Aristotelian Corpus*, transl. A. Preus. Berkeley: Univ. of CA Pr., 1986. Ar's efforts to devise a system of classification for animals had the unfortunate effect of blocking taxonomic progress because of his interest in identifying substances. Maintains Ar does not use *genus* and *eidos* in a fixed way and that the biological writings have a rigid syllogistic base. [3851]

——. "Logical Difference and Biological Difference: The Unity of Aristotle's Thought," in #3814, pp. 313-338. Summarizes argument of #3851. Throughout Ar's work, concepts of *genos* and *eide*, at each level of generality, express same logical/ontological relationship: *eide* are always forms of *kinds* arrived at by division of the kind. Extends argument to include concepts of "the more and the less," analogy, difference.   [3852]

PICKERING, F. R. "Aristotle on Walking." *AGPh* 59(1977), 37-43. Examines differing roles of *energeia* and *kinesis* in this physical process.   [3853]

PRATT, V. "Aristotle and the Essence of Natural History." *History and Philosophy of the Life Sciences* 4(1982), 203-223. In his biological work Ar aimed to identify the nature of a creature rather than establish a system of classification. This is the primary difference between Greek philosopher-scientists and modern naturalists.   [3854]

————. "The Essence of Aristotle's Zoology," *Phron* 29(1984), 267-278. When Ar speaks of "complex action" or "full activity" for which body of an animal exists, he is invoking not so much its "function" as its functioning. He sees animal as a working system.   [3855]

PREUS, A. "Aristotle's *Parts of Animals* 2.16.659b 13-19: Is It Authentic?" *CQ* 18(1968), 270-278. Section may be a later insertion into Ar's text. Such a reading allows for a more sensible theory of development of his notion of connate *pneuma*.   [3856]

————. "Biomedical Techniques for Influencing Reproduction in the Fourth Century B. C." *Arethusa* 8(1975), 237-263. Along with medical writers of the period, Ar thinks that restraint of the male is not an effective means of controlling population. He knows contraceptive methods described in Hippocratic literature, but doubts their effectiveness. He condones abortion, but only early in pregnancy, and endorses practice of "exposure," or killing of deformed or unwanted infants.   [3857]

————. "*Eidos* as a Norm in Aristotle's Biology." *Nat&Sys* 1(1979), 79-101; also in #42, pp. 340-363. Presents biological sense of *eidos* and compares uses of concept in normative passages. Examines how Ar appeals to concept to explain, in one instance, pleasure and kinds of pleasures and, in another instance, reasons for variations in kinds of government. Ar's classification system stresses comparison of similar characteristics rather than of types.   [3858]

————. "Reply to Jacobs' 'Preus on Aristotle's *Eide*.'" *Nat&Sys* 3(1981), 119-121. Response to #3825. Answers criticisms, argues that Ar's statements about the continuity of nature make distinctions into kinds non-obvious and problematic.   [3859]

————. *Science and Philosophy in Aristotle's Biological Works.* Hildesheim, Ger.: Olms, 1975. Investigates interpenetration of scientific and philosophical methods and goals in Ar's biological works. Discusses his sources and methods, central argument in *De gen anim*, principles of understanding organic parts and their variations, use of concept of necessity, and use of personalized concept of nature. Discusses sections in which Ar's philosophical principles and observed data are at variance.   [3860]

————. "Science and Philosophy in Aristotle's *Generation of Animals*." *JHistBiol* 3(1970), 1-52. Ar's concept of substantial or entitative change is crucial for his ontology. Presents new interpretation of his theory of sexual generation.   [3861]

————. cf. #1427.

RIST, J. M. "Some Aspects of Aristotelian Teleology." *TAPhA* 96(1965), 337-349. Idea that nature itself has goal or purpose, even if unconscious, did not raise problems for Ar. He viewed even inanimate things as having a desire to fulfil their own nature. **[3862]**

SAVARY, C. "About Aristotle and Evolutionism." *NewSchol* 47(1973), 248-252. Though Ar and French theologian Teilhard de Chardin both look at the world as undergoing a process of evolution, comparison between them is not easy. **[3863]**

SHARPLES, R. W. "Species, Form, and Inheritance: Aristotle and After," in #3809, pp. 117-128. Explores issue of what aspects of an individual can be attributed to his form, and what aspects to his matter, in context of Ar's discussion of inheritance. **[3864]**

SIWEK, P. "The *Parva Naturalia* of Aristotle. Reply to Prof. Drossaart Lulofs and Prof. G. E. R. Lloyd." *Sophia* 34(1966), 310-316. Reply to reviews of Siwek's earlier book on Ar's shorter biological treatises. **[3865]**

SOLMSEN, F. "The Fishes of Lesbos and Their Alleged Significance for the Development of Aristotle." *Hermes* 106(1978), 467-484. Reply to #3830. **[3866]**

SPRAGUE, R. K. "Models for the Practical Syllogism." *AncPh* 7(1987), 87-94. Principles of the practical syllogism, familiar in Ar's ethics, can be applied to his biology and physics as well. **[3867]**

WILLIAMS, B. "Hylomorphism." *OSAP* 4(1986), 189-199. Considers certain general features of Ar's view that relation of soul to body bears some illuminating resemblance to relation of form to matter. **[3868]**

WILLIAMS, C. J. F. *Aristotle's* De Generatione et Corruptione. Oxford: Clarendon Pr., 1982. Assesses strength of Ar's arguments regarding generation and corruption in light of modern developments in logic. **[3869]**

WITT, C. "Form, Reproduction and Inherited Characteristics in Aristotle's *Generation of Animals*," *Phron* 30(1985), 46-57. Response to Balme (#3782). Seeks to understand Ar's explanation of inherited resemblances in a way that gives a consistent account of form in *De gen anim* and in *Meta*. **[3870]**

CATEGORIES

The work known as the *Categories* may not be, in its present form, a composition of Ar but it displays the marks of his mind. It now stands as the first part of the logical works as they are collected under the title *Organon* ("The Tool"). In this early attempt to classify knowledge and determine how things can be said with precision, Ar developed a list of ten predicates or categories to describe Being. We can say that something is, how big it is, what sort it is, where it is, when it is, and so on.

Categories are predicates, i. e., statements about what a thing is or what qualities it has. In W. D. Ross's words, "the categories are a list of the widest predicates which are predicable essentially of the various namable entities, *i. e.,* which tell us what kinds of entity at bottom they are." Ar's list is given in several places, but in no two places is it exactly the same. Ten seems to be the maximum, not the standard, number of categories. Most of the terms apply best to individual humans or animals. Some, such as what clothing or equipment a thing has, can apply only to humans. Various interpretations of the categories have been advanced. Some maintain that the categories are linguistic, either nouns, verbs, or some other part of speech. Given the importance Ar accords to language, such a view is not surprising. Other scholars argue that Ar is classifying the things which the language symbolizes, the "main aspects of reality." This approach might be called ontological. Still others see the categories as logical devices.

Ar probably saw his categories as fulfilling all three functions. He uses them to criticize P's theory of forms and to introduce his own distinction between primary and secondary substance, a position which he gives up in *Meta*.

Users of this portion of the bibliography are advised to consult the sections on Logic and Metaphysics as well, as the lines dividing those topics from the Categories are not always clearly drawn.

ACKRILL, J. L. "Aristotle's *Categories*, Chapters I-V: Translation and Notes," in #3625, pp. 90-124. Offers new interpretations of certain key passages. **[3871]**

ALLEN, R. E. "Individual Properties in Aristotle's *Categories*." *Phron* 14(1969), 31-39. Critical response to Owen's (#3929) interpretation of *Cat*. **[3872]**

———. "Substance and Predication in Aristotle's *Categories*," in #65, pp. 362-373. Examines Ar's denial that secondary substances are in primary substances. **[3873]**

ANNAS, J. "Individuals in Aristotle's *Categories*: Two Queries." *Phron* 19(1974), 146-152. Criticizes Jones' (#3911) attempt to approach the problem of non-substantial individuals in *Cat* in terms of Ar's concept of 'one' in *Meta* 1 and to extend his account to explain role of paronymy in *Cat*. **[3874]**

ANTON, J. P. "The Aristotelian Doctrine of Homonyma in the *Categories* and its Platonic Antecedents." *JHPh* 6(1968), 315-326. For P homonymy is problem arising from different views people have of a word or name. For Ar homonymy can undermine validity of a syllogism. **[3875]**

———. "The Meaning of *O Logos tes Ousias* in *Categories* 1A." *Monist* 52(1968), 252-267. This phrase is not used imprecisely. *Ousia* is to be taken as substance in the sense of species. **[3876]**

———. "Some Observations on Aristotle's Theory of Categories." *Diot* 3(1975), 67-81. Ar does not confuse kinds of beings and categories. His theories rely on basic ontological and logical doctrines. **[3877]**

———. cf. #6326.

APOSTLE, H. G. "Ackrill on Aristotle's Categories." *NewSchol* 50(1976) 204-211. Challenges Ackrill's (1963) reading in *Cat* 6; argues Ackrill is not aware of Ar's method of dividing problems into kinds and that he uses Ar's terms not with scientific meaning specified by Ar.   [3878]

——. *Aristotle's Categories and Propositions.* Grinnell, Iowa: Peripatetic Pr., 1980.
Translations and commentaries, with glossary.   [3879]

BARNES, J. "Property in Aristotle's *Topics*." *AGPh* 52(1970) 136-155. Technical
discussion of: (1) definition of property found in *Topics* E, and (2) ways in which Ar
departs from this definition, a confusion that affects his discussion of property. Maintains
that *per se* accidents are not properties.   [3880]

——. cf. #4418.

BARNES, K. "Aristotle on Identity and its Problems." *Phron* 22(1977) 48-62. In Ar's
early writings, we find what seems to be a formulation of the view that identicals are
indiscernible. Examines Ar's solution to certain problems of identity.   [3881]

BENSON, H. H. "Universals as Sortals in the *Categories*." *PacPhQ* 69(1988), 282-306.
By reading Ar's concept of universals as based on a sortal analysis one can resolve the
difficulty of interpreting *Meta* Z, where Ar maintains that substances are not universals,
forms are substances and are predicated of more than one entity.   [3882]

BLACK, E. "Aristotle's 'Essentialism' and Quine's Cycling Mathematician." *Monist*
52(1968), 288-297. Quine's objection that Ar's doctrine of essences separates meaning
from reference cannot be supported by Quine's own examples. Ar's distinction between
essences and accidents is still a useful tool for organizing knowledge.   [3883]

BLAKELEY, T. J. "The Categories of Mtu and the Categories of Aristotle," in *African
Philosophy: An Introduction*, ed. R. A. Wright (Washington, DC: Univ. Pr. of America,
1979), pp. 149-156. Suggests that research into Bantu philosophy could profitably begin
with construction of table of categories and that can benefit from use of Ar's categories
(rather than those of Kant or Hegel).   [3884]

BROWNSTEIN, D. "Parmenides' Dilemma and Aristotle's Way Out." *SJPh* 24(1986),
1-7. In first five books of *Cat* Ar attempts to reply to the dilemma which Parmenides
poses in Plato's *Parm*, which results in the regress known as the Third Man Argument.
Like Plato, Ar is unable to offer valid objections to the TMA.   [3885]

CODE, A. "Aristotle: Essence and Accident," in *Philosophical Grounds of Rationality*,
ed. R. E. Grandy (Oxford Univ. Pr., 1986), pp. 411-439. Develops some of H. P. Grice's
ideas about predication in Ar's *Cat*; uses them to develop an ontological framework
neutral between Platonic and Aristotelian metaphysics.   [3886]

——. "On the Origins of Some Aristotelian Theses about Predication," in #45, pp. 101-
132. Response to G. E. L. Owen's argument in (#4778) regarding origins of Ar's views
on predication. Examines distinction between essense and predication and how it is
related to doctrine of substance and categories.   [3887]

——. "What Is It to Be an Individual?" *JPh* 75(1978), 647-648. Reply to M. Furth
(#4673).   [3888]

COHEN, S. M. "'Predicable of' in Aristotle's Analytics." *Phron* 18(1973), 69-70.

Addendum to #3920.   [3889]

CRESSWELL, M. J. "Aristotle's *Phaedo*." *AustlJPh* 65(1987), 131-155. The discussion of relative tallness in *Phaedo* 102d can be interpreted as teaching the same doctrine as Ar's *Cat* and providing the seed of Ar's philosophy. Both P and Ar seem to equate predicating and naming.   [3890]

DE RIJK, L. M. "On Ancient and Mediaeval Semantics (2)." *Vivarium* 16(1978), 81-107. Examines doctrine of substance in *Cat*, ontological character of Ar's classification and some problems arising from it. Ar was unsuccessful in his effort to eliminate P's Forms by telescoping genera and species into level of primary substance.   [3891]

———. "On Ancient and Mediaeval Semantics and Metaphysics (3)." *Vivarium* 18(1980), 1-62. Examines Ar's categories as classes of names.   [3892]

DRISCOLL, J. A. "The Platonic Ancestry of Primary Substance." *Phron* 24(1979), 253-269. Notes similarities between the spatial Receptacle of *Tim* 49-52 and five characteris-tics of primary substance listed in *Cat* 5.   [3893]

DUERLINGER, J. "Predication and Inherence in Aristotle's *Categories*." *Phron* 15(1970), 179-202. Ar distinguishes between predication and inherence to: 1) avoid problem in P's account of how many things come to have same name; 2) distinguish what P does not distinguish, namely how particulars such as an individual man and his bravery participate in Form of bravery; 3) oppose Platonic view that Forms could exist even if no particulars were to participate in them.   [3894]

EDEL, A. "Aristotle's Categories and the Nature of Categorical Theory." *RMeta* 29(1975), 45-65. Ar's views on categories changed over his lifetime, but he always con-sidered study of their application as important as categories themselves.   [3895]

EVANS, J. D. G. "Aristotle *Topics* E 5,135a20-b6: The Ontology of *Homoiomere*." *AGPh* 60(1978), 284-292. It is important to understand how Ar distinguishes between properties of homoiomerous things such as earth, where a part is similar to the whole, and things such as a hand, whose parts are not similar to the whole.   [3896]

FREDE, M. "Categories in Aristotle," in #57, pp. 29-48; also in #3631, pp. 1-24. Distinction of categories amounts to distinction of these various ways of being and corre-sponding various kinds of entities.   [3897]

———. "The Title, Unity, and Authenticity of the Aristotelian *Categories*," in #57, pp. 11-28. Argues for unity of treatise, but also maintains that we are not to project the universals of *Cat* into the ontology of *Meta*.   [3898]

GARVER, N. "Notes for a Linguistic Reading of the *Categories*," in #52, pp. 27-32. Ar's categories are linguistic as well as metaphysical. The most useful method of examining is distinctive feature analysis. Some passages in the *Cat* use what can be taken as an early version of this method.   [3899]

GILL, M. L. "Aristotle on the Individuation of Changes." *AncPh* 4(1984), 9-22. Ar's discussion of individual nonsubstances in *Cat* provides a background for his account, in *Phys* 5.4, of conditions affecting change in individual cases. The two passages require different types of analysis.   **[3900]**

GILLESPIE, C. M. "The Aristotelian Categories," in #4598, pp. 1-12. Considers how Ar makes his first attempt to distinguish a basic entity (substance) from all other kinds of entity. Focuses on how Ar arrives at classification given, and stresses influence which dialectical debate plays in Ar's recognition of need to make distinction between things of different sorts of categoies.   **[3901]**

GRANGER, H. "Aristotle on Genus and Differentia." *JHPh* 22(1984), 1-23. At different stages in his life Ar believed: 1) genus and differentia are essentially different and that genus was more significant element; 2) genus and differentia are very similar; 3) the two are similar but differentia is more significant in a definition.   **[3902]**

————. "A Defense of the Traditional Position Concerning Aristotle's Non-Substantial Particulars." *CanJPh* 10(1980), 593-606. Reply to G. E. L. Owen (#3929). Non-substantial particulars cannot be shared.   **[3903]**

————. "The Differentia and the *Per Se* Accident in Aristotle." *AGPh* 63(1981), 118-129. Presents an account of the *per se* accident and argues that the differentia is a type of *per se* accident.   **[3904]**

GRENE, M. "Is Genus to Species as Matter to Form? Aristotle and Taxonomy." *Synthèse* 28(1974), 51-69. Explores Ar's use of taxonomic terms by examining main differences in use of key terms, and then by looking at main import of Ar's usage in logic and metaphysics.   **[3905]**

HADGOPOULOS, D. J. "The Definition of the 'Predicables' in Aristotle." *Phron* 21(1976) 59-63. Tries to show that Barnes' (#3880) view that *per se* accidents are not properties is false.   **[3906]**

HEINAMAN, R. "Aristotle on Accidents." *JHPh* 23(1985), 311-324. Reply to #4908. Ar's views on accidents are too confused to be easily defended.   **[3907]**

————. "Non-Substantial Individuals in the *Categories*." *Phron* 26(1981), 195-307. Reply to G. E. L. Owen (#3929) and M. Frede (#3897).   **[3908]**

HETHERINGTON, S. C. "A Note On Inherence." *AncPh* 4(1984), 218-223. Ar's account of conceptual inherence is best understood in light of G. E. L. Owen's work (#3929), but Owen's comments can be clarified at several points.   **[3909]**

JONES, B. "An Introduction to the First Five Chapters of Aristotle's *Categories*." *Phron* 20(1975), 146-172. Analyzes first five chapters based on earlier argument (#3911) that satisfactory account of Ar's postulation of individuals, both substantial and non-substantial, can be achieved by taking seriously his characterization of these individuals as things that are "one in number" and by interpreting this characterization as "a unit in a possible act of enumeration."   **[3910]**

————. "Individuals in Aristotle's *Categories*." *Phron* 17(1972), 107-123. Ar's view of individuals is coherent and enables us to define more precisely distinction among synonyms, homonyms, and paranyms.   **[3911]**

KOSMAN, L. A. "Aristotle's First Predicament." *RMeta* 20(1967), 483-506; also in #4773, pp. 19-42. Asks if Ar's categories are classes of predicates or of things, and argues that Ar's remarks about the first category do not require a separation of these functions nor show a confusion in Ar's thought. [3912]

KUNG, J. "Aristotle on 'Being is Said in Many Ways'." *HPhQ* 3(1986), 3-18. The phrase "being . . . ways" means something like "being has different meanings." Ar takes the categories as knowable prior to the development of sciences. No revisions will be necessary as a result of discoveries in the sciences. [3913]

KUNKEL, J. C. "A New Look at Non-Essential Predication in the *Categories*." *NewSchol* 45(1971), 110-116. *Cat* 1b10-12 and 2a19-34 support a reading of Ar's concept of "predicated of" which goes against the majority view and encompasses both essential and non-essential predication. [3914]

LeBLOND, J. M. "Aristotle on Definition," in #4598, pp. 63-79. Surveys Ar's treatment of definition, and focuses on three kinds of definition: statement of essense, definition by genus and differentia, and definition by matter and form. Sees Ar's statements concerning role of definition as inconsistent; his view that definitions express scientific intuitions is unclear and unconvincing. [3915]

LLOYD, A. C. "Aristotle's Categories Today." *PhQ* 16(1966), 258-267. Discussion of Ackrill's translation and commentary (1963) and some issues raised by it. Reviews opinions of other scholars. [3916]

MALCOLM, J. "On the Generation and Corruption of the Categories." *RMeta* 34(1981), 662-681. Rejects view that an obvious way in which Ar determines list of categories is to take a primary substance as subject and classify its predicates. [3917]

MATTHEN, M. "The Categories and Aristotle's Ontology." *Dial*(Can) 17(1978), 228-243. Claims that recent assumptions about the ontological theory presented in *Cat* are misguided. Building on G. E. L. Owen's distinction between theory and *phainomena*, maintains that *Cat* is primarily designed to explain appearances. Ontological concerns are minimal. [3918]

MATTHEWS, G. B. "The Enigma of *Categories* 1a20 ff. and Why It Matters." *Apeir* 22(1989), 91-104. Response to interpretations of *Cat* 1a24-25 by Frede (#3897), Owen (#3929), and Ackrill (#3871) on what it means to be "in a subject." [3919]

——., and COHEN, S. M. "The One and the Many." *RMeta* 21(1968), 630-655. Sympathetic with general lines of Ar's account of predication, but argues that it is problematic because it relies on the notion of "unit quality" (e. g., this bit of wisdom in Socrates). Seeks to amend Ar's account by developing an account of quality attribution based on the notion of "quality individual." [3920]

McKIRAHAN, R. D. "Aristotelian Epagoge in *Prior Analytics* 2.21 and *Posterior Analytics* 1.1." *JHPh* 21(1983), 1-13. "Epagoge" has a broader meaning than has generally been given to it. For Ar it means recognition that a particular universal has one or more individuals under it. [3921]

MIGNUCCI, M. "Aristotle's Definitions of Relatives in *Cat.* 7." *Phron* 31(1986), 101-

127. Explores two meanings of "relative" and their logical consequences.   **[3922]**

MIKELADZE, Z. N. "Intensional Principles in Aristotle." *Acta Philosophica Fennica* 35(1982), 22-25. Discusses Ar's division of predicates into categories and predicables and into what is necessary, impossible, and contingent.   **[3923]**

MORAVCSIK, J. M. E. "Aristotle on Predication." *PhR* 76(1967), 80-96. Reviews Ackrill's (1963) commentary on *Cat* and *De Interp*, and focuses on Ar's discussion on certain features of predication.   **[3924]**

———. "Aristotle's Theory of Categories," in #3625, pp. 125-145. Seeks to understand theory or theories in which list of categories is embedded by investigating following questions: 1) What classes of expressions designate items each of which falls under only one category? 2) What is the list a list of? 3) What gives it unity?   **[3925]**

NOVAK, M. "Toward Understanding Aristotle's *Categories*." *Ph&PhenRes* 26(1965), 117-123. Three positions must be assumed in order to interpret first five chapters of *Cat*. This includes meaning and role of "present in a subject." These positions are: rejection of univocity; dual conception of accident; principle of discrimination.   **[3926]**

O'BRIEN, D. "Bibliographie annotée des études principales sur les *Categories* d'Aristote (1794-1975)," in *Concepts et Catégories dans la pensée antique*, ed. P. Aubenque (Paris: Vrin, 1980), pp. 1-22. Examines some of most important studies of this era.   **[3927]**

O'FARRELL, F. "Aristotle's Categories of Being." *Gregor* 63(1982), 87-131. Ar takes being as a plurality of categories in order to resolve Parmenides' dilemma about the reality of the multiple.   **[3928]**

OWEN, G. E. L. "Inherence." *Phron* 10(1965), 97-105. Maintains that items present in but not predicable of a subject are particular or individual, but argues that they are particular in being determinate in kind. Thus, holds that same individual property may be found in many subjects.   **[3929]**

OWENS, J. "Aristotle on Categories," in #3634, pp. 14-22. Inquires whether the notion of category instruction was intended in its beginnings to be an arbitrary procedure, whether it was meant to categorize words, and how it stands up to later examples of category mistakes.   **[3930]**

ROHR, M. D. "Aristotle on the Transitivity of Being Said of." *JHPh* 16(1978), 379-385. Idea that categories are highest types is not definitely asserted in either *Cat* or *Topics*. Ar does make it clear, though, that "being said of" is a transitive relation.   **[3931]**

SCALTSAS, T. "Numerical Versus Qualitative Identity of Properties in Aristotle's *Categories*." *Phil*(Athens) 10-11 (1980-81), 328-345. Reply to Owen's "Inherence" interpretation of *Cat* (#3929). Owen's view cannot account for the concept of oneness which Ar applies to non-substance particulars.   **[3932]**

SMITH, B. D. "Aristotle's Theory of Continuity." *Kinesis* 12(1982), 36-41. Ar does not see contintuity and discreteness as opposites but as extremes within a genus.   **[3933]**

STOUGH, C. L. "Language and Ontology in Aristotle's *Categories*." *JHPh* 10(1972), 261-

272. Use of language in the *Cat* affirms the category of substance as unique and special in relation to the other nine categories.   [3934]

THORP, J. W. "Aristotle's Use of Categories: An Easing of the Oddness in *Metaphysica* Delta 7." *Phron* 19(1974), 238-256. Explores Ar's claim that "being is said in many ways" and examines two quite different ways he explains this slogan. Sometimes Ar indicates that there a different *uses* of verb "to be," and sometimes that there are different *senses* of verb "to be" corresponding to the categories. Investigates how these divisions into uses and senses "mesh" with one another.   [3935]

WEDIN, M. V. "'Said of' and 'Predicated of' in the *Categories*." *PhResArch*, 5(1979), 418-432. Defends standard interpretation that "predicated of" marks a general relation of predication while "said of" is reserved for essential predication.   [3936]

WEDIN, V. E. "A Remark on Per se Accidents and Properties." *AGPh* 55(1973), 30-35. Reply to J. Barnes (#3880).   [3937]

WHITING, J. E. "Form and Individuation in Aristotle." *HPhQ* 3(1986), 359-377. Argues that 1) matter cannot be the principle of individuation and 2) Ar must introduce individual forms if he is to provide principles of individuation.   [3938]

WILSON, J. C. "Categories in Aristotle and in Kant," in #3625, pp. 75-89. By contenting himself with pointing out that Being is not a genus and therefore could not constitute essence of things, Ar seems to have missed true significance of his own list of categories.   [3939]

For related items see #4497, #4526, #4687.

EPISTEMOLOGY

   One of the issues on which Ar differs most from P is the question of how one knows something. The difference is based on their understanding of what is real and of the human desire to know it. Since P granted no reality to the changing, physical world, his epistemology is linked to perception of the Forms by the mind. The senses, in such a system, cannot provide any reliable knowledge, since what they perceive is not the same from one moment to the next. It is little better than an illusion. The real world can be known only by a philosophically enlightened elite. Ar, however, is more empirical in his approach to knowledge. Sense data, combined with the mind's ability to conceptualize, can provide trustworthy knowledge of the world. And this knowledge is something which all humans instinctively want, though to varying degrees. The opening sentences of the *Metaphysics* state his "credo": "All men by nature desire to know. An indication of this is the delight we take in our senses."
   To oversimplify the matter, P would look at two dogs and decide that, since they were not the same color or size and since their fur was different lengths and their barks sounded different, he could not know anything about those two dogs that applied equally to both of them, or to all dogs. To know what a dog is, one must understand the Form of Dogness, an ideal that is not discernible to the senses. Ar would look at the same two dogs and see that they had certain

characteristics that were the same: number of legs, presence of a tail, sharp teeth, etc. Those shared characteristics are what define a dog and allow us to talk about a concept of "dog" while recognizing that each individual dog will vary to a greater or less degree in such non-essential ("accidental") qualities as color of hair and pitch of the bark.

Ar thus does not assume separately existing Forms as objects of knowledge. All that is necessary for a person to know something is that he/she be able to observe a class of phenomena and abstract a concept which underlies and unifies all of them (a substratum). This is what he means when says that "though one perceives the particular, perception is of the universal" (*PostAn* 2.19, 100a17-b1). The physical senses enable us to perceive (*aisthesis*) sensible things (*aistheta*), but the mind (*nous*) must take us to the next step of perception of the universals (*noeta*). These universals do not exist except as objects of thought. To know them is to know the causes of things, not just to record data about observable phenomena. The organs of physical perception, the five senses, are bound up in the body and affected by it. Sight can be impaired by eyes which do not function properly or overwhelmed by excessively bright light. But *nous* is what Ar calls "unmixed," not linked to one physical organ. (As noted in the Biology section, Ar thought the brain served to cool the body.) Mind is separable from the body and remains unaffected by the *noeta*. (Some have argued that Ar thought of it as immortal, but that does not follow from his reasoning.)

Ar's concept of how we know was perhaps best summed up by J. H. Randall, Jr. (*Aristotle*, 1960, p.95): "For Aristotle, knowledge comes from observing the world and reflecting upon what can be observed, not, as the Platonists held, from an immediate inner "intuition" or intellectual vision of a supposed intelligible realm."

ANDRIOPOULOS, D. Z. "Did Aristotle Assume a Sense-Data Theory?" *PhilInq* 1(1979), 125-128. Ar's epistemology rests on his assumption that any object has an un-sensed and a sensed part and that perception depends on the existence of semi-autono-mous entities which mediate between perceiver and object. **[3940]**

———. "An Examination of Aristotle's Theory of Perception." *Platon* 19(1967), 45-76. For Ar perception is a two-stage process. Simple sensory perception precedes more complex intellectual comprehension. **[3941]**

ANNAS, J. "Aristotle on Memory and the Self." *OSAP* 4(1986), 99-117. Explores suggestion that Ar's memory and recollection are akin to "personal" and "non-personal" memory. **[3942]**

BARKER, A. "Aristotle on Perception and Ratios." *Phron* 26(1981), 248-266. In general Ar's theory of perception (*aisthesis*) is that it is achieved by comparisons and pro-portions. In *De anima* 426a27-b7, however, he describes a very specific type of percep-tion which does not seem to fit his earlier descriptions. **[3943]**

BARNES, J. "An Aristotelian Way with Scepticism," in #5374, pp. 51-76. Ar did not concern himself with epistemology to the extent that Hellenistic schools thought he did. He was certain of possibility of knowledge because of his teleological view of nature.

Rational creatures cannot achieve the good unless their senses are trustworthy. Nature does nothing in vain. Ergo, the senses are trustworthy.   **[3944]**

BAUMRIN, J. M. "Active Power and Causal Flow in Aristotle's Theory of Vision." *JHistBehavSci* 12(1976), 254-259. Ar's theory that vision results from something caused by the object is, with terminology updated, not far removed from modern understandings of the process.   **[3945]**

BEN-ZEEV, A. "Aristotle on Perceptual Truth and Falsity" *Apeir* 18(1984), 118-125. Ar holds that we determine what is true and false in perception by whether we are perceiving under normal circumstances.   **[3946]**

BLOCK, I. "Truth and Error in Aristotle's Theory of Sense Perception." *AustlJPh* 43(1965), 189-195. Discusses solutions to problem of why Ar says that common sensibles are susceptible to error while specific sensibles are not and concludes that Ar's meaning is teleological.   **[3947]**

BOS, A. P. "*Manteia* in Aristotle *De Caelo* II.1." *Apeir* 21(1988), 29-54. The phrase *he manteia he peri ton theon* refers not to human knowledge about God but to knowledge possessed by the cosmic gods from the one transcendent god which enables them to carry out the divine plan for the cosmos.   **[3948]**

BRUMBAUGH, R. S. "Aristotle: Education as Self-knowledge," in *Philosophers on Education: Six Essays on the Foundations of Western Thought* ed. R. S. Brumbaugh and N. M. Lawrence (Boston: Houghton Mifflin, 1986; rprt), pp. 49-75. Reacting against P's interest in mathematics, Ar sets up a program of studies. *Pol* 8 is his single most important text on education but his complete program must be culled from all his works.   **[3949]**

BURNYEAT, M. F. "Aristotle on Understanding Knowledge," in #5337, pp. 97-139. Discusses how Ar "goes a long way" toward segregating out and distinguishing elements of knowledge and of understanding, and his efforts to place philosophy of science at center of epistemology.   **[3950]**

BYNUM, T. W. "A New Look at Aristotle's Theory of Perception." *HPhQ* 4(1987), 163-178. Points up modernity of Ar's theory and its possible contributions to psychology, information theory, and other such disciplines.   **[3951]**

CASHDOLLAR, S. "Aristotle's Account of Incidental Perception." *Phron* 18(1973), 156-175. Argues that perception of individual qualities is a type of "pure" *aisthesis* and does not involve thought or memory.   **[3952]**

CATAN, J. R. "Recollection and *Posterior Analytics*." *Apeir* 4 #2(1970), 34-57. What is taken as a reference in *PostAn* 2.19 to P's doctrine of recollection actually describes a misinterpretation, among of his own students, of Ar's concept of *nous*.   **[3953]**

CHAMBLISS, J. J. "Aristotle: The Artful in Nature and the Natural in Art," in *Imagination and Reason in Plato, Aristotle, Vico, Rousseau, and Keats: An Essay on the Philosophy of Experience* (The Hague: Nijhoff, 1974), pp. 20-28. For Ar knowledge is a kind of activity related to productivity, aimed at producing a good person.   **[3954]**

CHARLTON, W. "Telling the Difference Between Sweet and Pale." *Apeir* 15(1981), 103-114. How one differentiates the objects of the different senses is taken by P as a function of intellect. Ar makes this function the key to distinguishing between perception and merely having sensation.   [3955]

CLEARY, J. "On the Terminology of 'Abstraction' In Aristotle." *Phron* 30(1985), 13-45. Terminology which some see as indicating that Ar's theory of knowledge relies on abstraction should be taken to refer to a logical method of subtraction.   [3956]

COHEN, S. M. "Sensations, Colors and Capabilities in Aristotle." *NewSchol* 52(1978) 558-568. Ar does not mean that faculty of sensation does not possess actual existence; rather, he means that it is a capacity, and not the exercise of a capacity.   [3957]

COOPER, J. C. "The Epistemological Order of Value and Fact." *OJRelStud* 5(1977), 78-83. Shows the idea that values are prior to facts in human cognition to be basis of Ar's view.   [3958]

DUNNE, J. "Aristotle After Gadamer: An Analysis of the Distinction Between the Concepts of *Phronesis* and *Techne*." *IrishPhJ* 2(1985), 105-123. Ar's "theory" of *phronesis* is essentially negative. It subtly reveals significance of *phronesis'* adherence to particulars, but it still remains an account of why an account in the more usual sense — be it *logos* or *techne* — is not possible.   [3959]

ELZINGA, A. "Some Remarks on a Theory of Research in the Work of Aristotle." *Zeitschrift fur Allgemeine Wissenschaftstheorie* 5(1974), 9-38. Ar had a dialectical method with two main phases: 1) doxographic induction — a form of recollecting ideas of previous generations, 2) organization of knowledge by classification.   [3960]

ENGBERG-PEDERSEN, T. "More on Aristotelian *Epagoge*." *Phron* 24(1979), 301-319. Considers various senses of *epagoge* (induction) and *epagein* and tries to find a proper place for *nous* in connection with *epagoge*.   [3961]

EVANS, J. D. G. "Aristotle on Relativism." *PhQ* 24(1974), 193-203. Ar attempts to find a mediating position between Protagorean relativism and Platonic realism. He grants a larger part to human faculties in determining the objects of truth, assuming that they are faculties of a good man.   [3962]

FEREJOHN, M. T. "Meno's Paradox and *De Re* Knowledge in Aristotle's Theory of Demonstration." *HPhQ* 5(1988), 99-117. Offers a description of different kinds of definitions which are involved in effort to reach causal definition in strictest sense. [3963]

GAUKROGER, S. "Aristotle on the Function of Sense Perception." *StudHist&PhSci* 12(1981), 75-89. Reply to Krips (#3977). Ar's view of perception must be analyzed in light of his teleological view of the sense organs.   [3964]

GLIDDEN, D. "Aristotelian Perception and the Hellenistic Problem of Representation." *AncPh* 4(1984), 119-131. Discusses misunderstanding of Ar's theory of perception in a passage in Sextus Empiricus. Hellenistic philosophers seem to have missed the ontological emphasis in Ar's theory of perception.   [3965]

GUERRIERE, D. "The Aristotelian Concept of *Episteme*." *Thom* 39(1975) 341-348.

For Ar *episteme* is knowledge organized so that we may move from our prior awareness of universals and particulars to see the relationships existing among them. [3966]

HALPER, E. "Aristotle on Knowledge of Nature." *RMeta* 37(1984), 811-836. Ar, unlike P, believes it is possible to know the physical world because he sees motion as an actuality. Like all actualities, it is complete and unchanging. This interpretation allows him to overcome P's objections to knowledge of the physical world. [3967]

HAMLYN, D. W. *"Koine Aisthesis."* Monist 52(1968), 195-209. Though used only once in his works, this phrase describes a potentiality which Ar saw as necessary to postulate in different sense organs in order to explain perception of objects or properties common to different senses. [3968]

————. cf. #5358.

HEINAMAN, R. "Knowledge of Substance in Aristotle." *JHS* 101(1981), 63-77. Ar maintains that universals are the only object of knowledge, but he also argues that universals are not substances. This leads to an apparent discrepancy between what is real and what can be known. [3969]

HOULIHAN, T. "A Point of Rapport Between Piaget and Aristotle." *LThPh* 26(1970), 233-262. Despite differences in their epistemologies, Piaget and Ar share a belief that human knowing is always a transition from vague to clear knowledge. [3970]

HYLAND, D. A. "Self-Reflection and Knowing in Aristotle." *GM* 23(1968), 49-61. Goal of philosophic life is resemblance to Unmoved Mover. But does that mean contemplating the same object as the Unmoved Mover (itself) or contemplating ourselves as the Unmoved Mover contemplates itself? Ar seems to take self-reflection as a beginning point in the process of knowledge. [3971]

INWOOD, B. "A Note on Commensurate Universals in the *Posterior Analytics*." *Phron* 24(1979), 320-329. Shows that commensurate universals are important to Ar in his scientific explanations because they are self-explanatory. Response to Barnes' comments on this topic in #4417. [3972]

KAL, V. *On Intuition and Discursive Reasoning in Aristotle.* Leiden: Brill, 1988. For Ar discursive reasoning consists of dialectic and demonstrative syllogisms and definitions. Any of these procedures rests upon a kind of knowledge, called intuition, which is based on experience and sense perception. *Post An* provides a complete statement of Ar's theory of knowledge. His remarks about cognition in *De anima* add little. [3973]

KELLY, M. J. "Aristotle as Sophist." *JTho* 3(1968), 253-257. P's basic concept of understanding was implicit in Presocratics' theories while Ar's view resembles Sophists' criticism of Presocratics. [3974]

KENNY, A. "The Argument from Illusion in Aristotle's *Metaphysics* Gamma, 1009-1010." *Mind* 76(1967), 184-197. Examines Ar's discussion and refutation of Protagoras' theory that things are what they appear to be. [3975]

KOSMAN, L. A. "Understanding, Explanation, and Insight in the *Posterior Analytics*," in #65, pp. 374-392. Examines how explanatory art presupposes another sort of understanding, *nous*, which is a disposition of soul. Investigates nature and connection of *nous* to *episteme*.   **[3976]**

KRIPS, H. "Aristotle on the Infallibility of Normal Observation." *StudHist&PhSci* 11(1980), 79-86. Contrary to the general view, Ar does not regard *normal* observational beliefs as infallible.   **[3977]**

LANG, H. S. "On Memory: Aristotle's Corrections of Plato." *JHPh* 18(1980), 379-393. The vocabulary of Ar's *De memoria* suggests that he was a Platonist when he wrote the treatise. Comparison with P's concept of memory in *Philebus* and *Theaet* suggests that Ar has incorporated P's vocabulary but is in fact decidedly anti-Platonic.   **[3978]**

LEAR, J. "Active *Episteme*," in #4575, pp. 149-174. For Ar, *episteme* is of the universal, but in *Meta* M, he appears to qualify this claim. In exploring this qualification, argues that paradigm of active *episteme* is substantial form, and that it is of substantial form. Offers an interpretation which in no way endorses thesis that there can be an *episteme* of particulars.   **[3979]**

————. cf. #3615.

LESZL, W. "Knowledge of the Universal and Knowledge of the Particular in Aristotle." *RMeta* 26(1972), 278-313. Commentators note what appears to be a contradiction in Ar's thought over whether universal is derived from particular or vice versa, and which of these can actually be known. Problem is perceived if Ar is approached with Platonic preconceptions. Ar's own view is somewhat dualistic but not inconsistent.   **[3980]**

LONG, A. A. "Aristotle and the History of Greek Scepticism," in #3631, pp. 79-106. Explores to what extent Ar is aware of the sceptical challenge to knowledge, and how far he attempts to answer it.   **[3981]**

LOWE, M. F. "Aristotle on Kinds of Thinking." *Phron* 28(1983), 17-30. Analysis of passages from *De anima* suggests that Ar wants to differentiate between thinking and sensation rather than assimilate the two.   **[3982]**

MANIOU-VAKALI, M. "Some Aristotelian Views on Learning and Memory." *JHistBehavSci* 10(1974), 47-55. Ar defines learning as acquisition and use of knowledge; memory is retention of things or ideas perceived in past. This distinction is important for him.   **[3983]**

MITCHAM, C. "A Non-Aristotelian Simile in *Metaphysics* 2.1." *CPh* 65(1970), 44-46. Comparison of mind blinded by objects of knowledge to bat blinded by daylight does not fit Ar's epistemology or what he says elsewhere about bats. Such details lend credence to arguments that *Meta* 2 is not by Ar.   **[3984]**

MOORE, F. C. T. "Evans Off Target." *PhQ* 25(1975), 58-59. Reply to #3962. **[3985]**

MOURELATOS, A. P. D. "Aristotle's Rationalist Account of Qualitative Interaction." *Phron* 29(1984), 1-16. Examines how causality is transmitted in the abstract context of qualitative interaction.   **[3986]**

NUSSBAUM, M. C. "The Discernment of Perception: An Aristotelian Conception of

Private and Public Rationality." *PBACAPh* 1(1985), 151-201. Starts by distinguishing practical wisdom from scientific understanding, and then explores three of the many dimensions to Ar's attack upon "the pseudo-scientific concept of rationality". [3987]

OEHLER, K. "Aristotle on Self-Knowledge." *PAPhS* 118(1974), 493-506. In Ar's cosmology of "graded forms of self-reference" each form is goal for lower forms. Unmoved Mover is highest form of self-reflection, the *telos* of all others. [3988]

OSBORNE, C. "Aristotle, *De anima* 3.2. How Do We Perceive What We See and Hear?" *CQ* 33(1983), 401-411. Discussion of how we know which sense we are using in perception. [3989]

OWENS, J. "Aristotle and Modern Epistemology," in #50, IV, pp. 848-851. Ar sees human cognition as arising from sensible things external to us. We do not reason from sense data to external reality. Without the external existents we could not be aware of our own existence. [3990]

———. "Aristotle: Cognition a Way of Being." *CanJPh* 6(1976), 1-11. Knowing or perceiving causes the agent to become different. [3991]

———. "Aristotle's Notion of Wisdom." *Apeir* 20(1987), 1-16. Ar uses *sophia*, which had meant skill in an art, to describe the highest sort of theoretical knowledge. Practical knowledge he classifies as *phronesis*. [3992]

———. "Form and Cognition in Aristotle." *AncPh* 1(1980-81), 17-28. Form causes cognition by making the person who is perceiving become, in some way, the thing being perceived. [3993]

———. "A Note on Aristotle, *De Anima* 3.4.429b9." *Philosophiques* 3(1976), 107-118; also in #3634, pp. 99-108. An emendation of the text suggested by Bywater in 1885 has been incorporated in some modern editions/translations. But the traditional reading has better ms. support and gives an important insight into Ar's view of human cognition. [3994]

———. "The Self in Aristotle." *RMeta* 41(1988), 707-722. Discusses problems in Ar's view that human agent of cognition has no direct knowledge of itself. [3995]

PATTARO, E. "'Wit' and 'Judgment' in Legal Thinking. Their Aristotelian Origin," in #72, pp. 54-58. Ar regards some faculties of the mind, such as wittiness and the ability to shape metaphors, as innate. Judgment and prudence, however, are faculties developed with age. [3996]

RINGBOM, M. "Thoughts and Facts — An Aristotelian Problem." *Ajatus* 34(1972), 7-25. Deals with problems Ar had to face in correlating conceptual relations and abstract concepts to factual relations and elements in the world which we perceive. [3997]

ROMANO, J. J. "Aristotle's Assumption of an Intelligible World." *Apeir* 7 #1(1973), 1-13. Examines Ar's basic assumption that things of world are intelligible and his theory of principles. Analyzes specific link between Ar's assumption and *archai* as found in *aporiai* of *Meta* B. [3998]

SCHOEN, E. L. "Wittgenstein and Aristotle on Knowledge from Perception." *SJPh*

21(1983), 435-451. Compares and contrasts main points of the two systems. **[3999]**

SCHOLAR, M. "Aristotle: *Metaphysics* Lambda 101b1-3." *Mind* 80(1971), 266-268. Reply to Kenney (#3975). Defends more radical interpretation of this passage by taking *phantasia* to mean "appearing" and by construing Ar's distinction as being between appearing and a particular act or episode of perception. **[4000]**

SODIPO, J. "The Universal and the Individual in Aristotle's Theory of Knowledge." *Platon* 22(1970), 181-193. Reply to #3872. Relationship between universal and particular in Ar's epistemology is more complex than Allan recognizes. **[4001]**

UPTON, T. V. "Infinity and Perfect Induction in Aristotle." *PACPhA* 55(1981), 149-158. Most interpreters take *PostAn* 2.23 to mean that Ar based his theory of scientific demonstration on concept of "perfect induction," i. e., enumeration of all possible cases. But Ar's concept of infinity conflicts with this. Human mind cannot go through an infinite series of things. Alternative translation of Greek phrase used here can resolve conflict. **[4002]**

———. "A Note on Aristotelian *Epagoge*." *Phron* 26(1981), 172-176. Reply to Engsberg-Pedersen (#3961). In context of scientific investigation, induction can lead to true, universal, and necessary propositions. **[4003]**

VANDERWEEL, R. L. "The *Posterior Analytics* and the *Topics*." *LThPh* 25(1969), 130-141. *PostAn* is not meant to replace *Topics*; rather, each treatise is meant to serve a special need in the direction of reasoning. The two treatises are not contrary, but complementary. **[4004]**

WATSON, G. "*Phantasia* in Aristotle, *De anima* 3.3." *CQ* 32(1982), 100-113. Ar uses this term consistently to describe our awareness of perception even after the event perceived is finished. **[4005]**

WEBB, P. "Bodily Structure and Psychic Faculties in Aristotle's Theory of Perception." *Hermes* 110(1982), 25-50. Survey of Ar's views on how perception is accomplished and the value of his theory. **[4006]**

For related items see #162, #1651, #1669, #1670, #1671, #6548.

ETHICS

Ethics and politics constitute, for Ar, the Practical Sciences, those areas of knowledge which concern human actions (*praxeis*). Because these fields are, more than any other aspect of his thought, bound up with the customs and outlook of his society, they remain "the most difficult part of Aristotle's thought to understand."

Ar's ethical thought is contained in three works, the *Nicomachean Ethics (NE)*, *Eudemian Ethics (EE)*, and *Magna Moralia (MM)*. The first has always been accepted by the majority of scholars as a genuine work of Ar's, but opinions have varied, and still do vary, about the other two. *EE* is generally accepted today, but the *MM* is considered by all but a minority of Aristotelian scholars as a work of the Peripatetic school. The study of these works is complicated by the fact that mss. of the *EE* state at the end of Book 3 that three books are missing and that those three books are identical with *NE* 5-7.

The uncertainty over the authorship of these works has led to some confusion over just what Ar's ethical theory was. In one of his early works, the *Protrepticus* (now lost except for fragments), Ar seems to have taken a highly Platonic approach to ethics as the comprehension of some absolute standard of right behavior. In that work he used the term *phronesis* to mean wisdom in both the theoretical and practical senses, i. e., knowing what the Right is and knowing how to do the right thing. In *EE* he admits that part of our knowledge of ethics is empirical but still uses *phronesis* in the general sense of wisdom. In *NE* 6 he uses *phronesis* to mean practical wisdom and *sophia* to express theoretical wisdom. If W. Jaeger's hypothesis of a development in Ar's thought over the course of his life is accepted, we can conclude that he moved from the Platonic view of the *Protrepticus* to an analysis in *NE* which is based on his own metaphysical and psychological theories.

In its maturest form Ar's ethical thought is not intended to provide people with definite guidelines for right behavior. He recognizes that circumstances determine what is the right or best thing to do, and circumstances can vary so widely that one cannot enunciate a theory to cover all cases. Ethics is a matter of *praxis* ("action"), not *theoria* ("contemplation"). What he hopes to do is enlighten those, in both the state and the family, who are responsible for guiding the development of the young. To this end he defines the concept of *eudaimonia* ("happiness" or "well-being") as the purpose of all human action. People will disagree, of course, over what constitutes happiness, and Ar does not try to arrive at some specific state or activity but stresses that *eudaimonia* is for a human being to live according to his/her highest purpose. But he defines that as a Greek intellectual of his time and place would define it, and the person he presents as embodying his ethical ideals, the "great-souled man" (*megalopsychos*), appears by our standards too self-centered and self-assertive.

If the "good" in life is to live according to our highest purpose, the next step is to define that purpose. Since, for Ar, the thing that separates humans from other animals is the ability to reason, the good life should be one in which a person lives most in accord with reason. The most precise definition of *eudaimonia* which he gives us is that it is "the active exercise of the faculties of the soul in conformity with excellence or virtue (*arete*); if there are several virtues, in conformity with the best and most perfect among them, during a complete lifetime."

In elaborating this definition Ar reveals his cultural conditioning. His ethics reflect the materialistic values of fourth-century Athens. He thinks that, in order to live such a life, a person must be born into a respectable family, have an attractive appearance, wealth, political power, friends, successful children, and a long life. Slaves, the poor, women (who could not own anything and had no political rights), and men who don't live in a democratic city would seem to be excluded from the possibility of attaining *eudaimonia*. It would also be difficult to know if a man was happy until he died, since his children might disappoint him, his city might be captured by some foreign power, or some other reversal of fortune might overwhelm him.

Given the right background, a person must strive to develop the rational part of the soul and bring the non-rational part under control. By means of *phronesis* one can discover what is the right action in a given situation. Virtue consists in living in conformity with that decision. It typically takes the form of following a mean between two extremes. Reaching such decisions is not an easy matter. It requires "conditioning" of the soul. Ar does believe that one becomes virtuous by living like a virtuous person, becoming habituated to such a life.

A number of topics are discussed in Ar's ethical writings which cannot be elaborated on here, for reasons of space. *NE* 3 treats the kinds of choices people must make and their responsibility for those which are not entirely voluntary. Justice is covered in *NE* 5 and pleasure in Book 7, where Ar refutes the notion that all pleasures are bad. Books 8 and 9 discuss aspects of friendship: is it based on altruism or self-interest? is it possible for socially unequal persons to be friends? is friendship necessary for happiness? Book 10 defines happiness and relates ethics to the larger topic of living in a community, i. e., politics.

ACHTENBERG, D. "The Role of the *Ergon* Argument in Aristotle's *Nicomachean Ethics.*" *AncPh* 9(1989), 37-48. Interprets *ergon* argument as "central" and one which does not assume we ought to exaggerate our specific human differences.   **[4007]**

ACKRILL, J. L. "Aristotle on Action." *Mind* 87(1978), 595-601; also in #4312, pp. 93-101. Asks: 1) how action can be good in itself if it is valued as a means to *eudaimonia* and 2) how action can be something done to bring about an outcome and yet be distinguished from a production because done for its own sake. Focuses on (2) and examines Ar's concept of action and his distinction between *praxis* and *poiesis*.   **[4008]**

————. "Aristotle on *Eudaimonia.*" *PBA* 60(1974), 339-359; also in #4312, pp. 15-33; also in #4255, pp. 335-355. Ar does not commit himself to thesis that actions are valuable only insofar as they promote *theoria*. Suggests why he does not address question of best combination of *theoria* and virtuous activity.   **[4009]**

————. "Aristotle on 'Good' and the Categories," in *Islamic Philosophy and the Classical Tradition: Essays Presented to Richard Walzer*, ed. S. M. Stern et al. (Oxford, 1972), pp. 33-40; also in #4036, pp. 17-24. Examines Ar's claim at *NE* 1096a23-29 that goodness is not a single common universal: if it were it would be "said" in only one category, but it is "said" in all the categories.   **[4010]**

————. *Aristotle's Ethics.* New York: Humanities Pr. 1973. Contains translations of most of *NE* and large part of *EE*, extracts from *De Anima* and *De Motu Animalium*, plus an introductory essay.   **[4011]**

ADKINS, A. W. H. "The Connection Between Aristotle's *Ethics* and *Politics.*" *PolTheo* 12(1984), 29-50. Ar's *Ethics* and *Pol* cannot be fully understood unless they are read together. A number of terms, such as *ergon* and *arete*, should be studied against background of earlier Greek to appreciate nuances of Ar's usage.   **[4012]**

————. "Paralysis and Akrasia in *Eth. Nic.* 1102 b 16 ff." *AJPh* 97(1976), 62-64. Ar compares doing things unwillingly to inability to control one's muscles.   **[4013]**

———. "Theoria versus Praxis in the *Nichomachean Ethics* and the *Republic*." *CPh* 73(1978), 297-313; also in #4255, pp. 427-443. The *theoretikos* or enlightened philosopher should not interrupt his contemplation to perform an action, no matter how moral. Neither P nor Ar can see any reason to abandon a superior kind of *eudaimonia* for an inferior.   **[4014]**

AGONITO, R. "The Paradox of Pleasure and Pain: A Study of the Concept of Pain in Aristotle." *Pers* 57(1976), 105-112. Ar's view of pleasure and pain is complicated by several paradoxes: 1) he rejects bodily pleasure as highest good; 2) he holds pleasure can be evil while pain can be good; 3) pleasure and pain can cause people to become evil, so virtue is contrary to nature; 4) pleasure is a movement but not a motion.   **[4015]**

ALLAN, D. J. "Aristotle's Account of the Origins of Moral Principles," in #4036, pp. 72-78. Practical wisdom must not only ensure that the means we adopt to chosen end are satisfactory but also give our choice of the end a foundation in reason.   **[4016]**

———. "The Fine and the Good in the *Eudemian Ethics*," in #4252, pp. 63-71. Ar distinguishes between the fine (*ta kala*) and the good (*ta agatha*) but does not make it clear who decides what the fine are. They are commended actions, but he does say who commends them or on what basis.   **[4017]**

———. "Individual and State in the *Ethics* and *Politics*," in *La Politique d'Aristote* (Geneva: Fond. Hardt, 1965), pp. 53-95. Ar's political philosophy does not negate individual autonomy. In his view a city's laws govern a person's external actions (*erga*) but not his ethical activities (*praxeis*).   **[4018]**

———. "Quasi-mathematical Method in the *Eudemian Ethics*," in #4255, pp. 185-200. Though Ar describes his method of proof at the beginning of *EE*, he does not make clear that he is using a mathematical model of deduction.   **[4019]**

———. "Rezension zu: Aristoteles, *Eudemische Ethik*, uebersetzt und erlaeutert von F. Dirlmeier, Berlin 1962," in #4255, pp. 225-236. Review essay (in English) of somewhat controversial translation and commentary on *EE*.   **[4020]**

ALPERN, K. D. "Aristotle on the Friendship of Utility and Pleasure." *JHPh* 21(1983),303-316. Challenges Cooper's (#4068) reading that disinterestedness plays no role in friendships of utility and pleasure. Argues that such friendships can exhibit trust and sharing.   **[4021]**

ANAGNOSTOPOULOS, G. "Aristotle on Function and the Attributive Nature of the Good," in #54, pp. 91-137. Elucidates some reasons that might have led Ar to argue that man has a function.   **[4022]**

ANDO, T. *Aristotle's Theory of Practical Cognition.* The Hague: Nijhoff, 1971; rprt. Examines the structure and functions of the soul and intellect to show how Ar's ethical theory is founded on and integrated with his biological and psychological works. Considers scientific formulations and positive foundations which Ar gives to material inherited from P.   **[4023]**

ANNAS, J. "Aristotle on Pleasure and Goodness," in #4312, pp. 285-299. Discusses Ar's view that pleasure is not a bad thing. What matters is not to avoid or minimize pleasure, rather what is important is to be right about pleasure.   [4024]

——. "Plato and Aristotle on Friendship and Altruism." *Mind* 86(1977), 532-554. Ar's discussion of *philia* in *NE* 8 and 9 is largely a response to two paradoxes about friendship put forth in P's *Lysis*.   [4025]

——. "Self-Love in Aristotle," in #4305, pp. 1-18. Ar explains friendship in terms of relations that are clearest in case of self-love without reducing former to latter in any way. Draws out certain paradoxical consequences of his discussion.   [4026]

ANSCOMBE, G. E. M. "Thought and Action in Aristotle: What is Practical Truth?" in #1268, pp. 143-158; also in #4036, pp. 61-71. Explores apparently inconsistent theses: 1) choice is what is determined by deliberation; 2) what the uncontrolled man does *qua* uncontrolled, he does not choose to do; 3) uncontrolled man, even when acting against his convictions, does on occasion determine what to do by deliberation.   [4027]

ARDLEY, G. "Is Aristotle an Immoralist?" *Prud* 15(1983), 77-85. Ar's ethical thought is more than a form of self-interest. It has its basis in his concept of a deity who is not remote and unconcerned for human beings.   [4028]

ARNOLD, M. B. "Historical Development of the Concept of Emotion." *PhilStud* (Ireland) 22(1974), 147-157. Examines Ar's idea of emotion as "man's recognition of something good or bad" and compares it with other ideas of emotion throughout history.   [4029]

ASSELIN, D. *Human Nature and 'Eudaimonia' in Aristotle*. New York: Lang, 1989. Explores connection Ar sees between human nature and *eudaimonia*, and how this connection reveals "true good" of man. Shows Ar to be arguing that man is unique in being both a philosopher and a citizen.   [4030]

AUSTIN, J. L. "*Agathon* and *Eudaimonia* in the *Ethics* of Aristotle," in #3625, pp. 261-296. Argues that *agathon* cannot mean "conducive to happiness."   [4031]

BAILLIE, H. W. "Learning the Emotions." *NewSchol* 62(1988), 221-227. Emotions, though not entirely reliable because not based on knowledge, do provide guidance and limitation for ethical decisions.   [4032]

BAMBROUGH, R. "Aristotle on Justice: A Paradigm of Philosophy," in #1268, pp. 159-174. Explores two questions about Ar's discussion of two senses of justice: 1) If justice in wider sense is equivalent to whole of virtue, why do we refer to it by means of two different expressions, sometimes calling it "justice" and sometimes "the whole of moral virtue"? 2) If justice in wider sense is something different from justice in second sense, why do we use same word to refer to both?   [4033]

BARDEN, G. "Aristotle's Notion of *Epieikeia*," in *Creativity and Method: Essays in Honor of Bernard Lonergan, S. J.*, ed. M. L. Lamb (Milwaukee, WI: Marquette Univ. Pr., 1981), pp. 353-366. Examines Ar's treatment of equity, and how he works with opposing philosophic and popular traditions.   [4034]

BARNES, J. "Aristotle and the Methods of Ethics." *RIPh* 34(1980), 490-511; also in #4255, pp. 461-482. Examines three components of Ar's method: 1) laying out opinions on a subject, 2) reviewing puzzles that arise from these opinions, and 3) puzzling through and resolving problems. Raises several questions about the method. [4035]

———., et al. *Articles on Aristotle, 2: Ethics and Politics*. New York: St. Martin's Press, 1977. Collection of essays with overall theme of showing relation of ethical and political thought in Ar's work. Each abstracted herein. [4036]

BASHOR, P. S. "Plato and Aristotle on Friendship." *JValInq* 2(1968), 269-280. Comparison of P's *Lysis* and Ar's *Ethics* shows that Ar's somewhat mechanical doctrine of causes of friendship is more limited than P's transcendent view. [4037]

BAUMRIN, B. H. "Aristotle's Ethical Intuitionism." *NewSchol* 42(1968), 1-17. Ar is a non-naturalist, an epistemological intuitionist; his ethic is not teleological. [4038]

———. "Classifying Aristotle's Ethics." *NewSchol* 44(1970), 153-161. Reply to Carlin (#4056) and King (#4194). Discussion of classification in ethical theory leads to clarification of views expressed in #4038. [4039]

BERTMAN, M. A. "Pleasure and the Two Happinesses in Aristotle." *Apeir* 6 #2(1972), 30-36. Functional examination of relationship between what Ar calls the *bios theoretikos* (life of contemplation) and the practically good life. Also investigates significance of potentiality for physical pleasure and for the sort of happiness which results from contemplation of eternal objects. [4040]

BLITS, J. H. "Privacy and Public Moral Education: Aristotle's Critique of the Family." *EducTheo* 35(1985), 225-238. Ar's critique of family shows that its greatest strengths in moral education prove also to be its essential limitations. [4041]

BODUNRIN, P. O. "Aristotle on Conduct and Human Happiness: *Nicomachean Ethics* I, II and X." *Phrontis* 5(1967), 28-33. Though his ethical doctrines have an empirical base, Ar never really broke away from Platonic influences. [4042]

———. "The Meaning and Definition of *Ethike Arete* in Aristotle's *Nicomachean Ethics*." *Dialogos* 16(1981), 115-117. By *ethike arete* Ar means "good manners" rather than "moral virtue." This definition avoids possible charge of ethical relativism. [4043]

BOGEN, J., and MORAVCSIK, J. "Aristotle's Forbidden Sweets." *JHPh* 20(1982), 111-127. Examines Ar's treatment of incontinence (lack of self-control) in *NE* by examining two related but ultimately different situations. [4044]

BONDESON, W. "Aristotle on Responsibility for One's Character and the Possibility of Character Change." *Phron* 19(1974), 59-65. Ar claims that only a "senseless person" does not see the link between one's activities and one's character (*NE* 1114A9-11). This claim is analyzed in a discussion of his views on the individual's responsibility for his character (which is great) and the possibility of changing it. [4045]

BOSTOCK, D. "Pleasure and Activity in Aristotle's Ethics." *Phron* 33(1988), 251-272. The only pleasurable activities are those of the soul. Pleasures of perception and of thinking are only kind Ar recognizes. [4046]

BRICKHOUSE, T. C. "A Contradiction in Aristotle's Doctrines Concerning the Alterability of Moral *Hexeis* and the Role of *Hexeis* in the Explanation of Action." *SJPh* 14(1976), 401-411. Ar holds that moral *hexeis* (habits) can be altered. But the role he assigns to them to explain any action requires that a person cannot habitually act contrary to his developed moral *hexeis*. Thus he can never fulfill a necessary condition for modifying an established moral *hexeis*.   **[4047]**

BRINTON, A. "Ethotic Argument." *HPhQ* 3(1986), 245-257. Examines Ar's conception of "ethical proof" in *Rhet*, and then turns to *NE* for a fuller conception of *ethos* (character) to develop a more adequate account of its role in argument.   **[4048]**

BROADIE, A. "Aristotle on Rational Action." *Phron* 19(1974), 70-80. Ar concludes that a practical syllogism, which results in an action, is parallel to theoretical reasoning, even though a theoretical syllogism issues in a judgment. This position is not inconsistent, since the relation between premises and conclusion in both types of syllogism is metaphysical.   **[4049]**

————. "The Problem of Practical Intellect in Aristotle's *Ethics*." *PBACAPh* 3(1987), 229-252. There are two reasons why we have difficulty understanding Ar's ethical reasoning: 1) our interest in justifying value judgments; 2) Ar's failure to clarify distinction between structure of deliberation and structure of reasons explaining an action.   **[4050]**

BROCK, D. "Commentary on Nussbaum's 'The Discernment of Perception: An Aristotelian Conception of Private and Public Rationality'." *PBACAPh* 1(1985), 202-208. Disputes Nussbaum's (#3987) assertion that theorists who defend commensurability of values must also accept metricity, i. e., that there is some one value which can be used as a standard.   **[4051]**

BROYER, J. A. "Aristotle: Is 'Happiness' Ambiguous?" *MidwJPh* 1(1973), 1-5. Alleged inconsistency in Ar's concept of happiness may result from taking particular distinctions out of context. Pleasure, politics, and contemplation are, in different ways, all necessary for attainment of happiness, but none is sufficient by itself.   **[4052]**

BRYANT, D. "Aristotle Didn't Heed the Tortoise." *NewSchol* 46(1972), 461-465. Reply to Palmer (#4275), who does not fairly represent prevailing opinion about practical syllogisms.   **[4053]**

BURNYEAT, M. F. "Aristotle on Learning to Be Good," in #4312, pp. 69-92. Reconstructs Ar's picture of the good man's development over time in order to illuminate certain features in his conception of what virtue is.   **[4054]**

BYRUM, C. S. "Aristotle's Concept of Individuality." *JValInq* 14(1980), 93-104. The *NE* can be interpreted axiologically on the basis of ethicist R. S. Hartman's work to show the importance of a concept of human individuality in Ar's thought.   **[4055]**

CARLIN, J. R. "Aristotle's Teleological Theory: A Reply." *NewSchol* 42(1968), 307-310. Criticizes Baumrin's (#4038) claim that Ar's ethical theory is not teleological. Baumrin's definition of what teleology in ethics means is too narrow; he doesn't take into account some of the ways that Ar would regard an action as having value.   **[4056]**

CARLSON, G. R. "Aristotle and Alcoholism: Understanding the *Nicomachean Ethics*."

TeachPh 9(1986), 97-102. Insights gained from the study of alcoholism can help us understand two of Ar's claims: 1) that an *akolastic* person "lacks right opinion in the form of a principle of reason" and that 2) a hedonist suffers from a disease but acts voluntarily. [4057]

CASHDOLLAR, S. "Aristotle's Politics of Morals." *JHPh* 11(1973), 145-160. Ar does not distinguish between the study of value in human action and in the activity of political bodies. [4058]

CELANO, A. J. "Aristotle on Beatitude." *AncPh* 5(1985), 205-214. Examines meaning of happiness (*eudaimonia*) and beatitude (*to makarion*) and their importance to Ar's ethics. Former depends partly on material goods and is variable. Latter is characteristic of gods and can be experienced when men contemplate the divine. [4059]

CHAMBERLAIN, C. "The Meaning of Prohaeresis in Aristotle's Ethics." *TAPhA* 114(1984), 147-157. "Commitment" is close to what Ar means by *prohairesis*. [4060]

——. "Why Aristotle Called Ethics Ethics. The Definition of *ēthos*. *Eudemian Ethics* 2,2." *Hermes* 112(1984), 176-183. Ar defines *ēthos* as the principle which a person uses to subject desire to reason. [4061]

CHARLES, D. "Aristotle: Ontology and Moral Reasoning." *OSAP* 4(1986), 119-144. Investigates two general problems: 1) Can something be a *praxis* under one description and a production under another? Or are *praxeis* and productions distinct actions? 2) What is relation between actions and results of actions which are not themselves actions, but are achieved by acting? These difficulties require a proper understanding of Ar's ontology for their resolution. [4062]

——. *Aristotle's Philosophy of Action.* Ithaca, NY: Cornell Univ. Pr., 1984. Examines Ar's discussions of ontology, intentional action, irrationality, and mental states, seeking to bring his contributions into contact with contemporary work in these areas. [4063]

CHROUST, A. H. "Some Comments on Aristotle's Major Works on Ethics." *LThPh* 21(1965), 63-79. Examines evidence regarding authenticity and dating of Ar's *MM* and surveys critical opinion on it. [4064]

CLARK, S. "The Use of 'Man's Function' in Aristotle." *Ethics* 82(1972), 269-283. Ar's concept of "man's function," by which he means the ability to choose, to come to ethical conclusions, cannot be faulted. [4065]

CLOUSER, R. A. "Aristotle's Theory of Incontinence." *PhRef* 33(1968), 90-99. Ar's view about weakness of will is not compatible with Socratic position that no one ever commits an act knowing it to be bad. [4066]

CODER, D. "A Small Point in Aristotle's *Ethics*." *Mind* (1969), 140. Ar offers a valid (if unsound) argument for the claim, "There is some, one, final, worthwhile end at which all reasonable actions aim." [4067]

COOPER, J. M. "Aristotle on Friendship," in #4312, pp. 301-340. Investigates Ar's theory of friendship and what role it plays in good person's life. Examines three basic kinds of friendship, and finds two important arguments to show that true friendship is essential constituent of flourishing human life.   **[4068]**

———. "Aristotle on the Forms of Friendship." *RMeta* 30(1977), 619-648. Examines Ar's views on what is essential to each form of friendship to determine if he really makes well-wishing and well-doing out of concern for the other person's good a condition of friendship.   **[4069]**

———. "Aristotle on the Goods of Fortune." *PhR* 94(1985), 173-196. Examines relation between *eudaimonia* and goods which Ar describes as external.   **[4070]**

———. "Contemplation and Happiness: A Reconsideration." *Synthèse* 72(1987), 187-216. Revised theory of happiness in *NE* 10 is "fully compatible" with accounts of moral virtues, practical reasoning, friendship, and other topics of the middle books.   **[4071]**

———. "Friendship and the Good in Aristotle." *PhR* 86(1977), 290-315. Ar sees friendship as intrinsically valuable and a psychological benefit to those who share it. He does not think any human being can live a good life without it.   **[4072]**

———. "The *Magna Moralia* and Aristotle's Moral Philosophy." *AJPh* 94(1973), 327-349; also in #4255, pp. 311-333. Defends view that *MM* is part of Aristotelian ethical corpus, earlier than *EE* or *NE*.   **[4073]**

———. *Reason and Human Good in Aristotle*. Cambridge, MA: Harvard Univ. Pr., 1975. Studies two central concepts: *eudaimonia* and practical reasoning. Argues that intellectualist interpretation of Ar's ethics cannot make sense of *NE* as a whole and the *EE's* doctrine of the best life as that of mixed moral virtue and theoretical excellence is preferable.   **[4074]**

———. "Some Remarks on Aristotle's Moral Psychology," in #4305, pp. 25-42. Focuses on Ar's distinction between non-rational desires and reason itself in generation of human action.   **[4075]**

———. cf. #1684.

COOPER, N. "Aristotle's Crowning Virtue." *Apeir* 22(1989), 191-205. The account of the *megalopsychos* is based on the methodology of *PostAn* 97b7-25. Ar was trying to produce a unitary account of the "great-souled" man but created a compromise between the types of Achilles and Socrates, even though he had the material at hand to produce an ethical ideal more in line with other aspects of his thought.   **[4076]**

CROMEY, R. D. "Aristotle on the Destruction of Dionysius I's Family." *RBPh* 57(1979), 5-17. Examines Ar's view that flaws of this family, which had dominated Syracuse, resulted partly from personal choices and partly from heredity.   **[4077]**

CROPSEY, J. "Justice and Friendship in the Nicomachean Ethics," in *Political Philosophy and the Issues of Politics* (Univ. of Chicago Pr., 1977), pp. 252-273. Justice is a virtue and a mean, while friendship is only doubtfully a virtue and not a mean. Discusses significance of justice and friendship for the philosopher.   **[4078]**

CURREN, R. "The Contribution of *Nicomachean Ethics* III 5 to Aristotle's Theory of Responsibility." *HPhQ* 6(1989), 261-277. Ar's limitation of responsibility to people whose carelessness results from their own action (such as those who are voluntarily drunk) should be taken seriously.   [4079]

DAHL, N. O. *Practical Reason, Aristotle, And Weakness of the Will.* Minneapolis: Univ. of MN Pr., 1984. Ar holds that what is called practical reason provides motivation for actions and moral decisions. Reason helps people decide what is good and, at the same time, see what they must do to reach the objective of the good. It is possible, however, for a person to know what is good but still not do it. Knowing something rationally is not quite the same as integrating it into one's character.   [4080]

DANCY J., et al., eds. *Human Agency : Language, Duty and Value: Philosophical Essays in Honor of J. O. Urmson.* Stanford, CA: Stanford Univ. Pr., 1988. Collection of essays, several of which deal with Ar's ethics and are abstracted herein.   [4081]

DAVENPORT, M. M. "The Military Virtues: From Aristotle to Skinner." *SwPhR* 3(1986), 161-177. Discusses how Ar and Skinner think that virtues are to be inculcated through positive reinforcement.   [4082]

DAVIES, J. C. "Internal and External Rationalism in Aristotle's Ethics." *Orpheus* 15(1968), 3-12. Ar derives his rationalistic view of ethics from P and finds external justification for his system.   [4083]

——. "The Justification of Aristotle's Ethics." *Euphro* 3(1969), 175-182. While Ar sees reason as dominant over emotions, it is not necessary for him to seek a rationalization of his ethics.   [4084]

DE FOURNY, P. "Contemplation in Aristotle's Ethics," in #4036, pp. 104-112. Analyzes Ar's argument that *eudaimonia* consists in contemplative activity, and concludes that the rational contemplative will engage in a type of theology.   [4085]

DE KIRCHNER, B. B. "On the Power of Practical Reason." *RMeta* 43(1989), 47-71. Situates Ar between Hume and Kant on the role of practical reason in the causation of moral action.   [4086]

——. "Aquinas as an Interpreter of Aristotle on the End of Human Life." *RMeta* 40(1986), 41-54. Aquinas' comments can help us to understand Ar's concept of *eudaimonia* as the goal of human life. Ar recognizes the impossibility of P's philosopher-king ideal. His views did develop from *EE* to *NE*.   [4087]

DESMOND, W. "Phronesis and the Categorical Imperative." *PhilStud* (Ireland) 27(1980), 7-15. Examines Ar's *phronesis* (practical wisdom) and Kant's Categorical Imperative for interpreting man's moral condition. *Phronesis* provides an image of human wholeness, capable of rectifying the deficiency of abstract universals, capable of intellectual alertness to the concrete.   [4088]

DEVEREUX, D. T. "Aristotle on the Active and Contemplative Lives." *PhResArch* 3(1977), no. 1138. Life devoted to practical activity has no place for philosophical contemplation. Challenges claim such a life is incompatible with moral virtue. [4089]

——. "Aristotle on the Essence of Happiness," in #3631, pp. 247-260. For Ar there are two forms of happiness, one associated with active life of moral virtue and the other with contemplative life. Both of these forms are implicitly inclusive.   **[4090]**

———. Comments on 'Good as Goal' by Nicholas P. White," in #4305, pp. 195-207. Challenges the way White (#4391) argues for his thesis that the best life is not one in which *theoria* is maximized.   **[4091]**

———. "Particular and Universal in Aristotle's Conception of Practical Knowledge." *RMeta* 39(1986), 483-504. *Phronesis* is name P gave to highest form of knowledge (knowledge of the good) that is at once practical and theoretical. Shows how Ar separates out of this Platonic mixture his own special concept of *phronesis*.   **[4092]**

DE VOGEL, C. J. "On the Character of Aristotle's Ethics," in #71, pp. 116-124; also in #4255, pp. 273-281. Ar's ethics are not validated by divine origin but are intimately connected with his concept that Nature provides the goal and the norms of behavior. This helps explain some characteristics which seem "unethical" to us.   **[4093]**

DIGBY, T. F. "Theoria and the Spontaneity of Right Action in Aristotle's Ethics." *NewSchol* 54(1980), 194-199. Ar's explanation of moral actions done spontaneously can only be understood in the context of relationships between the person, his environment, and the divine.   **[4094]**

DRYER, D. P. "Aristotle's Conception of the *Orthos Logos*." *Monist* 66(1983), 106-119. Examines what Ar says about deliberation in the practice of an art in order to explicate his conception of *orthos logos*.   **[4095]**

DUFF, A. "Aristotelian Courage." *Ratio* 29(1987), 2-15. Perhaps the best example of courage as Ar understood it would be that of a martyr who goes to his/her death willingly, showing a unity of reason, passion, and action.   **[4096]**

DWORKIN, G. "Reply to MacIntyre's 'How Moral Agents Became Ghosts'." *Synthèse* 53(1982), 313-318. Examination of text suggests that Ar's view of responsibility is not significantly different from Kant's, contrary to MacIntyre's claim.   **[4097]**

DYBIKOWSKI, J. C. "Is Aristotelian *Eudaimonia* Happiness?" *Dial*(Can) 20(1981), 185-200. Ar's theory of *eudaimonia* is not exactly what we mean by "happiness." But his concept does offer a suggestive theory about the nature of happiness.   **[4098]**

DYER, R. R. "Aristotle's Categories of Voluntary Torts (*E. N.* V,1135b8-25)." *CR* 15(1965), 250-252. Ar devises four categories of voluntary wrongs. The second, consisting of acts which are deliberately committed as injurious but without premeditation, is the most important group.   **[4099]**

EBERT, A. C. "Aristotle's Conception of Friendship as the Mirror of Happiness." *Dial*(PST) 29(1986), 23-29. Friendship functions epistemologically by enabling an individual to recognize himself as happy.   **[4100]**

ELDERS, L. J. "The Criteria of the Moral According to Aristotle." *Doctor Communis* 31(1978), 362-375. Examines Ar with respect to question of whether human nature is foundation of moral life.   **[4101]**

ENGBERG-PEDERSEN, T. *Aristotle's Theory of Moral Insight.* Oxford: Clarendon Pr.,

1983. First part examines how morally good actions lead to *eudaimonia*. The role of *theoria* (contemplation) is also examined. Second part looks at "the habituated state of the passions" and the cognitive role of moral virtue, which is concerned with the same objects as *phronesis* (practical wisdom) but on a different level.   [4102]

------. "Converging Arisotelian Faculties: A Note on *Eth. Nic.* VI, XI 2-3, 1143a25-35." *JHS* 99(1979), 158-160. Suggests textual emendation which clarifies Ar's argument that faculties of moral understanding, judgment, and practical wisdom ultimately focus on common concerns.   [4103]

------. "For Goodness' Sake: More on *Nicomachean Ethics* I vii 5." *AGPh* 63(1981), 17-40. Investigates relation in Ar's ethics between value of "acts proper" (*praxeis*) as opposed to "production" (*poiesis*), and *eudaimonia*.   [4104]

ERIKSEN, T. B. Bios Theoretikos: *Notes on Aristotle's* Ethica Nicomachea *X, 6-8.* Oslo: Universitetsforl., 1976. Examines relation of *phronesis* (practical wisdom) and *theoria* (contemplation) to the happy life. Ar felt a tension in his own life between the impulse toward solitary contemplation and his theoretical position that a human being is part of a community.   [4105]

ETEROVICH, F. H. *Aristotle's* Nicomachean Ethics: *Commentary and Analysis.* Washington DC: Univ. Pr. of America, 1980. Discusses the most important and most concise passages, emphasizing teleology, the virtuous mean, friendship, and other significant topics.   [4106]

ETHERIDGE, S. G. "Aristotle's Practical Syllogism and Necessity." *Philologus* 112(1968), 20-42. Ar considers even a voluntary act the outgrowth of necessity arising from force of a syllogism. Once terms of syllogism have been posed, conclusion follows inevitably. Ar is a determinist in his ethics and in his view of world.   [4107]

FANN, K. T. "Aristotle's Conception of Pleasure." *SJPh* 5(1967), 160-166. Analyzes Ar's discussion of pleasure and his claims that pleasures are not processes, but activities and ends.   [4108]

FISHER, N. R. E. "Hybris and Dishonor, I." *G&R* 32(1976), 177-193. Defines *hybris* based on Ar's *Rhet* 1378b23-25 and surveys its use from Homer to Ar. Its essential element is its link with honor and shame.   [4109]

FLASHAR, H. "The Critique of Plato's Theory of Ideas in Aristotle's Ethics," in #4036, pp. 1-16; transl. M. Schofield. Analyzes Ar's objections to P's attempt to ground moral philosophy on Theory of Forms. Discusses relationship between *EE* and *NE*.   [4110]

FORTENBAUGH, W. W. "Aristotle and the Questionable Mean-Dispositions." *TAPhA* 99(1968), 203-231. None of Ar's ethical works has a classification to cover character traits unconnected with choice and not directly linked to emotions.   [4111]

------. "Aristotle: Animals, Emotion, and Moral Virtue." *Arethusa* 4(1971), 137-165. Because animals lack ability to respond emotionally, they cannot be virtuous.   [4112]

------. "Aristotle: Emotion and Moral Virtue." *Arethusa* 2(1969), 163-185. Ar argues emotions involve apprehension and evaluation of information and behavior directed toward some end. Moral virtue insures emotions as well as reason are good. **[4113]**

———. "Aristotle's Analysis of Friendship: Function and Analogy, Resemblance, and Focal Meaning." *Phron* 20(1975), 51-62. Explores how different kinds of friendship are related, and argues that friendship does not admit a focal analysis. **[4114]**

———. "Menander's *Perikeiromene*: Misfortune, Vehemence, and Polemon." *Phoenix* 28(1974) 430-443. Discusses Menander's play with respect to Ar's definitions of misfortune and injustice as found in *NE*. **[4115]**

———. "*Nicomachean Ethics*, I, 1096b26-29." *Phron* 11(1966), 185-194. Examines Ar's analysis of "good," and argues that while Ar believes that predication of good may involve equivocation, it does not involve fortuitous equivocation. **[4116]**

———. "*Ta pros to telos* and Syllogistic Vocabulary in Aristotle's *Ethics*." *Phron* 10(1965), 191-201. This Greek phrase is borrowed from *Analytics* but does nothing more than indicate a relation. **[4117]**

———. cf. #5179.

FORTIER, T. L. "Aristotle on Social Friendships." *LThPh* 27(1971), 235-250. The concept of friendship in Ar's ethics, if restated in contemporary terms, could humanize our technocratic society and move us toward a balance between social and rational aspects of man. **[4118]**

FREELAND, C. A. "Aristotelian Actions." *Nous* 19(1985), 397-414. Examines Ackrill's claim (#4008) that Ar did not develop a concept of action that would enable us to define and distinguish individual actions. **[4119]**

———. "Moral Virtue and Human Powers." *RMeta* 36(1982), 3-22. Virtues are *dynameis*; examines their structure and operation. Examines *Meta* 9 in order to find room for virtues, and explains why Ar does not discuss virtues specifically, despite his implicit treatment of them as *dynameis* in *Ethics*. **[4120]**

FURLEY, D. J. "Aristotle on the Voluntary," in #4036, pp. 47-60 (revised portion of #5977). Places Ar's analysis in its historical setting. Ar's criterion of a voluntary act is not that it is "spontaneous" or "freely chosen" or that "he could have chosen otherwise," but that source of action cannot be traced to anything outside the agent. **[4121]**

———. "Self-Movers," in #4312, pp. 55-67. Examines Ar's claim that animals are self-movers in conjunction with certain passages in *Phys* that appear to deny that there can be self-movers, and explores Ar's theory of desire. **[4122]**

GARDNER, B. B. *Moral Responsibility: A Modern Aristotelian Analysis.* New York: Pageant, 1965. Exposition of Ar's concept of moral responsibility. His distinctions between voluntary and involuntary action and between voluntary action and choice are close to those of contemporary ethical theorists. **[4123]**

GARRETT, J. E. "Aristotle's Nontechnical Conception of *Techne*." *ModSch* 65(1987), 283-294. Ar does not understand *techne* as having only instrumental value and being value-neutral. A *techne* is perfection itself, causing perfection in its products. **[4124]**

GARSIDE, C. "Can A Woman be Good in the Same Way as a Man?" *Dial*(Can) 10(1971), 534-544. Comparison of Kierkegaard's and Ar's concepts of women indicates that, on the basis of their understanding of what it is to be a good person and what women are capable of, women cannot ultimately be good. **[4125]**

GARVER, E. "Aristotle on Virtue and Pleasure," in #54, pp. 157-176. Explores complications in distinction between *kinesis* and *energeia* through study of courage, and focuses on three questions: 1) What does it mean for an action to be its own end? 2) What is relation between activity and pleasure? 3) What is difference between virtue and self-control? **[4126]**

————. "Aristotle's Genealogy of Morals." *Ph&PhenRes* 44(1984), 471-492. Uses non-Aristotelian terminology to examine his concept that an action is its own end. **[4127]**

————. "Aristotle's Metaphysics of Morals." *JHPh* 27(1989), 7-28. Discusses how distinction between rational and irrational potencies in *Meta* is unable to explicate idea of moral virtue as a *hexis prohairetike*, a habit concerned with choice. **[4128]**

————. "The Meaning of *Thrasos* in Aristotle's *Ethics*." *CPh* 77(1982), 228-233. Rashness (*thrasos*) is the emotional vice connected with courage. Both are founded on confidence. **[4129]**

————. "The Moral Virtues and the Two Sides of *Energeia*." *AncPh* 9(1989), 293-313. Seeks to clarify connections between three aspects of moral virtues: they are *energeiai* of irrational but persuadable part of soul, are activities worth pursuing for their own sake, and coincide for most part with traditionally praised activities. **[4130]**

GASTALDI, S. "*Pathe* and *Polis*: Aristotle's Theory of Passions in the *Rhetoric* and the *Ethics*." *Topoi* 6(1987), 105-110. For Ar passions are natural and acceptable in human life if they can be controlled. That must be accomplished by the individual, not by state regulation. **[4131]**

GEORGIADIS, C. "Equitable and Equity in Aristotle," in #1283, pp. 159-172. Analyzes Ar's effort to reconcile the just and equitable while keeping their distinctions. **[4132]**

GIBBS, B. R. "Virtue and Reason." *PAS* Suppl. 48(1974), 23-41. Rejects Ar's ways of distinguishing virtue from art, and argues that right account of understanding art and virtue is found in P's *Rep*. **[4133]**

GILDIN, H. "Aristotle and the Moral Square of Opposition." *Monist* 54(1970), 100-105. Examines doctrine of mean and a particular logical pattern, an adaptation of traditional square of opposition. Shows how Ar's doctrine of mean offers an explanation of why it is easy to frame universally valid rules for various moral vices. **[4134]**

GOLD, H. B. "Praxis: Its Conceptual Development in Aristotle's *Nicomachean Ethics*." *GradFacPhJ* 6(1977), 106-130. To see Ar's ethical philosophy as based purely on inculcation of habits is to limit it unnecessarily. Delineates development of *praxis* in Ar's thought to add a new dimension to our understanding of his ethics. **[4135]**

GOMEZ-LOBO, A. "Aristotle," in *Ethics in the History of Western Philosophy*, ed. R. J. Cavalier (New York: St. Martin's, 1989), pp. 32-59. Overview of Ar's ethics, focusing on his concepts of practical knowledge, the good, and the right.   **[4136]**

———. "The Ergon Inference," *Phron* 34(1989), 170-184. Ar is not guilty of a fallacious inference from fact to value. Several key terms must be properly defined to understand what Ar really meant to say.   **[4137]**

GOOCH, P. W. "Aristotle and the Happy Dead." *CPh* 88(1983), 112-116. Reply to K. Pritzl (#4289).   **[4138]**

———. cf. #1062.

GOSLING, J. "More Aristotelian Pleasures." *PAS* 74(1973-1974), 15-34. Both Books 7 and 10 of *NE* offer similar accounts of nature of pleasure, which offer general conditions for occurrence of pleasure. However, Ar is interested in "real" pleasure, which is related to the nature of the relevant being.   **[4139]**

GOULD, T. "The Metaphysical Foundations for Aristotle's Ethics," in #41, pp. 451-461. Asks whether Ar tries to fit his treatment of ethics into his general metaphysical program: If there is not a single motion in universe which is not caused by a good striven for, then why do we treat strivings of men differently from strivings of rocks, trees, and horses?   **[4140]**

GREENWOOD, L. H. G. *Aristotle:* Nicomachean Ethics *Book Six*. New York: Arno Pr, 1973. Reprint of 1909 edition; notes, commentary.   **[4141]**

HALL, R. H. "The Voluntary and the Involuntary in Aristotle's *Nicomachean Ethics*." *Auslegung* 5(1977), 18-42. Ar specifically mentions four criteria for determining whether an action is voluntary or involuntary. However, he also uses a fifth criterion, control, which he never defines explicitly.   **[4142]**

HAMPSHIRE, S. *Two Theories of Morality*. Oxford Univ. Pr., 1977. Shows how Ar assigns an overriding value to established opinion whereas Spinoza sees philosophy as pointing the way to a radical moral conversion. Ar also stresses importance of good or bad performance of a single human life.   **[4143]**

HANTZ, H. D. "Aristotle's Theory of Man and Modern Counterparts." *Diot* 8(1980), 44-47. Important similarities exist in ethics of Ar and John Dewey.   **[4144]**

———. "Justice and Equality in Aristotle's *Nicomachean Ethics* and *Politics*." *Diot* 3(1975), 83-94. An assessment of role of equality in a larger view of Ar's theory of justice is needed. Shows that where problems of justice arise, if equality is not achieved, then generally justice is not realized.   **[4145]**

HANUS, J. G. "Friendship in Aristotelian Ethics." *ModSch* 50(1973), 351-365. Reason is the point of contact between human and divine and the basis of friendship. The person who contemplates truth becomes similar to the gods and can be their friend. Compares Ar's view with P's theory of contemplation of God.   **[4146]**

HARDIE, W. F. R. "Aristotle and the Freewill Problem." *Ph* 43(1968), 274-278. Response to Huby (#4163) who argues that Ar was unaware of problem of psychological determinism.   **[4147]**

———. "Aristotle on Moral Weakness," in *Weakness of Will*, ed. G. Mortimore (London: Macmillan, 1971), pp. 69-94. Detailed commentary on Ar's treatment of moral weakness, suggesting that his patterns of analysis may not cover all the facts.   [4148]

———. "Aristotle on the Best Life for a Man." *Ph* 54(1979), 35-50; also in #3625, pp. 297-322. Ar's ethical theory is more coherent than certain critics maintain but less fully integrated with other parts of the corpus than others believe.   [4149]

———. "Aristotle's Doctrine that Virtue is a 'Mean'." *PAS* 65(1965), 183-204; also in #4036, pp. 33-46. Examines central features of Ar's account of moral virtue; explores how close an analogy he wishes to suggest between ethical mean and types of means in mathematics. Argues that doctrine of mean is not grounded in ideas of *Phys.*   [4150]

———. *Aristotle's Ethical Theory*. Oxford: Clarendon Pr., 1988. Study of Ar's moral theory in *NE* aimed particularly at students. Addresses ambiguities and critical disagreements on topics such as definition and extension of happiness, embodiment of soul, the ethical mean, and initiation of action.   [4151]

———. "The Final Good in Aristotle's Ethics." *Ph* 40(1965), 277-295. Shows, using Ar's doctrine of the final good, that if moral philosophy has to search for one comprehensive principle of duty, that principle must be self-respect.   [4152]

———. "'Magnanimity' in Aristotle's Ethics." *Phron* 23(1978), 63-79. Explores Ar's meaning in saying that magnanimity is "a sort of crown." Investigates how the account does not confirm doctrine of the mean expounded in *NE* 3.6.   [4153]

HARE, J. "*Eleutheriotes* in Aristotle's Ethics." *AncPh* 8(1988), 19-32. Discusses Ar's account of *eleutheriotes*, which can mean "generosity" or "liberality." In *NE* he stresses the former sense; in *EE*, the latter.   [4154]

HEINAMAN, R. "Compulsion and Voluntary Action in the *Eudemian Ethics*." *Nous* 22(1988), 253-281. Examines those conditions in definition of voluntary action which are central to account of compulsion. Investigates certain difficulties in discussion of coercion and how Ar avoids them in *NE*.   [4155]

———. "*Eudaimonia* and Self-Sufficiency in the *Nicomachean Ethics*," *Phron* 33(1988), 31-53. Appeal to self-sufficiency at 1097b 14-21 as well as other arguments fails to prove that Ar is giving a "comprehensive" account of *eudaimonia*.   [4156]

———. "The *Eudemian Ethics* on Knowledge and Voluntary Action." *Phron* 31(1986), 128-147. Finds a number of shortcomings in Ar's account, and maintains *NE*'s account of role of knowledge represents an advance.   [4157]

HELD, G. F. "The Meaning of $\bar{E}$thos in the *Poetics*." *Hermes* 113(1985), 280-293. $\bar{E}$thos covers intellectual as well as moral qualities. Comparison of its use in *Poet* with use in other of Ar's works.   [4158]

HELSTROM, K. L. "The Mean." *Auslegung* 1-2(1973-75), 60-67. The mean and the practical categories do not provide rules for determining the virtues; rather they provide general characteristics of what practical reason judges to be virtuous.   [4159]

HOFFMAN, R. "Aristotle on Moral Virtue." *Phil*(Isrl) 1 (1971), 191-195. Seeks to correct standard interpretations that Ar views moral virtue as a mean. There are four faulty extremes with respect to which courage is a mean.   **[4160]**

HOMIAK, M. L. "The Pleasure of Virtue in Aristotle's Moral Theory." *PacPhQ* 66(1985), 93-110. Ar bases the connection between happiness and moral virtue on his claim that the happy person's pleasures are derived from the unrestricted activity of human nature.   **[4161]**

———. "Virtue and Self-Love in Aristotle's Ethics." *CanJPh* 11(1981), 633-652. The virtuous person, in Ar's view, loves himself and for that reason tends toward virtue rather than vice. Above all he loves practical reasoning.   **[4162]**

HUBY, P. "The First Discovery of the Freewill Problem." *Ph* 42(1967), 353-362. Argues that Ar approaches the problem but turns away every time without being aware that there is any genuine difficulty.   **[4163]**

HUDSON, S. D. "Reason and Motivation in Aristotle." *CanJPh* 11(1981), 111-135. Reason can guide our behavior because our recognition that an act is reasonable is motivation to perform it. Moral judgments have internal motivational power.   **[4164]**

HURSTHOUSE, R. "Acting and Feeling in Character: *Nicomachean Ethics* 3.i." *Phron* 29(1984), 252-266.   This section is often read too narrowly so that the *ouk hekousion/akousion* distinction gets ignored and inadequate accounts are given of acting under necessity. Sees the chapter as dealing with the relationship between character and actions, not just with responsibility.   **[4165]**

———. "Aristotle, *Nicomachean Ethics*," in #79, pp. 35-56. Ar maintains that ethics does have a point and recognizes as a constraint on his account of happiness that the flourishing life should contain advantages of (some) material wealth and pleasure.   **[4166]**

———. "A False Doctrine of the Mean." *PAS* 81(1980-81), 57-72. Reply to Urmson #4374. Ar does allow for possibility that a person's character could be both excessive and deficient in regard to a particular virtue.   **[4167]**

HUTCHINSON, D. S. *The Virtues of Aristotle.* New York: Routledge and K. Paul, 1987. Examines Ar's answer to question, "What is virtue?" and argues that his views are found in every part of his work and are systematically unified.   **[4168]**

———. cf. #1707.

IRWIN, T. H. "Aristotle on Reason, Desire, and Virtue." *JPh* 72(1975), 567-578. Examines similarities between Ar and Hume on the question of whether correct decisions and action depend on reason/thought. Finds the two thinkers not far apart.   **[4169]**

———. "Aristotle's Conception of Morality." *PBACAPh* 1(1985), 115-143. Ar has a concept of morality corresponding to the modern one. Focuses on taking even the most self-regarding excellences of character as moral virtues in our modern sense of being oriented toward the welfare of others.   **[4170]**

———. "Aristotle's Methods of Ethics," in #3631, pp. 193-223. Asks whether Ar's methods are right ones to express his moral epistemology, and whether his epistemology is reasonable. [4171]

———. "Disunity in the Aristotelian Virtues." *OSAP* Suppl. (1988), pp. 61-78. Examines three propositions which Ar has good reason to believe, but which together form an inconsistency: 1) if you have any one virtue of character, you have all of them; 2) large-scale virtues are distinct from their small-scale counterparts; 3) one can have small-scale virtues without having large-scale counterparts. [4172]

———. "First Principles in Aristotle's Ethics." *MidwStudPh* 3(1978), 252-272. Ar compares first principles in ethical reasoning to hypothesis of his scientific method. At some points he at least implies first principles can be logically justified. [4173]

———. "The Metaphysical and Psychological Basis of Aristotle's Ethics," in #4312, pp. 35-53. From Ar's metaphysical doctrines on natural substances, seeks to construct an argument for Ar's view of the soul and his basic ethical claims. [4174]

———. "Moral Science and Political Theory in Aristotle." *HPolTho* 6(1985), 150-168. Suggests that we can see from *Ethics* why empirical study of political systems might be intended to support Ar's ethical principles. [4175]

———. "Permanent Happiness: Aristotle and Solon." *OSAP* 3(1985), pp. 89-124. Examines Ar's remark that if someone is well off for most of his life, but then suffers some disaster and comes to a bad end, then no one counts him as happy. Explores problem that, if happiness is vulnerable to external hazards, Ar cannot claim that virtue ensures happiness. The virtuous man is, however, happier than others because virtue is the most significant, most stable element of happiness. [4176]

———. "Reason and Responsibility in Aristotle," in #4312, pp. 117-155. Asks if Ar's theory of voluntary action is a good theory of responsibility; argues that his account appears simple and basically negative, but he needs and assumes a positive account that raises more complex questions about general conditions of responsibility. [4177]

———. "Some Rational Aspects of Incontinence," in #4305, pp. 49-88. Shows that Ar thinks incontinence involves an error in practical reasoning, and specifically in deliberation, and examines the nature of that error in more detail. [4178]

———. cf. #5713.

JOST, L. J. "Aristotle's *Ethics*: Have We Been Teaching the Wrong One?" *TeachPh* 6(1983), 331-340. *NE* may not be best vehicle for teaching Ar's ethical thinking; *EE* might be a logical alternative. [4179]

———. "A 'Descriptivist' Reading of Aristotle's Treatment of Virtue-Terms." *Apeir* 13 #1(1979), 41-48. Analyzes terms "courage" and "liberality" as used in *NE* to show how Ar defined them and to describe their content. [4180]

———. "Is Aristotle an Ethical Intuitionist?" *Apeir* 10 #1(1976), 15-19. Reply to Baumrin (#4038). Close attention needs to be paid to the criteria by which moral phenomena are evaluated. [4181]

KAHN, C. H. "Aristotle and Altruism." *Mind* 90(1981), 20-40. Altruism and egoism need not be as contradictory as their modern implications suggest. What makes friendship possible is the Active Intellect working in every person. Two persons committed to love of this suprapersonal principle share the basis of a friendship.   **[4182]**

————. "Discovering the Will: From Aristotle to Augustine," in #5589, 234-259. Compares Ar and Augustine to identify several ways in which Augustine has and Ar lacks a concept of will; traces historical development of concept.   **[4183]**

KAPSOMENOS, S. G. "Hellenism and Humanism," in *Proceedings of the First International Humanistic Symposium at Delphi, Sept. 25 - Oct. 4, 1969* (Athens: Hellenic Soc. for Human. Stud., 1971), II, pp. 15-25. Greek ethical ideals developed over a long period of time. Sophists and Ar made significant advances.   **[4184]**

KEARNEY, J. K. "Happiness and the Unity of the *Nicomachean Ethics* Reconsidered." *PACPhA* 40(1966), 135-143. Problem of end of man can only be resolved by taking contemplation as highest good because it is a "god-like" activity and because the intellectual life and leisure are ends toward which political life is directed.   **[4185]**

KENNY, A. J. P. "Aristotle on Moral Luck," in #4081, pp. 105-119. Investigates how a moral matter can depend on luck within the tradition of Ar; suggests that his awareness of unfairness and contingency of the world makes for a better morality.   **[4186]**

————. *The Aristotelian Ethics: A Study of the Relationship Between the* Eudemian *and* Nicomachean Ethics *of Aristotle.* Oxford: Clarendon Pr., 1978. Attacks "dogma" that *EE* is to be relegated to inferior, provisional position in comparison with *NE*.   **[4187]**

————. *Aristotle's Theory of the Will.* New Haven, CT: Yale Univ. Pr., 1972. Challenges view that Ar has no theory of will. Satisfactory philosophical account of will must treat voluntariness, intentionality, rationality; examines Ar's discussions of each.   **[4188]**

————. "Happiness." *PAS* 66(1965-66), 93-102; revised version in *The Anatomy of the Soul: Historical Essays in the Philosophy of Mind* (New York: Harper & Row, 1973), pp. 51-61; rprt as "Aristotle on Happiness," in #4036, pp. 25-32. Ar's idea of happiness as activity is worth re-examining in light of modern interest in the *summum bonum.* He also sees happiness as self-sufficient but able to be increased by other goods.   **[4189]**

————. "The Practical Syllogism and Incontinence." *Phron* 11(1966), 163-184; also in *The Anatomy of the Soul: Historical Essays in the Philosophy of Mind* (New York: Harper & Row, 1973), pp. 28-50. At 1147a24ff. Ar acknowledges case in which someone knowingly commits a wrong act. When one does not recognize Ar's position, it is due to a faulty understanding of structure of practical syllogism.   **[4190]**

————. "The Stylometric Study of Aristotle's *Ethics.*" *Computing in the Humanities* (1977), 11-22. The three sections common to both *NE* and *EE* seem originally to have been part of *EE*.   **[4191]**

KEYT, D. "Intellectualism in Aristotle," in #42, pp. 364-387. Ar has a single, consistent ideal of human happiness throughout *NE*: "one should seek to immortalize oneself but only within the bounds of the life of practical wisdom and moral virtue."   **[4192]**

——. "The Meaning of *Bios* in Aristotle's *Ethics* and *Politics*." *AncPh* 9(1989), 15-22. Explores why theoretical life is always presented as an alternative to and a rival of the political life.   [4193]

——. cf. #5079.

KING, J. T. "Aristotle's Ethical Non-Intuitionism." *NewSchol* 43(1969), 131-142. Reply to Baumrin (#4038). For Ar, there is neither a special property of "rightness," nor a special faculty to intuit it. Thus he is not an intuitionist.   [4194]

KIRWAN, C. "Logic and the Good in Aristotle." *PhQ* 17(1967), 97-114. Technical discussion of several logical positions which can be attributed to Ar in regard to pursuit of *eudaimonia*.   [4195]

KLEIN, S. "An Analysis and Defense of Aristotle's Method in *Nicomachean Ethics* i and x." *AncPh* 8(1988), 63-72. In defining happiness Ar relies on two types of opinion (*endoxa*). One type, the substantive, states what happiness is. The other, regulative, evaluates and eliminates inappropriate *endoxai*.   [4196]

KORSGAARD, C. M. "Aristotle and Kant on the Source of Value." *Ethics* 96(1986), 486-505. Kant holds that the good will is a source of value in sense that other things acquire their value from standing in an appropriate relation to it. Ar holds a similar view about contemplation which explains his preference for contemplative life.   [4197]

——. "Aristotle on Function and Virtue." *HPhQ* 3(1986), 259-279. Without actualizing our potential for practical learning, we cannot experience the good life. The moral virtues are the qualities which enable us to reach that potentiality.   [4198]

KOSMAN, L. A. "Being Properly Affected: Virtues and Feelings in Aristotle's Ethics," in #4312, pp. 103-116. Ar's moral theory must be seen as a theory not only of how to act well, but how to feel well.   [4199]

——. "Predicating the Good." *Phron* 13(1968), 171-174. Ar claims (*NE* 1096a23-27) that predicating any quality which is characteristic of the Good is the same as predicating the Good.   [4200]

KRAUT, R. "Aristotle on Choosing Virtue for Itself." *AGPh* 58(1976), 223-279. Ar's claim that we choose virtue for itself, and not as a means to an end, is inconsistent with rest of his moral philosophy.   [4201]

——. *Aristotle on the Human Good*. Princeton Univ. Pr., 1989. Emphasis on contemplation as highest human good in *NE* 10 is fully consistent with focus on moral virtue in earlier books.   [4202]

——. "Comments on 'Disunity in the Aristotelian Virtues' by T. H. Irwin." *OSAP* Suppl. (1988), 79-86. Questions reality of conflict Irwin (#4172) identifies, and questions whether Ar has provided adequate grounding for view that if one has one virtue, one has all of them.   [4203]

——. "Comments on 'Self-Love in Aristotle' by Julia Annas," in #4305, pp. 19-23. Challenges Annas' (#4026) interpretations on competition and self-sacrifice.   [4204]

——. "The Importance of Love in Aristotle's Ethics," *PhResArch* 1(1975), no. 1060. If reason is the only basis for virtuous activity, then Ar's ethical theory is weakened, because unethical behavior can also be based on reason. But virtue is also an expression of love/friendship toward others.   **[4205]**

——. "The Peculiar Function of Human Beings." *CanJPh* 9(1979), 467-478. Ar asserts that happiness is based on an activity peculiar to humans, viz., contemplation. His view is not vitiated by the fact that God also contemplates. What he intends to emphasize is the function which separates us from all other animals and plants.   **[4206]**

——. "Two Conceptions of Happiness." *PhR* 88(1979), 167-197. "Happiness" and *eudaimonia* are similar enough in meaning that the traditional translation can be maintained. Both suggest a psychological state and a standard for evaluating lives. Ar's standard is objective, ours much more subjective.   **[4207]**

LAWRENCE, G. "Akrasia and Clear-Eyed Akrasia in *Nicomachean Ethics* VII." *RPhA* 6(1988), 77-106. Reply to #4063. Ar's views on intellectual adequacy in *NE* 7.1-10 will not support possibility of a person knowing better and choosing worse.   **[4208]**

LEIGHTON, S. R. "Aristotle and the Emotions." *Phron* 27(1982), 144-174. If courage is a virtue, and if virtues are based on self-control, then Ar is inconsistent. His theory of the passions in *Rhet* helps resolve the difficulty.   **[4209]**

——. "Aristotle's Courageous Passions." *Phron* 33(1988), 76-99. Explores how "the courageous feel on the battlefield," and argues that tensions in Ar's account arise not from carelessness but from particular theoretical commitments leading Ar in different directions.   **[4210]**

——. "*Eudemian Ethics* 1220b11-13." *CQ* 34(1984), 135-138. Examines why certain types of *pathe* are not accompanied by pain or pleasure.   **[4211]**

LLOYD, G. E. R. "The Role of Medical and Biological Analogies in Aristotle's *Ethics*." *Phron* 13(1968), 68-83; also in #4255, pp. 237-252. Examines most important texts where Ar uses biological or medical analogies to advance his own ethical doctrines, identifies ethical doctrines which derive their chief support from such analogies; tries to assess analogies. Discusses function of man, moral excellence, the mean, pleasure.   **[4212]**

LOSIN, P. "Aristotle's Doctrine of the Mean." *HPhQ* 4(1987), 329-341. Mean in moral behavior is not simply a point between two extremes. Many factors, including individual personalities, go into establishing a mean for which each person strives.   **[4213]**

LUCASH, F. "More Pleasure in Aristotle." *RFilNeo-Scol* 66(1974), 126-130. Reply to #4373. Ar distinguishes between pleasure involved in an activity and that accruing from it. Pleasure comes from a completed activity and is distinct from the activity.   **[4214]**

MacINTYRE, A. C. "Aristotle's Account of the Virtues," in *After Virtue: A Study in Moral Theory* (Notre Dame, IN: Univ. of Notre Dame Pr., 1984; 2nd ed.), pp. 146-164. Ar's account of ethics is undermined by three assumptions of his: the teleological nature of life, the connection of individual ethics with life in the *polis*, and his insistence on unity and harmony in the soul and the *polis*.   **[4215]**

——. "Practical Rationalities as Forms of Social Structure." *IrishPhJ* 4(1987), 3-19. Rational action is structured very differently in different times and places and Ar's theory is best understood as one which has a subject matter specific to one important mode of practical reasoning in classical Greece.   **[4216]**

MADIGAN, A. "Dimensions of Voluntariness in *EN* III 12:1119a21-33." *AncPh* 6(1986), 139-152. There are two aspects to voluntariness: an agent's response to natural inclination and the opportunity to make decisions.   **[4217]**

——. "*EN* IX 8: Beyond Egoism and Altruism." *ModSch* 63(1985), 1-20. Self-love and self-sacrifice are mutually exclusive aims which Ar tries to reconcile with concepts of nobility and intellectual satisfaction. Introduction of those concepts into ethical discussion moves him beyond egoism and altruism, rather than resolving the problem. **[4218]**

MAGNUS, B. "Aristotle and Nietzsche: '*Megalopsychia* and *Uebermensch*'," in #54, pp. 260-295. Discusses Ar's account of pride and the great-souled man.   **[4219]**

MANHOOD, G. H. "Human Nature and the Virtues in Confucius and Aristotle." *JChinPh* 1(1974), 295-312. Compares concept of "virtue" in Ar's *NE* and Confucius' *Analects* with aim of elucidating each thinker's views of human nature.   **[4220]**

MARTIN, R. "Intuitionism and the Practical Syllogism in Aristotle's *Ethics*." *Apeir* 11 #2(1977), 12-19. Reply to Baumrin (#4038) and Jost (#4181). Question of Ar's ethical intuitionism cannot be resolved by introduction of notion of "ethical perception." Ar's concept of the practical syllogism provides a key to settling the debate.   **[4221]**

McCONNELL, T. C. "Is Aristotle's Account of Incontinence Inconsistent?" *CanJPh* 4(1975), 635-651. Most scholars take Ar to say that one cannot act contrary to his knowledge of right behavior. But in several passages he indicates that one can knowingly act contrary to his moral principles. Contradiction is resolved by realization that for Ar "knowledge" means more than knowing one's moral principles propositionally.   **[4222]**

McDOWELL, J. "Comments on 'Some Rational Aspects of Incontinence' by T. H. Irwin," in #4305, pp. 89-102. Challenges Irwin's (#4178) interpretation that the incontinent's failure is that his particular judgment as to what is to be done here and now is not dictated by his correct general conception of "happiness."   **[4223]**

——. "The Role of *Eudaimonia* in Aristotle's Ethics." *PACA* 15(1980), 1-15; also in #4312, pp. 359-376. Explores two interpretations of Ar's evident thesis that *eudaimonia* (happiness) is chief good: 1) *eudaimonia* is that for sake of which all action is undertaken; 2) *eudaimonia* is that for sake of which all action ought to be undertaken. **[4224]**

McGINLEY, J. "Aristotle's Notion of the Voluntary." *Apeir* 14(1980). 125-133. Ar's concept of voluntary behavior in *NE* 3.1 attempts to combine two views which are irreconcilable.   **[4225]**

McINERNY, R. "Ultimate End in Aristotle," in *Vérité et ethos: Recueil commémoratif dédie à Alphonse-Marie Parent*, ed. J. Danek (Quebec: Univ. Laval Pr., 1982), pp. 43-55. For Ar man's ultimate end is *eudaimonia*, a set of virtuous activities.   **[4226]**

MELE, A. R. "Aristotle on *Akrasia* and Knowledge." *ModSch* 58(1981). 137-157. Some inconsistencies in Ar's account of *akrasia* in *NE* 7.3 can be resolved by rejecting some traditional assumptions about the epistemological foundations of the passage.   **[4227]**

――――. "Aristotle on *Akrasia, Eudaimonia*, and the Psychology of Action." *HPhQ* 2(1985), 375-393. In Ar's thought it is possible for a person to act akratically against what he knows logically to be a right course of action.   **[4228]**

――――. "Aristotle on the Justification of the Ends." *PACPhA* 56(1982), 79-86. Ar's position that practical ends are "assumed" rather than deliberated about is consistent with idea that practical *archai* are subject to justificatory reasoning.   **[4229]**

――――. "Aristotle on the Proximate Efficient Cause of Action," in #3637, pp. 133-155. Ar states that choice is origin of action. Investigates what choice is for Ar and what the proximate efficient cause is for non-chosen action.   **[4230]**

――――. "Aristotle on the Roles of Reason in Motivation and Justification" *AGPh* 66(1984), 124-147. Examines what role, if any, *phronesis* has in generation of occurrent desires for ends chosen by virtuous agents, and what role, if any, practical thought has in justifying ends of virtuous agents.   **[4231]**

――――. "Aristotle's Wish." *JHPh* 22(1984), 139-156. Elucidates role of wish (*boulesis*) in Ar's theory of human action. He claims that people wish only what they consider good and that *boulesis* is the only sort of desire in the rational part of soul and that a wish is a wish for some end.   **[4232]**

――――. "Choice and Virtue in the *Nicomachean Ethics*." *JHPh* 19(1981), 405-423. Ar uses only one notion of *prohairesis* (choice) in *NE*, and that is choice made toward an end. Various sorts of actions result, depending on the end.   **[4233]**

――――. "On Happiness and the Good Life." *SwJPh* 10(1979), 181-188. Defends Ar's view that happiness is an inclusive good. By this concept he tries to account for inconsistencies between acts and desires.   **[4234]**

――――. "The Practical Syllogism and Deliberation in Aristotle's Causal Theory of Action." *NewSchol* 55(1981), 281-316. Ar's theory of action is clarified by understanding that a person can deliberate and devise a practical syllogism without being aware of engaging in those processes. Causal interpretation of Ar's theory of action is plausible.   **[4235]**

MERLAN, P. "Studies in Epicurus and Aristotle," in #4255, pp. 161-171. Section of this article on Ar, which is reprinted here, discusses problems of dating and authenticity of *MM*, especially in light of controversy between Arnim and Dirlmeier.   **[4236]**

MILLER, A. B. "Aristotle on Habit (*ethos*) and Character (*ēthos*): Implications for the *Rhetoric*." *SM* 41(1974), 309-316. Ar bases character on habitual behavior.   **[4237]**

MILLER, F. D., Jr.   "Actions and Results." *PhQ* 25(1975) 350-354. Uses Ar's *energeia/kinesis* distinction to develop theory of identification of actions.   **[4238]**

――――. "Aristotle on Practical Knowledge and Moral Weakness," in #4282, pp. 131-144. Ar's approach to problem of moral weakness is comprehensible only when viewed in light of his theory of moral knowledge.   **[4239]**

———. "Aristotle on Rationality in Action." *RMeta* 37(1984), 499-520. Unlike modern moral philosophers, Ar sees action rather than knowledge as the end of ethical inquiries. Considering what to do should lead to a decision to do whatever is determined to be the right thing to do. [4240]

———. "Rationality and Freedom in Aristotle and Hayek." *Reason Papers* 9(1983), 29-36. Discusses Ar's theory of practical rationality and its implications for public policy. For Ar, deliberation is complete only at time of action when agent identifies particulars to implement a plan of action. [4241]

MILLGRAM, E. "Aristotle on Making Other Selves." *CanJPh* 17(1987), 361-376. In Ar's view a friend is one's product, an actualization of one's self. Friendship is thus self-oriented. [4242]

MILLS, M. J. "Aristotle's Dichotomy of *Eutuchia* (*Eudemian Ethics* Theta, 2,1247b18-1248a15." *Hermes* 111(1983), 280-295. This passage continues to puzzle scholars in terms of both text and meaning. [4243]

———. "The Discussions of *Andreia* in the *Eudemian* and *Nicomachean Ethics*." *Phron* 25(1980), 198-218. Account of *andreia* (manliness) in *EE* is less philosophically developed and closer to P's concept of this virtue. Its vocabulary more nearly matches other acknowledged early works of Ar, suggesting that *EE* is earlier than *NE*. [4244]

———. "*Eudemian Ethics*, Theta, 2,1247a7-013." *Hermes* 109(1981), 253-256. Proposed translation of passage which discusses relation between fortune and character. [4245]

———. "*Tyche* in Aristoxenus, Fr. 41, and *Eudemian Ethics* Theta 2." *AJPh* 103(1982), 204-208. Aristotle and Aristoxenus both believe men are born with innate good or bad fortune. Aristotle does not agree with Aristoxenus, however, that gods can also cause such conditions to exist. [4246]

———. cf. #1722.

MILO, R. D. *Aristotle on Practical Knowledge and Weakness of Will*. The Hague: Mouton & Co., 1966. Examines Ar's accounts of motivation of human action and of nature of practical knowledge. Ar is not as far from S's concept that no one does wrong willingly as some suspect. Examines a weakness in his account of relationship between practical knowledge and action. [4247]

MINGAY, J. "How Should a Philosopher Live? Two Aristotelian Views." *HPolTho* 8(1987), 21-32. Views of philosophic life presented in *NE* and *EE* are contradictory, and neither is satisfactory. They may have been written for different audiences. [4248]

MODRAK, D. K. "Aisthesis in the Practical Syllogism." *PhilStud* 30(1976), 379-392. Defends sense of practical syllogism as presented by Ar in *De Motu* and in *NE* as well as showing that it need not be construed as a logical mistake. Also suggests that it be seen as the first step in understanding Ar's doctrine of akrasia. [4249]

MOLINE, J. "Contemplation and the Human Good." *Nous* 17(1983) 37-53. Contradiction between different accounts of *eudaimonia* is real. Ar is engaging in irony in his discussion of contemplation in *NE* Book 10. [4250]

MONAN, J. D. *Moral Knowledge and Its Methodology in Aristotle.* Oxford: Clarendon Pr., 1968. Discusses views of Jaeger, Duering, et al. on Ar's doctrine regarding ideal of human life in three ethical treatises: *Protrepticus, NE,* and *EE.* Does not regard *MM* as genuine. Concludes *NE* 1 and 10 are early treatises, reflecting concept of man as *nous,* while books common to *EE* and *NE* represent more advanced stage in Ar's development, a development completed in *EE.* Ar's mature position takes into account moral and intellectual virtues as necessary for attaining moral knowledge.   **[4251]**

MORAUX, P., and **HARLFINGER, D.,** eds. *Untersuchungen zur* Eudemischen Ethik: *Akten des 5. Symposium Aristotelicum (Oosterbeek, Niederlande, 21.-29. August 1969).* Berlin: de Gruyter, 1971. Relevant essays in English are abstracted herein.   **[4252]**

MORAVCSIK, J. M. E. "On What We Aim at and How We Live," in #54, pp. 198-235. Claim of autonomy of morality is ill-founded; no sharp line exists between moral and non-moral in terms of choices, relevant considerations, and desirable character traits. Ethics of P and Ar offer a more adequate pattern for approaching morality.   **[4253]**

———. "The Perils of Friendship and Conceptions of the Self," in #4081, pp. 133-151. Defends possibility of those friendships Ar characterizes as transcending considerations of gratification or utility and being based on care and concern for other person in virtue of person he is.   **[4254]**

MUELLER-GOLDINGEN, C. *Schriften zur aristotelischen Ethik.* Hildesheim: Olms, 1988. Previously published essays; those in English abstracted herein.   **[4255]**

MULHERN, J. J. "*Mia monon pantaxou kata phusin he ariste (EN* 1135a5)." *Phron* 17(1972), 260-268. Explores how to interpret, "there is but one which is everywhere by nature the best." Ar seems to say that only one form of government is the best in any circumstance. What he probably means is that for each situation there is one constitution which is best.   **[4256]**

———. cf. #1112.

MULVANEY, R. J. "Action, Teaching, and the Limits of Practical Rationality: A Response to President Green." *EducTheor* 26(1976), 259-262. Appeals to Ar's account of practical syllogism to point out limitations on role of reason in action.   **[4257]**

NAGEL, T. "Aristotle on *Eudaimonia.*" *Phron* 17(1972), 252-259; also in #4312, pp. 7-14. Defends an "intellectualist" reading of Ar's account of happiness, and maintains that for Ar, "a person should seek to transcend not only his individual practical concerns but also those of society as a whole."   **[4258]**

NEWMAN, J. "Torture and Responsibility." *JVallnq* 8(1974), 161-174. In light of Ar's discussion of "mixed" acts, considers whether actions done under, or from fear of, torture are voluntary or not.   **[4259]**

NIKOLAIDIS, A. G. "Aristotle's Treatment of the Concept of *Praotes.*" *Hermes* 110(1982), 414-422. Discusses Ar's difficulties in defining and treating concept of gentleness (*praotes*).   **[4260]**

O'CONNOR, D. K. "Aristotelian Justice as a Personal Virtue." *MidwStudPh* 13(1988),

417-427. Response to B. Williams (#4402), whose focus on morality is somewhat different from Ar's. Ar's concept of justice is capable of expressing an excellence *and* correcting a defect. **[4261]**

OLMSTED, E. H. "The 'Moral Sense' Aspect of Aristotle's Ethical Theory," in #4255, pp. 59-78. Ar's ethical theory, which uses analogy between sense perception and ethics, is not entirely satisfactory because of imprecision about physiology. In its broad applications, however, the theory does show virtue is essentially a mean. **[4262]**

OLSHEWSKY, T. M. "The Ideal, the Actual and the Human Condition." *PhilInq* 1(1979), 129-140. Because P and Ar differ ontologically, they reach different conclusions about ethics and the human condition. P stresses ideals, Ar actualities. **[4263]**

ONYEWUENYI, I. C. "The Aristotelian Concept of Friendship." *ThoughtPrac* 2(1975), 125-134. Explores following questions about friendship: What is friendship? How does it originate? What are its concepts? What are conditions of genuine friendship and who are genuinely friends? **[4264]**

OWEN, G. E. L. "Aristotelian Pleasures." *PAS* 72(1971-1972), 135-152; also in #4036, pp. 92-103; also in #4255, pp. 293-310. Presents new exegesis of two apparently conflicting accounts of pleasure in *NE* Books 7 and 10. Ar is striving for a consistent and complex view of several notions which we loosely conjoin under pleasure. **[4265]**

OWENS, J. "The Acratic's 'Ultimate Premise' in Aristotle," in #3657, pp. 376-392. Someone who knows the better but does not do it is following passion rather than reason. The moral prohibition "I should not do this" remains a premise rather than a conclusion of such a person's logic. **[4266]**

———. "An Ambiguity in Aristotle, *EE* VII 2 1236a23-4." *Apeir* 22(1989), 127-137. Ar's concept of friendship is difficult to understand because he uses term "universal" in two different senses. In one it means something identical with any and all particulars; in the other it means something identical only with primary instance. **[4267]**

———. "Aristotelian Ethics, Medicine, and the Changing Nature of Man," in #3634, pp. 169-180. Examines Ar's claim at 1147b6-9 that to restore moral knowledge to the weak-willed man, we must turn to physiology. **[4268]**

———. "Aristotle on Leisure." *CanJPh* 16(1981), 713-724. Leisure can be enjoyed only after basic needs are met. Ar has no formal theory but does offer guidance for giving it purpose and making it contribute to development of moral fiber. **[4269]**

———. "Aristotle's Contribution on the Nature of Ethical Norms." *Listening* 18(1983), 225-234. Term "norms" does not easily apply to Ar's *Ethics*, because his moral assertions have an intrinsically flexible nature. **[4270]**

———. "The Grounds of Ethical Universality in Aristotle." *M&W* 2(1969), 171-193; also in #3634, pp. 148-164. Examines Ar's argument that starting point of anything done is choice made in mental activity of agent, and asks whether this view makes very notion of science in the practical order impossible. **[4271]**

———. "How Flexible is Aristotelian 'Right Reason'?" in #4282, pp. 49-66. Examines philosophical criterion for moral goodness — right reason — and asks how this standard can both be flexible enough to give rise to principles that hold only roughly and yet be strong enough to hold that some types of conduct are always right.   **[4272]**

——. "The *Kalon* in the Aristotelian Ethics," in #3631, pp. 261-277. Explores how notion of *kalon* ("beautiful, good") is to be expressed in English, what is its nature, how is it self-motivated, and how it is obligatory.   **[4273]**

——. "Nature and Ethical Norm in Aristotle," in #3634, pp. 165-168. Nature offers inclination and framework for community life, but these determinations enter into moral order only when free choice decides they are to be followed in human conduct. **[4274]**

——. cf. #3849.

PALMER, D. "What the Tortoise Said to Aristotle (about the Practical Syllogism)." *NewSchol* 46(1972), 449-460. Passages in *De anima* and *De motu animal* suggest Ar links perception and desire to action, i. e., result of practical syllogism is action.   **[4275]**

PARKER, F. H. "Contemplation in Aristotelian Ethics," in #4282, pp. 205-212. Relation of contemplation to life of moral virtue poses no philosophical problem.   **[4276]**

PATTANTYUS, J. E. "Aristotle's Doctrine of Equity." *ModSch* 51(1974), 213-222. Ar developed concept of equity as the connection between law and morality. It guarantees a legal system will function on an ontologically valid foundation.   **[4277]**

——. "Justice in General and General Justice according to Aristotle." *StudPh&HistPh* 5(1970), 79-137. Ar's theory of justice is psychologically based. The moral virtue of justice is guided by *phronesis*. Ar distinguishes justice from other virtues by its other-relatedness and objective mean of equality.   **[4278]**

PEARS, D. "Aristotle's Analysis of Courage." *Philosophical Exchange* 2(1976), 43-52; also in *MidwStudPh* 3(1978), 273-285. Examines Ar's analysis of courage and contrasts it with his analysis of temperance. Argues that "typical courage" is an "executive" virtue, practiced in service of further goals which vary from case to case.   **[4279]**

——. "Courage as a Mean," in #4312, pp. 171-186. Since courage involves two distinct feelings, fear and confidence, it does not fit the model of a mean in quite the same way as other virtues.   **[4280]**

PETERSON, S. "*Horos* (Limit) in Aristotle's *Nicomachean Ethics*." *Phron* 33(1988), 233-250. Argues that "the right reason" in *NE* 6.1 refers to "propositional content which makes some reference to the particular situation and which is true, and not merely true, but also relevant to the situation." *Horos* means not "criterion" but "limit or boundary of the intermediate outside which is the too much and the too little."   **[4281]**

PORRECO, R., ed. *The Georgetown Symposium on Ethics*. Lanham, MD: Univ. Pr. of America, 1984. Relevant essays in this collection are abstracted herein.   **[4282]**

PORTE, D. F. "Injustice and Tragedy in Aristotle," in #4282, pp. 175-184. Examines Ar's "moral taxonomy of pain" and central conceptions of injustice and tragedy. **[4283]**

PREUS, A. "Aristotle on Healthy and Sick Souls." *Monist* 69(1986), 416-433. Ar's theory of close connection between body and soul makes most mental illnesses, in his view, physical maladies. Examines *Ethics* and *Parva naturalia*. **[4284]**

———. "Intention and Impulse in Aristotle and the Stoics." *Apeir* 15(1981), 48-58. Early followers of Ar lost sight of his theory of action because they introduced the Stoic concept of *horme* (impulse) in place of Ar's *orexis* (intention). **[4285]**

———. "Reason in Aristotle's Ethics." *IntStudPh* 10(1978), 136-140. Reply to Cooper (#4074) and Eriksen (#4105). **[4286]**

———. cf. #1427.

PRICE, A. W. "Aristotle's Ethical Holism." *Mind* 89(1980), 338-352. Ar sees *eudaimonia* as consisting of judgments made on the basis of how they affect one's entire life. But, given our inability to see our entire lives, this holistic view is impractical. **[4287]**

———. cf. #1735.

PRICHARD, H. A. "The Meaning of *Agathon* in the *Ethics* of Aristotle," in #3625, pp. 241-260. By *agathon* Ar really means "conducive to our happiness." This means that when a man does an action deliberately, as distinct from impulsively, he does it from the desire to become happy, even when he does what is virtuous, or speculates. **[4288]**

PRITZL, K. "Happiness after Death: *Nicomachean Ethics* 1.10-11." *CPh* 78(1983), 101-111. Ar interprets popular views of life after death as consistent with his own understanding of happiness. **[4289]**

PROSEN, A. J. "Aristotle on Temperance." *CB* 44(1968), 73-75. Temperance is not merely moderation. It is use of things exercised under guidance of reason. **[4290]**

RADFORD, R. "Aristotle on Doing Evil." *JTho* 1(1966), 9-22. Examines Ar's analysis of Socratic understanding of wrongdoing, and then considers his analysis of vice, unjust acts, and incontinence. **[4291]**

REES, D. A. "'Magnanimity' in the *Eudemian* and *Nicomachean Ethics*, in #4252, pp. 231-243. Concept of *megalopsyche* in *NE* is more philosophically interesting than that in *EE* and suggests that the latter work is the earlier. **[4292]**

REILLY, R. "Weakness and Blameworthiness: The Aristotelian Predicament." *PhilStud* (Ireland) 28(1976), 148-165. In *NE* 6 Ar tries to take *akrasia* (moral weakness) as worthy of blame, as well as bad, because the akratic person is in a certain state of ignorance. But that interpretation conflicts with what Ar says in *NE* 3 about ignorance and compulsion as criteria of non-blameworthiness. **[4293]**

RICHARDSON, H. S. "Commentary on Broadie's 'The Problem of Practical Intellect in Aristotle's *Ethics*.'" *PBACAPh* 3(1987), 253-261. Reply to #4050. For Ar neither deliberation nor the practical syllogism is purely deductive. **[4294]**

RIEDEL, M. "Concerning Several *Aporiai* in Aristotle's Practical Philosophy." *AncPh* 1(1981), 148-159. Examines whether it is possible to use Aristotelian terminology and its systematic structure to re-establish practical philosophy.   **[4295]**

RING, M. "Aristotle and the Concept of Happiness," in #54, pp. 69-90. Employs distinction between concept and conception to show that happiness envisioned by citizens of twentieth-century liberal democracies does not differ radically from *eudaimonia* discussed by Ar. Concepts are the same, conceptions differ.   **[4296]**

RINGBOM, M. "Aristotle's Notion of Virtue." *Ajatus* 29(1967). 51-61. When Ar investigates wherein human *arete* consists, he faces three problems: 1) What is the ideal end for man? 2) What properties are needed for achievement of this end; 3) What are essential characteristics of a good man. Argues that Ar does not realize that (2) and (3) are different questions.   **[4297]**

──────. "Moral Relevance in Aristotle." *Ajatus* 27(1965), 83-96. Understands two different things by "moral relevance": 1) a certain act or activity becomes an object of moral value-judgments, and thus has moral relevance; 2) the relevance of an act to the passing of moral judgments on the person who performs it. Examines then those acts and activities Ar regards as morally relevant.   **[4298]**

RIST, J. M. "Aristotle: The Value of Man and the Origin of Morality." *CanJPh* 4(1974), 1-21. Investigates broader sense of "man," which refers to women and slaves as well as adult males, and narrower sense, which refers to those men who are naturally constituted in such a way as to be suited to form and to live as citizens in a city-state. Degree of intellectual development determines a man's value.   **[4299]**

ROBERTS, J. "Aristotle on Responsibility for Action and Character." *AncPh* 9(1989), 23-34. Ar's position on voluntary action is importantly different from P's.   **[4300]**

──────. "Political Animals in the *Nicomachean Ethics*." *Phron* 34(1989), 185-204. Offers an explanation for absence of any recognition on Ar's part of a possible conflict between self-interest and the common good by examining Ar's view that man is by nature a political animal.   **[4301]**

ROBERTS, R. C. "Aristotle on Virtues and Emotions." *PhilStud* 56(1989), 293-306. Explores two ways emotions relate to virtues: 1) virtues are dispositions to be properly affected; 2) emotional pleasure and pain are indices of virtue. Develops a schema that distinguishes types of virtue by their relations to emotions.   **[4302]**

ROBINSON, D. B. "Ends and Means and Logical Priority," in #4252, pp. 185-193. In *EE* 1 Ar treats *to agathon* as a telos and a means, but he considers them to be related hierarchically.   **[4303]**

ROBINSON, R. "Aristotle on Akrasia," in #4036, pp. 79-91; also in #74, pp. 139-169. Shows how Ar accepts opinion that *akrasia* occurs and also accepts S's opinion that knowledge cannot be overcome. Then shows how for Ar, by means of doctrines of potentiality and of the syllogism, the two opinions are consistent.   **[4304]**

ROCHE, T. D. *Aristotle's Ethics: Spindel Conference 1988*. *SJPh* 27 Suppl., 1988. Papers and commentaries, each abstracted herein.   **[4305]**

──────. "*Ergon* and *Eudaimonia* in *Nicomachaean Ethics*: Reconsidering the Intellectualist Interpretation." *JHPh* 26(1988), 175-194. Shows, contrary to many scholars, that Ar consistently adheres to some sort of "inclusive end" conception of good throughout first book of *NE*.   [4306]

―――. "On the Alleged Metaphysical Foundation of Aristotle's *Ethics*." *AncPh* 8(1988), 49-62. Challenges Irwin's view (#4174) that Ar's ethics are metaphysically based. Argues that Irwin has an inadequate conception of Ar's method of dialectical reasoning and gives problematic interpretations of several passages.   [4307]

―――. "The Perfect Happiness," in #4305, pp. 103-125. Challenges those interpretations which maintain that Ar's theory of the best life is consistently inclusive, that is, consisting of a plurality of goods.   [4308]

ROHATYN, D. A. "The Logic of Moral Paralysis." *JValInq* 7(1973), 61-64. Explores why Ar did not analyze or exploit notion of moral paralysis, since its logic poses an insoluble paradox for action-theory.   [4309]

RORTY, A. O. "Akrasia and Pleasure: *Nicomachean Ethics* Book 7," in #4312, pp. 267-284. Ar accepts one aspect of Socratic account of wrongdoing, namely that wrongdoer, and in particular the *akrates*, is not ignorant because he is misled by pleasure; rather his being misled by pleasure is an instance of a culpable ignorance.   [4310]

―――. "Aristotle on the Metaphysical Status of *Pathe*." *RMeta* 37(1984), 521-546. Locates the origins of contemporary discussions about passions and emotions through analysis of Ar's account of *pathe*. Sorts out various uses of *pathe* and reconstructs the rationale of Ar's shifting emphases.   [4311]

―――. *Essays on Aristotle's Ethics*. Berkeley: Univ. of CA Pr., 1980. Collection of essays on various topics in Ar's ethical writings; each is abstracted herein.   [4312]

―――. "The Place of Contemplation in Aristotle's *Nicomachean Ethics*." *Mind* 87(1978), 343-358; also in #4312, pp. 377-394; also in #4255, pp. 445-460. Investigates a way of reading Ar which shows how contemplative and comprehensive practical lives need not be competitors for the prizes of the best life.   [4313]

―――. "The Place of Pleasure in Aristotle's Ethics." *Mind* 83(1974), 481-497. Ar argues against both hedonists who think pleasure is a measure of goodness, and anti-hedonists who think pleasure cannot be a good at all.   [4314]

―――. cf. #1739.

ROWE, C. J. *The* Eudemian *and* Nicomachean Ethics: *A Study in the Development of Aristotle's Thought*. Cambridge Philological Soc. Suppl. 3, 1971. Investigates relationship between the two works in context of exploring development of Ar's ethical thinking. Sees *EE* as entirely Ar's work, written early when Ar was still under Platonic influences. *NE* is a revision — sometimes careless — of the *EE*.   [4315]

―――. "The Meaning of *Phronesis* in the *Eudemian Ethics*," in #4252, pp. 73-92; also in #4255, pp. 253-272. In *EE* Ar does not distinguish between practical and theoretical .thinking, as he clearly does in *NE*. *Phronesis*, used very generally in *EE*, means the *arete* of one part of the rational faculty in *NE*.   [4316]

———. "A Reply to John Cooper on the *Magna Moralia*." *AJPh* 96(1975), 160-172; also in #4255, pp. 371-383. Disputes Cooper's contention (#4073) that the *MM* is an early Aristotelian ethical treatise.   [4317]

RUSSELL, J. L. "The Concept of Natural Law." *HeythJ* 6(1965), 434-446. Discusses ethical applications of Ar's concept of nature. Examines aspects of his philosophy which are important for later developments in theory of natural law.   [4318]

RYAN, E. E. "Aristotle and A Refutation of Naturalism." *JValInq* 6(1972), 221-225. Attempts by G. E. Moore and C. Lewy to apply refutations of naturalism to Ar's *Ethics* are unconvincing.   [4319]

———. "Aristotle's *Rhetoric* and *Ethics* and the Ethos of Society." *GRBS* 13(1972), 291-308. Ar's ethics are based on notion that a society establishes its own customs (*ethe*). His awareness of the importance of persuasive techniques in creating or changing a social *ethos* led him to write the *Rhet*.   [4320]

SANTAS, G. "Aristotle on Practical Inference, the Explanation of Action and Akrasia." *Phron* 14(1969), 162-189. Examines importance of teleological explanations of practical inference in Ar's discussion of *akrasia* in *NE* 7.   [4321]

———. "Aristotle's Criticism of Plato's Form of the Good: Ethics without Metaphysics." *PhilPapers* 18(1989), 137-160. In *NE* 1.6 Ar criticizes P's theory of the Form of the Good but does not demonstrate that such a thing is impossible or impracticable.[4322]

SANTORO, L. "Greek 'Ethos' and Modern 'Morality'." *Diot* 7(1979), 171-177. In modern thought morality lies somewhere between freedom and obligation. For Ar *ethos* is above freedom and obligation, with its own teleological justification.   [4323]

SAUVE, S. M. "Why Involuntary Actions are Painful," in #4305, 127-158. Argues that Ar's account of involuntariness is not meant to to reveal conditions in which praise and blame are inappropriate, but rather to explain conditions in which attitudes such as pity and forgiveness are appropriate.   [4324]

SCALTSAS, T. "Weakness of Will in Aristotle's Ethics." *SJPh* 24(1986), 375-382. Ar's ethical theory allows for weak *akrasia* (agent makes only nominal choice) and for strong *akrasia* (agent makes a real choice but still acts contrary to it).   [4325]

SCHAEFER, D. L. "Wisdom and Morality: Aristotle's Account of *Akrasia*." *Polity* 21(1988), 221-251. Ar's agreement with the Socratic claim that no one does wrong willingly is linked to his understanding of practical wisdom, which is inseparable from philosophy.   [4326]

SCHOEMAN, F. "Aristotle on the Good of Friendship." *AustlJPh* 63(1985), 269-282. Weaknesses in Ar's theory of friendship arise largely because it fails to account for respect for the independence of one's friend. His belief that friends must possess certain moral qualities precludes the notion of altruism.   [4327]

SCHOFIELD, M. "Aristotelian Mistakes." *PCPhS* 19(1973), 66-70. Understanding of *NE* 5.8 depends on importance assigned to negligence.   [4328]

SCHOLLMEIER, P. "An Aristotelian Motivation for Good Friendship." *RMM* 91(1986), 379-388. Ar contends that good friendship is based on mental pleasure derived from bringing happiness to another. The happiness of another is a good, something created by us, in a sense. **[4329]**

———. "Aristotle on Practical Wisdom." *ZPhilForsch* 43(1989), 124-132. Discusses intuitive and discursive functions of Ar's practical wisdom. Intuitive function apprehends universal propositions about the ends of our actions and particular propositions concerned with means to those ends. Discursive function is deliberation. **[4330]**

SCHWARTZ, A. "Aristotle on Education and Choice." *EducTheor* 2a(1979), 97-107. There is no inconsistency between Ar's contentions that virtuous persons are decision-making agents and their primary desires arise from habituation. Position is consistent only because of limitations on education and choice which Ar posits. **[4331]**

SEDDON, F. A. "Megalopsychia: A Suggestion." *Pers* 56(1975), 31-37. Reexamines Ar's account of great-souled man, and suggests that such a man is a kind of composite picture of Socrates and Ar himself. **[4332]**

———. "A Problem at *Nicomachean Ethics* 1109a30-b13." *AncPh* 8(1988), 101-104. Shows that three rules Ar gives in this passage for attaining the mean are incompatible in certain special cases. **[4333]**

SEGVIC, H. "Deliberation, Wisdom, and the Self in the *Nicomachean Ethics*," in *Contemporary Yugoslav Philosophy: The Analytic Approach*, ed. A. Parkovic (Dordrecht, Nether.: Kluwer, 1988), pp. 283-309. Examines Ar's distinction between being guided by passion and by reason, and his characterization of deliberation as inquiry. **[4334]**

SEIDLER, M. J. "The Medical Paradigm in Aristotle's *Nicomachean Ethics*." *Thom* 42(1978), 400-433. Examines Ar's dependence in *NE* on ancient medical theory and practice, which leads to certain weaknesses and strengths of his ethics. **[4335]**

SHARPLES, R. W. "Responsibility and the Possibility of More than One Course of Action. A Note on Aristotle *De caelo* II,12." *BICS* 23(1976), 69-72. Humans can do more than one thing. This makes them inferior to heavenly bodies which move in regular patterns and superior to other creatures who cannot make choices. **[4336]**

SHEA, J. "The Commensurability of Theorizing and Moral Action in the *Nicomachean Ethics*." *Ph&PhenRes* 48(1988), 753-755. Reply to Ackrill (#4009) and Keyt (#4192). Ar regards theorizing and moral action as capable of being compared, but theorizing is inherently superior to any amount or type of moral action. **[4337]**

SHERMAN, N. "Aristotle on Friendship and the Shared Life." *Ph&PhenRes* 47(1987), 589-613. In Ar's view an individual can be happy only if others are happy. Humans have the rational ability to work for their own ends but also to identify common goals. This process involves extension of the self through attachments to friends. **[4338]**

———. "Character, Planning, and Choice in Aristotle." *RMeta* 39(1985), 83-106. Ar's theory of practical inference does allow an individual to deliberate on ways to improve his character and does explain how a person can intend now to act later. **[4339]**

------. "Commentary on Irwin's 'Aristotle's Conception of Morality'." *PBACAPh* 1(1985), 144-150. Response to Irwin's (#4170) critique of Williams (#4312). What distinguishes Ar's ethics from Williams' is the importance Ar assigns to the motives of partiality and friendship.   [4340]

------. *The Fabric of Character: Aristotle's Theory of Virtue.* Oxford: Clarendon Pr. 1989. Seeks to demonstrate that character is inseparable from the operations of practical reason.   [4341]

SHINER, R. A. "*Aisthesis, Nous,* and *Phronesis* in the Practical Syllogism." *PhilStud* 36(1979), 377-387. Disputes idea that *aisthesis* is propositional attitude appropriate to all three sentential components of Ar's practical syllogism. *Nous* must play a role because the major premise of a practical syllogism assumes awareness of universals.   [4342]

------. "Ethical Perception in Aristotle." *Apeir* 13(1979), 79-85. Ar's understanding of what is involved in making a moral judgment does not fit such modern categories as Naturalist or Intuitionist because it considers *orexis* (desire), *aisthesis* (perception), and *nous* (intuition) all essential.   [4343]

SIEGLER, F. A. "Voluntary and Involuntary." *Monist* 52(1968), 268-287. Examines Ar's definitions of involuntary and voluntary, and then explores how to reconcile claim that it is only for voluntary acts that a person is praised and blamed with fact that we do blame people for other than voluntary acts.   [4344]

SIFAKIS, G. M. "Aristotle, *E.N.*, IV, 2, 1123a19-24, and the Comic Chorus in the Fourth Century." *AJPh* 92(1971), 410-432. Explains meaning of Ar's statement that it is vulgar to provide a comic chorus "with purple in the parodos" using knowledge of common practices of the day.   [4345]

SNIDER, E. "*Akrasia* According to *EN* 1151a29-35." *ModSch* 63(1986), 267-274. Examines a type of *akrasia* which Ar did not discuss. Considers textual variants in *NE* 1151a29-33 to see how they relate to the treatment of *akrasia.*   [4346]

------. "Aristotle on Deliberation and the Practical Syllogism: Interpretations and Disputed Texts." *NewSchol* 62(1988), 179-209. Maintains that Mele (#4235) is wrong to claim that deliberation and practical syllogism are distinct phenomena.   [4347]

SOLOMON, R. C. "Aristotle, the Socratic Principle, and the Problem of Akrasia." *ModSch* 49(1971), 13-21. Argues that Ar's inquiry into problem of *akrasia* was not opposed to Socrates but rather was a more precise formulation of "Socratic principle" and that even with Aristotelian modifications, Socratic principle cannot explicate many cases of complex problem of *akrasia.*   [4348]

------. "Is there Happiness After Death?" *Ph* 51(1976), 189-193. Maintains that Ar's suggestion that no man can be called happy until he is dead is not absurd.   [4349]

SORABJI, R. "Aristotle on the Role of Intellect in Virtue." *PAS* 74(1973-4), 107-129; also in #4312, pp. 201-219. Commentators have minimized role of intellect in Ar's concept of virtue by de-rationalizing choice involved, reducing role of practical wisdom, and treating habituation as mindless process sufficient for making men good.   [4350]

SPARSHOTT, F. E. "Arisotle's *Ethics* and Plato's *Republic*: A Structural Comparison." *Dial*(Can) 21(1982), 483-499. Demonstrates fifteen-point structural correspondence between the two works and offers explanations for this correspondence.   [4351]

——. cf. #1752.

STACK, G. J. "Aristotle and Kierkegaard's Existential Ethics." *JHPh* 12(1974), 1-19. Shows that Ar's *Meta* and *Ethics* contributed to some of detailed ingredients of Kierkegaard's existential ethics.   [4352]

——. "Aristotle's Concept of Choice." *ModSch* 50(1973), 367-373. Teleology is important for Ar in both natural and moral processes. But choice exists only in moral decisions and is thus the key element in the ontological distinction between humans and other natural entities.   [4353]

STAHL, G. "The Function of Analytic Premises in Aristotle's Ethics." *IntPhQ* 10(1970), 63-74. Analyzes argument at *EN* I.1-7; maintains that it is convincing and coherent even if we interpret key propositions as analytic.   [4354]

STOCKER, M. "Affectivity and Self-Concern: The Assumed Psychology in Aristotle's *Ethics*." *PacPhQ* 64(1983), 211-229. Ar does not deal in his ethical writings with psychological problems such as depression and fear. Either the people around him were different or he based his theories on different psychological assumptions. Either possibility should make us cautious about applying his ethical views directly to the modern situation.   [4355]

——. "Dirty Hands and Conflicts of Values and of Desires in Aristotle's *Ethics*." *PacPhQ* 67(1986), 36-61. In Ar's view moral choices are difficult to make, even for good people.   [4356]

STRIKER, G. "Comments on 'Aristotle's Moral Psychology' by John M. Cooper," in #4305, pp. 43-47. Agrees with Cooper's (#4075) interpretation of Ar's moral psychology; compares Ar's and Stoic theory of moral virtue.   [4357]

SUITS, B. "Aristotle on the Function of Man." *CanJPh* 4(1974), 32-40. Ar's ethical theory relies heavily on arguments from analogy. Mankind's body parts and craft skills have special functions, so mankind in general must have a special function. Various interpretations have been offered to make these arguments appear convincing, but none succeeds.   [4358]

SULLIVAN, R. J. *Morality and the Good Life: A Commentary on Aristotle's* Nicomachean Ethics. Memphis, TN: Memphis State Univ. Pr., 1980. Provides an exposition for non-specialist, along with commentary and criticism.   [4359]

——. "Some Suggestions for Interpreting *Ethica Nicomachea* 10:7-8." *SJPh* 15(1977), 129-138. The arguments in this section summarize inconsistencies found throughout *NE*. They are evidence for Ar's incomplete rejection of Platonism.   [4360]

SWINDLER, J. K. "Subjects: A Consideration of the Ethics of Aristotle and Kant." *Auslegung* 3(1975), 3-19. Argues Ar's ethic is superior to Kant's in its concept of the soul and of voluntariness, its understanding of ends and desire of happiness.   [4361]

TAYLOR, C. C. W. "Urmson on Aristotle on Pleasure," in #4081, pp. 120-132. Challenges Urmson's (#4373) view that when a person engages in a certain activity for the sake of enjoyable sensation, that person's enjoyment is always to be described as enjoyment of sensation, and never as enjoyment of action itself.   **[4362]**

————. cf. #1753.

TELFER, E. "Leisure," in *Moral Philosophy and Contemporary Problems*, ed. J. D. G. Evans (Cambridge Univ. Pr., 1987), pp. 151-164. Discusses how Ar's conception of leisure values work only as productive of leisure, and how Ar fails to see how work which is useful can also be seen as valuable in itself. Explores certain shortcomings of Ar's conception of best way to spend leisure.   **[4363]**

TESSITORE, A. "Aristotle's Political Presentation of Socrates in the *Nicomachean Ethics*." *Interp* 16(1988), 3-22. Ar's portrait of S is more accurate and sympathetic than generally supposed. Ar knew that S represented a major failure for philosophy in conflict with politics. This awareness gives his *Ethics* an apologetic tone.   **[4364]**

————. "A Political Reading of Aristotle's Treatment of Pleasure in the *Nicomachean Ethics*." *PolTheo* 17(1989), 247-265. Argues that supposed major discrepancies in Ar's double accounts of pleasure in Books 7 and 10 can be made intelligible by paying attention to different educational aims of each book.   **[4365]**

THORNTON, M. T. "Aristotelian Practical Reason." *Mind* 92(1982), 57-76. Reply to several modern scholars who have questioned role of the practical syllogism in Ar's thought.   **[4366]**

TOBIN, B. M. "An Aristotelian Theory of Moral Development." *JPhEduc* 23(1989), 195-211. Ar's theory of moral development has cognitive, affective, and conative features. The individual must grasp certain principles intellectually but must also be able to translate that knowledge into action and sensitivity to others. Traces stages of development and shows where failure is possible.   **[4367]**

TRACY, T. "Perfect Friendship in Aristotle's *Nicomachean Ethics*." *ICS* 4(1979), 65-75. Perfect friendship can only occur if both parties possess and recognize one another's *arete*. This can happen only between equals.   **[4368]**

————. *Physiological Theory and the Doctrine of the Mean in Plato and Aristotle.* Chicago: Loyola Univ. Pr., 1969. Studies earlier medical writers' views of health as a mean and the applications which P and Ar made of their work. P sees a mean as proportionate blending. For Ar the mean is relative to each person.'   **[4369]**

TUTTLE, H. N. "The Problem of Natural Law in Aristotle." *SwPhSt* 3(1978), 75-78. Ar's use of *physis* in certain ethical, political, and legal texts does not always imply a natural law doctrine, as is commonly supposed. Interpreting *physis* in this way leaves much of his moral and legal philosophy incoherent.   **[4370]**

ULVANEY, R. J. "Action, Teaching and the Limits of Practical Rationality." *ProcPhEduc* 32(1976), 21-26. Emphasizes severe limitations on role of reason in action, and discusses Ar's theory of practical syllogism and difficult concept of imperative function of practical reason.   **[4371]**

UPTON, T. V. "Aristotle's Moral Epistemology: The Possibility of Ethical Demonstration." *NewSchol* 56(1982), 169-184. Response to Irwin (#4173). It is valid for Ar to compare ethical ends with scientific hypotheses. This means that he can construct ethical demonstrations comparable to those he uses in his scientific works.   **[4372]**

URMSON, J. O. "Aristotle on Pleasure," in #3625, pp. 323-333. Summarizes account of pleasure in *NE* 10 and discusses such problems as assimilation of enjoyment of feelings to enjoyment of activity.   **[4373]**

——. "Aristotle's Doctine of the Mean." *AmPhQ* 10(1973), 223-230; also in #4312, pp. 157-170. Examines the doctrine, and argues that Ar goes wrong not in his general account of nature of excellence of character, but in his account of its application to specific virtues.   **[4374]**

——. *Aristotle's Ethics.* Oxford: Blackwell, 1988. Examines Ar's detailed accounts of excellence of character, excellence of intelligence that is essential in practical affairs, and other problems of action.   **[4375]**

VEATCH, H. B. "Telos and Teleology in Aristotelian Ethics," in #3631, pp. 279-296. Explores very different way human telos is conceived and understood by Ar and by modern teleologists, and suggests that we return to something like an Aristotelian telos.   **[4376]**

VERBEKE, G. "Happiness and Chance in Aristotle," in #3809, pp. 247-258. Explores role of chance in realization of happiness and place of chance at end of list of factors (nature, learning, training, divine inspiration, chance) which contribute to attainment of highest good.   **[4377]**

——. "Moral Behaviour and Time in Aristotle's *Nichomachean Ethics*," in #67, pp. 78-90; also in #4255, pp. 161-171. Whereas in *Phys*, Ar's concept of time is rather pessimistic, in *Ethics*, appreciation of time is much more positive. Seeks to explain this new appraisal of time.   **[4378]**

VERDENIUS, W. J. "Human Reason and God in the *Eudemian Ethics*," in #4252, pp. 285-297. Translation of, and commentary on, *EE* 7.15. Concludes that God cannot be *nous* and that Ar values contemplation as highest human activity.   **[4379]**

VON FRITZ, K. "Aristotle's Anthropological Ethics and Its Relevance to Modern Problems." *JHI* 42(1981), 187-208. Individual attains greatest happiness by doing whatever he does as well as he can. Ar's account implies a radical condemnation of modern tendency to produce intentionally goods of inferior quality and assembly-line mode of production.   **[4380]**

WALKER, A. D. M. "Aristotle's Account of Friendship in the *Nicomachean Ethics*." *Phron* 24(1979), 180-196. Challenges Fortenbaugh's (#4114) claim that analogy provides connection between three kinds of friendship. Ar relates three types of friendship (of goodness, of pleasure, of utility) by a little noticed form of homonymy.   **[4381]**

WALKER, S. "The Natural Condition of the Soul and the Development of Virtue." *Dial*(PST) 29(1987), 39-44. Ar's theory of moral development cannot be understood by looking only at educational aspect, as most interpreters do. Since we are not virtuous by nature, we must first analyze Ar's view of natural condition of soul.   **[4382]**

WALUCHOW, W. J. "Weinrib on Corrective Justice," in #1283, pp. 153-157. Weinrib's interpretation (#4837) of Ar on nature and corrective justice is incorrect.   **[4383]**

WEBB, P. "The Relative Dating of the Accounts of Pleasure in Aristotle's *Ethics*." *Phron* 22(1977), 235-262; also in #4255, pp. 399-426. Account in *NE* 7 is actually later and more satisfactory than that in Book 10.   **[4384]**

WEDIN, M. V. "Aristotle on the Good for Man." *Mind* 90(1981), 243-262. Maintains validity of Ar's argument that human action has a single final good. Argues that treatment of *eudaimonia* in *NE* 1.7 is not inconsistent with *NE* 1.2,1094a18-22. Ar does not take an inclusivist view of the final good.   **[4385]**

————. "Critical Study: David Charles, *Aristotle's Philosophy of Action*." *AncPh* 6(1986), 161-167. Examines several points of Charles' interpretation (#4063) of Ar's views on intentionality, akrasia, and other issues. Charles' assertion of the superiority of Ar's theory of events over modern theories is insufficiently supported.   **[4386]**

WEINRIB, E. J. "Aristotle's Forms of Justice," in #1283, pp. 133-152. Corrective and distributive justice are, respectively, formal structures of rationality immanent to transactions and distributions. Corrective justice is formal cause of private law. **[4387]**

WEISS, R. "Aristotle's Criticism of Eudoxan Hedonism." *CPh* 74(1979), 214-221. Ar concedes three of Eudoxus' arguments about pleasure and the good and fails to refute the fourth, that pleasure is the ultimate good.   **[4388]**

WHITE, D. A. "Pleasure and the Continuum in the *Nicomachean Ethics*." *SJPh* 21(1983), 611-623. Analyzes relationship between pleasure and continuum and resolves an apparent inconsistency in Ar's account of divisibility of pleasure.   **[4389]**

WHITE, M. J. "Functionalism and the Moral Virtues in Aristotle's Ethics." *IntStudPh* 11(1979), 49-58. Explores apparent "lack of fit" between Ar's enunciation in *NE* 1.7 of functionalist schema as proper framework in which to conceive of human virtues and his actual account of moral virtues in Book 2.   **[4390]**

WHITE, N. P. "Good as Goal," in #4305, pp. 169-193. Right way to think of Ar's view is to construe him as telling us what the "ultimate goal" of a human life is.   **[4391]**

————. "Goodness and Human Aims in Aristotle's Ethics," in #3631, pp. 225-246. Investigates relationship in Ar's philosophy between various sorts of good and the aims and desires of human beings.   **[4392]**

WHITE, S. A. "Reasons for Choosing a Final End," in #4305, pp. 209-232. Examines what is involved in having a final end of any sort, whether our conception of its content is correct or not.   **[4393]**

WHITING, J. "Aristotle's Function Argument: A Defense." *AncPh* 8(1988), 33-48. Defends Ar's view that a good man has virtues and abilities which enable him to do well whatever it is man's function to do.   **[4394]**

———. "Comments on 'Why Involuntary Actions are Painful' by Susan Sauve," in #4305, pp. 159-167. Argues that Sauve's account (4324) fails to explain two features of Ar's account of involuntary action: 1) why Ar explicitly acknowledged possibility of non-voluntary action only in cases involving ignorance, and 2) why Ar formulates his requirement in terms of pain rather than contrariety. **[4395]**

———. "Human Nature and Intellectualism in Aristotle." *AGPh* 68(1986), 70-95. Argues against Cooper (#4074) that *NE* 10 does not restrict intellectualism by identifying the person exclusively with his theoretical *nous*. **[4396]**

WIGGINS, D. "Deliberation and Practical Reason." *PAS* 76(1975-76), 29-51; also in #4312, pp. 221-240. Book 3 is straightforwardly continuous with Book 6's account of deliberation, choice, and practical reasoning. Suggests that both accounts are dominated by Ar's "obsession" with situation of geometer who searches for means to construct a given figure with ruler and compass. **[4397]**

———. "Weakness of Will, Commensurability, and the Objects of Deliberation and Desire," in #4312, pp. 241-265. Offers an Aristotelian account of incontinence, and explains why it is superior to Ar's. **[4398]**

WILES, A. M. "The Acratic Man and the Acratic State." *PACPhA* 57(1983), 44-51. Ar's view of *akrasia* can be better understood in light of his distinction between having and using knowledge. This also helps explain the parallels between *akrasia* in the individual and in the state. **[4399]**

———. "Method in the *Nicomachean Ethics*." *NewSchol* 56(1982), 239-243. Ar's discussion of human conduct rests on two propositions: 1) that the *telos* of man is happiness; 2) human good is "activity of the soul in accordance with virtue." His methodology has empirical and *a priori* facets, which can be reconciled. **[4400]**

WILKES, K. V. "The Good Man and the Good for Man in Aristotle's Ethics." *Mind* 87(1978), 553-571; also in #4312, pp. 341-357. Discusses incompatibility of Ar's two accounts of *eudaimonia* (happiness), and explores extent to which notions of "the life of a good man" and "the life good for a man" can be successfully united in a single concept of *eudaimonia*. **[4401]**

WILLIAMS, B. "Justice as a Virtue," in #4312, pp. 189-199. Focuses on two aspects of what Ar calls "particular justice": 1) whether particular injustice as a vice is characterized by the motive of pleonexia; and 2) whether all acts that are unjust in the particular sense are motivated that way. **[4402]**

WOODS, M. "Intuition and Perception in Aristotle's Ethics." *OSAP* 4(1986), 145-166. Examines role Ar assigns to perception in his ethical theory. For Ar one's grasp of what the best life for a human being is largely consists in one's ability to discern what is required of the virtuous person in particular cases. **[4403]**

———., trans. *Aristotle's* Eudemian Ethics. Oxford: Clarendon Pr., 1982. Translation of Books 1, 2, and 8 with a philosophical commentary, and notes on the text used for translation. **[4404]**

YOUNG, C. M. "Aristotle on Justice," in #4305, pp. 233-249. Connect specific virtues of character to practical wisdom by focusing on Ar's view of justice.   **[4405]**

———. "Aristotle on Temperance." *PhR* 97(1988), 521-542. Ar's discussion of temperance in *NE* 3.10-11 cannot be supported by his doctrine of the mean. He must be taken as saying that temperate people can take pleasure in physical actions such as eating if they deem them wholesome, thus acknowledging their animal nature without giving in to it.   **[4406]**

———. "Virtue and Flourishing in Aristotle's *Ethics*," in *#54*, pp. 138-156. Ar never presents deliberative arguments which show why it is that a flourishing person will display virtues of character in circumstances that call for their display. Attempts to develop such an argument with respect to courage.   **[4407]**

ZEIGLER, G. M. "Aristotle's Analysis of *Akrasia*." *Pers* 58(1977), 321-332. Contrary to common belief, Ar agrees with Socratic thesis that no one voluntarily acts contrary to his/her best judgment.   **[4408]**

For related items see #191, #1695, #1703, #1715, #1733, #1744, #3286, #3867, #5033, #5044, #5727, #5731, #6014, #6764.

LOGIC/DIALECTIC/LANGUAGE

As noted in the general introduction to Ar, he did not consider logic a separate science, on a par with physics or theology. For him it was a technique, a tool (*organon* in Greek), something to be mastered prior to beginning one's philosophical studies. He would not have included it in the study of philosophy proper any more than a carpenter writing a how-to book would include the study of the principles of physics which govern the operation of a pair of pliers.

But Ar does talk about logic in some of his early works, which are collectively called the *Organon*. The *Topics* was probably the first of these to be written, since it does not use the syllogism, which came to be the foundation of Ar's logical system, as we will see. The *Categories*, the next in the series, is discussed above (p. 436) under its own heading, because the definitions Ar establishes there have significant implications for his metaphysics as well. *De interpretatione* is usually considered the next installment. Where the *Cat* deals with terms, *De interp* discusses how one establishes the truth of a proposition. Chapter 9 of this treatise raises the issue of future contingencies and the possibility/necessity of future actions. These problems have prompted so much discussion that they are treated separately below under the section called Modal Logic (pp. 533). The treatise called *De sophisticis elenchis* appears last in the *Organon* but was probably written after the *Topics* and before the *Analytics*. It discusses fallacious types of arguments and is sometimes called *On Fallacies* or *On Refutations of the Sophists*.

The core of Ar's logical system is found in his *Analytics* (which was his preferred term for what we call logic). There are two books of the *Analytics*, the *Prior* and the *Posterior*. Some scholars would argue that the *PostAn* is actually earlier than the *PrAn*, but that issue is by no means settled. It is in the *Analytics* that Ar develops his theory of the syllogism. The word "syllogism" comes from a Greek word meaning to "sum things up." Socrates uses it occasionally in Plato's dialogues, but not in any formal way. For Ar it becomes a means of demonstrating a truth, not of proving something new. The conclusion is always known in advance, before the premises are decided on.

In devising the syllogistic method Ar did not perfect something which earlier philosophers had worked on. He informs us rather proudly at the end of *De soph* that there had been no earlier efforts in this area. Ar actually recognizes three types of syllogisms, differentiated by the premises on which they are based. (One could even say he knows four if one counts the enthymeme, a type of argument used in rhetoric.) The first type of syllogism, discussed in the *Topics*, is the dialectic, in which the premises are propositions, often definitions, that everyone agrees on, or seems to agree on. Ar is willing to admit that in some types of inquiry, particularly in the practical sciences (ethics and politics), opinions held by many people for a long time are likely to have some validity and be worth examining. This may be one reason he typically begins an investigation into a subject by collecting the opinions of his predecessors. A second type of syllogism is eristic, or purely disputatious. The Megarians (cf. Chapter 11) were fond of such arguments, which had no point expect to demonstrate a supposed fallacy in an opponent's methodology. Diodorus Cronus originated one which ran: "You have whatever you have not lost. You have not lost any horns. Therefore, you have horns."

The most familiar form of the syllogism is the demonstrative: A is B; B is C; therefore A is C. This is a way of representing a statement such as "Socrates is a man; men are mortal; therefore Socrates is mortal." A valid syllogism rests on premises which require no further demonstration and has a conclusion which follows of necessity from the premises. The middle term (the B in the example) is the link, the more general term of which the first term is part and which is itself part of the third term. The beauty of the syllogism is that it can establish logical connections even if one does not know the meaning of the individual terms. One could say, "Qinram is a phebob; all phebobs are skagons; therefore Qinram is a skagon."

By using what are called "operators" (terms such as "all," "some," "no," and "not all") Ar is able to construct what are known as perfect first-figure syllogisms, which are true in every instance without any further statements added. He uses this technique to eliminate some forms which have no syllogistic consequences. If one says, for example, "No a's are b; all b's are c," no necessary conclusion follows. It is not a valid syllogism, in other words, to say, "No dogs are reptiles; all reptiles are cold-blooded." While each term of the syllogism is valid, no connection is established between them. There is no "adding up," to get back to the meaning of the term "syllogism."

Other syllogisms Ar regards as imperfect because the conclusion does not follow necessarily from the premises or because some other statement is necessary to establish the connection between the premises. These are called second or third figure syllogisms. He devised a technique of "perfecting" such syllogisms. In the Middle Ages commentators worked out a system of designating these syllogistic forms by Latin code words. In reading some of the items listed below one will find references to syllogisms "in Barbara" or "in Celarent." Explanation of this system is beyond the scope of this introduction. A helpful summary is provided by J. Lear (#3615, p. 226).

Many of the items in this section deal with Ar's theory of language, which is so closely tied to his logic that it proved impossible to separate them, as we had at first thought we might do. Language fits in here because Ar recognized that any logical arguments depend on the language in which they are expressed. Some problems of language are also problems of logic. One could say of a teacher, e. g., "He is a fair teacher." That introduces the problem of equivocation. Does the statement mean that the teacher grades fairly, or that he has only mediocre abilities? If we change the gender and say "She is a fair teacher," we could add another possible equivocation, using the old-fashioned meaning of "fair" as "beautiful." Homonyms and synonyms also raise problems which are ultimately logical in nature. How can two words mean the same thing? How can the same sound (e. g., "hear" and "here") mean two quite different things? Negation is another problem of both language and logic. If one says "The boy is not smart," what is being negated, the verb or the adjective? Should the sentence be understood as "The boy (is not) smart" or "The boy is (not smart)"? Since the Greeks attributed a certain sense of reality to words, these problems loomed larger for them than they do for us.

ALEXANDER, H. G. "Transformational Grammar and Aristotelian Logic." *SwJPh* 2(1971), 57-64. A system of logic tends to be shaped by the language in which it develops. Ar's logic is based on the transformational grammar implicit in Greek and other Indo-European languages.   [4409]

AL.-GEORGE, S. "On Negative Compounds: A Parallel Between Panini and Aristotle." *Dacoromania* 5(1979-80), 216-219. Examples similarities in linguistic concepts of Indian grammarian Panini (fifth century B. C.) and Ar. They differ in that Ar sees a negative compound as practically infinite while Panini confined it to a definite field.   [4410]

AMARAL, P., and ALLISON, J. "Aristotle *Metaphysics* 13.10. 1086b32-37." *CPh* 70(1975), 121-123. Word *syllogismos* should be translated "conclusion." Its meaning is unclear.   [4411]

ANTON, J. P. *Aristotle's Theory of Contrariety*. Lanham, MD: Univ. Pr. of America, 1987; rprt. Examines the concept of contrariety/opposition in Presocratic thought, then shows how Ar uses it in his categories, logic, and other areas of his thought. The concept has an ontological foundation. First published in 1957, the book shows the influence of J. Dewey's reading of Ar.   [4412]

———. "On Aristotle's Principle of Contradiction: Its Ontological Foundations and Platonic Antecedents." *Phil*(Athens) 2(1972), 266-280. P and Ar both place boundaries on the world and limits to possible changes. Their ontologies allow for false judgments and affirm the reality of the principle of contradiction.   [4413]

BAECK, A. "Syllogisms with Reduplication in Aristotle." *NDJFormLog* 23(1982), 453-458. Somewhat technical analysis of *PrAn* 1.33.   [4414]

BARKER, E. M. "Unneeded Surgery on Aristotle's *Prior Analytics*." *NDJFormLog* 25(1984), 323-331. Challenges Ross's description of 45a9-16 as "an elementary logical error." Lines in question are a crucial part of Ar's defense of this method. **[4415]**

BARNES, J. "Aristotle, Menaechmus, and Circular Proof." *CQ* 26(1976), 278-292. Ar attempted to answer arguments of Menaechmus (mathematician from Academy) about circularity of mathematic proofs with arguments based on cycles of nature. **[4416]**

———. *Aristotle's* Posterior Analytics. Oxford: Clarendon Pr., 1975. Influential translation and notes. **[4417]**

———. "Homonymy in Aristotle and Speusippus." *CQ* 21(1971), 65-80. Compares two thinkers' views on homonymy and synonymy as linguistic properties. **[4418]**

———. "The Law of Contradiction." *PhQ* 19(1969), 302-309. Argues on basis of Ar's *Meta* that no one can believe the conjunction of a proposition and its negation, and that in this sense law of contradiction is a law of thought. **[4419]**

———. cf. #5335.

BASU, D. K. "A Question of Begging." *InformLog* 8(1986), 19-26. Examines argument that Ar's two accounts of *petitio* in *PrAn* and *Topics* are incompatible. His concept is actually unitary. **[4420]**

BENARDETE, S. "The Grammar of Being." *RMeta* 30(1977), 486-496. Questions whether it is sufficient to understand *einai* solely as copulative, existential, and veridical. Some important subtleties of meaning are lost. The concept of negation needs to be considered as well. **[4421]**

BERKA, K. "The Fourth Figure in Aristotle's Syllogistics." *Eirene* 16(1978), 5-17. The three figures in *PrAn* do not actually conflict with four figures in Ar's other logical works. Difference represents a maturation of Ar's thought which most modern interpreters have not taken into account. **[4422]**

———. "What is the Nature of Aristotle's Syllogism?" *Acta Universitatis Carolinae Philosophica et Historica* 4(1977), 11-28. Work of J. Corcoran (#4442) and J. Lukasiewicz (#4500) on the syllogism does not recognize that it can be both an inference rule and an implicative proposition. **[4423]**

BLANCK, D. L. "Dialectical Method in Aristotle's *Athenaion Politeia*." *GRBS* 25(1984), 275-284. Ar's method of gathering and using source materials in this work is influenced by his understanding of history as not strictly a science. He uses a dialectical method rather than the analytic approach characteristic of his scientific works. **[4424]**

BOBOC, A. "Aporetic with Aristotle." *Philosophie et Logique*, 24(1980), 327-332. Aristotelian aporetic as a way of posing "metaphysical problematic" is superior to global dialectic of ancients and dialectic of Hegel. **[4425]**

BOSLEY, R. *Aspects of Aristotle's Logic.* Assen, Netherlands: Van Gorcum, 1975. Shows that the leading idea was teleological, and analyzes certain difficulties in Ar's use of modal notions and his procedure for resolving logical conflict. **[4426]**

BREKLE, H. E. "A Note on Aristotle's *De Interpretatione* 20b-21a." *Folia Linguistica* 4(1970), 167-173. Analyzes Ar's simple proposition and his understanding of accumulation of predicates in terms of modern linguistic theory. [4427]

BRESLIN, C. F. "The Logistic Interpretation of Aristotle's Categorical Syllogistic." *PACPhA* 42(1968), 99-109. Technical discussion of failure of several modern logicians to reinterpret Ar's syllogistic. His ontological premises cannot be overlooked in any analysis of his logic. [4428]

BUENO, A. A. "Aristotle, the Fallacy of Accident, and the Nature of Predication: A Historical Inquiry." *JHPh* 26(1988), 5-24. Gives a detailed consideration of Ar's original definition of the concept of fallacy of accident and an account of interpretations it has received down to the present day. [4429]

BUNCH, B. L. "Aristotle, The Laws of Thought." *Dial*(PST) 19(1977), 33-39. Contrary to Ar's claim, the three laws of thought can be demonstrated. [4430]

BURKE, R. J. "Aristotle on the Limits of Argument." *Ph&PhenRes* 27(1967), 386-400. Explores Ar's efforts at delineating characteristic features of informal argument, as opposed to formal demonstration and rhetoric. [4431]

BURNYEAT, M. F. "The Origins of Non-Deductive Inference," in #5599, pp. 193-238. Ar's theory of signs as non-deductive logic was taken up by rhetoricians. But influence of Stoics, with their formal deductive logic, blocked any further development. [4432]

BURRELL, D. "Aristotle: Inquiry and Its Method," in *Analogy and Philosophical Language* (New Haven, CT: Yale Univ. Pr., 1973), pp. 68-91. Ar stressed method and structure in logic and language at the expense of connecting them to life. [4433]

CASSIDY, J. R. "Aristotle on Definitions." *SJPh* 5(1967), 110-118. Shows that for Ar, definitions are functional by exhibiting his various definitions of "man"; outlines his theory of definition itself. A definition is a "statement of essence." [4434]

CATALDO, P. J. "Whitehead and Aristotle on Propositions." *ProcStud* 12(1982), 15-22. Ar and Whitehead differ in their view of the relationship of propositions to linguistic expressions and judgments. Ar identifies them while Whitehead separates them and avoids some logical problems. [4435]

———. cf. #1822.

CLEARY, J. J. "On the Terminology of Abstraction in Aristotle." *Phron* 30(1985), 13-45. Ar uses abstraction as more than an epistemological concept. It is closely connected to the logical process of subtraction. The results of this process he calls objects of mathematics. [4436]

COBB, R. A. "The Present Progressive Periphrasis and the *Metaphysics* of Aristotle." *Phron* 18(1973), 80-90. Ar is the first Greek writer to take the progressive sense of a verb ("the dog is running") as equivalent to the meaning "the dog runs." This allows him to assert that continuous activity is part of the being of a substance. [4437]

CODE, A. "Aristotle's Investigation of a Basic Logical Principle: Which Science

Investigates the Principle of Non-Contradiction?" *CanJPh* 16(1986), 341-357. To some extent the science of metaphysics is the discipline which covers the logical principle of non-contradiction. In *Meta* Gamma 4.4, Ar demonstrates by elenchus that the principle must be accepted, though it cannot be proved.   **[4438]**

————. cf. #4623.

CORCORAN, J. "Aristotelian Syllogisms: Valid Arguments or True Universalized Conditionals?" *Mind* 83(1974), 278-281. Argues against the view that Aristotelian syllogisms are true universalized conditionals.   **[4439]**

————. "Aristotle's Natural Deduction System," in #52, pp. 85-131. Ar conceived of his syllogistic as a natural deduction system and not as an axiomatic theory.   **[4440]**

————. "Completeness of an Ancient Logic." *JSymLog* 37(1972), 696-702. Ar's deductive system is complete in that any valid argument which can be formed in the system's language can be demonstrated by a formal deduction.   **[4441]**

————. "A Mathematical Model of Aristotle's Syllogistic." *AGPh* 55(1973), 191-219. Mistakes in logical method attributed to Ar by various scholars are shown to be invalid. He is a precursor of some modern trends in logic.   **[4442]**

DANCY, R. M. *Sense and Contradiction: A Study in Aristotle.* Dordrecht: Reidel, 1975. Seeks to clarify initial and most important part (*Meta* Gamma 1005b35-1007b18) of Ar's argument against those who deny law of non-contradiction. Ar himself does not regard the principle as capable of proof.   **[4443]**

DAVIES, J. C. "Aristotle's Theory of Definition." *Euphro* 7(1975-76), 129-135. Ar's theory of definition is closely linked to his understanding of Nature as a whole. **[4444]**

DONALDSON, J. "Aristotle's *Categories* and the *Organon*." *PACPhA* 46(1972), 149-156. Examines what Ar has to say about the syllogism.   **[4445]**

DUERING, I. "Aristotle's Use of Examples in the *Topics*," in #4517, pp. 202-232. Ar uses examples to expound his dialectical method and is not concerned with whether examples are valid.   **[4446]**

DUERLINGER, J. "Aristotle's Conception of Syllogism." *Mind* 77(1968), 480-499. Examines assumption that a syllogism contains three propositions, one of which is made necessary by the other two; offers a new account of Ar's syllogism.   **[4447]**

————. "Drawing Conclusions from Aristotelian Syllogisms." *Monist* 52(1968), 229-236. Ar did not conceive of syllogism as necessarily containing a conclusion. Some syllogisms can lead to more than one conclusion. Ar tends to discuss syllogisms which have conclusions with universal applications.   **[4448]**

————. "*Syllogismos* and *Syllogizesthai* in Aristotle's *Organon*." *AJPh* 90(1969), 320-328. Term *syllogismos* should be defined as "a pair of premises put forward in support of a conclusion which necessarily follows from that pair of premises." The verb *syllogizesthai* means "to prove by syllogism." It is important to note different connotations of prepositions *dia* and *ek* which may be used with these words.   **[4449]**

ELDERS, L. "The *Topics* and the Platonic Theory of Principles of Being," in #4517, pp. 126-137. Ar employs logical devices typical of P and Academy, but that does not necessarily mean that he accepted underlying ontology. [4450]

ENGEL, S. M. "Fallacy, Wit and Madness." *Ph&Rh* 19(1986), 224-241. Ar uses absurd examples from P to demonstrate points about flawed arguments. He and his audience must have recognized the absurdities and seen the humor, a connection forgotten today. [4451]

ENGLEBRETSEN, G. "Aristotle and Quine on the Basic Combination." *NewSchol* 56(1982), 244-249. Contrasts Quine's "basic combination" as sentence joining singular to general term with Ar's view of it as sentence joining subject and predicate. [4452]

————. "Aristotle on the Oblique." *PhilStud* (Ireland) 29(1982-83), 89-101. In *Organon*, Ar had basic elements for a syllogistic treatment of relationals, but he failed to distinguish between his two senses of "predicate." [4453]

————. "Aristotle on the Subject of Predication." *NDJFormLog* 19(1978), 614-616; also in *Formale und nicht-formale Logik bei Aristoteles*, ed. A. Menne & N. Oeffenberger. (Hildesheim, Ger.: Olms, 1985), pp. 128-130. Argues against using Ar's thesis that universals must always inhere in a primary substance as evidence that Ar rejects the predication of terms to universal subjects. [4454]

————. "A Journey to Eden: Geach on Aristotle." *GPhS* 14(1981), 133-141. Examines Ar's theory of logical syntax. Logician P. Geach accuses Ar of corrupting logic because Geach does not take into account the differences between his own concept of subjects and subject-terms and Ar's view. [4455]

————. "Noncategorical Syllogisms in the *Analytics*." *NDJFormLog* 21(1980), 602-608. Noncategorical syllogisms in *Analytics* do not appear to be subject to syllogistic laws being developed there. It may be possible to analyze them categorically. [4456]

————. "On Propositional Form." *NDJFormLog* 21(1980), 101-110; also in *Formale und nicht-formale Logik bei Aristoteles*, ed. A. Menne & N. Oeffenberger (Hildesheim, Ger.: Olms, 1985), pp. 131-140. Unlike modern logicians, Ar views subjects and predicates of sentences as logically complex. He holds asserted propositions cannot be contrasted with negated ones. Asserted propositions have meaning and truth or falsity. [4457]

————. "Singular Terms and the Syllogistic." *NewSchol* 58(1980), 68-74. Ar does use singular terms in his syllogistic, as either subjects or predicates. The work of F. Sommers on syllogistic logic helps explain how singulars can bè part of a syllogism. [4458]

————. *Three Logicians: Aristotle, Leibniz, and Sommers and the Syllogistic.* Assen, Netherlands: Van Gorcum, 1981. Argues that syllogistic logic is philosophically defensible, and starts with an examination of Ar's logic. [4459]

EVANS, J. D. G. "The Codification of False Refutations in Aristotle's *De Sophisticis Elenchis*." *PCPhS* 21(1975), 42-51. One cannot separate dialectic from logic in study of Ar. Theory of error in argument plays an important part in such a study. [4460]

————. *Aristotle's Concept of Dialectic.* Cambridge Univ. Pr., 1977. Place of dialectic in

Ar's philosophy is larger than has usually been appreciated. This study emphasizes his theory of dialectic more than his use of it. For Ar dialectic is a particular form of intellectual activity, not the sort of universal science which P believed it to be. **[4461]**

FALLON, R. J. "Engels, Aristotle and Non-Contradiction." *StudSovTho* 18(1978), 1-15. Ar's criticisms of dialectic as a tool for studying metaphysics are inadequate. But dialecticians must observe the principle of non-contradiction. **[4462]**

FEREJOHN, M. T. "Aristotle On Necessary Truth and Logical Priority." *AmPhQ* 18(1981), 285-293. Ar seems to have been dissatisfied with his definition, in *Cat*, of a certain kind of necessary truth. In *PrAn* 1.4 he develops the theory of *per se* predication to resolve his difficulty and finds it a useful tool for dealing with a variety of philosophical problems. **[4463]**

———. cf. #5351.

FURS, S. N. "Computation of Aristotle's and Gorgonne's Syllogisms." *Studia Logica* 46(1987), 209-225. Technical discussion of a connection between Ar's syllogistic and the calculus of relations. **[4464]**

GALSTON, M. "Aristotle's Dialectic, Refutation, and Inquiry." *Dial*(Can) 21(1982), 79-94. For Ar dialectic plays a crucial role in philosophic inquiry. He does not regard it as inferior to demonstrative reasoning. **[4465]**

GHOSE, A. "Singular Propositions and Aristotle's Conception of Logic." *IntPhQ* 15(1975), 327-331. Aristotelian and mathematical logic lack singular terms since they deal purely with thought. In Buddhist logic, singular terms are indispensable. **[4466]**

GIULIANI, A. "The Aristotelian Theory of the Dialectical Definition." *Ph&Rh* 5(1972), 129-142. In ethics and politics Ar uses dialectical definitions which rely on argumentation. In other fields he uses scientific demonstration. **[4467]**

GOMEZ-LOBO, A. "Aristotle's Hypotheses and the Euclidean Postulates." *RMeta* 30(1977), 430-439. Though Euclid did not use Ar's system of hypotheses, outlined in *PostAn* 1.2, there are similarities between their demonstrative methods. **[4468]**

GRYAZNOV, B. S. "On The Historical Interpretation of Aristotle's *Analytics*." *Organon* (1975), 193-203. Focuses on the theory of assertoric syllogism in the *PrAn* to examine the role of the methods of mathematical logic as applied to historical research. **[4469]**

GYEKYE, K. "Aristotle and a Modern Notion of Predication." *NDJFormLog* 15(1974), 615-618. Consideration of Ar's logic and ontology leads to the conclusion that his theory of predication is closer to the modern view than to the traditional one. **[4470]**

———. "Aristotle on Language and Meaning." *IntPhQ* 14(1974), 71-77. The distinction which Ar seeks to draw between proper and improper (accidental) predication is shown to be invalid. **[4471]**

———. "Aristotle on Predication." *IntLogRev* 7(1976), 102-105. Examines Ar's distinction between genuine and accidental predication, and argues that his analysis of "That large thing is (a) timber" is wrong. **[4472]**

――――. "Aristotle on Predication: An Analysis of *Anal. Post.* 83a." *NDJFormLog* 20(1979), 191-195. Examines distinction Ar draws between proper predication and improper (or accidental) predication.   [4473]

HADGOPOULOS, D. J. "A Note on Aristotle's Theory of Identity." *Ph&PhenRes* 35(1974), 113-114. Ar states principle of "transitivity of identity" in *PrAn* 67b13-23, though some scholars have not taken note of this.   [4474]

――――. "*Posterior Analytics* II,viii,93a36." *Apeir* 11 #2(1977), 32-39. Challenges Ross' (1949) reading of the expression *dia meson* ("through middle terms") because it gives rise to an interpretation which is inconsistent with distinction between syllogisms of fact and syllogisms of reasoned fact.   [4475]

――――. "Reduction to Immediate Premisses: *Post. Anal.* 79a29-31, I,xiv." *Apeir* 10 #2(1976), 29-37. Examines various interpretations of this passage. Ar is not concerned with reduction of imperfect syllogisms to perfect ones, but about reducing non-immediate premises to immediate ones.   [4476]

――――. "Substitution of Variables in Aristotle." *JHPh* 13(1975), 133-138. Challenges view that Ar was not aware of identification of two variables, i. e., that he never substituted variables for variables.   [4477]

――――. "The Syllogism and Aristotle's Notion of Validity." *PhilInq* 1(1979) 120-124. Claims that Ar's definition of syllogism is a definition of valid deductive arguments and that Ar views the "follows from" relation as an intensional one. Also tries to define Ar's notion of validity.   [4478]

――――. cf. #5357.

HANKINSON, R. J. "Improper Names: On Intentional Double Ententes in Aristotle's *De Interpretatione*." *Apeir* 20(1987), 219-225. While examining semantic significance of parts of words in *De interp* 2.16a19-26 Ar indulges in some puns which seem to have sexual overtones.   [4479]

HESSE, M. "Aristotle's Logic of Analogy." *PhQ* 15(1965), 328-340. There is an "essential continuity" between Ar's scientific metaphysical analogies; this insight is useful with respect to analogical uses of language implicit in growth of science.   [4480]

HINTIKKA, J. "Different Kinds of Equivocation in Aristotle." *JHPh* 9(1971), 368-371. Examines relations among several kinds of equivocation: 1) synonymy, 2) homonymy and 3) the middle group of *pollakos legetai* ("things said in many ways").   [4481]

IRWIN, T. H. "Aristotle's Concept of Signification," in #76, pp. 241-266. Explores whether Ar's concept of signification is really a concept of meaning, and whether his remarks about signification are about meaning. Argues that Ar's concept of signification does not primarily reflect an interest in meanings and concepts.   [4482]

――――. "Homonymy in Aristotle." *RMeta* 34(1981), 523-544. Examines Ar's conditions for homonymy and multivocity. Homonymy and multivocity are often the same, and neither is intended to mark different senses of words.   [4483]

JACOBS, W. "Aristotle and Nonreferring Subjects." *Phron* 24(1979), 282-300. *De interp* 11,21a25-28 and *Cat* 10,13b12-35 do not support the claim that Ar thought subjects could be without referents.   **[4484]**

―――――. "The Existential Presupposition of Aristotle's Logic." *PhilStud* 37(1980), 419-428. In order to assert something one must use subject and predicate terms which denote something. Compares Ar's view with that of several modern logicians.   **[4485]**

KAPP, E. "Syllogistic," in #5336, pp. 35-49, transl. M. H. Dill and P. Dill. Presents overview of Ar's logic as a whole, and discusses development of syllogistic as theory of "discourse in which, given certain suppositions, something other than those suppositions follows necessarily because of them." Shows how dialectical debate was source of Ar's theory of syllogism.   **[4486]**

KING-FARLOW, J. "Facts, Agency and Aristotle's 'Is': Logical Atomism in Early Metaphysics?" *Metaphil* 16(1985), 166-177. Investigates Matthen's (#4502) conclusion that Ar was frequently prepared to employ the existential *esti* to create linguistically deviant sentences which would be quite easily understood by Greeks of his day. **[4487]**

KIRWAN, C. "Aristotle and the So-called Fallacy of Equivocation." *PhQ* 29(1979), 34-46. Ar's analysis of equivocation in *De soph* is sufficient, but can be improved. **[4488]**

―――――. cf. #4195.

KOEHL, R. A. "The Janus Face of *Metaphysics*, Gamma." *Ph&Rh* 2(1969), 12-18. Discusses two mutually incompatible ways that the account of the law of non-contradiction has been taken: 1) to imply everyone who uses language in social intercourse is metaphysically committed to real existence of at least some publicly known objects of discourse; 2) to provide vantage point from which one may question the legitimacy of knowledge claims in (1).   **[4489]**

KOTERSKI, J. W. "Aristotle on Signifying Definitions." *NewSchol* 54(1980), 75-86. By distinguishing between "real" and "signifying" definitions Ar gets around Meno's paradox about knowledge. Definitions which signify only tell us what words mean. They say nothing about the essence of the thing named.   **[4490]**

KRETZMANN, N. "Aristotle on Spoken Sound Significant by Convention," in #52, pp. 3-21. *De interp* 16a3-8 is one of the most important texts in the history of semantics. Ar notes that written marks, spoken sounds, and mental impressions are not the same for everyone, but that actual things are the same. Spoken sounds are, therefore, significant only by convention.   **[4491]**

KUNG, J. "Aristotle on Thises, Suches, and the Third Man Argument." *Phron* 26(1981), 207-247. Reply to Owen (#4518).   **[4492]**

LANDOR, B. "Definitions and Hypotheses in *Posterior Analytics* 72a19-25 and 76b35-77a4." *Phron* 26(1981), 308-318. Some apparent contradictions in the meaning of definitions in these two passages can be resolved by taking hypotheses as types of definition with assertive force.   **[4493]**

LARKIN, M. T. *Language in the Philosophy of Aristotle.* The Hague: Mouton, 1971.

Examines Ar's theory of philosophical language in light of his theory of signification. Compares it to P's and discusses the meaning of sentences and parts of sentences and Ar's theory of reference.   [4494]

LEAR, J. *Aristotle and Logical Theory.* Cambridge Univ. Pr., 1980. Offers an interpretation of Ar's logical program to show that his philosophy of logic is still worth thinking about and arguing with.   [4495]

———. "Aristotle's Compactness Proof." *JPh* 76(1979), 198-215. Ar's syllogisms are of little philosophical interest today, but his compactness proof (*PrAn* 1.23 and 25) earns him the title of father of logic and "(grand)father of metalogic."   [4496]

LEWIS, D. "Quality Individuals?" *RMeta* 23(1969), 114-122. Rejects views of Matthews and Cohen (#3920) which tries to amend Ar's account of predication.   [4497]

LESZL, W. *Logic and Metaphysics in Aristotle: Aristotle's Treatment of Types of Equivocity and its Relevance to His Metaphysical Theories.* Padua, Italy: Ed. Antenore, 1970. Examines Ar's distinciton between homonymy and synonymy (i. e., equivocity and univocity). Surveys history of scholarship on this point and takes issue with those who maintain that Ar continued to be close to Plato throughout his life.   [4498]

LLOYD, A. C. "The Principle that the Cause is Greater than the Effect." *Phron* 21(1976), 146-151. What can be called the transmission theory of Hume and Descartes originates with Ar's assertion in *Post An* that a cause must be greater than its effect. It is unclear whether Ar originated it or drew from Plato's idea of Forms.   [4499]

LUKASIEWICZ, J. *Aristotle's Syllogistic from the Standpoint of Modern Formal Logic.* New York: Garland, 1987; rprt. Presents an exposition of texts, and explains some theories of modern formal logic needed to understand Ar's syllogistic.   [4500]

MATTHEN, M. "Aristotle's Semantics and a Puzzle Concerning Change," in #3637, pp. 21-40. Shows that within a certain standard framework for semantics of subject-predicate sentences, several things Ar wants to believe do not make sense. Then develops a new account of semantics for such sentences that is arguably Ar's and shows how Ar's proposals concerning change fit into that framework.   [4501]

———. "Greek Ontology and the 'Is' of Truth." *Phron* 28(1983), 113-135. Technical discussion of various ways Greek could assert that something "is" and application of the concept of predicative complex to the study of Ar.   [4502]

MAURODES, G. I. "Aristotle and Non-Contradiction." *SJPh* 3(1965), 111-114. While Ar claims that law of Non-Contradiction is self-evident, he also offers a "negative demonstration" of the law. Argues that this demonstration is fallacious.   [4503]

McLAUGHLIN, R. J. "Language and Man: Aristotle Meets Koko." *Thom* 45(1981), 541-570. In light of reports from studies of ape language examines Aristotelian arguments for uniqueness of man.   [4504]

MIGNUCCI, M. "Puzzles about Identity. Aristotle and his Greek Commentators," in #3657, pp. 57-97. Technical discussion of points in Ar's logic resembling "Leibniz' Law," assertion that if two things are identical, they share all the same properties.   [4505]

MORSINK, J. "The Mandate of *Topics* 1,2." *Apeir* 16(1982), 102-128. Examines Ar's claim that it is the proper task of dialectic to establish the fundamental principles of each of the sciences. [4506]

MOST, G. W. "Seming and Being: Sign and Metaphor in Aristotle," in *Creativity and the Imagination: Case Studies from the Classical Age to the Twentieth Century*, ed. M. Amsler (Newark: Univ. of DE, 1987), pp. 11-33. Somewhat technical discussion of Ar's views on metaphors and puns. [4507]

MULHERN, M. "Corcoran on Aristotle's Logical Theory," in #52, pp. 133-148. Finds Corcoran's interpretation (#4440) of Ar's logic closer to the original than Lukasiewicz's (#4500). [4508]

NEWELL, H. "Smith on Aristotle." *SwPhSt* 8(1982), 61-65. Reply to #4540. [4509]

NOVAK, J. A. "A Geometrical Syllogism: *Posterior Analytics*, II, 11." *Apeir* 12 #2(1978), 26-33. Discusses traditional interpretations of this passage and offers a new one which emphasizes connection between geometrical proof and syllogistic. This connection elucidates Ar's claim that syllogistic reasoning can be universally applied. [4510]

———. "Some Recent Work on the Assertoric Syllogistic." *NDJFormLog* 21(1980), 229-242. Summarizes scholarly efforts to translate Ar's syllogistic into the language of modern logic. [4511]

NUSSBAUM, M. C. "Saving Aristotle's Appearances," in #76, pp. 267-294. Investigates three issues: 1) What are Ar's *phainomena* (appearances)? How is term best translated? How are *phainomena* related to observation? 2) What exactly is Ar's philosophical method if his method is to set down *phainomena*? 3) Why should philosophers be committed to *phainomena*? [4512]

OCHS, D. J. "Aristotle's Concept of Formal Topics." *SM* 36(1969), 419-425; also in #5280, pp. 194-204. Ar sees dialectical topics as descriptions of relations between subject and predicate. [4513]

O'FARRELL, F. "Aristotle's, Kant's, and Hegel's Logic." *Gregor* 54(1973), 477-516. Investigates the task and its fulfillment which Ar, Kant, and Hegel set themselves in their logic, and what its relation is to the problem of what being is, and how the change in the conception of this problem changed the conception of logic. [4514]

OLSHEWSKY, T. S. "Aristotle's Use of *Analogia*." *Apeir* 2 #2(1968), 1-10. Analogy, a kind of proportionality, serves Ar as a way of explaining resemblances. [4515]

O'NEILL. P. D. and **WASHELL, R. F.** "Perfect and Imperfect Syllogism." *NewSchol* 40(1966), 190-198. Explores why Ar names "discourse in which necessity is not perfectly established" syllogistic. [4516]

OWEN, G. E. L., ed. *Aristotle on Dialectic:* The Topics. *Proceedings of the Third Symposium Aristotelicum.* Oxford: Clarendon, 1968. Collection of previously unpublished papers, abstracted herein. [4517]

———. "Dialectic and Eristic in the Treatment of the Forms," in #4517, pp. 103-125.

Examines and challenges "reductive" thesis that Ar's dialectic is no more than eristic. Ar's arguments against Forms are examples of technique rather than expressions of philosophical positions.   **[4518]**

———. cf. #5634.

OWENS, J. "Is Philosophy in Aristotle an Ideology?" in *Ideology, Philosophy and Politics*, ed. A. Parel (Waterloo, Ont.: Laurier Univ. Pr., 1983), 163-178. Explores point that ideological thought is for sake of practical activity, while in Aristotelian philosophy, practical activity is for sake of thought.   **[4519]**

PATZIG, G. *Aristotle's Theory of the Syllogism. A Logico-Philological Study of Book A of the* Prior Analytics, transl. J. Barnes.   Dordrecht, Netherlands: Reidel, 1968. Examines nature of Aristotelian syllogism, Ar's accounts of logical necessity, perfection, the figures, and reduction and deduction.   **[4520]**

———. "Logical Aspects of Some Arguments in Aristotle's *Metaphysics*," in #4594, pp. 37-48. Examines Ar's logical methodology in Book Zeta. He does not emphasize logic at all points but can use it to evaluate the success or failure of his arguments.   **[4521]**

PELLETIER, F. J. "Sameness and Referential Opacity in Aristotle." *Nous* 13(1979), 283-311. Semantic investigation of use of term "the same." Looks at some of his obscure arguments in *Meta* Z 6.   **[4522]**

PHILIPPE, M.-D. *"Analogon* and *Analogia* in the Philosophy of Aristotle." *Thom* 33(1969), 1-74. Examines texts in which Ar describes analogy and the relationship between his statements about "terms having manifold meanings" and their connection with analogy and metaphysics.   **[4523]**

QUANDT, K. "On the Programmatic Formula *Proton Apo Ton Proton* in Aristotle." *AJPh* 104(1983), 358-371. Though Ar uses the terms *archai* and *prota* for both the "first principles" of a subject and the theses on which he begins his investigation of the subject, he does not identify such theses with the first principles.   **[4524]**

RASMUSSEN, D. B. "Aristotle and the Defense of the Law of Contradiction." *Pers* 54(1973), 149-162. Ar's defense of law of contradiction is not circular, as many critics maintain, but is a form of "negative demonstration."   **[4525]**

RECK, A. J. "Aristotle's Concept of Substance in the Logical Writings." *SwJPh* 3(1972), 7-15. Ar's theory of categories was shaped more by logic than by the nature of the Greek language. He distinguished logical subjects from ontological substances. The key to understanding the theory of substances expounded in the logical writings is the concept of "primary substances with essential natures."   **[4526]**

ROHATYN, D. A. "Aristotle and the Limits of Philosophic Proof." *Nat&Sys* 4(1982), 77-86. None of Ar's seven proofs of the law of non-contradiction succeeds, but some worthwhile observations on Ar himself and on the nature of philosophy can be drawn from his attempts.   **[4527]**

———. "Some Notes on Aristotle's Logic." *Athenaeum* 52(1974), 349-351. Translating *aitia* in *Cat* 14b14-22 as "the reason for which" allows us to see clearly Ar's connection between act and language.   **[4528]**

ROSE, L. E. *Aristotle's Syllogistic*. Springfield, IL: Thomas, 1968. Explores the consequences of accepting the Aristotelian syllogism as a linear array of three terms, an approach that will provide new insights into purpose of *PostAn* and his logic.   **[4529]**

————. "Aristotle's Syllogistic and the Fourth Figure." *Mind* 74(1965), 382-389. Basic structure of an Aristotelian syllogism is three figures. Introduction of a fourth figure indicates misunderstanding of Ar's notation.   **[4530]**

————. "Premise Order in Aristotle's Syllogistic." *Phron* 11(1966), 154-158. Examines each of syllogisms in *PrAn* to discover whether any particular pattern could be discerned in premise order of three figures.   **[4531]**

RYAN, E. E. "Aristotle on Proper Names." *Apeir* 15(1981), 38-47. Ar was indeed aware of philosophical issues and problems connected with use of proper names.   **[4532]**

RYLE, G. "Dialectic in the Academy," in #4517, pp. 69-79; also in #1268, pp. 39-68. Examines exercise of dialectic during last ten to twelve years of P's life and first ten to twelve years of Ar's teaching life and investigates P's dialectic vis-a-vis eristic. Ar wrote *Topics*, with P's consent, while still a student.   **[4533]**

SCHOLZ, H. "The Ancient Axiomatic Theory," in #5336, pp. 50-64, transl. J. Barnes. Overview of Ar's contributions to development of axiomatic theory and some weakness of his method.   **[4534]**

SIMONS, P. "Aristotle's Concept of State of Affairs," in *Antike Rechts- und Sozial-philosophie*, ed. O. Gigon & M. W. Fischer (Frankfurt, Ger.: Lang, 1988), pp. 97-112. Semantic concept of "state of affairs" is implicit in Ar's definition of truth.   **[4535]**

SIMPSON, P. "Aristotle's Theory of Assertions: A Reply to William Jacobs." *Phron* 26(1981), 84-87. Response to #4485.   **[4536]**

SLATER, B. H. "Aristotle's Propositional Logic." *PhilStud* 36(1979), 35-49. Examines differences between Ar's predicate logic and that used by modern logicians.   **[4537]**

SMILEY, T. J. "What is a Syllogism?" *JPhilLog* 2(1973), 136-153. Response to Lukasciewicz's study (#4500). Ar's syllogisms are not conditional formulae but sequences of proof or methods of deduction.   **[4538]**

SMITH, R. "Aristotle as Proof Theorist." *Philosophia Naturalis* 21(1984), 590-597. Ar developed syllogistic theory in *PrAn* to resolve issues concerning demonstrative sciences of his time. In particular, he made proofs themselves objects of study.   **[4539]**

————. "The Axiomatic Method and Aristotle's Logical Methodology." *SwPhSt* 8(1982), 49-59. Ar's methodology proceeds from discussion of syllogism in *PrAn* to its application in *PostAn* to problem of whether every proposition can, or must, be proved. His method is similar to modern proof theory.   **[4540]**

————. "Immediate Propositions and Aristotle's Proof Theory." *AncPh* 6(1986), 47-68. Ar's main reason for developing theory of deductions was its use as a proof-theoretic instrument to solve problems about demonstrative sciences.   [4541]

———. "The Relationship of Aristotle's Two *Analytics*." *CQ* 32(1982), 327-335. Analysis of reasons for Ar's development of syllogism shows that *PostAn* is earlier than *PrAn*. It is not just a matter of adding the syllogism to an earlier work.   [4542]

———. "The Syllogism in *Posterior Analytics* I." *AGPh* 64(1982), 113-135. Ar probably wrote *PostAn* first, before he had developed idea of syllogism. He did not revise *PostAn* to any significant degree after *PrAn*.   [4543]

———. "What is Aristotelian Ecthesis?" *HPhLog* 3(1982), 113-127. *Ecthesis* is Ar's technique for "setting out" a problem for proof. He probably used letters in his demonstrations and had some knowledge of certain techniques of modern logic.   [4544]

———., trans. *Prior Analytics.* Indianapolis: Robin Smith, 1989. Translation and commentary.   [4545]

———. cf. #4582.

SOLMSEN, F. "Dialectic without the Forms," in #4517, pp. 49-68. Examines Ar's view that dialectic deals with arguments and propositions taken from realm of "opinion," and how this view of dialectic differs from P's.   [4546]

SPANGLER, G. A. "Aristotle on Saying Something." *Apeir* 10 #2(1976), 38-46. Discusses Ar's notion of contrariety and his combination theory of truth.   [4547]

SPRAGUE, R. K. "Aristotelian Periphrasis: A Reply to Mr. Cobb." *Phron* 20(1975), 75-76. Cobb's (#4437) analysis of Aristotelian periphrases should include a discussion of *Phys* 185b26ff. Ar is not involved in grammatical innovation at *Meta* 1017a22-30 and *De interp* 21b9-10.   [4548]

STEVENSON, J. G. "Aristotle and the Principle of Contradiction as a Law of Thought." *Pers* 56(1975), 403-413. Formalizes Ar's proof of his argument that no one can believe the same thing to be and not to be.   [4549]

SWIGGERS, P. "Cognitive Aspects of Aristotle's Theory of Metaphor." *Glotta* 62(1984), 40-45. Ar's concept of metaphor, which is surprisingly modern, has linguistic, cognitive, and cultural bases.   [4550]

TANNER, R. G. "Aristotle as a Structural Linguist." *TPhS* (1969), 99-164. *Topics* and *Cat* reveal Ar's efforts to analyze "interior relations within texts of a particular kind." He refined the method and applied it on another level in *Meta*.   [4551]

———. "Form and Substance in Aristotle." *Prud* 15(1983), 86-108. "Form" and "substance" are linguistic concepts arising from analysis of linguistic relations among certain kinds of texts which Ar began in *Topics* and *Cat*.   [4552]

TEJERA, V. "Dialogue and Dialectic," in #81, pp. 49-59. Examines how to approach Ar's systematic or categorical writings in light of views of S and P about writing. The "system" may have been imposed by Ar's editors. It is significant that the works published in his lifetime were dialogues.   [4553]

THOM, P. "Aristotle's Syllogistic." *NDJFormLog* 20(1979), 751-759. Technical study of a syllogistic without propositions, which proves to be closer to Ar's system than that elaborated by J. Lukasiewickz (#4500).   **[4554]**

THOMPSON, M. "On Aristotle's Square of Opposition," in #3625, pp. 51-72. Certain modern proposed qualifications of Ar's principle of excluded middle (advanced to save Ar's square of opposition) are of dubious value.   **[4555]**

THOMPSON, W. N. *Aristotle's Deduction and Induction: Introductory Analysis and Synthesis.* Amsterdam: Rodopi, 1975. Attempts to provide introductory analysis of Ar's system of deduction. Synthesizes scattered materials on induction, gives detailed citations and footnotes, and takes on some persistent issues.   **[4556]**

VAN BENNEKOM, R. "Aristotle and the Copula." *JHPh* 24(1986), 1-18. Examines question of how it is that Ar recognizes in several places distinction between copulative and existential senses of *einai* (to be), but ignores distinction at *Meta* IV.7 where he deals with ten different categories and corresponding senses of *einai*.   **[4557]**

VEATCH, H. B. "A Modest Word in Defense of Aristotle's Logic." *Monist* 52(1968), 210-228. Ar's logic focuses on what and why things are, not on epistemological or ontological problems. It is more efficient than some modern critics will admit.   **[4558]**

WEDIN, M. V. "Aristotle on the Existential Import of Singular Sentences." *Phron* 23(1978), 179-196. Ar's discussions of this matter in *Cat* 13b27-33 and *De Interp* 21a24-28 only appear to be contradictory.   **[4559]**

WEIL, E. "The Place of Logic in Aristotle's Thought," in #5336, pp. 88-112, transl. J. and J. Barnes. Explains how dialectical debates between two persons were conducted, and why solitary thought processes could also be called dialectical.   **[4560]**

WHITE, N. P. "A Note on 'Ekthesis'." *Phron* 16(1971), 164-168. Ar's account of TMA at *De soph* 178b is completely coherent when read correctly.   **[4561]**

WILLIAMS, K. J. "Aristotle's Theory of Truth." *Prud* 10(1978), 66-76. Interprets Ar's concept of truth, in several works, in terms of modern theories of logic.   **[4562]**

WOODS, J. and **WALTON, D.** "The *Petitio*: Aristotle's Five Ways." *CanJPh* 12(1982), 77-100. Examines Ar's different characterizations of the fallacy of arguing in a circle, and then specifies certain lessons to be drawn from the theory of fallacies.   **[4563]**

ZIRIN, R. "Aristotle's Biology of Language." *TAPhA* 110(1980), 325-347. Overview of Ar's use of terms such as sound, phoneme, and syllable.   **[4564]**

————. "Inarticulate Noises," in #52, pp. 23-25. Ar describes certain sounds not "unable to be written down" but "unable to be broken down into discrete units."   **[4565]**

For related items see #197, #1236, #1769, #2223, #3905, #4602, #4665, #5284, #5381, #5382, #5471.

MATHEMATICS

Ar distinguishes two types of mathematics: geometry and arithmetic. The former has more philosophic interest for him than the latter. His problem in this area is to explain how one can think of geometric concepts apart from the figures which contain them, without becoming a Platonist and espousing Forms of triangles and other figures. P had taught that mathematical concepts such as circularity and equality existed on a level where they could be comprehended by contemplation. Ar is too much of a realist to accept such a notion. He does hold, however, that one can "abstract" the concept of triangularity, for example, from a real figure which has three sides and angles whose sum equals two right angles. One can think about the properties of this figure without thinking that it actually exists. One can also draw a line, for purposes of demonstration, and say "Let this line be a foot long" and not fall into error if it is not precisely a foot long.

Mathematics, or geometry in particular, studies objects that exist in the natural world, but it does not study them as objects. It studies only the mathematical properties which can be abstracted from them. One of Ar's favorite illustrations is that the curve formed by Socrates' snub nose can be studied apart from the snub nose itself. This may have been brought to his mind by a bust of Socrates. Ar is interested only in those aspects of a geometrical figure which result from its nature as a geometrical figure. He applies what logicians call a "predicate filter" to cut out all the attributes or qualities of the figure which are not related to its shape. If the bust of Socrates was made of bronze or marble, that would have nothing to do with the *curve* of the nose.

Ar also addressed some problems of arithmetic, though geometry was of far more interest to him. The Greeks in general had so little interest in arithmetic that they never developed a system of numerals. They had the words for the numbers, many of which have come over into English in terms such as pentagon and hexagon, but they used the letters of the alphabet instead of some numeric symbol when writing numbers. (That is why some editions of Ar's longer works use Greek letters to designate the separate books, e. g., *Meta* B [for Beta] instead of *Meta* 2.)

Looked at arithmetically, a person can be one unit, but he/she can also be said to have two arms, two legs (or four members), ten fingers, ten toes (or twenty digits). Ar found it difficult to resolve these kinds of ambiguities, so he focuses on geometry, which he defines as the study of surfaces, points, lines, solids, and related matters, as these can be abstracted from natural objects.

ANDERSON, T. C. "Intelligible Matter and the Objects of Mathematics in Aristotle." *NewSchol* 43(1969), 1-28. Ar fails to apply his concept of intelligible matter to the objects of mathematical study.   [4566]

APOSTLE, H. G. "Aristotle's Theory of Mathematics as a Science of Quantities." *Phil*(Athens), 8-9(1978-9), 154-214. Ancient philosophers defined mathematics as a science of quantities. Modern philosophers, especially Logistic, Formalist, and Intuitionist, consider such a definition simplistic. Ar's work provides a definition of mathematics which accords well with modern views.   [4567]

BARNES, J. "Aristotelian Arithmetic." *RPhA* 3(1985), 97-133. Somewhat technical discussion of Ar's philosophy of mathematics, which is very sketchy. One may doubt whether he himself ever developed it fully.   **[4568]**

BRUMBAUGH, R. S. "Aristotle as a Mathematician," in #49, pp. 153-162. In the way he applies mathematics Ar is Pythagorean. His view of the nature and fundamentals of mathematics makes him an anti-Platonic intuitionist. His view of the relation between mathematical theory and practice reverses the modern understanding.   **[4569]**

BURNYEAT, M. F. "Platonism and Mathematics: A Prelude to Discussion," in #4575, pp. 213-240. Argues that choice between an Aristotelian account and a Platonic account of objects of mathematics is simultaneously a choice as to which sciences we should take as most fundamental to our understanding of the world and its goodness.   **[4570]**

CATALANO, J. S. "Aristotle and Cantor: On the Mathematical Infinite." *ModSch* 46(1969), 264-267. Ar did not accept potential infinite nor reject actual mathematical infinite, for he had no knowledge of contemporary meaning of these terms.   **[4571]**

CRAWLEY, C. B. *Universal Mathematics in Aristotelian-Thomistic Philosophy.* Washington, DC: Univ. Pr. of America, 1980. Ar did not implicitly hold for a universal mathematics prior to Arithmetic and Geometry. Such a position is contrary to his philosophical principles.   **[4572]**

GAUKROGER, S. "Aristotle On Intelligible Matter." *Phron* 25(1980), 187-197. Ar bases his mathematical concepts on the idea that numbers have intelligible matter, which is the same as that of geometrical figures.   **[4573]**

———. "The One and the Many. Aristotle on the Individuation of Numbers." *CQ* 32(1982), 312-322. Comparison with modern mathematical concepts can shed light on Ar's number theory, especially the sense in which they are "ones."   **[4574]**

GRAESER, A., ed. *Mathematics and Metaphysics in Aristotle.* Bern: Haupt, 1987. Collection of essays, abstracted herein.   **[4575]**

LEAR, J. "Aristotle's Philosophy of Mathematics." *PhR* 91(1982), 161-192. Examines *Phys* B2 and *Meta* M3 to show how Ar unified mathematical and knowledgeable truths. Mathematics is true because of its ability to describe structures and relations existing within and among physical objects.   **[4576]**

MIGNUCCI, M. "Aristotle's Arithmetic," in #4575, pp. 175-211. In criticizing P's philosophy of mathematics, Ar does not deny that mathematical objects exist, but wants to challenge the way P thinks they exist.   **[4577]**

MODRAK, D. K. W. "Aristotle on the Difference Between Mathematics and Physics and First Philosophy." *Apeir* 22(1989), 121-139. Examines contrast in *NE* 6.8 between mathematics on the one hand and physics and first philosophy on the other. The puzzle which this distinction raises is solved by recognizing that, unlike mathematics, first philosophy and physics both rely on principles which rest on sense perception.   **[4578]**

MUELLER, I. "Aristotle and the Quadrature of the Circle," in #64, pp. 146-164. Examines Ar's comments and those of his pupil Eudemus about the quadratures.   **[4579]**

――. "Aristole on Geometrical Object." *AGPh* 52(1970) 156-171; also in #4598, pp. 96-107. Describes how Ar's account of mathematical objects incorporates the role of human thinking in mathematics with the Platonic assumption that a correlation between the objects of reasoning and the real world must exist.   **[4580]**

――. "Aristotle's Approach to the Problem of Principles in *Metaphysics* M and N," in #4575, pp. 241-260. Examines Ar's discussion of what are principles of independently existing ideas and mathematical objects.   **[4581]**

――. cf. #5381.

SMITH, R. "The Mathematical Origins of Aristotle's Syllogistic." *AHES* 19(1978), 201-209. Ar's syllogistic is closer to modern mathematical theory than to logic.   **[4582]**

SORABJI, R. "Aristotle, Mathematics, and Colour." *CQ* 22(1972), 293-308. Different colors can be produced by mixing the four elements in different proportions, in a process analogous to mathematical ratios.   **[4583]**

TILES, J. E. "Why the Triangle Has Two Right Angles *Kath' hauto*." *Phron* 28(1983), 1-16. Ar considers theorem about sum of angles in a triangle to be important but does not integrate it effectively into his theory of demonstration.   **[4584]**

VASSILIOU, P. "Aristotle and the Philosophy of Mathematics." *Phil*(Athens) 8-9(1979), 144-153. Ar's contributions to philosophy of mathematics are most noteworthy in areas of induction, concepts of actual and potential infinity, continuity and syllogism.   **[4585]**

For related items see #242, #457, #4436, #5366, #5370, #5371, #5381, #5439.

METAPHYSICS

The word "metaphysics" does not appear in Ar's work, but the concept which it describes — the study of Being — is certainly at the core of his thought. Ar's usual names for the discipline are "first philosophy" or "theology." In the early seventeenth century philosophers coined the term "ontology." A persistent story relates that the term "metaphysics" came into being because that work was placed in Ar's corpus after the *Phys.* (In Greek *meta* means "after.") The *Meta* is not an easy read. Plutarch described it as "written in a style which makes it useless for those who wish to study or teach the subject from the beginning; the book serves simply as a memorandum for those who have already been taught its general principles" (*Alexander* 7).

The book we know as the *Metaphysics* was, in all likelihood, not composed by Ar as continuous lectures or a series of treatises. Rather, the work appears to be a number of separate tracts which were first collected under one title by Andronicus of Rhodes in the first century B. C. The collection may have received its title from being placed in the Aristotelian corpus after the *Physics*. The diversity of topics has given rise to a good bit of scholarly controversy about the structure and unity (or lack thereof) in the work. Nonetheless, at the beginning of Book 4, Ar writes, "There is a science which investigates being as being and the attributes which belong to this in virtue of its own nature"

(1003a21-22; all quotations in this section are from Ross' transl.). This study of being as such (Being *qua* Being) is frequently taken to be a central concern of Aristotelian metaphysics, and this introduction will focus on this topic, acknowledging its indebtedness to the account of J. Barnes in #3548, pp. 39-46. For definitions of some of the basic concepts involved in this study, the reader is referred to the section on Plato's metaphysics (p. 213).

Ar is keenly aware that certain terms are ambiguous, and one of the most significant, most ambiguous, terms is "being." "There are," he says, "several senses in which a thing may be said to 'be,' as we pointed out previously in our book on the various senses of words; for in one sense the 'being' meant is 'what a thing is' or a 'this,' and in another sense it means a quality or quantity or one of the other things that are predicated as these are" (1028a10-13). In the *Cat* Ar had classified ten different categories of predicates, which reflect linguistically ten categories of being. Thus being is said in many ways.

Yet while things are said to be in many ways, "all that 'is' is related to one central point, one definite kind of thing" (1003a-33-34). Ar first illustrates his point here with two non-philosophical examples, health and medicine:

> Everything which is healthy is related to health, one thing in the sense that it preserves health, another in the sense that it produces it, another in the sense that it is a symptom of health, another because it is capable of it. And that which is medical is relative to the medical art, one thing being called medical because it possesses it, another because it is naturally adapted to it, another because it is a function of the medical art. And we shall find other words used similarly to these (1003a35-b6).

We can say that John is healthy, that the right diet is healthy, that an exercise program is healthy. But John, the right diet, an exercise program are not all healthy in exactly the same way. Hence, the term "healthy" is ambiguous. Yet the different senses of "healthy" are indeed related, for they all refer to one thing, health.

Ar wants to make the same point with respect to "being."

> So, too, there are many senses in which a thing is said to be, but all refer to one starting-point; some things are said to be because they are substances, others because they are affections of substance, others because they are a process towards substance, or destructions or privations or qualities of substance, or productive or generative of substance, or of things that are relative to substance, or negations of one of these things or of substance itself (1003b6-10).

Socrates is or exists; a color, such as Socrates' whiteness, is or exists; a characteristic, such as Socrates' heaviness, is or exists. But Socrates, whiteness, and heaviness do not all exist in the same way. Despite this ambiguity Ar argues that everything said to be or to exist is done so with reference to substance. Colors such as white are or exist, but they are or exist in some substance. Weight is or exists, but it is or exists in some substance. In effect Ar has divided the constituents of the world into two kinds: 1) substances, and 2) the various characteristics and attributes of those substances. Substances are primary, for characteristics and attributes do not exist in themselves; they are dependent on the existence for their very being.

Given the primacy of substance in the study of being *qua* being, the question arises as to what it is to be a substance. In Book 5 Ar argues that things are called substance in two ways: "(A) the ultimate substratum, which is no longer predicated of anything else, and (B) that which, being a 'this', is also separable" (1017b23-25). What Ar seems to be suggesting is that a thing is a substance if it is both an individual (something that can be picked out and identified as an individual thing) and is not dependent on something else for its very existence. Hence, Socrates is a substance, but his whiteness is not.

With these criteria for something being a substance, we can then ask what in fact are substances. In addressing this question Ar criticizes several of his predecessors. He rejects those Presocratic thinkers who had taken the ultimate stuff of the world, such as earth or water or the like, to be substance. He argues against the atomists who had maintained that the ultimate parts of ordinary objects were substances. He criticizes the Pythagoreans who had taken number to be substance. Finally, he challenges Plato's theory of Forms, which posits universals as substances. Ar's own answer seems to be that persons, animals, plants, and other natural objects (such as the sun, moon, stars) are substances in the primary sense. However, in Book 7, the account of substance seems to be complicated by Ar's claim that "substance is of two kinds, the concrete thing, and the formula (I mean that one kind of substance is the formula taken with the matter, while another kind is the formula in its generality" (1039b20-22).)

This cursory review of Ar's discussion of being and substance by no means exhausts for him the topics which might fall under the heading of "Metaphysics." In the *Metaphysics* we also find him discussing the Unmoved Mover, the distinction between potentiality and actuality, the nature of mathematical realities, and many other subjects. Some of the liveliest debates in Aristotelian scholarship center around his metaphysics.

ACKRILL, J. L. "Aristotle's Distinction Between *Energeia* and *Kinesis*," in #1268, pp. 121-141. Ar distinguishes between getting, having, and using a (first-order) ability. Getting such an ability is undergoing a *kinesis*; using it is an *energeia*.   **[4586]**

ADDIS, L. "Aristotle and the Independence of Substances." *Ph&PhenRes* 33(1972), 107-111. Examines views of several scholars on Ar's concept of substances as "independent" and attributes as "dependent." Consideration of time must be part of a clarification of the problem.   **[4587]**

ANDERSON, J. F. "Teilhard's Cosmological Kinship to Aristotle." *NewSchol* 45(1971), 584-589. Examines points of similarity in thought of the ancient Greek philosopher and the modern French theologian.   **[4588]**

ANNAS, J. "Aristotle on Inefficient Causes." *PhQ* 32(1982), 311-326. Ar misunderstood P because he interpreted *Phaedo* too literally, but his arguments against Forms are cogent.   [4589]

——. "Aristotle on Substance, Accident and Plato's Forms." *Phron* 22(1977), 146-160. Examines Ar's argument that Platonists are guilty of a contradiction. They want to say that there are Forms not just of substances but also of accidents of substances. But they are committed to belief that there are Forms only of substances.   [4590]

——. *Aristotle's* Metaphysics, *Books M and N*. Oxford: Clarendon Pr. 1976. Translation with introduction and notes.   [4591]

——. cf. #1810.

ANSCOMBE, G. E. M. "The Principle of Individuation," in #4598, pp. 88-95. Shows why Ar could not allow matter simply to be substance, and yet why matter is what distinguishes one sensible substance from another.   [4592]

APOSTLE, H. G. *Aristotle's* Metaphysics. Bloomington: Indiana Univ. Pr., 1966. Translation and commentary, with glossary.   [4593]

AUBENQUE, P. *Études sur la* Métaphysique *d'Aristote.* *Actes du vi^e Symposium Aristotelicum.* Paris: Vrin, 1979. Previously unpublished essays. Those in English are abstracted herein.   [4594]

——. "The Origins of the Doctrine of the Analogy of Being." *GradFacPhJ* 11(1986), 35-45. Doctrine of analogy of being is not found explicitly or implicitly in Ar's works, but has its origins in medieval thought.   [4595]

BALME, D. M. "The Snub." *AncPh* 4(1984), 1-8. The snub nose paradox is used as an example of how difficult it is to define some things. The problem is discussed in *Meta* Z and a solution proposed in Book Eta. The solution is applied to the problem of reproduction in *De gen anim.*   [4596]

BARFORD, R. "A Proof from the *Peri Ideon* Revisited." *Phron* 21(1976), 198-218. Analysis of argument concerning relatives and Ar's refutation. Addresses what the argument contributes to our understanding of nature of predication in P, nature of relations, nature of paradigm, and character of Ar's criticisms of P.   [4597]

BARNES, J., et al. *Articles on Aristotle, 3: Metaphysics.* New York: St. Martin's Pr., 1979. Essays focusing on Ar's approach to metaphysics and conceptual tools he develops for addressing ontological questions; abstracted herein.   [4598]

BECHLER, Z. "Aristotle Corrects Eudoxus, *Met.* 1073b39-1074a16." *Centaurus* 15(1970), 113-123. In setting number of celestial spheres at 55 instead of 33, Ar is not correcting Eudoxus' theory but acting in accordance with physical laws which he had established.   [4599]

BERTI, E. "Logical and Ontological Priority Among the Genera of Substance in Aristotle," in #67, pp. 55-69. Examines relationship between three types of substance distinguished in *Meta* 12: terrestrial (mobile and corruptible), celestial (mobile and incorruptible), and supracelestial (incorruptible and immobile) and question of whether they are reducible to a common genus.   [4600]

BLAIR, G. A. "The Meaning of *Energeia* and *Entelecheia* in Aristotle." *IntPhQ* 7(1967), 101-117. Neither of these words should be translated "actuality." *Energeia* is "activity" and *entelecheia* means "having the end/goal internally." Ar created both words. In his later writings he tends to use *energeia*.   [4601]

BOLTON, R. "Existentialism and Semantic Theory in Aristotle." *PhR* 85(1976), 514-544. Ar's doctrine of nominal definition is his semantic theory of natural-kind terms; offers a new interpretation of that doctrine.   [4602]

BRAKAS, G. *Aristotle's Concept of the Universal.* Hildesheim, Ger.: Olms, 1988. Offers a systematic account of Ar's view on universals, which went through three stages, arriving at a developed view closer to what Socrates had first taught.   [4603]

BRENNAN, S. O. "Substance and Definition. Reality and *Logos*: *Metaphysics* ZH." *NewSchol* 59(1985), 53-62. Traces Ar's development from Platonic ideas to the concept of nature as concrete and real in an attempt to reconcile apparently contradictory statements about what sort of substance is definable.   [4604]

BRENTANO, F. *On the Several Senses of Being in Aristotle,* transl. R. George. Berkeley: Univ. of CA Pr., 1975. Edition of Brentano's 1862 dissertation, a work which influenced Heidegger and others. Finds that being in the sense of the categories, in particular substantial being, is the most basic. All other modes stand to it in a relation of well-founded analogy.   [4605]

BROADIE, S. "Problems of Aristotle's Concept of Form." *JPh* 84(1987), 679-681. Reply to Halper (#4694) and Witt (#4862).   [4606]

BRODY, B. A. "Natural Kinds and Real Essences." *JPh* 64(1967), 431-446. Suggests that differences found between Ar's and Kant's views of substantial change are based upon their understanding of permanence of predication.   [4607]

BROGAN, W. "Is Aristotle a Metaphysician?" *JBritSocPhen* 15(1984), 249-261. In light of Heidegger's interpretation, it can be shown that several aspects of Ar's concept of Being (universal, substance, induction, etc.) need to be re-evaluated.   [4608]

BRUMBAUGH, R. S. "The Unity of Aristotle's *Metaphysics*." *MidwJPh* 6(1978), 1-12; also in #49, pp. 141-156. In spite of stylistic differences and clumsy construction, the arrangement of the treatises in *Meta* reveals unity and a logical sequence.   [4609]

BURGER, R. "Is Each Thing the Same as its Essence?: On *Metaphysics* Z 6-11." *RMeta* 41(1987), 53-76. Explores Ar's apparently inconsistent responses to title question. His differing answers arise from changes in the meaning of the terms used.   [4610]

BURNS, A. "Ancient Greek Thought and the Missing Energy Concept." *C&M* 30(1969), 228-240. Ar's theory of *dynamis* and *energeia* overcomes P's body-soul dualism and provides a teleology within each individual which can be studied scientifically.   [4611]

BURNYEAT, M. F., et al. *Notes on Book Zeta of Aristotle's* Metaphysics. Oxford: Sub-Faculty of Philosophy, 1979. Contains seminar notes compiled from 1975-1979. There is also a discussion of "Universals as Potential Substances" by G. J. Hughes.   [4612]

BURRELL, D. B. "Substance: A Performatory Account." *PhilStud* (Ireland) 21(1973), 137-160; also in #4773, pp. 226-249. Many, perhaps all, of the paradoxes arising from Ar's discussion of substance can be resolved by taking sentences, not terms, as the basic unit of discourse. [4613]

CAPECCI, A. "Final Causality and Teleological System in Aristotle" in *The Teleologies in Husserlian Phenomenology* ed. A. T. Tymieniecka (Dordrecht, Netherlands: Reidel, 1979), pp. 33-62. Examines reciprocal implications and internal connections which subsist between discussion of value and possibility of final cause, the eventual ontological structure which it involves, and overall vision of the real. [4614]

CAREY, G. "A Mute Point in Aristotle." *MonStud* 8(1972), 133-142. Ar does not describe the unity of the four metaphysical causes (reality, act, existence, and being) but may have viewed them as analogous to the four elements of the material world. [4615]

CATAN, J. R. "Two Views on the Completeness of the *Metaphysics* of Aristotle." *RFilNeo-Scol* 73(1981), 388-398. Examines differing viewpoints of G. Reale and J. Owens on the interpretation of Ar's four causes and the connection between *Meta* Lambda and Books A-El. [4616]

CHAPPELL, V. "Matter." *JPh* 70(1973), 679-696. For Ar, matter can be differentiated on a theoretical level from things which it makes up, but it cannot actually exist without making up something. [4617]

CHEN, C. H. "Aristotle's Analysis of Change and Plato's Theory of Transcendent Ideas." *Phron* 20(1975), 129-145; also in #42, pp. 388-403. Argues that Ar did accept P's theory of transcendent ideas, but modified it by separating the two aspects of essence and ideal. Ar retains the aspect of essence for his substantial forms and leaves out the aspect of the ideal. Discusses views of C. J. de Vogel (#4641). [4618]

CHROUST, A.-H. "Aristotle, *Metaphysics* 981b13-25. A Fragment of the Lost Aristotelian *On Philosophy*." *RhM* 120(1977), 241-246. This passage, which discusses human progress after a natural catastrophe, is actually from Ar's *On Philosophy*. [4619]

CLEARY, J. J. *Aristotle on the Many Senses of Priority.* Carbondale: S. IL Univ. Pr., 1988. Analyzes different treatments of many senses of priority in *Cat* and *Meta*. Examines how Ar applies these to some typical metaphysical arguments. [4620]

———. "Science, Universals, and Reality." *AncPh* 7(1988), 95-130. Analyzes three arguments "from the sciences" in order to examine the unsuitability of sensible particulars as objects of scientific knowledge and to clarify why Platonic Forms were thought to serve that purpose. Examines Ar's criticisms of these arguments. Sketches conceptual development of universal as a sort of entity that is distinguished from substantial form. [4621]

CODE, A. "The Aporematic Approach to Primary Being in *Metaphysics* 2," in #3637, pp. 1-20. Explores the last *aporia* of *Meta* 3, "Are the principles of things universal or particular?" to see what it is we need to elaborate and explore, and then suggests how this *aporia* is treated in *Meta* 2. [4622]

———. "Metaphysics and Logic," in #5374, pp. 127-149. Part I explains why metaphysics deals with principle of non-contradiction. Part II discusses various objections to: 1) the argument at *Meta* 4.3 that principle of non-contradiction is most secure of all principles; 2) the elenchtic proof of principle of non-contradiction at *Meta* 4.4.   **[4623]**

————. cf. #4438.

COHEN, S. M. "Aristotle and Individuation," in #3637, pp. 41-65. While the claim that for Ar matter provides a principle of individuation is simplistic and only approximately correct, it still points us in basically the right direction.   **[4624]**

————. "Aristotle on the Principle of Non-Contradiction." *CanJPh* 16(1986), 359-370. Response to Code (#4623). Ar was not trying to construct an elenctic proof of Principle of Non-Contradiction. He manages to prove that every particular instance of PNC is inarguable, but that does not guarantee PNC itself.   **[4625]**

————. "Essentialism in Aristotle." *RMeta* 31(1978), 387-405. Various areas of Ar's thought cannot serve as sources of essentialism. Only the hylomorphic conception of substance put forth in late books of *Meta* could be taken as essentialist.   **[4626]**

————. "Proper Differentiae, The Unity of Definition and Aristotle's Essentialism." *NewSchol* 55(1981), 229-240. Examines how Ar distinguishes between *differentiae* (qualities by which things are defined as different) which entail membership in a genus and those which do not. A brown dog, e. g., is not a member of a separate genus. "Dog" is a proper *differentia*; "brown" is not.   **[4627]**

COLSON, D. D. "Aristotle's Doctrine of *Universalia in rebus.*" *Apeir* 17(1983), 113-124. Ar can rightly be described as a moderate realist, who conceives of particulars sharing universals in common.   **[4628]**

COOPER, J. M. "Chappell and Aristotle on Matter." *JPh* 70(1973), 696-698. Reply to #4617.   **[4629]**

————. "Hypothetical Necessity," in #3809, pp. 151-167. Explores how Ar's conception of hypothetical necessity unites two seemingly divergent ideas: the idea of matter making some outcomes necessary, and the idea of those outcomes as means to a natural goal. Examines Ar's challenge to Democritus' conception of necessity.   **[4630]**

CRESSWELL, M.J. "What is Aristotle's Theory of Universals?" *AustlJPh* 53(1975) pp. 238-247. Shows how P's reasons for postulating separate Forms do not apply to Forms in the way Ar conceives them.   **[4631]**

————. cf. #1829.

DANCY, R. M. "Aristotle and Existence." *Synthese* 54(1983), 409-442; also in #61, pp. 49-80. Examines Ar's concept of being, the difference between *einai ti* (being something) and *einai haplos* (being once), and Owen's (1960) comments on Ar's "being."   **[4632]**

————. "Matter: Aristotle and Chappell." *JPh* 70(1973), 698-699. Further discussion of #4617.   **[4633]**

————. "On Some of Aristotle's First Thoughts about Substances." *PhR* 84(1975), 338-

373. In his early work Ar maintained that something of which other things are predicated is most likely to be real. His later concept of matter conflicted with that view, and Ar never resolved the difficulty. [4634]

——. "On Some of Aristotle's Second Thoughts About Substances: Matter." *PhR* 87(1978), 372-413. Explores apparent contradiction in *Meta* Z.3 where Ar says that "matter" means the bronze of which a statue is made and which is something in its own right, and then where he says "matter" means "what is not in its own right called either something or so big or any of the things by which being is determined." [4635]

DEGROOD, D. H. "The Status of Essential Definition." *DarshInt* 6(1966), 5-10. Explains Ar's notion of "essential definition," and argues that his concepts of "essence," "definition," and "formal cause" can be subsumed in special cases under modern concept of formula. [4636]

DEMOSS, D. and DEVEREUX, D. T. "Essence, Existence, and Nominal Definition in Aristotle's *Posterior Analytics* II 8-10." *Phron* 33(1988), 133-154. Identifies fourteen points relating to Ar's theory of nominal definition, i. e., a definition which explains the meaning of a thing's name, but not its underlying cause. [4637]

DEVEREUX, D. T. "The Primacy of *Ousia*: Aristotle's Debt to Plato," in #1282, pp. 219-246. Focuses on question of how Ar understands relation between substance and other kinds of being in his earliest works. Sees important parallels between this relation and what Ar sees as relation between Platonic Forms and their participants. [4638]

——. "The Relationship between Theophrastus' *Metaphysics* and Aristotle's *Metaphysics Lambda*," in #5491, pp. 167-188. Theophrastus' *Meta* criticizes only Book Lambda of Ar's *Meta*. This particular book of Ar's *Meta* was probably written earlier than the rest. Theophrastus' reaction to it was probably written during Ar's lifetime. [4639]

DE VOGEL, C. J. "Aristotle's Attitude to Plato and the Theory of Ideas, According to the *Topics*," in #4517, pp. 91-102. Ar's attitude toward Ideas in *Topics* is inconsistent, suggesting that his own views had not matured when he wrote this book. [4640]

——. "Did Aristotle Ever Accept Plato's Theory of Transcendent Ideas: Problems Around a New Edition of the *Protrepticus*." *AGPh* 47(1965), 261-298. Examines and challenges Duering's (1958) denial of view that Ar accepted P's Theory of Forms for a significant part of his life. [4641]

DOMINO, B. "Form as Substance and Its Relation to Matter in *Metaphysics* Z 17." *Dial*(PST) 31(1989), 44-51. Substance is Form. The nature of substance, determined by at least one of the four causes, must be studied in relation to matter. The study has implications for Ar's concept of soul. [4642]

DRISCOLL, J. A. "*Eide* in Aristotle's Earlier and Later Theories of Substance," in #3631, pp. 129-159. Challenges view of Woods (#4864) and Owen (#4778) that the species which is a secondary substance in *Cat* is elevated to status of primary substance in *Meta* Z. [4643]

DUERING, I. "Did Aristotle Ever Accept Plato's Theory of Transcendent Ideas." *AGPh* 48(1966) 312-316. Criticizes De Vogel's interpretation (#4641) of Ar's philosophical development that claims that Ar accepted P's theory of transcendent ideas.   [4644]

DUNLOP, A. "Making Sense of Aristotelian Essentialism." *PhilStud* (Ireland) 29(1982-83), 68-88. Clarifies Aristotelian doctrine that certain entities have some of their properties essentially and others accidentally.   [4645]

DURRANT, M. "Aristotle's 'Second Substance' and Its Significance." *SecOrd* 3(1973), 40-53. Second-substance terms enable Ar to define particular things and to distinguish them. Other terms "provide criteria of continuous identity."   [4646]

DYBIKOWSKI, J. C. "Professor Owen, Aristotle and the Third Man Argument." *Mind* 81(1972), 445-447. Response to #4778. Owen's claim that Ar revised his theory of predication does not seem to be justified.   [4647]

DYE, J. W. "Aristotle's Matter as a Sensible Principle." *IntStudPh* 10(1978), 59-84. Matter's most important function for Ar is to be a principle of explanation.   [4648]

————. "The Sensibility of Intelligible Matter." *IntStudPh* 13(1981), 17-40. Shows Ar's use of intelligible matter to be a rational and economical explanation of certain features of mathematical knowledge, given presuppositions common to many Greek philosophers and the concept of (sensible) matter which Ar employs as an explanatory principle for physical entities and processes.   [4649]

ELDERS, L. "The *Topics* and the Platonic Theory of Principles of Being," in #4517, pp. 126-140. Explores whether *Topics* shows traces of an ontology modeled upon P's theory of principles of being.   [4650]

ELLROD, F. E. "*Energeia* and Process in Aristotle." *IntPhQ* 22(1982), 175-181. Fact that Ar uses concept of *energeia* does not make him a process philosopher.   [4651]

ELUGARDO, R. "Woods on *Metaphysics* Zeta, Chapter 13." *Apeir* 9 #1(1975), 30-42. Certain *aporiai* arise in Wood's (#4864) interpretation of Z 13 as claiming that "Nothing that is predicated universally can be substance."   [4652]

ENGLEBRETSEN, G. "Aristotelian Universals." *CPh* 73(1978), 17-23. Ar defines universals in broad terms but often restricts the notion to what is predicable essentially and of substance.   [4653]

————. cf. #4454.

ENGMANN, J. "Aristotle's Distinction Between Substance and Universal." *Phron* 18(1973), 139-155. Concludes that Ar does not provide adequate explanation and backing for his distinction between terms that are essentially predicative and terms that cannot occur predicatively.   [4654]

ETZWILER, J. P. "Being as Activity in Aristotle: A Process Interpretation." *IntPhQ* 18(1978) 311-334. Ar conceives of realities as activities, as events, or occurences, not as "things" or "objects." He explains physical objects not only as activities, but also as capacities exactly because they have the potential to change.   [4655]

FAY, T. A. "The Problem of Primary Substance in Aristotle's *Metaphysics* and Some

Recent Interpretations." *GM* 30(1975), 657-663. Surveys recent work on terms *ousia* and *hypokeimenon*.   [4656]

FELT, J. W. "Whitehead's Misconception of 'Substance' in Aristotle." *ProcStud* 14(1985), 224-236. Whitehead's reading of "substance" in Ar as something unchanging and self-contained is erroneous but has shaped process philosophy. For Ar, substance is actually something which develops internally with passage of time.   [4657]

FEREJOHN, M. T. "Aristotle on Focal Meaning and the Unity of Science." *Phron* 25(1980), 117-128. Reconstructs focal meaning of *to on* ("being") in order to explain how different applications of *to on* are all supposed to "point towards a one," and develops a line of reasoning which leads Ar to argue that there must be an all-encompassing field of inquiry which studies the totality of being.   [4658]

FINE, G. "Aristotle and the More Accurate Arguments," in #76, pp. 155-177. Investigates Ar's criticisms of Platonic arguments for Forms. Examines logic of these arguments and interconnections between them.   [4659]

————. "The Object of Thought Argument: Forms and Thoughts." *Apeir* 18(1984), 50-58. Discusses Ar's own doubts about ontological status of artifacts and the effect these reservations had on his concept of substance.   [4660]

————. "Owen, Aristotle, and the Third Man." *Phron* 27(1982), 13-33. Reply to #4778. Ar's only response to TMA is to draw a distinction between "this one" and "such a one." He makes no distinction between weak and strong predicables.   [4661]

————. "Plato and Aristotle on Form and Substance." *PCPhS* 29(1983), 23-47. Points out strengths and weaknesses of Ar's theory of substances and criticizes his refusal to admit Platonic Forms as substances.   [4662]

————. "Separation." *OSAP* 2(1984), 31-87. Argues 1) the separation Ar typically has in mind in connection with Forms is capacity for independent existence; 2) Ar is probably correct to say that at least some Forms, in some dialogues, are separate, but is wrong to indicate that P, beginning with *Phaedo*, specifies separation as a new feature of Forms; 3) Ar's account of basis of separation is incorrect; 4) Ar is probably correct to say Socrates is uncommitted to separation.   [4663]

————. "Separation: A Reply to Morrison." *OSAP* 3(1985), 159-165. While Morrison (#4762) is right to say that each substance is separate from every other, he is wrong to think this claim is incompatible with Fine's claim that separation consists in independent existence.   [4664]

————. cf. #1842-#1845.

FOSS, L. "Are There Substances? Another Look at the Classical Doctrine," in #4773, pp. 69-88. It is necessary to distinguish two competing senses of "substance": 1) formal or logical sense in which substance *must* be said to exist, and 2) empirical or material sense in which saying that substance exists entails many difficulties.   [4665]

————. "Substance and Two Theories of Natural Language," in #4773, pp. 213-223. Investigates whether Aristotelian concept of substance has application in an evolutionary universe from point of view of language.   **[4666]**

FRANK, D. H. *The Arguments "From the Sciences" in Aristotle's* Peri Ideon. New York: Lang; Vol. 1, 1982; Vol. 2, 1985. Focuses on first set of arguments against Platonic metaphysics in *Peri Ideon*, the so-called arguments "from the sciences." Ar's chief target in these arguments is P himself; we can evaluate arguments and "fairness" of Ar's objections against background of P's dialogues of middle period.   **[4667]**

FREDE, M. "The Unity of General and Special Metaphysics: Aristotle's Conception of Metaphysics," in #57, pp. 81-98. Proper reading of Ar's conception of metaphysics, and in particular his remark that first philosophy is universal because it is first, will restore metaphysics to its proper place, the first of the demonstrative sciences.   **[4668]**

FREELAND, C. A. "Aristotle on Possibilities and Capacities." *AncPh* 6(1986), 69-89. It is incorrect to link Ar's different treatment of *dynameis* in *De interp*, *Meta*, and *Ethics*. Discusses 1) contingencies and capacities for opposites in *De interp*; 2) Ar's account of rational and non-rational capacities in *Meta* 9.2 and 5; and 3) ethical topic of voluntariness and how *Meta* 9 is not about voluntariness.   **[4669]**

FURTH, M. "Aristotle on the Unity of Form." *PBACAPh* 2(1986) 243-267. In central books of *Meta*, Ar is guided by two leading assumptions: 1) that "kind" is best candidate for substance of a thing, and 2) that each kind has an internal structure which is open to rational analysis.   **[4670]**

————. "A Note on Aristotle's Principle of Non-Contradiction." *CanJPh* 16(1986), 371-381. Comments on Code's (#4438) argument, and suggests a better account of this argument that is still in conformity with the general line of Code's approach.   **[4671]**

————. *Substance, Form, and Psyche: An Aristotelian Metaphysics.* Cambridge Univ. Pr., 1988. Seeks to explain and to motivate a theory of essence, existence, and individuation to be found in Ar's later and more advanced works. Centers on a concept of what an individual material object is, looking at biological rather than inanimate objects. **[4672]**

————. "Transtemporal Stability in Aristotelian Substances." *JPh* 75(1978) 624-646. Suggests that the "cut-down concept of substance" found in *Cat* is "more radically undetermined by what is actually stated about it" than is normally realized. Considers some basic features of universe of substances mentioned in later parts of *Meta*.   **[4673]**

GEORGIADIS, C. "The Criteria of Substance in *Metaphysics* Delta 8,1017b 23-26, Zeta 3,1028b33-1029a3, and Alpha 1,1042a24-30." *BICS* 25(1978), 89-91. In these passages Ar does not distinguish different senses of substance.   **[4674]**

————. "The Individual Thing and its Properties in Aristotle." *Dial&Hum* 4(1977), 157-167. Discusses how substance is related to other categorical beings.   **[4675]**

————. "*Metaphysics* Z,1,1028a20-30." *RhM* 125(1982), 102-105. Interprets the passage on basis of close study of several Greek terms. Ar may mean to suggest possibility that all substances can be reduced to single ontological category of being.   **[4676]**

————. "Two Conceptions of Substance in Aristotle." *NewSchol* 47(1973), 22-37; in #4773, pp. 172-187. Contrasts two meanings of *ousia*: 1) sense in *Cat* in which it refers to an individual thing, and 2) sense in *Phys* and *Meta*, in which the substance is a principle of the individual thing. Exemplifies intimate connection between two conceptions in discussion of causality and predication. **[4677]**

GILL, M. L. *Aristotle on Substance: The Paradox of Unity.* Princeton Univ. Pr., 1989. Explores role of matter in generation and constitution of Aristotelian composite substances. Argues that matter seriously threatens intrinsic unity, and hence substantiality of object to which it contributes. **[4678]**

GLOUBERMAN, M. "Matter and Rationality." *Apeir* 11 #2(1977), 11-31. Examines whether matter's irrationality is inevitable in Aristotelian terms. In *Meta* 7 Ar seems to allow for rationality of "sensible matter" under certain conditions. **[4679]**

GOMEZ-LOBO, A. "Aristotle: *Metaphysics* H, 2." *Dialogos* 16(1981), 7-12. Challenges Owen's (#4775) interpretation of existential uses of verb "to be." Argues that in Eta 2, Ar is not dealing with existential use and its alleged multiplicity of senses. **[4680]**

——. "The So-Called Question of Existence in Aristotle, *An. Pos.* 2." *RMeta* 34(1980), 71-90. Offers an interpretation of Ar's statement that "it is one and the same thing to know what it is and to know the cause of the if (it) is" (93a4), and thus claims that essence does not explain existence. **[4681]**

——. cf. 3662.

GRAHAM, D. W. "States and Performances: Aristotle's Test." *PhQ* 30(1980) 117-130. Discusses Ar's division of actions into actualizations and movements in *Meta* 6. Accepts linguistic test used to divide actions and Ar's resulting classification. Argues that failure to appreciate actualization/movements distinction is based on two errors. **[4682]**

GRAM, M. S. "Substance," in #4773, pp. 120-143. In responding to challenges by A. N. Whitehead, argues that for Ar substance is not matter and substance exists by itself not as though it were sealed off from rest of world, but in contradistinction to existence of accidents. **[4683]**

——. "Two Concepts of Substance." *NewSchol* 51(1977), 75-89. Whitehead's attack on Aristotelian doctrine of substance seems to rest on a confusion of Ar's concepts of substance and accident with those of matter and form. **[4684]**

GRANGER, H. "Aristotle's Natural Kinds." *Ph* 64(1989), 245-247. Continuation of debate with Franklin over nature of "continuity" of Ar's natural kinds. Argues that Ar would not regard possible kinds as natural kinds. **[4685]**

——. cf. #3818-#3821.

GYEKYE, K. "Aristotle on the Universal." *MusAfr* 4(1975), 52-56. Ar realized that, philosophically and scientifically, universals were necessary. He did not believe, however, that one must derive universals from several examples. One will do. **[4686]**

——. "Substance in Aristotle's *Categories* and *Metaphysics*." *SecOrd* 3(1974), 61-65. Explores different treatments of concept of substance in *Cat* and *Meta*, and seeks "to discover the philosophical underpinnings . . . of the different conceptions of substance."   [4687]

———. "The Term *ta adiaphora* in Aristotle's *Posterior Analytics*." *MusAfr* 6(1977-78), 100-101. Addendum to #4686.   [4688]

HADGOPOULOS, D. J. "A Note on Aristotle's Notions of Universality and Necessity." *Log&An* 18(1975), 171-174. Provides evidence against the contention that Ar equates necessity with omnitemporal truth.   [4689]

HAGEN, C. T. "The *Energeia-Kinesis* Distinction and Aristotle's Conception of *Praxis*." *JHPh* 22(1984), 263-280. Reply to several scholars who maintain that Ar considers *energeiai* to be states. Argues that they are in fact activities, based in Ar's concept of teleology, which links them to the notion of *praxis*.   [4690]

HAHN, R. "Aristotle as Ontologist or Theologian: Or, Aristotelian Form in the Context of the Conflicting Doctrines of Being in the *Metaphysics*." *SJPh* 10(1979), 79-88. Examines scholarly controversy over apparent inconsistency in Ar's concept of being. It appears one of the conflicting views can be subsumed under the other.   [4691]

HALPER, E. C. "Aristotle On The Extention of Non-Contradiction." *HPhQ* 1(1984), 369-380. In *Meta* 4.4-8, Ar is not trying to argue for the principle of non-contradiction but to show that it applies universally to things which have essence.   [4692]

———. "Aristotle on the Possibility of Metaphysics." *RPhA* 5(1987), 99-131. The aporiai in *Meta* B provide a rationale for a non-Platonic metaphysics.   [4693]

———. "Aristotle's Solution to the Problem of Sensible Substance." *JPh* 84(1987), 666-672. By the terms "universal" and "individual," which he applies to Forms, Ar designates characteristics, not kinds of entities.   [4694]

———. "Being *qua* Being in *Metaphysics* Gamma." *Elenchos* 8(1987), 43-62. Being *qua* Being, in Ar's view, encompasses all Beings but is also a kind of substance.   [4695]

———. "*Metaphysics* Z 4-5. An Argument from Addition." *AncPh* 6(1986), 91-122. Ar shows that failures in definition result not from inadequacy of the definer but because certain features of accidents and accidental composites render them incapable of strict definition.   [4696]

———. "*Metaphysics* Z 12 and H 6: The Unity of Form and Composite." *AncPh* 4(1984), 146-159. Passages deal with somewhat different issues, but both relate to problems of form and definition, and how one form or one definition can consist of more than one thing. Defining form as actuality helps to resolve the issue.   [4697]

———. *One and Many in Aristotle's* Metaphysics: *The Central Books*. Columbus: OH State Univ. Pr., 1989. Ar recognizes that "one" is said in many says, and his complex treatment of one is key to understanding his metaphysical *aporia*, the antinomies that constitute Book B.   [4698]

———. "The Origin of Aristotle's Metaphysical *Aporiai*." *Apeir* 21(1988), 1-27. The fifteen difficulties which Ar discusses in *Meta* B arise not merely from opposition to Platonic metaphysics but because Ar believes they are fundamental to any effort to comprehend metaphysics.   [4699]

HAMLYN, D. W. "Aristotle on Form," in #3809, pp. 55-65. Examines implications of Ar's rejection of separately existing Forms for his attempts to explain how notion of *eidos* can have application.   [4700]

———. "Focal Meaning." *PAS* 78(1977-78), 1-18. While notion of homonymy by reference is an important discovery by Ar, it does not have quite the importance for philosophy in general within context of theory of meaning. "Focal meaning" involves a doctrine of primary and secondary meanings such that the secondary meaning is derivative from the primary. Ar uses this doctrine to establish an ontological dependence of the secondary on the primary. Notes the circularity in this approach.   [4701]

HARE, J. E. "Aristotle and the Definition of Natural Things." *Phron* 24(1979) 168-179. Explores puzzling feature of Ar's account of definition which suggests there is a sense in which naturally existing things do not, strictly speaking, have definitions.   [4702]

HARPER, A. W. J. "Substance as a Causal Principle in Aristotle's *Metaphysics*." *Eidos* 4(1985), 149-165. The apparent gap between universal and particular in Ar's thought is bridged by taking substance as a unifying causal principle.   [4703]

HARTMAN, E. "Aristotle on the Identity of Substance and Essence." *PhR* 85(1976), 545-561. Seeing essence as substance enables Ar to assert unity of substance over time in a way that answers Heraclitus' doctrine of flux but raises other problems.   [4704]

HATHAWAY, R. F. "Formal and Material Principles of Hierarchy," in *Jacob's Ladder and the Tree of Life*, ed. M. L. Kuntz (New York: Lang, 1987), pp. 31-40. Examines Ar's views about an internal hierarchic order within substance itself.   [4705]

HEINAMAN, R. "An Argument in *Metaphysics* Z13." *CQ* 30(1980), 72-85. Though passage is read differently by many scholars, Ar does seem to be denying that any universal can be substance.   [4706]

———. "Aristotle's Tenth Aporia." *AGPh* 61(1979), 249-270. Challenges view that Aristotelian substantial forms are universals by showing how solution to one of problems of *Meta* B requires that substantial forms be individuals and not universals.   [4707]

HINTIKKA, J. "The Varieties of Being in Aristotle," in #61, pp. 81-114. Identity, predication, existence, and class-inclusion are not different meanings of *estin* (is), merely different uses. This result elucidates *inter alia*, the role of existence assumptions in Aristotelian science and the essential-accidental distinction.   [4708]

HOCUTT, M. O. "Aristotle's Four Becauses." *Ph* 49(1974), 385-399. The "causes" might better be described as explanations, lacking productive force or necessity.   [4709]

HUSAIN, M. "The Multiplicity in Unity of Being *Qua* Being in Aristotle's *Pros Hen* Equivocity." *NewSchol* 55(1981), 208-218. Reply to Hamlyn (#4701) and Owen (#4777). Maintains that Ar did understand dependence of secondary on primary being in concrete terms.   [4710]

INCIARTE, F. "Metaphysics and Reification." *Ph* 54(1979), 311-327. In *Cat* Ar takes *ousia* as a substance. In *Meta* he understands it verbally. **[4711]**

IRWIN, T. H. "Aristotle's Discovery of Metaphysics." *RMeta* 31(1977), 210-229. Ar's desire to separate empirical sciences from dialectical theorizing led him to reject Platonic approach and establish his own principles, developed in answering questions raised in work now called *Meta*. **[4712]**

ITZKOWITZ, K. "Reaching Beyond Aristotle: A Note On Absolute or Ontological Difference." *NewSchol* 56(1982), 340-345. Starts with what Ar says about difference and greatest difference to try to understand what Kierkegaard and Heidegger say about inconceivable difference. **[4713]**

JONES, J. F. "Intelligible Matter and Geometry in Aristotle." *Apeir* 17(1983), 94-102. The phrase *hyle noete* should be understood as magnitude. **[4714]**

KAHN, C. H. "On the Intended Interpretation of Aristotle's *Metaphysics*," in #3657, pp. 311-338. Examines themes in work to understand Ar's intensions. Suggests chronology for the various books, while doubting it can be established. The *Meta* as a whole has more literary continuity and skill of composition than generally recognized. **[4715]**

KANE, W. H. "Aristotle and Moderate Realism: A Rejoinder." *NewSchol* 37(1965), 71-79. Challenges view that Ar's solution to problem of the universal is not metaphysical but purely logical. **[4716]**

KENNY, A. J. P. "A Stylometric Study of Aristotle's *Metaphysics*." *Assoc. for Literature & Linguistics Computing Bulletin* 7(1979), 12-21. Analyzes facets of Ar's language to establish chronology and authorship of individual books. **[4717]**

KIRWAN, C., transl. *Metaphysics Gamma, Delta, Epsilon*. Oxford: Clarendon Pr. 1971. Translation and notes. **[4718]**

KORCIK, A. "Existential Propositions in Aristotle." *Organon* 7(1970), 281-283. Discusses how Ar uses "is" in two senses, verbal, and copulative. **[4719]**

KOSMAN, L. A. "Substance, Being, and *Energeia*." *OSAP* 2(1984), 123-149. Ar's claim that actuality *dynamis* is more useful should suggest that discussion of actuality and actuality *dynamis*, and their distinction from motion and motion *dynamis*, serve an important purpose in development of account of *ousia*. **[4720]**

KOUTOUGOS, A. "The Relevancy of Aristotle's Theory of Change to Modern Issues (e. g. Conceptual Change)." *Phil*(Athens) 7(1977), 315-322. Discusses Ar as first to develop a theory of change through his concepts of primary matter, *entelecheia*, *energeia*, and *dynamis*. **[4721]**

KUNG, J. "Aristotle on Essence and Explanation." *PhilStud* 31(1977), 361-383. Taking essential properties as explanatory is an indispensable feature of Ar's view of essential properties. This position casts doubt on the claim that an essential property is such that it must belong to everything to which it belongs. **[4722]**

———. "Can Substance Be Predicated of Matter?" *AGPh* 60(1978), 140-159. Matter of living things, which is same as form, is classified as substance. Substance as form is predicated of particular matter in compound substance. [4723]

LACEY, A. R. "*Ousia* and Form in Aristotle." *Phron* 10(1965), 54-69. Ar does have a doctrine of pure form, and he is guilty of an inconsistency in that the notion of form only makes sense in conjunction with that of matter. Identifies eight tasks which *ousia* is at one time or another needed to fulfill, and discusses issue of unity of form. [4724]

————. cf. #590.

LANDOR, B. "Aristotle on Demonstrating Essence." *Apeir* 19(1985), 116-132. Examines Ar's identification of a thing's cause with its essence in *PostAn* 2.8,93b4-15. For Ar, knowing that X is Y means knowing why Y is. [4725]

LEHNER F. C. "The Lambda-Ennea Case." *Thom* 32(1968), 387-423. Argues for the historical probability that *Meta* Lambda consists, for the most part, of notes for Ar's final lectures at the Lyceum. [4726]

LESHER, J. H. "Aristotle on Form, Substance, and Universals: A Dilemma." *Phron* 16(1971), 169-178. Ar, because of his conception of forms as substance, falls prey to same sorts of criticism that he raised against Platonists. Surveys recent scholarship on question. [4727]

LESZL, W. *Aristotle's Conception of Ontology*. Padua, Italy: Ed. Antenore, 1975. Discusses Ar's conception of science of being *qua* being. Ar offers conception of ontology which attributes to it the character not of knowledge of truths that are inaccessible to non-philosophers, but of clarification of certain conceptual structures of our intellectual apparatus (especially of language) which are in principle accessible to everybody precisely because everybody makes use of them. [4728]

LEWIS, F. A. "Accidental Sameness in Aristotle." *PhilStud* 42(1982), 1-36. Examines the ontological implications of Ar's distinction between accidental compounds and substances. [4729]

————. "Form and Predication in Aristotle's *Metaphysics*," in #45, pp. 59-84. Examines progression from metaphysics of earlier logical works, where the individual is primary substance, to central books of *Meta*, where primary substance is form. Discusses Ar's efforts to specify what kinds of predication to include in metaphysical theory. [4730]

————. "Plato's Third Man Argument and the 'Platonism' of Aristotle," in #45, pp. 133-174. Ar has no satisfactory argument to show that P must accept a certain principle of predication. [4731]

————. "What is Aristotle's Theory of Essence," in #3637, pp. 89-131. A central feature of *Meta* 2 is distinction between primary and secondary cases of essence and a similar distinction in connection with related notions of substance and definition. [4732]

LLOYD, A. C. "Aristotle's Principle of Individuation." *Mind* 79(1970), 519-529. Matter, not form, is Ar's principle of individuation. [4733]

————. *Form and Universal in Aristotle*. Liverpool, UK: Cairns, 1981. Challenges conventional view that Ar replaces P's picture of universals as separately existing entities with an account of universals as "common natures" existing in individuals.   **[4734]**

LOBKOWICZ, N. "Substance and Reflection: Aristotle and Hegel." *RMeta* 43(1989), 27-46. These two present profound metaphysical alternatives. For Ar Being is a substance. Hegel's metaphysics emphasizes the self-awareness of Being.   **[4735]**

LOUX, M. J. "Aristotle on the Transcendentals." *Phron* 18(1973), 225-239. In *Meta* Ar maintains that universally true predicables cannot introduce genera and do not apply to all things univocally. First assertion seems defensible, but second is not.   **[4736]**

——. "Form, Species and Predication in *Metaphysics* Z, H and Theta." *Mind* 88(1979), 1-23. Begins considering view that substance-words are ambiguous or homonymous, then relates doctrine of homonymy of substance words to distinction between form- and species-predications, then clarifies central themes of Zeta-Theta.   **[4737]**

——. "*Ousia*: A Prolegomenon to *Metaphysics* Z and H." *HPhQ* 1(1984), 241-266. Suggests a picture of H.6 and all of Z and H of sustained dialectical treatment of a puzzle arising from Ar's own views about matter/form composition and the *ousia*-hood of form, on the one hand, and intuitions about the irreducibly real unity of ordinary objects on the other.   **[4738]**

LOWE, M. F. "Aristotle on Being and the One." *AGPh* 59(1977), 44-55. Takes issue with I. M. Bochenski's (1951) interpretation of *Meta* 2.3,998b22-27.   **[4739]**

——. "Aristotle's *De Somno* and Its Theory of Causes." *Phron* 23(1978), 279-291. Shows that a comparison of a fragment of *De Somno* with treatise reveals a development in Ar's theory of four causes which is confirmed by his *Meta*.   **[4740]**

LUDWIG, W. D. "Aristotle's Conception of the Science of Being." *NewSchol* 63(1989), 379-404. Ontology and theology are linked naturally in *Meta*. When one understands the nature of divine being, the nature of all other beings can be understood.   **[4741]**

LUKASIEWICZ, J. "On the Principle of Contradiction in Aristotle." *RMeta* 24(1971), 485-509, transl. V. Wedin; also in #4598, pp. 50-62 (under title "Aristotle on the Law of Contradiction") transl. J. Barnes. Discusses Ar's principle of contradiction, and shows how for Ar it is principally an ontological axiom, which is construed as a general truth about all beings, or at least all eternal beings. Principle is a valuable practical assumption, though Ar's arguments for it are invalid,.   **[4742]**

MacKINNON, D. M. "Aristotle's Conception of Substance," in #1268, pp. 97-119. Ar's doctrine of substance is a doctrine of relation of "the self-existent to that which is existentially derivative" and also a doctrine that involves such distinctions as that between essence and accident. Ar's doctrine of substance is an attempt to lay foundations of doctrine of degrees of beings at the level of the humdrum and every day.   **[4743]**

MADIGAN, A. "*Metaphysics* E3: A Modest Proposal." *Phron* 29(1984), 123-136. Obscurities in the passage are clarified by realizing that Ar presents an ambiguous thesis about causes of accidents and proceeds to analyze it dialectically, ending with a reformulation of his original position.   **[4744]**

MAMO, P. S. "*Energia* and *Kinesis* in *Metaphysics* Theta 6." *Apeir* 4 #2(1970), 24-33.

Ar's *energia-kinesis* distinction is not as confused as Ackrill maintains (#4586). **[4745]**

MANSION, S. "The Ontological Compostition of Sensible Substances in Aristotle (*Metaphysics* VII 7-9)," in #71, pp. 75-87; also in #4598, pp. 80-87, transl. J. and J. Barnes. Explains how Ar first decides that it is the form or essence of a thing which constitutes its being, and then examines his treatment of sensible substances and how form applies to them. **[4746]**

MARX, W. *Introduction to Aristotle's Theory of Being as Being.* The Hague: Nijhoff, 1977. Introduction that focuses on single theme of science of being *qua* being, the science which is foundation of traditional philosophy. **[4747]**

MATTHEN, M. "Individual Substances as Hylomorphic Complexes," in #5374, pp. 151-176. Discusses origin of concept of substance as subject; examines why Ar rejected P's view of substance. For Ar it is "a special sort of predicative complex." **[4748]**

——. cf. #4502.

MATTHEWS, G. B. "Accidental Unities," in #76, pp. 223-240. In *De interp*, Ar tries to explain why certain features of a thing make up a unity, whereas others do not. In *Meta* 5, he allows for accidental unity. The *musical* and the just make up an accidental unity because musicality and justice are accidents of one substance. **[4749]**

——. "Gender and Essence in Aristotle." *AustlJPh* Suppl. 64(1986), 16-25. Ar's view of women as defective men is partly accounted for by cultural factors, but his own metaphysics make it impossible for him to explain gender difference. **[4750]**

McMULLIN, E. "Cosmic Order in Plato and Aristotle," in *The Concept of Order*, ed. P. G. Kuntz (Seattle: Univ. of WA Pr., 1968), pp. 63-76. Discusses development of contrast between reason and sense in *Tim* as background for Ar, and examines differing accounts of matter. **[4751]**

MERLAN, P. "Hintikka and a Strange Aristotelian Doctrine." *Phron* 15(1970), 93-100. Studies Ar's explanation at *Meta* 1009a22-26 and 36-38, that some deny law of contradiction's validity because they pay exclusive attention to realm of sensible. **[4752]**

——. "On the Terms 'Metaphysics' and 'Being-*qua*-Being'." *Monist* 52(1968), 174-194. Argues that being-*qua*-being is not a universal concept, and argues that being-as-such is only different for what Ar otherwise calls the divine. Ar's being-*qua*-being is something transcendent. Discusses origins and meaning of term "metaphysics." **[4753]**

MILLER, F. D., Jr. "Did Aristotle Have the Concept of Identity?" *PhR* 82(1973), 483-490. Reply to N. P. White (#4855). Ar displays a concept of identity similar to ours but distinguishes between unitariness over time which characterizes a process (*kinesis*), and identity through time, characteristic of activities and substances. **[4754]**

MILLER, P. "What Aristotle Should Have Said: An Experiment in Metaphysics." *AmPhQ* 9(1972), 207-212. Attempts to reconstruct Ar's metaphysical system in a way that resolves difficulties he experienced in unifying substance, form, and act. **[4755]**

MISCEVIC, N. "In Defense of Ambiguity." *SynPhil* 1(1986), 153-161. Study of Ar's concept of focal meaning and *pros hen* equivocity and their usefulness in philosophy and history of science. [4756]

MODRAK, D. K. W. "Forms and Compounds," in #45, pp. 85-100. Response to Lewis' articulation (#4730) of problems in Ar's discussion of predication. First or metaphysical problem is whether acceptance of "Socrates is a man" as a well-formed sentence involves a commitment to a third type of metaphysical predication, the predication of a species or a form of a concrete individual. Second or linguistic problem concerns relationship between linguistic and metaphysical predication. [4757]

———. "Forms, Types, and Tokens in Aristotle's *Metaphysics*." *JHPh* 17(1979), 371-381. Argues that forms are universals, not particulars. [4758]

———. cf. #4578.

MORAVCSIK, J. M. E. "The Discernibility of Identicals." *JPh* 73(1976), 587-598. Shows how Aristotelian essentialism calls for changes in our normally accepted logical framework and how these concerns are important to assessment of recent work in linguistics by Kripke and Chomsky. [4759]

MORRISON, D. "The Evidence for Degrees of Being in Aristotle." *CQ* 37(1987), 382-401. In *Cat* Ar uses *mallon* ("more") and *malista* ("most") in ways that indicate he conceived of degrees of being. Several passages in *Meta* support this reading. [4760]

———. "Separation: A Reply to Fine." *OSAP* 3(1985), 167-173. Argues that if separation is as Fine's (#4663) view indicates, it should not be as important to Ar as it clearly is. [4761]

———. "Separation in Aristotle's Metaphysics." *OSAP* 3(1985), 125-157. Asks: 1) What was Ar's conception of separation as a criterion of substance? and 2) What are its consequences and how does it function? Argues that for Ar, for substance to be "separate" is to be separate from other substances, and Ar's use of "separate in definition" as means of saying that forms are after all "separate" is indefensible. [4762]

MOSER, P. K. "Two Notions of Substance in *Metaphysics* Z." *Apeir* 17(1983), 103-112. Ar is not inconsistent in his definitions of substance in *Meta* Zeta. [4763]

MOUKANOS, D. D. "Aristotle's Concept of First Philosophy (*Metaphysics*, A2)." *Diot* 13(1985), 72-77. Explores whether wisdom is basic meaning of first philosophy or one among three meanings in *Meta*: 1) science of first principles; 2) science which considers Being *qua* Being universally; 3) theoretical philosophy called "theological." [4764]

MOUTAFAKIS, N. J. "Aristotle's 'Metaphysics' (Book Lambda) and the Logic of Events." *Monist* 65(1982), 420-436. Reading Ar's *Meta* in terms of an event logic underlines connections among all areas of his thought. [4765]

MULHERN, J. J. "'Universally', 'Universal', 'the Universal'." *Teorema* 5(1975), 277-284. Ar's approach to question of universals differs from the traditional ones. Examines how he uses expressions translated "universally," "universal," and "the Universal." [4766]

MULHERN, M. M. "Types of Process According to Aristotle." *Monist* 52(1968), 237-

251. Reply to Ackrill (#4586). Argues that difficulties which Ackrill finds in Ar's distinctions arise from Ackrill's assumptions, not Ar's. Ar distinguishes clearly between *energeia* and *kinesis* but relates them systematically.   [4767]

MURE, G. R. G. "Cause and Because in Aristotle." *Ph* 50(1975), 356-357. Response to Hocutt (#4709). Ar's *aitia* (or *aition*) does not mean "a because" or "an explanation" but rather "a cause."   [4768]

NOGALES, S. G. "The Meaning of 'Being' in Aristotle." *IntPhQ* 12(1972), 317-339. Ar's metaphysic is incompletely developed but not incoherent.   [4769]

NOONAN, H. W. "An Argument of Aristotle on Non-Contradiction." *Analysis* 37(1977), 163-169. Uses contemporary notions of signification and reference to make suggestions about interpretation of Principle of Non-Contradiction.   [4770]

NOVAK, M. "A Key to Aristotle's 'Substance'," in #4773, pp. 190-208. Asks how Ar's substance can be both a universal essence and a singular individual, and seeks to offer a more developed doctrine of substance.   [4771]

O'BRIEN, J. F. "Teilhard and Aristotle: What is Radial and What is Tangential?" *NewSchol* 49(1975), 486-491. Develops further Anderson's arguments (#4588) about compatibility of the cosmologies of these two thinkers.   [4772]

O'HARA, M. L., ed. *Substances and Things: Aristotle's Doctrine of Physical Substance in Recent Essays*. Washington, DC: Univ. Pr. of America, 1982. Collection of essays, which are abstracted herein.   [4773]

OLDROYD, D. R. "The Doctrine of Property — Conferring Principles in Chemistry: Origins and Antecedents." *Organon* 12(1976-77), 139-155. Includes discussions of P's and Ar's views of substance or chemical principles.   [4774]

OWEN, G. E. L. "Aristotle on the Snares of Ontology," in #1268, pp. 69-95. Examines Ar's use of "to be" (*einai*) in light of his concern to show that the same expression may have many different senses. Sorts out three different existential uses of the verb: 1) as a predicate of individuals, 2) as a predicate of classes or universals, and 3) as a predicate of such things as time, place, the void, and mathematicals.   [4775]

——. "Logic and Metaphysics in Some Earlier Works of Aristotle," in #4598, pp. 13-32. Explores Ar's thesis that all entities can be studied by examining the basic entity (substance) to which others are related. Ar, despite his characteristic insight into ambiguity of notion of being, is able to argue his thesis by connecting various senses of "being" to a single primary sense.   [4776]

——. "Particular and General." *PAS* 79(1978-79), 1-21. Examines Ar's requirement that a substance be both a *this* and *what-is-it*, and how Ar attempts to hold these recalcitrants together in one focus.   [4777]

——. "The Platonism of Aristotle." *PBA* 51(1965), 125-150; also in #4598, pp. 14-34; also published separately by Oxford Univ. Pr., 1967. Contrary to Jaeger (1923), argues that Ar moves from sharp and rather schematic criticism of P to an avowed sympathy with P's metaphysical program.   [4778]

OWENS, J. "The Aristotelian Argument for the Material Principle of Bodies," in #3634, pp. 122-135; also in #5350, pp. 193-209. Examines Ar's argument for an ultimate material principle based on generation of natural bodies.   [4779]

——. *The Doctrine of Being in the Aristotelian* Metaphysics: *A Study in the Greek Background of Mediaeval Thought.* Toronto: Pontif. Inst. of Medieval Studies, 1978; 3rd ed. Analysis of *Meta* concludes that ancient commentators were basically correct in their readings of Ar. He cannot be forced into medieval or modern modes of thought. Treatises in *Meta* must be studied in order in which Ar intended them to be read, not in order of composition. Extensive bibliography, updated for 3rd ed.   [4780]

——. "The Doctrine of Being in the Aristotelian *Metaphysics* Revisited," in #68, pp. 33-59. Surveys trends on this question in the 1950's, '60's, and '70's, looking especially at relationship scholars have seen between Ar's ontology and his theology.   [4781]

——. "The Grounds of Universality in Aristotle." *AmPhQ* 3(1966), 162-169; also in #3634, pp. 48-58. Grounds for universality in Ar are twofold: 1) in every sensible thing there is a basic formal principle that, though individual, brings each instance into formal identity with all other instances, 2) in human intellectual cognition there is an active principle that raises knowledge above status of photographing or registering and actualizes what was only potential in the real thing.   [4782]

——. "Is There Any Ontology in Aristotle?" *Dial*(Can) 25(1986), 697-707. This term can be traced back only to 1613. As currently defined, it cannot be applied to Ar's metaphysical doctrine.   [4783]

——. "Matter and Predication in Aristotle," in #3634, pp. 35-47. Examines Ar's claim that a substance or substantial form can be predicated of matter in light of his position that matter is itself wholly undetermined and entirely unintelligible.   [4784]

——. "The Present Status of Alpha Elatton in the Aristotelian *Metaphysics*" *AGPh* 66(1984), 148-169. Book is useful introduction to later parts of *Meta*.   [4785]

——. cf. #791.

PAGE, C. "Predicating Forms of Matter in Aristotle's *Metaphysics*." *RMeta* 39(1985), 57-82. To speak of "form-matter" predication is actually to imply two types of predication, but both can be subsumed in Ar's ontology.   [4786]

PAMPAPTHY RAO, A. *Aristotle's First Philosophy in Proper Perspective* Part I. West Bengal: Centre of Advanced Study in Philosophy, 1968. Sees defense of science as primary theme of Ar's philosophizing.   [4787]

PECCORINI, F. L. "Does 'Being' Loom Behind Aristotle's 'Ousia'? An Essay on Ontology." *Filosofia Oggi* 5(1982), 457-483. Examines *Meta* 5, 8, 11 and 12 to trace how Ar unifies reality in the concept of *ousia*.   [4788]

PENNER, T. "Verbs and the Identity of Actions — A Philosophical Exercise in the Interpretation of Aristotle," in #3625, pp. 393-461; also in #82, pp. 393-460. The *energeia-kinesis* distinction should be understood by investigating what Ar means when he says in connection with walking that the *whence* and the *whither* constitute the form.   [4789]

PETERSON, J. "Aristotle's Incomplete Causal Theory." *Thom* 36(1972), 420-432. Weaknesses of Ar's theory of four causes include his failure to distinguish between the cause of something coming-to-be and its actual existence; incompatibility between his equation of efficient causes of Being with his idea that "actual causes are simultaneous with their effects."   [4790]

PETERSON, S. "Substitution in Aristotelian Technical Contexts." *PhilStud* 47(1985), 249-256. Response to Lewis (#4729) whose account does not do justice to Ar's account of primary and secondary substances.   [4791]

POLANSKY, R. "Aristotle's Treatment of *Ousia* in *Metaphysics* V 8." *SJPh* 21(1983), 57-66. *Meta* 5.8 provides a convenient summary of Ar's reading of earlier concepts of *ousia* and his own conclusions on the subject.   [4792]

——. "'*Energeia*' in Aristotle's *Metaphysics* IX." *AncPh* 3(1983), 160-170. Ar's distinction between *energeia* (activity) and *kinesis* (motion) can be defended if *energeiai* are understood to be "peculiar psychical operations."   [4793]

POTTS, T. C. "States, Activities, and Performances, Part I." *PAS* Suppl. 39(1965), 65-84. Examines Ar's distinctions between *kinesis* and *energeia*, *echein* and *energein*, *poiesis* and *praxis*.   [4794]

RANKIN, K. "The Complete Reality of Substance." *Mind* 91(1982), 377-397. Defends Ar's exclusive attribution of complete reality to substance.   [4795]

REALE, G. *The Concept of First Philosophy and the Unity of the* Metaphysics *of Aristotle*, trans. J. R. Catan. Albany, SUNY Pr., 1980. Reasserts unitary reading of *Meta*; argues it contains Ar's conception of first philosophy fully formed, consolidated in its structural lines. Also contains translation of Theophrastus' works on metaphysics.   [4796]

RECK, A. J. "Being and Substance." *RMeta* 31(1978), 533-554. Ar's concept of Being has not been improved upon by idealist, materialist, or process philosophers.   [4797]

REGIS, E. "Aristotle on Universals." *Thom* 40(1976), 135-152. Ar is not a moderate realist. In his view universals have their basis in things but they exist only in the mind.   [4798]

——. "Aristotle's 'Principle of Individuation'." *Phron* 21(1976), 157-166. Ar does not have to account for individuation by means of matter or form. Fact that numerically distinct individuals exist is primary for him, i. e., it does not require explanation. [4799]

ROMANO, J. J. "Aristotle's Assumption of an Intelligible World." *Apeir* 7 #1(1973), 1-13. Ar's assumption that world is intelligible is not circular reasoning.   [4800]

RORTY, R. "Genus as Matter: A Reading of *Metaphysics* Z-H," in #65, pp. 393-420. Plausibility of saying that substance is form only appears when this is taken together with claim that proximate matter and form are identical. Also, Ar's claim that genus is matter must be taken seriously.   [4801]

———. "Matter as Goo: Comments on Grene's Paper." *Synthèse* 28(1974), 71-77. Reply to #3905. Matter in Ar's definition must be some indiscriminate stuff if it is found in more than one kind of thing. But such a reading is inconsistent with other aspects of Ar's thought.   [4802]

ROSS, S. D. "Aristotle: The Heresy of Orthodoxy," in *Metaphysical Aporia and Philosophical Heresy* (Albany: SUNY Pr., 1989), pp. 89-116. Ar did not resolve the aporia between one and many. His concept that individual substances are always ontologically prior to other modes of being cannot be made compatible with his view of pluralism of principles and causes.   [4803]

ROWE, C. J. "The Proof From Relations in the *Peri Ideon*: Further Reconsideration." *Phron* 24(1979), 270-281. Evaluates three attempts to reconstruct an argument from Ar's lost work *Peri Ideon* (*On Ideas*). G. E. L. Owen's suggestion (1957) seems more likely than Barford's (#4597) or Leszl's (#4728).   [4804]

RYAN, E. E. "Pure Form in Aristotle." *Phron* 18(1973), 209-224. Challenges view that Ar subscribed to doctrine of pure form: there exist entities which are not only intelligible and free from matter, but also meet Ar's criteria for being forms.   [4805]

SACKSTEDER, W. "Some Words Aristotle Never Uses: Attributes, Essences, and Universals." *NewSchol* 60(1986), 427-453. Greek has no nouns that correlate to "attributes," "essences," and "universals." Ar is more likely to use a phrase which we translate by a word. He was investigating problems, not giving dogmatic answers.   [4806]

SCALTSAS, T. "Substratum, Subject, and Substance." *AncPh* 5(1985), 215-240. Examines Ar's "unity of substance" and the necessity for it in his system. The system requires a substratum, though it need not be a bare particular.   [4807]

SCHOFIELD, M. "*Metaph*. Z3: Some Suggestions." *Phron* 17(1972), 97-101. New reading of Ar's argument against the theory that a substance cannot be predicated of a substrate.   [4808]

SELLARS, W. "Aristotle's Metaphysics: An Interpretation," in #77, pp. 73-124. For Ar form of a thing *is* the thing itself. It can come to be and cease to exist.   [4809]

———. "Raw Materials, Subjects and Substrate," in #77, pp. 137-152. Substance and matter both have an internal teleology. Forms of material things are perishable, thus necessitating existence of pure, imperishable Forms.   [4810]

———. "Substance and Form in Aristotle," in #77, pp. 125-136. Ar seems to hold that souls are not only the essence of things to which they belong but that souls themselves have essence.   [4811]

SHARPLES, R. W. "Form in Aristotle — Individual or Universal?" *LCM* 5(1980), 223-229. For Ar forms exist in individuals but do not differ in any way except numerically. The form in the individual comprises only the essential features of the individual, not its accidental qualities.   [4812]

SKOUSGAARD, S. "Wisdom and Being in Aristotle's First Philosophy." *Thom* 40(1976), 444-474. Ar's concept of wisdom is linked to his ontology. Wisdom is dynamic, not dogmatic, because of the tension between Being-itself and the ways of being.   **[4813]**

SODDON, F. A., Jr. "The Principle of Contradiction in *Metaphysics Gamma*." *NewSchol* 55(1981), 191-207. Offers an historical examination of principle of contradiction with aim of showing it to be "true of being *qua* being."   **[4814]**

SOKOLOWSKI, R. "Matter, Elements, and Substance in Aristotle." *JHPh* 8(1970), 263-288; also in #4773, pp. 91-116. Explores whether simple bodies — earth, air, fire, and water — are substances and whether they are composed of substantial form and matter. Ar's idea of insubstantiality of elements is based on his theory of judgment as well as his chemistry.   **[4814a]**

——. cf. #5385.

SOMMERS, M. C. "Aristotle on Substance and Predication: A Mediaeval View." *PACPhA* 61(1987), 78-87. Some modern readings of Ar's four ways that something can be "in itself" (*kath'auto*) resemble views of medieval commentators.   **[4815]**

SORABJI, R. "Analyses of Matter, Ancient and Modern." *PAS* 86(1985-86), 1-22. Focuses on two recurrent themes in analysis of matter and body: body is extension endowed with properties, and bodies are solid, and discusses Ar's treatment of these themes.   **[4815a]**

SPELLMAN, L. "Specimens of Natural Kinds and the Apparent Inconsistency of *Metaphysics* Zeta." *AncPh* 9(1989), 49-65. Specimens have only the properties necessary for membership in a particular kind.   **[4816]**

SPRAGUE, R. K. "Aristotle and the Metaphysics of Sleep." *RMeta* 31(1977), 230-241. Applies concepts such as actuality/potentiality, matter, form, *hexis* (habit), etc., to analysis of sleep.   **[4817]**

——. "*Metaphysics* and Multiple Births." *Apeir* 20(1987), 97-102. Ar thought no act of generation, metaphysical or biological, should produce more than one offspring. **[4818]**

STACK, G. J. "Aristotle: The Conception of Substance in Book Zeta of the *Metaphysics*." *ModSch* 44(1967), 231-242. Discusses nature of *ousia* in *Meta* Z and analyzes relationship between logical conception of primary *ousia* and ontological conception of *ousia*.   **[4819]**

——. cf. #4353.

STAHL, D. "Stripped Away: Some Contemporary Obscurities Surrounding *Metaphysics* Z 3 (1029a10-26)." *Phron* 26(1981), 177-180. Attempts to interpret Ar's statement that "When all else is stripped off evidently nothing but matter remains."   **[4820]**

STARR, D. E. *Entity and Existence: An Ontological Investigation of Aristotle and Heidegger.* New York: Franklin, 1976. Assesses claims to ontological ultimacy of Ar's "substance" and "existence" as considered in Heidegger's early and middle works.**[4821]**

STEVENSON, J. G. "Being *Qua* Being." *Apeir* 9 #2(1975), 42-50. Ar's understanding of "being *qua* being" is broader than some have maintained. It includes all being, not just the divine. Metaphysics is more than theology.   **[4822]**

SUPPES, P "Aristotle's Concept of Matter and its Relation to Modern Concepts of Matter." *Synthèse* 28(1974), 27-50. Examines Ar's concept of matter, and defends correctness both scientifically and philosophically of the "central doctrine."   **[4823]**

SYKES, R. D. "Form in Aristotle." *Ph* 50(1975), 311-331. Asks whether form of a non-living sensible substance, such as "form of this house," is contradictory, and argues that Ar's position is self-contradictory.   **[4824]**

TALLON, A. "On the Confusion of *Modus Essendi* and *Modus Dicendi* in Aristotle's *Metaphysics*." *ModSch* 51(1974), 236-238. The source of confusion between these two modes is the role which matter plays in each.   **[4825]**

TARAN, L. "Aristotle's Classification of Numbers in *Metaphysics* M6, 108a 15-37." *GRBS* 19(1978), 83-90. Ar classifies numbers in this passage to facilitate argument against Platonic views of number and Form. What he says here cannot be applied to his concept of mathematical number.   **[4826]**

TAYLOR, C. C. W. "States, Activities, and Performances, Part II." *PAS* Suppl. 39(1965), 85-102. Examines Potts' (#4794) exegetical treatment of *kinesis* and *energeia*, *echein* and *energein*, *poiesis*, and *praxis*.   **[4827]**

TELOH, H. "Aristotle's *Metaphysics* Z 13." *CanJPh* 9(1979), 77-89. *Meta* Z 13 is not a discussion of Ar's views on universals and substances but a criticism of Platonic Forms.   **[4828]**

———. "The Universal in Aristotle." *Apeir* 13(1979), 70-78. In *Meta* Ar makes the apparently inconsistent assertions that form is universal and that it is substance, but that nothing universal is substance. The contradiction is resolved by realizing that he conceives of both particular and universal forms.   **[4829]**

———. "What Aristotle Should Have Said in *Metaphysics* Z." *SJPh* 20(1982), 241-256. While individual concretum is Ar's choice for primary substance in *Cat* and form is primary substance in *Meta*, he should have chosen an individual concretum in *Meta*. Concrete individual better satisfies six of his criteria for substance.   **[4830]**

THOBE, U. A. "Hylomorphism Revisited." *NewSchol* 42(1968), 226-253. For Ar, problem of establishing doctrine of a radical hylomorphic constitution of natural substance in face of physical and chemical theories is not a genuine problem.   **[4831]**

THORP, J. "Aristotle on Being and Truth." *De Philosophia* 3(1982), 1-9. To understand what Ar means in *Meta* 9.10 by attributing truth and falsity to things, we must realize connection between truth and existence, falsity and non-existence.   **[4832]**

TWEEDALE, M. M. "Aristotle's *Realism*." *CanJPh* 18(1988), 501-526. Although Ar is generally held to be a realist, his realism is tenuous and lacks numerical unity. Each universal is merely the various particulars which it encompasses.   **[4833]**

———. "Aristotle's Universals." *AustlJPh* 65(1987), 412-426. Claims that Ar was either a nominalist or a conceptualist in his theory of universals cannot be supported by careful reading of his text. He appears to have held to a form of realism.   **[4834]**

UPTON, T. V. "Aristotle on Existence: Escaping the Snares of Ontology?" *NewSchol* 62(1988), 373-399. Challenges Owen's claim in #4775 that Ar fails to recognize different uses of existence.   **[4835]**

────. "Aristotle on Hypothesis and the Unhypothesized First Principle." *RMeta* 39(1985), 283-301. Challenges interpretations by Kirwan (#4718) and Ross (publ. in 1924) of Ar's hypothesis in *Meta* 4, 1005b6 ff.   **[4836]**

────. "Naming and Non-Being in Aristotle." *PACPhA* 59(1985), 275-288. Ar indicates that it is possible to signify "non-beings" but it is not clear what he means by "non-beings." Reviews four most likely possibilities for "non-beings."   **[4837]**

────. "Psychological and Metaphysical Dimensions of Non-Contradiction in Aristotle." *RMeta* 36(1983), 591-606. Dialectical dimension of principle of non-contradiction should not be emphasized at expense of consideration of psychological and metaphysical grounds and dimensions.   **[4838]**

VAUGHT, C. G. "Categories and the Real Order." *Monist* 66(1983), 438-449. Criticizes Sellars' claim (#4811) that form and matter are identical with substance. They are identical, but only "according to different modes of being."   **[4839]**

VERBEKE, G. "Aristotle's Metaphysics Viewed by the Ancient Greek Commentators" in #3631, pp. 107-127. Shows various commentators' understanding of Ar's metaphysics with respect to relationship of metaphysics to physics and theology.   **[4840]**

────. "The Meaning of Potency in Aristotle," in #60, pp. 55-73. Concept of potency underlies Ar's philosophy. It expresses a dynamic, teleological world view, which sees things as more than what they are at any given time. Potency is not a creative power. It is ability to receive influences from outside.   **[4841]**

────. "Substance in Aristotle." *PACPhA* 61(1987), 35-51. Ar defines substance/Being on two levels. On the physical level substance is the form — the animating, organizing principle — of individual things. On the intelligible level, it is pure form, separate from any material being.   **[4842]**

VERDENIUS, W. J. "Hylozoism in Aristotle," in #60, pp. 101-114. Ar's concept of living matter helps to explain some difficult aspects of his general world view, his doctrine of four elements, and the connection between matter and form.   **[4843]**

VLASTOS, G. "The 'Two-Leveled Paradoxes' in Aristotle," in #1292, pp. 323-354. Examines those texts in which Ar exploits "two-leveled paradoxes" — sentences of the form, "the idea of F is P." Ar analyzes these as true if P is predicated of "the Idea *qua* Idea" or false if P is predicated of it "*qua* F."   **[4844]**

WATSON, G. "Aristotle's Concept of Matter." *PhilStud* (Ireland) 20(1972), 175-184. Ar recognizes three levels of substance: unmoved mover(s), heavenly bodies, bodies "under the moon." Explores how concept of matter applies to each level.   **[4845]**

WEDIN, M. V. "Aristotle on the Range of the Principle of Non-Contradiction." *Log&An*

25(1982), 87-92. Since Lukasiewicz (#4500) *Meta* Gamma 1006b28-34 has been taken to show that Ar applied the Principle of Non-contradiction to substances only, but it can be shown to have wider application.   **[4846]**

――. "Singular Statements and Essentialism in Aristotle," in #3637, pp. 67-88. Explores two competing interpretations of Ar's essentialism: essences are necessary for existence of objects; possessing a given essential property is only sufficient, but not necessary, for the existence of a given object.   **[4847]**

WEIDEMANN, H. "In Defence of Aristotle's Theory of Predication." *Phron* 25(1980), 76-87. Reply to Owen (#4784) and others. The distinctions which Ar makes between essential and accidental predication do not lead to confusion between statements which predicate essentially and statements of identity.   **[4848]**

WEIN, S. "Are Being and Unity of the Genera of All Things? A Note on *Metaphysics* 998b 21-26." *ModSch* 61(1983), 49-52. Whether or not the argument about being and unity in this passage is valid depends on whether Ar is discussing the nature of being and unity or their definition on a species/genus analogy.   **[4849]**

WHEELER, S. C. "The Theory of Matter from *Metaphysics* Zeta, Eta, Theta." *SIF* 9(1977), 13-22. Examines Ar's assertion that matter is potency and its implications for his theory of matter.   **[4850]**

WHITE, M. J. "Aristotle's Concept of *Theoria* and the *Energia-Kinesis* Distinction." *JHPh* 18(1980), 253-265. Depending on how one interprets verb forms in *Meta* 9.6, *energia* and *kinesis* can be taken as states, not activities. *Theoria* can also be a state, leading to conclusion that the connection between the contemplative and active life needs to be re-analyzed.   **[4851]**

――. "Causes as Necessary Conditions: Aristotle, Alexander of Aphrodisias, and J. L. Mackie," in #3637, pp. 157-189. Explores origin of conception of "causes" (*aitia*) as necessary conditions in Ar.   **[4852]**

――. "Genus as Matter in Aristotle?" *IntStudPh* 7(1975), 41-56. Reply to #4801. Interpretation of hylomorphic first substances needs to consider Ar's genus terms and matter terms as separate except in certain cases.   **[4853]**

――. "On Continuity: Aristotle Versus Topology?" *H&PhLog* 9(1988), 1-12. Compares Ar's account of continuity as something without seams or joints to modern topological theories.   **[4854]**

WHITE, N. P. "Aristotle on Sameness and Oneness." *PhR* 80(1971), 177-197. In *Topics*, but not in later works, Ar deals with the problem of identity. He seems to have turned his attention to some issues raised by P.   **[4855]**

――. "Origins of Aristotle's Essentialism." *RMeta* 26(1972), 57-85. Seeks to spell out Ar's essentialism with respect to sensible particulars, focusing on distinction between substance and non-substance.   **[4856]**

WHITING, J. E. "Commentary on Furth's 'Aristotle on the Unity of Form'." *PBACAPh* 2(1986), 268-273. Challenges Furth's argument (#4670) that Ar recognizes only one form for each species. Also suggests that division between male and female activity is made at a genus higher than that proposed by Furth.   **[4857]**

———. "Form and Individuation in Aristotle." *HPhQ* 3(1986), 359-377. Ar has to introduce the concept of individual forms as principles of individuation because matter cannot serve that function.   **[4858]**

WIENER, M. H. "Potency and Potentiality in Aristotle." *NewSchol* 44(1970), 515-534. By comparing Ar's logical and metaphysical vocabulary, one can see that the concepts of potency and potentiality are not interchangeable, even though Ar sometimes speaks of them as such.   **[4859]**

WILLIAMS, C. J. F. "Aristotle's Theory of Descriptions." *PhR* 94(1985), 63-80. Ar's accounts of accidental predication and accidental identity can be interpreted as putting forward the same view as B. Russell's theory of descriptives.   **[4860]**

WITT, C. "Aristotelian Essentialism Revisited." *JHPh* 27(1989), 285-298. Ar considers essences to be causes, not a means of classification. An essence is not a necessary property of the substance whose essence it is.   **[4861]**

———. "Hylomorphism in Aristotle." *JPh* 84(1987), 673-681. Examines relationship between form and matter in Aristotelian composite substance. Bases interpretation on two ideas: (1) matter and form should be understood in terms of potentiality and actuality; (2) potentiality and actuality should be understood as ways of being.   **[4862]**

———. *Substance and Essence in Aristotle: An Interpretation of* Metaphysics *VII-IX*. Ithaca, NY: Cornell Univ. Pr., 1989. Non-specialist study of this important facet of Ar's thought. Argues that substances are what cause things to exist. They are individual, not characteristic of species. Ar's theory of essences is significantly different from modern essentialism.   **[4863]**

WOODS, M. J. "Problems in *Metaphysics* Z, Chapter 13," in #3625, pp. 215-238. Clarifies Ar's theory of substance through an examination of his discussion of whether universal terms can be names of substances. Argues that Z13 supports thesis "Nothing that is predicated universally can be substance" rather than "no universal can be substance."   **[4864]**

———. "Substance and Essence in Aristotle." *PAS* 75(1974-75), 167-180. Ar's difficult doctrine of the identity of substance and essence developed from his need to reject self-predication and other difficulties similar to the TMA.   **[4865]**

For related items see #138, #821, #1232, #1822, #1824, #1898, #3667, #3905, #3984, #4000, #4412, #4437, #4566, #4581, #5323, #5428, #5503.

MODAL LOGIC

Modal logic deals with questions of probability, possibility/impossibility, necessity, free will and determinism. If one thing logically leads to another, will the second thing happen *of necessity*? If something *may* happen, *must* it happen? What is the relationship between true conditions and false conclusions in logical statements? The Megarian Diodorus tried to use such questions to ridicule the possibility of motion. His so-called "Master Argument" provoked lengthy rebuttals for centuries. Philo of Megara, in the fourth century B. C., formalized some of the propositions involved in the debate. Ar contributed to the controversy in Book 9 of his *De interpretatione*. Christian philosophers in late antiquity and the Middle Ages did not pursue the subject, probably because they answered questions about future contingency in theological terms. For them God, not logical probability, decided what would or could happen. The publication of A. O. Lovejoy's *The Great Chain of Being* in 1936 reawakened an interest in the subject which J. Hintikka and others have nurtured.

Let us take a statement of the form "If *x*, then *y*." That is to say, "If a certain proposition is true, then a certain conclusion results." Does that statement always, of necessity, hold? If we substitute real conditions for *x* and *y*, what might we learn? Let us say, "If it rains, the grass will grow." On the surface that statement appears inarguable to most people. But not to a philosopher, of course. Does it mean that rain forces the grass to grow? Does the grass have no choice but to grow? The verb "will" can have that implication, as in "You will clean your room before we go get ice cream." But it can also have a less definite meaning, as in "If your father gets a raise, we will buy a new car." In that context it means something less definite, a possibility, even a probability, but not a certainty.

Ar's concern with this problem of contingency probably grew out of his interest in logic in general but may have been heightened by claims made by the Megarians. Many thinkers of his day were concerned to combat the determinism of Diodorus, a philosopher who was given more attention in his own time than in ours. Ar examined the various permutations that we can work on a statement such as "If it rains, the grass will grow" (If *r*, then *g*). We can negate both parts of it: "If it does not rain, the grass will not grow" (If not *r*, then not *g*). We can negate only one part of it: "If it does not rain, the grass will grow" (If not *r*, then *g*) or "If it rains, the grass will not grow" (If *r*, then not *g*). Can those forms, any or all of them, be true? Another way of stating the problem is to ask if one thing entails another, i. e., makes it inevitable.

Consider these possibilities. What if we are in the midst of a drought but notice that our neighbor's lawn is lush and green? It could mean that he has been watering it on the sly, or that there is some sort of underground spring (or a leaky septic tank) under his property. Or perhaps he planted a type of hardy grass that requires very little water. Whatever the explanation, the proposition "If not *r*, then not *g*" does not seem to be *necessarily* true in every case. Or perhaps it rained, but only once this month. Lawns are turning brown all over town. The first proposition (If *r*, then *g*) appears not to be true in every case, or at least needs further definition about the adequacy of rainfall.

These examples of the problem of future contingencies are perhaps too simple, but they should serve to illustrate the issues that Ar is dealing with in his treatment of modal logic. Much of his argument centers around the example of a statement such as "A sea battle will take place tomorrow." Does that statement imply necessity, possibility, or some degree of probability? How can one judge the truth-value of such a statement until after the fact? Another aspect of the problem is the use of constructions such as "follows from." What does it mean to say that one statement "follows from" another? Does it imply necessity or simply logical progression? These problems have metaphysical implications for Ar because they are linked to the distinction he makes between potentiality and actuality.

ANSCOMBE, G. E. M. "Aristotle and the Sea Battle: *De Interpretatione*, Chapter 9," in #3625, pp. 15-33. Analyzes Ar's views on truth of future contingents. **[4866]**

BARKER, J. A., and **PAXSON, T. D.** "Aristotle vs. Diodorus: Who Won the Fatalism Debate?" *PhResArch* 11(1985), 41-75. Develops a modified system of standard logic to argue that both Ar and Diodorus presented valid arguments in their famous debate over necessity and fate. **[4867]**

BOSLEY, R. "Hintikka on Modalities and Determinism in Aristotle," in *Jaakko Hintikka*, ed. R. J. Bogdan (Dordrecht, Netherlands: Reidel, 1987), pp. 247-260. Examines Hintikka's work on Ar's modality and determinism in light of Hintikka's efforts to show Ar's tendency to blur distinctions between apodictic and assertoric propositions. **[4868]**

BRADIE, M., and **MILLER, F. D.** "Teleology and Natural Necessity in Aristotle." *HPhQ* 1(1984), 133-146. Teleology and natural necessity are linked by irreducible compatibilism. Ar's view of that relation raises some problems. **[4869]**

BRANDON, E. P. "Hintikka on *Akolouthein*." *Phron* 23(1978), 173-178. Reply to Hintikka's (#4888) comments against traditional reading of *De interp* 12-13 and his suggestion that this verb be translated "is compatible with," not "follows from." **[4870]**

BROADIE, S. W. "Necessity and Deliberation: Making Sense of *De Interpretatione* A 9." *CanJPh* 17(1987), 289-306. Seeks to justify Ar's assertion that "if everything were necessary there would be no need to deliberate." **[4871]**

BROGAN, A. P. "Aristotle's Logic of Statements about Contingency." *Mind* 76(1967), 49-61. Identifies the mistaken inference which Ar makes in his argument about contingencies and shows how this led him to deduce (validly but wrongly) that contingent statements are convertible. **[4872]**

———. "Modality and Quantification in Aristotle." *Mind* 82(1973), 123-124. Reply to Kosman (#4894). Ar does not "quantify" modal statements. **[4873]**

CODE, A. "Aristotle's Response to Quine's Objections to Modal Logic." *JPhilLog* 5(1976), 159-186. Some of Quine's objections to modal logic apply as well to notions used to explain temporal change. Ar's reaction involves concepts which lend themselves to kind of semantic analysis which has improved our understanding of modality. **[4874]**

DANCY, R. M. "Aristotle and the Priority of Actuality," in #4893, pp. 73-115. Ar did not satisfactorily resolve the dilemma of how potentiality can exist without being an actuality, or actuality without being a potentiality. **[4875]**

DICKASON, A. "Aristotle, the Sea Fight, and the Cloud." *JHPh* 14(1976), 11-22.

Considers most important commentaries, traces development of recent criticism, and concludes that Ar is concerned with problems of both truth and of necessity, but is not sure of their relation.   **[4876]**

FINE, G. "Aristotle on Determinism: A Review of Richard Sorabji's *Necessity, Cause and Blame.*" *PhR* 90(1981), 561-580. Challenges Sorabji's reading (#4908) of caused but unnecessitated actions with respect to idea of responsibility.   **[4877]**

———. "Truth and Necessity in *De interpretatione.*" *HPhQ* 1(1984), 23-47. Ar's rebuttal of fatalism is based on assumption that arguments for that position are not just unsound but invalid.   **[4878]**

FREDE, D. "Aristotle on the Limits of Determinism: Accidental Causes in *Metaphysics* E.3," in #3809, pp. 207-225. Examines Ar's claim that accidental causes must be "generable" and "destructible" without undergoing a proper process of coming to be or passing away, and various questions that arise as a result of this claim.   **[4879]**

———. "The Sea-Battle Reconsidered: A Defence of the Traditional Interpretation." *OSAP* 3(1985), 31-87. Ar encounters problem of Sea-Battle and problem of truth or falsity of future contingents when he develops distinction between *dunamis* and *energeia*, as seen in both his physical and metaphysical writings.   **[4880]**

GILL, M. L. "Sorabji and Aristotle Against Determinism." *AncPh* 2(1982), 122-133. Sorabji (#4908) is correct to say that Ar's theories allow for free will, but a somewhat different reconstruction of Ar's theory is suggested.   **[4881]**

HINTIKKA, J. "Aristotelian Infinity." *PhR* 75(1966), 197-218; also in #4890, pp. 114-134; also in #4598, pp. 125-139. For Ar the potential for infinite division always exists, and as long as something potentially exists, it will, in his view, come to exist. Thus infinity exists potentially.   **[4882]**

———. "Aristotle and the Ambiguity of Ambiguity," in #4890, pp. 1-26; also in #4893, pp. 57-72. Ar's concept of possibility is more easily grasped when one examines his comments on two types of ambiguity. He often bases his criticisms of other thinkers on ambiguities in their language which they failed to notice.   **[4883]**

———., et al. *Aristotle on Modality and Determinism.* Amsterdam: North Holland Publ., 1977. Some of Ar's ideas about necessity, potentiality, and actuality require an understanding of modality which Ar himself does not argue for, and could not. He was unable to resolve this dilemma and create a coherent system.   **[4884]**

———. "Aristotle on the Realization of Possibilities in Time," in #4890, pp. 93-113. Discussion of A. O. Lovejoy's view (1936) that everything which is possible will eventually be realized. Ar accepts this principle. This causes him to blur the distinction between modal logic and plain syllogistic.   **[4885]**

———. "Aristotle's Different Possibilities," in #4890, pp. 27-40. Analyzes concept of contingency in *PrAn* 1. Ar defines contingent as something (properly) possible but not necessary. "Contingent" and "possible" are not homonyms.   **[4886]**

———. "On Aristotle's Modal Syllogistic," in #4890, pp. 135-146. Somewhat technical discussion of Ar's reliance on different principles, not all of which are compatible, in different parts of his modal syllogistic.   **[4887]**

———. "On the Interpretation of *De Interpretatione* 12-13," in #4890, pp. 41-61. Understanding of this passage depends on meaning of: *symbainein* ("to follow logically"), *akolouthein* ("to be compatible with"), and *hepesthai* ("to go together with").   **[4888]**

———. "The Once and Future Sea Fight: Aristotle's Discussion of Future Contingents in *De Interpretatione* 9," in #4890, pp. 147-178. Discusses traditional attempts to resolve problem of future contingents. Ar's difficulties arise from trying to distinguish temporally qualified from temporally unqualified statements. Article contains useful bibliography on subject.   **[4889]**

———. *Time and Necessity. Studies in Aristotle's Theory of Modality.* Oxford: Clarendon Pr., 1973. Collection of previously published papers, some revised. All are abstracted herein.   **[4890]**

———. cf. #1234.

KARPENKO, A. S. "Aristotle, Lukasiewicz, and Factor-Semantics." *ActaPhFenn* 25(1982), 7-21. Discusses standard interpretation of Ar's solution to problem of status of propositions about future contingent events.   **[4891]**

KIRWAN, C. "Aristotle on the Necessity of the Present," *OSAP* 4(1986), 167-187. Investigates doctrine of Necessity of Present, which concerns relationship between necessity, or possibility, and time. Claims a proposition is possible at a time if and only if it is consistent with what is actual at that time.   **[4892]**

KNUUTTILA, S., ed. *Reforging the Great Chain of Being: Studies in the History of Modal Theories.* Dordrecht, Netherlands: Reidel, 1980. Collection of essays. Relevant items are abstracted herein.   **[4893]**

KOSMAN, L. A. "Aristotle on Incontrovertible Modal Propositions." *Mind* 79(1970), 254-258. Reply to #4872; technical defense of Ar's argument that, if something is contingently not true, then the reverse contingency is not true either.   **[4894]**

KUNG, J. "*Metaphysics* 8.4: Can Be But Will Not Be." *Apeir* 12 #1(1978), 32-36. Discusses translation of a phrase which may clear up confusion over whether something which is possible is also necessary.   **[4895]**

LOWE, M. F. "Aristotle on the Sea-Battle: A Clarification." *Analysis* 40(1980), 55-59. In his discussion of determinism Ar does not deny the Law of the Excluded Middle, but he does not infer from it the necessity of all events. The ancient and medieval commentators read him this way, in spite of what some modern scholars maintain.   **[4896]**

McCALL, S. *Aristotle's Modal Syllogisms.* Amsterdam: North Holland Publ., 1965. Technical discussion of the mathematical basis of this facet of Ar's work.   **[4897]**

McCLELLAND, R. T. "Time and Modality in Aristotle *Metaphysics* IX,3-4." *AGPh* 63(1981), 130-149. Denies that Ar equates possibility with sometime truth and necessity with omnitemporal truth.   **[4898]**

McKIM, V. R. "Fatalism and the Future: Aristotle's Out." *RMeta* 25(1971), 80-111. *De interp* 9 is actually Ar's effort to resolve some semantic, not metaphysical, difficulties. He shows fatalism to be an untenable doctrine not because its underlying assumptions are false, but because they are ambiguous. **[4899]**

MIGNUCCI, M. *On a Controversial Demonstration of Aristotle's Modal Syllogistic: An Enquiry on* Prior Analytics *A 15.* Padua, Italy: Ed. Antenore, 1972. Technical formal demonstration of the syllogism with one categorical and one possible premise. Ar's proof appears to be logically correct. **[4900]**

MULHERN, M. M. "Aristotle on Universality and Necessity." *Log&An* 12(1969), 288-299. Replies to claims that Ar (*PostAn* 73) equates modality and quantity. **[4901]**

PARKS, R. Z. "On Formalizing Aristotle's Theory of Modal Syllogisms." *NDJFormLog* 13(1972), 385-386. Technical analysis of attempts to formalize Ar's theory of modal syllogisms in response to S. McCall (#4897). **[4902]**

PREUS, A. "Aristotle's Natural Necessity." *SIF* 1(1969), 91-100. Examines distinction between material necessity and simple, forced, or mechanical necessity. Biological necessity must be seen as conditional. **[4903]**

RESCHER, N. and **PARKS, Z.** "A New Approach to Aristotle's Apodeictic Syllogisms." *RMeta* 24(1971), 678-689; also in *Studies in Modality,* ed. N. Rescher (Oxford: Blackwell, 1974), 3-17. Technical discussion of Ar's insistence that, given a valid first figure categorical syllogism, the corresponding modal syllogism must be valid. **[4904]**

SHARPLES, R. W. "Aristotle and Necessity: A Clarification." *BICS* 31(1984), 197-198. Somewhat technical addendum to #4906. **[4905]**

————. "'If What is Earlier, Then of Necessity What is Later'? Some Ancient Discussions of Aristotle, *De generatione et corruptione* 2.11." *BICS* 26(1979), 27-44. Tries to understand Ar's views on *a tergo* conditional necessity by looking at how later commentators understood the passage. **[4906]**

SMITH, R. "New Light on Aristotle's Modal Concepts." *AncPh* 5(1985), 67-75. Discussion of #4919. **[4907]**

SORABJI, R. *Necessity, Cause, and Blame: Perspectives On Aristotle's Theory.* Ithaca, NY: Cornell Univ. Pr., 1980. Modern discussions of contingency and necessity owe much to Ar, though they differ in significant ways. Ar, e. g., recognizes more types of necessity than modern logicians do. His emphasis is more on time than cause. He should be considered an indeterminist. **[4908]**

SPELLMAN, L. "*DI* 9: An Exegetical Stalemate." *Apeir* 14(1980), 115-124. Ar cannot refute determinists' arguments, but he does assert they are fallacious when they go beyond claiming truth-value for statements about the future and claim that they are necessary. **[4909]**

TAYLOR, R. "Aristotle's Doctrine of Future Contingencies," in #41, pp. 522-545. Examines and defends Ar's argument that all propositions are either true or false, with exception of a limited class of propositions about future, viz., those that assert occurrence or non-occurrence of some future contingency.   **[4910]**

TOMBERLIN, J. E. "The Sea Battle Tomorrow and Fatalism." *Ph&PhenRes* 31(1971), 352-357. Examines treatments of Sea Battle argument found in *De interp* and shows how Ar's solution "undermines the more complicated 'solutions' to the puzzle."   **[4911]**

TRUNDLE, R. "*De Interpretatione* IX: The Problem of Future Truth or of Infinite Past Truth." *ModSch* 59(1981), 49-54. Analyzes Ar's notion of logic of possibility, and argues that with respect to problem of future truth, several traditional and contemporary approaches are inadequate.   **[4912]**

UPTON, T. V. "The Principle of Excluded Middle and Causality: Aristotle's More Complete Reply to the Determinists." *HPhQ* 4(1987), 359-367. Ar's implicit references to causality in *De Interp* 9 offer an adequate response to the determinists. He sees particular events as grounded in matter and maintains that all causes do not always produce the same effects.   **[4913]**

VAN ECK, J. B. M. "Another Interpretation of Aristotle's *De Interpretatione* IX: A Support for the So-Called Second Oldest or 'Mediaeval' Interpretation." *Vivarium* 26(1988), 19-38. Interpretation of this chapter is easier when one realizes the importance of historical necessity and the different roles which the Principle of Bivalence plays in statements about the past and those about the future.   **[4914]**

VAN RIJEN, J. *Aspects of Aristotle's Logic of Modalities.* Dordrecht, Netherlands: Kluwer, 1989. No modern commentators have been able to demonstrate that Ar held a consistent modal theory. But neither can it be shown that he held no such theory. One must take into account his semantic and ontological assumptions in order to understand his theories of modality (as well as on time).   **[4915]**

———. "The Principle of Plenitude, the *de omni-per se* Distinction and the Development of Modal Thinking." *AGPh* 66(1984), 61-88. Discusses modal theories in *PostAn* in response to work of Hintikka (#4884, #4890).   **[4916]**

VON WRIGHT, G. H. "Time, Truth and Necessity," in *Intention and Intentionality*, ed. C. Diamond (Ithaca, NY: Cornell Univ. Pr., 1979), pp. 237-250. Ar's difficulties over refuting determinism arise in part over his confusion between two senses of "true," which depend on whether the word is used with or without regard to time.   **[4917]**

WATERLOW, S. "Aristotle's Now." *PhQ* 34(1984), 104-128. Discusses how Ar combines two disparate concepts under "Now": that of temporal present as opposed to past and future, and that of an instant, a durationless point of time.   **[4918]**

———. *Passage and Possibility: A Study of Aristotle's Modal Concepts.* Oxford: Clarendon Pr., 1982. Examines Ar's treatment of necessity and possibility, and investigates his endorsement of some form of equivalence between temporal quantifiers "always" and "at some time," and modal operators "necessarily" and "possibly."   **[4919]**

WHITE, M. J. "Aristotle and Temporally Relative Modalities." *Analysis* 39(1979), 88-93. Somewhat technical discussion of a solution to Ar's modal dilemmas based on modification of his semantics of time.   **[4920]**

———. "Aristotle's Temporal Interpretation of Necessary Coming-to-be." *Phoenix* 34(1980), 208-218. Examines modal doctrines of Ar and Megarians and compares them to Stoic idea of eternal recurrence.   **[4921]**

———. "Fatalism and Causal Determinism: An Aristotelian Essay." *PhQ* 31(1981), 231-241. Ar's understanding of time determines whether a proposition pertaining to a future event is true or false in the present.   **[4922]**

———. "Necessity and Unactualized Possibilities in Aristotle." *PhilStud* 38(1980), 287-298. Somewhat technical discussion of semantic base of Ar's modal theory, looking at such issues as the necessity of the past and the cyclical nature of time.   **[4923]**

———. cf. #1241.

WHITE, N. "Identity, Modal Individuation, and Matter in Aristotle." *MidwStudPh* 11(1986), 475-494. Focuses on those cases in which Ar takes certain objects to be distinct and thinks they can be discriminated, and raises questions about what Ar thinks makes for discriminability.   **[4924]**

WIDENMAN, R. "Some Aspects of Time in Aristotle and Kierkegaard." *Kierkegaardiana* 8(1971), 7-22. With respect to Ar, focuses primarily on structure of "now" and its relation to time and motion.   **[4925]**

WILLIAMS, C. J. F. "Aristotle and Corruptibility. A Discussion of Aristotle, *De Caelo* I,xii." *RelStud* 1(1965), 95-107. On the question of whether something which is corruptible will necessarily pass away Ar is "hopelessly muddled."   **[4926]**

———. "True Tomorrow, Never True Today." *PhQ* 28(1978), 285-299. Much confusion about future contingent statements has arisen from Ar's efforts to introduce the concept of truth into the discussion of fatalism in *De interp* 9.   **[4927]**

———. "What Is, Necessarily Is, When it Is." *Analysis* 40(1980), 127-131. Examines Ar's distinction between a) "One or the other of them is necessarily the case" and b) "Necessarily, one or the other is the case", and seeks to explain the purpose of the distinction.   **[4928]**

For related items see #5398, #5484.

PHYSICS

The word "physics" is derived from a Greek verb meaning to grow or produce. The noun *physis* describes nature, the "physical" world around us, the world that changes moment by moment. It is that change which is Ar's theme in the work called the *Physics*.

Philosophers before Ar had either denied that change was real (Parmenides and Zeno), had claimed that constant change made secure knowledge difficult if not impossible to obtain (Heraclitus), or had said that things which change cannot be appropriate objects of scientific study (Plato). But Ar is enough of a realist to know that change — any motion, growth, or passage from one state or condition to another — is undeniable. How, then, is one to explain it?

For Ar the explanation is an object's natural tendency toward something. To give a classic (if not hackneyed) example, an acorn has within itself the capacity to become an oak. That process of change, however, leads to numerous questions: What actually changes? What causes the change? Is the oak tree the same thing as the acorn?

Ar's answers to these and other questions about motion and change revolve around several concepts. Perhaps the most important is matter. Matter is what remains through any and all changes. It is sometimes called the substrate. In Ar's view matter is eternal, uncreated and indestructible. It is not identified with one particular element (earth, water, air, fire). It is the substrate underlying them all, and it can change from one to another. It may have shapes or appearances as different as oak and acorn, but it is essentially matter.

What gives different shapes to matter is form. By "form" Ar does not mean the independently existing Platonic Forms. Aristotelian form is a kind of pattern that directs change. It is what makes an acorn always become an oak and never a pine. Equally important is the concept of privation or lack of a form. An important type of change is thus movement from privation to form.

Change can also be movement from one place to another. This raises the question of what is meant by "place." And, since movement requires time, Ar must consider what time is. The latter was such an important question that it necessitates a separate section; cf. below, p. 592.

All natural objects (as opposed to things made by human craft) have a tendency toward movement, even if it is as slow and imperceptible as a tree's upward motion in growth. Other plants turn toward the sun. Even rocks have a tendency (potentiality) toward motion. If all obstacles are removed, a rock will move downward without anyone or anything assisting it. One purpose of the *Physics*, then is to analyze how these movements come about in terms of the matter-privation-form theory.

Part of the explanation of change developed in the *Physics* and *Metaphysics* (4.2) is the theory of the four causes. Matter and form are two causes of a thing coming to be something it was not. Ar has a teleological view of the universe, i. e., a view based on the assumption that everything has a goal or purpose (*telos*). The final cause of an oak tree's growth would be the production of the mature tree. But there are also factors, such as rain and sunshine, which bring about the growth. These Ar would call efficient causes. This gives him the classic "four causes": material, formal, efficient, and final. It also means that he has no place for pure chance in his system. Everything has a cause, however difficult it may be determine.

Ar's explanation of the causes of motion appears to have changed during his life. In the early work *On Philosophy* he mentions three causes of motion: nature, force, and free will. In *De caelo* he explains that air and fire naturally move upward, while earth and water naturally move downward. The stars, composed of a fifth element (in Latin the *quinta essentia*), aether, move in a circle around the edge of the cosmos.

In *Phys* 8 Ar attempts to answer the question of what makes living creatures move themselves. In his system even a creature which moves itself is motivated by some power outside itself. We could say that A's movement is caused by B.

But what causes B's movement? C? That puts us well on our way into an infinite regress. Ar posits a prime (or first) mover(s), which are themselves unmoved and cause things to move because other things desire to be as perfect as the unmoved mover(s). Considerable debate has arisen over the number and location of the Unmoved Mover. In *Meta* Lambda there is one Unmoved Mover, who is identified with God. In other passages Ar talks about numerous Unmoved Movers, associated with different kinds of objects or types of movement.

AIDUN, J. "Aristotelian Force as Newtonian Power." *PhiSci* 49(1982), 228-235. Develops an interpretation of factors of motion presented in *Phys* 7.5 that shows that Aristotelian *force* is Newtonian *power*.   **[4929]**

APOSTLE, H. G. *Aristotle's* Physics. Bloomington: Indiana Univ. Pr. 1969. Translation with commentaries and glossary.   **[4930]**

BALABAN, O. "Aristotle's Theory of *Praxis*." *Hermes* 114(1986), 163-172. Shows how Ar distinguishes *praxis* (doing) from *poiesis* (making). *Praxis*, like modern concept of energy, involves conservation of power.   **[4931]**

BERGSON, H. "Aristotle's Concept of Place." *StudPh&HistPh* 5(1970), 13-72. Translation, with introduction, of Bergson's 1889 dissertation on Ar's doctrine on place, focusing especially on *Phys* 4.   **[4932]**

BOGEN, J. "Moravcsik on Explanation." *Synthèse* 28(1974), 20-25. Reply to #4994. Discusses meaning of *kath' hauto* and *kata symbebekos* as applied to concept of change.   **[4933]**

BOLZAN, J. E. "Aristotle and the Concept of Density." *Scientia* 109(1974), 237-243. Much attention has been given to what the concepts "heavy" and "light" meant to Ar. But his concept of density — involving weight, volume, and gravity — has not been duly noted, perhaps because it is not explicitly stated.   **[4934]**

————. "From Aristotle's Fixed Earth to the Mobile Aristotelian Earth." *PhilInq* 1(1979), 154-159. Like any ancient philosopher, Ar conceives of the earth as immobile in the center of the universe. But the physical planet cannot occupy that space, since it is only an "earthy" thing. It must be always moving (in a spiral) toward its ideal central position.   **[4935]**

BOS, A. P. "Notes on Aristotle's *De Mundo* Concerning the Discussion of its Authenticity." *PhilInq* 1(1979), 141-153. Discusses several issues relevant to subject which have not been given enough attention and concludes that many arguments that claim inauthenticity of *De Mundo* are not convincing.   **[4936]**

BOSTOCK, D. "Aristotle on the Principles of Change in *Physics* I," in #76, pp. 179-196. In Book 1, what is introduced as if it were a continuation of the physicists' investigation of nature has instead become a meta-investigation of general form which any account of change must take. This creates problems for discussion in chapters 5 and 6.   **[4937]**

——. cf. #693.

BRENNAN, S. O. "Is Aristotle's Prime Mover a Pure Form?" *Apeir* 15(1981), 80-95. Nothing in Ar's work allows us to identify any immaterial substance with form. **[4938]**

BRENNER, W. "Prime Matter and Barrington Jones." *PhResArch* 1(1975), no. 1008. Jones (#4971) fails to take account of two meanings of "matter" in Ar. One applies to a particular individual, which may come to be and cease to exist. The other sense describes the "prime matter," which exists even after a substantial change. **[4939]**

CASPER, B. M. "Galileo and the Fall of Aristotle: A Case of Historical Injustice?" *AmJPhys* 45(1977), 325-330. The objections which Galileo and others posed to Ar's claim that falling bodies increase in weight can be resolved if one realizes that Ar defines weight in relation to motion up and down. **[4940]**

CHARLTON, W. "Aristotelian Powers." *Phron* 32(1987), 277-289. Examines Ar's distinctions between active and passive powers (*dynameis*) associated with movement, between two kinds of active power, and narrow and broad conceptions of power. **[4941]**

——. "Aristotle and the Principle of Individuation." *Phron* 17(1972), 239-249. Many scholars maintain that Ar explained differences in individuals by saying that they were composed of different matter. Closer examination of his text indicates that he solved the problem of individuation on the basis of form. **[4942]**

——. *Aristotle's Physics Books I and II.* Oxford: Clarendon Pr., 1970. Translation and commentary, notable for its attack on the view that Ar postulates the existence of prime matter. **[4943]**

——. "Prime Matter: A Rejoinder," *Phron* 28(1983), 197-211. Response to criticisms of the position set forth in #4943 that Ar does not postulate prime matter. **[4944]**

CHROUST, A.-H. "Aristotle's Doctrine of the Uncreatedness and Indestructibiltiy of the Universe." *NewSchol* 52(1978), 268-279. Objections by other philosophers indicate that Ar put forward idea that universe is uncreated and indestructible in his lost dialogue *On Philosophy.* **[4945]**

——. "Some Reflections on the *Aeternitas Mundi* in Aristotle's *On Philosophy.*" *AClass* 16(1973), 25-32. In his extant writings Ar says nothing about eternal existence of cosmos. He probably argued this point in his lost *On Philosophy.* **[4946]**

COHEN, S. "Aristotle's Doctrine of the Material Substrate." *PhR* 93(1984), 171-194. Examines Ar's numerous and apparently contradictory statements on common and prime matter. **[4947]**

COOK, K. C. "The Underlying Thing, the Underlying Nature and Matter: Aristotle's Analogy in *Physics* I 7." *Apeir* 22(1989), 105-119. Debate over whether Ar held a doctrine of prime matter center has centered on the analogy which he draws at the end of *Phys* 1.7. The analogy seems to call attention to the underlying nature but should not be taken as an argument for prime matter. **[4948]**

CORISH, D. "Aristotle's Attempted Derivation of Temporal Order from That of

Movement and Space." *Phron* 21(1976), 342-251. When Ar tries in *Phys* 4.11 to derive a temporal order of *proteron* ("before") and *husteron* ("after") from a similar order of movement and space, he begs the question. The "before" and "after" of movement cannot be pre-temporal, as he tries to make it. [4949]

DAVIES, J. C. "Motion and the Prime Mover in Aristotle's Philosophy." *Emerita* 40(1972), 51-58. Ar's concept of Nature as teleological constitutes a combination of contrasting views of Nature and God drawn from his predecessors. [4950]

DE LEY, H. "Aristotle, *De gen. et corr.* A8, 324b35-325b II: A Leucippean Fragment?" *Mnem* 25(1972), 56-62. This passage is not drawn from Leucippus. It reflects Ar's views on *physis* and motion. [4951]

DRUMMOND, J. J. "A Note on *Physica* 211b14-25." *NewSchol* 55(1981), 219-228. Ar's criticisms of Atomists' concepts of void apply as well to his own theory of prime matter. [4952]

EDEL, A. "'Action' and 'Passion': Some Philosophical Reflections on *Physics* III 3," in #5350, pp. 59-64. Contact is necessary for motion to occur, but Ar is uncertain whether the action which produces it happens successively or all at once. [4953]

ELDERS, L. *Aristotle's Cosmology: A Commentary on the* de Caelo. Assen, Netherlands: van Gorcum, 1965. Lengthy introduction deals with structure, date, and major themes of the work. Claims that *De Caelo* can be shown to contain certain clues to relation between P's later ontology and Ar's physics. Bibliography. [4954]

FRIEDMAN, R. "Matter and Necessity in *Physics* B9 200a15-30." *AncPh* 3(1983), 8-11. Nothing in this passage must be taken to mean that material causes necessitate the things which they cause. [4955]

FURLEY, D. J. "Aristotle and the Atomists on Motion in a Void," in #4986, pp. 83-100. Ar objected to idea of motion in a void because he held that motion must have a direction and a sense, neither of which exist in a void. Atomists argued all motion is directionally defined by observer's point of view and is caused by weight of atoms. [4956]

——. "The Rainfall Example in *Physics* II.8," in #3809, pp. 177-182. Examines role played by example of rainfall in Ar's first argument for teleology of nature. Argues that Ar rejects non-teleological account of regular rainfall. [4957]

——. "Self Movers," in #5199, pp. 165-180. Examines Ar's claim that animals are self-movers in light of certain passages in *Phys* which appear to deny that there can be self-movers. [4958]

GERSHENSON, D. E., and **GREENBERT, D. A.** "A Question of Identification." *PhFor* 1(1968), 217-218. Examines three statements at 187a29-30: 1) all things were in existence together; 2) physical change is qualitative change; 3) physical change is a process of dissociation and recombination. Offers new translation. [4959]

GILL, M. L. "Aristotle's Theory of Causal Action in *Physics* III.3." *Phron* 25(1980), 129-147. Interprets Ar's account of action and passion in connection with his concept of motion to show that "action" and "passion" are not separate events but two terms describing one continuous event in which both agent and patient are changed. **[4960]**

GOEHRING, G. D. "Aristotle and the Increasing Weight of Falling Bodies." *AmJPhys* 48(1980), 82-83. Reply to Casper (#4940).   **[4961]**

GOTTHELF, A. "Aristotle's Conception of Final Causality." *RMeta* 30(1976), 226-254. Though Ar never defined precisely what he meant by "to be" or "come to be" for sake of something, passages in *Phys* and *De part animal* suggest that he saw a thing's existence and development as comprehensible only by understanding its end. He did not approach the study of nature with his teleological view already formed.   **[4962]**

GRAHAM, D. W. "Aristotle's Definition of Motion." *AncPh* 8(1988), 209-215. Challenges accepted interpretation of *kinesis*, and offers a new interpretation that better fits the texts.   **[4963]**

———. "Aristotle's Discovery of Matter." *AGPh* 66(1984), 37-51. Ar seems not to have had a doctrine of matter in the earliest phase of his career. He developed such a concept of matter by the time he wrote *Phys* 1.   **[4964]**

———. "The Paradox of Prime Matter." *JHPh* 25(1987), 475-490. Ar holds paradoxically that prime matter as a substratum is ultimately real and, as a particular, is ultimately unreal.   **[4965]**

HAHM, D. E. "Weight and Lightness in Aristotle and His Predecessors," in #4986, pp. 56-82. Ar claims to have been first to define and discuss *absolute* weight and lightness as opposed to *relative* concepts put forth by his predecessors. Examination of ideas of earlier philosophers does not support his claim.   **[4966]**

HANSON, N. R. "Aristotle (and Others) on Motion Through Air." *RMeta* 19(1965), 133-147. Demonstrates that in account of projectile motion, Ar anticipated a cornerstone of modern aerodynamics.   **[4967]**

HEINAMAN, R. "Aristotle and the Identity of Actions." *HPhQ* 4(1987), 307-328. Discussion in *Phys* 5.4 presents conditions which must be satisfied when a change x is in number with a change y. This criterion has implications for questions that arise concerning identity of actions.   **[4968]**

———. "Aristotle on Housebuilding." *HPhQ* 2(1985), 145-162. Discusses Ar's distinction between action of building a house and the builder's movement, which is a type of change but has a different subject than change involved in building. Issue is important for understanding of Ar's distinction between change and activity.   **[4969]**

HUSSEY, E. *Aristotle's* Physics *Books III and IV*. Oxford: Clarendon Pr., 1983. Translation with notes.   **[4970]**

JONES, B. "Aristotle's Introduction of Matter." *PhR* 83(1974), 474-500. The term "matter" is a "philosophical category" which allows us to talk about change. It describes the stuff which begins a process of coming-into-being.   **[4971]**

KING-FARLOW, J. "The Actual Infinite In Aristotle." *Thom* 52(1988), 427-444. *Phys* illustrates that Ar, torn between competing views about actual and potential infinites, tried to bolster his arguments by appealing to other disciplines as authorities.   [4972]

KONSTAN, D. "A Note on Aristotle *Physics* 1.1." *AGPh* 57(1975), 241-245. Discusses possible interpretations of two terms: *to katholon* and *ta kath' hekasta*.   [4973]

―――. "Points, Lines, and Infinity: Aristotle's *Physics* Zeta and Hellenistic Philosophy." *PBACAPh* 3(1987), 1-32, Discusses Ar's view that discrete points could not be put together to form a line and that a "line" could thus potentially be divided infinitely. Stoics and Epicureans accepted his position on points but not on divisibility.   [4974]

KOSMAN, L. A. "Aristotle's Definition of Motion." *Phron* 14(1969), 40-62. Ar defines motion as actuality of a potentiality *qua* potentiality.   [4975]

KOSTMAN, J. "Aristotle's Definition of Change." *HPhQ* 4(1987), 3-16. "Actualization" may apply to an actualizing (process by which something is actualized) or to an actuality (state of being actual resulting from such a process). Defends process view.   [4976]

KULLMAN, W. "Different Concepts of the Final Cause in Aristotle," in #3809, pp. 169-175. Investigates how different instances of Ar's use of "final cause" differ from each other in order to determine how they are related systematically.   [4977]

LANG, H. S. "Aristotle's Immaterial Mover and the Problem of Location in *Physics* VIII." *RMeta* 35(1981), 321-336. By locating the Unmoved Mover on the circumference of the cosmos Ar is not moving outside the realm of physical science.   [4978]

―――. "Commentary on Konstan's 'Points, Lines, and Infinity'." *PBACAPh* 3(1987), 33-43. Examines Konstan's (#4974) construal of *Phys* 2, and argues that Ar raises problems concerning motion. These problems require that he define "the continuous" as infinitely divisible. Subject of points arises only within this definition.   [4979]

―――. "Why Fire Goes Up: An Elementary Problem in Aristotle's *Physics*." *RMeta* 38(1984), 69-106. Concept of natural place in *Phys* 8.3-10 is all that is needed to explain motion of fire. Ar did not consider how the motion is produced.   [4980]

―――. cf. #5421.

LEAR, J. "Aristotelian Infinity." *PAS* 80(1979-80), 187-210. In terms of space Ar argues that infinity is incomplete, though immanent in nature. He concedes that world had no beginning but denies that an infinite length of time has already elapsed.   [4981]

LENNOX, J. G. "Aristotle on Chance." *AGPh* 66(1984), 52-60. Discusses Ar's doctrine of chance in *Phys* 2.4-6 and focuses on relationship between processes which are due to chance and those which are for sake of something.   [4982]

LEWIS, F. A. "Teleology and Material/Efficient Causes in Aristotle." *PacPhQ* 69(1988), 54-98. For Ar, a chain of material/efficient causes can fully necessitate a given, particular effect that is also explained by formal/final causes.   [4983]

LOBKOWICZ, N. "*Quidquid Movetur Ab Alio Movetur*." *NewSchoL* 42(1968), 401-421. Three Aristotelian proofs for principle that everything in motion is necessarily moved by something other than itself are inconclusive.   [4984]

MACHAMER, P. K. "Aristotle on Natural Place and Natural Motion." *Isis* 69(1978), 377-387. Concept of natural place is related to rest, not motion, for an object. Four causes of natural motion are discussed in *Phys* and *De caelo*.   [4985]

————., and TURNBULL, R. G., eds. *Motion and Time, Space and Matter: Interrelations in the History of Philosophy and Science.* Columbus: Ohio St. Univ. Pr., 1976. Collection of essays (dedicated "to Zeno, who said it couldn't be done"). Four on Ar are abstracted herein.   [4986]

MAGRUDER, J. E. "Notes on Aristotle's View of 'Chance' and 'Fortune'." *Kinesis* 1(1969), 75-81. Ar does not consider chance as a cause in a primary sense.   [4987]

MANICAS, P. T. "Aristotle, Dispositions and Occult Powers." *RMeta* 18(1965), 678-689. Ar's science is not occult and his central concepts, such as *dynamis*, *energeia*, and *telos*, may be satisfactorily construed in language of dispositions.   [4988]

MARTINAS, K., and ROPOLY, L. "Analogies: Aristotelian and Modern Physics." *IntStudPhSci* 2(1987), 1-9. Relates Ar's physics to modern theories, such as second law of thermodynamics.   [4989]

MENDELL, H. "Topoi on *Topos*: The Development of Aristotle's Concept of Place." *Phron* 32(1987), 206-231. Discusses development of Ar's concept of place from its early stages to that found in *Phys* 4.   [4990]

MILLER, F. D., Jr. "Actions and Results." *PhQ* 25(1975), 350-354. Examines Ar's interpretation of actions and processes in terms of whether the result is achieved in stages (such as building a house) or simultaneously with the action (as in looking at something).   [4991]

MILLER, W. M. "Aristotle on Necessity, Chance and Spontaneity." *NewSchol* 47(1973), 204-213. Examines Ar's concepts of chance and spontaneity in comparison with his four causes, by which he thinks all events can be explained.   [4992]

MORAVCSIK, J. M. E. "*Aitia*: A Generative Factor in Aristotle's Philosophy." *Dial*(Can) 14(1975), 622-638. Ar intended his theory of causes to help us understand, not to explain how things are caused.   [4993]

————. "Aristotle on Adequate Explanations." *Synthèse* 28(1974), 3-17. The Aristotelian theory commonly known as "the doctrine of four causes" should really be understood as Ar's account of what constitutes an adequate explanation.   [4994]

MORKOVSKY, M. C. "The Elastic Instant of Aristotle's Becoming and Perishing." *ModSch* 46(1969), 191-217. Discusses relation of time to change of form in Ar's *Phys*, *On the Heavens*, and *De Gen et Cor*.   [4995]

MORROW, G. R. "Qualitative Change in Aristotle's *Physics*," in #5350, pp. 154-167. Ar's view of change as qualitative plays a less significant role in his thought than is generally realized, and its overall effect is to confuse some of his explanations.   [4996]

MOURELATOS, A. P. D. "Aristotle's 'Powers' and Modern Empiricism." *Ratio* 9(1967), 97-104. Ar's analysis of such dynamical concepts as *dynamis* and *physis* involves both more and less than modern empiricist analyses.   **[4997]**

———. cf. #5380.

OWEN, G. E. L. "Aristotelian Mechanics," in #3809, pp. 227-245. Investigates whether
in his physical writings Ar practices "a technique or techniques of 'abstraction'" connected
with use of mathematical explanations, and whether he applies these techniques to
empirical observations.   **[4998]**

———. "'*Tithenai ta Phainomena*'," in #4598, pp. 113-126; also in #3625, pp. 167-190.
Shows how dialectical thought processes helped Ar define some of key terms (e.g.,
place), and fashion some of main tools (e.g., matter and form) of his physics. Also challenges criticism that Ar promised and failed in his physics to work empirically. **[4999]**

OWENS, J. "The Aristotelian Argument for the Material Principle of Bodies," in #5350,
pp. 193-209. Ar's arguments that bodies have a material principle is a type of analogy.   **[5000]**

PECK, A. L. "Aristotle on *Kinesis*," in #41, pp. 478-490. Asks whether we can define
field in which Ar believes *kinesis* to operate. Is *kinesis* as pervasive in Ar's system as potentiality is: does it extend over same field, and reach its limit at same point? **[5001]**

PICKERING, F. R. "Aristotle on Zeno and the Now." *Phron* 23(1978), 253-257. When
Ar's comments about Zeno's arrow paradox are read in context, he seems to have understood Zeno's argument to rest on faulty reasoning.   **[5002]**

REDDING, J. L. "Aristotle's Theory of Falling Bodies." *AmJPhys* 46(1978), 689.
Addendum to #4940.   **[5003]**

ROBINSON, H. M. "Prime Matter in Aristotle." *Phron* 19(1974), 168-188. Defends
position that Ar believed in a prime matter and a bare "stuff," lacking in all positive
determinations, which is matter of elements and which makes elemental change possible.
Examines *De Gen et Corr.* 329a and *Meta* 2,3.   **[5004]**

ROSEN, S. "Dynamis, Energeia and the Megarians." *PhilInq* 1(1979), 105-119. Ar's
failure to solve the problem of non-being, because of a weakness in his doctrine of
predication, leaves him unable to offer a theoretical explanation of change which can
answer the Megarians.   **[5005]**

SCHLOSSBERGER, E. "Aristotelian Matter, Potentiality, and Quarks." *SJPh* 17(1979),
507-521. Ar's concept of primary matter and the union of form and matter can be used
to explain how subatomic particles called quarks can exhibit fractional changes. **[5006]**

SHARVY, R. "Aristotle on Mixtures." *JPh* 80(1983), 439-457. Discussion of conditions
necessary for a true mixture to occur.   **[5007]**

SORABJI, R. "Aristotle on the Instant of Change." *PAS* Suppl. 50(1976), 69-90; revised
version in #4598, pp. 159-177. To resolve the problem of whether a body, when starting
to move, is at rest or in motion, one can look to Ar's *Phys* 6 and 8, where he seems to
treat motion differently from rest.   **[5008]**

──. "Atom and Time Atoms," in #64, pp. 37-86. Reviews the four paradoxes regarding time in *Phys* 4, and shows how these paradoxes inspired some of most interesting theories of time in late antiquity. **[5009]**

──. cf. #5531.

SPANGLER, G. A. "Aristotle's Criticism of Parmenides in *Physics* I." *Apeir* 13(1979), 92-103. Explores Ar's investigations of Parmenides' claim that all things are one to see how Ar understands Eleatic monism and tactics Ar uses against Parmenides. **[5010]**

SPRAGUE, R. K. "The Four Causes: Aristotle's Exposition and Ours." *Monist* 52(1968), 298-300. Standard way of presenting doctrine of four causes by example of creation of a statue is quite non-Aristotelian and should be abandoned. **[5011]**

STONE, M. A. "Aristotle's Distinction Between Motion and Activity." *HPhQ* 2(1985), 11-20. Accounts for main differences between activity and motion. Focuses on temporal characteristics as an essential means for distinguishing activities from motions. **[5012]**

THORP, J. The Luminousness of the Quintessence." *Phoenix* 36(1982), 104-123. The interpretive problem in Ar's account of how heavenly bodies give light and heat arises because we read our own scientific views back into Ar. **[5013]**

TODD, R. B. "The Four Causes: Aristotle's Exposition and the Ancients." *JHI* 37(1976), 319-322. Reply to #5011. The image of a sculptor at work on a statue as an illustration of A's four causes, while not derived from Ar himself, does appear in some later ancient philosophical texts. **[5014]**

TURNBULL, R. G. "'Physics' I: Sense Universals, Principles, Multiplicity, and Motion," in #4986, pp. 28-55. First chapter is crucial to understanding Ar's arguments in rest of this book and in other works. Ar is arguing that there are three principles. **[5015]**

VERBEKE, G. "The Aristotelian Doctrine of Qualitative Change in *Physics* VII, 3," in #41, pp. 546-565. Finds in Ar two reasons why it is not possible to translate into terms of qualitative change most important activities of man, such as technical activities, care of body, moral conduct, and scientific knowledge. **[5016]**

VERDENIUS, W. J. "Hylozoism in Aristotle," in #60, pp. 101-114. Though Ar disagrees with many Presocratic ideas, he does accept concept of hylozoism or a spirit active in matter. Such a theory might explain some otherwise inexplicable phenomena which have been observed today. **[5017]**

──., and **WASZINK, J. H.** *Aristotle:* On Coming-to-be and Passing-Away: *Some Comments.* Leiden: Brill, 1968. Detailed commentary. **[5018]**

WATERLOW, S. "Instants of Motion in Aristotle's *Physics* VI." *AGPh* 65(1983), 128-146. Explores why Ar rejected "motion at an instant." Compares Ar's theory with Zeno's paradox of the arrow. **[5019]**

──. *Nature, Change, and Agency in Aristotle's* Physics: *A Philosophical Study.* Oxford Univ. Pr., 1982. Ar's philosophical system is linked together by his concept of a natural substance which is unified internally by a principle of change and stasis. Shows in detail just what in the conceptual apparatus of Ar's natural science is inimicial to physics and chemistry as they subsequently developed. One reviewer called the book "heavy going even for professional philosophers, let alone students." **[5020]**

WHITE, D. A. "Part and Whole in Aristotle's Concept of Infinity." *Thom* 49(1985), 168-182. Some recent studies of *Phys* 1 do not get to the heart of the problems raised there concerning parts, wholes, and the infinite. Some of Ar's comments later in *Phys* provide a basis for a solution. **[5021]**

WIELAND, W. "Aristotle's *Physics* and the Problem of Inquiry into Principles," in #4598, pp. 127-140. Challenges view that Ar employs methodology of syllogism to achieve an imposing self-consistent system. Ar never relies on pure immediate intuition to legitimize his doctrine of principles. **[5022]**

————. "The Problem of Teleology," in #4598, pp. 141-160. Challenges some of more "extravagant" interpretations of Ar's teleological method. Argues that his teleology is grounded in experience and that, for Ar, a theological foundation is not a prerequisite. **[5023]**

WILLIAMS, C. J. F. *Aristotle's* De Generatione et Corruptione. Oxford Univ. Pr., 1982. Translation and commentary. Contains an appendix defending view that Ar believes in prime matter. **[5024]**

WILSON, T. A. "On Time and Motion As Natural Phenomena." *Kinesis* 10(1980), 92-103. Ar, like Einstein, links motion and time and establishes the need for someone to perceive motion in order for time to pass. **[5025]**

YOUNG, J. "A Note on Falling Bodies." *NewSchoI* 41(1967), 465-481. Critically examines contributions of Ar's theory of motion which have been unfairly overshadowed by criticism of its serious faults. **[5026]**

For related items see #590, #670, #4578, #5363, #5434, #5443.

POLITICS

For Ar politics, along with ethics, constitutes the field of practical science, i. e., the branch which deals with how one acts. Ethics (cf. p. 450) is the study of how the individual acts, but no person acts entirely alone, so Ar must consider also the principles governing people's actions in groups. The group most familiar to any Greek was the *polis* (city-state), so Ar's examination of the larger context of human behavior centers on that organization. It seems so natural to him that he even defines a human being as "an animal that lives in a *polis*." This devotion to the city gives rise to the first criticism that is normally offered of Ar's political philosophy, that it was so intimately tied up in the organization of the *polis* ("city state) that it has little applicability today. It was, in fact, outmoded by Ar's death because Alexander the Great had conquered the Persian Empire by then and set in motion a process that led to the development of strong, centralized monarchies in place of the independent cities in which the Greeks had traditionally lived.

The practical sciences are not as important to Ar as the theoretical sciences (Metaphysics, Mathematics, and Physics), but he and his students did collect the constitutions of over 150 Greek city-states as data, similar to the biological material contained in the *Historia animalium*. Ar's usual approach to any problem is to begin by examining the opinions of those who have studied that problem before him. In the practical sciences, since one does not expect the sort of conclusive answers one is looking for in the theoretical sciences, anyone's opinion can have some value. We do not have any of those constitutions except that of Athens, which was rediscovered at the end of the nineteenth century. Exactly what use Ar made of the material we do not know.

One problem associated with the study of the *Politics* is the question of the order of the books. Some scholars maintain that Books 7-8 should come after Book 3. Others argue that as presently arranged the books demonstrate how the theory of four causes (cf. *Physics*) applies to the *polis* as well. The work does begin by elaborating the principle that a human being naturally belongs in a *polis*, explains how cities grew from people's need for one another, then describes and evaluates various ways of governing a city (Books 2-6). He thinks the various forms of government (monarchy, despotism, etc.) are modeled on the organization of families. As the father is head of the house, so the king is head of the city. Ar does not take a definite stand on what is the best form of government but seems to favor some sort of aristocracy. In Books 7-8 he discusses the objective of a *polis*, which is the happiness (*eudaimonia*) of all its citizens.

This category includes some topics, such as slavery, the status of women, business, and education, which might not seem "political" in the pure sense to us. For Ar they involve the life of the *polis* and are discussed at various points in the *Politics*.

ADSHEAD, K. "Aristotle, *Politics* V.2.7 (1302B34-1303A11)." *Historia* 35(1986), 372-377. The examples of political systems which Ar cites in this passage represent a gradual transformation, not a contrast or analogy.   **[5027]**

AMBLER, W. "Aristotle on Nature and Politics: The Case of Slavery." *PolTheo* 15(1987), 390-410. In course of investigating Ar's understanding of relationship between nature and politics, argues that his natural master and natural slave establish standards which deny rather than establish naturalness of actual slavery.   **[5028]**

ANTON, J. P. "Revolutions, Reforms and Educational Philosophy in Aristotle's Theory of Constitutional Law," in #72, pp. 58-62. Ar links education and political structure. States with normal constitutions want to educate their youth to be prepared to participate intelligently in life of community, even to become aware of ways to change the state. States with deviant constitutions fear such prospects and thus discourage widespread education.   **[5029]**

BAECK, L. "Aristotle as Mediterranean Economist." *Diogenes* 138(1987) 81-104. Ar's *NE* and *Pol* are the basis of economic thought in the Mediterranean world, even into the Muslim and Latin periods. The link which he established between ethics and economics is being studied seriously again.   **[5030]**

BAKSHI, O. P. *Politics and Prejudice: Notes on Aristotle's Political Theory.* Univ. of Delhi, 1975. Critical study of Ar's political theory, focusing in particular on its relation with democratic, humanitarian, and equalitarian tendencies of his time. **[5031]**

BARKER, E. *The* Politics *of Aristotle.* Oxford Univ. Pr., 1969. Edition with lengthy introduction. **[5032]**

BERNS, L. "Spiritedness in Ethics and Politics: A Study in Aristotelian Psychology." *Interp* 12(1984), 335-348. In *Pol* 1, Ar is seeking that which can justify rule of one man over another. Explores questions of why spiritedness (*thumos*) does not justify rule. Spiritedness accounts for feelings of concerns for whatever is one's own. **[5033]**

BOOTH, W. J. "Politics and the Household: A Commentary on Aristotle's *Politics* Book One." *HPolTho* 2(1981), 203-226. Examines Book 1 for Ar's view on whether political authority is an order whose "mode of being" is natural or conventional. **[5034]**

BROWN, W. R. "Aristotle's Art of Acquisition and the Conquest of Nature." *Interp* 10(1982), 159-195. Ar does not discuss economics or acquisition in separate works, but he seems to think that nature does not provide adequate circumstances for man. Desire to acquire things is thus natural and must be controlled. **[5035]**

CHAMBLISS, J. J. "Aristotle's Conception of Childhood and the Poliscraft." *EducStud* 13(1982), 33-43. Examines Ar's ideas on childhood and on poliscraft — craft whose goal is to develop a city that facilitates highest development of human nature. **[5036]**

CHARLES, D. "Perfectionism in Aristotle's Political Theory: Reply to Martha Nussbaum." *OSAP* Suppl. (1988), 185-206. Questions Nussbaum's (#5105) argument that Ar develops a distributive conception of justice, and asks whether Ar makes genuine progress in considering basic problems in perfectionist theory concerning value of liberty or place of fairness. **[5037]**

CHARNEY, A. P. "Spiritedness and Piety in Aristotle," in *Understanding the Political Spirit,* ed. C. H. Zuckert (New Haven, CT: Yale Univ. Pr., 1988), pp. 67-87. While Ar replaces Homeric courage with true courage derived from one's own reason, he remains silent about nature of piety and instead advocates an earthly justice. **[5038]**

CHEN, E. "Confucius, Aristotle, and Contemporary Revolutions," in *Person and Society,* ed. G. F. McLean (Lanham: Univ. Pr. of America, 1988), pp. 17-27. Reply to McKeon (#5095). Contains an analysis of Ar's theory of man and his views on slavery, women, and youth in light of contemporary liberation movements. **[5039]**

CHROUST, A.-H. "Aristotle's Criticism of Plato's Philosopher King." *RhM* 111(1968), 16-22. Ar's *On Monarchy,* which took a more realistic approach to role of monarch in government than did P, cannot have been published before 345 B. C. **[5040]**

————. "Aristotle's *Politicus*: A Lost Dialogue." *RhM* 108(1965), 346-353. Examines moral basis of Ar's view of statesman and P's influence on him in this regard. **[5041]**

CLARK, S. R. L. "Aristotle's Woman." *HPolTho* 3(1982), 177-192. Discusses Ar's views of women as imperfect males, incapable of achieving highest forms of *eudaimonia.* Their most appropriate arena of action, in his view, is a well-run household. **[5042]**

COLLINS, D. "Aristotle and Business." *JBusEthics* 6(1987), 567-572. Systematizes Ar's views to suggest that he supports business and profits. **[5043]**

CRISTI, R. "The Aristotelian Ethics: Ethics or *Politike*?" *ModSch* 47(1970), 381-389. Ar uses term *politike* instead of ethics for some aspects of his ethical investigations, suggesting that *politike* had rather broad connotations for him. That he titled his books *Ethics* indicates that he finally delineated ethics from politics. **[5044]**

DAVID, E. "Aristotle and Sparta." *AncSoc* 13-14(1982-83), 67-103. The Sparta of Lycurgus' era serves Ar well as an example of the problems plaguing fourth-century Greece. It is neutral because it is so far in the past. **[5045]**

——. cf. #2402.

DAVIES, J. C. "Characteristics of Aristotle's Political Theory." *Euphro* 12(1983-84), 189-197. Though Ar tries to strike an empirical pose, elements of Platonic idealism still play an important role in the *Pol*. **[5046]**

DAVIS, M. "Aristotle's Reflections on Revolution." *GradFacPhJ* 11(1986), 49-63. Ar, understanding revolution to be merely boldest revelation of character of political life, generally does not hold out much hope for fulfillment of its extravagant claims. **[5047]**

DEFOURNY, M. "The Aim of the State: Peace," in #4036, pp. 195-201. Considers Ar's views of state as natural institution which enables individuals to pursue their natural aim of *eudaimonia*. Discusses his view that war should be subordinate to peace. **[5048]**

DE LAIX, R. A. "Aristotle's Conception of the Spartan Constitution." *JHPh* 12(1974), 21-30. Books 2, 7, and 8 of *Pol* represent a later, more empirical stage in Ar's thinking concerning Spartan system, and Books 4 and 5 an earlier, more theoretical one. His view became more favorable with time. **[5049]**

DEVELIN, R. "The Good Man and the Good Citizen in Aristotle's *Politics*." *Phron* 18(1973), 71-79. For Ar, distinction between good man and good citizen is one between goodness of a sound, practical nature and a higher goodness informed by wisdom and approaching the moral. **[5050]**

DOWNEY, G. "Aristotle as an Expert on Urban Problems." *Talanta* 3(1971), 56-73. Examines Ar's view of close connection between individual and *polis*, especially their mutual responsibilities. **[5051]**

——. cf. #1969.

FERGUSON, J. "Teleology in Aristotle's Politics," in #3809, pp. 259-273. Argues for clear biological basis to Ar's political thought, and discusses how his teleology is not theoretical or abstract, given his continual insistence on actual existence of *telos*. **[5052]**

FINLEY, M. I. "Aristotle and Economic Analysis." *P&P* 47(1970), 3-25; also in #4036, pp. 140-158. Discusses Ar's view on natural and unnatural uses of money, and suggests that what is significant is mentality which adopts notion that what we call economy was properly exclusive business of outsiders. **[5053]**

FORTENBAUGH, W. W. "Aristotle on Prior and Posterior, Correct and Mistaken Constitutions." *TAPhA* 106(1976), 125-137. Ar, in *Pol* 3.1, is concerned to show that there is a norm by which forms of government are measured. Like some aspect of physical beauty, a constitution is either correct or not. It may become less and less mistaken until it is correct, but it cannot be more or less correct.   [5054]

———. "Aristotle on Slaves and Women," in #4036, pp. 135-139. Discusses Ar's thesis that some men are slaves by nature, and analyzes his attempt to connect women's status with their nature.   [5055]

———. cf. #2963.

FRANK, D. H. "Aristotle on Freedom in the *Politics*." *Prud* 15(1983), 109-116. Surveys his views on slavery, democracy, and aristocracy.   [5056]

FRISCH, M. J. "Aristotle's Understanding of the State." *Archeological News* 11(1982), 71-74. Ar sees the growth of states as determined by human choice and fortuitous events. He does not attempt to impose his system of biological classification onto his political concepts.   [5057]

GEORGIADES, C. "Aristotle's Perspectives on Human Technical Work." *Dial&Hum* 5(1978) 57-72. Discusses Ar's views of technical work from following perspectives: ontological, anthropological and social, and conceptual-analytic.   [5058]

GERSON, L. P. "Aristotle's *Polis*: A Community of the Virtuous." *PBACAPh* 3(1987), 203-225. Examines what Ar means by his claim that the state exists by nature. Primary sense of *polis* is a community of people whose aim is the good life. An important part of their common good is concept of justice. Ar's views are applicable to modern circumstances, though no modern state corresponds to his *polis*.   [5059]

GILLIARD, F. W. "Teleological Development in the *Athenaion Politeia*." *Historia* 20(1971), 430-435. Philosophical arguments in this treatise cannot be used to challenge its historicity.   [5060]

GOEDECKE, W. R. "Aristotle's Search for the Perfect State: The Methodology of the *Politics*." *SwJPh* 1(1970), 58-64. According to Ar, it is better to live in a less perfect state which acknowledges that different views of the good life can co-exist than to live in a state which adheres to an absolute conception of justice.   [5061]

HAMBURGER, M. *Morals and Law. The Growth of Aristotle's Legal Theory.* New York: Biblo & Tanner, 1965; revised ed. Survey of Ar's ethical and political works and the connections which he makes between voluntary action and responsibility. For Ar law and morals are the *telos* of the state.   [5062]

HARE, J. E. "Aristotelian Justice and the Pull to Consensus." *IntJAppliedPh* 3(1987), 37-49. Observation of contemporary politics allows us to compare tendency toward consensus in American Congress to what Ar says about harmony in political life.[5063]

HENNIS, W. "*Topics* and Political Science." *GradFacPhJ* 7(1978), 35-77. The *Topics*, as the specific method in realm of dialectics, has a particular meaning for the discipline of practical philosophy, and especially the discipline of political science.   [5064]

HUXLEY, G. L. "Aristotle as Antiquary." *GRBS* 14(1973), 271-286. Ar's political works are based on his acquaintance with many sources used by scholars today: coins, inscriptions, religious rituals, etc. His reliance on myths is the primary difference between himself and modern researchers. **[5065]**

————. "Aristotle on the Origin of the Polis," in *Stele: Tomos eis Mnemen Nikolaou Kontoleontos* (Athens: n. p., 1980), pp. 258-264. His studies of the constitutions of various states led Ar to see the origin of the *polis* in villages which eventually joined together. The purpose of a *polis* is to provide for life together, but Ar goes on to argue that its purpose is to provide for the good life. **[5066]**

————. *On Aristotle and Greek Society.* Belfast: Mayne, Boyd, 1979. Ar's political theories, emphasizing friendship and wisdom, have more of a moral base than modern versions, but he also had a sound historical base for his views. **[5067]**

————. "On Aristotle's Best State." *HPolTho* 6(1985), 139-149. Ar's ideal state is not any of those described in *Pol* 4-6. In practice, the weakness of his arrangements lies in rigid connection between age and function. Ar is perhaps unduly confident that judicial and executive citizens would gracefully leave their positions at onset of old age. **[5068]**

IRWIN, T. H. "Generosity and Property in Aristotle's *Politics*." *SocPh&Pol* 4(1987), 37-54. Examines Ar's argument for generosity by investigating defense of private property because it provides resources for exercise of beneficence. **[5069]**

————. cf. #4715.

JACKSON, M. W. "Aristotle On Rawls: A Critique of Quantitative Justice." *JValInq* 19(1985), 99-110. Comparison of *Pol* 2 with Rawls' book, *A Theory of Justice*. Rawls takes justice quantitatively, as an equitable sharing of material goods. Ar's view of justice combines identity, excellence, and capacity. For him material equality is neither a means to nor an end of justice. **[5070]**

JOHNSON, C. "Aristotle's Polity: Mixed or Middle Constitution?" *HPolTho* 9(1988), 189-204. Resolves difficulties surrounding the "polity" (in the strict sense of a constitution) regarding its definition and attainability. **[5071]**

————. "The Hobbesian Conception of Sovereignty and Aristotle's *Politics*." *JHI* 46(1985), 327-348. Hobbes maintains that Ar based his concept of sovereignty on the authority of laws rather than in people holding coercive power. But Ar's view in *Pol* is actually close to Hobbes'. **[5072]**

————. "Who is Aristotle's Citizen?" *Phron* 29(1984), 73-90. Ar tries for definitions which are based upon empirical data, describe an end or purpose, and help solve real dilemmas. His attempt at defining a "citizen" (*Pol* 3) is not completely satisfactory because the various Greek city-states provided so many different examples of what it meant to be a citizen. **[5073]**

JOHNSTONE, C. L. "An Aristotelian Trilogy: Ethics, Rhetoric, Politics, and the Search for Moral Truth." *Ph&Rh* 13(1980), 1-24. Ar connects ethics, rhetoric, and politics because of their concern with moral virtues, persuasive speech, and the process of deliberation in the *polis*. The *polis* serves as the arena in which individual moral opinions are verified and generalized.   [5074]

KEANEY, J. J. "Aristotle's *Politics* 2.12.1274a22-b28." *AJAH* 6(1981), 97-100. This passage, which is consistent with the rest of the treatise, should be attributed to Ar. It may have been composed while he was in Asia Minor.   [5075]

——. "The Date of Aristotle's *Athenaion Politeia*." *Historia* 19(1970), 326-336. Work was probably written in 334-333 and updated twenty years later to take into account changes in Athenian system.   [5076]

——. "Ring Composition in Aristotle's *Athenaion Politeia*." *AJPh* 90(1969), 406-423. Technique of ring composition is used with particular effect to distinguish most important phases of constitution's development.   [5077]

KELSEN, H. "Aristotle and Hellenic-Macedonian Policy," in #4036, pp. 170-194. Sets in historical context Ar's views on nature and merits of different forms of government. Explores his ambivalence to competing strengths of democracy and despotism. [5078]

KEYT, D. "Distributive Justice in Aristotle's Ethics and Politics." *Topoi* 4(1985), 23-46. Ar's political theory centers on problem of distributing authority justly. He seeks a middle ground between Protagoras' relativism and Plato's absolutism.   [5079]

——. "Injustice and Pleonexia in Aristotle: A Reply to Charles Young," in #4305, pp. 251-257. Challenges Young's (#4405) identification of political justice with both absolute and particular justice.   [5080]

——. "Three Fundamental Theorems in Aristotle's *Politics*." *Phron* 32(1987), 54-79. Examines Ar's arguments in defense of three theorems: 1) *polis* is a natural entity; 2) man is by nature a political animal; 3) by nature *polis* is prior to individual. The first theorem is primary, and the other two are its corollaries. Ar fails to establish the primary theorem and has good reasons for denying it.   [5081]

KRONMAN, A. "Aristotle's Ideas of Political Fraternity." *AmJJur* 24(1979), 114-138. For Ar survival of a *polis* is based on friendship as well as justice. Friendship is built up of marriage relations, religious groups, and sharing of social activities. Such groups are half way between family and *polis*.   [5082]

KULLMANN, W. "Equality in Aristotle's Political Thought," in #62, pp. 31-44. Ar does not believe in the fundamental equality of all persons because of his biological studies, which had convinced him that different sorts of animals had different degrees of understanding and intelligence.   [5083]

LABARRIERE, J.-L. "The Political Animal's Knowledge According to Aristotle," in *Knowledge and Politics*, ed. M. Dascal (Boulder, CO: Westview Pr., 1989), pp. 33-47. Man is not the only animal which engages in political activity, but he is the only one which can think through what he is doing and establish goals for his political actions. Politics is not a science because it is subject to deliberation and change.   [5084]

LORD, C. "Aristotle," in *History of Political Philosophy*, ed. by L. Strauss and J. Cropsey. (Univ. of Chicago Pr., 1987), pp. 118-154. Commentary on Ar's account of the best regime.   [5085]

——. *Aristotle, The Politics.* Univ. of Chicago Pr., 1984. Translation which strives to be literal without sacrificing readability. Introduction covers Ar's life, critical problems of *Pol*, including possibility that Books 7 and 8 might belong after Book 3.   **[5086]**

——. "The Character and Composition of Aristotle's *Politics*." *PolTheo* 9(1981), 459-478. Studies Ar's process of composition. Argues Books 7 and 8 belong after Book 3. Discusses weaknesses of Jaeger's views on Ar's move away from Platonism.   **[5087]**

——. *Education and Culture in the Political Thought of Aristotle.* Ithaca, NY: Cornell Univ. Pr., 1982. For Ar, as for P, art is not a private experience but one with political and moral implications. He sees education, based on music and poetry, as setting an individual's values and continuing into adulthood. Tragedy serves to purge emotions which can lead to political extremism.   **[5088]**

——. "Politics and Philosophy in Aristotle's *Politics*." *Hermes* 106(1978), 336-357. Point of *Pol* 7 is not to argue that philosophic life is superior but to demonstrate best manner of life for a *polis*. Ar's best regime is ruled by gentlemen, not philosophers.   **[5089]**

MACRAKIS, M. S. "*Epieikeia* and Satisficing." *AncPh* 5(1985), 53-57. Ar admits (*Rhet* 1374a26-b1) that a lawmaker cannot foresee all possible ramifications of his legislation. His comments resemble the modern concept of satisficing, meaning that a person makes decisions with the hope that the outcome will be acceptable, not perfect.   **[5090]**

MANSFIELD, H. C., Jr. "Commentary on Gerson's 'Aristotle's *Polis*: A Community of the Virtuous'." *PBACAPh* 3(1987), 226-228. Reply to #5059.   **[5091]**

MARA, G. M. "The Role of Philosophy in Aristotle's Political Science." *Polity* 19(1987), 375-401. Though Ar does not found politics upon a life of philosophic contemplation, he views philosophy as compatible with politics.   **[5092]**

McCARTHY, G. "German Social Ethics and the Return to Greek Philosophy: Marx and Aristotle." *StudSovTho* 31(1986), 1-24. Looks at specific instances of Ar's influence on Marx, especially in their concepts of ethics and social praxis.   **[5093]**

McCOY, W. J. "Aristotle's *Athenaion Politeia* and the Establishment of The Thirty Tyrants." *YCS* 24(1975), 131-145. Examines how essential Ar's account is for understanding events of 404 B. C. in Athens. But his theoretical biases must be kept in mind.   **[5094]**

McKEON, R. "Person and Community, Individual and Society, Reformation and Revolution," in *Person and Society*, ed. G. F. McLean (Lanham, MD: Univ. Pr. of America, 1988), pp. 3-16. Discusses Ar's positions on nature and family, on natural relations (property, slavery, youth, women), and shows how Ar establishes "the vocabulary of culture and philosophy in the West."   **[5095]**

——. cf. #1991.

MEIKLE, S. "Aristotle and the Political Economy of the Polis." *JHS* 99(1979), 57-73. Modern interpretations of Ar's economic ideas fail because they are based on modern assumptions which Ar did not share, and because his thought on the subject is not as systematic as one sometimes thinks. Ar's thought has some affinity to Marx's and mirrors changes taking place in Athenian life.   **[5096]**

MILLER, F. D., Jr. "Aristotle and the Natural Rights Tradition." *Reason Papers* 13(1988), 166-181. Comparison with Hobbes and Locke shows that Ar's work is a source for later views of "natural rights" because of his understanding of certain rights as based on natural justice.   **[5097]**

――――. "Aristotle's Political Naturalism." *Apeir* 22(1989), 195-218. Ar resembles Hobbes in holding that a political community is built upon human reason, but he also sees it as a natural thing because of the natural human potential for political life. Such a community is necessary for achieving the ends of human life.   **[5098]**

MOORE, J. M. *Aristotle and Xenophon on Democracy and Oligarchy.* London: Chatto & Windus, 1983. Translation of *Athenaion Politeia* and two other documents relating to government of Greek cities, with introductions, commentary, and bibliography. First published in 1975.   **[5099]**

MULGAN, R. G. "Aristotle and Absolute Power." *Antich* 8(1974), 21-28. Ar sees ruler as deserving power because of his relative merits compared to others in community, and not as being meritorious in some absolute sense, as Plato had maintained.   **[5100]**

――――. "Aristotle and the Democratic Conception of Freedom," in *Auckland Classical Essays Presented to E. M. Blaiklock*, ed. B. F. Harris (Auckland [New Zea] Univ. Pr., 1970), pp. 95-112. For Ar freedom is not simply doing what one pleases. Free men are concerned with common good and must restrain themselves accordingly. Only slaves have so little responsibility that they may act as they wish.   **[5101]**

――――. *Aristotle's Political Theory: An Introduction for Students of Political Theory.* Oxford: Clarendon Pr., 1977. Brings major themes and arguments into sharper focus. Examines Ar's conception of good life, his general theory of state, his account of household, and definitions of citizenships and constitutions.   **[5102]**

――――. "A Note on Aristotle's Absolute Ruler." *Phron* 19(1974), 66-69. An absolute ruler deserves to rule only if his merits are beyond comparison with those of other citizens.   **[5103]**

NICHOLS, M. P. "The Good Life, Slavery, and Acquisition: Aristotle's Introduction to Politics." *Interp* 11(1983), 171-184. Ar's failure to prove that slavery exists naturally underlines the basic issue of *Pol* 1: mankind's dependence on, or slavery to, nature. Ar sees trade and commerce as limiting a person's capacity for political activity.   **[5104]**

――――. cf. #1122.

NUSSBAUM, M. "Nature, Function, and Capability: Aristotle on Political Distribution." *OSAP* Suppl. (1988), 145-184. Ar enunciates a distributive conception of justice in which a political arrangement is good just in case it secures conditions necessary for people's realization of their basic capacities to fullest extent. Also identifies certain complications in Ar's approach.   **[5105]**

――――. "Reply to David Charles." *OSAP* Suppl. (1988), 207-214. Response to Charles' (#5037) comments on #5105.   **[5106]**

PECIRKA, J. "A Note on Aristotle's Conception of Citizenship and the Role of Foreigners in Fourth-Century Athens." *Eirene* 6(1967), 23-26. Ar's overly idealistic view of the *koinonia* ("fellowship") of citizens has distorted modern views of Athens in fifth and fourth centuries B. C. [5107]

PETERSON, F. H. *A Philosophy of Man and Society.* New York: Philosophical Library, 1971. Good coverage of Ar's political views. [5108]

POLANSKY, R. "The Dominance of *Polis* for Aristotle." *Dialogos* 14(1979), 43-56. Argues for Ar's true, moderate position regarding dominance of *polis* over individuals. Government has it place, and can be just, but is also open to abuse. Reply to D. J. Allan (#4018) and E. Barker (#5032). [5109]

PRICE, G. "Confrontation and Understanding in the Foundations of Political Philosophy." *Method* 1(1983), 114-133. Discusses tension between Platonic and Aristotelian traditions as seen through work of Voegelin (#1670). [5110]

QUINN, T. S. "Parts and Wholes in Aristotle's *Politics* Book III." *SJPh* 24(1986), 577-588. Examines Ar's efforts to discern relation between citizen and city in ways aiming to preserve humanity of political inquiry and role of deliberation. [5111]

RESNICK, D. "Justice, Compromise and Constitutional Rules in Aristotle's *Politics*," in *Compromise in Ethics, Law, and Politics*, ed. J. R. Pennock (New York Univ. Pr., 1979), pp. 69-86. Ar confronts issue of class conflict directly and attempts to work out a political theory that recognizes its inevitable presence. [5112]

RHODES, P. J. *A Commentary on the Aristotelian* Athenaion Politeia. Oxford: Clarendon Pr., 1981. Section-by-section commentary which is more historical than philosophical. Argues the work was composed by a member of Ar's school. [5113]

RITTER, J. "On the Foundations of Practical Philosophy in Aristotle," in *Contemporary German Philosophy, vol. 2*, ed. D. E. Christensen (University Park: PA State Univ. Pr., 1983), pp. 39-58. Explores foundation and substance of ethical and political order of city upon its breaking free from *nomos* of tradition. [5114]

ROMER, F. E. "The *Aisymneteia*: A Problem in Aristotle's Historical Method." *AJPh* 103(1982), 25-46. Ar's account of the "elective" tyranny of Pittacus of Mytilene appears to be historically reliable, though its structure and purpose are influenced by Ar's philosophical assumptions about politics. [5115]

ROSEN, F. "The Political Context of Aristotle's Categories of Justice." *Phron* 20(1975), 228-240. To understand Ar's concept of justice we must consider it in the context of *NE* 5 and study connections between his four categories of justice (universal, distributive, corrective, reciprocity) and the major political themes of *NE* and *Pol*. [5116]

ROWE, C. J. "Aims and Methods in Aristotle's *Politics*." *CQ* 27(1977), 159-172. Examines nature of contrast between Books 4-6 ("empirical" books) and Books 7-8 ("Utopian" books). Also questions application of genetic method to composition and structure of work. [5117]

RUTHERFORD, L. "Notes on Educational Theory." *JWVaPhSoc* 9(1974) 18-20. Compares Ar's and Dewey's theories of education for a democratic society. Both see education as moving people toward happiness by means of virtuous action or discipline. **[5118]**

SAUNDERS, T. J. "*Arete* and *Ergon* in Aristotle, *Politics* III,iv,1276b24-26." *Mnem* 33(1980), 353-355. Tries to correct weaknesses in standard translations, which do not convey the necessary connection between *arete* ("virtue" or "function") and *ergon* ("work" or "deed"). **[5119]**

————. "A Note on Aristotle, *Politics* I,1." *CQ* 26(1976), 316-317. Role of the *politikos* can be better understood if one understands parts of *polis*. Each part has its own nature and roles. **[5120]**

SCHALL, J. V. "Aristotelian Political Theory: Immortality and Happiness," in *Reason, Revelation and the Foundations of Political Philosophy* (Baton Rouge: LA State Univ. Pr., 1987), pp. 38-62. Because Ar believed that the soul could exist independent of the body, a kind of immortal happiness was possible. But happiness of the whole person requires common life and thus the science of politics. **[5121]**

————. "Nature and Finality in Aristotle." *LThPh* 45(1989), 73-85. Ar's view that everything has natural limits helps him to define politics as limited to itself, with narrower implications than metaphysics. **[5122]**

————. "On Natural Law — Aristotle." *Vera Lex* 7(1987), 11-12, 26. Concept of natural law is based on a notion of creation or revelation which is not found in Ar. His idea of stable essences underlying nature might, however, be capable of supporting a doctrine of natural law. **[5123]**

SCHOLLMEIER, P. "The Democracy Most in Accordance with Equality." *HPolTho* 9(1988), 205-209. Explores why Ar first divides democracy into five species, but then later twice distinguishes four species. Finds solution for this problem in difference between philosophical and ordinary uses of language. **[5124]**

SCHUETRUMPF, E. "Platonic Methodology in the Program of Aristotle's Political Philosophy: *Politics* IV.1." *TAPhA* 119(1989), 209-218. Ar based his comprehensive political theory not on the model of his scientific studies but on the program outlined in *Phaedrus* for the field of rhetoric, a scheme which includes law-giving. **[5125]**

SHINER, R. A. "Aristotle's Theory of Equity," in #1283, pp. 173-192. For Ar, equity does not serve to fill in "gaps" left by legislation, but written law "falls short of" the ideal standard of universality it has at face-value. **[5126]**

SMITH, N. D. "Aristotle's Theory of Natural Slavery." *Phoenix* 37(1983), 109-122. Ar bases his theory of natural slavery on two models: body/soul and reason/emotion. His argument requires both, but the two cannot be combined. **[5127]**

SMITH, S. B. "Goodness, Nobility, and Virtue in Aristotle's Political Science." *Polity* 19(1986), 5-26. Ar's only justification for political life is the improvement of human happiness and character. His views are more realistic than often recognized. **[5128]**

SPELMAN, E. V. "Aristotle and the Politicization of the Soul," in *Discovering Reality:*

Feminist Perspectives on Epistemology, Metaphysics, Methodology, and Philosophy of Science, ed. S. Harding and M. B. Hintikka (Dordrecht, Nether.: Reidel, 1983), pp. 17-30. Ar's argument that men are by nature rulers of women is said to be based on relations between rational and irrational elements of human soul. Examines this argument in order to explore whether metaphysical positions are politically innocent.   **[5129]**

SPRINGBORG, P. "Aristotle and the Problem of Needs." *HPolTho* 5(1984), 393-424. Ar sees needs and their satisfaction through production and exchange as the basis of society.   **[5130]**

STERN, S. M. *Aristotle on the World State.* Oxford: Cassirer, 1968. Arabic version of what purports to be a letter from Ar to Alexander the Great goes back to a Greek original; two passages may go back to Ar himself.   **[5131]**

STRAUSS, L. "Letter to Helmut Kuhn." *IndepJPh* 2(1978), 23-26. Focuses on Strauss' disagreement with Kuhn over Ar's doctrine of natural right.   **[5132]**

TAYLOR, D. "Flew, Aristotle and Usury." *Auslegung* 9(1982), 76-84. Challenges Anthony Flew's argument that Ar's economic concepts in *Pol* are based on three misconceptions.   **[5133]**

TEJERA, V. "On the Nature of Reflective Discourse in Politics." *Ph&Rh* 17(1984), 59-72. Discusses political reflection in context of Ar's view that if political science were entirely theoretical, then it would be a speculative discipline, like physics, and not addressed to practice.   **[5134]**

TSIRKIN, J. B. "Carthage and the Problem of Polis." *Rivista di Studi Fenici* 14(1986), 129-141. For Ar the city of Carthage, Phoenician in origin, conformed to the pattern of a (large) Greek polis. Archeological evidence bears him out.   **[5135]**

VANDER WAERDT, P. A. "Kingship and Philosophy in Aristotle's Best Regime." *Phron* 30(1985), 249-273. Discusses apparent inconsistency between Ar's willingness to support permanent rule of a king of outstanding virtue and his claim that it is just for natural freemen to share in ruling through rotation of office.   **[5136]**

————. "The Political Intention of Aristotle's Moral Philosophy." *AncPh* 5(1985), 77-89. Critical discussion of R. Bodeus' work, *Le philosophe et la cite* (1982).   **[5137]**

VER EECKE, W. "The State: Ethics and Economics," in #4282, pp. 195-204. Concept of "merit good" in economic theory could be resolved by paying attention to Aristotelian insights.   **[5138]**

VON FRITZ, K. *The Relevance of Ancient Social and Political Philosophy for Our Times: A Short Introduction to the Problem.* Berlin: De Gruyter, 1974. Surveys lessons to be learned from the past, especially from Ar, whose philosophy can be shown to have value for solving modern social and political problems.   **[5139]**

————., and **KAPP, E.** "The Development of Aristotle's Political Philosophy and the Concept of Nature," in #4036, pp. 113-134. Examines Ar's account of structure and purpose of political association and role of concept of nature. Focuses on his thesis that the state is a natural institution.   **[5140]**

VON LEYDEN, W. "Aristotle and the Concept of Law." *Ph* 42(1967), 1-19. Ar examines four aspects of the problem of the nature of law and why it has binding force: 1) general nature, 2) rationality, 3) moral nature, 4) antiquity.   **[5141]**

————. *Aristotle on Equality and Justice: His Political Argument.* New York: St. Martin's Pr., 1985. Examines Ar's discussion with goal of relating it to modern considerations of problems of how to render the principle of equality compatible with the idea of fairness and of how to combine facts of individual as well as social diversity in civil life with demands for political justice and cohesion.   **[5142]**

WAGNER, P. A. "The Aristotelian Notion of 'Nomos' and Educational Policy Studies." *Review Journal of Philosophy and Social Science* 5(1980), 219-227. Suggests that a closer look at Ar's notion of *nomos* would make us less eager for national policy initiatives by those in power.   **[5143]**

WALUCHOW, W. J. "Professor Weinrib on Corrective Justice," in #1283, pp. 153-158. Challenges Weinrib's view (#5145) that Corrective Justice inheres in and makes intelligible very nature of transactions, and hence that private law, as sphere of law which pertains to transactions, must be modelled on Corrective Justice.   **[5144]**

WEINRIB, E. J. "Aristotle's Forms of Justice," in #1283, pp. 133-152. Shows how Ar's account of justice is formal, not substantive. Distributive and Corrective Justice express abstract forms of organization or principles of intelligibility.   **[5145]**

WHEELER, M. "Aristotle's Analysis of the Nature of Political Struggle," in #4036, pp. 159-169. Studies notion of *stasis*. Compares Ar and Marx, and argues that while Ar is aware of class struggle between rich and poor, he is more impressed by struggle between good and bad classes in state.   **[5146]**

WILDER, A. "On the Essential Equality of Men and Women in Aristotle." *Angelicum* 59(1980), 200-233. In *Meta* Iota Ar argues for the essential identity of male and female. The designations "male" and "female" are only incidental. This does not mean, however, that Ar advocates political equality between the genders, any more than he does between various classes in society.   **[5147]**

WILSON, J. F. "Power, Rule and Politics: The Aristotelian View." *Polity* 13(1980), 80-96. For Ar political relationships are based not on power and force, but on the need to develop moral and intellectual virtue. The leaders in any primitive community are those most in possession of such virtues.   **[5148]**

WINTHROP, D. "Aristotle and Political Responsibility." *PolTheo* 3(1975), 406-422. Ordinary citizens presume that politics is a matter of their rational choices. Political scientists understand politics as a matter of choices which are arbitrary or based on preferences and bias. Ar proposes a resolution to this problem in *Pol* 3.   **[5149]**

————. "Aristotle on Participatory Democracy." *Polity* 11(1978), 151-171. Ar viewed participatory democracy as natural, but did not take all facets of a human being into consideration when he did so. Overview of his position on democracy.   **[5150]**

ZUCKERT, C. "Aristotle on the Limits and Satisfactions of Political Life." *Interp* 11(1983), 185-206. People reach their full potential only through political association,

Ar maintains. But several factors, such as lack of education and time, prohibit everyone from participating fully. Among those who can participate, it is difficult to recognize ones with particular capabilities before they are shaped by their environment. **[5151]**

For related items see #191, #1670, #1970, #1993, #2009, #3626, #3829, #3949, #4012, #4018, #4036, #4058, #4145, #4256, #4364, #4424, #5260, #5261.

PSYCHOLOGY

The first thing one must do to understand Ar's psychology, as with P's, is to abandon all preconceptions about the meaning of the word based on the modern use of it. Ar was not Freud in a tunic.

The word "psychology" literally means "study of the soul." As noted in the introduction to the section of P's psychology (p. 237), the word *psyche* had broader implications for the Greeks, something like "life force." It is the non-physical part of an animal, the part which animates it.

It is in *De anima* (*Peri psyches* in Greek) that Ar treats this subject most fully. J. H. Randall has suggested that this title should be translated *On Living and Knowing*, for Ar is examining the processes by which an organism moves itself and becomes aware of its environment. The first book of that treatise reviews earlier philosopher's opinions, as Ar frequently does, and shows that soul is not material, nor a "harmony," as the Pythagoreans maintained, nor is it something which permeates the material world, as P argued.

In Book 2 Ar defines soul as "substance in the sense of being, the form of a natural body, which potentially has life." It is the *arche*, the fundamental principle, which distinguishes this field of study from others. He goes on to discuss the functions of the soul in nutrition, perception, and other areas related to the five senses. Imagination is the faculty which provides the link between the five senses and the intelligence, making it possible for a creature to remember past occurrences similar to one it is experiencing at the moment and to draw conclusions from such experiences. There is also what he calls the "common sense" (*koine aisthesis*), which enables creatures to recognize similarities such as shape, number, and color, among things perceived by each of the five senses. Living creatures possess these functions of the soul in varying degrees, making it possible to arrange them in a hierarchy with mankind at the top as the only creature which has reasoning capacity. This reasoning capacity, or intelligence (*nous*), has no physical location in the body.

Ar creates some confusion about his concept of *nous* when, in *De anima* 3.5, he refers to an active and a passive *nous*, as though the two were separate. The passive *nous* is not mixed with the rest of the body. It serves to realize the potential of things, just as light makes colors. It is immortal. Whether it is somehow God dwelling in the human soul has been debated for centuries.

It is possible that Ar's view of the soul changed over his lifetime. Judging from fragments of his earliest works, he took an essentially Platonic stance, even arguing for the doctrine of *anamnesis* (recollection), which was based on the idea of the reincarnation of the immortal soul. In some of his biological works he seems to speak of soul and body as two substances.

ACKRILLL, J. L. "Aristotle's Definitions of *Psyche*." *PAS* 73(1972-1973), 119-133; also in #5158, pp. 65-75. Examines weaknesses of application to body and soul of metaphysical distinction between matter and form, and why Ar might have been unable to escape from the difficulties involved. **[5152]**

ADLER, M. J. "Sense Cognition: Aristotle vs. Aquinas." *NewSchol* 42(1968), 578-591. Explains why Thomistic position on sense cognition is either self-contradictory or untenable in its ability to explain the existence of knowledge. Elucidates Aristotelian position and defends its tenability. **[5153]**

ANDRIOPOULOS, D. Z. "Aristotle's Concept of *Sozesthai* in Terms of His Theory of *Antilepsis*." *Platon* 21(1969), 305-307. Ar's wide-ranging knowledge of biology served as a foundation for his psychology, which stresses activity as principal characteristic of all organisms. **[5154]**

————. "The Structuralistic Aspects in Aristotle's Theory of *Aisthesis* and *Antilepsis*." *Platon* 22(1970), 228-232. Compares Ar's explanation of various psychological *kineseis* to modern structuralist methods. **[5155]**

APOSTLE, H. *Aristotle's* On the Soul. Grinnell, IA: Peripatetic Pr., 1981. Translation with commentaries. **[5156]**

BARNES, J. "Aristotle's Concept of Mind." *PAS* 72(1971-1972), 101-114; also in #5158, pp. 32-41. Ar does not make the soul a non-physical substance, but he does postulate non-physical properties. Hence, the emotions and sense perception include a non-physical component. **[5157]**

BARNES, J., et al. *Articles on Aristotle, 4: Psychology and Aesthetics.* New York: St. Martin's Press, 1978. Collection of previously published essays, abstracted herein. Topics include Ar's treatment of soul, views on poetry and tragedy. **[5158]**

BERTI, E. "The Intellection of 'Indivisibles' According to Aristotle *De Anima* III.6," in #5199, pp. 141-164. Examines whether 3.6 can be interpreted in a non-intuitionist way so as to make this section more consistent with following chapters where Ar indicates that soul never thinks without images. **[5159]**

BERTMAN, M. A. "The Function of the Rational Principle in Aristotle." *Thom* 37(1973), 686-701. Explores teleological aspects of Ar's views of the world system, human decision-making, and animal movement. The exact role of *nous* in these processes is difficult to define. **[5160]**

BLOCK, I. "Aristotle on the Common Sense: A Reply to Kahn and Others." *AncPh* 8(1988), 235-249. Defends 1961 paper against Kahn (#5195). Discrepancies in account of relationship between specific senses and common sense that exist between *De Anima* and *Parva Naturalia* show that Ar wavered in his view and that *Parva Naturalia* offers a more sophisticated and adequate view. **[5161]**

BOLTON, R. "Aristotle's Definitions of the Soul: *De Anima* II 1-3." *Phron* 23(1978) 258-278. Studies structure of familiar definition of soul as Form of body and offers a new interpretation which makess definition consistent with doctrine of prime mover, with theory of separate intellect and with various types of mind-body dualism. **[5162]**

BRENNAN, S. O. "Sensing and the Sensitive Mean in Aristotle." *NewSchol* 47(1973), 279-310. Examines Ar's concept of the sensitive mean and how it functions in reception of form without matter. Some scholars take sensing as mere touch, but Ar rejected that possibility. The psychic aspect of sensing is what must be explained. **[5163]**

BRENTANO, F. *The Psychology of Aristotle: In Particular His Doctrine of the Active Intellect. With an Appendix Concerning the Activity of Aristotle's God.* Berkeley: Univ. of CA Pr., 1977. Translation and reprint of an 1867 work which exegetes *De anima* 3.5, defends Ar's concern for individuality, argues against certain mystical misinterpretations. Discusses Ar's theory of soul and of thought, perception, desire. **[5164]**

BRONIAK, C. "On Aristotle's Mind and Being." *Dial*(PST) 27(1985), 54-60. Considers how Ar treats mind and being as a single consideration. **[5165]**

BUFORD, T. O. "Knowing Conceptual Universals, Making Imaginative Universals." *ProcPhEd* 44(1988), 432-436. *De anima* 430a15-17 should not be interpreted to mean that mind makes imaginative universals. Ar's epistemology, as seen in *PostAn* 100a14-17, is more realistic and asserts that the mind finds conceptual universals. **[5166]**

CATAN, J. R. "The Aristotelian Aporia Concerning Separate Mind." *ModSch* 46(1968) 40-50. Analyzing *De anima* 3.5, argues that Ar views separate mind as partially fulfilling the role of P's Forms developed in *Rep* 6. **[5167]**

CHARLTON, W. "Aristotle's Definition of Soul." *Phron* 25(1980), 170-186. Examines importance of *dynamis* (power) and *entelechia* (possibility) in Ar's definition of soul. He stresses former in his discussion of bodies, latter when defining soul. **[5168]**

CHROUST, A.-H. "Aristotle's *Protrepticus* Versus Aristotle's *On Philosophy*: A Controversy Over the Nature of Dreams." *Theta Pi* 3(1974), 168-178. Attempts to reconcile two passages from Ar which talk about soul during sleep as either inactive or capable of experience. **[5169]**

————. "The Doctrine of the Soul in Aristotle's Lost Dialogue *On Philosophy*." *NewSchol* 42(1968), 364-373. Frags upon which reconstruction of *On Phil* rests present a doctrine of soul that possesses a spiritual nature similar to divine nature. **[5170]**

————. "*Eudemus* or *On the Soul*: A Lost Dialogue of Aristotle on the Immortality of the Soul." *Mnem* 19(1966), 17-30. This work, dating from 353 B. C., differs from Plato's *Phaedo* and from Ar's other discussions of soul because it is essentially a *consolatio* written upon the death of Eudemus. **[5171]**

————. "The Psychology in Aristotle's Lost Dialogue *Eudemus* or *On the Soul*." *AClass* 9(1966), 49-62. Looks at Platonic influences on Ar's concept of soul and differences between the lost *Eudemus* and the extant *De Anima*. **[5172]**

COHEN, S. M. "The Credibility of Aristotle's Philosophy of Mind," in #5374, pp. 103-125. Discusses controversy between those, such as Putnam and Nussbaum on the one hand and Burnyeat on the other, who disagree over interpretation of Ar's psychology. Ar's theory has more validity than some will allow, but this does not mean that functionalists have read Ar rightly. **[5173]**

DULIN, J. T. "Memory in Aristotle and Some Neo-Aristotelians." *PhilStud* (Ireland) 24(1976), 205-214. Provides an overview of Ar's theoretical model of memory and his notions of similarity, contrariety, and contiguity.   **[5174]**

EASTERLING, H. J. "A Note on *De Anima* 413a8-9." *Phron* 11(1966), 159-162. Examines several interpretations of *De Anima* 413a8-9 and suggests that concept of *psyche* as efficient cause need not be rejected, but can be "reinterpreted in terms of the *entelechy* doctrine."   **[5175]**

EBERT, T. "Aristotle on What is Done in Perceiving." *ZPhilForsch* 37(1983), 181-198. Focuses on active side to sense perception, and in particular, the sort of activity involved in judging.   **[5176]**

ENGMANN, J. "Imagination and Truth in Aristotle." *JHPh* 41(1976), 259-265. Identifies some inconsistencies in Ar's concept of imagination and attempts to explain them. He does not make clear his criteria for truth and falsity.   **[5177]**

FITZPATRICK, F. J. "Aristotle, Aquinas and Ryle: Thought Processes and Judgment." *PhilStud* (Ireland) 31(1986-87), 197-227. Defends insistence by Ar and Aquinas that acts of judgment are indispensable ingredients in all thought processes.   **[5178]**

FORTENBAUGH, W. W. *Aristotle on Emotion. A Contribution to Philosophical Psychology, Rhetoric, Poetics, Politics, and Ethics.* New York: Barnes & Noble, 1975. Emphasizes Ar's connection between emotion and cognition. His theory grew out of studies in Academy which are intimated in P's *Philebus* and led to Ar's theories of bipartite psychology, rhetoric as persuasion, need of education for young people, women, and slaves, and conception of moral virtue as perfection of man's alogical side. **[5179]**

————. "A Note on *De Anima* 412b19-20." *Phron* 13(1968), 88-89. Ar's claim that sight is "the essence of the eye," in some way defining the eye, contradicts his statements in *Parva Naturalia* about role of heart in perception.   **[5180]**

————. "On the Antecedents of Aristotle's Bipartite Psychology." *GRBS* 11(1970), 233-250; also in #42, pp. 303-320. One should be careful about asserting that Ar's bipartite psychology originated from a popular psychology exemplified in the works of Euripides. There is nothing to support the claim that his bipartite psychology develops out of tri-partition by combining the two lower elements of the tripartite theory.   **[5181]**

————. "Recent Scholarship on the Psychology of Aristotle." *CW* 60(1967), 316-327. Bibliography with critical discussion.   **[5182]**

FREELAND, C. "Commentary on Modrak's 'Aristotle on Thinking'." *PBACAPh* 2(1986), 237-242. Response to #5206. Asks how psychological and epistemic concerns are to be integrated in Ar's account of *nous*. Also if making inferences is characteristic of all thinking, how complex is the influential procedure built into our knowledge of essences?   **[5183]**

GRAESER, A. "On Aristotle's Framework of *Sensibilia*," in #5199, pp. 69-98. Examines division of all sensibilia into two kinds: "proper" sensibilia and "incidental" sensibilia, and asks whether these two classes are meant to be mutually exclusive.   **[5184]**

HAMLYN, D. W., trans. *De Anima, Books II & III*. Oxford Univ. Pr., 1968. Translation and notes. Intended for "Greekless readers." Also includes some passages from Book 1. Notes discuss theory of meaning and nature of perception in Ar. **[5185]**

HANKINSON, R. J. "Explanatory Powers." *Apeir* 21(1988), 181-196. Review and discussion of #5207. **[5186]**

HARDIE, W. F. R. "Concepts of Consciousness in Aristotle." *Mind* 85(1976), 388-411. Reviews recent work. **[5187]**

HARTMAN, E. *Substance, Body, and Soul: Aristotelian Investigations*. Princeton Univ. Pr., 1977. Examines Ar's concept of soul in terms of modern materialist philosophy and argues that Ar had such an understanding of consciousness that he can be described as having a concept of the person as substance. Useful bibliography. **[5188]**

HARVEY, P. "Aristotle on Truth and Falsity in *De Anima* 3.6." *JHPh* 16(1978), 219-220. Challenges view that Ar is inconsistent in his application of criteria of truth and falsity in this chapter. **[5189]**

HORNE, J. R. "Randall's Interpretation of the Aristotelian 'Active Intellect'." *Dial*(Can) 10(1971), 305-316. "Active Intellect" should not be interpreted, as J. H. Randall does in his book (*Aristotle*, 1960), as describing language functions but as the almost mystical experience of insight. **[5190]**

HUBY, P. M. "*De Anima* 404b17-27." *Apeir* 1 #2(1967), 14-15. Examines whether doctrines set forth in this passage refer to views of Plato or those of Xenocrates. The passage may be a later addition. **[5191]**

———. "The Paranormal in the Works of Aristotle and his Circle." *Apeir* 13 #1(1979), 53-62. Ar's reports of paranormal events (ghosts, visions, etc.) indicate that he was ambivalent about their veracity. **[5192]**

HUDSON, S. D. "Reason and Motivation in Aristotle." *CanJPh* 11(1981), 111-135. Focusing primarily on *De anima*, argues that Ar holds that reason can be practical in sense that it can govern and guide behavior in ways other than merely directing us to relevant means for satisfaction of some passion, desire, or need. **[5193]**

HYMAN, A. "Aristotle's Theory of the Intellect and Its Interpretation by Averroes," in #3631, pp. 161-191. In focusing on human intellect, discusses Ar's account of nature of soul, and since thinking rests on sensing and imagining, discusses these two cognitive acts while examining thinking. **[5194]**

KAHN, C. H. "Sensation and Consciousness in Aristotle's Psychology." *AGPh* 48(1966), 43-81; also in #5158, pp. 1-31. It is difficult for modern students of psychology to interpret Ar because terms which both use do not actually mean the same. Both Ar and moderns also have concepts for which the other has no equivalent term. **[5195]**

KOSMAN, L. A. "Perceiving That We Perceive: *On The Soul* III,2." *PhR* 84(1975), 499-519. If Ar is discussing self-consciousness in *De anima* 3.2, as many scholars maintain, his arguments are hard to follow. His topic actually seems to be the consciousness characteristic of *all* perception. **[5196]**

LESHER, J. H. "The Meaning of *Nous* in the *Posterior Analytics*." *Phron* 18(1973), 44-68. Examines how *nous* relates to *aisthesis*, *epagoge*, and *katholou* principles, and argues that *nous* is not properly thought of as intuition or intellectual intuition.   **[5197]**

LLOYD, A. C. "Was Aristotle's Theory of Perception Lockean?" *Ratio* 21(1979), 135-148. Ar did not view perceptible qualities as "secondary" qualities or sense data. He seems to have linked thinking to perception.   **[5198]**

LLOYD, G. E. R. and **OWEN, G. E. L.**, eds. *Aristotle on Mind and the Senses: Proceedings of the Seventh Symposium Aristotelicum.* Cambridge Univ. Pr. 1978.   Articles are abstracted herein.   **[5199]**

MANNING, R. "Materialism, Dualism and Functionalism in Aristotle's Philosophy of Mind." *Apeir* 19(1985), 11-23. Ar was not trying to answer the question of what souls are made of. He was concerned to describe what living things do. This qualifies him as a functionalist.   **[5200]**

MANSION, S. "Soul and Life in the *De Anima*," in #5199, pp. 1-20. Examines how the old approach — which asks what soul is — still interferes with the new approach — which decides first to investigate what life is and then to conceive of its principle, the soul, accordingly.   **[5201]**

MASIELLO, R. J. "A Note on Aristotle's Definition of the Soul." *NewSchol* 54(1980), 224-227. Examines Ar's definition of soul as "the form of a natural body having life potentially within it" and problems of interpretation over this definition.   **[5202]**

MAUDLIN, T. "*De Anima* III 1: Is Any Sense Missing?" *Phron* 31(1986), 51-67. Examines opening argument of *De anima* 3.1 (424b20-425a17). Offers a reinterpretation and re-translation which views the passage as dialectical, directed against Empedoclean doctrine, rather than simply expository.   **[5203]**

McKAY, R. "Touching the Bronze Sphere at a Point: A Note on *De Anima* I,1,403a10-16." *Apeir* 13(1979), 86-91. Challenges received view which takes Ar to be constructing analogy between inseparability of soul and physical body and inseparability of straight line from physical body.   **[5204]**

MODRAK, D. K. "An Aristotelian Theory of Consciousness?" *AncPh* 1(1981), 160-170. Ar recognizes four fundamental characteristics of human consciousness: unity, self-awareness, intentionality, and the recognition of relations between cognitive objects. His conception of a central sense could be used to give a rudimentary but relatively satisfactory account of consciousness.   **[5205]**

———. "Aristotle on Thinking." *PBACAPh* 2(1986), 209-236. Examines *De anima* 3.4-8, *Meta* 12.6-9, and *NE* 10.6-8 to discern what is Ar's conception of thought. Elucidates his concept of *nous*; argues that Ar bases his whole model of cognitive activity upon workings of perceptual faculty; that is why priority in explanation is given to object of cognition, in the sense that it both actualizes the faculty and determines its character. Concludes that Ar is not committed to dualism.   **[5206]**

———. *Aristotle: The Power of Perception.* Univ. of Chicago Pr., 1987. Analyzes common conceptual foundations underlying Ar's treatment of sense perception, apperception, imagination, dreaming, memory, thought and consciousness. [5207]

——. "*Koine Aisthesis* and the Discrimination of Sensible Differences in *De Anima* III.2." *CanJPh* 11(1981), 405-424. Ar attributes perception of common objects and discrimination of sensible differences to the same faculty of the soul, the common sense, which is made up of two or more special senses acting together. [5208]

——. "*Phantasia* Reconsidered." *AGPh* 68(1986), 47-69. Ar sees *phantasia* as sensory awareness under conditions when true perception is not possible. His theory is coherent. [5209]

NUSSBAUM, M. C. "Aristotelian Dualism: Reply to Howard Robinson." *OSAP* 2(1984), 197-207. Response to #5228. Offers an alternative characterization of Ar's background questions and motivations which show "great gulf" between Ar and the Cartesian view, and asks what Ar's general hylomorphism says about relationship of substances to their component materials. [5210]

O'MEARA, D. "Remarks on *Dualismus* and the Definition of Soul in Aristotle." *MH* 44(1987), 168-174. In *De anima* Ar defines soul as both a substance and a principle of different functions which inhabits a body. [5211]

OWENS, J. "Aristotelian Soul as Cognitive of Sensibles, Intelligibles and Self," in #3634, pp. 81-98. Ar argues that reception of a sensible form may take place in two ways. In non-cognitive reception of heat or cold, change is described as undergone "with the matter." In any sensation, form of sensible object is received "without the matter." Explores what this contrast means. [5212]

——. "Aristotle — Cognition a Way of Being." *CanJPh* 6(1976), 1-10; also in #3634, pp. 74-80. Examines Aristotelian tenet that to perceive or to know means that the cognitive agent has become and is something other than what he is physically. [5213]

——. "Aristotle on Common Sensibles and Incidental Perception." *Phoenix* 36(1982), 215-236. Ancient commentators took Ar to be opposing the idea that common sensibles are objects perceived incidentally by the various senses. The grammatical construction he uses in this passage supports that interpretation. [5214]

——. "Aristotle's Definition of Soul," in #71, pp. 125-145; also in #3634, pp. 109-121. Examines whether Ar's reasoning actually achieves a definition of soul in terms of "the strict cause" of *Analytics*. [5215]

——. "A Note on Aristotle *De Anima* 3:4,429b9." *Philosophiques* 3(1976), 107-118. A suggested textual emendation in this passage has been adopted in Ross' text and Hamlyn's translation (#5185). But the traditional reading gives a much clearer understanding of Ar's concept of cognition. [5216]

——. "The Universality of the Sensible in the Aristotelian Noetic," in #3634, pp. 59-73; also in #41, pp. 462-477. Explores whether in Aristotelian noetic the human mind may behold sensible things, a notion that is more universal than the sensible. [5217]

PECCORINI, F. L. "Aristotle's Agent Intellect: Myth or Literal Account?" *Thom* 40(1976), 505-534. Ar's expression "Active Mind" is not merely a mythic description of the cognition process. It seems to stand for a definite faculty.   **[5218]**

———. "Divinity and Immortality in Aristotle: A De-mythologized Myth?" *Thom* 43(1979), 217-256. Ar's belief in soul's divinity and immortality through *nous* goes beyond P's position and draws on Orphic mysteries.   **[5219]**

PHILIPPE, M.-D. "Phantasia in the Philosophy of Aristotle." *Thom* 35(1971), 1-42. Ar understands the importance and dangers of imagination. He considers it an intermediate stage between sense perception and intellectual knowledge.   **[5220]**

PREUS, A. "Aristotle's Three Theories of the Soul." *Proceedings of the Creighton Club* (1973), 16-31. Presents Ar's hylomorphic, noetic, and pneumatic theories, and compares them in terms of possible theories of Ar's development.   **[5221]**

———. "*On Dreams* 2,459b24-460a33 and Aristotle's *Opsis*." *Phron* 13(1968), 175-182. Explores order of Ar's psychological writings. Discovers purely physiological senses of words, like *opsis*, heretofore thought essentially psychological.   **[5222]**

———. cf. #4284.

PRITZL, K. "The Cognition of Indivisibles and the Argument of *De Anima* I,3.4-8." *PACPhA* 58(1984), 140-150. Stresses importance of cognition of indivisibles in main argument of this section. The concept of convertibility of being and unity allows Ar to encompass intelligible objects other than composites and their forms.   **[5223]**

———. "On Sense and Sense Organ in Aristotle." *PACPhA* 59(1985), 258-274. Challenges dualist and physicalist interpretations of Aristotelian sense perception, and offers a non-standard view of nature of physical change in the organ.   **[5224]**

REES, D. A. "Aristotle's Treatment of *Phantasia*," in #41, pp. 491-504. At times, *phantasia* signifies occurrence of a mental image, at others it is propositional in character. But even when it is propositional, sensation provides the essential basis.   **[5225]**

RIST, J. M. "Notes on Aristotle's *De Anima* 3.5." *CPh* 61(1966), 8-20; also in #41, pp. 505-521. Offers an interpretation of Ar's account of active and passive intellect. Suggests that Active Intellect is a power to induce thought which is itself some kind of self-thinking being.   **[5226]**

ROBINSON, D. N. *Aristotle's Psychology.* New York: Columbia Univ. Pr., 1989. Examines Ar's psychology from a variety of approaches in terms of: 1) ethology and psychology; 2) perception, learning, and memory; 3) emotion and motivation; 4) rationality and volition; 5) the relation of self to social order.   **[5227]**

ROBINSON, H. "Aristotelian Dualism." *OSAP* 1(1983), 123-144. Maintains that Ar is a dualist, and that this dualism can be approached in two ways: 1) as consequence of his account of *nous*, and 2) in context of emergentist theory of form to be found in the biological works. Argues that human soul is only most extreme case of emergent nature of biological forms.   **[5228]**

———. "Mind and Body in Aristotle." *CQ* 28(1978), 105-124. Ar held perception to be a mental act with a non-physical object. His doctrine of soul as form of body has dualistic implications. [5229]

ROBINSON, T. M. "Soul and Definitional Priority: *De Anima* 414a4-14." *Apeir* 4 #1(1970), 4-12. To read this passage correctly one must be aware of when Ar is referring to definitional priority and when to ontological. Part of the confusion in the passage, noted by W. D. Ross, arises from Ar's density of expression. [5230]

ROSEN, S. "Thought and Touch: A Note on Aristotle's *De Anima*," in #75, pp. 119-126. Argues Ar's account of process of thinking rejects Platonic interpretation of thinking as a kind of seeing and rests on analogy between thought and touch. [5231]

SCHILLER, J. "Aristotle and the Concept of Awareness in Sense Perception." *JHPh* 13(1975), 283-296. Shows how Ar attempts to explicate concept of awareness in sense perception. Takes his characterization of sense perception as reception of forms of sensible objects without matter, and indicates how his attempt to account for awareness breaks down. [5232]

SCHOFIELD, M. "Aristotle on the Imagination," in #5199, pp. 99-140; also in #5157, pp. 103-132. Examines Ar's attempts to distinguish imagination to be always active in perception, and dissociates him from common view that imagination always involves mental image. [5233]

SHIELDS, C. J. "Soul and Body in Aristotle." *OSAP* 6(1988), 103-137. Sorts out Ar's various characterizations of body and soul in light of recent developments in philosophy of mind in order to clarify his position on soul/body relations. [5234]

——. "Soul as Subject in Aristotle's *De anima*." *CQ* 38(1988), 140-149. Souls may be subjects but not of actions requiring motion *kath' hauto*. [5235]

SHINER, R. A. "More on Aristotle's *De Anima* 414a4-14." *Phoenix* 24(1970), 29-38. Examines in detail use of analogy in this passage alluding to complexity of *psyche* and nine elements contained in this analogy. Reply to Sprague (#5243). [5236]

SILVERMAN, A. "Color and Color-Perception in Aristotle's *De Anima*." *AncPh* 9(1989), 271-292. Seeks to explain sense in which, for Ar, colors have an objective existence. Also argues that the taking on in perceiving of the sensible form of the perceptual object does not entail that the matter of the eye becomes colored. [5237]

SKEMP, J. B. "*Orexis* in *De Anima* III.10," in #5199, pp. 181-190. Examines Ar's discussion of way animate beings are led by *orexis* to initiate movement in space. [5238]

SOLMSEN, F. "*Aisthesis* in Aristotelian and Epicurean Thought," in #6065, pp. 151-172. Ar and earlier philosophers took perception to be a function of the soul, quite distinct from the physical senses. Epicurus uses *aisthesis* to mean physical sensations, which he distinguishes from activities of the mind. [5239]

SORABJI, R. "Aristotle on Demarcating the Five Senses." *PhR* 80(1971), 55-79; also in #5158, pp. 76-92. Offers support for Ar's distinguishing four of the senses by reference to their objects — color, odor, sound, flavor; but he goes wrong in defining touch as the contact sense. [5240]

——. *Aristotle on Memory*. Providence, RI: Brown Univ. Pr., 1972. Translation of Ar's treatise *De memoria et reminiscentia*, with notes and an introductory essay.   **[5241]**

——. "Body and Soul in Aristotle." *Ph* 49(1974), 63-89; also in #5158, pp. 42-64. Examines how Ar sometimes thinks of soul as a set of capacities and sometimes views it biologically. Rejects various efforts to assimilate his theory to materialism, to behaviorism, and to intentionalism.   **[5242]**

SPRAGUE, R. K. "Aristotle *De Anima* 414a4-14." *Phoenix* 21(1967), 102-107. Examines Ar's inference at line 13, "therefore the soul is a sort of definition or form, not a matter or subject."   **[5243]**

——. "Aristotle on Red Mirrors (*On Dreams* II 459b24-460a23)." *Phron* 30(1985), 323-325. Explores what interested Ar in the supposed "fact" that the gaze of a menstruating woman can redden a mirror into which she looks. Argues that he uses this example to provide additional illustration of the phenomenon of persistence essential to his explanation of dreams.   **[5244]**

——. "A Parallel with *De Anima* III, 5." *Phron* 17(1972), 250-251. Ar may have based his comparison of active intellect to light on sun analogy in *Rep* 507a ff.   **[5245]**

——. cf. #4817.

TRACY, T. "Heart and Soul in Aristotle," in #42, pp. 321-339. Examines incompatibility of definition of soul at *De anima* 412b5-6 with notion of soul present "in the heart" and operating through the heart found in *Parva Naturalia* and in biological works.   **[5246]**

——. "The Soul-Boatman Analogy in Aristotle's *De Anima*." *CPh* 77(1982), 97-112. Examines importance of 413a8-9 for introducing this concept.   **[5247]**

VANDER WAERDT, P. A. "Aristotle's Criticism of Soul Division." *AJPh* 108(1987), 627-643. In *De anima* 3.9 Ar is not criticizing P's tripartite psychology but theories of some members of the Academy. His comments about bipartite soul are a refinement of his view of relationship between psychology of his ethical/political works and view of human soul as part of a *scala naturae* which he develops in *De anima*.   **[5248]**

WARD, J. K. "Perception and *logos* in *De Anima* ii.12." *AncPh* 8(1988), 217-234. Challenges materialist interpretation that for Ar, perception consists simply in physical changes of sense-organs. Shows how notion of *logos* is used as to explain how senses have capacity to be, and are actually, affected by sensible objects.   **[5249]**

WATSON, G. "*Phantasia* in Aristotle, *De Anima* 3.3." *CQ* 32(1982), 100-113. Ar is more consistent in his use of this term than generally recognized. It should be translated "imagination." It is not judgment or perception but lies between those two.   **[5250]**

WEDIN, M. V. "Aristotle on the Mechanics of Thought." *AncPh* 9(1989), 67-86. Investigates causal mechanics in actual episodes of thinking and role played by system's internal states in such episodes.   **[5251]**

——. *Mind and Imagination in Aristotle*. New Haven, CT: Yale Univ. Pr., 1988. Takes Ar's treatment as an early cognitive theory concentrating on relations between mind and imagination. Argues that imagination is not a standard faculty, but rather a "general representational capability subserving such faculties." [5252]

———. "Tracking Aristotle's *Nous*," in *Human Nature and Natural Knowledge*, ed. A. Donagan et al. (Dordrecht, Netherlands: Reidel, 1986), pp. 167-197. Drawing a functionalist distinction between mind as productive and as receptive enables one to understand Ar's description of the structure of the mind in *De anima* 3.5. [5253]

WEISS, F. G. *Hegel's Critique of Aristotle's Philosophy of Mind*. The Hague: Nijhoff, 1969. Explicates the philosophical psychology of Hegel and Ar simultaneously by interpreting the thought of each in terms of the other. [5254]

WHITE, K. "The Meaning of *Phantasia* in Aristotle's *De Anima* III 3-8." *Dial*(Can) 24(1985), 483-505. Examines theme of *phantasia* as prelude to analysis of *noein* and in context of significance of *phantasia* in human life. [5255]

WIESNER, J. "The Unity of the *De Somno* and the Physiological Explanation of Sleep in Aristotle," in #5199, pp. 241-280. Investigates position of middle set of works of *Parva Naturalia* on sleep, dreams, and divination through dreaming. [5256]

WIJSENBEEK-WIJLER, H. *Aristotle's Concept of Sleep, Soul and Dreams*. Amsterdam: Hakkert, 1978. Makes cursory examination of Ar's criticisms of Plato's psychology, then examines Ar's *De somno, De insomniis*, and *De divinatione per somnium*, quoting at length from each. [5257]

For related items see #1899, #2053, #3551, #3593, #3868, #3678, #5033, #5129, #5615.

RHETORIC

Something about the importance of rhetoric in ancient Greece has already been said in the introduction to the section on P's view of the subject (p. 242). The political circumstances had changed somewhat by the time Ar came to write his treatise on rhetoric. The Greek city-states had been conquered by Philip of Macedon, and independent political oratory had lost much of its importance. Speeches still formed the basis of cases before the courts, but the orators of the late fourth century were beginning to stress a less controversial type of rhetoric. Demetrius of Phalcron, a younger contemporary of Ar's, was reckoned by ancient students of rhetoric as "the first who altered the character of oratory, rendering it weak and effeminate, preferring that it be thought agreeable rather than dignified."

It is against this background that Ar wrote his *Rhetoric*, a handbook similar to a number of others composed in the fourth century. But he is not a rhetorician, nor is he philosophically opposed to rhetoric, as P had been. In his view rhetoric is a productive science. That means, first, that it is concerned with *how* one makes something, not with the value or meaning of the thing made, and, secondly, that it has principles, fundamental rules, like any other science. It has its *technai* ("skills," "techniques") which can be taught and learned. Ar seems to have introduced the teaching of rhetoric in the Academy before the death of P, perhaps in reaction to the opening of a school by the noted rhetorician Isocrates.

This handbook, then, is the distillation of his observations (though not practical experience) on the subject.

Book 1 of the *Rhetoric* analyzes the types of speeches and their objectives and the types of arguments which can be used in each case. The orator must know not only the techniques of speech-making but also the mind of his audience in order to select the appropriate arguments. Ethics and psychology play an important role in Ar's view of rhetoric. The two types of proof most useful in rhetoric are discussed: the enthymeme (a type of syllogism) and induction (collecting examples similar to the case under consideration).

In the second book Ar concentrates on the emotional side of rhetoric: gauging the audience's frame of mind, making oneself appear mild, pathetic, or possessing whatever other characteristic is likely to win the audience's sympathy. Book 3 deals with technical aspects of the delivery of a speech.

The *Rhetoric* was widely read in antiquity, but approaches to communication have changed so much that its technical material is of limited interest today. Ar's insight into the "manipulative" aspects of rhetoric, however, deserve further study.

ADAMIK, T. "Aristotle's Theory of the Period." *Philologus* 128(1984), 184-201. *Rhet* 3.9, in which Ar discusses rhetorical periods, is logical within itself and an integral part of his theory of style. Its originality is apparent when it is compared with other classical writers on the subject. **[5258]**

———. "Remarks on Aristotle's Period Theory," in #69, II, pp. 341-346. Reviews Ar's definition of a rhetorical period, providing translation of quoted passages, and studies his use of examples in periods. **[5259]**

ARNHART, L. *Aristotle On Political Reasoning.* Dekalb: Northern IL Univ. Pr., 1981. Interprets *Rhet* as an essential part of Aristotelian approach to political science insofar as it shows the fundamental significance of commonsense experience for reasoning about political matters. Shows that Ar's theory of rhetoric is a genuine form of reasoning with distinct political value. **[5260]**

———. "The Rationality of Political Speech: An Interpretation of Aristotle's *Rhetoric.*" *Interp* 9(1981), 141-154. Summary of arguments presented in #5260. **[5261]**

BATOR, P. G. "The 'Good Reasons Movement': A 'Confounding' of Dialectic and Rhetoric?" *Ph&Rh* 21(1988), 38-47. Response to Crusius (#5275). **[5262]**

BENOIT, W. L. "Aristotle's Example: The Rhetorical Induction." *QJS* 66(1980), 182-192. Discusses Hauser's study of example (#5297). Analyzes example as a rhetorical induction which does not examine every instance of the class being considered, applies the generalization obtained to another instance, and deals with contingencies. **[5263]**

———. "On Aristotle's Example." *Ph&Rh* 20(1987), 261-267. Explores Ar's phrase "part to part" in his discussion of proof by example. **[5264]**

BITZER, L. R. "Aristotle's Enthymeme Revisited," in #5280, pp. 141-155. Explores deficiencies of several proposed definitions of enthymeme and explains it as a syllogism composed by orator and audience together. Speaker must draw on audience's knowledge and attitudes for premises. Enthymeme's purpose is persuasion.   [5265]

BLETTNER, E. "One Made Many and Many Made One: The Role of Asyndeton in Aristotle's Rhetoric." *Ph&Rh* 16(1983), 49-54. The use of connectives in spoken language can make many things one. Deliberate omission of connectives (*asyndeton*) makes one thing many. This technique can appeal to a part of the soul which other techniques leave untouched. The rhythm of the *asyndeton* evokes pleasure and leads to recognition and learning.   [5266]

BRANDES, P. D. "The Composition and Preservation of Aristotle's *Rhetoric*." *SM* 35(1968), 482-491. Reviews current scholarship (with bibliography) on how this work was written and transmitted.   [5267]

CHRISTENSEN, J. "The Formal Character of *Koinoi Topoi* in Aristotle's Rhetoric and Dialectic. Illustrated by the List in *Rhetorica* II.23." *Cahiers de l'Institut du moyen-age grec et latin* 57(1988), 3-10. Somewhat technical study of the list of rules in *Rhet* shows that only one is a "commonplace" in the usual sense.   [5268]

CHROUST, A.-H. "Aristotle's Earliest 'Course of Lectures on Rhetoric'," in #5280, pp. 22-36. Ar's lectures on rhetoric, to which several sources refer, was probably delivered between 360-355 in the Academy, perhaps prompted by opposition to Isocrates' teaching of rhetoric. Ar's extant *Rhet* does not preserve portions of the lectures.   [5269]

————. "Aristotle's First Literary Effort: The *Gryllus*, a Lost Dialogue on the Nature of Rhetoric." *REG* 78(1965), 576-591; also in #5280, pp. 37-51. Ar's first serious work was not an encomium on Xenophon's son but a defense of Platonic views on rhetoric and an attack on Isocrates' techniques.   [5270]

CONLEY, T. M. "The Greekless Reader and Aristotle's *Rhetoric*." *QJS* 65(1979), 74-79. Analyzes some passages in Cooper's translation of *Rhet* which can mislead readers who do not know Greek.   [5271]

————. "*Pathe* and *Pisteis*: Aristotle *Rhet*. II,2-11." *Hermes* 110(1982), 300-315. Ar's purpose in this passage goes beyond discussing ways of playing on an audience's emotions. He is trying to devise a list of *topoi* for arguments.   [5272]

CONSIGNY, S. "Dialectical, Rhetorical, and Aristotelian Rhetoric." *Ph&Rh* 22(1989), 281-287. Reply to Holmberg (#900) and Gaines (#5286). Ar's rhetoric is neither dialectical nor rhetorical. It looks for persuasive elements without being committed to any particular ontology.   [5273]

CREM, T. M. "The Definition of Rhetoric According to Aristotle," in #5280, pp. 52-71. First two chapters of *Rhet* 1 contain Ar's definition of the art, which he approaches theoretically, not as a practitioner, like Cicero. Rhetoric's aim is not merely to succeed but to discover what means of persuasion are available in any particular case.   [5274]

CRUSIUS, T. W. "A Case for Kenneth Burke's Dialectic and Rhetoric." *Ph&Rh* 19(1986), 23-37. Burke's treatment of rhetoric and dialectic is the first significantly new approach to the problem since Ar. Compares the two on several points.   [5275]

———. "Response to Paul G. Bator on 'A Case for Kenneth Burke's Dialectic and Rhetoric.'" *Ph&Rh* 21(1988), 153-157. Reply to #5262. Ar sees rhetoric and dialectic as having different functions and techniques.   [5276]

CURRIE, H. M. "Aristotle and Quintilian: Physiognomical Reflections," in #3809, pp. 15-26. Explores Ar's references to physiognomy in context of discussing importance of delivery in speech.   [5277]

DE ROMILLY, J. "Logic versus Magic: Aristotle and Later Writers," in *Magic and Rhetoric in Ancient Greece* (Cambridge, MA: Harvard Univ. Pr., 1975), pp. 69-88. Ar removed the "magic" from rhetoric by defining it as a *techne* governed by rules of logic. He does not see its primary purpose as swaying an audience by the power of words or images but convincing them by logic.   [5278]

DOUGLASS, R. B. "An Aristotelian Orientation to Rhetorical Communication." *Ph&Rh* 7(1974), 80-88. A modern approach to rhetoric based on Ar's ideas would conceive of rhetoric as a process of deliberative interaction between persons. It is a complex, dynamic process.   [5279]

ERICKSON, K. V., ed. *Aristotle: The Classical Heritage of Rhetoric*. Metuchen, NJ: Scarecrow Pr., 1974. Previously published essays, abstracted herein.   [5280]

———. *Aristotle's Rhetoric: Five Centuries of Philological Research*. Metuchen, NJ: Scarecrow Pr., 1975. Brief introduction to *Rhet* and history of scholarship on it. Bibliography of over 1500 items, not annotated.   [5281]

FORTENBAUGH, W. W. "Aristotle's Platonic Attitude toward Delivery." *Ph&Rh* 19(1986), 242-254. Examines Ar's negative attitude toward delivery. His failure to do justice to role of voice in oratory is due to P's influence.   [5282]

———. "Aristotle's *Rhetoric* on Emotions." *AGPh* 52(1970) 40-70; also in #5158, pp. 133-153; also in #5280, pp. 205-234. Definitions of emotions constitute an analytical advance particularly in way Ar seeks to specify how emotions involve cognition. Thus anger is disturbance due to certain beliefs. Emphasis upon cognition helps distinguish emotions from bodily drives and thus helps to develop an adequate moral psychology.   [5283]

FOWLER, R. L. "Aristotle on the Period (*Rhet*. 3.9)." *CQ* 32(1982), 89-99. Ar defines a rhetorical period in terms of its logical structure.   [5284]

GABIN, R. J. "Aristotle and the New Rhetoric: Grimaldi and Valesio." *Ph&Rh* 20(1987), 171-182. Examines these two studies which reveal tendencies of the "new rhetoric" and analyzes their emphasis on Ar's "textuality."   [5285]

GAINES, R. N. "Aristotle's Rhetorical Rhetoric?" *Ph&Rh* 19(1986), 194-200. Reply to Holmberg (#900). Some scholars hold Ar disliked rhetoric for its ambiguity, both in type of speaking involved and reasoning on which it is based, the enthymeme. But for Ar, rhetoric is ability to observe and enthymeme is a valid syllogism.   [5286]

GARVER, E. "Aristotle's *Rhetoric* as a Work of Philosophy." *Ph&Rh* 19(1986), 1-22. First chapter is not simply another handbook on public speaking, but a philosophical inquiry into nature of persuasion.   [5287]

——. "Aristotle's *Rhetoric* on Unintentionally Hitting the Principles of the Sciences." *Rhetorica* 6(1988), 381-393. Discusses passages in *Rhet, NE,* and *Pol* where Ar refers to a speaker unintentionally hitting upon a scientific principle. **[5288]**

——. "The Human Function and Aristotle's Art of Rhetoric." *HPhQ* 6(1989), 133-145. Ar's rhetorical theory is not based on principles inferred from human behavior. **[5289]**

GRIMALDI, W. M. A. "The Aristotelian *Topics,*" in #5280, pp. 176-193. Ar differentiates particular from general topics more carefully in *Rhet* than in *Topics.* **[5290]**

——. *Aristotle,* Rhetoric *I, A Commentary.* New York: Fordham Univ. Pr., 1980. Detailed commentary. **[5291]**

——. "Rhetoric and Truth: A Note on Aristotle, *Rhetoric* 1355a21-24." *Ph&Rh* 11(1978), 173-177. For Ar the purpose of rhetoric is not to persuade or mislead, but to assure an explanation of the truth. Interpretation of this passage hinges on translation of the phrase *di' auton.* **[5292]**

——. "*Semeion, Tekmereion, Eikos* in Aristotle's Rhetoric." *AJPh* 101(1980), 383-398. Argumentation by sign (*semeion*) is more convincing than that by likeness (*eikos*) because there is a closer connection between a sign and its signate than between a likeness and the thing it resembles. **[5293]**

——. *Studies in the Philosophy of Aristotle's Rhetoric.* Wiesbaden, Ger.: Steiner, 1972. Sees the enthymeme as central to Ar's concept of rhetoric. Maintains that Ar found nothing objectionable about *ethos* and *pathos.* They are a natural part of the deliberative process. Some difficulties of interpretation in *Rhet* arise from the fact that it was composed over a long period of time and may even contain material not by Ar. Alleged inconsistencies in the work either can be resolved or are insignificant. **[5294]**

HARRIS, H. A. "A Simile in Aristotle's *Rhetoric* (III.9,6)." *CR* 24(1974), 178-179. This simile does not allude to the Peripatetic school but compares a listener to one who loses ground at the turn in a race. **[5295]**

HAUSER, G. A. "Aristotle's Example Revisited." *Ph&Rh* 18(1985), 171-180. Rhetorical examples set in motion a chain of associations in the listener, a kind of deduction which leads to drawing conclusions. **[5296]**

——. "The Example in Aristotle's *Rhetoric*: Bifurcation or Contradiction?" *Ph&Rh* 1(1968), 78-90; also in #5280, pp. 156-168. Examines two seemingly disparate doctrines on example: 1) Book 1 presents example as an independent mode of proof; 2) Book 2 presents example as merely a source of materials for proof. **[5297]**

——. "Reply to Benoit's 'On Aristotle's Example'." *Ph&Rh* 20(1987), 268-273. Reply to #5264. Discusses Ar's account of epistemological aspects of induction. **[5298]**

HEAM, H. R. "Philosophy as Ultimate Rhetoric." *SJPh* 19(1981), 181-195. Contains discussion of Ar's notion of rhetoric and argues that this notion served to extricate an expressive dimension of deliberative-political discourse from mainly technical-manipulative understanding of rhetoric predominant in his time. **[5299]**

HILL, F. I. "The Amorality of Aristotle's Rhetoric." *GRBS* 22(1981), 133-147. Reply to #4320. We need not require a work to have moral content in order to be taken seriously. That is P's view. Some of Ar's works are purely methodological.   **[5300]**

——. "The Rhetoric of Aristotle," in *A Synoptic History of Classical Rhetoric*, ed. J. J. Murphy (New York: Random House, 1972), pp. 19-76. Surveys Ar's organization and purpose. Stresses his syllogistic approach to rhetoric and the ethical foundation on which he builds his theory.   **[5301]**

HOWELL, W. S. "Aristotle and Horace on Rhetoric and Poetics." *QJS* 54(1968), 325-339. For Ar poetics and rhetoric differ in that the former aims at imitation and catharsis while the latter is non-mimetic and aims at persuasion. Both can lead to pleasure. Horace shares Ar's views.   **[5302]**

JORDAN, W. J. "Aristotle's Concept of Metaphor in Rhetoric," in #5280, pp. 235-250. Ar's concept of metaphor has a psychological basis. Listener derives pleasure from a metaphor and constructs a new meaning more efficiently than if it were given to him in literal language.   **[5303]**

KINNEAVY, J. "William Grimaldi — Reinterpreting Aristotle." *Ph&Rh* 20(1987), 183-200. Examines Grimaldi's commentary (#5291) and argues that his attempt "to rescue classical rhetoric from its general disregard" is too expansive.   **[5304]**

LEVIN, S. R. "Aristotle's Theory of Metaphor." *Ph&Rh* 15(1982), 24-46. Ar's purpose in developing theory of metaphor was to find ways of leading a reader to knowledge through unusual linguistic combinations. Some types of metaphors help us to see relations between genus and species. Analogy leads to knowledge of accidents. **[5305]**

LIENHARD, J. T. "A Note on the Meaning of *Pistis* in Aristotle's *Rhetoric*." *AJPh* 87(1966), 446-454; also in #5280, pp. 169-175. Examines scholarly debate over how this word should be translated. It is capable of a variety of meanings, all associated with "proof."   **[5306]**

LORD, C. "The Intention of Aristotle's *Rhetoric*." *Hermes* 109(1981), 326-339. *Rhet* is a practical book guided by a practical intention, that is, the work is not so much concerned with elaborating a satisfactory theory of the nature of rhetoric as it is with bringing about a transformation of contemporary attitudes toward rhetoric.   **[5307]**

McBURNEY, J. H. "The Place of the Enthymeme in Rhetorical Theory," in #5280, pp. 117-140. For Ar the enthymeme serves same purpose in rhetoric that syllogism performs in logic. Its premises, which are probable causes and signs, are intended to influence the listener's emotional state and inspire confidence in the speaker.   **[5308]**

MILLER, A. B. "Enthymemes: Body and Soul." *Ph&Rh* 5(1972), 201-214. Ar's concept of the effect which an enthymeme could have on an audience can be clarified by examining the etymology of the word, its use in his other works, and the relation between public speaking and enthymeme which he describes in *Rhet*.   **[5309]**

——. cf. #4237.

NIMIS, S. "Aristotle's Analogical Metaphors." *Arethusa* 21(1988), 215-226. Ar's views on figures in *Rhet* 3 can be compared to production of metaphors and similes interpreted in light of Marxist understanding of value.   **[5310]**

OATES, W. J. "Aristotle and the Problem of Value," in #5280, pp. 102-116. Though Ar tries to establish an ethical basis for rhetoric in early chapters of *Rhet*, he soon gives up the attempt and produces an amoral — at times immoral — handbook.   **[5311]**

OLIAN, J. R. "The Intended Uses of Aristotle's *Rhetoric*." *SM* 35(1968), 137-148. The work describes rhetorical techniques without discussing their ethical base. Ar could assume that people using his work and dominating the practice of rhetoric in Athens would share his views on ethics.   **[5312]**

ORAVEC, C. "'Observation' in Aristotle's Theory of Epideictic." *Ph&Rh* 9(1976), 162-174. Ar understood epideictic rhetoric (speeches praising or attacking someone) to depend for its effect in part upon the audience's ability to observe and comprehend the speaker's ability to make judgments.   **[5313]**

PRICE, R. "Some Antistrophes to the *Rhetoric*." *Ph&Rh* 1(1968), 145-164; also in #5280, pp. 72-89. Rhetoric and dialectic are "antistrophic" arts because both share the structure of such arts as are concerned with production of certain *logoi* useful for certain purposes. Rhetoric is an art with no obvious antecedents.   **[5314]**

RAPHAEL, S. "Rhetoric, Dialectic and Syllogistic Argument: Aristotle's Position in *Rhetoric* I-II." *Phron* 19(1974), 153-167. There are not two chronologically separate views of the relation between rhetoric and syllogism/dialectic in Ar's *Rhet*. Ar himself never clearly defined the relationship.   **[5315]**

ROBERTS, W. R., and BYWATER, J., trans. *The* Rhetoric *and the* Poetics *of Aristotle*. New York: Random House, 1984. Translation and notes.   **[5316]**

ROHATYN, D. A. "A Double Anticipation in Aristotle's *Rhetoric*." *Ph&Rh* 2(1969), 235-236. *Rhet* 1.11,1370a27-32 foreshadows two important themes in Western philosophy: the copy theory of truth and calculation of prospective pleasures.   **[5317]**

ROSENFIELD, L. W. *Aristotle and Information Theory: A Comparison of the Influence of Causal Assumptions on Two Theories of Communication.* The Hague: Mouton, 1971. Examines how one's theory of causation influences one's understanding of the communication process. First few chapters discuss Ar.   **[5318]**

——. "The Doctrine of the Mean in Aristotle's *Rhetoric*." *Theoria* 31(1965), 191-198. Shows that *Rhet* fits within synoptic context of Aristotelian philosophy by illustrating how doctrine of the mean contributes to shaping Ar's rhetorical theory.   **[5319]**

——. "Rhetorical Criticism and an Aristotelian Notion of Process." *SM* 33(1966), 1-16. Studies how application of Ar's rhetorical theory, especially in the area of interaction between speaker and auditor, would affect modern theories of rhetoric.   **[5320]**

RYAN, E. E. *Aristotle's Theory of Rhetorical Argumentation.* Montreal: Ed. Bellarmin, 1984. The *Rhet* should not be dismissed as a mere handbook. Ar's theory of argumentation is carefully worked out. It is not necessary to explain apparent inconsistencies as resulting from development of his thought. His theory of rhetoric is teleological, aimed at producing action. It can, therefore, rely on arguments that are persuasive rather than convincing.   **[5321]**

——. cf. #2346, #4320.

SELF, L. S. "Rhetoric and *Phronesis*: The Aristotelian Ideal." *Ph&Rh* 12(1979), 130-145. There is an "association of persuasion and virtue" in Ar's theory of rhetoric which derives from nature of rhetoric itself. Ideal practitioner of concepts taught in *Rhet* uses skills and qualities of Ar's man of practical wisdom.   **[5322]**

SMITH, C. R. "Actuality and Potentiality: The Essence of Criticism." *Ph&Rh* 3(1970), 133-140. Ar's concept of actuality and potentiality applies to productive sciences as well as theoretical. In rhetoric, ideas have potential and the form of the speech actualizes it. One reacting to a work of art can formulate a potential product to which he compares the actual art work.   **[5323]**

SOLMSEN, F. "The Aristotelian Tradition in Ancient Rhetoric," in #5280, pp. 278-309. Traces influence of Ar and Peripatetic school on later rhetorical theorists and tries to distinguish Aristotelian from Isocratean elements in ancient rhetoric.   **[5324]**

SONKOWSKY, R. P. "An Aspect of Delivery in Ancient Rhetorical Theory," in #5280, pp. 251-266. Examines Ar's views on gestures as integral part of composition and delivery of speech. These concerns were passed on to Cicero.   **[5325]**

SPANGLER, G. A. "Aristotle on Saying Something." *Apeir* 10 #2(1976), 38-46. In Ar's theory of truth anything that can be said singly or without combination means something. Combined items do not contain truth. To speak is to create combinations, analogous to weaving.   **[5326]**

SUTTON, J. "The Death of Rhetoric and Its Rebirth in Philosophy." *Rhetorica* 4(1986), 203-226. Discusses Ar's theory of rhetoric as source of conflict between rhetoric and philosophy, centering on terms common to both, such as *ethos, pathos, logos*.   **[5327]**

TARAN, S. L. "Aristotle *Rhetoric* 3.2-7: An Analysis." *GRBS* 15(1974), 65-72. In chapters 2-4 Ar's arguments concern individual words or names of things; in 5-7 he discusses arrangement of words. Two sections are not contradictory.   **[5328]**

THOMPSON, W. N. "*Stasis* in Aristotle's *Rhetoric*." *QJS* 58(1972), 134-141; also in #5280, pp. 267-277. Ar's comments on *stasis* are inconsistent, perhaps because *Rhet* 3 was written after Books 1 and 2, which pay little attention to the subject. His concepts are poorly defined, and it is unclear whether later writers on rhetoric based their work directly on his.   **[5329]**

VAN NOORDEN, S. "Rhetorical Arguments in Aristotle and Perelman." *RIPh* 33(1979) 178-187. Suggests that Ar's and Perelman's accounts of rhetorical reasoning, (C. Perelman and L. Olbrechts-Tyteca, *The New Rhetoric: A Treatise on Argumentation*, 1971), are complementary. Ar thinks that rhetorical argument is sound because it is strong inductive argument. Perelman, however, looks primarily at efficacy of an argument when determining its value.   **[5330]**

WEIDEMANN, H. "Aristotle on Inferences from Signs (*Rhetoric* I. 2, 1357b 1-25)."

Phron 34(1989), 343-351. Studies Ar's classification of signs and examples.   **[5331]**

WESTBURY, I. "The Aristotelian 'Art' of Rhetoric and the 'Art of Curriculum'."
ProcPhEduc 28(1972), 126-136. Ar's view of rhetoric as an art and his understanding of
topics could be applied usefully to discussions on modern education theory.   **[5332]**

For related items see #900, #2083, #2271, #4048, #4209, #5074, #6250.

SCIENCE

We must begin, once again, with a warning: the term "science" as we use it
does not accurately describe what Ar meant by that concept. Our word "science"
is a direct derivative from the Latin *scientia*, which means "knowledge" in a broad
sense, not just chemistry, biology, and other subjects taught in buildings with labs
and test tubes behind doors with warning signs on them. The use of this word
to translate Greek words, especially *gnosis*, has raised problems over the centuries. The King James translators of the Bible, in 1611, used "science" to translate
gnosis in their version of I Timothy 6.20. They knew the word meant "knowledge," but modern fundamentalists have taken it to mean the physical sciences
and have used this text as an argument for opposing the teaching of such subjects
in the schools. As used in the study of Ar, "science" means "knowledge," with an
emphasis on what we call the physical sciences but not excluding other fields.
The items in this section deal with Ar's scientific method, rather than with any
particular field.

While he emphasizes the syllogism in logic (with the related forms known as
the practical syllogism in ethics and the enthymeme in rhetoric), Ar uses a
method of definition and demonstration in his more strictly scientific works.
Every science must have its own *archai*, or fundamental principles. For the
practical sciences — ethics and politics — the *archai* are opinions which people
have expressed over the years. In other fields the *archai* are based on observation. Observation of repeated instances of a phenomenon leads to recognition
of a universal principle underlying the phenomenon. As Ar himself says, "When
the observation of instances is often repeated, the universal that is there becomes
plain" (*PostAn* 2.19 100a5). His own favorite example of this process is the discovery that eclipses of the moon are caused by the earth moving between the sun
and the moon. This requires recognition that the sun illuminates the moon and
the principle that, when something moves between an object and its source of
illumination, an eclipse results.

This method is called *epagoge* (induction). Both of those words are based
on roots, one Greek and one Latin, meaning "to lead." The inductive method
gathers examples and leads to conclusions based on comparing those examples.
If we can find ten occurrences of a phenomenon, and the result is the same in
every case, then we are justified in concluding that any number of other examples
would also have the same result. We work our way from the particular instance
to the general principle underlying it (the universal) and back to the particular.

ACKRILL, J. L. "Aristotle's Theory of Definition: Some Questions on *Posterior*

Analytics II 8-10," in #5337, pp. 359-384. Examines Ar's explanation of nature and structure of definitions, and how he specifies relation of definition to demonstration. His theory is neither "dangerous" nor "obscurantist." [5333]

BARNES, J. "Aristotle's Theory of Demonstration." *Phron* 14(1969), 123-152; revised version in #5336, pp. 65-87. Some scholars see a contradiction between methodology which Ar uses in his scientific and philosophical works and that which he employs in his treatises on logic. But in *PostAn* he is concerned not with method of acquiring scientific knowledge, but with method of teaching what has been acquired. [5334]

————. "Proof and Syllogism," in #5337, pp. 17-59. Explores relationship between Ar's theory of demonstration and ancient Greek mathematics; logic of *Analytics* is inadequate for formalization of even elementary geometrical proof. Also investigates relationship between *PostAn* and Ar's major treatises, discussing how logic of *Analytics* has little apparent effect on structure of Ar's scientific reasoning. [5335]

————., et al., eds. *Articles on Aristotle, 1: Science.* London: Duckworth, 1975. Collection of articles focusing on Ar's science and offering thorough reappraisal of his aims and achievement. Each abstracted herein. [5336]

BERTI, E., ed. *Aristotle on Science: The* Posterior Analytics. Padua, Italy: Ed. Antenore, 1981. Proceedings of the Eighth Symposium Aristotelicum in Padua, September 1978. Essays in English are abstracted herein. [5337]

BOGAARD, P. A. "Heaps or Wholes: Aristotle's Explanation of Compound Bodies." *Isis* 70(1979), 11-29. Elements cannot be simply piled together without some effect on one another. The resulting combination will follow its own natural tendencies unless obstacles are imposed from outside. [5338]

BOGEN, J., and McGUIRE, J. E. "Aristotle's Great Clock: Necessity, Possibility, and the Motion of the Cosmos in *De Caelo* 1:12." *PhResArch* 12(1986-87), 387-447. Ar's arguments for the eternity and perpetual motion of the cosmos are based on his scientific theories, not on his logical and linguistic premises. They raise questions about the role of the Unmoved Mover. [5339]

BOLZAN, J. E. "Chemical Combination According to Aristotle." *Ambix* 23(1976), 131-144. Examines mixtures as a type of mean. [5340]

BOS, A. P. *On the Elements, Aristotle's Early Cosmology.* Assen, Netherlands: van Gorcum, 1973. Finds earlier and later strata in *De caelo*. Concludes that Ar's development should be viewed as transition from independent, less detailed conception to later, biologically oriented, philosophy of his second Athenian period. [5341]

BOURGEY, L. "Observation and Experiment in Analogical Explanation," in #5336, 175-182. Challenges view that there are no experiments in Ar, but also challenges interpretation that Ar follows an experimental method. [5342]

BRODY, B. A. "Towards an Aristotelian Theory of Scientific Explanation." *PhiSci* 39(1972), 20-31. Considers objections against covering-law model of scientific explanation; shows Ar was aware of them and had correct solutions to them, involving notions of non-Humean causality and of essential properties. [5343]

CARTERON, H. "Does Aristotle Have a Mechanics?" in #5336, pp. 161-174, transl. R. Sorabji. Finds no science of mechanics developed in Ar. Formulae collected from various texts should not be seen as having single, definite goal and should not be given systematic arrangement. **[5344]**

COLE, R. "Nomos." *SwJPh* 10(1979), 7-21. Contrasts modern understanding of science, especially idea of physical law, with Ar's philosophy; argues scientific understanding has an Aristotelian-like typological character as well as a Newtonian-like nomological character. **[5345]**

DAVIES, J. C. "The Aristotelian Conception of Science." *SicGym* 29(1976), 163-171. Surveys what the term "science" means to Ar and contrasts his views with those of Empiricists. **[5346]**

——. "The Assumption of Aristotelian Science." *Euphro* 13(1983), 171-178. Ar's assumption of order in the universe is tied to his assumption of logical order. **[5347]**

DeMOSS, D., and **DEVEREUX, D. T.** "Essence, Existence, and Nominal Definition in Aristotle's *Posterior Analytics* II,8-10." *Phron* 33(1988), 133-154. Ar's theory of science and scientific research can be summed up under fourteen headings. **[5348]**

DICKS, D. R. *Early Greek Astronomy to Aristotle.* Ithaca, NY: Cornell Univ. Pr., 1970. Seeks to trace the development of astronomy as a science rather than that of cosmology or cosmogony. **[5349]**

DUERING, I., ed. *Naturphilosophie bei Aristoteles und Theophrast. Verhandlungen des 4. Symposium Aristotelicum veranstaltet in Goeteborg, August 1966.* Heidelberg, Ger.: Stiehm, 1969. Essays in English are abstracted herein. **[5350]**

FEREJOHN, M. T. "Definition and the Two Stages of Aristotelian Demonstration." *RMeta* 36(1982), 375-395. Reply to #5334 and #5359. Ar's theory of demonstration begins with Platonic division, which provides premises for syllogisms. **[5351]**

——. cf. #4463.

FOSS, L. "'Substance' and Aristotle's Theory of Science," in #4773, pp. 149-169. Argues that Ar uses self-authenticating *nous* or mind to grasp substances, and thus assures existence of substance for science. **[5352]**

FREDE, D. "Comment on Hintikka's Paper 'On the Ingredients of an Aristotelian Science'." *Synthèse* 28(1974), 79-89. Challenges Hintikka's (#5360) interpretation of first principles in terms of their role in syllogistic demonstration and his claim that Ar accepts four kinds of first principles. **[5353]**

FURLEY, D. J. "Aristotle and the Atomists on Infinity," in #5350, pp. 85-96. Examines Ar's view that space cannot be infinitely divided and does not extend infinitely, against the opposing views of the Atomists (including Epicurus). **[5354]**

GIRVETZ, H., et al. "Aristotle and Nature," in #13, pp. 112-151. Discusses Ar's view of nature as collection of ordered processes and his effort to encompass in his philosophy both "sacred" and "profane." **[5355]**

GOMEZ-LOBO, A. "Definitions in Aristotle's *Posterior Analytics*," in #3631, pp. 25-46. Describes different kinds of definitions which are involved in effort to reach causal definition in the strictest sense.   [5356]

HADGOPOULOS, D. J. "Demonstration and the Second Figure in Aristotle." *NewSchol* 49(1975), 62-75. Ar's second syllogistic figure is a better tool for scientific explanations than is generally recognized.   [5357]

HAMLYN, D. W. "Aristotelian Epagoge." *Phron* 21(1976), 167-184. New interpretation of Ar's induction and its use as a scientific tool in his thought. It is valid for demonstration, not proof, and applies to application of general principles to particulars, but not to principles themselves.   [5358]

HINTIKKA, J. "Aristotelian Induction." *RIPh* 34(1980), 422-440. Investigates how, according to Ar, we come to know first principles of a science, and examines different kinds of induction. Ar uses *epagoge* in two ways: 1) sometimes it is restricted to coming to know premises about atomic connections; 2) sometimes it applies to the way of coming to know generic premises.   [5359]

————. "On the Ingredients of an Aristotelian Science." *Nous* 6(1972), 55-69. Ar distinguishes three types of foundational assumptions in any science: common axioms, minimal syllogistic premises, existential assumptions about genus of the science. [5360]

————. "Reply to Dorothea Frede." *Synthèse* 28(1974), 91-96. Reply to #5353. Defends thesis of different kinds of starting points for an Aristotelian science, outlined in #5360.   [5361]

HORNE, R. A. "Aristotelian Chemistry." *Chymia* 11(1966), 21-27. Ar's science, like that of all Greek thinkers, emphasized abstraction over practical experiments. Studies effect of this attitude in encouraging pseudo-sciences such as alchemy and delaying development of genuine chemical science.   [5362]

JOPE, J. "Subordinate Demonstrative Science in the Sixth Book of Aristotle's *Physics*." *CQ* 22(1972), 278-292. *Phys* 6 provides the kind of deductive approach to scientific knowledge which is outlined in *PostAn* 1.   [5363]

KAHN, C. H. "The Role of *Nous* in the Cognition of First Principles in *Posterior Analytics* II 19," in #5337, pp. 385-414. Addresses two questions: Why does Ar focus only on cognition of universal terms or concepts when what is at issue is knowledge of primitive axioms or self-evident truths? and What is role of *nous* in the "inductive" process that leads from sense perception to apprehension of universals?   [5364]

KAKKURI-KNUUTTILA, M.-L. "Aristotelian Dialectic and Reasoning in *Das Kapital* of Marx," in *Argumentation: Analysis and Practices. Proceedings of the Conference on Argumentation 1986*, ed. F. H. van Eemeren et al. (Dordrecht, Nether.: Foris, 1987), III, pp. 308-316. Ar's concept of science involves both deduction and argumentation. A passage from Marx's work is analyzed to show application of this principle.   [5365]

KNORR, W. "Aristotle and Incommensurability. Some Further Reflections." *AHES* 24(1982), 1-9. Reply to Marrachia's discussion (in Italian) of Ar's demonstration of incommensurability of a side with the diagonal of the same square.   [5366]

———. "A Correction to My Article 'Aristotle and Incommensurability'." *AHES* 27(1982), 391-392. Addition to #5366.   [5367]

LANDOR, B. "Aristotle on Demonstrating Essence." *Apeir* 19(1985), 116-132. Argues that Ar introduces possibility of a "demonstration of the essence" only in secondary sense that he thinks it possible through scientific demonstration to "reveal" essence, without directly demonstrating it.   [5368]

LeCLERC, I. "Platonism, Aristotelianism and Modern Science." *IntPhQ* 16(1976), 135-149. To remain relevant in face of challenges from modern scientific worldview, philosophy must abandon P's dualism in favor of Ar's understanding of nature.   [5369]

LESZL, W. "Mathematics, Axiomatization and the Hypotheses," in #5337, pp. 271-328. Investigates view that in *PostAn*, mathematics provides paradigm for any well-organized science.   [5370]

———. "Unity and Diversity of the Sciences: The Methodology of the Mathematical and of the Physical Sciences and the Role of Natural Definition." *RIPh* 34(1980), 384-421. In discussing Ar's theory of science, explores whether Ar really attempted to provide a single uniform treatment for all the sciences by identifying features which all must possess if they are to be called "sciences" in a proper sense.   [5371]

LLOYD, A. C. "Necessity and Essence in the *Posterior Analytics*," in #5337, pp. 157-171. Analyzes place of necessity in knowledge and explanation, and question of whether individual substances have essential properties.   [5372]

LLOYD, G. E. R. "The Empirical Basis of the Physiology of the *Parva Naturalia*," in #5199, pp. 215-240. Examines relation between empirical data and theories in *Parva Naturalia*, to consider how theories advanced are suggested or supported by, or checked against, empirical observations.   [5373]

MATTHEN, M., ed. *Aristotle Today: Essays on Aristotle's Ideal of Science.* Edmonton, Alberta: Academic Printing, 1987. Original essays, abstracted herein.   [5374]

———., "The Structure of Aristotelian Science," in #5374, pp. 1-23. Provides overview of themes in Ar's science: demonstration and knowledge; causes; first philosophy; matter. Comments on other essays in collection.   [5375]

McKIRAHAN, R. D., Jr. "Aristotle's Subordinate Sciences." *BritJHistSci* 11(1978), 197-220. "Subalternation," which best describes the relation between certain pairs of sciences, can function on two or three levels. Though Ar does not describe a three-level arrangement, it can be found implicit in his work.   [5376]

MILLER, F. D. "Aristotle Against the Atomists," in #64, pp. 87-111. In establishing that physical reality is a continuous plenum, Ar upholds two principles of importance for his science of nature: 1) deep structure of movement is same as that of spatial and temporal magnitude, and 2) structure of a continuum, which is shared by movement, space, and time, is not reducible to any deeper structure.   [5377]

MORAUX, P. "Galen and Aristotle's *De Partibus Animalium*," in #3809, pp. 327-344. Investigates general influence of Ar's treatise on Galen and Galen's fundamental agreement with Ar.   **[5378]**

MORSINK, J. "The Mandate of *Topics* I,2." *Apeir* 16(1982), 102-128. In this passage Ar argues for dialectic's ability to establish basis of each of sciences.   **[5379]**

MOURELATOS, A. P. D. "Aristotle's Rationalist Account of Qualitative Interaction." *Phron* 29(1984), 1-16. Ar's concept of change, discussed in *Phys* 1.5 and in *De gen et corr*, requires that both the agent and the thing being affected undergo change. For this to happen, both entities must be of the same genus but not the same species.   **[5380]**

MUELLER, I. "Greek Mathematics and Greek Logic," in #52, pp. 35-70. Ar's effort to develop principles of science takes syllogism as primary logical instrument for organization of a science. Syllogism and mathematical proof do not go together.   **[5381]**

RICHARDS, R. J. "Substantive and Methodological Teleology in Aristotle and Some Logical Empiricists." *Thom* 37(1973), 702-733. Examines Ar's logical analysis of the teleological assumptions inherent in all scientific explanation and contrasts his view with that of several modern empiricists.   **[5382]**

RICHARDSON, W. F. "Aristotelian Chemistry." *Prud* 19 #2(1987), 1-15. Book 4 of the *Meteorologica* has nothing to do with meteorology and did not originally belong to the work. It is an effort at chemistry. Contents of the book are outlined.   **[5383]**

SCHMITZ, K. L. "Natural Value." *RMeta* 38(1984), 3-15. For Ar nature has value because of the intelligence which underlies matter, process, and form. This intelligence makes nature intelligible to us.   **[5384]**

SOKOLOWSKI, R. "Scientific and Hermeneutic Questions in Aristotle." *Ph&Rh* 4(1971), 242-261. Ar asks two sets of questions in investigating phenomena. One set ("whether"/"why") are scientific and seek causes. The other set ("whether it is"/"what it is") are hermeneutic, i. e. interpretive, seeking what names of things mean or refer to. This is how he links physical being and problems of human existence.   **[5385]**

SOLMSEN, F. "Platonic Values in Aristotle's Science." *JHI* 39(1978), 3-23. Examines Ar's account of the "unparalleled glories of the Heaven" to show that nature and the Cosmos, to become so wonderful, had to absorb many qualities previously associated with P's Forms, and in particular the Form of the Good. Also considers place of concern for human good in Ar's work.   **[5386]**

SORABJI, R. "Aristotle and Oxford Philosophy." *AmPhQ* 6(1969), 127-135. Ar was not an empiricist, though his work is undeniably scientific. His understanding of definition, essence, and other "scientific" terms is significantly different from ours.   **[5387]**

——. "Definitions: Why Necessary and In What Way?," in #5337, pp. 205-244. Explores sort of necessity Ar attributes to statements giving essences of kinds, and why he regards his scientific definitions as necessary, and not contingent.   **[5388]**

SPARSHOTT, F. "Aristotle's World and Mine," in #5374, pp. 25-50. Explains how Ar's world-view works as a system that includes the system-builder and shows how this system made sense. Also asserts that no system built on Galilean principles can replace an Aristotelian one.   **[5389]**

THAYER, H. S. "Aristotle on Nature: A Study in the Relativity of Concepts and Procedures of Analysis." *RMeta* 28(1975), 725-744. Ar's approach to science and to *physis* in general does not emphasize a rigid system but recognizes that the meaning and use of concepts can vary according to their context. **[5390]**

——. "Aristotle on the Meaning of Science." *PhilInq* 1(1979), 87-104. Ar did not understand science as a tightly organized system of explanations and truths, similar to mathematics. In *PostAn* he did not intend to set forth the content of scientific knowledge but a method of teaching it effectively. **[5391]**

——. "The Network of Concepts: A New View of Aristotle," in *Ethics, Science and Democracy: The Philosophy of Abraham Edel*, ed. H. S. Thayer and I. L. Horowitz (New Brunswick, NJ: Transaction Books, 1987), pp. 189-216. Ar's mechanical and teleological explanations do not mesh well, especially in his discussion of motion of primary and living bodies. Comments on Edel's work on Ar (#3597) in light of this problem. **[5392]**

UPTON, T.V. "Aristotle on Hypothesizing the Genus and Scientific Explanation." *Nat&Sys* 5(1983), 161-168. Reply to M. T. Ferejohn (#5351). **[5393]**

——. "Imperishable Being and the Role of Technical Hypothesis in Aristotelian Demonstration." *Nat&Sys* 2(1980), 91-100. What Ar says about hypotheses in *PostAn* should be given a traditional, existential interpretation. **[5394]**

——. "The Role of Dialectic and Objections in Aristotelian Science." *SJPh* 22(1984), 241-256. Reply to #5334. Stresses importance for Ar of dialectical objections which are used to test intermediate hypotheses. **[5395]**

——. cf. #4002 and 4003.

VANDER WEEL, R. L. "The *Posterior Analytics* and the *Topics*." *LThPh* 25(1969), 130-141. *PostAn* provides criteria for evaluating a scientific procedure; *Topics* expounds a scientific method of discovery. **[5396]**

VAN FRAASSEN, B. C. "A Re-examination of Aristotle's Philosophy of Science." *Dial*(Can) 19(1980), 20-45. Examines Ar's concepts of science and scientific explanation in order to explore what philosophically controversial theses would have to be defended today to accept an Aristotelian account of science. **[5397]**

WIANS, W. "Aristotle, Demonstration, and Teaching." *AncPh* 9(1989), 245-253. Various attempts, most notably by J. Barnes (#5334), have been put forth to explain methodological contradictions between *PostAn* and Ar's other treatises. Several weaknesses of Barnes' position can be delineated. **[5398]**

WILKINS, B. T. "Aristotle on Scientific Explanation." *Dial*(Can) 9(1970), 337-355. Discusses Ar's treatment of scientific exploration, its structure and its principles, as distinct from Ar's own principles of explanation. **[5399]**

WILSON, F. "Explanation in Aristotle, Newton, and Toulmin: Part I." *PhiSci* 36(1969), 291-310. Defends claim that scientific explanation is deductive by distinguishing between perfect and imperfect explanations. Discusses similarities and differences between Aristotelian explanations of particular facts and those of classical mechanics. **[5400]**

———. "Explanation in Aristotle, Newton, and Toulmin: Part II." *PhiSci* 36(1969) 400-428. Continues discussion of Ar's scientific explanation and argues that Aristotelian framework becomes incoherent when classical mechanics is fit in with it. Discusses how Aristotelian patterns fell as the new science developed.   **[5401]**

THEOLOGY

Ar's concept of God does not grow out of religious conviction. He found God necessary, even inevitable, in his scheme of things. In his *Phys* and *Meta* he expounds his theory that everything has a cause. Every motion, every change, is brought about by something acting on something else. Change or motion is potential in every individual thing but must be brought about (actualized) by something outside the thing which is being moved or changed. There must ultimately be something which is unmoved and unchanged, which causes all other motion and change. That thing must be eternal, since motion and change are eternal, but it must not be affected by the motion and change which it causes, or else it would not be the true cause. Since it must be eternal, it cannot be material, for matter changes over time.

What Ar's system requires is some ultimate source of movement or change which is real but not material, acting on the physical universe but unaffected by it, in fact not even aware of it. It must be pure intelligence, thought, or *nous*; it must, in Ar's words, "think itself." This Unmoved Mover is the subject of Book Lambda (or 12) of the *Meta*, probably originally a separate treatise.

But how can the Unmoved Mover cause motion if it has no contact with the cosmos? Ar's explanation is that it does this by causing desire to arise in lesser created things which then move toward the Unmoved Mover (or toward one of the intermediate Movers which is itself moving toward the Unmoved Mover). The Unmoved Mover remains on the edge of the cosmos, contemplating its own unchanging, immaterial thoughts.

ANDRIOPOLOUS, D. Z., and **HUMBER, J.** "Aristotle's Concept of *To Proton Kinoun Akineton*." *Platon* 21(1969), 113-120. Reply to earlier studies of the Unmoved Mover by D. Ross and J. H. Randall.   **[5402]**

———. "Aristotle's Concept of *To Proton Kinoun Akineton*: A Reexamination of the Problem." *CJ* 66(1971), 289-293. Unmoved Mover is an ideal, a metaphor, not an actual being. We can think of it, and it serves as the essence of the universe, but not as a primary substance.   **[5403]**

ARDLEY, G. "Aristotle's Creationism." *Prud* 13(1981), 25-31. Ar's doctrine of Unmoved Mover does not prevent him from thinking that God created the world without any sense of necessity.   **[5404]**

———. cf. #4028.

BAILLIE, H. W. "Noetic Activity in Aristotle's Thought — Man, God, and Ultimate Reality, A Philosopher's View." *UltR&M* 5(1982), 230-249. For Ar, ultimate reality is *energeia* (activity or actuality). Degree of reality of a thing increases as its nature more closely approximates pure activity. Highest degree of reality resides in God. Meaning is found in mind's ability to understand the nature and purpose of the world.   **[5405]**

BELL, K. "Causation, Motion, and the Unmoved Mover." *Auslegung* 8(1981), 157-173. Overview of Ar's arguments for the Unmoved Mover's existence and what it means to say that the Unmoved Mover is a final cause. The Unmoved Mover has a theological function, inspiring all living creatures to strive for their own actualization.   **[5406]**

BLYTH, D. "The Motion Primary in Actuality: A Note on *Metaphysics* Lambda 7.1072b5-8." *AJPh* 109(1988), 513-522. Argues for an interpretation of *Meta* 12, 1072b5-6, which is central to Ar's concept of the Unmoved Mover as immaterial actuality and unique perfection.   **[5407]**

BOS, A. P. "*Manteia* in Aristotle, *De caelo* II,1." *Apeir* 21(1988), 29-54. *Manteia* in *De caelo* 284b3 may refer to the gods' knowledge about *nous*, which they can, to some degree, impart to humans.   **[5408]**

——. "The Theological Conception in *De mundo* and the Relation Between this Writing and the Work of Plato and Aristotle." *TijdFil* 39(1977), 314-330. Theology of chapter 6 of this dubious work can be situated between P's later views and those of *Meta* 12. God is unmoved but moves all heavenly spheres.   **[5409]**

——. cf. #2133.

CATAN, J. R. "Aristotle, the Immobile Mover: Translation, Introduction and Commentary by Giovanni Reale." *PhResArch* 2(1976), no. 1135. Translation of Reale's work on *Meta* 12.   **[5410]**

CHROUST, A.-H. "The *Akatonomaston* in Aristotle's *On Philosophy*." *Emerita* 40(1972), 461-468. A passage from Cicero displays a mixture of Ar's ideas on the fifth element, which constitutes the nature of God, with Stoic ideas.   **[5411]**

——. "Aristotle's *On Philosophy*: A Brief Comment on 12 Rose, 13 Walzer, 13 Ross, 18 Untersteiner (Cicero *De natura deorum* 11, 37.95-96)." *LThPh* 29(1973), 19-22. Arguments for existence of God in Cicero are probably from Ar's lost dialogue. **[5412]**

——. "The Concept of God in Aristotle's Lost Dialogue *On Philosophy*." *Emerita* 33(1965), 205-228. On basis of passage in Cicero's *De nat deor* one can conclude that Ar distinguished between "god" and "the divine."   **[5413]**

——. "'Mystical Revelation' and 'Rational Theology' in Aristotle's *On Philosophy*." *TijdFilos* 34(1972), 500-512. In this lost dialogue Ar seems to have argued that knowledge of God could be gained by revelation (either direct or through a prophet) or by reasoning from the order evident in the cosmos.   **[5414]**

——. cf. #6241.

EASTERLING, H. J. "The Unmoved Mover in Early Aristotle." *Phron* 21(1976) 252-265. Doctrine of Unmoved Mover was not in original versions of *Phys* 2 and 3 or in *On Philosophy*. In Ar's early thought God appears to have been final cause.   **[5415]**

ELDERS, L. *Aristotle's Theology: A Commentary on Book Lambda of the* Metaphysics. Assen, Netherlands: Van Gorcum, 1972. Introductory essay discusses Ar's links to P and Academy and argues that Book Lambda consists of six separate essays written over a considerable period of time.   **[5416]**

GEORGE, R. "An Argument for Divine Omniscience in Aristotle." *Apeir* 22(1989), 61-74. Last sentence of *Meta* 12.4 should be taken to mean that *nous* (mind) and *noeton* (object of thought) are identical.   **[5417]**

KAHN, C. H. "The Place of the Prime Mover in Aristotle's Teleology," in #3809, pp. 183-205. Explores how general Ar's claim is that the Prime Mover causes motion as an object of love.   **[5418]**

KESSLER, G. E. "Aristotle's 'Theology'." *Sophia* 17(1978), 1-9. Though Ar's Unmoved Mover is not a personal, caring deity like the Judeo-Christian god, it does resemble concepts of divinity in some strands of mystic thought.   **[5419]**

KOSMAN, L. A. "Divine Being and Divine Thinking in *Metaphysics* Lambda" *PBACAPh* 3(1987), 165-188. The central books of *Meta* show that *ousia* ("substance-being") is what informs and explains being in general. Book Lambda shows how the divine *ousia* is the explanatory principle of substance-being.   **[5420]**

LANG, H. S. "Aristotle's First Movers and the Relation of Physics to Theology." *NewSchol* 52(1978), 500-517. Ar sets out three proofs of a first mover (*Phys* 7 and 8 and *Meta* 12). Despite difficulties of interpretation, all three lead to the same mover. The argument in *Meta* 12 establishes that the Unmoved Mover is God.   **[5421]**

――――. cf. #4978.

LAWRENCE, J. P. "The Hidden Aporia in Aristotle's Self-Thinking Thought." *JSpecPh* 2(1988), 155-174. Actuality, to be complete, must include potentiality. Similarly, pure thought must include the possibility of *aporia*. Philosophy is aporetic because God (who thinks himself) is aporetic.   **[5422]**

MERLAN, P. "Two Theological Problems in Aristotle's *Met* Lambda 6-9 and *De Caelo* A 9." *Apeir* 1(1966), 3-13. Examines difficulties that arise with introduction of fifty-five other unmoved movers. Ar's concept of aether rendered them unnecessary.   **[5423]**

MEYNELL, H. "Cybernetics, Aristotle, and Natural Theology." *HeythJ* 9(1968), 50-53. Science of cybernetics and Ar's metaphysical theories have in common a very wide generality and a preoccupation with things and aggregates in process of change, plus certain aspects involving Prime Mover.   **[5424]**

NORMAN, R. "Aristotle's Philosopher-God," *Phron* 14(1969), 63-74; also in #5158, pp. 93-102. Examines Ar's claim that "God thinks himself." This does not mean that God thinks about himself, but rather is connected with doctrine that thought is identical with its object. Abstract thought is highest kind of activity.   **[5425]**

OWENS, J. "The Relation of God to the World in the *Metaphysics*," in #4594, pp. 207-222. The *Meta*, outside Book Lambda, depicts God as having a free and sovereign nature, not to be feared but loved because of its goodness and generosity. Book Lambda describes God as immaterial substance, life and thought. God causes movement or change, but heavenly bodies are eternal. God does not seem to know the world, since that would imply change. **[5426]**

PATT, W. "Aristotle's Notion of Theology and the Meaning of *Ousia*." *PACPhA* 61(1987), 69-77. Ar can claim that theology is the science of being *qua* being. Knowing the highest kind of *ousia* implies knowing lower types as well. **[5427]**

PATZIG, G. "Theology and Ontology in Aristotle's Metaphysics," in #4598, pp. 33-49. Explains Ar's doctrine that God, or Prime Mover, is entity that exhibits characteristics of substances in their purest and most general form. Ar views other substances as related focally to a primary substance, God. **[5428]**

PECCORINI, F. L. "An Inquiring Response to Prof. Tracy's and Prof. Baillie's Essays on Aristotle." *UltR&M* 5(1982), 265-270. Reply to #5436, #5405. Shows how soul, with *logos* and First Mover, explains human existence and eternal motion. **[5429]**

PREUS, A. "Aristotle's 'Nature Uses . . .'." *Apeir* 3 #2(1969), 20-33. Ar does not conceive of nature as personal, though he is often interpreted that way. The teleology of his system does not require personal involvement of a deity. **[5430]**

SHIELDS, C. "Commentary on Kosman's 'Divine Being and Divine Thinking in *Metaphysics* Lambda'." *PBACAPh* 3(1987), 189-201. Argues against #5420 that *ousia* is not a category of entity but a mode of being, with result that a white human being is not a substance, though it is numerically identical with a human being. **[5431]**

SINNIGE, T. G. "Cosmic Religion in Aristotle." *GRBS* 14(1973), 15-34. Passages in several works, including *De caelo* and *Meta*, suggest that Ar was capable of genuine religious feeling, sometimes at expense of dialectic. **[5432]**

SKEMP, J. B. "The Activity of Immobility," in #4594, pp. 229-241. Studies Ar's rejection of personal attributes of God and concern for the world by the divinity. **[5433]**

SOLMSEN, F. "Plato's First Mover in the Eighth Book of Aristotle's *Physics*," in #71, pp. 171-182. *Phys* 8,259b1-28 refutes Platonic notion of a First Mover, though P is never named. It was probably composed for another context and later inserted at this point, whether by Ar or by a later editor cannot be determined. **[5434]**

STEWART, D. "Aristotle's Doctrine of the Unmoved Mover." *Thom* 37(1973), 522-547. Difficulties of reconciling what Ar says about number of unmoved movers in *Phys* 8 and *Meta* Lambda are complicated by tampering which texts suffered in antiquity. **[5435]**

TRACY, T. "Ultimate Reality and Meaning in Aristotle: A Classicist's View." *UltR&M* 5(1982), 210-229. Survey of Ar's conception of the ultimate reality as pure actuality and the implications for this idea on his political and ethical thought. The best persons and communities are modelled on the divine, though none approaches perfection. The divine itself does not create or control the world and is utterly self-contained. **[5436]**

WALLACE, W. A. "The Cosmological Argument: A Reappraisal." *PACPhA* 46(1972), 43-57. Tries to restate Ar's cosmological argument in *Phys* 7.1 in terms of causes, not forces, stressing material over efficient causality. **[5437]**

YAFFE, M. D. "Myth and 'Science' in Aristotle's Theology." *M&W* 12(1979), 70-88.
Ar's theology remains "scientific" as well as "mythical"; his argument aims primarily at
introducing and exhorting his reader to "science."   **[5438]**

For related items see #2149, #3547, #4741, #4805, #4938, #5339, #6123.

TIME

Part of a definition of motion, for Ar, is the fact that motion occurs during
time. That leads to serious questions about what time is, questions which
plagued Ar throughout his life, as they have many other philosophers before and
since. Seven centuries after Ar, Augustine was still trying to explain time. "If no
one asks me, I know what it is," he said. "If I wish to explain it to him who asks
me, I do not know." Ar faced something of the same dilemma. Is time a
motion? A number? Can it be said to exist apart from someone or something
to perceive it? Does it have a beginning or end?

The problem is discussed in *Phys* 4, in the context of his explanation of
motion and place and his denial that empty space exists. When we consider the
concept of time we realize that it consists of divisions such as "no longer," "now,"
and "not yet." The first and last of those (past and future) do not exist. If time
is composed of things which do not exist, how can time exist? Is time merely
"now"? If it is, what does it mean to say "now" when we sit down for supper and
again when we have breakfast? How can two different points in time be
designated by the same word? When does one "now" become another "now"?
We talk of time as though it were divisible. The Greeks divided the day into
twelve hours, whose length varied according to the season of the year, and they
also counted days, months, and years. If time is divisible, it must exist, and all
of it must exist at once. It is also the objective measurement of any kind of
motion, so it must exist in the objective world. But as to what it is, matter or
soul or something else, he cannot enlighten us.

Ar's answer to all these quandries is that "time is the number of motion in
relation to before and after." It is the standard by which we measure movement.
A person was in one place "before"; he/she is in another place "after." How do
we measure that movement? When a runner runs a race of a specified distance,
we do not measure how many steps he/she takes or how many times his/her heart
beats. We measure the motion in terms of time. Looking at it conversely, if two
runners run for an hour and one covers twelve miles and the other ten, one has
accomplished more motion. Can the same period of time, then, be different for
different people/animals? Ar was close to to a doctrine of relativity here, but he
did not pursue it and the discovery was left to Einstein.

If time is the measurement of motion, what kind of motion does it measure?
Ar thinks circular motion best describes the phenomenon. The passage of a year
is a cycle, though Ar did not realize just how literally it is a circular motion. He
and other Greek scientists knew that some sort of circular motion took place in
the heavens, since the sun rose at certain points on certain days of the year, and
the moon, stars and planets appear to move in a circular pattern. Circular
motion is also the most uniform kind of motion.

ANNAS, J. "Aristotle, Number and Time." *PhQ* 25(1975), 97-113. Examines Ar's account of time in *Phys* 4 and how he uses notion that time is a kind of number. Appeals to his treatment of counting and concept *one* in *Meta* Book Iota. Discusses problems which theory raises and which Ar never fully resolved.   **[5439]**

BOSTOCK, D. "Aristotle's Account of Time." *Phron* 25(1980), 148-169. Examines thesis that time is a quantity of movement; looks at inadequacies of Ar's account of its *temporal* nature, which is movement in terms of before and after.   **[5440]**

CORISH, D. "Aristotle on Temporal Order: Now, Before, and After." *Isis* 69(1978), 68-74. Ar's account of temporal order is inadequate because it uses neither an earlier-later nor a past-present-future order.   **[5441]**

FAKHRY, M. "Aristotle and Absolute Time." *Diot* 16(1988), 43-48. Examines Ar's view of time and considers whether it confirms absolutist thesis (time is separate from events occuring in it and also from space in which they take place) or relativist theories of time (time is not separate from events and from space.)   **[5442]**

KRETZMANN, N. "Aristotle on the Instant of Change." *PAS* Suppl. 50(1976), 91-114. Three of the four puzzles which Ar presents in *Phys* 4.10 are intended to demonstrate the reality of time and to show that time is not change or passage. The fourth puzzle confirms this reading of the first three.   **[5443]**

MERLEAU-PONTY, J. "Ideas of Beginning and Endings in Cosmology," in *The Study of Time*, ed. N. Lawrence (New York: Springer, 1978) pp. 333-350. Examines discussions of the beginning of cosmic time in Plato and Ar.   **[5444]**

MILLER, F. D. "Aristotle on the Reality of Time." *AGPh* 56(1974), 132-155. Ar tried to escape dilemma of time as lacking duration and thus unreal by positing an "enduring present," but this theory falls prey to earlier arguments against reality of time.   **[5445]**

OWEN, G. E. L. "Aristotle on Time," in #4986, pp. 3-27; also in #4598, pp. 140-158. Ar tries to draw parallel between space and time to solve problem of unreality of time and to show that spatial order is "conceptually prior to temporal order." He is caught in a paradox in *Phys* 4, where he recognizes that moments are mere limits to stretches of time, but also accepts that identification of a "now," an extensionless present moment, is prerequisite of understanding any talk of a period containing that now.   **[5446]**

SUMMERS, J. W. "Aristotle's Concept of Time." *Apeir* 18(1984), 59-71. Ar uses argument of motion to validate his concept of time.   **[5447]**

WHITE, M. J. "Aristotle on 'Time' and 'A Time'." *Apeir* 22(1989), 207-224. Ar's concept of time is based on two components. One is "topological," a continuous, linear structure. The other is "metrical," a unit of time.   **[5448]**

For related items see #4995, #5594, #6367, #6999.

Chapter 15

THE ACADEMY AND THE PERIPATETICS;
SKEPTICISM AND ECLECTICISM

THE ACADEMY
The term "Academy" implies a well-organized school, one perhaps where the students wear uniforms in the school colors. To read such connotations back into the institution which Plato founded would be to create an anachronism of the worst sort. Plato's Academy, named for the protective spirit of the site where it was located, was a loosely organized group of teachers and students whose numbers at any given time we cannot estimate beyond saying that they were small. Nor are we certain what was taught or what sort of "research" the teachers did. The curriculum described in book 7 of the *Rep* might provide some clue as to the subjects investigated, but the evidence presently available does not allow us to say more than that mathematics was the core of the curriculum.

When Plato died in 347 B. C., his nephew Speusippus became head of the Academy. Aristotle left Athens at that time, perhaps disappointed that he had not been chosen Plato's successor. Speusippus and his successor, Xenocrates, transformed — probably unintentionally — Plato's teaching, abandoning the theory of the Forms and emphasizing certain metaphysical and mathematical doctrines which appear more Pythagorean than Platonic. Not enough of their work survives to enable us to evaluate their thought in any depth. We do get outlines and summaries in later writers. Both wrote more on ethics than Plato did. Speusippus, in two books criticizing the hedonist philosopher Aristippus, took the extreme position that nothing pleasurable can be good, while Xenocrates formulated several doctrines that seem to have been influential on Stoic ethics.

Xenocrates, who became head in 339, seems to have systematized Plato's thought, creating a body of dogma which members of the Academy held to more tenaciously than Plato himself had. His work is characterized by groupings and categories: the division of philosophy itself into dialectic, physics, and ethics; the division of the cosmos into the sub-lunar world, the heavens, and the world beyond the heavens. He posited daimonic forces at work in all three regions, giving some philosophical sanction to popular religious ideas about demons which dominated the Hellenistic period. He was a serious man, whose demeanor and manner of life caused the dissolute Polemo to give up his hedonistic ways and devote himself to the study of philosophy. In 314 Polemo became the next head of the Academy. Polemo has been described as leaving evidence of "scarcely a single original thought." The Academy's importance declined under his leadership.

A few students of the early Academy deserve at the least the mention of their names, though their work is more scientific than philosophical. Philippus of Opus and Eudoxus of Cnidus both developed Plato's interest in mathematics. Heraclides of Pontus theorized that the earth rotated daily and may have held that Mercury and Venus revolve around the sun. His work is, however, uncritical and tinged with magical elements. Perhaps the most outstanding student of the early Academy is Crantor of Soloe, whose treatise on grief became the foundation of a consolatory tradition in philosophical writing that continued through Seneca to Boethius in the sixth century A. D.

Not until Arcesilaus became head of the Academy in 265 B. C. did it enjoy a revival of influence. This was a very different Academy, with a strongly skeptical view of the possibility of knowledge, derived in part from the teaching of Pyrrho of Elis (see below) and perhaps in part from the Socratic/Platonic tendency to leave questions unresolved. (Often in the dialogues Socrates and his interlocutors reach an *aporia*, a failure to settle on a definite answer.) Arcesilaus wrote nothing, so we cannot describe his ideas with any certainty, a fact which he would probably appreciate. He was so deeply skeptical that he would not even assert as believable his doctrine of the unattainability of knowledge.

Later heads of the Academy continued this skeptical tradition. Carneades, who succeeded to the position ca. 157 B. C., did not write anything either, but his teachings seem to be accurately expounded in the works of his students. Much of his thought seems to have developed in opposition to Stoic doctrine. He was particularly concerned to refute the idea that anything could be proved. Any premises of a system of proof, he said, would require proof, and so on, ad infinitum. He also argued against the idea of the existence of God. His most positive work was concerned with ethics, founded on the notion that life should be lived "according to nature" and in pursuit of natural goods.

By the first century B. C. the heads of the Academy had turned to a view which combined certain features of the Stoic and Peripatetic schools. This approach of selecting similar ideas from different schools was called Eclecticism (cf. below). The Stoics and Peripatetics tended during this period to modify their positions in response to the telling criticisms of Carneades and others who followed him.

Eclecticism itself moved away from the radical skepticism of Carneades and admitted at least the possibility of attaining some degree of knowledge. This is the tenor of the teachings of Philo of Larissa, head of the Academy until he fled to Rome in 88 B. C. to escape the wars racking the eastern Mediterranean at the time. Philo "sought something intermediate between mere probability and knowledge." Philo's successor, Antiochus of Ascalon (died 68 B. C.), moved the Academy decidedly from Skepticism to Eclecticism. He argued that truth was to be found where all major philosophies agree and tried to interpret the schools of his day as though they were consistent with one another. They disagreed, he claimed, only on minor points of semantics or emphasis.

BARNES, J. "Philodemus and the Old Academy." *Apeir* 22(1989), 139-148. Discussion of K. Gaiser's book (in German), first volume of planned collection of doxographic material dealing with Plato and Academy. In addition to text and commentary, Gaiser argues that Plato's dialogues were meant merely to entice students into Academy. His actual (oral) teaching was rather different. [5449]

———. cf. #4416, #4418.

BLUMENTHAL, H. J. "529 and its Sequel: What Happened to the Academy?" *Byzantion* 48(1978), 369-385. There is no convincing evidence that the Academy actually closed in 529. [5450]

BOWEN, A. C. "Menaechmus *versus* the Platonists. Two Theories of Science in the Early Academy." *AncPh* 3(1983), 12-29. Proclus is more accurate than Plutarch in his account of Plato's discussion with fourth-century geometers on whether proofs by figures generate new existents or describe eternal objects. [5451]

BROWN, M. "A Pre-Aristotelian Mathematician on Deductive Order," in *Philosophy and Humanism: Renaissance Essays in Honor of Paul Oskar Kristeller*, ed. E. P. Mahoney (New York: Columbia Univ. Pr., 1976), pp. 258-274. Examines work of Menaechmus, one of Plato's pupils, who based his thought mathematically, denying Forms. [5452]

BURNYEAT, M. F. "Tranquility without a Stop. Timon, Frag. 68." *CQ* 30(1980), 86-93. Interpretation of a frag quoted by Sextus Empiricus. [5453]

CAMERON, A. D. E. "The Last Days of the Academy at Athens." *PCPhS* 15(1969), 46-70. Justinian ordered Academy closed in 529, perhaps fearing its revival under strong leadership, but school continued to function for more than thirty years. [5454]

CARLTON, W. W. "Greek Philosophy and the Concept of an Academic Discipline." *HPolTho* 6(1985), 47-61. Notion of an academic discipline, with standards of argumentation and a distinction among philosophy, religion, and science, originated with the Academy and the Lyceum. [5455]

COUISSIN, P. "The Stoicism of the New Academy,", in #5550, pp. 31-63. Traces development of Skepticism in Academy from Arcesilaus' "orthodox" version to much weaker stands of Philo and Antiochus. Their opposition to Stoicism led them to formulate many of their ideas in terms designed mostly to refute Stoics. [5456]

DANCY, R. M. "Ancient Non-Being: Speusippus and Others." *AncPh* 9(1989), 207-243. Somewhat technical discussion, with extensive bibliography, of why S rejected Forms and held numbers to be the first things in universe. [5457]

DILLON, J. M. "The Academy in the Middle Platonic Period." *Dion* 3(1979), 63-77. Instruction in Academy during this period seems to have been largely by lecture. The school gained official recognition in 176 A. D. when Marcus Aurelius established professorships there. [5458]

———. "Speusippus in Iamblichus." *Phron* 29(1984), 325-332. Reply to Taran (#5471). [5459]

———. "What Happened to Plato's Garden?" *Hermathena* 134(1983), 51-59. Examines evidence for establishment of Academy as institution; argues against any formal establishment. Describes contents of Academy. Students did not reside in it. **[5460]**

——. cf. #275 and #6299.

DOTY, R. "Carneades, A Forerunner of William James's Pragmatism." *JHI* 47(1986), 133-138. Like James, Carneades denied possibility of truth and offered criterion of probability similar to James's pragmatism. **[5461]**

FOSS, O. "The Pigeon's Neck," in *Classica et mediaevalia F. Blatt septuagenario dedicata*, ed. O. S. Due et al. (Copenhagen: Gyldendal, 1973), pp. 140-149. Variation of colors in a pigeon's neck as argument for unreliability of sense perception is widely attributed to Protagoras. Carneades, however, seems to have originated it. **[5462]**

GLUCKER, J. *Antiochus and the Late Academy.* Goettingen, Ger.: Vandenhoeck & Ruprecht, 1978. Academy probably lost ownership of its grounds by end of fourth century B. C. and was housed in a gymnasium. Antiochus of Ascalon advocated a Stoicized type of Platonism which marked end of Academy. After 88 B. C. no such school existed. The Platonic school which re-opened much later in Athens had no connection to Academy. That school did, however, continue in existence after Justinian's edict closing it in 529. **[5463]**

GOTTSCHALK, H. B. *Heraclides of Pontus.* Oxford: Clarendon Pr., 1980. H was a student of Plato, not Aristotle. Analysis of frags., especially of *On Cessation of Breathing*, reveals his philosophic and scientific interests. Also examined: ethics, pleasure, divinity of stars, eschatology. **[5464]**

LONG, A. A. "Diogenes Laertius, *Life of Arcesilaus*." *Elenchos* 7(1986), 429-449. The *Life* is one of longest in Diogenes' collection. Its sources are easy to trace. It provides useful information on Arcesilaus' formative years, his relationship with Stoics and his dialectical method. **[5465]**

——. cf. #5733.

MUELLER, I. "On Some Academic Theories of Mathematical Objects." *JHS* 106(1986), 111-120. Critical discussion of #5472 regarding facets of mathematical philosophies of Plato and Speusippus. **[5466]**

PEIKOFF, L. "Platonism's Inference from Logic to God." *IntStudPh* 16(1984), 25-34. In Platonic tradition, from antiquity to modern times, God's existence can be inferred from observation "that the Law of Contradiction is an innately known truth." **[5467]**

RENEHAN, R. F. "The Platonism of Lycurgus." *GRBS* 11(1970), 219-231. Ancient sources maintain that orator L was student of P's. Analysis of his only extant speech finds Platonic influences, especially from *Laws*. **[5468]**

SCHNEIDER, I. "The Contributions of the Sceptic Philosophers Arcesilaus and Carneades to the Development of an Inductive Logic Compared with the Jaina-Logic." *IndianJHistSci* 12(1977), 173-180. Compares Greek philosophers' theories of degrees of probability to Indian school of Jaina. Similarity need not imply contact. **[5469]**

SEDLEY, D. "The End of the Academy." *Phron* 26(1981), 67-75. Reply to #5463.

Discusses reasons for split between Antiochus and Philo.   **[5470]**

TARAN, L. "Speusippus and Aristotle on Homonymy and Synonymy." *Hermes* 106(1978), 73-99. S seems to have made extensive classification of names. Homonymy and synonymy are attributes of linguistic terms, not of substances. S probably influenced Ar in this area.   **[5471]**

————. *Speusippus of Athens. A Critical Study with a Collection of the Related Texts.* Leiden: Brill, 1982. Survey of his life, doctrines under headings of "Substances and Principles," "Epistemology and Logic," "Ethics." Doxographic frags and allusions to his teachings (only one direct quotation survives) receive almost three hundred pages of commentary.   **[5472]**

TARRANT, H. "Academics and Platonics." *Prud* 12(1980), 109-118. Review essay of #5463.   **[5473]**

————. "Agreement and the Self-Evident in Philo of Larissa." *Dion* 5(1981), 66-97. P sees general agreement as a sufficient criterion of knowledge, provided one's senses and intellect are healthy.   **[5474]**

————. *Scepticism or Platonism? The Philosophy of the Fourth Academy.* Cambridge Univ. Pr., 1985. Study focuses on Philo of Larissa, whose somewhat sceptical views on the possibility of apprehending reality and whose notion that Ideas are thoughts of God, represented a break with more traditional Platonists.   **[5475]**

————. "Speusippus' Ontological Classification." *Phron* 19(1974), 130-145. Suggests connections between Plato's *Parmenides* and S's thought.   **[5476]**

TOBIN, T. H., transl. *Timaios of Locri, On the Nature of the World and the Soul.* Chico, CA: Scholars Pr., 1985. This cosmological treatise presents many problems of style, date, and authorship. Based loosely on Plato's *Timaeus*, it probably originated in Alexandria in the late first century B. C. or early first century A. D.   **[5477]**

WHITEHEAD, D. "Xenocrates the Metic." *RhM* 124(1981), 223-244. Discussion of X's status as resident-alien and implications for his work in Athens.   **[5478]**

WILKERSON, K. E. "Carneades at Rome. A Problem of Sceptical Rhetoric." *Ph&Rh* 21(1988), 131-144. Rhetoric usually has as its aim to persuade an audience to assent to speaker's proposition. C realized that persuasion can lead people to accept what appears to be true but may not actually be so.   **[5479]**

For related item see #6221.

PERIPATETICS

Aristotle's school is formally known as the Lyceum, from the grove outside Athens where it had its headquarters. Because he was a *metic* (resident alien) Ar could not own property in Athens. He probably rented the site. One story has it that the name was derived from his habit of teaching while walking around with his students, the school received the name Peripatetic. Another explanation is that the covered walkway where he taught was called the Peripatos.

Upon Aristotle's death the headship of the school passed to his student and friend Theophrastus, who provided competent if not brilliant leadership until his own death in ca. 287. The titles of over two hundred works composed by Theophrastus are known, but only a handful survive. These extant works "show industry and intelligence, but testify to a seemingly complete lack of speculative originality in their author."

The Peripatetic school remained more faithful to the founder's teachings than the Academy did, but its adherence to Aristotle's thought was not slavish. The most significant change was one of emphasis. Hellenistic scholars separated science from philosophy. Much of Aristotle's biological and zoological work fell into the domain of the scientists of the third and second century B. C. After the first century B. C. the Peripatetic school produced little beyond commentaries on Aristotle's works. The only author who stands out from the herd is Alexander of Aphrodisias, who wrote ca. 200 A. D. He claimed to be only an interpreter of Aristotle, but in recent years has come to be seen as a philosopher in his own right. Much of his work deals with the problem of free will or determinism. Because he attacks the Stoics (usually without naming them) his work helps us to reconstruct their thought.

BARKER, A. "Theophrastus on Pitch and Melody," in #5492, pp. 288-324. One of the few substantive frags of T's work on music is analyzed to determine what positions he is arguing against.   [5480]

BARNES, J. "Peripatetic Negations." *OSAP* 4(1986), 201-214. Somewhat technical analysis of Alexander of Aphrodisias' arguments on negation. Alexander does not seem to have had cohesive theory on subject but to have worked out responses to his opponents' arguments, responses which are not always adequate.   [5481]

——. "Terms and Sentences: Theophrastus on Hypothetical Syllogisms." *PBA* 69(1983), 279-326. Studies T's logic from citations in Alexander of Aphrodisias.   [5482]

——. "Theophrastus and Hypothetical Syllogistic," in #5492, pp. 125-141; also in #3657, pp. 557-576. Examines various ancient reports on what T wrote about syllogisms which contain hypothetical propositions. While T categorized such syllogisms, he did not create a single system which covered all types of valid inference. The Stoic Chrysippus accomplished that, perhaps starting from T's work.   [5483]

BERKA, K. "Remarks on the Relation Between the Peripatetic and Modern Theories of Modality." *Acta Logica* 12(1969), 261-267. In modal logic terms "necessary" and "possible" have a different ontological status from "true" and "false." Peripatetic tradition fully explored connection between these semantic and ontological concepts.   [5484]

BLUMENTHAL, H. J. "Themistius, the Last Peripatetic Commentator on Aristotle?" in #48, pp. 391-400. This early fourth-century A. D. commentator on Aristotle gave lip service to Plato but was a true Peripatetic.   [5485]

ELLIS, J. "The Aporematic Character of Theophrastus' *Metaphysics*," in #5491, pp. 216-

223. T seldom expresses a definite opinion in the antithesis sections of his work. If he sets a view against one of Aristotle's, for example, it does not necessarily mean that he endorses the opposing view.   [5486]

FORTENBAUGH, W. W. "Arius, Theophrastus, and the *Eudemian Ethics*," in #5611, pp. 203-223. Citation of T in Arius' comments on ethics suggests that T wrote something akin to Aristotle's *Eudemian Ethics*.   [5487]

———. "Theophrastus on Delivery," in #5492, pp. 269-288. Speculative discussion of rhetoric might have been contained in T's short work *On Delivery*. He probably connected oratorical delivery and literary style with analysis of emotions.   [5488]

———. "Theophrastus on Emotion," in #5492, pp. 209-229. T seems, like Aristotle, to have seen emotions (*pathe*) as complex and to have analyzed similar emotions in terms of degree ("more and less"). Neither Aristotle nor T arrived at a general definition of *pathe*.   [5489]

———. "Theophrastus on Fate and Character," in #48, pp. 372-375. For T the gods have given us a character which, if developed wisely, will lead to a moral, successful life. Our fate is determined only to that extent.   [5490]

———., and **SHARPLES, R. W.**, eds. *Theophrastean Studies. On Natural Science, Physics and Metaphysics, Ethics, Religion and Rhetoric*. New Brunswick, NJ: Transaction Books, 1988. Collection of essays, abstracted herein.   [5491]

———. et al., eds. *Theophrastus of Eresus. On His Life and Work*. New Brunswick, NJ: Transaction Books, 1985. Collection of essays on T's thought and the transmission of his text. Those of philosophical interest are abstracted herein.   [5492]

FOTINIS, A. P., ed. and transl. *The De Anima of Alexander of Aphrodisias*. Washington, DC: Univ. Pr. of America. Transl. omits several chapters, but is clear and helpful. Commentary.   [5493]

FRANK, D. H. "A Disproof in the *Peri Ideon*." *SJPh* 22(1984), 49-60. An Aristotelian objection to Platonic arguments "from the sciences" can be made intelligible.   [5494]

FREDE, D. "Could Paris (Son of Priam) Have Chosen Otherwise? A Discussion of R. W. Sharples, *Alexander of Aphrodisias: de Fato*." *OSAP* 2(1984), 279-292. Review essay of #5521.   [5495]

———. "The Dramatization of Determinism: Alexander of Aphrodisias' *De fato*." *Phron* 27(1982), 276-298. Attempts to reconstruct Stoic arguments on determinism which A was refuting. Real focus of debate is Stoic idea of panentheism.   [5496]

———. cf. #5694.

FURLEY, D. "The Greek Commentators' Treatment of Aristotle's Theory of the Continuous," in #64, pp. 17-36. Examines Ar's commentators and what they found problematic in his theory of the continuous and how they tried to clarify it.   [5497]

———. "Strato's Theory of the Void," in #3657, pp. 594-609. The Peripatetic Strato seems to have held that place was three dimensional and that void was only potential. He seems not to have been influenced by the Atomists or Epicurus.   **[5498]**

GIGON, O. "The Peripatos in Cicero's *De finibus*," in #5491, pp. 259-271. In Cicero's ethical treatise Peripatetic views are treated more favorably than Stoics or Epicureans, except that Theophrastus's biologic ethics cannot account for evil.   **[5499]**

GOERGEMANNS, H. "*Oikeiosis* in Arius Didymus," in #5611, pp. 165-189. What is usually thought of as a Stoic doctrine is treated by Arius as part of Peripatetic ethics. Translation and analysis of passage in which this occurs.   **[5500]**

GOTTHELF, A. "*Historiae I: plantarum et animalium*," in #5491, pp. 100-135. T modeled his *Historia plantarum* on Aristotle's *Historia animalium*. Both works seek to explore all the differences observable in the things under study, with the ultimate aim of discovering causes and the essential nature of animals and plants.   **[5501]**

GOTTSCHALK, H. B. "The *De audibilibus* and Peripatetic Acoustics." *Hermes* 96(1968), 435-460. This treatise is a significant advance beyond Aristotle's work on acoustics. It introduces the concept of vibrations for the first time.   **[5502]**

GRAYEFF, F. *Aristotle and His School: An Inquiry into the History of the Peripatos, with a Commentary on Metaphysics Alpha, Beta, and Gamma.* London: Duckworth, 1974. First part traces Ar's life and history of his school after his death. Second part argues that portions of the *Meta* were written by later Peripatetics and reflect controversies with Stoics and Epicureans.   **[5503]**

HUBY, P. M. "A Neglected Fragment of Peripatetic Logic." *LCM* 4(1979), 207-210. Analyzes a discussion of hypothetic syllogism which was attached to a medieval copy of Ar's *PostAn*. It seems to express Theophrastus' views.   **[5504]**

——. "Peripatetic Definitions of Happiness," in #5611, pp. 121-134. The definitions cited by Arius Didymus derive from Aristotle's esoteric (non-public) writings. Some closely resemble Stoic doctrines. Discussions of the definitions are independent of Aristotle.   **[5505]**

——. "Theophrastus in the Aristotelian Corpus, with Particular Reference to Biological Problems," in #3809, pp. 314-325. Examines contents of *Historia animalium*, Books 8 and 9 to consider whether T authored these texts.   **[5506]**

HUGHES, J. D. "Theophrastus as Ecologist," in #5491, pp. 67-75. Though he emphasized individual plants and animals instead of a system, T did study them in context. His philosophical outlook, which stressed efficient rather than final causes, was more congenial to development of an ecological view than was Aristotle's.   **[5507]**

INNES, D. C. "Theophrastus and the Theory of Style," in #5492, pp. 251-267. It is difficult to sort out T's particular contributions on literary style from those of the Peripatetic school in general. He does seem to have advocated a mean, between an overly plain and an overly emotive style.   **[5508]**

KUSTAS, G. L. "The Commentators on Aristotle's *Categories* and on Porphyry's *Isagoge*," in *Studia Byzantina II: Beitraege aus der byzantinischen Forschung der Deut-*

schen Demokratischen Republik zum XIV. Internationalen Byzantinisten-Kongress Bukarest 1971, ed. J. Irmscher and P. Nagel (Berlin: Akad.-Verlag, 1973), pp. 101-126. Alexandrians' reverence for Ar gave mystical cast to difficult passages from his work. This attitude carried over into Byzantine era. **[5509]**

LAKS, A., et al. "Four Notes on Theophrastus' *Metaphysics*," in #5491, pp. 224-256. 1) The work seems to have been written in the 330's, shortly after Aristotle's *Historia animalium*; 2) T uses the term *energeia* in several ways, as does Aristotle; 3) discussion of textual difficulties in *Meta* 4-6 illuminates the importance of certain Academic ideas for T; 4) suggests an emendation of a quotation of Heraclitus in T's *Meta*. **[5510]**

LENNOX, J. G. "Theophrastus on the Limits of Teleology," in #5492, pp. 143-163. T was not satisfied with two reasons Aristotle gave for finding teleological causes in natural processes. T's *Metaphysics* is aporetic, not intended to resolve the problem. **[5511]**

LYNCH, J. P. *Aristotle's School: A Study of a Greek Educational Institution*. Berkeley: Univ. of CA Pr., 1972. Examines the Lyceum from its origins to its demise in the early first century B. C. Looks at school's methodology more than its doctrine. **[5512]**

MADIGAN, A. "Alexander of Aphrodisias: The Book of Ethical Problems." *ANRW* II,36.2,1260-1279. The work is a mixture of exposition of Aristotelian doctrine, especially *NE*, and responses to Stoics. **[5513]**

MANSFELD, J. "*Diaphonia*. The Argument of Alexander *De Fato* Chapters 1-2." *Phron* 33(1988), 181-207. What are called chapters 1 and 2 are actually a prologue in which A thanks the emperor for his appointment and makes it clear that he has no sympathy with the Skepticism which some Peripatetics of his day were adopting. He does, however, use several Pyrrhonist techniques of argument. **[5514]**

MIGNUCCI, M. "Logic and Omniscience. Alexander of Aphrodisias and Proclus." *OSAP* 3(1985), 219-246. A statement such as "Socrates is sleeping" is called an indefinitely tensed statement. It may be true at one time but not at another. Such a logical possibility raises ontological problems when one considers possibility of divine omniscience. A denied that God could know everything about all individuals. P sees God as outside time and avoids this difficulty. **[5515]**

OBBINK, D. "The Origin of Greek Sacrifice: Theophrastus on Religion and Cultural History," in #5491, pp. 272-295. In his treatise *On Piety* T traced the development of the practice of animal sacrifice and presented philosophical arguments against it. Frags of the work suggest that aversion to such sacrifices was not widespread in the Greek world. **[5516]**

PODLECKI, A. J. "Theophrastus on History and Politics," in #5492, pp. 231-249. Sixteen or seventeen of T's works seem to have been largely historical in nature. He appears to have been methodical and conscientious in his compilation of historical information and may have collaborated with Aristotle on some works. The incomplete nature of his work does not allow us to evaluate his political writings. **[5517]**

PREUS, A. "Drugs and Psychic States in Theophrastus' *Historia plantarum* 9.8-20," in #5491, pp. 76-99. T is more interested in the nature and classification of plants, as was Aristotle, than in their medicinal properties. He does make note of some pharmacological effects and is puzzled when a plant can have more than one effect. [5518]

RIST, J. M. "On Tracking Alexander of Aphrodisias." *AGPh* 48(1966), 82-90. There are few direct references to A in Plotinus, who does not refute specific objections of his opponents but offers general and constructive criticism of their views. [5519]

SHARPLES, R. W. "Alexander of Aphrodisias, *De fato*. Some Parallels." *CQ* 28(1978), 243-266. Supposed parallels between A's work and Middle Platonic discussions of fate are actually common-places which could have been drawn independently from several sources. A shows more profound understanding of the problem of determinism than do Platonists. [5520]

------. *Alexander of Aphrodisias: On Fate*. London: Duckworth, 1983. Greek text, with translation, commentary and an introduction discussing A's contribution to debate on determinism vs. choice. Treatise has polemical overtones because A was arguing against Stoic notion of providence. Introduction discusses development of concept of fate/freewill before Alexander. [5521]

------. "Alexander of Aphrodisias 'On Time'." *Phron* 27(1982), 58-81. Translation of a Latin version of the treatise and discussion of its contents. [5522]

------. "Alexander of Aphrodisias: Scholasticism and Innovation." *ANRW* II,36.2,1177-1243. Survey with lengthy bibliography. [5523]

------. "Could Alexander (Follower of Aristotle) Have Done Better? A Response to Professor Frede and Others." *OSAP* 5(1987), 197-216. Reply to #5495. [5524]

------. "The Peripatetic Classification of Goods," in #5611, pp. 139-159. Classification scheme found in Arius Didymus has weaknesses but there are indications of connected sequences. Some of the divisions have parallels in Aristotle. [5525]

------. "Theophrastus on Tastes and Smells," in #5492, pp. 183-204. In good Aristotelian fashion T bases his account of tastes and smells on the four primary opposites — hot, cold, wet, dry. How closely he adhered to Aristotle's teaching on the matter cannot be determined because of the incompleteness of T's texts on the subject. [5526]

------. "Theophrastus on the Heavens," in #3657, pp. 577-593. Theophrastus may have viewed the heavens as made of fire, instead of Aristotle's aether. It is not clear whether he thought of a construction in spheres or how he explained motion. [5527]

------. "The Unmoved Mover and the Motion of the Heavens in Alexander of Aphrodisias." *Apeir* 17(1983), 62-66. A sees universe as eternal in its own nature rather than from divine will. Unmoved Mover is not a contradiction in this scheme because he causes the universe to fulfill its natural tendency. [5528]

------. cf. #4906.

SKEMP, J. B. "The *Metaphysics* of Theophrastus in Relation to the Doctrine of *Kinesis* in Plato's Later Dialogues," in #5350, pp. 217-223. The *Metaphysics* attributed to Theophrastus should be regarded as his. The explanation of the movement of the heavens does not seem to take cognizance of Plato's theory of *kinesis*. [5529]

SOLLENBERGER, M. G. "Identification of Titles of Botanical Works of Theophrastus," in #5491, pp. 14-24. Surveys problems of identifying works from lists such as Diogenes Laertius'. Portions of T's works are sometimes cited under separate titles.   **[5530]**

SORABJI, R. "Theophrastus on Place," in #5491, pp. 139-166. Outlines Aristotle's views on place, and then explores T's doubts about Ar's account, doubts which were carried over into writers of late antiquity and the Middle Ages.   **[5531]**

TODD, R. *Alexander of Aphrodisias on Stoic Physics: A Study of the* De mixtione *with Preliminary Essays, Text, Translation and Commentary.* Leiden: Brill, 1976. Examines problem of studying early Stoic physics on basis of text written by an opponent of the school. Treatise *De mixtione* deals with question of whether two bodies could occupy same place at same time. Translation and bibliography included.   **[5532]**

TWEEDALE, M. M. "Alexander of Aphrodisias' Views on Universals." *Phron* 29(1984), 279-303. A's views on universals became normative for western medieval philosophy through translations of Boethius and later Avicenna. A's view, unfortunately, is difficult to elucidate.   **[5533]**

VALLANCE, J. "Theophrastus and the Study of the Intractable: Scientific Method in *De lapidibus* and *De igne*," in #5491, pp. 25-40. The scientific method used in these and other minor works does not indicate that T was breaking with Aristotle. Many of T's remarks seem to be directed against the Academy and Plato's *Timaeus*.   **[5534]**

VAN DER BEN, N. "Theophrastus, *De Vertigine*, Chapter 9, and Heraclitus Fr. 125." *AJPh* 109(1988), 397-401. Reply to #530.   **[5535]**

VANDER WAERDT, P. A. "The Peripatetic Interpretation of Plato's Tripartite Psychology." *GRBS* 26(1985), 283-302. Peripatetic *Magna Moralia* distorts P's understanding of soul as tripartite into a bipartite theory that accords with Aristotle's views.   **[5536]**

———. "Peripatetic Soul-Division. Posidonius and Middle Platonic Moral Philosophy." *GRBS* 26(1985), 373-394. Study of how a Peripatetic doctrine was accepted and transmitted in Middle Platonism.   **[5537]**

VAN RAALTE, M. "The Idea of the Cosmos as an Organic Whole in Theophrastus' *Metaphysics*," in #5491, pp. 189-215. T's view of the cosmos as an organism uses Aristotle's methodology but denies his teleology. T is much closer to Heraclitus and the Stoics, whose founder, Zeno of Citium, could have heard T.   **[5538]**

WOEHRLE, G. "The Structure and Function of Theophrastus' Treatise *De odoribus*," in #5491, pp. 3-13. Outline of this fragmentary work and comparison of T's explanation of how odors are produced and perceived to Aristotle's view. The two agree in principle if not in terminology.   **[5539]**

For related items see #4639, #5747, #5756.

SKEPTICISM

The Skeptic school of philosophy, which predates the Stoic and Epicurean, taught that certainty in knowledge could never be achieved. They would probably appreciate the irony that today we do not know much about the founding of the school, what it was originally called, or how to spell Skeptic/Sceptic. (The former spelling is closer to the original Greek and will be used in our analysis. We will retain whichever spelling is used in titles in the bibliography.) The term "Skeptic" comes from the Greek *skeptesthai*, which means to look carefully at something, to examine, or consider. The earliest philosophers to take this cautious approach to knowledge were also called Aporetics (from *aporia*, an uncertain outcome) or Ephectics (from *epoche*, a suspension of judgment).

All of these terms point to an epistemology which could not advance beyond the problem of how reliable information could be obtained. Aristotle had taught that the philosopher must begin his quest for knowledge in a state of *aporia*, but that following the proper logical process would lead to the removal of that uncertainty. The Skeptics, however, found sense data unreliable and logic fallible. The only possible conclusion was that certain, indisputable knowledge was unobtainable.

Two distinct strains of Skepticism are discernible. One, already discussed above (p. 595), arose in the Academy between the third and first centuries B. C. By 80 B. C. it had merged with the older strain, also called Pyrrhonism after its founder Pyrrho of Elis (365-275 B. C.).

Trained to be a painter, Pyrrho accompanied Alexander the Great on his Eastern campaigns and may have become acquainted with the doctrines of the Elean-Megarian school and with the relativism of Protagoras, which clearly teaches a kind of skeptical attitude about the possibility of attaining absolute knowledge. He may also have known the teachings of the eastern Magi and Gymnosophists ("Naked Sages") of India (cf. #5559 and #5576). He did not write anything, so we have to rely on his student, Timon of Phlius, for a report of his teaching (cf. #5570) and on late doxographers for details about his life, all of which may be unreliable (cf. #5566).

Like the other Hellenistic philosophers, Pyrrho sought happiness. To live happily, a person must understand three things: 1) the nature of things; 2) the proper attitude toward them; 3) the benefits to be derived from this attitude.

Pyrrho was convinced, however, that one could not know anything certain about the physical world. All our knowledge of it is derived from sensory perceptions, which are so subjective as to be worthless for securing knowledge. Given this situation, we may never assert anything as true. We may say that something appears to us to be so-and-so, but it may appear to be slightly, or entirely, different to someone else. Our attitude must be one of observing things but reserving judgment about them, which is the basic meaning of "skepticism." We can thus see that there is some truth in Ambrose Bierce's description of Pyrrhonism as consisting of "an absolute disbelief in everything but Pyrrhonism."

But what benefit does one derive from this philosophy? Pyrrho claimed that one who did not expect to gain knowledge about things would place no value on them. Since definite assertions cannot be made about anything, no one thing can be judged to be better or worse than another. His teaching on this point is called the *ou mallon*, "not more [this than that]." The Skeptic abstains from judgment, basing his actions on appearances and social customs. But at least he knows their basis. Thus the true Skeptic can detach himself from worldly concerns and live in a state of *ataraxia* (tranquility) or *apathe* (indifference). Such a state of mind is the ultimate objective of Stoicism and Epicureanism as well. The Skeptic school never achieved the kind of organization and wide recognition that the Academy or the other Hellenistic schools gained. Once the Academy assumed a skeptical posture (cf. above), the Pyrrhonian school disappeared as an independent entity. When the Academy shifted to Eclecticism in the mid-first century B. C., Pyrrhonism was revived by Aenesidemus. None of Aenesidemus' work has survived, but several titles are known: *Pyrrhonic Discourses, On Investigation,* and *Against Wisdom* are typical. He developed ten "tropes" or forms of argument which demonstrated the necessity of *epoche*.

Because it is so difficult to separate the thought of Pyrrho and Sextus, we have grouped all entries on Skepticism together.

ANNAS, J. "Doing without Objective Values: Ancient and Modern Strategies," in #5643, pp. 3-29. Differences between ancient/modern approaches to skeptical views on law and value are noticeable in three areas: 1) ancient Skeptics thought suspension of judgment brought happiness; 2) ancient Skeptics saw rejection of objective values as passive; 3) modern Skeptics see no conflict between denying possibility of objective standards but see no effect on their actions. [5540]

————., and BARNES, J. *The Modes of Scepticism. Ancient Texts and Modern Interpretations.* Cambridge Univ. Pr., 1985. New translation of and commentary on one of most important texts of ancient Skeptical school, the Ten Modes. It compares ancient Skeptics with later philosophers, from Descartes to Nagel. Does not assume knowledge of Greek. [5541]

BARNES, J. "Ancient Skepticism and Causation," in #5550, pp. 149-204. Assembles Skeptics' arguments against idea of deliberate causation of events and, in a somewhat technical discussion, attempts to refute them. [5542]

————. "The Beliefs of a Pyrrhonist." *PCPhS* 28(1982), 1-29; also in *Elenchos* 4(1983), 5-43. Sextus seems to reject knowledge through phenomena as well as from philosophical theories, but not all Pyrrhonists recognized same degree of suspension of judgment. [5543]

————. "Proof Destroyed," in #5642, pp. 161-181. Study of Stoic demonstrations of proof and Skeptic refutations of them. [5544]

————. "Scepticism and the Arts." *Apeir* 21(1988), 53-77. Sextus Empiricus' *Against the Mathematicians* I-VI is not a philosophical attack on liberal arts. It is a collection of arguments which can be raised against the dogmatic philosophers. [5545]

BRUNSCHWIG, J. "Proof Defined," in #5642, pp. 125-160. Attempts to examine four definitions of proof in Sextus lead to conclusion that he may have been drawing upon early Stoics, especially Zeno, Cleanthes, Chrysippus. [5546]

BURNYEAT, M. F. "Can the Skeptic Live his Skepticism?" in #5550, pp. 117-148. One of most telling arguments against Skepticism, from antiquity to modern times, is inability of human beings to detach themselves from judgment completely enough to live consistently with this philosophy. [5547]

——. "Can the Sceptic Live his Scepticism?" in #5642, pp. 20-53. Constraints of human nature make it impossible for Skeptic to live a life devoid of all judgments and commitments. [5548]

——. "Protagoras and Self-Refutation in Later Greek Philosophy." *PhR* 85(1976), 44-69. Sextus maintains that P's doctrine that "as things appear to each they are for him" means that whatever appears to be true *is* true. But if it appears that not every appearance is true, then P's principle can be self-refuting. Study of this argument illuminates methods of controversy in Hellenistic philosophy. [5549]

——, ed. *The Skeptical Tradition.* Berkeley: Univ. of CA Pr., 1983. Seventeen essays, eight of which pertain to ancient philosophy, others to influence of Skepticism on thinkers down to Kant. Relevant items abstracted herein. [5550]

CHATTERJEE, D. "Skepticism and Indian Philosophy." *PhE&W* 27(1977), 195-209. Indian philosophy did not develop a full-fledged skeptical school, but cautions against dogmatism in Vedic literature display similarities to Skeptic suspension of judgment. Indian philosophy, however, never doubted possibility of knowing the real. [5551]

CHAUDHURI, S. "Pyrrhonian Scepticism and Epoche." *IndianPhQ* 3(1976), 235-244. Survey of process of suspension of judgment between two counter-balancing arguments. *Epoche* brings peace of mind and avoids pitfalls of dogmatism. [5552]

CHROUST, A. H. "Sextus Empiricus, *Adversus mathematicos*, IX,26-27 (*Adversus Physicos* I,26-27). A Fragment of Aristotle's *On Philosophy*?" *CF* 28(1974), 214-218. Passage has Platonic and Stoic overtones; not definitely attributable to Ar. [5553]

COHEN, A. "Sextus Empiricus. Skepticism as a Therapy." *PhFor* 15(1984), 405-424. Classical Skepticism is not the absurd failure it is often depicted as. It offers release from uncertainty and striving after absolute answers. Skeptic is able to consider all aspects of a question and is not disconcerted by inability to resolve contradictions or paradoxes. [5554]

COUISSIN, P. "The Origin and the Evolution of the Epoche." *GradFacPhJ* 11(1986), 47-66; transl. L. Bostar. The concept of suspension of judgment seems to have originated with Zeno the Stoic and was picked up, at first ironically, by Arcesilaus. Its precise usage became blurred in later Skeptics. [5555]

DE LACY, P. "*Ou mallon* and the Antecedents of Ancient Scepticism." *Phron* 3(1958), 59-71. Meanings of term *ou mallon* ("no more this than that") were refined, though never really changed, from its early appearance in Democritus to its full development in the Skeptical school. [5556]

EVERSON, S. "Apparent Conflict." *Phron* 30(1985), 305-313. Review essay of #5541. [5557]

FERRARRIA, L., and **SANTESE, G.,** eds. "Bibliografia sullo scetticismo antico (1880-1978)," in *Lo scetticismo antico. Atti del Convegno orginazzato dal Centro di studio del* *pensiero antico del C. N. R., Roma 5-8 novembre 1980*, ed. by G. Giannantoni (Naples: Bibliopolis, 1981), vol. II, pp. 753-850. Comprehensive but not annotated. **[5558]**

FLINTOFF, E. "Pyrrho and India." *Phron* 25(1980), 88-108. Scholars have not paid enough attention to Diogenes Laertius' claim of Indian influence on Pyrrho. His teaching as a whole bears some resemblance to Buddhism. **[5559]**

FOWLER, D. "Sceptics and Epicureans: A Discussion of M. Gigante, *Scetticismo e Epicureismo.*" *OSAP* 2(1984), 237-267. Review essay of an important work. **[5560]**

GLIDDEN, D. "Marcello Gigante and the Sceptical Epicurean." *AncPh* 6(1986), 169-176. Discussion of Gigante's book *Scetticismo e Epicureismo* (1981). **[5561]**

———. "Skeptic Semiotics." *Phron* 28(1983), 213-255. Mnemonic signs are based on circumstances; indicative signs establish a line of reasoning. Sextus juxtaposes them to disguise his rejection of the mnemonic. **[5562]**

GREAVES, D. D., ed. *Sextus Empiricus, Argument against the Musicians*. Lincoln: Univ. of NE Pr., 1986. Text, transl., commentary. Treatise disputes musical theorists, especially Stoics, who make claims about nature of music and its effects on soul. As a Skeptic, S does not believe that certain knowledge about music or its influence on soul (existence of which cannot be proved) is possible. **[5563]**

HALLIE, P. P., ed., and **ETHERIDGE, S. G.,** transl. *Sextus Empiricus: Selections from the Major Writings on Scepticism, Man, and God*. Indianapolis: Hackett, 1985; rprt. Introduction and notes stress that Skepticism is not a matter of systematic negation or indifference but that Skeptics were attempting to live "according to Nature," like Stoics and Epicureans. Bibliography. **[5564]**

HILEY, D. R. "The Deep Challenge of Pyrrhonian Scepticism." *JHPh* 25(1987), 185-213. Emphasizes Pyrrho's view that skepticism enables one to lead a tranquil life. Attempts to refute claim that Skeptic cannot live his skepticism. **[5565]**

HOUSE, D. K. "The Life of Sextus Empiricus." *CQ* 30(1980), 227-238. Evidence for S's date, place of birth, and every other detail of his life, cannot be trusted. **[5566]**

JANACEK, K. *Sextus Empiricus' Sceptical Methods*. Prague: Univ. Karlova, 1972. Technical study of a dozen terms which Sextus uses frequently. **[5567]**

JOHNSON, O. A. "Mitigated Skepticism." *Ratio* 18(1976), 73-84. Pyrrho's Skepticism is "mitigated." It admits at least knowledge of what appears to be so. Such a compromise results in ultimate failure of Skepticism, as Hume and others realized. **[5568]**

LONG, A. A. "Sextus Empiricus on the Criterion of Truth." *BICS* 25(1978), 35-49. *Outlines of Pyrrhonism* 2.13-79 is more formalistic in treatment of truth-criterion than is *Against the Dogmatists* 7.27-448. **[5569]**

———. "Timon of Phlius. Pyrrhonist and Satirist." *PCPhS* 24(1978), 68-91. Most biographical data on Pyrrho derives from Timon, who shows Cynic influences. **[5570]**

———. cf. #3981.

MANSFELD, J. *"De Melisso Xenophane Gorgia.* Pyrrhonizing Aristotelianism." *RhM* 131(1988), 239-276. Purpose of this anonymous treatise is to criticize earlier philosophers from standpoint of a pyrrhonized aristotelianism, rather than merely to describe earlier writers' thought. **[5571]**

McPHERRAN, M. L. "Skeptical Homeopathy and Self-Refutation." *Phron* 32(1987), 290-328. Sextus compares Pyrrho's self-refuting argument to purgative which is passed out by organism along with noxious material. Though treated seriously by Sextus, argument confounds modern logic. **[5572]**

MUELLER, I. "Geometry and Scepticism," in #5599, pp. 69-95. Skeptics opposed mathematics because of their contention that the objects of mathematical knowledge have no real existence but are mental creations. **[5573]**

NAESS, A. "Psychological and Social Aspects of Pyrrhonian Scepticism." *Inquiry* 9(1966), 301-321. Balancing claims and suspension of judgment which characterize Pyrrhonian Skepticism can have positive impact on individual's mental health. **[5574]**

——. "Pyrrho's Scepticism according to Sextus Empiricus," in *Scepticism* (New York: Humanities Pr., 1969), pp. 1-35. Attempts to define differences between Skepticism of Pyrrho and the Academy, between skeptical and dogmatic methods of teaching, and between *epoche* and doubt. **[5575]**

NANAJIVAKO, B. "The Indian Origin of Pyrrho's Philosophy of Epoche." *IndianPhQ* 12(1985), 319-340. Elements of Indian thought, perhaps from Alexander's time, are evident in P's work. **[5576]**

RIST, J. M. "The Heracliteanism of Aenesidemus." *Phoenix* 24(1970), 309-319. A rejected Academy's Stoic tendencies and combined Heraclitean doctrine of opposite characteristics in one subject with Skepticism. **[5577]**

SCHMITT, C. B. "The Rediscovery of Ancient Skepticism in Modern Times," in #5550, pp. 225-251. Humanists of Italian Renaissance first expressed interest in Skeptical texts. By 1500 they were more popular in northern Europe than in Italy. Sextus' work was better known in early sixteenth century than has previously been recognized. **[5578]**

SEDLEY, D. "The Motivation of Greek Skepticism," in #5550, pp. 9-29. Skeptics did not make their *epoche* a matter of dogma but left open possibility that some claim of knowledge might eventually be made which could withstand their arguments. **[5579]**

STOUGH, C. L. *Greek Skepticism. A Study in Epistemology.* Berkeley: Univ. of CA Pr., 1969. Survey from Pyrrho to Sextus Empiricus, focusing on basic concepts: knowledge, belief, experience, perception, and sensation. School's basic assumption is doubt about knowledge of the world, not denial of its possibility. Skepticism inherited reality/phenomena distinction. **[5580]**

——. "Knowledge and Belief." *OSAP* 5(1987), 217-234. Review of #5541 and #5475. **[5581]**

——. "Sextus Empiricus on Non-Assertion." *Phron* 29(1984), 137-164. Skeptic's daily behavior, while not necessarily different from average person's, is founded on opinions, not convictions. Truth is not necessary for *ataraxia*. Their claims of non-assertion have pragmatic, non-descriptive function.   **[5582]**

STRIKER, G. "Sceptical Strategies," in #5642, pp. 54-83. Skeptic thesis that nothing can be known is independent of their recommendation to suspend judgment. Carneades worked out counter-arguments against Stoics but does not appear to have believed them himself.   **[5583]**

————. "The Ten Tropes of Aenesidemus," in #5550, pp. 95-115. Discussion of structure of arguments in favor of suspension of judgment and against claims that sense impression can yield knowledge. Probably developed in first century B. C. in reaction against Stoic tendencies among later Academics.   **[5584]**

VISVADER, J. "The Use of Paradox in Uroboric Philosophies." *PhE&W* 28(1978), 455-467. Uroboric philosophies, so called after the ancient emblem of snake swallowing its tail, attempt to negate themselves. Thought of Sextus Empiricus, L. Wittgenstein, Buddhism and Taoism are examined, especially their use of paradox.   **[5585]**

WHITE, M. J. "The Fourth Account of Conditionals in Sextus Empiricus." *H&PhLog* 7(1986), 1-14. S's fourth account of conditional statements can be viewed in terms of modern "relevance" interpretations of entailment. The fourth account may be a reaction to Stoic arguments about validity of arguments in conditional statements.   **[5586]**

WILLIAMS, M. "Scepticism without Theory." *RMeta* 41(1988), 547-588. Ancient (Pyrrhonian) Skepticism recognized that some matters can never be resolved. One must avoid all theories/dogmas and get on with life. Modern Skepticism is theoretical, with little effect on daily life, largely due to increased scientific certainty.   **[5587]**

WRIGHT, R. "Greek Scepticism." *Pegasus* 11(1969), 13-24. Summary for non-specialists of origins and major tenets of the school and ancient objections to it.   **[5588]**

For related items see #5695, #6276, #6391.

ECLECTICISM

   With so many competing views in circulation it is not surprising that some people found themselves unable to choose one over the other. Some aspect, perhaps the physics, of one school might be appealing, while the ethics of another school might be more attractive. A "school" of philosophy soon arose which selected doctrines from various schools, reasoning that *all* philosophies were true to some degree. This approach is called Eclecticism, from a Greek word meaning to select or choose. Since it had no definite doctrines of its own, this "school" is difficult to describe. It would be more accurate to say that some post-Aristotelian philosophers in each of the schools took an eclectic approach, rather than adhering dogmatically to the principles of their respective founders.

DILLON, J. M., and **LONG, A. A.** *The Question of 'Eclecticism': Studies in Later Greek Philosophy.* Berkeley: Univ. of CA Pr., 1988. Essays written for conference in Dublin.

Greek/Latin terms translated, to make it accessible to wider audience. Relevant essays abstracted herein. **[5589]**

DONINI, P. "The History of the Concept of Eclecticism," in #5589, pp. 15-33. Though most ancient philosophers, as early as Socrates, admitted to choosing doctrines from their predecessors, term "eclectic" to describe a school is rare. At least six different interpretations of term are current today. **[5590]**

Chapter 16

HELLENISTIC PHILOSOPHY

Hellenistic philosophy arose in the wake of Alexander the Great's conquest of the eastern end of the Mediterranean Sea, the Mesopotamian valley, and India. His successors divided his territory into kingdoms of varying size. The Seleucids in Syria/Turkey and the Ptolemies in Egypt were the dominant rulers. It was an age productive of intellectual endeavors, if not of genius. Alexander had been taught by Aristotle, and the successor kings gave patronage to writers, philosophers, and scientists. Loss of political freedom seems to have created an aura of despair, defeatism, and withdrawal. The idea of some inexorable fate or indifferent chance (*Tyche*) governing everything became widespread. Though it was an impersonal force, this fate was seen as envious of persons who achieved too much or enjoyed too much prosperity.

The philosophical systems which developed in this new milieu emphasized ethics, primarily personal but also to some degree societal. They did not ignore questions of the nature of the world (drawing most of their answers from Heraclitus and Democritus), but they considered them only the foundation for the more important problem of developing guidelines for human behavior. In the Hellenistic era philosophy and science grew apart. Aristotle was the last to attempt to combine them. Neither he nor Plato had much direct impact on philosophy between the death of Alexander and the birth of Christ. The Academy moved to skepticism on the question of whether knowledge was even possible. Aristotle's works lay unpublished and unread until ca. 80 B. C. Systems which claimed to be based on their teaching were muddled rehashings which neither thinker would have claimed as legitimate offspring.

Dropping its scientific orientation, philosophy in the Hellenistic era took on a religious tinge, competing with the mystery religions which sought to offer consolation and hope to the masses in an age when old political and religious forms had lost all meaning. The Cynics and Stoics developed the diatribe, a forerunner of the Christian sermon, and won "converts" by their public proclamations of their doctrines. Many philosophers began to play the role of spiritual advisors to the rulers and the masses alike. In general, philosophy turned "away from disinterested speculation to the provision of security for the individual."

Stoicism and Epicureanism, the dominant Hellenistic schools, were efforts to help people cope with life under the new conditions. As J. A. Akinpelu says, "both are rooted in defeat; both are offspring of disillusionment and discomfiture. The Greek *polis* had failed; freedom as Pericles envisioned it had disappeared. The life of the individual, which was formerly inextricably twined with that of the state, had lost its roots; it had become meaningless." The doctrines of these schools will be studied in separate chapters, but it might be helpful to see how they fit into this mood of the Hellenistic era.

The Stoics offered what one might call a rationale for despair in their view that every thing and every event in the world has been pre-ordained by God. No human decision can make a difference. Happiness can be found only in acceptance of this state of affairs and in living up to the highest standards of conduct befitting the status which has been meted out to one. Both the slave Epictetus and the emperor Marcus Aurelius consoled themselves by the knowledge that they were not responsible for their respective conditions.

Epicureanism offered a different explanation for the state of the world, but happiness was its ultimate objective. Everything in the world, Epicurus held, resulted from the random movement of atoms, which collided and formed objects. There was no plan or purpose, rational or otherwise, in anything. There was, consequently, no point in involving oneself in the affairs of the world. Instead, one should withdraw and seek tranquility, the only sure source of happiness.

The Cynics, though originating somewhat earlier, found an eager audience for their message of disdain for worldly goods and standards. Their lifestyle required more of a commitment than that of the Stoics or Epicureans, but it attracted people who were more radically alienated than members of the other two schools.

For generations Hellenistic philosophy received scant scholarly attention, due to its presumed inferiority to Platonic and Aristotelian thought. It is still possible to find survey texts of ancient philosophy which stop with Aristotle, though they are becoming rare. Karl Marx was one of the first to attribute some importance to the Hellenistic schools. He maintained that they were the key to understanding Greek philosophy. As its ultimate outcome, they could provide clues to how earlier thinkers were understood by antiquity. There were no useful studies of those schools in his day, so he wrote his dissertation on Epicurus. Today there has been a blossoming of interest in post-Aristotelian philosophy, reflected in the bibliographies in this and succeeding chapters.

AALDERS, G. J. D. "The Hellenistic Concept of the Enviousness of Fate," in #5651, pp. 1-8. In classical period gods were thought to be envious of human prosperity or fortune. In Hellenistic era envy was attributed to Fate itself. **[5591]**

ANNAS, J. "The Heirs of Socrates." *Phron* 33(1988), 100-112. Survey of recent studies on dispute among Stoics, Skeptics, and Academy over which was true continuator of Socratic philosophy. **[5592]**

ANTON, J. P. "Ancient Interpretations of Aristotle's Doctrine of *Homonyma*." *JHPh* 7(1969), 1-18. Later thinkers platonized Ar's doctrine of *homonyma* because they failed to understand term *logos tes ousias*. They took *logos* to mean both definition and description. **[5593]**

ARIOTTI, P. "The Concept of Time in Late Antiquity." *IntPhQ* 12(1972), 526-552. Aristotle saw time as celestial reductionism, related to motions of celestial bodies. Alexander of Aphrodisias knew of more complex motions, so time was reduced to motion of fixed stars. Idea of relational time, found in Epicurus, can be traced down to Plotinus and Iamblichus. Augustine's internal time is also studied.   [5594]

ARMSTRONG, A. H., ed. *The Cambridge History of Later Greek and Early Medieval Philosophy*. Cambridge Univ. Pr., 1967. Survey, which perhaps suffers from compression, of Greco-Roman and Christian philosophers, on into Arabic era. Part I focuses on development of Platonism to Plotinus. Concludes with St. Anselm.   [5595]

BARNES, J. "Bits and Pieces," in #5597, pp. 223-294. Looks at efforts to explain relationship between parts and whole, beginning with Plato.   [5596]

————., and MIGNUCCI, M., eds. *Matter and Metaphysics. Fourth Symposium Hellenisticum*. Naples: Bibliopolis, 1988. Essays, abstracted herein.   [5597]

————. "Medicine, Experience and Logic," in #5599, pp. 24-68. The sorites argument ("when does a heap become a heap?") influenced observational techniques of Hellenistic doctors, who debated when they had amassed enough observation to determine treatment.   [5598]

————., et al., eds. *Science and Speculation: Studies in Hellenistic Theory and Practice*. Cambridge Univ. Pr., 1982. Essays from the second conference on Hellenistic philosophy, examining connections between philosophy and science. Those in English are abstracted herein.   [5599]

CHRONIS, N. "Post-Classical Philosophers' Concept of Man as a Social Animal." *Diot* 12(1984), 57-70. Although the city-state, which had served as a basis for Aristotle's definition of man as social animal, had been destroyed, Hellenistic philosophies still stressed relations between people as natural and axiomatic.   [5600]

CHROUST, A.-H. "Late Hellenistic 'Textbook Definitions' of Philosophy." *LThPh* 28(1972), 15-25. By late Hellenistic times six areas were believed to comprise "philosophy": knowledge of divine and human things; contemplation of death; desire to become godlike; aesthetics; scientific methodology; love of wisdom.   [5601]

DE LACY, P. "Some Recent Publications on Hellenistic Philosophy (1937-1957)." *CW* 52(1958), 8-15, 25-27, 37-39, 57. Bibliographic essay.   [5602]

DEN BOER, W. "Duty and Pleasure: Their Relative Value," in *Actes du VIIe Congrès de la Fédération Internationale des Associations d'Études Classiques*, ed. J. Harmatta (Budapest: Akademiae Kiado, 1984), II, pp. 327-343. Duty is a matter of will, while pleasure results from perception. Duty can be imposed; pleasure is self-regulated. Epicurean and Stoic concepts are combined in Christian thought.   [5603]

DIHLE, A. "Cosmological Conceptions in the Second Century A. D.," in #128, pp. 1-19. In late second century Greek thinkers became clearly aware of conflict between Biblical idea of God governing world by his will, which shows no evidence of rationality akin to human understanding, and Greek concept that God creates and governs world subject to certain rules. He can do nothing contrary to his nature or natural order.   [5604]

DILLON, J. M. "*Metriopatheia* and *Apatheia*: Some Reflections on a Controversy in Later Greek Ethics," in #42, pp. 508-517. Controversy between view that passions can be extirpated or merely controlled is basically a conflict between Platonic and Aristotelian views of soul. [5605]

DRAGONA-MONACHOU, M. "Philosophy and Culture in Hellenistic Times," in #50, III, pp. 780-784. Differences between Stoic and Epicurean schools arise not from social/political conditions of the day but from differing conceptions of what philosophy is. Posidonius has one of most expansive views of philosophy in this period. [5606]

DUERING, I. *Herodicus the Cratetean: A Study in the Anti-Platonic Tradition.* New York: Garland, 1987; rprt. Studies origins of various stories told to discredit Socrates and Plato. Greek passages are left untranslated. [5607]

DUMONT, L. "A Modified View of Our Origins. The Christian Beginnings of Modern Individualism." *Religion* 12(1982), 1-27. Hellenistic philosophers, especially Stoics, formulated concepts of wise man, detached from world around him, and of natural law. Early Christians adapted and modified these teachings. [5608]

FESTUGIERE, A. J. "Nature and Quietism in the Hellenistic Age." *Sileno* 1(1975), 125-141. Looks at Hellenistic attitudes under several headings: disenchantment with life; inclination to retirement; peace in country; communing with gods; last sleep. [5609]

FLASHAR, H., and **GIGON, O.** *Aspects de la Philosophie Hellenistique.* Geneva: Fond. Hardt, 1986. Collected essays. Those in English abstracted herein. [5610]

FORTENBAUGH, W. W., ed. *On Stoic and Peripatetic Ethics. The Work of Arius Didymus.* New Brunswick, NJ: Transaction Books, 1983. Collection of essays, abstracted herein, studying compendium attributed to Arius Didymus, philosopher residing in Augustus Caesar's household. [5611]

FREDE, M. "The Empiricist Attitude Towards Reason and Theory." *Apeir* 21(1988), 79-87. Comments on influence of earlier thinkers, such as Plato and Aristotle, on development of Empiricist attitudes toward reason and theory. [5612]

GILL, J. E. "Theriophily in Antiquity. A Supplementary Account." *JHI* 30(1969), 401-412. Theriophily (idea that humans and animals share traits) originated in Hellenistic thought, especially writings of Theophrastus, Cynics, and Stoics. [5613]

GOLDIN, J. "A Philosophical Session in a Tannaite Academy." *Trad* 21(1965), 1-21. Palestinian rabbis knew Greco-Roman philosophy, especially Stoicism. [5614]

GOTTSCHALK, H. B. "Soul as Harmonia." *Phron* 16(1971), 179-198. Survey of development by Aristotle and later thinkers of originally Platonic concept. New frag of Epicurus fits into discussion. [5615]

HAHM, D. E. "Early Hellenistic Theories of Vision and the Perception of Color," in #66, pp. 60-95. Theories of mathematicians, Epicureans, and Stoics are examined. All agree that color is not a primary quality and that all colors are intermediate on a scale between black and white. On question of how color was perceived, no significant advance was made beyond views of Plato and Aristotle. [5616]

HANKINSON, R. J. "Causes and Empiricism: A Problem in the Interpretation of Later

Greek Medical Method." *Phron* 32(1987), 329-348. Although sources make their attitude toward causes appear inconsistent and sometimes Pyrrhonist, later medical writers known as Empiricists did develop a coherent account of causes. **[5617]**

————. "Evidence, Externality and Antecedence. Inquiries into Later Greek Causal Concepts." *Phron* 32(1987), 80-100. Development of medical theory influenced philosophers' concepts of causality. **[5618]**

INWOOD, B., and **GERSON, L. P.** *Hellenistic Philosophy: Introductory Readings.* Indianapolis: Hackett, 1988. Selections from major writers and schools with brief introductions. **[5619]**

KRESS, R. L. "*Veritas rerum.* Contrasting Cosmic Truth in Hellenistic and Christian Thought." *Thom* 50(1986), 1-27. In Greek thought man is an object of similar substance with cosmos around him. In Christian thought man is subject, differing in nature from the cosmos. **[5620]**

LLOYD, G. E. R. "Observational Error in Later Greek Science," in #5599, pp. 128-164. Study of difficulties in trustworthiness of perceptions recognized by Hellenistic philosophers and scientists. **[5621]**

LONG, A. A. "Astrology: Arguments Pro and Contra," in #5599, pp. 165-192. Late philosophers found some value in astrology on basis of Plato's astral theology and Stoic determinism and idea of universal sympathy. **[5622]**

————. *Hellenistic Philosophy: Stoics, Epicureans, Sceptics.* London: Duckworth, 1973; 2nd ed., 1986. Concedes superiority of Plato and Aristotle but finds later philosophy "historically and conceptually fascinating." Shows separation of science from philosophy; sees empiricism as basis of Epicureanism. Treatment of Skeptics emphasizes their attack on philosophical theories, not common sense. Rates Stoicism as most important of the Hellenistic schools and gives it fullest coverage. **[5623]**

————. "Socrates in Hellenistic Philosophy." *CQ* 38(1988), 150-171. Hellenistic schools considered S's philosophy incomplete because it did not treat physics. He was not accorded authoritative position he held in Plato's thought. **[5624]**

————., and **SEDLEY, D. N.** *The Hellenistic Philosophers. Translations of the Principal Sources, with Philosophical Commentary.* Cambridge Univ. Pr., 1987. Vol. I contains translations of seven hundred Stoic, Epicurean, Skeptic texts, with commentary. Vol. II contains Greek and Latin originals with notes, bibliography. **[5625]**

MANCHESTER, P. "The Religious Experience of Time and Eternity," in #43, pp. 384-407. For religio-philosophical schools of Hellenistic era union with divine becomes a means of experiencing eternity, of knowing that eternity is more a matter of a presence than of durational time. **[5626]**

MANSFELD, J. *The Pseudo-Hippocratic Tract* Peri Hebdomadon *Ch. 1-11 and Greek Philosophy.* Assen, Netherlands: Van Gorcum, 1971. Technical discussion. This treatise, "On Sevens," should be dated to late first, not fifth, century B. C. It shows Stoic influences, especially from Posidonius. **[5627]**

MATTHEN, M. "Empiricism and Ontology in Ancient Medicine." *Apeir* 21(1988), 99-121. Like Skeptics, Empiricist physicians rejected notion of non-sensible entities. Other doctors held to philosophical view that reality is knowable by rationality. Discusses difference in treatments arising from different approaches. **[5628]**

MENDELS, D. "Hellenistic Utopia and the Essenes." *HThR* 72(1979), 207-222. Accounts of Essenes in Philo and Josephus seem to be historically accurate, not merely built up of philosophical *topoi* about ideal communities. **[5629]**

MILLER, J. *Measures of Wisdom: The Cosmic Dance in Classical and Christian Antiquity.* Univ. of Toronto Pr., 1986. Plato's image, in *Timaeus*, of planets and stars moving in a well-ordered dance became a favorite of later Platonic interpreters. Philosophical and poetic texts are examined to see how this image evolved in Gnosticism, Christianity, Stoicism, and Neoplatonism. **[5630]**

MUELLER, I. "Greek Mathematics and Greek Logic," in #52, pp. 35-70. Aristotle's logic and that of Stoics is independent of mathematical proof. Early mathematicians show no knowledge of logical theory. Posidonius and later Peripatetics attempted unsuccessfully to link mathematics and logic. **[5631]**

NATALI, C. "*Adoleschia, Leptologia* and the Philosophers in Athens." *Phron* 32(1987), 232-241. Lacking positions similar to professors today, ancient Greek philosophers, from fifth century B. C. on, were subject to charges of teaching useless, even harmful, ideas. They were especially vulnerable during times of public tension. **[5632]**

ONIANS, J. *Art and Thought in the Hellenistic Age: The Greek World View, 350-50 B. C.* London: Thames & Hudson, 1979. Attempts to show how Epicurean and Stoic thought fit in with art of Hellenistic period. Chapters on classification and criticism in art and allegory, images, and signs. For non-specialists. **[5633]**

OWEN, G. E. L. "Philosophical Invective." *OSAP* 1(1983), 1-25. Study of abuse aimed at philosophers in fourth century B. C., its origins in comedy and rhetoric. This tradition influenced accounts of Plato's and Aristotle's philosophical development. **[5634]**

PASSMORE, J. A. "The Godlike Man: Aristotle to Plotinus," in *The Perfectibility of Man* (New York: Scribner's, 1971), pp. 46-67. Surveys concepts of Aristotle, major Hellenistic schools, Philo, and Plotinus. **[5635]**

RANDALL, J. H., Jr. *Hellenistic Ways of Deliverance and the Making of the Christian Synthesis.* New York: Columbia Univ. Pr., 1970. Examines turn from rational philosophy to religio-philosophical mysticism between Alexander's death and closing of Academy in 529 A. D. Though no new concepts were introduced after Aristotle's death, new problems demanded reinterpretation of old ideas. Ultimately, Persia conquered Greece. **[5636]**

RIST, J. M. "Hypatia." *Phoenix* 19(1965), 214-225. This female philosopher (370-415 A. D.) seems to have been conservative Platonist, with strong mathematical interests, not influenced by Plotinus. Bishop Cyril of Alexandria was probably not responsible for her death. **[5637]**

———. "Pleasure, 360-300 B. C." *Phoenix* 28(1974), 167-179. Traces development of

Aristotle's view and its impact on Stoics and Epicureans.   **[5638]**

SANDERS, E. P., et al. *Jewish and Christian Self-Definition.* 3 vols. Philadelphia: Fortress Pr., 1980-1983. Relevant essays are abstracted herein.   **[5639]**

SAUNDERS, J. L., ed. *Greek and Roman Philosophy after Aristotle.* New York: Free Pr., 1966. Extensive selections from major Hellenistic schools, Philo, and several Christian Platonists. Brief introduction to each writer.   **[5640]**

SCHALL, J. V. "From the Stoics to Augustine: Practical Philosophy, Neo-Platonism, and Revelation," in *Reason, Revelation and the Foundations of Political Philosophy* (Baton Rouge: LA State Univ. Pr., 1987), pp. 63-92. Aristotle and Christian thinkers agree that human happiness depends on the inner state of the person. Stoics and Epicureans see humans as independent, a virtue which Christians turned into a vice. Augustine and Plotinus stress primacy of contemplation.   **[5641]**

SCHOFIELD, M., et al., eds. *Doubt and Dogmatism. Studies in Hellenistic Epistemology.* Oxford: Clarendon Pr., 1980. Introduction for non-specialists and ten essays, abstracted herein, on problem of how one knows anything, a topic for lively debate among Hellenistic schools. Select bibliography.   **[5642]**

————., and **STRIKER, G.,** eds. *The Norms of Nature. Studies in Hellenistic Ethics.* Cambridge Univ. Pr., 1986. Collection of previously unpublished essays, abstracted herein.   **[5643]**

SEDLEY, D. "The Protagonists," in #5642, pp. 1-19. Brief overview of major figures of Hellenistic philosophy. Contains chart comparing important dates for each figure/school.   **[5644]**

SHAPIRO, H., and **CURLEY, E. M.,** transls. and eds. *Hellenistic Philosophy. Selected Readings in Epicureanism, Stoicism, Skepticism and Neoplatonism.* New York: Modern Library, 1965. Readings from Epicurus, Lucretius, Seneca, Epictetus, Marcus Aurelius, Sextus Empiricus, Plotinus, and Cicero.   **[5645]**

STERTZ, S. A. "Themistius: A Hellenic Philosopher-Statesman in the Christian Roman Empire." *CJ* 71(1975-76), 349-358. Though a pagan, T was honored by Christian emperor Constantius and worked to blend old classical traditions with new Christian thought, whose eventual dominance he seems to have accepted.   **[5646]**

SWEENEY, L. "Foreign Books on Greek Philosophers: Aristotle and After." *ModSch* 50(1973), 219-232. Survey of recent publications.   **[5647]**

TARRANT, H. "Peripatetic and Stoic Epistemology in Boethus and Antiochus." *Apeir* 20(1987), 17-37. Boethus displays Peripatetic and Middle Stoic traits; Antiochus betrays Middle Stoic and Chrysippean influences.   **[5648]**

TAYLOR, C. C. W. "Hellenistic Ethics." *OSAP* 5(1987), 235-245. Review essay of #5643.   **[5649]**

VAN DEN BROEK, R., et al., eds. *Knowledge of God in the Graeco-Roman World.* Leiden: Brill, 1988. Collection of papers read at an international symposium. Those in

English with philosophical interest are abstracted herein. [5650]

VERMASEREN, M. J. *Studies in Hellenistic Religions.* Leiden: Brill, 1979. Thirteen essays. Those with philosophical implications are abstracted herein. [5651]

VON FRANZ, M.-L. "Daimons and the Inner Companion." *Parabola* 6 #4(1981), 36-44. Traces development of the ancient concept of spirits, especially among Stoics and Middle Platonists, and their relation to development of concept of self. [5652]

WHITE, M. J. *Agency and Integrality: Philosophical Themes in the Ancient Discussion of Determination and Responsibility.* Dordrecht, Netherlands: Reidel, 1985. Covers Aristotle to Plotinus. Studies the question of how human agency can be reconciled with the notion of universal causation. Also looks at concepts of necessity, possibility, impossibility. [5653]

————. "Time and Determinism in the Hellenistic Philosophical Schools." *AGPh* 65(1983), 40-62. Because of their "reductionist" conception of time, Stoics, Epicureans, and Peripatetics could accept that the idea of determinate truth or falsity (every proposition is either true or false at a particular time) implied determinism. The Academy, however, viewed time as a fixed linear phenomenon and did not believe in determinism. [5654]

WHITTAKER, J. "Moses Atticizing." *Phoenix* 21(1967), 196-201. Phrase *ho men ge on* ("the one who is") which Eusebius quotes from Neopythagorean Numenius is a reminiscence of Septuagint designation for God. Numenius was attracted to Judaism and other non-Greek religions. [5655]

WRIGHT, M. R. "Method and Argument after Aristotle: A Discussion of J. Barnes *et al* (eds), *Science and Speculation: Studies in Hellenistic Theory and Practice*." *OSAP* 2(1984), 269-277. Review essay of #5599. [5656]

Chapter 17

THE STOICS

INTRODUCTION

The Stoic school traced its origins back to Zeno of Citium, whose life will be discussed briefly under his own heading below. The school which he founded is generally treated in three periods: Early (represented by Zeno, Cleanthes, and Chrysippus), Middle (Panaetius and Posidonius), and Late (Seneca, Epictetus, and Marcus Aurelius). Though less formally organized than the Academy or other contemporary schools, the Stoa boasted an unbroken succession of official heads from Zeno until late in the third century A. D. The Stoics seem to have been "voluminous writers, with generally speaking a highly unattractive style." Because so little written material survives from the early Stoics themselves, we must depend on quotations in their critics and summaries by later writers for our knowledge of their doctrines. This makes it difficult to distinguish what Zeno thought from what later members of the school contributed, or to be certain that we have an accurate representation of Stoic thought.

The tripartite organization of knowledge which Zeno devised remained traditional for his school. He divided philosophy into logic (including epistemology and rhetoric), physics (including ontology, cosmology, and theology), and ethics. Stoics devised several similes to explain the relationship among these parts. Some likened philosophy to a garden in which physics was the soil (or plants), ethics the crop (or fruit), and logic a fence surrounding them. Others saw the discipline as an egg, with the yolk symbolizing ethics, the white, physics, and the shell, logic. Posidonius integrated the three somewhat better, comparing philosophy to a living creature. Physics was its blood and flesh, ethics its soul, and logic its bones and sinews. There was no consensus among Stoics about which area one should study first. We will look at some of these areas below.

LOGIC/EPISTEMOLOGY

Zeno approached knowledge on what we would call an empirical basis. The soul, which at birth is a clean slate, receives all knowledge from "presentations" (*phantasiai*), though the Stoics differed on how those presentations are received. Some thought they made an impression on the soul, like an imprint on wax. Others thought the soul was somehow altered by the presentations. The individual's contribution to the process was called by Zeno *katalepsis* (grasping). His image was of an open hand, representing the presentation. By partially closing his hand he symbolized an incomplete grasping of the presentation, which is assent to something without full understanding. Closing his hand tightly signified full apprehension.

Perception of these *phantasiai* gives rise to recollections and experience, which make up general concepts. These general concepts are the kinds of things self-evident to everyone, such as: if a wet cloth is left outside in the sunshine, it soon becomes dry. Common sense deduces that the sun's heat causes the water to leave the cloth. Disputes might arise as to *how* the action took place, but the fact that it happened would be called a "common concept" (*prolepsis*).

Proceeding from a body of such concepts by a rigorous dialectical method, one could build up an understanding of the structure and functioning of the universe. The Stoics did not, however, believe that the concepts were merely individual examples of some ideal or supra-sensible existent, such as Plato's Forms. For the Stoics only individual, particular things have real existence. It is important, therefore, to be certain that one's evaluation of sense perceptions is accurate, since it is that evaluation which is the basis of knowledge. Conceptions formed on the basis of sensory data must be validated by reason.

The wise man, then, is one who is able to gain the clearest, most accurate, sense perceptions and to have his mental conceptions correspond most closely with reality. Clarity of expression is crucial if one is to know with certainty what one knows and teach it to others, so various aspects of language (dialectic and grammar) and rhetoric loom large in Stoic epistemology.

It is difficult to reconstruct more than an outline of Stoic logic, which was developed largely by Chrysippus in works no longer extant (311 of them, according to one list). The only information left to us is found in the Skeptic Sextus Empiricus, in Diogenes Laertius, and in "scattered and often confused statements in other ancient authors, mostly unsympathetic." In brief, Stoics seem to have distinguished among the meaning (*lekton*) of articulate sounds, the sounds themselves, and the objects which they signified. A complete *lekton* had to be a complete thought, i. e., consisting of a subject and predicate. The *lekta* were divided into four categories, whose function is still a matter for debate.

Lekta could be combined to create propositions, either simple or compound. Depending on the word linking them, compound propositions could be either conditional ("if"), inferential ("since"), or causal ("because"). This propositional logic was regarded by later writers as inferior to Aristotle's logic of terms (cf. p. 488), but modern opinions of it are somewhat higher. A good example is a passage from Chrysippus, quoted by Cicero (*De divinatione* 1.82: "If (a) the gods exist and (b) do not foretell the future, either (c) they do not love us, or (d) they do not know what will happen, or (e) they do not think it would profit us to know or . . . ." and several more possibilities are listed. Objections to each option are then given, with the result that we conclude that the gods exist and that they do foretell the future. The weakness of the system is its reliance on premises which are often assumed without any justification.

PHYSICS

For the Stoics, physics includes the area which Aristotle would have called theology and we would call metaphysics, the study of what is, or actually exists. It also encompasses what is usually called cosmology, the study of the nature of the universe. In this, as in all else, Stoic thought is materialist. Only what acts or can be acted upon is real. Only bodies can act or be acted upon, so everything — including God and the human soul — is made of matter. It is a passive principle, somewhat like Ar's matter. Some things, such as God and the soul, are made of a finer kind of matter, but they are ultimately matter. Fire and air are also causal forces, more like Ar's form, while earth and water are passive, inert. Physical things must be animated by fire and air before they are alive, a notion drawn from observation of body heat and breath in living creatures.

All Stoic thought is ultimately based on their understanding of the nature, origin, and fate of the universe. The two original principles (active and passive) combine to produce the cosmos which we experience. Matter is essentially a by-product of fire that has lost its force. The cosmos is a sphere floating in empty space. It is held together and animated by soul. In a sense, the cosmos is an organism, similar to the relationship between the human body and its soul. Their doctrine allowed for the practice of astrology, because what happens in one part of an organism affects all other parts of it. Gods exist in the Stoic system, but over everything — gods, humans, and all the rest — is Fate. The cosmos is always in a process of decay, moving toward a conflagration which consumes everything and starts the cycle over again. Many Stoics found this doctrine difficult to accept and by the second century B. C. many had abandoned it. They stressed the idea that Logos (reason or the divine fire) governs the actions of the cosmos, giving everything its purpose. The gods became symbols for natural forces. The Stoics' allegorization of Homer and other early Greek poets became the inspiration for Christian treatment of the Old Testament and pagan literature.

ETHICS

Ethics holds the pre-eminent place in Stoic teaching, but it is not the easiest aspect of their thought to analyze. It has been called "the apparent labyrinth the Stoics so proudly proclaimed as their system." There is a Socratic element in their view that ethics must be based on knowledge. But there is also an inherent contradiction between their insistence on determinism and their desire to assert free will. How can people be responsible for their actions if they have no freedom of choice? If they have no choice, what incentive do they have to live a moral life? The Stoic resolution of the conflict between fatalism and free will was not wholly satisfactory. A person has a choice about his/her actions, they said, just as a dog tied to a chariot has a choice when the chariot begins to move. He can trot along behind or he can be dragged. He is going along with the chariot in any case.

The Stoic ideal is, like that of the Cynics who influenced early Stoic thought so heavily, the life lived "in accordance with nature." For the Cynics that meant despising worldly goods and striving for independence from what they saw as the materialistic culture around them. The Stoics reinterpreted this ideal and did not carry it quite so far. Since it is man's nature to be in harmony with the soul of the cosmos, living "in accordance with nature" was taken to mean living the most rational life possible, downplaying material goods but taking one's place in society. Where the Cynics sought *autarkeia* (self-sufficiency) the Stoics strove for *apatheia* (indifference).

An important element in living this life of reason and virtue is understanding the nature of the soul and thus being able to control its less rational elements. The emotions and feelings which we have (anger, jealousy, desire for material things) are *pathe* and must be eradicated — not just controlled but completely eliminated — before one can become a Sage or wise man. One cannot realize this ideal by degrees; he either attains it or doesn't. A popular saying among Stoics was that a person could drown a few inches beneath the surface of the water as easily as at the bottom of the sea. The person who is able to put aside emotions and desire for material things becomes, in Armstrong's words (#1, p. 126):

> the grim figure of the Stoic Sage, their ideal of humanity, who is utterly indifferent to all external things, to riches, health or power, and utterly without any trace of irrational affection for family or friends, whose every action and thought is pure reason and virtue, in complete accordance with his Ruling Principle.

The Stoics themselves admitted that this ideal was so difficult to attain that hardly anyone could.

Because of their concept of the cosmos as a unity, the Stoics looked beyond the narrow confines of the city-state at a time when large kingdoms were taking shape around the Mediterranean basin, from Rome and Carthage in the west to the Seleucid and Ptolemaic empires at the eastern end. Stoicism provided a theoretical foundation for the rule of a "best man" and was always more popular among an aristocratic elite than among the general public. The school's concept of a "natural law" which outranked the laws of various nations came to be accepted by most jurists by the second century A. D., and its notion of the brotherhood of all persons resulted in legislation improving the treatment of slaves. Some of its physical and ethical doctrines seem to have appealed to Paul and other early Christian writers.

Scholarly opinions of Stoicism have varied over the last century. In 1913 E. Bevan called it "a system put together hastily, violently, to meet a bewildered world." More recently, a more positive view of it has come to the fore, expressed by L. Edelstein, who called the philosophy "a new consciousness of man's power . . . the belief in the deification of the human being" (#5682, p. 13).

GENERAL

AKINPELU, J. A. "The Stoic *scala naturae*." *Phrontis* 5(1967), 7-16. Relationship between steps of ladder is illogical. Man occupies a disproportionate place. **[5657]**

——. "The Stoic *scala naturae*." *PACA* 10(1967), 29-35. Cicero's discussion of concept in *De nat. deor.* II. **[5658]**

——. "Stoicism and a Future Existence." *CB* 45(1969), 67-68, 76-77. Though it resembles Christianity at many points, Stoicism teaches no life after death. It retained strictly physical concept of soul and God. **[5659]**

ALGRA, K. "The Early Stoics on the Immobility and Coherence of the Cosmos." *Phron* 33(1988), 155-180. Stoic theory of centripetal force — idea that all elements move toward center of cosmos — is sufficient to explain immobility and coherence of cosmos at center of void. **[5660]**

ANDRIOPOULOS, D. "The Stoic Theory of Perceiving and Knowing." *Phil*(Athens) 2(1972), 305-326. Studies concepts of *aisthesis, oikeiosis, logos, prolepsis,* and *phantasia.* Latter is basis of Stoic criterion of truth. **[5661]**

ANNAS, J. "Truth and Knowledge," in #5642, pp. 84-104. Stoics distinguished between "truth" and "the true" but did not apply that distinction in their search for a criterion of truth. **[5662]**

ARTHUR, E. P. "The Stoic Analysis of the Mind's Reactions to Presentations." *Hermes* 111(1983), 69-78. *Katalepsis,* or apprehension, of what is presented to the mind can be performed by either a sage or a fool. The fool does not know, however, whether a presentation is real or false; he achieves only *doxa* (opinion). The sage knows the difference and his apprehension results in *episteme.* **[5663]**

BALCH, D. L. "I Cor. 7,32-35 and Stoic Debates About Marriage, Anxiety and Distraction." *JBL* 102(1983), 429-439. Paul uses technical terms often used in Stoic discussions of marriage. He agrees with normative Stoic position that marriage benefits some, but is not right for all. **[5664]**

BODUNRIN, P. O. "The Religion of the Ancient Stoics." *N&C* 11(1969), 17-25. Discusses Stoic views on God, worship, immortality, and several other topics. **[5665]**

BOTROS, S. "Freedom, Causality, Fatalism and Early Stoic Philosophy." *Phron* 30(1985), 274-304. Conflict between free will and determinism did not trouble early Stoics because two themes were treated separately. Modern interpreters have magnified inconsistency. **[5666]**

BRUNSCHWIG, J., ed. *Les Stoïciens et leur logique. Actes du colloque de Chantilly, 18-22 sept. 1976.* Paris: Vrin, 1978. Collection of essays of a somewhat technical nature. In the back of the volume are English abstracts for the essays written in other European languages. Those in English are abstracted herein. **[5667]**

BRUNT, P. A. "Aspects of the Social Thought of Dio Chrysostom and the Stoics." *PCPhS* 19(1973), 9-34. Dio's attitude toward manual labor, atypical for his time and class, betrays Stoic influences, especially of Cleanthes and Chrysippus. **[5668]**

————. "Stoicism and the Principate." *PapBritSchR* 43(1975), 7-35. Stoics had no preference for one form of government over another, so they had no philosophical objections to Roman monarchy. Person with natural endowments should participate in public life so long as it did not hamper his spiritual development. **[5669]**

CAMPBELL, K. "Self-Mastery and Stoic Ethics." *Ph* 60(1985), 327-340. Stoic ethics, emphasizing making up one's mind, is consistent with a philosophy that sees the self as a unity. Self-mastery is difficult at best. **[5670]**

————. *A Stoic Philosophy of Life.* Lanham, MD: Univ. Pr. of America, 1986.

Examines principles of Greco-Roman Stoicism, especially cardinal virtues and "those features of character and action which issue in a life well led." Second part applies Stoic principles to modern problems (careers, ecology, child-rearing, abortion). [5671]

CHRISTENSEN, J. "Equality of Man and Stoic Social Thought," in #62, pp. 45-54. Stoics based arguments for equality on mankind's rational nature, from which political equality can be deduced. Many Stoics were reform-minded, almost revolutionary, in their views on social equality. [5672]

CHROUST, A.-H. "Natural Law and 'According to Nature' in Ancient Philosophy." *AmJJur* 23(1978), 73-87. Stoics and Peripatetics shared idea that any living thing must exist in harmony with its own nature, but Stoics were reluctant to extend it to biological relations, as Peripatetics did. Stoic notion of *oikeiosis* (self-preservation) and Peripatetic *oikeiotes* (kinship of things) were synthesized in second century A. D. [5673]

COLISH, M. L. *The Stoic Tradition from Antiquity to the Early Middle Ages.* Leiden: Brill, 1985:
    vol. I: *Stoicism in Classical Latin Literature.*
    vol. II: *Stoicism in Christian Latin Thought Through the Sixth Century.*
First defines main tenets of Stoicism, then shows how these are preserved by Cicero, by poets from Horace to Silius Italicus, and by historians. Vol. II deals with Christian adaptation of Stoic ideas and influence of Neoplatonism on Stoicism. [5674]

CORCORAN, J. "Remarks on Stoic Deduction," in #52, pp. 169-181. For Stoics deduction consists of tree diagrams fanning out to simpler arguments. [5675]

DENYER, N. "Stoicism and Token Reflexivity," in #5597, pp. 375-396. Examination of Stoic theories of meaning/reference of grammatical terms when time or context changes. Is the truth of an utterance in the utterance itself or in the context? [5676]

DEVINE, F. E. "Stoicism on the Best Regime." *JHI* 31(1970), 323-336. Reflecting contemporary political realities, early Stoics favored republic, Middle Stoa a mixed government, while late Stoics regarded monarchy as best. [5677]

DOTY, R. "Ennoemata, Prolepseis, and Common Notions." *SwJPh* 7(1976), 143-148. These three terms mean basically same thing, but each has slightly different connotation or emphasis: prolepseis = process; ennoemata = content of mental notions; koine ennoia (common notion) = context. [5678]

DOWNING, F. G. "A Stoic Submission to Counter an Epicurean Resignation." *Ph* 61(1986), 124. One of most important points of divergence between schools and their modern counterparts is Stoic belief that one could achieve something in cooperation with Providence. [5679]

DRAGONA-MONACHOU, M. *The Stoic Arguments for the Existence and the Providence of the Gods.* Athens: Nation. and Capodistrian Univ. of Athens, 1976. Cleanthes and Seneca are most theological of Stoics. Seneca uses arguments of religious experience. Cleanthes and Marcus Aurelius rely on premonitions and apparitions as evidence. Zeno is source of fourfold theology and pantheism of Stoics. Stoics are indebted to Plato's late dialogues and early works of Aristotle. They may have been arguing not against non-existence of gods but in favor of religious attitude toward world. [5680]

EBERT, T. "The Origin of the Stoic Theory of Signs in Sextus Empiricus." *OSAP* 5(1987), 83-126. Sextus' description of a Stoic theory of signs should not be taken to mean that all Stoics held a single theory. The early Stoics (pre-Chrysippus) took up a theory of signs from such dialectical philosophers as Diodorus Cronus. **[5681]**

EDELSTEIN, L. *The Meaning of Stoicism.* Cambridge, MA: Harvard Univ. Pr., 1966. Though Stoics differed in doctrine among themselves, several common factors can be found to define Stoicism: image of sage; doctrine of living in accord with nature; concept of nature. Sees Stoicism not as defeatist philosophy of resignation but a type of moral idealism and optimism, teaching man's perfectibility. **[5682]**

EDLOW, R. B. "The Stoics on Ambiguity." *JHPh* 13(1975), 423-436. Stoics made subtle distinctions among various types of logical and linguistic ambiguities, which they used as criteria for identifying logical fallacies. **[5683]**

EGLI, U. "Stoic Syntax and Semantics," in #5667, pp. 135-154. Stoics gave much more attention to syntax than has been realized. Their work can be better understood now in light of work of Corcoran, Chomsky, and others. **[5684]**

ENGBERG-PEDERSEN, T. "Discovering the Good. *Oikeiosis* and *Kathekonta* in Stoic Ethics," in #5643, pp. 145-183. *Oikeiosis* (appropriation, valuation) leads a person to see that his goal is rational action without regard to personal interest. *Kathekonta* are what the sage sees as natural duties and obligations. Combination of the two produces evaluative insight into what is good. **[5685]**

EPP, R. H., ed. *Recovering the Stoics. Spindel Conference* (*SJPh* vol. 23 suppl). Memphis: TN St. Univ. Pr., 1985. Collection of essays, abstracted herein. **[5686]**

————. "Stoicism Bibliography," in #5686, pp. 125-171. Extensive bibliography of American and European work on Stoics in the twentieth century. Not annotated. **[5687]**

EVANS, J. D. G. "The Old Stoa on the Truth-Value of Oaths." *PCPhS* 20(1974), 43-47. Stoics evaluated oaths primarily on criterion of excellence-value. **[5688]**

FAJ, A. "The Stoic Features of the Book of Jonah." *Apeir* 12 #2(1978), 34-64. Stoic logic provides an explanation for main problem of book: was God's message to Nineveh false? Jonah seems to have been written from Stoic viewpoint ca. 300 B. C. **[5689]**

————. cf. #1773 and #1774.

FEARS, J. R. "Cyrus as a Stoic Exemplum of the Just Monarch." *AJPh* 95(1974), 265-267. From time of middle Stoa Stoics honored Persian king's memory. **[5690]**

FREDE, M. "The Original Notion of Cause," in #5642, pp. 217-249. Stoics stress causes as active and define them in a progressively narrower sense. **[5691]**

————. "Principles of Stoic Grammar," in #5772, pp. 27-75. Stoic doctrines of grammar must be dug out of their dialectic. Parts of speech and syntax received special attention. It is influenced by concepts such as meaning and reference, origin and rationality of language, and by Stoic views on logic. **[5692]**

------. "The Stoic Doctrine of the Affections of the Soul," in #5643, pp. 93-110. Stoic sage is *apathe* but not without emotions. There is no contradiction because Stoics saw soul as having only a rational part (not two parts, as did Plato and Aristotle). Rational emotions arise from this rational soul. Desires or concerns for honor, wealth, etc., are indifferent.
[5693]

------. "Stoic vs. Aristotelian Syllogistic." *AGPh* 56(1974), 1-32. Stoics and Peripatetics rejected each other's logic. It is not clear that the two schools actually debated the question of which type of syllogism was prior.
[5694]

------. "Stoics and Skeptics on Clear and Distinct Impressions," in #5550, pp. 65-93. Comparison of views of Stoics and Academy on cognitive impressions. Late Academy tried to reassert early Academy's radical skepticism on this question.
[5695]

GOSLING, J. "The Stoics and *Akrasia*." *Apeir* 20(1987), 179-202. Examination of Stoic theory of action and weakness of will and of criticism posed by Plutarch and Galen. Stoic position is seen as subtler than their opponents would allow.
[5696]

GOULD, J. B. "Being, the World and Appearance in Early Stoicism and Some Other Greek Philosophies." *RMeta* 28(1974), 261-288. A point of strong contrast between Stoicism and Platonic/Aristotelian thought is former's materialism and lack of concern with being. Stoicism emphasizes logic more than Plato did. It was a fully developed philosophy, not a type of folk wisdom.
[5697]

------. "Deduction in Stoic Logic," in #52, pp. 151-168. Notes close similarities between Stoic logic of propositions and Aristotle's syllogistic.
[5698]

------. "The Stoic Conception of Fate." *JHI* 35(1974), 17-23. No individual could act other than in accordance with nature and its *logos*. Thus, no one is responsible for his/her actions.
[5699]

GRAESER, A. "The Stoic Categories," in #5667, pp. 199-221. Standard Stoic categories, adapted from Aristotle, cannot cover linguistic and extra-linguistic items. Stoics developed another set of terms to classify basic types of existents.
[5700]

------. "The Stoic Theory of Meaning," in #5772, pp. 77-100. Stoic semantic theory rests on tripartite division (sign, significate, and external object referred to) which closely approximates theories of modern linguists such as Frege and Carnap.
[5701]

------. cf. #6457.

HAHM, D. E. "The Stoic Theory of Change," in #5686, pp. 39-56. Change occurs with a shift in the proportion of elements making up perceptible substances or by change in their density.
[5702]

------. *The Origins of Stoic Cosmology*. Columbus: OH St. Univ. Pr., 1977. Limited to discussion of corporealism and cosmology, excluding notions of god, fate, or providence. Sees Stoic doctrine as synthesis of ideas — especially Aristotelian — in circulation at time. Synthesis is original.
[5703]

HANKINSON, R. J. "Stoicism, Science and Divination." *Apeir* 21(1988), 123-160. Most

Stoics accepted ability of astrology and divination to foretell generalities. Cicero rejects them as sciences because they do not produce causal accounts.   **[5704]**

HAY, W. H. "Stoic Use of Logic." *AGPh* 51(1969), 145-157. Stoics used not only propositional logic but also syllogistic logic similar to Peripatetics'.   **[5705]**

HUNT, H. A. K. "Some Problems in the Interpretation of Stoicism." *JAULLA* 28(1967), 165-177. Overarching problem is conflict between free will and determinism. Views of Zeno, Panaetius, Posidonius, Cicero are examined.   **[5706]**

IMBERT, C. "Stoic Logic and Alexandrian Poetics," in #5642, pp. 182-216. Stoic idea of apprehension through *phantasia* explains how a poet or artist can receive an impression of something that does not really exist and communicate it to others through literature or art.   **[5707]**

INWOOD, B. "Commentary on Striker's 'Origins of the Concept of Natural Law'." *PBACAPh* 2(1986), 95-101. Reply to #5789. Early Stoic notion of natural law was less rigid than concept developed by Cicero. Stoic concept is squarely within Socratic, Platonic, Aristotelian tradition, though it differs in its view of relationship between morally right action and legislation of a rational divinity.   **[5708]**

———. *Ethics and Human Action in Early Stoicism.* Oxford: Clarendon Pr., 1985. Analyzes early Stoic concepts of reason, assent, impulses and their place in foundation of ethics, with questions about free will/determinism. Extensive bibliography.   **[5709]**

———. "Goal and Target in Stoicism." *JPh* 83(1986), 547-555. Discussion of the Stoic claim that virtue is craft of living well. Virtuous man has a goal, unlike someone, not yet wise, who is making moral progress.   **[5710]**

———. "Hierocles: Theory and Argument in the Second Century AD." *OSAP* 2(1984), 151-183. H may be ranked among the mediocre Stoics in terms of his acuity and ability to deal with challenges to Stoic doctrine. He tried to emphasize self-perception in *oikeiosis*. Like earlier Stoics, though, H never resolved problem between egoism and altruism which arises in an ethic based on *oikeiosis*.   **[5711]**

———. "The Stoics on the Grammar of Action," in #5686, pp. 75-86. Concepts of assent and command, taken as real mental events, provide insight into Stoic understanding of action as response to stimulus.   **[5712]**

IRWIN, T. H. "Stoic and Aristotelian Conceptions of Happiness," in #5643, pp. 205-244. Stoics' arguments for rejecting Ar's concept of happiness are of unequal merit.   **[5713]**

KAHN, C. H. "Stoic Logic and Stoic LOGOS." *AGPh* 51(1969), 158-162. Logic is not an end in itself but is part of complex of problems focused on rationality, which must be resolved in larger context of Logos, rational structure of universe.   **[5714]**

KERFERD, G. B. "The Origin of Evil in Stoic Thought." *BJRL* 60(1978), 482-494. In Stoicism there is only one force, Good, which sometimes produces things not entirely good, because uncontrolled activity of Good can be bad as well as good.   **[5715]**

———. "The Problem of *Synkatathesis* and *Katalepsis* in Stoic Doctrine," in #5667, pp.

251-272. Stoic epistemology is based on the *phantasia*, a mental impression which can arise from one of several causes. Assent to truth of impression (*katalepsis* or *synkatathesis*) is based on ability to describe it and find it coherent with previous impressions.   [5716]

——. "The Search for Personal Identity in Stoic Thought." *BJRL* 55(1972), 177-196. *Oikeiosis* describes process by which a person establishes his own identity and then extends his perception to make others part of himself.   [5717]

——. "Two Problems Concerning Impulses," in Fortenbaugh #5611, pp. 87-98. Some *pathe* arise when naturally good impulses go too far (*pleonasmos*). Others arise when good impulses fall short (*arrostemata*).   [5718]

——. "What Does the Wise Man Know?" in #5772, pp. 125-136. According to Stoic moral theory wise man knows what is right as well as what is fitting.   [5719]

KIDD, I. G. "Moral Actions and Rules in Stoic Ethics," in #5772, pp. 247-258. Stoics determined morality of an act by intent, not content. On basis of *logos*, one can determine not only what is morally good but also what is appropriate.   [5720]

——. "The Stoic Intermediates and the End for Man," in #5740, pp. 150-172. Examines scholarship on question of value of intermediates (category of things/actions that are neither good nor bad). Not all Stoics agreed but disagreements not major. These ethical problems must be evaluated in context of Stoic physics.   [5721]

KIMPEL, B. *Stoic Moral Philosophies: Their Counsel for Today.* New York: Philosophical Library, 1985. Stoicism is modification of Cynic teachings, which rest ultimately on Socrates. Analysis of major Stoic doctrines.   [5722]

KONSTAN, D. "Stoics and Epicureans on the Nature of Man." *IntStudPh* 14(1982), 27-34. Similarities between schools are noted: both stress importance of psychological stability, value of pleasure/attraction, mankind's ability to think rationally. Stoicism, however, allows for changes in human nature, especially as result of logical pursuit of happiness.   [5723]

LAPIDGE, M. "*Archai* and *Stoicheia*. A Problem in Stoic Cosmology." *Phron* 18(1973), 240-278. Three meanings of *hule* (matter) and its relationship to *theos*. Aristotelian influence on Stoic concept of two *archai*. Four elements (*stoicheia*) in cosmogonies of major Stoic thinkers.   [5724]

——. "Stoic Cosmology," in #5772, pp. 161-185. Stoics saw universe as a living organism, on a biological model rather than a mechanistic one. Later Stoics abandoned some facets of the theory, such as *ekpyrosis*. Roman Stoics paid little attention to cosmology and did not connect ethics to nature of world.   [5725]

——. "Stoic Cosmology and Roman Literature, First to Third Centuries A. D." *ANRW* II,36.3,1379-1429. Roman writers of the first century had detailed knowledge of Stoic cosmology. Some of them even drew from original Greek sources. By third century little was known beyond second-hand accounts, many of them incoherent, in work of pseudo-Censorinus.   [5726]

LLOYD, A. C. "Activity and Description in Aristotle and the Stoa." *PBA* 50(1970), 227-240. For Ar every act must have an end or goal which can be described. Stoics, in reaction to Ar, saw time as a function of language and resisted idea that actions in any but present tense could be described. **[5727]**

———. "Definite Propositions and the Concept of Reference," in #5667, pp. 285-295. In explaining how nouns and pronouns refer to things, Stoics did not allow for both *deixis* (physical act of points or facing) and *anaphora* (syntactical relation of pronoun to antecedent). **[5728]**

———. "Emotion and Decision in Stoic Psychology," in #5772, pp. 233-246. Stoic theories of emotion and decision were based on Aristotle, but Stoics did not believe emotions arose from a non-rational part of the soul. Decisions for Stoics are a series of overlapping aspects, not chronological stages. **[5729]**

———. "Grammar and Metaphysics in the Stoa," in #5740, pp. 58-74. Stoic categories, being *lekta* (utterances, or meanings), should be studied under dialectic and grammar, not physics. **[5730]**

LONG, A. A. "Aristotle's Legacy to Stoic Ethics." *BICS* 15(1968), 72-85. Aristotle had a stronger influence on Stoic ethics than generally recognized, especially in the doctrine of *eudaimonia* and external goods, in discussions of emotion and virtue. **[5731]**

———. "Arius Didymus and the Exposition of Stoic Ethics," in #5611, pp. 41-66. Material on Stoic ethics preserved by the Byzantine writer Stobaeus seems to originate with Arius, who was relying on a compendium of some sort. Arius' original contribution was to arrange materials along the lines of goods, evils, and indifferents. He ignores the doctrines of primary impulse and *oikeiosis*. **[5732]**

———. "Carneades and the Stoic Telos." *Phron* 12(1967), 59-90. Telos is defined; Stoics modified the doctrine somewhat in light of criticisms of C and his successors but never resolved certain conflicts in it. **[5733]**

———. "Dialectic and the Stoic Sage," in #5772, pp. 101-124. Stoics linked dialectic and rhetoric under logic. Philosopher will be proficient in dialectic not because he wants to play sophistic games but as a measure of progress toward living rational life. **[5734]**

———. "The Early Stoic Concept of Moral Choice," in #47, pp. 77-92. Evidence for early Stoic theory is sparse, but they seem to have assumed that humans have ability to make choices, based on their desires, needs, and educational conditioning. **[5735]**

———. "Freedom and Determinism in the Stoic Theory of Human Action," in #5740, pp. 173-199. Stoics never resolved contradiction between determinism and an individual's moral responsibility. They did advance beyond Aristotle's ethical theories by raising the problem of heredity and environment. **[5736]**

———. "Heraclitus and Stoicism." *Phil*(Athens) 5-6(1975-76), 133-156. H's thought is not foundation of Stoic cosmology, but he did exercise considerable influence on early Stoics, especially Cleanthes. **[5737]**

———. "Language and Thought in Stoicism," in #5740, pp. 75-113. In order to think, one must have a means of saying something about objects or ideas. Words used, however, are not regarded by Stoics as existing independently.   **[5738]**

————. "The Logical Basis of Stoic Ethics." *PAS* 71(1970-71), 85-104. Stoic ethics is based on premise of living according to Nature, i. e., obedient to reason. Only the Sage can do this, but Sages are rare. Stoics substituted sets of rules which, though admirable, provide no sure happiness for their practioners.   **[5739]**

————., ed. *Problems in Stoicism.* London: Athlone Pr., 1971. Essays, most original, on logic, metaphysics, determinism, natural law. All are abstracted herein.   **[5740]**

————. "Soul and Body in Stoicism." *Phron* 27(1982), 34-57. Mankind shares physical nature with all other things, but not the soul, which is God activating matter.   **[5741]**

————. "Stoa and Sceptical Academy. Origins and Growth of a Tradition." *LCM* 5(1980), 161-174. Conflict between these two schools is a dominant factor in Hellenistic philosophy. It ended when Antiochus of Ascalon moved the Academy from Scepticism to what he claimed was true Platonism but was in fact Stoicism.   **[5742]**

————. "The Stoic Concept of Evil." *PhQ* 18(1968), 329-343. People's ignorance of their own nature, and of nature of world, is cause of evil. Term "evil" should not be applied to human acts and things beyond human control.   **[5743]**

————. "The Stoic Distinction Between Truth (*hē aletheia*) and the True (*to alethes*)," in #5667, pp. 297-315. Sextus Empiricus is only writer to refer to Stoic distinction between "truth" and "the true." Stoics do seem to have differentiated between a true proposition and a broader concept of truth underlying a number of true propositions.   **[5744]**

————. "Stoic Eudaimonism." *PBACAPh* 4(1988), 77-101. Stoics draw their idea of happiness as virtue from Socrates, influenced by Cynic interpretation. The definition of happiness as a life lived in accordance with nature, however, is their own distinctive contribution.   **[5745]**

————. "The Stoics on World-Conflagration and Everlasting Recurrence," in #5686, pp. 13-37. These doctrines are not unreasonable but arise inevitably from several features of Stoic logic and physics. Concept has more than superficial resemblances to Nietzsche's doctrine of eternal recurrence   **[5746]**

————. cf. #5623.

LONGRIGG, J. "Elementary Physics in the Lyceum and Stoa." *Isis* 66(1975), 211-229. Aristotle's followers rejected his views on unmoved mover, fifth element, theory of weight. Stoic physics resembles Theophrastus'. Both schools were probably responding to Epicurean ideas.   **[5747]**

MANNING, C. E. "Stoicism and Slavery in the Roman Empire." *ANRW* II,36.3,1518-1543. There is no consistent pattern of Roman treatment of slaves which suggests any profound Stoic influence.   **[5748]**

MANSFELD, J. "Diogenes Laertius on Stoic Philosophy." *Elenchos* 7(1986), 295-382. Discussion of strengths and weaknesses of Diogenes' lives of Stoics. He links Cynics and

Stoics perhaps too closely.   [5749]

———. "Providence and the Destruction of the Universe in Early Stoic Thought, with Some Remarks on the 'Mysteries of Philosophy'," in #5651, pp. 129-188. Early Stoic doctrine of *ekpyrosis*, formulated in part against Platonic and Aristotelian arguments about indestructibility of matter, sees God as destructive agent as well as creative. This cyclical destruction can be seen as an act of Providence since it is the most desirable, most completely unified, state of existence.   [5750]

———. "Resurrection Added. The *Interpretatio christiana* of a Stoic Doctrine." *VigChr* 37(1983), 218-233. Hippolytus, Clement of Alexandria, Athenagoras, and Tatian thought that Stoics taught bodily resurrection.   [5751]

MARIETTA, D. E. "Conscience in Greek Stoicism." *Numen* 17(1970), 176-187. Notion of "conscience," an internal moral guide, is not earlier than Hellenistic period. Seems to have originated with Stoics and become widespread and popular.   [5752]

MIGNUCCI, M. "The Stoic Notion of Relatives," in #5597, pp. 129-221. References to a theory of relatives appear in only a few writers and are difficult to interpret. Biggest block is from Simplicius' commentary on Aristotle's *Categories*.   [5753]

MOST, G. W. "Cornutus and Stoic Allegoresis: A Preliminary Report." *ANRW* II,36.3,2014-2065. Study of Stoic allegorical techniques, using *Epidrome* of Cornutus as an example of an ancient text on subject. Etymology was his favorite method. [5754]

MUELLER, I. "An Introduction to Stoic Logic," in #5772, pp. 1-26. Stoic logic could not settle questions of metaphysics or epistemology. It aimed to provide a framework in which questions about validity of inferences could be resolved.   [5755]

———. "Stoic and Peripatetic Logic." *AGPh* 51(1969), 173-187. Stoic logic is purely propositional, though Stoics claim to be able to translate classical theorems into their own terms. Claim was challenged by Alexander of Aphrodisias. Views of W. H. Hay (#5705) are discussed.   [5756]

NEWMAN, R. J. "*Cotidie meditare.* Theory and Practice of the *Meditatio* in Imperial Stoicism." *ANRW* II,36.3,1473-1517. Meditation or contemplation is an important activity for Stoics from Seneca to Marcus Aurelius. Personal virtue and the ability to distinguish what is important from "indifferent" things had replaced civic virtue as objective of Stoicism. There is no set pattern to meditation, but it is regarded as exercise/training.   [5757]

NUSSBAUM, M. C. "The Stoics on the Extirpation of the Passions." *Apeir* 20(1987), 129-177. Chrysippus' analogy of medical treatment for soul became basis for Stoic doctrine that feelings such as greed, fear, envy, etc., must be not merely controlled but eradicated.   [5758]

PEMBROKE, S. G. "*Oikeiosis,*" in #5740, pp. 114-149. Term means "making well-disposed, endearment." Unclear whether idea originated with Stoics or Peripatetics, perhaps even with Plato or Cynics. It is a foundation of Stoic ethics.   [5759]

RABEL, R. J. "Diseases of Soul in Stoic Philosophy." *GRBS* 22(1981), 385-393. Passing emotions were not considered diseases; long-lasting dispositions were.   **[5760]**

——. "The Stoic Doctrine of Generic and Specific Pathe." *Apeir* 11 #1(1977), 40-42. Stoics distinguished clearly among four generic emotions (pain, pleasure, desire, and fear) and long lists of subheadings under each category.   **[5761]**

REESOR, M. E. "Fate and Possibility in Early Stoic Philosophy." *Phoenix* 19(1965), 285-297. Possibility and fate in physics correspond closely to the possible and necessary in logic. Possibility inheres in the Logos, which is God and the intelligence of the sage. Necessity is man's environment, over which he has no control.   **[5762]**

——. *The Nature of Man in Early Stoic Philosophy.* New York: St. Martin's, 1989. Focus is on Stoic epistemology, with chapters on man as a physical and metaphysical entity, the Stoic categories of being, the mind, the "presentation" and assent to it, and the criterion by which something may be judged to be true.   **[5763]**

——. "Necessity and Fate in Stoic Philosophy," in #5772, pp. 187-202. Things predicted by oracles/gods come to pass of necessity, but humans are still responsible for their roles in bringing them about. Their acceptance of the truth of the prophecy makes it an antecedent cause.   **[5764]**

——. "On the Stoic Goods in Stobaeus, *Eclogae 2*," in #5611, pp. 75-84. Discussion of distinction between *kathekonta* (appropriate things) and *kathorthomata* (necessary things). Appropriate things are those chosen by *logos*.   **[5765]**

——. "*Poion* and *Poiotes* in Stoic Philosophy." *Phron* 17(1972), 279-285. Discussion of interrelations of these concepts ("the thing made/done" and "the maker/doer") in light of Boethius' commentary on Aristotle's *De interpretatione.*   **[5766]**

——. cf. #984.

RIST, J. M. "An Early Dispute about *Right* Reason." *Monist* 66(1983), 39-48. In their critique of Aristotle's moral theory Stoics expanded concept of moral virtues to include practical wisdom. This was an attempt to overcome a weakness in Ar's theory. No matter how perfect one's reasoning, he can still make wrong moral choices.   **[5767]**

——. "Categories and Their Uses," in #5740, pp. 38-57. Stoic categories are examples of *lekta* (meaning of utterance). The four categories make up a set of philosophical questions enabling us to identify things ontologically. They refer to physical objects and are ways of describing/classifying reality.   **[5768]**

——. "The Stoic Concept of Detachment," in #5772, pp. 259-272. Detachment (*apatheia*) does not imply lack of pain or concern. In area of justice Stoics were criticized as severe, lacking mercy. But they see justice as an impartial evaluation of character and motives of person being judged, rather than of his actions. Stoics took such a stance because of high value they placed on human life.   **[5769]**

——. *Stoic Philosophy.* Cambridge Univ. Pr., 1969. It is difficult to reconstruct Stoicism because all the writings of the founder and earliest giants of the school are lost. Only through quotations in other writers (usually opponents) and works of lesser figures like Seneca do we know what Stoics originally thought. Rist works on selected topics: ethics, human action and emotion, personality, the soul.   **[5770]**

———. "Stoicism. Some Reflections on the State of the Art," in #5686, pp. 1-11. Survey of some of the most important work and trends since 1945.   **[5771]**

———., ed. *The Stoics*. Berkeley: Univ. of Calif. Pr., 1978. Collection of essays, abstracted herein.   **[5772]**

SANDBACH, F. H. *Aristotle and the Stoics*. Cambridge Philos. Soc. Suppl. vol X Cambridge, 1985. Sees little, if any, Aristotelian influence on Stoics. When Stoicism was developing, Ar's works were little read and his school not highly regarded.   **[5773]**

———. "*Ennoia* and *Prolepsis*," in #5740, pp. 22-37. The two terms are not identical. Neither refers to innate ideas of *a priori* concepts. Stoic empiricism resembles that of the Epicureans in some ways.   **[5774]**

———. "*Phantasia Kataleptike*," in #5740, pp. 9-21. *Phantasia kataleptike* is the test of a true presentation. Zeno and Chrysippus do not disagree on this subject.   **[5775]**

———. *The Stoics*. New York: Norton, 1975. Surveys individual Stoics and doctrines of the school.   **[5776]**

SCHOFIELD, M. "Preconception, Argument, and God," in #5642, pp. 283-308. Stoics tried to argue that intuitive preconceptions of idea of God are proof of God's existence. Argument is easily refuted and many later Stoics asserted only that preconceptions of God's existence but not his nature are widely shared.   **[5777]**

SEDLEY, D. "The Stoic Criterion of Identity." *Phron* 27(1982), 255-275. Academy rejected Stoic concept of identity; change, for them, means change of substance and/or identity. Stoic position, formulated by Chrysippus, is that identity resides in "particular quality" of a thing, not in its material substance.   **[5778]**

———. "The Stoic Theory of Universals," in #5686, pp. 87-92. Stoics had a theory of universals different from Plato's. They did not think of universals as existing. There were merely convenient concepts ranging over all individuals in a category, much like the "Average Man" in modern thought.   **[5779]**

SEIDLER, M. J. "Kant and the Stoics on Suicide." *JHI* 44(1983), 429-454. Kant was well acquainted with Stoic justifications of suicide but eventually rejected them. **[5780]**

SHARPLES, R. W. "Soft-Determinism and Freedom in Early Stoicism." *Phron* 31(1986), 266-279. Reply to #5666. Stoic position, a soft determinism, is internally self-consistent.   **[5781]**

———. "Aristotelian and Stoic Conception of Necessity in *De fato* of Alexander of Aphrodisias." *Phron* 20(1975), 247-274. Alexander's statements about necessity are confused by the fact that he criticizes Stoic views but in fact states their views in his own terms.   **[5782]**

———. cf. #5840.

SHAW, B. D. "The Divine Economy. Stoicism as Ideology." *Latomus* 44(1985), 16-54. Survey of Stoic system and evaluation of reasons for its success.   **[5783]**

SLOTE, M. "Stoicism and the Limits of the Human Good," in *Goods and Virtues* (Oxford: Clarendon Pr., 1983), pp. 131-142. Criticism of weaknesses of Stoic position of *autarkeia* (self-sufficiency).   **[5784]**

SORABJI, R. "Causation, Laws, and Necessity," in #5642, pp. 250-282. Not all ancient philosophers linked cause/explanation to law/necessity. Stoics were first to associate the two concepts. Early Stoics denied moral responsibility for actions, since they were determined. Chrysippus may have introduced idea of "soft" determinism, asserting compatibility of responsibility and determinism.   **[5785]**

STOUGH, C. "Stoic Determinism and Moral Responsibility," in #5772, pp. 203-231. External events and forces determine one's character but an individual is responsible for his actions.   **[5786]**

STRANGE, S. K. "Commentary on Long's 'Stoic Eudaimonism'." *PBACAPh* 4(1988), 102-112. Response to #5745. Stoic ethical arguments were naturalistic.   **[5787]**

STRIKER, G. "Antipater, or the Art of Living," in #5772, pp. 185-204. By their predilection for identity statements Stoics created difficulties for themselves defining the *telos* (goal) of life. Second-century writer Antipater resolved some of them.   **[5788]**

———. "Origins of the Concept of Natural Law." *PBACAPh* 2(1986), 79-94. Stoics introduced theory of natural law to provide a more objective basis for justice than the abstract ideas found in Plato or Aristotle.   **[5789]**

———. "The Role of *Oikeiosis* in Stoic Ethics." *OSAP* 1(1983), 145-167. *Oikeiosis* supports Stoic concept of *telos* and also is their foundation of justice. This dual role involves Stoics in some paradoxes.   **[5790]**

TANNER, R. G. "The Case for Neo-Stoicism Today." *Prud* 14(1982), 39-51. Review of Stoic positions on physics, logic, ethics; their application to modern problems.   **[5791]**

———. cf. #6797.

TODD, R. B. "Cleomedes and the Stoic Concept of the Void." *Apeir* 16(1982), 129-136. This late Stoic writer defines void as lacking dimensions and unable to be bounded by body. It is passive and only "capable of receiving body."   **[5792]**

———. "Monism and Immanence: The Foundations of Stoic Physics," in #5772, pp. 137-160. Monistic philosophy must explain how god can be immanent in world. Stoics relied on Presocratic notions of soul/nous/logos but went further to explain god's immanence as a matter of bringing himself into universe to structure it. Stoic moralists in Roman Empire used this doctrine as basis of their optimism about world.   **[5793]**

———. "The Stoic Common Notions. A Re-examination and Reinterpretation." *SO* 48(1973), 47-75 Chrysippus' doctrine of common notions was adopted outside his school, even by his opponents. But the doctrine is thoroughly Stoic.   **[5794]**

——. "The Stoics and Their Cosmology in the First and Second Centuries A. D." *ANRW* II,36.3,1363-1378. Cosmological interest did not decline among later Stoics, as is usually maintained. **[5795]**

——. "*Sunentasis* and the Stoic Theory of Perception." *GB* 2(1974), 251-261. *Sunentasis* is technical epistemelogical term, internal complement to *antiparektasis*. **[5796]**

TOWNSLEY, A. L. "Religious Tragedy and Stoic Morality." *Dioniso* 47(1976), 37-53. Stoic morality has features in common with fifth-century Greek tragedy. **[5797]**

TSEKOURAKIS, D. *Studies in the Terminology of Early Stoic Ethics.* Wiesbaden, Ger.: Steiner, 1974. Ethical terms used by early Stoics seem to come largely from Aristotle. Areas covered are: duties, the good, the *telos* (ultimate goal), the Sage. **[5798]**

VERSTEEGH, C. H. M. "The Stoic Verbal System." *Hermes* 108(1980), 338-357. Somewhat technical discussion of influence of Stoic understanding of past and future time and its influence on grammatical concept of tense. **[5799]**

VESSEY, D. W. T. C. "The Stoics and Nobility: A Philosophical Theme." *Latomus* 32(1973), 332-344. Surveys characteristics of nobility, its links with birth. **[5800]**

VON STADEN, H. "The Stoic Theory of Perception and its Platonic Critics," in #66, pp. 96-136. Survey of Stoic theory and Academic arguments against it reveals that the sceptical Academics were more Platonic than has been realized in their understanding of perception. **[5801]**

WATSON, G. "The Natural Law and Stoicism," in #5740, pp. 216-238. Though implicit in earlier Greek thought, concept of natural law was first formulated clearly by Stoics and passed on by Cicero to church fathers. **[5802]**

——. *The Stoic Theory of Knowledge.* Belfast: Queen's Univ., 1966. First chapter surveys physical theory, because theory of knowledge is based on the two principles: active (soul) and passive (matter). Mankind is a model of those elements. His ability to grasp an idea and express it is essential to his being human. Stoics stressed that words have different meanings in different contexts. Posidonius' theory of the passions had considerable impact on Stoic theory of knowledge. **[5803]**

WHITE, M. J. "Can Unequal Quantities of Stuffs Be Totally Blended?" *HPhQ* 3(1986), 379-389. Stoic doctrine of "blending throughout," fundamental to their concept of matter as continuous, may distinguish between quantity as "mass" or as "volume." **[5804]**

WHITE, N. P. "The Basis of Stoic Ethics." *HSCP* 83(1979), 143-178. Founders of Stoicism emphasized harmony and internal consistency. **[5805]**

——. "Nature and Regularity in Stoic Ethics. A Discussion of Anna Maria Ioppolo, *Aristone di Chio e lo Stoicismo Antico.*" *OSAP* 3(1985), 289-305. Review essay of an important European study. **[5806]**

——. "The Role of Physics in Stoic Ethics," in #5686, pp. 57-74. Surviving sources do not make it clear why early Stoics thought that physical doctrine was necessary basis of ethics. Later Stoics were able to omit the doctrine without feeling they had abandoned an essential tenet of the school.   **[5807]**

——. "Two Notes on Stoic Terminology." *AJPh* 99(1978), 111-119. Stoics distinguish between duties (*kathekonta*) under special and ordinary circumstances. Wise man's indifference (*apathe*) is passive parallel to his activity (*poiein*).   **[5808]**

WILKES, K. V. "Aspects of Stoicism: From Revisionary to Reactionary Ethics," in #69, I, pp. 183-188. By the Roman period Stoicism had lost interest in logic and physics. Roman Stoics converted ethical theory to a concern with duty.   **[5809]**

WOLFF, M. "Hipparchus and the Stoic Theory of Motion," in #5597, pp. 471-545. Hipparchus' theory of motion was not as close to the modern idea of impetus as Galileo and others have thought. Hipparchus seems to have accepted contemporary Stoic view that motion results from the medium surrounding a projectile acting on it every instant it is in motion.   **[5810]**

WRIGHT, G. "Stoic Midwives at the Birth of Jurisprudence." *AmJJur* 28(1983), 169-188. Roman legal practice had a Stoic, not Aristotelian, philosophical base.   **[5811]**

WYLLIE, R. "Views on Suicide and Freedom in Stoic Philosophy and Some Related Contemporary Points of View." *Prud* 5(1973), 15-32. Stoics counseled suicide only when option was loss of one's character. Also examines views of Heidegger, Camus, Merleau-Ponty, and Ricoeur.   **[5812]**

For related items see #531, #1231, #1684, #4285, #4432, #5544, #5842, #5995, #6083, #6124, #6511, #7004.

ZENO OF CITIUM (336-264 B. C.)

The founder of Stoicism was a native of Citium (or Kition) on the island of Cyprus. According to the doxographers, he was the son of a wealthy dealer in purple dye and had read deeply in philosophy before he was shipwrecked and washed up in the Piraeus, the port of Athens. Taking advantage of his lot, he acquainted himself with representatives of the various schools active in Athens at that time, particularly the Cynics and Megarians. Dissatisfied with their teachings, he resolved to create a more comprehensive system of thought. He attempted to incorporate so much of the thought of earlier philosophers that one critic likened him to a spider weaving an oversized web. His school took its name from the fact that he taught in a Stoa, or colonnade.

Because his works do not survive and his teaching was buried under the interpretations of later generations of Stoics, it is difficult to determine just what the genius of Z was. Bevan suggested that he combined the non-Hellenic approach of the prophet, exemplified by the statement "Thus saith the Lord," with the Hellenic love of reason. His approach was more dogmatic than other Greek philosophers. For him truth was not arrived at by Socratic conversation but by a teacher who had perceived it and taught it to his students. His dogmatism may have proved attractive in an age unsettled by the conquests of Alexander and the sense of powerlessness and vague dis-ease which many people seem to have felt then.

Z would not accept just anyone as a student, though his reputation for sincerity and a high moral sense drew potential learners from across the Greek world. Perhaps because of the Cynic influences under which he began his studies, he lived frugally for the rest of his life, wearing only one cloak year round and holding to a simple diet. His lifestyle earned him the mockery of the comic poets but the esteem of most other Athenians. Decrees were passed honoring him as "a virtuous man, who had made his life an example to all, for he followed his own teaching." He was awarded a crown of gold, and a bronze statue of him was erected. He declined the offer of Athenian citizenship, preferring, he said, to be a citizen of the world.

Ancient biographies of Z report that he starved himself to death, either because he was incurably ill or because old age prevented him from carrying on his work.

GANNON, J. F. "An Interpretation of Timon of Phlius Fr. 38D." *AJPh* 108(1987), 603-611. Timon compares Z to a Phoenician spider trying to tie every perception into its web. [5813]

HUNT, H. A. K. "The Importance of Zeno's Physics for an Understanding of Stoicism During the Late Roman Republic." *Apeir* 1 #2(1967), 5-14. States several problems in study of Z, rather than solution of them. His doctrine of physics was basis of later Stoic ideas on nature of God and doctrine that moral living is possible only through perfect knowledge. [5814]

————. *A Physical Interpretation of the Universe. The Doctrines of Zeno the Stoic.* Carlton, Australia: Melbourne Univ. Pr., 1976. Brief (79 pp.) attempt to reconstruct what can be known of Z's physics from citations in later writers. [5815]

MANSFELD, J. "Zeno and Aristotle on Mixture." *Mnem* 36(1983), 306-310. One fragment of Z is best understood as influenced by Aristotle *De gen. et corr.* 2.7. [5816]

————. "Zeno of Citium. Critical Observations on a Recent Study." *Mnem* 31(1978), 134-178. Comments on A. Graeser's *Zenon von Kition*. [5817]

RIST, J. M. "Zeno and Stoic Consistency." *Phron* 22(1977), 161-174. Z undoubtedly authored Stoic double imperative "live in conformity with oneself; live in conformity to nature." [5818]

————. "Zeno and the Origins of Stoic Logic," in #5667, pp. 387-400. Most themes of Stoic logic can be traced not to Chrysippus but to Z, who talks about detecting fallacies and inference but not about signs. He probably did not develop syllogisms. [5819]

SCHOFIELD, M. "Ariston of Chios and the Unity of Virtue." *AncPh* 4(1984), 83-96. Ariston developed Socrates' idea that virtue is a unity and emphasized *phronesis*, a central concept of Zeno, his teacher. [5820]

————. "The Syllogisms of Zeno of Citium." *Phron* 28(1983), 31-58. Z's syllogisms, criticized by Cicero and Seneca, served several functions: to gain attention in competition with other philosophers, to develop sense of logic, to epitomize complex arguments, and to provide kind of theological proof.   [5821]

SPARSHOTT, F. E. "Zeno on Art: Anatomy of a Definition," in #5772, pp. 273-290.
Neither Plato nor Aristotle arrived at satisfactory definition of art. For Zeno an art is
systemization of perceptions on a subject.   [5822]

TARRANT, H. "Zeno on Knowledge or on Geometry. The Evidence of Anon. *In
Theaetetum.*" *Phron* 29(1984), 96-99. The definitions referred to in this commentary
apply to knowledge, not to mathematics.   [5823]

CLEANTHES (331-232 B. C.)

The second head of the Stoa was born in Assos, in the northwestern corner
of modern Turkey, and listened to the lectures of Crates the Cynic and Zeno in
Athens. Known more for his industry than his brilliance, he is said to have
composed fifty works, but only fragments survive today. His lofty pantheistic
Hymn to Zeus is the only one of his works which is complete enough to allow us
to study his thought.

Cleanthes seems to have emphasized the materialistic aspect of Zeno's
teaching. Everything which exists can act and be acted upon. But only
body/matter can act on body/matter. Thus the cause of any action, motion, or
existence is material. This doctrine of "pansomatism" he coupled with the idea
of *tonos* (tension) to explain the structure of the universe. The concept was
elaborated by later Stoics.

Zeno's interests had been primarily ethical. Cleanthes turned to the problem
of defining the school's concept of the natural world. Later Stoics were thus able
to aim at the goal of "living according to nature."

DE ROSSI, A. "Cleanthes' Hymn to Zeus." *CB* 53(1976), 1-2. Biographical sketch and
translation of the hymn. C introduces element of religious fervor to Stoicism.   [5824]

DRAGONA-MONACHOU, M. "Providence and Fate in Stoicism and Prae-neoplatonism.
Calcidius as an Authority on Cleanthes' Theodicy (SVF 2,933)." *Phil*(Athens) 3(1973),
262-306. Discussion of views of early Stoics and value of Calcidius as source.   [5825]

JAMES, A. W. "The Zeus Hymns of Cleanthes and Aratus." *Antich* 6(1972), 28-38. C
seems to have been aware of "Presocratic philosopher-poets" in his prayer for philosophic
enlightenment. Aratus' astral poem, the *Phaenomena*, though not primarily philosophical, does show traces of Stoicism.   [5826]

KLEYGWEGT, A. "Cleanthes and the Vital Heat." *Mnem* 37(1984), 94-102. Reply to
#5828.   [5827]

MANSFELD, J. "The Cleanthes Fragment in Cicero, *De Natura Deorum* II 24," in
ACTUS: Studies in Honour of H. L. W. Nelson (Utrecht, Nether.: Talen, 1982), pp.
203-210. Much of frag actually comes from an author other than Cleanthes.   [5828]

MEIJER, P. A. "*Geras* in the Hymn of Cleanthes on Zeus." *RhM* 129(1986), 31-35.

The hymn is a *geras* (gift of honor) which people offer to God for gift of Logos which enables them to create a hymn. The hymn reflects Stoic ideas, as found in Chrysippus, about meaning of honor.   **[5829]**

SOLMSEN, F. *Cleanthes or Posidonius? The Basis of Stoic Physics.* Amsterdam: Noord-Holl. Vitg. Maats, 1961. Brief (24-page) booklet examining Cicero *De natura deorum* 2.23-32, which reflects teaching of Cleanthes, not Posidonius.   **[5830]**

CHRYSIPPUS (ca. 279-206 B. C.)

The third head of the Stoa, a native of Soli (in southeastern Turkey), was a more prolific writer and apparently a more original thinker than Cleanthes, though he expressed the highest admiration for his predecessor. He wrote over seven hundred books, none of which survive. Almost half of them, to judge from titles in catalogues, dealt with logic and language.

Epistemologically C was an empiricist. Knowledge is gained by reception of "presentations" of objects, which are produced by movements in the sense organs (eyes, ears, etc.) of the person receiving them. The crux of the problem of knowledge is to distinguish between true and false presentations. This is to be done by comparing the presentation to a fund of "common notions" or previously acquired presentations. If the new presentation is similar enough to the old, it is probably true. C admitted the possibility that false notions could be similar enough to true ones that it might be difficult to distinguish them.

C's logic is propositional rather than syllogistic. The truth of simple propositions ("the sky is blue") is demonstrated by the very occurence of what they assert. The truth of non-simple propositions ("the sky is blue because of sunlight reflected in the air") must be gauged by the truth-value of their component simple propositions. Antiquity recognized him as a clever dialectician, though Cicero found himself numbed by C's writing style.

In his ethics C adheres to the Stoic objective of life lived in accordance with nature. This requires knowledge of what is rational, and the origin of that knowledge is one point at which C seems ambivalent. In some passages moral knowledge seems to be derived, like knowledge in general, from conclusions based on experience and observation. In other passages, however, moral knowledge seems to be innate. The greatest barrier to human happiness is our emotions, which C described as false judgments about the goodness or badness of things. Emotions must be eradicated and the true sage will live indifferent to external circumstances.

C's physical theory is monistic and deterministic. The universe is made of one substance which undergoes a continuous cycle of growth and decay, with a periodic conflagration after which the cycle begins again. Every event occurs as a result of some previous event, even if the antecedent cause is not immediately evident. And yet Chrysippus taught that men are responsible for their actions and decisions.

DOTY, R. "Chrysippus' Theory of Education." *JTho* 20(1985), 70-75. Like all Stoics, C stressed early childhood education, so poor language habits would not lead to wrong thinking and behavior. For C language learning rests on observation, mimicry. Development arises from combining words to create new concepts.   [5831]

GILL, C. "Did Chrysippus Understand Medea?" *Phron* 28(1983), 136-149. C's Stoic interpretation of several crucial lines of Euripides' play takes full account of its psychological content and shows how Euripides' view of intentional weakness of will is significant for understanding of emotions.   [5832]

GOULD, J. B., Jr. "Chrysippus on the Criteria for the Truth of a Conditional Proposition." *Phron* 12(1967), 152-161. According to passage in Sextus Empiricus, C defended what is known as analytic definition of conditionals.   [5833]

———. *The Philosophy of Chrysippus.* Leiden: Brill, 1970. Effort to establish what C himself thought as distinct from summaries of Stoic doctrine generally attributed to him. Survey of his life and position in Stoa. Emphasizes four principal themes: monism, nominalism, providentialism, and psychological monism.   [5834]

HAGER. P. "Chrysippus' Theory of *Pneuma*." *Prud* 14(1982), 97-108. C adds to Stoic doctrine of *pneuma* ("spirit") the claim that it pervades entire cosmos.   [5835]

HAHM, D. E. "Chrysippus' Solution to the Democritean Dilemma of the Cone." *Isis* 63(1972), 205-220. C rejects atomistic basis of puzzle discussed by Plutarch.   [5836]

MANSFELD, J. "*Techne.* A New Fragment of Chrysippus." *GRBS* 24(1983), 57-65. Technical discussion of passaage in Olympiodorus which comes from C.   [5837]

———. cf. #288.

SCHOFIELD, M. "The Retrenchable Present," in #5597, pp. 329-374. Looks at Chrysippus' attempts to define "now" and at possible paradoxes in his theory. It contains part that is past and part that is future.   [5838]

SEDLEY, D. "The Negated Conjunction in Stoicism." *Elenchos* 5(1984), 311-316. New frag of Chrysippus and its implications for Stoic logic.   [5839]

SHARPLES, R. W. "Necessity in the Stoic Doctrine of Fate." *SO* 56(1981), 81-97. It is difficult to determine C's precise meaning of necessity and fate and relationship between them because we must rely on quotations in other, often hostile, authors. C seems to have held that what is fated is necessary in certain contexts. His critics neglected this finer point of his doctrine.   [5840]

TODD, R. B. "Chrysippus on Infinite Divisibility (Diogenes Laertius VII,150)." *Apeir* 7 #1(1973), 21-29. Textual emendation enables us to understand C as arguing that void can be extended indefinitely but bodies are not infinitely divisible.   [5841]

For related items see #751, #6267, #6860.

PANAETIUS (ca. 185-109 B. C.)
    A native of Rhodes, P came to Rome ca. 145 and was accepted into the

circle of *literati* around Scipio Aemilianus, patron of the playwright Terence and the historian Polybius. For fifteen years P split his time between Rome and Athens. Becoming head of the Stoa in 129, he spent the rest of his life in Athens. His brand of Stoicism borrowed liberally from Plato and Aristotle. He rejected the orthodox Stoic notion of a periodic conflagration of the universe and substituted instead the Peripatetic idea that the universe is eternal. He tried to make Stoic ethics more active than passive, stressing what one should do rather than what one should avoid doing.

DE LACY, P. H. "The Four Stoic Personae." *ICS* 2(1977), 163-172. Panaetius seems to be source of Cicero's discussion of four personae which correspond to four determinants of ethical choice (*De off.* I, 107-117). **[5842]**

DYCK, A. "On Panaetius' Conception of *Megalopsychia*." *MH* 38(1981), 153-161. P raises *megalopsychia* from subordinate virtue to rank with four cardinal virtues. **[5843]**

——. "On the Composition and Source of Cicero *De officiis*, I,50-58." *CSCA* 12(1979), 77-84. C used a somewhat theoretical work of Panaetius. **[5844]**

——. "The Plan of Panaetius' *Peri tou kathekontos*." *AJPh* 100(1979), 408-416. Order of topics can be seen from Cicero's treatment of same material in *De officiis*. **[5845]**

LUCK, G. "Panaetius and Menander." *AJPh* 96(1975), 256-268. P describes effects of love, cited by Seneca *Ep.* 116.5, in terms similar to comic playwright Menander, who influenced P's ethical thought. **[5846]**

VAN STRAATEN, M. "Notes on Panaetius' Theory of the Constitution of Man," in #47, pp. 93-109. P does not appear to have held that human personality consisted of separate rational and irrational parts. **[5847]**

WALBANK, F. W. "Political Morality and the Friends of Scipio." *JRS* 55(1965), 1-16. Panaetius attempted to justify Roman imperialism and answer questions raised by Polybius and others in the Scipionic circle. **[5848]**

POSIDONIUS (ca. 135-51 B. C.)

Born in Apamea, on the Orontes river in Syria, P came to Athens in his early twenties and heard Panaetius, the current head of the Stoa. He then travelled extensively, visiting the Atlantic coasts of Spain and North Africa and southern Gaul before settling on the island of Rhodes. He wrote a history of the Mediterranean world as it was coming under the domination of Rome. His interest in morality and ethics is clear in the fragments of this history, as he comments on the customs and traditions of various ethnic groups, often using the example of the "noble savage" to condemn the luxury and self-indulgence of Hellenistic society. His scientific interests prompted him to write about natural phenomena. Much of that material was passed through Seneca to the Middle Ages.

The fragments expressly attributed to P make only a small volume when collected, but in this century scholars have come to realize that his thought lies unattributed behind the work of Cicero, Philo of Alexandria, Seneca, and other thinkers of the Roman period. He was not a philosophical genius, but he seems to have been the most successful synthesizer and popularizer of some ideas which cut across the various schools. This characteristic of his work makes it even more difficult to identify what he himself taught and what later writers may have drawn from him and what from other sources which say the same things.

The point at which P differs most noticeably from orthodox Stoicism is his psychology. From the beginning the Stoics had rejected the Platonic dualism of body and soul. Human beings were seen as entirely material. Evil, seen as poor judgment, was caused by external forces. P grafted Platonic/Neopythagorean ideas of the soul (and its survival after death) onto Stoicism, except that he held the soul to be material and to reside in the air surrounding the earth after death. Souls of those who had lived pure lives (i. e., philosophers) would rise the highest to the realm of the stars. Souls of those who had muddied themselves with materialism would have less buoyancy, as it were, and would remain closer to the earth (the center of the cosmos).

P does stress that the world is a unity, with its various parts working in harmony with each other. The disembodied souls watch with interest the movements of the stars and the course of events on earth. They can even help persons who are struggling in their progress toward the liberation of the soul. Since all parts of the universe are in sympathy with one another, it is possible by observing one part to learn what may happen in another. P's work on divination seems to have been preserved in Cicero's book by that title.

The work of P paved the way for the syncretism of East and West which took place in Neoplatonism, Gnosticism, and Christianity.

CHERNISS, H. F. "Galen and Posidonius' Theory of Vision," in #51, pp. 447-454. Galen's theory of vision is derived from Plato and Aristotle and probably not from Posidonius. [5849]

DIHLE, A. "Posidonius' System of Moral Philosophy." *JHS* 93(1973), 50-57. Seneca's arguments in letters 94 and 95 derive from P, who divided moral life into *praxeis, ethe, pathe.* [5850]

EDELSTEIN, L., and KIDD, I. G., eds. *Posidonius, Vol. I: The Fragments; Vol. II, Commentary.* Cambridge Univ. Pr., 1972. Collection of all fragments of Posidonius, with notes and commentary. Vol. II, ed. by Kidd alone, looks at intellectual and historical background and stresses P's "idiosyncratic style." [5851]

HAHM, D. E. "Posidonius's Theory of Historical Causation." *ANRW* II,36.3,1325-1363. P wrote history as a guide for philosopher-statesmen. It was important he describe events and also demonstrate their causes. By rational action men control their destinies. [5852]

JONES, R. M. "Posidonius and Cicero's *Tusculan Disputations* I,17-81," in #6309, pp. 202-228. P probably exercised little influence on Cicero or later writers, and there is hardly any evidence for reconstructing P's doctrine of soul. [5853]

———. "Posidonius and Solar Eschatology," in #6309, pp. 113-135. Much of solar eschatology attributed to P is merely astrological theory.   [5854]

———. "Posidonius and the Flight of the Mind Through the Universe," in #6309, pp. 97-113. Figure of flight of mind, often used by late Hellenistic writers, was a philosophical commonplace, not an image drawn from P.   [5855]

KIDD, I. G. "*Euemptosia* — Proneness to Disease," in #5611, pp. 107-113. Discussion of two phrases in doxographer Arius Didymus which seem to derive from P.   [5856]

———. "Philosophy and Science in Posidonius." *A&A* 24(1978), 7-15. P was interested in science only as an ancilla to philosophy.   [5857]

———. "Posidonian Methodology and the Self-Sufficiency of Virtue," in #5610, pp. 1-28. P's original contribution to Stoic thought seems to have been his discussion of causes of moral weakness.   [5858]

———. "Posidonius and Logic," in #5667, pp. 273-283. Few of surviving frags of P refer to logic, but he seems to have considered it quite important. He views it as integral to philosophy, rather than as a tool, as other Stoics did.   [5859]

———. "Posidonius as Philosopher-Historian," in #6199, pp. 38-50. P seems to have written a history because, in his Stoic view of the world as an organic whole, it was important to examine what had happened to all parts of the whole.   [5860]

———. "Posidonius on Emotions," in #5740, pp. 200-215. Unlike other Stoics, P sees ethics as dependent on an understanding of the causes of emotions. This approach arose from his general interest in discovering causes of phenomena.   [5861]

STRASBURGER, H. "Poseidonius on Problems of the Roman Empire." *JRS* 55(1965), 40-53. P, in his history, saw Rome as cruel and not true to its word but still bringing peace and order to less civilized areas. Insisted on kindness and humane treatment of all men because of their innate dignity.   [5862]

For related items see #5537, #5830, #6248.

SENECA (3-65 A. D.)

Few ancient philosophers wrote in more genres or were more actively involved in the public life of their time than Lucius Annaeus Seneca. Born in Cordoba, Spain, son of a noted teacher of rhetoric (identified today as Seneca Rhetor or Seneca the Elder), he was one of three brothers, all of whom achieved a degree of fame. One brother was adopted by a friend of his father and took the name Lucius Junius Gallio. He became governor of Achaia (southern Greece) in 50/51 A. D. and appears in Acts 18, where he refused to hear charges brought by the Jews of Corinth against Paul. The other brother became the father of the poet Lucan, author of the Silver epic poem known as either *De bello civili* or the *Pharsalia*.

S's life is an object lesson in the vagaries of fortune, about which Stoic philosophy has so much to say. His fame as a political orator aroused the enmity of the psychotic emperor Caligula; only S's poor health and the prospect of his early death saved him from execution. In 41 he was banished by the emperor Claudius on a charge of adultery with Claudius' niece, Agrippina the Younger. In 49, after Agrippina had married Claudius, she summoned S to tutor her son (from a previous marriage), who had been adopted by Claudius and given the name Nero.

As advisor to the youthful Nero, S was one of the most powerful voices in Rome between 54 and 62. Apparently he cut no magisterial figure: he described himself as short, bald, with weak eyes and thin legs. He amassed a fortune almost incalculable by today's standards. Yet in his philosophical treatises and in epistolary essays addressed to his friend Lucilius, he frequently downplayed the importance of wealth, prompting complaints from modern scholars about his "irksome inconsistency." His surviving works also include: the *Natural Questions*; nine tragedies based on Greek models but probably designed for dramatic readings, not stage performances; and the *Apocolocyntosis*, a wicked satire on the deification of the emperor Claudius. No longer extant are several philosophical treatises on physics and ethics and his speeches.

S is, by and large, an orthodox Stoic, but he engages in the eclecticism which characterized philosophical thought in his age. He often quotes Epicurus and seems to have derived the earnest, almost evangelical tenor of his writing from the Cynic diatribe, the same source which nurtured the sermons of the early Christians. S does not present a comprehensive philosophical system. He seems to have understood his purpose as leading his readers to a knowledge of virtue, a far more important field of philosophy than physics, logic, or any other, in his view. The person who understands what is truly good will be indifferent to external goods and affairs. Social distinctions will be seen as meaningless and emotions as merely erroneous judgments of the value of externals.

Originality and profundity are not S's strong points. What marks him out from other Stoics is the power of his message and the keenness of his moral and psychological insights. Some passages in his writings, including references to a *sacer spiritus* and a form of the Golden Rule, led Christians to claim that he was a Christian in secret or at least had a "naturally Christian soul." Nero tired of his advice and forced him to retire in 62. Three years later he was implicated in a plot to assassinate Nero and committed suicide to escape any more horrendous death sentence.

AKINPELU, J. A. "'Logos' Doctrine in the Writings of Seneca." *CB* 44(1968), 33-37. S's doctrine of Logos as identical with God, Nature, and Fate is basis of his humanitarian and cosmopolitan philosophy. **[5863]**

BOAL, S. J. "Doing Battle with Grief. Seneca, *Dialogue* 6." *Hermathena* 116(1973), 44-51. S seems unduly harsh in his exhortations to Marcia to squelch her grief at her son's death. Stoic *apatheia* is hardly adequate to deal with child's death. **[5864]**

——. "Seneca's Dialogues." *Hermathena* 114(1972), 65-69. Structure of *Dial.* 3-5. Study of S's view on retirement (*Dial.* 8). **[5865]**

BOYLAN, M. "Seneca and Moral Rights." *NewSchol* 53(1979), 362-374. Examination of concept of "moral rights" shows that Seneca, in *De beneficiis*, was first to arrive at this notion. **[5866]**

BRADEN, G. "The Rhetoric and Psychology of Power in the Dramas of Seneca." *Arion* 9(1970), 5-41. S's plays demonstrate how the madman/ruler destroys whatever angers him while the philosopher ignores it. Radical Stoicism allows radical tyranny. **[5867]**

BRADLEY, K. R. "Seneca and Slavery." *C&M* 37(1986), 161-172. S's views on slavery are not as liberal, or as clearly expressed, as one might wish. **[5868]**

CAPONIGRI, R. A. "Reason and Death. The Idea of Wisdom in Seneca." *PACPhA* 42(1968), 144-151. Dread of death is as much part of it as physical death. Through reason sage overcomes all aspects of death. **[5869]**

CHAUMARTIN, F. R. "Quarante ans de recherche sur les oeuvres philosophiques de Sénèque (Bibliographie 1945-1985)." *ANRW* II,36.3,1547-1605. Thorough but not annotated. **[5870]**

COLAKIS, M. "Life after Death in Seneca's *Troades*." *CW* 78(1985), 149-155. Play's ghosts are real. Idea that person lives through descendants is emphasized. **[5871]**

COLEMAN, R. "The Artful Moralist. A Study of Seneca's Epistolary Style." *CQ* 24(1974), 276-289. S's use of various rhetorical and stylistic devices in presentation of ethical doctrine puts *Epistulae morales* in category of Hellenistic diatribe. **[5872]**

CURRIE, H. M. "Seneca as Philosopher," in *Neronians and Flavians: Silver Latin I*, ed. D. R. Dudley (London: Routledge & Kegan Paul, 1972), pp. 24-61. S is noteworthy for efforts to popularize Stoic doctrine. His concern is not development of philosopher-sage but encouragement to people trying to live under difficult circumstances. **[5873]**

DAVIS, P. J. "*Vindicat omnes natura sibi*. A Reading of Seneca's *Phaedra*." *Ramus* 12(1983), 114-127. Each of main characters in play defies a natural law. **[5874]**

FERRILL, A. "Seneca's Exile and the *Ad Helviam*. A Reinterpretation." *CPh* 61(1966), 253-257. This consolatory treatise is not intended for S's mother but for publication. It is a ploy on his part to convince the emperor's wife that he was ready to give up political ambition so that she might allow him to be recalled from exile. **[5875]**

GAMBET, D. G. "Cicero in the Works of Seneca Philosophus." *TAPhA* 101(1970), 171-183. S's unfavorable attitude toward C, whom he had read seriously, is contrary to critical consensus of his day. **[5876]**

GOULD, J. B. "Reason in Seneca." *JHPh* 3(1965), 13-25. For S reason is synonymous with God, cause and continuator of creation. In man reason is a binding force, the cause of right conduct. It is achieved by mind's increasing awareness of self. **[5877]**

GRIFFIN, M. T. *Seneca, a Philosopher in Politics.* Oxford: Clarendon Pr., 1976. Analyzes political content and philosophical background of S's writings. Shows how some of the apparent inconsistencies, e. g., his wealth and disparagement of it, fit into context of his times. **[5878]**

————. "Seneca on Cato's Politics. *Epistle* 14.12-13." *CQ* 18(1968), 373-375. Passage is drawn from standard Stoic *topoi* and does not indicate S changed his opinion about reasons for avoiding politics. **[5879]**

HIJMANS, B. L. "Conscientia in Seneca. Three Footnotes." *Mnem* 23(1970), 189-192. Reply to #5894. **[5880]**

————. "Drama in Seneca's Stoicism." *TAPhA* 97(1966), 237-251. Analysis of selected prose passages shows how S uses dramatic techniques and imagery even in philosophical discussion. **[5881]**

KING, C. M. "Seneca's *Hercules Oetaeus*. A Stoic Interpretation of the Greek Myth." *G&R* 18(1971), 215-222. Play should not be compared to Sophocles' *Trachiniae*. Seneca's purposes are so different his play is almost in another genre. Free will and control of passion are two major themes in Seneca's play. **[5882]**

LAVERY, G. B. "Metaphors of War and Travel in Seneca's Prose Works." *G&R* 27(1980), 147-157. S's use of images of war and travel are meant to encourage persons facing difficulties in their lives. But, with his uncertainty about life after death, and his doctrine of world cycles, S offers no real comfort to the beleaguered. **[5883]**

LAWALL, G. "*Virtus* and *Pietas* in Seneca's *Hercules Furens*." *Ramus* 12(1983), 6-26. Hercules defeats Juno not by strength but by submission. Importance of such ethical qualities as *pietas* and *fortitudo* defines S's humane Stoicism. **[5884]**

LEEMAN, A. D. "Seneca's *Phaedra* as a Stoic Tragedy," in *Miscellanea Tragica in Honorem J. C. Kamerbeek*, ed. J. M. Bremer et al. (Amsterdam: Hakkert, 1976), pp. 199-212. Examines how Phaedra's dramatic actions are more or less consistent with Stoic doctrine. **[5885]**

LEFEVRE, E. "A Cult without God or the Unfreedom of Freedom in Seneca Tragicus." *CJ* 77(1981), 31-36. Paradox between S's tragedies and philosophy. In former, person who makes himself a god is free; in latter, submitting to God's will is freedom. **[5886]**

MADER, G. "Paradox and Perspective. Two Examples from Seneca's Tragedies (*Thy.* 470; *Ag.* 869)." *AClass* 25(1982), 71-83. Stoic paradoxes of ruling and victory appear in these passages. **[5887]**

————. "Some Observations on the Senecan *Goetterdaemmerung*." *AClass* 26(1983), 61-71. S introduces a new element of ethicism into the Stoic concept of the process of cosmic destruction. **[5888]**

MANNING, C. E. "The Consolatory Tradition and Seneca's Attitude to the Emotions." *G&R* 21(1974), 71-81. In his *consolationes* S deals with emotions in terms inconsistent with Stoic doctrine. Influenced by Peripatetics and Epicureans, he concedes the inevitability of grief and the difficulty of coping with it. **[5889]**

————. *On Seneca's Ad Marciam*. Leiden: Brill, 1981. Commentary with introductory comments on several matters, including philosophical background of this *consolatio*. Though thoroughly Stoic, S uses arguments from other schools where they are useful in making a point. **[5890]**

———. "Seneca and the Stoics on the Equality of the Sexes." *Mnem* 26(1973), 170-177. Virtue is same in men and women. Those who succumb to vices betray weakness of their individual character, not of their gender.   **[5891]**

———. "Seneca's 98th Letter and the *Praemeditatio futuri mali.*" *Mnem* 29(1976), 301-304. Letter is more Cyrenaic than Epicurean in its view of contemplation of future ills. It expresses Stoic view that future ills are unreal; to fear them is irrational.   **[5892]**

MANS, M. J. "The Macabre in Seneca's Tragedies." *AClass* 27(1984), 101-119. As a Stoic, S tries to show dire consequences of losing control of emotions.   **[5893]**

MOLENAAR, G. "Seneca's Use of the Term *Conscientia.*" *Mnem* 22(1969), 170-180. Term is used frequently and typically in a positive sense.   **[5894]**

MOTTO, A. L. "The Idea of Progress in Senecan Thought." *CJ* 79(1984), 225-240. Though he accepted Stoic doctrine of periodic conflagration of world, S also believed that mankind was capable of making progress through philosophy.   **[5895]**

———. "Recent Scholarship on Seneca's Prose Work, 1940-1957." *CW* 54(1961), 13-18, 37-38, 70-71, 111-112. Annotated bibliographical survey.   **[5896]**

———. *Seneca.* New York: Twayne, 1973. Defense of S against charges of philosophical inconsistency between life and work. Emphasizes irony and wit in his literary works and sees tragedies as closer to Pindaric odes than to Greek drama.   **[5897]**

———. "Seneca on Trial. The Case of the Opulent Stoic." *CJ* 61(1966), 254-258. Charges that S's lifestyle was inconsistent with his teachings are examined.   **[5898]**

———. "Seneca on Women's Liberation." *CW* 65(1972), 155-157. S assumes intellectual and moral equality of both genders, disapproves of double standard in behavior.**[5899]**

———. *Seneca Sourcebook: Guide to the Thought of Lucius Annaeus Seneca, in the Extant Prose Works:* Epistulae Morales, *the* Dialogi De beneficiis, De clementia, *and* Quaestiones naturales. Amsterdam: Hakkert, 1970. Topical index of most important words and concepts.   **[5900]**

———, and CLARK, J. R. "Dramatic Art and Irony in Seneca's *De providentia.*" *AC* 42(1973), 28-35. S's literary techniques buttress his arguments.   **[5901]**

———. "*Epistle* 56. Seneca's Ironic Art." *CPh* 65(1970), 102-105. Reversals and turns of argument indicate S's literary artistry and the depth of his perception of the human condition.   **[5902]**

———. "*Hic situs est.* Seneca on the Deadliness of Idleness." *CW* 72(1978-79), 207-215. S urges meditative leisure as an ideal in a city consumed by commerce and busy-ness. But leisure (*otium*) must focus on philosophical pursuits.   **[5903]**

———. "*Paradoxum Senecae.* The Epicurean Stoic." *CW* 62(1968), 37-42. Though certainly a Stoic, S displays eclecticism in citations from earlier thinkers. Epicurus is quoted more than any other, often for refutation in a paradox.   **[5904]**

———. "Philosophy and Poetry: Seneca and Vergil." *ClassOut* 56(1978), 3-5. Though inconsistent in his attitude toward poetry, S quotes or alludes to Vergil numerous times, often putting his own, somewhat strained, interpretation on the passages. **[5905]**

———. "Scholarship on Seneca's Prose Works, 1968-1978." *CW* 77(1983), 69-116. Annotated bibliography. **[5906]**

———. *Seneca: A Critical Bibliography, 1900-1980.* Amsterdam: Hakkert, 1989. Evaluates most of the work done on Seneca during this period, including his philosophical treatises. **[5907]**

———. "Senecan Irony." *CB* 45(1968), 6-7, 9-11. Contradictions in S's life, teachings illustrate ability to combine opposites and serious irony similar to Socrates. **[5908]**

———. *Senecan Tragedy.* Amsterdam: Hakkert, 1988. Survey of scholarly trends in study of S's plays and analysis of seven generally acknowledged to be his. Vicious or degenerate characters often seem to triumph, but their victory is empty. Admirable characters are those who submit to fate without complaint. Philosophical themes are not touched upon separately but do appear *passim*. Useful bibliographies. **[5909]**

———. "Time in Seneca, Past, Present, and Future." *Emerita* 55(1987), 31-41. S's allusions to brevity and speed with which time passes are thoroughly Stoic. **[5910]**

NEWMAN, R. J. "*In umbra virtutis: Gloria* in the Thought of Seneca the Philosopher." *Eranos* 86(1988), 145-159. S. used term *gloria*, which had political, military, and egocentric connotations for Romans, but gave it Stoic meaning, so that a Roman could seek *gloria* by living a virtuous life. **[5911]**

NIETMANN, W. D. "Seneca on Death. The Courage to Be or Not to Be." *IntPhQ* 6(1966), 81-89. While not advocating suicide, S did teach that philosopher must be prepared for death when moment comes, whatever the circumstances. **[5912]**

NIKOLOVA-BOUROVA, A. "On the Chronology of Seneca's Philosophical Dialogues." *RELO* 2(1975), 1-30. S's style evolves from early to late dialogues. **[5913]**

NOYES, R. "Seneca on Death." *JRelHealth* 12(1973), 223-240. Death is not end of life but new vantage point. Committing suicide can bring escape from disgrace. **[5914]**

POE, J. P. "An Analysis of Seneca's *Thyestes.*" *TAPhA* 100(1969), 355-376. Violent passions are seen as natural human instincts, contrary to Stoic doctrine. **[5915]**

RIESER, M. "The Moral Basis of Seneca's Aesthetics," in *Actas del Congresso internacional de Filosofia en conmemoracion de Seneca, en el XIX centenario de su muerte. Ponencias y conferencias para las sesiones plenarias.* (Cordoba: Presidencia del Consejo ejecutivo del Congreso intern. de Filos., 1965), II, pp. 237-244. Examines connection between S's plays and comments on art and his philosophical views. **[5916]**

RIST, J. M. "Seneca and Stoic Orthodoxy." *ANRW* II,36.3,1993-2012. S adheres to standard Stoic thought in politics, diverges on suicide, is most unorthodox in his psychology. Most of his unorthodox ideas seem to derive from Posidonius. **[5917]**

ROSE, A. R. "Seneca and Suicide. The End of the *Hercules Furens*." *ClassOut* 60(1983), 109-111. Hercules' decision to live has philosophical and mythological import for S.   **[5918]**

ROSENMEYER, T. G. *Senecan Drama and Stoic Cosmology.* Berkeley: Univ. of CA Pr., 1989. S's drama is Stoic in its ethics and psychology and in its science.   **[5919]**

ROSS, G. M. "Seneca's Philosophical Influence," in *Seneca*, ed. C. D. N. Costa (London: Routledge & Kegan Paul, 1974), pp. 116-165. S had no appreciable influence on later philosophy, even on Stoics such as Epictetus, because he contributed nothing original but tried to popularize Stoic doctrine, especially ethics. Other factors were decline of Stoicism, rise of Platonism, fact that S wrote in Latin while all later philosophers used Greek.   **[5920]**

ROZELAAR, M. "Seneca: A New Approach to His Personality." *Psychiatry* 36(1973), 82-92; also in *Lampas* 7(1974), 33-42. From S's writings and descriptions of his activities one may conclude that an overprotective mother inculcated some of his less admirable qualities in him. His pursuit of philosophy helped him to control negative aspects of his personality and makes him seem almost a split personality.   **[5921]**

SORENSEN, V. *Seneca. The Humanist at the Court of Nero*, transl W. G. Jones. Univ. of Chicago Pr., 1984. General survey with some coverage of S's philosophy.   **[5922]**

STALEY, G. A. "Seneca's *Thyestes. Quantum mali habeat ira.*" *GB* 10(1981), 233-246. This play is best understood in light of philosophical views of *De ira*.   **[5923]**

TANNER, R. G. "Stoic Philosophy and Roman Tradition in Senecan Tragedy." *ANRW* II,32.2,1100-1133. S's plays can be seen as commenting on imperial abuses of Roman tradition. Soliloquies in the plays are often associated with Stoic *pathe*.   **[5924]**

THERON, L. "Progression of Thought in Seneca's *De Providentia* c.vi." *AClass* 13(1971), 61-72. S's literary style, focused on *sententiae* (pithy summarizing maxims), does not interfere with his development of themes.   **[5925]**

WATTS, W. "Seneca on Slavery." *DR* 90(1972), 183-195. S's humane treatment of slaves was not influenced by Christianity.   **[5926]**

WHITTAKER, J. "Seneca, *Ep.* 58.17." *SO* 50(1975), 143-148. Word *est* is used as substantive in passage inspired by *Timaeus*.   **[5927]**

For related items see #278, #407, #5850, #5954, #6005.

EPICTETUS (ca. 60-120 A. D.)

Very little is known about the life of E. He was a slave, probably born in Phrygia (part of modern Turkey). His sadistic master broke E's leg, leaving him a cripple for life. Freed when his master died, he supported himself for a time by teaching in Rome. The emperor Domitian, however, banished the philosophers from Rome in 89, driving E to Greece, where he lived in fame and poverty, equally indifferent to both.

His teachings were recorded by his disciple Arrian in two works, the *Discourses* and the *Encheiridion* or *Handbook*. In his prefatory remarks Arrian disclaims any literary or philosophical pretensions for E's thought. On paper, he says, the words may not have the impact they had when spoken by E. E's philosophical interests are purely ethical. He presents no organized physical or logical doctrine. Perhaps the most noteworthy feature of his interpretation of Stoicism is the almost Christian tone of many of his teachings. He has been called "a pagan practitioner of Christianity."

Even where his thought is purely Stoic, it carries the doctrine of *apatheia* (indifference to external things and events) to an extreme unmatched by any other Stoic writer. "Only cease to admire your clothes," he says, "and you are not angry with him who steals them; cease to admire your wife's beauty, and you cease to be angry with the adulterer. Know that the thief and adulterer have no place among things that are your own, but only among things that are another's and beyond your power." (*Discourses* I,18,11-21).

BRUNT, P. A. "From Epictetus to Arrian." *Athenaeum* 65(1977), 19-48. Though a student of E, Arrian does not display Stoic influences — particularly condemnation of power and wealth — in his history of Alexander the Great. [5928]

HERSHBELL, J. "The Stoicism of Epictetus: Twentieth-Century Perspectives." *ANRW* II,36.3,2148-2163. Survey of Anglo-American and continental scholarship on various facets of E's life and thought. [5929]

HIJMANS, B. L., Jr. "A Note on *Physis* in Epictetus." *Mnem* 20(1967), 279-284. For E *physis* can mean a universal principle, mankind as a whole, and process of individual development. These concepts are distinct for us, creating some difficulty in understanding E at times. [5930]

MILLAR, F. "Epictetus and the Imperial Court." *JRS* 55(1965), 141-148. Study of his comments on imperial policies and treatment of persons. [5931]

OLDFATHER, W. A. *Contributions toward a Bibliography of Epictetus*, ed. by M. Harman. Urbana: Univ. of IL Pr., 1952. Covers 1927-1946; not annotated. [5932]

PURTILL, R. L. "The Master Argument." *Apeir* 7 #1(1973), 31-36. *Discourses* 2,19 discusses three propositions of so-called master argument by Diodorus Cronus, Cleanthes, and Chrysippus. Dispute comes down to conflict between determinism and indeterminism. [5933]

SEVENSTER, J. N. "Education or Conversion. Epictetus and the Gospels." *NovTest* 8(1966), 247-262. "Education" implies development of reasoning faculty while conversion presumes human culpability. Christian education is thus impossible. [5934]

STANTON, G. R. "The Cosmopolitan Ideas of Epictetus and Marcus Aurelius." *Phron* 13(1968), 183-195. The two agree on many points, but E bases his teaching on idea of relationship between God and man and worldwide citizenship of all men. M abandons idea that man is intended to be communal creature. [5935]

WHITE, N. P. *The Handbook of Epictetus.* Indianapolis, IN: Hackett, 1983. Introductory essay, translation for non-specialist.   **[5936]**

XENAKIS, J. *Epictetus: Philosopher-Therapist.* The Hague: Nijhoff, 1969. While E's emphasis on ethics is generally recognized, one should realize his ethics aim at coping with daily problems. Individuals' difficulties arise from within, from their impulses and perceptions. Philosophy should be a method of controlling those impulses.   **[5937]**

———. "Logical Topics in Epictetus." *SJPh* 6(1968), 94-102. Like all Stoics, E saw importance of logic but subordinated it to ethics. Happiness, he felt, was more important than consistency.   **[5938]**

———. "Stoic Suicide Therapy." *Sophia* 40(1972), 88-99. E counsels suicide as means of freeing oneself from pain. It can be compared to seeing life as a child's game. When child tires of it, he quits playing.   **[5939]**

MARCUS AURELIUS (121-180 A. D.)

The Roman emperor Marcus Aurelius did not add anything new to the body of Stoic doctrine, but he did show how that doctrine could be lived out by a person who found himself in a position in life which he did not choose or enjoy. His *Meditations* allow us to listen in on his efforts to make sense of life, which he called "a warfare and a journey in a strange land." He also, almost unconsciously, put a different emphasis on the Stoic concept of God, moving away from the impersonal, mechanistic deity of earlier Stoics toward some unknown god who would feel some concern for humanity's problems and sympathy for their hopes.

One scholar has said that Marcus Aurelius' Stoicism grew out of his pessimism, just as surely as Epictetus' grew out of his optimism. And M's was surely not a happy life. Attracted from his youth to the life of a philosopher, he dressed the part and slept on a hard bench. However, his uncle, the emperor Antoninus Pius, had no son and turned to M as his heir and successor. The second-century emperors found it necessary to have an heir clearly designated and groomed in order to prevent civil war upon the death of a ruler. None of them (until M) had biological children who lived to adulthood, so they chose other members of their families or some trusted soldier to serve as heirs. The system worked so well that the second century is usually regarded as a kind of golden age in the history of western Europe. It came to an end when M's incompetent son Commodus became emperor in 180 A. D.

M himself must not have looked like a promising emperor when he took the throne at age forty. He hated the military campaigning which took up most of his reign. The *Meditations* were written in part to lighten that burden. Accepting rulership as his lot in life, just as Epictetus had accepted slavery, he did whatever was necessary to preserve Rome, whether it be persecuting Christians or squelching an assassination attempt.

His dissatisfaction with his lot brought him close to Cynicism at times. "The world is a vapor," he wrote in one passage. "Life is nothing but a . . . stranger's passing, and after fame is oblivion . . . ." Some scholars maintain that M also used opium to escape the despair which hung over his daily life.

ASMIS, E. "The Stoicism of Marcus Aurelius." *ANRW* II,36.3,2228-2252. M never identifies himself as a Stoic; wants only to be a philosopher. His ethics, however, are essentially Stoic, with some variations. His views seem to change over time in response to his personal situation, but reason is always exalted. **[5940]**

BIRLEY, A. *Marcus Aurelius: A Biography.* Boston: Little, Brown, 1987; 2nd ed. Survey, with a chapter on "The Stoic Prince," pp. 89-115. **[5941]**

BRUNT, P. A. "Marcus Aurelius in his *Meditations.*" *JRS* 64(1974), 1-20. *Meditations* were not intended for publication. One can trace emperor's preoccupation with certain themes: chief virtues, truthfulness, religion, his advisors and friends. **[5942]**

DRAGONA-MONACHOU, M. "God, the World and Man as a Social Being in Marcus Aurelius' Stoicism." *Diot* 12(1984), 86-96. Survey of M's use of terms relating to society, illustrating importance to him of Stoic idea of connectedness between God, world, and mankind. **[5943]**

FARQUHARSON, A. S. L. *Marcus Aurelius: His Life and His World.* Westport, CT Greenwood, 1975; rprt. Survey with chapter on "The Religion of Stoicism." **[5944]**

HENDRICKX, B. "Once Again Marcus Aurelius, Emperor and Philosopher." *Historia* 23(1974), 254-256. Reply to #5950. **[5945]**

OLIVER, J. H. "Marcus Aurelius and the Philosophical Schools at Athens." *AJPh* 102(1981), 213-225. M seems to have been considered a man of wisdom by contemporary philosophers and endowed chairs in the field in Athens. **[5946]**

PFLAUM, K. B. "Marcus Aurelius, Ruler-Philosopher." *Prud* 2(1970), 59-70. Examines coherence of his Stoic philosophy and his actions as emperor. **[5947]**

RIST, J. M. "Are You a Stoic? The Case of Marcus Aurelius," in #5639, III, pp. 23-45. M knows Stoic ethical teachings but not their physical and logical underpinnings. Some of his views reflect Atomism and Platonism. His "Stoicism" is more religion than philosophy. **[5948]**

RUTHERFORD, R. B. *The Meditations of Marcus Aurelius: A Study.* Oxford: Clarendon Pr., 1989; rprt. Gives a biography of M, summary of his thought and its relation to Stoicism in general, and a translation of the *Meditations.* **[5949]**

STANTON, G. R. "Marcus Aurelius, Emperor and Philosopher." *Historia* 18(1969), 570-587. M's legislation is no more or less philosophically influenced than that of his predecessors and successors. **[5950]**

STERTZ, S. A. "Marcus Aurelius as Ideal Emperor in Late-Antique Greek Thought." *CW* 70(1977), 433-439. For later Greek intellectuals M was embodiment of Platonic philosopher-king. Emperor Julian (361-363) esteemed him as a role model. **[5951]**

Chapter 18

EPICUREANISM

EPICURUS (341-270 B. C.)

Along with the Stoics, E offered the other most widely known solution to the malaise which beset the Hellenistic world. It is not a brilliant philosophy. One scholar calls it "the least philosophically interesting" of the Hellenistic schools, while A. H. Armstrong (#1, p. 132) says that "his system is even more obviously than that of the Stoics a structure hastily run up, out of what seemed to him the best available materials, to provide a secure refuge for the soul among the storms of this troublesome life."

E was less concerned than other philosophers to find some fundamental principle of the universe or solve the question of how one can attain certain knowledge. As Armstrong suggests, he wanted to provide some way for people to deal with the problems confronting them in a age of turmoil, when most people seemed to feel that they were losing whatever control they might once have had over their lives (cf. Chapter 16). If one cannot influence the course of events, he taught, cease to be concerned with them. Withdraw, seek tranquility (*ataraxia*). Pleasure is his keyword, his objective, and by it he means the absence of pain.

But life does not always present an individual with pleasant experiences. How is one to deal with the difficulties and anguish of life? E's answer was based on his understanding of the physical nature of the universe. In his own words, "It is not possible to gain unmixed happiness without natural science." It is doubtful, however, that he had done any deep study of the physics of the earlier philosophers. The atomism of Democritus (cf. p. 105) struck him as offering the best basis for an ethic of pleasure (hedonism). If the world is the result of the random movement of atoms, then there is no room for fate, determinism, or divine providence. Things happen by chance and without influencing other events.

The only drawback to adopting atomism as the basis of his ethics was that Democritus had taught that the atoms all fall through the void in straight lines at the same speed. How could they actually combine, then? E introduced the controversial notion of a spontaneous or random swerve in the motion of the atoms which caused them to collide and combine.

Everything which happens, everything which exists, was to E the result of this random movement of atoms. Anything could come to exist, whether a cat or a god (and E participated in the public festivals of the gods, as every good citizen was expected to do), but no creature — cat or god — could control or determine any other creature's destiny. Not even the individual being could control what happened to him. The only way he could be happy was to remove himself from situations in which he was likely to be unhappy.

Unhappiness arises from pain and fear, E taught. We experience various kinds of pain, both physical and mental. The first step toward happiness is to avoid the causes of such pain. Physical discomfort arises from overeating, drinking too much, exerting oneself too much. The true philosopher will refrain from such activities. E himself lived on a diet of bland foods, unlike the Epicures who misuse his name today.

Mental anguish results from various causes. If one becomes involved in political life, he will be disappointed over the loss of an election. If he wins, he will be burdened with the duties of office. The solution: withdraw from political life. One who loves someone else will be tormented constantly with doubts. Does the one I love, love me in return? What if she/he ceases to love me, or I cease to love him/her? Epicurus' advice would be to avoid falling in love with anyone. Sexual intercourse by itself is pleasurable, but don't fall in love.

The greatest mental anguish is that caused by fear of the gods and possible punishment in the afterlife. The mystery religions which were so popular in this era had developed the general public's awareness of the idea of rewards and punishments in the afterlife. Some temples had paintings of the Underworld which, to judge from descriptions like Pausanias', would rival anything Dante imagined on his worst day. Have no fear, E said. You will not be tormented in this life or the next for two reasons: 1) the gods do not concern themselves with judging your actions. They are the blessed immortals. If they paid any attention to the activities of lesser creatures, they would be troubled and would not be blessed; 2) there is no afterlife. When a person dies, the atoms which make up his/her soul are scattered as the body decomposes. There is no consciousness after death. One of E's most famous dicta was, "Death is nothing to us."

E's philosophy, like that of the Stoics, was organized into three sections: canonic, physics, and ethics. His ethics, as noted above, is hedonistic. Canonic, derived from the Greek word for a standard by which things are tested, establishes the criteria by which truth can be judged. It is not logic in the sense which Aristotle or the Stoics use that term; it does not analyze statements. E held that all knowledge was derived from sense perception. He follows Democritus on this point, too, in holding that sense perception is caused by images (*eidola*) of objects which are emitted by the objects and strike our sense organs. The criterion of truth, then, must be something which enables us to judge whether sensations are true. False judgments of the sensations result not from the sensations but from the judgments we form of them. Repeated observation and reliance on the experiences of others can correct our errors.

His physics is entirely materialistic. (It is not without significance that Karl Marx wrote his doctoral dissertation on E.) Matter is all that exists, and it is indestructible. The "soul" is only lighter atoms distributed throughout the body. One part of it, which directs the rest, is located in the chest.

E's wrote voluminously, some three hundred papyrus scrolls according to ancient lists, but only a handful of his work survives. There are three letters (epistolary essays might be a better term) to disciples of his. Two (to Herodotus and Menoeceus) seem to be genuine; the other (to Pythocles) is probably a later work of the Epicurean school. Some of his ethical maxims were collected into forty short statements called the "Principal Doctrines" (*Kuriai doxai*). Another collection is known as the "Vatican Sayings," from the location of the ms. in which they are contained.

ARKINS, B. "Epicurus and Lucretius on Sex, Love, and Marriage." *Apeir* 18(1984), 141-143. L follows E closely in approving of casual sexual relationships and marriage under certain circumstances, but rejecting sexual love.   [5952]

ASMIS, E. *Epicurus' Scientific Method*. Ithaca, NY: Cornell Univ. Pr., 1984. E's method of inquiry, derived from early Atomists, is unified and empirical.   [5953]

AVOTINS, I. "On Some Epicurean and Lucretian Arguments for the Infinity of the Universe." *CQ* 33(1983), 421-427. Arguments probably drawn from Atomists. [5954]

——. "Training in Frugality in Epicurus and Seneca." *Phoenix* 31(1977), 214-217. E taught self-sufficiency by practicing frugality on selected days, according to S's *Ep.* 18.9.   [5955]

BASTOMSKY, S. J. "The Talmudic View of Epicureanism." *Apeir* 7 #1(1973), 17-19. Talmudic scholars found a more serious challenge in Epicurean atheism than in standard polytheism.   [5956]

BICKNELL, P. J. "Atomic *Isotacheia* in Epicurus." *Apeir* 17(1983), 57-61. E's doctrine that all atoms move at same high speed may be response to Aristotle's discussion of motion in void. Inconsistencies in E's position have not been fully explored.   [5957]

BOLLACK, J., and LAKS, A., eds. *Études sur l'Épicurisme antique*. Université de Lille, 1976. Collection of essays on Epicurus, Lucretius, and Diogenes of Oenoanda. Relevant ones in English are abstracted herein.   [5958]

CHROUST, A.-H. "The Philosophy of Law of Epicurus and the Epicureans." *AmJJur* 16(1971), 36-83. Overview of Epicurean philosophy. E taught submission to law because it was a surer road to happiness than the chaos which would result without it. His views were in part drawn from Cynics and Sophists.   [5959]

CLARKE, M. L. "The Garden of Epicurus." *Phoenix* 27(1973), 386-387. Garden from which E's school took its name was probably outside Athens, near Academy.   [5960]

CLAY, D. "Epicurus' *Kuria doxa* XVII." *GRBS* 13(1972), 59-66. Concept of justice goes beyond dictates of polis. Justice calms soul; injustice disturbs it and is evil.   [5961]

——. "Epicurus' Last Will and Testament." *AGPh* 55(1973), 252-280. Letter to Herodotus is E's will, establishing how he wants his *dogmata* remembered.   [5962]

——. "Individual and Community in the First Generation of the Epicurean School," in #6037, pp. 255-279. E's authority was such that it is difficult to attribute doctrines or sayings to later Epicureans. The group's own tendency was to attribute everything to E, who was regarded as a founding hero.   [5963]

———. cf. #6067, #6162.

CONWAY, P. "Epicurus' Theory of Freedom of Action." *Prud* 13(1981), 81-89. The fullest account is found in Lucretius *De rer nat* 2.251-293. A reconstruction is not without problems.   [5964]

DE LACY, P. H. "Limit and Variation in the Epicurean Philosophy." *Phoenix* 23(1969), 104-113. Concept of limits serves as important unifying theme in E's thought. He is vague about where limits occur.   [5965]

———. "Some Recent Publications on Epicurus and Epicureanism (1937-1954)." *CW* 48(1955), 169-177. Bibliographic survey with brief annotations.   [5966]

DeWITT, N. W. *Epicurus and His Philosophy.* Westport, CT: Greenwood Pr., 1973; rprt. Tries to reconstruct a biography of E, interpret his doctrines without relying so heavily on emendations of text, and show importance of Epicureanism as bridge from classical philosophy to Christianity.   [5967]

DUBAN, J. M. "*Ratio Divina Mente Coorta* and the Mythological Undercurrent in the Deification of Epicurus." *Prud* 11(1979), 47-54. E is depicted by Lucretius as Venus' counterpart, then moves from being a "Greek man" to a *deus*. His intelligence is described as arising from a "divine mind."   [5968]

EARLE, W. J. "Epicurus: 'Live Hidden'!" *Ph* 63(1988), 93-104. Discusses arguments against E's advice to withdraw from society. It would be feasible for an entire society to live in such fashion under certain circumstances.   [5969]

ENGLERT, W. G. *Epicurus on the Swerve and Voluntary Action.* Atlanta, GA: Scholars' Pr., 1987. Examines E's sources of the doctrine, its nature and role in Epicurean physics, its role in psychology and ethics, especially in preservation of free will.   [5970]

FARRINGTON, B. *The Faith of Epicurus.* New York: Basic Books, 1967. Sees E as reformer working on "practical problems of his age" and opponent of Plato. He especially opposed the imposition of a state religion to control people. Written for non-specialists.   [5971]

———. cf. #6078.

FISCHEL, H. A. *Rabbinic Literature and Greco-Roman Philosophy. A Study of Epicurea and Rhetorica in Early Midrashic Writings.* Leiden: Brill, 1973. Somewhat technical study of knowledge of Epicurean philosophy among Palestinian rabbis.   [5972]

FRISCHER, B. "A Socio-Psychological and Semiotic Analysis of Epicurus' Portrait." *Arethusa* 16(1983), 247-265. Epicureans recruited new followers by descriptions of E himself.   [5973]

———. *The Sculpted Word. Epicureanism and Philosophical Recruitment in Ancient Greece.* Berkeley: Univ. of CA Pr., 1982. Epicureans, an alternative community without strong attachments to surrounding culture, recruited members by presenting as positive an image as possible, in keeping with their view that a perception motivates people to imitate it. Statues of E played important role in propagation of his message.   [5974]

FURLEY, D. J. "Knowledge of Atoms and Void in Epicureanism," in #41, pp. 607-619. E did not claim to have any intuitive knowledge of atoms and void. He presented his theories as contradictories and tried to disprove one of them.   **[5975]**

———. "Nothing to Us?" in #5643, pp. 75-91. Key to overcoming fear of death is to eliminate future possibilities, desires and plans of the human mind which give purpose to life. E failed to do this.   **[5976]**

———. *Two Studies in the Greek Atomists, I: Indivisible Magnitudes; II: Aristotle and Epicurus on Voluntary Action.* Princeton Univ. Pr., 1967. First essay traces development of idea of indivisible magnitudes, from Pythagoreans to E. Second traces E's effort to find some cause other than swerve of atoms to account for human actions; compares his conclusions to Aristotle's *Nichomachean Ethics.*   **[5977]**

GLIDDEN, D. K. "Epicurean *Prolepsis.*" *OSAP* 3(1985), 175-217. Somewhat technical discussion of Epicurean concepts of definitions and preconceptions.   **[5978]**

———. "Epicurean Semantics," in #6037, pp. 185-226. Epicurean linguistics emphasizes how acts of speech are used as labels of physical states. E is not much interested in meanings of words. His is a theory of behavior as much as of language.   **[5979]**

———. "Epicurus and the Pleasure Principle," in #54, pp. 177-197. Pleasure is the primary good of life, but so is *phronesis*. Thus pleasurable and virtuous life is one. One arrives at pleasure by reason. Pleasure is in self-interest of individual.   **[5980]**

———. "Epicurus on Self-Perception." *AmPhQ* 16(1979), 297-306. To understand E's theory of perception it is important to distinguish, as he does, between *pathe* (feelings) and *aisthesis* (sensation). Former applies to pain and pleasure only and cannot be foundation of knowledge. Latter provides information.   **[5981]**

GREEN, O. H. "Fear of Death." *Ph&PhenRes* 43(1982), 99-105. E was right to say death is no evil for one who dies. But it is reasonable to fear death because of desirability of continued life.   **[5982]**

HARRY, B. "Epicurus: Some Problems in Physics and Perception." *G&R* 17(1970), 58-63. Lucretius tries to correct E's mistaken argument about how lights appear at a distance. E may have been myopic.   **[5983]**

HIBLER, R. W. *Happiness Through Tranquility: The School of Epicurus.* Lanham, MD: Univ. Pr. of Amer., 1984. E's contributions to philosophy and education have been undervalued. He anticipated modern social adjustment theories of education.   **[5984]**

HOSSENFELDER, M. "Epicurus — Hedonist *Malgré Lui*," in #5643, pp. 245-263. E's concept of highest good is ambivalent and his doctrine of pleasure paradoxical. He is not a thorough-going hedonist.   **[5985]**

HUBY, P. M. "An Epicurean Argument in Cicero *De fato* xvii,40." *Phron* 15(1970), 83-85. Discussion of acts of assent in this passage may be from E.   **[5986]**

———. "The Epicureans, Animals, and Freewill." *Apeir* 3 #1(1969), 17-19. Wild animals have no freewill, in E's view, while domesticated ones do.   **[5987]**

———. "Epicurus' Attitude to Democritus." *Phron* 23(1978), 80-86. Contrary to general view, E considered D a holy man. [5988]

INWOOD, B. "The Origin of Epicurus' Concept of Void." *CPh* 76(1981), 273-285. Reply to #6033. E modified Democritus' concept of void on basis of Aristotelian criticisms. [5989]

KERFERD, G. B. "Epicurus' Doctrine of the Soul." *Phron* 16(1971), 80-96. E did not see soul as divided into two parts, made up of three elements. Soul consists of atoms of other elements recombined. Soul's patterns of movements — its mental activity — are determined by body containing it. [5990]

———. "On Diog. Laert. X,73." *RhM* 114(1971), 87-89. Suggested textual emendation and its implications for the meaning of a passage in E's *Letter to Herodotus*. [5991]

KLEVE, K. "Empiricism and Theology in Epicureanism." *SO* 52(1971), 39-51. Study of other sources, such as Cicero *De nat deor* 1, aids in understanding certain Epicurean teachings which rested on empirical data. [5992]

———. "The Epicurean Isonomia and its Sceptical Refutation." *SO* 54(1979), 27-35. Cotta, the Skeptic in Cicero's *De nat deor*, does not sum up E's doctrine of isonomia correctly before beginning to refute it. [5993]

———. "*Id facit exiguum clinamen.*" *SO* 55(1980), 27-31. Epicureans found it difficult to reconcile the concept of rational freewill with their view (necessary to avoid determinism) that the atoms of the soul made small random swerves. Epicurus himself seems to have thought that the soul had to struggle against numerous swerves and choose only beneficial ones. [5994]

———. "On the Beauty of God: A Discussion Between Epicureans, Stoics and Skeptics." *SO* 53(1978), 69-83. Cicero's *De nat deor* presents views of the three schools on anthropomorphic gods. Basic assumption is that human shape is most beautiful; gods, as perfect, must have this shape. [5995]

———. "*Scurra Atticus*: The Epicurean View of Socrates," in #6037, pp. 227-253. Epicureans disliked and disparaged Socrates because he professed to have no sure knowledge and to believe in an afterlife. His conduct was also thought unseemly. [5996]

KONSTAN, D. "Atomism and its Heritage: Minimal Parts." *AncPh* 2(1982), 60-75. A "minimal part," for Epicurus, is inverse of a quantity which is "incomprehensible but not strictly infinite." Idea is traced through Islamic and Renaissance philosophy. [5997]

———. "Epicurus on 'Up' and 'Down' (*Letter to Herodotus* 60)." *Phron* 17(1972), 269-278. Text, translation, and criticism of standard interpretation. [5998]

———. "Problems in Epicurean Ethics," in #42, pp. 431-464. Examines such concepts as collision, contact, weight; finds E's theory no more absurd than modern notions of subatomic particles. E's theory is bold and sophisticated but does not adequately describe any significant class of particles. [5999]

———. "Problems in Epicurean Physics." *Isis* 70(1979), 394-418. Epicurean physics is coherent model of mechanics. [6000]

———. *Some Aspects of Epicurean Psychology.* Leiden: Brill, 1973. Most people are trapped by irrational fears arising from frustrated desires for wealth, immortality. Hades is an exaggerated form of these fears and frustrations. Chapter on social theory looks at origins of false beliefs resting on images instead of objects themselves. Chapter on epistemology examines origin of concept of immortality in atomist world view. [6001]

LEE, E. N. "The Sense of an Object: Epicurus on Seeing and Hearing," in #66, pp. 27-59. E sees perception as a matter of receiving emanations from objects, but there is an element of perceptual awareness, a tendency of the perceiver to reach out toward external objects, which helps to account for perception as well. His physical theory is grounded in his philosophical objectives. [6002]

LONG, A. A. "*Aisthesis, Prolepsis* and Linguistic Theory in Epicurus." *BICS* 18(1971), 114-133. To explain perceptions we must have standardized vocabulary enabling us to relate new perceptions to prior ones and describe them accurately to others. [6003]

———. "Chance and Natural Law in Epicureanism." *Phron* 22(1977), 63-88. Chance (*tyche*) is involved in creation of world but not in its subsequent functioning. [6004]

———. "Epicureans and Stoics," in #43, pp. 135-153. For Epicureans gods are models of tranquility and friendship. We should learn from them to be free of pain and harm no one. Stoics saw world as organism. God, present everywhere in it, feels everything that we feel or experience. Humans should seek complete harmony of their rational faculty with the divine Reason. [6005]

———. "Pleasure and Social Utility: The Virtues of Being Epicurean," in #5610, pp. 283-324. For E, achievement of pleasure requires social justice and harmony. [6006]

LUPER-FOY, S. "Annihilation." *PhQ* 37(1987), 233-252. Discussion of weakness in E's claim that "death is nothing to us." [6007]

MacLEOD, C. W. "Ethics and Poetry in Horace's *Odes* (1.20 and 2.3)." *G&R* 26(1979), 21-29. Epicurean tone of these poems suits their subject matter and philosophical inclinations of person to whom they are addressed. Horace's own philosophical views seem eclectic. [6008]

METTE, H. J. "Epikuros 1963-1978." *Lustrum* 21(1978), 45-116. Bibliography and survey of current research (in German). [6009]

MILLER, F. D. "Epicurus on the Art of Dying." *SJPh* 14(1976), 169-177. Though death need hold no fear for a materialist, atheistic philosopher, it can lead to fear or frustration of leaving something incomplete. E holds that one should emphasize pleasure of doing a thing, not completing it. [6010]

MITSIS, P. *Epicurus' Ethical Theory: The Pleasures of Invulnerability.* Ithaca, NY: Cornell Univ. Pr., 1988. Focuses on E's effort to separate human happiness and chance. For E pleasure was not a subjective mental event but an objective natural goal. Tries to show how such an ethic can account for altruistic elements such as friendship, justice. Most difficult aspect of his theory is his insistence that chance plays a part in human happiness and morality. Aims for non-specialist audience.   **[6011]**

——. "Epicurus on Death and the Duration of Life." *PBACAPh* 4(1988), 303-322. Discusses E's two strategies for disarming fear of death: 1) death cannot harm us since we do not exist when dead; 2) death cannot detract from life's ultimate value.   **[6012]**

——. "Epicurus on Friendship and Altruism." *OSAP* 5(1987), 127-153. E's stress on importance of altruistic friendships seems inconsistent with his fundamental hedonism. His inability to resolve the problem is typical of a dilemma faced by Hellenistic moral philosophers.   **[6013]**

NUSSBAUM, M. C. "Therapeutic Arguments: Epicurus and Aristotle," in #5643, pp. 31-74. E thought philosophy useless if it did not result in a sort of "healing" for individuals. Aristotle saw value in scientific inquiry for its own sake. These objectives affected their methods and produced conflict between the two schools.   **[6014]**

PANCHERI, L. "Greek Atomism and the One and the Many." *JHPh* 13(1975), 139-144. E's doctrine of sensible least parts, indivisible at their level of perception but also a multiplicity in regard to next lower level, resolves problem of relation between unity and plurality.   **[6015]**

——. "Indivisibility and Epicurus: In Reply to Prof. Baldes." *Apeir* 13(1979), 49-52. Reply to #849. E conceived of atoms as indivisible.   **[6016]**

PANICHAS, G. A. *Epicurus*. New York: Twayne, 1967. Straightforward introduction, for non-specialist. Looks at traditional categories: atomism, cosmology, theology, happiness, friendship. Examines Epicurean influence on English thought.   **[6017]**

PETERS, E. "What Was God Doing Before He Created the Heavens and the Earth?" *Augustiniana* 34(1984), 53-74. Epicurean cosmogony and its critique by Irenaeus and Augustine.   **[6018]**

REESOR, M. E. "Anaxagoras and Epicurus," in #42, pp. 93-106. E seems to owe to Anaxagoras his sense of order and regularity, the idea that an entity emerging from something has same predominant parts as thing from which it emerges.   **[6019]**

RILEY, M. T. "The Epicurean Criticism of Socrates." *Phoenix* 34(1980), 55-68. Epicureans rejected Socratic behavior rather than teaching. They considered his life inconsistent with his doctrine.   **[6020]**

RIST, J. M. *Epicurus: An Introduction*. Cambridge Univ. Pr., 1972. Breaks Epicureanism down into: canonic; physics; man and cosmos; soul, mind, body; pleasure; friendship; gods and religion. Pleasure is unifying theme. It draws upon physics (knowledge of atomic swerve releases one from anxiety); upon friendship (to insure safety and security), and all other aspects of Epicurean doctrine.   **[6021]**

——. "Epicurus on Friendship." *GPhS* 5(1980), 121-129. Friendship is better able to make men happy than is wisdom. The wise man should avoid marriage but welcome friendship.   **[6022]**

ROSENBAUM, S. E. "Epicurus and Annihilation." *PhQ* 39(1989), 81-90. Clarification and defense of E's claim that death has no meaning to, or effect on, us.   **[6023]**

——. "The Harm of Killing. An Epicurean Perspective," in #44, pp. 207-226. Partial defense of Epicurean idea that "one's death is not bad for one." Since death is meaningless, killing another person is not harmful, nor can death be a punishment.   **[6024]**

——. "How to Be Dead and Not Care. Defense of Epicurus." *AmPhQ* 23(1986), 217-225. Defense of E's claim that one's own death is not bad for one; assessment of recent arguments against it.   **[6025]**

SAYERS, B. "Death as a Loss." *Faith&Ph* 4(1987), 149-159. Neither E's claim that death is no loss nor Christian claim that death is a gain is satisfactory.   **[6026]**

SEDGWICK, H. D. *The Art of Happiness, or the Teachings of Epicurus.* Freeport, NY: Books for Libraries Pr., 1970. rprt. For non-specialists, introduction to Epicurean ethics, with chapters on altruism, the gods, friendship, passions, leisure.   **[6027]**

SEDLEY, D. "Epicurean Anti-Reductionsim," in #5597, pp. 295-327. Though a materialist, E does not reduce non-physical states and perceptions to level of being physical states or properties.   **[6028]**

——. "Epicurus and His Professional Rivals," in #5958, pp. 119-160. Ancient accounts in which E is depicted as heaping abuse on other philosophers in order to mask his own lack of originality stem from Timocrates and should not be taken at face value. **[6029]**

——. "Epicurus and the Mathematicians of Cyzicus." *BCPE* 6(1976), 23-54. Influence of school of Cyzicus on Epicurean geometry and astronomy.   **[6030]**

——. "Epicurus' Refutation of Determinism," in #6037, pp. 11-51. Notion of atomic swerve has psychological, not physical, origins. E argues against determinism as self-defeating and untenable.   **[6031]**

——. "The Structure of Epicurus' *On Nature*." *BCPE* 4(1974), 89-92. Conjectural outline: Books 1-13, exposition of principal doctrines; 14-26, refutation of rival theories; 28, psychological and ethical ramifications; 32ff., Epicurean physics.   **[6032]**

SOLMSEN, F. "Epicurus on Void, Matter, and Genesis: Some Historical Observations." *Phron* 22(1977), 263-281. E's thought on these subjects has an originality approaching Aristotle's. One cannot deny, however, that Atomists also taught that nothing that is can pass into non-being.   **[6033]**

——. cf. #5239.

STERN, G. S. "Epicurus and Friendship." *Dial*(Can) 28(1989), 275-288. McIntyre's interpretation (in *After Virtue*, cf. #4215) of friendship in Hellenistic era does not do justice to E's view. When state's role in formation of moral self was de-emphasized, E stressed aspects of personal relations that earlier philosophers had overlooked. **[6034]**

STRIKER, G. "Epicurus on the Truth of Sense Impressions." *AGPh* 59(1977), 125-142. First in line of philosophers who sought sure knowledge in sense perception, E concluded that, if a proposition expressed no more nor less than what could be deduced empirically, it was true.   **[6035]**

STROZIER, R. M. *Epicurus and Hellenistic Philosophy.* Lanham, MD: Univ. Pr. of Amer., 1985. Examines background against which Epicureanism arose and looks at E's views on cognition and ethics.   **[6036]**

Suzetesis. Studi sull'epicureismo greco e romano offerti a Marcello Gigante. Naples: Macchiaroli, 1983. Essays in English are abstracted herein.   **[6037]**

TAYLOR, C. C. W. "All Perceptions are True," in #5642, pp. 105-124. Examines how Epicurus used atomic theory and theory of *eidola* to maintain his essentially indefensible thesis that all sense impressions are true.   **[6038]**

TODD, R. B. "Infinite Body and Infinite Void. Epicurean Physics and Peripatetic Polemic." *LCM* 7(1982), 82-84. Discussion of frags preserved in Alexander of Aphrodisias and Simplicius.   **[6039]**

TSINOREMA, V. "The Concept of Pleasure in Epicurus' Moral Philosophy." *Diot* 13(1985), 147-155. E's moral philosophy cannot be found guilty of pure sensualism if a dispositional account of pleasure is accepted. Other forms of criticism against it may be valid.   **[6040]**

VANDER WAERDT, P. A. "Hermarchus and the Epicurean Genealogy of Morals." *TAPhA* 118(1988), 87-106. Hermarchus' account of origin of justice and morality is quite polemical. He admits that Stoic doctrine of *oikeiosis* — natural kinship among members of a species — might be a secondary factor but that concept of justice arose because some saw it to their advantage.   **[6041]**

VAN UNNIK, W. C. "An Attack on the Epicureans by Flavius Josephus," in #6736, pp. 341-355. Josephus' *Antiquities* 10,277-281 shows evidence of some original arguments against Epicureans, especially in discussion of Providence.   **[6042]**

VLASTOS, G. "Minimal Parts in Epicurean Atomism." *Isis* 56(1965), 121-147. *Minima* are mathematically divisible. E's doctrine is meant "only as a physical statement about atoms."   **[6043]**

WASSERSTEIN, A. "Epicurean Science." *Hermes* 106(1978), 484-494. Epicurean science does not begin with theorems or principles and pursue them for sake of pure knowledge. It is designed to find freedom from fear and necessity.   **[6044]**

For related items see #978, #6201, #6239, #6686, #6760, #7046.

LUCRETIUS (ca 94-54 B. C.)

Most of our knowledge of Epicurean doctrine comes from a long, didactic poem, *De rerum natura (On the Nature of Things)*, written in Latin by Titus Lucretius Carus, who lived during the last chaotic half-century of the Roman Republic. L enjoyed the good education available to a member of any wealthy Roman family but seems to have avoided political involvement in a period when Rome was being torn apart by factional strife. One ancient source preserves a highly dubious story about him being driven mad by an aphrodisiac given to him by his mistress and eventually committing suicide.

Epicurean philosophy had not become enormously popular in Rome, perhaps because its quietism did not appeal to a nation which had spent a century and a half conquering the Mediterranean coastline and then turning its armies on itself. But L, possibly because of his intense dislike of Roman religion, found comfort in Epicureanism and attempted to "spread the gospel" among his countrymen. He had many models for choosing to write a philosophical treatise in poetic form. Parmenides and Empedocles had done the same. His decision to put his revered master's teaching into the form of an epic poem had the result of making the message accessible to far more people than would have read it had it been presented as a prose philosophical treatise.

The crucial interpretive question is how original L was. He claimed to be merely presenting Epicurus' doctrine without change or elaboration. But the process of translating Epicurus into Latin forced L to make some decisions about the meaning of the Greek text he was dealing with. Every translation is an interpretation, as someone has observed. Being a poet, L created images — metaphors and similes — which Epicurus had disdained. He also injected an element of emotional conviction into Epicurus' coldly rational philosophy.

L's contribution to Epicurean thought is most evident in his attitude toward the gods. Epicurus had sanctioned worship of the gods, but L denounced the traditional state cults because they seemed to encourage ambition and militarism. He went much further than Epicurus in personifying Nature and worshiping it, almost as a pantheist. L also built upon Epicurus' observations about the origins of language to create a concept of human society arising from a compact which some early humans entered into "not to hurt or be hurt." Not everyone, he admits, adhered to the conditions of such compacts. Those communities which did, on the whole, prospered while others were unable to develop beyond a primitive level.

L's Epicureanism is strongly materialistic, from his insistence on the doctrine of the atomic swerve (*clinamen*) to explain free will to his exposition of the doctrine that perception occurred as a result of images emanating from a body and striking the mind atoms. Epicurus had called these images *eidola*; in L's Latin they become *simulacra*.

In the Roman Empire, where Stoicism and Platonism dominated, L was read as a poet, not as a philosopher. The Christians found his arguments against the pagan gods useful ammunition in their own polemic, but after the Christians came to dominate the Empire in the fourth century they had no further use for L. His work languished in the Middle Ages and was not widely read again until the time of Galileo and Descartes.

Some modern critics still question how compatible poetry and philosophy are. Didactic (teaching) poetry is looked at as artificial today. As Samuel Taylor Coleridge said, "Whatever in Lucretius is poetry is not philosophical; whatever is philosophical is not poetry."

AMORY, A. "*Obscura de re lucida carmina.* Science and Poetry in *De rerum natura*."

YCS 21(1969), 145-168. Argues against dividing poem into poetic and scientific parts. Analyzes 2.333-380 to show how themes are interwoven.   **[6045]**

ANDERSON, W. S. "Discontinuity in Lucretian Symbolism." *TAPhA* 91(1960), 1-29. L changes meanings of his symbols as his poem progresses. Many which are positive at first become neutral, then destructive. Universe is eternal but mankind is not. Symbols applied to universe/atoms can be applied to human existence but take on different meanings.   **[6046]**

ASMIS, E. "Lucretius' Explanation of Moving Dream Figures at 4.768-76." *AJPh* 102(1981), 138-145. Transposition of several lines makes L's meaning clear.   **[6047]**

——. "Lucretius's Venus and Stoic Zeus." *Hermes* 110(1982), 458-470. Venus, symbol of world governed by impulse, is opposed to Zeus, who represents Stoic order and rationality.   **[6048]**

——. "Rhetoric and Reason in Lucretius." *AJPh* 104(1983), 36-66. Contrary to majority opinion, L does have control of logical sequence of his arguments. His structure follows rhetorical rules of the time.   **[6049]**

AVOTINS, I. "Notes on Lucretius 2.51-193." *HSCP* 84(1980), 76-79. Atomic swerves are responsible for unforeseen acts of will.   **[6050]**

——. "The Question of *Mens* in Lucretius 2.289." *CQ* 24(1979), 95-100. *Res* is correct reading here; it refers to atom.   **[6051]**

——. "Two Observations on Lucretius 2.251-2.257." *RhM* 126(1983), 282-291. Lines are directed not against Stoics but against Atomist criticism of Epicurean swerve. Two textual emendations are necessary.   **[6052]**

BAILEY, C. "The Mind of Lucretius," in #6065, pp. 3-16. L expressed Epicureanism in images because his pattern of thinking is visual rather than given to logical argument. He is more poet than philosopher, but term "visionary" might be most apt.   **[6053]**

BERNS, G. "Time and Nature in Lucretius' *De rerum natura*." *Hermes* 114(1976), 477-492. L's three metaphors of time (force, motion, and space of time) correspond to three aspects of nature (matter, motion, and space). Mankind is more concerned with change than permanence, thus more with time than nature.   **[6054]**

BETENSKY, A. "Lucretius and Love." *CW* 73(1980), 291-299. While stressing destructive powers of Venus, L advocates marriage more strongly than Epicurus did. For L, though, marriage is a form of friendship.   **[6055]**

BLICKMAN, D. R. "Lucretius, Epicurus, and Prehistory." *HSCP* 92(1989), 157-191. L's discussion of early stages of humanity's development foreshadows his introduction of E as a benefactor equal to gods. E seems to have held same view of himself.   **[6056]**

BRADLEY, E. M. "Lucretius and the Irrational." *CJ* 67(1972), 331-340. Pessimistic tone of *De rer nat* is due not to L's alleged insanity but to poem's philosophical aim. **[6057]**

BROWN, R. D. "Lucretian Ridicule of Anaxagoras." *CQ* 33(1983), 146-160. L's criticism of A is more pointed than his treatment of Heraclitus or Empedocles. **[6058]**

BURNYEAT, M. F. "The Upside-Down Back-to-Front Sceptic of Lucretius IV,472." *Philologus* 122(1978), 197-206. L's graphic picture of self-refuting skeptic is close translation of phrase from Epicurus.   **[6059]**

CABISIUS, G. "Social Metaphor and the Atomic Cycle in Lucretius." *CJ* 80(1985), 109-120. Poetic metaphor bridges gap between atoms' mechanical behavior and human social behavior.   **[6060]**

CASTNER, C. J. "*De Rerum Natura* 5:101-103. Lucretius' Application of Empedoclean Language to Epicurean Doctrine." *Phoenix* 41(1987), 40-49. Use of Empedoclean language to describe divinity of Epicurus and his doctrine is effort to overcome doctrine's inaccessibility to empirical proof and its unattractiveness to non-Epicureans.   **[6061]**

————. *Prosopography of Roman Epicureans Between the 2. Century B. C. and the 2. Century A. D.* Frankfurt: Lang, 1988. Introductory section on development of Epicureanism in Rome, followed by listing of persons known or thought to be Epicurean. Citations from ancient sources are included.   **[6062]**

CATO, B. A. "Venus and *Natura* in Lucretius: *De Rerum Natura* 1.1-23 and 2.167-74." *CJ* 84(1988-89), 97-104. Poetic images such as Venus help L disguise the bitterness of Epicurean philosophy, as he himself admits. But Venus is subordinated, as are other gods, to all-powerful Nature.   **[6063]**

CLASSEN, C. J. "Poetry and Rhetoric in Lucretius." *TAPhA* 99(1968), 77-118; also in #6065, pp. 331-373. L was not primarily a poet or an Epicurean philosopher but someone concerned with improving human welfare by teaching a means of achieving inner peace. His hortatory purpose led him to adopt a number of rhetorical techniques.   **[6064]**

————., ed. *Probleme der Lukrezforschung.* Hildesheim, Ger.: Olms, 1986. Collection of previously published essays. Those in English are abstracted herein.   **[6065]**

CLAY, D. "*De rerum natura.* Greek *Physis* and Epicurean *Physiologia* (Lucretius I,1-148)." *TAPhA* 100(1969), 31-47. L first equates *natura* to birth/genesis, then makes its meaning broader, borrowing from Presocratic notions of *physis* as much as from Epicurus.   **[6066]**

————. *Lucretius and Epicurus.* Ithaca, NY: Cornell Univ. Pr., 1984. Analysis of *De rer. nat.* as philosophical poem. Surveys L's sources and E's thought as propounded late in his life. Study of L's proem and handling of Euclidean "Master Propositions," treated in E's writing. Analysis of Epicurean methodology.   **[6067]**

————. "The Sources of Lucretius' Inspiration," in #5958, pp. 203-228. Empedocles and Epicurus are L's main literary sources. His aim is to bring readers to the point that they can contemplate the tragedy of the plague at the end of Book VI but draw on their inner tranquility and not be disturbed by the vision.   **[6068]**

COX, A. S. "Lucretius and His Message: A Study in the Prologues of the *De rerum natura.*" *G&R* 18(1971), 1-16. Prologues, taken together, impart poem's principal ideas and are integral part of its structure. Observations on L's interest in science. **[6069]**

DALZELL, A. "A Bibliography of Work on Lucretius, 1945-1972." *CW* 66(1973), 389-427; 67(1974), 65-112. Annotated survey broken down by topics. **[6070]**

———. "Lucretius' Exposition of the Doctrine of Images." *Hermathena* 118(1974), 22-32. Argument concerning *simulacra* in 4.26-215 conforms to Epicurus' view. **[6071]**

DE LACY, P. H. "Distant Views. The Imagery of Lucretius 2." *CJ* 60(1964-65), 49-55. Proem to Book 2 attacks philosophical commonplace of deducing order and purpose in universe from watching movements of armies or ships from a distance. **[6072]**

———. "Lucretius and Plato," in #6037, pp. 291-307. L seems to have had first-hand knowledge of P and to have consciously attacked his doctrines, sometimes even turning P's own arguments against him. **[6073]**

DUBAN, J. M. "Some Remarks on Lucretius' Pessimism, Distant View, and Images." *Epoche* 10(1982), 3-18. L is not pessimistic or detached from life. **[6074]**

———. "Venus, Epicurus, and *Naturae species ratioque*." *AJPh* 103(1982), 165-177. The several passages where this phrase occurs suggest that L is linking Venus, nature's outward face, with Epicurus as the one who understands its working. Awareness of both is necessary for *ataraxia*. **[6075]**

DUDLEY, D. R. *Lucretius.* New York: Basic Books, 1965. Collected essays. Relevant ones abstracted herein. **[6076]**

DUTRA, J. A. "Anticipations of Modern Science in Epicureanism." *ClassOut* 56(1978), 1-3. In methodology and in many specific theories L is quite contemporary. **[6077]**

FARRINGTON, B. "Form and Purpose in the *De Rerum Natura*," in #6076, pp. 19-34. In form the poem is a monologue addressed to Memmius, for Epicureans typically won converts by personal appeal. Its purpose is to acquaint him thoroughly with Epicurus' moral philosophy and win him over to it. **[6078]**

FITZGERALD, W. "Lucretius' Cure for Love in the *De Rerum Natura*." *CW* 78(1984), 73-86. By de-emphasizing the unique individuality of persons and stressing atomist view of people and their emotions, L hopes to overcome notion of love, just as he argues against fear of death and of the gods. **[6079]**

FOWLER, D. "Lucretius and Politics," in #6199, pp. 120-150. Surveys Epicurean views on political activity. L believes that only conversion of every individual to Epicureanism will solve Rome's political problems. **[6080]**

———. "Lucretius on the *Clinanem* and 'Free Will' (II 251-93)," in #6037, pp. 329-352. Only by *clinamen* ("swerve") of atoms can Epicureanism account for free will, which seems to be an observable fact. L's presentation of it is self-consistent. **[6081]**

FRIEDLAENDER, P. "Pattern of Sound and Atomistic Theory in Lucretius," in #6065, pp. 291-307. L views letters and individual sounds as atoms which make up his poetry. Concept gives him a rational link between his poetry and his philosophy. **[6082]**

FURLEY, D. F. "Lucretius and the Stoics." *BICS* 13(1966), 13-33. Examination of passages in which L is allegedly replying to Stoics shows that they need not be so interpreted. He seems to have been drawing directly from Epicurus.   **[6083]**

———. "Lucretius the Epicurean. On the History of Man," in #6087, pp. 1-37. In L's view mankind had been progressing materially but degenerating spiritually until Epicurus began to teach.   **[6084]**

———. "Variations on Themes from Empedocles in Lucretius' Proem." *BICS* 17(1970), 55-64. References to Empedoclean elements can be discerned in L's opening lines. L apparently saw some parallels between Empedocles and Epicurus as enlighteners of mankind.   **[6085]**

GALLOWAY, A. "Lucretius' Materialistic Poetics: Epicurus and the Flawed *Consolatio* of Book 3." *Ramus* 15(1986), 52-73. Discussion of mortality at end of Book 3. **[6086]**

GIGON, O., ed. *Lucrèce. Huit exposés suivis de discussions.* Geneva: Fondation Hart, 1977. Essays in English are abstracted herein.   **[6087]**

GLIDDEN, D. K. "*Sensus* and Sense Perception in the *De rerum natura.*" *CSCA* 12(1979), 155-182. L holds what we perceive is different from how we feel.   **[6088]**

GOAR, R. I. "On the End of Lucretius' Fourth Book." *CB* 47(1971), 75-77. Influenced by Roman experience, L is more positive about family life than Epicurus.   **[6089]**

GORDON, C. A. *A Bibliography of Lucretius*, with introd. and notes by E. J. Kenney. Winchester: St. Paul's Bibliographies, 1985.   Covers only editions of L's text, no secondary literature.   **[6090]**

GOTTSCHALK, H. B. "Lucretius on the 'Water of the Sun'." *Philologus* 110(1966), 311-315. L's account can be traced back to a Hippocratic treatise.   **[6091]**

———. cf. #5615.

HOLTSMARK, E. B. "Lucretius and the Fools." *CJ* 63(1968), 260-261. In 1.639-642 L refers to fools (*stolidi* and *inanes*) who don't comprehend atoms and void (*solidum* and *inane*).   **[6092]**

———. "Lucretius, the Biochemistry of Olfaction and Scientific Discovery." *Euphro* 9(1978-79), 7-18. Modern scientific discoveries verify L's conjectures.   **[6093]**

———. "On Lucretius 2.1-19." *TAPhA* 98(1967), 193-204. L says that pleasure comes not from observing others' misfortunes but from knowing what true security is.   **[6094]**

INGALLS, W. B. "Repetition in Lucretius." *Phoenix* 25(1971), 227-236. Repetition of formulaic phrases has didactic value, makes composition easier, and follows his model, the Roman epic poet Ennius.   **[6095]**

JEFFREYS, R. L. "Barking Nature. A Note on *De rerum natura* 2,17." *Latomus* 42(1983), 126-128. Verb *latrare* (to bark) alludes to the Cynic origins of the theme of the prologue to Book 2.   **[6096]**

JOPE, J. "The Didactic Unity and Emotional Import of Book 6 of *De Rerum Natura.*" *Phoenix* 43(1989), 16-34. Final book of poem is not as unstructured as it appears. While explaining principles of world's destruction, it tries to persuade reader to accept transitory nature of man and cosmos with detachment.   **[6097]**

———. "Lucretius, Cybele, and Religion." *Phoenix* 39(1985), 250-262. For L, Cybele's cult is just what Epicurus opposed: an effort to enforce morality through fear. **[6098]**

———. "Lucretius' Psychoanalytic Insight: His Notion of Unconscious Motivation." *Phoenix* 37(1983), 224-238. L's ideas on dreams, fear of death, other psychological states seem modern because he attributes them to unconscious motivation.   **[6099]**

KEEN, R. "Lexical Notes to the Epicurean Doctrine of Perception." *Apeir* 15(1981), 59-69. Study of L's adaptation of E's vocabulary of perception and truth criteria. **[6100]**

———. "Lucretius and His Reader." *Apeir* 19(1985), 1-10. Memmius as exemplary reader helps to make L's point that Epicurean philosophy can cure Rome's social and political ills.   **[6101]**

———. "Notes on Epicurean Terminology and Lucretius." *Apeir* 13(1979), 63-69. By altering meaning of certain Latin words, L could express Epicurus' ideas accurately for a Roman audience.   **[6102]**

KLEVE, K. "The Philosophical Polemics in Lucretius: A Study in the History of Epicurean Criticism," in #6087, pp. 39-75. Importance of L as source for opposing philosophical views of his day, which he represents in his polemics.   **[6103]**

———. "What Kind of Work Did Lucretius Write?" *SO* 54(1979), 81-85. *De rer nat* focuses on physics because Epicureans saw it as necessary prelude to ethics.   **[6104]**

KOLLMANN, E. D. "Lucretius' Criticism of the Early Greek Philosophers." *StudClass* 13(1971), 79-93. L imitates style of each earlier philosopher as he critiques his views. Only Anaxagoras is treated straightforwardly.   **[6105]**

LENAGHAN, L. H. "Lucretius 1.921-950." *TAPhA* 98(1967), 221-251. Passage fits in its present context after L's discussion of theories opposed to his.   **[6106]**

LIENHARD, J. T. "The Proemia of the *De Rerum Natura.*" *CJ* 64(1969), 346-353. Analysis of main themes of introductions to the six books. They do more than merely state the theme of a particular book; they convey a philosophical mood.   **[6107]**

LONGRIGG, J. "'Ice of Bronze'. (Lucretius I,493)." *CR* 20(1970), 8-9. This striking phrase may have been borrowed from Empedocles.   **[6108]**

———. "Melissus and the Mortal Soul (Lucretius III,510-522)." *Philologus* 119(1975), 147-149. L's seventh argument for the mortality of soul goes back to M.   **[6109]**

LOWENSTEIN, O. E. "The Pre-Socratics, Lucretius, and Modern Science," in #6076, pp. 1-17. Studies concept of atomism as developed by Democritus, transmitted by L, and compares it to twentieth-century understanding.   **[6110]**

MAGUINNESS, W. S. "The Language of Lucretius," in #6076, pp. 69-93. L criticizes Heraclitus and others for obscure language and is not afraid to use plain, even clumsy, language himself. Studies use of techniques such as simile, repetition.   **[6111]**

MINADEO, R. "The Formal Design of *De rerum natura*." *Arion* 4(1965), 444-461. Poem is organized around cycle of creation and destruction in nature. L intended it to end where it does.   **[6112]**

NETHERCUTT, W. R. "Anticipations of Modern Science in Lucretius: A Footnote." *ClassOut* 56(1978), 51-52. Addendum to #6077.   **[6113]**

NEUMANN, H. "The Unpopularity of Epicurean Materialism: An Interpretation of Lucretius." *ModSch* 45(1968), 299-311. People disliked Epicureanism because it isolated individuals from sense of community which most people seem to need.   **[6114]**

NICHOLS, J. H. *Epicurean Political Philosophy. The* De rerum natura *of Lucretius.* Ithaca, NY: Cornell Univ. Pr., 1976. Summary of poem and treatment of question of whether an Epicurean can participate in politics. Examines L's influence on Hobbes, Montesquieu, Rousseau.   **[6115]**

NUSSBAUM, M. C. "Beyond Obsession and Disgust: Lucretius' Genealogy of Love." *Apeir* 22(1989), 1-59. L's attack on love, especially in Book 4, is the first step in a kind of therapy designed to cure the reader who loves love. L himself may have had a quite ordinary sort of marriage.   **[6116]**

———. "Mortal Immortals: Lucretius on Death and the Voice of Nature." *Ph&PhenRes* 50(1989), 303-351. Explores tension between L's two main aims: to make readers equal to gods and make them aware of natural world and their connectedness to it.   **[6117]**

OWEN, W. H. "The Lacuna in Lucretius II,164." *AJPh* 89(1968), 406-418. Missing portion probably contained discussion of gravity.   **[6118]**

PACKMAN, Z. M. "Ethics and Allegory in the Proem of the Fifth Book of Lucretius' *De Rerum Natura*." *CJ* 71(1975-76), 206-212. Hercules served mankind by freeing him from physical dangers and fears. Result for Hercules himself was separation from mankind. Epicurus served mankind by freeing him from fear of supernatural. As a result he also is set apart from humanity, a model for his followers.   **[6119]**

PANCHERI, L. U. "On *De rerum natura* 2.289: A Philosophical Argument for a Textual Point." *Apeir* 8 #2(1974), 49-55. Text need not be emended if one properly understands Epicurean meaning of concept "weight."   **[6120]**

RANKIN, H. D. "The Adynaton as a Proof of *nullam rem e nilo* in Lucretius (I,150-70)?" *Emerita* 36(1968), 309-313. The *adynata* (things impossible or contrary to nature) are used by L to demonstrate that nothing can come from nothing. He introduced the argument himself, not drawing it from Epicurus.   **[6121]**

———. "Lucretius on 'Part of Everything is in Everything'." *AC* 38(1969), 158-161. L refutes Anaxagoras' argument by common sense. His claim that A's seeds would be visible while Epicurean atoms would not does not seem inconsistent to him.   **[6122]**

REICHE, H. "Myth and Magic in Cosmological Polemics: Plato, Aristotle, Lucretius." *RhM* 114(1971), 296-329. P and Ar mocked their materialist opponents' views of the cosmos. L dealt with their comments as though they were serious. In all three writers the materialists are compared to mythological figures. [6123]

ROBERTS, L. "Lucretius 1.857-58 and Stoic Logic." *CW* 65(1972), 215-217. As used here, *res* is equivalent to Stoic *pragmata*. L seems to be parodying Stoic logic. [6124]

ROSENBAUM, S. E. "The Symmetry Argument: Lucretius Against the Fear of Death." *Ph&PhenRes* 50(1989), 353-373. L argued that our non-existence after death can be likened to our non-existence before birth. It is no more reasonable to fear one than the other. Various objections to this argument, from ancient and modern writers, are examined. It deals with one aspect of death-anxiety but is not comprehensive enough to cover all aspects of the phenomenon. [6125]

SAUNDERS, T. J. "Free Will and the Atomic Swerve in Lucretius." *SO* 59(1984), 37-59. Study of several passages shows function of swerve is located not in will's formation but in its execution. Swerve helps will to control "physical processes" of mind. [6126]

———. "A Note on Lucretius III,240." *Mnem* 28(1975), 296-298. "Fourth nature" is essential to both *mens* and *anima*. The line under study describes the functions of the former, distinguishes them from the functions of the latter. [6127]

SCHOENHEIM, U. "The Place of *Tactus* in Lucretius." *Philologus* 110(1966), 71-87. L's doctrine of the senses does not treat touch adequately. [6128]

SCHRIJVERS, P. H. "Lucretius." *Lampadion* 7(1966-68), 5-32. Bibliography. [6129]

SEGAL, C. P. "*Delubra decora*. Lucretius II,352-366." *Latomus* 29(1970), 104-118. Lost calf image, which is drawn out farther than necessary, refers to some basic themes of Book 2, especially luxury-simplicity dichotomy. [6130]

———. "Poetic Immortality and the Fear of Death: The Second Proem of the *De Rerum Natura*." *HSCP* 92(1989), 193-212. Lines 922-930 of Book 1 present tension between Epicurean view of death as end of consciousness and L's hope for lasting fame. This poetic hope helps philosopher accept dissolution of consciousness in death. [6131]

SHARPLES, R. W. "Lucretius' Account of the Composition of the Soul (3.231ff.)." *LCM* 5(1980), 117-120. Epicureanism maintains that soul is composed of several types of atoms; rejects notion that fire-atoms are one of those types. [6132]

SMITH, F. M. "Some Lucretian Thought Processes." *Hermathena* 102(1966), 73-83. Studies three techniques: digression, reflection, and repetition, which L uses to make philosophical points. [6133]

SNYDER, J. M. "Lucretius and the Status of Women." *CB* 53(1976), 17-19. L concedes feminine qualities of earth and nature but considers women physically and mentally inferior to men. He is less progressive than Epicurus in this regard but not as misogynistic as Stoics. [6134]

———. "Lucretius' Empedoclean Sicily." *CW* 65(1972), 217-218. L's word play often serves a purpose, as when Empedocles' four elements are inserted into description of Sicily which occurs just before L's criticism of Empedoclean ideas.   **[6135]**

————. "The Significant Name in Lucretius." *CW* 72(1978-79), 227-230. L does not often play on proper names, but he finds two contradictory meanings in "Heraclitus."   **[6136]**

————. "The Warp and Woof of the Universe in Lucretius' *De rerum natura*." *ICS* 8(1983), 37-43. Loom imagery links L's view of world and his role as poet.   **[6137]**

SOLMSEN, F. "Lucretius' Strategy in *De Rerum Nature* I." *RhM* 131(1988), 315-323. Book 1 does discuss the doctrine of bodies, though not as fully as it does other points of Epicurean philosophy.   **[6138]**

SPRINGER, L. A. "The Role of *Religio, Solvo* and *Ratio* in Lucretius." *CW* 71(1977), 55-61. For L *religio* usually involves sense of binding. It refers to any teaching/thought which inhibits use of reason.   **[6139]**

STEWART, D. J. "The Silence of Magna Mater." *HSCP* 74(1970), 75-84. *De rer nat* 2,600-645 has philosophical implications. Cybele symbolizes mute nature of atomic universe. She also serves as contrast to Venus.   **[6140]**

STREBEROVA, T. "Necessity and Chance in Lucretius' *De rerum natura*." *GLO* 9-10(1977-78), 17-62. Discussion of most important passages on the subjects.   **[6141]**

TATUM, W. J. "The Presocratics in Book One of Lucretius' *De rerum natura*." *TAPhA* 114(1984), 177-189. L uses Heraclitus, Empedocles, and Anaxagoras to underscore his concern with philosophical language. Empedocles is his justification for presenting philosophy in poetic form.   **[6142]**

THURRY, E. M. "Lucretius' Poem as a *Simulacrum* of the *Rerum natura*." *AJPh* 108(1987), 270-294. L uses poetic images to enter reader's mind in same way that, according to Epicurus, images given off by physical objects impart knowledge of those objects. L's objective helps explain his otherwise puzzling use of Venus.   **[6143]**

WALLACH, B. P. *Lucretius and the Diatribe against the Fear of Death:* De rerum natura *III 830-1094.* Leiden: Brill, 1976. Along with philosophical influences, one must consider L's use of, and reaction against, literary genres in this passage.   **[6144]**

————. "Lucretius and the Diatribe: *De rerum natura* II,1-61," in *Gesellschaft. Kultur. Literatur. Rezeption und Originalitaet im Wachsen einer europaeischen Literatur und Geistigkeit. Beitraege L. Wallach gewidmet,* ed. K. Bosl (Stuttgart, Ger.: Hiersemann, 1975), pp. 49-77. Study of stylistic traits (especially antithesis), rhetorical devices, themes of passage show it to be poetic diatribe, modelled on sermons of Cynics.   **[6145]**

WARDY, R. "Lucretius on What Atoms are Not." *CPh* 83(1988), 112-128. L tries to combat "reductionist" argument against atomic theory by showing that atoms are completely lifeless and inanimate, and they must be so. Only in combination do they produce animation and sensation.   **[6146]**

WEST. D. A. "Lucretius' Methods of Argument (3.417-614)." *CQ* 25(1975), 94-116. Thirteen examples drawn from L's proofs of mortality of soul demonstrate essentials of his logic. [6147]

WIGODSKY, M. "A Pattern of Argument in Lucretius." *PacCPh* 9(1974), 73-78. L often anticipates objections to his points to avoid misinterpretation. Use of numerous metaphors is based on Epicurus' theory that words are congruent with thoughts they express or objects they describe. [6148]

WILTSHIRE, S. F. "*Nunc age*. Lucretius as Teacher." *CB* 50(1973-74), 33-37. By his empathy, clarity, and exhortation L hopes to persuade his readers of the truthfulness of his viewpoint. [6149]

WORMELL, D. E. W. "Lucretius: the Personality of the Poet," in #6065, pp. 17-28. Nothing in L's text substantiates charges that he was mentally unbalanced. Tries to identify some of his positive characteristics. [6150]

———. "The Personal World of Lucretius," in #6076, pp. 35-67. Surveys what can be known of L's life and shows how various themes of his poem relate to his own experience. Stresses his ability to blend science and poetry. [6151]

For related items see #5983, #6273, #6274.

PHILODEMUS (First century B. C.)
 Born in Gadara, in Syria, Philodemus came to Rome ca. 75 B. C. and made a name for himself as a poet and philosopher. His patron gave him a lavish villa at Herculaneum (a town near Pompeii which was also buried by the eruption of Vesuvius in 79 A. D.). P's work inspired other poets such as Horace and Virgil. Some two dozen of his poems are preserved. None of his philosophical works survive, but papyrus copies of part of his work have been unearthed at Herculaneum. Only portions of them are still legible.
 P's aim seems to have been to popularize Epicureanism. He wrote an outline of the main doctrines of Greek philosophy, from an Epicurean point of view. There is little noteworthy about his work, except his aesthetic theories. He argued that a work of art was independent of any moral or logical constraints and was defined by its aesthetic value, not its content.

BARNES, J. "Epicurean Signs." *OSAP* Suppl.(1988), 91-134. Analysis of papyrus from Herculaneum, apparently a notebook for P's private use, which treats Epicurean teaching on signs and their relation to real things. [6152]

———. cf. #5449.

HENRICHS, A. "Towards a New Edition of Philodemus' Treatise on Piety." *GRBS* 13(1972), 67-98. Discusses problems of reconstructing the text of this document and its importance as a source for study of Epicurean theology. [6153]

LONG, A. A. "Reply to Jonathan Barnes, 'Epicurean Signs'." *OSAP* Suppl.(1988), 135-144. Reply to #6152. [6154]

MURRAY, O. "Philodemus on the Good King According to Homer." *JRS* 55(1965), 161-182. Commentary on text from Herculaneum. Literary and historical setting, connection with Caesar and with Cicero's concept of *princeps*.   **[6155]**

SEDLEY, D. "On Signs," in #5667, pp. 239-272. P's opponents seem to have been Stoics. Stoic and Epicurean methods of sign-inference are compared.   **[6156]**

SIDER, D. "The Love Poetry of Philodemus." *AJPh* 108(1987), 310-324. Discussion of problems of an Epicurean marrying and writing poetry, both of which Epicurus himself frowned upon.   **[6157]**

SUTTON, D. F. "PHerc 1581: The Argument." *Phil*(Athens) 12(1982), 270-276. This frag of P seems to have been the source of Iamblichus' discussion of dramatic catharsis in *De mysteriis*.   **[6158]**

For related item see #6274.

DIOGENES OF OENOANDA (ca. 200 A. D.)

In one of his essays Plutarch tried to prove that a follower of Epicurus' teachings could not hope to live a pleasant life. One Epicurean, however, left a very public testimonial of his gratitude to the founder of the school, in the town of Oenoanda in southern Asia Minor. This man, known only as Diogenes, erected a colonnade where his fellow citizens could stroll or sit in the shade. On the wall of the structure, which was over 120 feet long, he put up an inscription outlining the physical and ethical doctrines which he felt had benefited him. The stones of the colonnade have been scattered/destroyed over the centuries. Recovering and reconstructing them has required considerable scholarly efforts in recent years.

CHILTON, C. W. *Diogenes of Oenoanda: The Fragments. A Translation and Commentary.* London: Oxford Univ. Pr., 1971. Critical text, translation, commentary.   **[6159]**

————. "The Epicurean Theory of the Origin of Language. A Study of Diogenes of Oenoanda, Fragments X and XI William." *AJPh* 83(1962), 159-167. Frags indicate Epicurus refuted theory of Cratylus.   **[6160]**

CLAY, D. "An Epicurean Interpretation of Dreams." *AJPh* 101(1980), 342-365. Diogenes criticizes Stoics and Democritus, tries to compromise between dreams as void and as psychic images.   **[6161]**

————. "Sailing to Lampsacus. Diogenes of Oenoanda, New Fragment 7." *GRBS* 14(1973), 49-59. Frag seems to be about Epicurus and his close brush with death at sea, a story also told by Plutarch (1090e and 1103e).   **[6162]**

————. "Philippson's 'Basilica' and Diogenes' Stoa (Diogenes of Oenoanda, fr. 51)." *AJPh* 99(1978), 120-123. D seems to have wanted sayings of Epicurus inscribed on walls of stoa in Oenoanda.   **[6163]**

HALL, A. S. "Who Was Diogenes of Oenoanda?" *JHS* 99(1979), 160-163. Author of recently discovered treatise was probably Flavius Diogenes, ca. 220 A. D.   **[6164]**

SMITH, M. F. "A Bibliography of Work on Diogenes of Oenoanda (1892-1981)," in #6037, pp. 683-695. Comprehensive listing, with some annotations.   **[6165]**

――. "Diogenes of Oenoanda, New Fragment 24." *AJPh* 99(1978), 325-328. Fragment comes from letter of Epicurus to his mother, probably written in 311 B. C. Represents his earliest urging to follow philosophy.   **[6166]**

――. "Diogenes of Oenoanda, New Fragments 115-121." *Prometheus* 8(1982), 193-212. Text, translation, commentary.   **[6167]**

――. "Diogenes of Oenoanda, New Fragments 122-124." *AS* 34(1984), 43-57. Text, translation, notes, indices.   **[6168]**

――. "Eight New Fragments of Diogenes of Oenoanda." *AS* 29(1979), 69-89. Text and commentary.   **[6169]**

――. "Epicureanism in a Stoa: The Philosophical Inscription of Diogenes of Oenoanda," in #69, I, pp. 241-244. Review of what has been learned about D through recovery of frags of his inscription and describes two new frags which discuss the gods.   **[6170]**

――. "Fifty-five New Fragments of Diogenes of Oenoanda." *AS* 28(1978), 39-92. Text, translations, and comments on further frags of the inscription.   **[6171]**

――. "Fragments of Diogenes of Oenoanda Discovered and Rediscovered." *AJA* 71(1970), 51-62. Four new frags analyzed.   **[6172]**

――. "More New Fragments of Diogenes of Oenoanda," in #5958, pp. 281-318. Description of new frags with photos of inscriptions, index of Greek words.   **[6173]**

――. "New Fragments of Diogenes of Oenoanda." *AJA* 75(1971), 357-389. Description of, and commentary on, several new pieces of D's Epicurean inscription.   **[6174]**

――. "Observations on the Text of Diogenes of Oenoanda." *Hermathena* 110(1970), 52-78. Analysis of inscription set up by this Epicurean thinker ca. 200 A. D.   **[6175]**

――. "Seven New Fragments of Diogenes of Oenoanda." *Hermathena* 118(1974), 110-129. Text, translation, commentary.   **[6176]**

――. *Thirteen New Fragments of Diogenes of Oenoanda*. Vienna: Oesterreichischen Akad. der Wissenschaft, 1974. Further publication of pieces of D's Stoa wall.   **[6177]**

――. "Two New Fragments of Diogenes of Oenoanda." *JHS* 92(1972), 147-155. One frag discusses Epicurean tenet of not fearing severe pain. The other belongs to a collection of E's private writings.   **[6178]**

Chapter 19

THE LATE HELLENISTIC AND ROMAN ERA

NEOPYTHAGOREANISM

The teaching of Pythagoras had all but died out by the fourth century B. C. The last writer who can be called a Pythagorean in anything like the original sense of the word is Lucanus Ocellus (or Okellos), author of *On the Nature of the Universe*, who lived in the second century B. C.

The loosely defined school (or "direction of thought," as one scholar has described it) known as Neopythagoreanism made its appearance in the first century B. C. in Rome and Alexandria. It derived some of its doctrine from the teachings of Pythagoras, but most of its knowledge of the earlier sage probably came from Aristotle (or one of his students), who had collected and discussed the *Akousmata* or oral doctrines attributed to him. This material consisted largely of scientific concepts, proverbial wisdom sayings, and ethical maxims.

Neopytyhagoreans adopted Pythagoras' dietary regulations (no beans or meat), his belief in reincarnation of the soul, and his fascination with numbers and their symbolism. To that basic stock they added a veritable stew of ideas from other sources: rules for ritual purity (wearing linen, shoes not made of animal skins, going barefoot in a temple, not shaving); elements of the salvation theology of the Orphic-Dionysiac mystery cults; strong Platonic overtones, especially in their dualism and their insistence on the reality of demons. Frank Thilly in his *History of Philosophy* described their methodology in these terms: "Whatever the Neopythagoreans accepted as truth, and whatever appealed to them in the writings of Plato, Aristotle, and the Stoics, they naively ascribed to the great teacher whose personality and work had been surrounded with the nimbus of mystery."

The resultant "philosophy" can best be described as eclectic. For example, intermediaries, modelled on the Platonic *daimones* or Demiurge, were thought to be responsible for the creation of the physical world. Such speculation led to the search for intuitive knowledge of God. No two writers in the school hold exactly the same views, and many of the ideas espoused in Neopythagorean literature also appear in the Jewish Platonist Philo of Alexandria, the Christian philosopher Justin Martyr, and other diverse sources from the early Roman Empire.

Two individuals most closely identified with this school can be examined briefly. Apollonius of Tyana, whose life spanned virtually the entire first century A. D., is best known because of the biography of him composed by Philostratus in the early third century. Claims of a miraculous birth and precocious knowledge are made for him. He denounced possession of material goods and took a vow of silence for five years. Travelling around the Roman world as well as to Persia and India, he visited with sages and hermits wherever he could find them. His public activities centered on exorcism of demons, healings of the sick, and preaching against animal sacrifices to the gods. He was widely denounced as a magician and charlatan and was arrested several times by the Romans, though apparently never brought to trial. One pagan writer, Hierocles of Nicomedia, tried to publicize Apollonius as a rival to Christ. The sage came to be venerated in several towns, and the emperor Alexander Severus set up a statue of Apollonius along with images of Alexander the Great, Orpheus, Abraham, and Christ.

Less flamboyant but perhaps more influential was Numenius of Apamea, who lived in the second century A. D. Substantial fragments of two of his works, a treatise *On the Good* and a history of Plato's Academy, survive. The latter shows how far the Academy had departed from Plato's teachings by Numenius' day. Numenius' own thinking borrowed Oriental elements and foreshadowed Plotinus' concept of three gods. He also taught that the human soul has the potential to become identified or united with its divine original, an idea that looms large in Plotinus. Some of Plotinus' critics, in fact, accused him of plagiarizing from Numenius. Numenius seems to have been familiar with certain points of Jewish and Christian doctrine, which he interpreted allegorically, a practice certainly not lost on Origen. Porphyry and later Neoplatonists also seem to have been influenced by him.

Neopythagoreanism illustrates the disappearance of the boundary between philosophy and religion which was occurring by the first century B. C. The gradual conquest of the Mediterranean world by Rome and the frightful civil wars which racked the late Republic before the rise of the emperor Augustus seem to have heightened a popular yearning for some secure promise of salvation, for revelation of a God who was assumed to be separate from and opposite to the created world. With its teaching of the immortality of the soul and its eventual release from a cycle of reincarnation, Neopythagoreanism sounded a note which many people wanted to hear. The school disappeared by the late second century A. D., being absorbed in the system of religious/philosophical mysticism known as Neoplatonism. It had a perceptible impact on the Christian heretical group known as Valentinians.

BOWIE, E. L. "Apollonius of Tyana: Tradition and Reality." *ANRW* II,16.2,1652-1699. Effort to separate historical A from Philostratus' account of him. Historical figure does seem to have had Pythagorean leanings. **[6179]**

CAMPBELL, F. W. G. *Apollonius of Tyana: A Study of His Life and Times.* Chicago: Argonaut, 1968; rprt. Survey for non-specialists. **[6180]**

CHESTNUTT, G. F. "The Ruler and the Logos in Neopythagorean, Middle Platonic, and Late Stoic Philosophy." *ANRW* II,16,2,1310-1332. Idea of ruler as embodiment of Law or Logos of God probably originated in Neopythagorean writings, which are difficult to date. It appears also in Middle Platonist Plutarch and Stoic Seneca. It survived changeover to Christianity in fourth century. **[6181]**

DZIELSKA, M. *Apollonius of Tyana in Legend and History*, transl. P. Pienkowski. Rome: "L'Erma" di Bretschneider, 1986. Chapters on Apollonius' philosophy, his reputation as a magician, and development of legends about him. **[6182]**

GORMAN, P. "The Apollonius of the Neoplatonic Biographies of Pythagoras." *Mnem* 38(1985), 130-144. Biographies of Pythagoras by Iamblichus and Porphyry do not rely on Apollonius of Tyana. **[6183]**

GUTHRIE, K., ed. *The Neoplatonic Writings of Numenius*. Kew Gardens, UK: Selene Books, 1986; rprt. Greek text and facing-page translation of Numenius' frags, with introductory essay. **[6184]**

———., and **TAYLOR, T.,** eds. *The Pythagorean Writings. Hellenistic Texts from the First Century B. C. - Third Century A. D. on Life, Morality, Knowledge and the World*, ed. R. Navon. Kew Gardens, UK: Selene Books, 1986; rprt. Introduction and outline of Pythagorean thought, with selections from Hellenistic writers such as Philolaus and Archytas. Grouped by subject: morals, science, mathematics, etc. **[6185]**

HARRIS, B. F. "Apollonius of Tyana: Fact and Fiction." *JRelHist* 5(1969), 189-199. Philostratus' biography of A grew out of imperial plans for a syncretistic religious cult. Against that background, it is possible to make allowances for propaganda in the account and get behind Philostratus' picture to some perception of the historical A. **[6186]**

HERSHBELL, J. P. "Plutarch's Pythagorean Friends." *CB* 60(1984), 73-79. Not as many of P's friends were Pythagoreans as some scholars have suggested. **[6187]**

LITTLE, D. A. "Non-Parody in *Metamorphoses* 15." *Prud* 6(1974), 17-21. Reply to Segal #6192. **[6188]**

MATHIESEN, T. J., transl. *Aristides Quintilianus. On Music in Three Books*. New Haven, CT: Yale Univ. Pr., 1983. Translation, with commentary, of important text in fields of ancient music and linguistics and in Neopythagorean and Neoplatonic philosophy. **[6189]**

MEAD, G. R. S. *Apollonius of Tyana: The Philosopher-Reformer of the First Century A. D.* New York: University Books, 1966. Survey of his life and teachings, stressing the universality of his ideas. **[6190]**

SCHATTENMANN, J. "Jesus and Pythagoras." *Kairos* 21(1979), 215-220. Iamblichus quotes a *dictum* of Pythagoras about cutting off "with fire and sword all that does not comply with right measure." This may be source of Jesus' statement in Matt. 5:29-30 about cutting off what offends and may have some connection with "eunuch saying" of Matt. 19:11-12. **[6191]**

SEGAL, C. "Myth and Philosophy in the *Metamorphoses*." *AJPh* 90(1969), 257-292. Pythagoras' speech in *Meta*. 15 is intended by Ovid as a parody of Pythagorean thought, especially vegetarianism. **[6192]**

TSEKOURAKIS, D. "Orphic and Pythagorean Views on Vegetarianism in Plutarch," in *International Plutarch Society, Sezioni Italiana. Miscellanea Plutarchea. Atti del I Convegno di Studi su Plutarcho (Roma, 23 Novembre 1985)*, ed. F. E. Brenk and I. Gallo

(Ferrara: n. p., 1986), pp. 127-138. Orphic-Pythagorean doctrines of the rationality of animals and the transmigration of souls into animal bodies have less impact on Plutarch's vegetarianism than do purely hygenic considerations. **[6193]**

VESSEY, D. W. T. "Horace's Archytas Ode: A Reconsideration." *ZAnt* 26(1976), 73-87. Poem, written as monologue by Archytas, is Epicurean reflection on death and futility of religio-mystical ideas, such as Pythagoreanism. **[6194]**

WHITTAKER, J. "Neopythagoreanism and the Transcendent Absolute." *SO* 48(1973), 77-86. Neopythagoreans saw the One as transcending any positive quality, even unity. It goes beyond any pairs of opposites (one and many, male and female). These arise from it but are not part of it. **[6195]**

For related item see #2449.

ROMAN PHILOSOPHY

The Romans first made contact with Greeks in southern Italy, which had been colonized by Greeks beginning ca. 800 B. C. But extensive Greek-Roman contact did not occur until after the end of the first Punic War (241 B. C.). This meant that the Greeks who passed their culture along to the Romans were not those of the "Golden Age" of Periclean Athens but their less ambitious, less accomplished successors. The Romans modelled their plays after the romantically superficial Menander and Epicharmus of the New Comedy, not the brilliantly satiric Aristophanes of the Old Comedy. Their poetic models were the Alexandrian poets, not Pindar or Bacchylides.

Philosophy did not have an auspicious beginning in Rome. Some Romans were suspicious of the new ideas and what they feared would be their demoralizing effect. The poet Ennius (second century B. C.) advised his countrymen to "bathe, but not to wallow" in philosophy. Two Epicureans were expelled in 173 B. C. and a general expulsion of philosophers and rhetoricians was decreed in 161. Neither action was permanent. When an embassy composed of several philosophers arrived from Athens early in 155 B. C. and spent several years in Rome, conservatives who objected to the new ideas — this being the age of Carneades and the Skeptical Academy — brought a resolution to the Senate to expel the philosophers from the city. The leader of this movement, Cato the Elder (also called the Censor), described Socrates as "a turbulent old windbag" who encouraged the Athenians to disobey the laws of their city. The fate he had suffered seemed a fitting one, in Cato's opinion.

Other Romans, such as Aemilius Paulus and Scipio Aemilianus, responded more favorably to this new intellectual stimulus. They assigned Greek slaves as tutors for their children and brought in philosophers as public lecturers and honored guests. Because Greeks were their teachers, the students learned the Greek language. More pragmatic than speculative by nature, the Romans did not develop an independent philosophical tradition. Just as they had taken over Greek comedy and poetry wholesale, they also imported the Hellenistic philosophical systems, finding Stoicism more congenial to their tastes than pessimistic Epicureanism or the self-doubting skepticism of the Academy. A people who had built an empire stretching from Spain to the eastern shore of the Mediterranean felt little attraction to philosophies which taught indifference, withdrawal, and uncertainty. Stoic ideas of divine destiny and acceptance of fate helped justify the Romans' position. Only small groups of Epicureans or Academics can be identified, mostly among the intellectual elite.

Greek philosophy filled an intellectual, even a spiritual, void for the Romans. Their native religious and moral traditions were meager, to put it kindly. The state, as an extension of the family, claimed all allegiance. Worship of the gods was a public obligation, a fulfilment of a contract between the state and the deities. A few hardy virtues, such as *pietas* (devotion to one's duty) and *gravitas* (seriousness), might have sufficed for the rude farmers of the early republic, but the sophisticated masters of a Mediterranean empire needed a broader world view.

Rome produced significant representatives of each of the three major Hellenistic schools. Seneca, Epictetus, and Marcus Aurelius have been discussed in the chapter on Stoicism. Lucretius' efforts to promote Epicureanism are so closely tied to what we know of Epicurus himself that it was necessary to present him along with his master. Cicero, the voice of the Academy in Rome, will be considered below.

The philosophers often voiced opposition to the government, particularly under the Empire. Few emperors lived up to the ideal of the Stoic ruler. Under Vespasian the philosophers were banished from the city of Rome, and again under Domitian. Philosophy seems to have had little impact on the general public in Rome, being limited to the aristocratic circles who had the education and the leisure time to spend in pursuit of wisdom. A letter from Pliny the Younger (1.10) describing a Stoic philosopher named Euphrates gives much insight into the pragmatic Romans' somewhat ambivalent attitude toward philosophy:

> His arguments are subtle, his reasoning profound, and his words well-chosen, so that he often seems to have something of the sublimity and richness of Plato. He talks readily on many subjects with a special charm which can captivate and so convince the most reluctant listener. He is moreover tall and distinguished to look at, with long hair and a flowing white beard, and though these may sound like natural advantages of no real importance, they help to make him widely respected . . . . his serious manner makes no show of austerity, so that your first reaction on meeting him would be admiration rather than repulsion. He leads a wholly blameless life, while remaining entirely human; he attacks vices, not individuals, and aims at reforming wrongdoers instead of punishing them . . . . Whenever I have the chance I complain about these [public] duties to Euphrates, who consoles me by saying that anyone who holds public office, presides at trials and passes judgment, expounds and administers justice, and thereby puts into practice what the philosopher only teaches, has a part in the philosophic life and indeed the noblest part of all.

AALDERS, G. J. D. "Ideas about Human Equality and Inequality in the Roman Empire. Plutarch and Some of his Contemporaries," in #62, pp. 55-71. As Platonist, P accepts basic equality of persons, distinguishing them on basis of moral character. He rejects democracy but holds men and women equal. Dio Chrysostom and Epictetus, from a Stoic viewpoint, differ on several of those points. Dio and P are influenced as much by contemporary social norms as by philosophical views. **[6196]**

ATTRIDGE, H. W. "The Philosophical Critique of Religion under the Early Empire." *ANRW* II,16.1,45-78. Few, if any, philosophical schools of early Empire acknowledged validity of state cults and mystery religions. Most recognized some sort of natural, rational piety. Epicurean critique tended to be negative; Stoics, Academics and Neopythagoreans stressed their positive theology; Cynics were divided. **[6197]**

BARNES, J. "Antiochus of Ascalon," in #6199, pp. 51-96. A's originality, influence on later thinkers have been overestimated. His importance lies in his skill as a syncretist in an age when philosophical debate had reached a stage of hopeless confusion. **[6198]**

————., and **GRIFFIN, M.** *Philosophia Togata: Essays on Philosophy and Roman Society.* Oxford Univ. Pr., 1989. Collection of essays on Posidonius, Philodemus, Cicero, Lucretius and others, focusing especially on philosophy's role in Roman politics and cultural life. All are abstracted herein. **[6199]**

BOND, R. P. "Aeneas and the Cardinal Virtues." *Prud* 14(1974), 67-91. In the first six books of *Aeneid* the title character displays the cardinal virtues of courage, justice, temperance, and wisdom. Virgil, originally an Epicurean, seems to have adopted an eclectic Stoicism in the poem. **[6200]**

BOURNE, F. C. "Caesar the Epicurean." *CW* 70(1977), 417-432. Roman version of Epicureanism allowed political involvement. Julius Caesar's career displays commitment to Epicurean teaching. **[6201]**

BOWERSOCK, G. W. *Greek Sophists in the Roman Empire.* Oxford Univ. Pr., 1969. By second century A. D. "Sophist" was very broad term, including many writers, orators, political figures. People identified as such held high posts in government and enjoyed friendship with philhellenic emperors such as Hadrian and Marcus Aurelius. **[6202]**

BRINTON, A. "Quintilian, Plato, and the *Vir bonus*." *Ph&Rh* 16(1983), 167-184. Q's statement that the orator must be a good person seems to mean that he is so by definition, an idea derived from Plato. **[6203]**

BROADIE, A., and **MacDONALD, J.** "The Concept of Cosmic Order in Ancient Egypt in Dynastic and Roman Times." *AC* 47(1978), 106-128. Analyzes Philo's concept of Logos and compares it with the Stoic notion. Finds some similarities between Philo's view and older Egyptian concept of *Maat* or cosmic order. **[6204]**

BRUNT, P. A. "Philosophy and Religion in the Late Republic," in #6199, pp. 174-198. There is no convincing evidence that Greek philosophical teaching drew Romans away from their religious practices or weakened their faith. Roman religion was largely mechanical even in days before contact with Greeks. **[6205]**

COX, A. S. "To Do as Rome Does?" *G&R* 12(1965), 85-96. Stoic *virtus* is narrower ideal than Christian *agape* and thus more attainable. This helps account for Stoicism's popularity in Rome. [6206]

DEN BOER, W. "Allegory and History," in #6736, pp. 15-27. Compares use of allegory, especially in a defensive way, by pagans and Christians of Roman period. Some pagans, e. g., Porphyry, insisted that Christians read their texts literally. Others, such as emperor Julian, wanted to use allegory on all old texts. [6207]

————. cf. #6736.

GOAR, R. J. "Horace and the Betrayal of Philosophy: *Odes* 1.29." *CJ* 68(1972-73), 116-118. H berates one Iccius for giving up philosophical ideals to go off on a military expedition in hopes of plunder. [6208]

GOTTSCHALK, H. B. "Aristotelian Philosophy in the Roman World from the Time of Cicero to the End of the Second Century A. D." *ANRW* II,36.2,1079-1174. Discusses revival of interest in A's work before triumph of Neoplatonism. Its ethical content, avoiding Epicurus' mechanism and Stoics' determinism, helps account for renewed popularity. Much of A's thought was taken over into Neoplatonism. [6209]

————. "Currents of Philosophical Thought in the First Two Centuries A. D." *Dodone* 16 #3(1987), 87-101. Philosophical ideas developed in this period were more religious than philosophical. They emphasize a system of thought and the importance of a written document containing founder's words. Aristotle's is the only school to exhibit any significant development. [6210]

GRASSI, E. "The Philosophical and Rhetorical Significance of Ovid's *Metamorphoses.*" *Ph&Rh* 15(1982), 257-261. Apollo and Daphne are at opening of work because Apollo symbolizes beginnings of poetic thought and speech, which were original form of philosophical discourse. [6211]

GRIFFIN, M. "Philosophy, Cato, and Roman Suicide." *G&R* 33(1986), 64-77, 192-202. Stoicism "glamorized" suicide, which had always been acceptable in Roman eyes, but regarded it as justified only in extraordinary circumstances. [6212]

————. "Philosophy, Politics, and Politicians at Rome," in #6199, pp. 1-37. Discusses popularity of various schools and evidence for influence of philosophy on Roman conduct, both personal and political. It is often difficult to distinguish specific tenets of philosophical schools from Roman tradition in general. [6213]

HARRIS, B. F. "Stoic and Cynic under Vespasian." *Prud* 9(1977), 105-114. Activities of philosophers in first-century Rome. Stoics took part in public life. [6214]

JOCELYN, H. D. "*Homo sum; humani nil a me alienum puto.*" *Antich* 7(1973), 14-46. Terence's line reflects Romans' suspicion of philosophy. Cicero takes it as statement of Stoic sage; Seneca and Augustine give it humanistic connotations. [6215]

LIND, L. R. "Roman Religion and Ethical Thought. Abstraction and Personification." *CJ* 69(1973), 108-119. Ethical poverty of Rome's religions is seen in deification of abstract concepts such as honesty and chastity. Participation in these cults amounted to little more than philosophical contemplation. [6216]

LYLE, E. B. "The Circus as Cosmos." *Latomus* 43(1984), 827-841. In its design the Roman race course (*circus*) has cosmological significance, representing cycle of the seasons. Pattern of races — a dash to a turning post and a return to the starting point — seems to symbolize the waxing and waning of moon, year, human life itself. **[6217]**

MAYER, R. "Horace's *Epistles* I and Philosophy." *AJPh* 107(1986), 55-73. H seems to have been searching for the good life apart from any philosophical school. **[6218]**

McKIM, R. "Myth against Philosophy in Ovid's Account of Creation." *CJ* 80(1984-85), 97-108. O's vague knowledge of philosophical cosmogonies comes from Stoics, Lucretius. Elevation of myth over reason is essential to impact of *Metamorphoses*. **[6219]**

MULGAN, R. G. "Was Caesar an Epicurean?" *CW* 72(1979), 337-339. A passage in Sallust, which is often taken as evidence for Caesar's Epicurean views, may represent no more than Sallust's recording of philosophical commonplaces of the day. **[6220]**

OLIVER, J. H. "The Diadoche at Athens under the Humanistic Emperors." *AJPh* 98(1977), 160-178. After hardships of Roman civil wars (first century B. C.), an orderly succession of leaders of philosophical schools was re-established under patronage of Roman emperors. **[6221]**

PELLING, C. "Plutarch: Roman Heroes and Greek Culture," in #6199, pp. 199-232. To understand P's intentions in the *Lives* one must distinguish between study of character and of personality. "Character" is more closely related to placing a person in a category; "personality" is what makes him unique. P concentrates on character and when he discusses Hellenic culture in a hero's life, connects it with character, not personality. **[6222]**

RAWSON, E. *Intellectual Life in the Late Roman Republic*. Baltimore: Johns Hopkins Univ. Pr., 1985. Survey, looking especially at Greek influences, with attention given to such fields as rhetoric, medicine, law, theology, and philosophy. **[6223]**

———. "Roman Rulers and the Philosophic Adviser," in #6199, pp. 233-257. Though Greek writers claim that Roman rulers as far back as Numa studied philosophy or were advised by philosophers, Roman sources show little appreciation for such a position. Romans expected their leaders to be generally well educated. **[6224]**

SEDLEY, D. "Philosophical Allegiance in the Greco-Roman World," in #6199, pp. 97-119. In Hellenistic and Roman eras allegiance in philosophical schools was directed to authority of founder figure, rather than to a body of doctrine. Philodemus exemplifies this approach. Seneca is an exception. **[6225]**

SIGSBEE, D. L. "The *Paradoxa Stoicorum* in Varro's *Menippeans*." *CPh* 71(1976), 244-248. Varro's fragments contain five references or allusions to Stoic paradoxes. Lack of context makes it difficult to judge whether his treatment was hostile. **[6226]**

THORNTON, A. H. F. "A Roman View of the Universe in the First Century B. C." *Prud* 1(1969), 2-13. Varro, Cicero, and Virgil illustrate blending of monotheism and polytheism which characterized Roman religious philosophy at this time. **[6227]**

VAN GEYTENBEEK, A. C. *Musonius Rufus and Greek Diatribe*, transl. B. L. Hijmans,

Jr. Assen, Nether.: van Gorcum, 1965. Little of his work survives, and that mediocre, but M was highly esteemed in antiquity. He seems to have had some originality and insight in treatises on obedience, equality of sexes, other ethical matters.   **[6228]**

VERSTRAETE, B. C. "The Implication of the Epicurean and Lucretian Theory of Dreams for *Falsa Insomnia* in *Aeneid* 6.896." *CW* 74(1980), 7-10. Aeneas is not a "false dream," as he might seem if passage is taken too literally. He is "false" inasmuch as all dreams are false in Epicurean thought, which influenced Virgil considerably.   **[6229]**

For related items see #888, #6008.

CICERO (106-43 B. C.)

Perhaps Rome's greatest orator, Marcus Tullius Cicero was not esteemed by his contemporaries as a philosopher. Not until a century and a half after his death would he be styled a "rival of Plato." His philosophical works, in fact, were composed in a flurry of activity in the last few years of his life, during a period of "retirement" forced on him by Julius Caesar, whom C had opposed politically for years. In the introduction to one of his dialogues, *De natura deorum (On the Nature of the Gods)*, C dealt with the complaints about "the large number of books that I have produced within a short space of time." His devotion to philosophy is no new thing, he claims.

> From my earliest youth I have devoted no small amount of time and energy to it, and I pursued it most keenly at the very periods when I least appeared to be doing so . . . . If again anyone asks what motive has induced me so late in the day to commit these precepts to writing, there is nothing that I can explain more easily. I was languishing in idle retirement, and the state of public affairs was such that an autocratic form of government had become inevitable. In these circumstances, in the first place I thought that to expound philosophy to my fellow-countrymen was actually my duty in the interests of the commonwealth, since in my judgment it would greatly contribute to the honor and glory of the state to have thoughts so important and so lofty enshrined in Latin literature also.

Though he came to philosophical writing late in life, C's assertion of lifelong interest in the subject does appear to have some validity. As a young man he had the opportunity to study under the leading representatives of the three major Hellenistic schools. Philo of Larissa, head of the Academy, Phaedrus the Epicurean, and the Stoic Diodotus all spent time in Rome during the 80's B. C. to escape the turmoil of the wars in the east between Rome and Mithridates of Pontus. Nor were these casual contacts. Diodotus lived as a guest in C's home until his death.

At the age of twenty-seven C withdrew from public life for two years and spent time in Athens, hearing Phaedrus again and also Philo's successor Antiochus of Ascalon, who (as noted in Chapter 15) moved the Academy from Skepticism to Eclecticism. During this "sabbatical" C also lived in Rhodes, where he studied with Posidonius, the leading Stoic after Diodotus' death.

Allusions and quotations scattered throughout his letters and speeches illustrate the influence that this philosophical study had on C. And he did not hesitate to claim that "in my public and private conduct alike I have practiced the precepts taught by reason and by theory." In his dialogues he attempted to pass on — to an audience which viewed Greek philosophy somewhat negatively — the views of the most important Greek schools on subjects such as the nature of the state, the laws, friendship, old age, fate, and the nature of the gods. Stoicism receives fair if not sympathetic treatment in his hands. Posidonius' teaching is evident in some of his works, especially *De officiis*. It is debatable how well he understood Epicureanism, but his opposition to it is unmistakable. His bias is always for the Academic position, which he set forth in his *Academica*. His defense of that position can be summed up briefly in his own words: "Our position is not that we hold that nothing is true, but that we assert that all true sensations are associated with false ones so closely resembling them that they contain no infallible mark to guide our judgment and assent." (*De nat. deor.* I.12) This accurately reflects the movement of the Academy away from Skepticism which had occured in C's lifetime.

C's contribution to philosophy is not a profound one, but appreciation of him has risen in the last generation or so. One scholar speaks of his "service to philosophy" while another credits him with some originality, at least of purpose. He may have been more successful than generally recognized in helping to create an ethic for a tumultous time.

ANNAS, J. "Cicero on Stoic Moral Philosophy and Private Property," in #6199, pp. 151-173. In *De Officiis* 1 and 2, C is not setting forth his own view of conflict between private property and moral obligation but showing how a Stoic ought to resolve it. He misinterprets earlier Stoics writing on the subject.   [6230]

ARDLEY, G. W. R. "Cotta and the Theologians." *Prud* 5(1973), 33-50. Cotta in *De nat deor* is not a skeptic but believes one can know only what God is not. He objects to philosophy taking place of religion.   [6231]

———. "Cicero on Philosophy and History." *Prud* 1(1969), 28-41. C's efforts to amalgamate two disciplines had been anticipated by Aristotle in works unknown to C.   [6232]

ARMLEDER, P J. "Cicero, Pioneer Philosopher of History." *CB* 41(1965), 76-80. C views history through philosophical lenses. States, like souls, function best when reason rules. One reasonable man should rule the state paternalistically. His primary duty is to constantly examine and improve himself.   [6233]

BARLOW, J. J. "The Education of Statesmen in Cicero's *De Republica*." *Polity* 19(1987), 353-374. By C's day philosophy had abandoned ethics and politics and returned largely to physics (nature). In the *De Rep* Scipio sets out to re-establish a philosophical basis for the study of law and politics.   [6234]

BARNES, J. "Cicero's *De fato* and a Greek Source," in *Histoire et structure. A la mémoire de Victor Goldschmidt*, ed. J. Brunschwig et al. (Paris: Vrin, 1985), pp. 229-239.

C is translating Chrysippus in at least one section. In general he deserves more credit for being an independent thinker, though writing for popular consumption.   **[6235]**

BENARDETE, S. "Cicero's *De Legibus* I: Its Plan and Intention." *AJPh* 108(1987), 295-309. On the basis of a passage in Plato's *Laws*, C tries to relate law as "right reason" to law as "civil law."   **[6236]**

BUCKLEY, M. J. "Philosophic Method in Cicero." *JHPh* 8(1970), 145-154. C combines methods of New Academy and Peripatetics (antitheses with debate) in method with overtones of rhetoric. Testing theories in debate leads at least to probability.   **[6237]**

CARTER, J. M. "Cicero: Politics and Philosophy," in #6272, pp. 15-36. C's actions during last few years of his life contrast noticeably with philosophical tenets of *humanitas* which he expounds in treatises written during that period. Roman philosophical theories had little impact on daily life.   **[6238]**

CASTNER, C. J. "Difficulties in Identifying Roman Epicureans. Orata in Cicero *De fin.* 2.22,70." *CJ* 81(1986), 138-147. C's description of C. Sergius Orata as Epicurean is inaccurate, since C's purpose was to refute Epicureanism.   **[6239]**

CHROUST, A. H. "Some Comments on Cicero, *De natura deorum* II,15,42-16,44. A Fragment of Aristotle's *On Philosophy*." *CF* 29(1975), 103-113. Only a portion of this section is Aristotelian. Rest was written by C or an earlier Stoic author.   **[6240]**

————. "Some Comments to Cicero, *De natura deorum* II 37, 95-96. A Fragment of Aristotle's *On Philosophy*." *Emerita* 43(1975), 197-205. This discussion of the order and beauty of the cosmos as evidence for God's existence is drawn from A's lost work. It is used by several other writers as well.   **[6241]**

————. cf. #3567.

CLARK, M. E., and **RUEBEL, J. S.** "Philosophy and Rhetoric in Cicero's *Pro Milone*." *RhM* 128(1985), 57-72. In the published version of the speech C uses charged terms such as *tyrannis* to justify violence against citizens.   **[6242]**

COPLEY, F. O., transl. *Cicero*: On Old Age *and* On Friendship. Ann Arbor: Univ. of MI Pr., 1967. Two important philosophical works, transl. with introduction.   **[6243]**

DAVIES, C. "Cicero." *HT* 21(1971), 99-106. Survey of his life with some attention to importance of his philosophical works.   **[6244]**

DAVIES, J. C. "The Originality of Cicero's Philosophical Works." *Latomus* 30(1971), 105-119. C's philosophical works served three purposes: moral guide to young people; creation of new literary genre; presentation of coherent political message.   **[6245]**

DENYER, N. "The Case against Divination: An Examination of Cicero's *De divinatione*." *PCPhS* 31(1985), 1-10. C's arguments against divination cannot defeat Stoic rationale, which does not claim to be scientific.   **[6246]**

DiLORENZO, R. "The Critique of Socrates in Cicero's *De Oratore*: *Ornatus* and the Nature of Wisdom." *Ph&Rh* 11(1978), 247-261. Ideal orator embodies wisdom and or-

nate style of speaking. C uses an idealized Licinius Crassus much as Plato used
Socrates.
[6247]

DOUGLAS, A. E. "Cicero the Philosopher," in *Cicero* ed. T. A. Dorey (London:
Routledge & Kegan Paul, 1965), pp. 135-170. Examines C's method, themes of his
works. He is more interested in moral upbuilding of society than were Hellenistic Greek
philosophers. This tendency made his work popular until nineteenth century. [6248]

DYCK, A. R. "Notes on Composition, Text and Sources of Cicero's *De officiis.*" *Hermes*
112(1984), 215-227. Posidonius was a major source for the work. [6249]

FANTHAM, E. "*Aequabilitas* in Cicero's Political Theory and the Greek Tradition of
Proportional Justice." *CQ* 23(1973), 285-290. *Aequitas* means political equality of upper
and lower classes. C, drawing from Plato, conceived of *aequabilitas* as higher concept
of innate fairness.
[6250]

————. "Ciceronian *conciliare* and Aristotelian Ethos." *Phoenix* 27(1973), 262-275.
Discusses C's efforts — largely unsuccessful — to translate Aristotelian concepts into
Latin; implications of various words he used. [6251]

FORTENBAUGH, W. W., and **STEINMETZ, P.,** eds. *Cicero's Knowledge of the
Peripatos.* New Brunswick, NJ: Transaction Bks, 1989. Relevant essays in English are
abstracted herein.
[6252]

FREDE, D. "Constitution and Citizenship: Peripatetic Influence on Cicero's Political
Conceptions in the *De re publica,*" in #6252, pp. 77-100. Theophrastus seems to have
been C's source for idea of mixed constitution. [6253]

FURLEY, D. J. "Aristotelian Material in Cicero's *De natura deorum,*" in #6252, pp. 201-
219. Dialogue contains direct reference to Ar and also allusions to his views on cosmology, elements, and gods. C seems to have know Ar's lost *On Philosophy.* [6254]

GILL, C. "Personhood and Personality: The Four-*Personae* Theory in Cicero, *De
Officiis* I." *OSAP* 6(1988), 169-199. C borrows heavily from Panaetius for his discussion
of what is appropriate behavior. But he also demonstrates interest in preservation and
enhancement of personal individuality.
[6255]

GLUCKER, J. "Cicero's Philosophical Affiliations," in #5589, pp. 34-69. In the 50's B.
C. Cicero rejected Skepticism in his philosophical writings, perhaps from optimism over
Rome's political situation. By the mid-40's, however, he had returned to Skepticism,
except in religious matters.
[6256]

HATHAWAY, R. F. "Cicero, *De re republica* II, and his Socratic View of History." *JHI*
29(1968), 3-12. Inconsistency in C's treatment of history in the dialogue results from the
fact that his true model is Socrates, not Stoic philosophy. [6257]

HECK, V. C., and **REECE, B. R.** "A Statistical Study of the Philosophical Vocabulary
of Cicero." *Furman University Bulletin* 12 #3(1965), 12-30. Of more interest to statis-
ticians than philosophers.
[6258]

HEIBAGES, U. "Cicero, a Hypocrite in Religion?" *AJPh* 90(1969), 304-312. The skep-

ticism displayed in C's philosophical works is not necessarily at variance with his support
of state religion in his orations.   **[6259]**

HOLLIS, M. "Reasons of Honour." *PAS* 87(1986-87), 1-19. Discussion of C's example
of man whose decision to kill himself was not irrational solely because it was based on
his sense of duty.   **[6260]**

HOWES, J. R. "Cicero's Moral Philosophy in the *De Finibus*," in #6272, pp. 37-59. Although C occasionally exaggerates or misses an opponent's point, his moral philosophy
has some original facets which merit further study.   **[6261]**

HUBY, P. M. "Cicero's *Topics* and its Peripatetic Sources," in #6252, pp. 61-76. C's
Topics seems to be derived from some Peripatetic source other than Aristotle's work by
that title.   **[6262]**

———. "An Epicurean Argument in Cicero, *De fato* XVII,40." *Phron* 15(1970), 83-85.
The *assensio* argument which Chrysippus criticizes probably originated with Epicurus.
It does not go back farther than Zeno.   **[6263]**

JOCELYN, H. D. "Greek Poetry in Cicero's Prose Writings." *YCS* 23(1973), 61-111.
Quotations from Greek poetry are more frequent in C's philosophical writings than in
other genres, especially where he is following Academic sources, as in *De off, De fin, De
nat deor,* and *De div.* Quotations probably appeared in his sources.   **[6264]**

KANY-TURPIN, J., and **PELLEGRIN, P.** "Cicero and the Aristotelian Theory of
Divination by Dreams," in #6252, pp. 220-245. C uses only one facet of Ar's theory of
divination and he has reinterpreted it to a considerable degree. C disagrees with Ar that
there is a connection between world of dreams and reality.   **[6265]**

KERFERD, G. B. "Cicero and Stoic Ethics," in #6272, pp. 60-74. Stoics maintained that
intention of an action mattered more than its content. C reports their view accurately
and maintains that to *attempt* to live in accordance with nature and reason is same as
living in that fashion.   **[6266]**

KLEYWEGT, A. J. "Fate, Free Will, and the Text of Cicero." *Mnem* 26(1973), 342-349.
Chrysippus sees destiny as equal to causality, not necessity. C, in *De fato*, uses different
terminology and methodology but reaches same conclusion.   **[6267]**

KWAPISZEWSKI, J. "Roman Philosophers in the Philosophical Works of Cicero."
SPhP 1(1973), 65-75. In C's works appear philosophers from all major schools of the
time: Eclectics, Stoics, and Epicureans.   **[6268]**

LONDEY, D. "An Open Question Argument in Cicero." *Apeir* 18(1984), 144-147. In
De fin 2.15 C argues, against Epicurus, that moral integrity is not what is popular or
pleasant. His argument has structure of an Open Question argument.   **[6269]**

LUCK, G. "On Cicero *De fato* 5 and Related Passages." *AJPh* 99(1978), 155-158.
Discussion of several terms which C uses as equivalent of Stoic *sympatheia*.   **[6270]**

MANDEL, J. "State Religion and Superstition as Reflected in Cicero's Philosophical
Works." *Euphro* 12(1983-84), 79-110. C rejected superstition and irrationality personally

but approved of them as a magistrate.   **[6271]**

MARTYN, J. R. C. *Cicero and Virgil: Studies in Honour of Harold Hunt.* Amsterdam: Hakkert, 1972. Essays with philosophical themes are abstracted herein.   **[6272]**

MASLOWSKI, T. "The Chronology of Cicero's Anti-Epicureanism." *Eos* 62(1974), 55-78. C's opposition to Epicureanism was strongest when he was politically active. In later works, possibly after reading Lucretius, he became largely indifferent.   **[6273]**

———. "Cicero, Philodemus, Lucretius." *Eos* 66(1978), 215-226. Italian Epicureans, led by P, seem to have disdained didactic poetry and to have allowed for political activity. C is rather tolerant of them, despite his antipathy to Epicurean philosophy. L fits the more traditional Epicurean mold and C attacks him without ever naming him.   **[6274]**

MEADOR, P. "Rhetoric and Humanism in Cicero." *Ph&Rh* 3(1970), 1-12. Committed philosophically to justice, C sees rhetoric as way to attain this ideal in society.   **[6275]**

———. "Skeptic Theory of Perception. A Philosophical Antecedent to Ciceronian Probability." *QJS* 54(1968), 340-351. C derives his theory from Philo of Larissa and Pyrrhonism. He does not think we can perceive reality. Our actions must be based on clearest image we can perceive.   **[6276]**

MITCHELL, T. N. "Cicero on the Moral Crisis of the Late Republic." *Hermathena* 136(1984), 21-41. C's solution to Rome's problems, appearing in his philosophical treatises, stressed education and *humanitas*, to overcome corrupt politicians who were dragging the Republic down.   **[6277]**

NICGORSKI, W. "Cicero's Paradoxes and His Idea of Utility." *PolTheo* 12(1984), 557-578. Inconsistencies in his political and philosophical pronouncements lead to questions about C's intellectual integrity. Paradoxes are resolved by noting Socratic basis of his thought and stress on principle of utility.   **[6278]**

PLEZIA, M. "The First of Cicero's Philosophical Essays," in *Ciceroniana. Hommages à K. Kumaniecki*, ed. A. Michel and R. Verdiere (Leiden: Brill, 1975), pp. 196-205. First letter in collection to brother is actually discussion of art of governance.   **[6279]**

RAWSON, E. "The Consolations of Philosophy," in *Cicero: A Portrait* (London: Allen Lane, 1975), pp. 230-248. Examines themes of C's philosophical works and the stage of life at which he wrote most of them.   **[6280]**

———. "The Interpretation of Cicero's *De Legibus*." *ANRW* I,4,334-356. Discusses problems of work's date and purpose. Main influence is Stoic, but no one author can be cited as a source. Pythagorean/Platonic ideas are clear in some passages.   **[6281]**

ROWLAND, R. J. "A Survey of Selected Ciceronian Bibliography, 1953-1965." *CW* 60(1966), 51-65, 101-115. Annotated essay.   **[6282]**

———. "A Survey of Selected Ciceronian Bibliography (1965-1974)." *CW* 71(1978), 289-327. Annotated essay.   **[6283]**

RUNIA, D. T. "Aristotle and Theophrastus Conjoined in the Writings of Cicero," in

#6252, pp. 23-38. C connects these two because of his own interest in successions of philosophical schools and to use them as a model in his own effort to inform a Roman audience about history of philosophy. He always makes T the less important. **[6284]**

SCHMIDT, P. L. "Cicero's Place in Roman Philosophy: A Study of His Prefaces." *CJ* 74(1978), 115-127. C's efforts to develop secular ethic in age when morality was breaking down were philosophically based. Seems to have been more successful in communicating his ideas to his generation than generally recognized. **[6285]**

SHARPLES, R. W. "Plato's *Phaedrus*-Argument for Immortality and Cicero's *Somnium Scipionis*." *LCM* 10(1985), 66-67. C twice quotes P's argument for immortality of soul in *Phaedrus* 245c. For both of them the point of the argument seems to be that soul's status as self-moving *arche* renders debate over its immortality absurd. **[6286]**

SMETHURST, S. E. "Cicero's Rhetorical and Philosophical Works. A Bibliographic Survey." *CW* 51(1957), 1-4, 24, 32-41. Annotated. **[6287]**

———. "Cicero's Rhetorical and Philosophical Works, 1957-1963." *CW* 58(1964-1965), 36-45. Annotated bibliography. **[6288]**

———. "Cicero's Rhetorical and Philosophical Works, 1964-1967." *CW* 61(1967), 125-133. Annotated bibliography. **[6289]**

SWEENEY, R. D. "*Sacra* in the Philosophical Works of Cicero." *Orpheus* 12(1965), 99-131. C sees religion as one element in the civic order. In the ideal republic, religious laws rank higher than civil. **[6290]**

TANNER, R. G. "Cicero on Conscience and Morality," in #6272, pp. 87-112. C defines conscience as right reasoning, expressed in decisions made without bias, with regard to others. Wise man must seek greatest good for the most fellow-citizens. **[6291]**

WALLACH, B. P. "Cicero's *Pro Archia* and the *Topics*." *RhM* 132(1989), 313-331. Examines C's treatment of rhetorical *topoi* and Aristotle's influence on him. **[6292]**

WELLMAN, R. R. "An Argument in *De Officiis*." *CJ* 60(1964-65), 271-272. At end of Book 1 C maintains that social obligations, derived from wisdom, rank as highly as purely philosophical duties. **[6293]**

For related items see #2076, #5658, #5853, #5876, #5992, #6646.

Chapter 20

MIDDLE PLATONISM
NEOPLATONISM: PLOTINUS, PORPHYRY, IAMBLICHUS, PROCLUS. PHILO OF ALEXANDRIA

SURVEY

All great thinkers eventually attract disciples or students who claim to revere the master and to be studying and passing on his teachings. The next generation begins to wonder what the master meant by a particular word or phrase, and they begin to explain to others the doctrines of their teacher. But, as Socrates cautioned in the *Phaedrus*, words on paper cannot explain the intent of their author. The reader must decide what they mean, and the words cannot protest if the reader misinterprets them. In this way every system of thought finally comes to have only a degree of resemblance to what its creator first propounded. The parables of Jesus become the theology of Paul, Augustine, Aquinas, and Luther. The social reform theories of Karl Marx become Marxism-Leninism or Maoism. Few and fortunate are the teachers who avoid this fate.

Plato did not avoid it. Throughout antiquity we encounter "Platonists." Augustine said he had read some "books of the Platonists." But when we examine what these latter day Platonists taught, it seems so different from Plato's thought that we have come to designate it Neoplatonism (a term coined in the nineteenth century). A transitional form of Platonic thought, which flourished from the first century B. C. to the early second century A. D. is designated Middle Platonism. Some scholars do not insist on a firm delineation between the two. As Andresen says, "we today, in contrast to earlier generations, do not stress so much the distinction between so-called Middle-Platonism and Neo-platonism; we focus rather upon the unity of development." (#6720, p. 399)

For the purposes of this bibliography, we will separate items designated Middle Platonic from Neoplatonic. Our discussion will not attempt to draw any finer distinction between them than to say that Middle Platonism generally lacks the intense religious mysticism of Neoplatonism.

These Platonists — whether Middle or Neo- — had no doubt that they were teaching what Plato had taught. His writings, especially the dialogue called the *Parmenides*, were the basis of their thought. But the Hellenistic world's fascination with mystery religions — which promised their initiates union with a deity and eternal life — had a strong impact on the "mainline" philosophical schools.

The writings of Plotinus, and the interpretations by his pupil Porphyry, form the base of Neoplatonism. The most important tenets, which must be culled from Plotinus' obscure prose, can be outlined as follows:

1. reality is immaterial.
2. what is perceived by the senses refers to a higher level of being.
3. intuitive knowledge is preferred to empirical.
4. the soul is immortal.
5. the universe, on its ultimate (i. e., non-physical) level, is good.
6. the true, the beautiful, and the good are one and the same.

These ideas are not immediately evident in Plato or any other earlier writer. How could Plotinus and his followers justify their interpretation? The answer was allegory, which had long since become a common interpretive tool in the philosophical schools, especially at Alexandria. By the first century A. D. people's sensibilities were refined enough that they found early works like Homer's crude, offensive. But such documents were the foundation of Greek education. How could one bring Homer up to modern standards? Rewriting the text was out of the question. The only answer was to read it in a different way, looking for subtle meanings, for symbolism where Homer had just tried to tell a story.

Applied to other writers, this technique became widespread and was eventually adopted by Christians who found the Old Testament difficult to deal with on a literal level. Those who read Plato allegorically and with the mystery cults in the background, claimed to find in him a kind of philosophical religion which looked to a higher spiritual plane.

Neoplatonism actually blends Platonic and Aristotelian thought. Some scholars suggest it could more accurately be called Neo-Aristotelianism. Plotinus preferred Aristotle's dialectical methods to Plato's but rejected Aristotle's logic and substituted his own categories for Aristotle's. Later Neoplatonists, beginning with Plotinus' own student Porphyry, derived their logic from Aristotle.

The essence of Neoplatonism is difficult to define because it uses terms and concepts alien to the pragmatic, empirical frame of mind which characterizes modern western education. Its general outlook is more comparable to some forms of eastern thought, especially Buddhism, which stress the unimportance of matter and the need to seek union with the divine but cannot actually define this One or Absolute, except to say that it is not like any of the "gods" people have traditionally worshiped.

For the Neoplatonists the One (a term drawn ultimately from Pythagoras and Parmenides) is Plato's transcendent Good and Aristotle's First Principle, only so completely transcendent as to be incomprehensible. It is "nothing because it is everything." To describe it is to put limits on it, so most Neoplatonists favor what is called apophatic speech or the *via negativa*, i. e., putting their statements about the One in the form "the One is not . . . ."

But the One must have some connection with the world. This the Neoplatonists establish by the process of emanation. From the One, like light radiating from the sun, other "beings," called *hypostases*, come to exist. This is not a creative process so much as an inevitable result of the nature of the One. By extending itself below its normal level the One becomes Mind (*nous*). By in turn extending itself below its normal level Mind becomes Soul, which is what we perceive as the material world.

The purpose of philosophy, for Neoplatonists, is to work our way back up this scale. Dialectical reasoning allows us to perceive the true nature of reality and to purify ourselves from attachment to the material. The individual's soul turns inward and comes to see itself as essentially *nous*. The ultimate step of enlightenment, however, takes place when the soul sees itself as One, losing its identity as soul or mind. This the Neoplatonists equated with salvation. It resulted from an arduous discipline of philosophical contemplation and happened only rarely. Plotinus claimed to have accomplished it only a few times in his life.

Neoplatonism exercised a profound influence on Christian thought in the third and fourth centuries, a process to be commented on in Chapter 21. It resurfaced in the Renaissance in the Platonic academy established in Florence by Marsilio Ficino and again in the nineteenth century among a group called the Cambridge Neoplatonists. Traces of this school of thought have been delineated in the work of Robert Browning, C. S. Lewis, and J. R. R. Tolkien.

MIDDLE PLATONISM

BERCHMAN, R. M. *From Philo to Origen: Middle Platonism in Transition.* Chico, CA: Scholar's Pr., 1984. Middle Platonism had two tendencies: Antiochus of Ascalon introduced Stoic concepts which blurred distinction between Being and Becoming; Eudorus of Alexandria took a Pythagorean approach; Philo combined the two. **[6294]**

BRENK, F. E. "An Imperial Heritage: The Religious Spirit of Plutarch of Chaironeia." *ANRW* II,36.1,248-349. Looks at P's concept of God, demonology, attitude toward Isis cult, dreams, portents, other topics, all as influenced by Middle Platonism. **[6295]**

———. "A Most Strange Doctrine: *Daimon* in Plutarch." *CJ* 69(1973-74), 1-11. Wide-ranging survey of Plutarch's work shows his concept of *daimon* as higher part of soul, capable of virtue, held truer to Plato's concept than did Neoplatonists. **[6296]**

DEITZ, L. "Bibliographie du Platonisme impérial antérieur à Plotin: 1926-1986." *ANRW* II,36.1,124-182. Extensive bibliography, not annotated. **[6297]**

DE LACY, P. "Plato and the Intellectual Life of the Second Century A. D.," in *Approaches to the Second Sophistic. Papers Presented at the 105th Annual Meeting of the American Philological Association*, ed. G. W. Bowersock (University Pk: PA St. Univ. Pr., 1974), pp. 4-10. Knowledge of P was widespread, while few other philosophers were read, either for content or style. **[6298]**

DILLON, J. *The Middle Platonists: A Study of Platonism, 80 B. C. to A. D. 220.* London: Duckworth, 1977. Discusses ethics, physics, logic of Antiochus of Ascalon, Philo, Plutarch, and several minor figures. Dismantles idea of two schools or groups, Athenian and school of Gaius. Middle Platonism contributes little to philosophical development, primarily reacting against Stoics and preserving Plato's thought. Shows relationship of some Gnostics and other figures of a "Platonic underworld." **[6299]**

———. "Plutarch and Second Century Platonism," in #43, pp. 214-229. For Plutarch

Apollo is the symbol of divinity. His name is taken to mean "not many," i. e., "One." Though a dualist, Plutarch does not entirely negate the physical world. Other Platonists of his era seem to have been more dualistic and pessimistic.   **[6300]**

————. cf. #5458.

DOERRIE, H. *"Formula analogiae*: An Exploration of a Theme in Hellenistic and Imperial Platonism," in #6339, pp. 33-49. Plato thought that analogies from physics allowed one to describe the metaphysical realm. Celsus is last Platonist to uphold this method. Neoplatonist idea of emanation rules it out entirely.   **[6301]**

GERSH, S. *Middle Platonism and Neo-Platonism: The Latin Tradition.* 2 vols. Notre Dame, IN: Univ. of Notre Dame Pr., 1986. Vol. I examines Middle Platonists and Stoics and doxographical matters. Plotinus and other Greek Neoplatonists are considered only to extent that they were sources for Latin writers.   **[6302]**

HELLER, S. "Apuleius, Platonic Dualism, and Eleven." *AJPh* 104(1983), 321-339. Eleven-book structure of *Golden Ass* is neither odd nor accidental. It symbolizes A's Platonism. Ten books stand for the cosmos in Pythagorean symbolism, the one for the One God (to whom Isis in Book 11 leads initiates). Several occurences of groups of eleven in novel underline importance of this number.   **[6303]**

HENRY, P. "Plutarch and Origen on Theology and Language." *StudPatr* 15(1984), 453-457. For P all forms of worship are basically the same. O asserts historicity and uniqueness of Christianity, especially in his later writings.   **[6304]**

HERSHBELL, J. P. "Plutarch's 'De animae procreatione in Timaeo': An Analysis of Structure and Content." *ANRW* II,36.1,234-247. Outlines and summaries of chapters of work reveal how devoted a Platonist P is. He opposes Stoics and Epicureans at many points because of his adherence to Platonism.   **[6305]**

HIJMANS, B. L., Jr. "Apuleius, Philosophus Platonicus." *ANRW* II,36.1,396-475. A was not a professional philosopher/teacher but adopted Plato as a model for his lifestyle and attempted to combat popular ignorance.   **[6306]**

JOHANSON, C. "Was the Magician of Madaura a Logician?" *Apeir* 17(1983), 131-134. Oldest extant Latin treatise on logic, *Peri Hermeneias*, is attributed to Apuleius. Despite rejection of claim by nineteenth-century scholars, attribution should stand.   **[6307]**

JONES, R. M. "The Ideas as the Thoughts of God," in (cf. #6309), pp. 317-326. Concept that Ideas and God are not independent realities probably arose from an Aristotelian reading of certain Platonic texts.   **[6308]**

————. "The Platonism of Plutarch," in *The Platonism of Plutarch and Selected Papers*, ed. L. Taran (New York: Garland, 1980), pp. 1-153. Reprint of Jones's dissertation. Discusses Plutarch's relationship to Academy, views on demonology, creation of world soul, his eschatological myths. Lists parallel passages from the two authors.   **[6309]**

KLEVE, K. "Albinus on God and the One." *SO* 47(1972), 66-69. In *Didascalikos* 10.3 the One is clearly equated with God.   **[6310]**

LONDEY, D., and JOHANSON, C. "Apuleius and the Square of Opposition." *Phron* 29(1984), 165-173. Heuristic diagram known as Square of Opposition first appears in logical treatise attributed to A. Figure's original form can be deduced. Change from Greek to Latin required re-thinking of diagram's substance and shift in focus. **[6311]**

MANSFELD, J. "Compatible Alternatives. Middle Platonist Theology and the Xenophanes Reception," in #5650, pp. 92-117. Middle Platonists often speak of God in terms of paired polar opposites, e. g.: "God is neither large nor small." But they also describe him as unlimited, spherical, and having other positive attributes. These contradictory terms may have originated with Theophrastus' borrowing from Xenophanes. **[6312]**

MORTLEY, R. "Apuleius and Platonic Theology." *AJPh* 93(1972), 584-590. God of Middle Platonists could not be named. This, and not being a Christian in secret, is A's reason for refusal to name his god in *Apol.* 64.8. **[6313]**

PRATT, K. J. "Plutarch's Formal and Animal Psychology," in *Panhellenica: Essays in Ancient History and Historiography in Honor of Truesdell S. Brown*, ed. S. M. Burstein and L. A. Okin (Lawrence, KS: Coronado Pr., 1980), pp. 171-186. P's interest in psychology is stimulated and hampered by his Platonism. He presents strong arguments against Epicurean and Stoic theories of the soul and argues for the reality of the soul and perception in animals. **[6314]**

RUNIA, D. T. "Redrawing the Map of Early Middle Platonism: Some Comments on the Philonic Evidence," in *Hellenica et Judaica. Hommage à Valentin Nikiprowetzky*, ed. A. Caquot (Leuven, Netherlands: Ed. Peters, 1986), pp. 85-104. Attempt to re-evaluate our knowledge of early phases of this movement, for which scant sources are available. Philo does not seem to know the philosophical digression in Plato's seventh letter. The anonymous *Commentary on Theaetetus* is probably earlier than assumed. **[6315]**

SCHNEEWEISS, G. "History and Philosophy in Plutarch," in #48, pp. 376-382. P applies Platonic idealism to historical accounts, looking for moral and educative value, rather than historical truth. **[6316]**

SULLIVAN, M. *Apuleian Logic: The Nature, Sources and Influence of Apuleius' Peri Hermeneias*. Amsterdam: North Holland Publ. Co., 1967. Somewhat technical analysis of the treatise and study of influences on it. **[6317]**

SWAIN, S. "Plutarch: Chance, Providence, and History." *AJPh* 110(1989), 272-302. Study of concepts such as *tyche, daimones*, and God/gods. P's belief in determinism may have come from Stoics such as Posidonius. **[6318]**

TARRANT, H. "Middle Platonism and the *Seventh Epistle*." *Phron* 28(1983), 75-103. Philosophical digression in the letter seems to be a Middle Platonist or Neopythagorean interpolation. **[6319]**

TSEKOURAKIS, D. "Pythagoreanism or Platonism and Ancient Medicine? The Reasons for Vegetarianism in Plutarch's 'Moralia'." *ANRW* II,36.1,366-393. Some of P's arguments for vegetarianism are drawn from Platonic as well as Pythagorean sources. Others come from medical literature or P's own sense of what is human. **[6320]**

WALSH, P. G. "Apuleius and Plutarch," in #6339, pp. 20-32. Both writers wanted to reconcile Platonism with cult of Isis. Plutarch's essay *De Iside* seems a direct source of inspiration for Apuleius, as do his *De curiositate* and several other treatises dealing with themes which also occur in *Golden Ass.*   **[6321]**

WHITTAKER, J. "Platonic Philosophy in the Early Centuries of the Empire." *ANRW* II,36.1,81-123. Challenges two assumptions about development of Middle Platonism: 1) the work known as the *Didaskalikos* was written by Albinus; 2) this document is derived from same source as Apuleius' *De Plat dogm.* Also examines influence of Aristotelian, Stoic, and Neopythagorean thought on Middle Platonism.   **[6322]**

————. "Plutarch, Platonism and Christianity," in #6339, pp. 50-63. Platonism, as formulated by Plutarch, is so close to Christian thought on a number of points that some later Christian writers maintained that Plutarch had read the gospels.   **[6323]**

WITT, R. E. *Albinus and the History of Middle Platonism.* Amsterdam: Hakkert, 1971; rprt. Examines A's *Didaskalikos*, a summary of Plato's teaching highly respected in late antiquity. Considers background of work including developments in Academy under Xenocrates and Antiochus. Thorough analysis of *Didaskalikos* itself.   **[6324]**

YOUNG, M. O. "Did Some Middle Platonists Deny the Immortality of the Soul?" *HThR* 68(1975), 58-60. Interpretation of certain passages in Hippolytus and Origen as evidence for Middle Platonic denial of soul's immortality is incorrect.   **[6325]**

NEOPLATONISM: GENERAL

ANTON, J. P. "Ancient Interpretations of Aristotle's Doctrine of Homonyma." *JHPh* 7(1969), 1-18. Early Neoplatonists misconstrued Ar's meaning of *ousia*; created concept of homonymy (*Cat* 1,1a) picked up by Ammonius, Porphyry, and others.   **[6326]**

ARMSTRONG, A. H. "Dualism Platonic, Gnostic and Christian," in #6530, pp. 29-52. Discusses four possible types of dualism and extent to which each can be discerned in various representatives of these groups.   **[6327]**

————. "Man in the Cosmos: A Study of Some Differences Between Pagan Neoplatonism and Christianity," in #6736, pp. 5-14. Christians and pagans seldom tried to understand each other. When they did, they recognized differences in nature of divinity and God's manifestation in cosmos. Christianity was more anthropocentric.   **[6328]**

————. "The Negative Theology of *Nous* in Later Neoplatonism," in #6335, pp. 31-37. Christian thinkers who adopted Neoplatonist apophatic theology often went on to define God, usually because of need to exclude theological opponents' positions.   **[6329]**

————. "Neoplatonic Valuations of Nature, Body and Intellect. An Attempt to Understand some Ambiguities." *AugStud* 3(1972), 35-59. Neoplatonism was less other-worldly and interested in mundane matters, much like Christianity of late imperial era.   **[6330]**

————. "Platonic Mirrors." *Eranos-Jb* 45(1986), 147-181. Considers Platonic and Neoplatonic views on mimesis and relation between Being and appearances.   **[6331]**

———. cf. #6721.

ATHERTON, J. P. "The Neoplatonic 'One' and the Trinitarian 'ARCHE'," in #6360, pp. 173-185. Neoplatonists were never specific about nature of *arche*, the inaccessible and unknowable which lay at root of their entire system. Christians saw *arche* as manifested in the sensible. Debate has a bearing on identity of the absolute in thought of Schilling and Hegel.   **[6332]**

Atti del Convegno internazionale sul tema: Plotino e il Neoplatonismo in Oriente e in Occidente (Roma, 5-9 Ottobre, 1970). Rome: Acad. naz. dei Lincei, 1974. Twenty-nine essays. Those in English abstracted herein.   **[6333]**

BEIERWALTES, W. "The Love of Beauty and the Love of God," in #43, pp. 293-313. For Plato Beauty is an aspect or manifestation of God. Love of Beauty is thus a step toward love of God. For Plotinus and Proclus this becomes Neoplatonic ascent toward union with the One, a process Christianized by Dionysius the Areopagite.   **[6334]**

BLUME, H., and **MANN, F.,** eds. *Platonismus und Christentum: Festschrift fuer Heinrich Doerrie.* Muenster: Aschendorf, 1983. Relevant essays in English are abstracted herein.   **[6335]**

BLUMENTHAL, H. J. "Neoplatonic Elements in the *De anima* Commentaries." *Phron* 21(1976), 64-87. Most Neoplatonic commentators held that Plato, Aristotle, Plotinus all taught the same thing. This lessens value of their work for modern scholars.   **[6336]**

———. "Some Platonist Readings of Aristotle." *PCPhS* 27(1982), 1-16. Neoplatonists harmonized Platonic and Aristotelian texts, wherever possible, by reading the earlier philosophers as Neoplatonists.   **[6337]**

———. "Some Problems about Body and Soul in Later Pagan Neoplatonism. Do they Follow a Pattern?" in #6335, pp. 75-84. Earlier Neoplatonists thought soul could ascend to the One through philosophical effort. Later Neoplatonists found magic and theurgy necessary aids to the ascent.   **[6338]**

———. and **MARKUS, R. A.,** eds. *Neoplatonism and Early Christian Thought. Essays in Honour of A. H. Armstrong.* London: Variorum, 1981. Abstracted herein.   **[6339]**

BORMANN, K. "The Interpretation of Parmenides by the Neoplatonist Simplicius." *Monist* 62(1979), 30-42. In his commentary on Aristotle's *Physics* S discusses P's thought at length. He takes P to mean that there are two large regions, sensible and non-sensible. Non-sensible is divided into levels of soul, intellectual, and intelligible. Being is identical with the intelligible.   **[6340]**

BRECKENRIDGE, J. "Julian and Athanasius. Two Approaches to Creation and Salvation." *Theology* 76(1973), 73-81. Emperor Julian championed Neoplatonic view of creation of world and search for salvation within creation that was close to heretic Arius' view of Jesus as creature less than God. Bishop Athanasius opposed both, finding Arianism a more subtle foe.   **[6341]**

CORRIGAN, K. "Amelius, Plotinus and Porphyry on Being, Intellect and the One. A Reappraisal." *ANRW* II,36.2,975-993. The three writers do not agree in details but for all three "soul and the physical universe are contained from within by the power of Intellect which is grounded in the pure identity of the One." **[6342]**

COULTER, J. A. *The Literary Microcosm. Theories of Interpretation of the Later Neoplatonists.* Leiden: Brill, 1976. Proclus' commentaries on *Timaeus* and *Parmenides* and his discussion of Plato's comments on Homer in *Republic* are primary texts for study of Neoplatonists' allegorizing interpretation of literature. They were concerned with unity and coherence within a work and with its several levels of meaning. **[6343]**

DE VOGEL, C. J. *"Aeterna Veritas*: Present-Day Problems Concerning Neoplatonism and Christianity," in #1338, pp. 128-155. Attitudes toward created world/cosmos were biggest difference between Christians and Neoplatonists. Plotinus' three-fold concept of God is not analogous to trinity. **[6344]**

DILLON, J. "The Concept of Two Intellects: A Footnote to the History of Platonism." *Phron* 18(1973), 176-185. Several passages in later Platonists suggest a doctrine of two intellects, one governing the noetic world, the other the sensible world. Two horses of the soul in *Phaedrus* are interpreted in this way by Iamblichus and Proclus. **[6345]**

———. "Self-Definition in Later Platonism," in #5639, III, pp. 60-75. In spite of internal conflicts between Skeptical (Academic) Platonists and the "Old Academy" of Antiochus of Ascalon, Platonism retained its identity, without any central leader or authority to define an orthodox position. **[6346]**

DOMBROWSKI, D. A. *"Lumen est Umbra Dei, Deus est Lumen Luminis."* *CB* 60(1984), 18-19. H. D. Thoreau cites this quotation from Sir Walter Raleigh and connects it to Plato's myth of the sun, which was taken by Neoplatonists to mean knowledge of what is good is impossible without the Good, but the Good itself is unknowable. **[6347]**

FINDLAY, J. N. "The Logical Peculiarities of Neoplatonism," in #6359, pp. 1-10. Neoplatonist logic fits generally into Plato's scheme, but Plotinus carried some aspects much further by emphasizing the *"unbroken continuity* of the eidetic system." **[6348]**

———. "The Neoplatonism of Plato," in #6360, pp. 23-40. Plotinus' philosophy is logical extension and fulfilment, not distortion, of Plato's, liberating Plato's ontology from its Socratic shell. **[6349]**

———. "The Three Hypostases of Platonism." *RMeta* 28(1974-75), 660-680. Ammonius should be credited with doctrine of three hypostases. Plotinus wrote about it but *Enneads* show little development. Hypostases are a series of principles emerging from one another by necessity, not desire or need. Development of doctrine was in part an effort to reconcile Platonic and Aristotelian ideas. **[6350]**

FOWDEN, G. "The Platonist Philosopher and his Circle in Late Antiquity." *Phil*(Athens) 7(1977), 359-383. Philosophical circles of third and fourth centuries A. D. differ from classical schools in religious character of their teaching and reverence accorded Plato. **[6351]**

FRANK, R. M. "The Neoplatonism of Gahm ibn Safwan." *Museon* 78(1965), 395-424. Connection is based on Plotinus' work. **[6352]**

GOTTSCHALK, H. B. "Boethus' Psychology and the Neoplatonists." *Phron* 31(1986), 243-257. Fragmentary work by Porphyry was directed against Boethus, Peripatetic philosopher of late first century B. C. **[6353]**

HACKER, P. "*Cit* and *Nous*," in #6358, pp. 161-180. Both terms can be translated "spirit." Though no historical influence of one culture on the other can be established, both seem to point in different ways to same concepts. **[6354]**

HADOT, P. "Neoplatonist Spirituality, I: Plotinus and Porphyry," in #43, pp. 230-249. For Plotinus and Porphyry the philosopher must constantly separate himself from the world and strive for union with God. When that experience comes, however, it is gratuitous and unexpected. **[6355]**

HARDRE, J. "Camus' Thoughts on Christian Metaphysics and Neoplatonism." *SPh* 64(1967), 97-108. Study of Camus' dissertation, which examined Plotinus' and Celsus' influence on early Christian philosophy. **[6356]**

HARRIS, R. B. "A Brief Description of Neoplatonism," in #6360, pp. 1-20. Defines the school, identifies its major documents and briefly introduces major Neoplatonists, including medieval and modern. **[6357]**

——., ed. *Neoplatonism and Indian Thought*. Albany: SUNY Pr., 1982. Nineteen essays, only two of which were previously published, comparing and contrasting the two systems of thought. Essays are abstracted herein. **[6358]**

——. ed. *The Structure of Being: A Neoplatonic Approach*. Albany: State Univ. of NY Pr., 1982. Essays, abstracted herein, focusing on logic and methodology. **[6359]**

——. ed. *The Significance of Neoplatonism*. Norfolk, VA: Old Dominion Univ., 1976. Collection of essays; those dealing with ancient period are abstracted herein. **[6360]**

HATHAWAY, R. "The Neoplatonist Interpretation of Plato. Remarks on its Decisive Characteristics." *JHPh* 7(1969), 19-26. Neoplatonism moved far from Platonic thinking because it lost sight of Socratic element, especially *aporia*, in dialogues. **[6361]**

IGAL, J. "The Gnostics and 'the Ancient Philosophy' in Porphyry and Plotinus," in #6339, pp. 138-149. It is not clear whether Porphyry, in his *Life of Plotinus* 16.1-3 intends by the phrase "ancient philosophy" to refer to Greek or Persian thought, or both. Porphyry distinguishes Gnostics from other Christians because they had their own thought, derived from ancient philosophy. **[6362]**

JONES, J. D. "A Non-Entitative Understanding of Be-ing and Unity. Heidegger and Neoplatonism." *Dion* 6(1982), 94-110. For most Neoplatonists, as for Heidegger, Being and Unity are not themselves beings. This approach renders invalid the "what-is-it?" question, the basis for Aristotelian thought and much that comes after him. **[6363]**

JONES, R. M. "Chalcidius and Neo-Platonism," in (cf. #6309), pp. 194-208. In spite of some resemblances between the Christian Chalcidius and Neoplatonism, differences between them are greater. One cannot assume a Neoplatonist commentary or treatise as Chalcidius' source. **[6364]**

KENNEDY, G. A. "Later Greek Philosophy and Rhetoric." *Ph&Rh* 13(1980), 181-197. Survey of rhetorical theory after second century A. D., when an effort was made to combine Platonism and Aristotelianism.   **[6365]**

LAMBERTON, R. *Homer the Theologian: Neoplatonist Allegorical Readings and the Growth of the Epic Tradition.* Berkeley: Univ. of CA Pr., 1986. Neoplatonist interpreters did not tamper with text of Homer but created a method of reading it which became inextricably interwoven with the text. Later generations of readers were conditioned to expect levels of meaning in epic text.   **[6366]**

MANCHESTER, P. "Time, Soul, Number: Late Platonic Light on an Obscurity in Aristotle," in *The Philosophy of Order: Essays on History, Consciousness and Politics,* ed. P. J. Opitz and G. Sebba (Stuttgart, Ger.: Klett-Cotta, 1981), pp. 110-124. Though Aristotle describes time as a kind of number, he seems to suggest that it is imaginary. Neoplatonists elaborate and shed light on his essentially physical concept.   **[6367]**

MEIJERING, E. P. *"En pote hote ouk en ho huios.* A Discussion on Time and Eternity." *VigChr* 28(1974), 161-168. Athanasius' arguments against Arians on eternity of Son are similar to Neoplatonist arguments on eternity of world, especially in Proclus.   **[6368]**

———. cf. #6774.

MILLER, D. L. "Through a Looking-Glass: The World as Enigma." *Eranos-Jb* 45(1986), 394-402. This metaphor illustrates illusionary character of world. It is also used by Christians to explain relationship between world and God. In studying such passages we must recall that glass mirrors were not invented until sixteenth century. Ancients used polished metal or pans of water to see their reflections.   **[6369]**

MORTLEY, R. A. *Ancient Mysticism. Greek and Christian Mysticism and Some Comparison with Buddhism.* North Ryde, Austral.: Macquarie Univ., 1981. Pamphlet (12 pp.) surveying early Greek views of rationality as only means to knowledge. Skeptic and Middle Platonist questioning of reason led to "negative theology," defining God by what he is not. Intellectual ascent of this sort leads to an encounter with a "conceptual blank space," not unlike Buddhist concept of God.   **[6370]**

———. "The Fundamentals of the *Via Negativa*." *AJPh* 103(1982), 429-439. Use of abstraction, often by negating alpha-privative, to express the transcendental.   **[6371]**

———. "Review-Article: Recent Work on Neoplatonism." *Prud* 7(1975), 47-62. Surveys a number of books. Appendix of works on Christianity and Neoplatonism.   **[6372]**

Le neo-platonisme. Colloque de Royaumont, 9-13 juin, 1969. Paris: Centre National de la Recherche Scientifique, 1971. Essays in English are abstracted herein.   **[6373]**

O'MEARA, D. J., ed. *Neoplatonism and Christian Thought.* Albany: SUNY Pr., 1982. Essays pertinent to ancient period are abstracted herein.   **[6374]**

OWENS, J. "The Neoplatonic Leaven in Western Culture," in #50, V, pp. 181-185. Survey of Neoplatonic influences on Augustine, Aquinas, Ficino, et al.   **[6375]**

PEPIN, J. "The Platonic and Christian Ulysses," in #6374, pp. 3-18. Unlike Cynics and

Stoics, who saw Ulysses as moralistic symbol or clever speaker and statesman, Neoplaton-ists viewed him as metaphysical symbol of soul's journey. Christians added specifically Christian features to the interpretation, e. g., his ship as image of church.   **[6376]**

PLASS, P. C. "Timeless Time in Neoplatonism." *ModSch* 55(1977-78), 1-19. Iamblichus introduced concept of transcendent time, which differs from eternity in having serial structure but also containing all moments of ordinary time simultaneously.   **[6377]**

RIST, J. M. "Pseudo-Ammonius and the Soul/Body Problem in Some Platonic Texts of Late Antiquity." *AJPh* 109(1988), 402-415. Neoplatonist efforts to explain how soul was united to body were no more cogent than Plato's. Plotinus did use phrase "without confusion" to describe this mixture. Through works of pseudo-A the phrase came into Christian thought to describe how divine and human were joined in Christ.   **[6378]**

SAFFREY, H. D. "Neoplatonist Spirituality,II: From Iamblichus to Proclus and Damascius," in #43, pp. 250-265. Later Neoplatonists turned philosophy into a kind of daily liturgy. The gods were seen as emanating from the One/Good. To worship the gods was to progress up a ladder toward union with the One.   **[6379]**

SAMBURSKY, S. *The Concept of Place in Late Neoplatonism.* Jerusalem: Israel Academy of Sci. & Human., 1982. Texts from Iamblichus, Proclus, et al.; facing-page transl. Introduction on history of concept of place in ancient philosophy.   **[6380]**

————. "Place and Space in Late Neoplatonism." *StudHist&PhSci* 8(1977), 173-187. Surveys concept of *topos*, which can mean "place" or "space" from Democritus and Aristotle. Neoplatonic theory of space is a synthesis of Stoic, Jewish, and Neopythag-orean concepts. Surveys various Neoplatonist thinkers on this point.   **[6381]**

————. "The Theory of Forms. A Problem and Four Neoplatonic Solutions." *JHPh* 6(1965), 327-340. *Timaeus* 30c-31b claims that there is only one physical world. But some objects (e. g., sun, moon) exist in only one form while others (trees, dogs) have many forms. Analysis of how Proclus, Porphyry, Iamblichus, and Syrianus resolved the problem shows "anticipation of scholastic modes of thought."   **[6382]**

————., and **PINES, S.** *The Concept of Time in Late Neo-Platonism.* Jerusalem: Israel Acad. of Sciences and Humanities, 1971. Selected texts with translation, introductions, notes, focusing on late Neoplatonic idea that static, intelligible time is a real, transcen-dent entity, on which the moving time of our world depends.   **[6383]**

SCHROEDER, F. M. "Ammonius Saccas." *ANRW* II,36.1,493-526. Little can be known of this shadowy teacher of Plotinus apart from details in Porphyry's writings, and their reliability is highly questionable. A was not Origen's teacher.   **[6384]**

SWEENEY, L. "Are Plotinus and Albertus Magnus Neoplatonists?" in #60, pp. 177-202. Much has been made of differences between Plotinus and later Neoplatonists on various points. What defines a Neoplatonist, however, are basic metaphysical assumptions. On those points thinkers from Plotinus to Albertus Magnus are in accord.   **[6385]**

TIGERSTEDT, E. N. *The Decline and Fall of the Neoplatonic Interpretation of Plato: An Outline and Some Observations.* Helsinki: Soc. Scient. Fennica, 1974. Traces history of western attitudes (Augustine to Hegel) toward relationship between P, the Academy, and Neoplatonism. Some have held that P's teachings were accurately passed on, others that we should ignore later interpretations and study only P's works. **[6386]**

TRIPATHI, C. L. "The Influence of Indian Philosophy on Neoplatonism," in #6358, pp. 273-292. Brief sketches of both systems. Indian philosophy appears to have exercised some direct influence on Neoplatonism. **[6387]**

TRIPATHI, R. K. "Advaita Vedanta and Neoplatonism," in #6358, pp. 233-242. Two systems share characteristics of an absolutist, not merely monist, philosophy: the One is infinite, unchangeable, transcendent. Beyond expression, it grounds everything and thus is immanent. It is knowable because one with our real (spiritual) self. **[6388]**

WALLIS, R. T. "Divine Omniscience in Plotinus, Proclus, and Aquinas," in #6339, pp. 223-235. Neither Aquinas nor Neoplatonists could reconcile divine knowledge of world with Aristotle's description of divine perfection. **[6389]**

————. *Neoplatonism.* London: Duckworth, 1972. Survey of development, aims of movement, emphasizing religious aspects. It probably had less Eastern influence than sometimes suggested. Various individuals in school are treated, with some emphasis on Porphyry's and Iamblichus' divergence from Plotinus. Last two chapters survey Athenian Neoplatonists, especially Proclus, and influence of movement on medieval Christian thought, Islamic philosophy, and Renaissance. **[6390]**

————. "Scepticism and Neoplatonism." *ANRW* II,36.2,911-954. Consideration of Skeptics' epistemological critique and its impact on Plotinus' concept of *nous*, the influence of their anti-theological statements on his view that incorporeal beings do not feel/suffer. Lack of Skeptic sources makes study difficult. **[6391]**

WALZER, R. "Lost Neoplatonic Thought in the Arabic Tradition," in #6373, pp. 319-328. Al-Farabi preserves ideas on soul, active intellect, other subjects. **[6392]**

WHITTAKER, J. "*Epekeina Nou kai Ousias.*" *VigChr* 23(1969), 91-104. Later Platonists differed widely on question of whether the ultimate principle (or the One) was *nous* or beyond *nous*. Uncertainty on this issue is already evident in Early Academy. **[6393]**

————. "Philological Comments on the Neoplatonic Notion of Infinity," in #6360, pp. 155-172. Term *apeiron* comes ultimately from Plato's *Parm.*, but the meaning is expanded to mean infinitely small. Ambiguity of term gave considerable range for development of Neoplatonic doctrine. Neoplatonists also stress opposites as characteristic of the One (e. g. "everywhere/nowhere"). **[6394]**

WHITTEMORE, R. C. "Panentheism in Neo-Platonism." *TulStudPh* 15(1966), 47-70. Survey from Plotinus to Proclus, trying to surmount obstacle of Christian readings of Neoplatonism. **[6395]**

WITT, R. "Platonism After Plotinus." *Diot* 4(1976), 87-97. Adaptations of Platonism by Christians and humanists. **[6396]**

YOUNG, F. M. "The Idea of Sacrifice in Neoplatonic and Patristic Texts." *StudPatr* 11(1967), 278-281. Christians and Neoplatonists borrowed their arguments from same sources. **[6397]**

PLOTINUS (205-270 A. D.)

Virtually nothing is known about the birth and early life of P, generally reckoned as the founder of Neoplatonism. According to his pupil and biographer, Porphyry, he would not talk about such things, almost as if he was ashamed of having a physical existence at all. When, in his late twenties, he became interested in philosophy, he could not find a satisfactory teacher in Alexandria until he heard Ammonius Saccas. (This Ammonius may have been a former Christian and may also have been the teacher of Origen of Alexandria.)

After studying with Ammonius for eleven years, P joined a military expedition against Persia, perhaps out of a desire to investigate Eastern philosophy first hand. The expedition, however, did not get beyond the Tigris-Euphrates valley, and there is no evidence that P ever had close acquaintance with Indian or Persian philosophy. Modern scholars differ widely on the question of whether he was influenced by those schools, to what degree, or how the contact might have come about. It has been pointed out that Alexandria had extensive commercial contacts with the East and that Indian or Persian communities may have existed within the city.

Cutting short his military career, P moved to Rome, where he taught for about ten years and became a close friend of the emperor Gallienus and other high officials. Some scholars maintain that he began to write only late in his life. According to Porphyry, however, the treatises vary in quality because they were written at different stages of P's life: "According to the time of writing — early manhood, vigorous prime, worn-out constitution — so the tractates vary in power." Porphyry also tells us (*Life of Plotinus* 8), that P wrote his treatises "as if he was copying from a book," without revising or looking them over. This may account for some inconsistencies. Porphyry arranged the treatises according to subject matter and in groups of nine, hence the title *Enneads*. R. B. Harris admits that "the *Enneads* probably deserves to be called the world's worst written book since Plotinus seems to presume that the reader already has a complete knowledge of his system when he discusses any topic." (#6360, p. 2)

Much of what was said about Neoplatonism in general is derived from P's work, which remained the primary resource for later thinkers in the school. Notice should be taken of P's theory of knowledge, which has been described as a "rather radical development" of Plato's epistemology. Plato thought that only the universals, the Forms, could be known. We cannot really know something, such as individual tree, which changes from day to day. It is only the concept of Tree which we can know. P goes farther than this to say that the knower is not separate from the known, that the process of knowing is a matter of recognizing whatever is like us in the thing we are trying to know.

The goal of P's philosophy was union with God. He claimed to have achieved this mystical triumph himself four times during the last seven years of his life. Porphyry managed it only once, at the age of sixty-eight (*Life* 23). According to Porphyry, P's last words were to describe man's task as "bringing back the god in oneself to the divine in the all." (*Vita Plot.* 2.26)

P "has been receiving considerable attention in the past three decades" (#6385, p. 177), but he is, in the words of another scholar, "a notoriously difficult philosopher."

ALFINO, M. R. "Plotinus and the Possibility of Non-Propositional Thought." *AncPh* 8(1988), 273-284. Reply to #6548. P's model of intellection which explains *nous'* nondiscursive activity leaves no room for propositional thought.   **[6398]**

ANTON, J. P. "Plotinus' Approach to Categorical Theory," in #6360, pp. 83-99. P's different ontology caused him to re-define Aristotle's categories before criticizing them.   **[6399]**

------. "Plotinus' Conception of the Functions of the Artist." *JAAC* 26(1967), 91-101. The source of beauty is the artist's *nous*, which is an emanation from the One. Artistic creation is prompted by awareness (and memory) of nature's beauty. Art, though not as exalted as philosophy, does imply a quest for being.   **[6400]**

------. "Some Logical Aspects of the Concept of Hypostasis in Plotinus." *RMeta* 31(1977), 258-271; also in #6359, pp. 24-33. Reply to J. N. Deck (#6435). The One must be first hypostasis, not a "quasi-hypostasis."   **[6401]**

ARMSTRONG, A. H. "The Apprehension of Divinity in the Self and Cosmos in Plotinus," in #6360, pp. 187-198. Though "apprehension" cannot be defined or explained, it is clear that the process is the same in the self and the cosmos, since individual and cosmos are not separated by any wide gap in Neoplatonic thought.   **[6402]**

------. ""Elements in the Thought of Plotinus at Variance with Classical Intellectualism." *JHS* 93(1973), 13-22. Against Plato and Aristotle, P holds that we do not and cannot notice many things about ourselves and our experiences. His concept of *nous* differs from classical definitions in that he does not see divine intellect as planning things.   **[6403]**

------. "Eternity, Life and Movement in Plotinus' Accounts of *Nous*," in #6373, pp. 67-76. P's accounts of eternal life, in different passages, are inconsistent.   **[6404]**

------. "Form, Individual and Person in Plotinus." *Dion* 1(1977), 49-68. P sees individual as a limited, identifiable part of a universal whole.   **[6405]**

------. *Plotinian and Christian Studies.* London: Variorum, 1979. Twenty-four essays, reprinted from journals.   **[6406]**

------. "Tradition, Reason and Experience in the Thought of Plotinus," in #6333, pp. 171-194. In this context "tradition" is Neoplatonic teaching passed on to P, "reason" is his methodology, and "experience" is religio-mystical aim of his work. Also discussed are soul and its fall, nature of intelligible world, and transcendence of the One. **[6407]**

------, and **RAVINDRA, R.** "The Dimensions of Self. Buddhi in the Bagavad-Gita and Psyche in Plotinus." *RelStud* 15(1979), 327-342. In both systems of thought self moves away from ego to being centered in the One/Krishna. *Buddhi* and *psyche* do not correspond on all levels but are quite similar on highest level.   **[6408]**

ATKINSON, M. *Plotinus: Ennead V.1, On the Three Principal Hypostases.* Oxford: Clarendon Pr., 1983. Translation and commentary.   **[6409]**

BALES, E. F. "A Heideggerian Interpretation of Negative Theology in Plotinus." *Thom*

47(1983), 197-208. It is not accurate to say that P sees the One as pure nothingness or as merely Being. Heidegger's interpretation is closer to mark.   [6410]

——. "Plotinus' Theory of the One," in #6359, pp. 40-50. To describe the One P uses meontological and ontological language in a way that is not merely paradoxical but intrinsically self-contradictory. The One and *Nous* may both be real but their unity cannot be demonstrated by causal language.   [6411]

BARNES, T. D. "The Chronology of Plotinus' Life." *GRBS* 17(1976), 65-70. Difficult to establish precise dates for P because he lived in a chaotic era of Roman history. Recent papyrus finds clear up some confusion about emperors' reigns and establish P's dates as 204/5-270.   [6412]

BAZAN, F. G. "Matter in Plotinus and Samkara," in #6358, pp. 181-207. For both Greek and Indian thinker matter exists only as reflection of the One/Brahman, which is the only true reality.   [6413]

BLUMENTHAL, H. J. "Did Plotinus Believe in Ideas of Individuals?" *Phron* 11(1966), 61-80. P seems to have acknowledged existence of ideas of individuals but did not admit infinity into intelligible world.   [6414]

——. "*Nous* and Soul in Plotinus: Some Problems of Demarcation," in #6333, pp. 203-219. P does not always clearly distinguish soul from *nous*, as in *Enn* 4,3-4.   [6415]

——. "Plotinus' Adaptation of Aristotle's Psychology: Sensation, Imagination and Memory," in #6360, pp. 41-58. P's view of soul's nature is Platonic, but his understanding of its function is Aristotelian, though P criticized Ar's theory of soul.   [6416]

——. "Plotinus' *Ennead* IV,3:20 1 and Its Sources: Alexander, Aristotle and Others." *AGPh* 50(1968), 254-261. P seems to have used *De anima* of Alexander of Aphrodias and works of Aristotle and other Peripatetics.   [6417]

——. "Plotinus in Later Platonism," in #6339, pp. 212-222. Later Neoplatonists were not as mystical and irrational as sometimes presented. Surveys how various Neoplatonists regarded Plotinus.   [6418]

——. "Plotinus in the Light of Twenty Years' Scholarship, 1951-1971." *ANRW* II,36.1,528-570. Bibliography with comments and discussion.   [6419]

——. "Plotinus' Psychology. Aristotle in the Service of Platonism." *IntPhQ* 12(1972), 340-364. P's dualistic, Platonic view of soul takes many facets from Ar.   [6420]

——. *Plotinus' Psychology. His Doctrines of the Embodied Soul.* The Hague: Nijhoff, 1971. Unlike other studies of P's doctrine of soul, this book stresses the human being and his relationship with sensible world. Weakness of P's psychology is his attempt to combine an Aristotelian understanding of functions of soul with a Platonic view of soul-body relationship.   [6421]

——. "Soul, World-Soul and Individual Soul in Plotinus," in #6373, pp. 55-66. Effort to find some coherence in P's doctrine that all souls are one and that the world soul can behave very differently from individual souls.   [6422]

BOOT, P. "Plotinus' *On Providence (Ennead* III,2-3). Three Interpretations." *Mnem* 36(1983), 311-315. New readings of three passages.   **[6423]**

BOS, A. P. "World Views in Collision: Plotinus, Gnostics and Christians," in #6530, pp. 11-28. P represents pure theoretical science, dominant world view since time of Plato and Aristotle. Gnostics considered Neoplatonists superficial interpreters of Plato. P rejected Gnostics as false Platonists. Christians put forward their philosophy as ultimately reasonable.   **[6424]**

BUSSANICH, J. "Plotinus on the Inner Life of the One." *AncPh* 7(1987), 163-189. The One should not be viewed as sterile or inactive. A number of passages in *Enn* suggest that the inner life of the One, incomprehensible to humans, is rich.   **[6425]**

CHATTERJI, P. "Plotinus and Sri Aurobindo: A Comparative Study," in #6358, pp. 257-272. Though separated by sixteen centuries, P and Sri Aurobindo faced similar situations and tried to offer their respective generations a means of salvation from their malaise and despair.   **[6426]**

CORRIGAN, K. "Body's Approach to Soul. An Examination of a Recurrent Theme in the *Enneads*." *Dion* 9(1985), 37-52. Image of an external nature approaching and surrounding core of soul should not be interpreted spatially or metaphorically.   **[6427]**

————. "The Internal Dimensions of the Sensible Objects in the Thought of Plotinus and Aristotle." *Dion* 5(1981), 98-125. P rejects Ar's categories but his analysis of internal dimensions of sensible objects develops from Ar's thought.   **[6428]**

————. "The Irreducible Opposition Between the Platonic and Aristotelian Conceptions of Soul and Body in Some Ancient and Medieval Thinkers." *LThPh* 41(1985), 391-401. Discusses Plotinus' efforts to reconcile the two thinkers.   **[6429]**

————. "Is There More Than One Generation of Matter in the *Enneads*?" *Phron* 31(1986), 167-181. Reply to H. R. Schwyzer (in German), who argues that matter is not generated but is eternal. P distinguishes three stages of generation of matter.   **[6430]**

————. "A Philosophical Precursor to the Theory of Essence and Existence in Thomas Aquinas." *Thom* 48(1984), 219-240. P's distinction between Being and Existence, developed by later Neoplatonists, is basis of Thomas' theory of essence and existence in created immaterial substances.   **[6431]**

————. "Plotinus, *Enneads* 5,4[7],2 and Related Passages. A New Interpretation of the Status of the Intelligible Object." *Hermes* 14(1986), 195-203. Despite some ambiguity, these passages do not seem to teach consciousness of the One or to view the One as mere object of thought.   **[6432]**

————., and **O'CLEIRIGH, P.** "The Course of Plotinian Scholarship from 1971-1986." *ANRW* II,36.1,571-622. Discussion and bibliography.   **[6433]**

COSTELLO, E. B. "Is Plotinus Inconsistent on the Nature of Evil?" *IntPhQ* 7(1967), 483-497. Separating P's ethics from his metaphysics reconciles his teaching about matter. It is good metaphysically and evil only if it becomes object of desire for soul.   **[6434]**

DECK, J. N. *Nature, Contemplation and the One: A Study in the Philosophy of Plotinus.* Univ. of Toronto Pr., 1967. In *Enn.* 3.8 P maintains that Nature produces things by contemplation. In other passages, such as *Enn* 6.4 and 5, he seems to account for the production of the world by the activity of *Nous.* The doctrine of contemplative production, though, surprising, is a synthesizing principle. **[6435]**

——. "The One, or God, is not Properly Hypostasis. A Reply to John P. Anton," in #6359, pp. 34-39. Reply to #6401. Hypostasis is mind; the One is quasi-hypostasis, not hypostasis in the proper sense. **[6436]**

——, and **ARMSTRONG, A. H.** "A Discussion on Individuality and Personality." *Dion* 2(1978), 93-99. Further comments on #6405. **[6437]**

DE VOGEL, C. J. "Plotinus' Image of Man: Its Relationship to Plato as Well as to Later Neoplatonism," in #47, pp. 147-168; revised version in #1338, pp. 213-232. Plotinus' doctrine of the soul entering the body does not accurately reflect Plato's teaching. It is more akin to Aristotle's idea. Later Neoplatonists refined Plotinus' view without ultimately changing it. **[6438]**

——. cf. #1339.

DILLON, J. M. "*Enn.* III,5. Plotinus' Exegesis of the *Symposium* Myth." *Agon* 3(1969), 24-44. P does not seem comfortable with exegetical form he used to analyze the myth. His system of hypostases may have been moving into more elaborate theory. **[6439]**

——. "The Mind of Plotinus." *PBACAPh* 3(1987), 333-358. P's difficulty was to explain operation of *nous* in intelligible world. He may have posited a "quasi-mathematical formula subsisting in the Intellect" which can be projected into matter. **[6440]**

——. "Plotinus, *Enn.* 3.9.1 and Later Views of the Intelligible Word." *TAPhA* 100(1969), 63-70. Analysis of passage shows how later interpretations, e. g., those of Porphyry, Iamblichus, and Proclus, could have been based on P's. **[6441]**

——. "Plotinus, Philo and Origen on the Grades of Virtue," in #6335, pp. 92-105. Plotinus is first to articulate a doctrine of levels of virtue. For him, courage in a true philosopher is different from courage in an ordinary person. Philo and Origen demonstrate earlier steps toward this view. **[6442]**

DOMBROWSKI, D. A. "An Anticipation of Hartshorne: Plotinus on 'Daktylos' and the World-Soul." *HeythJ* 29(1988), 462-467. Examination of P's use of analogy of body parts to explain how individuals are connected to the World-Soul. Among modern philosophers C. Hartshorne is singular in his use of similar language. **[6443]**

——. "Asceticism as Athletic Training in Plotinus." *ANRW* II,36.1,701-712. For P asceticism is not so much self-denial as a kind of training which enables one to achieve moderation in order to reach the One. **[6444]**

EMILSSON, E. K. *Plotinus on Sense-Perception: A Philosophical Study.* Cambridge Univ. Pr., 1988. First two chapters examine P's metaphysics and psychology. In treating sense-perception Emilsson argues that P does not see light as the medium of transmission. Images are passed by *sympatheia* from object to viewer. P is a realist, i. e., he does not believe that one perceives a representation but the external object itself. **[6445]**

EVANGELIOU, C. "The Ontological Basis of Plotinus' Criticism of Aristotle's Theory of Categories," in #6359, pp. 73-82. P rejected Ar's categories because they were concrete and individual, restricted to realm of phenomena. **[6446]**

FERWERDA, R. "Man in Plotinus' Anthropology and Its Influence on the Western World." *Diot* 8(1980), 35-43. Study of P's interest in man as a complete human being and influence of his ideas on later thinkers, from Eckhardt to Jung. **[6447]**

———. "Pity in the Life and Thought of Plotinus," in #6530, pp. 53-72. In some passages of *Enn* P rejects pity as a vice, in line with Plato, Aristotle, Stoics. In others he speaks of it favorably, and Porphyry's biography stresses his kindness to others. P seems to have been prompted to pity (*sympatheia*) by his sense of union with the One. **[6448]**

———. "Plotinus on Sounds. An Interpretation of Plotinus' *Enneads* v,5.5,19-27." *Dion* 6(1982), 43-57. P's analogy between origins of sound and being was not popular in Greek thought. A parallel occurs in ancient Indian literature. **[6449]**

FIELDER, J. H. "*Chorismos* and Emanation in the Philosophy of Plotinus," in #6360, pp. 101-120. Study of P's use of metaphors of growth and development, especially that of emanation of light from a luminous source, derived from Stoic Posidonius. **[6450]**

———. "A Plotinian View of Self-Predication and TMA." *ModSch* 57(1980), 339-348. P accepted notion of self-predication but his view of Copy Theory and participation makes it possible for him to avoid objections of Third Man Argument and maintain theory of Forms. **[6451]**

———. "Plotinus and Self-Predication," in #6359, pp. 83-89. P finds it valid to make statement of the form "Justice is just" as epsilon rather than Pauline predications, terms which are discussed in this essay. Though this approach has difficulties, it is not as absurd as Vlastos and others have claimed. **[6452]**

———. "Plotinus' Copy Theory." *Apeir* 11 #2(1977), 1-11. Likeness can be defined as shared characteristics instead of analogical similarity. **[6453]**

———. "Plotinus' Reply to the Arguments of *Parmenides* 130a-131d." *Apeir* 12 #2(1978), 1-5. P resolves one objection to theory of Forms presented in *Parm* by distinguishing between things insignificant in themselves but part of a valuable whole and things which mirror sensible world's imperfection. The first have Forms; the second don't. **[6454]**

———. "Plotinus' Response to Two Problems of Immateriality." *PACPhA* 52(1978), 98-101. What is immaterial can be two places at once. Only distinction between form and image is objects. Intelligible pattern is shared between form and image. **[6455]**

GORDON, C. "His Name is 'One'." *JNES* 29(1970), 198-199. Near Eastern thought on oneness of God and its relation to concept in Aristotle and Plotinus. **[6456]**

GRAESER, A. *Plotinus and the Stoics: A Preliminary Study.* Leiden: Brill, 1972. Examines Stoic influences on P, especially in concept of sympathy, important in understanding friendship, providence, and influence of stars on human life. **[6457]**

GURTLER, G. M. "Plotinus and Byzantine Aesthetics." *ModSch* 66(1989), 275-284. P's view on perception taking place at the point of the object, not the subject, seems coherent with Plato's views and seems to have influenced Byzantine technique of inverse perspective.   **[6458]**

────. *Plotinus: The Experience of Unity.* New York: Lang, 1988. P's cognitive vocabulary is not inconsistent. Each word used (consciousness, perception, etc.) has three meanings, one a transcendent source. This technique provides experiential and metaphysical unity to his thought.   **[6459]**

────. "Sympathy in Plotinus." *IntPhQ* 24(1984), 395-406. Derived from Stoic sources, concept of sympathy does not seem to fit P's isolationist system, but levels of being within cosmos are related to one another on this basis.   **[6460]**

GUTHRIE, K. S. *Porphyry's* Launching-Points to the Realm of the Mind. *An Introduction to the Neoplatonic Philosophy of Plotinus.* Grand Rapids, MI: Phanes Pr., 1989. Rprt of early twentieth-century transl. with introductory essay by M. Hornum. Porphyry attempted to summarize Plotinus' most important teachings.   **[6461]**

HADOT, P. "Ouranos, Kronos and Zeus in Plotinus' Treatise Against the Gnostics," in #6339, pp. 124-137. Myth of first three gods, so horrifying to Plato, is for P a symbol of progression of Intellect from the One and Soul from Intellect.   **[6462]**

HARRINGTON, K. W. "Plotinus' Allegorical Approach to Platonic Myth in *Ennead* III,5 and Its Antecedents." *Diot* 3(1975), 115-125. The mystic tone of P's vision of love distinguishes his thought from Plato's.   **[6463]**

HATAB, L. J. "Plotinus and the Upanishads," in #6358, pp. 27-43. Comparison of elements of Plotinus' thought with Indian texts, especially on four-fold structure of reality. Similarity need not, however, imply dependence.   **[6464]**

HELLEMAN-ELGERSMA, W. *Soul Sisters. A Commentary on Enneads IV,3(27) 1-8 of Plotinus.* Amsterdam: Rodopi, 1980. Translation and commentary with introductory material on P's life, his concept of the soul and of the soul as sister of the World-soul. Also reviews modern scholarship on P's concept of the soul.   **[6465]**

HENRY, P. "The Oral Teaching of Plotinus." *Dion* 6(1982), 4-12. Discussion of transmission of P's oral criticism (*Enn.* 6.1-3) of Aristotle's *Categories*.   **[6466]**

HUNT, D. P. "Contemplation and Hypostatic Procession in Plotinus." *Apeir* 15(1981), 71-79. The soul does not contemplate a higher pattern before ascending by imitation. Ascent occurs before contemplation and ends at level of intelligence.   **[6467]**

JACKSON, B. D. "Plotinus and the *Parmenides*." *JHPh* 5(1967), 315-327. Studies P's relation to dialogue, especially in terms of argumentation, third hypostasis.   **[6468]**

JEVONS, F. R. "Lumping Plotinus' Thought." *AGPh* 47(1965), 132-140. P is better at synthesis than analysis. He moves toward doctrine of Unity by denying spatial and temporal extensions.   **[6469]**

JONAS, H. "The Soul in Gnosticism and Plotinus," in #6373, pp. 45-53. P's description of soul's escape from intellect avoids dialectic and uses psychological and emotional terms. His language is close to that of Gnostic myth. Study analyzes connection between Plotinus and Gnostics. **[6470]**

JUFRESA, M. "Basilides, a Path to Plotinus." *VigChr* 35(1981), 1-15. The God of the Gnostic Basilides bears a strong resemblance to P's One. **[6471]**

KORDIG, C. R. "The Mathematics of Mysticism. Plotinus and Proclus," in #6359, pp. 114-121. The One must have properties, but not those applicable to finite objects. Logic which describes the One cannot be ordinary. **[6472]**

KOUTRAS, D. N. "The Essence of the Work of Art According to Plotinus." *Diot* 14(1986), 147-153. A work of art is an imitation of an Idea and inspires one who contemplates it to seek union with the One. **[6473]**

LEE, J. S. "The Doctrine of Reception According to the Capacity of the Recipient in *Ennead* VI,4-5." *Dion* 3(1979), 79-97. P's use of doctrine of reception does not run counter to Platonism's assertion that nature of sensible world can be elucidated by comparison to Forms. **[6474]**

———. "Omnipresence and Eidetic Causation in Plotinus," in #6359, pp. 90-103. *Enn.* VI,4-5 are not outside the mainstream of Greek philosophy, as E. Brehier has claimed. Treatises deal with a basic problem of Platonism: description of relationship between intelligible and sensible worlds. Theory of monopsychism helps explain how one sensible world can be equally accessible to all subjects which experience it. **[6475]**

LLOYD, A. C. "Non-Propositional Thought in Plotinus." *Phron* 31(1986), 258-265. Reply to #6548. **[6476]**

———. "Plotinus on the Genesis of Thought and Existence." *OSAP* 5(1987), 155-186. P refers to the beginnings of thought and existence in at least eight of the *Enneads*. Thought arises from the One's contemplation of itself. Existence is not a hypostasis or a category of Being. It seems to develop as an extension of thought. **[6477]**

LOUNIBOS, J. "Plotinus: Pagan, Mystic, Philosopher," in *Pagan and Christian Anxiety. A Response to E. R. Dodds*, ed. R. C. Smith and J. Lounibos (Lanham, MD: Univ. Pr. of Amer., 1984), pp. 131-166. Survey of P's work, emphasizing aspects of it which interested E. R. Dodds, who saw him as a lonely rationalist in an irrational age. **[6478]**

MacKENNA, S., transl. *Plotinus, the Enneads*, transl. and rev. by B. S. Page. London: Faber, 1969. Translation with introductory essay. **[6479]**

MAMO, P. S. "Forms of Individuals in the *Enneads*." *Phron* 14(1969), 77-96. Reply to #6415. Resolves alleged contradictions by noting theory of forms of individuals may refer to Plato's theory of Ideas or to individuals other than humans or animals. **[6480]**

———. "Is Plotinian Mysticism Monistic?" in #6360, pp. 199-215. P's mysticism is not theistic, i. e., insisting on a complete otherness of God and the human soul, but it is not purely monistic either, i. e., claiming complete union of soul and God. **[6481]**

MANCHESTER, P. "Time and the Soul in Plotinus III,7 [45],11." *Dion* 2(1978), 101-

136. While providing evidence for P's doctrine of soul, this passage is also important for his concept of time.   **[6482]**

MARTIN, R. M. "On Logical Structure and the Plotinic Cosmos," in #6359, pp. 11-23. Highly technical discussion of P's logic in terms that bring it into harmony with modern science and mathematics.   **[6483]**

MARTINICH, A. "The Descent of the Soul in the Philosophy of Plotinus." *Kinesis* 3(1970), 34-42. P's explanation, like Heidegger's "falling," is ultimately dualistic. **[6484]**

McCUMBER, J. "Anamnesis as Memory of Intelligibles in Plotinus." *AGPh* 60(1978), 160-167. P limits nature and function of anamnesis. Soul recovers memory of forms as it approaches the intelligible realm.   **[6485]**

McEVILLEY, T. "Plotinus and Vijnanavada Buddhism." *PhE&W* 30(1980), 181-193. P's concept of three hypostases (One, Mind, and Soul) with two forces binding them together and bringing about transitions is similar to some aspects of Buddhist thought. But P is chronologically earlier than Buddhists who espouse similar ideas.   **[6486]**

McGUIRE, J. E., and STRANGE, S. K. "An Annotated Translation of Plotinus' *Ennead* iii 7: *On Eternity and Time*." *AncPh* 8(1988), 251-257. Transl. and commentary on a treatise important for its introduction of idea of eternity as a life spent in a present without time or duration. P's arguments are complex.   **[6487]**

MEREDITH, A. "Emanation in Plotinus and Athanasius." *StudPatr* 16(1985), 319-323. P's doctrine of emanation was an attempt to refute Gnostics. He is very cautious about its metaphors. Athanasius, in combatting Arian doctrine of origin of world, does not use term "emanation" but does use metaphors similar to P's.   **[6488]**

———. cf. #6876.

MICHAELIDES, C. P. "Plotinus and Jaspers: Their Conception and Contemplation of the Supreme One." *Diot* 4(1976), 37-46. Examines similarities based on Neoplatonist traditions, especially notion of unity of all forms of the "encompassing." Our speech about this unity is not irrational but supra-rational.   **[6489]**

MILLER, C. L. "Union with the One: *Ennead* 6,9,8-11." *NewSchoI* 51(1977), 182-195. Discusses images describing mystical union: center of all centers, dancing chorus and leader, beloved. By its nature soul contains what enables it to achieve union.   **[6490]**

MODRAK, D. K. W. "Realism in Rough Water." *Phron* 34(1989), 111-113. Review essay of #6445.   **[6491]**

MORTLEY, R. "Love in Plato and Plotinus." *Antich* 14(1980), 45-52. In *Symp* and *Enn* 5 love is viewed as a lack.   **[6492]**

———. "Negative Theology and Abstraction in Plotinus." *AJPh* 96(1975), 363-377. By describing the One in terms of negations instead of affirmation and predication P avoids problem of multiplicity.   **[6493]**

MOUTSOPOULOS, E. "Dynamic Structuralism in the Plotinian Theory of the Imaginary." *Diot* 4(1976), 11-22. P seems to have been first representative of dynamic structuralist conception of imagination and the imaginary. He holds that phantoms are real. They inspire imagination by substituting images for reality.   **[6494]**

MURAJI, P. *Providence, Destiny and Free Will.* Tokai Univ. Pr., 1974. Compares P's treatises "On Destiny" and "On Providence" to show that Necessity and Destiny are bound up with evil, while Liberty and Providence are connected to Good.   **[6495]**

MYERSCOUGH, A. "The Nature of Man in Plotinus." *StudPh&HistPh* 5(1970), 138-177. Man is midway between the One and formless matter. His essence is his soul, which by accident occupies a body but which is immortal.   **[6496]**

NABI, M. N. "Union with God in Plotinus and Bayazid," in #6358, 227-232. Neither thinker saw union with God as becoming identified with God but as being absorbed in God, the self being annihilated.   **[6497]**

O'BRIEN, D. "J. M. Narbonne on Plotinus and the Generation of Matter: Two Corrections." *Dion* 12(1988), 25-26. Corrects two misinterpretations of O'Brien's thought in an article (in French) by Narbonne.   **[6498]**

――――. "Plotinus and the Gnostics on the Generation of Matter," in #6339, pp. 108-123. Though their views on generation of matter and its evil nature are similar, P maintains that the soul which eternally generates matter also eternally illumines it.   **[6499]**

――――. "Plotinus on Evil: A Study of Matter and the Soul in Plotinus' Conception of Human Evil," in #6373, pp. 113-146. Neither matter nor soul alone is cause of evil. Baseness of matter and weakness of soul must combine to produce evil.   **[6500]**

――――. "Plotinus on Evil." *DR* 87(1969), 68-112. Evil is failure of a thing to achieve its proper nature.   **[6501]**

O'BRIEN, E., transl. *The Essential Plotinus: Representative Treatises from the Enneads.* Indianapolis: Hackett, 1981; rprt. Translation of ten treatises dealing with "The Good or the One," "The Soul," "The Three Primal Hypostases," and other topics essential to understanding Plotinus. Introductory essay and commentary.   **[6502]**

O'DALY, G. J. P. *Plotinus' Philosophy of the Self.* Dublin: Irish Univ. Pr., 1973. Study of development of concept of individual self, a central idea in P. Self is distinct from soul and capable of union with the One.   **[6503]**

――――. "The Presence of the One in Plotinus," in #6333, pp. 159-169. When P speaks of union of self with the One in *Enn.* 4.8,1, it is unclear whether the self is active or passive.   **[6504]**

O'MEARA, D. J. "Being in Numenius and Plotinus. Some Points of Comparison." *Phron* 21(1976), 120-129. Though they differ in many respects, N's account of true Being may have influenced *Enn* VI,4,2 and VI,5,3 and may have prompted P's use of *Parm* in these essays.   **[6505]**

――――. "Gnosticism and the Making of the World in Plotinus," in #6688, pp. 365-378. P's concept of creation of world in a manner excluding Demiurge of Plato's *Tim* seems largely a reaction to Gnostics' overly literal reading of Demiurge passages.   **[6506]**

——. "Plotinus on How Soul Acts on Body," in #1282, pp. 247-262. By using Aristotle's distinction between actuality and change, P resolves the Platonic problem of explaining the relation of soul to body.   **[6507]**

——. "The Problem of Omnipresence in Plotinus *Ennead* VI,4-5. A Reply." *Dion* 4(1980), 61-73. Reply to #6475.   **[6508]**

——. cf. #7025.

PECORINO, P. "Evil as Direction in Plotinus." *PhResArch* 7(1981), no. 1450. Evil does not exist in the metaphysical realm. It results from soul's "misdirected orientation toward its own completeness in matter."   **[6509]**

PHILLIPS, J. F. "*Enneads* V.1.2. Plotinus' Hymn to the World Soul and its Relation to Mystical Knowledge." *SO* 58(1983), 133-146. Hymn reflects rituals of sun worship. Soul is a creative demiurge and divine force immanent in world.   **[6510]**

——. "Stoic 'Common Notions' in Plotinus." *Dion* 11(1987), 33-52. Examination of P's view of common or widely held ideas as innate suggests that some scholars go too far in equating these innate ideas with Stoic "common notions."   **[6511]**

——. "The Universe as Prophet. A Soteriological Formula in Plotinus." *GRBS* 22(1981), 269-281. In reaction to a Gnostic doctrine P claims that universe serves role of prophet, pointing mankind to the One.   **[6512]**

PLASS, P. "Plotinus' Ethical Theory." *ICS* 7(1982), 241-259. Distinction between civic and true virtue. Former is restraint of physical passions; latter is acknowledgement of providence and assimilation of lower to higher self.   **[6513]**

——. "Porphyry, *Life of Plotinus*, 8: On Philosophical Thinking." *IntPhQ* 27(1987), 243-247. Plotinus' ability to recapture a line of philosophical reasoning after an interruption suggests only intense concentration required by philosophical thinking, not Neoplatonic doctrine of two levels of awareness.   **[6514]**

RANDALL, J. H. "The Intelligible Universe of Plotinus." *JHI* 30(1969), 3-16. P's philosophy is more rational than generally recognized.   **[6515]**

REMUS, H. E. "Plotinus and Gnostic Thaumaturgy." *LThPh* 39(1983), 13-20. While criticizing Gnostic ideas in *Enn* 2,9, P seems to recognize continuing tension within his own thought. He wrote not to win over Gnostics but to inform his students.   **[6516]**

RICH, A. N. M. "Body and Soul in the Philosophy of Plotinus," in #41, pp. 620-636. P's thought here is influenced by dualism he found in Plato and by Aristotle's *De anima*. His work displays profound distrust of the body. His effort to explain soul-body relationship rejects Aristotle's account, along with Epicurean and Stoic views. Best explanation of connection is an analogy with air and light. The soul exists separately from the body, before and after it.   **[6517]**

RIST, J. M. "Back to the Mysticism of Plotinus: Some More Specifics." *JHPh* 27(1989),

183-197. Reviews discussions of whether P's mysticism is monistic or theistic. The key to understanding his mysticism is process of ascension to the One through *nous*, which must be translated in a way to stress its beauty.   **[6518]**

――――. *Eros and Psyche: Studies in Plato, Plotinus, and Origen.* Univ. of Toronto Pr., 1967; rprt. Examines love and knowledge in the three authors, showing how Plotinus systematized Plato and how Origen attempted to personalize Plato's concepts.   **[6519]**

――――. "Ideas of Individuals in Plotinus. A Reply to Dr. Blumenthal." *RIPh* 24(1970), 298-303. Reply to #6414. Examination of treatises in chronological order suggests that P did believe in ideas of individuals.   **[6520]**

――――. "Integration and the Undescended Soul in Plotinus." *AJPh* 88(1967), 410-422. It is possible, P believes, for philosopher to understand his own immortality and advance toward union with the One.   **[6521]**

――――. "Metaphysics and Psychology in Plotinus' Treatment of the Soul," in #60, pp. 135-151. It is better for the soul to be capable of sinning than for it not to exist. In his consideration of sin and the soul Plotinus never resolved Plato's difficulty of the difference between the soul of a god and that of a person.   **[6522]**

――――. "Monism: Plotinus and Some Predecessors." *HSCP* 69(1965), 329-344. Survey beginning with Parmenides, focusing on Pythagorean influences on P.   **[6523]**

――――. "The One of Plotinus and the God of Aristotle." *RMeta* 27(1973-74), 75-87. Ar held that person could experience, though briefly, the sort of intellectual existence which God enjoys. P views fundamental activity of the One as something more than just exaggerations of human attributes and powers.   **[6524]**

――――. *Plotinus: The Road to Reality.* Cambridge Univ. Pr., 1967. Discusses life of the sage, the One, its knowledge, the Beautiful and the Good, Logos, Descent of soul, free will, P's originality. P is optimistic about human capacity to know the One.   **[6525]**

――――. "Plotinus and Augustinus on Evil," in #6333, pp. 495-508. Reply to #6500. For P matter is not a sufficient cause of evil.   **[6526]**

――――. "Plotinus and Moral Obligation," in #6360, pp. 217-233. P does not discuss moral obligation explicitly but examines it as part of broader concept of good life and theory of virtue.   **[6527]**

――――. "The Problem of 'Otherness' in the *Enneads*," in #6373, pp. 77-87. P's doctrine of the "otherness" distinguishing one Form from another is not clearly articulated. Motion, arising from lack of the One and desire for it, is key to his definition. **[6528]**

――――. cf. #5519.

RODIER, D. F. T. "The Problem of the Ordered Chaos in Whitehead and Plotinus," in #6360, pp. 301-317. Sympathy unifies the cosmos. It is predictive, uniting each part with the whole, and operative, referring to the mutual relationship of part to part.   **[6529]**

RUNIA, D. T., ed. *Plotinus Amid Gnostics and Christians. Papers Presented at the*

Plotinus Symposium Held at Free University, Amsterdam, on 25 January 1984. Amsterdam: Free Univ. Pr., 1984. Four essays, abstracted herein, on interaction of the three philosophical systems. **[6530]**

SAGET, A. C. "The Limit of Self in Plotinus." *Antich* 19(1985), 96-101. Images, as reflections, derive beauty from their source. Value is in their transparency. **[6531]**

SCHALL, J. V. "Plotinus and Political Philosophy." *Gregor* 66(1985), 687-707. P's political philosophy abandons Aristotle's tenet that man is political by nature. P's emanation theory is applied to politics, which becomes aspect of metaphysics. **[6532]**

SCHIBLI, H. S. "Apprehending Our Happiness: *Antilepsis* and the Middle Soul in Plotinus, *Ennead* I 4.10." *Phron* 34(1989), 205-219. The "middle soul" is ordinary consciousness. Participating in both the intelligible and the sensible, it knows true happiness. It must be guarded against physical and psychic disturbances. **[6533]**

SCHILLER, J. P. "Plotinus and Greek Rationalism." *Apeir* 12(1978), 37-50. P is not entirely mystic. Three hypostases are effort to resolve problems in Plato's epistemology and other areas. **[6534]**

SCHROEDER, F. M. "Conversion and Consciousness in Plotinus, *Enneads* 5,1[10],7." *Hermes* 114(1986), 186-195. Argues that power of the One is subject of a crucial sentence in this passage. The power (*dynamis*) is located in the One, not the *Nous*, as other interpretations have maintained. **[6535]**

————. "Light and the Active Intellect in Alexander and Plotinus." *Hermes* 112(1984), 239-248. A of Aphrodisias and P use light as analogy for relationship of *nous*/Intellect to the One, but their analogies vary as do details of their theories of light. **[6536]**

————. "The Platonic *Parmenides* and Imitation in Plotinus." *Dion* 2(1978), 51-73. Plotinus tries to define form to preclude opposing arguments of *Parm*. True understanding of language of imitation is key to effort. **[6537]**

————. "Representation and Reflection in Plotinus." *Dion* 4(1980), 37-59. Man can comprehend or reflect on the creative source only when the soul is at peace. **[6538]**

————. "Saying and Having in Plotinus." *Dion* 9(1985), 75-84. It is impossible to "have" the One in knowledge, but a relationship is possible by speaking about the One. **[6539]**

————. "Synousia, Synaisthaesis and Synesis: Presence and Dependence in the Plotinian Philosophy of Consciousness." *ANRW* II,36.1,677-699. This vocabulary, borrowed from Plato's *Parm*, links ontological categories to states of consciousness. Human awareness is not immediate. It depends on the presence of a superior source. **[6540]**

SELLS, M. "Apophasis in Plotinus: A Critical Approach." *HThR* 78(1985), 47-65. P refused to make a "thing" of the One. The One is what cannot be spoken of. But even using the term "the One" delimits it to some degree. The infinite regress resulting from *apophasis* may have been one reason Plotinus disliked writing down his doctine and refused to edit/change a treatise once he had composed it in one sitting. **[6541]**

SHARMA, I. C. "The Plotinian One and the Concept of *Paramapurusa* in the *Bhagavad-*

716 PLOTINUS

gita." *OJRelStud* 6(1978), 3-12. Plotinian One and Supreme Being of the Gita are same metaphysically. Approach to them (buddhi yoga or philosophic contemplation) is also essentially the same. [6542]

SIMONS, J. "Matter and Time in Plotinus." *Dion* 9(1985), 53-74. P maintains that matter causes both becoming and evil. Cause of soul's decline is passage of time. Time and matter seem to be manifestations of same principle. [6543]

SINARI, R. "The Concept of Human Estrangement in Plotinism and Samkara Vedanta," in #6358, pp 243-255. For both thinkers man's awareness of separation from One/Brahman leads to quest for transphenomenal being which forms core of his life. [6544]

SINNIGE, T. G. "Gnostic Influences in the Early Works of Plotinus and in Augustine," in #6530, pp. 73-97. Gnostic ideas appear especially in P's writings about the soul and its fate. Concept of emanation is also close to Gnostic views. Some of the more pessimistic aspects of A's thought seem to come from Gnosticism. [6545]

SMITH, A. "Potentiality and the Problem of Plurality in the Intelligible World," in #6339, pp. 99-107. P seems to have had difficulty explaining concept of plurality in unity without recourse to experience. Whether or not one can explain the idea, it can be known through experience. [6546]

———. "Unconsciousness and Quasiconsciousness in Plotinus." *Phron* 23(1978), 292-301. A person can operate on two levels, unaware of, or oblivious to, the lower one, because of presence of soul in the body. Ascent of soul involves being as little aware as possible of external world. [6547]

SORABJI, R. "Myths About Non-Propositional Thought," in #76, pp. 295-314. Examples of non-propositional thought do not occur in Plato and Aristotle but are common in Plotinus. [6548]

STRANGE, S. K. "Plotinus, Porphyry, and the Neoplatonic Interpretation of the 'Categories'." *ANRW* II,36.2,955-974. Plotinus and Porphyry do not differ as much as is usually thought in their attitudes toward Aristotle's theory of categories. [6549]

THESLEFF, H. "Notes on *Unio mystica* in Plotinus." *Arctos* 14(1980), 101-114. P borrows Platonic terminology of love to describe mystic experience, but changes the direction of soul's movement in ecstasy. It is not moving toward a higher sphere, but to the interior. Thus arise some inconsistencies of P's thought. [6550]

WAGNER, M. F. "The Contribution of Plotinian Metaphysics to the Unification of Culture," in #50, V, pp. 192-195. In P's thought the ascent of the soul does not imply separation from earthly life but provides a means by which all persons can be purified, regardless of their cultural context. [6551]

———. "Plotinus' Idealism and the Problem of Matter in *Enneads* vi,4 and 5." *Dion* 10(1986), 57-83. P's account of "recipient capacities" in things is not inconsistent with his Neoplatonic idealism. [6552]

———. "Plotinus' World." *Dion* 6(1982), 13-42. An examination of P's views on perception, imagination, and memory, including his distinction between what is intelligible and what is perceptible. [6553]

——. "Realism and the Foundations of Science in Plotinus." *AncPh* 5(1985), 269-292. For P, sensible world is an "image of being" to extent that certain of its characteristics can be shown to derive from the Forms. Mathematics and dialectic, bases of science, are tools he uses. [6554]

——. "Vertical Causation in Plotinus," in #6359, pp. 51-72. The Forms, and not other bodies, are causes of bodies. Forms determine order of our concepts. [6555]

WALLIS, R. T. "*Nous* as Experience," in #6360, pp. 121-153. Plotinus' intelligible world is grasped empirically, through psychological experiences, which are then elevated to metaphysical realities. [6556]

——. "Plotinus and Paranormal Phenomena," in #42, pp. 495-507. For non-specialists. P did not discount the paranormal, but it could affect only lower soul and body. Philosophers, living in the intelligible realm, could be free of such things. [6557]

——. "Phraseology and Imagery in Plotinus and Indian Thought," in #6358, pp. 101-120. Are similarities in these areas merely parallels or result of cultural contact? Though certainty cannot be achieved, P seems to be the more original thinker, arguing his positions in detail while Indian documents state them dogmatically. [6558]

WARREN, E. W. "Imagination in Plotinus." *CQ* 16(1966), 277-285. Discusses relation of imagination to objects and ideas and functioning of human consciousness. [6559]

——. "Memory in Plotinus." *CQ* 15(1965), 252-260. Examines concepts of conscious and unconscious memory. [6560]

WIJSENBEEK, H. "Man as a Double Being. Some Remarks on Plotinus." *Diot* 13(1985), 172-191. Examines importance of P's recognition of conscious self-awareness, critical for development of concept of free will. [6561]

WOLTERS, A. M. "Igal's Translation of Plotinus." *Dion* 7(1983), 33-42. Review essay of an important Spanish translation with commentary. [6562]

——. "A Survey of Modern Scholarly Opinion on Plotinus and Indian Thought," in #6358, pp. 293-308. Though opinion is divided, P does not seem to have been directly influenced by Indian thought. One should not discount element of genius. [6563]

For related items see #336, #2149, #7002.

PORPHYRY (ca. 232-304 A. D.)

P can be credited with the survival and propagation of Plotinus' works, but also with modifications to his system of thought. He wrote treatises expounding Plotinus' obscurely worded ideas and introduced Aristotelian motifs which gave an entirely different slant to some of Plotinus' main points. He put more emphasis on ethics and daily life than did his teacher. He also introduced the concept of *daimones* into his philosophy. Plotinus had admitted the existence of such beings but denied that they had any influence on human activities. P believed that nature was affected by the unpredictable actions of these bodiless spirits.

His other works include a defense of vegetarianism, and a commentary on Aristotle's *Categories* which was translated into Latin and widely read in the Middle Ages. About 270 A. D. he wrote a book entitled *Against the Christians*. He had studied the Bible more carefully than most pagans of that era, who considered it inferior in style and content to their own religious and philosophical texts. P argued against the divinity of Christ and pointed out inconsistencies in the Biblical accounts, such as the two creation stories in Genesis 1 and 2 and the two variant versions of the Christmas story. He also concluded that the prophecies in the book of Daniel were accurate because the book was written after the fact, ca. 165 B. C. (a position that most modern Biblical critics hold). Some stories claim that he was attacked by Christian gangs after this book was published. The work was condemned by Christian emperors in the early fifth century.

ANASTOS, M. V. "Porphyry's Attack on the Bible," in #80, pp. 421-450. P knew Bible well, though he was over-literal in his interpretation. [6564]

BARNES, T. D. "Porphyry, *Against the Christians*: Date and the Attribution of Fragments." *JThS* 24(1973), 424-442. Work may have been composed early in fourth century rather ca. 270. We cannot be certain that all frags currently attributed to it do in fact come from it. [6565]

BEHR, C. A. "Citations of Porphyry's *Against Aristides* Preserved in Olympiodorus." *AJPh* 89(1968), 186-199. Study of eight passages which seem to be drawn from Porphyry's work. [6566]

DEN BOER, W. "A Pagan Historian and His Enemies. Porphyry, *Against the Christians*." *CPh* 69(1974), 198-208. Using principles of Greek historiography, P attacked chronological problems in Bible and inconsistencies between multiple accounts, e. g., those of the Passion. [6567]

DOMBROWSKI, D. A. "Porphyry and Vegetarianism: A Contemporary Philosophical Approach." *ANRW* II,36.2,774-791. If same rights are to be extended to all sentient beings, vegetarianism becomes a duty. A certain heroism is required of those who adhere to it. [6568]

———. "Vegetarianism and the Argument from Marginal Cases in Porphyry." *JHI* 45(1984), 141-143. On basis of *De Abstinentia* 2.19-20 P was first to advocate vegetarianism on argument from marginal cases. [6569]

EVANGELIOU, C. *Aristotle's* Categories *and Porphyry*. Leiden: Brill, 1988. Study of Porphyry's commentary on Ar's *Cat* and Plotinus' critique of Aristotle's doctrine of categories (*Enn* 6.1-3). Sees Porphyry as trying to reconcile Plato and Aristotle in face of challenges from Christian and Gnostic thought. [6570]

———. "Aristotle's Doctrine of Predicables and Porphyry's *Isagoge*." *JHPh* 23(1985), 15-

34. P did not distort Ar's doctrine of predicables. *Isagoge* is more than mere introduction to Ar's work.   **[6571]**

GRANT, R. M. "Porphyry Among the Early Christians," in #6736, pp. 181-187. Before 268 A. D. P's work was admired by Christians. Only after that year did he begin his criticisms of church.   **[6572]**

MEREDITH, A. "Allegory in Porphyry and Gregory of Nyssa." *StudPatr* 16(1985), 423-427. P, a Platonist, took over the historically Stoic practice of allegory. He gives several possible meanings of a passage, whereas Gregory sticks to one. Both, however, have a similar moral aim.   **[6573]**

———. "Porphyry and Julian against the Christians." *ANRW* II,23.2, 1119-1149. Julian, like Celsus before him, fought Christianity from a pagan philosophical standpoint. P emphasizes inconsistencies of Bible. Julian and P object to Christian god as arbitrary and unpredictable, unlike impersonal, impassive god of Neoplatonism.   **[6574]**

O'MEARA, J. J. "Indian Wisdom and Porphyry's Search for a Universal Way," in #6358, pp. 5-25. P seems to have found Greek philosophy inadequate as means of releasing soul from cycle of reincarnation. He found more practical approaches to problem in Indian philosophy.   **[6575]**

———. "Porphyry's *Philosophy from Oracles* in Eusebius' *Praeparatio evangelica* and Augustine's Dialogues of Cassiciacum." *RecAug* 6(1969), 103-139. Passage from E can be identified as coming from P's work on philosophy derived from oracles. Work can also be identified with one referred to by A in *City of God*.   **[6576]**

PLASS, P. "Porphyry, *Life of Plotinus*, 8: On Philosophic Thinking." *IntPhQ* 27(1987), 243-247. Description of Pl's intellectual activity in this passage does not suggest a pattern of non-discursive thought. Abstraction and distance from those around him need indicate nothing more than intense concentration.   **[6577]**

PREUS, A. "Biological Theory in Porphyry's *De Abstinentia*." *AncPh* 3(1983), 149-159. P's vegetarianism rests on two arguments: ecological balance is preserved by God/Nature; there is no real difference between human and animal rationality.   **[6578]**

SMITH, A. "Did Porphyry reject the Transmigration of Human Souls into Animals?" *RhM* 127(1984), 276-284. Evidence is inconclusive.   **[6579]**

———. "Porphyrian Studies Since 1913." *ANRW* II,36.2,719-773. Bibliography by subjects with brief discussions.   **[6580]**

———. *Porphyry's Place in the Neoplatonic Tradition. A Study in Post-Plotinian Neoplatonism.* The Hague: Nijhoff, 1974. P incorporated religious and mystical concepts into Plotinus' metaphysics, forming transition to later Neoplatonists. He differs from Plotinus in believing in escape from cycle of rebirth. Does not think philosopher can live true philosophical/mystical life on earth. Extensive bibliography.   **[6581]**

SMITH, M. "A Hidden Use of Porphyry's *History of Philosophy* in Eusebius' *Praeparatio Evangelica*." *JThS* 39(1988), 494-504. Eusebius quotes passages from P without acknowledging his source in order to make it appear that he had read the original and to avoid the embarrassment of citing an anti-Christian writer.   **[6582]**

TAYLOR, T., transl. *Porphyry, On the Cave of the Nymphs.* Grand Rapids, MI: Phanes Pr., 1989. Rprt of nineteenth-century transl. of P's philosophical and allegorical commentary on passage in *Odyssey* 13 in which Homer describes a cave with two openings, taken by P as a symbol of the cosmos. Introductory essay by K. Raine.   **[6583]**

ZIMMERN, A., transl. *Porphyry's* Letter to His Wife Marcella, Concerning the Life of Philosophy and the Ascent to the Gods. Grand Rapids, MI: Phanes Pr., 1988. P explains why he chose Marcella as his wife and expounds on the preparatory stages for the philosophical life. Introductory essay by D. Fideler.   **[6584]**

For related items see #5509, #6461, #7054.

IAMBLICHUS (250-326 A. D.)

After studying with Porphyry, Iamblichus returned to his native Syria to teach. His most distinctive contribution to Neoplatonic thought was the creation of a One beyond Plotinus' One. Iamblichus' One was utterly without attributes and absolutely unknowable. The Plotinian One was assigned the role of creator of the world. From the intelligible world came the intellectual world, which was divided into three parts, one of which was the Demiurge. Even such a Platonic concept, however, was given seven divisions.

Iamblichus' primary difference with his predecessors was his emphasis on theurgy, or practice of religio-magical rituals. For Iamblichus these rituals, and not Plotinian contemplation, were the route to union with the gods. Contemplation was not without value, but theurgy was the ultimate route to salvation.

ALLAN, D. J. "A Passage from Iamblichus in Praise of the Contemplative Life." *AGPh* 57(1975), 246-268. Section of Iam's *Protr.* (34.5-36.26) is based on Aristotle but with ideas borrowed as well from Plato. Iam's source is probably Stoic Posidonius.   **[6585]**

BLUMENTHAL, J. H. "Did Iamblichus Write a Commentary on the *De anima*?" *Hermes* 102(1974), 540-556. It seems unlikely that Iam wrote a commentary. He probably did treat selected passages in some detail.   **[6586]**

CAMERON, A. "The Date of Iamblichus' Birth." *Hermes* 96(1968), 374-376. Argues for 250 A. D. instead of 265.   **[6587]**

DE VOGEL, C. J. "On Iamblichus V. P. 215-219." *Mnem* 18(1965), 388-396. Passage is from Heraclides of Pontus through Nicomachus or Apollonius of Tyana.   **[6588]**

DILLON, J. M. "Iamblichus and the Origin of the Doctrine of Henads." *Phron* 17(1972), 102-106. For Iam each henad represents the highpoint of a series of emanations at different levels.   **[6589]**

———. "Iamblichus of Chalcis (c. 240-325 A. D.)." *ANRW* II,36.2,862-909. Biography and survey of works, with brief bibliography.   **[6590]**

DUNN, M. "Iamblichus, Thrasyllus, and the Reading Order of the Platonic Dialogues," in #6360, pp. 59-80. Iam proposed a reading order for twelve dialogues, designed to lead reader systematically through Plato's thought. Thrasyllus (30's A. D.) proposed a grouping of nine tetralogies, which remained popular into the Renaissance. **[6591]**

FINAMORE, J. F. *Iamblichus and the Theory of the Vehicle of the Soul.* Chico, CA: Scholars Pr., 1985. Study of dispute between Iam and Porphyry over vehicle of the soul. Also discusses Neoplatonist interpretation of Plato and Aristotle. **[6592]**

JOHNSON, T. *Iamblichus:* The Exhortation to Philosophy. Grand Rapids, MI: Phanes Pr., 1987. Iamblichus' description of the philosophic life, an introduction to the study of Plato, containing comments on teachings of Pythagoras. **[6593]**

KRILL, R. M. "Aspects of the Philosophical Priesthood in Iamblichus' *De mysteriis*." *CB* 47(1971), 89-94. To displace Christianity, emperor Julian (361-363) wanted to create a group of priestly theosophists of sort described by Iam. **[6594]**

O'MEARA, D. J. "New Fragments from Iamblichus' Collection of Pythagorean Doctrines." *AJPh* 102(1981), 26-40. Byzantine source for selections from Iam. **[6595]**

SHAW, G. "Theurgy as Demiurgy: Iamblichus' Solution to the Problem of Embodiment." *Dion* 12(1988), 37-59. Plato's inconsistent views on condition of soul in the body led Plotinus to resolve problem through mysticism. Iam did not attempt a conceptual solution but turned to theurgy, acting out in ritual the soul's union with God. **[6596]**

STEEL, C. G. *The Changing Self: A Study on the Soul in Later Neoplatonism. Iamblichus, Damascius and Priscianus.* Brussels: Palais des Acad., 1978. Iam took radical position that soul's nature changed when it fell and was embodied. Later Neoplatonists followed him, rather than Plotinus, on this point. **[6597]**

TAYLOR, T. *Jamblichus of Chalcis:* Life of Pythagoras. London: Watkins, 1965. Rprt of a nineteenth-century translation of Iam with frags of Pythagorean writings and some previously unpublished excerpts. **[6598]**

WATERFIELD, R., transl. The Theology of Arithmetic: *On the Mystical, Mathematical and Cosmological Symbolism of the First Ten Numbers.* Grand Rapids, MI: Phanes Pr., 1987. First English translation of a work, the longest from antiquity on number symbolism, attribued to Iamblichus. Notes, bibliography, and an introductory essay by K. Critchlow. **[6599]**

For related item see #3584.

PROCLUS (ca. 410-485 A. D.)

A native of Constantinople, Proclus came to Athens to study at about age nineteen and eventually became head of the Academy. He gained a reputation as an enthusiastic and energetic scholar who lectured five times a day, wrote copiously, and still found time for conversations with his students and participation in municipal life. He also practiced theurgy and considered it a superior way to union with the Ultimate. The effects of these practices and Proclus' own deep beliefs in Pythagorean mysticism on his recasting of Neoplatonic thought was to produce an "amazing metaphysical museum" in which Plotinus' concepts were fossilized.

Two of Proclus' works, *Plato's Theology* and *Elements of Theology*, had considerable influence on Arabic and medieval Latin Christian thought. The latter consists of 217 propositions defended logically, each building upon what went before. Proclus seems to have been the first to attempt such a methodological study in philosophy or theology. Two works attributed to the Christian Dionysius the Areopagite were actually derived from Proclus' work.

BLUMENTHAL, H. J. "Marinus' *Life of Proclus*. Neoplatonist Biography." *Byzantion* 54(1984), 469-494. Compares M's biography with Porphyry's *Life of Plotinus*. **[6600]**

———. "Plutarch's Exposition of the *De anima* and the Psychology of Proclus," in *De Jamblique à Proclus*, ed. H. Doerrie (Geneva: Fond. Hardt, 1975), pp. 123-151. Plutarch and Proclus represent two steps in development of doctrine of soul. For both, *doxa* plays an important role in function of soul. **[6601]**

———. "Proclus on Perception." *BICS* 29(1982), 1-11. Looks especially at views on *aisthesis*. **[6602]**

BRUMBAUGH, R. S. "Cantor's Sets and Proclus' Wholes," #6359, pp. 104-113. Plato's proposal in *Rep* 7 for a science uniting all branches of mathematics could not be realized as long as mathematics was geometrically based. Proclus' mathematics puts forth theorems about parts, wholes, elements, which are more general than Plato's or Aristotle's. They most closely resemble G. Cantor's set theory. Combination of Cantor's and Proclus' theories could lead to new understandings of science of reality. **[6603]**

GERSH, S. E. *Kinesis Akinetos. A Study of Spiritual Motion in the Philosophy of Proclus.* Leiden: Brill, 1973. Problem raised is how can non-durational and changeless nature of Intellect be reconciled with dynamic aspect of Intellect? Spiritual motion for Proclus is "a dynamic logical relation." **[6604]**

HATHAWAY, R. "The Anatomy of a Neoplatonist Metaphysical Proof," in #6359, pp. 122-136. P's first theorem, that "every multitude partakes in some way of unity," is basis of all that follows in his *Elements of Theology*. His proof is not Euclidean but has a Euclidean element in it. His proof is inadequate because of its weak notion of the infinite and its failure to state a logically necessary postulate. **[6605]**

LLOYD, A. C. "Procession and Division in Proclus," in *Soul and Structure of Being in Late Neoplatonism: Syrianus, Proclus, and Simplicius* (Liverpool [UK] Univ. Pr., 1982), pp. 18-42. Discusses P's views on changeability of soul once it has fallen from its original state and been embodied. **[6606]**

LOWRY, J. M. P. *The Logical Principles of Proclus' "Stoicheiosis Theologike" as Systematic Ground of the Cosmos.* Amsterdam: Rodopi, 1980. Examines Aristotelian basis of this systematization and its influence on late Neoplatonic thought. **[6607]**

MORROW, G. R. *Proclus, A Commentary on the First Book of Euclid's Elements.*

Princeton Univ. Pr., 1970. New translation, with introduction, notes, of an important source of insight into how ancients understood Euclid and how a Neoplatonist like P interpreted mathematics in philosophical terms.   [6608]

———., and **DILLON, J. M.** *Proclus' Commentary on Plato's* Parmenides. Princeton Univ. Pr., 1987. Introduction and notes, text and transl. of surviving portions.   [6609]

MOUTSOPOULOS, E. A. "The Idea of False in Proclus," in #6359, pp. 137-139. Nothing is true or false except in relation to something else. Even if something contains some falsehood, this only means it has been damaged and can be restored.   [6610]

NIARCHOS, C. G. "The Concept of [Participation] According to Proclus, With Reference to the Criticism of Nicolaus of Methone." *Diot* 13(1985), 78-94. Participation, a pivotal ontological term, was used by Plato and given a different interpretation by Christian thinkers, e. g., Nicolaus of Methone.   [6611]

———. "Nicolaus of Methone's Criticism on Proclus' Theory of Participated or Unparticipated Intelligence (Nous)." *Phil*(Athens) 13-14(1983-84), 324-345. For P *nous* refers primarily to divinity, source of existence of all other thing, a view later criticized by Nicolaus of Methone.   [6612]

ROSAN, L. J. "Proclus and the *Tejobindu Upanishads*," in #6358, pp. 45-62. Comparison of approaches to mystical union with the One in Neoplatonism and Indian thought. P displays movement from objectivism of earlier Neoplatonism to subjectivism similar to Eastern views.   [6613]

SAMBURSKY, S. "Plato, Proclus, and the Limitations of Science." *JHPh* 3(1965), 1-11. Proclus's pessimism about limits of science is an outgrowth of negative philosophy of his day and belief that matter is evil.   [6614]

SCHRENK, L. P. "Proclus on Space as Light." *AncPh* 9(1989), 87-94. P's ontology emphasizes the Law of Mean Terms. Light serves this function as connector between intelligible and sensible worlds.   [6615]

SHELDON-WILLIAMS, I. P. "Henads and Angels: Proclus and the Ps.-Dionysius." *StudPatr* 11(1972), 65-71. P and Ps.-Dionysius were probably both students of Syrianus in Athens and adapted his doctrine of henads, which was based on a poor reading of passages from Plato's *Philebus* and *Tim.*   [6616]

SHEPPARD, A. D. R. *Studies on the Fifth and Sixth Essays of Proclus' Commentary on the* Republic. Goettingen, Ger.: Vandenhoeck & Ruprecht, 1980. The two essays, discussing poetry, differ in their conclusions. Fifth seems to be more elementary, sixth for experts. Much of the material may be drawn from P's master, Syrianus.   [6617]

SWEENEY, L. "Participation and Structure of Being in Proclus' *Elements of Theology*," in #6359, pp. 140-155. P's world-view is cosmogony rather than cosmology. There are two types of participation. Except for the One, every monad participates in higher monads. Ultimately everything proceeds from and returns to the One.   [6618]

WATSON, G. "Unfair to Proclus?" *Phron* 17(1982), 101-106. Reply to Beierwaltes (in German) and Blumenthal (#6601). P's view of *phantasia* expressed in commentary on

Tim does not differ from that in his later works. More frequent use of term *doxa* does not imply change of thinking.   **[6619]**

WESTERINK, L. G. "Proclus on Plato's Three Proofs of immortality," in #83, pp. 296-306. English translation of and commentary on several Latin and Arabic passages from which Proclus's views can be reconstructed.   **[6620]**

WHITTAKER, J. "The Historical Background of Proclus' Doctrine of the *Autupostata*," in *De Jamblique à Proclus* (Geneva: Fondation Hardt, 1975), pp. 193-230. Neoplatonic idea of a "self-constituting" Nous seems to develop from Stoic concept of a self-creating world. It also appears in Gnosticism. P refutes Stoic, Plotinian idea of self-creation of the One. Question of freedom of human will arose from other sources.   **[6621]**

PHILO OF ALEXANDRIA (ca. 20 B. C. - 40 A. D.)

Philo, who has been called "the most complex personality known to us from antiquity," is the best surviving example of the amalgamation of Jewish and Greek thought associated with, but by no means confined to, the city of Alexandria. But he did not spring full-grown from the head of Zeus/Yahweh. Early in the Hellenistic era Judaism, in both Palestine and the Diaspora, came into close contact with elements of Greek culture. Historians still debate the extent of the influence but its presence, in whatever degree, is undeniable.

One measure of the degree of Hellenization of Diaspora Jews is the appearance, by the mid-third century B. C., of a Greek translation of the Jewish scriptures. This document, known as the Septuagint (LXX), was acclaimed by Hellenistic Jews as a "sister version" to the original, equally inspired. Translating their scriptures into Greek meant that the Jews came to share a common vocabulary with the Greek philosophers. The word *nomos*, for example, was used to translate *torah*, though the equivalence is not exact. But a Jew accustomed to reading about the *nomos* of God in his own scriptures could not see the word in a Greek philosophical text without assuming that they meant the same thing. And if a prophet said that the "word" (*logos*) of the Lord came to him, could that be anything but the *logos* which Heraclitus, Plato, and other philosophers talked about?

Conversely, the Greeks were quick to interpret Judaism as a kind of philosophical school. It had a founder, whom some identified with the legendary Athenian sage Musaeus, and it had a code which defined its adherents' daily life, much as the Pythagoreans did. The essence of its teaching was ethical, in line with the emphases of the Greek philosophies of the time. Its extreme monotheism was not really offensive to most Greek intellectuals of the third century B. C. The Olympian gods embarrassed them far more and were widely regarded by then as patent nonsense but too difficult to eradicate from the minds and hearts of simpler folk.

The first literary product of this Hellenistic-Jewish amalgamation appeared between 200 and 150 B. C. The *Wisdom of Jesus Ben Sirach*, or *Ecclesiasticus* in the Septuagint, contains ethical maxims, psalms, and didactic poetry. Its author appears to have been an aristocrat from Jerusalem, a diplomat and active in a school, "rather like a Greek philosopher." The book's overall outlook inclines toward Stoicism, seeing the world as arranged according to a divine purpose. The Jewish law is equated with the wisdom of the Greeks.

Slightly later than *Ben Sirach* is the book of *Qoheleth*, better known by its Greek title, *Ecclesiastes*. Probably because of its alleged authorship by king Solomon, it was taken into the canon of Jewish scriptures while *Ben Sirach* was not. But it reflects profound doubts about the justice of the natural order and seems convinced of the futility of life and the oblivion which death brings ("the dead know nothing"), themes more familiar from Euripides and the school of Epicurus. An orthodox editor had to add the epilogues of chapter 12 and occasional comments in the text to bring the book up to canonical standards.

The theme of Jewish law and Greek wisdom appears in another Palestinian work of the early Hellenistic period, *First Baruch*. Its middle section is a poetic speech urging Israel to embrace wisdom, which is defined as the law, Israel's peculiar possession.

The next step in the development of a Hellenistic-Jewish philosophy was for Jewish writers to assert that their law was not merely equivalent to Greek wisdom, but that it was in fact the origin of Hellenic philosophy, of all learning, for that matter. The *Epistle of Aristeas* (ca. 150 B. C.) presents a philosophical defense of the Torah and depicts a group of Jewish wise men holding a symposium in the presence of Ptolemy II, king of Egypt. Perhaps at about the same time an anonymous Jewish poet wrote a didactic poem of just over two hundred lines combining Jewish proverbial wisdom with Greek. It circulated under the name of an early Greek poet, Phocylides of Miletus. Another second-century writer, Aristobolus, wrote an allegorical interpretation of the Pentateuch, combining Platonic cosmogony with Pythagorean number symbolism and making Moses a combination of prophet and philosopher.

This trend continued into the first century B. C., when the *Wisdom of Solomon* and *Fourth Maccabees* demonstrate how "Jewish wisdom is dissolved into Greek popular philosophy." Both make a stronger case for the immortality of the soul than any Old Testament book.

Philo's work, then, should come as no great surprise. The leading exponent of a Platonic interpretation of the Old Testament was born in Alexandria of a Hellenistic Jewish family which had Roman citizenship. He received an education in the best Greek fashion and could quote tragedians, historians, and philosophers with ease. He does not appear to have had any extensive background in Hebrew language or Judaic traditions.

Philo's writings fall generally into two categories: apologies which present Judaism to a non-Jewish audience as a philosophical school and Biblical commentaries which interpret the Pentateuch in allegorical, largely Platonic terms.

The fullest of Philo's apologetic works, his *Apology*, is no longer extant. We can sample the basis of his arguments for Judaism in a treatise called *On the Contemplative Life* and in a fragment, preserved in Eusebius, which describes a Jewish monastic sect called the Therapeutai, sometimes identified with the Essenes.

Annual bibliographies on Philo, as well as abstracts of some articles from other journals, appeared in *Studia Philonica* from 1972 to 1980.

ALEXANDRE, M. "Rhetorical Argumentation as an Exegetical Technique in Philo of Alexandria," in *Hellenica et Judaica. Hommage à Valentin Nikiprowetzky*, ed. A. Caquot (Leuven: Ed. Peters, 1986), pp. 13-27. Studies fundamental importance of rhetoric to Philo as an exegetical tool. It is closely related to definitions of truth and morality and thus to philosophy.   **[6622]**

AMIR, Y. "Philo and the Bible." *StPhilon* 2(1973), 1-8. Examines P's allegorical interpretation. His view of Moses as a philosopher links his system to Greek philosophy, but religious nature of his thought does not fit easily with Greek speculation.   **[6623]**

ARGYLE, A. W. "Philo. The Man and His Work." *ExposT* 85(1974), 115-117. Survey, noting Hellenistic influences. Sees P as: statesman, philosopher, theologian.   **[6624]**

BAER, R. A. *Philo's Use of the Categories Male and Female.* Leiden: Brill, 1970. P substitutes a higher dualism of sexual/asexual for the male/female duality. To say that humans are "in the image" of God thus means that they transcend sexuality altogether. Use of masculine terms such as *nous* and *logos* should not disguise P's meaning that masculinity is the first step toward a higher, asexual level of being.   **[6625]**

BARNES, E. J. "Petronius, Philo, and Stoic Rhetoric." *Latomus* 32(1973), 787-798. Several passages in these two, roughly contemporary, authors deal with same themes from similar points of view. Their common source is Stoic rhetoric.   **[6626]**

BILLINGS, T. H. *The Platonism of Philo Judaeus.* New York: Garland, 1979; rprt. Chapters look at Plato's influence on Philo's concept of ultimate reality, intermediary powers, soul, ethics, and literary influences.   **[6627]**

BORGEN, P. "Philo of Alexandria: A Critical and Synthetical Survey of Research Since World War II." *ANRW* II, 21.1,98-154. Sections on Philo's social and cultural background, interpretation of Pentateuch, place in development of philosophy and religion. Analysis of most important studies.   **[6628]**

CARSON, D. A. "Divine Sovereignty and Human Responsibility in Philo: Analysis and Method." *NovTest* 23(1981), 148-164. Question of free will is an aspect of tension between divine sovereignty and human responsibility. For Philo there are some limits on providence. God is active and man can collaborate with him.   **[6629]**

CHROUST, A.-H. "A Fragment of Aristotle's *On Philosophy* in Philo of Alexandria, *De Opificio Mundi* I,7." *Divus Thomas* 77(1974), 224-235. In this passage Philo criticizes idea that the world is ungenerated and indestructible. This would reduce God and nature to passivity and impotence.   **[6630]**

———. "'Mystical Revelation' and 'Rational Theology' in Aristotle's *On Philosophy.*" *TijdFil* 34(1972), 500-512. Philo's idea of knowledge coming by revelation from God has a precedent in Ar's lost work on philosophy.   **[6631]**

———. "Some Remarks about Philo of Alexandria, *De aeternitate mundi*, V,20-24. A Fragment of Aristotle's *On Philosophy.*" *CF* 28(1974), 83-88. P's alterations of passage can be detected, allowing us to reconstruct genuine fragment of Ar's work.   **[6632]**

———. cf. #3586.

DEY, L. K. K. *The Intermediary World and Patterns of Perfection in Philo and Hebrews.* Missoula, MT: Scholars Pr., 1975. Technical study of concepts such as Logos, Sophia, heavenly man, and their use in P and New Testament epistle to the Hebrews. **[6633]**

DILLON, J. "Ganymede as the Logos. Traces of a Forgotten Allegorization in Philo." *StPhilon* 6(1979-80), 37-40. P is only source of an allegorization of Zeus' cupbearer Ganymede as the Logos, poured out for mankind. **[6634]**

——. "Philo Judaeus and the *Cratylus*." *LCM* 3(1978), 37-42. Plato in the *Cratylus* advances the theory that names of things are natural. Philo applies this theory to his interpretation of the Old Testament, concluding that the purest form of language is an archaic Hebrew. **[6635]**

——., and **TERIAN, A.** "Philo and the Stoic Doctrine of *Eupatheiai*. A Note on *Quaes. Gen.* 2.57." *StPhilon* 4(1976-77), 17-24. P does not create a fourth *eupatheia*, compunction. He merely uses the term for symmetry. **[6636]**

FELDMAN, L. H. "Philo's View on Music." *Journal of Jewish Music and Liturgy* 9(1986), 36-54. P's descriptions of music do not reflect practices of synagogues in Alexandria but are based on Greek theory, especially from Pythagoras and Plato. **[6637]**

——. "Scholarship on Philo and Josephus (1937-1959)." *CW* 54(1961), 281-291. Annotated bibliography. **[6638]**

——. "Scholarship on Philo and Josephus (1937-1959). Supplement to Philo." *CW* 55(1962), 299-301. Addendum to preceding item. **[6639]**

GOODHART, H. L., and **GOODENOUGH, E. R.** "A General Bibliography of Philo Judaeus," in *The Politics of Philo Judaeus: Practice and Theory,* ed. E. R. Goodenough (New Haven, CT: Yale Univ. Pr., 1938), pp. 125-321. Not annotated. **[6640]**

HALL, E. "Philo and Alexandria." *Hermes* (Santa Barbara) 5(1979), 232-239. Nonspecialist introduction to Philo's theosophical writing. **[6641]**

HAMERTON-KELLY, R. G. "Sources and Traditions in Philo Judaeus. Prolegomena to an Analysis of his Writings." *StPhilon* 1(1972), 3-26. Surveys various views held of Philo in recent years and suggests that analysis of his sources and his composition techniques is still needed. **[6642]**

HARVEY, W. Z. "Hebraism and Western Philosophy in H. A. Wolfson's Theory of History." *Immanuel* 14(1982), 77-85. Wolfson maintained that Philo remolded Greek philosophy into a Hebrew image. **[6643]**

HAY, D. M. "Philo's Treatise on the Logos-Cutter." *StPhilon* 2(1973), 9-22. For P, Logos is a cutting blade which separates mankind from *hamartia*. Resemblances to Old and New Testaments and to Gnostic views. **[6644]**

HILGERT, E. "Bibliographia Philoniana 1935-1981." *ANRW* II,21.1,47-97. Bibliography, not annotated. **[6645]**

HORSLEY, R. A. "The Law of Nature in Philo and Cicero." *HThR* 71(1978), 35-59.

Idea is found in C, but P is first to use phrase; both show Stoic influence.   **[6646]**

JOBLING, D. "'And Have Dominion . . .': The Interpretation of Genesis 1,28 in Philo Judaeus." *JSJ* 8(1977), 50-82. In his somewhat disorganized comments on this passage P draws upon Stoicism and Middle Platonism for his anthropology and ethics, and Sophism and Cynicism for his negative view of human culture.   **[6647]**

KOESTER, H. "*Nomos Physeos*: The Concept of Natural Law in Greek Thought," in *Religions in Antiquity: Essays in Memory of Erwin Ramsdell Goodenough* ed. J. Neusner (Leiden: Brill, 1983), pp. 521-541. P is first Greek writer to use term "law of nature." He combines Greek concept of nature with Jewish idea of a perfect law. Roman idea of *lex naturalis* developed independently.   **[6648]**

LaPORTE, J. "The Ages of Life in Philo of Alexandria." *SocBiblLitSemPapSer* 25(1986), 278-290. Analysis of Greek philosophical sources which influenced P in this area.   **[6649]**

MANSFELD, J. "Heraclitus, Empedocles, and Others in a Middle Platonist Cento in Philo of Alexandria." *VigChr* 39(1985), 131-136. Examines Philo's use of passages from Greeks to illustrate theme of vicissitudes and condition of human soul.   **[6650]**

———. "Philosophy in the Service of Scripture: Philo's Exegetical Strategies," in #5589, pp. 70-102. P can use different philosophical techniques to interpret different passages because he finds different levels of meaning in those passages. He neutralizes philosophical criticism of scriptural teaching by arranging teachings of philosophers in opposite pairs. Choices between them are made on basis of Mosaic teaching, from which they all originated.   **[6651]**

MEALAND, D. L. "Philo of Alexandria's Attitude to Riches." *ZNTW* 69(1978), 258-264. In his criticism of riches P displays influences of Stoicism and Cynicism as well as Platonic and Aristotelian strains.   **[6652]**

MENDELSON, A. *Secular Education in Philo of Alexandria.* Cincinnati, OH: Hebrew Union College Pr., 1982. Philo absorbed not only Greek philosophical ideas but also more ordinary aspects of a Hellenistic education.   **[6653]**

MOEHRING, H. R. "Moses and Pythagoras: Arithmology as an Exegetical Tool in Philo." *Journal for the Study of the Old Testament* Suppl. 11(1979), 205-208. Moses supposedly set down instructions for building tabernacle and ordering Israelites in numbers/ratios, which are actually symbols of secret cosmic harmony. Pythagoras rediscovered what Moses had found. Philo saw significance of Pythagoras' work.   **[6654]**

OSBORN, E. "Philo and Clement." *Prud* 19 #1(1987), 34-39. P is not a philosopher, strictly speaking, but an exegete who does attempt to resolve contradictions in his sources other than by allegorizing the sources. Clement is a philosopher because he had to make Christianity intellectually respectable in face of persecution of attacks from other philosophical schools.   **[6655]**

PEARSON, B. A. "Philo and Gnosticism." *ANRW* II,21.1,295-342. Compares P's views on Gen. 1-3, which are drawn from *Tim* and commentaries on it, with Gnostic ideas on creation and finds them similar. P and Gnostics seem to depend on common sources.

Surveys recent scholarship on the problem.   [6656]

RADICE, R., and RUNIA, D. T. *Philo of Alexandria: An Annotated Bibliography, 1937-1986.* Leiden: Brill, 1988. Thorough coverage of work in all European languages and in Hebrew. Includes works in which P is only referred to.   [6657]

RHEINHARTZ, A. "The Meaning of *Nomos* in Philo's *Exposition of the Law.*" *SR* 15(1986), 337-345. Translating "Torah" as *nomos* does not necessarily limit the meaning of the original term. Rather, it broadens the meaning of the Greek word.   [6658]

RIST, J. M. "The Use of Stoic Terminology in Philo's *Quod Deus Immutabilis Sit* 33-50." *Center for Hermeneutical Studies in Hellenistic and Modern Culture* 23(1976), 1-12. Stoic terminology used in this work seems to be derived from the Academy of Philo of Larissa and Antiochus of Ascalon rather than from the Stoa proper.   [6659]

RUNIA, D. T. "God and Man in Philo of Alexandria." *JThS* 39(1988), 48-75. P thinks of beings in quasi-Aristotelian terms but draws his relational concepts from Platonism. Only man's rational soul is related to God, and that part can be called divine.   [6660]

——. "Mosaic and Platonist Exegesis. Philo on Finding and Refinding." *VigChr* 40(1986), 209-217. In his explanation of Gen. 6.1-12 Ph uses the verb *heuriskein* to designate two distinct activities. He may have derived the idea from the anonymous commentary on the *Theaet.*   [6661]

——. "Naming and Knowing: Themes in Philonic Theology with Special Reference to the *De Mutatione Nominum*," in #5650, pp. 69-91. P's work marks shift from direct experience of God to one resulting from philosophical contemplation of God's nature. Naming and Knowing become important for him and for those he influences.   [6662]

——., ed. *Philo of Alexandria and the* Timaeus *of Plato.* Leiden: Brill, 1983. Survey of current research on P's philosophy; examines his background and interpretation of *Tim* from Plato's time to P's. Commentary on all passages from dialogue which P cites. Evaluates P's use of *Tim* and its influence on his concept of creation and Logos. He sees Plato and Moses making many of same points in their creation accounts. Draws conclusions about impact of philosophy on P's scriptural exegesis.   [6663]

——. "Philo's *De aeternitate mundi*: The Problem of its Interpretation." *VigChr* 35(1981), 105-151. Surveys history of scholarship from rejection of treatise as Philonic in late nineteenth century to present-day interest in re-evaluation of all of P's philosophical dialogues. Several interpretive principles are suggested which help to show place of the work in his overall thought.   [6664]

——. cf. #6315.

SANDMEL, S. "The Confrontation of Greek and Jewish Ethics. Philo, *De Decalogo*." *Central Conference of American Rabbis Journal* 15(1968), 54-63. P's ethics are deistic, not naturalistic. Mosaic law is a written copy of the Ideal Law. P makes comparison with Platonic and Stoic ethics. Greek and Jewish ethics do not blend well because one is based on speculative analysis, the other on divine revelation.   [6665]

——. "Philo Judaeus: An Introduction to the Man, His Writings and His Significance."

ANRW II,21.1,3-46. General survey of life and background, theology, ethics, and other facets of his thought.   **[6666]**

——. *Philo of Alexandria. An Introduction.* Oxford Univ. Pr., 1979. First describes contents of his works, then outlines main points of his thought. Stresses his success at blending Hellenism and Judaism so that neither predominates. His theology and philosophy point toward mystical communion with God.   **[6667]**

——. "The Rationalist Denial of Jewish Tradition in Philo," in *A Rational Faith: Essays in Honor of Levi A. Olan* (New York: Ktav, 1977), pp. 137-143. For non-specialists, to show how P balances philosophical knowledge and religious faith. He even seems to affirm religiously what he denies philosophically.   **[6668]**

——. "Virtue and Reward in Philo," in *Essays in Old Testament Ethics: J. Ph. Hyatt in Memoriam*, ed. J. L. Crenshaw and J. T. Willis. (New York: Ktav, 1974), pp. 215-223. P claims deeds are of little interest to him in connection with virtue. Good deeds do seem, in his view, to lead to virtue, and a spiritual, not material, reward.   **[6669]**

TERIAN, A. "A Critical Introduction to Philo's Dialogues." *ANRW* II,21.1,272-294. Two dialogues with his nephew are little studied because of poor preservation of text. They seem to be later works of P's, heavily influenced by Stoic thought.   **[6670]**

——. "The Implications of Philo's Dialogues on His Exegetical Works." *SocBiblLitSem-PapSer* 13(1978), 1.181-190. P's work develops from exegesis to philosophy.   **[6671]**

VAN DEN BROEK, R. "Jewish and Platonic Speculations in Early Alexandrian Theology: Eugnostus, Philo, Valentinus, and Origen," in *The Roots of Egyptian Christianity*, ed. B. A. Pearson and J. E. Goehring (Philadelphia: Fortress Pr., 1986), pp. 190-203. P's view of Logos as revealing royal and creative powers of God is comparable to concept of heavenly Adam in Gnostic treatise *Eugnostos the Blessed*. P seems to have been adapting a Jewish myth with Gnostic overtones.   **[6672]**

VAN WINDEN, J. C. M. "The World of Ideas in Philo of Alexandria: An Interpretation of *De opificio mundi* 24-25." *VigChr* 37(1983), 209-217. Philo's arguments are coherent but not fully spelled out. They are based on the double image relation between God, Logos and cosmos-man.   **[6673]**

WAGNER, W. H. "Philo and Paideia." *Cithara* 10(1971), 53-64. With other Hellenistic philosophers P shares view that people are educable. He relegates traditional stages of philosophical learning (logic, ethics, and physics) to a lower level, using *philosophia* to describe his second stage and *sophia* for the highest stage.   **[6674]**

WALLIS, R. T. "The Idea of Conscience in Philo of Alexandria." *StPhilon* 3(1974-75), 27-40. P has no clear metaphysical doctrine of conscience. He sees it at times in Epicurean terms as something that hurts. His clearest view of it is as a transcendent being, much like the guardian daemon of late Stoics.   **[6675]**

WILSON, R. M. "Philo of Alexandria and Gnosticism." *Kairos* 14(1972), 213-219. Despite significant differences between them, P and Gnosticism both stand in the tradition of Platonic philosophy.   **[6676]**

WINSTON, D. S. "Freedom and Determinism in Philo of Alexandria." *StPhilon* 3(1974-75), 47-70. P is basically deterministic, with concept of divine Logos penetrating everything. Stoic idea of relative free will has some impact on him.   [6677]

———. *Logos and Mystical Theology in Philo of Alexandria.* Cincinnati: Hebrew Union College Pr., 1985. Three lectures, tracing P's life and intellectual influences. He is a devout Jew as well as a Platonist. His mysticism anticipates Plotinus.   [6678]

———. "Philo's Ethical Theory." *ANRW* II,21.1,372-416. Looks at freedom and determinism, natural law, conscience, *philanthropia*, *apatheia/eupatheia*, and asceticism. He is Platonic in his desire to ignore physical, worldly things, somewhat Stoic in emphasis on acting appropriately.   [6679]

———. "Philo's Theory of Eternal Creation: *De Prov.* 1,6-9." *Proc of the Amer. Acad. for Jewish Research* 46-47(1980), 593-606. P's doctrine of creation is adapted from *Tim* but with original elements. He seems to have held that God's thought and creative act are identical. God created world of ideas directly and sensible world indirectly.   [6680]

———. "Was Philo a Mystic?" *SocBibLitSemPapSer* 13(1978), 161-180. P's mysticism is genuine, not just a literary *topos*. This factor needs to be understood in the study of his philosophy.   [6681]

WOLFSON, H. A. "Greek Philosophy in Philo and the Church Fathers," in *The Crucible of Christianity*, ed. A. J. Toynbee (New York: World, 1969), pp. 309-316; also in *Studies in the History of Philosophy and Religion* 1(1973), 71-97. P is the path of transmission between Greek philosophy and Origen, Clement, and Justin. Most important elements that were passed on: analogy between human and divine wisdom; divine origin of virtue; use of allegorical interpretation; subordination of philosophy to faith; concepts of Ideas and Logos.   [6682]

For related items see #685, #5972, #6294.

Chapter 21

GNOSTICISM AND CHRISTIAN PHILOSOPHY

GNOSTICISM

One does not quite know where, or how, or whether, to treat Gnosticism in a book on ancient philosophy. Some studies ignore it, but it seems to us to have a place. It has Neoplatonic elements, and its influence on Christian philosophy makes it difficult to ignore. We will not attempt to treat it in detail as a phenomenon in its own right, but merely as one more variation of the development in ancient philosophy and as a bridge to the late Neoplatonic and Christian schools.

Different groups of Gnostics are called by a bewildering variety of names, sometimes based on the founder of a sect, sometimes from a peculiar practice, or from a derogatory epithet applied by their enemies. All sects, however, have in common a belief in *gnosis*, knowledge revealed to them about mankind's true spiritual origins and the way of redemption from the physical world in which we are now trapped.

Whether Gnosticism predates Christianity is unclear. Some Gnostics found in Jesus a messenger from God, sent to lead us from physical corruption to life. ("I am the Way, the Truth, the Life." "You shall know the truth and the truth shall make you free.")

Much attention has been given to possible contact between Plotinus and the Gnostics. Plotinus did write a lengthy essay *Against the Gnostics*, but his philosophical vocabulary, which talks about creation as a process of emanation and describes the divine as "hypostases" or essences, bears a close resemblance to Gnostic terminology. Several essays listed below or in the section on Plotinus discuss the complex question of relationships and influences.

Gnosticism is essentially self-centered. Knowledge of one's true self is an all-important first step in the return to God. The parable of the Prodigal Son (Luke 15) became for them a symbol of the soul's journey. Different groups interpreted this self-knowledge in different ways. For some it meant release from conventions of the world, indulgence in any activity, no matter how shameful others might consider it. For others it meant ascetic rejection of contact with the world for fear of strengthening the hold of the material upon their spiritual natures.

ARMSTRONG, A. H. "Gnosis and Greek Philosophy," in *Gnosis: Festschrift fuer Hans Jonas*, ed. B. Aland et al. (Goettingen, Ger.: Vandenhoeck & Ruprecht, 1978), pp. 87-124. Surveys state of question and concludes that influence of philosophy on Gnosticism was slight, superficial. [6683]

BETZ, H. D. "The Delphic Maxim *Gnothi Sauton* in Hermetic Interpretation." *HThR* 63(1970), 465-484. "Holy word" of tractate *Poimandres* is Delphic maxim "know thyself," reinterpreted as call to potentially divine man to acknowledge his true nature. **[6684]**

DILLON, J. "The Descent of the Soul in Middle Platonic and Gnostic Theory," in #6688, pp. 357-364. Platonists and Gnostics display considerable range of explanations for soul's presence in body. For some it results from a transgression; for others, from the very existence of the universe. **[6685]**

GAGER, J. G. "Marcion and Philosophy." *VigChr* 26(1972), 53-59. Marcion's critics attribute to him ideas closely associated with Epicurus. **[6686]**

KENT, S. A. "Valentinian Gnosticism and Classical Samkhya: A Thematic and Structural Comparison." *PhE&W* 30(1980), 241-259. No direct borrowing can be established in either direction, but contact through Egypt is likely. Two traditions share similar views on question of immanence against transcendence and other points of doctrine. Both see cosmological structure reflected in individual's psychological structure. **[6687]**

LAYTON, B., ed. *The Rediscovery of Gnosticism. Proceedings of the International Conference on Gnosticism at Yale, New Haven, Connecticut, March 28-31, 1978, I: The School of Valentinus.* Leiden: Brill, 1980. Collection of essays; relevant ones abstracted herein. **[6688]**

――――. *Ibid., II: Sethian Gnosticism.* Leiden: Brill, 1981. Collection of essays; relevant ones abstracted herein. **[6689]**

――――. "Vision and Revision. A Gnostic View of Resurrection," in *Colloque international sur les textes de Nag Hammadi (Quebec, 22-25 août 1978),* ed. B. Barc (Quebec: Pr. de l'Univ. Laval & Louvain Peeters, 1981), pp. 190-217. *Treatise on Resurrection* displays Middle Platonic influences in interpretation of resurrection, which is taken as detachment from physical world. **[6690]**

MANSFELD, J. "Hesiod and Parmenides in Nag Hammadi." *VigChr* 35(1981), 174-182. Author of one Gnostic treatise alludes to *Theogony* and several frags of Parmenides, but knows them only through Hellenistic extracts. **[6691]**

MARTIN, L. H. "The Anti-Philosophical Polemic and Gnostic Soteriology in *The Treatise on the Resurrection* (CG I,3)." *Numen* 20(1973), 20-37. Treatise equates philosophers and their teaching with acceptance of life in physical world. **[6692]**

MATSUMOTO, M. "Sophia and Philosophia. Are They the Same?" *Diot* 11(1983), 119-129. Gnosticism exalts a mystical wisdom with roots in Indian thought and Plotinus. It is not sought by the intellect, as is true in traditional Greek philosophy. **[6693]**

MILLER, B. F. "A Study of the Theme of Kingdom: The Gospel According to Thomas, Logion 18." *NovTest* 9(1967), 52-60. Examination of this saying and comparison with New Testament version shows how Jesus' sayings were reshaped under influence of Greek philosophy and theology. **[6694]**

PEARSON, B. A. "Gnosticism as Platonism: With Special Reference to Marsanes (NHC 10,1)." *HThR* 77(1984), 55-72. Tractate Marsanes, from Nag Hammadi, demonstrates profound influence of Middle Platonism on later, better developed Gnosticism. **[6695]**

———. "The Tractate Marsanes (NHC X) and the Platonic Tradition," in *Gnosis: Festschrift fuer Hans Jonas*, ed. B. Aland et al. (Goettingen, Ger.: Vandenhoeck & Ruprecht, 1978), pp. 373-384. Overview of Platonic influences on this tract. **[6696]**

PEEL, M. L., and **ZANDEE, J.** "'The Teachings of Silvanus' from the Library of Nag Hammadi (CG VII,84,15-118,7)." *NovTest* 14(1972), 294-311. Describes document's literary form, content; studies influences on it: Biblical, Platonic, Stoic. **[6697]**

PERKINS, P. "On the Origin of the World (CG II,5). A Gnostic Physics." *VigChr* 34(1980), 36-46. Four main themes (biological metaphors, myth of Eros, providence, end of the world), suggesting an Athenian provenience. **[6698]**

———. cf. #6788.

QUISPEL, G. "The Demiurge in the Apocryphon of John," in *Nag Hammadi and Gnosis: Papers Read at the First International Congress of Coptology (Cairo, December 1976)*, ed. R. M. Wilson (Leiden: Brill, 1978), pp. 1-33. Influence of Plato's *Tim* can be traced here, but it is not determinative factor. **[6699]**

———. "From Mythos to Logos." *Eranos-Jb* 39(1970), 323-340. Gnosticism developed from efforts to rationalize myths, just as Greek philosophy did. **[6700]**

———. "The Origins of the Gnostic Demiurge," in #6749, I, pp.. 271-276. The idea is Jewish rather than Greek. **[6701]**

SAMUEL, A. "How Many Gnostics?" *BASP* 22(1985), 297-322. Downplays influence and importance of Gnosticism. **[6702]**

SCHENKE, H. M. "The Problem of Gnosis." *SCent* 3(1983), 73-87. Surveys origins of Gnosticism and its relation to mystery religions and philosophies of the time. **[6703]**

SCHOLER, D. N. *Nag Hammadi Bibliography, 1948-1969.* Leiden: Brill, 1971. Not annotated. **[6704]**

SMITH, M. "The History of the Term 'Gnostikos'," in #6689, pp. 796-807. Term is first used by Plato and later only by Platonic-Pythagorean writers. It means "leading to knowledge," "capable of knowing." Clement is first Christian to use it. **[6705]**

STEAD, G. C. "The Valentinian Myth of Sophia." *JThS* 20(1969), 75-104. Concept of Sophia is derived from eastern sources as well as Platonic, Stoic, and Pythagorean elements. **[6706]**

THOMASSEN, E. "The Structure of the Transcendent World in the Tripartite Tractate (NHC I,5)." *VigChr* 34(1980), 358-375. With its two levels (Silence and Logos) and three hypostases (Father, Son, and Church) Gnostic thought resembles Neoplatonic and that of Marius Victorinus. **[6707]**

TURNER, J. D. "The Gnostic Threefold Path to Enlightenment. The Ascent of Mind and the Descent of Wisdom." *NovTest* 22(1980), 324-351. Five treatises from Nag Hammadi illustrate Platonic origins of concept of enlightenment. **[6708]**

VAN DEN BROEK, R. "The *Authentikos Logos*: A New Document of Christian Platonism." *VigChr* 33(1979), 260-286. Treatise from Nag Hammadi presents thoroughly Platonic doctrine of soul and gives evidence of familiarity with Philo. **[6709]**

——. "The Present State of Gnostic Studies." *VigChr* 37(1983), 41-71. Survey of several collections of essays in Gnostic studies under such headings as Gnosticism and Judaism, Gnosticism and philosophy. **[6710]**

——., and VERMASEREN, M. J., eds. *Studies in Gnosticism and Hellenistic Religions Presented to Gilles Quispel on the Occasion of his 65th Birthday.* Leiden: Brill, 1981. Relevant essays abstracted herein. **[6711]**

VAN GRONINGEN, G. *First-Century Gnosticism: Its Origins and Motifs.* Leiden: Brill, 1967. Judicious survey with some attention given to Philo and Greco-Roman philosophy as background influences. Finds them superficial. **[6712]**

VAN UNNIK, W. C. "The 'Wise Fire' in a Gnostic Eschatalogical Vision," in #6749, I, pp. 277-288. Phrase, based on Heraclitus, probably originated with a second-century Stoic. It denotes divine character of fire; Christians also used it. **[6713]**

WHITTAKER, J. "Basilides on the Ineffability of God." *HThR* 62(1969), 367-371. Reply to Wolfson (1957) on whether or not God can be spoken of. **[6714]**

——. "Self-Generating Principles in Second-Century Gnosticism," in #6688, pp. 176-193. Self-generating principles may be an influence from some Platonic school, from Neopythagoreanism, or from some other currently unsuspected source. Notion was widespread in theologizing philosophies of first-century A. D. **[6715]**

WILSON, R. M. "Jewish Christianity and Gnosticism." *RecSR* 60(1972), 261-272. Origins of Gnosticism remain very difficult to determine. J. Danielou has argued for Judeo-Christianity as channel for apocalyptic ideas into religio-philosophical setting of Gnosticism. **[6716]**

——. "Jewish Gnosis and Gnostic Origins. A Survey." *HUCA* 45(1974), 177-190. Organized system which could be called Gnosticism did not exist before second century A. D. General gnostic tendencies can be traced as far back as Philo. Such tendencies were strong in Hellenistic Judaism, where distinctions between Judaism and Greek philosophy were not always observed. **[6717]**

——. cf. Philo #6676.

For related items see #6362, #6425, #6471, #6499, #6876.

CHRISTIAN PHILOSOPHY

Most textbooks on ancient philosophy give scant attention, if any, to Christianity, but as Irwin says (#23, p. 202), "we would leave a serious gap in an account of Greek philosophy if we said nothing about Christianity."

Though it began from a tradition and principles quite antithetical to Greek philosophy, Christianity soon adopted terminology and modes of thought from Stoicism and Neoplatonism. The process may have been half conscious or unintentional. Other philosophical schools had absorbed their opponents' views while attempting to refute them. The Academy became Skeptical; Neoplatonists became Neo-Aristotelians while avowing their adherence to Plato's teaching.

This process usually happens without any malicious intent on the part of those who are modifying their views. Their intent is to keep up with a predominant intellectual trend. When Aristotle's works were recovered during the Crusades, Christian thinkers all over western Europe began adapting their teaching to the new syllogistic methodology, certain that it was the best way to express the truths they had taught for centuries. In the twentieth century many conservative Christians have interpreted the first twelve chapters of Genesis as scientifically accurate, because a positivist, scientific mentality now undergirds our educational system and, consequently, our worldview. Any system of thought which wants to appear respectable needs to be scientifically up-to-date.

Christianity, arising from Judaism, had no intellectual respectability in Greco-Roman eyes. It was new, in a world which valued religions and philosophies for their antiquity. If a system of thought was new, the reasoning ran, its merits were unknown. Only systems which time had proved could be recognized as legitimate. Christianity survived at first as a sub-group under Judaism, but once those two groups had broken apart, Christianity needed legitimation. It also needed an intellectual framework. If it wasn't a type of Judaism, what was it?

The presentation of Christianity as a philosophical school was not as far-fetched a notion as it might now seem. The Romans admired Judaism more as a philosophy than as a religion. As a religion Judaism appeared to them atheistic, exclusivist, and — with its demand for circumcision — extremist. But Judaism had a revered teacher and a set of rules for living day by day. The Pythagoreans and Epicureans had such things, along with dietary peculiarities and restrictions on dress. To the Roman mind those were characteristics of a philosophical school. It is not too surprising, then, that Christians began to explain their faith in terms intelligible to people who found more value in philosophy than in religion. Jesus, the Palestinian rabbi, became the incarnate Christ, the *Logos* of God.

This interpretation of Christianity may not have been universal. Paul expressed his distrust of philosophy in no uncertain terms in Colossians 2.8: "Beware of philosophy." At the same time his cosmology shows Stoic influences (#6797) and his preaching technique seems to have been modelled on the Cynic diatribe (#1243). The composition of parts of the gospels may have been influenced by literary productions of Greek philosophical schools (#6728 and #6729).

We must be careful, however, to remember that literary resemblances between two ancient texts need not prove that one was derived from the other. Samuel Sandmel once decried the tendency toward "parallelomania" which he saw running rampant in modern academe. It was quite possible, he pointed out, for two writers to draw upon terms or images which were common intellectual coin in a society (cf. #6758). If Paul refers to the "elements (*stoicheia*) of the world" (Colossians 2.8), it does not necessarily mean that he has read Plato or Aristotle or any other philosopher who uses the term. Any educated person of that day (which Paul certainly was) would have known the term and could have used it without endorsing the meanings given to it by earlier writers.

By the early second century Christianity had gained enough of a beachhead in the Roman Empire that Christian intellectuals became more aggressive and outward looking in their writings. They began to address Apologies or defenses of their position to persons in authority, sometimes even to the emperor himself. Justin Martyr (ca. 150 A. D.), who is discussed below, made perhaps the most straightforward equation of Christianity with earlier philosophical schools.

Since the dominant philosophical school of the Roman imperial period was Platonism, it is not surprising that traces of Platonic thought have been discerned in Christianity by numerous modern scholars. J. Dillon assumes that it is "generally agreed that Christian thinkers were profoundly influenced in the development of their theology by their growing acquaintance with contemporary Greek philosophy, and in particular with Platonism"(#6740, p. 1). This blending may have resulted from a common Platonic and Christian opposition to Manicheism (#6720). Or perhaps early Christian writers were simply most familiar and most comfortable with this widespread mode of thought. Paul was obviously alive to Platonic views; II Cor. 4.18 has been called "Platonism in a nutshell." But some of his writing also shows Stoic influence (cf. I Cor. 2.5).

The entries in this section focus on these philosophical influences on Christianity and not on theological developments within the faith. That division, however, is not always so clear-cut.

ALTMANN, A. "*Homo imago Dei* in Jewish and Christian Theology." *JR* 48(1968), 235-259. Looks at Jewish background of idea with emphasis on role of Neoplatonism from Philo's day on. **[6718]**

AMUNDSEN, D. W. "Suicide and Early Christian Values," in *Suicide and Euthanasia: Historical and Contemporary Themes*, ed. B. A. Brody (Dordrecht, Nether.: Kluwer, 1989), pp. 77-153. Augustine is not first Christian writer to condemn suicide. Earlier patristic sources based opposition to it on NT. They approved of it only in case of virgins trying to protect their chastity. Augustine prohibits suicide even then. **[6719]**

ANDRESEN, C. "The Integration of Platonism into Early Christian Theology." *StudPatr* 15(1984), 399-413. Discusses gradual blending of the two schools, encouraged by their common opposition to Manicheism. **[6720]**

ARMSTRONG, A. H. "On Not Knowing Too Much About God: The Apophatic Way of the Neoplatonists and Other Influences from Ancient Philosophy which Have Worked Against Dogmatic Assertion in Christian Thinking," in #6805, pp. 129-145. Surveys conflict between traditions of assertion and negation in Christian thought. **[6721]**

———. "Pagan and Christian Traditionalism in the First Three Centuries A. D." *StudPatr* 15(1984), 414-431. Pagans and Christians both accepted authority of some body of tradition, whether Scripture or teachings of some philosopher, because they found it coherent and providing an adequate explanation of the human situation. **[6722]**

——. "Greek Philosophy and Christianity," in *The Legacy of Greece: A New Appraisal*, ed. M. I. Finley (Oxford: Clarendon Pr., 1981), pp. 347-375. Focuses on influence of Platonism and Neoplatonism.   [6723]

——. "Reason and Faith in the First Millenium A. D." *PACPhA* 40(1966), 104-109. Christians were always concerned that their message be intelligible to world around them. By late classical period they did not distinguish religion from philosophy.   [6724]

——. "The Self-Definition of Christianity in Relation to Later Platonism," in #5639, I, pp. 74-99. Platonic influence was especially felt in concept of God as spirit, but Christians differed from Platonists in understanding of God as distinct from created world and as omnipotent. In their negative theology (defining God by what he is not), Christians remained more Middle than Neoplatonist.   [6725]

——. cf. #6406.

BALAS, D. L. "Christian Transformation of Greek Philosophy Illustrated by Gregory of Nyssa's Use of the Notion of Participation." *PACPhA* 40(1966), 151-157. His doctrine of divine participation in world is designed to resolve problem of change or stability. View of divine hierarchy is inherited.   [6726]

BAUCKHAM, R. "The Fall of the Angels as the Source of Philosophy in Hermias and Clement of Alexandria." *VigChr* 39(1985), 313-330. Author of the *Irrisio Gentilium Philosophorum*, an attack on philosophical schools, is probably a contemporary of Clement.   [6726a]

BETZ, H. D. "Matthew VI.22f and Ancient Greek Theories of Vision," in *Text and Interpretation: Studies in the New Testament Presented to Matthew Black*, ed. E. Best and R. M. Wilson (Cambridge Univ. Pr., 1979), pp. 43-56. Eye-as-lamp saying assumes a theory of vision based on Empedocles and Plato.   [6727]

——. "The Sermon on the Mount. Its Literary Genre and Function." *JR* 59(1979), 285-297. Sermon resembles Epicurus' *Kyriai Doxai* in form and function. It systematically epitomizes Jesus' teaching.   [6728]

BLAIKLOCK, E. M. "The Irony of Paul." *Prud* 3(1971), 1-14. First four chapters of I Cor. allude to contemporary philospohical teaching, especially Stoicism. Paul approaches the Corinthians with an almost Socratic irony and seems to consider Christianity a philosophy.   [6729]

BRANDON, S. G. F. "B. C. and A. D. The Christian Philosophy of History." *HT* 15(1965), 191-199. Greco-Roman view is that history is cycle. Christians saw it as gradual unfolding of God's purpose. Best expressed in Augustine.   [6730]

CHERNISS, H. F. *The Platonism of Gregory of Nyssa*. New York: Burt Franklin, 1971; rprt. Gregory does not draw his knowledge of Plato from intermediaries but knew P's works well enough to quote them from memory. He also knew Philo and Origen and draws Stoic terminology from common philosophical vocabulary of his day.   [6731]

CIHOLAS, P. "Plato, the Attic Moses? Some Patristic Reactions to Platonic Philosophy." *CW* 72(1978-79), 217-225. Christian writers pointed to three areas to demonstrate

P's dependence on Old Testament: creation, monotheism, universal law.   [6732]

CLARKE, G. W. "The Literary Setting of the *Octavius* of Minucius Felix." *JRH* 3(1965), 195-211. Minucius attempts to heighten respectability of Christian apologetics by adapting form of philosophical dialogue.   [6733]

CUMMING, A. "Pauline Christianity and Greek Philosophy: A Study of the Status of Women." *JHI* 34(1973), 517-528. Greco-Roman society never accorded women a status anywhere near that which Plato, Aristotle, or other thinkers granted them. Paul's admonitions in I Cor. against women speaking in church were aimed at a local situation, but overly literal interpreters made him seem to be a misogynist.   [6734]

DEANE, H. A. "Classical and Christian Political Thought." *PolTheo* 1(1973), 415-425. Discusses different conceptions of role that political activity plays in realization of human potentialities and in fostering of men's moral qualities.   [6735]

DEN BOER, W., et al., eds. *Romanitas et Christianitas: Studia I. H. Waszink a. d. vi kal. Nov. a MCMLXXIII XIII lustra complenti oblata.* Amsterdam: North Holland Publ., 1973. Collection of essays, most abstracted in this volume, on cross-fertilization of two systems.   [6736]

DE VOGEL, C. J. "Platonism and Christianity. A Mere Antagonism or a Profound Common Ground?" *VigChr* 39(1985), 1-62. Platonism provided rational foundation which Christians believed compatible with Biblical teaching. Platonism influenced development of trinitarian and christological doctrine in fourth and fifth centuries and spiritual life of Christians beginning in second century.   [6737]

──. cf. #1339 and #6344.

DIHLE, A. "Philosophy and Religion in Late Antiquity," in #128, pp. 99-122. Various schools of thought tried to resolve discrepancy between ideas of man's free will and divine providence. Marius Victorinus adapted Porphyry's three-fold definition of God (to be/to live/to know) to make second person of the trinity the divine will.   [6738]

──. "St. Paul and Philo," in #128, pp. 68-98. Neither Old Testament nor Greek philosophy developed a clear concept of will. Philo and Paul, with their doctrine of conscience, flirt with the idea, but neither coined a term to mean "will."   [6739]

DILLON, J. "Logos and Trinity: Patterns of Platonist Influence on Early Christianity," in #6805, pp. 1-13. Christian theologians found in Platonic thought a well developed theory of relation between God and a subordinate principle (*logos*) and a system of three principles. Porphyry provides clearest explication of these concepts.   [6740]

DODDS, E. R. *Pagan and Christian in an Age of Anxiety.* Cambridge Univ. Pr., 1965. Examines the intellectual milieu of the late Roman Empire, showing how religious and philosophical traditions were blended in an effort to answer people's needs for security and salvation.   [6741]

DOWINING, F. G. *Christ and the Cynics: Jesus and Other Radical Preachers in First-Century Tradition.* Sheffield, UK: JSOT Pr, 1988. Book of readings with notes pointing up close similarities between Cynics and Christians. Bibliography.   [6742]

———. cf. #1243.

DROGE, A. J. "*Mori lucrum*: Paul and Ancient Theories of Suicide." *NovTest* 30(1988), 263-286. Paul's views on suicide resemble those of Plato and Epictetus.   **[6743]**

DUMONT, L. "A Modified View of Our Origins. The Christian Beginnings of Modern Individualism." *Religion* 12(1982), 1-27. Hellenistic philosophers, especially Stoics, formulated concepts of wise man, detached from world around him, and of natural law. Early Christians adapted and modified these teachings.   **[6744]**

EMMET, D. "Theoria and the Way of Life." *JThS* 17(1966), 38-52. "Theoria" implies unity of theory and practice, an important concept among Greek and Christian philosophers.   **[6745]**

FERGUSON, J. "Athens and Jerusalem." *RelStud* 8(1972), 1-13. Survey of contributions of Greek thought and Judaism to development of Christianity.   **[6746]**

FORTIN, E. L. "Christianity and Hellenism in Basil the Great's Address *Ad Adulescentes*," in #6339, pp. 189-203. Basil criticizes Greek orators as skilled liars, but urges young Christian students to read Greek classics and offers some examples of how pagan authors teach virtue. He distorts meaning of virtually every passage he cites.   **[6747]**

GAERTNER, B. E. "The Pauline and Johannine Idea of 'To Know God' against the Hellenistic Background. The Greek Philosophical Principle 'Like by Like' in Paul and John." *NTS* 14(1968), 209-231. For Stoics and other Hellenistic philosophers the principle that things are known only by like things is important epistemologically. Paul uses it in I Cor. 2.6-16 and John in several passages in his Gospel to explain how the Logos knows the Father and how the Christian apprehends the Spirit.   **[6748]**

GRANFIELD, P., and **JUNGMANN, J. A.,** eds. *Kyriakon: Festschrift Johannes Quasten.* Muenster: Aschendorff, 1970. Relevant essays abstracted herein.   **[6749]**

GRANT, R. M. "Early Alexandrian Christianity." *ChHist* 40(1971), 133-144. Christian school at Alexandria adapted contemporary eclectic philosophy to explain their faith. Pythagorean influences are especially prominent.   **[6750]**

———. "Paul, Galen, and Origen." *JThS* 34(1983), 533-536. Discussion of attitudes toward logical proof in these writers and in Clement of Alexandria.   **[6751]**

———. "The Prefix auto- in Early Christian Theology," in *The Impact of the Church upon its Culture. Reappraisals of the History of Christianity,* ed. J. C. Brauer (Univ. of Chicago Pr., 1968), pp. 5-16. Gnostics, Origen, Plotinus use words with prefix auto- to describe God. Patristic writers, influenced by later Neoplatonists, used such words when talking about all three persons of Trinity, creating a more philosophical theology.   **[6752]**

———. cf. #445.

GREGG, R. C. *Consolation Philosophy: Greek and Christian Paideia in Basil and the Two Gregories.* Cambridge, MA: Philadelphia Patristic Foundation, 1975. Study of influence of Greek thought on early Christian efforts to deal with death and grief. Main problem for Christians was contradiction between *apatheia* and *metriopatheia*.   **[6753]**

HAUCK, R. J. "'They Saw What They Said They Saw': Sense Knowledge in Early Christian Polemic." *HThR* 81(1988), 239-249. Studies Christian efforts to rebut philosophical arguments against doctrines based on apostolic accounts. *Clementine Homilies*, Origen are important sources in debate over reliability of sense data. [6754]

HENRICHS, A. "Philosophy, the Handmaiden of Theology." *GRBS* 9(1968), 437-450. Discussion of idea that philosophy should be subordinated to theology. Authors included: Philo, Clement of Alexandria, and Origen. [6755]

HORSLEY, R. A. "The Background of the Confessional Formula in I Kor. 8:6." *ZNTW* 69(1978), 130-135. Background of the phrase is Platonic, not Stoic. Paul's immediate source may have been Philo. [6756]

———. "Spiritual Marriage with Sophia." *VigChr* 33(1979), 30-54. Book of Wisdom and Philo speak of "marriage" between divine Sophia and an individual soul, with resulting sexual asceticism. Similar motif is found in Isis worship and in I Cor. [6757]

HURST, L. D. "How 'Platonic' are Heb. vii.5 and ix.23f?" *JThS* 34(1983), 156-168. Several words which are often cited as evidence of Platonism in this letter can be shown to have had a much wider currency. [6758]

JACKSON, B. D. "Socrates and Christianity." *CF* 31(1977), 189-206. Most church fathers considered S a Christian. His asceticism influenced monasticism. [6759]

JUNGKUNTZ, R. "Fathers, Heretics and Epicureans." *JEH* 17(1966), 3-10. Heresies were often explained as influences of Greek philosophical schools. "Epicurean" was a term of disparagement for anyone expressing unorthodox views. [6760]

KINDSTRAND, J. F. "The Date and Character of Hermias' *Irrisio*." *VigChr* 34(1980), 341-357. The document may have originated as a Cynic diatribe. Its only Christian imprint is in the title and introduction. [6761]

KLASSEN, W. "A Child of Peace. Luke X,6 in First-Century Context." *NTS* 27(1981), 488-506. Compares concept of peace in Stoics Musonius Rufus and Epictetus with Luke's Gospel. [6762]

KORTEWEG, T. "The Reality of the Invisible. Some Remarks on St. John XIV,8 and Greek Philosophic Tradition," in #5651, pp. 50-102. In this passage Jesus is visible image of God, as wisdom or Logos is image of God in Stoicism and Platonism. [6763]

KURSCHWITZ, R. B. "Christian Virtues and the Doctrine of the Mean." *Faith&Ph* 3(1986), 416-428. Against many philosophers, argues that doctrine of the mean correctly describes a significant range of virtues, including many Christian virtues. [6764]

MALHERBE, A. J. "Antisthenes and Odysseus, and Paul at War." *HThR* 76(1983), 143-173; also in #6771, pp. 91-119. In II Cor. 10.3-6 P draws an image of the reasoning facilities as an inner fortification. [6765]

———. "The Beasts at Ephesus." *JBL* 87(1968), 71-80; also in #6771, pp. 79-89. Paul's image of fighting with beasts is probably taken from Cynic literature, in which the passions are likened to wild animals against which the sage must struggle. [6766]

———. "'Gentle as a Nurse': The Cynic Background to 1 Thess. 2." *NovTest* 12(1970), 103-117; also in #6771, pp. 35-48. Comparison with descriptions of Cynic philosophers in Lucian of Samosata and Dio Chrysostom and with Cynic descriptions of true philosopher as opposed to charlatan suggests that Paul had such concepts in mind when writing this passage.   [6767]

———. "Medical Imagery in the Pastoral Epistles," in *Texts and Testaments: Critical Essays on the Bible and Early Christian Fathers*, ed. W. E. March (San Antonio, TX: Trinity Univ. Pr., 1980), pp. 19-35; also in #6771, pp. 121-136. References to false teachers and their followers in the letters are couched in terms of disease. Stoics often described the passions in such terms, and the Cynics considered themselves physicians who could lead the soul to a state of health, which they identified with virtue.   [6768]

———. "*Me Genoito* in the Diatribe and Paul." *HThR* 73(1980), 231-240; also in #6771, pp. 25-33. P's use of the phrase resembles Epictetus. It is more characteristic of teaching than of Cynic diatribe.   [6769]

———. "'Not in a Corner': Early Christian Apologetic in Acts 26:26." *SCent* 5(1985-86), 193-210; also in #6771, pp. 147-163. The language which Luke depicts Paul as using is borrowed from the moral philosophers of the day. The insistence on the public character of the Christian proclamation is an important aspect of that picture.   [6770]

———. *Paul and the Popular Philosophers*. Minneapolis: Augsburg Fortress, 1989. Collection of previously published papers. Those demonstrating Paul's acquaintance with Greek philosophical schools, especially Stoics and Cynics, are abstracted herein. [6771]

———. "Paul: Hellenistic Philosopher or Christian Pastor?" *AngThR* 68(1986), 3-13; also in #6771, pp. 67-77. Hellenistic philosophic influences are not the core of Paul's theology, but they do shape his concept of himself as leader/pastor of a group. [6772]

MEALAND, D. L. "Community of Goods and Utopian Allusions in Acts II-IV." *JThS* 28(1977), 96-99. Vocabulary used to describe pooling of goods in these chapters can be traced to Plato's *Rep* 424a and 449c.   [6773]

MEIJERING, E. P. "God, Cosmos, History: Christian and Neo-Platonic Views on Divine Revelation." *VigChr* 28(1974), 248-276. Comparison of Irenaeus' and Plotinus' arguments against the Gnostics on various topics.   [6774]

———. "Irenaeus' Relation to Philosophy in the Light of his Concept of Free Will," in #6738, pp. 221-232. In attacks on Gnostics I asserts free will in language borrowed from Greek philosophers, whom he condemns in other contexts. His description of eternity of God is couched in Platonic language.   [6775]

———. "Mosheim on the Difference between Christianity and Platonism: A Contribution to the Discussion about Methodology." *VigChr* 31(1977), 68-73. Tries to determine whether Calcidius was Christian, Platonist, or Eclectic.   [6776]

———. *Orthodoxy and Platonism in Athanasius. Synthesis or an Antithesis?* Leiden: Brill, 1968. The supposed antithesis between Biblical and Platonic thought in Athanasius is over-emphasized. Athanasius does express his faith largely in Platonic terms, but only in his ontology is he more Platonic than Biblical.   [6777]

MILLER, D. L. "Between God and the Gods." *Eranos-Jb* 49(1980), 81-148. Christian idea of trinity was influenced by Neoplatonic and Pythagorean ideas. **[6778]**

MURPHY, F. X. "The Moral Doctrine of St. John Chrysostom." *StudPatr* 11(1972), 52-57. John uses "philosophy" to mean a virtuous way of life, uses philosophical arguments and rhetorical techniques in his construction of a Christian ethic. **[6779]**

NASH, R. H. *Christianity and the Hellenistic World.* Grand Rapids, MI: Zondervan, 1983. Examines Hellenistic philosophy and mystery religions and denies that NT writers were influenced by either. **[6780]**

NORRIS, R. A. *God and World in Early Christian Theology. A Study in Justin Martyr, Irenaeus, Tertullian, and Origen.* London: Black, 1966. Introductory chapter on Greek and Hellenistic cosmology (*Tim* and the Stoics); chapter-length studies of Justin and Platonism, Irenaeus and the Gnostics, Tertullian, Origen and Platonism. Stresses that Christian thinkers were Greek in language and outlook at a subconscious level as well as being influenced by Greek philosophical speculation. **[6781]**

OSBORN, E. F. *The Beginning of Christian Philosophy.* Cambridge Univ. Pr., 1981. Early Christians developed philosophy to deal with several problems in their encounter with their environment: nature of God and our ability to talk about him; man and his freedom; cosmology; history and continuity; Logos and incarnation. **[6782]**

————. *Ethical Patterns in Early Christian Thought.* Cambridge Univ. Pr., 1976. Sees four main patterns: righteousness (justice), discipleship, faith, love. Greek philosophy (especially Plato, Aristotle, and Stoics) informs all of these to some degree. **[6783]**

————. "From Justin to Origen: The Pattern of Apologetic." *Prud* 4(1972), 1-22. Despite individual differences Apologists show common development, dealing with same logical themes, moving from apologetic to protreptic discourse, and shifting from large themes to individual points. **[6784]**

————. "The Platonic Ideas in Second-Century Christian Thought." *Prud* 12(1980), 31-45. Transcendence, especially in Justin, Clement, and Tertullian. The Forms are absorbed in concept of God. Demons fill void between God and man. **[6785]**

————. "Problems of Ethics in Early Christian Thought." *Prud* 7(1975), 11-19. Christians emphasized ethics because their moral behavior provided evidence of the truth of their claim to change lives by their doctrine. They gave new meanings to terms which Stoics and others had been using for centuries. **[6786]**

PALMER, D. W. "Atheism, Apologetic and Negative Theology in the Greek Apologists of the Second Century." *VigChr* 37(1983), 234-259. Primary source for this approach is Middle Platonism as passed along by Hellenistic Judaism. **[6787]**

PERKINS, P. "Ordering the Cosmos: Irenaeus and the Gnostics," in *Nag Hammadi, Gnosticism, and Early Christianity,* ed. C. W. Hedrick and R. Hodgson, Jr. (Peabody, MA: Hendrickson, 1986), pp. 221-238. Irenaeus' arguments against Gnosticism take form of anti-Platonic polemic common in Christian apologetics of second century. There are Platonist strains in Gnosticism, but Irenaeus probably overemphasizes them to make his refutations seem more effective. **[6788]**

POKORNY, P. "Greek Philosophy in the Apostle Paul's Letter to the Colossians," in #69, I, pp. 286-291. This letter, regardless of authorship or date, shows that Christianity inherited from Greek philosophy a concept of the world as good, in contrast to Gnostic anti-materialism. **[6789]**

RIST, J. M. *Platonism and its Christian Heritage.* London: Variorum Rprts, 1985. Essays originally published between 1962 and 1983. **[6790]**

SHIEL, J. *Greek Thought and the Rise of Christianity.* London: Longmans, Green, 1968. Chapters on Greek rationalism, its religious roots, rise of Christianity and the synthesis of the two. Introductory essays with excerpts from primary and modern secondary sources. **[6791]**

SIMON, M. "Early Christianity and Pagan Thought. Confluences and Conflicts." *RelStud* 9(1973), 385-399. One reason for Christianity's triumph was lack of coherence among pagan philosophies and religions. While mocking new cult, various pagan thinkers, from Seneca to Julian, imitated one aspect or another of it. Some tried to establish competing cult around some figure. **[6792]**

SMITH, E. W. "The Form and Religious Background of Romans VII 24-25a." *NovTest* 13(1971), 127-135. In this passage Paul reflects a Hellenistic lamentation tradition comparable to passages in Epictetus. **[6793]**

STEAD, G. C. "The Freedom of the Will and the Arian Controversy," in #6335, pp. 245-257. Earlier thinkers had regarded free will as a mark of human rationality, given by God. During Arian controversy of early fourth century it came to be viewed as a mark of weakness and corruption and not part of divine nature. **[6794]**

———. "Knowledge of God in Eusebius and Athanasius," in #5650, pp. 229-242. Mankind can contemplate and know abstract ideas and even angels, but not God. Contemplation is a more active process than it is in Greek philosophers from whom it is borrowed. **[6795]**

TANNER, R. G. "The Epistle to Diognetus and Contemporary Greek Thought." *StudPatr* 15(1984), 495-508. Survey of textual and interpretive problems. Document is an exhortation (of mid-second century) for an unknown recipient to convert from the old philosophy to the new Christian philosophy. **[6796]**

———. "S Paul and Stoic Physics." *Studia Evangelica* 7(1982), 481-490. Evidence of influences of Middle Stoa can be found in P's concept of persistence of baptized believers, bodily resurrection, and second coming of Christ. Stoic views on epistemology and the *pneuma* (spirit) also seem to have had some impact on his thought. **[6797]**

TeSELLE, E. "*Regio dissimilitudinis* in the Christian Tradition and Its Context in Late Greek Philosophy." *AugStud* 6(1975), 153-179. Numerous Christian writers recount myth from Plato's *Rep* 269c-274d. Plutarch, Origen, and Porphyry passed it on to the Middle Ages. **[6798]**

THOM, J. C. "The Journey Up and Down: Pythagoras in Two Greek Apologists." *ChHist* 58(1989), 299-308. Theophilus and Hermias refer to P's investigations of natural phenomena by the phrase "journey up and down." P is a symbol of the speculations of

Greek natural philosophers about heavenly and earthly things. [6798a]

THOMPSON, J. W. *The Beginnings of Christian Philosophy: The Epistle to the Hebrews.* Washington, DC: Catholic Biblical Assoc. of Amer., 1982. Author of letter was not a philosopher but his arguments reflect an effort to construct a Christian philosophy. He sees two stages of instruction and rejects animal sacrifice, themes common to Hellenistic philosophy. [6799]

———. "Hebrews 9 and Hellenistic Concepts of Sacrifice." *JBL* 98(1979), 567-578. Inadequacy of animal sacrifice is widespread notion by early Christian era. Passage in Hebrews 9.11-14 shows Platonic influence. [6800]

TIMOTHY, H. B. *The Early Christian Apologists and Greek Philosophy, Exemplified by Irenaeus, Tertullian and Clement of Alexandria.* Assen, Netherlands: Van Gorcum, 1973. Describes conditions in Hellenistic era, after city states' loss of power. Many philosophies and religions grew up in response to people's needs. Christianity, Gnosticism, Greek philosophy proved most popular. Christians consistently opposed Gnosticism but diverged in their attitude toward philosophy. Ir was defensive, T hostile, C accomodating. Last position triumphed, contributing to Christian church's success. [6801]

VAN DEN BELD, A. "Romans 7:14-25 and the Problem of *Akrasia.*" *RelStud* 21(1985), 495-515. After analysis of problem of *akrasia* (weakness of will), a crucial passage in Romans is interpreted to mean that one can do evil intentionally or involuntarily, but not from free will. [6802]

VAN DEN BROEK, R. "Eugnostus and Aristides on the Ineffable God," in #5650, pp. 202-218. Comparison of concept of God in apologist Aristides and in *Eugnostus the Blessed*, which is not a Gnostic treatise but a Christianized Jewish work. Its theology most closely resembles that of Presocratic philosopher Xenophanes. [6803]

———. cf. #6709.

VAN WINDEN, J. C. M. "'An Appropriate Beginning': The Opening Passage of Saint Basil's *In Hexaemeron,*" in #6335, pp. 307-311. Basil sees opening lines of Genesis as intended to refute philosophical schools which taught a spontaneous beginning to cosmos. Term *arche* is taken as equivalent to its use by Greek philosophers. [6804]

VESEY, G. *The Philosophy in Christianity.* Cambridge Univ. Pr., 1989; *Philosophy* Suppl. 25. Collection of essays; relevant ones are abstracted herein. [6805]

WALKER, D. P. *The Ancient Theology. Studies in Christian Platonism, from the Fifth to the Eighteenth Century.* London: Duckworth, 1972. Studies ancient pseudonymous texts of patristic era, ascribed to Orpheus, Pythagoras, Hermes Trismegistus, and others, which formed basis of Christian apologetics in first four centuries. Doctrines of monotheism and creation through Logos loomed large in these writings and let Christians argue that Greek philosophy was derived from Old Testament. [6806]

WHITTAKER, J. *Studies in Platonism and Patristic Thought.* London: Variorum Rprts, 1984. Collection of twenty-eight previously published articles. Many are textual or paleographic. [6807]

WILES, M. "The Philosophy in Christianity: Arius and Athanasius," in #6805, pp. 41-52. Philosophical influences are more evident in form of debate over Jesus' nature than in particular answers. Orthodox position is essentially a Platonic ontology.   **[6808]**

WILKEN, R. L. "Collegia, Philosophical Schools, and Theology," in *The Catacombs and Colosseum: The Roman Empire as the Setting of Primitive Christianity*, ed. S. Benko and J. J. O'Rourke (Valley Forge, PA: Judson Pr., 1971), pp. 268-291. Second-century Christians identified themselves with philosophical schools only partly because of similarities of thought. Such an identification brought recognition and higher status than that associated with new religious cults.   **[6809]**

————. "Justification by Works. Fate and Gospel in the Roman Empire." *CTM* 40(1969), 379-392. To combat fatalistic determinism of Hellenistic philosophy, early Christian apologists taught justification by works.   **[6810]**

WOLFSON, H. A. "The Identification of *Ex Nihilo* with Emanation in Gregory of Nyssa." *HThR* 63(1970), 53-60. Earlier Christian writers distinguished Neoplatonic emanation from Biblical creation. Former was seen as eternal process arising from necessity. Gregory, however, equates "nothing" of *ex nihilo* with ineffability of God and can see Biblical creation as equivalent to Neoplatonic emanation.   **[6811]**

————. "Patristic Arguments against the Eternity of the World." *HThR* 59(1966), 351-367. Discussion of six arguments used by Christian writers to refute Greek philosophical concept that world was not created but has always existed.   **[6812]**

————. "Plato's Pre-Existent Matter in Patristic Philosophy," in #80, pp. 409-420. Most church fathers interpreted Plato to mean that pre-existent matter was created. They denied that world was created from pre-existent, uncreated matter.   **[6813]**

————. cf. #6682.

For related items see #167, #237, #5620, #5664, #6376, #6424

JUSTIN MARTYR (died ca. 165 A. D.)

All that is known of Justin's life is what can be gleaned from his own writings, especially the *Dialogue with Trypho*, in which he relates the intellectual odyssey which carried him through various philosophical schools until he arrived at the true philosophy, Christianity. He was born in the Roman colony of Flavia Neapolis in Samaria, apparently of Greco-Roman ancestry, and as an adult lived and studied in Ephesus, on the Aegean coast of Turkey. While contemplating the inadequacies of Greek philosophy one day, he tells us, he encountered an old man, who pointed him toward the true philosophy, Christianity.

Justin is fundamentally a Platonist, thinking of God as transcendent and creating the world through the Logos, who serves an intermediary role something like that of the Demiurge. Justin does not reject all Greek philosophies out of hand, nor does he resort to the theory that the Greeks had borrowed from Jewish scriptures to account for some points of resemblance which both pagan and Christians saw between their two systems. Instead, Justin adapts a Stoic idea, the *logos spermatikos* ("seedlike reason"), to explain the relationship among the different schools of thought and the superiority of Christianity. The *logos*, according to the Stoics, was present in all men, though better used by some than others. Justin concedes that point and claims that all earlier philosophers had been able to grasp some facet of the truth. Christians, he maintains, have not just seeds or fragments of the *logos* but the *Logos*, the incarnate word of God revealed to them. This makes the Christian philosophy superior to any other. After his conversion (ca. 130 A. D.) Justin continued to live the life of a philosopher, devoting himself to a simple lifestyle and always wearing the plain cloak typical of a philosopher. He was martyred, probably during a persecution which broke out in the mid-160's. His extant works consist of the *Dialogue with Trypho* and two *Apologies*.

BARNARD, L. W. *Justin Martyr. His Life and Thought.* Cambridge Univ. Pr., 1967. Survey, emphasizing Greek philosophy in J's background and development of his doctrine of Logos; importance of *logos spermatikos*.   [6814]

———. "Justin Martyr's Eschatology." *VigChr* 19(1965), 86-98. J's language varies with circumstances of his writing. *Second Apology* is directed against Stoics.   [6815]

———. "The Logos Theology of St. Justin Martyr." *DR* 89(1971), 132-141. J seems not to have borrowed idea of *logos spermatikos* from Philo but to have taken core of it from Stoicism and developed it himself.   [6816]

CHADWICK, H. *Early Christian Thought and the Classical Tradition. Studies in Justin, Clement and Origen.* London: Oxford Univ. Pr., 1966. Survey of the three writers with close attention given to influences of Greek philosophy, especially Plato.   [6817]

———. "Justin Martyr's Defence of Christianity." *BJRL* 47(1965), 275-297. Review of J's intellectual background, including influence of Greek philosophy.   [6818]

DAVIDS, A. *Justinus Philosophus et Martyr. Bibliographie 1923-1973.* Nijmegen: Kathol. Univ. der Godgeleerheid, 1983. Not annotated.   [6819]

DENNING-BOLLE, S. "Christian Dialogue as Apologetic. The Case of Justin Martyr Seen in Historical Context." *BJRL* 69(1986-87), 492-510. For Greek philosophers dialogue was a technique for discovering truth. Christians such as J used the dialogue form to display the truth which they believed they already knew.   [6820]

DE VOGEL, C. J. "Problems Concerning Justin Martyr. Did Justin Find a Certain Continuity Between Greek Philosophy and Christian Faith?" *Mnem* 31(1981), 360-388. J saw common metaphysical base in Platonism, Christianity. They seemed to him to have same truth as their ultimate object.   [6821]

DROGE, A. J. "Justin Martyr and the Restoration of Philosophy." *ChHist* 56(1987), 303-319. Like Numenius tracing Platonism and Pythagoreanism back to oriental sources, J claims that Platonism was derived only from Moses and prophets, who recorded their reception of the *Logos* in scripture.   [6822]

KERESZTES, P. "Justin, Roman Law and the Logos." *Latomus* 45(1986), 339-346. As a defense against Roman persecution of Christianity J, in his *Second Apology*, describes Jesus as incarnation of philosophical Logos, making Christianity greater than any other philosophical school. **[6823]**

OSBORN, E. F. *Justin Martyr.* Tuebingen: Mohr, 1973. Survey for non-specialists. J's presentation of Christianity as a philosophical system in face of a morally bankrupt world has implications for modern situation. **[6824]**

PRICE, R. M. "Hellenization and Logos Doctrine in Justin Martyr." *VigChr* 42(1988), 18-23. To speak of "hellenization" of J's thought implies too strong a distinction between Judaic and Greek traditions by second century A. D. J's ideas do not resemble those of Middle Platonism as closely as sometimes maintained. **[6825]**

SKARSANNE, O. "The Conversion of Justin Martyr." *StudTheol* 30 (1976), 53-73. Two accounts of J's conversion (*Dial.* 1-8 and *2 Apol.* 12) appear contradictory. Old Man in former account, a kind of angelic Socrates, may be J's teacher. **[6826]**

VAN WINDEN, J. C. M. *An Early Christian Philosopher: Justin Martyr's Dialogue with Trypho, Chapters One to Nine.* Leiden: Brill, 1971. Greek text with lengthy commentary. Justin does not see Christianity as continuation of Greek philosophy but as reversion to a primordial philosophy. **[6827]**

ATHENAGORAS (ca. 175 A. D.)

Athenagoras is a shadowy figure, whose very existence is doubted by some. One of the works attributed to him is an apology for the Christian faith, the other a treatise on the resurrection. A heading on one ms. describes him as "the philosopher of Athens." His *Apology* defends Christians against charges of cannibalism, incest, and other heinous crimes. His treatise *On the Resurrection* shows strong philosophical influences, especially Platonic, as he argues the necessity of a resurrection from the nature of God and the nature of man. The *Apology* is addressed to the emperor Marcus Aurelius and his son Commodus, providing the only clue to when A lived.

BARNARD, L. W. "Notes on Athenagoras." *Latomus* 31(1972), 413-432. A was familiar with M. Aurelius' philosophy before he presented his *Legatio* to emperor. His manner of presentation shows influence of Galen. **[6828]**

————. "The Philosophical and Biblical Background of Athenagoras," in *Epektasis. Mélanges patristiques offerts à Jean Danielou*, ed. by J. Fontaine and C. Kannengiesser (Paris: Beauchesne, 1972), pp. 3-16. A drew his philosophical arguments from collections of texts used in philosophical schools in his day. His Biblical citations are intended as a base for Christianization of Hellenistic philosophy. **[6829]**

GRANT, R. M. "Five Apologists and Marcus Aurelius." *VigChr* 42(1988), 1-17. Survey of apologetic works addressed to emperor by Apollinaris, Melito, Tatian, Miltiades, and A. All refer to Christianity as a philosophy, an equation accepted by M's court physician

Galen.   [6830]

MALHERBE, A. J. "Athenagoras on Christian Ethics." *JEH* 20(1969), 1-5. A's discussion of Christian ethics in *Supplicatio* 11 and 12 uses Platonist and anti-Epicurean arguments.   [6831]

———. "Athenagoras on the Location of God." *ThZ* 26(1970), 46-52. Middle Platonist definitions of space and gods as occupying it are basis of A's claim that God must be one because more than one thing cannot occupy a space simultaneously.   [6832]

———. "Athenagoras on the Poets and Philosophers," in #6749, I, pp. 214-225. In his *Supplicatio* A criticizes poets and myths on basis of Middle Platonic dialectical criteria. Philosophers had some ability to perceive noetically but were confined to material forms. Plato, however, is quoted with approval. Except for one quotation from Empedocles, he is only philosopher quoted verbatim.   [6833]

———. "The Holy Spirit in Athenagoras." *JThS* 20(1969), 538-542. For A the Spirit resembles World Soul of Middle Platonism.   [6834]

———. "The Structure of Athenagoras, *Supplicatio pro Christianis*." *VigChr* 23(1969), 1-20. Argument follows Middle Platonist lines, probably from an epitome.   [6835]

MARCOVICH, M. "Athenagoras, *De Resurrectione*, 3.2." *JThS* 29(1978), 146-147. In his argument for bodily resurrection A attempts to deal with three Greek theories of matter as put forth by Presocratics, Anaxagoras, and Plato.   [6836]

TERTULLIAN (ca. 165-220 A. D.)

Quintus Septimius Tertullianus Florens was born in Carthage, in North Africa. Educated as a lawyer, he converted to Christianity at about age forty. He argued against the priority of reason over faith and coined the dictum "I believe because it is absurd." Some would argue, however, that he is not irrational (#6842). Though critical of philosophy, he was "one of the first men to have done philosophy in a Christian sense."

His philosophical grounding is largely Stoic. Like the Stoics, he is materialist, i. e., he conceives of God and the soul (and anything that is real) as bodies. What he knows of Greek philosophy he derives from earlier Christian writers (Justin Martyr, Tatian, Theophilus, Irenaeus) and from the Greek physician Soranus, who wrote in the early second century. T is able to cite Heraclitus and Democritus among the Presocratics, Plato, Aristotle, and several Stoics. His own thought is expressed in a love of paradox and absurdity. His best known statement on the relationship of philosophy to Christianity is his famous rhetorical outburst: "What has Athens to do with Jerusalem? What has the Academy to do with the Church? . . . . Away with all attempts to produce a Stoic, Platonic, and dialectical Christianity."

Most of his works contain passing references (largely critical) to earlier philosophers or schools, but only two could be classed as philosophical treatises. The *Against Hermogenes* attempts to refute the claims of one of his opponents that matter is eternal. In another treatise, *On the Soul*, he attacks the Platonic concept of the soul, its pre-existence, and its transmigration. In his writings, however, he uses the emanation metaphors (stream from source, light from sun) for God which pagan philosophers were so fond of.

T eventually aligned himself with a puritanical and heretical Christian sect, the Montanists. We know nothing of his life after 220 A. D. An annual bibliography of work on him appears in *REAug*.

AYERS, R. H. *Language, Logic and Reason in the Church Fathers. A Study of Tertullian, Augustine and Aquinas.* Hildesheim, Ger.: Olds, 1979. T and Aug both betray strong influences of rhetoric, which built its logic on Aristotle and Stoics. View that T was irrational and paradoxical is not borne out by close study of his work. He borrows from Stoicism. Aug. draws from Neoplatonism. Both regarded philosophy as a means of expressing truths found in revelation. **[6837]**

———. "Tertullian's 'Paradoxes' and 'Contempt for Reason' Reconsidered." *ExposT* 87(1976), 308-311. Invective and vituperative language are more likely to be found in T's conclusions than in the bodies of his works. Such *indignatio* is a rhetorical technique and does not indicate any anti-rationalism in T. **[6838]**

BARNES, T. D. *Tertullian. A Historical and Literary Study.* Oxford: Clarendon Pr., 1971. Begins by refuting standard biographical and chronological data. Attempts to trace his intellectual and literary development. Chapter on "The Christian Sophist." Lengthy bibliography. **[6839]**

BOUGHNER, R. "Tertullian and the Satiric." *CF* 32(1978), 21-28. In themes and compositional technique T shows influence of satire and diatribe. **[6840]**

BRAY, G. "The Legal Concept of *Ratio* in Tertullian." *VigChr* 31(1977), 94-116. Term is used juridically, with no apparent influence from Stoic philosophy. **[6841]**

GONZALEZ, J. L. "Athens and Jerusalem Revisited. Reason and Authority in Tertullian." *ChHist* 43(1974), 17-25. T is not irrational. He converted to Montanism after deciding logically that catholic church had abandoned true faith. **[6842]**

HOUSE, D. K. "The Relation of Tertullian's Christology to Pagan Philosophy." *Dion* 12(1988), 29-36. T regarded Plato as originator of all heresies. His concept of *logos* is closest to Stoic idea. **[6843]**

SIDER, R. D. *Ancient Rhetoric and the Art of Tertullian.* Oxford Univ. Pr., 1971. Study of influence of Aristotle, Cicero, Quintilian on T's rhetorical techniques. His use of those techniques affects his interpretation of Biblical passages and suggests he was seeking some integration of Christian and classical world views. **[6844]**

———. "On Symmetrical Composition in Tertullian." *JThS* 24(1973), 405-423. T's use of this technique suggests that classical culture influenced nature as well as form of his thought. **[6845]**

VANDER LOF, L. J. "Tertullian on the Continued Existence of Things and Beings." *REAug* 34(1988), 14-24. Philosophically and theologically, continued existences of things is of tremendous importance for T. He argues that it can take one of four forms: derivation of the whole from part; evolution; procreation; resurrection. [6846]

CLEMENT OF ALEXANDRIA (ca. 150-215 A. D.)

Clement, a teacher in a catechetical school in Alexandria, was the first Christian thinker after Justin to consciously build his religious faith upon a philosophical system. He may have been a pupil of the same Ammonius who taught Plotinus. C does not despise Greek philosophy, as Tertullian did, and sees it as more than just a "seed" of the truth, to use Justin Martyr's image. For C, Greek philosophy can be a preparation for understanding truths revealed by God. While stressing biblical ideas, such as the grace of God, he phrases them Platonically. His moral teaching is close to the Stoics of the Roman era, especially Musonius Rufus.

C adapted ideas of Plato and eastern mystics and also borrowed some Stoic elements, especially in ethics. His most non-Christian idea is his division of believers into two groups: ordinary believers and gnostics. Ordinary Christians live strictly by faith, without any deeper understanding. The "gnostics," or enlightened Christians, have access to a secret tradition handed down to the apostles by Jesus, perhaps during the time between his resurrection and his ascension. This view of Christ's oral teaching fit well with Plato's distrust of writing (*Phaedrus, Letter* 7).

For C knowledge (*gnosis*) leads to salvation, and reason is the basis of faith. His thought is expressed in three books: the *Protrepticus* (*Exhortation to the Greeks*); the *Paedagogus* (*The Instructor*), a guide to daily life and morals; and the *Stromateis* (*Miscellanies*), a discussion of philosophy and religion intended for the general public. The three are intended as a connected series.

BRADLEY, D. J. M. "The Transformation of the Stoic Ethic in Clement of Alexandria." *Augustinianum* 14(1974), 41-66. C was interested in Stoic ethics but could not allow dependence of ethics on physics. [6847]

CLARK, E. *Clement's Use of Aristotle: The Aristotelian Contribution to Clement of Alexandria's Refutation of Gnosticism.* New York: Mellen, 1977. C uses some Aristotelian themes, especially relating to volition and choice, in his arguments against the Gnostics. C did not acknowledge his debt to Ar in every instance. [6848]

FERGUSON, J. *Clement of Alexandria.* New York: Twayne, 1974. Introductory chapter, exposition of each of his major works. [6849]

FLOYD, W. E. G. *Clement of Alexandria's Treatment of the Problem of Evil.* Oxford Univ. Pr., 1971. C's approach to problem of evil was result of his reaction to Gnosticism and his Neoplatonism. Dualism and blind determinism appear to him as particular problems for Christian thinkers. But evil has its place in God's providence. [6850]

FORTIN, E. L. "Clement of Alexandria and the Esoteric Tradition." *StudPatr* 9(1966), 41-56. Comparison of C's claim of secret knowledge with some of Plato's comments, especially *Epist.* 7,340b-345a. [6851]

LILLA, S. R. C. *Clement of Alexandria: A Study in Christian Platonism and Gnosticism.* Oxford Univ. Pr., 1971. C's theology/philosophy derives from three sources: Alexandrian Jewish thought, Platonism, and Gnosticism, but he evaluates the rest from Platonic viewpoint. His ethics are a mixture of Platonism, Aristotelianism, and Stoicism. Philo was the source of his cosmogony and his understanding of *logos.*   **[6852]**

McLELLAND, J. C. "The Alexandrian Quest of the Non-historical Christ." *ChHist* 37(1968), 355-364. Platonism, passed on by Philo and Albinus, raised problem of Being and Becoming for Alexandrian theologians attempting to explain incarnation.   **[6853]**

――――. *God the Anonymous: A Study in Alexandrian Philosophical Theology.* Cambridge, MA: Philadephia Patristic Foundation, 1976. Western thought is a blend of Greek, Jewish, and Christian elements. Philosophical theology of Alexandria is ultimate product of these elements. It stresses that God is nameless, immutable, and impassible. Mystical union with him is highest form of knowledge.   **[6854]**

MORTLEY, R. "The Theme of Silence in Clement of Alexandria." *JThS* 24(1973), 197-202. For C silence demonstrates mastery over physical nature and is highest form of contemplation. It is thus part of his ethic and epistemology.   **[6855]**

OSBORN, E. F. "Paul and Plato in Second-Century Ethics." *StudPatr* 15(1984), 474-485. C's *Stromateis* synthesize Paul and Plato. C understood Paul better than Plato. **[6856]**

――――. *The Philosophy of Clement of Alexandria.* Cambridge Univ. Pr., 1978; rprt. Survey under headings: God, Goodness, and Truth. C's "eclectic enthusiasm" leads him to select any doctrine from an earlier school which he feels has some validity. In reading him one must be mindful that he wrote his works in a deliberately abstruse style to frustrate opponents and superficial readers.   **[6857]**

――――. cf. #6655.

PAULSEN, D. "Ethical Individualism in Clement of Alexandria." *CTM* 43(1972), 3-20. Unlike most Christian writers, C stresses individual perfection over such collective ideals as love, justice. Reflects Stoic doctrine of *apatheia.*   **[6858]**

PROCOPE, J. F. "Quiet Christian Courage: A Topic in Clemens Alexandrinus and its Philosophical Background." *StudPatr* 15(1984), 489-494. For C, influenced by Socrates and Stoics, courage is virtue which confronts external trials, inner temptations. **[6859]**

RICHARDSON, W. "The Basis of Ethics: Chrysippus and Clement of Alexandria." *StudPatr* 9(1966), 87-97. C cites Chrysippus often, drawn to him perhaps due to his doctrine of *oikeiosis.* There is a natural tendency, C believes, to strive for good.   **[6860]**

SOLMSEN, F. "Early Christian Interest in the Theory of Demonstration," in #6736, pp. 281-291. C's theory of demonstration (*apodeixis*) in *Strom.* 8 is derived from Aristotle and resembles frag of Galen on same subject.   **[6861]**

――――. "Providence and the Souls. A Platonic Chapter in Clement of Alexandria." *MH* 26(1969), 229-251. In treating this subject C follows *Laws* 10 closely. Unlike Origen, he makes no effort to reconcile Platonism and Christian thought.   **[6862]**

VAN DEN HOEK, A. *Clement of Alexandria and his Use of Philo in the* Stromateis: *An Early Christian Reshaping of a Jewish Model.* Leiden: Brill, 1988. Inventory of all passages from Philo which appear in C, designed as a research tool. **[6863]**

ZANDEE, J. *"The Teachings of Silvanus" and Clement of Alexandria: A New Document of Alexandrian Theology.* Leiden: Ex Oriente Lux, 1977. Comparison of the more popular "Teachings" with the more sophisticated C shows similar influences of Stoicism in ethics and Platonism in theology. **[6864]**

For related item see #6726a.

ORIGEN OF ALEXANDRIA (ca. 185-253 A. D.)

Origen was head of the catechetical school in Alexandria from 204-231. Because of a difference of opinion with the bishop of the city he went to Caesarea, in Palestine, where he spent the rest of his life. His textual studies of the Bible resulted in the monumental *Hexapla*, an edition of the Old Testament in which different translations (Hebrew, Greek, Latin, et al.) are displayed in six columns. One of his first philosophical works was the *De principiis (On First Principles).* His doctrine of the soul in this work is largely Neoplatonic. He read the scriptures on three levels (literal, moral, and allegorical), corresponding to the three parts of a human being (flesh, soul, and spirit), the three persons of the Trinity, and the three Neoplatonic hypostases. Only fragments of the original work survive, but it can be read in a Latin translation made in the fourth century.

In his *Contra Celsum* O rebuts arguments against Christianity put forth by a pagan critic. He displays a wide acquaintance with Greek philosophical writing and, like Celsus, rejects anthropomorphism, worship of images, and overly literal readings of scripture. Celsus' work no longer survives, so the quotations in Origen are our only source for reconstructing it.

Philosophical influences on O show up in concepts rather than in direct quotations. The Neoplatonists exercised the strongest influence on his thought, though he knows the Stoics and Peripatetics as well. Some scholars even find elements of Gnosticism and Indian philosophy in his thought. He has been called "the first Christian to be a genuinely philosophical theologian." He was considered heretical by later church authorities.

COX, P. "Origen and the Bestial Soul. A Poetics of Nature." *VigChr* 36(1982), 115-140. Discusses allegorical and metaphorical interpretations of animals. **[6865]**

CROUZEL, H. *Bibliographie critique d'Origene.* The Hague: Nijhoff, 1971. Chronologically arranged bibliography, covering 1468-1968. It has been called "the necessary starting-point for Origen studies." Updated annually in *BLE.* **[6866]**

——. "The Literature on Origen, 1970-1988." *ThS* 49(1988), 499-516. Essay emphasizing books but taking note of some articles. Trend is away from Origen as a philosopher in theologian's garb to seeing him as man of the church. **[6867]**

——. *Origen,* transl. A. S. Worrall. San Francisco: Harper & Row, 1989. Looks at life

and personality, exegesis, spirituality (including doctrine of knowledge), and theology.
References to philosophical influences throughout.   [6868]

DANIELOU, J. *Origen*, transl. W. Mitchell. New York: Sheed & Ward, 1972; rprt.
Four parts: O and his times; O and the Bible; O's system; O's theology of the spiritual
life. O knew Plato's works, especially *Tim* and *Phaedrus*, knew Aristotle and Chrysippus.
Does not seem to have known Plotinus. He is fundamentally eclectic.   [6869]

DILLON, J. "Knowledge of God in Origen," in #5650, pp. 219-228. O uses light imagery drawn from Platonist writings to describe God. His nature is unknowable, but his
existence can be known, through his Logos and his works.   [6870]

——. "Origen's Doctrine of the Trinity and Some Later Neoplatonic Theories," in
#6374, pp. 19-23. O's doctrine of different levels of activity of persons of trinity
resembles Proclus' idea of range of activity of causal principles. Both seem to draw from
originally Platonic concept.   [6871]

FARINA, R. "Bibliografia Origeniana 1960-1970." *Salesianum* 32(1970), 619-702.
Bibliography, thematically arranged.   [6872]

GAMBLE, H. Y. "Euhemerism and Christology in Origen, *Contra Celsum* III, 22-43."
VigChr 33(1979), 12-29. Celsus seems to have used Euhemerus' theory of gods as
glorified humans against claims for Christ's divinity. O refutes him here.   [6873]

HOVLAND, C. W. "The Dialogue between Origen and Celsus," in *Pagan and Christian
Anxiety: A Response to E. R. Dodds*, ed. R. C. Smith and J. Lounibos (Lanham, MD:
Univ. Pr. of Amer., 1984), pp. 191-216. E. R. Dodds favored rationalist approach to the
world and presented conflict between O and C in a way that favored C. This survey
stresses that basic difference between them was Greek philosophical emphasis on rational
argument and Christian insistence on belief.   [6874]

McNAMEE, K. "Origen in the Papyri." *CF* 27(1973), 28-51. Eleven Egyptian papyri
preserve frags of O which have textual as well as philosophical/theological value. Two
recently discovered texts, *Dialogue with Heracleides* and *On Easter*, are particularly important in latter regard.   [6875]

MEREDITH, A. "Origen, Plotinus and the Gnostics." *HeythJ* 26(1985), 383-398. Like
the Gnostics, O and P de-emphasize the material and stress God's transcendence. They
differ from Gnostics in their emphasis on human freedom and from one another on
matter of resurrection and degree of personality they attribute to God.   [6876]

O'CLEIRIGH, P. M. "The Meaning of Dogma in Origen," in #5639, I, pp. 201-216. O
presents his teachings systematically, as truths or tenets (*dogma*), not opinion. Earlier
philosophical schools had used term in this way. O knows and uses Greek philosophical
thought whenever it will support his reading of Scripture.   [6877]

——. "Prime Matter in Origen's World's Picture." *StudPatr* 16(1985), 260-263. O
affirms existence of prime matter, as did most Platonists of his time, but he uses it only
as a basis for a genuine dualism between visible and invisible reality.   [6878]

OSBORN, E. F. "The Intermediate World in Origen's *On Prayer*," in *Origeniana secunda*.

Second colloque international des études origèniennes (Bari, 20-23 septembre 1977), ed. H. Crouzel and A. Quacquarelli (Rome: Ed. dell'Ateneo, 1980), pp. 95-103. Intermediaries such as saints, angels, and Christ, do not constitute stages leading to contact with God but aid in establishing such contact.   **[6879]**

RIST, J. M. "Beyond Stoic and Platonist: A Sample of Origen's Treatment of Philosophy (*Contra Celsum* 4.62-70)," in #6335, pp. 228-238. O does more than merely pass on ideas from earlier schools. He has mastered and integrated them. This passage, on origin of evil, sheds light on Stoic views on *daimones* and cosmic cycles.   **[6880]**

———. "The Importance of Stoic Logic in the *Contra Celsum*," in #6339, pp. 64-78. O seems to have known Stoic logic directly, not from Clement or some other intermediary. He seems to regard Stoics as masters of logic.   **[6881]**

———. cf. #6519.

ROBERTS, L. W. "Origen and Stoic Logic." *TAPhA* 101(1970), 433-444. Looks at three problems: relation between O's use of *pragmata* and Stoic definition of axiom; Stoic distinction between "truth" and "the true"; O's use of so-called Lazy Argument and syllogism of two conditionals.   **[6882]**

TOWNSLEY, A. L. "Origen's *ho theos*, Anaximander's *to theion* and a Series of Worlds. Some Remarks." *RSC* 23(1975), 5-13. Notes parallels between the two thinkers, but does not think O knew A. O may have derived his ideas from some source earlier than Middle or Neoplatonism, the usual sources suggested.   **[6883]**

TRIGG, J. W. *Origen: The Bible and Philosophy in the Third-Century Church.* Atlanta, GA: John Knox Pr., 1983. First three chapters look at O's intellectual and social background. Chapters 4-9 deal with his major works.   **[6884]**

VON BALTHASAR, H. U. *Origen: Spirit and Fire. A Thematic Anthology of His Writings*, transl. R. J. Daly. Washington, DC: Cath. Univ. of Amer. Pr., 1984. Introduction to O's thought and extracts from his writings organized around several themes: soul, word, spirit, God.   **[6885]**

WALTER, V. L. "A Reassessment of the Tension Between the Biblical Sources and Greek Philosophy as it is Expressed in the Play Between Biblical and Philosophical Concepts in the Development of Trinitarian Thought in Origen of Alexandria," in *Origeniana: Premier colloque international des études origèniennes (Montserrat 18-21 septembre 1973)*, ed. H. Crouzel et al. (Bari: Inst. di lett. crist. ant., 1975), pp. 289-295. Studies influences, especially Neoplatonic, on development of idea of Trinity.   **[6886]**

For related items see #6294, #6304, #7059.

MARIUS VICTORINUS (died ca. 363)

A teacher/philosopher, probably in Rome, who converted to Christianity around 357. He understood Christianity in terms of Neoplatonism, which he had studied for some years. He wrote commentaries on the works of Aristotle and the Neoplatonists, which he translated into Latin. His Christian works attacked the Arian heretics (who denied the identity of God the Son with the Father) and attempted to found Christian thought on Neoplatonic concepts. Most of his treatises are lost, except for commentaries on some of Paul's letters, a four-volume *Against Arius* and a treatise *On the Generation of the Divine Word*. His possible influence on later Christians such as Augustine is difficult to trace.

BELL, D. N. *"Esse, vivere, intelligere*. The Noetic Triad and the Image of God." *RecTh* 52(1985), 5-43. Idea of tripartite human personality becomes, in V, an analogy of Trinity.   [6887]

CLARK, M. T. "The Earliest Philosophy of the Living God. Marius Victorinus." *PACPhA* 41(1967), 87-94. Basically Neoplatonist, V applied Platonic categories to God in new ways.   [6888]

———. "Marius Victorinus Afer, Porphyry, and the History of Philosophy," in #6360, pp. 265-273. V and other Latin Neoplatonists drew upon Porphyry, not Plotinus.   [6889]

———. "A Neoplatonic Commentary on the Christian Trinity. Marius Victorinus," in #6374, pp. 24-33. V's views on Trinity were scripturally based, but he adduced Platonic ideas as philosophic defense of doctrine. Seems to have drawn from Porphyry more than from Plotinus.   [6890]

———. "The Neoplatonism of Marius Victorinus." *StudPatr* 11(1972), 13-19. V argues for Trinity by stressing active meaning of *hypostasis*. He remains Neoplatonist in insistence on incomprehensibility of first person of Trinity.   [6891]

———. "The Neoplatonism of Marius Victorinus the Christian," in #6339, pp. 153-159. V saw Neoplatonic theology as essentially correct.   [6892]

———. "The Psychology of Marius Victorinus." *AugStud* 5(1974), 149-166. V's concept of nature of soul is basis for his view of possibility of Trinity.   [6893]

For related items see #6707.

AUGUSTINE (354-430 A. D.)

Aurelius Augustinus (hereafter Aug) was born in the Roman province of Numidia, in North Africa, the child of a pagan father and a Christian mother, Monica. His father wanted him to become a teacher; Monica urged him to become a priest. Aug seems to have been confused, pulled in opposite directions, by these parental forces. He allowed himself to indulge in the debaucheries of imperial Roman society, taking a mistress (who gave him a son), luxuriating in the games and baths. All of this he later agonized over in his *Confessions*. He did teach rhetoric, first in Africa, then in Rome and Milan. Though he expressed no interest in Christianity at this early stage, it is noteworthy that that influence was always in his life, even before he began to read Greek philosophy.

At eighteen he read the *Hortensius*, a dialogue of Cicero's which is no longer extant. It inspired him to a search for some framework for his life. He was attracted to various schools which offered "wisdom." For a time he was a follower of the Persian teacher Mani, in spite of some misgivings about his doctrines. In Milan he came under the influence of Ambrose, the bishop of that city. Among Ambrose's circle of friends he became acquainted with Neoplatonist writings which seemed to him to answer many of the dissatisfactions he felt with Manichean ideas. Years later, reflecting on his spiritual journey, he claimed to have found in the "books of the Platonists" a foreshadowing of the doctrines of Christianity, except for the incarnation and resurrection of Christ.

After his conversion to Christianity in 386 Augustine's life centered on the question of the relation of his new faith to his lifelong interest in philosophy. For him philosophy was a search for the Good in human life. As he himself said, "Men have no reason to pursue philosophy except that they may be blessed (*beatus*)." Part of the problem in studying Aug as philosopher or theologian is the tight inter-weaving of these two strands. As J. M. Rist says, "it must still be emphasized that for Augustine it is impossible to demarcate the boundary between philosophy and theology." (#7037, p. 421). A. H. Armstrong agrees: "There is not and cannot be . . . any separation in St. Augustine between philosophy and theology" (#1, p. 205).

Neoplatonism is the primary philosophical influence on Aug. In Plotinus he found arguments that God was purely spirit and transcendent which seemed to be saying what the Gospel of John said. Plotinus' divine *Nous* also seemed to Aug another way of talking about John's Logos. The essential difference between Neoplatonism and Aug's thought (and all orthodox Christian thought) is the Christian insistence that God is absolutely One (though a trinity), not simply the greatest of a series of divine beings. In terms of cosmology Aug adheres to a fairly strict Platonic view, except that creation does not occur as a natural emanation or something inevitable from the nature of God. It is his free and gracious act. Matter exists as a substance capable of receiving a form. The Forms are ideas in the mind of God which are imposed on matter. The resulting copies are imperfect and Aug speaks of them as "numbers." Human beings are as imperfect as any created thing, but from the fact that they exist and are capable of knowing the truth, one can derive a proof for the existence of God, the source of all truth.

The end of Aug's philosophical quest, as noted above in his own words, is happiness, which he defines as union with God. This union is possible only by the ascent of the mind, which one achieves through philosophy. An important element in this ascent is the choices one makes, and Aug talks a great deal about freedom of the will. He believes that people do have free will, which can be moved by God's grace toward the desired end. His doctrine of the soul has Platonic elements, both in its separateness from the body and its role in perceiving and knowing. Unlike the Platonists, however, he views the soul as a creature, not a part of God.

Aug wrote voluminously, especially during the last thirty years of his life while he was bishop of Hippo, a town in North Africa, near the Mediterranean coast. His thought must be culled from sermons, Biblical commentaries, and treatises on varous topics, as well as from his autobiographical *Confessions* and the *City of God*, which sets forth his philosophy of history in the aftermath of the

Visigoths' sacking of Rome in 410.

ALEXANDER, W. A. "Sex and Philosophy in Augustine." *AugStud* 5(1974), 197-208. His effort to combine Platonism and Biblical thought leads Aug to argue that sex for procreation is good but that abstinence for higher, rational reasons is better. **[6894]**

ANDERSON, J. F. *St. Augustine and Being: A Metaphysical Essay.* The Hague: Nijhoff, 1965. Emphasizes Aug's existentialism as much as his essentialism. Looks at proofs for existence of God, creation, and nature of participation. Many of Aug's views which are supposedly Neoplatonic he thought he was drawing from Scripture. **[6895]**

ANDRESEN, C. *Bibliographia Augustiniana.* Darmstadt, Ger.: Wissenschaftliche Buchgesellschaft, 1973. Not annotated. **[6896]**

ARMSTRONG, A. H. *Saint Augustine and Christian Platonism.* Philadelphia: Villanova Univ. Pr., 1967; also in #6969, pp. 3-37. First section shows why Aug rejected Platonic contention that man's soul is naturally divine. Second part looks at differences between the two systems in regard to the body and material world. Third section discusses Aug's view of selective predestination and its detrimental effects. Platonism stressed God's goodness; Aug stressed his immutability and power. **[6897]**

BAKER, P. H. "Liberal Arts as Philosophical Liberation: St. Augustine's *De magistro*," in *Arts libéraux et philosophie au moyen âge. Actes du 4e Congres international de philosophie médiévale, Université de Montreal, Canada, 27 août-2 septembre 1967.* (Paris: Vrin, 1969), pp. 469-479. This dialogue, written in subdued style which Aug learned from Cicero, aims to show that words themselves do not teach. He is particularly concerned to refute Stoic doctrine of signs. **[6898]**

BEARDSLEY, P. "Augustine and Wittgenstein on Language." *Ph* 58(1983), 229-239. Wittgenstein seems to have understood Aug and to have recognized deep differences between them in theory of language and meaning. He does not seem to have known Aug's *De Magistro*, his fullest statement on subject of language. **[6899]**

BOOTH, E. G. T. "St. Augustine's *de Trinitate* and Aristotelian and Neo-Platonist Noetic." *StudPatr* 16(1985), 487-490. By a Neoplatonist critique of transcendent structuring Aug was able to resolve the *aporia* of Aristotle's views in *De anima* and *Meta* on the one hand and *NE* and *Parva naturalis* on the other. **[6900]**

——. "St. Augustine's *notitia sui* Related to Aristotle and the Early Neoplatonists." *Augustiniana* 27(1977), 70-132; 364-401; 28(1978), 183-221; 29(1979), 97-124. Study of development of idea of *noesis noeseos* from Ar to Aug. Evidence drawn from *De trinitate*. **[6901]**

BOURKE, V. J. "Augustine and the Roots of Moral Values." *AugStud* 6(1975), 65-74. For Aug, source of moral values is mind's innate ability to recognize right and good. Aug contrasted Christian value system with that of Epicureans and Stoics. **[6902]**

——. "Augustine of Hippo. The Approach of the Soul to God," in *The Spirituality of Western Christendom*, ed. E. R. Elde (Kalamazoo, MI: Cistercian Publ., 1976), pp. 1-12.

Though his views on spiritual development changed over time, Aug always maintained a threefold pattern of withdrawal from the world, focus on the soul, and rising above the soul to God. His writings, with emphasis on ultimate peace of the soul, suggest a mystical experience, not unlike that of Neoplatonists.   **[6903]**

——. *Wisdom from St. Augustine.* Houston, TX: Center for Thomistic Studies, 1984. Fourteen chapters, most previously published in journals, on various aspects of Aug's philosophical thought, e. g., theories of knowledge and reality, ethics, moral illumination, and world soul.   **[6904]**

BROWN, P. R. L. "Political Society," in #6969, pp. 311-335. Aug's political thought continues to be relevant because it is based on his rejection of "rational myth" that state is derived from rational aspects of human personality and experience. What makes a society for Aug is the "love" its people have for a certain object or goal.   **[6905]**

BUBACZ, B. *St. Augustine's Theory of Knowledge. A Contemporary Analysis.* New York: Mellen Pr., 1981. Aug's epistemology, which must be deduced from his writing, is pragmatic. His discussion of necessary truth is no mere restatement of Plato.   **[6906]**

BURKHILL, T. A. "St. Augustine's Notion of Nothingness in the Light of Some Recent Cosmological Speculation." *AugStud* 5(1974), 15-17. Aug sees God as a presence which prevents world from devolving into nothingness. From Neoplatonist background he conceives of nothingness as total absence of existence, not just a lower form.   **[6907]**

BURNYEAT, M. F. "Wittgenstein and Augustine *De Magistro.*" *PAS* Suppl. 61(1987), 1-24. In *De Magistro* Aug argues no person can teach another. Wittgenstein set this view over against Aug's description in *Conf.* of how he learned to speak as a child.   **[6908]**

CALLAHAN, J. F. *Augustine and the Greek Philosophers.* Philadelphia: Villanova Univ. Pr., 1967. Looks at Aug's formulation of a doctrine quite close to Anselm's ontological argument, flight of soul (a Plotinian concept), and relation of time to soul.   **[6909]**

CAMPION, E. "Defences of Classical Learning in St. Augustine's *De doctrina christiana* and Erasmus' *Anti-barbari.*" *HistEurIdeas* 4(1983), 467-472. Aug, and later Erasmus, argued that Christians should use pagan philosophy and literature to undergird their own beliefs and to argue against non-believers.   **[6910]**

CATON, H. "St. Augustine's Critique of Politics." *NewSchol* 47(1973-74), 433-457. Desire for domination estranges man from God and from himself because it puts him in conflict with natural laws. Withdrawal into one's self to love one's soul rejects the earthly city and creates disunity in it.   **[6911]**

CHADWICK, H. *Augustine.* New York: Oxford Univ. Pr., 1986. Stresses importance of Platonism and Neoplatonism in development of Aug's thought. He saw world as developing, based on "seminal principle" provided by God, who is Thought. Neoplatonist concepts of hierarchies of powers provide part of Aug's vocabulary.   **[6912]**

CHIDESTER, D. "The Symbolism of Learning in St. Augustine." *HThR* 76(1983), 73-90. Learning is analogous to pattern of cosmogony; brings eternal word and light in human existence.   **[6913]**

CHROUST, A.-H. "The Fundamental Ideas in St. Augustine's Philosophy of Law." *AmJJur* 18(1983), 57-79. Aug's views on law, not stated in one treatise but dispersed throughout his writings, are based on a combination of Plato's Ideas and Stoic concept of natural law. Natural law can be known by reasoning.   **[6914]**

COOPER, J. C. "The Basic Philosophical and Theological Notions of St. Augustine." *AugStud* 15(1984), 93-113. Aug sees Christian experience as a kind of philosophical quest, except that Christian undertakes a quest initiated by God, not by man.   **[6915]**

CRAIG, W. L. "Augustine on Foreknowledge and Free Will." *AugStud* 15(1984), 41-63. Aug seems not to have known Aristotle's views on determinism but to have been influenced by Cicero's *De fato*. Neoplatonic idea of realm of intelligible essences as object of *Nous* allows *Nous* to know everything while intelligibles act on their own.   **[6916]**

CRANZ. F. E. "*De Civitate Dei* XV,2, and Augustine's idea of the Christian Society," in #6969, pp. 404-421. Aug sees Christian society as still separate from the society of this world, even when secular society is dominated by Christians. Other Christian writers, such as Eusebius, did not share this view.   **[6917]**

————. "The Development of Augustine's Ideas on Society Before the Donatist Controversy," in #6969, pp. 336-403. Traces Aug's progress from thinking of society in terms borrowed from Greco-Roman philosophy to a more thoroughly Biblical view.   **[6918]**

CROUSE, R. D. "'*In aenigmate trinitas*' (*Confessions* XIII,5,6). The Conversion of Philosophy in St. Augustine's *Confessions*." *Dion* 11(1987), 53-62. Relationship between Christianity and Platonism in Aug's thought is not one of confrontation but of interpenetration.   **[6919]**

————. "*In Multa Defleximus*: *Confessions* X,29-43, and St. Augustine's Theory of Personality," in #6339, pp. 180-185. The "philosophical discovery of the person" cannot be credited to Aug. It goes back at least to Plato. His concept of a tripartite personality has influenced all subsequent western thought.   **[6920]**

————. "St. Augustine's *De Trinitate*. Philosophical Method." *StudPatr* 16(1985), 501-510. Argument of treatise *is* philosophical, against views of some European scholars. **[6921]**

DIHLE, A. "St. Augustine and His Concept of Will," in #128, pp. 123-144. Aug's theory seems unrelated to earlier philosophical concepts. Will, both divine and human, exists prior to and separate from any act of cognition.   **[6922]**

DiLORENZO, R. D. "Ciceronianism and Augustine's Conception of Philosophy." *AugStud* 13(1982), 171-176. Aug's assertion that acceptance of scriptural authority is beginning of search for truth grows out of effects of Cicero's thought, directly from the *Hortensius* and indirectly through Ambrose. For Cicero reason must submit to persuasion and authority.   **[6923]**

————. "'*Non pie quaerunt*.' Rhetoric, Dialectic, and the Discovery of the True in Augustine's *Confessions*." *AugStud* 14(1983), 117-128. Philosophical reasoning can find truth about God if it is guided by dialectic and recognizes necessity of piety.   **[6924]**

DOMBROWSKI, D. A. "Starnes on Augustine's Theory of Infancy: A Piagetian

Critique." *AugStud* 11(1980), 125-133. Examines epistemological issues in Aug's account of infancy. Reply to #7050.   [6925]

DOULL, J. A. "Augustinian Trinitarianism and Existential Theology." *Dion* 3(1979), 111-159. Aug's trinitarian doctrine was influenced by Neoplatonism.   [6926]

EVANS, G. R. "*Alienatio* and Abstract Thinking in Augustine." *DR* 98(1980), 190-200. Mathematics lies between matter and abstraction. Separation of the two is a gradual progression toward truth.   [6927]

———. *Augustine on Evil.* Cambridge Univ. Pr., 1982. For Aug evil has the effect of preventing the mind from perceiving higher, abstract ideas. Neoplatonist concept of mind becoming free of body provided an escape from this difficulty. Evil is not static but is a constantly moving state of disorder.   [6928]

FAY, T. A. "*Imago dei.* Augustine's Metaphysics of Man." *Antonianum* 49(1974), 173-197. Man can know God because soul is image of God. Decision to turn toward God is first step in quest which produces wisdom and purity of heart, which enables soul to perceive God in contemplative vision.   [6929]

FERWERDA, R. "Two Souls. Origen's and Augustine's Attitude toward the Two Souls Doctrine. Its Place in Greek and Christian Philosophy." *VigChr* 37(1983), 360-378. Aug's rejection of the idea is not anti-Manichean but anti-Gnostic. Examination of O and Neoplatonism on the subject.   [6930]

FLOOD, E. T. "The Narrative Structure of Augustine's *Confessions*: Time's Quest for Eternity." *IntPhQ* 28(1988), 141-162. Substituting memory for events remembered, time for memory, etc., Aug moves up a "chain of causal antecedents" toward God.   [6931]

FORTIN, E. L. "Augustine and the Problem of Christian Rhetoric." *AugStud* 5(1974), 85-100. While relying on classical theories of rhetoric, Aug emphasizes orator's teaching function over elegant style and persuasiveness.   [6932]

GERSON, L. "Saint Augustine's Neoplatonic Argument for the Existence of God." *Thom* 45(1981), 571-584. Argument is inconsistent with Aug's theology.   [6933]

GILSON, E. *The Christian Philosophy of St. Augustine*, transl. L. E. M. Lynch. New York: Octagon Pr., 1983; rprt. Traditional Catholic interpretation of Aug's system. Part I: Search for God through Understanding (i. e., soul and epistemology); II: Search for God through the Will (human agency and determinism); III: Contemplating God in His Works (Cosmology). Useful bibliography.   [6934]

GRANT, P. "Polanyi: The Augustinian Component." *NewSchol* 47(1973-74), 438-463. Study of Aug's impact on Polanyi in topics such as: illumination, amnesia, skepticism, referral, and others.   [6935]

HAGENDAHL, H. *Augustine and the Latin Classics, I: Testimonia; II: Augustine's Attitude.* Goeteborg, Sweden: Almqvist & Wiksell, 1967. Vol. I contains passages quoted by Aug and the texts in which he cites them. Vol. II discusses his methodology, accuracy of his quotations (usually high), increasing hostility to pagan thought. [6936]

HEIL, J. "Augustine's Attack on Skepticism, the *Contra Academicos*." *HThR* 65(1972), 99-116. Aug concentrates on ethical basis of Skepticism. By challenging goal of quietude he is able to undermine their position. [6937]

HENDLEY, B. "Saint Augustine and Cicero's Dilemma," in #1277, pp. 195-204. Aug refused to resolve dilemma of God's foreknowledge versus man's free will by denying the former, as Cicero did. [6938]

HENRY, P. *The Path of Transcendence. From Philosophy to Mysticism in Saint Augustine*, transl. F. F. Burch. Pittsburgh, PA: Pickwick Pr., 1981. Studies Neoplatonist influence on Aug's visionary experience at Ostia. Plotinus' vocabulary informs Aug's account throughout. [6939]

HOELSCHER, L. *The Reality of the Mind. St. Augustine's Philosophical Arguments for the Human Soul as a Spiritual Substance*. London: Routledge & Kegan Paul, 1987. Soul is a spiritual substance, different from, but part of, body. It has positive characteristics, e. g., rationality. The soul-body difference and unity is best explanation of nature of man. [6940]

HOPKINS, J. "Augustine on Fore-Knowledge and Free Will." *IntJPhRel* 8(1977), 111-126. Reply to W. L. Rowe #7039. [6941]

HOUSE, D. "St. Augustine's Account of the Relation of Platonism to Christianity in the *De civitate dei*." *Dion* 7(1983), 43-48. Aug saw Platonists' failure to become Christians as arising from their unwillingness to follow their own teachings to their necessary conclusion. [6942]

HOWIE, G. *Educational Theory and Practice in St. Augustine*. London: Routledge & Kegan Paul, 1969. Chapters discuss faith before understanding, Aug's doctrine of knowledge, mechanism of perception, Platonic bases of his understanding of mind. [6943]

JACKSON, B. D. "The Theory of Signs in St. Augustine's *De doctrina christiana*." *REAug* 15(1969), 9-49; also in #6669, pp. 92-147. Basis of Aug's understanding of signs is Stoic logic, but he is original in calling words signs and in using theory to interpret Scripture. [6944]

JOHNSON, D. W. "*Verbum* in the Early Augustine (386-397)." *RecAug* 8(1972), 25-53. As used by Aug during this period the word *verbum* is not Neoplatonic in origin nor does it equate to *sapientia*. Its closest meaning is Christian concept of God. [6945]

JORDAN, R. "Time and Contingency in St. Augustine," in #6969, pp. 255-279. Aug sees time as related to creation of ordered world. Original inchoate mass of matter needed no time because there was no change in it. Once matter was separated out and change and motion became observable, time could be measured. [6946]

KEYES, G. L. *Christian Faith and the Interpretation of History. A Study of St. Augustine's Philosophy of History*. Lincoln: Univ. of NE Pr., 1966. Aug's skepticism about possibility of knowledge through senses leads him to accept religious principles on which he views history. Causes of a particular event cannot be fully known, but he posits an overall teleological view of history. Study of history has only apologetic value. [6947]

KIRWAN, C. *Augustine.* London: Routledge, 1989. Examines Aug strictly as a philosopher, especially on topics of free will and time. Looks at evil, skepticism, language, morals. **[6948]**

――――. "Augustine Against the Skeptics," in #5550, pp. 205-224. In *Contra Academicos* Aug argues that only search for truth produces happiness and that if there is no knowledge, there is no wisdom. Much of his argument centers on what is called the Stoic criterion of truth. **[6949]**

KONDOLEON, T. "Augustine's Argument for God's Existence: *De Libero Arbitrio*, Book II." *AugStud* 14(1983), 105-115. Aug's proof, which relies on Plotinus' doctrine of mind's direct access to a superior light, is inconclusive. **[6950]**

――――. "Divine Exemplarism in Augustine." *AugStud* 1(1970), 181-195. For Aug ideas are identical with divine wisdom. Word of God is exemplar/archetype of all created things. **[6951]**

KOTERSKI, J. W. "St. Augustine on the Moral Law." *AugStud* 11(1980), 65-77. Aug's view of how man knows moral law changed. At first he thought it was known through reason, later by grace of God. **[6952]**

KRETZMANN, N. "Faith Seeks, Understanding Finds: Augustine's Charter for Christian Philosophy," in *Christian Philosophy*, ed. T. Flint (Notre Dame, IN: Univ. of Notre Dame Pr., 1989), pp. 1-36. Aug's arguments for a Christian philosophy appear to present several difficulties because of the priority of faith over understanding in his thought. But Aug is trying to establish a link between religious faith (a way of life) and propositional understanding. **[6953]**

KUNTZ, P. G. "Augustine. From *Homo erro* to *Homo viator*." *AugStud* 11(1980), 75-89. *Conf* records Aug's search for truth, seen as progression from disorder to order. **[6954]**

LACEY, H. M. "Empiricism and Augustine's Problems about Time." *RMeta* 22(1968-69), 219-245; also in #6969, pp. 280-308. In *Conf* 11.20 Aug argues coherently that time is subjective. His premises and conclusions are examined and similarities to Reichenback's causal theory of time are noted. **[6955]**

LANGAN, J. P. "Augustine on the Unity and the Interconnection of the Virtues." *HThR* 72(1979), 81-95. Aug's ethical theory holds that only one's relation to God and his intentional will can make acts virtuous. All virtues are united in chastity. **[6956]**

LAWLESS, G. P. "Interior Peace in the *Confessions* of St. Augustine." *REAug* 26(1980), 45-61. The Neoplatonic categories *kinesis* and *stasis* are basis of Aug's teaching on peace, but Biblical ideas of creation and sabbath contribute to its development. **[6957]**

――――. "On Understanding Augustine of Hippo." *DR* 100(1982), 31-46. Non-specialist survey of important themes. **[6958]**

LEIGH, D. J. "Augustine's *Confessions* as a Circular Journey." *Thought* 60(1985), 73-88. Books I-IV of *Conf* form a chiasmus with VI-IX. Book V provides pivot. Aug drew upon symmetry of classical epics and Neoplatonic and Biblical stories of departure and return. **[6959]**

LLOYD, A. C. "On Augustine's Concept of a Person," in #6969, pp. 191-205. Basic element in Aug's definition of a person is mind's knowledge of itself. In *De Trin* he applies Aristotelian categories of relation and substance to definition of a person, without complete success.   **[6960]**

MacDONALD, S. "Augustine's Christian-Platonist Account of Goodness." *NewSchol* 63(1989), 485-509. Aug interprets God's statement (Gen. 1:31) that everything created is good as equivalent to P's equation of Being and goodness. Aug's explanation of the relationship between Being and goodness depends on the conceptual link between corruptibility and goodness.   **[6961]**

MACKEY, L. H. "The Mediator Mediated. Faith and Reason in Augustine's *De magistro*." *FranStud* 42(1982), 135-165. Nothing can be learned from signs, and nothing taught without them. Divine illumination through mediator is only resolution. **[6962]**

MacQUEEN, D. J. "Augustine on Free Will and Predestination. A Critique of J. M. Rist." *MusAfr* 3(1974), 17-28. Reply to #7037. Investigation of several terms associated with this doctrine: *voluntas, liberum arbitrium*, and *libertas*.   **[6963]**

———. "Saint Augustine on Philosophy: Its Uses and Misuses." *SecOrd* 3(1974), 53-74. For Aug true philosophy is based on Christian revelation, but he never maintains that the truth of his deductions is based on revelation. All wisdom is part of an indivisible whole, made up of authority, faith, and reason. The operations of the intellect, in his view, are not hampered by reliance on revelation.   **[6964]**

MAKER, W. A. "Augustine on Evil. The Dilemma of the Philosophers." *IntJPhRel* 15(1984), 149-160. Aug, philosopher and theologian, developed his treatment of problem of evil in part in response to inadequacies of Platonism and Manicheism.   **[6965]**

MANN, W. E. "Dreams of Immorality." *Ph* 58(1983), 378-385. Aug worried about sinning in dreams because he believed one has control over them.   **[6966]**

———. "The Theft of the Pears." *Apeir* 12(1978), 51-58. This youthful peccadillo is important to Aug because it is an example of sinning purely for the sake of sinning. He found it difficult to explain an act for which he could find no formal cause.   **[6967]**

MARKUS, R. A. "*Alienatio*: Philosophy and Eschatology in the Development of an Augustinian Idea." *StudPatr* 9(1966), 431-450. In his early writings Aug's thought in this area scarcely goes beyond Stoic commonplaces. In later works Neoplatonist elements have given it more precise place in his theory of knowledge.   **[6968]**

———., ed. *Augustine: A Collection of Critical Essays.* New York: Doubleday, 1972. Collection of journal reprints; relevant ones are abstracted herein.   **[6969]**

———. "The Eclipse of a Neo-Platonic Theme: Augustine and Gregory the Great on Visions and Prophecies," in #6339, pp. 204-211. Aug's views on the three types of visions and division between *spiritus* and *mens* clearly reflect Neoplatonic influences. Two hundred years later pope Gregory, though he knew Aug's theory, had developed his own which reflects an inner-outer duality.   **[6970]**

———. *Saeculum: History and Society in the Theology of St. Augustine.* Cambridge Univ.

Pr., 1970. Aug sees Roman Empire as theologically neutral. His interpretation allows for a pluralistic society. [6971]

──. "Saint Augustine on History, Prophecy, and Inspiration," in *Strenas Augustinianas V. Capanaga oblatas, I: Theologica*, ed. by I. Oroz-Reta (Madrid: Ed. Augustinus, 1967), pp. 271-280. Aug's view of revelation is elaborated philosophically. [6972]

MARROU, H.-I. *The Resurrection and St. Augustine's Theology of Human Values*, transl. M. Consolata. Villanova, PA: Villanova Univ. Pr., 1966. Aug's doctrine of embodiment makes him precursor of modern personalism. [6973]

MARTIN, R. "The Two Cities in Augustine's Political Philosophy." *JHI* 33(1972), 195-216. Aug does not identify heavenly or earthly city with particular institutions on earth, but some earthly institutions serve as their agents. [6974]

MATTHEWS, A. W. *The Development of St. Augustine. From Neoplatonism to Christianity, 386-391 A. D.* Washington, DC: Univ. Pr. of Amer., 1980. Sees Aug as trying to understand Christian doctrine on a rational basis during this period and being willing to use a Neoplatonic framework to do so. (Publication of dissertation done in early 1960's. Bibliography not updated.) [6975]

──. "Philosophical Concepts and Religious Concepts. Some Problems Illustrated in St. Aurelius Augustine and Professor Paul Tillich." *REAug* 17(1971), 143-154. These two faced similar problems in trying to reconcile Christian faith to dominant philosophical systems of their days in such areas as: scripture, concept of God, nature of man, salvation. [6976]

MATTHEWS, G. B. "Augustine on Speaking from Memory." *AmPhQ* 2(1965), 157-160; also in #6969, pp. 168-175. Aug claims that when asked about things we are familiar with but not in the presence of, we talk about our memory images and not the objects. He is unsuccessful in explaining how we can speak from memory about sensible things because he fails to distinguish between two possible meanings of the question. [6977]

──. "The Inner Man," in #6969, pp. 176-190. In Aug's basically dualist view of man's nature the concept of an inner man who is separate from the body provides a coherent way of describing mental functions and psychological episodes. [6978]

──. "*Si fallor, sum*," in #6969, pp. 151-167. Aug's argument that it is impossible to be mistaken if one does not exist all, is not to be taken as an exact forerunner of Descartes' *cogito, ergo sum*. [6979]

McEVOY, J. "*Anima una et cor unum*. Friendship and Spiritual Unity in Augustine." *RecTh* 53(1986), 40-92. Aug's concept of Christian friendship is based on Greek notion of *philia*. Such a relationship is most nearly possible in a monastery. [6980]

MAERTENS, G. "Augustine's Image of Man," in #47, pp. 175-198. Aug combines his trinitarian concept with Plotinian view of man as a fallen soul in a body. But soul is image of God, and it is God's will that soul find its way back to him. [6981]

MIETHE, T. L. *Augustinian Bibliography, 1970-1980. With Essays on the Fundamentals of Augustinian Scholarship*. Westport, CT: Greenwood Pr., 1982. Not annotated but includes section on philosophical issues. Also lists dissertations and theses and earlier bibliographies. Somewhat marred by numerous typographical errors.   **[6982]**

————. "St. Augustine and Sense Knowledge." *AugStud* 8(1977), 11-20. Aug's views are derived from Plotinus.   **[6983]**

MILES, M. "Vision: The Eye of the Body and the Eye of the Mind in Saint Augustine's *De trinitate* and *Confessions*." *JR* 63(1983), 125-142. Aug's philosophical understanding of physics of vision was model for spiritual vision of "that which is."   **[6984]**

MONAGLE, J. F. "Friendship in St. Augustine's Biography." *AugStud* 2(1971), 81-92. Friendship for Aug is brotherly goodwill among Christians, concept developed from Greek idea of *philia* and Cicero's observations on *amicitia*.   **[6985]**

MORANO, D. V. "Augustine's Linguistic Success in *De quantitate animae*." *AugStud* 5(1974), 101-111. After reading Plotinus, Aug was able to shape vocabulary for talking about God and soul in non-materialistic terms.   **[6986]**

MORRISON, J. L. "Augustine's Two Theories of Time." *NewSchol* 45(1971), 600-610. In *Conf* Aug says that time depends on soul's existence, while in *City of God* he asserts that time is objective. His concept of angels as created beings placed at time's beginning may offer a resolution to the inconsistency.   **[6987]**

MOSHER, D. L. "The Arguments of St. Augustine's *Contra Academicos*." *AugStud* 12(1981), 89-113. Platonic ideas led Aug to Christianity. This work is not designed to refute Academic Skeptics but to counter Manichees.   **[6988]**

MOURANT, J. A. "Augustine and the Academics." *RecAug* 4(1966), 67-96. Aug used Academic doctrine to refute materialism. Its teaching led to his rejection of Manicheism, but he objected to its skepticism.   **[6989]**

————. *Augustine on Immortality*. Philadelphia: Villanova Univ. Pr., 1968. The *De immortalitate animae* is purely philosophical in form, without prayers or scriptural references. Terminology is Platonist. "God" is mentioned explicitly only once. Argued for immortality of soul on basis of immortal nature of mind and knowledge.   **[6990]**

————. "The Emergence of a Christian Philosophy in the Dialogues of Augustine." *AugStud* 1(1970), 69-88. From 386-395 Aug wrote several dialogues which became increasingly superficial in form as he became aware of dialectic's inadequacies for the task of reaching absolute truth. Later dialogues are little more than essays.   **[6991]**

————. "Remarks on the *De immortalitate animae*." *AugStud* 2(1971), 213-217. Dialogue is unique among Aug's early works for its Platonic and Plotinian reasoning about identity of spiritual soul with nature of man.   **[6992]**

MUNDLE, C. W. K. "Augustine's Pervasive Error Concerning Time." *Ph* 41(1966), 165-168. Aug is wrong to assume only the present exists, and without duration.   **[6993]**

MUNOZ-ALONSO, A. "The Idea and the Promise of Philosophy in St. Augustine." *PACPhA* 48(1974), 14-24, transl. A. LeMay. For Aug, reason necessarily precedes faith. God would not despise the faculty given to distinguish us from animals. Philosophy is primarily a desire to know, whether truth is revealed or arrived at deductively. **[6994]**

NASH, R. H. *The Light of the Mind. St. Augustine's Theory of Knowledge.* Lexington: Univ. of KY Pr., 1969. Non-Thomistic view. First part of book gives overview of Aug's epistemology. Latter portion discusses how man can know forms in the divine mind, rejecting views of Thomas Aquinas, the Franciscans, and modern scholars such as Gilson and Copleston. Aug's modified ontologism seems the best solution. **[6995]**

———. "St. Augustine on Man's Knowledge of the Forms." *NewSchol* 41(1967), 223-234. Argues against interpretation of Aug's illumination theory put forth by Gilson, Copleston, and Bourke, who maintain that it implies no content but merely regulates. **[6996]**

———. "Some Philosophic Sources of Augustine's Illumination Theory." *AugStud* 2(1971), 47-66. Aug derives his ideas from Plato and Aristotle. **[6997]**

NEWTON, J. T. "The Importance of Augustine's Use of the Neoplatonic Doctrine of Hypostatic Union for the Development of Christology." *AugStud* 2(1971), 1-16. Aug compares union of divine and human in Christ with link between body and soul in humans. Idea had far-reaching impact on later Christian thinkers. **[6998]**

NIARCHOS, C. "Aristotelian and Plotinian Influences on St. Augustine's Views of Time." *Phil*(Athens) 15-16(1985-86), 332-351. Aug differs dramatically from Ar and P but borrows vocabulary from them and their sources (Presocratics and Plato). **[6999]**

O'CONNELL, R. J. "Action and Contemplation," in #6969, pp. 38-58. Aug saw life in Plotinian terms, as a progression away from action toward liberation from the physical body. He later retreated somewhat from this stance but never entirely. **[7000]**

———. *Art and the Christian Intelligence in St. Augustine.* Oxford: Blackwell, 1978. *De musica* is Aug's only work on aesthetics. He views beauty as a "relation," with a structure open to rational analysis. This formal beauty is transcended as soul is led to ascend to a plane where beauty and truth are one. His view is utilitarian, more in line with Plato than Aristotle. Art must contribute to soul's climb toward perfection. **[7001]**

———. "Augustine and Plotinus. A Reply to Sr. Mary Clark." *IntPhQ* 12(1972), 604-608. Reply to review of #7009, #7010. **[7002]**

———. "Augustine's Rejection of the Fall of the Soul." *AugStud* 4(1973), 1-32. Aug may have held to doctrine of pre-existent soul and its fall early in his life. *Retractions* condemn such a view without admitting that he held it. He clearly rejects any cyclical version of it. **[7003]**

———. "De libero arbitrio I. Stoicism Revisited." *AugStud* 1(1970), 49-68. Though much is made of Neoplatonic influences on Aug in early phase of his career, in this work he bases his arguments against Manichees on Stoic principles. In Book 2, written some time later, his approach is Neoplatonic. **[7004]**

———. *Imagination and Metaphysics in St. Augustine.* Milwaukee, WI: Marquette Univ. Pr., 1986. For Aug, as for Aristotle, universe is ordered according to weight of each element, though Aug spiritualizes the elements. Spiritual progress results when one is freed from reliance on sense perceptions and the "phantasms" which senses produce. **[7005]**

———. *The Origin of the Soul in Augustine's Later Works.* New York: Fordham Univ. Pr., 1987. Aug debates four views of soul's origin in later works. He modifies his view as he becomes aware of Origen's ideas and in reaction to Pelagius' teachings.   **[7006]**

———. "Pre-existence in Augustine's Seventh Letter." *REAug* 15(1969), 67-73. Reply to R. A. Markus in #5595.   **[7007]**

———. "Pre-existence in the Early Augustine." *REAug* 26(1980), 176-188. Reply to G. J. P. O'Daly (#7014).   **[7008]**

———. *St. Augustine's Confessions. The Odyssey of Soul.* Cambridge, MA: Harvard Univ. Pr., 1969. Doesn't attempt to find connections between Books 1-10 and 11-13. Believes that Aug accepts pre-existence of souls. Tries to see Aug in *Conf* as a symbol of Everyman in his quest for union with God.   **[7009]**

———. *St. Augustine's Early Theory of Man, A. D. 386-391.* Cambridge, MA: Harvard Univ. Pr., 1968. Argues that Aug's doctrines of fall and potential union of soul with God are based on his reading of Plotinus, not Porphyry.   **[7010]**

O'DALY, G. J. P. "Augustine on the Measurement of Time: Some Comparisons with Aristotelian and Stoic Texts," in #6339, pp. 171-179. Aug does not seem dependent on either Aristotelian or Stoic concepts of time. He stresses memory as indispensable function in all calculations of time.   **[7011]**

———. "Augustine on the Origin of Souls," in #6335, pp. 184-191. Aug begins his study of this issue in Scripture, uses philosophical concepts to compensate for lack of scriptural statements on nature and origin of soul; ultimately fails to resolve problem.   **[7012]**

———. *Augustine's Philosophy of Mind.* Berkeley: Univ. of CA Pr., 1987. Analyzes Aug's arguments ("particularly his more intricate and obscure ones") on soul, sense-perception, imagination, memory, time, and psychology of knowledge. Sources are not stressed but Cicero and Stoics are seen as more important and Neoplatonists less so than most studies suggest.   **[7013]**

———. "Did St. Augustine Ever Believe in the Soul's Pre-Existence?" *AugStud* 5(1974), 227-235. Reply to R. J. O'Connell (#7003).   **[7014]**

———. "Memory in Plotinus and Two Early Texts of St. Augustine." *StudPatr* 14(1976), 461-469. In *De ordine* II,ii,6-7 Aug's account of memory is only superficially similar to P's view.   **[7015]**

———. "Predestination and Freedom in Augustine's Ethics," in #6805, pp. 85-97. Aug maintains that one who is predestined to do something has the ability not to do it, even if he does not use it. His theory is philosophically indefensible.   **[7016]**

———. "*Sensus interior* in St. Augustine, *De libero arbitrio* 2.3.25-6.51." *StudPatr* 16(1985), 528-532. In this treatise Aug uses term *sensus interior* to describe faculty of sense perception. In other works *intentio* or *memoria* describe same function.   **[7017]**

O'DONNELL, J. J. *Augustine.* Boston: Twayne, 1985. Survey for non-specialists, focusing on several works representative of facets of Aug's thought.   **[7018]**

———. "Augustine's Classical Readings." *RecAug* 15(1980), 144-175. Grouping of authors whom Aug cited from memory, consulted occasionally, and read closely. [7019]

O'DONOVAN, O. *The Problem of Self-Love in St. Augustine.* New Haven, CT: Yale Univ. Pr., 1980. Analyzes types of self-love and examines Stoic and Platonic influences. Concept moves beyond eudaimonism in Aug. [7020]

———. "*Usus* and *Fruitio* in Augustine, *De Doctrina Christiana* I." *JThS* 33(1982), 361-397. In *De Doctr* Aug classified love of neighbor as a type of "use" of the world. He does not use term as Stoics would and in his later writings reclassifies love of neighbor as something enjoyable (*fruitio*). [7021]

O'LOUGHLIN, T. "Knowing God and Knowing the Cosmos: Augustine's Legacy of Tension." *IrishPhJ* 6(1989), 27-58. Examines tension Aug sees between impulse to study created world because it is God's work and recognition that as matter and in comparison with God it does not deserve attention and may distract us from higher goal. [7022]

O'MEARA, J. J. "Augustine and Neo-Platonism." *RecAug* 1(1958), 91-111. Survey of scholarly debate from 1888 to 1957. Lists passages from Aug which are focal point of controversy. [7023]

———. "The Neoplatonism of Saint Augustine," in #6374, pp. 34-41. Aug rejected Neoplatonism but used some aspects of its doctrine to support his arguments. He was particularly drawn to Plotinus' account of soul's turning toward God. Includes review of scholarship in this area. [7024]

———. "Plotinus and Augustine. Exegesis of *Contra Academicos* II,5." *RIPh* 24(1970), 321-337. Resemblances between P and Aug are undeniable but should not be stressed too strongly. They are due to Aug's knowledge of a few particular passages rather than familiarity with P's thought as a whole. [7025]

———. "St. Augustine's Attitude to Love in the Context of his Influence on Christian Ethics." *Arethusa* 2(1969), 46-60. Aug's concept of spiritual love is influenced by his classical background. [7026]

———. "Time as *Distentio* and St. Augustine's Exegesis of Philippians 3,12-14." *REAug* 23(1977), 265-271. Aug's reference in *Conf* 11.23,30 and 26,33 to time as *distentio* is not allusion to philosophical concept but to a New Testament text. [7027]

PEGIS, A. C. "The Second Conversion of St. Augustine," in *Gesellschaft. Kultur. Literatur. Rezeption und Originalitaet im Wachsen einer europaeischen Literatur und Geistigkeit. Beitraege L. Wallach gewidmet*, ed. (Stuttgart: Hiersemann, 1975), pp. 79-93. Book 10 of *Conf* marks point in Aug's spiritual progress when he made Platonism subservient to his faith. [7028]

PENASKOVIC, R. "An Analysis of Saint Augustine's *De immortalitate animae*." *AugStud* 11(1980), 167-176. Aug is less negative toward the body than is Plato's *Phaedo* but he had not read Plotinus' positive view in *Enn* 4.7. [7029]

———. "The Fall of the Soul in Saint Augustine: A *Quaestio Disputata*." *AugStud* 17(1986), 135-145. Summarizes scholarly controversy over R. J. O'Connell's view of soul as fallen (#7009). Finds O'Connell "on target."   **[7030]**

PERRICONE, C. "St. Augustine's Idea of Aesthetic Interpretation." *AncPh* 9(1989), 95-107. Interpretation of a work of art begins with an intuition that it is art. One then considers the artist's meaning and whatever other meanings one can find. The work must be viewed or read with charity.   **[7031]**

PRESS, G. A. "*Doctrina* in Augustine's *De doctrina christiana*." *Ph&Rh* 17(1984), 98-120. Conflict between Christianity and paganism brought new meanings to the word *doctrina*, which was already capable of a variety of interpretations.   **[7032]**

PREUS, M. C. *Eloquence and Ignorance in Augustine's* On the Nature and Origin of the Soul. Atlanta: Scholars Pr., 1985. This relatively minor work of Aug actually epitomizes conflict between Christian and classical views on rhetoric and philosophy.   **[7033]**

PRUFER, T. "Notes for a Reading of Augustine, *Confessions*, Book X." *Interp* 10(1982), 197-200. Discusses contrasts between Aristotle's and Aug's concepts of mind.   **[7034]**

QUINN, J. M. "Augustine's View of Reality." *Augustinianum* 8(1968), 140-146. Reply to V. J. Bourke, *Augustine's View of Reality* (1964).   **[7035]**

———. "The Concept of Time in St. Augustine." *Augustinianum* 5(1965), 5-57. Analysis of *Conf* 11,14-28 lets us see that, for Aug, time is a distention of the soul. His ideas can be compared to those of Aristotle and H. Bergson.   **[7036]**

RIST, J. M. "Augustine on Free Will and Predestination." *JThS* 20(1969), 420-447; also in #6969, pp. 218-252. Aug defines freedom as obedience to God. Mankind's choices are his own, but without aid of God they will be wrong choices. Being free does not imply being freed from sin.   **[7037]**

———. cf. #6526.

ROBERTS, L. D. "Augustine's Version of the Ontological Argument and Platonism." *AugStud* 9(1978), 93-102. Aug's argument for God's existence is more Platonic than is Anselm's.   **[7038]**

ROWE, W. L. "Augustine on Foreknowledge and Free Will." *RMeta* 18(1964-65), 356-363; also in #6969, pp. 209-215. In *De libero arbit* 3.2,4, Aug argues God's foreknowledge does not limit man's free will, but his reasoning is faulty.   **[7039]**

RUDEBUSCH, G. "Aristotelian Predication, Augustine and the Trinity." *Thom* 53(1989), 587-597. Aug modifies somewhat a nonstandard form of predication drawn from Aristotle to defend the doctrine of the trinity.   **[7040]**

RUSSELL, R. P. "Cicero's *Hortensius* and the Problem of Riches in Saint Augustine," in *Scientia Augustiniana. Studien ueber Augustinus, den Augustinismus und den Augustinerorden. Festschrift Adolar Zumkeller zum 60. Geburtstag*, ed. C. P. Mayer and W. Eckermann. (Wuerzburg: Augustinus-Verl., 1975), pp. 12-21. Aug claims to have resolved to give up worldly goods and honors upon reading *Hortensius*. He did not, however, implement that resolve until some years later, when he had reached a degree of certitude in his faith.   **[7041]**

———. "The Role of Neoplatonism in St. Augustine's *De civitate Dei*," in #6339, pp. 160-170. Platonic philosophy provided Aug with the intellectual framework which enabled him to accept Christian teachings he found otherwise intellectually repugnant. But he had to point out the system's weaknesses in *De Civ* in order to win over intellectual pagans and keep wavering Christians in the fold.   [7042]

SCHALL, J. V. "St. Augustine and Christian Political Philosophy," in *The Politics of Heaven and Hell. Christian Themes from Classical, Medieval, and Modern Political Philosophy* (Lanham, MD: University Pr. of Amer., 1984), pp. 39-66. Aug sees Plato's Good as God. But the crucifixion of Christ at the hands of the Roman government severed any connection between the city and the Good. Political and social philosophy is thus directed toward the individual.   [7043]

SCHUETZINGER, C. E. "Franz Koerner's Existential Interpretation of the Young Augustine." *AugStud* 1(1970), 19-29. Survey of German scholar's work on "interiority" of Aug's search for God and his conversion experience.   [7044]

SCIACCA, M. F. *Augustinus*. Bern, Switzerland: Francke, 1948. Bibliography by subjects; not annotated.   [7045]

SIMPSON, D. "'Epicureanism in the *Confessions* of St. Augustine'." *AugStud* 16(1985), 39-48. Though Epicureanism was the most despised of Greek philosophies among Christians, Aug found some its doctrines could bring men closer to divine peace.[7046]

SOLOMON, R. C. "I Can't Get It Out of My Mind (Augustine's Problem)." *Ph&Phen-Res* 44(1984), 405-412. Discussion of problem of voluntary or involuntary nature of thoughts and impulses, exemplified in Aug's *Conf*.   [7047]

SONTAG, F. "Augustine's Metaphysics and Free Will." *HThR* 60(1967), 297-306. Aug's attempt to answer problem of freedom of will must be read in context of his metaphysics, which is Neoplatonic coupled with doctrine of necessity and God as personal.   [7048]

STARNES, C. "Saint Augustine and the Vision of Truth." *Dion* 11(1977), 85-126. Discusses *Conf* 7. Anyone seeking truth cannot ignore Christianity.   [7049]

———. "Saint Augustine on Infancy and Childhood: Commentary on the First Book of Augustine's *Confessions*." *AugStud* 6(1975), 15-43. Aug's story of his childhood is not an account of a particular childhood but of the universal state of infancy. It emphasizes the child's preference for his own good but his relationship to the whole of humanity through his possession of being.   [7050]

STEAD, C. "Augustine's Philosophy of Being," in #6805, pp. 71-84. Aug uses the term "Being" existentially and as a symbol of the nature of God. Like other Platonists, he organizes his theory of the created world much more coherently than his explanation of the intelligible world.   [7051]

STEWART, A. C. "The *De peccatorum meritis* and Augustine's Rejection of Pre-Existence." *REAug* 34(1988), ':74-279. The work, written before 412, does not refute Origen but refuses to consider incarnation of soul as punishment.   [7052]

STOB, H. "Notes on the Philosophy of St. Augustine." *Calvin Theological Journal*

8(1973), 117-130. Looks at problem of gleaning Aug's views from his writings; examines religious, inward and Neoplatonic character of Aug's philosophy.   [7053]

TeSELLE, E. "Porphyry and Augustine." *AugStud* 5(1974), 113-147. Aug seems to have owned and read some of P's works and, from 395-405, to have given close attention to utility of his writing in interpreting Christianity and opposing paganism.   [7054]

TESKE, R. J. "The Aim of Augustine's Proof that God Truly Is." *IntPhQ* 26(1986), 253-268. Even before his conversion Aug did not doubt God's existence. In *De libero arbitrio* 2 he aims to prove not that God exists but that he is an immutable and eternal spiritual substance.   [7055]

———. "Augustine's Use of *substantia* in Speaking about God." *ModSch* 62(1985), 147-163. Aug's use of term *substantia* in discussions of God's predicates or nature, while problematic, is intelligible.   [7056]

———. "Divine Immutability in Saint Augustine." *ModSch* 63(1986), 233-249. Aug's insistence on God's immutability derives from his Platonism as well as from his opposition to Manichees.   [7057]

———. "The World-Soul and Time in St. Augustine." *AugStud* 14(1983), 75-92. Aug conceived of individual souls as identical with World-soul. Like Plotinus, he sees time as a distention of the soul.   [7058]

TZAMALIKOS, P. "Origen: The Source of Augustine's Theory of Time." *Phil*(Athens) 17-18(1987-88), 396-418. Aug's concept of time is Neoplatonic. He did not appreciate some important modifications of time theory made by O. Aug retains the concept that time is dependent on changes in the soul. O's theory is more objectivist.   [7059]

VAN BAVEL, T., and VANDERZEE, F. *Repertoire bibliographique de saint Augustin, 1950-1960.* Steenbrugge, Nether.: Abb. S. Petri, 1963. Thorough coverage.   [7060]

VAN DER HORST, P. W. "A Pagan Platonist and a Christian Platonist on Suicide (Macrobius and St. Augustine)." *VigChr* 25(1971), 282-288. Both M and Aug agree that suicide defiles soul. M rejects suicide as an unreasonable act, Aug as a sin.   [7061]

VAN FLETEREN, F. E. "Augustine's Ascent of the Soul in Book VII of the *Confessions.* A Reconsideration." *AugStud* 5(1974), 29-72. Aug may have tried some kind of mental ascent to God in 386. Emphasis which he places on ascent or return of soul to God probably grew out of such Platonist meditation.   [7062]

———. "Authority and Reason, Faith and Understanding in the Thought of St. Augustine." *AugStud* 4(1973), 33-72. Manicheism taught Aug to value reason over authority. The Christian view reverses that priority. He came to see reason as object of man's intellectual pursuit, with authority having greater temporal importance.   [7063]

VERHEIJEN, L. M. J. "The Straw, the Beam, the *Tusculan Disputations*, and the Rule of Saint Augustine. On a Surprising Augustinian Exegesis." *AugStud* 2(1971), 17-36. Aug draws his concept of anger (*ira*) from Cicero's *Tusc. Disput.* 4.9,21.   [7064]

VERSFELD, M. "The Notions of Pride and Imitation in St. Augustine." *SAfrJPh*

2(1983), 180-186. Pride is imitation of divinity by creature. Doctrine of analogy must be used cautiously, since it implies a kind of imitation.   **[7065]**

VIGNA, G. S. *A Bibliography of St. Augustine's* De Civitate Dei. Evanston, IL: Garrett-Evangelical Theological Library, 1978. Not annotated.   **[7066]**

VON JESS, W. G. "Augustine: A Unitary and Consistent Theory of Time." *NewSchol* 46(1972), 337-351. Reply to #6987. We must distinguish time from history.   **[7067]**

VON RINTELEN, F. J. "Augustine: The Ascent in Value Towards God." *AugStud* 2(1971), 155-178. Good is inherent in every stage of being. This leads Aug to develop a hierarchy of values which ascends to incomprehensible value of God.   **[7068]**

WARD, K. "God as Creator," in #6805, pp. 99-118. Discusses Aug's consideration of the problem of God's relationship to time. To place God beyond time does not make him immutable.   **[7069]**

WARFIELD, B. B. "Augustine's Doctrine of Knowledge and Authority," in *Studies in Tertullian and Augustine* (Westport, CT: Greenwood Pr., 1970; rprt.), pp. 135-225. Aug saw knowledge as originating in God's presentation to us of ideas which constitute intellectual world. We each perceive those ideas as our abilities allow.   **[7070]**

WATSON, G. "Crime and Punishment in Augustine and the Philosophical Tradition." *Maynooth Review* 8(1983), 32-43. Aug combined Neoplatonism and Christian thought on this subject but does not seem to have known Plato or Aristotle directly.   **[7071]**

———. "St. Augustine's Theory of Language." *Maynooth Review* 6 #2(1982), 4-20. Aug made contributions of his own to Stoic base of language theory.   **[7072]**

WETZEL, J. "The Recovery of Free Agency in the Theology of St. Augustine." *HThR* 80(1987), 101-125. Divine calling does not obviate human freedom and responsibility. Aug's arguments are theological and philosophical.   **[7073]**

WOOD, N. "*Populares* and *Circumcelliones*. The Vocabulary of 'Fallen Man' in Cicero and St. Augustine." *HPolTho* 7(1986), 33-51. Compares Aug's description of the troublemakers he knew in his youth with Cicero's description of the political gangs which terrorized Rome in the 50's B. C.   **[7074]**

YOUNG, A. M. "Some Aspects of St. Augustine's Literary Aesthetics, Studied Chiefly in *De Doctrina Christiana*." *HThR* 62(1969), 289-299. Discussion of images as signs and beings.   **[7075]**

ZUM BRUNN, E. *St. Augustine: Being and Nothingness in the Dialogs and* Confessions. New York: Paragon House, 1988. Aug has forged a unity between Platonic ontology and Christian faith. One cannot distinguish in his thought between essence and existence. Instead Aug shows soul growing or atrophying, depending on whether it looks inward or outward.   **[7076]**

For related items see #1969, #6018, #6545, #6837.

INDEX

Computers can generate an index in a relatively short time. They lack the philosophical sophistication, however, to distinguish between, for example, "being" as a metaphysical concept and the participle of a verb. We have tried to be certain that the items in this index are used only as ancient philosophers used them. We have tried to strike a middle ground by including terms which will interest non-specialist users as well as some of the basic technical terms. Numbers refer to the numbers in bold brackets at the end of each item.

abortion 113, 1976, 5671
absolutes 28, 991, 1834
Academy 21, 34, 247, 458, 1323, 1464, 1964, 2010, 2095, 2136, 2532, 2601, 3554, 3560, 3561, 3564, 3787, 4416, 4450, 4533, 5179, 5248, 5269, 5416, 5449-5479, 5534, 5575, 5577, 5592, 5636, 5654, 5695, 5742, 5778, 5960, 6237, 6309, 6324, 6346, 6386, 6393, 6659
accidents 1953, 2642, 3880, 3883, 3906, 3907, 3937, 4590, 4683, 4696, 4744, 4749, 5305
Achilles 691, 697, 698, 701, 704, 709, 710, 712, 713, 728, 2251, 2258, 4076
aesthetics 247, 248, 251, 432, 682, 1326, 1443, 1500, 1509, 1532, 1540, 1547, 1573, 1583, 1587, 1592, 2363, 2783, 2960, 3616, 3659, 3661, 3667, 3686, 3690, 3742, 3751, 3759, 5158, 5601, 5916, 6458, 7001, 7075
afterlife 502, 1094, 1691, 5996
agape (cf. also: *eros*, love, *philia*) 1678, 1713, 1728, 1755, 6206
aisthesis (cf. also: perception) 3943, 3952, 3968, 4249, 4342, 4343, 5155, 5197, 5208, 5239, 5661, 5981, 6003, 6602
aitia 1348, 1415, 1498, 2247, 2723, 4528, 4768, 4852, 4993
akrasia 1143, 1210, 1734, 1739, 1754, 2043, 2866, 2875, 3027, 4013, 4208, 4227, 4228, 4249, 4293, 4304, 4310, 4321, 4325, 4326, 4346, 4348, 4386, 4399, 4408, 5696, 6802
allegory/allegorical 261, 444, 895, 909, 1308, 1615, 2040, 2146, 2782, 2971, 2977, 2986, 3001, 3035, 3038, 3110, 3136, 3168, 5633, 5754, 6119, 6207, 6366, 6463, 6573, 6583, 6623, 6682, 6865
altruism 950, 1227, 1728, 1735, 4025, 4182, 4218, 4327, 5711, 6013, 6027
analogy 185, 769, 1080, 1189, 1307, 1427, 1435, 1445, 1518, 1540, 1611, 1618, 1662, 1860, 2179, 2210, 2328, 2333, 2491, 2566, 2659, 2817, 2895, 2897, 2969, 2980, 2982, 2988, 2991, 2993, 2994, 3035, 3044, 3051, 3056, 3057, 3068, 3095, 3100, 3123, 3124, 3133, 3150, 3165, 3169, 3255, 3308, 3352, 3458, 3476, 3493, 3680, 3852, 4114, 4150, 4262, 4358, 4381, 4480, 4515, 4523, 4595, 4605, 4849, 4948, 5000, 5027, 5204, 5231, 5236, 5245, 5247, 5305, 5758, 6443, 6449, 6517, 6536, 6682, 6887, 7065
anamnesis (cf. also: memory, recollection) 1214, 1411, 1618, 1635, 1654, 1661, 1666, 1670, 1672, 2488, 2507, 2521, 2623, 2652, 2664, 2681, 2689, 2759, 6485
animal 1737, 2104, 3452, 3492, 3779, 3781, 3784, 3808, 3812, 3829, 3833, 3840, 3844, 3850, 3855, 4275, 4301, 4406, 5081, 5084, 5160, 5516, 5600, 5613, 6193, 6314, 6578, 6799, 6800
anthropology 584, 858, 3038, 3590, 6447, 6647
apathy/*apatheia* 5605, 5693, 5769, 5808, 5864
apeiron 307, 374, 380, 406, 411, 413, 468, 2801, 2810, 6394
apophasis/apophatic (cf. also: *via negativa*) 6329, 6541, 6720
aporetic 1372, 1444, 1916, 2310, 2189, 2539, 2614, 4425, 5422, 5511

aporia 1495, 1555, 1634, 1916, 2511, 3389, 3640, 3998, 4295, 4622, 4652, 4693, 4698, 4699, 4707, 4803, 5167, 5422, 6361, 6900

appearance 140, 245, 633, 650, 678, 1589, 2409, 3032, 3285, 3373, 5549, 5697

arche 137, 243, 1810, 2050, 6286, 6332, 6804

art 116, 117, 495, 522, 529, 560, 1137, 1291, 1373, 1435, 1510, 1512, 1519, 1521, 1523, 1525, 1527, 1533, 1534, 1539, 1544, 1547, 1548, 1550, 1553, 1562, 1563, 1564, 1567, 1568, 1570, 1571, 1578, 1579, 1581, 1584, 1593, 1595, 1602, 1604, 1681, 1748, 1978, 2074, 2273, 2340, 2351, 2371, 2372, 2389, 2420, 2729-2731, 2757, 2972, 2974, 3125, 3145, 3398, 3667, 3669, 3684, 3689, 3694, 3707, 3713, 3724, 3728, 3731, 3732, 3737, 3743, 3749, 3751, 3757, 3761, 3778, 3824, 3954, 3992, 4095, 4133, 5088, 5274, 5289, 5314, 5323, 5332, 5633, 5707, 5822, 5901, 5902, 5916, 6400, 6473, 7001, 7031

asceticism 6444, 6679, 6757, 6759

astronomy 126, 183, 321, 342, 422, 434, 459, 2094, 2115, 2117, 2118, 2126, 2128, 5349, 6030

ataraxia 5582, 6075

atheism 198, 279, 982, 1104, 5956, 6787

atoms 353, 854, 855, 864, 866, 870, 875, 4956, 5009, 5957, 5975, 5977, 5990, 5994, 6016, 6043, 6046, 6060, 6081, 6082, 6092, 6122, 6132, 6146

auta ta isa 2625, 2647, 2706, 2718

autarkeia 5784

axiology 1640, 1881

axiomatic 3811, 4440, 4534, 4540, 5600

beauty/beautiful 248, 348, 1133, 1506, 1510, 1521, 1555, 1560, 1567, 1573, 1576, 1577, 1606, 1635, 1677, 1730, 1860, 1944, 2109, 2218, 2284, 2360, 2363, 2675, 2759, 2818, 2996, 3179, 3277, 3284, 3290, 3299, 3308, 3318, 3321, 3336, 3342, 3343, 3344, 3349-3351, 3778, 4273, 5054, 5995, 6241, 6334, 6400, 6518, 6525, 6531, 7001

becoming 501, 635, 670, 1211, 1232, 1602, 1818, 1828, 1849, 1909, 2037, 2055, 2100, 2132, 2287, 2491, 2575, 3326, 3382, 3423, 3526, 3535, 4995, 6294, 6497, 6543, 6853, 6928

being (cf. also metaphysics, non-being, ontology) 18, 61, 78, 155, 163, 170, 171, 261, 359, 379, 488, 590, 597, 598, 608, 614, 616, 618, 623, 627, 629, 634, 635, 642, 645-647, 659, 667, 670, 678, 685-687, 697, 706, 721, 737, 754, 759, 776, 797, 812, 825, 900, 938, 972, 989, 994, 1007, 1037, 1114, 1121, 1163, 1221, 1258, 1315, 1375, 1392, 1437, 1449, 1489, 1812, 1818, 1828, 1837, 1846, 1849, 1851, 1863, 1866, 1880, 1890, 1905, 1909, 1913, 1915, 1923, 1949, 2063, 2088, 2132, 2152, 2287, 2541, 2575, 2584, 2602, 2613, 2786, 2804, 2806, 3128, 3179, 3181, 3182, 3190, 3192, 3196-3200, 3203, 3205, 3208, 3209a, 3212, 3218, 3225, 3226, 3231, 3233, 3236, 3237, 3240, 3242, 3259, 3303, 3343, 3345, 3391, 3475, 3493, 3520, 3535, 3539, 3553, 3728, 3826, 3848, 3897, 3913, 3928, 3935, 3939, 3991, 4139, 4421, 4437, 4450, 4507, 4514, 4595, 4605, 4608, 4615, 4622, 4632, 4635, 4638, 4650, 4655, 4658, 4676, 4691, 4695, 4708, 4710, 4720, 4728, 4735, 4739, 4741, 4746, 4747, 4753, 4760, 4764, 4769, 4776, 4780, 4781, 4788, 4790, 4797, 4803, 4813, 4814, 4822, 4832, 4839, 4842, 4849, 4862, 4875, 4893, 4971, 4976, 5165, 5213, 5223, 5226, 5385, 5394, 5403, 5420, 5427, 5431, 5697, 5763, 5943, 6294, 6331, 6340, 6342, 6359, 6363, 6400, 6410, 6431, 6449, 6460, 6477, 6505, 6544, 6554, 6561, 6618, 6781, 6853, 6895, 6961, 6975, 7037, 7050, 7051, 7068, 7076

belief (cf. also: *doxa*) 56, 97, 166, 641, 719, 953, 999, 1121, 1136, 1201, 1461, 1619, 1620, 1625, 1628, 1641, 1646, 1663, 1704, 1739, 2034, 2038, 2205, 2312, 2313, 2321, 2340, 2341, 2349, 2396, 2497, 2812, 2961, 2980, 2986, 3035, 3351, 3371,

3379, 3380, 3397, 3399, 3415, 3418, 3424, 3433, 3487, 3797, 3970, 4327, 4408, 4590, 5219, 5580, 5581, 5679, 6318, 6614, 6874
Bergson, H. 320, 696, 1358, 4932, 7036
bibliography 9, 10, 24, 37, 65, 119, 249, 251, 303, 355, 356, 363, 365, 374, 455, 553, 562, 568, 668, 669, 789, 838, 885, 892, 910, 920, 1217, 1270, 1273, 1277, 1279, 1286, 1290-1292, 2070, 2082, 2216, 2217, 2379, 2417, 2803, 2902, 3163, 3542, 3597, 3695, 3780, 3809, 4780, 4889, 4954, 5099, 5182, 5188, 5267, 5281, 5457, 5523, 5532, 5564, 5602, 5625, 5642, 5687, 5709, 5870, 5906, 5907, 5932, 5966, 6009, 6070, 6090, 6129, 6165, 6282, 6283, 6287, 6288, 6289, 6297, 6419, 6433, 6580, 6581, 6590, 6599, 6638, 6640, 6645, 6657, 6704, 6742, 6819, 6839, 6866, 6872, 6934, 6975, 6982, 7045, 7060, 7066
biography 26, 36, 517, 777, 1162, 1219, 1354, 3594, 3609, 5941, 5949, 5967, 6186, 6448, 6590, 6600, 6985
biology 777, 2110, 2946, 3470, 3590, 3597, 3661, 3779, 3782, 3787, 3790, 3791, 3804-3806, 3814, 3821, 3822, 3823, 3824, 3827, 3829, 3834, 3835, 3837, 3842, 3843, 3851, 3858, 3867, 4564, 5154
birth 328, 784, 791, 1027, 1538, 1976, 2106, 2698, 2888, 3847, 4818, 5566, 5800, 5811, 6066, 6125, 6587
body 118, 212, 220, 252, 309, 314, 448, 781, 855, 880, 1036, 1059, 1152, 1339, 1466, 1523, 1899, 2053, 2054, 2070, 2178, 2637, 2644, 2725, 3267, 3328, 3331, 3444, 3630, 3855, 3868, 4284, 4358, 4611, 5008, 5016, 5121, 5127, 5152, 5162, 5188, 5202, 5204, 5211, 5229, 5234, 5242, 5309, 5741, 5792, 5990, 6021, 6039, 6330, 6338, 6378, 6421, 6427, 6429, 6438, 6443, 6496, 6507, 6517, 6547, 6557, 6596, 6685, 6897, 6928, 6940, 6978, 6981, 6984, 6998, 7000, 7029
Buddhism 5559, 5585, 6370, 6486

Cantor, G. 716, 738, 2099, 4571, 6603
categories 92, 108, 1314, 2152, 3050, 3528, 3539, 3652, 3661, 3747, 3871-3879, 3882, 3884, 3887, 3892, 3894, 3895, 3897-3899, 3901, 3908, 3910-3914, 3916, 3917-3919, 3923, 3925-3928, 3930-3932, 3934, 3935, 3936, 3939, 4010, 4099, 4159, 4343, 4412, 4445, 4526, 4557, 4605, 4687, 4839, 5116, 5509, 5700, 5730, 5753, 5763, 5768, 6017, 6399, 6428, 6446, 6466, 6540, 6549, 6570, 6625, 6888, 6957, 6960
catharsis cf. *katharsis*
causality 101, 1939, 2646, 3469, 3523, 3808, 3810, 3986, 4614, 4677, 4913, 4962, 5343, 5437, 5618, 5666, 6267
cause(s) 2906, 3520, 3840, 4616, 4636, 4642, 4740, 4744, 4768, 4790, 4955, 4960, 4977, 4983, 4987, 4992-4994, 5011, 5014, 5375, 5437
cave 1307, 1308, 1437, 1490, 1615, 1665, 1858, 1865, 2129, 2146, 2897, 2941, 2942, 2962, 2971, 2977, 2986, 2987, 2987a, 3001, 3005, 3014, 3035, 3050, 3056, 3110, 3133, 3136, 3153, 3168, 6583
censorship 1705, 3155
chance (cf. also fortune, *tyche*) 18, 861, 880, 3836, 4377, 4982, 4987, 4992, 6004, 6011, 6141, 6318
change 55, 178, 225, 230, 234, 334, 345, 409, 488, 489, 496, 525, 545, 558, 590, 690, 754, 797, 810, 874, 880, 1019, 1071, 1315, 1333, 1408, 1486, 1504, 1620, 1746, 1784, 1818, 1971, 2037, 2544, 2946, 3196, 3197, 3215, 3552, 3652, 3667, 3861, 3900, 4045, 4501, 4514, 4607, 4618, 4655, 4721, 4874, 4933, 4937, 4939, 4959, 4968, 4969, 4971, 4976, 4995, 4996, 5004, 5005, 5008, 5016, 5020, 5029, 5084, 5212, 5224, 5380, 5424, 5426, 5443, 5702, 5778, 5940, 6054, 6311, 6507, 6541, 6619, 6726, 6786, 6946
children 994, 1090, 1394, 1467, 1577, 2405

Chinese (cf. also: Confucius) 132, 2014, 3038

chronology 20, 819, 820, 831, 1135, 1326, 1354, 1360, 1388, 1397, 1446, 1457, 1479, 1480, 1784, 2607, 4715, 4717, 5913, 6273, 6412

civil disobedience 1003, 1038, 1160, 2240, 2249, 2267

clepsydra 762, 769, 787

clinamen (cf. also: swerve) 5994, 6081

commensurability 1706, 1727, 4051, 4337, 4398

common notions 5678, 5794

community 188, 209, 496, 896, 945, 950, 959, 1125, 1611, 1708, 1747, 1966, 1991, 2009, 2535, 2907, 2941, 2986, 3089, 3105, 3107, 4105, 4274, 5029, 5059, 5091, 5095, 5098, 5100, 5148, 5963, 5974, 6114, 6773

computer 733, 1397, 1502, 2448, 2450a, 3487

Confucius (cf. also: Chinese) 1030, 1096, 1167, 1485, 1547, 4220, 5039

contemplation 167, 181, 203, 1558, 1690, 1738, 1740, 2323, 2654, 2886, 3667, 4014, 4040, 4052, 4071, 4085, 4089, 4102, 4105, 4146, 4185, 4197, 4202, 4206, 4250, 4276, 4313, 4379, 5092, 5601, 5641, 5757, 5892, 6216, 6435, 6467, 6477, 6489, 6542, 6662, 6795, 6855, 7000

contractarian 2023, 2244, 2878

copulative 649, 1863, 1869, 2578, 4421, 4557, 4719

cosmogony 84, 307, 354, 395, 409, 424, 468, 633, 789, 798, 805, 824, 836, 840, 5349, 6018, 6618, 6852, 6913

cosmology 200, 338, 390, 415, 423, 459, 468, 508, 519, 527, 586, 607, 608, 612, 618, 644, 673, 719, 777, 778, 798, 1556, 2092, 2112, 2113, 2140, 3228, 3272, 3440, 3443, 3461, 3988, 4954, 5341, 5349, 5444, 5703, 5724-5726, 5737, 5795, 5919, 6017, 6254, 6618, 6781, 6782, 6934

cosmos 373, 393, 412, 478, 496, 527, 761, 775, 793, 800, 809, 833, 841, 854, 865, 1128, 1730, 1839, 2086, 2110, 2116, 2164, 2776, 3235, 3267, 3268, 3273, 3439, 3458, 3500, 3508, 3559, 3948, 4946, 4978, 5339, 5386, 5414, 5538, 5620, 5660, 5835, 6021, 6097, 6123, 6217, 6241, 6303, 6328, 6344, 6402, 6460, 6483, 6529, 6583, 6607, 6673, 6774, 6788, 6804, 7022

craftsman (cf. also: Demiurge) 1057, 1749, 2107, 2144, 3473, 3486

creativity 190, 1333, 1526, 1591, 3155, 3156, 4034, 4507

curriculum 1314, 1613, 2105, 2485, 5332

cycle/cyclical 129, 550, 581, 763, 765, 770, 778, 785, 788, 789, 2131, 2672, 2725, 3795, 4923, 5750, 6060, 6112, 6217, 6575, 6581, 6730, 7003

daimon 498, 500, 760, 765, 1011, 1086, 5652, 6296, 6880

daimonion 997, 1029, 1163

death 176, 502, 513, 537-539, 555, 764, 775, 923, 991, 1011, 1013, 1027, 1041, 1046, 1056, 1058, 1059, 1064, 1094, 1127, 1146, 1156, 1169, 1212, 1238, 1459, 1532, 2041, 2054, 2151, 2152, 2159, 2250, 2251, 2624, 2627, 2643-2645, 2649, 2663, 2665, 2669, 2688, 2705, 2725, 2769, 3064, 3284, 3386, 3502, 3565, 3577, 3584, 3628, 4096, 4289, 4349, 5171, 5327, 5503, 5601, 5636, 5637, 5659, 5864, 5869, 5871, 5883, 5912, 5914, 5976, 5982, 6007, 6010, 6012, 6023-6026, 6079, 6099, 6117, 6125, 6131, 6144, 6162, 6194, 6753

definition 197, 1005, 1030, 1060, 1121, 1145, 1252, 1648, 1732, 2275, 2284, 2290, 2489, 2512, 2519, 3915, 3963, 4444, 4493, 4602, 4604, 4627, 4636, 4637, 4696, 4697, 4702, 4732, 4762, 5243, 5333, 5348, 5351, 5356, 5371, 5387, 5593

demiurge 189, 1901, 1947, 2037, 2110, 2144, 2148, 3228, 3235, 3267, 3272, 3484, 3496, 3515, 3520, 3523, 3526, 3536, 3537, 6506, 6510, 6699, 6701

democracy 885, 1078, 1196, 1218, 1220, 1376, 1964, 1977, 1992, 2008, 2024, 2167, 2827,

2857, 3039, 3100, 5056, 5078, 5099, 5124, 5150, 5392, 6196

Derrida, J. 964, 1311, 1622, 1968, 3182

desire 160, 254, 876, 990, 1109, 1118, 1176, 1368, 1378, 1391, 1421, 1678, 1706, 1709, 1727, 1734, 1739, 1996, 2033, 2034, 2066, 2137, 2147, 2324, 2339, 2343, 2347, 2458, 2475, 2809, 2878, 2920, 2973, 3015, 3084, 3087, 3131, 3139, 3266, 3305, 3309, 3336, 3344, 3362, 3564, 3615, 3862, 4061, 4122, 4169, 4232, 4275, 4288, 4343, 4361, 4398, 4712, 5035, 5164, 5193, 5601, 5761, 6350, 6434, 6528, 6679, 6911, 6994

determinism (cf. also: fatalism, necessity) 264, 1234, 1238, 4147, 4868, 4877, 4879, 4881, 4884, 4896, 4917, 4922, 5496, 5520, 5521, 5622, 5654, 5666, 5706, 5709, 5736, 5740, 5781, 5785, 5786, 5933, 5994, 6031, 6209, 6318, 6677, 6679, 6810, 6850, 6916, 6934

deuteros plous 2696, 2701, 2702

Dewey, J. 90, 93, 1004, 1703, 3690, 4144, 4412, 5118

diaeresis (cf. also: division) 1784, 3674

dialectic 70, 102, 193, 197, 494, 526, 587, 634, 904, 991, 1066, 1144, 1274, 1319, 1351, 1362, 1364, 1375, 1384, 1386, 1405, 1411, 1477, 1489, 1522, 1580, 1581, 1641, 1690, 1691, 1758, 1760, 1764, 1766, 1767, 1768, 1770, 1772, 1775, 1777, 1778, 1782, 1783, 1785, 1786, 1791, 1800, 1803, 1948, 2075, 2083, 2089, 2091, 2097, 2119, 2122, 2233, 2318, 2330, 2331, 2345, 2393, 2443, 2475, 2506, 2519, 2563, 2571, 2607, 2656, 2689, 2729, 2734, 2737, 2767, 2804, 2814, 2822, 2863, 2867, 2892, 2894, 2905, 2906, 2915, 2917, 3193, 3195, 3204, 3205, 3241, 3263, 3282, 3302, 3314, 3468, 3611, 3789, 3973, 4409, 4425, 4460-4462, 4465, 4506, 4517, 4518, 4533, 4546, 4553, 5262, 5268, 5275, 5276, 5314, 5315, 5365, 5379, 5395, 5432, 5692, 5730, 5734, 6470, 6554, 6924, 6991

diatribe 1264, 5872, 6144, 6145, 6228, 6761, 6769, 6840

dike 224, 330, 615, 659, 2851

dine/dinos (cf. also vortex) 141, 323, 811, 866

Diotima 1635, 3280, 3281, 3287, 3290, 3299, 3307, 3310, 3317, 3321, 3322, 3325, 3326, 3328, 3347, 3350

disobedience 1003, 1031, 1038, 1080, 1099, 1100, 1106, 1160, 1202, 2240, 2241, 2243, 2249, 2255, 2257, 2267, 3119

Dissoi Logoi 894, 910, 911, 918, 921, 923, 1091

divided line 1312, 1490, 1581, 1611, 1627, 1642, 1665, 1858, 2098, 2897, 2904-2906, 2914, 2919, 2962, 2985, 3044, 3045, 3075, 3117, 3172, 3352, 3469

divine 84, 88, 96, 163, 216, 241, 248, 258, 397, 454, 478, 486, 500, 565, 580, 625, 775, 796, 800, 872, 880, 1011, 1086, 1098, 1102, 1163, 1305, 1333, 1367, 1564, 1601, 1606, 1690, 1970, 2055, 2068, 2133, 2145, 2282, 2307, 2372, 2399, 2494, 2696, 2771, 2798, 3547, 3948, 4059, 4093, 4094, 4146, 4377, 4741, 4753, 4822, 5170, 5413, 5417, 5420, 5431, 5436, 5515, 5528, 5601, 5626, 5783, 5968, 6005, 6378, 6389, 6403, 6510, 6629, 6660, 6665, 6677, 6682, 6684, 6712, 6725, 6738, 6757, 6774, 6794, 6897, 6922, 6951, 6962, 6995, 6998, 7046, 7057, 7073

divinity 96, 340, 393, 680, 792, 1652, 2147, 2148, 2761, 3492, 5219, 5419, 5433, 5464, 5708, 6061, 6300, 6328, 6402, 6612, 6873, 7065

divisibility 701, 716, 721, 751, 849, 2576, 4389, 4974, 5841

division 99, 220, 277, 692, 698, 849, 1656, 1763, 1767, 1782, 1784, 1785, 1787, 1796, 1803, 1804, 1886, 1958, 2034, 2066, 2125, 2428, 2600, 2751, 2815, 2932, 2958, 3176, 3205, 3229, 3263, 3264, 3274, 3473, 3663, 3674, 3784, 3852, 3923, 4682, 4857, 4882, 5184, 5248, 5351, 5537, 5701, 6606, 6970

doxa (cf. also: belief) 605, 608, 611, 632, 634, 638, 644, 648, 660, 663, 676, 678, 679, 1625, 1646, 1668, 2980, 3133, 3377, 3441, 5663, 5961, 6601, 6619

doxographic 288, 405, 822, 828, 3960, 5449, 5472
doxography 267, 277, 287, 482, 1440
dream 493, 1667, 2196, 2251, 3001, 3244, 3363, 3367, 3378, 3383, 3396, 3410, 3412, 3416,
6047, 6229
dualism 90, 143, 441, 464, 613, 1299, 1704, 1816, 2043, 2814, 3593, 4611, 5162, 5200,
5206, 5210, 5228, 5369, 6303, 6327, 6517, 6625, 6850, 6878
duty (cf. also: *kathekonta*) 127, 882, 1101, 1202, 2129, 2246, 2254, 2260, 2927, 3114,
3307, 4081, 4152, 5603, 5809, 6233, 6260, 6568

eclectic 543, 2108, 5590, 6008, 6200, 6750, 6776, 6857, 6869
eclipses 364, 472, 839, 840
ecology 165, 5671
economics 5030, 5035, 5138
education 331, 859, 895, 901, 945, 949, 956, 959, 1081, 1122, 1184, 1277, 1306, 1314,
1344, 1373, 1383, 1417, 1432, 1447, 1462, 1467, 1472, 1511, 1520, 1536, 1548,
1553, 1579, 1598, 1599, 1607, 1613, 1615, 1646, 1647, 1702, 1705, 1707, 1733,
1764, 1921, 2001, 2030, 2079, 2137, 2270, 2385, 2425, 2485, 2496, 2517, 2529,
2832, 2858, 2889, 2890, 2947, 2975, 3025, 3035, 3036, 3040, 3059, 3071, 3084,
3110, 3137, 3357, 3393, 3435, 3578, 3658, 3684, 3712, 3949, 4041, 4331, 5029,
5088, 5118, 5151, 5179, 5332, 5831, 5934, 5984, 6234, 6277, 6653
eidola 844, 857, 6038
eidos 134, 676, 1181, 1381, 1936, 3220, 3394, 3819, 3851, 3858, 4700, 4703
einai 619, 649, 1864, 2578, 3224, 3237, 4421, 4557, 4632, 4775
eironeia (cf. also: irony) 89, 1062, 1206, 2920
elements 329, 334, 335, 350, 352, 413, 420, 424, 449, 520, 561, 587, 618, 757, 759, 760,
768, 776, 783-785, 790, 809, 996, 1134, 1191, 1251, 1401, 1425, 1651, 1833, 2066,
2161, 2288, 2326, 2362, 2519, 2709, 2876, 2984, 3168, 3266, 3268, 3318, 3372,
3395, 3412, 3415, 3416, 3500, 3510, 3653, 3672, 3724, 3729, 3756, 3762, 3763,
3817, 3950, 3997, 4453, 4583, 4615, 4814a, 4843, 5004, 5046, 5129, 5181, 5236,
5273, 5324, 5338, 5341, 5576, 5660, 5702, 5724, 5803, 5990, 6011, 6085, 6135,
6254, 6336, 6403, 6464, 6603, 6605, 6608, 6618, 6680, 6682, 6706, 6854, 6968,
7005
elenchus 197, 998-1000, 1020, 1023, 1066, 1089, 1141, 1144, 1145, 1157, 1159, 1194,
1201, 1204, 1205, 1214, 1302, 1410, 1486, 1788, 1791, 1804a, 2012, 2171, 2186,
2188, 2316, 2341, 3063, 3138, 3279, 4438
empiricism 476, 3390, 3592, 3841, 4997, 5617, 5623, 5628, 5774, 5992, 6955
energeia 1744, 3554, 3593, 3853, 4126, 4130, 4238, 4586, 4601, 4611, 4651, 4690, 4720,
4721, 4767, 4789, 4793, 4794, 4827, 4880, 4988, 5005, 5405, 5510
entail/entailment 2178, 2764, 4627, 5237, 5586
episteme cf. epistemology, knowledge
epistemology 57, 76, 162, 247, 267, 519, 904, 952, 967, 1290, 1326, 1360, 1608, 1614,
1628, 1635, 1639, 1640, 1642, 1647, 1651, 1656, 1663, 1881, 1897, 1982, 2049,
2479, 2789, 2938, 3084, 3133, 3371, 3421, 3475a, 3476, 3661, 3829, 3940, 3944,
3950, 3984, 3990, 4001, 4171, 4372, 5129, 5166, 5472, 5580, 5642, 5648, 5716,
5755, 5763, 6001, 6534, 6797, 6855, 6906, 6934, 6995
epoche 203, 5552, 5555, 5575, 5576, 5579, 6074
eponymous 1814, 1951, 1952
equality 62, 230, 902, 2009, 2102, 2625, 2634, 2647, 2657, 2679, 2718, 2925, 3014, 3026,
3036, 3045, 3073, 3115, 4145, 4278, 5070, 5083, 5124, 5142, 5147, 5672, 5891,
5899, 6196, 6228, 6250
equivocal 2228, 2606, 3823

equivocation 2316, 2367, 2368, 3012, 3167, 4116, 4481, 4488
equivocity 1822, 4498, 4710, 4756
eristic 999, 1066, 2503, 2849, 4518, 4533
eros 681, 683, 780, 1192, 1318, 1373, 1378, 1424, 1430, 1647, 1678, 1679, 1686, 1713,
    1728, 1730, 1755, 2052, 2460, 2764, 2771, 2955, 3090, 3139, 3277, 3279, 3280,
    3283, 3285, 3287, 3290, 3292, 3295, 3299, 3300, 3303, 3305, 3309, 3314, 3317,
    3318, 3332, 3335-3337, 3350, 6519, 6698
essence 258, 489, 1151, 1185, 1223, 1562, 1792, 1829, 1840, 2045, 2145, 2311, 2443,
    2638, 2642, 3221, 3414, 3746, 3801, 3812, 3817, 3854, 3855, 3886, 3939, 4090,
    4434, 4490, 4610, 4618, 4636, 4637, 4672, 4681, 4692, 4704, 4722, 4725, 4732,
    4743, 4746, 4750, 4771, 4811, 4861, 4863, 4865, 5180, 5323, 5348, 5368, 5372,
    5387, 5403, 6431, 6473, 6496, 7076
esti (cf. also: einai) 627, 629, 645, 1863, 1892, 4487
eternal 55, 406, 413, 454, 531, 590, 653, 667, 797, 872, 1163, 1241, 1885, 1905, 1916,
    1934, 1956, 2099, 3483, 3486, 3831, 4040, 4742, 4921, 4946, 5426, 5429, 5451,
    5528, 5746, 6046, 6404, 6430, 6680, 6811, 6913, 7055
eternity 177, 636, 667, 685, 1473, 1488, 1885, 1956, 3483, 3496, 3559, 5339, 5626,
    6368, 6377, 6404, 6487, 6775, 6812, 6931
ethics 8, 22, 29, 38, 54, 84, 113, 131, 149, 164, 191, 211, 221, 228, 247, 277, 448, 548,
    856, 869, 876, 879, 880, 898, 952, 1149, 1291, 1427, 1457, 1500, 1540, 1674, 1683,
    1690, 1694, 1698, 1699, 1703, 1704, 1707, 1714, 1722, 1724, 1731, 1745, 1746,
    1750, 1987, 1991, 2013, 2296, 2304, 2830, 2944, 3084, 3121, 3265, 3280, 3475a,
    3590, 3604, 3652, 3658, 3659, 3867, 4007, 4011, 4012, 4014, 4017-4019, 4031,
    4035, 4036, 4037, 4039, 4042, 4043, 4046, 4050, 4056, 4057, 4059-4061, 4064,
    4065, 4067, 4074, 4078, 4079, 4081, 4083-4085, 4093, 4094, 4104, 4106, 4107,
    4110, 4116-4118, 4120, 4129, 4131, 4135, 4136, 4140-4142, 4144-4146, 4152-4157,
    4162, 4165, 4166, 4171, 4173-4175, 4179, 4185, 4187, 4191, 4193, 4196, 4197,
    4199, 4205, 4208, 4211, 4212, 4215, 4221, 4224, 4233, 4243-4246, 4253, 4262,
    4263, 4268, 4270, 4273, 4276, 4281, 4282, 4284, 4286, 4288, 4289, 4292, 4294,
    4301, 4305, 4306, 4307, 4310, 4312-4316, 4319, 4320, 4322, 4325, 4333-4335, 4337,
    4340, 4351, 4352, 4354, 4355, 4356, 4359, 4361, 4364, 4365, 4368, 4375, 4376,
    4378-4381, 4384, 4389, 4390, 4392, 4400, 4401, 4403, 4404, 4407, 4467, 4669,
    5030, 5033, 5044, 5074, 5079, 5093, 5109, 5112, 5138, 5179, 5312, 5392, 5464,
    5472, 5487, 5491, 5499, 5500, 5605, 5611, 5643, 5649, 5670, 5685, 5709, 5720,
    5725, 5731, 5732, 5739, 5759, 5770, 5790, 5791, 5798, 5805-5807, 5809, 5861,
    5919, 5920, 5937, 5938, 5940, 5970, 5977, 5999, 6008, 6027, 6036, 6104, 6119,
    6234, 6266, 6299, 6434, 6627, 6647, 6665, 6666, 6669, 6674, 6786, 6831, 6847,
    6852, 6856, 6860, 6864, 6904, 7016, 7026
eudaimonia 1744, 4008, 4009, 4014, 4030, 4031, 4059, 4070, 4074, 4085, 4087, 4098,
    4102, 4104, 4156, 4195, 4207, 4224, 4226, 4228, 4250, 4258, 4287, 4296, 4306,
    4385, 4401, 5042, 5048, 5731
eudaimonism 1725, 5745, 5787, 7020
Eudoxus 839, 2136, 2601, 2802, 3482, 4388, 4599
eugenics 1976
evil 18, 189, 972, 1011, 1016, 1118, 1156, 1167, 1729, 2031, 2046, 2050, 2248, 2409, 2760,
    2812, 2866, 2928, 3267, 3495, 4015, 4291, 5499, 5715, 5743, 5961, 5982, 6434,
    6495, 6499-6501, 6509, 6526, 6543, 6614, 6802, 6850, 6880, 6928, 6948, 6965
existence 68, 172, 279, 359, 373, 638, 639, 657, 665, 823, 865, 960, 1032, 1320, 1438,
    1640, 1792, 1829, 1840, 1847, 1861, 1863, 1881, 1902, 1906, 2039, 2049, 2050,
    2143, 2254, 2409, 2575, 2608, 2627, 2689, 2770, 2793, 2965, 3144, 3149, 3208,
    3209a, 3225, 3269, 3310, 3436, 3515, 3940, 3957, 3990, 4489, 4615, 4632, 4637,

4663, 4664, 4672, 4681, 4683, 4708, 4790, 4810, 4821, 4832, 4835, 4847, 4943, 4946, 4959, 4962, 5052, 5153, 5237, 5348, 5352, 5385, 5406, 5412, 5429, 5463, 5467, 5563, 5573, 5659, 5680, 5750, 5777, 6046, 6125, 6241, 6414, 6431, 6477, 6524, 6612, 6685, 6846, 6870, 6878, 6895, 6907, 6913, 6933, 6950, 6987, 7007-7009, 7014, 7038, 7052, 7055, 7076

existential 231, 619, 627, 649, 1115, 2061, 2301, 3224, 3231, 3303, 4352, 4421, 4485, 4487, 4557, 4559, 4680, 4719, 4775, 5360, 5394, 6926, 7044

fatalism (cf. also: determinism, necessity) 1241, 4867, 4878, 4899, 4911, 4922, 4927, 5666
feminism 2883, 2940, 2963, 3026, 3074
fire 368, 407, 489, 493, 507, 508, 540, 543, 556, 558, 576, 583, 584, 586, 1563, 3497, 3796, 4980, 5527, 5746, 5750, 6132, 6191, 6712, 6885
flux 507, 545, 574, 585, 586, 1640, 1859, 1881, 2200, 2220, 2231, 2377, 2633, 2814, 3373, 3432, 3436, 3451, 3465, 3493-3495, 3540, 4704
forms 16, 49, 110, 114, 138, 347, 579, 660, 682, 791, 928, 962, 1175, 1259, 1261, 1313, 1315, 1333a, 1345, 1390, 1404, 1443, 1460, 1510, 1533, 1541, 1550, 1558, 1583, 1610, 1613, 1617, 1619, 1631, 1640, 1652, 1653, 1672, 1698, 1702, 1709, 1710, 1713, 1738, 1748, 1755, 1766, 1773, 1783, 1784, 1805, 1807, 1808, 1810, 1811, 1813, 1814, 1817, 1820, 1823, 1825, 1826, 1827, 1831, 1833, 1842, 1843, 1844, 1849, 1850, 1852, 1856, 1857, 1859-1862, 1873-1875, 1878, 1881, 1882, 1884-1887, 1889, 1895, 1896, 1898, 1900-1906, 1908, 1909, 1912-1914, 1916, 1917, 1918, 1919, 1923-1925, 1927, 1927a, 1930-1934, 1937, 1939-1941, 1946, 1949, 1950, 1952-1957, 1959, 2054, 2063, 2099, 2100, 2105, 2111, 2120, 2121, 2144, 2148, 2149, 2200, 2210, 2214, 2215, 2226, 2230, 2274, 2300, 2305, 2314, 2363, 2366, 2377, 2484, 2488, 2542-2544, 2546, 2548, 2551, 2553, 2554, 2556-2559, 2562-2564, 2566, 2567, 2571, 2572, 2574, 2576, 2580, 2586, 2587, 2588-2591, 2593, 2595, 2596, 2598, 2606, 2608, 2611, 2617, 2620, 2622, 2626, 2633, 2636, 2638, 2640, 2641, 2647, 2653, 2654, 2682, 2683, 2692, 2696, 2697, 2703, 2709, 2711, 2715, 2718, 2721, 2751, 2764, 2767, 2789, 2791, 2794, 2795, 2798, 2800, 2801, 2811, 2815, 2818, 2821, 2823, 2906, 2935, 2937, 2953, 2961, 2987, 2987a, 3002, 3029, 3042-3044, 3050, 3069, 3084, 3099, 3101, 3117, 3160, 3161, 3182, 3184, 3193, 3195-3197, 3201, 3202, 3205, 3209, 3210, 3213, 3220, 3222, 3227, 3233, 3239, 3241, 3246, 3248, 3253, 3255, 3256, 3272, 3299, 3308, 3389, 3413, 3414, 3428, 3434, 3436, 3461, 3473, 3475, 3479, 3483, 3484, 3489, 3491, 3492, 3496, 3499, 3512, 3521, 3523, 3553, 3627, 3652, 3669, 3740, 3810, 3827, 3834, 3842, 3864, 3868, 3870, 3891, 3882, 3894, 3915, 3938, 3979, 3988, 3993, 4069, 4110, 4216, 4322, 4387, 4499, 4518, 4546, 4552, 4589, 4590, 4606, 4618, 4621, 4631, 4638, 4641, 4642, 4659, 4660, 4662, 4663, 4670, 4672, 4684, 4691, 4694, 4697, 4700, 4707, 4723, 4724, 4727, 4730, 4733, 4734, 4737, 4738, 4746, 4755, 4757, 4758, 4762, 4784, 4786, 4805, 4809-4812, 4817, 4826, 4828-4830, 4839, 4842-4844, 4857, 4858, 4862, 4938, 4942, 4995, 4999, 5006, 5152, 5162, 5163, 5167, 5212, 5223, 5228, 5232, 5243, 5384, 5386, 5452, 5457, 6040, 6304, 6382, 6405, 6451, 6454, 6455, 6474, 6480, 6485, 6489, 6528, 6537, 6554, 6555, 6697, 6728, 6733, 6785, 6788, 6793, 6833, 6995, 6996
fortune (cf. also chance, *tyche*) 141, 433, 1182, 3642, 3677, 4070, 4245, 4246, 4987, 5591
free will (cf. also: determinism) 167, 264, 1238, 4881, 5666, 5706, 5709, 5882, 5970, 6081, 6126, 6267, 6495, 6525, 6561, 6629, 6677, 6738, 6775, 6794, 6802, 6916, 6938, 6941, 6948, 6963, 7037, 7039, 7048
friendship 121, 147, 164, 1305, 1735, 2261, 2265, 2324, 2455, 2459, 2462, 2463, 2465, 2466, 3335, 4021, 4025, 4026, 4037, 4068, 4069, 4071, 4072, 4078, 4100, 4106, 4114, 4118, 4146, 4182, 4205, 4242, 4254, 4264, 4267, 4327, 4329, 4338, 4340,

4368, 4381, 5067, 5082, 6005, 6011, 6013, 6017, 6021, 6022, 6027, 6034, 6055, 6202, 6243, 6457, 6980, 6985

gender 262, 630, 814, 944, 1456, 1735, 2902, 3115, 3303a, 3843, 4750, 5891
genesis (cf. also: birth) 595, 757, 784, 1501, 1507, 6033, 6066, 6477, 6647, 6804
genus 3817, 3819, 3832, 3851, 3902, 3905, 3915, 3933, 3939, 4600, 4627, 4801, 4849, 4853, 4857, 5305, 5360, 5380, 5393
geometry 242, 381, 736, 1617, 2130, 2491, 2524, 2525, 3071, 4572, 4714, 5573, 5823, 6030
gnosis 521, 528, 3396, 6683, 6696, 6699, 6703, 6716
God (cf. also: *theos*) 155, 202, 216, 227, 248, 258, 264, 380, 473, 476, 484, 527, 556, 683, 685, 765, 1014, 1057, 1098, 1109, 1128, 1155, 1213, 1258, 1535, 1541, 1677, 1969, 2127, 2141, 2143, 2145, 2164, 2166, 2263, 2293, 2637, 2693, 2746, 2929, 3315, 3344, 3452, 3461, 3547, 3574, 3630, 3660, 3948, 4146, 4185, 4206, 4379, 4950, 5164, 5404, 5405, 5409, 5411-5415, 5419, 5421, 5422, 5425, 5426, 5428, 5433, 5467, 5475, 5515, 5564, 5604, 5650, 5655, 5659, 5665, 5689, 5703, 5741, 5750, 5762, 5777, 5793, 5814, 5829, 5863, 5877, 5886, 5935, 5943, 5995, 6005, 6018, 6181, 6231, 6241, 6295, 6303, 6308, 6310, 6312, 6313, 6318, 6328, 6329, 6334, 6341, 6344, 6355, 6369, 6370, 6436, 6456, 6471, 6481, 6497, 6522, 6524, 6574, 6576, 6578, 6596, 6625, 6629-6631, 6660, 6662, 6667, 6672, 6673, 6680, 6714, 6721, 6725, 6730, 6738, 6740, 6748, 6752, 6763, 6774, 6775, 6778, 6781, 6782, 6785, 6794, 6795, 6803, 6811, 6832, 6850, 6854, 6857, 6870, 6876, 6879, 6885, 6887, 6888, 6895, 6897, 6903, 6907, 6911, 6912, 6915, 6924, 6929, 6931, 6933, 6934, 6938, 6945, 6950-6952, 6956, 6961, 6976, 6981, 6986, 6987, 6990, 6994, 7009, 7010, 7022, 7024, 7037-7039, 7043, 7044, 7048, 7051, 7055, 7056, 7057, 7062, 7068-7070
gods 261, 279, 475, 682, 824, 872, 901, 904, 982, 1028, 1128, 1231, 1373, 1594, 1897, 2022, 2145, 2164, 2227, 2276, 2278, 2281, 2290, 2292, 2297, 2298, 2302, 2313, 2315, 2877, 3181, 3426, 3486, 3948, 4059, 4146, 4246, 5408, 5490, 5591, 5609, 5680, 5764, 5995, 6005, 6021, 6027, 6056, 6063, 6079, 6117, 6170, 6254, 6318, 6379, 6462, 6584, 6778, 6832, 6873
good 54, 133, 149, 178, 180, 191, 211, 248, 255, 490, 856, 942, 950, 966, 972, 989, 1018, 1034, 1037, 1118, 1124, 1182, 1192, 1195, 1254, 1292, 1304, 1368, 1371, 1443, 1445, 1493, 1506, 1508, 1558, 1575, 1652, 1665, 1677, 1685, 1690, 1691, 1693, 1695, 1696, 1698, 1714, 1730, 1733, 1737, 1741, 1745, 1748, 1749, 1750, 1753, 1812, 1833, 1966, 1990, 1999, 2046, 2147, 2148, 2248, 2252, 2273, 2325, 2337, 2339, 2357, 2368, 2406, 2430, 2453, 2461, 2496, 2541, 2626, 2653, 2704, 2723, 2736, 2760, 2792, 2793, 2802, 2810-2813, 2815, 2816, 2818, 2824, 2834, 2865, 2866, 2871, 2877, 2894, 2906, 2921, 2940, 2973, 2982, 3002, 3026, 3029, 3031, 3032, 3042, 3044, 3078, 3095, 3099, 3101, 3152, 3158, 3162-3164, 3313, 3321, 3336, 3349, 3374, 3384, 3536, 3581, 3599, 3642, 3717, 3738, 3798, 3809, 3844, 3944, 3954, 3962, 4008, 4010, 4015, 4017, 4022, 4029, 4030, 4040, 4043, 4054, 4068, 4069, 4072, 4074, 4080, 4091, 4092, 4102, 4113, 4116, 4125, 4136, 4140, 4143, 4152, 4172, 4177, 4185, 4195, 4197, 4198, 4200, 4202, 4224, 4232, 4234, 4246, 4250, 4273, 4297, 4301, 4306, 4314, 4322, 4327, 4329, 4350, 4356, 4359, 4377, 4385, 4388, 4391, 4392, 4394, 4400, 4401, 5050, 5059, 5061, 5066, 5081, 5101, 5102, 5104, 5105, 5108, 5138, 5146, 5262, 5386, 5526, 5685, 5715, 5718, 5720, 5721, 5784, 5798, 5980, 5985, 6155, 6203, 6218, 6291, 6347, 6379, 6434, 6495, 6502, 6525, 6527, 6669, 6789, 6860, 6894, 6902, 6961, 7043, 7050, 7068

hamartia 2705, 3672, 3681, 3692, 3734, 3738, 3748, 3756, 3767, 6644 happiness (cf. also: *eudaimonia*) 164, 859, 876, 1018, 1088, 1195, 1227, 1244, 1318, 1679, 1701, 1704, 1723, 1745, 1750, 1756, 2007, 2322, 2461, 2886, 2890, 2893, 2910, 2931, 4031, 4040, 4042, 4052, 4059, 4071, 4090, 4098, 4100, 4151, 4161, 4166, 4176, 4185, 4189, 4192, 4196, 4206, 4207, 4223, 4224, 4234, 4258, 4288, 4289, 4296, 4308, 4329, 4349, 4361, 4377, 4380, 4400, 4401, 5118, 5121, 5128, 5505, 5540, 5641, 5713, 5723, 5739, 5745, 5938, 5959, 5984, 6011, 6017, 6027, 6533, 6949

harmony 147, 436, 575, 585, 775, 859, 1349, 1675, 1708, 1723, 2072, 3070, 3146, 3148, 3158, 3170, 3309, 3481, 4215, 5063, 5673, 5805, 6005, 6006, 6483, 6654

Hebrew (cf. also: Jewish) 120, 154, 1098, 1513, 6635, 6643, 6653, 6657, 6678

hedonism 1742, 1750, 2790, 2830, 2834, 2837, 2873, 2875, 4388, 6013

Hegel, G. W. F. 197, 260, 494, 572, 587, 1305, 1441, 1708, 1775, 1965, 1973, 2913, 2964, 3884, 4425, 4514, 4735, 5254, 6332, 6386

Heidegger, M. 105, 121, 333, 337, 509, 510, 516, 533-535, 570, 571, 572, 616, 635, 938, 1358, 1423, 1437, 1503, 1504, 1604, 1741, 1806, 1837, 1851, 1865, 1926, 1949, 2184, 2315, 2971, 3181, 3182, 3303, 4605, 4608, 4713, 4821, 5812, 6363, 6410, 6484

hermeneutics 146, 1357, 1438, 1439, 1572

Hesiod 131, 163, 173, 176, 215, 224, 307, 331, 354, 369, 370, 382, 642, 651, 658, 773, 980, 1380, 1516, 6691

hexis 1744, 4128, 4817

Hindu 671, 2126, 3129

history 2, 3, 6, 7, 12, 14, 17, 23-27, 30, 32, 38, 39, 45, 57, 66, 72, 73, 77, 91, 125, 132, 143, 158, 163, 199, 218, 219, 241, 248, 251, 257, 260, 271, 310, 319, 345, 346, 441, 463, 807, 867, 914, 979, 1046, 1067, 1191, 1319, 1345, 1351, 1484, 1487, 1498, 1670, 1674, 1748, 1772, 1913, 1993, 2092, 2126, 2129, 2472, 2520, 2545, 2651, 2902, 3134, 3276, 3446, 3459, 3555, 3575, 3586, 3595, 3619, 3630, 3638, 3655, 3660, 3681, 3687, 3726, 3777, 3780, 3854, 3981, 4029, 4136, 4424, 4491, 4498, 4756, 4854, 4893, 4986, 5085, 5281, 5301, 5503, 5516, 5517, 5590, 5595, 5852, 5860, 5862, 5928, 6084, 6103, 6182, 6207, 6232, 6233, 6257, 6284, 6314, 6316, 6318, 6324, 6345, 6367, 6380, 6386, 6412, 6582, 6643, 6664, 6682, 6705, 6730, 6752, 6774, 6782, 6889, 6947, 6971, 6972, 7067

Hobbes, T. 2023, 2398, 5072, 5097, 5098, 6115

Homer 23, 85, 86, 118, 126, 142, 159, 176, 209, 215, 261, 314, 327, 331, 370, 382, 642, 768, 843, 909, 980, 1515, 1674, 1676, 2375, 3107, 3108, 3718, 3720, 3724, 3769, 3770, 4109, 6155, 6343, 6366, 6583

homoiomere 817, 821, 837, 3896

homosexual 1430, 1496, 3286

humanism 341, 898, 933, 957, 3635, 4184, 5452, 6275

hylomorphism 3868, 4831, 4862, 5210

hylozoism 382, 4843, 5017

hypostasis 6401, 6436, 6468, 6477, 6891

hypothesis 351, 377, 1765, 1768, 1789, 1791, 1793, 1795, 1796, 1799, 1801, 2122, 2478, 2489, 2498, 2511, 2518, 2530, 2554, 2560, 2585, 2591, 3410, 3442, 3622, 3681, 3768, 4173, 4836, 5394

idealism 494, 548, 1469, 1470, 1687, 1920, 3203, 5046, 5682, 6316, 6552

ignorance 148, 655, 1012, 1015, 1023, 1040, 1069, 1095, 1118, 1159, 1166, 1374, 1465, 1609, 1625, 1641, 1745, 1758, 2163, 2282, 2344, 2354, 2376, 2414, 2475, 2837, 2898, 2920, 2934, 3138, 3206, 3380, 3681, 3767, 4293, 4310, 4395, 5743, 6306, 7033 image 177, 246, 343, 574, 648, 846, 1252, 1307, 1316, 1339, 1395, 1425, 1437, 1642, 1755, 1855, 1889, 1904, 1927a, 2098, 2511, 2659, 2970, 2986, 3005, 3045, 3065, 3091, 3139, 3171, 3244, 3245, 3280, 3449, 3479, 3486, 3488, 3491, 3494, 4088, 5014, 5225, 5233, 5630, 5682, 5855, 5974, 6130, 6276, 6376, 6427, 6438, 6455, 6554, 6625, 6643, 6673, 6763, 6765, 6766, 6887, 6929, 6981

imagination 169, 779, 1546, 1599, 1616, 1637, 2093, 3463, 3954, 4507, 5177, 5207, 5220, 5233, 5250, 5252, 6416, 6494, 6553, 6559, 7005, 7013

imitation (cf. also: *mimesis*) 1518, 1533, 1539, 1552, 1561, 1566, 1580, 1590, 2372, 3667, 3669, 3712, 3713, 3728, 3730, 3758

immortality 88, 563, 584, 1026, 1190, 2039, 2042, 2050, 2054, 2060, 2068, 2070, 2149, 2627, 2630, 2636, 2637, 2643, 2648, 2649, 2655, 2657-2659, 2661, 2665, 2666-2669, 2672, 2677, 2688, 2700, 2703, 2707, 2711, 2721, 2725, 2727, 2773, 2774, 3296, 3299, 3307, 3321, 3326, 3840, 5121, 5171, 5219, 5665, 6001, 6131, 6286, 6325, 6521, 6620, 6990

Indian philosophy 2014, 6387

individuals 303, 322, 1829, 1891, 1953, 2405, 2697, 2890, 2994, 3024, 3033, 3139, 3609, 3777, 3828, 3874, 3908, 3910, 3911, 3921, 4497, 4707, 4734, 4775, 4799, 4812, 4942, 5048, 5109, 5515, 5779, 5937, 6014, 6114, 6390, 6414, 6443, 6480, 6520

infinite 318, 419, 584, 597, 693, 697, 698, 701, 705, 706, 709, 716, 748, 754, 776, 865, 1821, 1825, 1903, 1958, 3069, 3818, 4002, 4410, 4571, 4882, 4912, 4972, 4981, 5021, 5841, 5997, 6039, 6388, 6541, 6605

infinity 64, 374, 380, 694, 705, 710, 733, 809, 818, 826, 2540, 4002, 4585, 4882, 4974, 4979, 4981, 5021, 5354, 5954, 6394, 6414

injustice 1090, 1143, 1218, 1720, 2355, 2414, 2838, 2941, 2942, 3126, 3170, 4115, 4283, 4402, 4940, 5080, 5961

inquiry 165, 171, 314, 650, 1051, 1098, 1159, 1265, 1312, 1317, 1330, 1597, 1613, 1617, 1760, 1816, 2032, 2108, 2283, 2476, 2478, 2481, 2482, 2484, 2501, 2503, 2511, 2527, 2626, 2650, 2914, 3192, 3263, 3379, 3458, 3470, 3492, 3749, 4334, 4348, 4429, 4433, 4465, 4658, 5022, 5111, 5287, 5503, 5574, 5953, 6014

inspiration 399, 1316, 1513, 1522, 1558, 1573, 1587, 1601, 1606, 2653, 2770, 2771, 3682, 4377, 6068, 6321, 6972

interlocutor 999, 1400, 1984, 2188, 2330, 2833, 3588

intuition 181, 1637, 1671, 1764, 1958, 3973, 4343, 4403, 5022, 5197, 7031

involuntary 2354, 2414, 4123, 4142, 4324, 4344, 4395, 7047

irony (cf. also: *eironeia*) 988, 1023, 1058, 1062, 1115, 1131, 1144, 1206, 1259, 1424, 1542, 2153, 2270, 2494, 2500, 2515, 2630, 2731, 2734, 2782, 2920, 3007, 3078, 3107, 3115, 3636, 4250, 5897, 5901, 5908, 6729

irrationalism 130, 2038

Isocrates 915, 2076, 2728, 2734, 2735, 2740, 2756, 2782, 3560, 5269, 5270

isonomia 2474, 5993

Jewish (cf. also: Hebrew) 212, 226, 264, 443, 449, 1251, 1263, 5639, 6381, 6637, 6648, 6665, 6668, 6672, 6680, 6701, 6715, 6716, 6717, 6803, 6852, 6854, 6863

Jung, C. 1386, 6447

justice 85, 122, 159, 859, 898, 927, 929, 931, 932, 945, 1002, 1070, 1200, 1203, 1218, 1226, 1283, 1391, 1445, 1589, 1675, 1682, 1697, 1749, 1827, 1862, 1943, 1944, 1974, 1986, 2002, 2016, 2023, 2190, 2236, 2259, 2280, 2297, 2298, 2307, 2312, 2852, 2853, 2860, 2864, 2868, 2872, 2884-2886, 2889, 2892, 2893, 2900, 2917, 2927, 2933, 2944, 2945, 2952, 2964, 2969, 2973, 2988, 2989, 2993-2995, 3008, 3012, 3013, 3015, 3018, 3021, 3023, 3028, 3030-3032, 3034, 3041, 3042, 3046, 3047, 3061, 3068, 3077, 3084, 3092, 3095, 3097, 3100, 3104, 3105, 3114, 3116,

3118, 3120, 3132, 3134, 3140, 3141, 3146, 3148, 3149, 3152, 3158, 3166, 3263, 3264, 3297, 4033, 4078, 4145, 4261, 4278, 4383, 4387, 4402, 4405, 4749, 4791, 5037, 5038, 5059, 5061, 5063, 5070, 5079, 5080, 5082, 5097, 5105, 5112, 5116, 5142, 5144, 5145, 5282, 5769, 5789, 5790, 5961, 6006, 6011, 6034, 6041, 6200, 6250, 6275, 6452, 6783, 6858

K'ang 3072
Kant, I. 197, 2693, 3017, 3884, 3939, 4086, 4088, 4097, 4197, 4361, 4514, 4607, 5550, 5780
katalepsis 5663, 5716, 5775
katharsis 94, 432, 1350, 1626, 1691, 2138, 2397, 2666, 3671, 3675, 3679, 3680, 3682, 3693, 3696, 3702, 3704, 3707-3710, 3721, 3740, 3753, 3760, 3762, 3764, 3765, 3776, 5302, 6158
kathekonta (cf. also: duty) 5685, 5765, 5808, 5845
Kierkegaard, S. 1086, 1109, 1115, 1151, 4125, 4352, 4713, 4925
kinesis 648, 1327, 1979, 2089, 2175, 2382, 2637, 2666, 3009, 3302, 3373, 3648, 3853, 3933, 4126, 4238, 4586, 4690, 4745, 4754, 4767, 4789, 4793, 4794, 4827, 4851, 4963, 4987, 5001, 5025, 5529, 6484, 6604, 6957
knowledge 13, 133, 143, 144, 156, 161-164, 169, 171, 173, 388, 476, 486, 574, 580, 587, 598, 605-607, 615, 625, 629, 655, 777, 845, 879, 897, 912, 946, 980, 1002, 1034, 1066, 1075, 1092, 1103, 1105, 1112, 1113, 1118, 1121, 1147, 1152, 1156, 1159, 1198, 1201, 1214, 1329, 1357, 1367, 1368, 1379, 1400, 1410, 1425, 1435, 1443, 1490, 1509, 1540, 1549, 1558, 1563, 1564, 1581, 1595, 1606, 1608-1612, 1616, 1617-1620, 1622, 1624, 1628-1636, 1638, 1641, 1645, 1646, 1649, 1650, 1652, 1655, 1656, 1657-1659, 1661-1663, 1667, 1673, 1698, 1710, 1729, 1738, 1745, 1756, 1758, 1789, 1817, 1823, 1861, 1925, 1937, 1952, 1963, 1977, 2002, 2013, 2049, 2057, 2063, 2116, 2134, 2141, 2144, 2163, 2171, 2174, 2176, 2185-2187, 2195, 2196, 2222, 2226, 2231, 2314, 2323, 2327, 2340, 2343, 2383, 2384, 2391, 2392, 2423, 2451, 2475, 2481, 2488-2491, 2494, 2499, 2505, 2510, 2516, 2528, 2530, 2586, 2596, 2607, 2631, 2635, 2652, 2654, 2666, 2679, 2680, 2698, 2707, 2712, 2751, 2766, 2767, 2814, 2821, 2822, 2824, 2829, 2835, 2837, 2861, 2863, 2865, 2873, 2874, 2882, 2894, 2898, 2914, 2927, 2934, 2961, 2973, 2979, 2980, 3045, 3047, 3056, 3131, 3144, 3150, 3161, 3284, 3311, 3313, 3316, 3358, 3362, 3364, 3366, 3371, 3372, 3375-3381, 3386, 3387, 3389-3391, 3394, 3396, 3398, 3402, 3412, 3413, 3414, 3415, 3417, 3421, 3424, 3428, 3429, 3432, 3434, 3439, 3487, 3492, 3553, 3574, 3597, 3630, 3665, 3666, 3720, 3732, 3737, 3780, 3815, 3883, 3944, 3948, 3950, 3954, 3956, 3960, 3963, 3966, 3967, 3969-3971, 3973, 3980, 3981, 3983, 3984, 3992, 3995, 3999, 4001, 4032, 4092, 4136, 4157, 4222, 4227, 4239, 4240, 4247, 4251, 4268, 4304, 4367, 4399, 4489, 4490, 4621, 4649, 4728, 4782, 5016, 5084, 5153, 5154, 5183, 5220, 5305, 5334, 5363, 5364, 5372, 5375, 5391, 5414, 5474, 5543, 5563, 5568, 5573, 5579-5581, 5584, 5601, 5650, 5662, 5803, 5814, 5823, 5975, 5981, 5996, 6035, 6044, 6143, 6185, 6347, 6370, 6389, 6510, 6519, 6525, 6539, 6631, 6668, 6705, 6754, 6795, 6851, 6854, 6868, 6870, 6904, 6906, 6943, 6947, 6949, 6960, 6968, 6983, 6990, 6995, 6996, 7013, 7025, 7070
kosmos cf. cosmos
Kubler-Ross, E. 2041
Kukai 2209

language 76, 87, 92, 150, 171, 203, 268, 369, 371, 510, 523, 551, 637, 654, 712, 736, 772, 871, 889, 893, 903, 904, 908, 916, 964, 971, 976, 987, 1074, 1119, 1295, 1319, 1352, 1542, 1576, 1577, 1589, 1664, 1719, 1759, 1760, 1765, 1781, 1782, 1795,

1802, 1813, 1922, 1927, 2195, 2196, 2198, 2206, 2207, 2208, 2209, 2212, 2213, 2218, 2220, 2222, 2226, 2227, 2230, 2232, 2233, 2457, 2493, 2610, 2653, 2764, 2785, 2919, 3183, 3193, 3236, 3659, 3850, 3934, 4081, 4409, 4433, 4441, 4471, 4480, 4489, 4494, 4504, 4511, 4526, 4528, 4564, 4666, 4717, 4728, 4883, 4988, 5124, 5190, 5266, 5303, 5692, 5727, 5738, 5831, 5979, 6061, 6111, 6142, 6160, 6304, 6411, 6443, 6470, 6537, 6635, 6770, 6775, 6781, 6815, 6837, 6838, 6899, 6948, 7072

laughter 1342, 1431, 3360

law 72, 88, 164, 215, 330, 415, 565, 890, 898, 929, 930, 934, 985, 1003, 1027, 1031, 1038, 1042, 1080, 1090, 1099, 1106, 1165, 1168, 1225, 1283, 1300, 1692, 1970, 1994, 1995, 2002, 2007, 2019, 2024, 2085, 2158, 2170, 2236, 2240-2243, 2246-2248, 2254, 2255, 2264, 2266, 2285, 2333, 2410, 2411, 2425, 2531, 2532, 2534-2536, 2860, 2979, 3041, 3286, 4277, 4318, 4370, 4387, 4419, 4443, 4489, 4503, 4505, 4525, 4527, 4549, 4742, 4752, 4896, 4989, 5029, 5062, 5112, 5123, 5125, 5126, 5141, 5144, 5343, 5345, 5467, 5540, 5608, 5673, 5708, 5740, 5785, 5789, 5802, 5874, 5959, 6004, 6181, 6223, 6234, 6236, 6615, 6646, 6648, 6658, 6665, 6679, 6732, 6744, 6823, 6914, 6952

legislation 1300, 1301, 5090, 5126, 5708, 5950

lie 1508, 1515, 1694, 1978, 2617

light 143, 364, 421, 454, 659, 874, 3124, 3182, 4934, 5013, 6445, 6450, 6517, 6536, 6615, 6870, 6913, 6950, 6995

limit 2324, 2567, 2792, 2801, 2808, 3155, 4135, 4281, 5001, 5965, 6531, 6658, 7039

literary style 20, 109, 560, 582, 785, 1372, 5488, 5508, 5925

logic 22, 29, 38, 40, 52, 57, 61, 70, 132, 139, 204, 354, 367, 533, 597, 624, 640, 723, 985, 1149, 1229, 1238, 1259, 1329, 1360, 1386, 1451, 1758, 1759, 1762, 1773, 1774, 1781, 1791, 1793, 1794, 1797, 1799, 1802, 1924, 1925, 2270, 2288, 2339, 2435, 2457, 2505, 2549, 2583, 2598, 2608, 2618, 2825, 2862, 3024, 3186, 3207, 3235, 3281, 3488, 3601, 3616, 3630, 3659, 3869, 3905, 4195, 4266, 4309, 4409, 4412, 4426, 4428, 4432, 4433, 4441, 4442, 4455, 4458-4460, 4466, 4469, 4470, 4480, 4485, 4486, 4495, 4496, 4498, 4500, 4505, 4508, 4511, 4514, 4521, 4526, 4528, 4529, 4537, 4544, 4558, 4560, 4562, 4582, 4623, 4659, 4765, 4776, 4854, 4866, 4867, 4872, 4874, 4885, 4912, 4915, 5278, 5308, 5334, 5335, 5381, 5467, 5469, 5472, 5482, 5484, 5504, 5515, 5572, 5598, 5631, 5689, 5692, 5694, 5697, 5698, 5705, 5707, 5714, 5734, 5740, 5746, 5755, 5756, 5762, 5791, 5809, 5819, 5821, 5839, 5859, 5938, 6124, 6147, 6299, 6307, 6317, 6348, 6359, 6472, 6483, 6674, 6837, 6881, 6882, 6944

logos 76, 106, 130, 178, 203, 298, 489, 500, 507, 525, 532, 533, 534, 540, 541, 543, 546, 552, 554, 556, 559, 561, 605, 632, 965, 1170, 1449, 1507, 1589, 1648, 1817, 1831, 1970, 2021, 2221, 2223, 2450, 2456, 2644, 2697, 3064, 3218, 3248, 3332, 3363, 3378, 3381, 3383, 3387, 3389, 3415, 3477, 3602, 3876, 3959, 4095, 4604, 5249, 5327, 5429, 5593, 5661, 5699, 5714, 5720, 5762, 5765, 5793, 5829, 5863, 6181, 6204, 6525, 6625, 6633, 6634, 6644, 6663, 6672, 6673, 6677, 6678, 6682, 6700, 6706, 6708, 6740, 6748, 6763, 6782, 6806, 6814, 6816, 6822, 6823, 6825, 6843, 6852, 6870

love (cf. also: *agape, eros, philia*) 160, 164, 765, 773, 786, 788-790, 798, 986, 1034, 1131, 1378, 1414, 1418, 1426, 1606, 1677, 1678, 1687, 1709, 1713, 1726, 1728, 1735, 1736, 1755, 1985, 2052, 2072, 2084, 2281, 2290, 2457, 2460, 2607, 2653, 2681, 2730, 2734, 2736, 2747, 2760, 2770, 2779, 2786, 3048, 3064, 3122, 3281, 3290, 3298, 3305, 3307, 3311, 3314-3316, 3319, 3321, 3323, 3324, 3327, 3335, 3336, 3339, 3342, 3344, 3348, 3349, 3350, 3735, 4026, 4162, 4182, 4204, 4205, 4218, 5418, 5601, 5846, 5952, 6055, 6079, 6116, 6157, 6334, 6463, 6492, 6519,

6550, 6783, 6858, 6905, 6911, 7020, 7021, 7026
Lyceum 14, 235, 3571, 4726, 5455, 5512, 5747
lying 2662, 3175, 3277

madness 1771, 2055, 2063, 2435, 2761, 2783, 3323, 4451
magic 182, 184, 254, 433, 451, 966, 998, 1302, 2078, 2643, 3837, 5278, 6123, 6338
mania 2779
many 86, 231, 379, 1815, 1830, 1844, 2540, 2550, 2791, 2794, 2981, 3159, 3920, 4574,
    4803, 5266, 6015, 6195, 6300
Marx, K. 4747, 5093, 5096, 5146, 5365
master argument 1234, 1235, 1237, 1240, 5933
materialism 16, 376, 494, 779, 873, 1265, 5200, 5242, 5697, 6114, 6789, 6989
mathematics 38, 52, 67, 139, 242, 381, 433, 436, 457, 463, 464, 713, 728, 741, 1351, 1408,
    1438, 1486, 1581, 1652, 1764, 1772, 1801, 2092, 2094, 2096, 2097, 2105, 2106,
    2109, 2119, 2120, 2122, 2123, 2396, 2596, 2894, 2905, 2906, 3014, 3168, 3178,
    3368, 3534, 3949, 4150, 4436, 4566-4570, 4572, 4575, 4576, 4577, 4578, 4580,
    4583, 4585, 5335, 5370, 5381, 5391, 5573, 5631, 5823, 6185, 6472, 6483, 6554,
    6603, 6608, 6927
matter 122, 145, 205, 238, 273, 336, 347, 374, 382, 406, 694, 810, 815, 821, 828, 835, 838,
    865, 868, 928, 1013, 1581, 1819, 1900, 1901, 1916, 2036, 2053, 2054, 2103, 2123,
    2127, 2287, 2363, 2402, 2931, 3155, 3414, 3441, 3465, 3501, 3519, 3553, 3652,
    3731, 3803, 3842, 3864, 3868, 3905, 3915, 3938, 4014, 4186, 4216, 4542, 4559,
    4566, 4573, 4592, 4617, 4624, 4629, 4630, 4633-4635, 4642, 4648, 4649, 4678,
    4679, 4683, 4684, 4714, 4721, 4723, 4724, 4733, 4738, 4751, 4784, 4786, 4799,
    4801, 4802, 4805, 4810, 4814a, 4815a, 4817, 4820, 4823, 4825, 4839, 4843, 4845,
    4850, 4853, 4858, 4862, 4913, 4924, 4939, 4942-4944, 4947, 4948, 4952, 4955,
    4964, 4965, 4971, 4986, 4999, 5004, 5006, 5017, 5024, 5149, 5152, 5163, 5212,
    5232, 5237, 5243, 5375, 5384, 5526, 5564, 5579, 5597, 5603, 5626, 5724, 5741,
    5750, 5767, 5793, 5803, 5804, 6002, 6008, 6033, 6054, 6413, 6430, 6434, 6440,
    6496, 6498, 6499, 6500, 6509, 6526, 6543, 6552, 6614, 6813, 6836, 6876, 6878,
    6927, 6946, 7022
mean 115, 314, 569, 617, 639, 737, 791, 799, 802, 810, 854, 957, 1002, 1034, 1081, 1164,
    1206, 1223, 1236, 1543, 1707, 1960, 2019, 2150, 2181, 2197, 2221, 2410, 2635,
    2700, 3051, 3208, 3288, 3370, 3434, 3444, 3496, 3702, 3708, 3819, 3957, 3971,
    4000, 4002, 4031, 4078, 4098, 4106, 4111, 4126, 4134, 4150, 4151, 4153, 4154,
    4159, 4160, 4167, 4212, 4213, 4262, 4278, 4280, 4333, 4369, 4374, 4406, 4450,
    4490, 4676, 4768, 4955, 5147, 5163, 5166, 5173, 5195, 5239, 5319, 5340, 5385,
    5417, 5425, 5486, 5508, 5593, 5678, 5681, 5930, 6203, 6300, 6340, 6347, 6381,
    6394, 6615, 6739, 6764, 6779, 6802, 6813
medicine 140, 144, 182, 350, 432, 440, 1137, 1528, 1707, 2318, 2333, 3815, 4268, 5598,
    5628, 6223, 6320
memory (cf. also: *anamnesis*, recollection) 71, 222, 1622, 2058, 2514, 2809, 3277, 3417,
    3942, 3952, 3978, 3983, 5174, 5207, 5227, 5241, 5690, 6400, 6416, 6485, 6553,
    6560, 6648, 6731, 6931, 6977, 7011, 7013, 7015, 7019
metaphilosophy 1371, 1853
metaphysics (cf. also: being, ontology) 29, 57, 70, 76, 109, 121, 123, 179, 180, 267, 275,
    353, 411, 464, 543, 552, 629, 631, 845, 938, 1256, 1290, 1296, 1326, 1329, 1378,
    1408, 1437, 1500, 1672, 1719, 1773, 1805, 1806, 1809, 1822, 1824, 1832, 1836,
    1858, 1897, 1900, 1904, 1909, 1910, 1917, 1921, 1933, 1939, 1947, 1953, 2608,
    2684, 2726, 2933, 2938, 2960, 3084, 3186, 3194, 3207, 3237, 3305, 3413, 3476,
    3479, 3574, 3590, 3601, 3604, 3616, 3659, 3662, 3667, 3686, 3785, 3807, 3823,

3829, 3886, 3892, 3905, 3975, 3984, 4000, 4128, 4322, 4411, 4437, 4438, 4462, 4487, 4489, 4498, 4521, 4523, 4575, 4581, 4586, 4591, 4593, 4598, 4604, 4609, 4610, 4612, 4616, 4619, 4622, 4623, 4639, 4642, 4652, 4656, 4667, 4668, 4672, 4674, 4676, 4680, 4687, 4691, 4693, 4695, 4696, 4697-4699, 4703, 4706, 4711, 4712, 4715, 4717, 4718, 4730, 4735, 4737, 4738, 4744-4746, 4750, 4753, 4755, 4758, 4762-4765, 4776, 4780, 4781, 4785, 4786, 4792, 4793, 4796, 4801, 4809, 4814, 4816-4820, 4822, 4825, 4826, 4828, 4830, 4840, 4849, 4850, 4863, 4864, 4879, 4895, 4898, 5122, 5129, 5407, 5416, 5420, 5426, 5428, 5431, 5486, 5491, 5503, 5510, 5511, 5529, 5538, 5597, 5730, 5740, 5755, 6356, 6434, 6445, 6522, 6532, 6551, 6581, 6929, 7005, 7048

methodology 38, 196, 282, 879, 1157, 1310, 1329, 1385, 1475, 1791, 2303, 2387, 2463, 2825, 3555, 3664, 3745, 3791, 3822, 3829, 3833, 4076, 4251, 4400, 4521, 4540, 5022, 5061, 5125, 5129, 5334, 5371, 5512, 5538, 5601, 5858, 6067, 6077, 6267, 6359, 6407, 6776, 6936

mimesis (cf. also: imitation) 94, 1382, 1526, 1533, 1539, 1540, 1547, 1552, 1566, 1580, 1593, 1626, 2896, 3128, 3689, 3697, 3710, 3713, 3714, 3730, 3752, 3763, 3824, 6331

mind 22, 25, 88, 92, 142, 212, 345, 428, 481, 642, 647, 710, 716, 718, 725, 730, 743, 750, 752, 843, 855, 901, 918, 966, 1072, 1122, 1144, 1236, 1328, 1332, 1339, 1398, 1466, 1540, 1610, 1640, 1688, 1700, 1729, 1754, 1784, 1881, 1900, 1925, 1938, 1947, 2029, 2032, 2047, 2053, 2118, 2212, 2409, 2422, 2439, 2447, 2514, 2588, 2591, 2626, 2715, 2811, 2937, 2953, 2977, 3043, 3247, 3328, 3353, 3375, 3418, 3480, 3630, 3643, 3794, 3975, 3984, 3996, 4000, 4002, 4008, 4025, 4067, 4182, 4189, 4190, 4287, 4313, 4314, 4366, 4385, 4401, 4439, 4447, 4530, 4647, 4663, 4733, 4737, 4795, 4798, 4872, 4873, 4894, 5094, 5157, 5162, 5165-5167, 5173, 5187, 5199, 5200, 5217, 5218, 5229, 5234, 5239, 5252, 5253, 5254, 5352, 5405, 5417, 5552, 5663, 5670, 5763, 5855, 5877, 5968, 5976, 6021, 6053, 6126, 6143, 6436, 6440, 6461, 6486, 6707, 6767, 6902, 6928, 6940, 6943, 6950, 6960, 6984, 6990, 6995, 7013, 7034, 7047

minima 1238, 6043

mixture 672, 771, 785, 826, 919, 2383, 2580, 2818, 3273, 3472, 3503, 4092, 5007, 5411, 5513, 5816, 6378, 6852

moderation 1002, 1154, 2173, 3166, 4290, 6444

monism 329, 379, 441, 507, 599, 614, 626, 649, 695, 758, 5010, 5793, 5834, 6523

moon 293, 422, 471, 839, 4845, 6217, 6382

morality 158, 341, 563, 950, 990, 1070, 1098, 1368, 1485, 1599, 1675, 1680, 1682, 1689, 1692, 1699, 1705, 1780, 1970, 2056, 2244, 2299, 2302, 2323, 2327, 2348, 2495, 2693, 2979, 3024, 3175, 3293, 4143, 4170, 4186, 4253, 4261, 4277, 4299, 4323, 4326, 4340, 4359, 5720, 5797, 5848, 6011, 6041, 6098, 6185, 6285, 6291, 6622

motion 141, 145, 205, 595, 598, 602, 688, 692, 695, 702, 706, 709, 710, 714, 720, 723, 725, 728, 734, 737, 738, 788, 810, 861, 866, 875, 877, 1233, 1398, 1402, 1669, 2037, 2050, 2105, 2115, 2287, 2429, 3180, 3235, 3241, 3257, 3267, 3480, 3503, 3519, 3520, 3524, 3528, 3659, 3806, 3844, 3967, 4015, 4140, 4720, 4793, 4925, 4929, 4940, 4950, 4951, 4953, 4956, 4960, 4963, 4967, 4975, 4979, 4980, 4984, 4985, 4986, 5008, 5012, 5015, 5019, 5025, 5026, 5235, 5296, 5339, 5392, 5406, 5407, 5418, 5429, 5447, 5527, 5528, 5594, 5810, 5957, 6054, 6528, 6604, 6946

movement 16, 259, 434, 494, 598, 655, 690, 697, 711, 730, 789, 866, 896, 902, 904, 917, 1232, 1398, 1405, 1453, 1812, 2055, 2519, 3480, 3520, 3654, 3844, 4015, 4941, 4949, 4969, 5160, 5238, 5262, 5377, 5426, 5440, 5529, 6315, 6390, 6404, 6550, 6613

music 427, 432, 434, 998, 1511, 1530, 1588, 2788, 2907, 3684, 3696, 5088, 5480, 5563,

6189, 6637
mysticism 155, 192, 437, 466, 504, 631, 779, 2063, 2135, 5636, 6370, 6472, 6481, 6518, 6596, 6678, 6681, 6939
myth 215, 217, 339, 354, 383, 386, 1107, 1319, 1375, 1380, 1401, 1408, 1412, 1462, 1507, 1520, 1531, 1538, 1589, 1596, 1664, 1837, 1865, 1922, 2022, 2116, 2131, 2140, 2141, 2284, 2644, 2688, 2734, 2746, 2747, 2759, 2766, 2829, 2855, 2874, 2888, 2960, 2990, 3037, 3048, 3080, 3082, 3094, 3108, 3136, 3142, 3151, 3267, 3268, 3273, 3274, 3276, 3446, 3463, 3464, 3468, 3484, 3516, 3522, 3524, 3550, 3577, 5218, 5219, 5438, 5882, 6123, 6192, 6219, 6347, 6439, 6462, 6463, 6470, 6672, 6698, 6705, 6798, 6905

Nagarjuna 720, 737
name 328, 622, 660, 687, 871, 1242, 1394, 1425, 1696, 1781, 1844, 2195, 2203, 2205-2207, 2211, 2217, 2225, 2235, 2469, 2543, 2596, 2787, 2908, 3344, 3875, 3894, 4092, 4637, 5960, 6136, 6300, 6313, 6456
naming 656, 687, 1016, 1167, 1862, 1951, 2205, 2232, 2469, 3567, 3890, 4837, 6274, 6662
nature (cf. also: *physis*) 8, 58, 88, 96, 116, 117, 146, 164, 165, 217, 227, 259, 315, 340, 382, 397, 401, 448, 637, 760, 779, 871, 872, 880, 896, 914, 930, 939, 1258, 1329, 1670, 1959, 2002, 2108, 2195, 2323, 2372, 2490, 2526, 2669, 2712, 2726, 2793, 2815, 2951, 3273, 3305, 3456, 3497, 3498, 3519, 3604, 3653, 3728, 3797, 3808, 3825, 3848, 3849, 3854, 3859, 3860, 3862, 3944, 3954, 3967, 3976, 4015, 4030, 4093, 4161, 4220, 4268, 4274, 4301, 4318, 4377, 4382, 4383, 4396, 4406, 4416, 4444, 4604, 4937, 4948, 4950, 4957, 4962, 4981, 5020, 5028, 5035, 5095, 5104, 5105, 5122, 5123, 5140, 5141, 5170, 5355, 5369, 5377, 5384, 5386, 5390, 5430, 5564, 5604, 5609, 5643, 5673, 5682, 5699, 5739, 5745, 5806, 5818, 5863, 6032, 6054, 6063, 6075, 6096, 6112, 6117, 6121, 6134, 6234, 6266, 6330, 6400, 6427, 6435, 6501, 6578, 6630, 6646, 6648, 6855, 6865, 7051, 7056
necessity 18, 141, 435, 861, 880, 882, 1057, 1241, 1305, 1986, 1996, 2254, 3119, 3316, 3462, 3498, 3503, 3513, 3523, 3526, 3804, 3805, 3810, 3860, 4107, 4165, 4516, 4520, 4630, 4689, 4709, 4807, 4867, 4869, 4871, 4876-4878, 4884, 4890, 4892, 4896, 4898, 4901, 4903, 4905, 4906, 4908, 4914, 4917, 4919, 4923, 4955, 4992, 5339, 5372, 5388, 5404, 5653, 5762, 5764, 5782, 5785, 5840, 6044, 6141, 6267, 6350, 6495, 6811, 6924, 7048
Nietzsche, F. 151, 250, 348, 531, 1032, 1153, 1508, 2032, 2146, 2649, 2888, 4219, 5746
noesis 1671, 1764, 2061, 2689, 6901
noetic 951, 1558, 1823, 5217, 5221, 5405, 6345, 6887, 6900
nominalism 1906, 5834
nomos 660, 904, 926, 2002, 2199, 2225, 2851, 5114, 5143, 5345, 6648, 6658
non-being 622, 639, 646, 654, 826, 970, 976, 1315, 1375, 1562, 1838, 2552, 2840, 3187, 3189, 3199, 3212, 3219, 3226, 3231, 3236-3238, 3249, 3252, 3260, 3468, 3469, 4837, 5005, 5457, 6033
non-existence 2575, 4832, 5680, 6125
non-propositional 1645, 6398, 6476, 6548
non-rational 2038, 2343, 2397, 4075, 4669, 5729
nous 130, 216, 385, 473, 647, 809, 823, 829, 833, 834, 843, 852, 1398, 1671, 1841, 1901, 1924, 2065, 2105, 2142, 2308, 2682, 2779, 3246, 3272, 3480, 3523, 3547, 3777, 3794, 3953, 3961, 3976, 4119, 4155, 4250, 4251, 4342, 4343, 4379, 4396, 4522, 5160, 5183, 5197, 5206, 5219, 5228, 5253, 5352, 5360, 5364, 5408, 5417, 5793, 6329, 6354, 6391, 6393, 6398, 6400, 6403, 6404, 6411, 6415, 6435, 6440, 6518, 6535, 6536, 6556, 6612, 6621, 6625, 6916
number theory 434, 459, 2111, 3602, 4574

obedience 1038, 1042, 1098, 1106, 1165, 1202, 1226, 2238, 2242, 2248, 2264, 2266, 6228, 7037

Odysseus 229, 622, 1045, 3048, 6765

oikeiosis 5661, 5673, 5685, 5711, 5732, 5790

one 231, 379, 579, 580, 1506, 1815, 1830, 1838, 1841, 1844, 1879, 1889, 2540, 2541, 2544, 2550, 2560, 2563, 2570, 2572, 2584, 2586, 2590, 2593, 2596, 2602, 2609, 2791, 2794, 2811, 2906, 3187, 3874, 3910, 3920, 4803, 6015, 6195, 6310, 6332, 6334, 6338, 6379, 6382, 6388, 6393, 6394, 6400, 6401, 6407, 6408, 6410, 6411, 6413, 6425, 6432, 6435, 6436, 6448, 6456, 6462, 6471-6473, 6477, 6486, 6489, 6490, 6493, 6496, 6502-6504, 6512, 6518, 6521, 6524, 6525, 6528, 6535, 6536, 6539, 6541, 6542, 6544, 6613, 6618, 6621,

ontology (cf. also: being, metaphysics) 61, 68, 170-172, 247, 482, 593, 597, 618, 629, 695, 784, 1295, 1411, 1535, 1562, 1665, 1803, 1840, 1854, 1858, 1879, 1918, 1955, 2208, 2274, 2366, 2468, 2789, 2813, 3194, 3199, 3222, 3492, 3512, 3553, 3861, 3896, 3898, 3918, 3934, 4062, 4063, 4450, 4470, 4502, 4650, 4728, 4741, 4775, 4781, 4783, 4786, 4788, 4813, 4835, 4954, 5273, 5428, 5628, 6349, 6399, 6615, 6777, 6808, 7076

oracle 493, 499, 1014, 1044, 2156, 2157

orality 87, 299, 326, 345, 371, 372, 477, 1071, 2075, 3193

Orphism 97, 433

ousia 241, 1423, 1892, 3876, 4638, 4656, 4677, 4711, 4720, 4724, 4738, 4788, 4792, 4819, 5420, 5427, 5431, 6326

painting 1518, 1529, 1540, 1552-1554, 1566, 2895, 2970, 3684

pangenesis 756, 3799

panspermia 756, 3799

paradeigma 1908, 3080

paradigms 109, 1908, 2590, 2937

paradox 348, 518, 529, 541, 587, 691, 692, 697, 698, 703, 704, 706, 708-713, 722, 725, 728, 730, 735, 738, 745, 748, 752, 943, 1015, 1112, 1113, 1118, 1143, 1156, 1159, 1198, 1225, 1259, 1356, 1583, 1585, 1693, 1941, 1966, 2158, 2315, 2339, 2423, 2481, 2487, 2489, 2500, 2502-2505, 2507, 2516, 2527, 2663, 2762, 2764, 2909, 2910, 2970, 3118, 3215, 3247, 3252, 3356, 3361, 3399, 3427, 3671, 3963, 4015, 4309, 4490, 4596, 4678, 4965, 5002, 5019, 5446, 5585, 5886, 5887, 5904

parody 1039, 1049, 1082, 1158, 1572, 2554, 6188, 6192

particles 709, 868, 870, 3501, 3510, 3612, 5006, 5999

particular(s) 1610, 1814, 1820, 1878, 1893, 1913, 1952-1955, 2234, 2365, 2544, 2633, 2635, 2638, 2682, 2715, 2718, 2721, 2813, 2818, 3157, 3159, 3161, 3484, 3638, 3665, 3894, 3903, 3926, 3932, 3959, 3966, 3979, 3980, 4001, 4241, 4267, 4402, 4621, 4628, 4703, 4758, 4816, 4829, 4833, 4856, 5290, 5358

passions 211, 1743, 3740, 4102, 4131, 4209, 4210, 4311, 5605, 5758, 5803, 5915, 6027, 6513, 6766, 6768

Pater, W. 545, 1284, 1592

pathe 1722, 4131, 4211, 4311, 5272, 5489, 5718, 5761, 5850, 5924, 5981

pathos 3746, 5294, 5327

pedagogy 996, 1399, 2340

peras 468, 2801, 2804, 2810

perception (cf. also: *aisthesis*) 66, 150, 519, 607, 613, 657, 759, 779, 792, 846, 847, 848, 851, 1581, 1620, 1623, 1669, 2088, 2220, 2664, 2689, 2817, 3189, 3352, 3364, 3369, 3373, 3375, 3379, 3382, 3391, 3401, 3404, 3409, 3417, 3420, 3423, 3429, 3432, 3439, 3707, 3761, 3940, 3941, 3943, 3946, 3947, 3951, 3952, 3955, 3964, 3965,

3968, 3973, 3987, 3989, 3999, 4000, 4005, 4006, 4046, 4051, 4221, 4262, 4275, 4343, 4403, 4578, 5157, 5164, 5176, 5180, 5185, 5196, 5198, 5207, 5208, 5209, 5214, 5220, 5224, 5227, 5229, 5232, 5233, 5237, 5239, 5249, 5250, 5364, 5462, 5580, 5603, 5616, 5711, 5717, 5796, 5801, 5813, 5902, 5974, 5981, 5983, 6002, 6015, 6035, 6088, 6100, 6186, 6276, 6314, 6445, 6458, 6459, 6553, 6602, 6943, 7013, 7017

Persia 2, 88, 143, 5636

personality 86, 309, 1840, 1921, 2879, 5770, 5847, 5921, 6150, 6222, 6255, 6437, 6868, 6876, 6887, 6905, 6920

persuasion 603, 916, 968, 1492, 1984, 2012, 2085, 2091, 2340, 2771, 3498, 3694, 5179, 5265, 5274, 5287, 5302, 5322, 5479, 6923

phaenomena 3918, 4512, 4999, 5826

phenomenology 570, 768, 1308, 3603, 4614

philia 121, 1678, 1686, 1713, 1728, 1730, 1755, 2324, 2460, 3500, 4025, 6980, 6985

philosopher-king 1472, 1966, 2885, 2886, 2941, 3037, 3070, 3125, 3127, 3137, 3166, 4087, 5951

phren 473, 765, 800

phronesis 65, 521, 3603, 3959, 3992, 4088, 4092, 4102, 4105, 4231, 4278, 4316, 4342, 5322, 5820, 5980

physics 38, 256, 329, 350, 398, 411, 453, 541, 670, 738, 753, 868, 879, 880, 928, 939, 2100, 2197, 3273, 3509, 3510, 3521, 3616, 3659, 3867, 4578, 4840, 4929, 4930, 4937, 4943, 4948, 4953-4955, 4957, 4960, 4970, 4973, 4974, 4978, 4980, 4989, 4996, 4999, 5010, 5015, 5016, 5019, 5020, 5022, 5134, 5363, 5421, 5434, 5491, 5532, 5624, 5721, 5730, 5746, 5747, 5762, 5791, 5793, 5807, 5809, 5814, 5815, 5830, 5970, 5983, 6000, 6021, 6032, 6039, 6104, 6234, 6299, 6301, 6340, 6674, 6698, 6797, 6847, 6984

physis (cf. also: nature) 28, 146, 359, 395, 515, 660, 791, 802, 876, 904, 926, 1214, 1823, 2002, 2133, 2199, 2225, 2741, 2784, 3792, 4370, 4951, 4997, 5390, 5930, 6066

planets 306, 351, 422, 2094, 2429, 5630

pleasure (cf. also: hedonism) 149, 173, 253, 876, 879, 880, 883, 1304, 1373, 1443, 1517, 1576, 1687, 1742, 1747, 2325, 2334, 2425, 2792, 2793, 2796, 2802, 2805, 2806, 2811, 2812, 2816, 2817, 2824, 2865, 2866, 2871, 2898, 3678, 3686, 3703, 3753, 3757, 3764, 3858, 4015, 4021, 4024, 4040, 4046, 4052, 4108, 4126, 4139, 4161, 4166, 4211, 4212, 4214, 4265, 4302, 4310, 4314, 4329, 4362, 4365, 4373, 4381, 4384, 4388, 4389, 4406, 5266, 5302, 5303, 5464, 5603, 5638, 5723, 5761, 5980, 5981, 5985, 6006, 6010, 6011, 6021, 6040, 6094

pluralist 826, 863

plurality 86, 688, 702, 719, 721, 727, 729, 738, 747, 789, 810, 2039, 2200, 2553, 2575, 3928, 4308, 6015, 6546

poetry 59, 75, 114, 119, 133, 140, 173, 248, 327, 560, 676, 794, 967, 1171, 1392, 1438, 1509, 1511, 1514, 1515, 1517, 1518, 1520, 1521, 1531, 1532, 1536, 1537, 1540, 1541, 1543, 1544, 1549, 1550, 1561, 1564, 1565, 1566, 1572, 1574-1577, 1585, 1590, 1594, 1596, 1598, 1600, 1601, 1603-1605, 2080, 2283, 2375, 2376, 2378, 2734, 2738, 2768, 2877, 2881, 2895, 2968, 3006, 3128, 3136, 3638, 3669, 3670, 3674, 3684, 3687, 3693, 3712, 3726, 3745, 3751, 3758, 3771, 3777, 5088, 5158, 5905, 6008, 6045, 6064, 6082, 6151, 6157, 6264, 6274, 6617

poiesis 1837, 3277, 3458, 4008, 4104, 4794, 4827, 4931

political 34, 125, 154, 194, 202, 207, 218, 225, 265, 343, 387, 455, 524, 540, 565, 883, 1066, 1100, 1125, 1133, 1174, 1202, 1228, 1328, 1354, 1360, 1379, 1396, 1456, 1474, 1577, 1704, 1740, 1747, 1897, 1962, 1963-1965, 1967, 1968, 1971-1974, 1977-1985, 1987-1991, 1993-2001, 2003, 2005, 2011, 2012, 2013-2016, 2020, 2027,

2032, 2035, 2057, 2089, 2102, 2184, 2192, 2261, 2351, 2356, 2400, 2410, 2431, 2434, 2440, 2444, 2447, 2453, 2472, 2736, 2745, 2828, 2878, 2883, 2901, 2913, 2923, 2927, 2938, 2964, 2967, 2988, 2991, 2993, 2994, 3009, 3010, 3016, 3025, 3060, 3062, 3067, 3083, 3098, 3102, 3113, 3118, 3131, 3134, 3144, 3262, 3273, 3337, 3342, 3435, 3440, 3453, 3464, 3467, 3626, 4018, 4036, 4058, 4078, 4175, 4185, 4193, 4301, 4364, 4365, 4370, 5027, 5029, 5031, 5034, 5037, 5038, 5046, 5047, 5052, 5057, 5062-5065, 5067, 5079-5085, 5088, 5092, 5096, 5098, 5102, 5104, 5105, 5108, 5110-5112, 5114, 5116, 5121, 5125, 5128, 5134, 5137, 5139, 5140, 5142, 5146-5149, 5151, 5248, 5260, 5261, 5299, 5436, 5517, 5606, 5641, 5672, 5677, 5848, 5875, 5878, 5911, 6080, 6101, 6115, 6201, 6202, 6213, 6245, 6250, 6253, 6256, 6274, 6278, 6532, 6735, 6905, 6974, 7043, 7074

politics 22, 163, 315, 455, 936, 1047, 1125, 1174, 1215, 1291, 1326, 1393, 1408, 1460, 1485, 1509, 1521, 1670, 1960, 1961, 1964, 1966, 1967, 1975, 1980, 1982, 1990, 1992, 2002, 2009, 2010, 2020, 2022, 2173, 2245, 2265, 2331, 2398, 2442, 2726, 2736, 2901, 2927, 2986, 3000, 3103a, 3010, 3107, 3112, 3123, 3151, 3166, 3262, 3273, 3275, 3280, 3338, 3339, 3601, 3621, 3658, 3669, 3847, 4012, 4018, 4036, 4052, 4058, 4078, 4145, 4193, 4364, 4467, 4519, 5027, 5028, 5031-5034, 5044, 5050, 5052, 5056, 5061, 5063, 5069, 5072, 5074, 5075, 5079, 5081, 5084, 5086, 5087, 5089, 5092, 5104, 5111, 5112, 5115, 5117, 5119-5122, 5125, 5134, 5148, 5149, 5179, 5517, 5878, 5879, 5917, 6080, 6115, 6199, 6213, 6234, 6238, 6367, 6532, 6640, 6911, 7043

Popper, K. 349, 366, 547, 1346, 1961, 1979, 1981, 2004, 2005, 2008, 2020, 2121, 2978, 3009, 3096, 3181, 3511

positivist 1692, 3730

poverty 2406, 2966, 2967, 6216

precognition 852, 853

predication 45, 124, 648, 1261, 1807, 1814, 1827, 1857, 1871, 1875-1877, 1882, 1894, 1896, 1907, 1924, 1929, 1935, 1942, 1944, 1945, 1951, 1952, 2305, 2552, 2587, 2589, 2591, 2606, 2615, 2620, 2639, 2652, 2673, 2677, 2691, 2692, 2953, 3190-3192, 3210, 3213, 3231, 3873, 3886, 3887, 3894, 3914, 3920, 3924, 3936, 4116, 4429, 4454, 4463, 4470-4473, 4497, 4597, 4607, 4647, 4677, 4708, 4730, 4731, 4737, 4757, 4784, 4786, 4815, 4848, 4860, 4865, 5005, 6451, 6452, 6493, 7040

procreation 3290, 3296, 3307, 6846, 6894

progress 56, 129, 136, 934, 1004, 1186, 1331, 1361, 1446, 2106, 3331, 3366, 3387, 3576, 3643, 3851, 4619, 5037, 5710, 5734, 5895, 6379, 6918, 7005, 7028

prolepsis 5661, 5774, 5978, 6003

properties 940, 1814, 1827, 1878, 1883, 1895, 1952, 2100, 2361, 2396, 2537, 2572, 2638, 2721, 3265, 3872, 3880, 3896, 3906, 3932, 3937, 3968, 4297, 4418, 4505, 4645, 4675, 4722, 4816, 5157, 5343, 5372, 5518, 6028, 6472

proposition 210, 1241, 4419, 4423, 4427, 4540, 4892, 4922, 5479, 5654, 5744, 5833, 6035

pros hen 1822, 4710, 4756

Proteus 2284, 2370

protreptic 168, 2189, 2267, 3644, 6784

psyche (cf. also: soul) 86, 118, 314, 500, 501, 515, 522, 554, 555, 561, 580, 584, 1841, 1933, 2037, 2043, 2051, 2059, 2062, 2065, 2369, 2764, 2776, 2879, 3070, 3148, 3652, 3689, 3691, 4672, 5152, 5175, 5236, 6408, 6519

psychoanalysis 738, 3689

real 150, 240, 361, 374, 457, 627, 638, 646, 647, 662, 663, 716, 736, 849, 886, 952, 958, 1060, 1114, 1425, 1499, 1515, 1521, 1564, 1623, 1637, 1655, 1742, 1753, 1820,

1831, 1866, 1884, 1905, 1940, 1941, 2117, 2199, 2268, 2517, 2780, 2826, 2973,
3428, 3454, 3515, 3969, 4139, 4250, 4325, 4489, 4490, 4580, 4604, 4607, 4614,
4634, 4738, 4782, 4839, 4965, 5073, 5496, 5551, 5573, 5663, 5712, 5871, 5883,
6152, 6383, 6388, 6411, 6494, 6578
realist 586, 1673, 3611, 4628, 4798, 4833, 6445
reality 92, 101, 112, 150, 245, 254, 361, 481, 522, 596, 613, 647, 650, 675, 739, 833, 971,
1232, 1304, 1329, 1425, 1495, 1533, 1539, 1540, 1550, 1562, 1589, 1602, 1610,
1625, 1673, 1711, 1730, 1818, 1834, 1866, 1890, 1904, 1907, 1932, 1940, 1959,
2055, 2086, 2140, 2213, 2217, 2218, 2361, 2821, 2882, 2898, 2970, 3258, 3285,
3462, 3528, 3652, 3667, 3688, 3829, 3928, 3990, 4203, 4413, 4604, 4615, 4621,
4788, 4795, 5129, 5377, 5405, 5436, 5443, 5445, 5475, 5580, 5628, 5768, 6179,
6265, 6276, 6314, 6413, 6464, 6494, 6525, 6603, 6627, 6763, 6878, 6904, 6940,
7035
recollection (cf. also: *anamnesis*, memory) 1214, 1404, 1410, 1411, 1452, 1618, 1631,
1635, 1642, 1644, 1654, 1661, 1672, 1709, 1710, 2475, 2476, 2478, 2479, 2489,
2491, 2492, 2502, 2512, 2519, 2521, 2527, 2528, 2626, 2652, 2653, 2657, 2664,
2680, 2681, 2689, 3414, 3942, 3953
regress 1821, 1825, 1903, 1927a, 1958, 2602, 2617, 2953, 3069, 3381, 3491, 3885, 6541
reincarnation 237, 6575
relations 244, 785, 825, 1450, 1564, 1824, 1825, 1891, 1899, 1903, 1927a, 1954, 1991,
2270, 2305, 2361, 2544, 2569, 2622, 2637, 2639, 2641, 2642, 2673, 2686, 2721,
3131, 3149, 3256, 3459, 3997, 4026, 4302, 4464, 4481, 4513, 4551, 4552, 4576,
4597, 4804, 5082, 5095, 5205, 5234, 5252, 5305, 5600, 5673, 6034
relativism 171, 660, 886, 904, 935, 937-940, 942, 947, 1326, 1921, 2533, 2859, 3354, 3362,
3384, 3385, 3404, 3411, 3599, 3962, 4043, 5079
religion 10, 38, 148, 198, 217, 251, 279, 376, 395, 396, 402, 475, 477, 480, 775, 997, 1057,
1248, 1291, 1328, 2131, 2134, 2137, 2141, 2143, 2286, 2295, 2302, 2425, 5432,
5455, 5491, 5516, 5608, 5665, 5942, 5944, 5948, 5971, 6021, 6098, 6197, 6205,
6216, 6231, 6259, 6271, 6290, 6628, 6682, 6724, 6738, 6744
rhetoric 10, 152, 194, 195, 440, 731, 885, 889, 893, 900, 907, 966, 967, 977, 980, 1048,
1049, 1114, 1136, 1148, 1158, 1160, 1352, 1438, 1533, 1575, 1707, 2046, 2071,
2072, 2074, 2075, 2077-2084, 2087, 2088, 2089-2091, 2259, 2262, 2325, 2329, 2331,
2335, 2340-2342, 2345-2347, 2351, 2470, 2471, 2520, 2729, 2730, 2737, 2752, 2756,
2757, 2760, 2764, 2767, 2771, 2780, 2783, 2785, 3077, 3125, 3347, 3601, 3731,
4131, 4237, 4320, 4431, 5074, 5125, 5179, 5258, 5260-5262, 5266-5271, 5273-5276,
5278-5281, 5283, 5285-5289, 5291-5295, 5297, 5299-5304, 5306-5308, 5311-5317,
5319-5324, 5327-5332, 5479, 5488, 5491, 5634, 5734, 5867, 6049, 6064, 6223, 6237,
6242, 6275, 6365, 6622, 6626, 6837, 6844, 6924, 6932, 7033
Rig Veda 1375, 3468
Rousseau, J. J. 1616, 1654, 2023, 2958, 3954, 6115
Russell, B. 320, 708, 713, 1093, 1699, 2036, 2061, 2109, 2964, 3094, 3254, 4318, 4860,
7041

Santayana, G. 320, 1640, 1704, 1881
science 13, 38, 45, 66, 70, 107, 140, 146, 157, 179, 183, 184, 186, 206, 226, 251, 265, 318,
321, 342, 349, 376, 377, 396-399, 430, 434, 437, 441, 706, 1001, 1136, 1137, 1310,
1329, 1368, 1839, 1959, 1963, 1977, 2002, 2092, 2098, 2108, 2121, 2123, 2128,
2129, 2192, 2341, 2398, 2712, 3123, 3125, 3262, 3435, 3440, 3463, 3547, 3600,
3660, 3662, 3663, 3811, 3822, 3829, 3837, 3845, 3860, 3861, 3950, 4175, 4271,
4424, 4438, 4461, 4480, 4567, 4621, 4658, 4708, 4728, 4741, 4747, 4756, 4764,
4787, 4978, 4986, 4988, 5020, 5064, 5084, 5092, 5121, 5128, 5129, 5134, 5143,

5260, 5333, 5336, 5337, 5344, 5345-5349, 5352, 5353, 5359-5363, 5365, 5369, 5370, 5371, 5374, 5375, 5377, 5381, 5386, 5390, 5391, 5392, 5395, 5397, 5401, 5424, 5427, 5438, 5451, 5455, 5491, 5599, 5621, 5623, 5656, 5704, 5857, 5919, 6044, 6045, 6069, 6077, 6110, 6113, 6151, 6185, 6424, 6483, 6554, 6603, 6614

scientist 183, 364, 2108, 3548

second best (cf. also: *deuteros plous*) 2701, 2712

secret 3280, 3373, 6313, 6654, 6851

seed 814, 842, 3890

seeming 579, 651, 675, 676, 753, 935

self-consciousness 1441, 1653, 5196

self-knowledge 209, 1154, 1298, 1429, 1441, 1609, 1615, 1653, 2055, 2172, 2173, 2185, 2750, 2751, 2968, 3110, 3949, 3988

self-moving 2037, 2773, 4958, 6286

self-predication 1807, 1827, 1857, 1875, 1894, 1896, 1907, 1924, 1935, 1944, 1945, 2587, 2589, 2606, 2620, 2652, 2691, 2953, 3190, 3210, 4865, 6451, 6452

self-reference 2351, 3988

sema 368, 1339

semantics 123, 124, 1875, 2199, 2543, 3194-3196, 3238, 3485, 3891, 3892, 4491, 4501, 4891, 4920, 5684, 5979

sensibles 1669, 1842, 1918, 2566, 2617, 2961, 3489, 3947, 5212, 5214

sex 814, 1430, 1736, 3036, 3115, 3829, 5952, 6894

simile 423, 518, 762, 787, 1858, 2897, 3172, 3984, 5295, 6111

simulacrum (cf. also: *eidola*) 6071, 6143

size 104, 747, 830, 846, 874, 1669, 1991

slave 512, 1647, 2482, 2509, 2525, 5028

slavery 2021, 2411, 2566, 2926, 3082, 3147, 5028, 5039, 5056, 5095, 5104, 5127, 5748, 5868, 5926

sleep 491, 537-539, 2151, 4817, 5169, 5256, 5257, 5609

soma 1339, 2204

sophia 223, 343, 515, 534, 1092, 1915, 2191, 3633, 3865, 3992, 5419, 5939, 6633, 6674, 6693, 6705, 6757

sophist 19, 536, 746, 884, 896, 911, 920, 922, 925, 929, 930, 931, 932, 935, 955, 968, 986, 1061, 1129, 1932, 2552, 2580, 2832, 2842, 2858, 3005, 3176, 3177, 3178-3180, 3184-3193, 3197-3200, 3202-3208, 3210-3214, 3216-3229, 3232, 3236, 3237, 3239, 3240-3243, 3245-3249, 3251, 3255-3258, 3261, 3266, 3275, 3376, 3383, 3393, 3579, 3621, 3974, 6202, 6839

sophistic 245, 315, 886, 895-897, 902-904, 907, 912, 917, 918, 922, 981, 1091, 1124, 1161, 1260, 1400, 1618, 1658, 1986, 2081, 2090, 2270, 2470, 2833, 2858, 2860, 2863, 3136, 3218, 5734, 6298

sophistry 885, 944, 1122, 1779, 1798, 2191, 2271, 2272, 3125, 3220, 3229

sophos 343

sophrosyne 208, 209, 1154, 1653, 2183, 2185, 2189, 2838, 2853

sorites 1231, 1236, 5598

soul (cf. also: *psyche*) 20, 100, 118, 212, 216, 220, 252, 261, 288, 309, 314, 373, 389, 393, 454, 459, 501, 515, 538, 539, 561, 563, 584, 775, 796, 872, 880, 1059, 1092, 1133, 1179, 1198, 1327, 1339, 1373, 1410, 1413, 1443, 1463, 1489, 1500, 1508, 1523, 1569, 1574, 1630, 1715, 1738, 1749, 1819, 1897, 1899, 2030, 2031, 2034, 2037-2040, 2042-2050, 2054-2057, 2060, 2062, 2063, 2064-2068, 2070, 2105, 2110, 2113, 2139, 2142, 2149, 2151, 2175, 2178, 2293, 2317, 2336, 2357, 2382, 2394, 2488, 2529, 2570, 2627, 2630, 2636, 2637, 2644, 2648, 2649, 2655, 2657, 2661, 2667, 2668, 2688, 2694, 2697, 2703, 2711, 2714, 2721, 2725, 2727, 2730, 2750,

2751, 2771, 2773, 2801, 2809, 2888, 2921, 2932, 2944, 2968, 2969, 2987a, 2991, 2993, 3005, 3019, 3027, 3030, 3042, 3063, 3065, 3087, 3100, 3105, 3106, 3126, 3128, 3165, 3167, 3169, 3228, 3235, 3267, 3272, 3277, 3284, 3321, 3326, 3336, 3439, 3444, 3461, 3488, 3490, 3503, 3524, 3551, 3659, 3696, 3762, 3847, 3868, 3976, 4023, 4046, 4130, 4151, 4174, 4189, 4190, 4215, 4232, 4284, 4361, 4382, 4400, 4611, 4642, 5121, 5127, 5129, 5152, 5156-5159, 5162, 5164, 5168, 5169-5172, 5188, 5194, 5196, 5201, 5202, 5204, 5208, 5211, 5212, 5215, 5219, 5221, 5228, 5229, 5230, 5234, 5235, 5239, 5242, 5243, 5246, 5247, 5248, 5257, 5266, 5309, 5429, 5477, 5536, 5537, 5563, 5605, 5615, 5659, 5693, 5729, 5741, 5758, 5760, 5770, 5793, 5803, 5853, 5961, 5990, 5994, 6021, 6109, 6132, 6147, 6286, 6296, 6309, 6314, 6325, 6338, 6340, 6342, 6345, 6367, 6376, 6378, 6392, 6407, 6415, 6416, 6420-6422, 6427, 6429, 6434, 6438, 6443, 6462, 6465, 6467, 6470, 6481, 6482, 6484-6486, 6490, 6496, 6499, 6500, 6502, 6503, 6507, 6509, 6510, 6517, 6521, 6522, 6525, 6533, 6538, 6543, 6545, 6547, 6550, 6551, 6557, 6575, 6592, 6596, 6597, 6601, 6606, 6627, 6650, 6660, 6685, 6708, 6757, 6768, 6834, 6865, 6885, 6893, 6897, 6903, 6904, 6909, 6911, 6929, 6934, 6940, 6981, 6986, 6987, 6990, 6992, 6998, 7001, 7003, 7006, 7009, 7010, 7012-7014, 7024, 7030, 7033, 7036, 7052, 7058, 7059, 7061, 7062, 7076

space 214, 238, 239, 318, 383, 506, 697, 715, 725, 754, 809, 878, 1652, 3454, 3494, 4935, 4949, 4981, 4986, 5238, 5354, 5377, 5442, 5446, 6054, 6370, 6381, 6615, 6832

species 496, 1882, 3782, 3783, 3792, 3795, 3801, 3802, 3808, 3817, 3819, 3820, 3825, 3828, 3831, 3832, 3850, 3864, 3876, 3891, 3905, 4643, 4737, 4757, 4849, 4857, 4863, 5124, 5305, 5380, 6041, 6075

sphere 214, 310, 776, 786, 865, 2114, 5144, 5204, 6550

spirit 336, 448, 499, 1405, 2054, 2067, 2247, 3060, 3315, 5017, 5038, 5835, 6295, 6354, 6724, 6748, 6797, 6834, 6885

strife 335, 558, 765, 773, 786, 788-790, 798, 1971

stylometrics 2439, 3466

subjectivism 850, 904, 2049, 2850, 3400, 3422, 6613

substance(s) 241, 823, 837, 3803, 3826, 3851, 3873, 3882, 3969, 4174, 4526, 4587, 4590, 4612, 4634, 4635, 4662, 4665, 4673, 4676, 4678, 4723, 4727, 4729, 4737, 4743, 4746, 4748, 4754, 4755, 4762, 4773, 4791, 4795, 4797, 4801, 4803, 4811, 4814a, 4824, 4828-4831, 4846, 4853, 4863, 4864, 5210, 5352, 5372, 5428, 5471, 5472, 5702, 6431

suicide 174, 990, 1041, 1056, 1140, 1212, 1684, 2663, 2665, 2693, 2710, 2713, 2720, 3577, 5780, 5812, 5912, 5914, 5917, 5918, 5939, 6212, 6718, 6743, 7061

sun 351, 414, 421, 422, 472, 538, 808, 830, 836, 1351, 1563, 1665, 1772, 1858, 2897, 2962, 3124, 5245, 6091, 6347, 6382, 6510

Sundiata 2772

swerve (cf. also: *clinamen*) 5970, 5977, 6021, 6031, 6052, 6081, 6126

syllogism 192, 3739, 3867, 3875, 4049, 4107, 4190, 4221, 4235, 4249, 4257, 4275, 4294, 4304, 4342, 4347, 4366, 4371, 4423, 4445, 4447-4449, 4458, 4469, 4478, 4486, 4510, 4516, 4520, 4529, 4530, 4538, 4540, 4542, 4543, 4585, 4900, 4904, 5022, 5265, 5286, 5308, 5315, 5335, 5381, 5504, 5694, 6882

Tao 1386

techne 1137, 1434, 1435, 1489, 1578, 1638, 1706, 2017, 2078, 2179, 2327, 2331, 2822, 2827, 2972, 3141, 3603, 3748, 3752, 3959, 4124, 5278, 5837

teleology 22, 165, 1731, 2107, 2723, 3592, 3717, 3788, 3790, 3792, 3797, 3798, 3804, 3808, 3813, 3824, 3836, 3840, 3849, 3862, 4056, 4106, 4353, 4376, 4611, 4690, 4810, 4869, 4957, 4983, 5023, 5052, 5382, 5418, 5430, 5511, 5538 *telos* 1195, 2941, 3002, 3785, 3988, 4117, 4303, 4376, 4400, 4988, 5052, 5062, 5733, 5788, 5790, 5798

theology 340, 478, 482, 486, 541, 1535, 2131-2133, 2140, 2143, 2144, 2149, 2299, 3547, 3553, 3659, 4085, 4741, 4781, 4822, 4840, 5402, 5409, 5414, 5416, 5419, 5421, 5424, 5427, 5428, 5438, 5622, 5680, 5992, 6017, 6153, 6197, 6223, 6304, 6312, 6313, 6329, 6341, 6370, 6410, 6493, 6599, 6605, 6618, 6631, 6662, 6666, 6667, 6672, 6678, 6694, 6717, 6719, 6724, 6752, 6755, 6772, 6781, 6787, 6803, 6806, 6809, 6816, 6852, 6854, 6864, 6868, 6869, 6892, 6926, 6933, 6971, 6973, 7073

theos (cf. also: God, gods) 479, 760, 792, 1128, 2139, 2164, 5724, 6883

therapy/therapeutic 178, 1392, 1400, 1523, 3682, 3684, 3760, 5554, 5939, 6014, 6116

Third Man Argument 1762, 1821, 1850, 1852, 1871, 1924, 1930, 1936, 1947, 1951, 2542, 2555, 2558, 2564, 2565, 2574, 2587, 2588, 2591, 2592, 2598, 2606, 2616, 2619, 2620, 2640, 3069, 3491, 3512, 3885, 4492, 4561, 4647, 4661, 4731, 4865, 6451

Thoreau, H. D. 1160, 6347

Thrasyllus 1323, 1420, 6591

thumos 501, 1192, 5033

Tibetan 2645

Tillich, P. 1915, 6976

time 37, 95, 112, 130, 154, 162, 177, 200, 212, 222, 239, 240, 290, 339, 399, 454, 458, 461, 494, 581, 617, 636, 650, 667, 685, 690, 697, 704, 705, 710, 715, 726, 748, 754, 809, 857, 916, 1052, 1277, 1315, 1322, 1396, 1402, 1437, 1457, 1474, 1488, 1529, 1602, 1652, 1689, 1885, 1936, 1960, 2106, 2185, 2298, 2334, 2400, 2544, 2612, 2888, 2919, 2925, 3154, 3276, 3453, 3455, 3481, 3483, 3485, 3496, 3506, 3515, 3524, 3538, 3554, 3733, 3772, 3780, 3787, 3830, 4054, 4080, 4163, 4184, 4241, 4378, 4539, 4587, 4657, 4704, 4724, 4754, 4775, 4841, 4885, 4890, 4892, 4898, 4908, 4915, 4917-4920, 4922, 4923, 4925, 4964, 4981, 4986, 4995, 5009, 5025, 5031, 5049, 5151, 5294, 5299, 5377, 5416, 5439, 5440, 5442-5448, 5502, 5515, 5522, 5532, 5576, 5594, 5626, 5654, 5668, 5676, 5690, 5703, 5727, 5799, 5910, 5940, 6049, 6054, 6209, 6227, 6268, 6367, 6368, 6377, 6383, 6424, 6482, 6487, 6543, 6663, 6703, 6878, 6903, 6909, 6931, 6946, 6948, 6955, 6987, 6993, 6999, 7004, 7011, 7013, 7027, 7036, 7058, 7059, 7067, 7069

TMA cf. Third Man Argument

transcendental 591, 685, 1487, 1660, 1884, 2609, 3109, 6371

transmigration 459, 2028, 2034, 6193, 6579

trinity 241, 2145, 6344, 6738, 6740, 6752, 6768, 6778, 6871, 6886, 6887, 6890, 6891, 6893, 7040

truth 133, 162, 163, 167, 171, 210, 316, 378, 579, 580, 605, 609, 623, 626, 633, 646, 657, 659, 663, 675, 676, 677, 741, 800, 891, 930-932, 939, 1011, 1015, 1049, 1065, 1070, 1114, 1155, 1204, 1241, 1374, 1421, 1423, 1483, 1504, 1516, 1521, 1538, 1573, 1581, 1594, 1604, 1605, 1622, 1655, 1656, 1671, 1711, 1760, 1851, 1864, 1949, 2061, 2076, 2084, 2090, 2146, 2213, 2219, 2287, 2289, 2338, 2370, 2376, 2443, 2450, 2476, 2479, 2797, 2799, 2805, 2806, 2818, 2971, 3004, 3118, 3122, 3188, 3247, 3266, 3277, 3344, 3347, 3361, 3404, 3420, 3516, 3599, 3750, 3946, 3947, 3962, 4027, 4146, 4457, 4463, 4502, 4535, 4547, 4562, 4689, 4742, 4832, 4866, 4876, 4878, 4880, 4898, 4909, 4912, 4917, 4927, 5074, 5177, 5189, 5292, 5317, 5326, 5461, 5467, 5569, 5582, 5620, 5654, 5661, 5662, 5676, 5688, 5716, 5744, 5764, 5833, 6035, 6100, 6316, 6622, 6786, 6820, 6821, 6857, 6882, 6906, 6923, 6924, 6927, 6949, 6954, 6964, 6991, 6994, 7001, 7049

tyche 219, 4246, 6004, 6318

unity of virtue 1051, 1138, 1693, 5820

universal 88, 106, 133, 213, 255, 330, 341, 548, 826, 1617, 1766, 1858, 1893, 2039, 2246, 2499, 2937, 3667, 3707, 3757, 3921, 3979, 3980, 4001, 4003, 4010, 4092, 4267, 4330, 4448, 4454, 4461, 4572, 4603, 4608, 4621, 4622, 4654, 4668, 4686, 4694, 4703, 4706, 4716, 4734, 4753, 4766, 4771, 4812, 4829, 4833, 4864, 5116, 5217, 5364, 5622, 5653, 5930, 6405, 6575, 6732, 7050

universals 1125, 1808, 1831, 1833, 1883, 1893, 2274, 3050, 3355, 3638, 3882, 3898, 3966, 3969, 3972, 4088, 4342, 4454, 4603, 4612, 4621, 4628, 4631, 4653, 4686, 4707, 4727, 4734, 4758, 4766, 4775, 4798, 4806, 4828, 4834, 5015, 5166, 5364, 5533, 5779

universe (cf. also cosmos) 100, 104, 145, 233, 240, 251, 318, 353, 397, 399, 411, 415, 522, 527, 598, 621, 798, 865, 1324, 1409, 1506, 1819, 2127, 2608, 2908, 3522, 3537, 3590, 3807, 4140, 4666, 4673, 4935, 4945, 5347, 5403, 5457, 5528, 5714, 5725, 5750, 5793, 5815, 5855, 5954, 6046, 6072, 6137, 6140, 6227, 6342, 6512, 6515, 6685, 7005

univocal/univocity 1991, 3926, 4498

unjust 994, 1697, 1719, 2240, 2241, 2247, 2886, 2918, 2973, 2982, 3032, 3119, 4291, 4402

unmoved mover 3988, 4845, 4978, 5402-5404, 5406-5410, 5415, 5418, 5419, 5423, 5424, 5428, 5429, 5434, 5435, 5528, 5747

utilitarian 1077, 1685, 1724, 2327, 3031, 7001

utopia 254, 1983, 2375, 2430, 2884, 2926, 2928, 2930, 2965, 3058, 5629

vegetarianism 131, 2951, 6192, 6193, 6320, 6568, 6569, 6578

via negativa 6371

virtue 188, 208, 435, 904, 913, 945, 989, 1018, 1024, 1034, 1040, 1050, 1051, 1066, 1092, 1101, 1103, 1105, 1112, 1113, 1118, 1121, 1123, 1137, 1138, 1147, 1157, 1159, 1182, 1195, 1198, 1203, 1209, 1223, 1227, 1244, 1404, 1576, 1608, 1615, 1629, 1680, 1693, 1698, 1707, 1712, 1716, 1729, 1740, 1745, 1750, 1752, 1756, 1989, 2105, 2181, 2187, 2190, 2310, 2315, 2322, 2323, 2328, 2343, 2391, 2397, 2423, 2425, 2461, 2476, 2478, 2484, 2486, 2489, 2490, 2494, 2498, 2499, 2508, 2511, 2517, 2518, 2522, 2529, 2530, 2620, 2634, 2663, 2674, 2707, 2719, 2829, 2833, 2844, 2860, 2874, 2931, 2952, 2957, 2963, 2974, 3008, 3017, 3024, 3051, 3068, 3114, 3132, 3145, 3150, 3167, 3829, 4015, 4033, 4043, 4054, 4074, 4076, 4078, 4089, 4090, 4102, 4112, 4113, 4120, 4126, 4128, 4133, 4150, 4160, 4161, 4162, 4167-4169, 4172, 4176, 4180, 4192, 4198, 4201-4203, 4205, 4209, 4215, 4220, 4233, 4244, 4254, 4261, 4262, 4276, 4278, 4279, 4297, 4302, 4341, 4350, 4357, 4382, 4400, 4402, 4407, 5119, 5128, 5136, 5148, 5179, 5322, 5641, 5710, 5731, 5745, 5757, 5820, 5843, 5858, 5891, 6034, 6296, 6442, 6513, 6527, 6669, 6682, 6747, 6768, 6859

vision 94, 232, 682, 787, 822, 844, 857, 1108, 1364, 1618, 1635, 1662, 2145, 2450, 2924, 3080, 3088, 3298, 3378, 3452, 3655, 3659, 3945, 4614, 5616, 5849, 6068, 6463, 6690, 6712, 6727, 6929, 6984, 7049

void 84, 214, 318, 878, 3457, 4775, 4952, 4956, 5498, 5660, 5792, 5841, 5957, 5975, 5989, 6033, 6039, 6092, 6161, 6785

voluntary 113, 2414, 4099, 4107, 4121, 4123, 4142, 4155, 4157, 4177, 4225, 4259, 4300, 4344, 4395, 5062, 5970, 5977, 7047

vortex (cf. also: *dine*) 801, 866

wealth 986, 1182, 2077, 2733, 2966, 4166, 5693, 5878, 5928, 6001

will 127, 128, 167, 254, 264, 963, 979, 1143, 1238, 1721, 1734, 1748, 1754, 2315, 2399, 2837, 2843, 2861, 4066, 4080, 4183, 4188, 4197, 4247, 4325, 4398, 4881, 4882, 5528, 5603, 5604, 5666, 5696, 5706, 5709, 5832, 5882, 5886, 5962, 5970, 6050,

6081, 6126, 6267, 6495, 6525, 6561, 6621, 6629, 6677, 6738, 6739, 6775, 6794, 6802, 6916, 6922, 6934, 6938, 6941, 6948, 6956, 6963, 6981, 7037, 7039, 7048

wisdom 208, 213, 223, 254, 264, 484, 515, 557, 560, 683, 880, 1014, 1092, 1305, 1387, 1417, 1418, 1444, 1451, 1551, 1560, 1693, 1711, 1741, 2157, 2317, 2383, 2441, 2531, 2666, 2674, 2719, 2733, 2757, 2862, 2870, 3633, 3661, 3920, 3987, 3992, 4016, 4088, 4102, 4103, 4105, 4192, 4326, 4330, 4334, 4350, 4405, 4764, 4813, 5050, 5067, 5322, 5601, 5630, 5697, 5767, 5869, 5946, 6022, 6200, 6247, 6293, 6575, 6682, 6693, 6708, 6757, 6763, 6904, 6929, 6949, 6951, 6964

women 108, 143, 186, 199, 208, 230, 257, 262, 487, 1306, 1365, 1366, 1456, 1463, 1466, 1496, 2000, 2009, 2011, 2069, 2400, 2413, 2883, 2902, 2922, 2925, 2940, 2946, 2963, 2976, 3011, 3025, 3066, 3073, 3074, 3076, 3103a, 3337, 3591, 3648, 3650, 3829, 4125, 4299, 4750, 5039, 5042, 5055, 5095, 5129, 5147, 5179, 5891, 5899, 6134, 6196, 6734

world-soul 216, 796, 1819, 2037, 2113, 2142, 3267, 3490, 6422, 6443, 6465, 7058

writing 57, 98, 109, 222, 316, 1081, 1311, 1334, 1356, 1357, 1383, 1384, 1388, 1493, 1507, 1569, 1761, 2168, 2435, 2441, 2451, 2574, 2607, 2730-2732, 2754, 2757, 2762, 2766, 2772, 2782, 2802, 3358, 3714, 3738, 4553, 5409, 6067, 6157, 6230, 6235, 6541, 6641, 6767, 6815, 6906, 7054

Zarathustra/Zoroaster 88, 2136, 2146

ALBERT A. BELL, Jr., is Associate Professor of Classics and History at Hope College, in Holland, Michigan. He received his Ph. D. from the University of North Carolina at Chapel Hill, where he worked for four years as an abstracter for *Annee Philologique*, covering philosophical and religious journals. His publications include articles and book reviews in *New Testament Studies, Classical Journal, Classical World, American Journal of Philology, Revue Bénédictine, Church History, Religious Studies Review*, and other periodicals. He is also the author of a novel, *Daughter of Lazarus*, set in Rome in the first century A. D.

JAMES B. ALLIS is Assistant Professor of Philosophy at Hope College, in Holland, Michigan. He received his Ph. D. from the University of Pittsburgh. He was selected as the outstanding professor-educator at Hope in 1990 and has published reviews of books in ancient philosophy and in political thought in journals such as *Ancient Philosophy* and *Christian Scholars Review*. He is on the editorial board of the *History of Philosophy Quarterly*.